THE GAELIC OTHERWORLD

John Gregorson Campbell (painted from a photograph)   © Catrìona Black

THE GAELIC OTHERWORLD

JOHN GREGORSON CAMPBELL'S

Superstitions of the Highlands & Islands of Scotland and
Witchcraft & Second Sight in the Highlands & Islands

Edited with commentary by

RONALD BLACK

Birlinn

This edition published in 2008 by
Birlinn Limited
West Newington House
10 Newington Road
Edinburgh EH9 1QS

www.birlinn.co.uk

The Gaelic Otherworld first published by Birlinn Ltd in 2005

Originally published as *Superstitions of the Highlands & Islands of Scotland* (1900)
and *Witchcraft & Second Sight in the Highlands & Islands of Scotland* (1902)
by James MacLehose & Sons, Glasgow

ISBN10 1 84158 7338
ISBN13: 978 1 84158 7332

British Library Cataloguing-in-Publication Data
A catalogue record for this book is available from the British Library

Typesetting and maps by Edderston Book Design, Peebles
Printed and bound by Antony Rowe Ltd, Chippenham

CONTENTS

MAPS

EDITOR'S PREFACE

This book shows that there was not a single Gaelic otherworld but three, peopled respectively by Fairies, spirits and witches.

Chapters 1–3 speak of the Fairies. This is a secular otherworld, demonstrating little of magic beyond what science has now given us – the ability to fly, for example. Notwithstanding the author's remark about the 'tinge of the ludicrous' (p. 27), stories about the Fairies are to be taken seriously, for they can be shown to represent pre-Freudian psychiatry, and to provide an appropriately fictionalised setting for discussion of everyday moral dilemmas. In terms of twenty-first-century culture they are soap.

This 'first otherworld' is nothing if not complete. Chapter 4 shows that in addition to the Fairies there is the domesticated glaistig or gruagach, the offspring of unions between humans and Fairies – the indigenous equivalent of the brownie, who also appears in his own right. There is an animal kingdom, too, described in chapters 5 and 6, which the author arranges for us in what appears to be descending order, biologically speaking: the urisk (a sort of Highland monkey), blue men, streamers, mermaid, water-horse, water-bull, etc.

Chapters 15–17 speak of spirits, ghosts and the second sight. This 'second otherworld' is the simplest of the three. It is the abode of the dead and of omens of death. It is sad, morbid and violent, and clearly in terms of entertainment it has the same function (and the same allure) as horror movies. In a sense it is the most immediate of the three otherworlds because it deals with something faced at one time or another by all of us, and because the phenomenon of second sight forced it repeatedly and involuntarily upon people's attention.

Chapters 11–14 speak of witchcraft and the devil. This is the religious otherworld, influenced by Protestantism but full of magic and the machinery of magic. It is a study in polarities – God and the devil; healing and harming; human beings who voluntarily partake of the supernatural, as opposed to those in Fairy stories who may wander into the *sithein* or be captured by the Fairies but nevertheless retain their humanity. In terms of science it represents primitive medicine; with regard to genre, the best present-day analogy is probably television news, documentaries and satire. Stories about it tend to be peopled with real celebrities rather than fictionalised ordinary folk, and their purpose is to inform and entertain rather than to discuss. Of the three otherworlds, it is the funniest; *taghairm nan cat* (pp. 167–68) is a pantomime with a strong message about cruelty to animals. That this was necessary is demonstrated by the custom of burying a cat alive to get a favourable wind (p. 189); for another memorate about cruelty to animals, not at all funny, see p. 191.

Each of these otherworlds represents a different attempt to probe the mysteries of time and space. The Fairies and their fellow-creatures live mainly in the visible world below the ground and in lochs and streams, and enjoy the suspension of the normal rules of time – death exists among them only in a limited way, and a visit to the first otherworld appears to take just a minute or two, but it always transpires that a year or more has gone by in the real world before the visitor returns to it. Rip Van Winkle is a migratory legend of Celtic origin, claimed by Orcadians to have come from Washington Irving's father, who was born and bred in Shapinsay (Bruford 1997, p. 128). Under the promptings of second sight, tales of the second otherworld peer anxiously forward into the physical reality of death in all its horror, and ask if it is not possible for the dead to return. As for the third otherworld, it seems to represent the Christian choice between eternal life in heaven and eternal damnation in hell, but is really just borrowing Christian imagery for everyday practical purposes – healing, identifying scapegoats when things go wrong, keeping children safe, and providing hilarious entertainment.

In the main, the three otherworlds are clearly distinguished. They are parallel universes which provide alternative solutions. After reading countless stories of how sickness and mortality in infants was accounted for by the belief in changelings from the first otherworld, it comes as a shock to be told at p. 202 that 'when a healthy and thriving child is seized with unaccountable illness, and becomes uneasy and sickly, it is suspected of being struck with the evil eye', and that the solution lies in white witchcraft – all this being part of the third otherworld. With the exception of the glaistig (p. 82), typified by Lionnag (pp. 324–25), there is a clear distinction between creatures (such as the water-horse) which are permanent denizens of the first otherworld and animal wraiths which appear as *manaidhean* or omens from the second. JGC does not confuse the two, but in my notes I provide some evidence to suggest that his 'Big Beast of Loch Awe' (p. 117) may be a creature of the second otherworld rather than of the first. For his own reasons, twentieth-century man chose to look for the Loch Ness monster (which JGC does not even mention) in the domain of flesh and blood rather than in the second otherworld where she lives. I hope twenty-first-century men and women will be more sensible; perhaps this book will help.

On the rare occasion when one otherworld actually intrudes upon another, as when we meet a banshee (or banshi, as the author spells it) in a tale of the second otherworld at p. 237, or a deathly apparition on a Fairy mountain at p. 251, we gain an immediate sense of something odd and interesting at work. Charms and amulets (except perhaps for Fairy arrows) belong so exclusively to the third otherworld that it comes as a surprise when the Fairies are mentioned at p. 230. *Mac mollachd*, the devil, turns into Meg Mholach, a glaistig – but then, that is far away in the north-eastern Highlands, not mentioned by the author at all and only introduced by myself in the way of commentary. Exactly the same is true of Isobel Gowdie, who claimed that the devil was involved in the throwing of Fairy arrows. She appears to have been a simple-minded young woman trapped between two cultures, seeing witchcraft as fun in the way described above and failing to understand the trouble it could get her into. She was like the young tailor in Rannoch called Cumming whose 'imagination was disordered by the many tales of witchcraft he had heard' (p. 196).

Four further chapters and an appendix furnish important additional context. Chapters 7 and 8 are on general superstitions, beginning with those about animals in order to lead on smoothly from chapter 6. Many of these are cross-cultural or global in nature, differing only in points of minor detail from practices and beliefs found elsewhere. Chapters 9 and 10 pick up the key issue of time, examining different ways of peering into the future. (It is a pity that JGC does not devote a section to traditional weather-forecasting.) Finally, 'The Celtic Year' offers a brief sketch of the complex matrix of time in which all the above-mentioned beliefs and practices are set, including Celtic quarter-days, Gaelic wind-names, Roman months, Latin weekdays and Christian feasts.

With one or two minor adjustments, I have retained the structure of chapters and sections in the original books. I have divided chapter 2 of *SHIS*, 'Tales Illustrative of Fairy Superstition' (which was very long), into chapters 2, 'Tales Illustrative of Fairy Superstition', and 3, 'Tales of Fairy Women, etc.' This should aid approaches from the perspective of women's studies. To compensate, as it were, I have amalgamated *SHIS* chapters 8, 'Augury', and 9, 'Premonitions and Divination', to form a new chapter 9, 'Augury, Premonitions and Divination'. *WSS* chapters 1–5 have now become chapters 13–17, while *WSS* chapter 6, 'The Celtic Year', has been set apart and given its own sequence of endnotes. This is entirely logical, as the Gaelic calendar is a subject in its own right which transcends superstitions, witchcraft, second sight and the otherworlds. I have adhered pretty strictly to JGC's sectional titles, with three exceptions: 'Fairy Dogs ('Cu Sith')', *SHIS* 141, which as a translator I felt would be more logically expressed 'Fairy Dog (*Cù Sìth*)' (p. 75); 'Struck by the Fairy Arrow Spade', *SHIS* 154, which I think is in error for 'Spade Struck by the Fairy Arrow' (p. 81); and 'Christmas Rhymes (*Rann Calluinn*)', *WSS* 233, which again I felt would be more logically 'Christmas Rhymes (*Rannan Callainn*)' (p. 518). For the change from *Calluinn* to *Callainn* see p. xiv. Where JGC did not allocate sectional titles, e.g. at the start of chapters, I have fallen back on his running heads or my imagination.

The main alteration to the structure of the two books lies in the prioritisation of Gaelic (where it occurs) over English. This is in fact the primary aim of the present edition. JGC's habit was to cite Gaelic originals of names, words and phrases in brackets following the English version – there is an example at p. lxxxiv, as I have purposely left JGC's preface unedited – and Gaelic originals of sentences and rhymes in footnotes. This often led to a confusing clutter at the foot of a page. Wherever appropriate, I have now put the originals first, followed by translations in brackets; as stated above, however, I have left almost all sectional titles as they were. I have eliminated all footnotes, incorporating the information given in them either at the relevant point in the text or (in a small number of cases where this was impractical, e.g. note 140 on p. 321) in my commentary, marking the information as having been provided by JGC. In a few such cases I have thought it better to paraphrase JGC's words than to cite them verbatim, e.g. in note 933 on p. 520 where JGC's text (*WSS* 200) was stuffed with misprints – *Camsrhron, Camsrhronach, Camsrhronaich*.

JGC's style of writing in *SHIS* and *WSS* swings back and forth from brilliant clarity to nightmarish muddle. The books were published posthumously, and, unusually for that time, were poorly edited. My aim has been to achieve clarity through sensitive editing and the use of Chambers' and Dwelly's dictionaries. I have tried to identify JGC's conventions and apply them consistently, updating English, Gaelic and punctuation to meet twenty-first-century requirements without losing the meaning or style of the original. I have altered punctuation, paragraphing and use of italicisation as far as seemed appropriate to elucidate his text. Occasionally his meaning is locked up in impenetrable syntax and I have had to recast his sentence structure to liberate it – the paragraph beginning 'The Fairies' at p. 12 (*SHIS* 22–23) is an example. In one case, JGC's poetic 'between Loch Maddy and Dïusa in Merivale, there is a well that cures the toothache' (p. 229), his punctuation (or rather the lack of it) affects the geography which he is attempting to describe, but as my interpretation is itself uncertain I have refrained from removing the comma after Merivale and placing it after Dïusa, see note 800. Sometimes where text is quoted in one language but not in the other I have added some material to correct the imbalance, usually from another source, occasionally by means of translation or reconstruction, see e.g. note 158 on p. 327. JGC often writes 'whenever' to mean 'as soon as', e.g. at p. 34; in one or two particularly ambiguous cases (e.g. 'whenever he observed the American', *WSS* 203) I have emended this to 'when' (p. 282). Similarly I have changed 'if they found no water in' (*SHIS* 20) to 'if they found no water indoors' (p. 10) and 'the Cairbre's feast' (*SHIS* 44) to 'Cairbre's feast' (p. 23).

I have maintained and regularised JGC's preference for upper-case E and F in the words Elf, Elves, Elfin, Fairy (both noun and adjective), Fairies and Fairylike, as these may be argued to denote the otherworld people as 'a race of beings' (p. 1). He is less consistent with regard to capitalisation of 'People' and 'Folk' when applied to the Fairies, and in these cases I have decided that quotation marks are sufficient: 'people', 'folk'. I have maintained his preference for lower-case *s* in the Gaelic equivalents *sìth*, *sìthche*, etc., the logic being simply that these have so many variants that it would be difficult to know where to draw the line. Although he also writes 'shi' and 'shi-woman' (pp. 1, 78), he capitalises 'banshi'; this I have overruled, but I have respected his use of *Shi* in 'The Origin of the Fairy Creed', which was written later. With respect to other terms denoting otherworld beings and creatures he shows a broad, but inconsistent, preference for lower-case, and on the grounds that these may be argued to denote species, not races, I have regularised this practice, except in the case of foreign terms borrowed from works such as Keightley's *Fairy Mythology* where they appear with upper-case initial (e.g Alfs, Duergar, Elle, Elle-maid, see for example the list based on Keightley and Grimm at p. 6).

JGC awards an upper-case initial not only to the glaistig but to her offspring and to her cousin the gruagach (*SHIS* 161, p. 85 below); this I have denied them all, except where the terms may be regarded as titles, e.g. 'the Glaistig of Glenduror'. Similarly, at pp. 100–01 'brownie' is now printed with upper-case initial only when used as a name, e.g. 'in character Brownie was harmless'. With respect to religious terminology, where JGC is again inconsistent, I have applied the principles outlined in Black 2002, pp. 26–27: God, Christianity etc. are capitalised, but the angels, the devil, paganism, death, etc., are not. 'King of grace' (*WSS* 75) becomes 'King of Grace' (p. 213), but 'King of Terrors' meaning death (*WSS* 109) becomes 'king of terrors' (p. 234). I print the adjective with upper-case in 'Outer Isles', 'Outer Hebrides', 'West Highlands', 'Western Isles' and 'Western Islands', but with lower-case in *ad hoc* usages like 'north Hebrides'. Following the practice which he encountered in Portree, JGC refers to places in the district now called Staffin (the parish of Kilmuir) as 'on east side', 'on East-side', 'in East-side' or 'on the east side'; I have regularised the last two words in each case as 'East Side'. In general however I have followed our twenty-first-century preference for lower case, e.g. 'Fairy Tale' becomes 'Fairy tale', 'the Isle of Man' becomes 'the isle of Man', 'the Duke of Argyll' becomes 'the duke of Argyll'.

In his eagerness to explain Gaelic terminology to English readers JGC indulges occasionally in spellings which are neither Gaelic nor English but phonetic. I have put these in bold, e.g. **saït hee** (p. 223), **MacCuïl** (p. 276), **kasg** (p. 541). In line with mid-nineteenth-century practice he is fond of using diacritics more generally to indicate the pronunciation of words and names; these I have retained, but without going so far as to use bold, e.g. 'Gaël' (p. 74), 'Gaïck' (pp. 164–65), 'Ballychroän' (pp. 165–66), 'Oär' (pp. 167–68), 'Doïni' (p. 190), 'Cuäl' (p. 217), 'Cragganoür' (p. 282). Where he (or his publisher) has used macrons to show long vowels, e.g. *an spōrs a līonas brū* (*WSS* 58), *ōisgean* (*WSS* 254), I have emended these to graves (*an spòrs a lìonas brù*, p. 201; *Òisgean*, p. 544).

JGC's spelling of 'Mac' names was totally inconsistent, e.g. M'Leod, McLeod, Macleod, MacLeod, Mac-Leod, Mac Leod. In line with preferred modern usage in the Highlands and Islands I have regularised the 'MacLeod' type. Exceptions: (1) where a particular name is well established by historical convention, such as 'Ossian' Macpherson, Lord Macaulay, Lord Macdonald, John Mackenzie of *Sàr Obair*; (2) direct quotations; (3) bibliographic citations, where I am obliged to follow the style adopted on the title-page of the book in question, unless there is more than one book and the spelling varies between them; (4) where the element following 'Mac' derives from the Gaelic article *an* I prefer lower case, e.g. Macintyre, Mackintosh; (5) patronymics, e.g. *Dòmhnall mac Iain*, Fin mac Coul; (6) some instances of the Gaelic genitive, e.g. *Clann 'ic Codrum*, p. 156. In direct quotations and bibliographic citations I regularise M' as Mc. I have rendered JGC's 'clan Maclachlan' (*WSS* 110) as 'Clan MacLachlan' (p. 234). At p. 276 I have left 'Macdonall' exactly as it stands in *WSS* 191; it is probably a misprint, but whether for 'Macdonell', 'Macdonald' or 'Macdouall' I have no idea.

I have generally expanded JGC's contractions, e.g 'plur.' to 'plural' and 'fem.' to 'feminine'. I have expanded his 'Scot.' to 'Scots' although he probably intended 'Scotice' or 'Scotch' – in fact 'Scotch' appears at *WSS* 272 (p. 554). I have generally left his bibliographic references unedited while providing fuller information in my notes. Where he provides a cross-reference I have altered the page number to refer to the present edition; very occasionally (e.g. at p. 22) I have added a cross-reference to the text.

In *SHIS* '-ize(d), -izing, -yze(d), -yzing' predominates, e.g. 'baptize, paralyzed', while in *WSS* '-ise(d), -ising, -yse(d), -ysing' predominates, e.g. 'baptise, paralysed', presumably because MacLehose allocated a different in-house editor. I have regularised '-s-'.

Without any particular consistency, JGC sometimes uses spellings which have an antique charm, e.g. 'insured' for 'ensured', 'phantasies' for 'fantasies', 'phrenzy' for 'frenzy', 'shewing' and 'shewn' for 'showing' and 'shown', 'staid' for 'stayed', 'whiskey' for 'whisky'. Where they occur, I have retained these as adding to the character of the book; more humdrum words I have simply modernised, e.g. 'to-day' to 'today'. 'Dyke' predominates over 'dike', so I have regularised the former. For an osier etc. he consistently uses 'withe', plural 'withies'; I have kept these spellings.

With regard to grammar and syntax I have tried to draw a line between solecisms and Highland English, e.g. in 'work began on Friday was said to be always hurriedly done' (*WSS* 300) I have corrected 'began' to 'begun' (p. 568), but I have allowed the infinitive to stand in 'The aversion of sea-faring men to leave' and 'aversion to disturb . . . the earth' (*WSS* 299, pp. 567–68 below). Sir Walter Scott's usage was similar (2001, p. 98): "Hector . . . evaded . . . to present her to trial."

Obviously 'in Tiree' (*passim*) comes into the 'Highland English' category, as do the likes of 'lifting with them', p. 18 (*a' togail leotha*); 'though they came', p. 57 (*ged a thigeadh iad*); 'in the smallpox', pp. 71, 259 (*anns a' bhric*); 'the dog sprang from him', p. 86 (*leum an cù bhuaithe*); 'bare naked', p. 100 (*lomnochd*); 'to snatch her seducer with her', p. 183 (*a fear-meallaidh a thoirt leatha*); 'as good luck did not direct him', p. 192 (*mar nach d'òrdaich sealbh e*); 'not looking well before him', p. 246 (*gun amharc gu math roimhe*); 'on the up side of him', p. 247 (*air a' cheann shuas dheth*); 'when it reached, her husband fell dead', p. 250 (*an uair a ràinig e, thuit a fear marbh*); 'no answer is given though he speak', p. 255 (*cha toirear freagairt ged a bhruidhneas e*); 'a coffin and men carrying it', p. 257 (*ciste 's daoine ga giùlan*); 'there was a bad chance of her going away', p. 280 (*gun robh droch theans gum falbhadh i*); 'near hand', p. 283 (*faisg air làimh*). Particularly characteristic of JGC's Highland English is confusion between 'though' (often used for 'even if'), 'if not' and 'unless', e.g. 'though he made a hole . . . and hid' for 'even if he made a hole . . . and hid' (p. 95), 'unless he . . . had been friendly' for 'if he . . . had not been friendly' (p. 111).

In regard to place-names, I have retained Arasaig as well as Arisaig, Argyle and Argyleshire as well as Argyll and Argyllshire, Athole as well as Athol (nowadays it is usually Atholl), Cantyre as well as Kintyre, Cnapdale as well as Knapdale, Cnoydart as well as Knoydart, and Raasa as well as Raasay; thus also one personal name, Ferchar as well as Farquhar. With some names JGC is perfectly consistent – Amhulaich (nowadays Aulich), Balachulish (Ballachulish), Breacacha (Breacachadh), Dowart (Duart), Glen Erochty (Glen Errochty), Glenevis (Glen Nevis), Lorn (often Lorne), Loscantire (Luskentyre), Strowan (Struan), Wigtonshire (Wigtownshire) – all of these I have kept. He spells Tiree in the modern way, even though many of his contemporaries still wrote Tyree. Where he mentions a name only once (e.g. Cashieville, now Coshieville, p. 285; Dunbuck and Dunbarton, p. 71; Funery, now Fiunary, p. 247; Glen Lochy, now Glen Lochay, p. 287; Loch Erne, now Loch Earn, p. 135; Tarnsa, now Taransay, p. 150) I have preferred to retain his spelling as being of interest, and have provided cross-references in the index where appropriate. Michael Scot he consistently spells Michael Scott; this, too, I have respected.

In other cases I have been a little less happy. He occasionally writes Caolis as well as Caolas, Kingerloch as well as Kingairloch, Maligeir as well as Màiligeir, Morven as well as Morvern, Oisian as well as Ossian. For various reasons I have regularised the latter form in each case. 'Morven' is a misleading spelling taken from James Macpherson's work – the name is *a' Mhorbhairne*, probably meaning 'Sea Gap', and has nothing to do with *mór* 'big' or *beinn* 'mountain'.

JGC allows some Tiree place-names to vary widely, and I have tried to reduce these to a single English and a single Gaelic spelling: Balefetrish, *Baile Pheudrais*; Balephuil, *Baile Phuill*; Balevullin, *Baile Mhuilinn*; Kennavara, *Ceann a' Bhara*. For *Haoidhnis* he prefers Heynish, although the form cited throughout the 'Life of John Gregorson Campbell' is Hynish. For *Tràigh a' Bhàigh* I have allowed both Trabay and Travay. I have kept his 'Loch Basibol' in the text but refer to it in my commentary as Loch Bhasapol (see however note 196). Heylipol is generally referred to in Gaelic in the east of Tiree as *an Cruaidh-Ghoirtean* and abbreviated in the west to *an Cruairtean* (cf. Brownlie 1995, pp. 102–03); JGC gives it as 'Croy-Gortan' (*SHIS* 108, see p. 58) and *Cruaidh-ghortain* (*SHIS* 108, see note 196; *WSS* 204, see p. 282). Pennygown in Mull he gives as *Peigh'nn-a-ghobhann, Peighinn-a-ghobhann, Peighinn-a-ghobhan*, so I have regularised *Peighinn a' Ghobhann*, although *Peighinn a' Ghobhainn* would be more correct. Rigg in Skye he gives as Rigg and *Ruig*, and I have kept these. The name of the saint whom we know in Gaelic as *Calum Cille* appears variously in JGC's English as Columba, Colum-Kil, Colum-Cill and Colum-cill; to all of these except the last I say 'stet'.

In Gaelic, it has to be said that despite the warm endorsement of the Very Rev. Dr John MacLeod of Morvern (see p. 626), JGC's spelling and grammar leave much to be desired. It seems clear from his frequent dropping of vocalic endings that he did not speak 'pure Argyleshire Gaelic' but was influenced by his mother's Perthshire dialect (cf. note 499). I have emended *Maighdean Bhuan* (*SHIS* 20) to *maighdeann bhuana* (p. 11), *Na Fir Ghorm* (*SHIS* 199) to *na Fir Ghorma* (p. 107), and *Sruth nam Fear Gorm* (*SHIS* 200) to *Sruth nam Fear Gorma* (p. 107), but I have kept *Macillduinn* (*WSS* 37, p. 190) rather than emending it to *MacilleDhuinn*, and I am content to leave 'Dùn Can' (*SHIS* 209, p. 112 below) as it stands. He has a habit of dropping proclitics as well as enclitics, e.g. *chiad* for *a' chiad*, and I have generally thought it best not to interfere with this. It is no surprise that he writes *seach gun leum* for *seach gun do leum* (p. 548). On the whole I have tried to adjust the spelling and grammar of the portions of Gaelic cited in the text to make it as accessible as possible to the modern reader without obliterating JGC's identity. This means maintaining his accenting system and retaining certain orthographic features which represent valid phonological distinctions, e.g. for 'mouth' I have allowed both *beul* and *bial*. I have emended his *Apuinn na Meinearach* (*WSS* 154) only as far as *Apainn nam Meinearach* (p. 256), although it should surely read *Apainn nam Mèinnearach* (cf. Macbain 1896–97, p. 325, and Dwelly 1977, p. 1023); on the following page I have allowed *tòrradh mo sheanamhair* ('my grandmother's funeral') to stand as best representing what was probably said (as opposed to *tòrradh mo sheanmhar*, which would represent good grammar and spelling). At some points in 'The Celtic Year' JGC's grammar deserts him completely (see especially pp. 540, 542, 544, 564), and as this presumably reflects his field-notes I have thought it best to let his words stand and discuss them in my commentary.

JGC is every bit as careless with the apostrophe as is the average Gaelic writer today. This simply had to be fixed, e.g. *eòlas a chronachaidh* becomes *eòlas a' chronachaidh*. In a single paragraph at *WSS* 141 he writes both *Fionnaghal a Mhoir* and *Fionnghal a Mhoir*; I have emended in each case to *Fionnaghal a' Mhòir*, but as pointed out in note 855, the correct reading is probably *Fionnaghal Iain Mhòir*. Where JGC commits a grammatical error which would be common nowadays and which it would seem pedantic to correct, e.g. *beagan piseach* (*SHIS* 278) as opposed to *beagan pisich*, I leave it uncorrected (p. 153).

JGC often writes *sd* even though this represents no distinction in sound from *st*;

in line with best modern practice, I have emending it to *st*, e.g. Alastair (p. 50), *Biast* (p. 116), *Traosta* (p. 539), except where *d* derives from Norse *dalr*, e.g. Scalasdal (p. 67). He appears to favour the grave accent on *a*, *i*, *o* and *u* but the acute on *e* (irrespective of sound), and often omits accents altogether. I have retained his accents as they stand (except when clearly wrong, e.g. *a tháillear*, WSS 196, and *óganach*, WSS 200), and have inserted missing ones according to his own system. His preference for *bò* over *bó* 'cow' and *mòr* over *mór* 'big' presumably reflects his own dialect (*bò* and *mòr* are the normal pronunciations in Lismore to this day). He was willing to write *ó* when it conveyed the sound intended – at WSS 216 we meet *mo theóghadh* (twice) and *Teóghan*, see p. 289. He usually spells *crodh* 'cattle' as *cro*, *dubh* 'black' as *du*, *inbhear* or *inbhir* as *inbher*, *rubha* 'headland' as *rutha*, and *tobhta* 'thwart, roofless wall' as *tota*; most of these are a form of shorthand, and I have updated or expanded them. At SHIS 274 he writes of *Uigh an du tuath* in Harris; *du* here is not *dubh* but an eclipsed and unstressed form of *taobh* 'side', and I have chosen to render the name in full as *Uidh an Taoibh Tuath*, 'the Isthmus of Northton', see p. 150 and note 511. Similarly, at WSS 26 he refers to the East Side as *Du-sear*; this represents the pronunciation of *'n Taobh Sear* and that is therefore how I render it at p. 184. Also deriving ultimately from field-notes, I think, is his tendency to omit lenition, e.g. *de glas darach* (SHIS 299), 'A mhuireartach maol, ruadh, muing-fhionn' (WSS 188); this, too, I have corrected wherever it seemed reasonable to do so, e.g. *de ghlas dharach* (p. 164), *A' Mhuireartach mhaol, ruadh, mhuing-fhionn* (p. 274). In *an Fhéill Mhoire mòr* (WSS 280) lenition is not so much omitted as transposed, and I have emended to *an Fhéill Moire mhòr* (p. 558).

With regard to vowels, JGC is fond of *'us* or *us* for *agus*; this is logical (as well as possessing antique charm), but after some hesitation I have updated to *is*. Like many another before and after him he writes schwa in unstressed syllables indifferently as *a*, *u* or even *o*, e.g. *Calluinn* 'New Year', *balgum* 'dram', *iarunn* 'iron', *dòruinneach* 'painful'; in line with modern practice I have, with some exceptions, emended to *a*, e.g. *Callainn, balgam, iarann, dòrainneach*. For 'rowan, mountain ash' (Irish *caorthann*) he writes sometimes *caorunn*, sometimes *caorrunn*; I have regularised *caorann*. Among the exceptions are *agus* 'and', *Calum* 'Malcolm', and some less usual words and names with which I felt it wrong to interfere: *rathum* (p. 111), *dòduman* 'a teetotum' (p. 144), *MacCodrum* (p. 156), *Bladrum* (pp. 190–91), *pàilliun* (p. 546). The same applies to certain words and names whose meaning is the subject of an endnote: *Loch Àluinn* 'Loch Aline' (note 151), *ùruisg* (note 350), *Mà-Cònuill* (note 625), 'Àirigh mhic Mharoich', which I have emended only slightly from 'Airidh-mhic-mharoich' (note 638), Bla-sguinn (note 650). Castlebay Harbour in Barra appears as *Bàgh Chiòsamul* at SHIS 264 and *Bàgh Chiòsamuill* at WSS 18, so I have regularised it to *Bàgh Chìosamuil*.

In writing *-un* for plural *-an* JGC produces an outstanding orthographic innovation which could usefully be adopted today, though my hopes are not high – it serves very importantly to distinguish the obscure vowel of the plural from the open vowel of the derivative, e.g. *creagan* 'a little rock' (see p. 100), *creagun* 'rocks'; *criosan* 'a little girdle', *criosun* 'girdles'; *casan* 'a path', *casun* 'feet'; *slabhagan* 'sea sloke' (note 577), *slabhagun* 'sockets'. This confusion is impossible in Irish, where the derivative is *án* and the plural is *-a*; where necessary it may be mitigated in Scottish Gaelic by the use of *án* for the derivative (as in note 344 on p. 363, where W. J. Watson is quoted), but even this option is being closed off by the disastrous modern tendency to use the grave in all circumstances. I have retained JGC's -*un* wherever it appears (e.g. at pp. 14, 18, 40), but he does not use it with complete consistency, and after long reflection I have decided not to impose it where it does not appear in *SHIS* or *WSS*. Thus we have *cuiseagan* 'stalks' at pp. 11 and 13 below (*SHIS* 22, 25) but *creuchdun* 'wounds' at p. 14 (*SHIS* 27); *casan* 'feet' at p. 202 (*WSS* 61), *creagan* 'rocks' at p. 203 (*WSS* 63); and at p. 571 we cannot be quite sure what word is intended by JGC's *slabhagan* 'pith'.

Moving now from general principles to miscellaneous items of vocabulary, I have allowed different spellings of the word for 'gateway' to stand: *cachla* (p. 75), *cachlaidh* (p. 570). JGC spells the word for 'steep mountain path' in three different ways: *càth* twice at *SHIS* 274 (p. 150), *catha* four times at *WSS* 136 (p. 247), *cadha* once on the same page; I have let *càth* stand but have emended *catha* to *cadha*, which is the correct spelling. On the odd occasion when he writes *co* for 'so' (e.g. 'co farranach', *SHIS* 303, *co dorcha*, *WSS* 289) I emend to his customary *cho*. Usually (but not always) he writes *croggan* even though there is no double *g* in Gaelic, and I emend to *crogan*. A word that gives him difficulty, as it did Carmichael, is *ortha* 'a charm'; the only traditional pronunciation which I have heard is *òra*, and this must apply to JGC also, because he spells it *Oradh* (*WSS* 56, 80) or *òradh* (*WSS* 278) and introduces it as meaning 'gilding' before settling for 'charm' or 'charms' (pp. 200, 216, 557). I have therefore regularised *òradh*. The verb 'freeze' is consistently spelt *reoth* with one exception, *reodh*; this I have regularised to *reoth*. Where *roi, roi'* or *roimh* occurs in the meaning 'before' or 'through' I have regularised *roimh*. I have let *roluig* 'graveyard' stand as it only occurs once (*WSS* 97, p. 226 below); it reflects a pronunciation *roilig*. For 'clanking' JGC writes both *straoilich* and *straighlich*, so I have regularised the latter.

Three related terms which come up more than once are *farcluais* 'eavesdropping' (*far* + *cluais* 'over-ear'), *fàrdoras* 'lintel' (*far* + *doras* 'over-door') and *fàrlus* 'smoke-hole' (*far* + *leus* 'over-light'). JGC gives the first twice as *farcluais*, which I adhere to, and the second as *san àrd dorus* and *san àrd-dorus* 'on the lintel'; I regularise these to *san àrd-doras*. The other he gives as *fàr-leus* and *fàr-lus*, and as both are good spellings I let them stand. The lengthening of *far-* to *fàr-* in two of the three cases is caused by the following consonant. See *CG2*, pp. 289, 293, and cf. *farrabheann* (for *far-bheann*), note 713 on p. 462.

I have tried to approach Gaelic names in the same way. Bo-chaoil in Glenorchy (*SHIS* 171) I have made Both Chaoil (p. 92). JGC gives Kylerhea as *Caol-Redhinn* (*WSS* 207), which looks odd but is intentional – in Campbell 1907–08, p. 201, he spells it *Caol Redhinn* and says that it commemorates an Ossianic hero called *MacRethinn*. I have made it *Caol Reidhinn* (p. 284). On the other hand, there is a battery of peculiar names in the section 'Charm to Keep Away Harm in a Lawsuit' (pp. 218–19), and these I have left exactly as they stand in *WSS* 83. *Mac Iain Ghiarr* (*SHIS* 181) and 'MacIain Ghiarr' (*WSS* 47) become *Mac Iain Ghiorr* (pp. 97, 195). JGC usually writes *Eoghan*, in only one case *Eòghan*, so I regularise the former; in English he has it variously as Hugh, Ewen, Evan, and all of these I have kept. He writes both *Pàdruig* and *Pàruig*; I have preserved the variation while modernising the spelling of the unstressed vowel (*Pàdraig, Pàraig*).

Moving on to the calendar terminology employed in 'The Celtic Year', I have basically followed JGC's usage of writing 'old style' and 'new style' except following a date, where they appear as 'Old Style', 'OS', 'New Style', 'NS'. I have preferred lower-case for 'day', 'night' and 'eve' other than in hyphenated compounds (e.g. 'New Year's day', 'St Finan's eve', 'May-Day'), but upper-case for *féill* ('feast, festival, vigil', from Latin *vigilium*), thus *an Fhéill Pàdraig* or *latha na Féill Pàdraig* 'St Patrick's day'. Modern Gaelic writers should note that the word *naomh* does not occur in these terms at all. I have capitalised traditional terms like *faoilleach* and *gearran* only when they are used as calendar months, but have thought it best to follow JGC's usage exactly with regard to capitalisation or otherwise of *Màrt*, which can mean Tuesday, March or a season of agricultural labour. With regard to the principal quarter-days, JGC adheres strictly to *Bealltainn*, but is torn between *Samhain* and *Samhainn*; I have let these stand, emending *Samhuinn* (which appears once) to *Samhainn*.

JGC's practice is inconsistent with regard to days of the week: *Di-luain*, *Di-Ciadain*, etc. In line with my policy that capitalisation of the unstressed part of a hyphenated compound should also apply to the stressed element, I have regularised upper-case as well as hyphen: *Di-Luain*, *Di-Ciadain*, etc. He consistently writes *Di'rdaoin* for Thursday; this I emend to the more familiar *Diar-Daoin* without doing too much violence, I hope, to his theory that it is somehow derived from *Thor, Tor, Thordan*, son of the Norse god Odin (p. 566). Presumably the masculine gender of *an t-aoine* 'Friday' (WSS 301, emended to *an t-Aoine*, p. 568) comes with great honesty from the pages of JGC's field-notes, as it goes against not only the conventional derivation of the name but also his own explanation that it derives from *Venus* and is cognate with *bean* 'a wife'. He writes indifferently *Sathurna* and *Sathuirne*; I have kept them both, merely emending to *Satharna* and *Sathairne*.

I am grateful to Professor John F. A. Sawyer, San Savino, Italy, for checking JGC's Greek quotations. He recommended one major emendation (ἔας and ἦς in WSS 226 to ἔαρ and ἦρ at p. 528 below) and some minor ones, all of which have been made. In certain cases JGC's spelling – or the printer's interpretation of his handwriting – gives us such a serious textual headache that I have thought it best to leave the offending word or phrase as it is and discuss it in an endnote. In English the most obvious instance is the confusion between 'wine' and 'urine' (p. 203, cf. p. 687). In Gaelic there is *(s)(g)rogag* (note 373), *faoire* (note 462), *ach sùil an t-saighdeir* (note 577), *an lorg ohn* (note 590), *Easa suc Con* (note 795), *Corra-lòigein* (note 908), *cruth an crios* (note 62 on pp. 585–86), *ioma-sguaba* (note 76 on pp. 586–87), *a chlaisich* (note 110 on p. 590), *Buigeuisg* (note 209 on p. 606). And in an unknown language there is 'the Macgnanean' (note 486).

In a much larger number of cases it has simply been a matter of correcting misprints. As the correction of misprints is one of the fundamental aims of this edition, I list the main ones opposite. It will be noticed that in many cases further changes have been made in line with the editorial principles described above.

No work of this kind can be done without occasional help from a lot of people and more sustained help from a few. I am deeply grateful to them, above all to Niall M. Brownlie, Joina MacDonald and Iain Thornber, who kindly read and commented on portions of my text related to Tiree, Harris and Morvern respectively. Many of

SHIS			GO
9	*ciree*	5	*circe*
57	*cleoch ort*	30	*Deoch ort*
70	*Mhàrtiunn*	37	*Mhàrtainn*
70	*taibhseis*	38	*taibhseir*
71	*sithehean*	38	*Sìthchean*
72	*Sasory*	38	*Savary*
72	*Invererragan*	38	*Inveresragan*
73	*Coira Bhaeaidh*	39	*Coire Bhacaidh*
74	*Dunruilg*	39	*Dunvuilg*
76	*Dunsuirv*	40	*Dunvuirv*
86	*Heynist*	45	*Heynish*
87	*Uaiue*	46	*Uaine*
95	*studied*	51	*studded*
96	*fhuais*	51	*fhuair*
105	*Baile-phendrais*	56	*Baile Pheudrais*
117	*retain*	62	*regain*
122	*Jain*	65	*Iain*
134	*Kianish*	71	*Hianish*
159	*artizans*	84	*artisans*
162	*Faschan*	85	*Faochan*
172	*Cairnbeulach*	92	*Caimbeulach*
176	*Goean, Goean*	94	*Gocan, Gocan*
179	*bò àd dheighinn*	96	*bò ad' dhéidhinn*
182	*Réiscapol*	98	*Réiseapol*
189	*triuthar*	101	*triubhas*
196	*Beinn Doohrain*	105	*Beinn Dòbhrain*
216	*Tarbh Uirge*	115	*TARBH UISGE*
216	*Carc-chluasach*	115	*corc-chluasach*
224	*beithis*	121	*beithir*
227	*everbody*	123	*everybody*
228	*a ghobachain*	124	*a ghobhachain*
229	*Gisvagun*	125	*GISREAGUN*
230	*an duigh*	126	*an-diugh*
241	*pearlswort*	132	*pearlwort*
243	*The cum-iochd*	133	*The leum-iochd*
244	*La u Bhrochain*	134	*LÀ A' BHROCHAIN*
245	*Làirig Isle*	135	*Làirig Isle*
246	*Luckd-Ceaird*	135	*luchd ceàird*
248	*Gaining Straw*	136	*SAINING STRAW*
256	*motaeilla*	141	*motacilla*
259	*nharbh*	142	*mharbh*
264	*Chìòsamul*	144	*Chìòsamuil*
268	*mas a dùrachd*	147	*mar a dùrachd*
269	*the fhéin*	147	*thu fhéin*
272	*Meair thig*	149	*Nuair thig*
272	*s fheum*	149	*o fheum*
275	*laimh*	151	*làimh*
278	*sheamar; toabh*	153	*sheanar; taobh*
283	*sigh*	156	*rìgh*
284	*ròm*	156	*ròn*
297	*storàch*	163	*stòrach*
298	*Squrra-side*	164	*Sgurra-side*
307	*a'a bhróig*	168	*ad' bhròig*
308	*seirreach; douus*	169	*seisreach; donas*
309	*b'fhaid aid*	169	*b' fhaid' iad*

WSS			GO
11	*Mac-Shiomoun*	177	*Mac Shìomoin*
23	*ni'a Dò'uill*	183	*nighean Dòmhnaill*
24	*tota shílidh*	183	*tobhta shilidh*
32	*airidh-Leòid*	187	*Àirigh Leòid*
54	Beand	199	Brand
59	go without	201	go out with
63	*an otm*	203	*an tom*
86	*meall èochd*	220	*meall càchd*
96	*an triugh*	225	*AN TRIUGH*
106	*aisneam*	231	*aisnean*
107	*Neghinn Righ*	232	*NIGHEAN RÌGH*
108	*A'v; Um; Un*	232	*A'r; Am'; An*
108	*m' athur no momhathar*	232	*m' athar no mo mhàthar*
108	*thré*	233	*thrì*
112	*avi amadan*	235	*air amadan*
113	*Siòlachadh*	236	*Sìolachadh*
114	*còiricheaa*	236	*còirichean*
116	*gobun cheare*	237	*gobun chearc*
117	*Onoc nan Sgolb*	238	*Cnoc nan Sgolb*
118	*Port-nan-amhn'*	238	Port na h-Amhn
136	Correi-Vulin	248	Corrie-Vulin
140	*tabhsearachd*	249	*taibhsearachd*
140	lying	249	laying
152	person	255	persons
165	Lights began	262	Sights began
188	*tiòm*	274	*tiom*
191	*eòmach mòr chlach*	276	*càrnach mòr chlach*
195	*à thàillear*	278	*a thàilleir*
196	*a tháillear*	278	*a thàilleir*
205	the Moas	283	the Moss
212	*fiòn*	286	*fion*
216	and then add	289	and then added
219	The burning peats	290	Then burning peats
229	*Chaneil*	295	*Chan eil*
245	*mhiòs*	305	*mhìos*
247	*mhàthiar*	306	*mhàthar*
249	corrections	307	correctness
252	at the season	309	at this season
255	*màs fheudar*	311	*mas fheudar*
260	*Chaneil*	314	*Chan eil*
264	Peneas	316	Pencas
265	*Chìòsamul*	316	*Chìòsamuil*
265	Vassius	316	Vossius
265	in expression	316	an expression
266	*Cáisg mhòr*	317	*Càisg Mhòr*
274	Clonfest	321	Clonfert
276	*Maighsthir*	322	*Maighstir*
279	*fiuchaeh*	323	*fiuchach*
279	*tomhaís*	324	*tomhais*
281	*Di-ciadain*	325	*Di-Ciadain*
282	in name or practices	325	in the name or practices
290	*S' oidhche*	329	*'S oidhche*
296	do nothing,	332	do nothing.
297	*DIES VENORIS*	333	*DIES VENERIS*
297	Gael, bean	333	Gaelic bean
300	*Sathnrna*	334	*Satharna*

Misprints and how they have been corrected (*GO* = *The Gaelic Otherworld*) those who provided help in specific areas are named at the appropriate point in my commentaries, but I would also like to thank Chrissie Bannerman, John Brady (Newberry Library, Chicago), Seon C. Caimbeul, Dr David H. Caldwell (National Museums of Scotland), Dr Christopher Cameron, Sandy Carmichael, Dr Richard Cox, Mrs Catherine Fagg, Nancy Gatz, Professor William Gillies, Mrs Fiona Gunn, Dr Andy Halpin (National Museum of Ireland), Dr Sheila Kidd, Mrs Marilyn Kristiansen, Ronnie Laing, Bill Lawson, Cathlin MacAulay, Alastair McIntosh, Dr Margaret A. Mackay, Fiona Mackenzie, Roddy Maclean, Nicholas Maclean-Bristol, Dennis MacNeil, Paddy McNicol, Professor Donald Meek, Donald R. Morrison, John Murdo Morrison, Peadar Ó Donnghaile, David Potts, Seumas Simpson, Mrs Mairi Smith (Oban and Australia), the late Insa Thierling, Ian Weir and Alex Woolf. For all surviving errors (other than JGC's!) I take full responsibility.

I am indebted to the staffs of the National Library of Scotland, Edinburgh Central Library, Edinburgh University Library, the General Register Office for Scotland, the National Archives of Scotland, Glasgow University Library, the Mitchell Library, New College Library, Moray House Library and Edinburgh City Archives for their unending patience and courtesy. I should like to thank Donnie Munro for the sketch at p. 491, my daughter Catrìona for her painting of JGC, and my wife Màire for many things, especially genealogical research.

I am grateful to Edinburgh University Library (Department of Special Collections), Glasgow University Library, the National Archives of Scotland, the School of Scottish Studies and the Trustees of the National Library of Scotland for permission to quote from manuscripts (or tapes) in their care, to the editors of *The Scottish Historical Review* for permission to reprint 'The Origin of the Fairy Creed', to Angela Bourke and Pimlico for so graciously allowing me to quote at length from *The Burning of Bridget Cleary* (see p. lxi), and to Ian McCormack, editor of the *West Highland Free Press*, for inviting me to contribute the fortnightly articles which furnished the basis for my introduction. Last but not least, I would like to express my debt of gratitude to Margaret Bennett, who first introduced me to the work of John Gregorson Campbell, and to Linda Gowans, in whose publications I found the clues that brought me to his 'Lost Appendix'.

Regrettably, vol. 62 of the *Transactions of the Gaelic Society of Inverness*, which contains a remarkable quantity of material relevant to the present work (on the MacCrimmons and Cremona, the Blind Piper and *Call Ghàig*) appeared too late to be taken into consideration. Nevertheless, I hope the fairly wide range of reference to printed sources which I have provided will be useful.

I wish I could say the same for manuscripts. At the end of this two-year darg I am left with the overwhelming feeling that something must be done to make the manuscript resources for the study of Gaelic folklore more accessible – by which I mean catalogues and indexes for scholars, leading to a series of attractive publications for the general reader, based on islands and districts. As a start, I look forward to seeing the fruits of Dr Allan Turner's analysis of R. C. Maclagan's magnificent collection.

If JGC's splendid work serves as a model for such approaches, and if my commentaries on it are helpful, it will have been well worth the trouble. JGC's and mine.

Ronald Black
Peebles, February 2005

INTRODUCTION

John Gregorson Campbell's *Superstitions of the Highlands and Islands of Scotland* (*SHIS*) and *Witchcraft and Second Sight in the Highlands and Islands of Scotland* (*WSS*) are surely among the most important folklore collections ever published. The closest comparison is with Alexander Carmichael's magnificent *Carmina Gadelica* (*CG*), which came out in six volumes between 1900 and 1974. In *CG*, however, primacy was given to the Gaelic texts, which appeared with facing English translation, Carmichael's notes on traditions being strictly secondary; JGC's books consisted of a discourse in English organised in chapters, Gaelic originals appearing only in the form of key phrases in brackets and slightly more extended quotations in footnotes.

Does this mean that JGC's work is less reliable than Carmichael's, or less useful? After all, the authenticity of Carmichael's work has itself been called into question, indeed the debate about it formed the most important academic controversy in Scottish Gaelic studies in the twentieth century. *Carmina* took three quarters of the century to come out, then the last quarter was spent debating it.[1] The late Alan Bruford included JGC in his criticisms: "John Gregorson Campbell . . . very likely never took down a complete Gaelic prose text, but rewrote stories from English summaries with notes of the more unusual Gaelic words and phrases, such as make up most of his posthumous publications. *Sir Uallabh O'Corn* . . . reads like a complete repertoire of descriptive 'runs' – far too many for any storyteller to use in a single tale – linked by a few sentences of narrative."[2]

This is a sweeping judgement and a serious accusation, although I doubt if it can be substantiated, and indeed, after making a detailed comparison of JGC's manuscript and printed texts of 'Sir Uallabh O Corn' Linda Gowans concluded (1998, p. 40) that the working-up of the story as a *tour de force* could be imputed largely to the teller Donald Cameron. The authenticity of JGC's work is an issue that goes well beyond the matter of narrative style, however, as *SHIS* and *WSS* are frequently the only source for some fundamental point, such as the description of the water-horse as having 'a sharp bill (*gob biorach*), or, as others describe it, a narrow brown slippery snout' (p. 109), or the name in Skye for Handsel Monday being *Di-Luain Traosta* (p. 539). It is particularly worrying that the books came out a decade after JGC's death in 1891. Are they the work of a champion of folklore scholarship – or of a charlatan?

In 1871 JGC corresponded with the great pioneer of scientific folktale collection, John Francis Campbell of Islay (JFC). "I am much obliged by your promise to put some one to write for me," JFC wrote on 28 March that year (Campbell 1895, pp. 139–40). "If he writes from dictation will you kindly *beg him to follow the words spoken* without regard to his own opinion, or to what they ought to be. I speak English, but when I come to read Chaucer I find words that I am not used to. So it is when men who speak Gaelic begin to write old stories . . . If you are sceptical I hold to my creed of the people. But creed or no creed I want to get the tradition as it exists and I would not give a snuff for 'cooked' tradition."

JGC's translations were sometimes too literal, sometimes too interpretative, but he never ceased to stress that what he printed in Gaelic was what he had heard. Bad grammar such as *gas feur* (p. 544) suggests to me the opposite of Bruford's point, and even when I make emendations to JGC's text as conventional as '*Mhàrt*, SEED-TIME' (*WSS* 255) to '*MÀRT*, SEED-TIME' (p. 545), I am left with the uncomfortable feeling that I have done a little bit of cooking myself. JGC wrote *SHIS* and *WSS* in the period immediately following his correspondence with JFC, and when he published 'The Muileartach' in 1881 he said (Campbell 1881b, p. 117, cf. 1891, p. 135): "For archæological or other scientific purpose, it is essential that ballads of this kind, and indeed everything got from oral sources, should be presented to the reader 'uncooked', that is, without suppression or addition, or alteration, which is not pointed out."

In his preface (pp. lxxxiii–lxxxiv below) JGC pays tribute to the intelligence of his informants, and stresses that he uses no sources but the mouths of the people – no books, no letters. Three years before his death he said of himself, spurning the newfangled term 'folk-lore' in favour of the more familiar 'antiquities' (Campbell 1888–89, p. 50): "The object of the writer has always been, in all matters affecting Celtic antiquities, to make whatever he deems worthy of preservation, as available and reliable to the reader as to himself, without addition, suppression, or embellishment."

Accuracy and authenticity were clearly of great importance to JGC. He lectures Carmichael on the need to be faithful to his materials (p. 678 below), and even turns upon his master (p. 275). He can no longer be accused of omitting the Gaelic originals of quoted texts from *SHIS* and *WSS*, because my evidence suggests that this was done by his publisher after his death (pp. 687–88). My systematic comparisons between his texts of charms and those in *CG* exonerate him completely of any charges of fabrication, but leave one wondering exactly how Carmichael achieved *his* renderings, which tend to be larger and fuller. Perhaps it is no coincidence that *SHIS* and *WSS* appeared right on the heels of *CG*, as if as a corrective.

JGC was one of a number of folklorists active in Gaelic Scotland during the second half of the nineteenth century. Each has his distinctive legacy. We think of JGC for superstitions just as we think of JFC and his assistants (Hector MacLean, John Dewar) for tales and ballads, of Sheriff Nicolson and the Rev. Duncan Campbell for proverbs, of Alexander Carmichael for charms and incantations; and there were others of great importance – such as Fr Allan McDonald, Dr Robert Craig Maclagan, Lady Evelyn Stewart-Murray and the Rev. Neil Campbell – whose regional collections of general folklore have yet to be published in their own right. Their era was the high noon of scientific folklore, and the richness and abundance of the harvest which they reaped put Gaelic Scotland right at the forefront of what was then an international movement. It had begun in Germany with the brothers Grimm, in Scotland with Sir Walter Scott (who put folklore at the service of fiction, but kept it separate through a structure of introductions and notes), and in Ireland with Thomas Crofton Croker (who simply fictionalised folklore). The first work of Highland folklore was William Grant Stewart's *Popular Superstitions and Festive Amusements* of 1823; we can see JGC imitating its structure, more or less, for Stewart presented ghosts, Fairies, brownies, water-kelpies, spunkies, witchcraft and 'festive amusements' (the traditional calendar) in that order. Lowland superstitions were collected by James Napier in the south-west and the Rev. Walter Gregor in the north-east, Gregor's work being built upon in turn by J. M. McPherson in the following century. "As Gregor advanced over Napier," says Dorson (1968, p. 417), "so John Gregorson Campbell advanced over Gregor . . . by printing texts of narratives embodying beliefs rather than simply enumerating the bare beliefs. In this respect the mistitled *Superstitions* resembled the *Fairy Legends* of Croker, save that Campbell properly gave the exact words of the tellers."

We may take Dorson's point one step further. JGC thought, read and wrote deeply about the meaning of what he had collected. Not only in 'The Origin of the Fairy Creed', but also in *SHIS* and *WSS* themselves, he was careful to place his stories, customs, beliefs and traditions in their intellectual context. When he refers to Phoenician deities, to 'personifications of the generative and receptive powers of nature', to myths of the sun and moon, and to human sacrifice, as he does for example at pp. 552–53 and 570, he is responding vigorously to the debates of his day, particularly those engendered by the solar theories of Max Müller as expounded in such erudite works as *Comparative Mythology* (1856), *Lectures on the Science of Language* (1861–64), *Chips from a German Workshop* (1867–75) and *Introduction to the Science of Religion* (1873). Müller found the sun, moon and stars in everything, seeing JFC's frog king, for example, as a solar hero traceable back to the Sanskrit, even though JFC himself, as Dorson points out (1968, p. 401), thought the story to be of Gaelic origin, given that the utterances of the enchanted frog sounded like the 'gurgling and quarking' of real frogs in springtime. JGC, who knew a thing or two about the king frog himself (see pp. 221–22), was polite but sceptical (see p. 552 especially), and Müller's ideas have few adherents today.

STORIES

The Gaelic Otherworld is full of stories. Many of them ask more questions than they answer. In the ceilidh-house there would be silence after some one told stories like these, then others would speak, one by one, some with opinions, some with facts, some with fresh stories and songs as well – one at the back perhaps who knew a man who knew the man it was about, another who only knew his genealogy, one at the front who had sailed the seven seas and brought a knowledge of the world to bear, a woman who denounced the appalling treatment of her sex, a sceptic who pointed out that until people stopped blaming Fairies for social ills the world could never be made better, another who retorted that as Fairies are mentioned in the Bible, disbelief in them is tantamount to disbelief in God.

JGC collected his material in the period 1850–74, which suggests that many of his informants were born in the eighteenth century, and indeed many of the stories have an eighteenth-century atmosphere. We are told that in Highland Perthshire before 1745 each farm or village had a *bodachan sabhail* (p. 102), and that *MacChaluim a' Chrònain* lived in Glen Etive after 1745 (p. 48). The American War of Independence is mentioned at p. 58. Corn appears more often than potatoes, which did not become the basis of subsistence in the Highlands until after 1770 (Fenton 1976, p. 116). A story is told of an eighteenth-century factor's son (p. 113), and one about a Fairy cow is placed 'about the end of last century' (p. 71). Land is described as under runrig, a form of tenure abolished in the early nineteenth century ('the village in these days was in common, ridge about', p. 50). Tales are told at p. 176 of Donald Livingstone (1728–1816) and the Rev. Lachlan MacKenzie (1754–1819). And so on.

In this essay I will seek explanations for the stories. This means exploring the eighteenth-century Highland dimension, placing JGC's 'Origin of the Fairy Creed' in its historiographical context, adding breadth and depth from his own period by making particular reference to the work of Yeats and Lady Gregory, and pulling these threads together using the sociological approach preferred by twenty-first-century folklorists. I will begin with Robert Kirk and traditional Fairy aetiologies, then move on to JGC's and other nineteenth-century readings of these. I will consider Fairies as the product of dreams and, conversely, as ways of visualising the unseen. This raises the issue of how – especially for women and children – the Fairies serve as a code for dealing with difficult aspects of everyday life, which I will discuss in turn: housekeeping; childcare; relocation, migration, separation, bereavement; pregnancy, sickness, death; alcohol addiction; sex (homosexual, heterosexual); murder; other types of violence – physical, mental, spiritual, male-on-female, female-on-male, self-inflicted. This leads to the aetiology of changelings and to the sadistic methods employed to get rid of them. Finally, before reaching conclusions, I will argue that fear of kidnapping should be regarded as one of the aspects of everyday life which were codified into Fairy belief, and briefly consider the role of the alternative cosmologies presented by JGC – the otherworlds of spirits and of witches.

WHO ARE THE FAIRIES? ROBERT KIRK

During the Middle Ages witches were not persecuted, the idea not yet having taken root that the practice of charms involved a compact with the devil; neither was there a clear view with regard to Fairies. The beginnings of the problem of their origins are summed up by JGC's contemporary Edwin Sidney Hartland (1891, p. 341): "Mediæval writers (especially ecclesiastics) were in a difficulty in describing fairies. They looked upon them as having an objective existence; and yet they knew not how to classify them. Fairies were certainly neither departed saints nor holy angels. Beside these two kinds of spirits, the only choice left was between devils and ghosts of the wicked dead, or, at most, of the dead who had no claims to extraordinary goodness. They did not believe in any other creatures which could be identified with these mysterious elves. It is no wonder, therefore, if they were occasionally perplexed, occasionally inconsistent, sometimes denouncing them as devils, at other times dismissing them as ghosts."

In the early modern era the task of finding the Fairies a respectable place in theology was left to the Rev. Robert Kirk of Aberfoyle (1644–92). Kirk and his 'Secret Commonwealth' have been reassessed many times (see for example Henderson and Cowan 2001, pp. 171–76), but no one has done more than Michael Hunter to place them in the intellectual context of their time. Hunter's *The Occult Laboratory* (2001) demonstrates how academics of the late seventeenth century in both England and Scotland recognised the Highlands and Islands as an area in which the occult was extraordinarily close to the surface of people's lives. It was a laboratory in which searching questions could be asked, evidence collected, theories tested. In 'The Secret Commonwealth', however, they received not an objective report by an independent observer but a misguided attempt to please them by rationalising the irrational.

Kirk has been called a 'walker between two worlds', and this is true, but not in the sense in which it was intended. His parents were Edinburgh people through and through. His father, James Kirk (1609–58), had the misfortune to be appointed to the Perthshire parish of Aberfoyle in 1639, during an era in which the Protestant church, divided into Presbyterian and Episcopalian factions, was struggling to extend its sway across the Highlands. James Kirk appears not to have been accepted by the people of Aberfoyle at first, and no wonder – he would have been incapable of making himself understood in the pulpit, because in his day and for long afterwards the parish was entirely Gaelic-speaking.[3] Robert, the youngest of his seven sons, was born in this period, and there is every sign that he made a conscious decision to continue his father's heroic attempt to bring the Gospel to this part of Perthshire. After all, there was nothing that the Church needed more than Lowland ministers who spoke the Highland tongue. His siblings by no means felt the same way – his elder brother George, for example, was apprenticed to a tailor in Edinburgh in 1658 and became a burgess of the city in 1667.[4]

Probably George was born too early in his father's career to accept the dangerous and incomprehensible Gaelic-speaking world which lay outside the manse of Aberfoyle. Robert, by contrast, with his sense of adventure and his intellectual curiosity, 'went native', made friends, willingly accepted a call to the neighbouring parish of Balquhidder at the age of 19, and moved just as happily to his late father's parish at the age of 40. It is in this sense that he became a 'walker between two worlds'. When asked to transliterate the Irish Bible into Roman script he obliged with enthusiasm, even appending a vocabulary, the first makings of a Scottish Gaelic dictionary. Had he then been asked to write a primer of Scottish Gaelic according to the conventions of Latin grammar, he would happily have done so. What he was asked to do, however, was even more interesting: he was invited by Oxford dignitaries to write the spooks who surrounded him in Aberfoyle into the system of theology which he had studied at St Andrews and which he now preached from his pulpit. As an Episcopalian and a believer in religious tolerance he must have seen his commission as an appropriate metaphor for political inclusion. Equally, the story that he himself did not die but went to Fairyland is itself a metaphor for the extraordinary way in which, as an outsider, he had integrated himself into the Gaelic community in which his father's profession had placed him.

Kirk has sometimes been associated with the anonymous 'Collection of Highland Rites and Customes'. As one of the most valuable ethnographic accounts of the Highlands in the early modern period, I refer to it repeatedly in my notes on JGC's text. The late John Lorne Campbell (1975, pp. 5, 58, 85) regarded the Rev. James Kirkwood, a native of Dunbar in East Lothian who became parson of Astwick in Bedfordshire, as the author of the text, while also pointing out that 'the possibility that Kirk was the original author of most of the *Collection* cannot be ignored'. Michael Hunter rejected both (2001, pp. 36–37), suggesting as alternatives William Houston, David Abercromby and the earl of Perth. To my mind, the text yields four clues as to authorship: (1) it is by a Gaelic speaker; (2) being written entirely in the third person ('They borrow . . .', 'They reckon . . .', 'They have . . .'), it is not by a native Gael; (3) it is by a person with particular knowledge of Teviotdale, the Merse and East Lothian; (4) it is by a person with particular knowledge of south Perthshire. Point (4) relates to the very first paragraph (Hunter 2001, p. 54, cf. Campbell 1975, p. 17): "They borrow the names of Feasts moveable & immovable from the Christian Account; onely they have mercat days held in Saints names unknown in other Languages as Feil Seirbh (thought to be St. Serf or Serbanus) Feil Domhingart, makessag, haden, moden &c."

This is not a list produced by a traveller who had roamed the length and breadth of the Highlands, nor by a scholar deeply learned in religious history, for it excludes all the great saints in whose names prayers were said, charms muttered, days kept and fairs held across a wide area – Patrick of Armagh, Calum Cille of Iona, Ma-Ruibhe of Applecross, Mo Luag of Lismore, Michael the Archangel, Brendan the Navigator, Fillan of Strathfillan, Finnan of Lochaber, Donnan of Eigg. No, it is a list produced by one who had heard the names of minor saints spoken on market days in some restricted locality. Serf is patron of Culross, and my only other source for the Gaelic name *Féill Seirbh* is a Balquhidder one (Black 1996, p. 48). 'Domhingart' is the Pictish name Domangart. There was such a saint (Macbain 1897–98, p. 163), but the last syllable is marked in the manuscript as doubtful (Campbell 1975, p. 17; Hunter 2001, p. 54), and probably what the writer heard was *Féill Domhnaigh*, *Féill Dòmhnaich* 'the Sunday Festival'.[5] He claims later that 'they think the Lords Day is consecrat to ane Angel called Domhin' (Hunter 2001, p. 72), and this can only be *Dòmhnach*, Dominicus, the Lord. 'Makessag', *Mo Cheasag*, is patron of Luss and Callander, and 'Haden' and 'Moden' will be for *Th' Aodhan* and *M' Aodhan* – Aidan, patron of Roseneath and Glendaruel (Watson 1926a, pp. 277–78, 289). The area delineated is relatively small and has Kirk's two parishes of Balquhidder and Aberfoyle at its centre. I would conclude therefore that Kirk is the principal author of the text. He had no known connection with Teviotdale, the Merse or East Lothian, however; that looks like Kirkwood, and it is noticeable that information referring to these areas is always given at the end of the sections into which the text is divided – with the exception of the final section, no. 47, 'Rarities', which consists entirely of material from these three districts. No. 14, 'Their Monuments', ranges from Iona through Stormond and Meigle in east Perthshire to Galloway, leaving it impossible to guess where Kirk's contribution breaks off and Kirkwood's begins. This, then, explains why the 'Highland Rites and Customes' are anonymous – they were written by Kirk but added to by Kirkwood, who in his day was the better known of the pair. As references to this text in my notes involve Highland material only, I cite 'Kirk(?)' as the author.

What Kirk(?) says about the beliefs of the Gael in the 'Rites and Customes', as opposed to the 'Secret Commonwealth', may be regarded as the more valuable for being unprovoked and unostentatious: "They'l not sleep on a Fayry hill . . . They say the Elfs feed on the faison of our corn whereof they make an Excellent Liquor. Others of Grosser Bodies are heard to take Bread . . . The *Second Sight* descends from Father to Son for some Generations. These who have it can prevent the Evil which doth threaten others, but cannot save themselves. It's so very troublsome to many, that theyd be gladly free from it. These persons observe that Spirits are great Lovers of Flesh & they see them sometimes taking Flesh out of the pots, putting that which is worse in its place, of whilk they'l not taste. Those who have this foresight by compact give Responses being ask'd. Sometymes they bring back to life these who are giving up the Ghost; but an other dies in his place, & it always provs fatal . . . In the night time they will not call upon children by their name, least the Devil get power over them. When persons of elder years are called on in the night by their name, they'l not answear unless they be called 3 times, fearing that it is a Spirit."[6]

In the 'Secret Commonwealth' Kirk tells us much that we know from other sources about otherworld beings and second sight, much that is abstract and philosophical, and also, admittedly, much that is of interest. On the origin of the Fairies he comments guardedly that some speak of them as 'departed souls', some as 'Astral Bodies', some as 'a numerous people by themselves, having their own polities'. As we emerge into a more modern critical atmosphere, we come to recognise these as three distinct strands of belief, all of which will appear here and there in the discussion that follows: Fairies as souls of the dead, as fallen angels or gods, and as an underground race. This means that in any more general discussion of the Fairies their mortality will be uncertain, as when Dalyell remarks (1834, pp. 536, 538): "The *Siths* vanished at the name of God or Jesus. They were of both sexes, and like mankind, they were mortal . . . They were believed to be skilful in the medical art, which they sometimes imparted to mortals."

The belief in Fairies as fallen angels (the motif 'Fall with Lucifer', MacDonald 1994–95, p. 43) derives ultimately from Rev. 12: 7-9: "And there was war in heaven: Michael and his angels fought against the dragon; and the dragon fought and his angels, and prevailed not; neither was their place found any more in heaven. And the great dragon was cast out, that old serpent, called the Devil, and Satan, which deceiveth the whole world: he was cast out into the earth, and his angels were cast out with him." The people knew from personal experience, however, that every war has its non-combatants. They must also have been conscious that they themselves possessed many beliefs which could not be comprehended by a simple choice between Christian good and Satanic evil. This traditional view is crisply presented by Carleton (1854, pp. 72–73). "The general opinion, at least in Ireland, is, that during the war of Lucifer in Heaven, the angels were divided into three classes. The first class consisted of those faithful spirits who at once, and without hesitation, adhered to the standard of the Omnipotent; the next consisted of those who openly rebelled, and followed the great apostate, sharing eternal perdition with him; the third and last consisted of those who, during the mighty clash and uproar of the contending hosts, stood timidly aloof, and refused to join either power. These, says the tradition, were hurled out of Heaven, some upon Earth, and some into the waters of the Earth, where they are to remain, ignorant of their fate, until the day of judgment. They know their own power, however, and it is said that nothing but their hopes of salvation prevent them from at once annihilating the whole human race . . . It is generally supposed by the people that this singular class of fictitious creatures enjoy, as a kind of right, the richest and best of all the fruits of the earth, and that the top grain of wheat, oats, &c., and the ripest apple, pear, &c., all belong to them, and are taken as their own exclusive property."

In Wales, by contrast, which had lost sight of its medieval Catholic tradition, the 'fallen angels' explanation ceased to be widely heard. The Celtic scholar Sir John Rhŷs (1840-1915) subscribed to a formula which accepted the theories of the gods and of the underground race, and chose to define the elusive x-factor simply as 'imagination' (Wentz 1911, p. 137): "Some characteristics of the fairies seem to argue an ancient race, while other characteristics betray their origin in the workshop of the imagination; but generally speaking, the fairies are heterogeneous, consisting partly of the divinities of glens and forests and mountains, and partly of an early race of men more or less caricatured and equipped by fable with impossible attributes."

'THE ORIGIN OF THE FAIRY CREED'

JGC's 'Origin of the Fairy Creed' was written about 1880 (see pp. lxxxv–xciii below). In it he rightly stresses the universality of Fairy beliefs, and could have gone much further. He also (again correctly in my view) points out the similarity of the Fairies to the deities of Greece and Rome; had he been more familiar with Irish mythology, he would no doubt have extended the comparison in that direction. As at p. 104, he dismisses theories that would derive Fairies from Lamiae, Fauns and Druids (cf. MacRitchie 1909–10b and Wentz 1911, p. 432), while finding that the idea of the Fairies as an alien race has much in its favour. He is cautious of hypotheses such as MacRitchie's (1890) which identify the race or races in question – Finns, Lapps, Eskimos – and prefers to fall back on the term 'allophylian'. In conversation with Alexander Carmichael he went only so far as to acknowledge his belief that 'a race similar to the Lapps lived in Scotland about the Glacial period' (*CG2*, p. 232). But he is well on the way to accepting that belief in the Fairies provides a mechanism for confronting issues of race.

To proponents of the racial theory such as MacRitchie (1890, 1907–08, 1909–10a), W. C. Mackenzie (1905) or the Hon. Stuart Ruaraidh Erskine of Mar ('Sithiche'), the Fairies were a primitive people, a conquered clan who lived in holes in the ground (see Bord 1997, pp. 142–45). MacRitchie (1912–13, pp. 290, 293, 295) seized on JGC's translation of *amhuisgean* as 'dwarfs, pygmies' (Campbell 1889–90) with delight. 'Sithiche' points out (1912, p. 351) that JGC shows in *SHIS* that running streams could be crossed by Fairies, but not by evil spirits, ghosts or apparitions; that evil spirits fled at cock-crow, while Fairies could be seen by day as well as night; and that 'a well-marked characteristic is the tinge of the ludicrous that pervades the creed'. He concludes that, although JGC 'gives no hint of any knowledge of any pygmy theory', Fairies can only be explained as folk memories of a race of black pygmies, 'memories that is to say, of a human race, a race of flesh and [blood], not of spirits, nor yet of imaginary creatures evolved by man out of his own innate animism'. This scarcely serves to explain the magnificence of their palaces, however, nor the strength of their hold over human beings, and JGC points to the difficulty of explaining their relationship with iron – they have smithies of their own, yet are cowed by that metal in any shape or form. "It is anomalous," says JGC (p. xci), "that they should have this wonderful knowledge, and have smithies in their brughs, while at the same time they had the simplicity of Arcadians and were kept away by iron."

This leads JGC to place ambiguity at the very centre of his argument. "The Fairy Creed . . . is of ethical rather than ethnical origin. It is moral and instructive, and not historical or mythological . . . The Fairy Creed is a polished and amusing satire on the vanity of human pleasures and the emptiness of what is commonly called 'life'."

This is our pastor talking, and it is a pity that he does not speculate further upon the coded nature of the stories. At p. 183 he is willing to see a gull as a head wind and a cormorant as a favourable tide, but in the 'Fairy Creed' he fails to extend this principle into codes of human behaviour. Instead he continues to worry about the anomalous place of iron in his theory, and ultimately falls back on an incremental approach (p. xciii): "Perhaps when the creed first arose, and the Fairies were made a race dwelling by themselves, the traditions of the stone savages still remained. The whole of the rest of the creed is explained by the Elves being appearance and nothing else, the semblance of mankind without the reality . . . In giving form and expression to this truth or teaching, the traditions and existence of an alien race may have been taken advantage of, and the ethical explanation of the superstition may include the ethnical."

Before suddenly breaking off the argument – his essay looks unfinished – JGC reinforces his new-found methodology by pointing out that 'the moral teaching became a superstition'. From race to ethics to superstition: these are not necessarily the correct elements, but the emphasis on organic development rings true, and one feels a sense of relief that at last a writer who knows the Fairies as intimately as JGC has invited us to think of them as an ethical and moral construct.

At the time of its writing 'The Origin of the Fairy Creed' was at the forefront of understanding. In *The Science of Fairy Tales*, published in the year of JGC's death, Hartland came down firmly against the ethnic theory, rejected that of the 'spectres of the dead', and pronounced in favour of an anthropological explanation which saw Fairies, ghosts and witches as survivors of an archaic system of belief in spirits, transformations and witchcraft common to all 'savage tribes', modified in subtly different ways by different cultures.[7] Even as he reached this comforting conclusion, however, Hartland revealed gnawing uncertainty as to how it might – or might not – nibble at the pillars of Western civilisation. Did the Biblical account of creation depict a race of savages? Not necessarily. Would over-zealous investigation reveal a canker under the surface of modern society? This must be avoided. Picking his words with great care, he declared: "It is not asserted that the status of savagery was the primitive condition of men. Of course it may have been. But if not, there is work to be done in endeavouring to ascertain what lies behind it. The questions started from this point wander across the border of folklore into pure psychology; but it is a psychology based not upon introspection and analysis of the mind of the civilized man, developed under the complex influences that have been acting and reacting during untold years of upward struggling, always arduous and often cruel, but a psychology which must be painfully reconstructed from the simplest and most archaic phenomena disclosed by anthropological research. Who can say what light may not thus be thrown as well on the destiny as on the origin of mankind?"

Hartland's 'psychology' represents a logical step forward from JGC's 'ethics', and is much more helpful than Rhŷs's 'imagination', but 'psychology' did not mean quite the same in the nineteenth as it does in the twenty-first century. Aided by the highly-respected folklorist Andrew Lang (1844–1912), W. Y. Evans Wentz concluded, after extensive fieldwork and research (1911, pp. 477, 491), that 'the living Fairy-Faith depends not so much upon ancient traditions, oral and recorded, as upon recent and contemporary psychical experiences, vouched for by many "seers" and other percipients among our witnesses'. He added that 'since the residuum or x-quantity of the Fairy-Faith, the folk-religion of the Celtic peoples, cannot be explained away by any known scientific laws, it must for the present stand, and the Psychological Theory of the Nature and Origin of the Belief in Fairies in Celtic Countries is to be considered as hypothetically established in the eyes of Science'.[8] Fortunately the search for the truth about the Fairies was pushing spiritualism to one side and moving in a sociological direction – even Wentz touched upon it accidentally (1911, p. 136) when he spoke of how 'some of these stories suggest how weak and sickly children became the objects of systematic cruelty at the hands of even their own parents'.

YEATS AND LADY GREGORY

Hartland would doubtless have been relieved that a breakthrough was about to be made by examination of a society which was not 'civilized' in the sense in which he intended the word. The researches of Lady Gregory and the young W. B. Yeats in the west of Ireland yielded phenomena that were 'simple' and 'archaic' enough to fulfil his demands. In *The Life of W. B. Yeats* Terence Brown writes (1999, p. 20): "When Yeats came at the end of the 1890s to do the fieldwork which gave him an even more intimate knowledge of such Irish folklore as the changeling motif, the six articles he wrote subsequently on the subject (drawing on Lady Gregory's manuscript, which deals with County Clare as well as County Galway) reinforce the impression . . . that such beliefs have social and psychological significance. They seem to be ways of explaining and coping with the manifold shocks and sorrows of a rugged rural life of peasant poverty in an unrelenting environment. The accidents, drownings, mysterious illnesses, sudden deaths (particularly of children), in which the church and the local healer, a redoubtable woman, compete for social power, are given some kind of meaning for the people in the narratives of the supernatural world interacting with the natural . . . Yeats seems aware of the sociological and psychological import of what he has been observing."

Yet Yeats, too, was of his time. It is insufficient to point out that he was a lyric poet with an idealised vision of rural Ireland. When he confronts the changeling motif, says Brown (1999, p. 20), he 'emphasizes the magical, even religious, significance of the occurrences he reports'. Magic and religion were the bread and butter of the anthropologists of Yeats's time – Frazer, Hartland, Lang – and it takes a late-twentieth-century mind to state, as does Brown (*ibid.*): "It is perfectly clear in these detailed accounts of personality changes, which are attributed to a changeling being left by the fairies, that such tales of the 'taken' and of those who are 'away' deal with the onset and the course of mental illnesses of one kind or another – depression, madness."

After that it seems almost superfluous to point out that in Scotland to be 'away with the Fairies' is slang for bizarre or insane behaviour, or, as JGC puts it (p. 20), when a person does a senseless action, he is said to have been 'taken out of himself' (*air a thoirt ás*) by the Fairies. Yeats himself comments (Welch 1993, pp. 316–17): "The ancient peoples from whom the country people inherit their belief had to explain how, when you were 'away', as it seemed to you, you seemed, it might be, to your neighbours or your family, to be lying in a faint upon the ground, or in your bed, or even going about your daily work. It was probably one who was himself 'away' who explained, that somebody or something was put in your place, and this explanation was the only possible one to ancient peoples, who did not make our distinction between body and soul. The Irish country people always insist that something, a heap of shavings or a broomstick or a wooden image, or some dead person, 'maybe some old warrior', or some dead relative or neighbour of your own, is put in your place, though sometimes they will forget their belief until you remind them, and talk of 'the others' having put such and such a person 'into a faint', or of such and such a person being 'away' and being ill in bed."

A good example of a story noted by Yeats and Lady Gregory which is best put down to psychosis, poverty, hunger, physical illness and family discord is the autobiography of an old man from the borders of Clare and Galway (Welch 1993, pp. 264–65, cf. Gregory 1970, pp. 63–68). "When I went to look for a wife, I went to the house, and there was a hen and a brood of small chickens before the door. Well, after I went home, one of the chickens died. And what do you think they said, but that it was I overlooked it."

By 'overlooked' he means destroyed by the evil eye, just as eighty hens were killed at a glance by Gilbride Macintyre (p. 203 below). Yeats points out that in due course Langan (as he calls him) married the woman anyway, but that the Fairies tried to take her the day after the marriage, using his feelings about her as their link between her and them. By this he is referring to the 'eye', just as was alleged by his in-laws about the chickens, for if a person looks at anybody or anything with envy, desire or admiration, it may be used by the Fairies as a link between them and the thing or person they covet. "They take a child through the eye of its father, a wife through the eye of her husband."

That is what happened to Langan – or 'Saggarton', as Lady Gregory chose to call him. "My wife got a touch from them, and they have a watch on her ever since. It was the day after I married, and I went to the fair of Clarenbridge. And when I came back the house was full of smoke, but there was nothing on the hearth but cinders, and the smoke was more like the smoke of a forge. And she was within lying on the bed, and her brother was sitting outside the door crying."

It may sound to us at best like poor housekeeping, at worst like a failed attempt by a sad woman to burn the house down, but Yeats chooses instead to point out that the Fairies are well known for their skill as smiths; what follows he describes as a test for hypnosis rather than (as we might assume today) for fear, madness or abuse. Langan tells him: "I took down a fork from the rafters, and asked her was it a broom, and she said it was. So then I went to the mother and asked her to come in, and she was crying too, and she knew well what had happened, but she didn't tell me, but she sent for the priest. And when he came, he sent me for Geoghagan, and that was only an excuse to get me away, and what he and the mother tried was to get her to face death. But the wife was very stout, and she wouldn't give in to them. So the priest read mass, and he asked me, would I be willing to lose something. And I said, so far as a cow or a calf, I wouldn't mind losing that. Well, she partly recovered, but from that day no year went by, but I lost ten lambs maybe, or other things. And twice they took my children out of the bed, two of them I have lost. And the others they gave a touch to. That girl there, see the way she is, and she is not able to walk. In one minute it came on her, out in the field, with the fall of a wall."

Yeats describes how Langan told his daughter to come out from where she sat in the corner of the chimney. She had the same dazed, vacant look as on the faces of the other children. She staggered for a foot or two, then sat down again. "From our point of view," says Yeats, "her body was paralysed and her mind gone. She was tall and gentle-looking, and should have been a strong, comely, country girl."

Langan continued: "Another time the wife got a touch, and she got it again, and the third time she got up in the morning, and went out of the house and never said where she was going. But I had her watched, and I told the boy to follow her, and never to lose sight of her. And I gave him the sign to make if he'd meet any bad thing. So he followed her, and she kept before him, and while he was going along the road, something was up on top of the wall with one leg. A red-haired man it was, with a thin face and no legs. But the boy got hold of him and made the sign, and carried him till he came to the bridge. At first he could not lift him, but after he had made the sign he was quite light. And the woman turned home again, and never had a touch after.

"It's a good job the boy had been taught the sign. It was one among them that wanted the wife. A woman and a boy we often saw coming to the door, and she was the matchmaker. And when we would go out, they would have vanished."

The sign is one with the thumb that Langan had demonstrated to Yeats (Welch 1993, p. 261), saying that a person who held out his hand like that would come to no harm from the Fairies. Yeats met Langan's wife, and found her to be 'a big, smiling woman'. It is a strange and disturbing story.

SOULS OF THE DEAD, FALLEN ANGELS, OR AN UNDERGROUND RACE?

In Yeats's world, who exactly *are* the Fairies? First of all, he makes it clear that the three main possible origins mentioned above all remain in the field, for he speaks of 'the gentry, or "the others", or "the fairies", or "the sidhe", or the "forgetful people", as they call the dead and the lesser gods of ancient times' (Welch 1993, p. 308). A man in Co. Galway said, "Fallen Angels they are, and after the fall God said, 'Let there be Hell,' and there it was in a moment!"[9]

This is in line with the native Catholic tradition of Scotland as noted by Fr Allan McDonald, who got it from Fr Alexander Campbell, who had got it *c.* 1825 from Iain mac Iain 'ic Iain 'ic Aonghais, 'Bàrd Laisgeir', at Askernish in South Uist (EUL MS CW 58A, f. 21v, cf. Watson 1908–09, pp. 56–57). "The fairies are supposed to belong to the angelic order of beings. It is thought that they remained neutral in the revolt of the Angels, & that they had to go through a second trial on earth to testify their fidelity. Many say that their time has now elapsed, the date of the cessation of their trial being within the last 50 years. This however is disputed ...

"In Harris two men were engaged at the tillage. While so engaged at 12 o'clock noon one was observed to fix his gaze always in a certain direction. His companion asked the reason of his gazing so persistently every day at the same hour in the same direction. He then told that he saw every day at this hour a countless multitude of people travelling east one day & west the next. His companion desired to see them also. 'If you wish to see them, place your foot on my foot when you see me standing & gazing at them, & the vision will be imparted to you.'"[10]

The man did this, saw the people, and at once set off towards them and asked them who they were. One of them broke ranks and declared:

Chan ann de shìol Àdhaimh sinn
'S chan e Àbraham ar n-athair,
Ach tha sinn de mhuinntir an aingil uaibhrich
Chaidh fhuadach a-mach á flathas.

("We are not of Adam's race / And Abraham is not our father, / But we're descended from the proud angel / Who was expelled from paradise.")

Fr Allan also appears to have been told that when God ordered the angels to stop fighting, those who fell upon the land became the Fairies, those who remained in the sky became the *fir-chlis, fir-chlisneach* or northern lights, and those who fell among the rocks became the *mac talla* or echo (Freer 1902, p. 44). This corresponds fairly closely to what JGC heard in Skye (p. 107 below); JGC also noted a particular connection between the fallen angels and Beltane (p. 554). In Caithness, he says, the angels became seals (p. 156); this belief also exists in Rathlin, where Linda-May Ballard was told that when the angels were cast out of heaven 'some fell on the land, some fell in the sea, and the seal, he's the one that fell in the sea' (1997, p. 53).

One old man whom Yeats and Lady Gregory met divided the Fairies into the *Tuatha Dé Danann* who were good, or at least 'like ourselves', and the *Fir Bolg* who were 'more wicked and more spiteful' (Gregory 1970, p. 67; Welch 1993, p. 262). There is an echo of this at p. 74 below, where two banshis come upon a sleeping piper, one of them blinds one of his eyes, and the other asks that the second eye be spared – but it, too, is blinded. Another echo may be found in a tale from Berneray (*Tocher* 9, pp. 30–33) of good and bad Fairies who fight until the good ones kill the bad ones and eat their leader, whose name is *Ceann Suic*.[11] Both the *Tuatha Dé Danann* or 'Peoples of the Goddess Danu' and the *Fir Bolg* or 'Men of Bags' are described in the *Leabhar Gabhála* ('Book of Invasions') as races who inhabited Ireland before the Gael. The *Fir Bolg* will be the tribe known to Caesar as the Belgae, who gave their name to Belgium, while, as their name suggests, the *Tuatha Dé Danann* were gods. Lady Gregory wrote (1970, p. 10):

> There are two races among the Sidhe. One is tall and handsome, gay, and given to jesting and to playing pranks, leading us astray in the fields, giving gold that turns to withered leaves or to dust. These ride on horses through the night-time in large companies and troops, or ride in coaches, laughing and decked with flowers and fine clothes. The people of the other race are small, malicious, wide-bellied, carrying before them a bag.

A *sporan*, perhaps? A professor in a Catholic college in the west of Ireland gave Wentz his personal opinion (1911, p. 70) that 'the fairies of any one race are the people of the preceding race – the Fomors for the Fir Bolgs, the Fir Bolgs for the Dananns, and the Dananns for us'. He added: "The old races died. Where did they go? They became spirits – and fairies."

Henderson and Cowan claim (2001, pp. 19, 112) that the Highland bishop John Carswell identified the Fairies as the *Tuatha Dé Danann* in the introduction to his Gaelic Prayer Book of 1567. This is not so. Carswell simply made the point that, for the sake of passing worldly gain, Gaelic writers preferred to 'the precise words of God and the perfect paths of truth' (*briathra dìsle Dé agas slighthe foirfe na fìrinde*) stories 'about the Tuatha Dé Danann, the Milesians, the champions, and Fionn mac Cumhaill with his Fianna, and much else besides' (*ar Thuathaibh Dé Dhanond, agas ar Mhacaibh*

Mīleadh, agas ar na curadhaibh, agas [ar] Fhind mhac Cumhaill gona Fhianaibh, agas ar mhóran eile). This is as good a description as any of the characters with which the Gaelic manuscripts of Carswell's day were filled. They always appear in their original mythological context, without links to sixteenth-century Scotland; nor does Carswell make such a link (Thomson 1970, pp. 11, 125). Internal evidence that the *Tuatha Dé Danann* turned into the Fairies may certainly be found in abundance in such texts, however (Wentz 1911, pp. 59, 82, 283–307), and as Kuno Meyer once remarked (1885, p. xiv), there is a tendency to give the favourite heroes – Fionn, for example – some relation with them. "The greatest among them," says Yeats himself of the Fairies, "were the gods and goddesses of ancient Ireland, and men have not yet forgotten their glory."[12]

There are certainly souls of the dead amongst the Fairies too.[13] Calum Maclean tells (1975, p. 61, cf. *Tocher* 17, pp. 28–29) of an elderly native of Camusdarrach in Morar who had fought under his chief, the late Colonel Simon Macdonald, in the Napoleonic Wars. Threatened with eviction by a new proprietor, Aeneas Macdonell, he went to the burial-ground at Arisaig and was seen by the factor kneeling on the old landlord's grave, beating it with his hands and calling: *Éirich is cuidich mi! Nach ioma latha lean mi thusa? Lean mise thusa eadar an Éipheit agus Éirinn agus tha mi 'n-diugh am' éiginn, agus éirich ás an uaigh agus cuidich mi!* "Arise, arise out of there, Colonel Simon! Arise and help me! Many a day I followed you in Egypt and in Ireland, and today I am in dire need! Arise out of your grave and help me!"

The terrified factor decided to leave the old man in possession of his home, for, as Maclean remarks, 'not even the direst necessity would force the Highlanders of old to call upon the dead to help them'. It is notable that this rare Scottish instance of a belief in the benign power of the spirits of the dead should come from a Catholic area. Yeats wrote (Welch 1993, pp. 309–10): "Almost all that go 'away' among them are taken to help in their work, or in their play, or to nurse their children, or to bear them children, or to be their lovers, and all fairy children are born of such marriages . . . But sometimes one hears of people taken for no reason, as it seems, but that they may be a thing to laugh at. Indeed, one is often told that unlike 'the simple' who would do us an evil, 'the gentle' among 'the others' wish us no harm but 'to make a sport of us'."

With 'the simple' and 'the gentle' we are again, it seems, meeting the *Fir Bolg* and the *Tuatha Dé Danann*, or some such contrasting pair. Yeats amplifies the point elsewhere. The young are taken, he says (Welch 1993, pp. 155–56), the good and the handsome, the useful and the pious, and he adds (*ibid.*, p. 172): "The most of the Irish country people believe that only people who die of old age go straight to some distant Hell or Heaven or Purgatory. All who are young enough for any use, for begetting or mothering children, for dancing or hurling, or even for driving cattle, are taken, I have been told over and over again, by 'the others', as the country people call the fairies; and live, until they die a second time, in the green 'forts', the remnants of the houses of the old inhabitants of Ireland, or under the roots of hills, or in the woods, or in the deep of lakes."

This is truly a 'secret commonwealth' with a discernible organisational principle, and indeed the traditions of the Church upon which the Roman Catholic doctrine of purgatory is based were themselves substantially inherited from eschatologies of this kind, including those of the Celts and of the Greeks. To put it very simply, the Gaelic otherworld *is* purgatory (Wentz 1911, p. 452; Black 2002, pp. 357–58). "It is, I think," says

Yeats (Welch 1993, pp. 168, 180), "a plausible inference that, just as people who are taken grow old among them, so unripe grain and fruits and plants that are taken grow ripe among them. Everything, according to this complex faith, seems to have a certain power of life it must wear out, a certain length of life it must live out, in either world, and the worlds war on one another for its possession . . . I have been told about Gort that nobody is permitted to die among 'the others', but everybody, when the moment of their death is coming, is changed into the shape of some young person, who is taken in their stead, and put into the world to die, and to receive the sacraments."

As JGC was told about the Fairies at Largs (p. 41), 'they never took anything without making up for it some other way'.

VISUALISING THE UNSEEN

Every so often in Gaelic literature we notice a poet or writer groping for familiar words to express an alien concept. In the sixteenth century a MacGregor woman calls a gun *fùdar caol neimhe*, 'a slender powder of poison', as if it were a snake (Watson 1959, p. 243). An eighteenth-century church elder in Badenoch describes quadrilles as *cluich air an ùrlar / bha sgùirte le siabann* – 'playing on the floor / that was scoured with soap', that is, I suppose, dancing on a deal floor polished with 'French chalk' or soapstone (Black 2001, pp. 330, 514). A twentieth-century writer explains that the trolley of a Glasgow tram is *mar gu 'm biodh stiùir giomaich*, 'like a lobster's antennae' (MacRury 1901–03, p. 52). Similarly, two of JGC's stories appear to show the Fairies being used as a kind of linguistic device to help visualise something heard of but never seen. The first (p. 51) explains: "A person who had a green knoll in front of his house, and was in the habit of throwing out dirty water at the door, was told by the Fairies to remove the door to the other side of the house, as the water was spoiling their furniture and utensils."

Gardyloo!

'Gardyloo' was what people shouted in Edinburgh before throwing slops out of the window into the street. It is supposed to have something to do with the French words *gare l'eau* or *garde d'eau*, 'beware of the water'. Even today the tenements of Edinburgh's Old Town are amazing for their height, and in the eighteenth century they were one of the wonders of the world. For every Gaelic speaker of those days who had seen them with his or her own eyes there were many who simply had to guess. Every Highland home had its cow in the byre, its dunghill at the door, its chickens on the thatch and its well of water, so even Dunvegan Castle could not have prepared people for the concept of families stacked in little stone cages, soaring a dozen storeys into the air. How could anyone live like that? This anecdote was one way to make sense of it. Change the question to 'Who would want to live like that?' and the answer would come. *Tà, sann mar sin a tha na sìthichean beò.* "Well, the Fairies live like that."

A Mhoire, sann da-rìribh. "Oh, so they do."

The more one tries to think about what life might be like in a tenement, the more problems one sees. This leads to JGC's next story at p. 51. "In the evening a man was tethering his horse on a grassy mound. A head appeared out of the ground and told him to drive his tether pin somewhere else, as he was letting the rain into their house, and had nearly killed one of the inmates by driving the peg into his ear."

Notice that the word 'Fairy' is not mentioned this time. Belief in Fairies could be justified, however, by interpreting dreams as the revelation of a spirit world normally unseen. JGC himself interprets his story 'Witches as Whales' as a dream (p. 194 below). Sir Walter Scott devoted the first of his 'Letters on Demonology and Witchcraft' to this kind of hypothesis (2001, pp. 9–35). The relationship between Fairy beliefs and Sigmund Freud's analysis of dreams was discussed by Wentz, who drew particular attention to the 'supernatural lapse of time' which is such a distinctive feature of both.[15] I will demonstrate the validity of the hypothesis by moving from a simple story to a more complex one. The simple story is at p. 41. "In another instance, a band of four was heard crossing over the bedclothes, two women going first and laughing . . ."

These appear to be tiny fairies like those mentioned in *Romeo and Juliet*, not the man-sized ones usual in Gaelic tradition. If we accept JGC's anecdote as a tentative admission that Fairies are the stuff of dreams, it helps us understand the more complex one which appears at p. 78 from the words 'On another day the husband was with his wife in the fields' to the bottom of the page. It seems to be a love story, but operates on different levels. It could be said to be about dealing with grief. Alternatively, it may have been designed to justify the actions of a man whose wife had disappeared in suspicious circumstances. If a Marxist interpretation of the 'great company of riders on white horses' in which the woman is carried away is preferred to a Freudian one, it becomes a nightmarish memory of the time after Culloden when Cumberland's army went on a spree of murder, rape and pillage. Yet another issue is whether it is a man's story or a woman's. One way or another it has a dream-like quality not common in Scottish Gaelic stories, and it may have started life as a dream. As for the white horses, they are a common supernatural motif. In a tale told by Alexander Macdonald, 'Gleannach' (1982, p. 223), a man is advised to retrieve his wife from otherworld capture by riding around the *sìthein* a specific number of times on a pure white horse, calling on her to join him; he must then deposit a live lamb beside a large stone that lies against the *sìthein*, and on returning next day the lamb's place will have been taken by his wife.

In modern times the Fairies have been associated with powers of mind and memory (see note 11 on p. 296). Dòmhnall Chaluim Bàin told Eric Cregeen (*Tocher* 18, p. 47):

> There was a man round here not very long ago, and he called on me and he said, "Where did you get all your folklore?" "Oh, well," says I, "seeing that you ask about it I'll tell you that. In every machaire," says I, "there's knolls, but there is a machaire over there and there's a big, big knoll, and they call it 'The Fairies' Knoll'. Well, I happened to be six months in that knoll along with the fairies. That's where I got all my information."

Another collector, Dr John MacInnes (1994–96, p. 10), recalls a friend who would say, when producing songs or legends that he had not previously seemed to know, *Bha mi sa chnoc o chunnaic mi thu*. "I've been in the hill since I saw you last."

CODES FOR SOCIAL ISSUES

It gradually strikes the twenty-first-century eye that the stories collected by JGC, Lady Gregory and Yeats speak of a spectrum of social issues – the fears and perils of marriage (forced and otherwise), sex, illness, domestic violence, murder, abduction, rape, physical decay, death, famine, abuse (physical, mental and sexual), worry, stress, phobia, drunkenness and alcoholism, schizophrenia, guilt, heaven, hell and purgatory. Angela Bourke has pointed out (1999, pp. 34, 36) that Fairy legends 'provided a way of understanding congenital and other disabilities, or at least an imaginative framework which could accommodate them', and that they 'express the anxiety which can surround the whole question of human fertility', while another commentator has referred to them as 'a discourse in which forms of social control, gender inequalities, psychosomatic illness and sexual abuse were symbolically articulated' (Ó Crualaoich 2003, p. 214). A contemporary Irish tradition-bearer, Mrs Jenny McGlynn, points to the connection between the Fairy beliefs and marital discord (Lysaght 1997, p. 36): "Some women can be good wives and mothers. Others can't take it and they are irritated and they break up their own happiness. So I think it is just like today's broken marriages; you hear more about them today than you did then. They would say that she [the wife] was a demon, that she wasn't from this earth at all, that she was one of the changelings. I think that's what it was all about."

Fairy stories offered a way of explaining such things to children, the explanations becoming so much part of the adult consciousness that new Fairy stories might be told which had no function other than entertainment. Equally the storyteller may launch into what can only be called evangelistic mode – showing us a sceptic who insists that his wife is dead, but is eventually persuaded that if he tries hard enough he can rescue her from the Fairy mound. He succeeds in doing so and they live happily together again (Ó Duilearga 1981, p. 254). Belief in Fairy assistance might be what sustained a person through a difficult life, as in the case of a man whom Yeats called Tierney who lived on the road to Kinvara in south Co. Galway – he used to be with the Fairies every night for seven years, he and his pony being brought together into the sky: "And if his wife had a clutch of geese, they'd be ten times better than any other one, and the wheat and the stock and all they had was better and more plentiful than what any one else had. Help he got from them of course. And at last the wife got the priest in to read a Mass and to take it off him. But after that all that they had went to flitters."[16]

A story like that might not be about what happened but about what people *said* happened – it may tell us less about Tierney than about his neighbours. In any event, Fairy tales are not so much a way of making life better as of coping with a bad one. Ó Crualaoich points out (2003, pp. 223–24) that 'it would appear that pre-modern vernacular culture in Ireland shows a grasp of the psychodynamic of therapy, making it available, however, in the public domain of oral narrative performance rather than in the private domain of the professional individual consultation', while Bourke (1999, p. 206) describes Fairy legends as 'resonant with awareness of mental and emotional turmoil'; the model of society they offer, she says, is 'firm, yet forgiving: flexible enough to accommodate transgression'. The following, told by a man from Co. Clare, appears to justify wife-beating, for example (Welch 1993, p. 319, cf. Gregory 1970, p. 105):

> I heard of a woman brought back again. It was told me by a boy going to school there at the time it happened, so I know there's no lie in it. It was one of the Lydons, a rich family in Scariff, whose wife was sick and pining away for seven years. And at the end of that time one day he came in, he had a drop of drink taken, and he began to be a bit rough with her. And she said, "Don't be rough with me now, after bearing so well with me all these seven

years. But because you were so good and so kind to me all the time," says she, "I'll go away from you now, and I'll let your own wife come back to you."

And so she did, for it was an old hag she was. And the wife came back again and reared a family. And before she went away she had a son that was reared a priest, and after she came back she had another that was reared a priest, so that shows a blessing came on them.

In this respect Fairy stories represent not a health service but self-help. As a system, it was entirely self-regulating. Says Yeats (Welch 1993, p. 319): "The country people seldom do more than threaten the dead person put in the living person's place, and it is, I am convinced, a sin against the traditional wisdom to really ill-treat the dead person."

Yeats may have been reluctant to draw direct conclusions from his anthropological data, especially perhaps about madness, since his own unhappy mother, Susan Pollexfen, was herself 'away' for the last years of her life. He did not shrink from experiment, however. On one occasion he tried to test the belief in the *sluagh* (Welch 1993, p. 313): "I have already told of Whelan and his nightly rides. I got a friend, with whom I was staying, to ask Whelan's father, who is a carpenter, to make a box and send it by his son. He promised to 'try and infatuate him to come', but did not think it would be of any use. It was no use, for the boy said, 'No, I won't go, I know why I am wanted.' His father says that he did not tell him, but that 'the others' told him, when he was out with them."

What JGC calls the 'doctrine' of Fairy belief was a psychic construct, then, that allowed people to make sense of what they could not understand, explain away what they did not want to acknowledge, and provide a set of rules for living. We still need to do all of these things today, but we do them differently. In JGC's Highland communities, as in Yeats's Irish ones, people faced many of the same issues that we face nowadays – crime and social control, stress in the workplace, community relations, marital problems, childcare, loneliness and so on – but they dealt with them differently. Let me begin with a simple example, housekeeping. Nowadays advice can be picked up from 'home economics' classes in school, magazines like *Good Housekeeping*, daytime TV. What did young women have who had no school, no magazines, no TV? They heard in the ceilidh-house what we may now read at p. 39 in the paragraph beginning 'The Elves came to a house at night'. Over and over in these stories Fairies, witches and evil spirits get into people's houses because nobody has thrown out the water in which the family have washed their feet. And JGC concludes: "This is a tale not localised anywhere, but universally known."

As if that were not enough, the entire horror-story 'Hugh of the Little Head' (pp. 235–38), which contains elements of both the first and second otherworlds, carries one simple message: the appalling consequences of a woman being a bad housewife. Áine O'Neill shows (1991, pp. 194–96) that good housekeeping is a prime function of Irish versions of the 'The Fairy Hill is on Fire!' (pp. 39–40 below), while Bourke makes the point more broadly (1999, p. 165): "In the benign environment of neighbourly story-telling, there is nothing dangerous about fairy-legends; on the contrary, they serve many of the purposes for which the modern world uses warning signs and safety regulations. Television programmes on health-education and childcare often use narrative too, to communicate their messages. However, fairy-belief is a powerful imaginative tool, with the same potential for misuse as mind-altering drugs and other therapies."

From housekeeping, then, to childcare. At p. 44 JGC tells the following as if it were simple fact: "A child was taken by the Fairies from Killichrenan (*Cille Chreunain*) near Loch Awe to the **shï-en** in Nant Wood (*Coill' an Eannd*). It was got back by the father drawing a furrow round the hillock with the plough . . ." This is a story with a purpose. Children attended the ceilidh-house and were expected to listen carefully and keep quiet. They would have been terrified by some of what they heard. Special little stories like that one were needed to reassure them so that they could go to sleep.

There is nothing more traumatic than an accident to a child. Several of JGC's stories deal with this problem, e.g. p. 45: "A boy, a mere child, was left alone for a few minutes in the islet of Soa, near Tiree. The mother was making kelp there at the time, and in her absence the Fairies came and gave the child's legs such a twist that it was lame (*liùgach*) ever after."

Notice that it is not described as an accident. The Fairies have done it, and as Fairies are not mortal, no human being can be blamed. The child is lame now, and that is that, for as Bourke points out (1999, pp. 187), Fairy legends 'claimed no monopoly on morality, but instead represented moral decisions as negotiations between rival claims'.

There is a longer story of the same type in the two paragraphs at p. 42 beginning 'Some seventy or eighty years ago' and ending 'The old woman, it is said, had the second sight.' We cannot be quite sure whether this remark about the second sight is relevant to the anecdote. If it is, does it mean that Fairies were drawn to people like her, in this case to try to steal her granddaughter? Or that it allowed her at least to try to counteract the Fairies' power? At any rate, in modern terms, it is fair to say that something happened that night that left the child a little bit brain-damaged – but, we are told, it was not the father's fault; nor was it the grandmother's, for she did her best.

A snatch of song at p. 269 reveals a community's concern at the plight of motherless children being brought up by a violent father. Discreetly placed in the mouth of his dead wife, it threatens him not with the 'first otherworld' of Fairies but with the 'second otherworld' of ghosts. Also in the 'childcare' category is the tale at p. 45 headed 'Kindness to a Neglected Child'. In it the Fairies are evoked again, and the fact that they sometimes opted to do good rather than harm is entirely within their character as set out by JGC in Chapter 1. But if we were to seek a rational explanation for what happened, one springs to mind very quickly. The members of a traditional Highland community quietly look out for each other but have no desire to be accused of meddling. This would especially have been the case when a child was in the care of its father. A female neighbour must have discreetly brought the child home to its own front door, then whispered in the herd's ear on her way home.

Many of our stories reflect a set of issues relating to relocation, migration, separation and bereavement. This is especially true of women who had married outside their locality. *Is fada cobhair o mhnaoi 's a muinntir an Éirinn* (Nicolson 1951, p. 235): "Far is help from a wife whose kinsfolk are in Ireland." Not all such stories concern women pining away in a *brugh*, however. *Dòmhnall Ruadh nan Sìthchean* (p. 38 below) was a homesick young boy who used the *sluagh* to visit his parents, and Wentz met a man in Ireland who had done the same (1911, p. 73): "From near Ederney, County Fermanagh, about seventy years ago, a man whom I knew well was taken to America on Hallow Eve Night; and *they* (the *good people*) made him look down a chimney to see his own daughter cooking at a kitchen fire. Then *they* took him to another place in America, where he saw a friend he knew. The next morning he was at his own home here in Ireland. This man wrote a letter to his daughter to know if she was at the place and at the work on Hallow Eve Night, and she wrote back that she was."

What kind of daughter would have said otherwise?

We now move on to pregnancy, sickness and death. Hugh Miller wrote of the genius of smallpox taking the form of a wandering green lady (1994, pp. 68–69, cf. Dorson 1968, p. 146). Disease and death, at least, could be rationalised as the touch of the *saighead shìth* or Fairy arrow, a topic to which Isobel Gowdie returned again and again when on trial in 1662.[18] As a native of Auldearn in Nairnshire, she lived right on the Highland line, a turbulent place socially, culturally and linguistically, and it is no surprise to discover that in her mind the imagery of pregnancy, sickness and death should be informed by that of violence. In her second confession, taken at Auldearn on 3 May 1662, she allegedly told her tormentors (Pitcairn 1833, vol. 3, p. 607):

> As for Elf-arrow-heidis, THE DIVELL shapes them with his awin hand, (and syne deliueris thame) to Elf-boyes, who whyttis and dightis [shapes and trims] them with a sharp thing lyk a paking neidle; bot (quhan I wes in Elf-land?) I saw them whytting and dighting them. Quhan I wes in the Elfes howssis, they will haw werie . . . . them whytting and dighting; and THE DIVELL giwes them to ws, each of ws so many, quhen . . . . Thes that dightis thaim ar litle ones, hollow, and boss-baked [?hunchbacked]! They speak gowstie [gruffly] lyk. Quhen THE DIVELL giwes them to ws, he sayes,

> > 'SHOOT thes in my name,
> > And they sall not goe heall hame!'

> And quhan ve shoot these arrowes (we say)—

> > 'I SHOOT yon man in THE DIVELLIS name,
> > He sall nott win heall hame!
> > And this salbe alswa trw;
> > Thair sall not be an bitt of him on lieiw [alive]!'

> We haw no bow to shoot with, but spang [jerk] them from of the naillis of our thowmbes. Som tymes we will misse; bot if thay twitch [touch], be it beast, or man, or woman, it will kill, tho' they haid an jack [coat of mail] wpon them.

Isobel's introduction of the Christian devil into the Gaelic otherworld is symptomatic of her position on the cusp of two belief-systems. As Ronald Hutton has noted (2002, p. 32), she is in every way a liminal figure. Not entirely a Gael, she imagines herself in Gaelic terms to be a Fairy. Not entirely a Gall, she imagines herself in Lowland terms to be a witch. She has no difficulty imagining herself in the devil's company, for he is a prominent character in both traditions (see Chapter 12 below), figuring largely in the preaching of the day and brought to life in rituals such as the expulsion of evil from the community at New Year ('*Callainn*', pp. 530–31). In her third confession, taken at Auldearn on 15 May 1662, she says (Pitcairn 1833, vol. 3, pp. 611–12):

> That quhich troubles my conscience most, is the killing of severall persones, with the arrowes quhich I gott from THE DIVELL. The first woman that I killed wes at *the Plewgh-landis*; also I killed an [one] in the East of *Murrey*, at *Candlmas* last . . . *Bessie* and *Margaret*

Wilsones in Aulderne, *Johne Taylor* and his wyff, *Margrat Brodie* and I, and THE DIVELL, wer together, and *Mr Harie Forbes*, Minister at Aulderne, goeing to *Moynes*. THE DIVELL gaw *Margret Brodie* an arrow to shoot at him, quhilk she did; bot it cam short; and *the Divell* cawsed tak it wp again. We desiret to shoot again, bot *the Divell* said, 'No; we wold not gett his lyff at that tyme!' *The Divell* cawsed me to shoot at *the Laird of Park*, as he was croceing *the Burne of the Boath*; bot I missed him.

What exactly Isobel means by 'kill' is an open question. She was, after all, not being accused of murder but of witchcraft. In her fourth confession, taken at Auldearn on 27 May 1662, she says (*ibid.*, p. 615):

I haw sein the Elf-arrowes maid. The *Divell* dights [dresses] them, and *the Elf-boyes* quhytes them [blocks them out]. We got ewerie on (of) ws so many of thaim from *the Divell*, to shoot at men. I my self killed on *William Bower*, at Miltoun of Moynes. This griewis me mor than any thing that I ewer did . . . I shot at *the Laird of Park*, as he ves crossing the Burn of Boath; bot, thankis to God now, that he preserwit him. *Bessie Hay* gaw me a great cuffe, becaus I missed him.

Pitcairn comments wrily that Isobel and her master 'ought to have known, that the Laird was out of their power while crossing a running stream'.

Let us move on to the more specific issue of alcohol dependency. That drinking bouts can be encoded into otherworld intervention is clear from JGC's story at p. 54 about the gardener in Glenorchy who saw a little man in his boat, spoke to him, received no answer, struck at him, and fell overboard. "Now, asked the old woman who told this story, what could the little man be but a *brughadair* (i.e. one that came from the Fairy dwelling, an Elf)? To the reader the case will appear one of simple hallucination produced by ardent spirits, but it is of interest as shewing the interpretation put upon it under a belief in the Fairies."

What it really shows is a woman who is not willing to accept that this man has a drink problem. Probably she was related to him. I think we have all known women like that. I am tempted to remark that had the Fairies not existed, she would have had to invent them.

I suspect, although it is not specifically mentioned, that drink also has something to do with the story from Largs at p. 41 about a man who cut a slip from an ash-tree growing near a Fairy dwelling and finished up next morning 'in the byre, astride on a cow, and holding on by its horns'. The phraseology would fit a binge very well: '. . . way home in the evening . . . stumbled and fell . . . heard . . . a laugh at his mishap . . . hoisted away . . .' This man has come home, reached the byre, fallen over the cow (whose warmth is attractive anyway) and ended up astride her. We are not told that she actually stood up with him on top, but the storyteller allows us to imagine it if we wish, although in JGC's work as a whole 'hoisted away' usually means 'brought flying through the air by the Fairies'. *Pace* John Sands (p. 655 below), this is the only case in *The Gaelic Otherworld* of a man sitting on a cow.

What then are we to make of 'cut a slip from an ash-tree'? This will be the rowan or mountain ash, which was sacred to the Fairies, and we can well understand that if a bit of rowan were wanted to safeguard property, it should be taken from a tree well away from a Fairy dwelling. Is it possible then that 'cutting a slip from an ash-tree growing near a Fairy dwelling' was a metaphor for having too much to drink? Imagine the scenario. *Dé tha ceàrr air Dòmhnall?* "What's the matter with Donald?"

Ù, says some woman like the one related to the gardener, *cha d'rinn e ach sliseag a ghearradh á caorann an t-sìthein.* "Oh, he's just cut a slip from an ash-tree growing near a Fairy dwelling."

We may first of all note Bourke's intriguing analysis (1999, p. 106): "The whole Irish tradition of fairies is preoccupied with boundaries, including those of the human body. Visits to the fairy realm may be presented as illicit penetrations of the earth's orifices, when curiosity and lack of caution make human characters, who are usually young and male, explore caves, rock clefts, or other hidden openings which unexpectedly appear in the familiar landscape. Young women taken by the fairies bear in their bodies the marks of their adventures: some are unable to speak until the fairies' *biorán suain*, a kind of tranquilliser-dart or 'slumber-pin', is discovered and removed; others are immobilized by painful swellings, caused by invasion of their flesh by some foreign body, and cured only when the offending matter is expelled."

The *biorán suain* has its Scottish equivalent in the *saighead shìth* or Fairy arrow. If we wish to ponder the relevance of this to Isobel's ramblings, it becomes an open question whether we should visualise her 'Divell' as a flesh-and-blood pimping innkeeper or some imaginary little cupid with his arrows. Fairy arrows or Elfshot wounded the muscle without piercing the skin, and the cure appears to have consisted simply of finding this subcutaneous lesion by searching the body with the fingers (Sutherland 1937, pp. 126–27). The equivalent of Elfshot in the Fairy lore of Newfoundland is the 'blast', where the flesh is infested with foreign matter – bits of rag, felt or string, rabbit's bones, needles, moths, stones, hare's teeth, pins, any old rubbish – and it has been wisely pointed out that 'like most powerful elements in folk narrative, the blast is simultaneously old and modern, expressive both of specific cultural concerns and widespread human tendencies, and amenable to multiple interpretations' (Rieti 1997, p. 284).

In a tale at p. 111 headed 'Island of Coll' a herdsman has a regular male visitor whose identity is unknown to the community. Rather than probe into their activities around what we may call the swimming-pool – Loch Annla, 'Olaf's Loch' – people are content simply to say that the visitor is a water-horse. If we now examine the tale that JGC tells at pp. 245–46 about the *Bigein* (for whom see pp. 646–47) we find, first, that he is a landless cottar with a nickname that means 'Chicken'; second, that over several months he is subjected by the farmer for whom he works to a series of physical assaults; third, that the pretext of these assaults is that he has 'disregarded his master's call' the night before; fourth, that his master is alleged to come in the form of a 'spectre' or 'phantom'. Most modern analyses would conclude that this is a case of homosexual abuse.

The source of the *Bigein* story is not hard to guess. "The person whose spectre it was, on being spoken to on the subject, got very angry, but the visits of the spectre ceased." The man who had a word in his ear will have been JGC's predecessor Neil Maclean, minister of Tiree from 1817 until his death in 1859; the man who told JGC the story will have been 'Old Archibald', who was 'for half a century servant to the ministers of Tiree', and who could not be persuaded by minister or elder that there were no Fairies, for he had heard them 'with his own ears' (p. 79 below).

Heterosexual relationships are also codified when necessary. The following story was told by Donald Mackinnon, who was born in South Uist about 1810 and moved to Barra in 1836 (Wentz 1911, pp. 106–07): "I heard of an apprentice to carpentry who was working with his master at the building of a boat, a little distance from his house, and near the sea. He went to work one morning and forgot a certain tool which he needed in the boat-building. He returned to his carpenter-shed to get it, and found the shed filled with fairy men and women. On seeing him they ran away so greatly confused that one of the women forgot her gird (belt), and he picked it up. In a little while she came back for the gird, and asked him to give it her, but he refused to do so. Thereupon she promised him that he should be made master of his trade wherever his lot should fall without serving further apprenticeship. On that condition he gave her the gird; and rising early next morning he went to the yard where the boat was a-building and put in two planks so perfectly that when the master arrived and saw them, he said to him, 'Are you aware of anybody being in the building-yard last night, for I see by the work done that I am more likely to be an apprentice than the person who put in those two planks, whoever he is. Was it you that did it?' The reply was in the affirmative, and the apprentice told his master the circumstances under which he gained the rapid mastership of his trade."

If we approach this story by reminding ourselves that there is no such thing as Fairies, it will be clear what was going on in the boatshed. The 'gird (belt)' will be a *crios* or *criosan*, for which see note 8 on pp. 294–95. It will have been of silk. Such articles were imported and distinctive (partly no doubt thanks to women's fondness for embroidery), as is clear from this young Rannoch woman's song to her idealised lover (Watson 1959, p. 193):

Nuair a ruigeadh tu 'n fhéill	*When you'd arrive at the fair*
Se mo ghear-*sa thig dhachaigh:*	*It's my gear will come home:*
Mo chriosan 's mo chìre	*My girdle and combs*
'S mo stìomag chaol cheangail,	*And narrow hairband for tying,*
Mo làmhainne bòidheach	*My beautiful gloves*
'S déis òir air am barraibh,	*With gold ears of corn on their fingertips,*
Mo sporan donn iallach	*My brown purse of thongs*
Ma' ri sgian nan cas ainneamh —	*With the rare-handled knife —*
Thig mo chrios á Dùn Éideann	*My gird will come from Auld Reekie*
'S mo bhréid á Dùn Chailleann.	*And my marriage-kertch from Dunkeld.*

The apprentice, who is clearly a good but undervalued workman, uses the *crios* or *criosan* to blackmail the girl, who pressurises his master – her father or uncle, presumably – into giving him the promotion he so richly deserves, and his sudden advancement is explained to the rest of the men as the result of supernatural intervention.

Curiously, on a fishing trip to Argyll, Andrew Lang was told a similar story – replete with phallic imagery and the codification of sex as violence – without recognising it for what it was (1891, pp. 57–58). "The Highland fairies are very vampirish," he remarks quizzically. "The Loch Awe boatman lives at a spot haunted by a shadowy maiden. Her last appearance was about thirty years ago. Two young men were thrashing corn one morning, when the joint of the flail broke. The owner went to Larichban and entered an outhouse to look for a piece of sheepskin wherewith to mend the flail. He was long absent, and his companion went after him. He found him struggling in the arms of a ghostly maid, who had nearly murdered him, but departed on the arrival of his friend. It is not easy to make out what these ghoulish women are – not fairies exactly, nor witches, nor vampires."

Too true, but this brings us to real murder and other types of serious crime. Some things in JGC's stories are very perturbing, provided we can make the assumption that the Fairies are being used as a code for certain inconvenient moral issues that society does not fully wish to face, and does not possess the vocabulary to describe, although I have to say that in the Gaelic original the meaning of these stories would have been clear enough to those hearers equipped to understand them, for they operate on different levels. If you, as a reader, disagree with any of my interpretations, it means that they are still operating on different levels today. Such stories, with their codes and allomotifs, provide 'a discussion forum for varying opinions and attitudes' (Almqvist 1991a, p. 40). Bourke is careful to point out (1999, pp. 139, 145) that Fairy belief is 'a question of idiom and world-view, not of intelligence', and that 'a willingness to forego natural scepticism paid rich dividends in terms of access to a shared symbolic universe'. Thus, at the level of metaphor, 'to make a Fairy' of a person (*ibid.*, p. 67) is to isolate and repudiate him (or her, as in the sad case of Bridget Cleary, where it went too far), while 'to see the Fairies' is to act strangely, to do mysterious or at least unusual things, to have hidden depths, to know more than others (Ó Crualaoich 2003, p. 174). Similarly, although Yeats was coy about the contemporary social significance of the Fairy stories which he and Lady Gregory had collected, he was fully alive to their coded nature with respect to Gaelic literature (Welch 1993, pp. 187–88): "The stories of the country people, about men and women taken by 'the others', throw a clear light on many things in the old Celtic poems and romances, and when more stories have been collected and compared, we shall probably alter certain of our theories about the Celtic mythology . . . When the country men and country women tell of people taken by 'the others', who come into the world again, they tell the same tales the old Celtic poets and romance writers told when they made the companions of Fionn compel, with threats, the goddess Miluchra to deliver Fionn out of the Grey Lake on the Mountain of Fuad; and when they made Cormac, the son of Art, get his wife and children again from Mananan, the son of Lir."

The balance between neighbourliness and meddling was a difficult one. It still is, with one important difference: if a man is beating his partner or if someone thinks a child is being molested, there is someone to call. But what if there were no police, no social services? "Another," says JGC (p. 44), "somewhere on the mainland of Argyllshire, suspecting his wife had been stolen by Fairies, hauled her by the legs from bed, through the fire and out at the door. She there became a log of wood, and serves as the threshold of a barn in the place to this day."

Strong stuff. What does it mean? First set aside the fiction that the wife has been stolen and a sort of shadow – a changeling – left in her place. I would read the tale as a whispered accusation in which crimes are spoken of mainly in symbols. The wife's being stolen by Fairies is her alleged adultery, her becoming a log of wood is murder. Think of the English expression 'dead as a doorpost'. The log, along with many other codes in such stories, can, I believe, be shown to an allomotif as defined by Carroll (1992, p. 226), that is, an incident which can be freely substituted for another without alteration to the symbolic meaning of the tale – the identification of allomotifs thus leading us to a psychoanalytical understanding of its purpose. So, for example, 'log', 'semblance of woman' and 'dead woman' seem to be in free variation in stories of Fairy abduction. The principle at work is of the theft by the Fairies of the fusion or life-force of the human being, exactly as they steal the *toradh* or substance from the milk, exactly indeed as the distiller 'steals' the spirit or vital spark from the barley. Sometimes an allomotif takes shape before our eyes (or ears), as in one of Yeats's stories where the log is clearly a code for death (Welch 1993, p. 121): "A woman of the sidhe (the faeries) came in, and said that the child was chosen to be the bride of the prince of the dim kingdom, but that as it would never do for his wife to grow old and die while he was still in the first ardour of his love, she would be gifted with a faery life. The mother was to take the glowing log out of the fire and bury it in the garden, and her child would live as long as it remained unconsumed. The mother buried the log, and the child grew up, became a beauty, and married the prince of the faeries, who came to her at nightfall."

The identity and function of the 'log' (or 'stock', or 'block of wood') is crucial. It is a Fairy changeling, or it is a live human being at the point of cure or of slaughter, or it is his or her coffin. It is interesting, therefore, to see how it is implausibly subverted for public consumption into an 'image' when Aberdeenshire tradition is moderated by the Rev. Walter Gregor (1883, p. 56): "When a child was to be taken away by the fairies, a 'stock' was some times substituted. It was an image of the child, and was made of wood. A man's child was carried off, and a 'stock' left. On discovering what had been done, the father hung it in the 'crook' over the fire. In a moment it flew out by the 'lum'. He rushed out to look after it, and found his own child lying under the gable of the house."

In between being 'stolen by Fairies' and 'becoming a log of wood', then, what the husband does to the woman in JGC's story at p. 44 is entirely real. In a house in which the fire was in the middle of the floor, domestic violence was always likely to include a woman being dragged through the fire. As for 'the threshold of a barn', we are being told where to dig if we wish to establish her husband's guilt.

If that story were unique, it would be possible to explain it otherwise. But there is more than enough of the kind to suggest a pattern. At pp. 114–15 JGC tells a story which is good enough to deserve a spot of scene-setting all of its own. I refer to the first three paragraphs of 'The Water-Horse at Loch Basibol, Tiree', which personally I would have called 'Man Murdered by Brothers for Dating their Sister'. One can imagine the mafia doing something like this to someone who had 'dishonoured' a member of their clan. Similarly, Lady Gregory collected a story in the Burren about a girl who was to be married (Welch 1993, pp. 213–14). The girl cried when the day was coming, and refused to go with the man. "Get into the bed, then," said her mother, "and I'll say that you're sick."

This the girl did, and when the man came the mother said to him: "You can't get her, she's sick in the bed."

He looked in and said, "That's not my wife that's in the bed, it's some old hag."

The mother began to cry. The man went out and got two hampers of turf and made a fire, and they thought he was going to burn the house down. "Come out now," says he, "and we'll see who you are, when I'll put you on the fire."

When the girl heard that, with one bound she was out of the house, and they saw she was an old hag. The man asked the advice of an old woman, who told him to go to a nearby Fairy bush where he might get some word of her. He went there at night, and saw all sorts of grand people, in carriages or riding horses. Among them was the girl. He went again to the old woman, who said, "If you can get the three bits of blackthorn out of her hair, you'll get her again."

So that night he went back again, but he only got hold of a bit of her hair. The old woman told him that he was no use, and that it might be twelve nights now before he got her. But on the fourth night he got the third bit of blackthorn, and she came away with him. He never told the mother he had got her, but one day the mother recognised her at a fair even though she had a shawl about her head. "That's my daughter," she said. "I know her by the smile and by the laugh of her."

The husband said, "You're right there, and hard I worked to get her."

The girl spoke often of the grand things she saw underground. She had wine to drink, and drove out in a carriage with four horses every night. She was able to see her husband when he came to look for her, and she was greatly afraid that he would get a drop of the wine, for then he would never have gone away again. "And she was glad," the story ends, "to come to earth again, and not to be left there."

I would interpret this as follows. A young woman refuses to accept the marriage which has been arranged for her, presumably by her father. Her 'suitor' comes to the house. In his fury, he threatens to burn her alive. She disappears. Perhaps he has killed her. No one is seen in the vicinity that night but an old hag. Four days later he is found to be living with a young woman who appears to be 'touched'. He keeps the mother of the *disparue* well away, but she sees his mistress at a fair with a shawl over her head and convinces herself that it is her daughter. This woman lives in fear of her partner's drinking bouts. As Bourke points out (1999, p. 37): "Fairy-legends carry disciplinary messages for women as well as for children, warning them about behaviour considered by a patriarchal society to be unacceptable. Undoubtedly, too, some of them have been used as euphemisms for domestic violence ... A woman in nineteenth-century rural Ireland who had obviously been beaten might explain the marks of violence as having been inflicted by fairy abductors, while a violent husband might account for his actions as loss of patience with a fairy interloper.

"This is not to say that such explanations would normally be accepted, or taken literally. Fairy-legend charts the territory of no man's land. It carries with it an air of the preposterous, the nod and wink, that allows one thing to be said, while another is meant. It permits face-saving lies to be told, and disturbing narratives to be safely detoured into fiction if children are found to be listening, or if the complex web of family relationships means that someone may take offence, or threaten retaliation."

In a one-sentence anecdote at p. 44 JGC says simply: "A woman taken by the Fairies was seen by a man who looked in at the door of a *brugh*, spinning and singing at her work." The *brugh*, he points out at p. 7, is in essence the interior of a Fairy residence, as opposed to the *sìthein* (*sìthean, sìdhean, sìdhein*) or exterior. What we have here is another case in which a young woman has disappeared. Yet we are being told that there is no need to look for her – she is safe and sound and in a happier place. Whether she has been murdered by a drunken partner, molested and killed by a relative, or seduced and done away with by a stranger, society does not want to know. The same 'tolerance' may be noted in a story told to Lady Gregory by 'The Old Man Who Is Making a Well' (1970, p. 262). It appears to describe an act of domestic violence ending in murder, but involves an interesting inversion: it is alleged to happen accidentally in the course of rescuing the woman from abduction. "There was a man and his wife was brought away at Cruachmaa and he was told to go dig, and he'd get her out. And he began to dig, and when he had a hole made at the side of the hill he saw her coming out, but he couldn't stop the pick that he had lifted for the stroke, and it went through her head."

It is obvious to the cynic that this woman's body was found in a shallow grave with a pickaxe wound in her head, and that this tale was told by her husband to explain it.

A more complex structure of codes is discernible in JGC's story at p. 77 beginning 'A gentleman of the name of Evan Cameron' and ending: "None of the terriers was ever heard of more." Several things come across quite clearly. The sexual nature of the encounter – 'a woman sitting by the fire, all wet and combing her hair'. Alleged provocation – *Nach d'thig thu 'n dèidh do shùil, Eoghain?* The possible presence of a code-word meaning more than it says – 'conversation'. The astonishing use of 'obliged' to defend the man's appalling action in setting his dogs on the woman – he has, after all, been stated to be a 'gentleman'. And finally, to exonerate him completely from what sounds like sexual assault followed by sadistic murder, we have the claim that the greyhound came home without any hair on its body – a motif that denotes a narrow escape from the Fairies or the devil, found in many stories in this book and also in Sorley MacLean's long poem 'Uamh an Òir', see note 913.

Three different points deserve to be made. First, we have the definition of a 'gentleman' as a person who murders women by setting his hunting-dogs on them rather than by the vulgar method of punching them and dragging them through the fire. Second, the woman is nowhere called a Fairy – merely a 'strange creature'. She is mortal. Third, I am by no means claiming that all Fairy stories can be interpreted in this way. Many Fairy stories have no discernible social implications whatever – which is why I am able to say what 'without any hair on its body' is intended to imply. But that such things happened in Gaelic society is a matter of record. Yeats speaks of a contemporary case of domestic violence in Conamara which involved a man who believed that his wife's sister was a Fairy (Welch 1993, p. 320). "When I was last in Western Galway a man had just been arrested for trying to kill his sister-in-law, because he thought she was one of 'the others', and was tempting him to murder his cousin. He had sent his cousin away that she might be out of his reach in case he could not resist the temptation. This man was merely out of his mind, and had more than common reasons for his anger besides."

If there are stories about attacks on women, it is logical to assume that there will be stories about how women can defend themselves. An example may be found, I believe, in the three paragraphs at p. 114 below beginning 'A water-horse in man's shape came to a house in which there was a woman alone'. Water-horse my foot. This was a real man, except that it was impolite to say so. The story is a very common one, and is told not merely of the water-horse but of every supernatural creature in the Gaelic bestiary. It is a woman's-eye view of self-defence against a predatory male. Conversely, in her study of the Cleary case (see below, p. lxi) Bourke suggests how the changeling belief offered a more subtle mode of self-defence (1999, p. 67): "Bridget Cleary, well versed in fairy-lore, would have found in its stories a language through which to resist her husband's negative assessment of her. A wife who could persuade a violent husband that she was a fairy changeling might even be able to convince him that he was damaging his chances of getting his 'real' wife back."

Curiously JGC gives us a string of man's-eye stories about predatory females. Take 'Donald Thrashed by the Fairy Woman' at pp. 56–57. The likely code-word in this story is 'thrashing' – it comes up three times, and we will meet it again shortly. In this story there are more questions than answers. Once again the woman is wet when the man first sees her, but she is specifically said to be a Fairy and the middle of a boundary stream sounds like the sort of in-between place a Fairy would be; JGC calls the relationship an 'affair', but I would not make too much of that.

So read on through the story at p. 57, 'Iona Banshi'. Here, following some shenanigans with a fishing-rod, God's name proves ineffective, and after two 'thrashings' and a 'drubbing' this extraordinary woman (who is specifically called 'his Fairy mistress') does the hero to death. I would like to know what Gaelic words lie behind 'thrashing' and 'drubbing'. *Bualadh? Slaiceadh? Collainn? Làdach?* In successive paragraphs at p. 105 JGC uses the same verb 'thrash' to denote how the urisk assaults passers-by in lonely places and threshes a farmer's corn; cf. also *làd*, p. 93. Another clue is provided in JGC's own hand in the kirk session records of Tiree (NAS CH2/482/1, p. 448):

Moss Church 26th April 1865.

Compeared before the Session, Sarah Kennedy, wife of Donald McLean, Ballevullin, complaining that Sarah Kennedy, wife to Neil Kennedy, Ballevullin, had accused her of improper intercourse with John Beatoun, a person whom she had seen once at harvest time in the south, but otherwise unknown to the Complainant. The said Mrs Neil Kennedy acknowledged having when quarrelling called her "Sgiursair a Bheatonuich," having once heard Mary Bhàn Cameron, Kilmoluag, call her so, but having no other authority. The oath of purgation was administered to the above Mrs McLean, when she declared herself free of the said John Beatoun.[19]

John G. Campbell
Modr.

The Gaelic words, nowadays more likely to be spelled *Sgiùrsair a' Pheutanaich*, mean 'Beaton's Scourger'. As I will show below, the Gaelic tradition of spiritual experience is full of physical wrestlings (usually at night), often resulting in actual injury. In 'Iona Banshi' we are offered a 'top shelf' version in which the devil comes in female form, and if there is any lingering doubt about the sexual nature of the relationship, note that the next anecdote (p. 58) speaks of 'a native of Tiree, similarly afflicted and wishing to escape from his Fairy love'.

'Thrashing' reappears in the story at p. 188 beginning 'A young man in the island of Lismore'. It reads so like the plot of *The Graduate* that one feels the hero must have been called Dustin. It belongs, however, to a strand introduced to Gaelic literature by the hero tales of Iron Age warriors. Yeats points out that in 'Serglige Con Culainn' ('The Wasting Sickness of Cu Chulainn') the hero sinks into trauma after an unsuccessful hunt (Welch 1993, pp. 323–24): "He lay down in great sorrow ... and fell asleep and dreamed that two women, one dressed in green and one dressed in red, came to him, and first one and then the other smiled and struck him with a whip, and that they went on beating him until he was nearly dead. His friends came while he was still dreaming, but only saw that he slept and must not be awakened, and when at last he awoke, he was so weak that he made them carry him to his bed ... The after madness of Cuchulain reminds me of the mystery the country people, like all premature people, see in madness, and of the way they sometimes associate it with 'the others'."

Female-on-male violence is to the fore in JGC's story about the mail-gig driver in *Coill an Eannd*, the Wood of Nant (p. 250). It dates apparently from 1870, and is the kind of story that lends authority to the concept that a living person could have a spectre or phantom (Kirk's *coimimechd*), for its *doppelgänger* is not so easily dismissed as a fraud as in the sad tale of the *Bigein*. The concept, which also appears at p. 561 ('a woman once saw herself coming after her'), was discussed in Eilidh Watt's book *Gun Fhois* (1987, pp. 12–13, cf. MacInnes 1994–96, pp. 16–17): *Their cuid gu bheil coimeas dhinn, ach neo-chorparra, daonnan ceangailte rinn* ... "Some say a copy of ourselves, albeit incorporeal, always goes with us, though some people's tether is longer than others'. The belief is pretty common around the world. In the Highlands and Islands it is called the *co-choisiche* ('co-walker'). Around the world it is better known as the *doppelgänger*. They say this shadow can reveal itself in our shape, our form, our clothing."

Mrs Watt, who died aged 88 in 1996, was from Skinidin in Skye and was herself second-sighted. Janet Bord has pointed to the possibility (1997, p. 147) that, especially in the Celtic lands, the 'old religion' has somehow 'imprinted itself on to the natural landscape in such a way that especially sensitive people may at times experience visions incorporating the main elements of the rites that used to be performed there', and Mrs Watt cites a first-hand instance of it (1989, pp. 35–36): "Once when I was motoring in Fife with a friend we decided to stop and drink from our flasks of tea at the first attractive spot we found. There was one with groups of trees, two streams converging and an air of tranquillity which seemed admirably suited to our purpose, and leaving the car we made for the clearing. My friend was unpacking the basket when I cried out in a panic: 'I can't stay here! There have been blood sacrifices here!' and fled.

"In the car I asked her what the place was called. 'Shank of Navitie', was the answer. From the name it may have had early Christian associations, but I am unable to account for my panic and for my declaration. I have been affected by other places but never to such a degree."

'Navitie' represents early Celtic *nemeto* 'sacred wood', whose origins lie beyond early Christianity in druidism (Watson 1926a, p. 247). Tacitus and Lucan refer to human sacrifice being carried out in *nemeto* sites, the former speaking of a grove in Anglesey whose altars were heaped with entrails, the latter of one near Marseille where every tree was sprinkled with blood (Green 1992, pp. 108, 183).

Mrs Watt was a splendid lady and a wonderful Gaelic writer. Her short stories, published as *Gun Fhois* ('Restless'), come to my mind when I am faced with the task of explaining the physical aspect of spiritual experience. In her introduction she quotes William James's *Varieties of Religious Experience* on how it feels to be confronted with evil (Watt 1987, p. 17). "Fear came upon me and trembling made all my bones to shake. To all appearances it was a perfectly insane and abject terror without ostensible cause, and only to be accounted for, to my perplexed imagination, by some damned shape, squatting invisible to me within the precincts of the room and raying out from his foetid personality influences fatal to life. The thing had not lasted ten seconds before I felt myself a wreck, reduced from a state of firm, vigorous, joyful manhood to one of almost helpless infancy . . ."

This typifies the experience of many of Mrs Watt's characters. In one story (1987, pp. 87–90) Seòras, a deacon and former seaman, has been visiting the minister. Despite the latter's entreaties, he insists on going home rather than staying overnight. As he walks, he wonders why the minister said: *Na rach an greim riutha. Na toir dùbhlan daibh. Na biodh nàire ort teicheadh. Till 'na àm.* "Don't tackle them. Don't challenge them. Don't be afraid to run away. Come back in time."

Seòras becomes very tired – as if walking into a wind, though there is none. "It was neither tiredness nor wind that drove him off the crown of the road, yet the ditch was his choice of pathway when he wasn't stumbling and crawling."

Back he goes to the manse, where the minister pulls him in as if he has swum through the sea from a shipwreck. They fall to prayer, the minister sweating with effort till eventually he says: *Dh'eug e, ach faodaidh gum bi tròcair Dhé éifeachdach. Cha deach agam air caim a chur mu thimcheall. Bha e ro fhad' ás. Ach dòcha fhathast.* "He has died, but perhaps God's mercy will be effectual. I didn't manage to put a circle round him. He was too far away. But perhaps yet."[20]

Next morning all is explained. *Is math nach do chum thu ort. Bha Iain Dubh ris a' bhàs is feachdan an dorchadais a' cruinneachadh gus aoigheachd a thoirt dha. Ach is motha cumhachd Dhé.* "It's as well you didn't keep going. Iain Dubh was on his death-bed with the powers of darkness gathering to take him in. But God's power is greater."

In another story (Watt 1987, pp. 52–58) we meet an intended victim of the powers of darkness at first hand. 'Ain Mór, a big bully of a shepherd, arrives at the manse demanding to be allowed the protection of communion. He has just spent the night in a lonely bothy where he was woken by his dead father's voice. He sensed a presence – as did his dog, a collie bitch. *Thàinig biùg fann geur bhuaipe is phlùisg i aig mo chasan.* "She uttered a pathetic little whine and expired at my feet."

He saw nothing, but kept his back to the wall and his eyes upon where a man's face would be on coming in the door. "I can't describe to you how the Spirit of Evil took control of my mind. *Bhuail gach drabasdachd is gach truaillidheachd orm is mise a' sabaid 'nan aghaidh.* All kinds of obscenity and corruption assaulted me as I fought against them. I believe that my soul parted from my body, from which the strength had completely melted, and that another spirit had come to fortify me, another mind to guide me. If it weren't for that I'd have collapsed like the dog.

"*Bha mi 'nam bhlàr cogaidh aig feachdan uabhasach nach faca mi . . .* I was a battlefield fought over by terrible unseen forces. Then I was left alone, and thanked

God – I who had no need of God. Though the awful forces had gone, I thought I could smell them as when in July I stumble across a dead sheep infested with worms. But worse, worse even than if every sheep I had ever lost were piled on top of each other in a pit."

The minister lets him take communion, though it takes some explaining to the Session. 'Ain Mór's life is not greatly changed, the minister tells us drily, except that when he rises to the Question on Men's Day he speaks with an authority that roots his hearers to the spot.

Another of Mrs Watt's stories (1987, pp. 37–46) concerns an old soldier called Pàdraig. It is put in the mouth of his neighbour Alasdair 'Ain Òig, who lives fifteen minutes' walk away. Three times this walk is described. The first time, Alasdair is seeing Pàdraig home after an evening's visit. "I felt a thickness of mist creeping clammily round my legs and making it difficult to walk. I glanced at Pàdraig. Have you ever seen a man walking on a shore where there is any depth of seaweed? Or walking through mud? Though Pàdraig was on the hard crown of the road, that is how he was walking."

On the way back Alasdair feels that the woods on either side are full of eyes and paws.

Two weeks later Pàdraig comes again. He looks sick. "Some people say there is no such place as Hell," Alasdair tells us. "I disagree. Whatever place or condition is Hell, Pàdraig's soul at that time had been pulled and sucked into it."

On the way through the trees the powers of darkness are out in force. "In the darkness I could see Pàdraig reeling like a boxer on whom punches were raining down."

Coming home, Alasdair feels that he is walking in a shell. "Though my body was on the road it was as if it wasn't my mind guiding it."

The third time, Alasdair wakes up at night sensing that Pàdraig is calling for help. Seizing a Bible, he goes up the road in his shell to find Pàdraig's wife cowering in a corner while Pàdraig stands with his back to the wall, foaming at the mouth, fists flailing, grunting every so often as if he has given or taken a punch. Alasdair leaps to his side, holds up the Bible and shouts, *Cobhair ann an ainm na Trianaid!* "Help in the name of the Trinity!"

A punch from Pàdraig sends the book flying. *Rinn mi air mo mhàgan gus an leabhar a thogail, ach bha mo làmhan 's mo cheann air am bualadh mar gum biodh le spògan móra anns nach robh cnàimh ged a bha neart annta.* "As I crawled to retrieve the book, my hands and head seemed to be struck by big paws which had strength without bones."

He tries again. Pàdraig is now using his hands to protect his throat and face. Repeatedly calling on the Trinity, Alasdair puts his arms around Pàdraig. Alasdair's strength drains out of his body, and he calls to Pàdraig's wife. She comes as if wading through deep water, and they embrace Pàdraig until he says, "They've gone. They won't attack me again. You came in time."

Pondering how the driver of the mail-gig was thrashed by the *co-choisiche* of his sweetheart as he passed through the Wood of Nant, I suspect it represented nothing more or less than the terrors of his own conscience, arrived from Hell to torment him. Had fever really broken out in the house at his journey's end, or was it a rival attraction? *Bhuail gach drabasdachd is gach truaillidheachd orm . . .*

These stories of Mrs Watt's are reworkings of a traditional theme. In general terms, their model can be found in Alexander Macdonald's account from Lochness-side of a man who met something one night which left him a physical and mental wreck, but who kept going back to meet it, with the same result, until one evening, after enjoying a quiet glass with some friends, he slipped off as usual, and his body was found next day 'in a bruised and mutilated condition' (1982, pp. 232–36). Physical violence of this kind is an integral part of spiritual experience in both Protestant and Catholic traditions – the Perthshire poet and evangelist Dugald Buchanan (1716–68) tells how, aroused by the preaching at a communion service, 'I remained a considerable part of the night upon the road, sometimes crying, sometimes praying, and at other times throwing myself upon the ground, careless of the hurting of my body'.[21] In Lewis, Kenneth Macdonald was often told by his mother to keep to the side of the road when he went out at night in case he met a funeral, as these always moved along the crown or middle of the road; spirit funerals were commonly encountered in the dark, but so were real ones, as bodies arriving by boat had to be carried home whatever the time, and it was hard to tell one kind from another (2003, p. 120). The Rev. George Sutherland speaks of a man walking along a road at night who felt a malignant presence and was afflicted by the greatest fear he had ever known; if he stepped aside upon the heather the fear left him, and when he returned to the road it came back (1937, pp. 20–21). This struggle to get along a road at night in the face of unseen or imperfectly-seen forces is touched upon again and again in JGC's stories (pp. 178, 244, 271, 281–82, 284), and a man in Inishmaan speaks of it to Lady Gregory (1970, p. 79): "Down by the path at the top of the slip from there to the hill, that's the way they go most nights, hundreds and thousands of them. There are two old men in the island got a beating from them; one of them told me himself and brought me out on the ground, that I'd see where it was. He was out in a small field, and was after binding up the grass, and the sky got very black over him and very dark. And he was thrown down on the ground, and got a great beating, but he could see nothing at all. He had done nothing to vex them, just minding his business in the field. And the other was an old man too, and he was out on the roads, and they threw him there and beat him that he was out of his mind for a time. One night sleeping in that little cabin of mine, I heard them ride past, and I could hear by the feet of the horses that there was a long line of them."

We might expect the sufferer to have a guilty conscience, but it is not always as simple as that. *Taibhse Choimhlig* (pp. 287–88 below), the ghost of a man who had hidden a ploughshare from his neighbours, regularly doles out beatings to innocent wayfarers, presumably in order to frighten them into finding the ploughshare and so releasing him from torment. In Lewis, says MacPhail (1896, p. 401), the ghost of a murdered man haunted the spot where he died, wrestling with all who passed by until it met someone who could throw it down and force it to speak. Only then could it tell its story and thus obtain everlasting rest. Wentz spoke of a man in Inisheer who was giving his cow some water at a well one evening when he saw some strange people playing hurley (1911, p. 41). One of them came up and struck the cow a hard blow, then turned on him and cut his face and body; he 'might not have been so badly off', but returned to the well to look for his cow 'and got five times as bad a beating'. Yeats pointed out (Welch 1993, pp. 178–79): "People indeed come back for all sorts of purposes. I was told at Sligo about four years ago of a man who was being constantly beaten by a dead person. Sometimes it was said you could hear the blows as he came along the road, and sometimes he would be dragged out of bed at night and his wife would hear the blows, but you could never see anything. He had thought to escape the dead person by going to a distant place, Bundoran I think, but he had been followed there. Nobody seemed to give him any pity, for it was 'an old uncle of his own that was beating him'."

Yeats draws attention to a remarkable series of stories (Welch 1993, pp. 168–71, 325–26) about the sound of violent struggle amongst the Fairies that may be heard about dying persons, 'thought to come of fighting between their dead friends who would prevent their being taken, and those who would take them' (*ibid.*, p. 168). He also points to a shorter series (*ibid.*, pp. 313–15) in which the violence is dealt out to the individuals themselves. Lady Gregory devotes a chapter to the subject, 'The Fighting of the Friends' (1970, pp. 185–89). She was told by a man in Corcomroe Abbey, Co. Clare: "There was one Delvin, that lies under a slab yonder, and for seven years he was brought away every night, and into this abbey. And he was beat and pinched, and when he'd come home he'd faint; but he used to say that the place that he went to was grander than any city. One night he was with a lot of others at a wake, and they knew the time was coming for him to go, and they all took hold of him. But he was drawn out of the door, and the arms of those that were holding him were near pulled out of their sockets."[22]

CHANGELINGS

The concept of the changeling is based on 'theft of substance'. The Fairies steal a real, healthy, growing child, and leave the unreal shadow of a child in its place – old, obnoxious, all the sap dried out of it.[23] No particular word is used: the changeling is a Fairy like any other, and *tàcharan* is not so much a description as an insult, see p. 242 and note 839. A remark made by a woman near Ardrahan, noted by Lady Gregory, helps us understand how the belief could have arisen (Welch 1993, pp. 317–18): "There was a cousin of my own was said to be 'away', and when she died I was but a child, and my mother brought me with her to the house where she was laid out. And when I saw her I began to scream and to say, 'That's not Mary that's in it, that's some old hag.' And so it was, I know well it was not Mary that was lying there in the bed."

In the same way we may observe an accident to a child, leading to sickness and to death, comprehensively rationalised in terms of the changeling belief. A woman near Loughrea told Lady Gregory about a child to whom something had happened close to what she and Yeats call a 'forth' – a fort, cashel, rusheen, *ráth, lios, bruíon, sí, cathair* or Fairy dwelling.[24] "Sure there was a fairy in a house at Eserkelly fourteen years. Bridget Collins she was called . . . She never kept the bed, but she'd sit in the corner of the kitchen on a mat, and from a good stout lump of a girl that she was, she wasted to nothing, and her teeth grew as long as your finger, and then they dropped out. And she'd eat nothing at all, only crabs and sour things. And she'd never leave the house in the daytime, but in the night she'd go out and pick things out of the fields she could eat. And the hurt she got, or whatever it was touched her, it was one day she was swinging on the Moneen gate, just there by the forth. She died as quiet as another, but you wouldn't like to be looking at her after the teeth fell out."

We may compare this sinister little children's taunt preserved by R. C. Maclagan (1901, p. 252):

Ma mà, ia ià, ha hà,
Is thusa a' chaileag bheag
Thàinig ás an ràth.

"Ma maa, ya yaa, ha haa, / You are the little girl / That came out of the fort." Sometimes the encoded nature of the belief slips out almost unawares, as when JGC points out at p. 5 that *brughadair*, applied to men, means 'one who does a stupid or senseless action', or a Kiltartan woman remarks to Lady Gregory (1970, p. 132, cf. Welch 1993, p. 180): "You might notice it's always the good they take. That's why when we see a child good for nothing we say, 'Ah, you little faery.'"

Stripped of its supernatural associations, 'changeling' becomes a euphemism for a mentally handicapped person, and Spence says straightforwardly (1948, p. 233) that 'whenever a cretinous or diseased child made its appearance in a family, it was usually regarded as a changeling'. In Lewis and elsewhere Dr Arthur Mitchell, Deputy Commissioner in Lunacy for Scotland, observed for himself the connection between Fairy belief and cretinism; he draws particular attention to the phenomenon of the old head on the young body, which is also a symptom of malnutrition (1860–62, p. 286). "I saw at M——, in Uig, an emaciated, shrivelled, helpless idiot, a dwarf with that puzzling expression of face – a compound of senility and babyhood – which is not rare. He is believed to be a changeling of the fairies, who are supposed to steal away the human child, and leave for it one of their own *young-old* children to be nursed. (I know two idiots in one of the Western Islands exactly of the same character, and also believed to be changelings of the fairies.) The only remedy for this of which I heard, is to place the changeling on the beach by the water side, when the tide is out, and pay no attention to its screams. The fairies, rather than suffer their own to be drowned by the rising waters, spirit it away, and restore the child they had stolen. The sign that this has been done is the cessation of the child's crying."

This is precisely the remedy stated by John Sands to have been practised in Tiree about the year 1876 (see below, p. 655); unfortunately he omits to tell us the result. In Cornwall the child was allegedly placed not on the beach but on a tree (Deane and Shaw 1975, p. 93).

> On 14 July 1843 the *West Briton* reported the case of J. Trevelyan of Penzance who was charged with ill-treating one of his children. It appears that the young boy was frequently starved, kicked and beaten by the servants and that at Christmas 1841, when the child was only 15 months old, he had been placed outside on a tree and left to remain in the cold for two-and-a-half-hours. The parents believed that he was a changeling and that their own child had been taken away by the fairies. The case was dismissed for lack of evidence.

Perhaps the most celebrated account of changelings outside the Gaelic world of Scotland and Ireland is that given to Wentz, in writing (1911, pp. 198–99), by Goulven Le Scour from Finistère in Lower Brittany. He describes a woman of the village of Kergoff, in Plouneventer, who bore three children in a row, all of whom were perfect at first – or so she claimed – but turned into wizened, evil-minded little hunchbacks. In addition,

Wentz was personally acquainted with a dwarf at Plouharnel-Carnac (*ibid.*, p. 251): "His own mother declares that he is not the child she gave birth to. He once said to me with a kind of pathetic protest, 'Did M. —— tell you that I am a demon?'"

In a superb summary of the potential relationships between changeling descriptions and medical diagnosis, Susan Eberly specifies three relevant conditions found in infants – PKU, homocystinuria and progeria (1997, pp. 239–42). A child with PKU, an inherited metabolic disease, will appear normal – not to say beautiful – at birth, with light skin, light hair and blue eyes, but within six months it will begin to display such symptoms as seizures, tremors, hyperactivity and irritability; it will grow slowly but will live to a normal age despite severe mental retardation. The symptoms of homocystinuria appear around the age of two months: rosy cheeks, fine sparse hair, limbs and digits that are long and thin, and a tendency to mental retardation, cerebral palsy, encephalitis, paralysis and seizures. Finally, a child with progeria looks old, has mottled brown skin and fine hair, and dies of heart disease before adulthood.

Joyce Munro supplements Eberly's analysis with one of her own (1997) in which the changeling is seen as an articulation of the 'failure to thrive' syndrome. Unlike Eberly she links her thesis closely to motifs in the narratives themselves, noting some particularly intriguing connections between the polydipsia and 'strange relationship with food' which are so characteristic of emotionally deprived children and the widespread eggshell motif which is described below at p. 21 and note 83. She would, I am sure, have been keenly interested in the parting words of a changeling threatened with being placed on a hot griddle over the fire in a story recorded by Maurice Fleming (2002, p. 41): "I wish I had 'a kent my mither! If I had 'a been longer wi' my mither, I would have kent her better."

To deal with the problem of changelings who survived childhood, Eberly spreads her net to include what she calls 'the solitary fairies, both domestic and reclusive' and 'the solitary "nature" fairy who lived, usually, by a well or stream; who hunted, fished, or scavenged for sustenance; and who was a sort of *genius loci* to a particular place'. These she names (1997, p. 242, retaining her spelling and order) as the Brownie (see pp. 100–02); the Gille Dubh (see Dixon 1886, pp. 160–61, Campbell 1940–60, vol. 1, pp. 480–85, and Mackenzie 1980, pp. 186–87); Meg Moulach (see note 549); the Brown Man of the Muirs (see Briggs 1976, pp. 44–45); the Urisk (see pp. 105–07); the Grogan (see Briggs, 1976, p. 206); and the Fenoderree (see p. 102 and note 336). Pointing out that many of these appear to represent human beings who are both mentally retarded and physically 'different', she cites two sets of congenital disorders which may help to explain them (Eberly 1997, pp. 242–43).

The first of these disorders are the syndromes that cause dwarfing. Achondroplastic or short-limbed dwarfism occurs in about 1:20,000 births; children born with this syndrome will have normally sized trunks, large heads, and very short limbs. Costovertebral dwarfing results in limbs of normal size, a very short trunk, frequent occurrence of clubfoot, and, in some cases, mental retardation. Anterior hypopituitary dwarfing, the most common dwarfing syndrome, leads to normal body proportions but overall small size. The second set of disorders that comes to mind are the mucopolysaccharidosis syndromes . . . These also affect growth, cause hair to grow over much of the body, and may lead to a darkening of the skin. Children with these syndromes are often mentally retarded.

Referring specifically to the 'brownie', while also including the more liminal 'urisk' and 'Fenoderree', she concludes (*ibid.*, pp. 244–45):

> While some have interpreted these solitary fairies to be representative of a shaggy aborigine, hanging about the farm, attached to its service by food and kindness, a theory first suggested by MacRitchie, it seems to me that they are more likely to represent persons with mental retardation and often physical disabilities as well; persons who made their living through labor, receiving in payment a cubbyhole, loft, or warm hearth that would shelter them from the weather.

Eberly's survey, based mainly on folklore data from Gaelic Scotland, allows us to flesh out a theory of the 'first otherworld' which relates Fairies, brownies and other creatures to timeless social issues of mental and physical disability. Such a theory runs somewhat as follows. Firstly, the Fairies themselves relate principally to mental illness, stress, fear, delusion, and the need to cope somehow with whatever was unseen or imperfectly understood – those who were mad, dead or disabled could be seen as Fairies, and those who were young or sane were well advised to respect and fear them. Secondly, given restricted gene pools, rudimentary health care, poor personal hygiene, recurrent famine, social inequality, rough justice and lawlessness, I see no reason to believe that the incidence of mental and physical disability was lower in traditional Highland communities than in the modern world. Some disabled persons were no doubt institutionalised in the way suggested by Eberly for the brownie, and some would have been driven out of the community to survive in the wild as best they could. This was practicable in parts of the Highland mainland where wood and fresh water were easily obtainable; where there was acute competition for resources (as in most of the islands) or density of settlement (as in most of Ireland) it was a less likely solution, and solitaries are correspondingly less prominent in the traditions of those places. In the Western Isles they appear to be principally associated with the smallest habitable islands (Cara, Shuna, Gunna, etc.), no doubt reflecting a 'Devil's Island' form of incarceration. JFC, who interpreted gifts laid out for brownies and *gruagaichean* as the benefices of ancient druids, remarked that they were 'still supposed to haunt many a desolate island in the far west', and quoted a Mrs MacTavish, 1859, Islay (Campbell 1890, vol. 1, pp. lxxxvii–lxxxviii):

> The small island of Inch, near Easdale, is inhabited by a brownie, which has followed the Macdougalls of Ardincaple for ages, and takes a great interest in them. He takes care of their cattle in that island night and day, unless the dairymaid, when there in summer with the milk cattle, neglects to leave warm milk for him at night in a knocking-stone in the cave, where she and the herd live during their stay in the island. Should this perquisite be for a night forgot, they will be sure in the morning to find one of the cattle fallen over the rocks with which the place abounds. It is a question whether the brownie has not a friend with whom he shares the contents of the stone, which will, I daresay, hold from two to three Scotch pints.

The case of Gunna, between Tiree and Coll, is particularly interesting. It was described by Dean Monro in 1549 as 'ane mile lang from the eist to the west, manurit and inhabite, gude for corn, store and fishing' (Munro 1961, p. 65), but appears to have been abandoned, as subsequent writers such as Martin Martin fail to mention it, and JGC duly records a tradition of a brownie called Gunna who was loose in Tiree (pp. 101–02). It has to be said however that Carmichael's previously unpublished account of this brownie (note 334) would lead us to suspect that that his name derives not so much from the island as from a tendency to priapism.

Eberly extends her thesis further to pick out some of the more detailed physical characteristics associated with otherworld beings (1997, pp. 245–46). The most common of all congenital malformations, she says, is webbed digits. "Webbing may join only two digits, or three, four, or all." This could be used to back up stories such as those of the seal-men at p. 157 below, and indeed Alan Bruford has pointed out (1997, p. 122) that a hereditary disability which takes the form of a thickening and hardening of the skin on the palms of the hands is attributed in Orkney to descent from a union between a mortal woman and a seal man. As for the mermaid's covering or *cochall* (p. 156 below), it may derive ultimately from ichthyosis. "Fishscale skin, or *ichthyosis*," says Eberly (1997, p. 246), "may occur in the newborn (as ichthyosis fetalis), may cover part or all of the body, may be fatal or may be only slightly disfiguring. Exfoliation, resulting in thick, platy masses of keratin in the skin, may be localized, as on the hands and feet, or may be found all over the body."

So, too, the creatures of the land. As pointed out in note 16 (pp. 297–98 below), the Elle-woman of Denmark is 'hollow like a dough-trough' behind; this, says Eberly, 'may recall spina bifida or a condition known as craniospinal rachischisis, in which there is an open trough along the spine'. Conversely, I try to show in note 549 that *Meg Mholach* ('Hairy Meg') is in origin a misunderstanding of *mac mollachd* ('son of cursing'), one of the devil's names, but this simply underlines the point that solitaries were assumed to be shaggy: "Hairy Meg (Meg Moulach) and other Gruagachs and suchlike furry fairy folk," says Eberly (1997, pp. 246–47), "exhibit the hirsutism found in a variety of congenital disorders, among them X-linked syndrome, Hunter's and Hurler's syndromes."

Under the heading 'The Defects of Fairies' JGC says at p. 8 that 'in Mull and the neighbourhood they are said to have only one nostril, the other being imperforate'; Eberly points out (*ibid.*, p. 246) that 'an imperforate nostril, a characteristic of the Mull fairies, occurs in human births'. Referring specifically to the female of the species, JGC speaks not only of her 'web foot' and 'entire want of a nostril' but also of her 'frightful front tooth'; Eberly comments (*ibid.*) that 'the single nostril and great front tooth of the *Bean Sidhe* is found with cleft palate'. The rest of the defects of Fairy women mentioned by JGC in that section – voracity, long breasts, inability to suckle – are less likely to be congenital, however, than the result of hunger. In a society which portrayed itself in words and music instead of oils, they represent women's paintings of themselves in their pain. In particular, the woman who is prevented by stress from breastfeeding her own children is 'away with the Fairies', a burden upon her sisters in the community.

It looks like being some time before Eberly's thesis is fully squared with pathology, given the opposition of scholars like Ann Skjelbred, who has stated categorically (1997, pp. 220–21) that 'the folklore of the changeling ... cannot be interpreted within the frame of folk medicine and definitely not within the frame of scientific medicine'. One reason for this is that changeling beliefs comprehended not only disability but such issues as precocity and illegitimacy – as Narváez has pointed out for Newfoundland, 'fairy explanations could be used by participants to mask actual deviant behaviors such as extreme tardiness, premarital sexual relations, infidelity, incest, child molestation, wife battering, and sexual assault' (1997, p. 357). A good Highland example of this is *Calum nighinn Eoghain* from Luing, for his name ('Hugh's daughter's Malcolm') suggests strongly that his mother was unmarried, and he possessed gifts of second sight, prophecy and healing (Mac a Phì 1938, p. 141). *Is e an t-iomradh a bha aca air mar a fhuair e an cumhachd so gu'n do ghoideadh e leis na sìthichean 'nuair a bha e 'na leanabh. Bha e fad cheithir bliadhna 's a'bhrùth; chaidh fidilean-finndinn, seann sìogaidh sean-athair Chloinn Chròig fhagail aig a mhàthair, ach mhothaich ise gu'm b'e am fleasgach sin fhéin a bha aice, is le cuideachadh Griosal Mhóir rinn i braid-a-gill air Fidilean is sgiùrsadh e do'n dùn as an d'thàinig e. Is ann mar sin a fhuair i Calum aice fhéin. B'iad na sìthichean a chuir an t-seunmhorachd ud air Calum.* "The explanation they had for how he got this power was that he was stolen by the Fairies when he was a child. He spent four years in the otherworld (*brugh*); his mother was left with a little fiddle-faddle, some old grandfather Fairy of the Clan MacClaw, but she noticed what a mighty warrior had been dumped upon her, and with the help of Big Grizel she got the better of Fiddlesticks, who was banished to the *dùn* from which he had come. That's how she got her own Malcolm. It was the Fairies who gave Malcolm that magic power of his."

Let us now consider a basic changeling story (MacDougall and Calder 1910, pp. 116–19). There was a widow in Glengarry who had a baby boy. One day when he was sleeping quietly in his cradle she went to the well for water, and when she got back he was screaming as if in great pain. She gave him a drink as quickly as she could. That calmed him down for a bit, but he soon broke out again as badly as ever. She gave him another drink, and this time while he was at her breast she noticed that he had two teeth, each more than an inch long, and that his face was looking old and withered. She said to herself: *Tha mi deas a-nis. Ach fuirichidh mi sàmhach fiach am faic mi ciod a thig ás a-seo.* "I'm finished now. But I'll keep quiet and see what comes of this."

Next day she picked up the baby, covered him with a shawl and set off *mar gum biodh i dol don ath bhaile leis* – as if she were bringing him to the next township. There was a big burn in the way, and as she was wading through the ford the wizened creature stuck his head out of the shawl and said: *Is iomadh buaile mhór a chunnaic mise air dà thaobh an uillt seo!* "Many a big fold have I seen on the banks of this stream!"

She did not wait to hear any more. She threw the baby into a deep pool below the ford, where he tossed about in the swirling water, screaming that 'if he had known in advance that was the trick she was going to play on him, he would have shown her another' (*nan robh fhios aige ro làimh gum b'e siud an cleas a bha i dol a chluich air, gun d'fheuch esan cleas eile dhi*). Then she heard a sound like a flock of birds, but saw nothing until she looked at her feet, and there was her own baby 'with his bones as bare as the tongs' (*gun mhìr air cnàimh dheth nas motha na air a' chlobha*). She brought him home, and he gradually got better, and in the end he was as healthy as any other child.

What are the main points of the story? Firstly, the woman is a widow. That means she and her child are at risk. At best she is a cottar. To have a cow she must pay rent for grazing; can she generate goods or services enough to do so? Probably not. More likely she has sold the cow, or it has died, and she is trying to manage with goats alone.

Secondly, the changeling is substituted for her baby while she is at the well. As JGC tells us, superstition provided various ways of safeguarding against this, involving the strategic placing of iron (such as a horseshoe), rowan, or coloured threads, or the sprinkling of *maistir*, urine, which was collected for use in waulking cloth, but which the Fairies much disliked. Who can blame them?

Thirdly, the changeling reveals its age in two different ways, both of which are common in such stories. One is having prominent teeth and being wizened. The other is more entertaining – being old, the Fairy cannot resist droning on about the old days.

The fourth point is that the woman tries to kill her baby – that is, the Fairy changeling – by drowning him. We are not told that she leaves the house with the intention of doing this. Motivation takes place in three stages. First she discovers her baby's physical condition. Then she sets off towards the next township, where presumably relief for it can be obtained. Finally the baby speaks.

But there is more. The Fairy host come around her in the form of birds which she cannot see. (We are reminded of the stork.) They deposit her own baby at her feet. Then a detail which the late Alan Bruford pointed out was 'quite unusual' in changeling stories (MacDougall 1978b, p. 105): the real baby seems starved even though he has only been a short time away, his bones being 'as bare as the tongs'.

My own interpretation of the story, a Marxist one, is this. The woman is pregnant, destitute, starving. She has nothing to give her son but breast milk. She comes back from the well to find he is teething. She has been a long time because she was foraging for food. "He looks so old," she says to herself. This is because he is malnourished. The teeth being 'more than an inch long' is an exaggeration. No doubt it feels like that as the baby sucks. She gets labour pains and sets off to find help. The swollen burn blocks her way. Her son is fretting and screaming. She tries to wade across, loses her footing, drops the baby into the water. He drowns. On reaching the bank she goes into labour and gives birth to a healthy son. She gets to the township, where she and the child are well taken care of. Perhaps because it is more than nine months since her husband died, she allows the women to believe that her new-born child is the one she bore many months before. That is why it strikes them that 'his bones are as bare as the tongs'.

This then is a case where the changeling may be identified as a troublesome year-old child, and the 'real' baby as a new-born one. Changeling stories should be seen in the perspective of a society in which famine was endemic, as was the case in the Highlands down to the nineteenth century. Changelings are always voracious, and one of Lady Gregory's stories from south Co. Galway offers a coded account of famine (1970, p. 261, cf. Welch 1993, p. 310). Again it concerns a 'forth'.

There was one Leary in Clough had the land taken that's near Newtown racecourse. And he was out there one day building a wall, and it was time for his dinner, but he had none brought with him. And a man came to him and said, "Is it home you'll be going for your dinner?" And he said, "It's not worth my while to go back to Clough, I'd have the day lost." And the man said, "Well, come in and eat a bit with me." And he brought him into a forth and there was everything that was grand, and the dinner they gave him of the best, so that he ate near two plates of it. And then he went out again to build the wall. And whether it was with lifting the heavy stones I don't know, but (with respects to you) when he was walking the road home he began to vomit, and what he vomited up was all green grass.

It was a tradition among my late father-in-law's people in Hollyford, Co. Tipperary, that victims of the Great Famine passed through the townland in the 1840s with their faces smeared green from eating grass. Thomas Pennant famously said of the people of Rum that 'they are a well-made and well-looking race, but carry famine in their aspect' (1998, p. 277); we catch a glimpse of such hunger in JGC's stories at pp. 39 and 97 below, and, as he says at pp. 172–73, 'we must remember that in days of scarcity and famine, poverty with icy hand and slow-consuming age will make people resort to shifts of which they would never dream when food was abundant'.

I have been quite charitable to the young widow, for she may have deliberately murdered her child. The evidence for changeling stories as a cover for infanticide is strong. Consider the following tale told by the Rev. Malcolm MacPhail (1900, pp. 443–44) in which an exhausted mother throws her child into the fire. This mother, he explains, was nursing a Fairy instead of her own child. He neither grew nor developed, and cried without cease (*cha robh ìre no piseach a' tighinn air, agus cha robh ràn a' dol ás a cheann*), till one day she said: *Is mì tha seachd sgìth dhìot.* "I'm seven times tired of you."

To her amazement the infant replied: *Ma-tà, nan dèanadh tu rùn maith ormsa, bheirinnse faochadh dhuit, agus dhèanainn greis dannsa dhuit.* "Well, if you would keep it a secret, I'd give you some relief and dance for you for a bit."

She promised to keep the secret, and in the shape of a smart little old man (*bodach beag sgiobalta*), he set to. When tired from his dancing he returned to her lap, exactly as before. She told her friends what had happened, and they advised her to put on a good fire, coax the Fairy to dance again, then take the first chance she got to throw him into the fire. She took their advice, and at the first touch of the flames the Fairy ran screaming out of the house. "No sooner did it do so," concludes MacPhail, "than her own child was at once imperceptibly restored."

In the last paragraph on p. 20 below JGC lists the ways in which (according to tradition) such children could be got rid of. In a serious Freudian slip, he describes the process as conversion into, not out of, the stock of a tree, which means murder. Clearly Mitchell's remedy of leaving a changeling on the beach to be drowned is a case in point, and JGC's grisly catalogue is corroborated by other sources.[25] Circumstantial accounts are harder to come by, however. William Grant Stewart speaks of a woman in the Speyside parish of Abernethy who, when a child, was identified by her parents as a changeling when she was unaccountably found one night on the outside of a window (1823, pp. 115–16). She was brought to the junction of the counties of Inverness, Moray and Banff and left there for the night. She came to no harm as she was well wrapped up, and her parents were well pleased with the result. Similarly, Kenneth Macdonald speaks (2003, p. 125) of a man, well known to him in Lewis, whose mother went out to put some clothes on the bleaching-green (this would have been about 1890). When she came back she saw 'that her baby had disappeared and that a baby with a wizened old face had been left in its place'. The wise men of the township were consulted, and advised that the changeling be placed under an umbrella on the highway where three roads met. Again, it worked.

The Rev. James Rust of Slains in Aberdeenshire adds a few extra details. When a baby suspected of being a changeling was laid overnight at the Lykar Cairn near his church – he was personally acquainted with the last person to whom this was done,

Mary Findlay, who died 'at a great age' in the 1860s – a 'peace-offering' of bread, butter, cheese, milk, eggs or chicken was 'presented at the same time with some incantations'. The relatives watched the child 'at a distance', and if the 'peace-offering' had disappeared by morning, it was taken as evidence 'that the Elfs had been propitiated, and prevailed upon to restore the human children, and take back their own sickly changelings' (1871, pp. 32–33, 35). The Rev. Charles Rogers describes the use of fire in a case at Louisburgh near Wick in 1845; he calls the victim a 'girl' three times and says that she was 'suspected of witchcraft', but from his description of what took place it seems that she was only a baby, and that the alleged witchcraft was merely a suspicion that she was a changeling, presumably because she was dwining, refusing to suck (1886, p. 329):

> To cure her, a neighbour placed her in a basket along with shavings of wood, and in this manner suspended her over a fire. The shavings were ignited, but the girl was removed from the flames uninjured. In handing her to her friends, the operator remarked that the girl was 'not half so witch-like since she had been singed'.

In only one Scottish case are we told that the 'treatment' ended in death. At Ardersier, according to E. J. Guthrie (1885, p. 121), it was believed that the Fairies lived in 'a conical knoll in the carse called *Tom Earnais*, or Henry's Knoll', and that if a changeling were left on it overnight the real child would be there in the morning. "About 1730, it is said, a man of the name of Munro had a sickly attenuated child, which he and his neighbours considered to be a changeling ... The infatuated father actually subjected his ailing offspring to this ordeal, and in the morning found it a corpse."

What this black litany appears to be telling us is that children with severe disabilities were routinely subjected to treatments so extreme that only two outcomes were possible: submissiveness to discipline (perhaps through maiming) or death. Elsewhere in Europe, even as close to the Highlands as the burghs of Inverness, Chanonry and Dornoch, this was applied to witches; the principal means of putting to the proof, fire and water, were the same. If death resulted, its cause was not murder but unsuccessful medical treatment. In Ireland, as I will show, such treatments persisted into the nineteenth century and surface in the records of courts of justice. In Scotland the folklore record appears to be identical, yet the strictly historical record appears to be blank. It is not clear to me why this should be the case, but some points come to mind. In many mainland districts, as we have seen, abandonment may have been a more popular option than murder. In some cases on the western seaboard people with disabilities may have been abandoned on uninhabited islands; this was not humane, but neither was it murder. Also, by and large, the Irish folklore record of the late nineteenth century appears to describe nineteenth-century experience, while the Highland folklore record of the same period (as exemplified by JGC's work) appears to describe eighteenth-century experience. During much of the eighteenth century the ordinary people of the Highlands and Islands were beyond the reach of the civil law. They were not, however, beyond the reach of ecclesiastical courts, and it is to eighteenth-century kirk session and presbyterial records that we must look for answers. It might be possible to argue that kirk sessions took no interest in abandonment, regarding it as the correct way to deal with mental and physical disability. Although eager to root out witchcraft in the seventeenth century and domestic violence in the eighteenth, they may have been aware of Martin Luther's advice with regard to a twelve-year-old changeling (*Wechselbalg*) in a house at Dessau which ate as much as four ploughmen, screamed when touched, laughed when things went wrong and cried when all was well (Bennett 1992, p. 27): "I said to the Prince of Anhalt, 'If I were prince or ruler here I would have this child thrown into the water, into the Moldau, that flows by Dessau, and would run the risk of being a homicide.' But the Elector of Saxony, who was then at Dessau, and the Prince of Anhalt, would not follow my advice. I then said: 'They ought to cause a Pater noster to be said in the church, that God would take the devil away from them.' This was done daily at Dessau, and the said changeling died two years after."

Let me turn now, as promised, to my Irish examples. A policeman's wife from the Burren told Lady Gregory of a little girl near Ballyvaughan who was believed to be 'away'.[26] Her mother used to hear horses coming about the door every night. "One day the mother was picking flax in the house and of a sudden there came in her hand an herb with the best smell and the sweetest that ever anyone smelled. And she closed it into her hand and called to the son that was making up a stack of hay outside, 'Come in, Denis, for I have the best smelling herb that ever you saw.' And when he came in she opened her hand and the herb was gone, clear and clean.

"She got annoyed at last with the horses coming about the door, and some one told her to gather all the fire into the middle of the floor and to lay the little girl upon it, and to see would she come back again. So she did as she was told, and brought the little girl out of the bed and laid her on the coals, and she began to scream and to call out, and the neighbours came running in, and the police heard of it, and they came and arrested the mother and brought her to Ballyvaughan, before the magistrate, Mr Macnamara, and my own husband was one of the police that arrested her. And when the magistrate heard all, he said she was an ignorant woman, and that she did what she thought right, and he would give her no punishment. And the girl got well and was married, and it was after she married I knew her."

Bourke cites the following (1999, pp. 33–34). A man in Kerry roasted his child to death, believing that it was a Fairy. He was not brought to trial, as the Crown prosecutor mercifully looked upon him as insane. A four-year-old child in Kerry, Michael Leahy, could neither stand, walk nor speak, and was thought to be 'fairy struck'. An old woman called Ann Roche drowned him in the River Flesk. In July 1826 she was indicted for murder at Tralee assizes. On cross-examination a witness said that it was 'not done with intent to kill the child, but to cure it – *to put the fairy out of it*'. Roche was found not guilty.

According to *The Daily Telegraph* of 19 May 1884 a three-year-old boy in Clonmel, Philip Dillon, did not have the use of his limbs. In the mother's absence Ellen Cushion and Anastatia Rourke entered the house and placed the lad naked on a hot shovel, believing that this would break the charm. He 'was severely burned, and is in a precarious condition'. Cushion and Rourke were arrested on a charge of cruelly ill-treating him. (See also Anon. 1884b.) In January 1888 Joanna Doyle, 45, murdered her 'imbecile' or 'epileptic idiot' son Patsy, 13, with a hatchet, with the help of her husband and three older children. One of them, Mary, 18, said: "I was not shocked when I heard my mother kill him, as I had heard people say he was a fairy, and I believed them." Joanna, whose next son, Denis, 12, was also described as an imbecile, insisted that

Patsy 'was not my son, he was a devil, a bad fairy'. On 30 January she was admitted to Killarney Asylum, where a canvas camisole was used to restrain her from tearing her clothing. She was later transferred to Dundrum Mental Hospital in Dublin.

On Thursday evening 14 March 1895, in Ballyvadlea, Co. Tipperary, a cooper's wife, Bridget Cleary, 26, who was attractive, successful and intelligent but childless, was in bed with bronchitis. Relatives and neighbours, including her husband, Michael Cleary, her father, Patrick Boland, and her cousins Patrick and James Kennedy, agreed that she must be a changeling. They fed her herbs boiled in new milk and held her over the fire, repeatedly demanding: "Are you Bridget Boland, wife of Michael Cleary, in the name of God?"

Michael Cleary was sick with worry and had hardly slept for several nights, having had to go to persuade the doctor and the parish priest to visit his wife. On the following evening, 15 March, following an argument about the Fairies, he tried to make her eat three bits of bread and jam, knocked her to the floor in a rage, tore off her clothes, seized a burning stick from the fire and demanded that she answer her name three times. She answered, but he was not satisfied. Then he took a can of oil, threw it over her and set her alight. "For the love of God," James Kennedy said, according to his own testimony, "don't burn your wife!"

"She's not my wife," Cleary replied. "She's an old deceiver sent in place of my wife."

Cleary forced Patrick Kennedy to help him bury the body, and on Sunday morning he put it about that his wife was at Kylenagranagh Fort, that they would go for her that night, that she would be on a grey horse, and that if they could cut the cords tying her to the animal they would get her back again. The body was found, however, and Cleary and the two Kennedy brothers were arrested, along with the murdered woman's father, aunt, two other cousins and two neighbours, all of whom had been in the house on the Thursday evening at least.

They were tried for murder at Clonmel in July. The jury found Cleary guilty of manslaughter and he was sentenced to five years' penal servitude. Of the rest, one was acquitted, while the other seven were found guilty of wounding and received sentences varying from five years' penal servitude to nothing at all. The case is the subject of perhaps the best analysis of Gaelic Fairy belief ever written, Angela Bourke's *The Burning of Bridget Cleary*. Bourke explains (1999, pp. 28–30, 183):

Fairies belong to the margins, and so can serve as reference points and metaphors for all that is marginal in human life. Their underground existence allows them to stand for the unconscious, for the secret, or the unspeakable, and their constant eavesdropping explains the need sometimes to speak in riddles, or to avoid discussion of certain topics. Unconstrained by work and poverty, or by the demands of landlords, police, or clergy, the fairies of Irish legend inhabit a world that is sensuously colourful, musical and carefree, and as writers from Yeats to Irish-language poet Nuala Ní Dhomhnaill have observed, legends about them richly reflect the imaginative, emotional and erotic dimensions of human life . . .

As Danish folklorist Bengt Holbek remarks: "What matters is not their artistic impact, but their function as arguments about reality . . . Legends *debate* the relation between our daily reality and some kind of possibly real 'otherworld'." One feature which makes fairy-legends so tenacious in a changing cultural environment is the concision and vivid memorability of their central themes. Another is their connection to real, named, people, and to real places in a known landscape. Yet another reason why they survive is that their narratives interact so intimately with the practicalities and the emotional realities of daily life.

Viewed as a system of interlocking units of narrative, practice and belief, fairy-legend can be compared to a database: a pre-modern culture's way of storing and retrieving information and knowledge of every kind, from hygiene and childcare to history and geography. Highly charged and memorable images like that of a woman emerging on a white horse from a fairy dwelling are the retrieval codes for a whole complex of stored information about land and landscape, community relations, gender roles, medicine, and work in all its aspects: tools, materials and techniques. Stories gain verisimilitude, and storytellers keep their listeners' attention, by the density of circumstance they depict, including social relations and the technical details of work. Most stories, however, are constructed around the unexpected, and therefore memorable, happenings in people's lives. Encounters with or interference by the fairies in these stories remind listeners (and readers) of everything in life that is outside human control. It is not surprising, then, that death and illness are among the preoccupations of fairy legends. Almost any death, other than a gentle and gradual departure in old age, is open to interpretation as the work of the fairies . . .

The overwhelming message of the fairy-legends is that the unexpected may be guarded against by careful observance of society's rules. These stories are important components of child-rearing practice, establishing the boundaries of normal, acceptable behaviour, and spelling out the ways in which an individual who breaches them may forfeit his or her position. They recognize, however, that rules may be in conflict with each other, or with other imperatives in certain circumstances, and that accidents may happen. When accidents do happen, or when inexperience or inattention has led to a breaking of the rules, remedies are available . . .

The legal system found in western societies today, which was also the one at work in Clonmel in 1895, endeavours to identify culprits and apportion blame. The legal systems of oral cultures, on the other hand, are more concerned with restoring equilibrium. It may be useful to view fairy-belief in Ireland as a sort of vernacular system of ethics: a way of laying down rules, defining sanctions, and, very occasionally, implementing them. Belonging, as it does by definition, to groups of people whose economic and family ties constrain them to live almost within sight and earshot of each other, it resists strict codification and invasive exegesis; its terms of reference are fluid, slippery and often ambiguous. Nevertheless, as long as the system is not discredited, everything in the environment, from landscape features to calendar custom to household hygiene, illness, birth and death, works to reinforce it. Attributing tragic events or criminal actions to the fairies could work as a face-saving mechanism which would allow ordinary, indispensable social interaction to proceed, something that could not be achieved through accusation and confrontation. Bridget Cleary's economic or sexual behaviour may have been causing offence to her neighbours and relatives, but the strategy they had employed to discipline her was not indictment, but diagnosis.

Yeats tells of a woman from Mayo who heard of the Tipperary case. "She had no doubt that they only burned some dead person, but she was quite certain that you should not burn even a dead person. She said: 'In my place we say you should only threaten. They are so superstitious in Tipperary.'"[27]

This is what throws into such stark relief the question of whether 'changeling murder' can be found in the historical record for the Highlands and Islands of Scotland. The clerical contributors to one source of general information, the 'Statistical Accounts' of the 1790s and 1840s, appear actively to discourage such inquiry, despite the fact that one of the questions specifically posed by Sir John Sinclair in 1790 was: "Have any murders or suicides been committed?" To take the parish of JGC's birth, Lismore and Appin, for example, the Rev. Donald McNicol wrote: "There has been no instance of child murder in the parish in the memory of man. This is a crime hardly known in the west Highlands."[28]

So why did he single it out, one wonders? If we then take the parish of Tiree and Coll, we find that the Rev. Archibald McColl says that 'for generations back, there has been no robbery, murder, or suicide', which we might well believe were it not for his statement that 'they are free of superstition'.[29]

Cases of changeling abuse or murder would have come, in the first instance, to the notice of kirk sessions, by whom they would statutorily be referred to the Presbytery (see p. 632 below) and, where appropriate, to the civil authorities. So far I have failed to find any such cases in published kirk session or presbytery records, although of course it is not always possible to know what underlies cases of infanticide.[30] By contrast, it is startling to find the term 'changeling' used quite routinely in the kirk session register of Ardnamurchan. On 26 November 1789, when £5 7s is distributed among forty-one persons designated as 'the most destitute Poor on both sides of the country, from Girgadal to Tarbert inclusive', a table is drawn up with columns for name, place of abode, age, remarks and the sum allocated, the 'age' and 'remarks' columns being used principally to justify the allocation of unusually large amounts. The 'remarks' column contains 'Cripple' twice and 'Changeling' twice. One changeling, Archibald McArthur, Kilchoan, receives 4s 6d. Only two other persons receive as much, and only one, aged 77, receives more (5s). The other changeling, Duncan McLauchlan, Achnaha, receives 3s; his grandmother, Christian McDonald, who lives in the same house, is given the same amount. Glancing again at the 'age' column we find that a 78-year-old receives 4s 6d and a 70-year-old 2s 6d.

A year later, on 3 December 1790, £8 11s 6d falls to be distributed, and a very similar table showing forty-three individuals is drawn up. Archibald McArthur, again shown as a changeling, receives 10s, by far the largest amount given to any individual. Duncan McLauchlan – again shown as a changeling – and his grandmother each receive 4s. This time the 'remarks' column is a little more informative, and we may note its contents by way of comparison. Two cripples and John Henderson, Girgadal, who is totally disabled, receive 5s each. Angus McNaughtan, Tarbert, who is blind, receives 4s. Mary Cameron, Glenmore, who has a sore leg, Angus McDonald, Suordail Chaol, who is deaf, and Mary McDonald, Achatenny, who is a 'convert from Popery', receive 3s each, the last being a blatant case of proselytism. The smallest amount disbursed, 2s 6d, is received by four persons – Mary McPherson, Glenboradale, a widow with an orphan; Donald Cameron, Goirtenfern, who 'has a dr. lame of a hand'; a child called McPhie in Glendrain; and Alexander Cameron, Bayhead Kintra, a cripple child. In addition, seven persons aged between 83 and 78 receive amounts ranging from 8s down to 2s 6d. All in all we may see in this the beginnings of a system of social security, with 'changelings' – presumably those who are at risk of abandonment due to mental and physical disability – regarded as among the most deserving. After 1790, however, changelings disappear from the register.[31]

Some relevant discussion is provided by Mitchison and Leneman from their study of Scottish kirk session records (1989, 1998), although it has to be said that there is no mention of euthanasia, mercy-killing or changelings in either edition of their book. Out of 8,429 instances of illegitimacy they found only 78 cases of abandoned children, mostly during 1680–1720, a time of economic hardship (1998, pp. 110, 112). They noted only four for the central and eastern Highlands and none at all for the western Highlands, but it has to be pointed out that although their sources for the central and eastern Highlands are fairly representative (Golspie, Petty, Croy, Alvie, Blair Atholl, Moulin, Kenmore, Kilmadock), their study included no West Highland parishes between Inveraray in the south and Durness in the north, and no island parishes at all outside Bute and Arran (1989, pp. 244–45; 1998, p. 127). Nevertheless, their explanation is of great interest (1989, p. 217): "The rarity of abandonment in the Highlands might indicate a society tolerant of single lapses by unmarried girls, or alternatively one where it was relatively easy for an unmarried mother to gain support. But it is also possible that geography played a part. In a society made up of small hamlets and joint farms, the only way to leave a child for others to find without being identified was to take it to another settlement or, preferably, to leave it at the manse door, which would ensure prompt care. In the Highlands, particularly in the west, parishes were large and settlements far from each other. A nocturnal and secret march to deposit a child may have been simply too great an enterprise for a mother weakened by childbirth. On the other hand, the more ruthless procedure of abandoning the child in the wild to die would have been relatively easy: there may well have been cases of murderous abandonment of which we have no evidence."

They add in a footnote: "It was usually the minister who reported to the session the existence of a foundling, which suggests that he was the first member to know of it. A minister would be the best informed in the parish on who had recently lost a child and would be able to nurse another: for this reason leaving the child at his door gave it the best prospect of survival."

So we are thrown back into the cycle of hearsay and anecdote. Youngson tells a story (2001, pp. 495–96, cf. Campbell 1890, vol. 2, pp. 368–69) of a woman in Jura, *cailleach mhór Dhainnsgeir*, who is a terror to all who pass by and 'when it was discovered that she had killed her own child, there was only one thing to be done in those days and that was to put her to death'. A man called Buie wrestles with her, and eventually he 'managed to draw his dirk and stabbed her to the heart'. In the end, we begin to realise that, *pace* McColl, there is a mindset at work which prefers to ascribe almost anything to the supernatural than to aberrant human behaviour, even if, for example, it means saddling a young girl with a reputation for witchcraft. Take this little tale from the Western Isles (MacIain 1884–85), a variant of JGC's 'Witch as Cormorant', p. 193 below. A man breaks off courting a particular girl. A waulking is to take place one evening, and on his way there in the darkness he is fiercely attacked from behind by an otter. He is horribly lacerated, but by invoking the help of St Mary and St Peter he is able to fight back until the creature runs away. When he reaches the house where the waulking is to take place, he finds his former sweetheart in agony from a blow which a man has given her on the way there. Eventually she confesses to having turned herself into an otter.

It seems from this the community as a whole is more willing to believe that human beings can turn themselves into animals than to confront the uncomfortable truth that one of its own young women is capable of attacking a man out of jealousy and injuring him with her fingernails.

Let me return finally to JGC's grisly catalogue at p. 20. It might be thought that the one thing missing from it is the most obvious way of getting rid of an unwanted child – suffocation. The threats, shock treatments and tortures which he lists are not the ways in which an exhausted modern mother silences a screaming child, or an unbalanced one carries out a mercy-killing. They are more like the ways in which a psychopathic father, stepfather or other male will systematically torture a baby under the guise of 'punishment' while the helpless mother looks on. Today's cigarette-butt is yesterday's gridiron. What then is the position of adult males in changeling stories?

The spotlight repeatedly picks out tailors, who enjoyed a unique role in Gaelic society. Other trades were carried on either by the people themselves in or around their own homes (dyeing, rope-making, butchering) or by craftsmen in their own workshops (metal-working, shoemaking, milling, weaving). With the partial exception of peddling – and the pedlar did not stay long – the tailor was the only craftsman who plied his trade in his customers' own homes, staying in the same house night after night if need be until his task was completed. This means that the reputation of tailors is of unheroic men, often crippled (cf. p. 149), not highly regarded, as JGC points out (p. 135), but wonderful gossips, poets, storytellers, tradition-bearers. And baby-sitters. Lady Gregory quotes a woman in the Burren: "There was one time a tailor, and he was a wild card, always going to sprees. And one night he was passing by a house, and he heard a voice saying, 'Who'll take the child?'

"And he saw a little baby held out, and the hands that were holding it, but he could see no more than that. So he took it, and he brought it to the next house, and asked the woman there to take it in for the night. Well, in the morning the woman in the first house found a dead child in the bed beside her. And she was crying and wailing and called all the people. And when the woman from the neighbouring house came, there in her arms was the child she thought was dead. But if it wasn't for the tailor that chanced to be passing by and to take it, we know very well what would have happened to it."[32]

Consider now the following from Argyll.[33] At Kentallen (*Ceann an t-Sàilein*) in Duror lived a woman whose baby son ate far more than was natural but never stopped crying. It was harvest-time, and everyone in the township was out with their sickles – everyone, that is, except the woman (who was afraid to go out for fear her son broke his heart crying) and a tailor (who was busy making clothes). The tailor was a shrewd, observant man, and he soon became suspicious of the baby. *Faodaidh tusa dol thun na buana*, he said, *agus gabhaidh mise cùram den phàist.* "You can go to the reaping, and I'll take care of the child."

He stared at the withered object (*cranndas*) in the cradle as it shrieked and bellowed. Eventually he lost patience and cried in a sharp, angry voice: *Stad, 'ille, den cheòl sin, air neo cuiridh mi air an teine thu.* "Stop that music, my lad, or I'll put you on the fire."

The crying stopped, then after a while it began again. *An ann fhathast, a phìobaire an aon phuirt? Cluinneam an ceòl sin agad tuilleadh agus marbhaidh mi thu leis a' bhiodaig.* "Still at it, piper of the one tune? If I hear any more of your music I'll kill you with the dirk."

When the Fairy saw the tailor glaring at him, dirk in hand, he took fright and kept quiet for a good while. But the tailor was a cheerful man, and began to hum a tune (*port a channtaireachd*) as he worked. That set the Fairy howling once more, so, picking up the dirk again, the tailor said: *Tha gu leòir againn den cheòl ud. Glac a' phìob-mhór cheart agus thoir dhuinn aon phort math oirre, air neo cuiridh mi a' bhiodag annad.* "We've had enough of that music. Take the proper pipes and give us one good tune on them, or I'll put the dirk in you."

The Fairy sat up in the cradle, took the pipes and played the sweetest music the tailor had ever heard. The reapers heard it too, dropped their sickles and ran towards it. But before they reached the house the tune had stopped; they did not know who was playing or where it was coming from.

I cannot rationalise that episode, other than by remarking that the tailor clearly tried to make the child do something – walk, perhaps? – at the point of a dirk, that it was common for harvest workers to be entertained with pipe music, and that skill in piping was universally believed to be one of the Fairies' gifts.

Anyway, in the evening the tailor took the woman aside and told her the child was a changeling. She should bring him to the Ardsheil side of the bay, he said, and throw him into the loch.

She took his advice. As soon as he hit the water he became a big grey-haired old man and swam to the other side of the bay. When he got to dry land he shouted that if he had known beforehand what she was going to do he would have made her never think of doing such a thing again. She returned home and found her own child at the door, safe and sound.

What are we to make of this? That the child was abused and survived? That the child was abused and died, but that the woman had another in due course? That the tailor was a hero? That the tailor was a villain, and is being set up as a scapegoat to take the blame off a local man's shoulders?

KIDNAPPING

If we wish to understand the taking by Fairies of adults and children we cannot avoid the subject of kidnapping. In the twenty-first century, girls and young women are kidnapped in many different parts of the world to be sold into prostitution, boys are kidnapped in parts of Africa to be reared as fighters, young men are kidnapped in parts of India as husbands who require no dowry. Significantly however, the Gaelic word which formerly denoted the practice now means other things: *fuadach* has become a euphemism for a disastrous drowning (see notes 634 and 653), while *Fuadach nan Gaidheal* and (in the plural) *na Fuadaichean* are 'the Highland Clearances'. For 'kidnap' Mackenzie's dictionary gives *goid clann no daoine* 'steal children or people' (1930, p. 412); Thomson's gives *goid air falbh* 'steal away' (1981, p. 102), and so does Robertson's and MacDonald's (2004, p. 207). In English the opposite applies. According to the *OED* 'kidnap' does not appear until the seventeenth century, being a sort of slang which means basically what it says – 'nab kids'. In *Pilgrim's Progress* (1684) Bunyan says: "Thou practisest the craft of a Kidnapper, thou gatherest up Women, and Children, and carriest them into a strange Countrey."

Through being used of women, the word came to apply to adults generally, but its primary association with children did not go unnoticed by nineteenth-century scholars, and a 'kidnap theory' was put forward to explain the changeling belief. Unfortunately all of those who subscribed to it saw the kidnapping as a phenomenon of a dim and distant past, the kidnappers as long-lost druids or an underground aboriginal race. For his part, Wentz became so convinced that Fairy belief was primarily animistic – that is, that Fairies were souls and spirits – that, having come close to this sensibly sociological explanation, he rejected it as limited and inadequate (1911, pp. 245–46, 251). However, Bunyan's words could be used unaltered of the Fairies. As JGC points out at p. 19: "Most frequently it was women (not yet risen from childbed) and their babes that the Fairies abducted. On every occasion of a birth, therefore, the utmost anxiety prevailed to guard the mother and child from their attacks. It is said that the Fairy women are unable to suckle their own children, and hence their desire to secure a human wet-nurse. This, however, does not explain why they want the children . . ."

Now nobody is going to steal a woman in childbed. The kidnapping of women and new-born babies by the Fairies is likely to be a metaphor for their death, although, as Angela Bourke points out (1999, p. 86) with regard to Bridget Cleary, 'stories about her abduction by fairies could have been a euphemistic way of noting her extra-marital activities', with which Gearóid Ó Crualaoich concurs (2003, p. 74): "Stories of otherworld fairy abduction and its consequences are now being revealed as coded discourse concerning such matters as post-natal depression, child and marital abuse, sexual non-conformity and psychic disturbances."

Where we are told (as we often are) that the woman or child is turned into a block of wood, the metaphor is clearer. It is, I believe, their coffin (even when, as at p. 46 below, it is found in conjunction with an actual coffin).[34] Consider this Manx story (Wentz 1911, p. 127): "I heard of a man and wife who had no children. One night the man was out on horseback and heard a little baby crying beside the road. He got off his horse to get the baby, and, taking it home, went to give it to his wife, and it was only a block of wood. And then the old fairies were outside yelling at the man: *'Eash un oie, s'cheap t'ou mollit!'* (Age one night, how easily thou art deceived!)"

For children, then, the metaphor is simple, but for women it is both complex and dangerous. A man in Islay is out looking for whisky to celebrate the birth of his child when his wife drops out of the sky (*Tocher* 14, p. 220). She had been taken by the Fairies, but the smell of his plaid as he threw it over his shoulder had brought her down! When they go home there is the appearance of another woman in the bed. He puts her in the fire and she turns out to be a block of wood. What has happened to the child we are not told. Mrs Katherine Whyte Grant says (1925, p. 29) that the threshold of Glenstockdale House in Appin, 'once the dower-house of Stewart ladies', was supposed to be made of a block of wood which had been left there to simulate a young woman whom the Fairies had carried off. We may perhaps conclude that to men at least, the block of wood symbolises the absolute power of husbands over their wives, while to women it may also signify the chilling presence of a rival for their partner's attentions.[35]

Once a birth is safely over, both woman and child become valuable commodities. Not to Fairies – there is no such thing, we must remind ourselves – but to those kindreds in the Highlands who lived outside the law, coming out of the mist to lift cattle and other booty and then disappearing back into the hills:

Bonny Babby Livingstone
Gaed out to see the kye,
And she has met with Glenlyon,
Who has stolen her away.[36]

Why should they want nursing women? Presumably, given their unsettled lifestyle, because their own women had a higher-than-normal incidence of perinatal mortality. Why should they want children? Because they had so many cattle to herd, and *buachailleachd* was a job for children of five and over. And why should people blame Fairies for things that evil men do? That is the big question which opens up the issue. Cattle-lifting then (like poaching now) had always been part of everyone's lives. The world was ever thus. How else could anyone live in a place like Rannoch? Camerons, Stewarts, MacDonalds – they all had relatives who were 'broken men'. They stole from the Lowlands as far as they could. That benefitted the whole Highland economy. How could they be denied their right to women?

A simple example is provided by Calum Maclean (1975, p. 110). The poet and cattle-lifter Dòmhnall Donn of Bohuntine captures a pretty young girl in Sutherland and he and his men are bringing her home to Lochaber. On the way they rest at a house where a waulking is in progrress. Dòmhnall joins in the fun with an impromptu song about the girl he has taken. The women take up the refrain as they work and the men drink, but meanwhile the girl steals out of the house and escapes. All famous thieves stole women, it seems, no matter how much trouble it might be. The laird of Boisdale in South Uist had a beautiful daughter, and the pirate who built the castle on Stack Island south of Eriskay, a man remembered as the *Breabadair* ('Weaver') or *Reubadair* ('Robber'), decided to take her (Mac a Phì 1938, p. 130). He carried her on his back from Boisdale to Taobh a' Chaolais, swam with her across the Sound of Eriskay, dragged her through that island from one end to the other, swam with her to the Stack, then brought her up to his castle. The old man who told the story said: *Gu dearbh cha robh cus an-asgaidh aige dhith.* "He didn't get much of her for nothing."

John MacPherson, 'the Coddy', told the story differently (1960, pp. 81–82). The Weaver needed a wife, so he headed for the nearest shieling (at Loch Eynort), knowing he would find plenty of young women there. Making a quick decision, 'without much debating he flung this young lady on his shoulders and made a bee-line for the boat, which carried them both safely to the castle'. In due course he trained her to go fishing and raiding with him. Then there is the Aberdeenshire legend of Leslie of Balquhoyn in the Garioch, who 'built a strong dyke round the highest top of Bennochie, and because the passage to it lay through a great moss he built a long Causey through the moss up to the fort; whither he brought such handsom Girles whom he fancied, and could forcibly carry away from their parents and friends defending himself by means of this fort and straitness of the place, against such as pursued after him to recover their ravished relations' (Macfarlane 1906–08, vol. 1, pp. xxix, 18). It is of great interest that Walter Macfarlane (*c.*1699–1767) chose to insist on the truth of the Leslie story even though, as he himself admitted, the people of his day spoke merely of 'a giant'. A similar mix of fear and fantasy may be noted in the story of Screuchag (note 815 below), which describes a young girl so traumatised that she bears her kidnapper three children before her mother-in-law can get her to utter a word; JGC says that her nickname means 'a shrill-voiced female', but 'Little Screamer' or 'She of the Scream' would be more accurate, suggesting that for seven years her vocal chords were employed for purposes other than speech. 'The Daughter of the King of Enchantments' (pp. 232–33), in which Screuchag disappears to be replaced by a real princess, is a slightly sanitised version, presumably aimed at children.

Tales of this kind, be they fact or fiction, helped keep the younger females in check; as for married women, a ritual was available to underline their status as property. In 1905 the Rev. Charles Robertson noticed that 'certain observances in connection with marriage at Little Lochbroom point very clearly to the primitive institution of marriage by capture'. These observances he described as follows:

> The marriage party, to take a typical instance, has to walk several miles to meet the minister who is to perform the desired ceremony, and he has to come perhaps an equal distance. The trysting-place for the performance of the ceremony may be the bank of a stream or some other well-known spot, and may be out of sight of all human habitation. All this and perhaps more of our tale is common in different parts of the west of Ross-shire. The bridegroom's house is a little further away than the bride's home from the trysting place.
>
> While the bride's party is at breakfast on the morning of the wedding day, a scout is sent out every few minutes to see what is doing at the bridegroom's house, and to guard against surprise by him and his party. The bridegroom's party, in the same way, are watching the bride's home.
>
> When the bride and her party set out, there immediately arises an appearance of great stir and bustle about the bridegroom's house. Presently he and his party are seen to come out, and, as though they were in hot haste to overtake the bride's party, they take a straight line through fields and over streams and fences. They do not overtake the party in front, however, but keep about two hundred yards behind. When the bride's party sits down to partake of a refreshment by the way, the pursuers still keep at the same respectful distance, and sit down to take their refreshments by themselves.
>
> While waiting for the minister at the trysting place, the two parties keep at a distance the one from the other, and even when they are obliged to approach for the performance of the ceremony, they still keep distinct. Immediately on the conclusion of the ceremony by which bride and bridegroom are made one, the two parties mingle together and are associated throughout the remainder of the day's proceedings.[37]

Marriage by capture is discussed by Sir Walter Scott in his revised edition of *Rob Roy*.[38] The Highlanders' imagination, he says, was less shocked at the idea of 'this particular species of violence' than might be expected from their kindness to their own families – but, he explains, 'all their views were tinged with the idea that they lived in a state of war', and in such a state the female captives are 'the most valuable part of the booty'. He goes on: "The annals of Ireland, as well as those of Scotland, prove the crime to have been common in the more lawless parts of both countries; and any woman who happened to please a man of spirit who came of a good house, and possessed a few chosen friends, and a retreat in the mountains, was not permitted the alternative of saying him nay."

> *Four-and-twenty Hieland men*
> *Came doun by Fiddoch side,*
> *And they have sworn a deadly aith,*
> *Jean Muir suld be a bride:*

> *And they have sworn a deadly aith,*
> *Ilke man upon his durke,*
> *That she should wed with Duncan Ger,*
> *Or they'd make bloody worke.*

Citing the ballad, Scott quotes the view of 'a respectable woman' on marriages like Jean Muir's.[39] He was told 'that there was no use in giving a bride too much choice upon such occasions; that the marriages were the happiest lang syne which had been done off hand'. And she averred that her 'own mother had never seen her father till the night he brought her up from the Lennox, with ten head of black cattle, and there had not been a happier couple in the country'. Whenever I read JGC's words at p. 13 below about 'the folk' travelling in an 'eddy wind', I have a mental picture of tartan-clad men on Highland ponies urging a stolen herd of black cattle towards the hills. JGC says: "By throwing one's left (or *toisgeul*) shoe at it, the Fairies are made to drop whatever they may be taking away – men, women, children, or animals. The same result is attained by throwing one's bonnet (saying, *Is leatsa seo, is leamsa sin*, 'This is yours, that's mine'), or a naked knife, or earth from a molehill. In these eddies, people going on a journey at night have been 'lifted', and spent the night careering through the skies."

That word 'lifted' is the very one used for stealing cattle by the likes of Rob Roy. Which confirms my feeling that when in a state of moral denial, the people resorted to the Fairies. Imagine a rat-tat at the door. It is the factor in his three-cornered hat. "Donald, I hear your daughter has gone off with that blackguard Robert MacGregor."

"Indeed sir no, the Fairies took her."

"Fairies be damned, there is no such thing."

"Indeed sir there is not, but they took her all the same."

In order to prove the case, what is required is a circumstantial account from oral tradition about a woman being kidnapped by Fairies, along with a circumstantial account from the historical record about a woman being kidnapped by cattle-lifters, the detail of one matching that of the other. This is not quite so unlikely as it sounds. A splendid traditional yarn, known as far away as Cape Breton, tells how the 'Black Officer' of Ballachroan in Badenoch was in league with the devil and lured men to their deaths, but materials exist to demonstrate how a true story of natural disaster became one of diabolical intervention – see 'The Gaïck Catastrophe (*Mort Ghàthaig*)', pp. 164–66 and note 567. I have failed as yet to find a story of Fairy kidnap paralleled in this way by sober documentary evidence, so I will do the next best thing. I will tell a series of six stories, beginning with two where the kidnappers are alleged to be Fairies, moving on through one where the Fairy kidnappers work with a human hit-man to one where the kidnapping is done by a human being with supernatural associations, and ending with two which contain no supernatural elements at all. By showing how arbitrary these classifications are, I will hope to prove that Fairy kidnapping is real kidnapping.[40]

My first story, 'John Roy', picks up on that custom of saying: *Is leatsa seo, is leamsa sin!* It was told by a Strathspey man, William Grant Stewart (1823, pp. 116–21). John Roy, who lived in Glenbrown in the parish of Abernethy, was out 'traversing the hills for his cattle' one night when 'he happened to fall in with a fairy banditti, whose manner of travelling indicated that they carried along with them some booty'. Stewart goes on: "John Roy took off his bonnet, and threw it towards them, demanding a fair exchange in the emphatic Gaelic phrase, *Sluis sho slumus Sheen.*"

It is Strathspey dialect – *Is leibhs' seo, is leamas sin.* "They abandoned the burden, which turned out to be nothing more or less than a fine fresh lady, who, from her dress and language, appeared to be a *Sasonach.*"

John Roy brought her home where she was 'treated with the utmost tenderness for several years' and gradually integrated into his family and community. When soldiers came to build roads he accommodated an English captain and his son under his own roof. They got on well, but the pair kept staring at 'his English foundling'. One day the son remarked how much she resembled his late mother, and the father replied that she did indeed look like his late wife, mentioning her name – upon which the lady 'instantly recognised her tender husband and darling son'. What had happened, Stewart explains, was that 'some of the hordes of fairies, inhabiting the "Shian of Coir-laggack"' had gone to the south of England and kidnapped the woman in childbed, depositing in her place a 'stock' which died a few days later and was buried 'in the full persuasion of *its* being the lady in question, with all the splendour which her merits deserved'. He concludes: "Thus would the perfidious fairies have enjoyed the fruits of their cunning, without even a suspicion of their knavery, were it not for the 'cleverness and generosity of John Roy, who once lived in Glenbrown'."

The first point to consider is whether John Roy could be the swashbuckling Jacobite poet Col. John Roy Stewart (1700-49), who fought at Culloden – a relative of the author's, perhaps? But I think not. Glenbrown is near Tomintoul, far away over the hills from the Colonel's stamping-ground by Aviemore, and the military road through Tomintoul, part of the link between Coupar Angus and Fort George, was built during 1748-57 (Taylor 1996, pp. 71–75, 148–53). Glenbrown and Tomintoul were wild country, full of broken men, especially MacGregors, who lifted cattle from far and wide and grazed them around the Cairngorms. These were real, not Fairy, banditti, and our John Roy would have been related to some of them. The south of England is only mentioned to put us off the scent. My guess is that they had lifted their *ban-Shasannach* at Coupar Angus or some such place when the army arrived there in 1748 to make a start on the road; that they took her because they thought she might be worth something; that they disposed of her to John Roy for the price of a bonnet because she was a lot of trouble; and that John Roy was happy to have her because he could use an extra pair of hands to fetch his water and milk his cows. As for her husband and son thinking that they had buried her, it must have been because a corpse or skeleton was found in the hills after she was lifted, and assumed to be hers. The broken men of the Highlands were not in the habit of murdering women – but try explaining that to a redcoat after Culloden.

My second story is JGC's 'The Woman Stolen from France' (p. 48). It begins: "*MacChaluim a' Chrònain*, 'MacCallum of the Humming Noise', who resided in Glen Etive subsequent to the '45, was the last to observe the habits of the Fairies and ancient hunters."

JGC does not mean that MacCallum watched the Fairies' habits but that he practised them. Such habits included not only hunting with arrows but living in caves, stealing into people's homes, and, as we have seen, kidnapping human beings for one purpose or another. The precise relevance of MacCallum to the story is uncertain, however. It is basically about a woman who was found running with the deer, who was caught by a sort of posse and brought to his house. Perhaps they believed that she was his woman, kidnapped from somewhere and gone mad. In this case the 'posse' would have been the kirk session of Ardchattan in its determination to assert its moral laws, their aim being to set up a public confrontation between MacCallum and the woman in order to oblige him to marry her and accept his duty of care. But what happens? While MacCallum is vociferously denying any connection with her, women are brought in to scrub her down. They remove many layers of clothing and grime, and lo and behold! "There were rings on her fingers, from which it was ascertained that she came from France."

Since we are not told that the woman has lost the power of speech, we have to assume that she speaks French to her captors and tells them who she is. I suppose it is obvious to the elders that these revelations are as much of a surprise to MacCallum as to themselves. "Inquiries were made, and she was sent home by a ship from Greenock."

This suggests to me that the company which runs the nearby iron smelter at Bonawe is asked to consult its records with regard to visiting French ships. When it is clear which ship was in Loch Etive around the time the woman appeared, a letter is written to the owner, and he in turn makes inquiries. To try to find out how likely it is that a French ship in West Highland waters in the decades following 1745 would have been carrying a woman, and why such a woman might have wanted to escape, I have consulted Suzanne J. Stark's *Female Tars: Women Aboard Ship in the Age of Sail* (1996). Stark concentrates on the Royal Navy, but France had a navy like Britain's. Like Britain, too, she had privateers (privately-owned armed vessels licensed to capture enemy ships) as well as merchantmen, armed and otherwise, and no doubt the same three categories of women associated with the Royal Navy were associated with naval ships, privateers and merchantmen of all nations.

The first category is prostitutes. From the seventeenth to the early nineteenth centuries, whenever a British naval ship was in port the crew shared their hammocks with hundreds of them. There were two reasons why the practice was condoned – the crews were of pressed men, who would promptly disappear if allowed ashore, and if not provided with females they might fall back upon homosexuality, which was a capital offence. The women were brought out in bumboats and often lived on board for weeks at a time. Many were children, the age of consent being twelve (Stark 1996, pp. 5–46).

The second category consists of the wives of such people as the master, purser, chaplain, surgeon, boatswain, gunner, carpenter, cooper, sailmaker and cook, sometimes even of petty officers and leading seamen. They regularly accompanied their husbands to sea, and often brought their maids and children as well. Despite this, Stark finds little evidence in naval records of sexual harassment, and only one case each of attempted adultery and rape. Such women played a valiant part in naval engagements, assisting the gunners and the surgeon (*ibid.*, pp. 47–81). Wives went to sea with the French navy too. When the seventy-four-gun *Achille* sank at Trafalgar (1805) Nelson's men pulled two Frenchwomen from the water. One, Jeannette, had been handing up powder to the gun decks when the ship caught fire. She climbed through a gunport and leapt into the sea just before the ship exploded. By a miracle her husband was also safe and sound, and they were set ashore at Gibraltar. The other woman was naked when fished out, having shed her clothing to stay afloat. A Marine subaltern gave her 'a large cotton dressing-gown' to wear and she, too, was released at Gibraltar (*ibid.*, pp. 75–77).

The third category comprises women who joined the Navy or Marines disguised as men. According to Stark (*ibid.*, p. 82) there are more than twenty verified cases of this from the late seventeenth to the early nineteenth century. Why women should join voluntarily when men had to be pressed takes some explaining; it has mainly to do with the frustration of being female in a time when women had no rights and could not own property. They had to like cross-dressing, of course. Being agile, women could do well on a sailing-ship, and they also enjoyed two advantages over men – they could leave without fuss whenever they liked, simply by confessing their identity, and lesbian behaviour was treated not as a crime but a joke (*ibid.*, pp. 82–167).

To which category did the woman who ran with the deer belong? "She had been taken away in childbed, doubtless by the Fairies." I would tentatively suggest that she had been snatched from a French port by a skipper who needed a wet-nurse for his child (as in the second category), then hired out to the crew (as in the first). If so, no wonder she absconded. Perhaps, like Jeannette, she climbed through a gunport and leapt into the sea.[41] That such things happened need not be doubted: Calum Maclean tells (1975, p. 61) how a party of Highland sailors met a girl in a port on the west coast of Sweden who recited to them a Gaelic rhyme about the islands and reefs at the mouth of Loch nan Cilltean – Arisaig Bay. She had been abducted from there by Swedish sailors many years before. She had 'probably married one of her captors', and the Gaelic-speaking men were able to bring to her kinsfolk the news that she was alive and well. Frances Tolmie had a similar story about a girl taken by a ship's crew while she was gathering dulse on the shore outside Loch Bracadale in Skye; Tolmie does not name the country where she was found, but gives the rhyme in full (MacDonald 1934–36a, pp. 199–200). In Rathlin this was the fate assumed to have befallen many young men as well as girls, until one night a midwife was taken by the Fairies into the Fairy hill and recognised a number of the people in it (Ballard 1997, p. 54): "Nobody ever knew what was happening, they thought that they were maybe being kidnapped, you know somebody coming to the island by boat and taking them off it. It was put down to this."

My third story, 'Throwing the Arrow', is told by JGC at p. 47. A weaver by the Bridge of Awe (near the smelter at Bonawe) is left a widower with three or four children. One moonlit night when thatching he hears the rushing sound of a high wind, and a multitude of little people settle on the roof and the ground like a flock of starlings. He is told that he must accompany them to Glen Cannel in Mull, where they are going for a woman. He refuses to go unless he gets whatever is foraged to himself. As MacDougall and Calder say of a tailor whom the Fairies had in their power (1910, p. 123): "They could not hurt any human being except by means of another; and for that reason they used to take him with them, and make him throw the fairy arrows at the person to whom they bore ill-will." It can be explained as a *geas* or tabu imposed in specific circumstances on a particular tribe of Fairies, in the same way that certain tabus were imposed from time to time on Cú Chulainn and the Ulaidh, or on Fionn and the Féinn.

On arriving at Glen Cannel the weaver is given an arrow to throw (see pp. 305–06, note 57). Pretending to aim at the woman, he throws it through the window and kills a pet lamb. The animal at once comes out through the window, but he is told that this will not do: he must throw again. He does so, and the woman is taken away and a log of alder-wood (*stoc feàrna*) left in her place.

This sounds like murder to me. A log of wood here can only mean a coffin. Alder is the worst kind of timber. If a Mullman has taken out a contract with some mainland ruffians for them to murder his wife and make it look like robbery (the lamb), he is likely to pick alder for her coffin. She has cost him enough as it is.

What comes next? "The weaver claimed his agreement, and the Fairies left the woman with him at the Bridge of Awe, saying they would never again make the same paction with any man. She lived happily with him and he had three children by her."

In other words JGC is claiming that the woman is not murdered at all, but kidnapped and given to the weaver. My own judgement is that she *is* murdered (it is hard to get around that log of wood), and by the weaver at that. So it must be some other woman who is kidnapped. The gang do not like this one bit, because they want to get away with a clean pair of heels, but the weaver is already in it up to the neck. What he wants is not blood money but a young wife, and what girl in Lorne will take on a shady character with four children?

Fortunately there is a twist in the tale which reveals the kidnapped woman's identity, for she is recognised by a passing traveller. "He said he had at one time been a farmer in Glen Cannel in Mull, comfortable and well-to-do, but his wife having died, he had since fallen into poverty till he was now a beggar, and that the weaver's wife could be no other than the wife he had lost."

The man's wife has died – yet here she is. So she has not died. It is a lie. She left him, or so he assumed. Men do not fall into poverty because their wives die, unless they turn to the bottle – it is usually the other way round, their wives leave them because they are falling into poverty. The Mullman stares at the woman, yet we are not told that she acknowledges him. But what happens in the end? "Explanations were entered into, and the beggar got his choice of the wife or the children. He chose the former, and again became prosperous in the world."

I do not know any other story that calls for so much argument.[42] Fairies are gangsters. Tabus are blackmail. Arrows are guns. Kidnap by shooting is murder. Logs are coffins. A man's wife dying is his wife leaving him. If each of these equations can be proved valid in other instances, however, they are likely to be valid here, for in Gaelic stories of the supernatural there is a code of symbols no less complex than the one that operates in Gaelic poetry (see Black 2001, pp. xix–xxvii, 525–27). Take the first equation, for example, 'Fairies are gangsters'. According to the *Dublin Evening Mail* of 18 April 1827, a schoolmaster in Co. Sligo named Connor was found hanged. He and his whole family had turned Protestant, it seems, but he had changed his mind and decided to 'read his recantation' in church the following Sunday. Warrants were issued for his father and two brothers on suspicion of murder. "These persons," declares the paper, "endeavoured to circulate a report that he had been hanged by the *fairies*."[43]

My fourth story concerns Ewen MacPhie (*c*.1784–1850) who is the subject of 'The Water-Horse at Loch Cuaich' (pp. 112–13 below). We know a good deal about him from different sources. He was an army deserter of heroic stamp who had been captured. He escaped while being brought in irons to Fort George, lived rough for a while on Loch Arkaig-side, and finally decamped to an island in Loch Quoich at the head of Glen Garry. JGC describes his kidnapping exploit at p. 112. The girl whom he abducted is said to have been twelve, the legal age of consent. Edward Ellice tells us (1931, p. 98) that Ewen was already living in Loch Quoich when he took her, but does not mention her age. "His bothy built, he must needs have a wife; so one fine morning he stepped across the hill to Glen Dulochan, where he had previously made the acquaintance of a girl, and, without much more courting, popped her on his back, and returned to his island, where they were duly married."

If he really 'popped her on his back', she cannot have been a grown woman.

Another source for Ewen MacPhie is an article published in *Cuairtear nan Gleann* in 1841, during Ewen's own lifetime. Probably written by the Rev. Dr Norman MacLeod, *Caraid nan Gaidheal*, it tells us that Ewen was living in a shieling bothy in the Coire Buidhe south of Loch Quoich (Anon. 1841–42b, p. 73). *Thug e a chridhe do dh-ainnir òg àluinn, aois cheithir-bliadhn'-deug – ruith e air falbh leatha, phòs iad, agus a nis tha cóigear chloinne aca.* "He gave his heart to a lovely young girl, aged fourteen – he ran away with her, they married, and now they have five children."

Subsequently they moved to the island, where they are now living off their goats, says the *Cuairtear*, with plenty of fish and venison to supplement their diet. Mutton too, we may add, when the neighbours moved out and the sheep moved in, but that was Ewen's undoing, for he ended his days in jail.

All accounts agree that there was something uncanny about him. JGC says that a water-horse was often seen in Loch Quoich. Ewen himself claimed that one stormy night there was a rattle at the door; knowing that it was a water-horse in the shape of a man, he fired at it using real bullets and a silver coin (p. 113 below). Ellice tells us that Ewen's wife once fired at two sheriff's officers who were rowing across to the island. Could this be another version of the same incident? Ellice also says that the people looked up to Ewen as a seer, a curer of cows and a maker of charms, while the *Cuairtear* says that 'the local people hold him in a kind of awe' (*tha seòrsa do sgàth air muinntir an àite roimhe*), some on account of his heroic reputation, others 'thinking he has some knowledge not of the best kind, the type of witchcraft and second sight (*fiosachd*) which it is unlucky to offend'. We cannot prove that the water-horses and the sheriff's officers are one and the same; what we can say is that in these stories about Ewen MacPhie, kidnapping is linked with the supernatural in a fully historical personage.

My fifth story, 'Raghnall na Ceapaich', brings us face to face with the kind of outlaws who lifted both cattle and women. Some time around 1600 Rachel, daughter of MacGregor of Dunan (the outermost settlement in the Braes of Rannoch), is being courted by an old bachelor from Lochaber, Raghnall na Ceapaich, whom she despises. One day he and a dozen comrades abduct her while she is walking in a birch wood. They take her to a lonely bothy where Raghnall demands that she accept him. She refuses. One of the men proposes that she be 'dishonoured' and allowed to go back to her father if that is what she wants. Cameron of Blàr a' Chaorainn objects and suggests she be given the choice of all present. Someone says: *Am boireannach nach toir a roghainn á triùir, bheir i a deòin ás a dhà dheug.* "The woman who can't choose between three will take what she wants out of twelve."

She chooses Cameron, and they are married next day in Lochaber. Her father pitches in with a dowry of twenty cows and a bull. The marriage, by all accounts, is a happy one.[44]

My final set of kidnappers are the sons of Rob Roy, and their crime – committed sixteen years after their father's death – is very much on the record.[45] The victim is Jean Key, Kay or Wright, 19, two months a widow, whose property is estimated at 18,000 merks. In today's values that is £100,000 or €150,000, enough to buy a house and a couple of acres. She is living with her mother at Edinbellie near Drymen. On the night of 8 December 1750 Rob Roy's three surviving sons, Seumas Mór, Raghnall and Roban Òg, force their way into the house with swords and pistols. They demand that Jean be handed over because, says Seumas, his little brother Roban is determined to make his fortune. Jean is dragged out, mounted on a horse behind Roban, and carried off, in the words of Sir Walter Scott, 'in spite of her screams and cries, which were long heard after the terrified spectators of the outrage could no longer see the party retreat through the darkness'. In an effort to escape, she throws herself off the horse and wrenches her side, so they lay her over the pommel and bring her through the moors and bogs until she is forced by pain to sit upright.

They call at several houses. No one tries to stop them. One witness is the future Professor William Richardson of Glasgow University, who was to describe to Scott the 'terrible dream' of their 'violent and noisy' arrival at the house where he was staying. Scott wrote: "The Highlanders filled the little kitchen, brandishing their arms, demanding what they pleased, and receiving whatever they demanded. James Mohr, he said, was a tall, stern, and soldier-like man. Robin Oig looked more gentle; dark, but yet ruddy in complexion – a good-looking young savage. Their victim was so dishevelled in her dress, and forlorn in her appearance and demeanour, that he could hardly tell whether she was alive or dead."[46]

They bring her to Rowardennan, where Seumas holds Jean up by force while an obliging priest marries her, protesting loudly, to Roban. They lock the pair up in a house, then bring them to Balquhidder parish church, where the minister only asks if they are married. Roban says yes; Jean says nothing.

This time there is no happy ending. The Court of Session sequesters Jean's estate. She dies of smallpox in Glasgow on 4 October 1751. The brothers are declared fugitives from justice and put to the horn. Seumas's trial begins in 1752, but he escapes from Edinburgh Castle with the help of his daughter, and dies of fever in Paris in 1754. Raghnall escapes arrest, probably by lying low in Balquhidder, and dies of old age about 1786. Roban is tried in 1754 and hanged.

Fairies?

To sum up: in 'John Roy' the alleged Fairy banditti are real banditti. In 'The Woman Stolen from France' the alleged Fairies are likely to have been sailors, the only supernatural associations being those of the mortal wrongly suspected of the kidnap. In 'Throwing the Arrow', where the Fairies are gangsters and the human hero is their hit-man, a supernatural atmosphere is created by the proliferation of symbols. In 'Ewen MacPhie' the kidnapper is a historically attested human being with supernatural associations. In 'Raghnall na Ceapaich', by contrast, there is neither a supernatural element nor any proof of historical authenticity. The presence of a supernatural element does not demonstrate that an anecdote is unhistorical, any more than the absence of one demonstrates it to be historical. Finally, 'Rob Roy's Sons' has an atmosphere of Gothic horror – an eye-witness describes the abduction as a 'terrible dream' and the young victim is dead within a year – but enjoys complete historical authenticity.

We have come full circle, I think. The last of these six crimes is very like the first, and probably committed in the same period. The only difference is that the first has come to us encoded by Gaelic oral tradition, the last through legal documentation in English.

THE THREE OTHERWORLDS

In my preface (p. vii) I distinguished the parallel otherworlds that emerge from JGC's work. I described the Fairies as the secular otherworld, spirits and second sight as the otherworld of death, and witches and the devil as belonging to the Christian otherworld. I have concentrated on the 'first otherworld' in this essay because Gaelic tradition is widely acknowledged to represent a primary source for the study of the Fairies, but a secondary one when it comes to spirits and witches. To put it another way, in Gaelic Scotland the Fairies are our indigenous friends and neighbours, being intimately connected with our landscape and with how it is named; ghosts and spirits, on the other hand, are common to all peoples as an instinctive way of coping with death, while witches and the devil have an umbilical connection to monotheistic ways of thought which have crept in over two millennia from Mediterranean lands.

JGC is careful to distinguish between 'black witchcraft' and 'white witchcraft'. The former is *sgoil dhubh* ('black schoolcraft') or *buidseachd* (an imported term derived from the English word, as is *buidseach* 'a witch'). In so far as there is a native term for a maleficent witch it appears to be *doideag*, perhaps connected with *dod* 'peevishness'. The historicity of the great Highland witches is hard to establish, but when we examine one of their greatest achievements, the drowning of Iain Garbh (p. 184), we find that, in the words of the Rev. James Fraser (note 628), "Drunkness did the [mischeife]." Similarly, the drowning of Captain Forrest (pp. 185–86) appears to derive from an eighteen-hour storm that sank three ships in 1653 (note 632), and it can be seen that black witchcraft serves the same function as the Fairy creed, that is, to provide scapegoats and metaphors for what man and nature do; it is interesting that witchcraft is even associated with *Fuadach Bhaile Phuill*, the Balephuil Drowning of 1856 (note 653). Perhaps the nearest we come to a biographic profile of a Highland witch is of *Cré Mhór Inbhir Nis*, and although she appears to have been burnt for her crimes in 1695, she was clearly no more than a 'white witch' or *cailleach* who scraped out a living on the Mill Burn by providing the women of Inverness with whatever charms they wished to buy, but who could curse with the best – or worst – of them (note 669). With Isobel Gowdie, who lived and died only fifteen miles away, albeit a generation earlier, the position is roughly the opposite: documentary evidence from her trial is *all* we have, and popular oral memory of her is lacking.

JGC's work appears to show the three otherworlds operating in balance. This is not illusory. The Fairies and second sight are parts of the legacy of a northern European cosmology of shamans, spirit flight and nocturnal battles, in which uncanny misfortune is inflicted not by mortal witches but by 'ancestral or nature-spirits, which must be defeated or propitiated' (Hutton 2002, pp. 27–28). This cosmology survived intact in Siberia, 'the largest witch-free area of the whole inhabited planet' (*ibid.*, p. 27), and more fragmentarily among the Sami and the Celts. MacRitchie was right to draw attention to the Lapps – not however because they *are* the Fairies, but because they *saw* the Fairies in the same way as ourselves. In Ireland there were hardly any witchcraft trials at all, while in Iceland and Finland the dynamic of persecution was curiously different from that in most of Europe, where on average eighty per cent of those accused were women. In Iceland only ten of the 120 people tried between 1604 and 1720 were women, while in Finland 'a clear majority of the accused were male until the great panic of the 1670s, when a Western European stereotype of witchcraft was introduced and women began to be denounced in significant numbers' (*ibid.*, pp. 26–27).

It is noticeable that Ronald Hutton, as a historian of witchcraft, asks a question very different from the one I have asked at p. lxii above. Approaching Gaelic Scotland from a Lowland and Renaissance perspective, he would like to know (*ibid.*, p. 31) whether any trials for witchcraft took place in the Highlands and Islands while legal administration was in the hands of chiefs of kindreds who possessed heritable jurisdictions but left no records. Approaching Gaelic Scotland from an Irish and Celtic perspective, I would like to know whether any trials for changeling murder took place in any period at all. The fact that both of us are in difficulty suggests that the people of Gaelic Scotland may have enjoyed peaceful equipoise between two ancient cosmologies.

To explain the existence of *three* otherworlds, we have to postulate a sort of cosmological nuclear fission. If the Fairies include in their ranks the spirits of the dead, why should the spirits of the dead also have a second otherworld all to themselves? The answer, it seems to me, lies in the emergence of a Christian otherworld to rival the Celtic one. The first otherworld is flexible enough to admit the angels expelled from paradise, but Christian eschatology refuses to have anything to do with the spirits of the dead. During the long, long move from the old religion to the new, these spirits remain a reality and have to be accommodated somewhere. In the cosmology of a Celtic Christian, therefore, they come to occupy a space of their own in the no-man's-land between the first and third otherworlds.

So the Fairies are . . .

. . . a psychological and metaphorical construct designed to help ordinary people struggle through a difficult life from day to day, deriving from the gods of the Celts and the fallen angels of Revelation, from chatter about other races and fear of kidnappers, reinforced every winter's night in the ceilidh-house by the power of oral narrative, believed by children, necessary for women, and used by men. Of Lady Gregory's collection Elizabeth Coxhead has written (Gregory 1970, p. 8): "It is obvious that these stories are myths and symbols, and that through them we look directly at a life of much fear and hardship, with a high maternal and child mortality, mysterious sicknesses (typhoid fever was endemic all along the western seaboard), sudden disasters by land and sea, and the ever-present memory of the Great Famine, when the Sidhe had turned the potatoes black in the ground . . . We too are 'away' when the tension grows too much for us, though we call it by names like nervous breakdown and neurosis. And we too seek shelter from our human condition behind a barrier of symbols . . ."

When we use these symbols to inquire into the social significance of a given story, the answer can be startling. The tale at p. 280 of a man who 'tapped a skull in the church window, saying to it every word the minister said to the couple marrying' seems innocent enough till viewed in the context of an anecdote about James Clow, miller, joiner and farmer at Kilmuir in Skye, told by William MacKenzie (1930, p. 133): "It is said that at the marriage of Dr. Matheson, while the ceremony was being gone through, James Clow and the bride's sister stood beside or behind with the others, and by signs, whispering, and hand pressures took the same vows as the contracting parties, though, at that time, it was not known that there was any such feeling between them." This suggests that the tapping of the skull was a piece of black magic designed to bring about the death of a spouse.

At pp. 44–45 below is a classic story of the type that operates on several different levels of meaning. It begins 'A trampling as of a troop of horses came round a house in which a woman lay in childbed' and ends with a piece of verse. According to a strict interpretation this young woman is married to a Fairy, but she does not claim to be unhappy, and in fact her words *bean mo choltais riamh chan fhacas* ('no wife like me has ever been seen') could be a very appealing line to a teenage girl – she is, she implies, admired as exotic, beautiful, unique, something special.

So what are the possible elements in this story? It could be a dream of teenage *angst*. It could reflect post-Culloden atrocities. It could be a way of coping with the death of a sister. It could show how women have always gone away to marry, but if so, there seems to be a twist in the tale. Did she elope? Was she abducted? Was she, perhaps, in Edinburgh or elsewhere in the Lowlands? It was in the late eighteenth century that young Highland people began to find their way there, attracted by harvest work on Lothian farms.

Whatever the answer, it is worth remembering that, given the nature of education, communication between women was the kind most likely to be 'oral'. Some men could read and write, very few women could. So the verse at p. 44 can be seen as an eighteenth-century text-message, passed on through the ceilidh-houses by a chain of Gaelic singers, perhaps from as far away as Edinburgh. Like a message on some abandoned mobile phone, we have no idea whether it ever reached the little sister. But it has reached us.

I hope I have succeeded in showing that JGC's conclusion that the 'Fairy creed' was of 'ethical rather than ethnical origin' was entirely correct, even if we would call it 'therapeutic' nowadays in preference to 'moral and instructive'. Janet Bord's view (1997, p. 160) is that 'traditional fairy lore has developed from various stimuli, namely belief in nature spirits, primitive races, pagan gods and the spirits of the dead', and that 'personal sightings, on the other hand, could be the result of imagination, fabrication, or the externalization of unconscious archetypes', to which I would add that poverty and deprivation in marginalised communities has made belief in the real existence of Fairies entirely necessary for day-to-day survival. Such a sociological interpretation is instinctive to our age – as a Scottish journalist has written (McGinty 2004), "What is *Hansel and Gretel* but a terrible tale of a child murderer or *Snow White* but a foul example of parental neglect?"

On Fairies as psychological constructs I refer the reader to Bord 1997, pp. 154–58. She speaks, for example, of a psychoanalyst, Nandor Fodor, one of whose patients claimed in 1948 to have enjoyed the company of the guardian spirit of her family, a leprechaun called Murgatroyd who claimed in turn to be of the Tuatha Dé Danann. Fodor concluded that the leprechaun was a 'successful device' who fulfilled his patient's need to belong to a family. Such Fairies, says Bord (*ibid.*, p. 158), are 'unlikely to have been independent beings but to have originated deep within the minds of the witnesses and to have been externalized by them'. In JGC's world, talk of the Fairies was so omnipresent that we do not have to prove psychological need; environmental influence is sufficient, and the psychological effect may even be harmful, as Henderson points out (1911, p. 57): "Take the case of a boy who goes to an evening's entertainment in Highland hamlets, where he hears lots of ghost stories; he stays until it is late and very dark; if he must come home alone and have to pass lonely roads and places shadowed with trees, or streams where he has heard it said at the *céilidh* that dogs were seen which tore such and such folks in former times to death, the chances are that he will see more than is good for him."

Henderson was right. Katherine Whyte Grant paints a picture of young folk so 'winged with terror', despite having only a few yards to go, that they had to be lighted home by a fir candle held aloft by a friend standing in the ceilidh-house door (1925, p. 3), and in 1985 an elderly informant from Harris recalled very similar fears to Margaret Bennett (1992, p. 75). What of those beyond the torch-bearer's reach?

Belief in Fairies must of course be validated occasionally by sightings, both alleged and 'real'. Traditionally the latter were supplied by second-sighted people. Fr Allan McDonald noted in 1896 or 1897 (GUL MS Gen. 1090/29, p. 220): "Christina McInnes says that Roderick Ban McKinnon & he was a truthful man told her that he himself saw a fairy dwelling open and a light in it & beings passing to & fro. [Roderick died 2 years ago & I knew him very well & he probably believed what he was telling)."

In the twentieth century – as is well documented by Bord (1997, pp. 106–29) in an engrossing chapter 'UFO Entities and Fairies: Are They the Same?' – UFOs and aliens gradually took the place of *sitheanan* and Fairies, while in the twenty-first century terrorism has taken the place of witchcraft, and terrorists of witches. The late Alan Bruford summarised the Fairies of Orkney and Shetland like this (1997, p. 133): "They serve a useful purpose as scapegoats, to be blamed for changing sickly or handicapped babies, stealing women who die in childbirth, or shooting cattle with unexplained ailments . . . To children, however, fairies might be bogeys to keep them from straying at night; for housewives, a warning to keep fresh water in the house overnight; for fiddlers, an explanation for tunes that suddenly came into their heads, or for anyone an excuse for things inexplicably lost, or found . . . But in a general way, they stood for both wild nature and the supernatural and everything inexplicable, good or bad, which modern society feels it can explain in more scientific terms like 'greenhouse effect' or 'chaos theory'."

In the end, as Kirk would have had us believe, the Fairies are a necessary spiritual construct, like God; but then, as I point out in note 151 below, so is *Niseag*, the Loch Ness Monster, and that has not deterred self-appointed men of science from spending millions of dollars on submarines and sonar equipment to try and locate her. It would make just as much sense for them to set their equipment to work in search of the living Gaelic otherworld inside the countless Fairy mansions which bestrew our landscape. But there are other ways of looking at it. The Fairies disappeared, said Fr Allan, about 1825. This was when the first of an unending series of discoveries was beginning to be made – photography, film, sound recording, the telegraph, the telephone, electric power, air travel, radio, television, computers – which have altered our relationship with time and space. Indeed at p. 176 JGC calls counter-charms 'disinfectants', just as we refer to anti-virus computer programs today. Our images, our voices, our thoughts can be projected in an instant or preserved for ever; this used to be the prerogative of the Fairies, who lived in an otherworld where time did not exist and who could bring human beings to America and back in a night. Should we in fact see belief in the Gaelic otherworld as prophetic? This view was best expressed, to my mind, by Sophia Morrison of the Manx Language Society,[47] who wrote to Wentz (1911, p. 119): "Even let it be granted that nine out of every ten cases of experiences with fairies can be analysed and explained away – there remains the tenth. In this tenth case one is obliged to admit that there is something at work which we do not understand, some force in play which, as yet, we know not. In spite of ourselves we feel 'There's Powers that's in'. These Powers are not necessarily what the superstitious call 'supernatural'. We realize now that there is nothing supernatural – that what used to be so called is simply something that we do not understand at present. Our forefathers would have thought the telephone, the X-rays, and wireless telegraphy things 'supernatural'. It is more than possible that our descendants may make discoveries equally marvellous in the realms both of mind and matter, and that many things, which nowadays seem to the materialistically-minded the creations of credulous fancy, may in the future be understood and recognized as part of the one great scheme of things."

NOTES

1 See Robertson 1976; Campbell 1978 and 1978–81; Bruford 1983; MacilleDhuibh 29.5.92 and 24.6.94; MacInnes 1994; Black 1999, pp. 709–12.
2 Bruford 1983, p. 3; his earlier view (1969, p. 205) had been that 'it could be the story-teller, Donald Cameron, Tiree, rather than the editor, J. G. Campbell, who worked up the story as a *tour de force*'.
3 Macfarlane 1906–08, pp. xxxi, 344; Scott 1915–50, vol. 4, p. 334; Maclean 1922–24, p. 329.
4 Grant 1906, p. 106; Boog Watson 1929, p. 293.
5 Curiously, a modern Gaelic writer from Lewis, Aonghas Caimbeul (1903–82), does something very similar in his autobiography, recalling (1973, p. 46): *Bha na faoiltich gheamhraidh is earraich, Féill-Mhàrtainn, Féill-Phàdruig, Féill-Bhrìghde, agus Féill-Dòmhnaich.* ("There were the winter and spring wolftimes, Martinmas, St Patrick's day, St Brigid's day, and the Sunday Festival.") The editor, John Murray, queried it (*ibid.*, p. 362): *Tha an t-ùghdar ag radh nach e aon fhéill àraidh a tha seo, ach làithean féille a bha air an cumail air Dì-Dòmhnaich, mar Féill-Dòmhnaich Càisg no Féill-Dòmhnaich Caingis.* ("The author says that this is not one particular festival, but feast-days that were kept on a Sunday, like Easter Sunday or Whit Sunday.")
6 Hunter 2001, pp. 56, 59, 60, 69. The 'faison' or 'fusion' of a product is its substance or essence, Gaelic *toradh*, see for example McPherson 1929, pp. 186–87.
7 For a full account of Hartland and his views see Dorson 1968, pp. 239–48.
8 For a useful summary of Lang's views on the Fairies and of his involvement with Wentz see Kathleen Raine's introduction to the 1977 edition of Wentz's *Fairy Faith*, pp. xiii–xiv. Lang caused Wentz much agony by remarking, not unreasonably, that 'if the researcher did find modern cases of fairy visions alleged by sane and educated percipients, he [Lang] would be apt to explain them by suggestion acting on the subconscious self' (Wentz 1911, p. 476).
9 Welch 1993, p. 293, cf. pp. 8, 24. On Fairies as fallen angels see Gregory 1970, pp. 212, 225, 238, 240, 241, and Bord 1997, pp. 149–50. Wentz found the belief in Ireland, Scotland, Man, Wales and Brittany (1911, pp. 67, 85, 109–10, 129–30, 154, 205). Margaret Bennett has found it among Gaelic-speaking settlers in Newfoundland (1989, pp. 124–25; *Tocher* 42, pp. 401–02).
10 See p. 244 and note 845.
11 *Ceann suic* is a 'share-beam' or 'ploughshare head', from *soc*, a 'sock' or ploughshare (Dwelly 1977, p. 180). I can see no reason why a Fairy leader should have such a name, but I can see every reason why he should

be called *ceann stuic*, the head of a 'stock' or family, this being the traditional term for the captain of a shinty team (Anon. 1959). For another 'head fairy' in action see p. 642 below.

12 Welch 1993, p. 249 and cf. pp. 8, 24–25. On Fairies as gods or *Tuatha Dé Danann* see Spence 1948, pp. 87–92, 130; Bord 1997, pp. 146–47.

13 On Fairies as the dead see Wentz 1911, pp. 74–75, 109, and Bord 1997, pp. 151–54.

14 Wentz 1911, p. 452; Black 2002, pp. 357–58.

15 Wentz 1911, pp. 464–69. The supernatural lapse of time in Fairyland was comprehensively discussed by Hartland (1891, pp. 161–254) and Spence (1948, pp. 303–06).

16 Gregory 1970, p. 142, cf. Welch 1993, p. 318.

17 Miller 1994, pp. 68–69, cf. Dorson 1968, p. 146.

18 Cf. Scott 2001, pp. 169–73; on Fairy arrows see pp. 14, 81 and 223 below.

19 For an oath of purgation see note 24 on p. 691.

20 For the *caim* or circle see p. 455 below (note 694).

21 Buchanan 1836, p. 50, quoted in Black 2001, p. 482.

22 Gregory 1970, p. 117, cf. *ibid.*, pp. 134–35, and Welch 1993, pp. 313–14.

23 For a substantial but old-fashioned discussion of the changeling belief see Spence 1948, pp. 228–54. He follows this with a chapter on 'The Abduction of Adults by Fairies' (pp. 255–75) in which he helpfully categorises the theories on Fairy abduction as 'Stealing the Soul', 'Reincarnation', 'The Increase of the Fairy Community' and 'The Theory of Sacrifice' (pp. 269–74). For an earlier discussion of changelings see Brand 1849, vol. 2, pp. 73–75; for more recent work see Mac Philib 1991, Bennett 1992, pp. 11–31, and Henderson and Cowan 2001, pp. 94–100; and for some further references see Ó Duilearga 1981, p. 398.

24 Welch 1993, p. 318, cf. Gregory 1970, p. 110; Bourke 1999, p. 47.

25 See for example Macbain 1887–88, pp. 244–45; Anon. 1908–09a, pp. 159–63, 169–70; *Tocher* 27, p. 174; *Tocher* 38, pp. 20–23.

26 Welch 1993, p. 320, cf. Gregory 1970, p. 146.

27 Welch 1993, p. 319, cf. Gregory 1970, p. 360, and Bourke 1999, p. 143.

28 McNicol 1790, p. 502 = new edn, p. 365.

29 McColl 1792, pp. 413–14 = new edn, pp. 275–76.

30 See for example Mackay 1896, pp. xxx, 92, 254, 255; Gray 1987, p. 136; Forsyth 1999, p. 95.

31 The current whereabouts of the kirk session register for the parish of Ardnamurchan (1775–1902) is uncertain. I am grateful to Iain Thornber for faxing me the relevant pages from a photocopy in his possession. In recent times the book has been circulating amongst the homes of the parish, which is how it comes to be quoted in Maclean 1984, p. 39, cf. also Henderson and Cowan 2001, p. 96.

32 Gregory 1970, pp. 116–17, cf. Welch 1993, p. 173.

33 MacDougall and Calder 1910, pp. 148–53, cf. Wentz 1911, pp. 110–12.

34 For an intriguing example see *Tocher* 14, p. 220.

35 For an interesting discussion of the 'stock' see Fleming 2002, pp. 46–48.

36 Scott 1830, vol. 1, Introduction, p. 77 = 1993, p. 224.

37 Robertson 1904–07, p. 298, cf. Henderson 1911, pp. 247–48, and p. 300 below, note 29.

38 Scott 1830, vol. 1, Introduction, p. 55 = 1993, pp. 190–91.

39 Scott 1830, vol. 1, Introduction, pp. 55–56, 78 = 1993, pp. 191, 225.

40 I exclude the notorious 'first marriage' (*c.* 1696) of Simon Lord Lovat of the '45. As Dr Johnson pointed out, it was not an abduction but a rape (McLaren 1957, pp. 42–48; Chapman 1970, p. 77).

41 I have discussed this story more fully in MacilleDhuibh 20.9.02.

42 The technique of telling a story of the supernatural and then analysing it from a rational point of view is well established. It was pioneered by Sir Walter Scott (2001, pp. 178–79) and has been put to good use by Gearóid Ó Crualaoich (2003, pp. 100–225).

43 Quoted in Croker 1825–28, vol. 2, pp. viii–ix.

44 Anon. 1885–86b, pp. 287–88; Cameron 1887–88, pp. 182–84; MacMillan 1971, pp. 22–23.

45 Scott 1830, vol. 1, Introduction, pp. 54–68 = 1993, pp. 190–209; Stevenson 2004, pp. 248–64.

46 Scott 1830, vol. 1, Introduction, p. 57 = 1993, p. 193.

47 For Morrison see Maddrell 2002.

PREFACE

BY JOHN GREGORSON CAMPBELL

This is unedited, exactly as it stands in *Superstitions of the Highlands & Islands of Scotland*. As is demonstrated at p. 686 below, JGC wrote that book and *Witchcraft & Second Sight* as a single work, an intention which is fulfilled in the present edition for the first time. — R.B.

The object aimed at in the following pages is to put before the reader a statement, as complete and accurate as the writer can attain to, of the Superstitions and Antiquities of the Scottish Highlands and Islands. In other words, the writer has endeavoured to gather full materials relating to that subject, and to arrange them in a form that may prove of some scientific value.

In pursuit of this object, it has been deemed advisable to derive information solely from oral sources. Books have been purposely avoided as authorities, and a rule has been laid down, and strictly adhered to, not to accept any statement in print regarding a Highland belief, unless also found current among the people. In the few books there are, having any reference to Gaelic lore, the statements have been so frequently found at variance with popular beliefs that this rule has been a necessity. There are a few honourable exceptions, but in general what is to be found in print on this subject is not trustworthy.

A want of acquaintance with the Gaelic language or with Highland feelings and modes of thought, is usually the cause of error. The writers think in English, and are not careful to eliminate from their statements thoughts derived from English or classical literature, or to keep from confusing with Celtic beliefs ideas derived from foreign sources, and from analogous creeds existing elsewhere. This gives an unconscious tinge to their statements, and (what is more to be regretted) sometimes makes them fill up with extraneous and foreign elements what seems to them gaps or blanks in beliefs they but imperfectly understand.

The writer's information has been derived from widely separated districts in the North, West, and Central Highlands, and from the Islands. Naturally, the bulk of the information was obtained in Tiree, where the writer had most opportunity of making inquiries, but information from this or any other source has not been accepted without comparison with the same beliefs in other districts. The writer has not been able personally to visit all parts of the Highlands, but his informants have spent their lives in districts far apart. The reader will fall into a mistake who supposes that the whole information is within the belief, or even knowledge, of any one individual, or of any one district.

The beliefs of one district do not differ essentially from those of another. In one or two cases several versions of a tale are given to show to some extent the nature of the variations of popular tradition.

The writer has thankfully to acknowledge, and he cannot but remember with pleasure, the readiness and courtesy, and in very many cases the great intelligence with which his inquiries have been answered. Some of his informants have shown a quickness and retentiveness of memory which he could not but envy, and an appreciation of, and an acquaintance with ancient lore that seemed to him to indicate in those who were strangers to the world of letters powers of mind of a high order.

The objection to books and print as authorities has also been extended to written correspondence. No doubt much that is additional and interesting could be obtained through these channels, but if the account given is to serve any purpose higher than that of mere amusement, strict accuracy is of such importance that all these sources of possible error have been avoided; they cannot be sifted by cross-examination and further inquiry so readily or thoroughly as information obtained by word of mouth. The whole has thus passed through the writer's own hands directly from what he has found current among the people.

Care has been taken that no statement be made conveying an idea different in the slightest from what has been heard. A popular Gaelic saying can be quoted as applicable to the case: "If it be a lie as told by me, it was a lie as told to me." (*Ma's breug bh'uam e, is breug dhomh e.*) It is as free to another as it has been to the writer, to draw his inferences from the statements given, and it is thought no genuine tale or oral tradition will be found to contradict the statements made in the following pages.

In the translations given of Gaelic, the object aimed at has been to give the corresponding English expression, that is, one conveying the same meaning to the English reader that the Gaelic expression conveys to the Gaelic reader. Accuracy has been looked to on this point rather than grace of diction. Where there is anything striking in the Gaelic idiom the literal meaning is also given. In poetry there is consequently a baldness, to which the original is a stranger; but this, it may be urged, is a fault inherent in all translations, however carefully executed. The transference of ideas from one language to another weakens the force and beauty of an expression; what is racy and witty, or musical and expressive in one, becomes tame and insipid in another.

This trite observation is made to deprecate unfavourable opinions being formed of the genius and force of the Gaelic language from the translations given.

THE ORIGIN OF THE FAIRY CREED

This paper by JGC was first published in *The Scottish Historical Review*, vol. 7, 1909–10, pp. 364–76. The editor, James Maclehose, stated that it was written 'about thirty years ago', that is, *c.* 1880. It therefore serves very well as JGC's introduction to the present work, which he wrote *c.* 1874 (see pp. 643–44 below). I have re-edited it lightly in line with the principles stated in my preface, and corrected a number of misprints – especially in the Gaelic words quoted, e.g. *gamhnain* appears in *SHR* for *gamhainn*, and *Cannan* twice for *Leannan*. — R.B.

In inquiring into the origin of the Fairy Creed, the first thing that arrests attention is the identity of the Celtic and Teutonic creeds. The differences are only such as arise from diversity of locality and society, and do not affect their spirit and essential characteristics. Both among Celts and Teutons, the Fairies are the counterparts of mankind in actions, enjoyments, dwellings, size, and modes of life. They live in families and societies, some communities being very rich and having magnificent dwellings, while others are poor and borrow food; they have children, dwell underground, and go about invisibly; bake and brew, confer prosperity, strength and skill upon their favourites; and steal women and children. They have delightful music and singing, and are fond of dancing. In fact, every tale regarding them to be found among the one tribe can be matched by a tale to be found among the other.

This correspondence cannot have originated from any intercourse of which history makes mention as existing between Celts and Teutons: the creed is known among every branch of the Celts in Scotland, Ireland, the isle of Man, Wales and Brittany, and of the Teutonic race in Scandinavia, Germany, and Britain, so that we are compelled to the conclusion that it originated in times anterior to history. The known intercourse between these widespread tribes will not account for this common creed on the subject. The *Shi* people of the Celts, the trolls and *Duergar* of Scandinavia and the still-folk of Germany so closely resemble each other that we are led to believe them to have been at one time identical. But at what time and under what circumstances the superstition spread from the one tribe to the other, it is not now possible to determine. After both tribes entered Europe, there was a long period antecedent to history during which we know nothing of their doings. We only know that like all other barbarians they were roving, unsettled, and seldom at peace, and we know also that among savage nations superstition is strangely infectious. Barbarians are unsettled in their creeds, as well as in their habits, and ready to accept the superstitions of their neighbours.

At the dawn of authentic history, the Celts were situated on the shores of the Atlantic. They were the first wave of Aryan immigration from the east, and a colony of them was found wherever the Teutons, who formed the succeeding wave, settled. A belief like the Fairy mythology is very likely to have been among the first things to spread from the one family to the other.

The superstition may be even older than the entry of these races into Europe. The Arabs, a Shemitic race, when they see a whirlwind in the desert, believe it to be caused by the flight of an evil spirit or jinn, and cry: "Iron! Iron!" So the Celt believed the Fairies travel in eddy winds, and that iron is a defence against them. Possibly the resemblance here, however, is merely accidental. Eddy winds must ever be a cause of wonder to the untutored mind, and the Arab, to whom they bring danger and mischief, has associated them with the evil spirits of his creed, while the Celt, in whose regions they cause little damage, has connected them with 'the little people', a class of beings of a different and better type than demons and evil spirits. Long after the days of Tubal Cain, iron was rare and highly prized, and it is not surprising to find it trusted to by any of the races of mankind, as possessed of divine power. In the Highlands it was a defence against the Fairies generally, but was not deemed more efficacious to scatter an eddy wind than a shoe, earth from a molehill, or other handy missile.

The Greek and Roman languages have a large element in common with the Gaelic and in a less degree with the Teutonic. We argue the antiquity of the Fairy Creed from its existence among all the branches of Celts and Teutons, and consequently are prepared to turn to the mythologies of Greece and Rome for any trace of its peculiarities. The mythology and modes of thought prevailing on the shores of the Mediterranean, from difference of climate, civilisation, etc., necessarily became divergent from those remaining among the wild northern nations, and any traces of identity now to be found must be indistinct. They are, however, perhaps as clear as is to be expected.

The anthropomorphic deities of Greece and Rome, in their manner of appearing, their influence over men, and the class of actions ascribed to them, frequently remind us of the Fairies, the counterparts of humanity. They conduct themselves more like the *Shi* people than like deities, who were objects of worship or adoration. The Fairy mistress, or *leannan sìth,* who compelled her mortal lover to hold nightly assignations, and gave him wonderful information, strongly reminds us of Numa and the nymph Egeria, with whom he held nightly meetings, and who gave him divine knowledge. His place of meeting with his divine mistress was at a well, and at such places the Fairy women were often encountered. The Highland 'Wife of Ben Breck' is called, in the popular song devoted to her memory, 'the big wife of the high fountain' (i.e. of the fountain high in the hill), and those who had Fairy mistresses frequently came in all draggled and wet from their nocturnal meetings. The Muses, 'sisters of the sacred well', were *nine* in number, and in Highland lore there is common mention of the 'nine slim Fairy women' (*na naoi mnathan seanga sìth*). The expression has remained in what is evidently an old class of compositions, the winter evening fireside tales, but without explanation of its origin or meaning. The nympholepts were seized with frenzy on seeing any of the nymphs, and Cybele, 'the wandering mountain mother', afflicted men with madness. Those over whom the Fairies got power became passionately fond of their Fairy loves, to an extent which could be construed as nothing else than the madness of the nympholept. Their ardent attachment overpowered every natural and human affection. The 'roaming wandering Elfin dame' (*na mnatha sìthe siùbhlacha seachranach*), also mentioned in the same class of popular tales, put men under enchantments and afflicted them with a wandering frenzy (*seachoran*) which allowed them no rest till they found the object of their bewitched search. The wandering of those 'lifted' by the Fairies (*air a thogail le sluagh*) was of a kindred character, the wandering of people under enchantments (*fo gheasaibh*). They knew not where they were going, nor felt how they were being conveyed.

The explanation which derives the Fairies from the Lamiae, who took away young children and slew them, and from the Fauns, the gods of the woods, is hardly an explanation at all. The Lamiae were the common bugbear, and all bugbears worthy of the name take away children. That is the object for which they exist. The Fauns and Fairies have nothing in common, and supposing them to be identical the question of their origin is still unsolved. The deduction of the Elves from the *lares* and *larvae* is not more satisfactory. What they have in common, every other supernatural being has also.

A theory is to be met with in Gaelic books that the Fairies were the druids, driven into remote and lonely places on the introduction of Christianity, and stealing children to keep up their numbers. There is no evidence that the druids continued their peculiar observances in retired places after the breaking up of their system, that they kidnapped children, or that the Fairy superstition resembles the druidic system. Very likely the belief in Fairies was part of the druid's teaching, and some points of it, as the days on which Fairy dwellings are open, the charming of querns etc. against the Elves by the *deiseal* turn, indicate a pagan or druidic origin, but it is not likely that the latter peculiar observance came to be used as a charm against the druids themselves.

There is much that is undoubtedly of ecclesiastical origin in the superstition. Friday was the day on which the 'little people' had most power of interference with men, and on which they were most given to entering houses. The bare mention of its name was sufficient to excite their wrath, the reason being that which has caused the day to be deemed unlucky throughout the rest of Christendom, that it was the day of the Crucifixion. Children were considered less liable after baptism to being taken away by Fairies, and the name of the deity was powerful to put an end to Fairy work and disenchant Fairy food.

In the Highlands of Scotland there has existed a belief in other supernatural beings besides the Fairies, such as gruagachs, glastigs, water-horses, etc., the origin of which cannot be traced to any doctrine (or perversion of doctrine) of the Christian religion, and which was but nurtured by the Church during the long period of the Middle Ages, when the principal weapons of the churchman were holy water and charms, and his principal duties the exorcising of devils, the counteracting of witches, and the laying of ghosts. The origin of these beliefs must be looked for in the pagan creeds which Christianity displaced. It is known that the heathen deities, which the Christian religion degraded from their high position as objects of worship, were not utterly eradicated. In early times ecclesiastics reduced them to the rank of devils and made them subordinates of Satan. It is, therefore, within the bounds of possibility that the Fairies are the deities of an effete religion. Heathen gods are, however, gloomy, and do not become more amiable when seen in the light of a purer faith. The feelings with which the Fairies were regarded, and their character and actions, do not warrant the supposition that they were ever objects of religious reverence. They had too little malignity ascribed to them, and were regarded too much with contempt and too little with fear. There is, besides, no resemblance on which any weight can be laid between the superstition and what classic or Celtic writers have told us was the old heathen Celtic faith.

But suppose all this to be granted, that the Fairies existed as part of the druidic teaching (which very likely they did), and that traces of them are to be found in the mythologies of Greece and Rome, the question still remains, what is the origin or meaning of the Fairy Creed?

Resemblances, real or imaginary, can be laid hold of to support any theory with which we are in love, and a creed which has been so widespread and tenacious of life must present many features which can be so construed. The tribes whose inheritance it has been have undergone the greatest changes in their social circumstances and modes of life: they have migrated, conquered and been conquered, they have been taught a higher faith, and science has opened her stores to them, yet the Fairies – sadly deprived, it is true, of their original vitality, and serving no higher purpose than ornaments of poetry – still survive, and, bearing traces of the ages, have found a permanent place in the world's literature. Their character has been altered, and the teaching of which they are the embodiment has been lost sight of, but their features (though disfigured) can be still recognised.

The supposition that the Fairies were originally an alien race presents many points to be urged in its favour. The main characteristics of the superstition – the Elves being counterparts of the human race and their fondness for alliances with mankind, the dwellings assigned to them, their dogs and cattle, love of music and dancing, borrowing and lending of meal and other articles, stealing of hand-mills, etc. – may be said to point, as clearly as the traces of a remote age can do, to a rude tribe of savages living in proximity to a superior race, while the making of trash their food, attributing to their women an imperforate nostril or other defect unnatural to humanity, and representing them as thievish and attacking the weakest of the race (women in childbed and their babes) and as being driven away by the smell of burning leather or a drop of urine, are the natural offspring of that ridicule which we may suppose the stronger race endeavoured to cast upon a feeble and despised enemy.

The most curious point in the superstition is that iron was all-powerful against the Fairies, and that the Fairy arrow and spade were of stone. In all popular tales to be met with in the Highlands, iron bears a different relation to the Fairies from what it does to any other supernatural being. Against ghost, or water-horse, or bugbear of that kind, an edged weapon was a defence, as it might be against a mortal enemy, but only against the Fairies was iron, or still better steel (*cruaidh*) in any shape or form, a specific guard. A bunch of keys or a rusty nail was as effective as the most lethal weapon.

It is no matter of surprise that a sword or dirk or knife should have miraculous powers ascribed to it. It is a valuable possession, a trusty friend in danger and in the presence of an enemy, and the wonder would be if popular imagination had *not* invested the 'touch of cold steel' with supernatural powers. In the form of arms and offensive weapons, steel was used by the Highlander in encounters with unearthly enemies, but not in any other way than as great personal strength or a good cudgel were available. Against the *Shi* people alone, iron and steel as such, whether manufactured into weapons of offence or not, were a defence; and the belief is one so remarkable that it forces us into some such explanation as this – it was the distinguishing difference in prehistoric times between the tribes inheriting the creed and the stone savages who were the first Fairies.

It is not a sufficient explanation that when iron was rare and valuable, miraculous powers were ascribed to it. Of that belief another Highland superstition is a memory. No one who hid iron – especially the ploughshare – during his life and died without telling his secret could rest in his grave, a belief afterwards transferred to the secreting of other metals that became more precious. If the efficacy of iron against the Fairies had no other origin, the metal would be equally efficacious against water-horses, water-bulls, brownies, ghosts, and all that sort. Except as arms it was not so.

It is now considered a well-ascertained fact in science that the Celts were preceded in Europe by a race unacquainted with iron, and using bone, flint and stone weapons or implements. Traces of this race are found over the greater part of Europe in caves, drift and mounds, from which it is inferred to have been similar to the races now found in the regions of the extreme north – Finns, Lapps and Esquimaux – in dwellings, habits, arts and social condition. It is at the same time so open to question whether it was the same as any of these races that the learned have preferred to give it a name to itself.

In the early times of these allophylians (as this race has been called), the rhinoceros, elephant, hyæna, tiger and other animals long since extinct in these latitudes were found in what are now the temperate regions of Europe. The Celts, forming the first wave of Aryan or Indo-European migration, either exterminated this race or drove it to its present inhospitable abodes, and they may in part have absorbed it. The water-bull and other mystic animals of Celtic superstition may be but indistinct memories, preserved through this alliance, of the animal forms of the remoter period.

It is not necessary to suppose that intermarriage prevailed to any great extent, and it is not likely that in these savage times the proud nomade Celt would tolerate, within his hunting or pasture grounds, an alien race requiring extent of ground for its support as much as himself. It is seldom that a conquered race is totally exterminated, and the few remaining in remote retirements are likely enough to form at times alliances with the superior race. This is only conjecture, but it explains the part of the superstition which relates to the *leannan shi* or Fairy love, and the disfavour with which alliances with the *Shi* race were looked upon. It also explains why dogs bark at, and give chase to, the Fairies, and the Fairies run away. Dogs, as 'it is their nature to', bark at strangers and people of uncouth appearance to the present day, and the allophylian, knowing the risk he ran when he approached an enemy's abode, fled in terror when he found himself discovered. His hiding himself readily gave rise to stories of his disappearance in the earth.

At the dawn of history the tribes of Europe occupied much the same places they now do, and the position of the Arctic tribes on the extreme outskirts of the continent argue them to be the oldest of the present possessors of the soil of Europe. Only hard necessity and the pressure of more powerful tribes could have sent them to the dreary and forbidding Arctic regions. The Celts, by all accounts, were a formidable and warlike horde, armed, as their language denotes, from the earliest times with sword and shield. It has not been settled among antiquarians whence Europe derived its knowledge of the smelting and working of iron, and historically it is considered highly probable that the Celts were acquainted with this branch of metallurgy before they came into contact with Rome. An invaded race, destitute of those weapons that would enable it to make a successful resistance, must be driven to remote fastnesses, and naturally seeks by treachery to make up for the want of strength. Hence the noiseless approach, and the Fairy arrow launched from an unseen hand.

There is evidence that the climate of Europe was much more rigorous in primeval days than it is now, and the aboriginal inhabitants, ignorant of iron, must have lived in much the same way as those now live who reside near to, and within, the Arctic Circle. On the supposition that the Fairies were these aborigines, an easy explanation of a great part of the superstition is furnished. In addition to the resemblances already pointed out, it is noticeable that the Fairies dwelling together and shifting their quarters in companies and societies, the 'wandering, roaming' Fairy women, the 'little men', the underground dwellings, the association with deer (*which were the Fairy cattle*), the dogs, the magic knowledge and the enchanting glitter of Fairy dwellings all find their counterpart in the migratory habits of the diminutive Lapp, his round hat, his reindeer and dogs, his practice of witchcraft and divination, and the glitter of ice.

The Fairy *brugh* was a round hillock or mound; the gammie of the shore Laplander is generally of a circular form, 'having the appearance of a large, rounded hillock'. The reindeer is everything to the Lapp – cow, horse, food and clothing – and it was the shape of deer the Fairy women assumed on every occasion on which they changed shape. They were often surprised in that form by the hunter, and his seeing them milking the hinds was followed by his being unsuccessful in the chase that day. The 'pretty striped yearling calf' (*gamhainn bòidheach breac*) promised by the Fairy lover to his mistress, and the 'hornless dun cow' (*bò mhaol odhar*) which the changeling said he had so often seen milked 'in yonder dun glen' are more likely the dappled fawn and the hind of the red deer than the polled or speckled dairy stock of modern days. The Fairy cat finds its prototype in the cave tiger, or some such feline animal of prehistoric times.

It can hardly be a meaningless tradition that the first hand-mill was got from the Fairies. The stone quern is one of the most common objects in the cyclopean underground dwellings of the savages of the stone period.

A further confirmation of this allophylian theory is to be found in the existence of a belief to the same effect among the Celts themselves. Waldron, in his *Description of the Isle of Man*, 1731, says, "They (the Manx people) confidently assert, the first inhabitants of their island were Fairies."

In the isle of Skye there is a tradition that the first inhabitants were a very, very small race, who formed their houses of branches placed leaning against each other, and who disappeared when the Norsemen came. This dwarfish race is not, however, said to be the Fairies. Every inquiry in the writer's power was made into this curious tradition, and the same account was heard from several people. The little people were called *Drunaich* or *Druinnich*, and were red-haired (*ruadh*). They never came near other houses, and their own were round bothies, formed of young trees and boughs placed leaning against each other, Skye being at the time covered with wood. They disappeared when the *Lochlannaich* came, and no one knows what became of them.

Many parts of the creed are at variance with this view of its origin, and so far as the historical meaning of the superstition is concerned, the figure of the allophylian becomes again indistinct. The eye is strained to pierce the darkness that has settled on these remote ages, and turns with eagerness to whatever promises to throw the slightest light on the obscurity. Like one who sees figures on a distant horizon in an imperfect light, and is doubtful whether they are men, or trees, or stones, the archæologist may be sometimes in doubt whether the figures which he sees are an allophylian race, or shadows thrown by succeeding ages.

There are, as we see, many features of the Fairy Creed to create a probability that the original Fairies were such a race. There are, however, other points that forbid it. The supposition does not explain the anomalies of Fairy lore. The Elves had great skill in handicraft of all kinds, and taught their favourites to perform all kinds of tradesmen's work, weaving, dyeing, and especially smith work, in a wonderfully short time and in a skilful manner. It is anomalous that they should have this wonderful knowledge, and have smithies in their brughs, while at the same time they had the simplicity of Arcadians and were kept away by iron.

Of the same class were the anomalies that the *Shi* people were as large as mortals, yet of pigmy stature; a puny race, yet able to lift men with them through the air; that they had great knowledge of the healing art, yet were laid up with disease; could be killed, and yet were invisible at will; had hand-mills of their own, and yet stole those of mortals. Neither does it satisfactorily explain how the Elves are associated with curious natural appearances and aerial phenomena, or their music is enchanting.

Another explanation suggests itself. The Fairy Creed teaches the difference between semblance and reality in the occupations and enjoyments of men, and is of ethical rather than ethnical origin. It is moral and instructive, and not historical or mythological. The Elves are the representation of appearance and show, as distinguished from substance and reality, in the affairs of men. Their doings are thus identical with what is now called illusion of the senses, and they are connected with natural appearances that bear a resemblance to the work and possessions of men. Thus Fairy hillocks are houses in appearance, but are useless for any of the purposes for which houses are erected; they give no shelter, nor even allow admission; they look as if they were houses, but they are not such in reality. People who were Elf-smitten, or taken away by the Fairies or struck by the Fairy arrow, remained in appearance as before, but the essence – the most valuable attribute of their humanity – was taken away. Their health was suddenly and unaccountably gone, their reason was clouded, and in many cases their existence as human beings terminated in sudden death.

The changeling had none of the fresh life and little winning ways that of themselves more than repay the parents' care and trouble in the rearing of children. Its appetite was inordinate, and its fretful peevish temper allowed no rest night or day. It gave all possible trouble, but no pleasure; it occupied the place and had the semblance but none of the reality of childhood, nor those attributes that make children dear to men. Women in childbed are liable to diseases that cause sudden death or affect their reason and urge them to wander. By either calamity, they are no longer what they were, and as wives and mothers cease to exist among mankind. Elf-smitten cattle retain the appearance of cattle, but none of their uses: they yield no milk, and their flesh is unfit for food. Cows are not kept to eat provender and be attended to, but for the supply of milk and beef. The Elf-smitten cow is, therefore, only a cow in appearance, its value and reality as a cow are gone.

So goods taken by the Fairies remain ostensibly in their owner's possession, but he derives no benefit from them. The farmer, for instance, has a plentiful harvest, but if he be of a discontented and mean spirit, decrying and concealing his good fortune, his little mind makes him blind to his prosperity, and he sees himself poor in the midst of plenty; or else after spending labour on his land, the crop, through what is now deemed want of skill or defect of the ground, proves a failure and useless for man or beast. The Fairies have taken away the goods; the trouble and expense have remained, but the advantages have mysteriously disappeared. It is not, however, a plentiful increase of the world's goods nor want of skill that is condemned in the Fairy Creed, but churlishness, discontentment, meanness, and niggardly concealment of prosperity.

The same distinction between appearance and reality holds good with regard to Fairy work. There is semblance, glitter and outward show, but nothing substantial and genuine. A plain cup, for example, is as good to quench thirst from as one loaded with ornaments. The benefit of design is to hold drink and appease thirst; elegance and beauty of shape may be desirable; but mere ornament is superfluous, of no use, existing only for the sake of appearance. Hence a highly ornamented cup or other article is of the character of Fairy work; the ornament contributes nothing towards the practical use for which the article is intended.

Again, many articles of workmanship are quickly made, to ordinary eyes showy, and as good as other work of the same kind on which time and labour have been spent, but they do not stand the test of use; they prove counterfeit; the senses have been illuded by mere appearance; the work is only Fairy work. This same doctrine has been revived in a different form in the present day by Carlyle in his denunciation of shams. Counterfeit work and articles that are not genuine, however gaudy to the sight, ought not to be considered the productions of true man at all; they are but the work of his shadowy counterparts, of beings who ought to be invisible; they are in short only Elfin work, having appearance but no reality.

The Fairy Creed is a polished and amusing satire on the vanity of human pleasures and the emptiness of what is commonly called 'life'. Young men who entered Fairy dwellings without taking precautions how to get out again joined the Fairy festivities, became unmindful of the passage of time, and lost all desire ever to return to the haunts of men. When brought to the open air, and on becoming conscious of the lapse of time, they crumbled into dust. In the same way, many enter on a round of festivities, and forgetting alike their sorrows and their duties, and unobservant of the passage of time, waste their days in frivolity and folly and giddiness. Sometimes they are disenchanted when too late, and have barely realised the misuse made of their means, health, and days when the end of their life comes upon them. The Fairy castle, which they in their inconsideration supposed to be the abode of pleasure and happiness, closes against them; their life is wasted, and they crumble into dust. The true enjoyments of man do not lie in a round of festivities, in exquisite music, grandeur of dwellings or apparel, dancing and outward show; these are merely specious, and better is he who is contented with the ordinary lot of man, a lot in which there are anxieties and labour.

So also, true travelling does not consist in being whirled from one place to another, heedless of everything but going over the ground. That is merely 'being lifted by the people'; it is travelling in appearance but not in reality, travelling in the company of the Fairies, and not as true men travel.

It also explains why *green* was the Fairy dress. Green is 'smiling nature's universal robe' (as the poet calls it), and the Elves, being the appearance of mankind but in reality illusions of the senses and interpretations of natural phenomena, were clothed in the same colour. So also their association with natural appearances led to physical objects, such as reddish coloured stones, Fairy butter, etc., and curious phenomena resembling the works of men, being referred to them.

It does not, however, explain why iron was a defence against the Elves. Iron is the most easily oxidised of the metals, and there is nothing in its nature to account for its being a better security against powers that take away the substance, while they leave the appearance, than gold or silver. Perhaps when the creed first arose, and the Fairies were made a race dwelling by themselves, the traditions of the stone savages still remained. The whole of the rest of the creed is explained by the Elves being appearance and nothing else, the semblance of mankind without the reality. Seeming work is quickly done; the most miserable noise becomes the finest music when listened to by an excited and fond imagination; the faint and weary hunter sees human forms where there are none – in everything Fairy there is appearance, semblance, outward form, such as are found among men, but there is nothing solid and true. In giving form and expression to this truth or teaching, the traditions and existence of an alien race may have been taken advantage of, and the ethical explanation of the superstition may include the ethnical.

The cause of Fairy aversion to ordure is that it is matter out of which the substance has been already taken. Hence also their objection to dirt of every kind, and the reward given by them, according to the Teutonic creed, to tidy servants. That the original meaning of the creed was not entirely lost sight of, when it degenerated into a superstition, may be inferred from faintness being ascribed to the Elves; from oatmeal being a protection against them; from their stealing the substance of men's goods; or their being associated with whatever is mere empty unprofitable show.

It is unobserved by themselves too often, that men lose the benefit of their labours and increase; and it is an amusing and instructive allegory which has ascribed their loss to the shadowy Elfin race. When the moral teaching became a superstition, it accumulated to itself many things not to be explained by the original creed, such as shedding the blood of the Elfin lover, or the detailed accounts of the hunter's adventures with Fairy women, etc.

But these are only the natural offspring of the unfettered imagination at work upon such a subject. The fate of those who married Fairy wives finds ample illustration in the issue of alliances for the sake of wealth and mere show. The veracity of the Elfin wife is fully matched by the extravagance of the showy wife.

John Gregorson Campbell

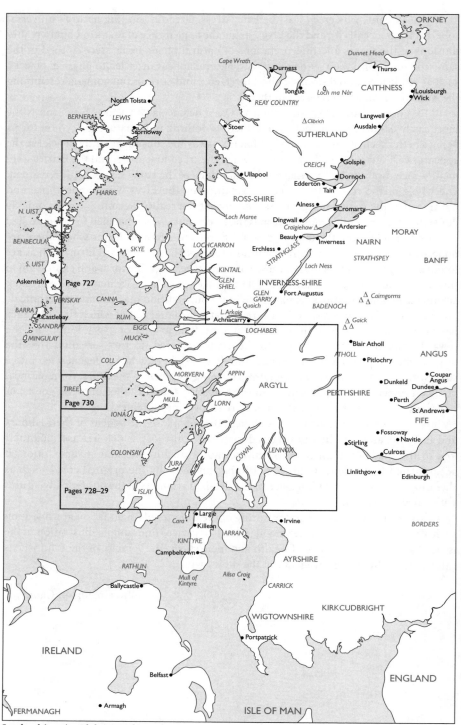

Scotland (west) with key to other maps

1

THE FAIRIES

Fairies and Elves

In any account of Gaelic superstition and popular belief, the first and most prominent place is to be assigned to the Fairy or Elfin people, or, as they are called both in Irish and Scottish Gaelic, the *sith* people, that is, 'the people of peace', the 'still folk' or 'silently-moving' people. The words Elfin and Fairy are, in these pages, used indifferently as equivalents of the Gaelic names *sith* (or shi) people, etc.[1]

The antiquity of the belief is shown by its being found among all branches of the Celtic and Teutonic families, and in countries which have not, within historical times, had any communication with each other. If it be not entirely of Celtic origin, there can be no doubt that among the Celtic races it acquired an importance and influence accorded to it nowhere else.

Of all the beings with which fear or fancy peopled the supernatural, the Fairies were the most intimately associated with men's daily life. In the present day, when popular poetical ideas are extinguished in the universal call for 'facts' and by 'cold material laws', it is hard to understand how firm a hold a belief like this had upon men in a more primitive state of society, and how unwillingly it is surrendered.

Throughout the greater part of the Highlands of Scotland the Fairies have become things of the past. A common belief is that they existed once, though they are not now seen. There are others to whom the Elves have still a real existence, and who are careful to take precautions against them. The changes which the Highlands are undergoing have made the traces of the belief fainter in some districts than in others, and in some there remains but a confused jumbling of all the superstitions. It would be difficult to find a person who knows the whole Fairy creed, but the tales of one district are never contradictory of those of another. They are rather to be taken as supplemental of each other, and it is by comparison and such supplementing that the following statement has been drawn out. It is thought that it will not be found at variance with any genuine Highland Fairy tale.

The Fairies, according to the Scoto-Celtic belief, are a race of beings, the counterparts of mankind in person, occupations and pleasures, but unsubstantial and unreal, ordinarily invisible, noiseless in their motions, and having their dwellings underground, in hills and green mounds of rock or earth. They are addicted to visiting the haunts of men, sometimes to give assistance, but more frequently to take away the benefit of their goods and labours, and sometimes even their persons. They may be present in any company, though mortals do not see them. Their interference is never productive of good in the end, and may prove destructive. Men cannot therefore be sufficiently on their guard against them.

NAMES GIVEN TO FAIRIES

The names by which these dwellers underground are known are mostly derivative from the word *sìth* (pronounced **shee**). As a substantive (in which sense it is ordinarily used) *sìth* means 'peace', and, as an adjective, is applied solely to objects of the supernatural world, particularly to the Fairies and whatever belongs to them. Sound is a natural adjunct of the motions of men, and its entire absence is unearthly, unnatural, not human. The name *sìth* without doubt refers to the 'peace' or silence of Fairy motion, as contrasted with the stir and noise accompanying the movements and actions of men. The German 'still folk' is a name of corresponding import. The Fairies come and go with noiseless steps, and their thefts or abductions are done silently and unawares to men. The wayfarer resting beside a stream, on raising his eyes, sees the Fairy woman, unheard in her approach, standing on the opposite bank. Men know the Fairies have visited their houses only by the mysterious disappearance of the substance of their goods, or the sudden and unaccountable death of any of the inmates or of the cattle. Sometimes the Elves are seen entering the house, gliding silently round the room, and going out again as noiselessly as they entered. When driven away they do not go off with tramp and noise and sounds of walking (such as men make) or melt into thin air (as spirits do) but fly away noiselessly like birds or hunted deer. They seem to glide or float along rather than to walk. Hence the name *sìthche* and its synonyms are often applied contemptuously to a person who sneaks about or makes his approach without warning.[2]

Sometimes indeed the Elves make a rustling noise like that of a gust of wind, or a silk gown, or a sword drawn sharply through the air, and their coming and going has been even indicated by frightful and unearthly shrieks, a pattering as of a flock of sheep, or the louder trampling of a troop of horses. Generally, however, their presence is indicated at most by the cloud of dust raised by the eddy wind, or by some other curious natural phenomenon, by the illumination of their dwellings, the sound of their musical instruments, songs, or speech.

For the same reason *sìth* is applied not merely to what is Fairy, but to whatever is Fairylike, unearthly, not of this world. Of this laxer use of the term the following may be given as illustrations.

Breac shìth, 'Elfin pox', hives, are spots that appear on the skin in certain diseases, as hooping-cough, and indicate a highly malignant stage of the malady.[3] They are not ascribed to the Fairies, but are called *sìth* because they appear and again disappear as it were 'silently', without obvious cause, and more mysteriously than other symptoms. Cows said to have been found on the shores of Loscantire in Harris, Scorrybreck in Skye and on the island of Bernera were called *crodh sìth*, 'Fairy cows', simply because they were of no mortal breed, but of a kind believed to live under the sea on *meillich*, seaweed.[4] Animals in the shape of cats, but in reality witches or demons, were called *cait shìth*, 'Elfin cats', and the water-horse, which has no connection whatever with the Elves, is sometimes called *each sìth*, unearthly horse. The cuckoo is an *eun sìth*, a 'Fairy bird', because, as is said, its winter dwelling is underground.[5]

A banner in the possession of the family of MacLeod, of MacLeod of Skye, is called 'MacLeod's Fairy Banner' (*Bratach Shìth MhicLeòid*) on account of the supernatural powers ascribed to it. When unfurled, victory in war (*buaidh chogaidh*) attends it, and it relieves its followers from imminent danger. These virtues it is to have only thrice, and it has been already unfurled twice. Many of the common people wanted it brought out at the time of the potato failure.[6] Every pregnant woman who sees it is taken in premature labour (a misfortune which happened, it is said, to the English wife of a former chief in consequence of her irrepressible curiosity to see the banner), and every cow casts her calf (*cha bhi bean no bò nach tilg a laogh*).[7] Others, however, say the name is owing to the magic banner having been got from an Elfin sweetheart.[8]

A light seen among the Hebrides, a sort of St Elmo's light or Will-of-the-Wisp, is called *teine sìth*, 'Fairy light', though no one ever blamed the Fairies as the cause of it.[9] In a semi-satirical song 'Long aig Calum Mac Shìomain', of much merit for its spirit and ease of diction, composed in Tiree to the owner of a crazy skiff that had gone to the Ross of Mull for peats and staid too long, the bard, in a spirited description of the owner's adventures and seamanship, says:

> *Seachad air Grianaig*
> *Mar fhiadh nam beann fuara,*
> *Dìreadh ri uchd garbhlaich*
> *'S an sealgair ga ruagadh,*
> *Ise 's siubhal sìth aice,*
> *Sìnteagan uallach,*
> *Sgoltadh nan tonn uaine*
> *'S a fuaradh air chàch.*

("Onward past Greenock / Like the deer of the cold high hills, / Breasting the rugged ground / With the hunter in pursuit, / She sailed with Fairy motion, / Bounding smoothly in her pride, / Cleaving the green waves / And passing to windward of the rest.")[10] By *siubhal sìth* ('Fairy motion') the poet means not rising and falling on the waves but gliding smoothly along.[11]

This latitude in the use of the word has led some writers on the subject to confound with the Fairies beings having as little connection with them as with mankind. A similar laxness occurs in the use of the English word Fairy. It is made to include kelpies, mermaids and other supernatural beings having no connection with the true Fairy or Elfin race.

The following are the names by which the 'folk' are known in Gaelic. It is observable that every one of the names, when applied to mortals, is contemptuous and disparaging.

Sìthche (pronounced **sheeche**) is the generic and commonest term. It is a noun of common gender, and its plural is *sìthchean* (**sheechun**).[12] In Graham's *Highlands of Perthshire*, a work more than once quoted by Sir Walter Scott, but unreliable as an authority, this word is written *shi'ich*.[13]

Sìreach, plural *sìrich*, also *sìbhrich*, is a provincial term: *an sìriche dubh* 'the black Elf', i.e. the veriest Elf.

Sìthbheire (pronounced **sheevere**), a masculine noun, is mostly applied to changelings, or the Elf substituted for children and animals taken by the Fairies. Applied to men it is very contemptuous.[14]

Sìochaire is still more so. Few expressions of scorn are more commonly applied to men than *sìochaire grànda*, 'ugly slink'.[15]

Duine sìth (plural *daoine sìth*), 'a man of peace, a noiselessly moving person, a Fairy, an Elf'; feminine *bean shìth* (genitive *mnà sìth*, plural *mnathan sìth*, genitive plural with the article *nam ban shìth*), 'a woman of peace, an Elle woman', are names that include the whole Fairy race.[16] *Bean shìth* has become naturalised in English under the form 'banshi'. The term was introduced from Ireland, but there appears no reason to suppose the Irish belief different from that of the Scottish Highlands. Any seeming difference has arisen since the introduction of the banshi to the literary world, and from the too free exercise of imagination by book-writers on an imperfectly understood tradition.

The *leannan sìth*, 'Fairy sweetheart, familiar spirit', might be of either sex. The use of this word by the translators of the Bible into Gaelic is made a great handle of by the common people to prove from Scripture that Fairies actually exist. The Hebrew word so translated is rendered 'pythons' by the Vulgate, and 'consulters of the spirits of the dead' by modern scholars.[17] Those said to have familiar spirits were probably a class of magicians who pretended to be media of communication with the spirit world, their 'familiar' making himself known by sounds muttered from the ground through the instrumentality, as the Hebrew name denotes, of a skin bottle.

Brughadair 'a person from a *brugh*, or fairy dwelling', applied to men, means one who does a stupid or senseless action.

Other names are *sluagh* 'folk, a multitude'; *sluagh eutrom*, 'light folk'; and *daoine beaga*, 'little men', from the number and small size ascribed to the Elves.

Daoine còire, 'honest folk', had its origin in a desire to give no unnecessary offence. The 'folk' might be listening, and were pleased when people spoke well of them, and angry when spoken of slightingly. In this respect they are very jealous. A wise man will not unnecessarily expose himself to their attacks, for 'better is a hen's amity than its enmity' (*is fheàrr sìth circe na h-aimhreit*). The same feeling made the Irish Celt call them *daoine matha*, 'good people', and the Lowland Scot 'gude neighbours'.

THE SIZE OF FAIRIES

The difference in size ascribed to the race, though one of the most remarkable features in the superstition, and lying on its surface, has been taken little notice of by writers.[18] At one time the Elves are small enough to creep through keyholes, and a single potato is as much as one of them can carry; at another they resemble mankind, with whom they form alliances, and to whom they hire themselves as servants; while some are even said to be above the size of mortals, gigantic hags in whose lap mortal women are mere infants.

In the Highlands the names *sìthche* and *daoine sìth* are given to all these different sizes alike, little men, Elfin youth, Elfin dame, and Elfin hag, all of whom are not mythical beings of different classes or kinds, but one and the same race, having the same characteristics and dress, living on the same food, staying in the same dwellings, associated in the same actions, and kept away by the same means. The easiest solution of the anomaly is that the Fairies had the power of making themselves large or small at pleasure. There is no popular tale, however, which represents them as exercising such a power, nor is it conformable to the rest of their characteristics that it should be ascribed to them. The true belief is that the Fairies are a small race, the men 'about four feet or so' in height, and the women in many cases not taller than a little girl (*cnapach caileig*).

Being called 'little', the exaggeration which popular imagination loves has diminished them till they appear as Elves of different kinds. There is hardly a limit to the popular exaggeration of personal peculiarities. Og, King of Bashan, was a big man, and the Rabbis made his head tower to the regions of perpetual snow, while his feet were parched in the deserts of Arabia.[19] Fin mac Coul was reputed strong – at least he thrashed the devil, and made him howl.[20] A weaver in Perthshire known as 'the weaver with the nose' (*figheadair na sròine*) had a big nose, at least he carried his loom in it. Similarly the 'little men' came down to the 'size of half an ell', and even the height of a quart bottle.

The same peculiarity exists in the Teutonic belief. At times the Elf is a dwarfish being that enters through keyholes and window-slits, at other times a great tall man. In different localities the Fairies are known as Alfs, Huldra-Folk, Duergar, Trolls, Hill Folk, Little Folk, Still Folk, Pixies, etc.[21] A difference of size, as well as of name, has led to these being described as separate beings, but they have all so much in common with the Celtic Fairies that we must conclude they were originally the same.

Fairy Dwellings

The Gaelic, as might be expected, abounds in words denoting the diversified features of the scenery in a mountainous country. To this the English language itself bears witness, having adopted so many Gaelic words of the kind, as strath, glen, corrie, ben, knock, dun, etc. From this copiousness it arises that the round green eminences which were said to be the residences of the Fairies are known in Gaelic by several names which have no synonym in English.

Sìthein (pronounced **shï-en**) is the name of any place in which the Fairies take up their residence. It is known from the surrounding scenery by the peculiarly green appearance and rounded form. Sometimes in these respects it is very striking, being of so nearly conical a form, and covered with such rich verdure, that a second look is required to satisfy the observers it is not artificial. Its external appearance has led to its being also known by various other names.

Tolman is a small green knoll or hummock of earth; *bac*, a bank of sand or earth; *cnoc*, knock, Scots 'a knowe', and its diminutive *cnocan*, a little knowe; *dùn*, a rocky mound or heap, such for instance as the Castle rock of Edinburgh or Dumbarton, though often neither so steep nor so large; *òthan*, a green elevation in wet ground;[22] and *ùigh*, a provincial term of much the same import as *tolman*.[23] Even lofty hills have been represented as tenanted by Fairies, and the highest point of a hill having the rounded form characteristic of Fairy dwellings is called its **shï-en** (*sìthein na beinne*).[24] Rocks may be tenanted by the Elves, but not caves. The dwellings of the race are below the outside or superficies of the earth, and tales representing the contrary may be looked upon with suspicion as modern. There is one genuine popular story in which the Fairy dwelling is in the middle of a green plain, without any elevation to mark its site beyond a horse-skull, the eye-sockets of which were used as the Fairy chimney.

These dwellings were tenanted sometimes by a single family only, more frequently by a whole community. The Elves were said to change their residences as men do, and when they saw proper themselves, to remove to distant parts of the country and more desirable haunts. To them, on their arrival in their new home, are ascribed the words:

Ged as math an cala dh'fhàg sinn,
Gum b' fheàrr an cala fhuair sinn.

("Though good the haven we have left, / Better be the haven we have found.")[25]

The Fairy hillock might be passed by the strangers without suspicion of its being tenanted, and cattle were pastured on it unmolested by the 'good people'. There is, however, a common story in the Western Isles that a person was tethering his horse or cow for the night on a green *tolman* when a head appeared out of the ground and told him to tether the beast somewhere else, as he let rain into 'their' house, and had nearly driven the tether-pin into the ear of one of the inmates. Another who was in the habit of pouring out dirty water at the door was told by the Fairies to pour it elsewhere, as he was spoiling their furniture. He shifted the door to the back of the house, and prospered ever after.[26]

The Fairies were very grateful to any one who kept the **shï-en** clean, and swept away cow- or horse-droppings falling on it. Finding a farmer careful of the roof of their dwelling, keeping it clean, and not breaking the sward with tether-pin or spade, they showed their thankfulness by driving his horses and cattle to the sheltered side of the mound when the night proved stormy. Many believe the Fairies themselves swept the hillock every night, so that in the morning its surface was spotless.

Brugh (**brŭ**) denotes the Fairy dwelling viewed as it were from the inside – the interiors – but is often used interchangeably with *sìthein*. It is probably the same word as burgh, borough or bro', and its reference is to the *number* of inmates in the Fairy dwelling.[27]

Few villages in the Highlands of Scotland are without a **shï-en** in their neighbourhood, and often a number are found close to each other. Strontian, well known to geologists from the mineral which bears its name, is *Sròn an t-Sìthein*, 'the Nose of the Fairy Hillock'.[28]

Fairy Dresses

The Fairies, both Celtic and Teutonic, are dressed in green. In Skye, however, though Fairy women (as elsewhere) are always dressed in that colour, the men wear clothes of any colour like their human neighbours. They are frequently called *daoine beaga ruadh*, 'little red men', from their clothes having the appearance of being dyed with the lichen called *crotal*, a common colour of men's clothes in the north Hebrides.[29]

The coats of Fairy women are shaggy or ruffled (*caiteineach*), and their caps curiously fitted or wrinkled. The men are said, but not commonly, to have blue bonnets, and in the song to the murdered Elfin lover the Elf is said to have a hat bearing 'a smell of honied apples'.[30] This is perhaps the only Highland instance of a hat, which is a prominent object in the Teutonic superstition, being ascribed to the Fairies.[31]

THE DEFECTS OF FAIRIES

Generally some personal defect is ascribed to them by which they become known to be of no mortal race. In Mull and the neighbourhood they are said to have only one nostril, the other being imperforate (*an leth choinnlein aca druidte*).[32] The Elfin smith who made Fin mac Coul's sword, 'the son of Lun that never asked a second stroke' (*Mac an Luin nach d'fhàg riamh fuigheall bheum*), had but one gloomy eye in his forehead.[33]

The *bean shìth* was detected by her extraordinary voracity (a cow at a meal), a frightful front tooth, the entire want of a nostril, a web foot, praeternaturally long breasts, etc.[34] She is also said to be unable to suckle her own children, and hence the Fairy desire to steal nursing women.

THEIR OCCUPATIONS

The Fairies, as has been already said, are counterparts of mankind. There are children and old people among them; they practise all kinds of trades and handicrafts; they possess cattle, dogs, arms; they require food, clothing, sleep; they are liable to disease, and can be killed. So entire is the resemblance that they have even been betrayed into intoxication. People entering their brughs have found the inmates engaged in similar occupations to mankind, the women spinning, weaving, grinding meal, baking, cooking, churning, etc., and the men sleeping, dancing and making merry, or sitting round a fire in the middle of the floor (as a Perthshire informant described it) 'like tinkers'. Sometimes the inmates were absent on foraging expeditions or pleasure excursions.

The women sing at their work, a common practice in former times with Highland women, and use distaff, spindle, hand-mills, and suchlike primitive implements. The men have smithies, in which they make the Fairy arrows and other weapons.[35]

Some Fairy families or communities are poorer than others, and borrow meal and other articles of domestic use from each other and from their neighbours of mankind.

FESTIVITIES

There are stated seasons of festivity, which are observed with much splendour in the larger dwellings. The *brugh* is illumined, the tables glitter with gold and silver vessels, and the door is thrown open to all comers. Any of the human race entering on these occasions are hospitably and heartily welcomed; food and drink are offered them, and their health is pledged. Everything in the dwelling seems magnificent beyond description, and mortals are so enraptured they forget everything but the enjoyment of the moment. Joining in the festivities, they lose all thought as to the passage of time. The food is the most sumptuous, the clothing the most gorgeous ever seen, the music the sweetest ever heard, the dance the sprightliest ever trod. The whole dwelling is lustrous with magic splendour.

All this magnificence, however, and enjoyment are nothing but semblance and illusion of the senses. Mankind, with all their cares and toils and sorrows, have an infinitely more desirable lot, and the man is greatly to be pitied whom the Elves get power over, so that he exchanges his human lot and labour for their society or pleasures. Wise people recommend that, in the circumstances, a man should not utter a word till he comes out again, nor on any account taste Fairy food or drink. If he abstains he is very likely before long dismissed, but if he indulges he straightway loses the will and the power ever to return to the society of men. He becomes insensible to the passage of time, and may stay, without knowing it, for years, and even ages, in the *brugh*. Many who thus forgot themselves are among the Fairies to this day.

Should they ever again return to the open air, and their enchantment be broken, the Fairy grandeur and pleasure prove an empty show, worthless and fraught with danger. The food becomes disgusting refuse, and the pleasures a shocking waste of time.

The Elves are great adepts in music and dancing, and a great part of their time seems to be spent in the practice of these accomplishments. The changeling has often been detected by his fondness for them. Though in appearance an ill-conditioned and helpless brat, he has been known, when he thought himself unobserved, to play the pipes with surpassing skill and dance with superhuman activity.

Elfin music is more melodious than human skill and instruments can produce, and there are many songs and tunes which are said to have been originally learned from the Fairies. The only musical instrument of the Elves is the bagpipes, and some of the most celebrated pipers in Scotland are said to have learned their music from them.

FAIRY RAIDS

The Gaelic belief recognises no Fairyland or realm different from the earth's surface on which men live and move. The dwellings are underground, but it is on the natural face of the earth the Fairies find their sustenance and pasture their cattle, and on which they forage and roam.

The seasons on which their festivities are held are the last night of every quarter (*h-uile latha ceann ràidhe*), particularly the nights before Beltane, the first of summer, and Hallowmas, the first of winter. On these nights, on Fridays, and on the last night of the year they are given to leaving home and taking away whomsoever of the human race they find helpless or unguarded or unwary. They may be encountered any time, but on these stated occasions men are to be particularly on their guard against them.

On Fridays they obtrusively enter houses, and have even the impudence, it is said, to lift the lid off the pot to see what the family have on the fire for dinner. Any Fairy story told on this day should be prefixed by saying: *Beannachd 'nan siubhal 's 'nan imeachd! Se 'n-diugh Di-Haoine 's cha chluinn iad sinn.* "A blessing attend their departing and travelling! This day is Friday and they will not hear us."[36] This prevents Fairy ill-will coming upon the narrator for anything he may chance to say. No one should call the day by its proper name of *Di-Haoine* (Friday) but *latha bhail' ud thall* ('the day of yonder town'). The Fairies do not like to hear the day mentioned, and if anyone is so unlucky as to use the proper name their wrath is directed elsewhere by the bystander adding *air crodh a' bhail' ud thall* ('on the cattle of yonder town') or 'on the farm of So-and-So', mentioning anyone he may have a dislike to.[37] The fear of Fairy wrath also prevented the sharpening of knives on this day.

They are said to come always from the west. They are admitted into houses, however well guarded otherwise, by the little hand-made cake, the last of the baking (*bonnach beag boise*),[38] called the *fallaid* bannock, unless there has been a hole put through it with the finger, or a piece is broken off it, or a live coal is put on the top of it. The Elfin call is:

> *Bonnach beag boise*
> *Gun bhloigh gun bheàrn,*
> *Éirich 's leig sinne a-staigh!*

("Little cake / Without gap or fissure, / Rise and let us in!")[39] They are also admitted by the water in which men's feet have been washed; by the fire, unless it be properly 'raked' (*smàladh*), i.e. covered up to keep it alive for the night; or by the band of the spinning-wheel, if left stretched on the wheel.[40]

The reason assigned for taking water into the house at night was that the Fairies would suck the sleeper's blood if they found no water indoors to quench their thirst. The water in which feet were washed (unless thrown out, or a burning peat were put in it) let them in, and was used by them to plash about in (*gu'n loireadh fhéin ann*) all night.[41]

Unless the band was taken off the spinning-wheel, particularly on the Saturday evenings, they came after the inmates of the house had retired to rest and used the wheel. Sounds of busy work were heard, but in the morning no work was found done, and possibly the wheel was disarranged. In the north of Ireland the band was taken off the spinning-wheel to prevent the Fairies spoiling the linen.

On the last night of the year they are kept out by decorating the house with holly; and the last handful of corn reaped should be dressed up as a harvest maiden (*maighdeann bhuana*) and hung up in the farmer's house to aid in keeping them out till next harvest.[42]

WHEN SEEN

There seems to be no definite rule as to the circumstances under which the Fairies are to be seen. A person whose eye has been touched with Fairy water can see them whenever they are present; the seer, possessed of second sight, often saw them when others did not; and on nights on which the **shï-en** is open the chance passer-by sees them rejoicing in their underground dwellings.

A favourite time for their encounters with men seems to be the dusk and wild stormy nights of mist and driving rain, when the streams are swollen and 'the roar of the torrent is heard on the hill'. They are also apt to appear when spoken of and when a desire is expressed for their assistance; when proper precautions are omitted, and when those whose weakness and helplessness call for watchfulness and care are neglected; when their power is contemned; and when a sordid and churlish spirit is entertained.

Often, without fault or effort (in places the most unexpected), mortals have been startled by their appearance, cries, or music.

FOOD

Fairy food consists principally of things intended for human food, of which the Elves take the *toradh*, i.e. the substance, fruit, or benefit, leaving the semblance or appearance to men themselves. In this manner they take cows, sheep, goats, meal, sowens, the produce of the land, etc.

Cattle falling over rocks are particularly liable to being taken by them, and milk spilt in coming from the dairy is theirs by right. They have, of food peculiar to themselves and not acquired from men, the root of silverweed (*brisgein*), the stalks of heather (*cuiseagan an fhraoich*), the milk of the red deer hinds and of goats, weeds gathered in the fields, and barleymeal.

The *brisgein* is a root plentifully turned up by the plough in spring, and ranked in olden times as the 'seventh bread'.[43] Its inferior quality and its being found underground are probably the cause of its being assigned to the Fairies. It is a question whether the stalks of heather are the tops or the stems of the plant. Neither contain much sap or nourishment. The banshi Fairy, or Elle woman, has been seen by hunters milking the hinds, just as women milk cows.[44]

Those who partake of Fairy food are as hungry after their repast as before it. In appearance it is most sumptuous and inviting, but on grace being said turns out to be horse-dung. Some, in their haste to partake of the gorgeous viands, were only disenchanted when 'returning thanks'.

Gifts Bestowed by Fairies

The Fairies can bestow almost any gift upon their favourites, e.g. great skill in music and in work of all kinds. They can give them cows and even children stolen for the purpose from others, they can leave them good fortune, keep cattle from wandering into their crops at night, assist them in spring and harvest work, etc.

Sometimes their marvellous skill is communicated to mortals, sometimes they come in person to assist. If a smith, wright, or other tradesman catches them working with the tools of his trade (a thing they are addicted to doing), he can compel them to bestow on him the *ceàird-chomainn* or 'association craft', that is, to come to his assistance whenever he wants them.[45] Work left near their hillocks overnight has been found finished in the morning, and they have been forced by men, entering their dwellings for the purpose, to tell the cure for diseases defying human skill.

In every instance, however, the benefit of the gift goes ultimately to the Fairies themselves, or, as it is put in the Gaelic expression, 'the fruit of it goes into their own bodies' (*théid an toradh 'nan cuirp fhéin*). Their gifts have evil influence connected with them, and, however inviting at first, are productive of bad luck in the end.

No wise man will desire either their company or their kindness. When they come to a house to assist at any work, the sooner they are got rid of the better. If they are hired as servants their wages at first appear trifling, but will ultimately ruin their employer. It is unfortunate even to encounter any of the race, but to consort with them is disastrous in the extreme.

Loans

Bha toirt is gabhail an iasad dol riamh feadh an t-saoghail. "The giving and taking of loans," according to the proverb, "always prevailed in the world," and the custom is one to which the 'good neighbours' are no strangers. They are universally represented as borrowing meal, from each other and from men. In the latter case when they returned a loan, as they always honestly did, the return was in *barleymeal*, two measures for one of oatmeal; and this, on being kept in a place by itself, proved inexhaustible, provided the bottom of the vessel in which it was stored was never made to appear, no question was asked, and no blessing was pronounced over it. It would then neither vanish nor become horse-dung!

When a loan is returned to them, they accept only the fair equivalent of what they have lent, neither less nor more. If more is offered they take offence, and never give an opportunity for the same insult again.

We hear also of their borrowing a kettle or cauldron, and, under the power of a rhyme uttered by the lender at the time of giving it, sending it back before morning.[46]

EDDY WIND

When 'the folk' leave home in companies, they travel in eddies of wind. In this climate these eddies are among the most curious of natural phenomena. On calm summer days they go past, whirling about straws and dust, and as not another breath of air is moving at the time their cause is sufficiently puzzling. In Gaelic the eddy is known as *oiteag sluaigh* ('the people's puff of wind') and its motion as *falbh air chuiseagan treòrach* ('travelling on tall grass stems').[47]

By throwing one's left (or *toisgeul*) shoe at it, the Fairies are made to drop whatever they may be taking away – men, women, children, or animals.[48] The same result is attained by throwing one's bonnet (saying, *Is leatsa seo, is leamsa sin*, 'This is yours, that's mine'),[49] or a naked knife, or earth from a molehill.

In these eddies, people going on a journey at night have been 'lifted', and spent the night careering through the skies. On returning to the earth, though they came to the house last left, they were too stupefied to recognise either the house or its inmates. Others, through Fairy despite, have wandered about all night on foot, failing to reach their intended destination though quite near it, and perhaps in the morning finding themselves on the top of a distant hill, or in some inaccessible place to which they could never have made their way alone.

Even in daylight some were carried in the Elfin eddy from one island to another, in great terror lest they should fall into the sea.[50]

RAIN AND SUNSHINE, WIND AND RAIN

When there is rain with sunshine the 'little people', according to a popular rhyme, are at their meat.

> *Rain and sun,*
> *Little people at their meat.*

When wind and rain come from opposite directions (which may for an instant be possible in a sudden shift of wind), by throwing some horse-dung against the wind the Fairies are brought down in a shower!

FAIRY ARROWS, ETC.

Natural objects of a curious appearance, or bearing a fanciful resemblance to articles used by men, are also associated with the Fairies. The reed-mace plant is called *cuigeal nam ban shìth* ('the distaff of the Fairy women'),[51] the foxglove *miaran nan cailleacha sìth* ('the thimble of the Fairy old women'), though more commonly *miaran nan cailleacha marbh* ('the thimble of dead old women').[52]

A substance found on the shores of the Hebrides, like a stone, red (*ruadh*) and half dark (*leth dhorcha*), holed, is called *fuil sìochaire* ('Elf's blood'). Similarly, in Dorsetshire fossil belemnites are called colepexies' fingers, and in Northumberland a fungous excrescence growing about the roots of old trees is called Fairy butter.[53] So, in Ireland, the round towers are ascribed to them.[54]

The Fairy arrow (*saighead shìth*) owes its name to a similar fancy. It is known also as 'Fairy flint' (*spor shìth*), and consists of a triangular piece of flint bearing the appearance of an arrow-head.[55] It probably originally formed part of the rude armoury of the savages of the stone period. Popular imagination, struck by its curious form and ignorant of its origin, ascribed it to the Fairies.[56] It was said to be frequently shot at the hunter, to whom the Elves have a special aversion, because he kills the hinds on the milk of which they live. They could not throw it themselves, but compelled some mortal (*duine saoghalta*) who was being carried about in their company to throw it for them. If the person aimed at was a friend, the thrower managed to miss his aim, and the Fairy arrow proved innocuous. It was found lying beside the object of Fairy wrath, and was kept as a valuable preservation in future against similar dangers, and for rubbing to wounds (*suathadh ri creuchdun*). The man or beast struck by it became paralysed, and to all appearance died shortly after. In reality they were taken away by the Elves, and only their appearance remained. Its point being blunt was an indication that it had done harm.[57]

The *caibe sìth* ('Fairy spade') is a smooth, slippery black stone, in shape 'like the sole of a shoe'. It was put in water given to sick people and cattle.[58]

CATTLE

Everywhere in the Highlands the red deer are associated with the Fairies, and in some districts, as Lochaber and Mull, are said to be their only cattle. This association is sufficiently accounted for by the Fairylike appearance and habits of the deer. In its native haunts, in remote and misty corries, where solitude has her most undisturbed abode, its beauty and grace of form, combined with its dislike to the presence of man, and even of the animals man has tamed, amply entitle it to the name of *sìth*. Timid and easily startled by every appearance and noise, it is said to be unmoved by the presence of the Fairies. Popular belief also says that no deer is found dead with age, and that its horns, which it sheds every year, are not found because hid by the Fairies. In their transformations it was peculiar for the Fairy women to assume the shape of the red deer, and in that guise they were often encountered by the hunter.

The Elves have a particular dislike to those who kill the hinds, and, on finding them in lonely places, delight in throwing Elf-bolts at them. When a dead deer is carried home at night the Fairies lay their weight on the bearer's back till he feels as if he had a house for a burden. On a penknife, however, being stuck in the deer it becomes very light.

There are occasional allusions to the Fairy women having herds of deer. *Cailleach Beinne Bhric horò*, the 'Carlin Wife of the Spotted Hill' who, according to a popular rhyme, was 'large and broad and tall', had a herd which she would not allow to descend to the beach, and which 'loved the water-cresses by the fountain high in the hills better than the black weeds of the shore'.[59]

The old women of Ben-y-Ghloe in Perthshire and of Clibrich in Sutherlandshire (Campbell's *West Highland Tales*, ii. 46) seem to have been *sìth* women of the same sort. "I never," said an old man (he was upwards of eighty years of age) in the island of Mull, questioned some years ago on the subject, "heard of the Fairies having cows, but I always heard that deer were their cattle."[60]

In other parts of the Highlands, as in Skye, though the Fairies are said to keep company with the deer, they have cows like those of men. When one of them appears among a herd of cattle the whole fold of them grows frantic and follows, lowing wildly. The strange animal disappears by entering a rock or knoll, and the others, unless intercepted, follow and are never more seen. The Fairy cow is dun (*odhar*) and 'hummel' or hornless. In Skye, however, Fairy cattle are said to be speckled and red (*crodh breac ruadh*), and to be able to cross the sea.

It is not on every place that they graze. There were not above ten such spots in all Skye. *Achadh na h-Annaid*, the 'Field of Annat' in the Braes of Portree, is one. When the cattle came home at night from pasture, the following were the words used by the Fairy woman, standing on *Dùn Ghearra-Seadar*, Dun Gerra-Sheddar near Portree, as she counted her charge:

> *Crooked one, dun one,*
> *Little wing grizzled,*
> *Black cow, white cow,*

Little bull black-head,
My milch kine have come home,
O dear! that the herdsman would come![61]

HORSES

In the Highland creed the Fairies but rarely have horses. In Perthshire they have been seen on a market day riding about on white horses; in Tiree two Fairy ladies were met riding on what seemed to be horses, but in reality were ragweeds; and in Skye the Elves have galloped the farm horses at full speed and in dangerous places, sitting with their faces to the tails.

When horses neigh at night it is because they are ridden by the Fairies and pressed too hard. The neigh is one of distress, and if the hearer exclaims aloud, *Do shrathair 's do phillein ort!* ("Your saddle and pillion be upon you!"), the Fairies tumble to the ground.[62]

DOGS

The Fairy dog (*cù sìth*) is as large as a two-year-old stirk, a dark green colour, with ears of deep green. It is of a lighter colour towards the feet. In some cases it has a long tail rolled up in a coil on its back, but others have the tail flat and plaited like the straw rug of a pack-saddle. Bran, the famous dog that Fin mac Coul had, was of Elfin breed, and from the description given of it by popular tradition, decidedly parti-coloured:

> *Casan buidhe bha aig Bran,*
> *Dà thaobh dhubh agus tàrr geal,*
> *Druim uaine mu'n suidhe sealg,*
> *Cluasan corrach cròidhearg.*

("Bran had yellow feet, / Its two sides black and belly white; / Green was the back of the hunting hound, / Its two pointed ears blood-red.")[63] Bran had a venomous shoe (*bròg nimhe*) with which it killed whatever living creature it struck, and when at full speed and 'like its father' (*dol ri athair*) was seen as three dogs, intercepting the deer at three passes.

The Fairy hound was kept tied as a watch-dog in the *brugh*, but at times accompanied the women on their expeditions or roamed about alone, making its lairs in clefts of the rocks. Its motion was silent and gliding, and its bark a rude clamour (*blaodh*). It went in a straight line, and its bay has been last heard, by those who listened for it, far out at sea. Its immense footmarks, as large as the spread of the human hand, have been found next day traced in the mud, in the snow, or on the sands.

Others say it makes a noise like a horse galloping, and its bay is like that of another dog, only louder. There is a considerable interval between each bark, and at the third (it only barks thrice) the terror-struck hearer is overtaken and destroyed, unless he has by that time reached a place of safety.

Ordinary dogs have a mortal aversion to the Fairies, and give chase whenever the Elves are sighted. On coming back, the hair is found to be scraped off their bodies, all except the ears, and they die soon after.[64]

CATS

Elfin cats (*cait shìth*) are explained to be of a wild, not a domesticated, breed, to be as large as dogs, of a black colour, with a white spot on the breast, and to have arched backs and erect bristles (*crotach agus mùrlach*). Many maintain these wild cats have no connection with the Fairies, but are witches in disguise.[65]

FAIRY THEFT

The Elves have got a worse name for stealing than they deserve. So far as taking things without the knowledge or consent of the owners is concerned, the accusation is well-founded – they neither ask nor obtain leave; but there are important respects in which their depredations differ from the pilferings committed among men by jail-birds and other dishonest people. The Fairies do not take their booty away bodily: they only take what is called in Gaelic its *toradh*, i.e. its substance, virtue, fruit, or benefit. The outward appearance is left, but the reality is gone. Thus, when a cow is Elf-taken, it appears to its owner only as suddenly smitten by some strange disease (*chaidh am beathach ud a ghonadh*).[66] In reality the cow is gone, and only its semblance remains, animated it may be by an Elf, who receives all the attentions paid to the sick cow, but gives nothing in return. The seeming cow lies on its side, and cannot be made to rise. It consumes the provender laid before it, but does not yield milk or grow fat. In some cases it gives plenty of milk, but milk that yields no butter. If taken up a hill and rolled down the incline, it disappears altogether. If it dies, its flesh ought not to be eaten – it is not beef, but a stock of alder wood, an aged Elf, or some trashy substitute.[67]

Similarly when the *toradh* of land is taken, there remains the appearance of a crop, but a crop without benefit to man or beast – the ears are unfilled, the grain is without weight, the fodder without nourishment.

A still more important point of difference is that the Fairies only take away what men deserve to lose. When mortals make a secret of (*cleth*), or grumble (*ceasad*) over, what they have, the Fairies get the benefit, and the owner is a poor man in the midst of his abundance. When (to use an illustration the writer has more than once heard) a farmer speaks disparagingly of his crop, and, though it be heavy, tries to conceal his good fortune, the Fairies take away the benefit of his increase. The advantage goes away mysteriously *'na phrìneachan 's 'na shnàdun* ('in pins and needles'), *'na alm 's 'na mhàdair* ('in alum and madder'), as the saying is, and the farmer gains nothing from his crop. Particularly, articles of food the possession of which men denied with oaths (*air a thiomnadh*) became Fairy property.[68]

The Elves are also blamed for lifting with them articles mislaid. These are generally restored as mysteriously and unaccountably as they were taken away. Thus, a woman blamed the Elves for taking her thimble. It was placed beside her, and when looked for could not be found. Some time after, she was sitting alone on the hillside and found the thimble in her lap. This confirmed her belief in its being the Fairies that took it away. In a like mysterious manner a person's bonnet might be whipped off his head, or the pot for supper be lifted off the fire, and left by invisible hands on the middle of the floor.

The accusation of taking milk is unjust. It is brought against the Elves only in books, and never in the popular creed. The Fairies take cows, sheep, goats, horses, and it may be the substance or benefit (*toradh*) of butter and cheese, but not milk.

Many devices were employed to thwart Fairy inroads. A burning ember (*éibhleag*) was put into *cabhraich* (sowens), one of the weakest and most unsubstantial articles of human food and very liable to Fairy attack.[69] It was left there till the dish was ready for boiling, i.e. about three days after. A sieve should not be allowed out of the house after dark, and no meal unless it be sprinkled with salt. Otherwise the Fairies may, by means of them, take the substance out of the whole farm produce.

For the same reason a hole should be put with the finger in the little cake (*bonnach beag 's toll ann*) made with the remnant of the meal after a baking, and when given to children, as it usually is, a piece should be broken off it. A nail driven into a cow killed by falling over a precipice was supposed by the more superstitious to keep the Elves away.[70]

One of the most curious thefts ascribed to them was that of querns or hand-mills (*brà, brathainn*). To keep them away these handy and useful implements should be turned *deiseal*, i.e. with the right hand turn, as sunwise.[71]

What is curious in the belief is that the hand-mill is said to have been originally got from the Fairies themselves. Its sounds have often been heard by the belated peasant as it was being worked inside some grassy knoll, and songs sung by the Fairy women employed at it have been learned.[72]

The use of some kind of mill, generally a hand-mill, is as universal as the growth of grain, and the necessity for reducing the solid grain into the more palatable form of meal no doubt led to its early invention. The Gaelic *meil* (or *beil*) 'to grind', the

English *mill*, the Latin *mola* and the Greek μύλη show that it was known to the Aryan tribes at a period long anterior to history. The hand-mill mentioned in Scripture, worked by two women, seems the same with that still to be found in obscure corners in the West Highlands.

An instrument so useful to man in the less advanced stages of his civilisation could not fail to be looked upon with much respect and good feeling. In the Hebrides it was rubbed every Saturday evening with a wisp of straw 'for payment' of its benevolent labours (*sop ga shuathadh ris a' bhrài ga pàigheadh*).[73] Meal ground in it is coarser than ordinary meal, and is known as *gairbhein*.

STEALING WOMEN AND CHILDREN

Most frequently it was women (not yet risen from childbed) and their babes that the Fairies abducted. On every occasion of a birth, therefore, the utmost anxiety prevailed to guard the mother and child from their attacks. It is said that the Fairy women are unable to suckle their own children, and hence their desire to secure a human wet-nurse. This, however, does not explain why they want the children, nor indeed is it universally a part of the creed.

The first care was not to leave a woman alone during her confinement. A house full of women gathered and watched for three days, in some places for eight. Various additional precautions against the Fairies were taken in various localities. A row of iron nails were driven into the front board of the bed; the smoothing iron or a reaping hook was placed under it and in the window; an old shoe was put in the fire; the door posts were sprinkled with *maistir*, urine kept for washing purposes – a liquid extremely offensive to the Fairies;[74] the Bible was opened, and the breath blown across it in the face of the woman in childbed;[75] mystic words of threads were placed about the bed; and, when leaving at the end of the three days, the midwife left a little cake of oatmeal with a hole in it in the front of the bed.

The father's shirt wrapped round the new-born babe was esteemed a preservative, and if the marriage gown was thrown over the wife she could be recovered if, notwithstanding (or from neglect of) these precautions, she were taken away.[76] The name of the Deity solemnly pronounced over the child in baptism was an additional protection.

If the Fairies were seen, water in which an ember was extinguished – or the burning peats themselves – thrown at them, drove them away. Even quick wit and readiness of reply in the mother has sent them off.[77]

It is not to be supposed that these precautions were universally known or practised. In that case such a thing as an Elf-struck child would be unknown. The gathering of women and the placing of iron about the bed seem to have been common, but the burning of old shoes was confined to the Western Isles. If it existed elsewhere, its memory has been forgotten. That it is an old part of the creed is evident from the dislike of the Fairies to strong smells being also part of the Teutonic creed. The blowing of the breath across the Bible existed in Sunart, part of the west of Inverness-shire.[78]

Other charms used on the occasion were the taking of the woman to be delivered several times across the byre-drain (*inne*), the opening of every lock in the house,[79] and ceremonies by means of

> *A grey hank of flax and a cockscomb,*
> *Two things against the commandments.*[80]

These practices seem to have been known only to the very superstitious, and to have been local. The first belonged to Ross-shire, the second to the north-west mainland of Argyllshire, and the last to Tiree.

CHANGELINGS

When they succeeded in their felonious attempts, the Elves left (instead of the mother, and bearing her semblance) *stoc maide*, a stock of wood, and (in place of the infant) an old mannikin of their own race.[81] The child grew up a peevish misshapen brat, ever crying and complaining. It was known, however, to be a changeling by the skilful in such matters from the large quantities of water it drank (a tubful before morning, if left beside it), from its large teeth, from its inordinate appetite, from its fondness for music and its powers of dancing, and from its unnatural precocity, or from some unguarded remark as to its own age.

It is to the aged Elf, left in the place of child or beast, that the name *sìthbheire* (pronounced **sheevere**) is properly given, and, as may well be supposed, to say of one who has an ancient manner or look, "He is but a *sìthbheire*," or, "He is only one that came from a *brugh*," is an expression of considerable contempt. When a person does a senseless action, it is said of him that he has been 'taken out of himself' (*air a thoirt às*), that is, taken away by the Fairies.

The changeling was converted into the stock of a tree by saying a powerful rhyme over him, or by sticking him with a knife. He could be driven away by running at him with a red-hot ploughshare; by getting between him and the bed and threatening him with a drawn sword; by leaving him out on the hillside, and paying no attention to his shrieking and screaming; by putting him sitting on a gridiron, or in a creel, with a fire below; by sprinkling him well out of the *maistir* tub; or by dropping him into the river. There can be no doubt these modes of treatment would rid a house of any disagreeable visitor, at least of the human race.[82]

The story of the changeling who was detected by means of eggshells seems in some form or other to be as widespread as the superstition itself. Empty eggshells are ranged round the hearth, and the changeling, when he finds the house quiet and thinks himself unobserved, gets up from bed and examines them. Finding them empty, he is heard to remark sententiously, as he peers into each, "This is but a windbag (*Chan eil an-seo ach balg fàs*); I am so many hundred years old, and I never saw the like of this."[83]

DEFORMITIES

Many of the deformities in children are attributed to the Fairies. When a child is incautiously left alone by its mother, for however short a time, the Fairies may come and give its little legs such a twist as will leave it hopelessly lame ever after. To give them their due, however, they sometimes took care of children whom they found forgotten, and even of grown-up people sleeping incautiously in dangerous places.[84]

NURSES

The Elves have children of their own, and require the services of midwives, like the human race. 'Howdies', as they are called, taken in the way of their profession to the Fairy dwelling, found on coming out that the time they had stayed was incredibly longer or shorter than they imagined, and none of them was ever the better ultimately of her adventure.[85]

THE MEN OF PEACE

The Gaelic *sìthche*, like the English 'Elf', has two ideas, almost amounting to two meanings, attached to it. In the plural *sìthchean* it conveys the idea of a diminutive race, travelling in eddy winds, lifting men from the ground, stealing, and entering houses in companies; while in the singular *sìthche* the idea conveyed is that of one who approaches mankind in dimensions. The 'man and woman of peace' hire themselves to the human race for a day's work or a term of service, and contract marriages with it. The Elfin youth (*gille sìth*) has enormous strength, that of a dozen men it is said, and the Elfin women (or banshis) are remarkably handsome. The aged of the race were generally the reverse, in point of beauty, especially those of them substituted for Fairy-abducted children and animals.

Mortals should have nothing to do with any of the race. No good comes out of the unnatural connection. However enchanting at first, the end is disaster and death. When, therefore, the *sìthche* is first met, it is recommended by the prudent to pass by without noticing; or (if obliged or incautious enough to speak, and pressed to make an appointment) to give fair words, saying, *Ma gheallas mi sin, co-gheallaidh mi e* ("If I promise that, I will fulfil it"), still sufficiently near houses to attract the attention of the dogs. They immediately give chase, and the Fairy flies away.

The *gille sìth* (or Elfin youth) is very solicitous about his offspring when his mortal mistress bears him children, and the love that women have to him as their lover or familiar spirit (*leannan sìth*) is unnaturally passionate. The Elfin mistress is not always so secure of the affections of her human lover. He may get tired of her and leave her. On meeting her first he is put under spells to keep appointments with her in future every night. If he dares for one night to neglect his appointment, she gives him such a sound thrashing the first time she gets hold of him that he never neglects it again. She disappears at the cock-crowing. While he remains faithful to her, she assists him at his trade as farmer, shepherd, etc., makes him presents of clothes, tells him when he is to die, and even when he is to leave her and get married. She gives *sian* (a magic belt or other charm) to protect him in danger. If offended, however, her lover is in danger of his life.[86] The children of these alliances are said to be the 'urisks', see p. 105.

Those who have taken Elfin women for wives have found a sad termination to their mesalliance. The defect or peculiarity of the fair enchantress, which her lover at first had treated as of no consequence, proves his ruin. Her voracity thins his herds, he gets tired of her or angry with her, and in an unguarded moment reproaches her with her origin. She disappears, taking with her the children and the fortune she brought him. The gorgeous palace – fit for the entertainment of kings – vanishes, and he finds himself again in his old black dilapidated hut, with a pool of rain-drippings from the roof in the middle of the floor.

THE *BEAN NIGHE* OR WASHING WOMAN

At times the Fairy woman (*bean shìth*) is seen in lonely places, beside a pool or stream, washing the linen of those soon to die, and folding and beating it with her hands on a stone in the middle of the water. She is then known as the *bean nighe* or washing woman; and her being seen is a sure sign that death is near.[87]

In Mull and Tiree she is said to have praeternaturally long breasts, which are in the way as she stoops at her washing. She throws them over her shoulders, and they hang down her back. Whoever sees her must not turn away, but steal up behind and endeavour to approach her unawares. When he is near enough he is to catch one of her breasts, and, putting it to his mouth, call herself to witness that she is his first nursing- or foster-mother (*muime cìche*).[88] She answers that he has need of that being the case, and will then communicate whatever knowledge he desires. If she says the shirt she is washing is that of an enemy he allows the washing to go on, and that man's death follows; if it be that of her captor or any of his friends, she is put a stop to.

In Skye the *bean nighe* is said to be squat in figure (*tiugh ìosal*), or not unlike a 'small pitiful child' (*pàiste beag brònach*). If a person caught her she told all that would befall him in after life. She answered all his questions, but he must answer hers. Men did not like to tell what she said. Women dying in childbed were looked upon as dying prematurely, and it was believed that unless all the clothes left by them were washed they would have to wash them themselves till the natural period of their death. It was women 'dreeing this weird' who were the washing women.[89] If the person hearing them at work beating their clothes (*slacartaich*) caught them before being observed, he could not be heard by them; but if they saw him first, he lost the power of his limbs (*lùgh*).

In the Highlands of Perthshire the washing woman is represented as small and round, and dressed in pretty green. She spreads by moonlight the linen winding sheets of those soon to die, and is caught by getting between her and the stream.

She can also be caught and mastered and made to communicate her information at the point of the sword. Oscar, son of the poet Ossian, met her on his way to Cairbre's feast, at which the dispute arose which led to his death.[90] She was encountered by Hugh of the Little Head on the evening before his last battle, and left him as her parting gift (*fàgail*) that he should become the frightful apparition he did after death, the most celebrated in the West Highlands.[91]

Song

The song of the Fairy woman foreboded great calamity, and men did not like to hear it. Scott calls it 'the fatal Banshi's boding scream',[92] but it was not a scream, only a wailing murmur (*torman mulaid*) of unearthly sweetness and melancholy.

Glaistig

The banshi is sometimes confounded with the glaistig, the apparition of a woman acting as tutelary guardian of the site to which she is attached. Many people use banshi and glaistig as convertible terms, and the confusion thence arising extends largely to books.

The true glaistig is a woman of human race who has been put under enchantments and to whom a Fairy nature has been given. She wears a green dress, like Fairy women, but her face is wan and grey, whence her name glaistig, from *glas*, grey. She differs also in haunting castles and the folds of the cattle, and confining herself to servant's work.[93]

ELFIN QUEEN

The banshi is, without doubt, the original of the queen of Elfland, mentioned in ballads of the south of Scotland. The Elfin queen met Thomas of Ercildoune by the Eildon tree, and took him to her enchanted realm, where he was kept for seven years. She gave him the power of foretelling the future, 'the tongue that never lied'. At first she was the most beautiful woman he had ever seen, but when he next looked –

> *The hair that hung upon her head,*
> *The half was black, the half was grey,*
> *And all the rich clothing was away*
> *That he before saw in that stead;*
> *Her eyes seemed out that were so grey,*
> *And all her body like the lead.*[94]

In Gaelic tales seven years is a common period of detention among the Fairies; the *leannan sìth* communicates to her lover the knowledge of future events, and in the end is looked upon by him with aversion. There is no mention, however, of Fairyland, or of an Elfin king or queen, and but rarely of Fairies riding. True Thomas, who is as well known in Highland lore as he is in the Lowlands, is said to be still among the Fairies, and to attend every market on the lookout for suitable horses. When he has made up his complement he will appear again among men, and a great battle will be fought on the Clyde.[95]

PROTECTION AGAINST FAIRIES

The great protection against the Elfin race (and this is perhaps the most noticeable point in the whole superstition) is iron, or preferably steel (*cruaidh*). The metal in any form (a sword, a knife, a pair of scissors, a needle, a nail, a ring, a bar, a piece of reaping-hook, a gun-barrel, a fish-hook: and tales will be given illustrative of all these) is all-powerful. On entering a Fairy dwelling, a piece of steel, a knife, needle or fish-hook, stuck in the door, takes from the Elves the power of closing it till the intruder comes out again. A knife stuck in a deer carried home at night keeps them from laying their weight on the animal. A knife or nail in one's pocket prevents his being 'lifted' at night. Nails in the front bench of the bed keep Elves from women 'in the straw' and their babes.[96]

As additional safeguards, the smoothing iron should be put below the bed and the reaping-hook in the window. A nail in the carcase of a bull that fell over a rock was believed to preserve its flesh from them.[97] Playing the Jew's harp (*tromb*) kept the Elfin women at a distance from the hunter, because the tongue of the instrument is of steel.[98] So also a shoemaker's awl in the door-post of his bothy kept a glaistig from entering.

Fire thrown into water in which the feet have been washed takes away the power of the water to admit the Fairies into the house at night;[99] a burning peat put in sowens to hasten their fermenting (*greasadh gortachadh*) kept the substance in them till ready to boil. Martin (*Western Islands*) says fire was carried round lying-in women, and round about children before they were christened, to keep mother and infant from the power of evil spirits.[100] When the Fairies were seen coming in at the door burning embers thrown towards them drove them away.

Another safeguard is oatmeal. When it is sprinkled on one's clothes or carried in the pocket no Fairy will venture near, and it was usual with people going on journeys after nightfall to adopt the precaution of taking some with them. In Mull and Tiree the pockets of boys going any distance after nightfall were filled with oatmeal by their anxious mothers, and old men are remembered who sprinkled themselves with it when going on a night journey. In Skye oatmeal was not looked upon as proper Fairy food, and it was said if a person wanted to see the Fairies he should not take oatmeal with him; if he did he would not be able to see them. When 'the folk' take a loan of meal they do not appear to have any objections to oatmeal. The meal returned, however, was always barleymeal.

Oatmeal taken out of the house after dark was sprinkled with salt, and unless this was done, the Fairies might through its instrumentality take the substance out of the farmer's whole grain. To keep them from getting the benefit of meal itself, housewives, when baking oatmeal bannocks, made a little thick cake with the last of the meal between their palms (not kneading it like the rest of the bannocks) for the youngsters to put a hole through it with the forefinger. This *bonnach boise* ('palm bannock') is not to be toasted on the gridiron, but placed to the fire leaning against a stone (*leac nam bonnach*), well known where a 'griddle' is not available.

Once the Fairies were overtaken carrying with them the benefit (*toradh*) of the farm in a large thick cake, with the handle of the quern (*sgonnan na brà*) stuck through it and forming a pole on which it was carried. This cannot occur when the last bannock baked (*bonnach fallaid*) is a little cake with a hole in it (*bonnach beag 's toll ann*).[101]

Carleton (*Tales and Stories*, p. 74) mentions an Irish belief of a kindred character connected with oatmeal. When one crossed *fair gurtha* or hungry grass (Scottish Gaelic *feur gorta*, famine grass), a spot on which the Fairies had left one of their curses, he was struck with weakness and hunger, but 'if the person afflicted but tasted as much meal or flour as would lie on the point of a penknife, he will instantaneously break the spell of the Fairies, and recover his former strength'.[102]

Maistir, or stale urine, kept for the scouring of blankets and other cloth, when sprinkled on the cattle and on the door-posts and walls of the house, kept the Fairies (and indeed every mischief) at a distance. This sprinkling was done regularly on the last evening of every quarter of the year (*h-uile latha ceann ràidhe*).[103]

Plants of great power were the *mòthan* (*sagina procumbens*, trailing pearlwort) and *achlasan Chaluim Chille* (*hypericum pulcrum*, St John's wort). The former protected its possessor from fire and the attacks of the Fairy women. The latter warded off fevers and kept the Fairies from taking people away in their sleep. There are rhymes which must be said when these plants are pulled.[104]

Stories representing the Bible as a protection must be of a recent date. It is not so long since a copy of the Bible was not available in the Highlands for that or any other purpose. When the Book did become accessible, it is not surprising that (as in other places) a blind, unmeaning reverence should accumulate round it.[105]

CONCLUSION

Such are the main features of the superstition of the *sìthchean*, the still-folk, the noiseless people, as it existed (and in some degree still exists) in the Highlands, and particularly in the Islands, of Scotland. There is a clear line of demarcation between it and every other Highland superstition, though the distinction has not always been observed by writers on the subject. The following Fairy characteristics deserve to be particularly noticed.

It was peculiar to the Fairy women to assume the shape of deer, while witches became mice, hares, cats, gulls or black sheep, and the devil a he-goat or gentleman with a horse's or pig's foot. A running stream could not be crossed by evil spirits, ghosts and apparitions, but made no difference to the Fairies. If all tales be true, they could give a dip in the passing to those they were carrying away; and the stone on which the 'washing woman' folded the shirts of the doomed was in the middle of water.

Witches took the milk from cows; the Fairies had cattle of their own, and when they attacked the farmer's dairy, it was to take away the cows themselves, i.e. the cow in appearance remained, but its benefit (the real cow) was gone. The Elves have even the impertinence at times to drive back the cow at night to pasture on the corn of the person from whom they have stolen it. The phrenzy with which Fairy women afflicted men was only a wandering madness (φοιταλέα μανία), which made them roam about restlessly without knowing what they were doing, or leave home at night to hold appointments with the Elfin women themselves; by druidism (*druidheachd*) men were driven from their kindred and made to imagine themselves undergoing marvellous adventures and changing shape.

Dogs crouched, or leapt at their master's throat, in the presence of evil spirits, but they gave chase to the Fairies. Night alone was frequented by the powers of darkness, and they fled at the cock-crowing; the Fairies were encountered in the daytime as well. There was no intermarriage between men and the other beings of superstition, but women were courted and taken away by Fairy men, and men courted Fairy women (or rather were courted by them), married, and took them to their houses.

A well-marked characteristic is the tinge of the ludicrous that pervades the creed. The Fairy is an object of contempt as well as of fear, and, though the latter be the prevailing feeling, there is observably a desire to make the Elves contemptible and ridiculous. A person should not unnecessarily provoke the anger of those who cannot retaliate, much less of a race so ready to take offence and so sure to retaliate as the Fairies. In revenge for this species of terror, the imagination loves to depict the Elves in positions and doing actions that provoke a smile. The part of the belief which relates to the banshi is comparatively free from this feeling, but the 'little people' and changelings come in for a full share of it. Perhaps this part of the superstition is not entirely to be explained as the recoil of the mind from the oppression of a belief in invisible beings that may be cognizant of men's affairs and only wait for an opportunity to exert an evil influence over them, but its existence is striking.

2

TALES ILLUSTRATIVE OF FAIRY SUPERSTITION

LURAN

This is a tale diffused in different forms over the whole West Highlands. Versions of it have been heard from Skye, Ardnamurchan, Lochaber, Craignish, Mull, Tiree – differing but slightly from each other.

Beinn Shianta (the 'Charmed Hill'), from its height, greenness, or pointed summit, forms a conspicuous object on the Ardnamurchan coast at the north entrance of the Sound of Mull. On the 'shoulder' of this hill were two hamlets, Sgìnid and Corryvulin, the lands attached to which, now forming part of a large sheep farm, were at one time occupied in common by three tenants, one of whom was named Luran Black (*Luran MacilleDhuibh*).[106]

One particular season a cow of Luran's was found unaccountably dead each morning. Suspicion fell on the tenants of the Culver (*an Cuilibheir*), a green knoll in Corryvulin having the reputation of being tenanted by the Fairies.[107] Luran resolved to watch his cattle for a night and ascertain the cause of his mysterious losses.

Before long he saw the Culver opening and a host of little people pouring out. They surrounded a grey cow (*mart glas*) belonging to him and drove it into the knoll. Not one busied himself in doing this more than Luran himself; he was, according to the Gaelic expression, 'as one and as two' (*mar a h-aon 's mar a dhà*) in his exertions.

The cow was killed and skinned. An old Elf, a tailor sitting in the upper part of the *brugh* with a needle in the right lappel of his coat, was forcibly caught hold of, stuffed into the cow's hide, and sewn up. He was then taken to the door and rolled down the slope.[108] Festivities commenced, and whoever might be on the floor dancing, Luran was sure to be. He was 'as one and as two' at the dance, as he had been at driving the cow. A number of gorgeous cups and dishes were put on the table, and Luran, resolving to make up for the loss of the grey cow, watched his opportunity and made off with one of the cups (*còrn*).[109] The Fairies observed him and started in pursuit. He heard one of them remark:

> *Cha bu luath Luran*
> *Mura bhith cruas arain.*

28

("Not swift would be Luran / If it were not the hardness of his bread.") His pursuers were likely to overtake him, when a friendly voice called out:

> *Lurain, Lurain MhicilleDhuibh,*
> *Thoir ort clacha dubh' a' chladaich!*

("Luran, Luran Black, / Betake thee to the black stones of the shore!") Below high water mark no Fairy, ghost or demon can come, and acting on the friendly advice Luran reached the shore, and keeping below tide-mark made his way home in safety. He heard the outcries of the person who had called out to him (probably a former acquaintance who had been taken by 'the people') being belaboured by the Fairies for his ill-timed officiousness.

Next morning the grey cow was found lying dead with its feet in the air at the foot of the Culver, and Luran said that a needle would be found in its right shoulder. On this proving to be the case, he allowed none of the flesh to be eaten, and threw it out of the house.

One of the fields tilled in common by Luran and two neighbours was every year, when ripe, reaped by the Fairies in one night, and the benefit of the crop disappeared. An old man was consulted, and he undertook to watch the crop. He saw the **shï-en** of Corryvulin open, and a troop of people coming out. There was an old man at their head who put the company in order – some to shear, some to bind the sheaves, and some to make stooks. On the word of command being given the field was reaped in a wonderfully short time.

The watcher, calling aloud, counted the reapers. The Fairies never troubled the field again.[110]

Their persecution of Luran did not, however, cease. While on his way to Inveraray Castle with his Fairy cup he was lifted mysteriously with his treasure out of the boat in which he was taking his passage, and was never seen or heard of after.

According to another Ardnamurchan version Luran was a butler boy in Mingarry Castle. One night he entered a Fairy dwelling and found the company within feasting and making merry. A shining cup called *an cupa cearrarach* was produced, and whatever liquor the person having it in his hand wished for and named came up within it.[111] Whenever a dainty appeared on the table, Luran was asked, "Did you ever see the like of that in Mingarry Castle?"

At last the butler boy wished the cup to be full of water and, throwing its contents on the lights and extinguishing them, ran away with it in his hand. The Fairies gave chase. Someone among them called out to Luran to make for the shore. He reached the friendly shelter, and made his way below high-water mark to the castle, which he entered by a stair leading to the sea. The cup remained long in Mingarry Castle, but was at last lost in a boat that sank at Mail Point (*Rubha Mhàil*).[112]

A Tiree version of the tale says that Luran entered an open Fairy dwelling (*brugh*), where he found the inmates asleep and a large cauldron or copper standing on the floor. He took up the kettle and made off with it. When going out at the door, the cauldron struck one of the door-posts and made a ringing noise. The Fairies, sixteen men in number, started out of sleep and gave chase. As they pressed on Luran, one of them (probably a friend who had at one time been 'taken') called out, "Luran, Luran, make for the black stones of the shore."

He did so, and made his escape. It was then the Fairies remarked: "Luran would be swift if it were not the hardness of his bread. If Luran had warm milk and soft barley bread, not one among the sixteen of us could catch him."

According to the Lochaber story, the Fairies stole a white cow from a farmer, and every night took it back again to pasture on his corn. He chased them with his dog Luran, but they threw bread behind them, which the dog loitered to devour, so that it never overtook the white cow. The Fairies were heard saying among themselves, "Swift would be Luran if it were not the hardness of his bread. If Luran got bread singed and twice turned, it would catch the white cow."

The field where this occurred is known as *Acha na Bò Bàin* ('the Field of the White Cow'), above Brackletter in Lochaber.[113]

According to a Skye version, the Fairies came to take with them the benefit (*toradh*) of the farmer's land, but his dog Luran drove them away. One night they were overheard saying, "Swift would be Luran if it were not the hardness of his bread. If thin porridge were Luran's food, deer would not overtake Luran."[114]

Next day thin porridge or crowdie was given to Luran, and it ate too much, and could not run at all. The Fairies got away, laughing heartily at the success of their trick.

In Craignish, Argyllshire, Luran was a dog – old and unable to devour quickly the bread thrown it by the Fairies. There are, no doubt, many other versions of the story current, but these are sufficient to show the want of uniformity in popular tales of this kind.[115]

THE CUP OF THE MACLEODS OF RAASA

In Raasa a man named Hugh entered a Fairy dwelling where there was feasting going on. The Fairies welcomed him heartily and pledged his health. *Deoch ort, Eoghain!* was to be heard on every side. "Here's to you, Hugh!" "I drink to you, Hugh!"

He was offered drink in a fine glittering cup. When he got the cup in his hands he ran off with it. The Fairies let loose one of their dogs after him. He made his escape, and heard the Fairies calling back the dog by its name of 'Farvann' – *Farbhann! Farbhann!*

The cup long remained in the possession of the MacLeods of Raasa.[116]

THE FAIRIES ON FINLAY'S SANDBANK

The sandbank of this name (*Bac Fhionnlaigh*) on the farm of Balevullin in Tiree was at one time a noted Fairy residence, but has since been blown level with the ground. It caused surprise to many that no traces of the Fairies were found in it.[117]

Its Fairy tenants were at one time in the habit of sending every evening to the house of a smith in the neighbourhood for the loan of a kettle (*iasad coire*). The smith, when giving it, always said:

> *Dlighe gobhainn gual*
> *Is iarann fuar a chur a-mach,*
> *'S dlighe coire cnàimh*
> *'S e thighinn slàn gu taigh.*

("A smith's due is coals / And to send cold iron out, / A cauldron's due is a bone / And to come safe back.")[118] Under the power of this rhyme the cauldron was restored safely before morning.

One evening the smith was from home, and his wife, when the Fairies came for the usual loan, never thought of saying the rhyme. In consequence the cauldron was not returned. On finding this out the smith scolded savagely, and his wife, irritated by his reproaches, rushed away for the kettle. She found the *brugh* open, went in, and (as is recommended in such cases), without saying a word, snatched up the cauldron and made off with it. When going out at the door she heard one of the Fairies calling out:

> *A Gheur bhalbh ud, 's a Gheur bhalbh,*
> *Thàinig oirnn a tìr na marbh,*
> *Dh' fhuadaich an coire o'n bhrugh,—*
> *Fuasgail an dul is leig an Garbh.*

("Thou dumb sharp one, thou dumb sharp, / That came from the land of the dead, / And drove the cauldron from the brugh – / Undo the Knot, and lose the Rough.")[119] She succeeded in getting home before the Rough, the Fairy dog, overtook her, and the Fairies never again came for the loan of the kettle.

This story is given in a slightly different form by Mr Campbell in his *Tales of the West Highlands* (vol. ii., p. 44), and the scene is laid in Sanntrai, an island near Barra.[120]

The above version was heard in Tiree by the writer several years before he saw Mr Campbell's book. There is no reason to suppose the story belongs originally either to Tiree or Barra. It is but an illustration of the tendency of popular tales to localise themselves where they are told.

PENNYGOWN FAIRIES

A green mound near the village of Pennygown (*Peighinn a' Ghobhann*) in the parish of Salen, Mull, was at one time occupied by a benevolent company of Fairies.[121] People had only to leave at night on the hillock the materials for any work they wanted done (as wool to be spun, thread for weaving, etc.), telling what was wanted, and before morning the work was finished.

One night a wag left the wood of a fishing-net buoy – a short, thick piece of wood – with a request to have it made into a ship's mast. The Fairies were heard toiling all night and singing:

> *Diomaich is mì-bhuaidh*
> *Air an fhear a dh'iarr oirnn*
> *Crann mòr luinge fada dhèanadh*
> *De mhaide bhola lìon.*

("Short life and ill-luck / Attend the man who asked us / To make a long ship's big mast / From the wood of a fishing-net buoy.") In the morning the work was not done, and these Fairies never after did anything for anyone.

BEN LOMOND FAIRIES

A company of Fairies lived near the Green Loch (*Lochan Uaine*) on Ben Lomond. Whatever was left overnight near the loch – cloth, wool, or thread – was dyed by them of any desired colour before morning. A specimen of the desired colour had to be left at the same time.

A person left a quantity of undyed thread, and a piece of black and white twisted thread along with it, to show that he wanted part of the hank black and part white. The Fairies thought the pattern was to be followed, and the work done at one and the same dyeing. Not being able to do this, they never dyed any more.[122]

CALUM CLARK AND HIS SORE LEG

Some six generations ago there lived at Port Vista (*Port Bhiosta*) in Tiree a dark, fierce man known as *Calum Mòr Mac a' Chléirich*, Big Malcolm Clark. He was a very strong man, and in his brutal violence produced the death of several people. Tradition also says of him that he killed a water-horse and fought a banshi with a horse-rib at the long hollow, covered in winter with water, called the *Léig*. In this encounter his own little finger was broken. When sharpening knives old women in Tiree said, *Di-Haoine am baile Mhic a' Chléirich* ("Friday in Clark's town"), with the object of making him and his the objects of Fairy wrath.[123]

One evening as he was driving a tether-pin into a hillock, a head was popped up out of the ground and told him to take some other place for securing his beast, as he was letting the rain into 'their' dwelling. Some time after this he had a painfully sore leg – *bha i gu dòrainneach doirbh*.[124] He went to the **shï-en** where the head had appeared and, finding it open, entered in search of a cure for his leg. The Fairies told him to 'put earth on the earth': *Cuir an talamh air an talamh*. He applied every kind of earth he could think of to the leg, but without effect.

At the end of three months he went again to the hillock, and when entering put steel (*cruaidh*) in the door. He was told to go out, but he would not, nor would he withdraw the steel till told the proper remedy. At last he was told to apply *criadh ruadh Lochan Ni'n Shomhairle*, the red clay of a small loch in the neighbourhood.[125]

He did so, and the leg was cured.

The Young Man in the Fairy Knoll

Two young men coming home after nightfall on Hallowe'en, each with a jar of whisky on his back, heard music by the roadside and – seeing a dwelling open and illuminated, and dancing and merriment going on within – entered. One of them joined the dancers without as much as waiting to lay down the burden he was carrying. The other, suspecting the place and company, stuck a needle in the door as he entered, and got away when he liked.

That day twelve months he came back for his companion, and found him still dancing with the jar of whisky on his back. Though more than half dead with fatigue, the enchanted dancer begged to be allowed to finish the reel. When brought to the open air he was only skin and bone.

This tale is localised in the Ferintosh district and at *Leathad nan Clacha Mòra* ('the Slope of Big Stones') in Harris. In Argyllshire people say it happened in the north. In the Ferintosh story only one of the young men entered the *brugh*, and the door immediately closed. The other lay under suspicion of having murdered his companion, but, by advice of an old man, went to the same place on the same night the following year, and by putting steel in the door of the Fairy dwelling – which he found open – recovered his companion. In the Harris story the young men were a bridegroom and his brother-in-law, bringing home whisky for the marriage.[126]

Two young men in Iona were coming in the evening from fishing on the rocks. On their way, when passing, they found the **shï-en** of that island open, and entered. One of them joined the dancers without waiting to lay down the string of fish he had in his hand. The other stuck a fish-hook in the door, and when he wished made his escape. He came back for his companion that day twelve months, and found him still dancing with the string of fish in his hand. On taking him to the open air the fish dropped from the string, rotten.

Donald, who at one time carried on foot the mails from Tobermory in Mull to *Rubh' an Fhiarain* (Grass Point ferry, where the mail service crosses to the mainland), was a good deal given to drink, and consequently to loitering by the way. He once lay down to have a quiet sleep near a Fairy-haunted rock above Drimfin. He saw the rock open and a flood of light pouring out at the door. A little man came to him and said in English, "Come in to the ball, Donald." But Donald fled, and never stopped till he reached the houses at Tobermory, two miles off. He said he heard the whizz and rustling of the Fairies after him the whole way.

The incident caused a good deal of talk in the neighbourhood, and Donald and his fright were made the subject of some doggerel verse, in which the Fairy invitation is thus given:

> *Rise, rise, rise, Donald,*
> *Rise, Donald, was the call;*
> *Rise up now, Donald,*
> *Come in, Donald, to the ball.*

It is well known that Highland Fairies who speak English are the most dangerous of any.

A young man was sent for the loan of a sieve and, mistaking his way, entered a *brugh* which was that evening open. He found there two women grinding at a hand-mill, two women baking, and a mixed party dancing on the floor. He was invited to sit down: *Fhearchair 'ic Nèill, bi 'd shuidhe.* "Farquhar MacNeill, be seated."[127] He thought he would first have a reel with the dancers. He forgot all about the sieve, and lost all desire to leave the company he was in.

One night he accompanied the band among whom he had fallen on one of its expeditions, and after careering through the skies, stuck in the roof of a house. Looking down the chimney (*fàr-leus*), he saw a woman dandling a child, and, struck with the sight, exclaimed: *Dia gu d' bheannachadh!* "God bless you!" Whenever he pronounced the Holy Name he was disenchanted and tumbled down the chimney.

On coming to himself he went in search of his relatives. No one could tell him anything about them. At last he saw, thatching a house, an old man so grey and thin he took him for a patch of mist resting on the house-top.

He went and made inquiries of him. The old man knew nothing of the parties asked for, but said perhaps his father did. Amazed, the young man asked him if his father was alive, and on being told he was, and where to find him, entered the house.

He there found a very venerable man sitting in a chair by the fire, twisting a straw-rope (*snìomh sìomain*) for the thatching of the house. This man also, on being questioned, said he knew nothing of the people, but perhaps his father did.

The father referred to was lying in bed, a little shrunken man, and he in like manner referred to his father. This remote ancestor, being too weak to stand, was found in a purse (*sporan*) suspended at the end of the bed. On being taken out and questioned, the wizened creature said, "I did not know the people myself, but I often heard my father speaking of them."

On hearing this the young man crumbled in pieces, and fell down a bundle of bones (*cual chnàmh*).

The incident of the very aged people forms part of some versions of the story 'Mar a Chaidh an Tuairisgeul Mòr a Chur gu Bàs' – 'How the Great Description (a man's name) Was Put to Death'.[128]

Another form is that a stranger came to a house, and at the door found an old man crying because his father had thrashed him. He went in, and asking the father why he had thrashed his aged son, was told it was because the grandfather had been there the day before, and the fellow had not the manners to put his hand in his bonnet to him!

BLACK WILLIAM THE PIPER

William MacKenzie was weaver to the Laird of Barcaldine. He and a friend were going home with two gallons of whisky in jars strapped on their backs. They saw a hillock open and illuminated, and entered. William's companion stuck a knife in the door when entering.

They found inside an old man playing the bagpipes and a company of dancers on the floor. William danced one reel, and then another, till his companion got tired waiting and left.

When, after several days, MacKenzie did not turn up, the other was accused of having murdered him, and was advised, if his story was true, to get spades and dig into the hillock for his missing friend. A year's delay was given, and when the hillock was entered MacKenzie was found still dancing on the floor. After this adventure he became the chief weaver in the district; he did more work in a shorter time than any other. At the first throw of the shuttle he said, *Mise 's fear eile an-seo!* "I and another one are here!"

He also began to make pipes, but though a better weaver and piper than he had been before, he never prospered. He became known as *Uilleam Dubh na Pìoba*, 'Black William of the Pipes'.

It is said in Sutherlandshire that a weaver getting a shuttle from the Fairies can go through three times as much work as another man, cf. 'MacCrimmon' in chapter 3, p. 74 below.

The Harris Woman and her Baking

A woman in Harris was passing *Creag Mhànais*, a rock having on its face the appearance of a door, which she saw opening, and a woman dressed in green standing before it, who called to her to come in to see a sick person.[129] The woman was very unwilling to go, but was compelled, and went in without taking any precaution.

She found herself among a large company, for whom she was immediately to begin baking bread, and was told that when the quantity of meal (not very large) given her was entirely used she would be allowed to go away. She began to bake, and made all possible haste to finish the work, but the more she strove the less appearance there was of the labour being finished, and her courage failed when day after day passed, leaving her where she began.

At last, after a long time, the whole company left for the outer world, leaving her, as she thought, alone. When the last tramp of their footsteps could no longer be heard, she was startled by hearing a groan. On looking through an opening which she found in the side of the dwelling, she saw a bedridden old man, who, on seeing her head in the opening, said, "What sent you here?"

"I did not come by my own will," she replied. "I was made to come to attend to a sick person."

He then asked what work was given her to do. She told him, and how the baking was never likely to be finished. He said she must begin again, and that she was not to put the dusting meal (*an fhallaid*) at any time back among the baking. She did as he told her, when she found her stock of meal soon exhausted, and she got out and away before the others returned, much to their discomfiture.[130]

A woman in Skye was taken to see a sick person in a *dùn*, and after attending to her patient, she saw a number of women in green dresses coming in and getting a loan of meal. They took the meal from a skin bag (*balgan*) which seemed as if it would never be exhausted. The woman asked to be sent home, and was promised to be allowed to go on baking the meal left in the bag and spinning a tuft of wool on a distaff handed to her. She baked away, but could not exhaust the meal bag; and spun, but seemed never nearer the end of her task. A woman came in and advised her: *Cuir an fhallaid anns a' bhalgan, agus snìomh an toban mar a chriomas a' chaora an tom* – that is to say, she had to put the remnant of the meal she baked into the little bag, and to spin the tuft upon the distaff as the sheep bites the hillock, i.e. to draw the wool in small tufts, like sheep-bites, from the distaff.

On doing this, the task was soon finished, the Fairies saying, *Beannachd dhuitsa ach mollachd do bheul t' ionnsachaidh*. "A blessing rest on you, but a curse on the mouth that taught you."[131] On coming out, the woman found she had been in the *dùn* for seven years.

LIFTED BY THE FAIRIES

Dòmhnall Dubh an t-Sluaigh ('Black Donald of the Multitude'), as he was ever afterwards known, was ploughing on the farm of Baile Pheutrais, in the island of Tiree, when a heavy shower came on from the west. In these days it required at least two persons to work a plough – one to hold it, and one to lead the horses.

Donald's companion took shelter to the lee of the team. When the shower passed, Donald himself was nowhere to be found, nor was he seen again till evening. He then came from an easterly direction with his coat on his arm. He said the Fairies had taken him in an eddy wind to the islands to the north – Coll, Skye, etc. In proof of this, he told that a person (naming him) was dead in Coll, and people would be across next day for whiskey for the funeral to Kennovay, a village on the other side of Baile Pheutrais, where smuggling was carried on at the time.[132]

This turned out to be the case. Donald said he had done no harm while away, except that the Fairies had made him throw an arrow at (and kill) a speckled cow in Skye. When crossing the sea he was in great terror lest he should fall.

Niall Sgrob (Neil the Scrub), a native of Uist, was on certain days lifted by the Fairies and taken to Tiree and other islands of the Hebrides, at least so he said himself. Once he came to **Saälun**, a village near the north-east end of Tiree, and at the fourth house in the village was made to throw the Fairy arrow.[133] There is an old saying:

> *Dùin an uinneag a-tuath*
> *'S gu luath an uinneag a-deas*
> *'S dùin uinneag na h-àird' an-iar —*
> *Cha d'thàinig olc riamh on àird' an-ear.*

("Shut the north window / And quickly close the window to the south / And shut the window facing west – / Evil never came from the east.") And the west window was this night left open. The arrow came through the open window, and struck on the shoulder a handsome, strong, healthy woman of the name of MacLean, who sat singing cheerfully at her work. Her hand fell powerless by her side, and before morning she was dead.

Neil afterwards told that he was the party whom the Fairies had compelled to do the mischief. In this and similar stories it must be understood that, according to popular belief, the woman was taken away by the Fairies, and may still be among them; only her semblance remained and was buried.

About twenty years ago a cooper employed on board a ship was landed at *Eilein Mhàrtainn* – Martin's Isle near Coigeach in Ross-shire – to cut brooms. He traversed the islet, and then somehow fell asleep. He felt as if something were pushing him, and, on awakening, found himself in the island of Rona, ten miles off. He cut the brooms, and a shower of rain coming on, again fell asleep. On awaking he found himself back in Martin's Isle. He could only, it is argued, have been transported back and forward by the Fairies.

A *taibhseir* (seer gifted with the second sight) resident at Bousd, in the east end of Coll, was frequently lifted by Fairies that staid in a hillock in his neighbourhood. On one occasion they took him to the sea-girt rock called *Eileirig*, and after diverting themselves with him for an hour or two took him home again. So he said himself.

A man who went to fish on Saturday afternoon at a rock in *Beinn Chinn a' Bhara* (Kennavara Hill, the extreme west point of Tiree) did not make his appearance at home until six o'clock the following morning. He said that after leaving the rock the evening before he remembered nothing but passing a number of beaches. The white beaches of Tiree, from the surrounding land being a dead level, are at night the most noticeable features in the scenery. On coming to his senses, he found himself on the top of the Dùn at Caolas in the extreme *east* end of the island, twelve miles from his starting point.

A few years ago a man in Lismore, travelling at night with a web of cloth on his shoulder, lost his way, walked on all night without knowing where he was going, and in the morning was found among rocks where he could never have made his way alone. He could give no account of himself, and his wanderings were universally ascribed to the Fairies.

Dòmhnall Ruadh nan Sìthchean ('Red Donald of the Fairies'), as he was called (and the name stuck to him all his life), used when a boy to see the Fairies. Being herd at the Spital (*an Spideal*) above Dalnacardoch in Perthshire, he was taken by them to his father's house at Ardlàraich in Rannoch – a distance of a dozen miles – through the night. In the morning he was found sitting at the fireside, and as the door was barred, he must have been let in by the chimney.[134]

An old man in Achabeg, Morvern, went one night on a gossiping visit (*céilidh*) to a neighbour's house. It was winter time, and a river near the place was in flood – which in the case of a mountain torrent means that it was impassable. The old man did not return home that night, and next morning was found near the **shï-en** of *Luran na Leaghadh* in Savary, some distance across the river. He could give no account of how he got there, only that when on his way home a storm came about him, and on coming to himself he was where they had found him.[135]

When Dr MacLaurin was tenant of Inveresragan near Connal Ferry in Benderloch, at the end of last century, Calum Clever – who derived his name from his skill in singing tunes and expedition in travelling, gifts given him by the Fairies – stayed with him whole nights. The doctor sent him to Fort William with a letter, telling him to procure the assistance of 'his own people' and be back with an immediate answer.

Calum asked as much time as one game at shinty (*aon tadhal air a' bhall*) would take, and was back in the evening before the game was finished. He never could have travelled the distance without Fairy aid.[136]

FAIRIES COMING TO HOUSES

Ewen son of Alastair Òg was shepherd in *Coire Bhacaidh*, the 'Dell of Banks' at the south end of Loch Ericht (*Loch Eireachd*), and stayed alone in a bothy far away from other houses. In the evenings he put the porridge for his supper out to cool on the top of the double wall (*anainn*) of the hut.[137] On successive evenings he found it pitted and pecked all round on the margin, as if by little birds or heavy rain-drops.

He watched, and saw little people coming and pecking at his porridge. He made little dishes and spoons of wood, and left them beside his own dish. The Fairies, understanding his meaning, took to using these, and let the big dish alone.

At last they became quite familiar with Ewen, entered the hut, and stayed whole evenings with him. One evening a woman came with them. There was no dish for her, and she sat on the other side of the house, saying never a word, but grinning and making faces at the shepherd whenever he looked her way. Ewen at last asked her, *Am bi thu mar sin daonnan, a bhuineagag?* "Are you always like that, my lively maid?"[138]

Owing to the absurdity of the question, or Ewen's failure to understand that the grinning was a hint for food, the Fairies never came again.

The Elves came to a house at night, and finding it closed, called upon *uisge nan cas* ('feet-water', i.e. water in which the feet had been washed) to come and open the door. The water answered from somewhere near that it could not, as it had been poured out. They called on the Band of the Spinning-Wheel to open the door, but it answered it could not, as it had been thrown off the wheel. They called upon Little Cake, but it could not move, as there was a hole through it and a live coal on the top of it. They called upon *smàladh an teine*, the 'raking' coal, but the fire had been secured in a proper manner to keep it alive all night. This is a tale not localised anywhere, but universally known.[139]

A man observed a band of people dressed in green coming toward the house, and recognising them to be Fairies, ran in great terror, shut and barred the door, and hid himself below the bed. The Fairies, however, came through the keyhole and danced on the floor, singing. The song extended to several verses, to the effect that no kind of house could keep out the Fairies, not a turf house (*taigh phloc*), nor a stone house (*taigh cloiche*), etc.

The Fairies staying in Dunvuilg came to assist a farmer in the vicinity in weaving and preparing cloth, and, after finishing the work in a wonderfully short space of time, called for more work. To get rid of his officious assistants, the farmer called outside the door that Dunvuilg was on fire.[140] The Fairies immediately rushed out in great haste, and never came back.

Of this story several versions are given in *Tales of the West Highlands* (ii. 52–4).[141] In some form or other it is extensively known, and in every locality the scene is laid in its own neighbourhood. In Mull the Fairy residence is said to have been the bold headland in the south-west of the island known as *Tun Bhuirg*. Some say the Elves were brought to the house by two old women who were tired spinning, and incautiously said they wished all the people in Tòn Bhuirg were there to assist.[142] According to others, the Elves were in the habit of coming to Tàpull House in the Ross of Mull, and their excessive zeal made them very unwelcome.[143]

In Skye the event is said to have occurred at Dùn Bhuirbh. There are two places of the name – one in Lyndale, and one in Beinn an Ùine, near Druim Uighe, above Portree.[144]

The rhyme they had when they came to Tapull is known as 'Rann Gillean Fir Thàbaill' ('The Rhyme of the Goodman of Tapull's Servants').

> *Cìream, càrdam, tlàmam, cuigealam,*
> *Beairt fhighe gu luath*
> *'S bùrn luadh air teine,*
> *Obair, obair, obair.*

("Let me comb, card, tease, spin, / Get a weaving loom quick, / Water for fulling on the fire, / Work, work, work.")[145] The cry they raised when going away, in the Skye version, runs:

> *Dùn Bhuirbh ri theine*
> *Gun chù, gun duine,*
> *Mo chearslagan snàth*
> *'S mo phocannan mine.*

("Dunvuirv on fire / Without dog or man, / My balls of thread / And my bags of meal.")

A man on the farm of Kennovay in Tiree saw the Fairies about twelve o'clock at night enter the house, glide round the room, and go out again. They said and did nothing.

THE LOWLAND FAIRIES

The 'people' had several dwellings near the village of Largs on the coast of Ayrshire (*na Leargun Gallta*, 'the Slopes-near-the-Sea of the Strangers' – the natives preserve the true name of the place when they call it 'the Lairgs'). See introduction to

Campbell's *Tales of the West Highlands*.[146] Knock Hill was full of Elves, and the site of the old Tron Tree, now the centre of the village, was a favourite haunt.

A sow belonging to the man who cut down the Tron Tree was found dead in the byre next morning. A hawker with a basket of crockery was met near the Noddle Burn by a Fairy woman. She asked him for a bowl she pointed out in his basket, but he refused to give it. On coming to the top of a brae near the village his basket tumbled, and all his dishes ran on edge to the foot of the incline. None were broken but the one which had been refused to the Fairy. It was found in fragments.

The same day, however, the hawker found a treasure that made up for his loss. That (said the person from whom the story was heard) was the custom of the Fairies: they never took anything without making up for it some other way.

On market days they went about stealing here and there a little of the wool or yarn exposed for sale. A present of shoes and stockings made them give great assistance at outdoor work. A man was taken by them to a pump near the Haylee Toll, where he danced all night with them. A headless man was one of the company.

They often came to people's houses at night, and were heard washing their children. If they found no water in the house they washed them in 'kit' (sowen water). They were fond of spinning and weaving, and if chid or thwarted, cut the weaver's webs at night. They one night dropped a child's cap, a very pretty article, in a weaver's house, to which they had come to get the child washed. They, however, took it away the following night.[147]

In another instance, a band of four was heard crossing over the bedclothes, two women going first and laughing, and two men following and expressing their wonder if the women were far before them.

A man cut a slip from an ash-tree growing near a Fairy dwelling. On his way home in the evening he stumbled and fell. He heard the Fairies give a laugh at his mishap. Through the night he was hoisted away, and could tell nothing of what happened till in the morning he found himself in the byre, astride on a cow, and holding on by its horns.

These are genuine popular tales of the south of Scotland which the writer fell in with in Largs. He heard them from a servant girl, a native of the place. They are quoted as illustrations of the vitality of the creed. They are not stories of the Highlands, but are quite analogous. The student of such mythologies will recognise in them a semblance to the Fairy tales of the north of Ireland.

FAIRIES STEALING WOMEN AND CHILDREN

The *machair* (or links) adjoining the hill of Kennavara, the extreme south-west point of Tiree, is after sunset one of the most solitary and weird places conceivable. The hill on its northern side, facing the Skerryvore lighthouse twelve miles off, consists of precipices descending sheer down for upwards of a hundred feet, with frightful chasms where countless sea-birds make their nests, and at the base of which the Atlantic rolls with an incessant noise, which becomes deafening in bad weather. The hill juts into the sea, and the coast, from each side of its inner end, trends away in beaches which – like all the beaches in the island – have after nightfall, from their whiteness and loneliness, a strange and ghostly look.

On the landward side, the level country stretches in a low dark line towards the horizon; little is to be seen, and the stillness is unbroken, save by the sound of the surf rolling on the beach and thundering in the chasms of the hill. It is not, therefore, wonderful that these links should be haunted by the Fairies, or the timid wayfarer there meet the big black Elfin dog prowling among the sand-banks, hear its unearthly baying in the stormy night wind, and in the uncertain light and the squattering of wildfowl, hear in wintry pools the banshi washing the garments of those soon to die.

Some seventy or eighty years ago the herdsman who had charge of the cattle on this pasture went to a marriage in the neighbouring village of Balephuil ('Mud-Town'), leaving his mother and a young child alone in the house. The night was wild and stormy; there was heavy rain, and every pool and stream was more than ordinarily swollen. His mother sat waiting his return, and two women – whom she knew to be Fairies – came to steal the child.

They stood between the outer and inner doors and were so tall their heads appeared above the partition beam. One was taller than the other. They were accompanied by a dog, and stood one on each side, having a hold of an ear and scratching it. Some say there was a crowd of 'little people' behind to assist in taking the child away. For security the woman placed it between herself and the fire, but her precautions were not quite successful. From that night the child was slightly fatuous, 'a half idiot' (*leth òinseach*). The old woman, it is said, had the second sight.

A shepherd, living with his wife in a bothy far away among the hills of Mull, had an addition to his family. He was obliged to go for assistance to the nearest houses, and his wife asked him, before leaving her and her babe alone, to place the table beside the bed, and a portion of the various kinds of food in the house on it, and also to put the smoothing iron below the front of the bed and the reaping-hook (*buanaiche*) in the window.

Soon after he had left, the wife heard a suppressed muttering on the floor and a voice urging someone to go up and steal the child. The other answered that butter from the cow that ate the pearlwort (*mòthan*) was on the table, that iron was below the bed, and the 'reaper' in the window – how could he get the child away? As the reward of his wife's providence and good sense the shepherd found herself and child safe on his return.[148]

A man in Morvern known by the nickname of *am Mor'aire* ('the Marquis') left a band of women watching his wife and infant child. On returning at night he found the fire gone out and the women fast asleep. By the time he had rekindled the fire he saw a banshi entering and making for the bed where his wife and child were. He took a faggot from the fire and threw it at her. A flame gleamed about his eyes, and he saw the Fairy woman no more. His wife declared that she felt at the time like one in a nightmare (*troma-lidhe*); she heard voices calling upon her to go out, and felt an irresistible inclination to obey.

A woman from Rahoy (*Rath Thuaith*) on Loch Sunart-side was taken with her babe to *Beinn Iadain* (Ben Iadain), a lofty hill in the parish of Morvern, rising to a height of above 2,000 feet, and at one time of great note as an abode of the Fairies. Her husband had laid himself down for a few minutes' rest in the front of the bed and fallen asleep. When he awoke his wife and child were gone.

They were taken, the woman afterwards told, to *a' Chòmhla Dhubh* ('the Black Door'), as the spot forming the Fairy entrance into the interior of the mountain is called. On entering, they found a large company of men, women, and children. A fair-haired boy among them came and warned the woman not to eat any food the Fairies might offer, but to hide it in her clothes. He said they had got his own mother to eat this food, and in consequence he could not now get her away.

Finding the food offered her was slighted, the head Fairy sent off a party to bring a certain man's cow. They came back saying they could not touch the cow as its right knee was resting on the plant *bruchorcan* (dirk grass). They were sent for another cow, but they came back saying they could not touch it either, as the dairymaid, after milking it, had struck it with the shackle or cow-spancel (*buarach*).[149]

That same night the woman appeared to her husband in his dreams, telling him where she was, and that by going for her and taking the black silk handkerchief she wore on her marriage day, with three knots tied upon it, he might recover her.[150] He tied the knots, took the handkerchief and a friend with him, entered the hill at the Black Door, and recovered his wife and child. The white-headed boy accompanied them for some distance from the Black Door, but returned to the hill, and is there still in all probability.

Another wife was taken from the neighbourhood of Castle Lionnaig – near Loch Aline (*Loch Àluinn*, 'the Pretty Loch'), in the same parish – to the same hill. She was placed in the lap of a gigantic hag, who told her it was useless to attempt escaping; her arms would close round her

> *Mar an eidheann ris a' chreig*
> *'S mar an iadhshlat ris an fhiodh,*
> *Mar an fheòil mun chnàimh*
> *'S mar an cnàimh mun smior.*

'As the ivy to the rock / And as the honeysuckle to the tree, / As the flesh round the bone / And as the bone round the marrow'.

The woman answered that she wished it was an armful of dirt the Fairy held. In saying so, she made use of a very coarse, unseemly word, and as no such language is tolerated among the Fairies, the big woman called to take the vile wretch away, and leave her in the hollow in which she had been found (*an lag 'san d'fhuaradh i*), which was done.[151]

A man in Balemartin on the south side of Tiree (*air an léige deas*) whose wife had died in childbed was sitting one night soon after with a bunch of keys in his hands. He saw his wife passing and repassing him several times. The following night she came to him in his dreams, and reproached him for not having thrown the bunch of keys at her, or between her and the door, to keep the Fairies from taking her back with them. He asked her to come another night, but she said she could not, as the company she was with was removing that night to another *brugh* far away.[152]

Another, somewhere on the mainland of Argyllshire, suspecting his wife had been stolen by Fairies, hauled her by the legs from bed, through the fire and out at the door. She there became a log of wood, and serves as the threshold of a barn in the place to this day.

A woman taken by the Fairies was seen by a man who looked in at the door of a *brugh*, spinning and singing at her work.

A wife taken in childbed came to her husband in his sleep, and told him that by drawing a furrow thrice round a certain hillock sunwise (*deiseal*) with the plough, he might recover her. He consulted his neighbours, and in the end it was deemed as well not to attend to a dream of one's sleep (*bruadar cadail*). He consequently did not draw the furrow, and never recovered his wife.

A child was taken by the Fairies from Killichrenan (*Cille Chreunain*) near Loch Awe to the **shï-en** in Nant Wood (*Coill' an Eannd*). It was got back by the father drawing a furrow round the hillock with the plough. He had not gone far when he heard a cry behind him, and on looking back found his child lying in the furrow.

A trampling as of a troop of horses came round a house in which a woman lay in childbed, and she and the child were taken away. At the end of seven years her sister came upon an open Fairy hillock, and thoughtlessly entered. She saw there her lost sister with a child in her arms, and was warned by her, in the lullaby song to the child, to slip away out again.

> *A phiuthrag, 's a phiuthrag chaidreach,*
> *An cuimhne leat oidhche nan capall?*
> *Seachd bliadhn' on thugadh ás mi*
> *'S bean mo choltais riamh chan fhacas.*
> > *Ialai horro, horro,*
> > *Ialai horro hì.*

"Little sister, little loving sister, / Rememberest thou the night of the horses? / Seven years since I was taken / And one like me was never seen. / Ialai horro, horro, / Ialai horro hì."[153]

Ready Wit Repulses the Fairies

A Fairy woman came to take away a child and said to its mother, *Is glas do leanabh.* "Grey is your child."

Is glas am fiar, 's fàsaidh e. "Grey is the grass, and it grows," was the ready answer.

Is trom do leanabh. "Heavy is your child," said the banshi.

Is trom gach torrach. "Heavy is each fruitful thing," the mother replied.

Is eutrom do leanabh. "Light is your child," said the banshi.

Is eutrom gach saoghaltach sona. "Light is each happy worldly one," said the mother,[154] bursting into singing and saying:

> *Is glas an duilleach, is glas am feur,*
> *Is glas an tuagh am bheil a' chas,*
> *'S chan eil nì thig roimh thalamh*
> *Nach eil gnè ghlaise 'na aoraibh.*[155]

"Grey is the foliage, grey the flowers, / And grey the axe that has a handle, / And nought comes through the earth, / But has some greyness in its nature."[156]

On finding herself outwitted the banshi left.

A boy, a mere child, was left alone for a few minutes in the islet of Soa, near Tiree. The mother was making kelp there at the time, and in her absence the Fairies came and gave the child's legs such a twist that it was lame (*liùgach*) ever after.[157]

Kindness to a Neglected Child

The Elves sometimes took care of neglected children. The herd who tendered the Balephuill cattle on Heynish Hill sat down one day on a green eminence (*cnoc*) in the hill which had the reputation of being tenanted by the Fairies. His son, a young child, was along with him.

He fell asleep, and when he awoke the child was away. He roused himself, and vowed aloud that unless his boy was restored he would not leave a stone or clod of the hillock together.

A voice from underground answered that the child was safe at home with its mother, and they (the 'people') had taken it lest it should come to harm with the cold.

THE BRIDEGROOM'S BURIAL

A young woman in Islay was promised in marriage to a rich neighbour, and the marriage day was fixed. She had a sweetheart who, on hearing this, said to a brother older than himself that if he had means to keep a wedding feast he would run away with the bride.

His brother promised him all he had, being thirty-five gallons of whisky. On getting this, the young man took the bride away, and gave a nuptial feast himself that lasted a month.

At the end of that time, when he was taking a walk with his wife, an eddy wind was seen coming. As it passed, the young man was seized with sickness, which in a short time ended in his death. Before his death his wife said to him, *Ma tha tùr aig marbh, tha mi 'g òrdachadh nach bi thu oidhche dhìth do leapa.* "If the dead have feeling, I ordain that you be not a night absent from your bed."[158]

The night after the funeral he came back, to the consternation of his wife. He told her not to be alarmed, that he was still sound and healthy (*slàn fallain*), that he had only been taken in the eddy by *Baintighearna 'n Eilein Uaine* ('the Lady of the Green Island'), and that by throwing a dirk at the eddy wind when next she encountered it, she would get him back again.

The wife threw a dirk at the next eddy wind she saw, and her husband dropped at her feet. He told he had been with the *sluagh eutrom* ('light people') and in the tomb in which they supposed him buried would be found only a log of alder wood (*maide feàrna*).

His wife's relatives were sent for, and they came, thinking the young widow had lost her wits through grief. The grave was opened and an alder stick, found in the coffin instead of the body, proved the husband's account of his disappearance.[159]

THE CROWING OF THE BLACK COCK

A woman in Islay (the story was heard in Tiree) was taken by the Fairies, leaving an infant who was baptised by the name of *Sìle* (Julia). To appearance the mother died and was buried. Every night, however, she came back and was heard singing to her child.

Her husband watched one night and caught her. She told that by going to a hillock (which she named) on a certain night he might recover her.

He went, taking with him according to her instructions *coileach dubh màirt* (a black cock born in the busy time of year) and a piece of steel (*cruaidh*). He found the door of the *brugh* open, put steel in one of the posts, entered (having the cock in his arms) and hid himself in a corner.[160]

Towards morning the cock crew. The head or principal Fairy caused a search to be made, and *Màrtainn Mòr gun iochd gun tròcair* ('Big Martin without clemency or mercy') was found in the *brugh*. On withdrawing the steel he was allowed to go home, and his wife along with him.

My informant could not say whether *màrt* was seed-time (*màrt cur an t-sìl*) or harvest (*màrt buain*); probably the former, cf. Campbell's *West Highland Tales*, ii., p. 98.[161]

THROWING THE ARROW

A weaver at the Bridge of Awe (*Drochaid Atha*) was left a widower with three or four children.[162] He laboured at his trade all day, and when the evening came, being a hard-working, industrious man, did odd jobs about the house to maintain his helpless family.

One clear moonlight, when thatching his house with fern (*ranach*), he heard the rushing sound of a high wind, and a multitude of little people settled on the housetop and on the ground like a flock of black starlings. He was told he must go along with them to Glen Cannel in Mull, where they were going for a woman.[163] He refused to go unless he got whatever was foraged on the expedition to himself.[164]

On arriving at Glen Cannel the arrow was given him to throw. Pretending to aim at the woman he threw it through the window and killed a pet lamb. The animal at once came out through the window, but he was told this would not do, he must throw again. He did so, and the woman was taken away and a log of alder-wood (*stoc feàrna*) was left in her place. The weaver claimed his agreement, and the Fairies left the woman with him at the Bridge of Awe, saying they would never again make the same paction with any man. She lived happily with him and he had three children by her.

A beggar came the way and staid with him that night. The whole evening the beggar stared at the wife in a manner that made his host at last ask him what he meant.

He said he had at one time been a farmer in Glen Cannel in Mull, comfortable and well-to-do, but his wife having died, he had since fallen into poverty till he was now a beggar, and that the weaver's wife could be no other than the wife he had lost.

Explanations were entered into, and the beggar got his choice of the wife or the children. He chose the former, and again became prosperous in the world.

It may interest the reader that the man from whom this story was heard (a shrewd enough person in ordinary life) adduced it as proof of the existence of Fairies, of which he said there could be no doubt; he had heard the story from his father, who knew the weaver.[165]

THE WOMAN STOLEN FROM FRANCE

MacChaluim a' Chrònain, 'MacCallum of the Humming Noise', who resided in Glen Etive subsequent to the '45, was the last to observe the habits of the Fairies and ancient hunters.[166] He ate three days' allowance of food before setting out on his hunting expeditions, and when he got hungry merely tightened his belt another hole. The Indians of Labrador are said to do the same at the present day. These hunters can go for nine days without food, merely tightening their belts as they get thin.

In MacCallum's time, a woman was for seven years observed among the deer of Ben Cruachan, as swift of foot and action as the herd with which she consorted. A gathering was made to catch her. The herd was surrounded by men and dogs, and on her being caught she was taken to Balinoe, where MacCallum resided. There were rings on her fingers from which it was ascertained that she came from France.

Inquiries were made, and she was sent home by a ship from Greenock. She had been taken away in childbed, doubtless by the Fairies. This story was believed by the person from whom it was heard. He had heard it from good authority, he said.

CHANGELINGS

A young lad was sent for the loan of a corn sieve to a neighbour's house. He was a changeling, and in the house to which he went there was another like himself. He found no one in but his fellow-Elf. A woman in a closet close by overheard the conversation of the two. The first asked for the sieve, and the other replied, *Iarr air chòir e, 's gun agam ach mi fhìn.* "Ask it in an honest way (that is, in Fairy language), seeing I am alone."

The first then said (and his words have as much sense in English as in Gaelic):

> *Dh'iarr a' mhugaill a' mhagaill*
> *Iasad an dubh-lugaill lagaill*
> *Thoirt a' mhagaill ás an t-sìol.*

("The muggle maggle / Wants the loan of the black luggle laggle / To take the maggle from the grain.") The words are a ludicrous imitation of the sound made by the fan in winnowing corn, and several versions of them exist.[167]

A child in Skye ate such a quantity of food people suspected it could not be canny. A man of skill was sent for, and on his saying a rhyme over it, the changeling became an old man.

A changeling in Hianish (some say Sanndaig), Tiree, was driven away by a man of skill who came and, standing in the door, said:

Muc dhearg, muc dhearg,
Muc leathchluasach dhearg
Mharbh Fionn le Mac an Luin
'S a thug e air a mhuin gu Druim Dearg.

("Red pig, red pig, / Red one-eared pig / That Fin killed with the Son of Luin / And took on his back to Druim Dearg.")

Druim Dearg, or the Red Ridge, is a common in the neighbourhood of Hianish. Fin's sword, 'the son of Luin', was of such superior metal that it cut through six feet of whatever substance was struck by it, and an inch beyond. Its peculiar virtue was 'never to leave a remnant from its blow'.[168]

When the changeling heard the bare mention of it, with the aversion of his race to steel, he jumped like a fish out of the water (*thug e iasg-leum ás*), rushed out of the house and was never seen again. The real child was found outside the house.[169]

A woman was told by her neighbours that her child, which was not thriving, was a changeling, and that she ought to throw it in the river. The imp, frightened by the counsel, advised the contrary in an expression which is now proverbial: *Air dha bhith reamhar na caol, is mairg nach beathaicheadh laogh dha fhéin.* "Whether it be fat or lean, every man should rear a calf for himself."[170]

TAKING AWAY COWS AND SHEEP

A farmer had two good cows that were seized one spring with some unaccountable malady. They ate any amount of food given them, but neither grew fat nor yielded milk. They lay on their sides and could not be made to rise.

An old man in the neighbourhood advised that they should be hauled up the hill and rolled down its steepest and longest incline. The brutes, he said, were not the farmer's cows at all, but two old men (*bodaich*) the Fairies had substituted for them.[171]

The farmer acted on this advice, and at the bottom of the descent down which the cows were sent rolling nothing was found – neither cow nor man, either dead or alive.

There are old people still living in Iona who remember a man driving a nail into a bull that had fallen over a rock to keep away the Fairies.[172]

A man in Ruaig, Tiree, possessed of the second sight, saw a wether sheep (*molt*) belonging to himself whirled through the sky, and was so satisfied the Fairies had taken it in their eddy wind that he did not, when the animal was killed, eat any of its mutton.

DWELLINGS

An old man kept a green hillock near his house (on which he frequently reclined in summer) very clean, sweeping away any filth or cow- or horse-droppings he might find on it. One evening, as he sat on the hillock, a little man, a stranger to him, came and thanked him for his care of the hillock, and added that if at any time the village cattle should leave their enclosure during the night, he and his friends would show their gratitude by keeping them from the old man's crops. The village in these days was in common, ridge about, and the Fairy promise, being tested, was found good.

Of hills having the reputation of being tenanted by Fairies may be mentioned, in Perthshire, Schiehallion (*Sìth Chailleann*) and Ben-y-Ghloe (*Beinn a' Ghlotha*), and in Argyllshire, *Sìthein na Rapaich* ('the Fairy Dwelling of Tempestuous Weather') in Morvern and Dunniquoich (*Dùn Cuaich*, 'the Bowl-Shaped Hill'), *Dùn Deacainn* and Shien-Sloy (*Sìthein Sluaigh*, 'the Multitude's Residence') near Inveraray.[173] The three latter hills are in sight of each other, and the preference of the Fairies for the last is mentioned in a popular rhyme:

> *Dùn Deacainn is Dùn Cuaich,*
> *Sìthein Sluaigh as àirde slios —*
> *Nam faighinn-sa mo roghainn den triùir*
> *B'e mo rùn a bhith san t-slios.*

"Dùn Deacainn and Dunniquoich, / Shien-Sloy of steepest shore – / Had I my favourite of the three / I would love to be in the shore."[174]

At the head of Glen Erochty (*Gleann Eireachdaidh*, the 'Shapely Glen') in Athol in Perthshire there is a mound known as *Càrn na Sleabhach*, which at one time was of much repute as a Fairy haunt.[175] Alastair Chaluim, a poor harmless person who went about the country making divinations for his entertainers by means of a small four-sided spinning top (*dòdaman*), was asked by a widow where her late husband now was. Alastair spun round his teetotum and, examining it attentively, said, *Tha e 'na each bagais aig na sìthchean an Càrn na Sleabhach, agus gad seilich 'na bhialthaobh.* "He is a baggage horse to the Fairies in Slevach Cairn, with a twisted willow withe in his mouth."

Alastair used to say the men of the present day were very small compared to their ancestors, and to prophesy with his teetotum that they would continue growing smaller and smaller till at last it would take six of them to pull a wisp of hay.

A native of the island of Coll went to pull some wild-briar plants (*fearra-dhris*). He tried to pull one growing in the face of a rock. The first tug he gave he heard some one calling to him from the inside of the rock, and he ran away without ever looking behind. To this day he says no one need try to persuade him there are no Fairies, for he heard them himself.

A shepherd at Lochaweside, coming home with a wedder sheep on his back, saw an open cave in the face of a rock where he had never noticed a cave before. He laid down his burden, and stepping over to the entrance of the cave, stuck his knife into a fissure of the rock forming a side of the entrance. He then leisurely looked in, and saw the cave full of guns and arms and chests studded with brass nails, but no appearance of tenants.[176] Happening to turn his head for a moment to look at the sheep, and seeing it about to move off, he allowed the knife to move from its place. On looking again at the rock, he only saw water trickling from the fissure from which the knife had been withdrawn.

A person who had a green knoll in front of his house, and was in the habit of throwing out dirty water at the door, was told by the Fairies to remove the door to the other side of the house, as the water was spoiling their furniture and utensils. He did this, and he and the Fairies lived on good terms ever after.

In the evening a man was tethering his horse on a grassy mound. A head appeared out of the ground and told him to drive his tether pin somewhere else, as he was letting the rain into their house, and had nearly killed one of the inmates by driving the peg into his ear.

Beinn Feall is one of the most prominent hills in the island of Coll. It is highly esteemed for the excellence of its pasture, and was of old much frequented by the Fairies. A fisherman going to his occupation at night saw it covered with green silk, spread out to dry, and heard all night the sound of a quern at work in the interior. On another occasion similar sounds were heard in the same hill, and voices singing:

> *Ged bu mhath an cala dh'fhàg sinn,*
> *Seachd feàrr an cala fhuair sinn.*

"Though good the haven we left, / Seven times better the haven we found."[177]

A man who avoided tethering horse or cow on a Fairy hillock near his house, or in any way breaking the green sward that covered it, was rewarded by the Fairies driving his horse and cow to the lee of the hillock in stormy nights.

Fairy Assistance

A man in Flodigarry, an islet near Skye, expressed a wish his corn were reaped though it should be by Fairy assistance.[178]

The Fairies came and reaped the field in two nights. They were seen at work, seven score and fifteen, or other large number. After reaping the field they called for more work, and the man set them to empty the sea.

One of the chiefs of Dowart was hurried with his harvest, and likely to lose his crop for want of shearers. He sent word through all Mull for assistance. A little old man came and offered himself. He asked as wages only the full of a straw-rope he had with him of corn when the work was over. MacLean formed no high opinion of the little man, but as the work was urgent and the remuneration trifling, he engaged his services. He placed him along with another old man and an old woman on a ridge by themselves, and told them never to heed though they should be behind the rest, to take matters easy and not fatigue themselves. The little man, however, soon made his assistants leave the way, and set them to make sheaf-bands. He finished shearing that ridge before the rest of the shearers were halfway with theirs, and no fault could be found with the manner in which the work was done.

MacLean would not part with the little reaper till the end of harvest. Fuller payment was offered for his excellent services, but he refused to take more than had been bargained for. He began putting the corn in the rope, and put in all that was in the field, then all that was in the stackyard, and finally all that was in the barn. He said this would do just now, tightened the rope, and lifted the burden on his back. He was setting off with it when MacLean in despair cried out:

> *Màrt a threabh mi,*
> *Màrt a chuir mi,*
> *Màrt a bhuain mi;*
> *Fhir a dh'òrdaich na trì Màirt,*
> *Na leig na bheil san ròp' uamsa.*

"Tuesday I ploughed, / Tuesday I sowed, / Tuesday I reaped; / Thou who didst ordain the three Tuesdays, / Suffer not all that is in the rope to leave me."[179]

Làmh t' athar 's do sheanar ort, said the little man, *bha feum agad labhairt!* "The hand of your father and grandfather be upon you, it is well that you spoke!"[180]

Another version of the tale was current in Morvern. A servant, engaged in spring by a man who lived at *Aodann Mòr* ('Big Face') in Liddesdale, when told to begin ploughing, merely thrust a walking-stick into the ground, and, holding it to his nose, said the earth was not yet ready – *cha robh an talamh air dàir fhathast*.[181] This went on till the neighbours were more than half finished with their spring work. His master then peremptorily ordered the work to be done. By next morning the whole *Aodann Mòr* was ploughed, sown and harrowed. The shearing of the crop was done in the same mysterious and expeditious manner. The servant had the 'association-craft', which secured the assistance of the Fairies. When getting his wages he was like to take away the whole crop, and was got rid of as in the previous version.[182]

An old man in Còrnaig, Tiree, went to sow his croft (or piece of land). He was scarce of seed oats, but putting the little he had in a circular dish made of plaited straw called *plàdar*, suspended from his shoulder by a strap (*iris*), commenced operations. His son followed, harrowing the seed.[183]

The old man went on sowing long after the son expected the seed corn was exhausted. He made some remark expressive of his wonder, and the old man said, "Evil befall you, why did you speak? I might have finished the field if you had held your tongue, but now I cannot go further." And he stopped. The piece sown would properly take four times as much seed as had been used.

A man in the Ross of Mull, about to sow his land, filled a sheet with seed oats and commenced. He went on sowing, but the sheet remained full. At last a neighbour took notice of the strange phenomenon and said, "The face of your evil and iniquity be upon you, is the sheet never to be empty?"

When this was said a little brown bird leapt out of the sheet, and the supply of corn ceased. The bird was called *Torc Sona*, i.e. 'Happy Hog', and when any of the man's descendants fall in with any luck they are asked if the *Torc Sona* still follows the family.[184]

A man in the Braes of Portree in Skye, with a large but weak family, had his spring and harvest work done by the Fairies. No one could tell how it was done, but somehow it was finished as soon as that of any of his neighbours. All his family, however, grew up 'peculiar in their minds'.

THE BATTLE OF TRAI-GRUINARD

On 5th August, 1598, one of the bloodiest battles in the annals of clan feuds was fought at the head of Loch Gruinard, in Islay, between Sir Lachlan Mor MacLean of Dowart and Sir James MacDonald of Islay for possession of lands forfeited by the latter's uncle, of which the former had received a grant.

Of the MacLeans, Sir Lachlan and eighty of his near kinsmen and two hundred clansmen were killed; and of the MacDonalds, thirty were killed and sixty wounded. See Gregory's *West Highlands and Islands*, p. 285. According to tradition, a trifling looking little man came to Sir Lachlan and offered his services for the battle. The chief, who was himself of giant frame and strength, answered contemptuously he did not care which side the little man might be on. The Elf then offered himself to MacDonald, who said he would be glad of the assistance of a hundred like him.

All day Sir Lachlan, who was clothed from head to foot in armour of steel, was followed by the little man, and on his once lifting the vizor of his helmet an arrow struck him in the forehead at the division of the hair and came out at the back of his head. It proved to be one of those arrows known as Elf-bolts. MacDonald was sorry for the death of his rival, and after the battle made enquiry as to who had killed him. "It was I," said the little man, "who killed your enemy; and unless I had done so he would have killed you."

"What is your name?" asked MacDonald.

"I am called," he said, "Dubh-Sìth (i.e. 'Black Elf'), and you were better to have me with you than against you."

Tradition is pretty uniform that Sir Lachlan was killed by the arrow of a little man, and the above is probably only a superstitious version of the real circumstances.[185] The story of powerful warriors, however, struck in the forehead by the arrows of little men, like the stories of Tell and the apple and Alfred and the cakes, is told of too many persons to be above the suspicion of being a popular myth.

The natives of one of the villages in Tiree are known by the nickname of *Clann Dubh-Shìth* and *Sìthbheirean*. The assertion that Dubh-Sìth was the ancient name of Duncan is incorrect, as one of those from whom the village nickname was derived was called Donnchadh Mòr mac Dhubh-Shìth. The little man who killed Lachann Mòr is also known as *an t-ochdaran bodaich*, 'the eighth part measure of a carle'.[186]

DUINE SÌTH, MAN OF PEACE

A wright in the island of Mull, on his way home in the evening from work, got enveloped in a mist. He heard someone coming towards him whistling. He entered into talk with the stranger, and was told a legacy would be left him and would continue in the line of his direct descendants to the third generation. His grandson is unmarried and well advanced in years, to the credit of the whistler's prophecy.

Davie, a south country ploughman or grieve, was brought to Tiree about the beginning of the present century by the then chamberlain or 'baillie' of the island. Ploughing one day on Crossapol farm, he saw before him in the furrow a very little man. Not understanding that the diminutive creature was a Fairy, Davie cried out in broken Gaelic, "What little man are you? Get out of that."

A former gardener in *Tìr Mhine* ('Meal Land') in Glenorchy, a good deal given to drinking, was crossing Loch Awe one night in a boat alone. He saw a little man sitting in the stern of the boat, and spoke to him several times but received no answer. He at last struck at the little man, and himself tumbled overboard. Now, asked the old woman who told this story, what could the little man be but a *brughadair* (i.e. one that came from the Fairy dwelling, an Elf)? To the reader the case will appear one of simple hallucination produced by ardent spirits, but it is of interest as shewing the interpretation put upon it under a belief in the Fairies.

3

TALES OF FAIRY WOMEN, &c.

Bean Shìth, Elle Woman, or Woman of Peace

While supper was being prepared in a farmer's house in Morvern, a very little woman, a stranger to the inmates, entered. She was invited to share the supper with the family, but would take none of the food of which the meal consisted, or of any other the inmates had to offer. She said her people lived on the tops of heather, and in the loch called *Lochan Fasta Litheag*. There does not seem to be any loch of the name in Morvern. The name is difficult to translate, but indicates a lakelet covered with weeds or green scum.[187] The little woman left the house as she came, and fear kept every one from following her or questioning her further.

A woman at Kinloch Teagus (*Ceann Loch Téacais*) in the same parish was sitting on a summer day in front of the house, preparing green dye by boiling heather tops and alum together. This preparation is called *ailmeid*. A young woman whom she had never seen before came to her and asked for something to eat. The stranger was dressed in green and wore a cap bearing the appearance of the king's-hood of a sheep (*currachd-an-rìgh caorach*). The housewife said the family were at the shielings with the cattle, and there was no food in the house: there was not even a drink of milk. The visitor then asked to be allowed to make brose of the dye, and received permission to do what she liked with it. She was asked where she stayed, and she said, "In this same neighbourhood."

She drank off the compost, rushed away throwing three somersaults, and disappeared.[188]

A young man named Calum, when crossing the rugged hills of *Àrd Meadhonach* (Middle Height) in Mull, fell in with some St John's wort (*achlasan Chaluim Chille*), a plant of magic powers if found when neither sought nor wanted.[189] He took some of it with him. He had *dùcun* (small swellings below the toes) on his feet, and on coming to a stream sat down and bathed them in the water. Looking up, he saw an ugly little woman, having no nostrils, on the other side of the stream, with her feet resting against his own. She asked him for the plant he had in his hand, but he refused to give it. She asked him to make snuff of it then and give her some. He answered, "What could you want with snuff, when you have no nostril to put it in?"[190]

He left her and went further on. As he did not come home that night his friends and neighbours next day went in search of him through the hills. He was found by his father asleep on the side of a *cnoc*, a small hillock, and when awakened he thought, from the position of the sun, he had only slept a few minutes. He had, in fact, slept for twenty-four hours.

His dog lay sleeping in the hollow between his two shoulders, and had 'neither hair nor fur' on. It is supposed it had lost the hair in chasing away the Fairies and protecting its master.[191]

In what seems to be only another version of this story, a herd-boy was sitting in the evening by a stream bathing his feet. A beautiful woman appeared on the other side of the stream, and asked him to pull a plant she pointed out and make snuff of it for her.

He refused, asking what need had she of snuff when she had no nostrils. She asked him to cross the stream, but he again refused. When he went home his stepmother gave him his food and milk as usual. He gave the whole of it to his dog, and the dog died from the effects.[192]

A herdsman at Balephuill, in the west end of Tiree, fell asleep on *Cnoc Ghrianal*, at the eastern base of Heynish Hill, on a fine summer afternoon. He was awakened by a violent slap on the ear. On rubbing his eyes and looking up, he saw a woman – the most beautiful he had ever seen – in a green dress, with a brooch fastening it at the neck, walking away from him. She went westward and he followed her for some distance, but she vanished, he could not tell how.

A person in Mull reported that he saw several Fairy women together washing at a stream. He went near enough to see that they had only one nostril each.

The places in Tiree where *cailleacha sìth* (Fairy hags) were seen were at streams and pools of water on *Druim Buidhe* ('the Yellow Back'), the links of Kennavara, and the bend of the hill (*lùbadh na beinne*) at Baile Pheudrais. They have long since disappeared, the islanders having become too busy to attend to them.[193]

A Skyeman was told by one of these weird women never to put the burning end of a peat outside when making up the fire for the night.[194]

DONALD THRASHED BY THE FAIRY WOMAN

A man in Mull, watching in the harvest field at night, saw a woman standing in the middle of a stream that ran past the field. He ran after her, and seemed sometimes to be close upon her, and again to be as far from her as ever. Losing temper, he swore himself to the devil that he would follow till he caught her. When he said the words the object of his pursuit allowed herself to be overtaken, and showed her true character by giving him a sound thrashing.

Every night after, he had to meet her. He was like to fall into a decline through fear of her, and becoming thoroughly tired of the affair, he consulted an old woman of the neighbourhood, who advised him to take with him to the place of appointment the ploughshare and his brother John. This would keep the Fairy woman from coming near him.

The Fairy, however, said to him in a mumbling voice, "You have taken the plough-share with you tonight, Donald, and big, pockmarked, dirty John your brother," and catching him she administered a severer thrashing than ever.

He went again to the old woman, and this time she made for his protection a thread which he was to wear about his neck. He put it on, and, instead of going to the place of meeting, remained at the fireside. The Fairy came and, taking him out of the house, gave him a still severer thrashing. Upon this, the wise woman said she would make a chain to protect him against all the powers of darkness, though they came. He put this chain about his neck, and remained by the fireside. He heard a voice calling down the chimney, "I cannot come near you tonight, Donald, when the pretty smooth-white is about your neck."[195]

IONA BANSHI

A man in Iona, thinking daylight was come, rose and went to a rock to fish. After catching some fish he observed he had been misled by the clearness of the moonlight, and set off home.

On the way, as the night was so fine, he sat down to rest himself on a hillock. He fell asleep, and was awakened by the pulling of the fishing-rod which he had in his hand. He found the rod was being pulled in one direction and the fish in another. He secured both, and was making off when he heard sounds behind him as of a woman weeping. On his turning round to her, she said, "Ask news, and you will get news."

He answered, "I put God between us." When he said this, she caught him and thrashed him soundly.

Every night after, he was compelled to meet her, and on her repeating the same words and his giving the same answer, was similarly drubbed.

To escape from her persecutions he went to the Lowlands. When engaged there cutting drains he saw a raven on the bank above him. This proved to be his tormentor, and he was compelled to meet her again at night, and, as usual, she thrashed him.

He resolved to go to America. On the eve of his departure, his Fairy mistress met him and said, "You are going away to escape from me. If you see a hooded crow when you land, I am that crow."

On landing in America he saw a crow sitting on a tree, and knew it to be his old enemy. In the end the Fairy dame killed him.

Tiree Banshi

At the time of the American War of Independence, a native of Tiree, similarly afflicted and wishing to escape from his Fairy love, enlisted and was drafted off to the States. On landing he thanked God he was now where the hag could not reach him. Soon after, however, she met him. "You have given thanks," she said, "for getting rid of me, but it is as easy for me to make my appearance here as in your own country."

She then told him what fortunes were to befall him, that he would survive the war and return home, and that she would not then trouble him any more. "You will marry there and settle. You will have two daughters, one of whom will marry and settle in Croy-Gortan, the other will marry and remain in your own house. The one away will ask you to stay with herself, as her sister will not be kind to you. Your death will occur when you are crossing the *Léige*." All this in due course happened.[196]

About four generations ago a native of Cornaig in Tiree was out shooting on the Reef plain, and returning home in the evening, at the streamlet which falls into Balefetrish Bay (near Kennovay) was met by a Fairy dame. He did not at first observe anything in her appearance different from other women, but, on her putting over her head and kissing him, he saw she had but one nostril. On reaching home he was unable to articulate one word.

By the advice of an old man he composed, in his mind, a love song to the Fairy. On doing this, his speech came back.

MacPhie's Black Dog

This tale was taken down in Gaelic from the dictation of Donald Cameron, Ruaig, Tiree, in 1863, and is here given in his words as closely as a translation will allow.[197] It is a very good specimen of a class of tales found in the Highlands, and illustrates many remarkable traits of the belief regarding the Fairy women, their enmity to the hunter, their beauty and powers of enchanting men at first, their changing their shape to that of deer, and the aversion dogs have to them; also the size and character of the Fairy hound.

Mac Mhic Ailein of Arasaig, lord of Moidart, went out hunting in his own forest when young and unmarried. He saw a royal stag before him, as beautiful an animal as he had ever seen. He levelled his gun at it, and it became a woman as beautiful as he had ever seen at all. He lowered his gun, and it became a royal stag as before. Every time he raised the gun to his eye, the figure was that of a woman, and every time he let it down to the ground, it was a royal stag.

Upon this he raised the gun to his eye and walked up till he was close to the woman's breast. He then sprang and caught her in his arms. "You will not be separated from me at all," he said. "I will never marry any but you."

"Do not do that, Mac Mhic Ailein," she said. "You have no business with me, I will not suit you. There will never be a day while you have me with you but you will need to kill a cow for me."

"You will get that," said the lord of Moidart, "though you should ask two a day."

But Mac Mhic Ailein's herd began to grow thin. He tried to send her away, but he could not. He then went to an old man who lived in the townland and was his counsellor. He said he would be a broken man, and he did not know what plan to take to get rid of her. The honest old man told him that unless MacPhie of Colonsay could send her away, there was not another living who could.

A letter was instantly sent off to MacPhie. He answered the letter, and came to Arasaig. "What business is this you have with me," said MacPhie, "Mac Mhic Ailein?"

Mac Mhic Ailein told him how the woman had come upon him, and how he could not send her away. "Go you," said MacPhie, "and kill a cow for her today as usual; send her dinner to the room as usual; and give me my dinner on the other side of the room."

Mac Mhic Ailein did as he was asked. She commenced her dinner and MacPhie commenced his. When MacPhie got his dinner past he looked over at her.

"What is your news, Elle-maid?" said he.

"What is that to you, Brian Brugh?" said she.

"I saw you, Elle-maid," said he,
"When you consorted with the Fingalians,
When you went with Diarmaid O Duibhne
And accompanied him from covert to covert."

"I saw you, Brian Brugh," she said,
"When you rode on an old black horse,
The lover of the slim Fairy woman,
Ever chasing her from brugh to brugh."[198]

"Dogs and men after the wretch!" cried MacPhie. "Long have I known her."

Every dog and man in Arasaig was called and sent after her. She fled away out to the point of Arasaig, and they did not get a second sight of her.

Upon this MacPhie went home to his own Colonsay. One day he was out hunting, and night came on before he got home. He saw a light and made straight for it. He saw a number of men sitting in there, and an old grey-headed man in the midst. The old man spoke and said, "MacPhie, come forward."

MacPhie went forward, and what should come in his way but a bitch, as beautiful an animal as he had ever seen, and a litter of pups with it. He saw one pup in particular, black in colour, and he had never seen a pup so black or so beautiful as it. "This dog will be my own," said MacPhie.

"No," said the man, "you will get your choice of the pups, but you will not get that one."

"I will not take one," said MacPhie, "but this one."

"Since you are resolved to have it," said the old man, "it will not do you but one day's service, and it will do that well. Come back on such a night and you will get it."

MacPhie reached the place on the night he promised to come. They gave him the dog. "And take care of it well," said the old man, "for it will never do service for you but the one day."

The Black Dog began to turn out so handsome a whelp that no one ever saw a dog so large or so beautiful as it. When MacPhie went out hunting he called the Black Dog, and the Black Dog came to the door and then turned back and lay where it was before. The gentlemen who visited at MacPhie's house used to tell him to kill the Black Dog, it was not worth its food. MacPhie would tell them to let the dog alone, that the Black Dog's day would come yet.

At one time a number of gentlemen came across from Islay to visit MacPhie and ask him to go with them to Jura to hunt. At that time Jura was a desert, without anyone staying on it, and without its equal anywhere as hunting ground for deer and roe. There was a place there where those who went for sport used to stay, called the Big Cave.

A boat was made ready to cross the sound that same day. MacPhie rose to go, and the sixteen young gentlemen along with him. Each of them called the Black Dog, and it reached the door, then turned and lay down where it was before. "Shoot it," cried the young gentlemen.

"No," said he, "the Black Dog's day is not come yet."

They reached the shore, but the wind rose and they did not get across that day. Next day they made ready to go; the Black Dog was called and reached the door, but returned where it was before. "Kill it," said the gentlemen, "and don't be feeding it any longer."

"I will not kill it," said MacPhie. "The Black Dog's day will come yet."

They failed to get across this day also from the violence of the weather, and returned. "The dog has foreknowledge," said the gentlemen.

"It has foreknowledge," said MacPhie, "that its own day will come yet."

On the third day the weather was beautiful. They took their way to the harbour, and did not say a syllable this day to the Black Dog. They launched the boat to go away. One of the gentlemen looked and said the Black Dog was coming, and he never saw a creature like it, because of its fierce look. It sprang, and was the first creature in the boat. "The Black Dog's day is drawing near us," said MacPhie.

They took with them meat, and provisions, and bedclothes, and went ashore in Jura. They passed that night in the Big Cave, and next day went to hunt the deer. Late in the evening they came home. They prepared supper. They had a fine fire in the cave, and light. There was a big hole in the very roof of the cave through which a man could pass.

When they had taken their supper the young gentlemen lay down. MacPhie rose and stood warming the back of his legs to the fire. Each of the young men said he wished his own sweetheart was there that night. "Well," said MacPhie, "I prefer that my wife should be in her own house; it is enough for me to be here myself tonight."

MacPhie gave a look from him and saw sixteen women entering the door of the cave. The light went out and there was no light except what the fire gave. The women went over to where the gentlemen were. MacPhie could see nothing from the darkness that came over the cave. He was not hearing a sound from the men. The women stood up and one of them looked at MacPhie. She stood opposite to him as though she were going to attack him. The Black Dog rose and put on a fierce bristling look and made a spring at her. The women took to the door, and the Black Dog followed them to the mouth of the cave. When they went away the Black Dog returned and lay at MacPhie's feet.

In a little while MacPhie heard a horrid noise overhead in the top of the cave, so that he thought the cave would fall in about his head. He looked up and saw a man's hand coming down through the hole and making as if to catch himself and take him out through the hole in the roof of the cave. The Black Dog gave one spring, and between the shoulder and the elbow caught the Hand, and lay upon it with all its might.

Now began the play between the Hand and the Black Dog. Before the Black Dog let go its hold it chewed the arm through till it fell on the floor. The Thing that was on the top of the cave went away, and MacPhie thought the cave would fall in about his head. The Black Dog rushed out after the Thing that was outside. This was not the time when MacPhie felt himself most at ease, when the Black Dog left him.

When the day dawned, behold the Black Dog had returned. It lay down at MacPhie's feet, and in a few minutes was dead.

When the light of day appeared MacPhie looked, and he had not a single man alive of those who were with him in the cave. He took with him the Hand and went to the shore to the boat. He went on board and went home to Colonsay, unaccompanied by dog or man. He took the Hand up with him that men might see the horror he had met with, the night he was in the cave. No man in Islay or Colonsay ever at all saw such a hand, nor did they imagine that such existed.

There only remained to send a boat to Jura and take home the bodies that were in the cave. That was the end of the Black Dog's day.

A short tale similar to the first part of the above legend is given in Campbell's *Tales of the West Highlands* (ii. 52). A Fairy changeling in Gaolin Castle, Kerrera, is detected by a visitor from Ireland as the Fairy sweetheart of a countryman – Brian mac Braodh. On being detected, the Elle woman ran into the sea from the point since called *Rubha na Sirich*. The name *Brian Brugh* of the one tale and *Brian mac Braodh* of the other renders it probable the two tales had originally more in common.[199]

The expression *Thig latha a' Choin Duibh fhathast*, 'The Black Dog's day will come yet', has passed into a proverb to denote that a time will yet come when one now despised will prove of service. The English proverb 'every dog has its day' means that everyone has his own time of enjoyment.[200]

The MacPhies or MacDuffies were lairds of Colonsay till the middle of the seventeenth century. In 1623 the celebrated Colkitto was delated for the murder of umquhill Malcolm MacPhie of Colonsay; one of the race lies buried in Iona, with the inscription on his tomb 'Hic Jacet Malcolumbus MacDuffie de Colonsay'.[201] If the same Malcolm is referred to in both cases, these traces of his fame, slight though they be, create some presumption that he may be the person round whom romance has gathered the incidents of the above tale.

In 1615 Malcolm MacPhie joined Sir James MacDonald of Dunyveg in Islay in the last and unsuccessful attempt made by the once powerful Clan Donald of Islay and Cantyre to regain their possessions from the Campbells. He was one of the principal leaders of the rebels and a remarkable man. The family was one of the oldest and most esteemed in the West Highlands.

The following are other versions of the tale in circulation. They are of interest when compared with each other in showing the growth and character of a popular tale.

MacPhie of Colonsay was kept captive by a mermaid in a cave by the shore. She supplied him with whatever he needed or desired, but he was not happy, and took advantage of her absence to make his escape. She missed him on her return and went in pursuit.

He had with him a large black dog which he had kept in spite of everyone's remonstrances. When the mermaid overtook him he threw it into the water and it fought the mermaid. The end of the battle was that the dog killed the mermaid and the mermaid killed the dog.

This version is the one which supplied the groundwork of Leyden's beautiful ballad 'The Mermaid'. Considerable changes must have been made by him upon the legend as it came to his hand. The dog, which in all the versions is the principal character, is left out; MacPhie's name is changed to Macphail; a magic ring (a thing unknown in Highland lore) is introduced; etc. Leyden fell in with the version of which he made use in his travels in the Highlands in 1801.[202]

MacPhie of Colonsay was in an island hunting, and in the course of his ramblings came to a hut, which he entered. He found no one in, and threw himself on a bed for a little rest. He was accompanied by a dog as large as a year-old calf. A dark object (*dùthra*) came to the door and the dog attacked it.[203] The Thing made a hideous screaming. When MacPhie saw the dog's hair beginning to smoke, he made his escape to the boat that had come with him to the island. Before long the dog came rushing after him like a mad beast, with a green flame issuing from its jaws.

MacPhie had prepared himself for this by loading his double-barrelled gun with two crooked sixpences.[204] He fired the two shots at the dog as it rushed to attack him, and killed it. The banshi it had fought with was left cruelly mauled, and she crawled or dragged herself to the shore, throwing rocks and stones out of her way. Her track is still known as *Sgrìob na Caillich* ('the Carlin's Furrow').[205] The boat left the shore before she reached it. She tried to bring it back by throwing a ball of thread after it, but without success. This was in Islay.

MacPhie of Colonsay, when he went hunting, was met in a particular glen by a man who accompanied him during the rest of the excursion. His companion had a brindled bitch (*galla riabhach*) to which MacPhie took a fancy. He asked the man to sell it. "I will not," said the man, "sell it to you or any one else, but as you have rested your eye upon it, I will give it to you for a while. It will have two pups, one like itself and one black. The brindled one you can keep, but the black one must be returned along with its mother. You will meet me at this same spot on such a day."

MacPhie took the brindled bitch home, and in due time the animal had two pups, both very pretty. When the time came MacPhie went back, according to promise, to the place appointed, but instead of taking the black pup, took the brindled one. The man said to him, "You have not brought the Black Dog; it would have been better for you if you had; but keep it. It will give you but one night's service; you will not gain much by the Black Dog."

After this the Black Dog began to wither; it grew large and tall but lank and lean. The servants thrashed and kicked it about, as if it never was likely to come to any good. MacPhie himself seemed to have an unaccountable regard for it, and was very angry when he saw it abused.

Two gentlemen came to see him with the intention of taking him with them to hunt in some neighbouring islet. On the morning of their intended expedition they rose early, and were getting the guns ready when the Black Dog rose and whined and fawned upon MacPhie. On reaching the boat the Black Dog was the first to spring on board.

The night became stormy, and the party were not able to get home that night. They passed the night in a cave. A noise as of walking was heard overhead, and a Hand appeared through the roof as if to grasp one of MacPhie's friends. All the dogs fled into the corners of the cave.

MacPhie himself had a Jew's harp (which is said to be the holiest kind of musical instrument), and when he played fast upon it the Hand drew back; when he played slow the Hand came nearer.[206]

At last he was almost exhausted. He called upon the Black Dog, and the Black Dog rose. "My Black Dog," said MacPhie, "if you cannot do it now, I am undone."

The Dog attacked the Hand, and made it disappear. It then rushed out and gave chase. It came back, spotted and speckled, with its hair stripped off. When the hunters got home on the following night the Dog disappeared.

MacPhie from Colonsay was cast ashore at Ormsaig, in the district of Brolas in Mull, clinging to a log of wood. He stayed for some time at Ormsaig, and was in the habit of going to the hill with his gun. A Fairy woman met him there, and from her he received the present of a young dog, which she said would yet be of service to him, but only for one day.

He had seventeen foster-brothers, and on his return home they came and asked him to go with them to shoot cormorants at the Paps of Jura. The dog, which had by this time grown very large and had never before given any indication of being useful, this day eagerly accompanied the hunters. MacPhie's wife had often urged him to kill the dog, but he had insisted on keeping it.

When Jura was reached, a servant was left in charge of the boats, and the company passed the night in a cave. As they reclined round the cave, each expressed a wish that his sweetheart were there. MacPhie, who was standing by the fire, said he had no such wish, it was better for his mistress to be at home.

Before long, seventeen women in green dresses entered the cave, and went over to the beds of heather where MacPhie's foster-brothers were, and MacPhie heard the crackling sound of breaking bones. The seventeen women then came up as if to attack himself. Afraid of their number, he called to the Black Dog: "If you assist me not now, I am a lost man."

The dog attacked the women, drove them out of the cave, and went off in pursuit. MacPhie fled to the boat, and he and the servant left in charge quitted the shore with all haste. When they were well out to sea, the servant said there was a fiery star coming after them. MacPhie said it was the Black Dog, and its heart had taken fire. He made ready, and when the dog overtook them, cut off its head.

THE CARLIN OF THE SPOTTED HILL (*CAILLEACH BEINNE BHRIC*)

The Fairy wife who owned the deer of Ben Breck is well known in the Highlands.[207] It is told of her that on one occasion, as she milked a hind, the animal became restive and gave her a kick. In return she struck the hind with her open palm and expressed a wish that the arrow of Donald the son of John (a noted hunter in his day) might come upon it. That very day the restive hind fell to Dòmhnall mac Iain's arrow.[208]

It is also told of this Elfin wife that while three hunters were passing the night in a bothy on Ben Breck the carlin wife came to the door and sought admittance. A dog that accompanied the hunters sprang up to attack her. She retreated and asked one of the men to tie up his dog. He refused. She asked him again, and a second time he refused. She asked a third time, and he replied he had nothing to tie it with. She pulled a hair out of her head and told him to tie his dog with that – it was strong enough to hold a four-masted ship at anchor.

He pretended to consent, and the hag, on trying again to enter, found the dog was not secured. She then went away, saying it was well for the hunter the dog had not been tied, and threatening to come again. It does not appear, however, that she ever came back.[209]

She was last seen about twenty years ago in Lochaber.[210] Age had told severely upon her. Instead of being 'broad and tall' she had become no bigger than a teapot! She wore a little grey plaid or shawl about her shoulders.

DONALD SON OF PATRICK

Donald the son of Patrick (*Dòmhnall mac Phàraig*) or, as others say, the son of Lachlan, was a *brocair* – that is, a foxhunter or destroyer of ground vermin – in Lorn. Persons following this profession were employed by the hill farmers, and had generally long tracts of country to travel over. Their companions were their gun, a pack of terriers, and perhaps a wiry deerhound. With these they led as lonely a life as anyone who had at all to descend to the strath and men's houses could do. Many a lonely night they watched by the fox's cairn in some remote corrie for an opportunity 'to put a hole in the red rogue's hide', and they often passed the night in bothies and shielings far from the haunts of men.

One day Donald the son of Patrick killed a roe and took it to a bothy in the hills. He kindled a fire with the flint of his gun, and having cut up the roe, roasted pieces of the flesh by a large fire. As he helped himself, he threw now and then a piece to his dogs.

Before long he observed, the night being moonlit, a large dark shadow coming about the door, and then a woman snatching at the pieces of flesh he threw to the dogs. She had one tooth as big as a distaff projecting from her upper gum. The dogs prevented her entering the hut, so that she got but little of the food. She asked Donald to leash up his dogs, and on his refusing, cried out, "This is poor hospitality for the night, Donald son of Patrick."

Donald answered, "It will be no better and no worse than that."

"You proved expert at raising a fire," she said.

"How do you know?" he asked.

"I was," she said, "on the top of the Cruach of Rannoch (a hill far away) the first click you gave to the flint, and this is poor hospitality for the night, Donald son of Patrick."[211]

"It will," he said, "be no better and no worse than that."

In a while again she said, "This is poor hospitality for the night, Donald son of Patrick."

"Take," he said, "as you are able to win."

She remained all night, and repeatedly asked him to leash up his dogs, which he refused to do. The dogs kept her at bay till she left.

Another version says that the foxhunter's name was Iain mac Phàraig, that he was accompanied by sixteen dogs, that his strange visitant disappeared at the cock-crowing, and that she then told she was *Cailleach Féith Chiarain* ('the Wife of Fe-Chiarain'). Some identify her with the Carlin of Ben Breck.[212]

THE WIFE OF BEN-Y-GHLOE

Donald and Big John (*Dòmhnall 's Iain Mòr*) were out deer-hunting on the lofty mountain of Ben-y-Ghloe, in Atholl in Perthshire, when a heavy snowstorm came on, and they lost their way.[213]

They came to a hut in a hollow and entered. The only one in was an old woman, the like of whom they said they had never seen. Her two arms were bare, of great length, and grizzled and sallow to look at. She neither asked them to come in nor go out, and being much in need of shelter, they went in and sat at the fire. There was a look in her eye that might 'terrify a coward', and she hummed a surly song the words of which were unintelligible to them. They asked for meat, and she set before them a fresh salmon trout, saying, "Little you thought I would give you your dinner today."

She also said she could do more, that it was she who clothed the hill with mist to make them come to her house. They stayed with her all night. She was very kind and hospitable. She told her name to them when leaving, that she was 'the wife of Ben-y-Ghloe'.[214]

They could not say whether she was *sìth* or *saoghalta* (Elfin or human), but they never visited her again.

FAIRY WOMEN AND DEER

On the lands of Scalasdal in Mull a deer was killed which turned out afterwards to be a woman. It is perhaps this belief in the metamorphosis of Fairy women and deer that was the origin of the tradition that Ossian's mother was a deer. In Skye it is said that after the poet's birth his mother could touch him but once with her tongue on the temple. On that corner (*air an oisinn sin*) a tuft of fur like that of a deer grew, hence the poet's name.[215]

An informant in the centre of Argyllshire said he did not hear Ossian's mother was a deer, but he had heard the poet was nurtured by a deer.

In the northern Hebrides a song is sometimes heard which Ossian is said to have composed to the deer. Several versions of the song will be found in Campbell's *Leabhar na Féinne*, p. 198.[216] According to the Skye tradition, the secret of Ossian's birth was not known till notice was taken of his never eating venison like the rest of the host. On being questioned he said, "When everyone picks his mother's shank bone, I will pick my own mother's slender shank bone."

O'CRONICERT'S FAIRY WIFE

The following was originally taken down in Gaelic from the recitation of Malcolm Sinclair, Balephuill, Tiree. The tale was known in Ireland, and the reputation of it still survives very extensively throughout the Highlands.[217]

There was a man in Ireland whose name was O'Cronicert, and his dwelling place was Corr-Water,[218] and he spent all he had on the great nobles of Ireland, bringing them for days' entertainment and for nights' entertainment till he had nothing left but an old tumbledown black house, and an old wife, and an old lame white horse.

The thought that came into his head was to go to the King of Ireland for assistance to see what he would give. He cut a cudgel of grey oak in the outskirt of the wood, and sat on the back of the old lame white horse, and set off at speed through wood and through moss and through rugged ground till he reached the King's house.

The custom was that a man should be a year and a day in the King's house before being asked the object of his journey. After being there a year and a day the King said, "O'Cronicert, it is not without a cause for your journey you have come here."

"It is not," said O'Cronicert. "It is for assistance I have come here. You know it was for yourself and your great nobles I spent my property entirely."

"You will wait," said the King, "till I bring in the children." And they were there, as men called them, Murdoch mac Brian and Duncan mac Brian and Torgill mac Brian and Brian Borr mac Cimi, and his sixteen foster-brothers with every one of them.[219]

"I will give," said Murdoch mac Brian, "a hundred milch cows to him."

"I will give," said Duncan mac Brian, "a hundred farrow cows to him, in case they should be in calf all in one year."

"I will give him," said Torgill mac Brian, "a hundred brood mares."

"I will give him," said Brian Borr mac Cimi, "a hundred sheep."

After O'Cronicert got this, he was not going away. The King told him to go away, that it was difficult to keep his herd separate from the King's own, and to take it away. He said to the King that he had one thing in view, and if he got it from the King, he would prefer it to all he had already got. "It is certain," said the King, "it must be some bad thing or other; you had better tell it, that I may let you away."

"It is," he said, "the lapdog that is out and in after the Queen that I wish for." And the King gave him permission to take it with him.

He took the lapdog, leapt on the back of the old lame white horse, and went off at speed, without one look at the herd, through wood and through moss and through rugged ground. After he had gone some distance through the wood, a roebuck leapt out of the wood, and the lapdog went after it, and in an instant they were out of sight.

Close upon the evening, he saw the lapdog coming and a royal stag before it, and the deer started up as a woman behind O'Cronicert, the handsomest that eye had ever seen from the beginning of the universe till the end of eternity. O'Cronicert caught her, and she asked him to let her go, and he said there would be no separation in life between them. "Well," said she, "before I go with you, you must come under three conditions to me."

And he promised to come under the conditions. "The first condition is that you will not go to ask the King of Ireland or his great nobles for a day's or a night's entertainment without telling me. The next condition is that you will not go to a change-house without putting it in my option; and the third thing, that you will never cast up to me that you found me an unwise animal (*beathach mì-chéillidh*) in the wood."

They reached the old tumbledown black house, and the wife he had left there was a faggot-bundle of bones in a pool of rain-drip in the middle of the floor. They cut grass in clefts and ledges of the rocks, and made a bed, and laid down.

O'Cronicert's wakening from sleep was the lowing of cattle and the bleating of sheep and the neighing of mares, while he himself was in a bed of gold on wheels of silver, going from end to end of the Tower of Castle Town, the finest eye had ever seen from the beginning of the universe till the end of eternity.[220] "It is no wonder," he said, "the like of this should happen to me, when I found you an unwise animal in the wood."

"As well as you broke that condition you will break the rest; rise, and drive the cattle away to pasture."

When he went out there was no number to the multitude of his flock, and on a day of the days after that, while looking at the flock, he thought he would go to ask the King of Ireland for a day and night's entertainment. He sat on the back of the old lame white horse, and went through wood and moss and rugged ground till he reached the King's house. The King said to him, "Do you at all intend, O'Cronicert, to take your flock with you? They are today so numerous that the herdsmen do not know them from my own."

"No, I have no need of them. I have a larger stock than yourself, and what has brought me is to ask yourself and nobles for a day and night's entertainment."

The King said to him, "We are ready, my good fellow, to go."

And there were there, as men called them, Murdoch mac Brian and Duncan mac Brian and Torgill mac Brian and Brian Borr mac Cimi, and his sixteen foster-brothers with every one of them. It was when they were near the house O'Cronicert remembered he had left without telling her. He told them to make their way slowly, and he himself would go before to tell they were coming. "You did not need, I knew very well that you went; let them come on, everything is ready."

When the King thought he had been seven days and seven nights drinking there, he said to Murdoch, his son, that it was time for them to be going. She then said to the King that it was high time for him – "You have been seven days and seven years in this place."

"If I am," said he, "I need not go back; there is not a man or living creature awaiting me."

Murdoch had a foster-brother whose name was Keyn the son of Loy (*Cian mac an Luaimh*), and he fell in love with O'Cronicert's wife. He pretended to be ill and remained behind the rest. She made a drink for him and went with it to him, but instead of taking the drink he laid hold of herself. She suddenly became a filly and gave him a kick and broke his leg. She took with her the tower of Castle Town as an armful on her shoulder and a light burden on her back, and left him in the old tumbledown black house, in a pool of rain-drip in the middle of the floor.

In the parting O'Cronicert went to the change-house to bid the party goodbye, and it was then Murdoch mac Brian remembered he had left his own foster-brother, Keyn the son of Loy, behind, and said there would be no separation in life between them, and he would go back for him. He found Keyn in the old tumbledown black house, in the middle of the floor, in a pool of rain-water, with his leg broken; and he said the earth would make a nest in his sole, and the sky a nest in his head, if he did not find a man who would cure Keyn's leg.

The rest of the tale consists principally of *true* tales, necessary to be told before Keyn will consent to stretch his leg for a salve to be applied to it. The King of Lochlin, or, according to others, the King of Ireland, who is bound not to allow anyone to remain in distress when he can relieve, tells a series of marvellous adventures that befell himself, all jointing into one another, before Keyn stretches his foot. The composition is of a kindred character with the *Arabian Nights' Entertainment*.[221]

The reader will observe that in this tale, as in that of 'MacPhie's Black Dog', the Fairy wife is first encountered in the shape of a deer, that (as is alleged of her race in other tales) she dislikes being reproached with not being of mortal race, and that she calls up in one night a palace of enchanting magnificence, in which time passes unobserved, and which in the end disappears, leaving matters worse than at the beginning.

THE *GRUAGACH BÀN*

In Campbell's *West Highland Tales* (ii. 410) will be found a tale also highly illustrative of this part of the superstition.[222] The hero of the tale, the Fair Long-Haired One, son of the King of Ireland, encounters a woman with a narrow green kirtle (the Fairy dress), and after playing cards with her, is placed under the following spell: "I place thee under enchantments and crosses, under the nine shackles of the roaming, wandering Fairy dame, that the most stunted and weakliest little calf take off your head, and your ears, and your livelihood, if you rest night or day; where you take your breakfast, that you will not take your dinner, and where you take your dinner, you will not take your supper, till you find out the place I am in, under the four red divisions of the world."

This rendering of the popular incantation differs somewhat from that given by Mr Campbell himself. The Gaelic version is the best the writer has been able to fall in with. There is a variation *an laogh maol carrach as miosa na ainm* . . . 'the polled scabbed calf that is worse than its name take off your head, etc.'[223]

There is also in the tale an Elfin old woman, 'the Carlin of the Red Stream', who is of the same class with the old wife of Ben Breck. She has a wonderful deer which she can restore to life if she can get any of its flesh as juice to taste, and her yells split the iron hoops the prudent Fin had put round his men's heads in anticipation of her outcries.[224]

DEER KILLED AT NIGHT

Eoghan Mòr Àird a' Chaoil, Big Hugh of Ardchyle in the east of the island of Mull, a noted deer-hunter in his day, killed a deer at Torness (*Tòrr an Eas*, 'the Eminence by the Ravine'), some seven miles away in Glenmore, and conveyed it home at night. He was accompanied by a man of the name of Sinclair. Sinclair asked him if the deer was heavy, and Big Hugh said he felt as if he had a house on his back.

Sinclair then stuck his penknife in the deer, and asked again if the burden felt heavy. Big Hugh said it was now so light he could hardly believe he had a burden on his back at all. The weight had been laid on by the Fairies.[225]

FAIRIES AND GOATS

In Breadalbane and the Highlands of Perthshire it is said the Fairies live on goats' milk.[226] A goat was taken home by a man in Strathfillan, in Perthshire, to be killed. In the evening a stranger dressed in green came to the door. He was asked to enter and rest himself. He said he could not, as he was in a hurry and on his way to Dunbuck (a celebrated Fairy haunt near Dunbarton), an urgent message having come for him.[227] He said that many a day that goat had kept him in milk. He then disappeared. He could be nothing but a Fairy.

FAIRIES AND COWS

A strong-minded headstrong woman in Hianish, Tiree, had a cow, the milk of which strangely failed. Suspecting that the cow was being milked by someone during the night, she sat up and watched. She saw a woman dressed in green coming noiselessly and milking the cow. She came behind and caught her. In explanation the Fairy woman said she had a child lying in the smallpox,[228] and as a favour asked to be allowed to milk the cow for one month till the child got better.[229] This was allowed, and when the month was out, the cow's milk became as plentiful as ever.

That the Fairies took away cows at night in order to milk them, and sent them back in the morning, was a belief in Craignish, Morvern, Tiree, Lochaber, and probably in the whole Highlands. When milk lost its virtue, and yielded neither cream, nor butter, nor cheese, the work was that of witches and suchlike diabolical agencies. When the mischief was done by the Fairies the whole milk disappeared.

FAIRY COWS

A strong man named Dugald Campbell was one night, about the end of last century, watching the cattle on the farm of Baile Phuill, in the west of Tiree.[230] A little red cow came among the herd and was attacked by the other cows. It fled and they followed. Dugald also set off in pursuit. Sometimes the little red cow seemed near, sometimes far away. At last it entered the face of a rock, and one of the other cows followed and was never again seen. The whole herd would have followed had not Dugald intercepted them.

A poor person's cow in Skye was by some act of oppression taken from him. That night the Fairies brought him another cow, remarkable only in having green water weeds upon it. This cow throve.

Some four generations ago cows came ashore on Nisibost beach, on the farm of Loscantire (*Losg an Tìr*) in Harris. The people got between them and the shore with such weapons as they could get, and kept them from returning to the sea again. Even handfuls of sand thrown between the cows and the shore kept them back. These sea-cows were in all respects like ordinary Highland cattle but were supposed to live under the sea on the seaweed called *meillich*.[231] They were called Fairy cows (*crodh sìth*), and the superiority of the Loscantire cattle was said to have originated from them. It is more probable the superiority of the stock was the origin of the Fairy cattle.

Cows of the same kind were also said to have come ashore in Bernera in Uist and at *Creag Mhòr Mhic Neacail*, 'MacNicol's Big Rock' on the farm of Scorrybreck in Skye.[232] In the latter place they were kept from returning by tossing earth between them and the sea. Earth from a burying-ground was thought to be the most effective in such cases. On the evening of the day on which the cows came ashore a voice was heard from the sea calling them by name. From the rhyme in which this was done we learn the cows were of different colours – one black, another brown, brindled, red, white-faced, etc.:

> Sisgein, Brisgein,
> Meangan, Meodhran,
> Bò dhubh, bò dhonn,
> Bò chrom riabhach,
> Sliochd na h-aona bhà maoile ruaidhe
> Nach d'fhàg buaile riamh 'na h-aonar,
> Bò chionnan thonn —
> É Bhlàrag!

"Droughty, Frisky, / Dodgy, Prancy, / Black cow, brown cow, / Brindled crook-cow, / Tribe of the single hornless red cow / That never left a fold by herself, / White-headed cow of the waves – / Hey Whiteface!"[233]

THE THIRSTY PLOUGHMAN

A ploughman while engaged at his work heard (or fancied he heard) a sound of churning, and said he wished his thirst 'was on the dairymaid'. In a short time after, a woman appeared and offered him a drink of buttermilk. Her green dress and sudden appearance made him refuse the offer, and she said that next year he would not need the drink. When the twelve months were nearly out the man died.

This version of the story is from Skye. A version from Uist is given in Campbell's *Tales of the West Highlands*, ii. 68. It varies merely in representing the thirsty man as a traveller who, in consequence of refusing from the Fairy the drink for which he had wished, was drowned at the next ferry.[234]

THE FAIRY CHURNING

A woman near Portree in Skye was coming home in the evening with her milk-pails from the cattle-fold, accompanied by a dog, which went trotting along before her. Suddenly the dog was observed to run to a green hillock, fall down on its knees, and hold its ear to the ground. The woman went up to see what the matter was, and on listening heard a woman inside the hillock churning milk and singing at her work. At the end of every verse there was a chorus or exclamation of *hŭ*. The song was learnt by the listener, and became known as 'Òran a' Chnuic' ('The Song of the Hillock'). The writer has not been able to fall in with a copy of it. The incident occurred three generations ago.[235]

MILK SPILT

There was a Fairy hillock near Dowart in Mull, close to the road which led from the cattle-fold to the village. If any milk was spilt by the dairymaids on their way home with the milk-pails, it was a common saying that the Fairies would get its benefit.

FAIRY MUSIC

Two children, a brother and sister, went on a moonlight winter's night to Kennavara Hill to look after a snare they had set for little birds in a hollow near a stream. The ground was covered with snow, and when the two had descended into the hollow, they heard most beautiful music coming from underground, close to where they were standing. In the extremity of terror both fled.

The boy went fastest, and never looked behind him. The girl was at first encumbered by her father's big shoes, which she had put on for the occasion, but, throwing them off, she reached home with a panting heart not long after her brother. The story was told by her when an old woman. She had never forgot the fright the Fairy music gave her in childhood.

In the Braes of Portree there is a hillock called *Sìthein Beinne Bòidhich* ('the Fairy Dwelling of the Pretty Hill'). A man passing near it in the evening heard from underground the most delightful music ever heard. He could not, however, tell the exact spot from which the sound emanated.[236]

Sounds of exquisite music, as if played by a piper marching at the head of a procession, used to be heard going underground from the Harp Hillock to the top of the Dùn of Caolas in the east end of Tiree. Many tunes of little poetical (whatever be their musical) merit said to have been learned from the Fairies are to be heard. One of these which the writer heard seemed to consist entirely of variations upon the word 'do-leedl'em'.[237]

MacCrimmon

The MacCrimmons were pipers to MacLeod of MacLeod, and the most celebrated musicians among the Scottish Gaël. The founder of the family is said to have been an Italian harper from Cremona who came with MacLeod to Dunvegan and took the surname from his native town.[238]

There are several versions of the story which ascribes the excellence of the MacCrimmons in music to the Fairies. The following two will suffice.

The first of the MacCrimmons, when a young lad, was sent to a music master to learn bagpipe playing. There was to be a competition of pipers at a wedding in the neighbourhood, and MacCrimmon asked from his master permission to attend, but was refused. He resolved to go notwithstanding, and set off alone, taking a short cut across the hills. On the way he fell in with a Fairy dwelling, which he entered. He found no person in but an old woman, who spoke kindly to him, saying she knew the object of his journey, and, on his promising to go half loss and gain with her, gave him a black chanter, which, placed in his pipes, would enable him to excel his master and every other performer. She added that she and her people were about to remove from their present dwelling, but if he came on a certain night (naming one near at hand) they would have time to give him some lessons.

To this one night's instruction and the magic chanter (which remained in the family as an heirloom) the MacCrimmons were indebted for their acknowledged superiority as pipers. Their fame will last 'while wind is blown into sheepskin'.[239]

Am Pìobaire Dall (the Blind Piper) was the first of the MacCrimmons who acquired fame as a piper. Two banshis found him sleeping in the open air, and one of them blinded one of his eyes. The second banshi asked that the other eye might be spared. It, however, was blinded also. The benevolent Fairy then suggested that some gift should be given that would enable the poor man to earn his living. On this the Fairy carlin gave MacCrimmon a brindled chanter, which, placed in the bagpipes, enabled the player to out-rival all pipers.[240] When the laird of Dungallon obtained the brindled chanter for his own piper Macintyre, the MacCrimmons never did well after. The chanter was last known to be at Callart.[241]

Mac an Sgialaiche pipers at Taymouth Castle were also said to have got their pipes from the Fairies.[242]

Fairy Dog (*Cù Sìth*)

A large black dog, passing by with a noiseless and gliding motion, was a common object of terror in the Hebrides on winter nights. The coil in the animal's tail was alone sufficiently alarming. Much of its shape depended, no doubt, on how his own hair hung over the eyes of the frightened spectator.

A man, coming across the links near Kennavara Hill in Tiree, came upon a large black dog resting on the side of a sandbank. On observing it he turned aside and took another road home. Next day he recovered courage and went to examine the spot. He found on the sand the marks of a dog's paw as large as the spread of his palm. He followed these huge footmarks till he lost them on the plain. The dog had taken no notice of him, and he felt assured from its size it could be no earthly hound.

On the north shore of Tiree there is a beach of more than a mile in length called *Cladach a' Chrògain*, well calculated to be the scene of strange terrors. The extensive plain (about 1,500 acres in extent) of which it forms the northern fringe is almost a dead level, and in instances of very high flood-tides, with north-west gales of wind, the sea has been known to overflow it and join the sea on the south side three miles away, dividing Tiree into two islands. The upper part of the beach consists of loose round stones, a little larger than a goose's egg, which make – when the tide is in, and under the influence of the restless surf – a hoarse rumbling sound, sufficiently calculated, with the accompaniment of strange scenery, to awaken the imagination.

An old woman, half a century ago, asserted that when a young girl she had heard on this beach the bark of the Fairy hound. Her father's house was at a place called Fidden, of which no trace now remains beyond the name of *Cachla nam Fidean* (the Fidden Gate) given to a spot where there is no gate. It was after nightfall, and she was playing out about the doors when she was suddenly startled by a loud sound like the baying of a dog, only much louder, from the other end of the shore. She remembered her father having come and taken hold of her hand and running with her to the house, for if the dog was heard to bark thrice it would overtake them. It made a noise like a horse galloping.[243]

At the foot of Heynish Hill, in the extreme south-west of Tiree, there is one of those small forts to be found in great numbers in the Hebrides (and said to have been intended, by fires lighted upon them, to give warning of the approach of the Danes), called Shiadar Fort. In former days a family resided, or was out at the summer shielings, near this fort. The byre in which the milch cows were kept was some distance from the dwelling-house, and two boys of the family slept there to take care of the cows. One night a voice came to the mother of the family that the two best calves in the byre were at the point of death, and as a proof of the warning, she would find the big yellow cow dead at the end of the house. This proved to be the case, and on reaching the byre the anxious woman found her two boys nearly frightened to death. They said they heard Fairy dogs trampling and baying on the top of the house.

There is a natural recess in the rocks of the shore at Baluaig in Tiree to which tradition has given the name of the Bed of the Fairy Dog. It is not far from Crogan beach, already mentioned as a place where the Fairy dog was heard, and opposite the *Gràdor*, a low-water rock over which the sea breaks with terrible violence in stormy weather. The loneliness and wildness of the spot might well cause it to be associated with tales of superstition.[244]

A shepherd in Lorn came to the top of a rock, and in a nest or lair below him he saw two pups about two months old with green backs and sides. They were larger and longer than his own dogs. He got afraid and fled before the old hound made her appearance. His dogs also were afraid. So the tradition says.

DOGS CHASING FAIRIES

Two men from Mull were engaged building a march dyke across the hills in Kintail. To be near their work, they took up their residence by themselves in a hut among the hills. One night, before retiring to rest, they heard a horrible screaming coming in the direction of the hut. They went out with sticks of firewood in their hands. Though they could see nothing, they knew something was approaching.

The shrieks came nearer and nearer, and at last a large dark object passed. A little dog, 'Dun-Foot' by name, which accompanied the men, gave chase. When it returned there was no hair on any part of it but on its ears, and no hair ever grew after but a sort of down.[245]

A number of young men were out at night on the moorlands of Cornaigbeg farm in Tiree, watching the cattle to keep them from wandering into the crop lands. They went to the moss about a mile away for peats, which at the time (some sixty years ago) were plentiful in Tiree, but becoming in some way alarmed they turned back on the road.[246] When returning they heard strange noises coming towards them, and a dog that accompanied them began to course round and round between them and the noise. At last the noise passed, with sounds like the trampling of a herd of sheep, and the dog went off in pursuit.

On its return its hair was found scraped off, as if by long sharp nails, and the whole skin was left bare and white, except where here and there it was torn and bloody. It died in a short time after.

A man in Mull was sent on a journey after nightfall, and about midnight, when crossing the hills from *Loch Tuath* (the North Loch) and *Loch Cumhan* (**Loch Cuän,** the Narrow Loch), saw a light in the face of a hillock.[247] He was accompanied by his dog, and before long he heard the noise of dogs fighting, mixed with sounds of lovely music. He made off as fast as he could, and on arriving at the house to which he had been sent was offered supper. He was unable to take any.

Before bed-time his dog came with every hair on its body pulled off. It smelt its master's clothes all over, lay down at his feet, and was dead in a few minutes.

A gentleman of the name of Evan Cameron (it does not appear where) on his way home across the hills was overtaken by nightfall and lost his way. He was accompanied by a greyhound and three terriers. He saw a light in a bothy or hut, used in summer when the cattle were at pasture among the hills but deserted during the greater part of the year. He made towards it, and on looking in at the door, saw a woman sitting by the fire, all wet and combing her hair. She looked towards him and said, *Nach d'thig thu 'n déidh do shùil, Eoghain?* "Will you not come after your eye, Evan?"

Cha d'thig an-dràst', he replied. "Not just now."

After some further conversation he was obliged to allow his dogs to attack the strange creature. He himself held on his way, and in a few hours reached home. The greyhound found its way home, but without any hair upon its body. None of the terriers was ever heard of more.[248]

This creature, haunting the pastures of the cattle, partakes more strongly of the character of the *glaistig*, afterwards to be described, than of the Fairy women.

FAIRIES AND HORSES

At Ruig at the foot of the Storr Rock in Skye, at the time it was occupied by small farmers (sixteen in number), all the horses on the farm, numbering as many as a hundred, were seen ridden by the Fairies – sitting with their faces to the tail – on Hallowmas night. The shoreline of the farm consists of frightful precipices, and the horses, as if very madness (*an cuthach dearg*) had taken possession of them, went off at their utmost speed towards the shore. Everyone thought they would be lost, but no harm arose after all from the stampede.

Near Killin in Perthshire a man entered a Fairy knowe and found inside a woman making porridge. The dish boiled so fiercely that a spark from the porridge flew and struck him in the eye. He saw the Fairies ever after with that eye. At the *Féill Fhaolain* (St Fillan Market) at Killin he saw them in great numbers riding about the market on white horses.[249] Meeting one whom he recognised he remarked: "What a number of you are here today!"

The Fairy asked which eye he saw 'the folk' with, and on being told put it out.[250]

A young wife had not, as was customary at that time, learned to spin and weave.

She tried in every way to learn, but try as she might she made no progress till one noon-day she wished some one would come to help her. She then saw a woman standing in the door, who said she would help her on condition that she would give her her first child when born, but if she could tell the shi-woman's name when she came to take away the child she would be free from her promise.

The young woman rashly agreed to this, and in a short time could make *clò* (cloth) better than anyone around her. After some time, however, she began to be afraid her visitor would return, and she went about eagerly listening to hear the name, when suddenly one day she saw an opening in a grassy hillock beside her, and on looking in saw the same woman standing inside, and heard another one calling to her. She went home joyously repeating the name all the way, and told her husband how she heard it.

When the *bean shìth* came again the mother of the child called out to her by the name she had heard, and invited her to come in, but she only said, "A blessing on the name, but banning on the mouth that taught you."[251] And she never afterwards darkened the door.

On another day the husband was with his wife in the fields working and looking about when they saw a great company of riders on white horses coming where they were, and as they came near one of the riders caught hold of her and took her away. Her husband did not know what to do. He went wandering about looking for her but never finding her, till one day – to his great wonderment – he saw a glimmer of light on the side of the hill.

He reached it and saw an opening. He put a pin in the side and went in, and saw a great company feasting and dancing, with his lost wife in the middle of the dancers. She saw him also, and began to sing loudly:

> *Take no food here Ialai o horro horro,*
> *Ask no drink here Ialai o horro hee.*[252]

No one took any notice of him. He got near her, and putting his arm around her, whisked her out of the circle of dancers. He took her home, but she became discontented, and was never the same being as she had been before.

At last it happened when they were again out together that the riders on white horses came their way. On parting with him this time she said, if at any time he wished her to come back, he was to throw her marriage dress, which had *craobh uaine* (i.e. green tracery) on the right shoulder, after her when he saw her passing in the company, and she would return home.

Thinking she did not belong to this world, he did nothing, and she passed and never returned to him.[253]

FAIRIES AND THE HAND-MILL

The invention of the hand-mill or quern, in the infancy of the arts, must have formed an era in the history of human progress. Whoever first found out a handy way of reducing the solid grain into meal bestowed an inestimable blessing on the human race. The instrument is still to be occasionally met with in the Hebrides, in houses not convenient to mill or market. It is usually worked by two women, like the mills in use in the East.

> *Paidhir de na cailean guagach*
> *Cur mun cuairt na brathainn-òran.*

"A pair of thick-set hussies / Winding round a quern."[254] It is a common practice with women to sing at their work – as indeed they did in the Highlands in olden times at most of their labours, such as reaping, sowing, milking.

Old Archibald, for half a century servant to the ministers of Tiree, would insist to his dying day that, coming home at night with a cart from the parish mill, he heard the hand-mill at work inside *na Cnocana Ruadha*, the 'Red Knolls' near the road.[255] He could put his foot on the very spot where he heard the noise. To ask him if he was naturally troubled with singing in the ears, or show any other symptom of unbelief, was resented as an affront, and neither minister nor elder, nor a whole synod, would persuade him there were no Fairies. He had heard them himself 'with his own ears'.

The man who first got the loan of a quern from the Fairies never sent it home. In revenge, the Elves took away all substance from his crop that year, and he derived no benefit from grain or fodder. His is the fate of many inventors. The benefit is not immediate. It seems the Elves had no power but over the year's crop.

FAIRIES AND OATMEAL

A man in Islay got a loan of oatmeal from the Fairies, and when returning it he (out of gratitude) left at the hole which led to the Fairy residence – and where he had been in the habit of getting and leaving such loans – more meal than he had borrowed. The Fairies are a just race; they take no more than their exact due; they were offended by more being offered, and never after gave that man a loan of meal.

A kind-hearted woman, the wife of a well-to-do farmer in the rugged district of Kingairloch, was one day visited by a young woman, a stranger to her, who asked for – and got – a loan of meal. In answer to the housewife's inquiries, the visitor said she came from the hillock above the house, on which a rowan-tree or mountain ash was growing. She wore an upper dress like a grey tippet. This event took place shortly before Beltane, when ploughing and other farm operations were being proceeded with. In a week after, Grey Tippet came back with the meal, but it was barleymeal, and she told the goodwife to bless this every time she took any of it. This direction was carefully attended to, and the meal never got less.

One day a scatterbrain member of the family asked if that cursed barleymeal was never to be done. The next time the mistress went to the chest there was no more barleymeal.

The house of one MacMillan, at the foot of Ben Iadain in Morvern – a high hill already mentioned for its reputation as a Fairy residence – was visited by a stranger, a woman, who asked for a loan of meal. She said she stayed in that same neighbourhood, that the men were away just now in Lismore, and that the meal would be sent back on their return.

This was done in due course, as promised, and MacMillan's wife was told never to allow anyone but herself to bend over the chest in which the meal was kept, and the meal would prove inexhaustible. At last, however, when Mrs MacMillan was ill, another opened the chest, and the meal disappeared.[256]

Hector, son of Ferchar, in the Ross of Mull, was an easygoing, kind-hearted man, a weaver by trade, who would give away the last of his goods to anyone he saw in distress. So weak was he in this respect that his wife did not care to trust him with anything – he was sure to give it away to the first poor man that came his way.

Having occasion to go to the summer pastures in the hill, and leave Hector alone in charge of the house, she measured out enough meal to last him for the fifteen days she expected to be away, and gave it to him in a skin bag. When returning, she met a beggar who said he had got a handful of meal from her husband, and Hector himself, when questioned, said he had given away sixteen such handfuls. Yet the bag was found to be quite full.

FAIRIES AND IRON

In Mull, a person encountered by a *bean shìth* was told by her that she was kept from doing him harm by the iron he had about him. The only iron he had was a ring round the point of his walking stick.

In the north of Ireland an iron poker, laid across the cradle, kept away the Fairies till the child was baptised.

The writer remembers well that, when a schoolboy, great confidence was put in a knife of which he was the envied possessor, and in a nail which another boy had, to protect us from a Fairy (*sìthche*) which was said to have made its appearance at a spot near which the road to school passed *an Crògan Sgithich eadar an t-Sròn Dubh 's Bealach nam Marbh* (the Hawthorn Bush between the Black Nose and the Pass of the Dead). This was in Appin, Argyllshire.[257]

The efficacy of iron in warding off Fairy attacks has already been illustrated.[258]

NAME OF THE DEITY

The Fairies were building a bridge across Loch Rannoch between Camaghouran and Innis Droighinn when a passer-by wished them God-speed. Instantly the work stopped, and was never resumed. (Cf. p. 34.)

FAIRY GIFTS

A smith, the poorest workman in his trade, from his inferior skill only got coarse work to do, and was known as *Gobhainn nan Soc* ('the Smith of Ploughshares'). He was, besides, the ugliest man and the rudest speaker. One day he fell asleep on a hillock, and three Fairy women, coming that way, left him each a *fàgail* (parting gift). After that he became the best workman, the best looking man and the best speaker in the place, and became known as *Gobhainn nan Sgial*, 'the Smith of Tales'.

A man, out hunting, fell asleep in a dangerous place, near the brink of a precipice. When he awoke a Fairy woman was sitting at his head, singing gently.

SPADE STRUCK BY THE FAIRY ARROW

Donald, who lived in Gortan Dubh in Lorn, was working in a drain with a pointed spade. One evening, having left the spade standing in the drain, he was startled by something striking it with a loud knock. He found the noise was made by the blow of a smooth, polished, flint-like stone. He put this in his pocket and took it home.

Some evenings after, 'Calum Clever' – already mentioned as frequently carried about by the Fairies – was shown the stone. He declared that it had been thrown by himself at the instigation of the Fairies, who wanted to take Donald himself. Donald of Gortan Dubh was a cooper, and was wanted to make a barrel for a cow the Elves had just killed. (Cf. 'Fairy Arrows, etc.', p. 14 above.)[259]

4

TUTELARY BEINGS

The Glaistig

The glaistig was a tutelary being in the shape of a little woman who was thin and grey (*tana glas*), with long yellow hair reaching to her heels, dressed in green, haunting certain sites or farms, and watching in some cases over the house, in others over the cattle. She is called *a' ghlaistig uaine* ('the green glaistig') from her wan looks and dress of green, the characteristic Fairy colour.[260]

She is said to have been at first a woman of honourable position, a former mistress of the house, who had been put under enchantments and now had a Fairy nature given her. She disliked dogs, and took fools and people of weak intellect under her particular charge. She was solitary in her habits, not more than one – unless when accompanied by her own young one – being found in the same haunt. Her strength was very great, much greater than that of any Fairy, and one yell of hers was sufficient to waken the echoes of distant hills. Strong men were said to have mastered her, but ordinarily people were afraid of meeting her. She might do them a mischief and leave them a token by which they would have cause to remember the encounter.

She made herself generally useful, but in many cases was only mischievous and troublesome. She seems in all cases to have had a special interest in the cows and the dairy, and to have resented any want of recognition of her services. A portion of milk was set apart for her every evening, in a hole for the purpose in some convenient stone, and unless this was done something was found amiss in the dairy next morning. Others left milk for her only when leaving the summer pastures for the season.

She was seldom seen, oftenest when anything was to happen to the house she followed. She might then be seen making her way in the evening up the slope to the castle, herding the cattle on the pastures, sunning herself on the top of a distant rock, or coming to the fold at dusk for her allowance of milk. Her cries, and the noise she made arranging the furniture, shouting after the cattle, or at the approach of joy or sorrow, were frequently heard.

In the south Highlands, the glaistig was represented as a little wan woman, stout and not tall, but very strong. In Skye, where most of her duties were assigned to a male deity, the *gruagach*, she was said to be very tall, 'a lath of a body' like a white reflection or shade.[261]

Her name is derived from *glas*, grey, wan, or pale-green, and *stig*, a sneaking or crouching object, probably in allusion to her invisibility, noiseless motions, or small size.[262] In the Highland Society's Dictionary she is called 'a she-devil, or hag, in the shape of a goat', and the definition is accepted by MacLeod and Dewar.[263] This, however, is a mistake. The shape of a goat, in the Highlands as elsewhere, has been assigned to the devil only, and there was nothing diabolical or of the nature of an evil spirit – seeking the perdition of mankind – ascribed to the poor glaistig. She occupied a middle position between the Fairies and mankind; she was not a *bean shìth* (Fairy woman) but one of human race who had a Fairy nature given to her.

The Fairies themselves are much nearer in character to the race of man than to that of devils. Of course all unearthly beings are to be avoided, but of all the beings with which fear or fancy has peopled the unseen world, the glaistig and her near relation the brownie are among the most harmless.

The house- or castle-haunting glaistig was also known by the names of *maighdeann sheòmbair* (i.e. chambermaid), *gruagach* (young woman, literally 'long-haired one'), and *gruagach sheòmbair* ('fille de chambre'), and her attachment was not to the family but to the site or stance (*làrach*). It was always the abodes of the affluent in which she resided, and she continued her occupancy after a change of tenants, and even after the building was deserted and had become a nesting place for wild birds.

In olden times there was a perpetuity of tenure enjoyed by large tenants, and it is not surprising that writers have fallen into the mistake of supposing the tutelary guardian of the house to be that of its tenants. The glaistig had sympathy with the tenant so far that she broke out into loud expressions of joy or sorrow, or made her appearance more frequently, when happiness or misfortune were to come upon the family; but her real attachment was to the building or site. Indeed, none of these beings of superstition were tutelary to the human race, or had anything about them of the character of the Genius or δαίμων. When the house was to be levelled, even though the family remained on the land and a new house (on another site) was built, the glaistig made a lamentable outcry, left, and was never afterwards seen or heard.

Her usual occupation consisted in 'putting things in order' at night, sweeping the floor, drawing chairs and tables about, and arranging the furniture. After the household had retired to rest she was heard at work in apartments that were locked and in which no human being could be. It was then known there would shortly be an arrival of strangers. In the morning the furniture was found in most cases untouched or disarranged. In other cases the house was found tidied up, and work which had been left for the glaistig – such as washing – was found finished.

She was fond of working with the spinning-wheel, and, according to some, it was to prevent her coming to the house and working with it on Sundays that old women were careful to take off the band every Saturday night.[264] She had a similar fondness for working with tradesmen's tools, and artisans were often much annoyed at hearing her working at night, and finding in the morning their tools spoiled or mislaid.

When the servants neglected their work or spoke disrespectfully of herself, or did anything to her favourites, she played pranks to punish them. She knocked down the water-stoups, disarranged the bedclothes, put dust in the meat, led the objects of her resentment a fool's chase about the house, or in the dark gave them a slap to be remembered on the side of the head. When happiness or misfortune, a marriage or a death, was to occur in the household, she was heard rejoicing or wailing long before the event occurred.

It was, however, to the being of this class that haunted the folds of the cattle that the name of glaistig is most commonly given. Her occupation consisted in a general superintendence of the sheep, cows and horses of the farm. When the family was at dinner, or the herdsman had fallen asleep and neglected his charge, she kept the cattle out of mischief; and, though not seen, was heard shouting after them and driving them to their proper pastures. In this respect she behaved like an old and careful herdsman. If the cows were not clean milked she punished the dairymaid by some unchancy prank. At night she kept the calves from the cows (a needful and useful occupation before the days of enclosures and plentiful farm accommodation) and its substance in the milk. In summer she accompanied the cattle to the hill pastures, and there had her portion of milk duly poured out for her in the evening in a stone near the fold. Unless this was done the calves were found next morning with the cows, the cream not risen from the milk, a cow was found dead, or some other mischance occurred.

She was not supposed ever to enter a house, but to stay in some ravine (*eas*) near a Fairy residence. She disliked dogs very much, and if a present of shoes or clothes were made to her, she was offended and left.[265] She is not generally spoken of as appearing in any shape but her own, but in some localities and tales is said to assume the shape of a horse as 'old grey mare', and even of a dog.

The glaistig resembled the Fairies in being invisible and in having a noiseless gliding motion; in her dislike of dogs; in affecting green in her dress; in being addicted to meddling at night with the spinning-wheel and tradesmen's tools; in her outcries being a premonition of coming events; in being kept away by steel; and in her ability to give skill in handicrafts to her favourites. The Fairies bestowed this skill on those who had the *ceàird-chomainn* or 'association craft', i.e. the assistance of the 'folk'.[266] The glaistig gave the choice of *ealdhain gun rath* ('ingenuity without advantage') or *rath gun ealdhain* ('advantage without ingenuity'). Those who chose the former proved clever workmen but never prospered, and those who chose the latter turned out stupid fellows who made fortunes.

She differed in being more akin to ordinary women than the true Fairy wife (*bean shìth*); she was stronger, and as it were more substantial; it was true woman's work which, as chambermaid or dairymaid, she performed. Though her 'bed' was near a Fairy dwelling, and she could command the services of the Elves, she did not engage in Fairy employments or recreations. The Fairies punished people of a discontented, grumbling disposition by taking away the substance of their goods. The glaistig was also offended at littleness and meanness of mind, but meanness of a different kind. Those who looked down on fools and people of weak intellect, or ill-treated them, she paid off by putting dust or soot in their meat. Akin to this was her punishment of neglect in servants.

In some parts of the Highlands the glaistig is called *glaisrig*. The name of her young one is *méilleachan*, a name probably derived from its bleating or whimpering after the old one. It is also called *isein*, a chicken, and *gocan*, a little plug.[267]

THE GLAISTIG AT GLENDUROR

The being which attached herself to the farmhouse of Achindarroch (*Acha nan Darach* 'the Field of Oaks') in Glenduror, Appin, Argyleshire, was variously known as the 'Glaistig' and as the 'Gruagach' of Glenduror. She attended to the cattle, and took particular charge of keeping the calves from the cows at night. She followed the house (not the family), and was alive not many years ago. A portion of milk was poured out for her every evening on a stone called *Clach na Glaistig* ('the Glaistig Stone'), and once this was neglected by a new tenant, the calves were found next morning with the cows.

Her face was described by those who professed to have seen her as being like a grey stone overgrown with lichens. A servant girl, going on a dark evening to draw water from a stream flowing past the house, was asked by her fellow-servants if she was not afraid of the glaistig. In her reply she spoke contemptuously of that being, and on her way to the stream received a slap on the cheek that twisted her head to one side. The following evening, going on the same errand, she got a slap on the other cheek that put her head right.

The same incident is related of the Sron-Charmaig glaistig.[268]

THE GLAISTIG AT SRON-CHARMAIG

The glaistig attached to this house on Loch Faochan-side in Lorn was known as *NicilleMhìcheil* (i.e. a woman of the surname of Carmichael), and was said to have been a former mistress of the house. She lived in a ravine called Eas Ronaich near the mansion, and, when any misfortune was about to befall the family, set up a loud wailing. On sunny days she was to be seen basking on the top of *Creag Ghrianach* (the 'Sunny Rock'), also in the neighbourhood.[269]

Before the old house was levelled and the present mansion was built, she set up an unusually loud wailing, and then left. Fully a year before the event she seemed greatly disturbed; her step up and down stairs, and the noise of chairs and tables being moved about, was frequently heard after people had gone to bed. At Glen Iuchair, a man who was in the evening convoyed across the glen by a grey sheep was firmly of opinion his strange convoy could have been no other than NicilleMhìcheil. No real sheep could have been so attentive to him.[270]

This attachment to particular individuals was also shown in the case of a poor old woman named *Mòr* (i.e. Sarah), resident on the farm. When Mor fell sick, the glaistig used to come to the window and wail loudly.

One evening at the cattle-fold, after the cows had been milked and before the herd and dairymaids had started home with the milk-pails, a woman dressed in green was seen coming and trying the udders of the cows as if to see whether they had been properly milked. The herd had his dog with him, and happened at the time to be sitting with it in his arms. The dog sprang from him and gave chase, and the woman fled like a bird. This was at a place called *Doire nan Each* ('the Wood of the Horses') several miles from the mansion, and the woman was believed to be NicilleMhìcheil.

AT INVERAWE HOUSE

This mansion-house has long been haunted by a glaistig known as *Maighdeann Inbhir Atha* ('the Maiden of Inverawe'), who was to be heard (at least till very recently) rustling (*srannail*) through the house. Stoups full of water, left in the house at night, were found in the morning upset by her, and chairs (left however neatly arranged) were turned round.

She is said to have been some former mistress of the house who had proved unfaithful and had been buried alive.[271]

AT DUNSTAFFNAGE CASTLE

This castle (*Dùn Sta'innis*), once a seat of the kings of Scotland, was haunted by a woman known as the *Sianag* (or Elle-maid) of Dunstaffnage. She broke into outcries of joy or sorrow (*mulad no aighear*) according as a happy or unfortunate event was to befall the inmates. A stranger who accompanied one of the servants to the castle and remained there that night had his bedclothes twice pulled off by her, and heard her all night walking through the room and in the adjoining passages. Her footsteps were heavy like those of a man.[272]

In Tiree

A *gruagach* haunted the 'Island House' (*Taigh an Eilein*, so called from being at first surrounded with water, the principal residence in the island) from time immemorial till within the present century.[273]

She was never called *glaistig* but *gruagach* and *gruagach mhara* ('sea-maid') by the islanders. Tradition represents her as a little woman with long yellow hair, but a sight of her was rarely obtained. She staid in the attics, and the doors of the rooms in which she was heard working were locked at the time.

She was heard putting the house in order when strangers were to come, however unexpected otherwise their arrival might be. She pounded the servants when they neglected their work.

At Sleat, Skye

The glaistig of the old Castle of Sleat (*Sléibhte*, 'Mountain Pastures'), once the residence of the Lords of the Isles, was often seen at dusk standing near the 'Gruagach Stone', where her allowance of milk was placed. Her appearance was that of a young woman with long hair.

In the Island of Coll

The glaistig that haunted old Breacacha Castle, the family seat of the MacLeans of Coll, was in size 'like a lump of a lassie' (*cnapach caileig*), and had white hair like a tuft of flax (*gibeag lìn*), as long as herself.[274]

She put the house in order when strangers were to come, and guests getting up through the night were led astray by her, so that they could not find their way back to bed again. Indeed she is even accused of maltreating strangers, while she let those she knew alone.

At Dunolly Castle

The glaistig of this castle made herself very useful. The family washing had only to be left for her at night and it was done before morning. Glimpses of her were seen in the evening on her way up to the castle. During the night she tidied up the house and swept the floors.

The fool (*amadan*) attached to the castle was taken under her special protection, and he often had his meat clean when others had it full of 'stour'.[275]

AT MEARNAIG CASTLE

This ancient ruin is on the summit of a conical rock, above a hundred feet high, close to the shore in Glen Sanda on the Kingairloch coast. About three or four hundred feet from it there is a beautiful and curious echo. A call of eight or nine syllables is distinctly repeated from the castle after the speaker has ceased. The only reminiscence of the castle's former tenants is the call usually given when rousing the echo, *Am bheil thu staigh, a mhaighdeann?* "Are you in, maiden?"

The maiden is the tutelary glaistig that haunted all such buildings.

IN STRATHGLASS

The gruagach or glaistig that haunted the house of *Mac 'ic Alastair* (the patronymic of the chiefs of Glengarry) in Strathglass was never seen, but was commonly heard at night putting dishes in order. She was given, like many of her sort in the old hospitable Highland days, to leading strangers astray through the house.[276]

A shepherd from Morvern came some forty years ago to the neighbourhood, and the glaistig took a great fancy to staying with him. He suffered a great deal of annoyance from her, though no ultimate loss. If he left his jacket on the paling (*staing*) to dry, it might be away the first time he went to look for it, but the next time he might – and ultimately would – find it all safe. At times cheese disappeared for a while from the 'amry'.[277] At night the shepherd felt the coverlet being hauled off, and heard the glaistig giggling with a short sort of laugh: "Hĭ, hĭ, hĭ."

He might leave their calves all night with the two cows he owned – the glaistig kept them from sucking. Before being reconciled to her he tried to keep her away by putting the New Testament above the door and round the walls, but without effect.

A party of young men came one evening to hear the mysterious noises. They saw and heard nothing till they were going away. The pot was then lifted off the fire without any visible agency and left on the floor, while they themselves had their eyes nearly knocked out at the door with 'tough clods from the marsh' (*pluic ruighinn réisg*).

AT LIANACHAN

A strong man of the name of Kennedy or MacCuaric,[278] residing at Lianachan in Lochaber, was coming home in the evening from setting a salmon net in the river when a glaistig met him on the bank of the stream. He locked his arms round her (*ghlas e làmhun*),[279] took her with him to the house, and would not let her go till she built for him a large barn of six couples (*sia suidheachun*). This she did in one night.

As her parting gift she left a blessing and a curse to the MacCuarics, that they should grow like rushes but wither like ferns. This proved to be the case – the man's family grew up tall and straight and handsome, but when they attained their full strength and growth they wasted prematurely away.[280]

The following is a close translation of a much fuller and slightly different version of the legend, headed 'Glaistig Lianachain' (see volume of Gaelic poems called *An Duanaire*, p. 123). It is a pity that the author of the piece, if known to the collector, is not given.[281]

Oidhche dh'an robh an Gille Dubh mór MacCuaraig a' dol dachaigh ás a' cheàrdaich, tachrar a' Ghlaistig air mar a bha e 'dol thar Cùrr aig Bial Àth' Chroisg. 'One night the big black lad MacCuaric was going home from the smithy;[282] the Glaistig met him as he was crossing *Curr* at the ford of Croisg:[283]

"Fàilt' ort, 'Ille Dhuibh mhóir," os ise,	*"Hail to thee, Big Black Lad," said she,*
"Am b' fheàirrd' thu cùlag?"	*"Would you be the better of a rider behind?"*
"B'eadh agus bialag," os esan,	*"Yes, and a rider before," said he,*
'S thug e togail bheag mhór oirre	*And he gave her a little big lift*
Far lom a' chladaich	*From the bare beach*
'S cheangail e i air a bhialaibh	*And tied her before him*
Gu tiarainte daingeann	*Safely and surely*
Air muin an eich sgiamhaich	*On the back of the mettlesome horse*
Le sian-chrios Fhaolain,	*With the wizard belt of Fillan,*[284]
'S bhóidich is bhriathraich e	*And he swore and asseverated*
Gu dian 's gu h-ascaoin	*Vehemently and stubbornly*
Nach leigeadh e slàn á 'ghlaic i	*He would not let her whole from his grasp*
Gus an nochdadh e 'n làthair dhaoin' i.	*Till he showed her before men.*
"Leig ás mi," os ise, "'s gheibh thu uam	*"Let me go," said she, "and I will give*
Mar chumhlaid 's mar dhochair	*For loss and damage*
Làn buaile de chrodh breac,	*A fold full of speckled cattle,*
Bailgionn, dubh, cean-fhionn,[285]	*White-bellied, black, white-headed,*
Buaidh cnuic agus còmhalach	*Success on hill and in company*[286]
Ort fhéin 's air do sheòrs' ad' dheaghaidh."	*To yourself and your sort after you."*
"S leam sin ad' ainneoin," os esan,	*"That is mine in spite of you," said he,*
"'S chan fhoghainn gu d' fhuasgladh."	*"And it suffices not to set you free."*
"Leig ás mi, 's fàgaidh mi d' fhonn	*"Let me go, and I will leave your land*

89

'San robh mi san tom a thàmh	Where in the knoll I stayed
Agus togaidh mi dhut a-nochd	And I will build thee tonight
Air an Fhoich ud thall	On yonder field[287]
Taigh mór daingeann dìge —	A big strong dyke house —
Taigh air nach drùidh teine,	A house fire will not pierce,
Uisge, no saighead, no iarann,	Water, nor arrow, nor iron,
'S a ghléidheas tu gu tioram seasgair	And will keep thee dry and comfortable
Gun fhiamh gun eagal, 's bidh sian ort	Without dread or fear, and charmed
O nimh, o cheathairn 's o shìth'chean."	Against poison, caterans and Fairies."

"Coimhlion do bhriathran," os esan,	"Fulfil your words," said he,
"Is gheibh thu do chead uam."	"And from me get your leave."

Leig ise sgal aiste le tùrsa	She gave a shriek with wailing
A chluinnt' thar sheachd beannan!	That was heard over seven hills!
Shaoilte gum b'e Còrn na Fiùbh	It seemed as if the Horn of Worth[288]
A bh' aig Fionn a thug fead ás;	Owned by Fionn had whistled;
'S cha robh sìthean no stùc	Every Fairy dwelling and beetling cliff
Nach do dhùisg 's nach d'ath-fhreagair,	Wakened and echoed,
'S chruinnich iad taobh thall an Lòin	And 'they' gathered round the Meadow[289]
'S iad ri h-òrdugh a' feitheamh.	Waiting her orders.

Chuir i 'n greim iad le cabhaig,	She set them to work speedily,
Gu farasta, rianail,	Calmly, orderly,
'S thug iad leacan is clachan	And they brought flags and stones
Á cladach Steall Chlianaig,	From the shore of Clianaig Waterfall,[290]
Gan sìneadh o làimh gu làimh.	Reaching them from hand to hand.

'N Tom Innis a' Chladaich	From the Knoll of Shore Islet[291]
Ghearradh cabair is taobhain	Were cut beams and rafters
Agus suidheachan fada	And supports long,
Réidh reamhar sa Chaor'naich'	Straight, and thick in the Rowan Wood[292]
'S ise gun aon tàmh ag ràdh:	While she herself unceasing said:

"Aon chlach air muin dà chloich	"One stone above two stones
'S dà chloich air muin aon chloich;	And two stones above one stone;
Bior, fòid, fair sgolb —	Fetch stake, clod, thatching-pin —
Gach fiodh sa choill	Every timber in the wood
Ach fiodhagach;	But mulberry;[293]

S mairg nach faigheadh mar a chuireadh	Alas for him who gets not as he sows
'S nach cuireadh mar a gheibheadh."	And sows not as he gets."
'S an glasadh an latha	And at the grey dawning
Bha fòid thar a dhruim	There was divot on the roof
Agus smùid deth!	And smoke from it!
Chum es' an coltar a's teine	He kept the coulter in the fire
G'a ghléidheadh o mhìostath	To keep him from mischance
On a b' eòl da mu chleasan	Since he knew the pranks
'S mu gheasan nan sìth'chean.	And enchantments of the Fairies.
Nuair bha 'n taigh a-nis ullamh	When the house was now finished
'S a dhìol i gach cumhlaid	And she had made up each loss
Gun d'fhuasgail e 'n t-suire[294]	He loosened the maid
'S cha d'fhuilig e dìobhail.	And suffered no harm.
Seach an uinneag mu 'chomhair	Going past the window in front
Gun do shìn i dha 'crodhan	She stretched him her crooked palm
A ghabhail leis soiridh —	To bid him farewell —
Ach gu 'thoirt don t-sìthean!	But (truly) to take him to the **shï-en**!
Ach shìn es' an coltar	But he stretched out the coulter
'S lean craiceann a bois' ris,	And the skin of her palm stuck to it,[295]
Is leum i air cloich ghlais	She sprang then on a grey stone
Na Foich' a thoirt binn air.	Of the Field to pronounce his doom.
Thug i mollachd an t-sluaigh air	She brought the curse of the 'people' on him
Is mollachd nan uamhlach,[296]	And the curse of the goblins,
'S ma chreidear na chualas	And if we may believe as we hear
Gun d'fhuair i a h-impidh:	She obtained her request:
"Fàs mar an luachair,	"Grow like rushes,
Crìonadh mar rainich,	Wither like fern,
Liathadh 'nur leanbain,	Turn grey in childhood,
Caochladh an treun ur neart;	Change in height of your strength;
Cha ghuidh mi gun mhac 'nur n-àite!	I ask not a son may not succeed!
S mis' a' ghlaistig bhròin	I am the sorrowing glaistig
Bha 'm Fearann an Lòin a thàmh,	That staid in the Land of the Meadow,[297]
Thog mi taigh mór air an Fhoich;	I built a big house on the Field

Cuiridh mi fuil mo chridhe 'mach	*Which caused a sore pain in my side;*
Air Sgùrr Finisgeig gu h-àrd,	*I will put out my heart's blood*
Air trì tomanan luachrach	*High on the Peak of Finisgeig,*
'S bidh iad ruadh gu Là 'Bhràth'."	*Which will be red for evermore."*[298]

'S leum i 'na lasair uaine	*And she leapt in a green flame*
Thar gualainn na Sgurra.'	*Over the shoulder of the Peak.'*

The last two lines suggest this to be a modern composition, and not a popular tradition. Supernatural beings do not go away in flames in Highland superstition.[299]

In Glenorchy

The glaistig living at the waterfall (*eas*) of Both Chaoil in Glenorchy came behind a man of the name of Campbell, riding home in the evening to the adjoining farmhouse, and, jumping up behind him, urged the horse to greater speed by crying now and then, *Huis! air each le dithis.* ("Hoosh! for a horse with two.") Campbell put back his hands and caught her. He was going to take her home, but she managed to get away, and left as her parting gift that no Campbell should ever be born alive (*nach gineadh 's nach goireadh Caimbeulach*) above Both Chaoil.[300]

The water before breaking over the fall is curiously split by an unseen pinnacle of the rock, and the glaistig is said to cause the appearance with her foot.

MacMillan of Knap

The *Cnap* (that is, the Lump) is opposite Shuna Island in Appin, and the name still remains in *Taigh a' Chnaip* ('the House of the Lump'), the Gaelic name of Balachulish Hotel on the road to Glencoe, well known to tourists. It was regarding the ownership of Knap by the MacMillans that the oral charter ran:

> *Còir Mhic Mhaoilein air a' Chnap*
> *Fhads a bhuaileas tonn air creig.*

"MacMillan's right to Knap / While wave strikes rock."[301]

A glaistig once came behind a kilted chief of this sept and caught him so that he could not struggle or escape. She asked him if he had ever been in greater straits – *Mhic Mhaoil a' Chnaip, an robh thu riamh an airc as mò?*

He said he had; she asked when; and he said, *Eadar féill is aimbeairt.* "Between plenty and penury."

On this she let go her hold. He said, *Bheir mise mo bhriathrun nach d'théid mis' air na sgàlun ciadna rithis.* "I give my word I will not be weighed on the same scales again" – and, stabbing her with his dirk, killed her.

The Glaistig at Craignish

A weaver, going home in the evening with a web (*còrn*) of cloth on his shoulder, was met by a glaistig at a stream. She caught hold of him and pummelled him (*làd i e*) all night in the stream with his own web of cloth, saying to all his remonstrances, *Figheadair fighe, 's fheàirrd' thu do nigheadh.* "Weaving weaver, you are the better of being washed."

On Garlios, Morvern

The lonely and rugged mountain tract known as the Garlios (*an Garbh-Shlios* 'the Rough Country Side'), extending along the coast of Morvern from the Sound of Mull to Kingairloch, a distance of about seven miles, was at one time haunted by a glaistig whose special employment was the herding (*buachailleachd*) of the sheep and cattle that roamed over its desert pastures. Tradition represents her as a small but very strong woman, taking refuge at night in a particular yew tree (*craobh iubhair*), which used to be pointed out, to protect herself from wild animals that prowled over the ground.

In a cave in the same locality lived a man known as *Dùghaill Buidhe na h-Uamh* ('Yellow Dougall of the Cave') who supported himself and wife by taking a sheep or goat, when he required it, from the neighbouring flocks. It was said of Dougall that when he wanted a sheep he drove a whole flock through a particular gap in the rocks, while his wife stood in waiting to catch the animal fixed upon. Once she allowed this sheep to pass, and Dougall asked her what she meant. "How," she said, "could I take the sheep of my own *goistidh* (godfather)?"

Dougall replied, "The man might be your godfather, but the sheep was not your godfather."

One day when about to row himself across to the opposite island of Lismore in his coracle (*curachan*), a woman came and asked for a passage. She took the bow oar, and before long cried out, *Hùg oirre, Dhùghaill.* ("A hearty pull, Dougall.")

Hùgan seo eil' oirre, bhean chòir! cried Dougall. "Another hearty pull then, honest woman!"[302]

Every now and then she repeated the same cry, and Dougall answered in the same way. He thought himself a good rower, and was ashamed to be beat by a woman. He never rowed so hard in his life. When the boat touched the Lismore shore, he for the first time turned round his head, and no woman was anywhere to be seen. She who was so strong and disappeared so mysteriously could only be the glaistig.

Other accounts say that the boatman was *Sealbhach Mac Shealbhaich* (Selvach Mac Selvach), a native of Lismore, and the woman against whom he pulled for the three miles from Kingairloch to Lismore, a glaistig that stayed in the ravine of *Alltaogain* in the latter place.[303] Her cry was *Hùg oirre, Shealbhaich* ("Pull away, Selvach"), and his answer, *Hùg oirre, ghalghad!* "Pull away, my lass!"[304]

AT ARDNADROCHIT, MULL

The glaistig that followed the house of Lamont at Ardnadrochit ('the Height of the Bridge') in Craignure parish, Mull, was commonly seen in the shape of a dog, and was said to carry a pup at the back of her head.[305]

A band came across from Lorn, the opposite mainland, to 'lift' Lamont's cattle. The glaistig, whose charge they were, drove them up the hill out of the way to a place called *Meall na Lìre*. Here, in a dell called *Glaic nan Gaisgeach* ('the Heroes' Hollow'), the freebooters were like to overtake her. On seeing this she struck the cows and converted them into grey stones, which are to be seen to this day.

On coming up, the plunderers stood at these stones, and one of them, tapping with his broadsword the stone near him, said he felt sure this was the bed of the white cow (*bò bhàn*). On his saying this, the tap of his sword split the stone in two. The glaistig broke her heart, and was afterwards taken by Lamont and buried in a small plot of ground near the Sound of Mull, where in those days the bodies of unbaptised children were put.

ON BAUGH, TIREE

The tenants of this farm once got the benefit of seven years' superintendence of their cattle from a glaistig. There is a place on the farm, still called 'the Glaistig's Bed', where she died by falling in the gap of a dyke. She was seldom seen, but was often heard. When driving the horses to pasture she called out, "Get along, get along, thou son of a mare! Betake thee to yonder white bank!" And when the herd-boy was at his dinner she was heard shouting to the cattle, "Horo va ho whish! Did ever any one hear of cattle without a herdsman but these?"

She prepared food for herself by dragging a bunch of eels (of which there is an overabundance in the small lochs on the farm) through the fireplace of a kiln used for preparing corn for the hand-mill. One night, when engaged at this work along with Gocan (i.e. 'a Perky Little Fellow', her son as is supposed), some one came behind and gave her a rap on the head with a stick. She and her son fled, and as they were going away, Gocan was overheard saying to his mother, "Your old grey pate has been rapped, but see that you have the bunch of eels."[306]

In appearance this glaistig is said to have been a thin sallow-looking little object, with ringletted yellow hair that reached down to her heels. She had short legs, and in person was not unlike a dwarf.

At Strontian

An incident similar to that of the bunch of eels is told of a glaistig that came at nights and worked in the smithy at Strontian. The smith was very much annoyed at the noises in the smithy at night, and at finding in the morning tools mislaid and the smithy in confusion. He resolved to stay up and find out the cause. He stood in the dark behind the door with the hammer on his shoulder ready to strike whatever should enter. The glaistig came to the door, accompanied by her bantling or *isein* (i.e. 'a young chicken').[307] The chicken thought he heard a noise, and said, "Something moving, little woman."

"Hold your tongue, wretch," she said. "It is only the mice."

At this point the smith struck the old one on the head with his hammer, and caught hold of the little one. On this the *isein* reproached his mother by saying, "Your old grey pate has got a punching; see now if it be the mice."

Before the smith let his captive go, the glaistig left a parting gift – that the son should succeed the father as smith in the place till the third generation. This proved to be the case, and the last was smith in Strontian some forty years ago.[308]

On Hianish, Tiree

About a hundred years ago one of the tenants of this farm, which adjoins Baugh, wondering what made his cows leave the fank (or enclosure) every night, resolved to watch. He built a small turf hut near the fold to pass the night in, and sat mending his *cuarain* (shoes or moccasins of untanned hides), when a woman came to the door. Suspicious of her being an earthly visitant, he stuck his awl in the door-post to keep her out.[309] She asked him to withdraw the awl and let her in, but he refused.

He asked her questions which much troubled him at the time. He was afraid of a conscription which was then impending, and he asked if he would have to go to the army. The glaistig said he would; that though he made a hole in the rock with his awl and hide himself in it, he would be found out and taken away, but if he succeeded in mounting a certain black horse before his pursuers came, he might bid them defiance; and he was to tell the wife who owned the white-faced yellow cow to let the produce of the cows home to their master.

The man was caught when jumping on the back of the black horse to run away from the conscription, and, after service abroad, came back to tell the tale.[310]

In Ulva

The glaistig of Ardnacallich, the residence of the MacQuarries of Ulva, used to be heard crying, "Ho-hò! Hò-ho! MacQuarrie's cattle are in the standing corn near the cave! The bald girl has slept! The bald girl has slept! Hò-hò, ho-hò."

The 'bald girl' was no doubt a reference to her own plentiful crop of hair.[311]

In Iona

The common of this island is called Staonnaig, and in former times the cattle of the east- and west-end people of the place came to it in summer for fourteen days alternately. In those days a glaistig stayed in a hole of the rocks in Staonnaig, and the people, when at the summer pastures (*àirigh*), poured milk every night in a stone for her.[312]

She once entered, on a very rainy day, a house where there was a woman of the name of Livingstone – alone and at dinner. She dried herself at the fire, holding her clothes spread out and turning round from side to side. Her clothes took fire, and she left as her parting gift that no fire can be kindled at dinner-time by a woman of the name of Livingstone.

In Ross, Mull

A herd in this district, whenever he moved the cattle at night, heard a voice shouting after him, *Mhic Iain Duibh Mhòir, tha bò ad' dhéidhinn!* "Son of Big Black John, there is a cow behind you!"

He shouted in reply, *Ma tha h-aon am' dhéidh, tha ceud romham!* "If there is one behind, there are a hundred before!"

Neil, who lived in Saorbheinn, went to fish on the rocks. Coming home in the dusk of the evening, a voice (that of the glaistig) followed him begging for a fish. *Thoir dhomh cudainn, a Nèill.* "Give me a cuddy fish, Neil."

This occurred every evening, and if he gave a fish the glaistig became more and more importunate, and one by one, to get rid of her solicitations, the fish were given away, the last at the door. In this way, Neil often returned empty-handed from the fishing.

Hector son of Ferchar lived at *Cnoc na Feannaig* ('Hoodie-Crow Hillock'), and, as was common in olden times, the door of his house was made of bunches of heather, tied together and made more wind-tight by straw stuffed between them. One cold frosty night he heard a scraping at the door, as if some animal were trying to pull out the straw. He rose and went out, and drove away an old white horse he found nibbling at the straw.

In a while he was disturbed again by the same noise. He went out, and, taking up a big stick, chased away the old white mare. When he almost overtook her the mare became a woman and, laughing at Hector, said: "I have played a trick upon you, Hector son of Ferchar."[313]

In Corry-na-Henchor

The glaistig of *Coire na Sheanchrach*, a valley on the Mull coast halfway up the sound between that island and the mainland, met a poor fisherman of the neighbourhood every evening when he came ashore from the fishing, and always got a fish for herself.[314]

One evening he caught nothing but lythe, and when the glaistig came and looked at them she said, "They are all lythe tonight, Murdoch."

Whatever offence was taken by her in consequence, she never came any more.

Mac Ian Year

This man *Mac Iain Ghiorr*, whose name is proverbial in the West Highlands for that of a master thief, was one of the MacIans of Ardnamurchan, a persecuted race.[315] He had a boat for going on his thieving expeditions, painted black on one side and white on the other, so that those who saw it passing would not recognise it on its return. Hence the proverb:

> *One side black and one side grey*
> *Like Mac Ian Year's boat.*[316]

Many tales are told of his skill in thieving, and the accomplishment is said to have been bestowed upon him by a glaistig.

He and his brother Ronald (his own name was Archibald) were out hunting, and having killed a roe, took it to a bothy and prepared it for supper. He threw himself on a bed of heather, and Ronald sat by the fire, roasting pieces of the roe on his dirk. A woman entered the hut, and made an effort now and then to snatch from him some of the roasted flesh. Ronald threatened unless she kept over her paw (*sall*) he would cut it off with his knife.[317] She appealed to Archibald: "Ho, Archibald, will you not put a stop to Ronald?"

"I will put a stop to him, poor creature," he said.

He told Ronald to allow the poor woman – that they had plenty, and perhaps she was hungry. When leaving, the glaistig asked him to the door, and it is supposed then bestowed upon him his wonderful gift of theft. He built a large byre when he had not a single 'hoof' to put in it, and before long it was amply stocked. He hired the glaistig to herd for him, and she was to be heard at night on the tops of the cliffs crying, "Ho hŏ, ho hŏ," to keep the cattle from wandering too near the verge.

Her wages were to be a pair of brogues of untanned leather, and when she got these, like the rest of her kind, she disappeared. She seems, however, only to have returned to her former haunts, which extended all over Ardnamurchan from the Point to Loch Sunart. When her former master died, she gave a shriek that roused the echoes of Ben Resipol (*Réiseapol*). The same night she was seen in the Coolin hills in Skye, and after that neither her shadow nor her colour (*a du no dath*) were anywhere seen.[318]

During her period of service with Mac Ian Year she made her appearance whenever he raised his standard, however far away she might be. Ronald's dog had a great aversion to her, and chased her whenever she came near. She was then to be heard calling out, *Hó, 'Lasbaig, nach caisg thu 'n cù?* "Ho, Archibald, will you not call off the dog?" – a common phrase in Ardnamurchan and the Small Isles to this day.

It is related of her that to escape from her attentions Mac Ian Year and his brother resolved to remove to the Outer Hebrides. They had barely kindled a fire in their new dwelling when the glaistig called down the chimney they had forgot the old harrow, but she had brought it, and that she was only on the top of the Coolin Hills when the first clink (*snag*) was given to the flint to kindle the fire.[319] There was nothing for it but to return to Ardnamurchan.

This story of glaistig officiousness is an appropriation of a floating tale that had its origin long previous to Mac Ian Year's time.[320]

AT ERRAY, MULL

At Erray (*an Eirbhe*, the outlying part of a farm) near Tobermory there was a glaistig that paid attention principally to the barn.[321] The herd slept in the byre, and he often heard trampling (*tartaraich*) in the adjoining barn. Whatever had been left there at night was found in the morning all in confusion, topsy-turvy (*turrach air tharrach*), one leg over the other (*cas mu seach*). All this was the glaistig's work.

The glaistig of Fernach on Loch Awe side conveyed persons of the name of Macintyre across a dangerous stream in the neighbourhood. She assumed the shape of a foal.[322]

THE GRUAGACH

Gruagach, i.e. long-haired one, from *gruag*, a wig, is a common Gaelic name for a maiden, a young woman. In old tales and poems, particularly those relating to the times of Murchard mac Brian, who was king of Ireland *c.* AD 1100, the term means a chief or some person of consequence, probably a young chief.[323] Thus in a conversation between that king and a young woman whose nine silk-clad brothers he had killed in battle she says:

> *Inghean oighre Bhaile Cliath —*
> *Cha cheilinn, a thriath nan lann;*
> *'S do ghruagach Eilein nan Eun*
> *Sann a rug mi féin mo chlann.*

"I am daughter of the heir of Dublin – / I would not hide it, lord of swords; / And to the gruagach of the Isle of Birds / I, in truth, bore my children."[324]

The name evidently refers to the length of the hair, which it seems to have been a custom in ancient times for men of rank and freemen to allow to grow long.[325]

In Argyllshire, and commonly in Gaelic, the name *gruagach* (applied to the tutelary being haunting farms and castles) means the same as *glaistig*, and the idea attached to it is that of a long-haired female, well-dressed like a gentlewoman, looking after the servants and particularly after the cattle. In parts of Skye, however, the fold-frequenting gruagach is a tall young man with long yellow hair in the attire of a gentleman of a bygone period, having a little switch (*slatag*) in his hand, and with a white breast as if he wore a frilled shirt. One of the writer's authorities described him as in appearance like a young man fashionably dressed in a long coat and knee-breeches, with a white breast like that of a frilled shirt and having a cane in his hand. He had even heard that the gruagach wore a beaver hat – a head-dress which in the Highlands was at one time believed to indicate a gentleman.

This gruagach was attentive to the herds and kept them from the rocks. He frequented certain places in the fields where the cattle were. A gruagach was to be found in every gentleman's fold (*buaile*), and, like the glaistig, milk had to be set apart for him every evening in a hollow in some particular stone called *clach na gruagaich* ('the gruagach stone') kept in the byres. Unless this was done no milk was got at next milking, or the cream would not rise to the surface of the milk. Some say milk was placed in the 'gruagach stone' only when going to and returning from the summer pastures and when passing with milk.

The gruagach amused himself by loosing the cattle in the byre at night, and making people get out of bed several times to tie them up. The cattle loosened did not fright or gore one another, as they did when they broke loose themselves or were untied by another person. On entering the byre, the gruagach was heard laughing and tittering in corners. Beyond this diversion he seems to have been ordinarily harmless. He sometimes walked alongside of people, but was never known to speak.

A woman was driving calves into the byre at Tota Roam in Scorrybreck. The gruagach amused himself inside by keeping them out. The woman, in a great rage, hastily cursed him. He gave her a slap on the cheek and killed her. All that night, however, he kept the fire alive for the woman that sat up watching the body.

Dr Johnson mentions a 'Greogaca' in Troda, an islet off the east coast of Skye.[326] This gruagach seems long since to have disappeared, but old people say the place is a very likely one for a being of the class to be in. At Holm (East Side) and Scorrybreck (near Portree) the stones where the libations were poured out may still be seen. In Braes the gruagach that followed the herds was a young woman with long hair; she was also known as the glaistig, and the rock in which her portion of milk was poured is in MacQueen's Big Rock – *Creagan na Glaistig an Creag Mhòr Mhic Cuinn*.[327]

BROWNIE

The term *brùnaidh*, signifying a supernatural being haunting the abodes of the affluent and doing work for the servants, seems to have made its way into the Highlands only in recent times and along with south country ideas. It is generally applied only to a big, corpulent, clumsy man, 'a fine fat fodgel wight', and in many districts has no other reference.[328] Its derivation is Teutonic and not Celtic, and brownies are mostly heard of in places to which (as in the south of Argyllshire) southern ideas have penetrated, or where (as in the Orkneys and Shetland) a Teutonic race is settled.

In the islet of Càra, on the west of Cantyre, the old house once belonging to the MacDonalds was haunted by a brownie that drank milk, made a terrific outcry when hurt, and disliked the Campbell race. In the old castle of Largie on the opposite coast of Cantyre,[329] which belonged to the same MacDonalds, there was also a brownie, supposed to be the same as the Càra one. Since the modern house was built Brownie has not been seen or heard.

In Càra he *is* still occasionally heard. It is not known exactly what he is like, no one having ever seen more than a glimpse of him. Before the arrival of strangers he put the house in order. He disliked anything dirty being left in the house for the night. Dirty bedclothes were put out by him before morning. Dogs had to be put outside at night, as he often killed those left in the house. He was much addicted to giving slaps in the dark to those who soiled the house; and there are some still alive who can testify to receiving a slap that left their faces black. He tumbled on the floor waterstoups left full overnight. A man was lifted out of bed by him and found himself 'bare naked', on awakening, at the fire.[330] A woman, going late in the evening for her cows, found Brownie had been before her, and tied them securely in the barn.

In one of the castles in the centre of Argyllshire, Brownie came to the bedside of a servant woman who had retired for the night, arranged the clothes and, pulling them above her, said: *Dèan cadal, a chreutair.* "Take your sleep, poor creature." He then went away.

In character Brownie was harmless, but he made mischief unless every place was left open at night. He was fed with warm milk by the dairymaid.

A native of the Shetland Isles writes me that Brownie was well known in that locality. He worked about the barn, and at night ground with the hand-mill for those to whom he was attached. He could grind a bag or two of grain in a night. He was once rewarded for his labours by a cloak and hood left for him at the mill. The articles were away in the morning, and Brownie never came back. Hence the byword, such a man is like Brownie –

> *When he got his cloak and hood,*
> *He did no more good.*

The same story is told of the 'Cauld Lad of Hilton' in the valley of the Wear in England (Keightley's *Fairy Mythology*, p. 296),[331] of brownies in the Scottish Lowlands (p. 358),[332] and of one in Strathspey (p. 395) who said, when he went away,

> *Brownie has got a coat and cap,*
> *Brownie will do no more work.*[333]

It also made its way to Tiree, and was there told as follows:

GUNNA

In olden times the tillage in Tiree was in common, the crop was raised here and there throughout the farm, and the herding was in consequence very difficult to do. In Baugh, or some farm in the west of the island (tradition is not uniform as to the locality), the cows were left in the pastures at night and were kept from the crops by some invisible herdsman. No one ever saw him or knew whence he came – nor, when he went away, whither he went.

A *taibhsear* or seer (i.e. one who had the second-sight or sight of seeing ghosts) remained up to see how the cattle were kept. He saw a man without clothes after them, and taking pity upon him made him a pair of trews (*triubhas*) and a pair of shoes. The trews went into the shoe, close-fitted to the legs, and was fastened with a buckle at the waist. When the ghostly herdsman put the trews on, he said (and his name then, for the first time, became known):

> *Triubhas air Gunna*
> *'S Gunna ris a' bhuachailleachd,*
> *'S na na mheal Gunna 'n triubhas*
> *Ma nì e tuille cuallaich.*

("Trews upon Gunna / Because Gunna does the herding, / But may Gunna never enjoy his trews / If he tends cattle any more.")[334]

When he said this he went away and was never more heard of.

Beings of this class seem to have had a great objection to presents of clothes. A pair of shoes made the glaistig at Unimore leave;[335] a cap, coat, and breeches the Phynnodderee in the isle of Man (Keightley, *Fairy Mythology*, p. 203);[336] in the Black Forest of Germany, a new coat drove away a nix, one of the little water-people with green teeth that came and worked with the people all day (*ibid.*, p. 261);[337] and Brownie, as already mentioned, in several places.

THE OLD MAN OF THE BARN

In the Highlands of Perthshire previous to the '45, each farm or village had its own *bodachan sabhail* ('little old man of the barn') who helped to thresh the corn, made up the straw into bundles, and saw that everything was kept in order. These brownies had the appearance of old men and were very wise. They worked always at night, and were never mischievous, but highly useful.

The *glaisein* (literally 'grey-headed man') of the isle of Man bears a strong resemblance to them. He was very strong, frequented farms, threshed corn, and went to the sheepfolds (Campbell's *West Highland Tales*, introduction, p. liii).[338]

CONCLUSION

These house-spirits have many relations – the Nis of Scandinavia, Kobold of Germany, Niägruisar of the Faroe Islands, and it is said the English Hobgoblin.[339] The Hinzelman that haunted Hudemühlen Castle in Lüneberg had 'curled yellow hair', also a characteristic of the glaistig; and the difference between one household tutelary being and another is only such as might be expected from differences of country and society.[340]

The oldest member of the family is the *lar familiaris* of the Romans. There is a noticeable resemblance between *lar*, the Roman household deity, and *làrach* (from *làr*, the ground), the Gaelic for the stance or site of a building, to which – and not to the tenants – the Celtic household apparition attached itself. The *lares* of the Romans were the departed spirits of ancestors, which were believed to watch over their dependents. The glaistig was held to have been a woman of honourable position, a former mistress of the house, the interests of the tenants of which she now attended to. Small waxen images of the *lares*, clothed with the skin of a dog, were placed in the hall. The glaistig had the Fairy aversion to dogs (an aversion which was reciprocal), but many of the actions ascribed to her savour strongly of her being in some way identical with the herdsman's dogs. This would very well explain the pouring of milk for her in the evening in the hollow of a stone. The glaistig of Ardnadrochit had the shape of a dog (see 'At Ardnadrochit, Mull', p. 94).

A satisfactory explanation of the origin of the superstition does not readily suggest itself. In days when men did not know what to believe in regarding the spirit world, and were ready to believe anything, a fancy may have arisen that it secures the welfare of a house (and adds to its dignity) to have a supernatural being attached to it and looking after its interests. It had its origin after the tribes among whom it is to be found ceased to be roving and unsettled barbarians.

In a large establishment a being of the kind was very useful. The master would not discredit its existence, as it helped to frighten idle and stupid servants into attending to their work and into clean and tidy habits. Shrewd servants would say as little against it when it served so well to screen their own knavery or faults, and to impose on a credulous and facile (or careless) master. Unless it was sometimes seen or heard, or some work was mysteriously done, the delusion – either of master or servant – could not be long continued; and, when men have little else to do, there are many who take a pleasure in imposing on their more simple-minded fellows, and are quite ready, as much from sport as interest, to carry on a delusion of the kind.

Besides, when the mind is nervously anxious, engrossed with the fear of a coming misfortune or the hope of a coming joy, it is apt to listen to the whispers of fancy and the confidently-told tales of others. When it broods alone, during the sleepless night, over the future, it is not surprising if the imagination converts the weird sounds of night – the melancholy moaning of the wind, its fitful gusts in the woods and round the house, the roar of the waterfall, the sound of the surf-beaten shore, and many noises of which the origin is at the time unknown and unsought – into the omens of that which makes itself sleepless, or hears in them the song of the house-spirit, prescient of the coming event. It must also be remembered that there are people who will see and hear anything if their story is believingly listened to, and they are themselves at the time objects of interest.

Pennant (*Tour*, p. 330) says Brownie was stout and blooming, had fine long flowing hair, and went about with a switch in his hand. He cleaned the house, helped to churn, threshed the corn, and belaboured those who pretended to make a jest of him. He says (p. 331) the gruagach was in form like the brownie, and was worshipped by libations of milk; and 'milkmaids still retain the custom of pouring some on certain stones, that bear his name'. He is thought, it is added, to be an emblem of Apollo and identical with χρυσοκόμος.[341]

Mr Campbell (*Tales of the West Highlands*, I. xciii) supposes the gruagach of superstition to be a druid fallen from his high estate, and living on milk left for him by those whose priest he had once been. In another place (ii. 101) he supposes him to be a half-tamed savage, hanging about the house, with his long hair and skin clothing.[342]

These explanations are not satisfactory. The character, dress and actions ascribed to the gruagach and his congeners are incongruous to the idea of druid, heathen deity, or savage wild or reclaimed.

5

THE URISK, THE BLUE MEN AND THE MERMAID

THE URISK

The urisk was a large lubberly supernatural, of solitary habits and harmless character, that haunted lonely and mountainous places. Some identify him with Brownie, but he differs from the fraternity of tutelary beings in having his dwelling not in the houses or haunts of men but in solitudes and remote localities. There were male and female urisks, and the race was said to be the offspring of unions between mortals and Fairies – that is, of the *leannan sìth*.

The urisk was usually seen in the evening, big and grey (*mòr glas*), sitting on the top of a rock and peering at the intruders on its solitude. The wayfarer whose path led along the mountain-side whose shattered rocks are loosely sprinkled, or along some desert moor, and who hurried for the fast approaching nightfall, saw the urisk sitting motionless on the top of a rock and gazing at him, or slowly moving out of his way. It spoke to some people, and is even said to have thrashed them, but usually it did not meddle with the passer-by. On the contrary, it at times gave a safe convoy to those who were belated.

In the Highlands of Breadalbane the urisk was said, in summer-time, to stay in remote corries and on the highest part of certain hills. In winter-time it came down to the strath and entered certain houses at night to warm itself. It was then it did work for the farmer, grinding, thrashing, etc. Its presence was a sign of prosperity; it was said to leave comfort behind it. Like Brownie, it liked milk and good food, and a present of clothes drove it away.[343]

An urisk haunting *Beinn Dòbhrain* (a hill beloved of the Celtic muse, on the confines of Argyllshire and Perthshire) stayed in summer-time near the top of the hill, and in winter came down to the straths. A waterfall near the village of Clifton at Tyndrum, where it stayed on these occasions, is still called *Eas na h-Ùruisg* ('the Urisk's Cascade'). It was encountered by St Fillan, who had his abode in a neighbouring strath, and banished to Rome.

The urisk of Ben Loy (*Beinn Laoigh* the 'Calf's Hill'), also on the confines of these counties, came down in winter from his lofty haunts to the farm of Sococh in Glen Orchy, which lies at the base of the mountain. It entered the house at night by the chimney, and it is related that on one occasion the bar from which the chimney chain was suspended – and on which the urisk laid its weight in descending – being taken away, and not meeting its foot as usual, the poor supernatural got a bad fall. It was fond of staying in a cleft at Moraig waterfall, and its labours in keeping the waters from falling too fast over the rock might be seen by anyone. A stone on which it sat with its feet dangling over the fall is called *Clach na h-Ùruisg* ('the Urisk Stone'). It sometimes watched the herds of Sococh farm.[344]

A man passing through Srath Dubh-Uisg (near Loch Sloy at the head of Loch Lomond) on a keen frosty night heard an urisk on one side of the glen calling out: *Reoth, reoth, reoth.* "Frost, frost, frost."

This was answered by another urisk calling from the other side of the glen: *Ceige-reoth, ceige-reoth, ceige-reoth.* "Kick-frost, kick-frost, kick-frost."

The man, on hearing this, said, "Whether I wait or not for frost, I will never while I live wait for kick-frost." And he ran at his utmost speed till he was out of the glen.[345]

The urisk of the 'Yellow Waterfall' in Gleann Màili, in the south of Inverness-shire, used to come late every evening to a woman of the name of Mary, and sat watching her plying her distaff without saying a word.[346] A man who wished to get a sight of the urisk put on Mary's clothes and sat in her place, twirling the distaff as best he could. The urisk came to the door but would not enter. It said:

> *I see your eye, I see your nose,*
> *I see your great broad beard,*
> *And though you will work the distaff*
> *I know you are a man.*

Graham (*Highlands of Perthshire*, p. 19, quoted by Sir Walter Scott in his notes to *The Lady of the Lake*) says the urisk 'could be gained over by kind attentions, to perform the drudgery of the farm; and it was believed that many families in the Highlands had one of the order attached to it'. He adds that the famous *Coire nan Ùruisgean* derives its name from the solemn stated meetings of all the urisks in Scotland being held there.[347]

The urisk, like the brownie of England, had great simplicity of character, and many tricks were played upon it in consequence. A farmer in Strathglass got it to undergo a painful operation that it might become fat and sleek like the farmer's own geldings. The weather at the time being frosty, it made a considerable outcry for some time after.

From its haunting lonely places, other appearances must often have been confounded with it. In Strathfillan (commonly called simply *Strathaibh*, the Straths) in the Highlands of Perthshire, not many years ago a number of boys saw what was popularly said to be an urisk.[348] In the hill, when the sun was setting, something like a human being was seen sitting on the top of a large boulder-stone and growing bigger and bigger till they fled. There is no difficulty in connecting the appearance with the circumstance that some sheep disappeared that year unaccountably from the hill, and a quantity of grain from the barn of the farm.

In the Hebrides there is very little mention of the urisk at all. In Tiree the only trace of it is in the name of a hollow, *Slochd an Aoirisg*, through which the public road passes near the south shore.[349] The belief that it assisted the farmer was not common anywhere, and all over the Highlands the word ordinarily conveys no other idea than that which has been well defined as 'a being supposed to haunt lonely and sequestered places, as mountain rivers and waterfalls'.[350]

THE BLUE MEN (*NA FIR GHORMA*)

The fallen angels were driven out of Paradise in three divisions. One became the Fairies on the land, one the blue men in the sea, and one the nimble men (*fir chlis*), i.e. the northern streamers or merry dancers in the sky.

This explanation belongs to the north Hebrides, and was heard by the writer in Skye. In Argyllshire the blue men are unknown, and there is no mention of the merry dancers being congeners of the Fairies. The person from whom the information was got was very positive he had himself seen one of the blue men. A blue-coloured man with a long grey face (*aodann fada glas*), and floating from the waist out of the water, followed the boat in which he was for a long time, and was occasionally so near that the observer might have put his hand upon him.

The channel between Lewis and the Shant Isles (*na h-Eileinean Siant'*, 'the Charmed Islands') is called *Sruth nam Fear Gorma* ('the Stream of the Blue Men'). A ship passing through it came upon a blue-coloured man sleeping on the waters. He was taken on board, and being thought of mortal race, strong twine was coiled round and round him from his feet to his shoulders till it seemed impossible for him to struggle or move foot or arm.

The ship had not gone far when two men were observed coming after it on the waters. One of them was heard to say, "Duncan will be one man," to which the other replied, "Farquhar will be two."[351]

On hearing this, the man who had been so securely tied sprang to his feet, broke his bonds like spider threads, jumped overboard, and made off with the two friends, who had been coming to his rescue.

THE STREAMERS

When the streamers (*na fir chlis*, literally the 'active' or 'quickly-moving' men) have 'a battle royal' (as they often have), the blood of their wounded falling to the earth and becoming congealed forms the coloured stones called 'blood stones', known in the Hebrides also by the name of *fuil siochaire*, Elf's blood.[352]

THE MERMAID

The mermaid (*muir-òigh, maighdeann mhara*) of the Scottish Highlands was the same as in the rest of the kingdom – a sea-creature, half fish half woman, with long dishevelled hair, which she sits on the rocks by the shore to comb at night. She has been known to put off the fishy covering of her lower limbs. Any one who finds it can by hiding it detain her from ever returning to the sea again. There is a common story in the Highlands, as also in Ireland, that a person so detained her for years, married her, and had a family by her. One of the family fell in with the covering, and telling his mother of the pretty thing he had found, she recovered possession of it and escaped to the sea.[353]

She pursues ships and is dangerous. Sailors throw empty barrels overboard, and while she spends her time examining these they make their escape.

A man in Skye (*MacMhannain*) caught a mermaid and kept her for a year. She gave him much curious information. When parting he asked her what virtue or evil there was in egg-water (i.e. water in which eggs had been boiled). She said, "If I tell you that, you will have a tale to tell," and disappeared.[354]

A native of *Eilein Anabaich* (the 'Unripe Island'), a village in North Harris, caught a mermaid on a rock, and to procure her release she granted him his three wishes.[355] He became a skilful herb-doctor who could cure the king's evil and other diseases ordinarily incurable, and a prophet who could foretell (particularly to women) whatever was to befall them; and he obtained a remarkably fine voice. This latter gift he had only in his own estimation; when he sang, others did not think his voice fine or even tolerable.

6

THE WATER-HORSE

THE WATER-HORSE (*EACH UISGE*)

The belief in the existence of the water-horse is now in the Highlands generally a thing of the past, but in olden times almost every lonely freshwater lake was tenanted by one – sometimes by several – of these animals.[356]

In shape and colour it resembled an ordinary horse, and was often mistaken for one. It was seen passing from one lake to another, mixing with the farmers' horses in the adjoining pastures, and waylaid belated travellers who passed near its haunts. It was highly dangerous to touch or mount it. Those whom it decoyed into doing so were taken away to the loch in which it had its haunt, and there devoured. It was said to make its approaches also in other guises – as a young man, a boy, a ring, and even a tuft of wool (*ribeag clòimhe*); and any woman upon whom it set its mark was certain at last to become its victim.

The cow-shackle round its neck, or a cap on its head, completely subdued it, and as long as either of these was kept on it, it could be as safely employed in farm labour as any other horse. In Skye it was said to have a sharp bill (*gob biorach*), or, as others describe it, a narrow brown slippery snout. Accounts are uniform that it had a long flowing tail and mane.

In colour it was sometimes grey, sometimes black, and sometimes black with a white spot on its forehead. This variation arose, some say, from the water-horse being of any colour like other horses, and others say from its having the power of changing its colour as well as its shape.

When it came in the shape of a man, it was detected by its horse-hoofs and by the green water weeds or sand in its hair. It was then very amorous, but the end of those who were unfortunate enough to encounter it was to be taken to the loch and devoured.

However much benefit the farmer might at first derive from securing one with the cap or cow-shackle, he was ultimately involved by it in ruinous loss.

The following tales will illustrate the character of the superstition better than a lengthened dissertation.

FARMERS AND WATER-HORSES

Stories to the following effect are common in Mull and the neighbourhood. A strange horse which cannot be driven away is seen all winter among the rest of the farm horses. (In olden times horses were little housed during winter; the stable door was left open, and the horses, after eating the little straw allowed them, went out to pick up what they could.) When spring work comes on the strange horse is caught like the rest and made to work. Perhaps for greater security the cow-shackle is put round its neck. It proves as docile and easily managed as any horse could be. It is the best horse the farmer has, and is fat and sleek when the rest are lean and ragged.

It works thus all spring, and in summer is employed to take home peats from the moor. It is placed foremost in a string of three or seven horses which have creels on their backs, in ancient fashion, and are tied each to the tail of the horse before it. The farmer rides the foremost of the team.

On the way it becomes restive and unmanageable, and sets off at full speed, followed by the rest, towards the loch. Observing that the shackle has slipped off, the man, in passing through a narrow gateway, plants a foot against each pillar and throws himself off its back – or he tumbles on the sands of the shore, and jumping up, cuts the halter of the hindmost horse. Those that remain tied are dragged into the loch, and next day their entrails or livers come ashore.

The most celebrated tale of this class was that of the son of the tenant of Aros, in Mull.

MAC FIR ÀROIS

The heir of Aros, a young man of great personal activity – and, it is said, of dissolute manners – having an opinion of himself that there was no horse he could not ride, was taken by a water-horse into Loch Frisa, a small lake about a mile in length in the north-west of Mull, and devoured. This occurred between his espousal and marriage, and the lament composed by his intended bride is still and deservedly a popular song in Mull.[357] There seems to be this much truth in the story, that the young man was dragged into Loch Frisa by a mare which he was attempting to subdue, and drowned. It would appear from the song that his body was recovered. The popular details of the incident vary considerably, and are of interest as illustrative of the growth of tales of superstition.

One account has it that a remarkably handsome grey mare came among horses belonging to the tenant of Aros pasturing on the rushes at the end of Loch Frisa. One day his son haltered and mounted it. The grey stood quite quietly till it got the young man on its back. It then rushed into the loch.

Another account says the young man found a mare in the hills, which he took to be one of those belonging to his father. He caught it with the intention of riding home, but the mare took out to Loch Frisa, and he was there devoured by water-horses.

A third account says the water-horse was kept all winter with the cow-shackle about its neck, and remained so quiet and steady that at last the shackle was neglected. The son of the tenant rode it one day to the peat-moss, three other horses following behind in usual form, when it suddenly rushed away to the lake, and nothing was ever seen of the youth or the horses but the livers.

A fourth account says: in spring a band of men went to the hill to catch a young horse wanted for harrowing or to send to market. They were unable to catch it, and next day Aros's son himself went with them. He caught what he supposed to be the horse wanted and jumped on its back. The horse rushed at full speed towards the loch, and the young man found he could not throw himself off. The horse's liver came ashore next day, the animal, it is supposed, having been killed by the other water-horses tenanting the lake when they felt the smell of a man off it.

There is still another account, that *Mac Fir Àrois* was twice taken away by the water-horse. The first time, he managed to put a foot on each side of a gate in passing through, and allowed the horse to pass on. The second time, a cap which hitherto had kept the horse was forgotten. In the terrible career of the steed to the loch, the young man clasped his arms round its neck, and could not unclasp them. His lungs came ashore next day.

THE TALKING HORSE AT CRU-LOCH

This is a lonely little lake above Ardachyle (*Àird a' Chaoil*, 'the Height of the Sound') in the north-east of Mull.[358] A person passing it late at night on his way home saw a horse with a saddle on, quietly feeding at the loch-side. He went towards it with the intention of riding it home, but in time he observed green-water herbs (*liaranaich*) about its feet and refrained from touching it. He walked on, and before long was overtaken by a stranger who said that unless he (the water-horse, who was also the speaker) had been friendly and a well-wisher, he would have taken him to the loch. Among other supernatural information it told the man the day of his death.

ISLAND OF COLL

At noontide, while the cattle were standing in the loch, the herdsman near Loch Annla was visited by a person in whose head he observed *rathum*, that is, water weeds. When going away the stranger jumped into the loch and disappeared without doing any harm. People used to hear strange noises about that loch, no doubt caused by the water-horse which was the herdsman's visitor.[359]

THE NINE CHILDREN AT SUNART

A number of children went on a Sunday to amuse themselves in the neighbourhood of *Loch na Dunach* ('the Loch of Disaster') in this district. They fell in with a horse, caught it, and in their thoughtless sport mounted it. Its back got longer till they were all mounted – except one, who had a Bible in his pocket. He touched the horse with his finger, and had to cut it off to save himself. The horse rushed into the lake, and the children, nine in number, were never more seen. The liver of one of them came ashore next day.

This tale is widely spread, and is obviously a pious fraud to keep children from wandering on Sundays to play in lonely places, and from meddling with any horse they may find.

KILLING THE RAASAY WATER-HORSE

Loch na Mnà, the 'Woman's Loch' near Dùn Can, the highest hill in this island, derives its name from having been the scene of the abduction of a woman by the water-horse that haunted it. *An Gobha Mòr*, the 'Big Smith' who lived in the neighbourhood, resolved to kill the horse, and by his success he earned himself the title of *Alastair na Béiste* ('Alexander of the Monster').

He built a hut close by with an opening like the syver of a drain, leading towards the loch. When he got the wind favourable, he killed and roasted a wether-sheep in the hut. The wind blew the savoury smell towards the loch, and the water-horse, attracted by it, made its way into the hut by the entrance left for it. The smith had his irons ready in the fire, and rushing with them at the water-horse killed it. On examination the monster proved to be merely grey turves (*pluic ghlas*), or, as others say, a soft mass (*sgling*) like jellyfish (*muir-tiachd*).[360]

THE WATER-HORSE AT LOCH CUAICH

Some thirty years ago, a small islet in this lake, of about an half an acre in extent, was tenanted by a strange specimen of the Highland freebooter, named MacPhie. He was a deserter from the army who at first took refuge in a cave in the neighbourhood. He took away by force a girl of twelve years of age, and, coming next day to her parents, said if it would give any satisfaction he would marry her, but refusing to part with her. A sort of ceremony of marriage was gone through, but MacPhie seems for several years to have looked upon the girl merely as his daughter. Her first child was born when she was eighteen years of age, and she had several more of a family.

After his marriage MacPhie removed to the islet mentioned, and remained there undisturbed for many years. He supported himself by fishing, hunting, and taking now and then a sheep or goat from the lands surrounding the loch. Such was his terror of being surprised by soldiers that he always carried arms about him and slept with a bayonet and loaded gun beside his bed. The country people were afraid of him, and he was commonly reported to be not 'canny'. He was at last evicted by a south country farmer, when he removed with his family to Fort William.

In his time a water-horse was quite commonly seen in Loch Cuaich, floating on its side, or as it is called, 'making a film' (*dèanadh sgleò*) and 'making a salmon of itself' (*dèanadh bradain dheth fhéin*), disporting itself and then disappearing.

One stormy night MacPhie, by his own account, was roused by a loud rattling noise at the door, as if some one were trying to enter. It stood in the door, and MacPhie knew it to be the water-horse in the shape of a man. He fired twice at it, but it did not move. He called to his wife to bring a silver coin, and when he put this in the gun and fired, the figure went away and was heard plunging into the loch.

The people round the loch heard three shots from the islet that night, for whatever cause they may have been fired.[361]

THE WATER-HORSE AT TIREE

A man working in the fields in Caolas, in the east end of the island, saw a water-horse coming from *Loch an Àir*, a small marshy lake full of reeds. He ran off in terror and left his coat behind. The water-horse tore the coat into shreds and then made after the man. The dogs came out when it came near the house and drove it away.

A son of one of the chamberlains of the island, last century, found a horse on the moors, and being struck with its excellence mounted it. The horse tore away at full gallop and could not be stopped. It galloped all round the country, till at last one side of the reins broke, and the horse rushed out on Loch Basibol, carrying its ill-fated rider with it.[362]

WATER-HORSE AND WOMEN

A young woman herding cattle drove her charge to a sequestered part of the hill, and while there a young man came her way, and reclining his head on her lap fell asleep. On his stretching himself she observed that he had horse-hoofs, and lulling him gently managed to get his head rested on the ground. She then cut out with her scissors the part of her clothes below his head and made her escape. When the water-horse awoke and missed her it made a dreadful outcry.

This tale, with unimportant variations, is known over the whole Highlands. Sometimes the young woman is sitting on the turf wall (*tobhta*) forming the end of the house when the water-horse, in the shape of a handsome young man, comes her way; sometimes she is one of a band of women assembled at the summer shieling – the rest are killed and she makes her escape. She detects the character of the youth by the water-weeds or the sand in his hair.

Many of the stories add that the young man (or water-horse) came for her on a subsequent Sunday after dinner, or to church – to which, as in the story of the water-horse of Loch Assapol in the Ross of Mull, she went for security rather than keep an appointment previously made with him – and took her to the loch.[363]

In Sutherlandshire the scene of the incident is laid at Loch Meudaidh in Durness, and the descendants of the woman to whom it occurred are still pointed out. She detected the young man by the sand in his hair and, on looking back after she had got to some distance, she saw him tearing up the earth in his fury. Such was the terror inspired a few years ago by a report that the water-horse of Loch Meudaidh had made its reappearance that the natives would not take home peats that they had cut at the end of the loch by boat (the only way open to them), and the fuel was allowed to go waste.[364]

A water-horse in man's shape came to a house in which there was a woman alone; at the time she was boiling water in a clay vessel (*crogan*) such as was in use before iron became common. The water-horse, after looking on for some time, drew himself nearer to her, and said in a snuffling voice, "It is time to begin courting, Sarah, daughter of John, son of Finlay."

"It is time, it is time," she replied, "when the little pitcher boils."

In a while it repeated the same words and drew itself nearer. She gave the same answer, drawing out the time as best she could, till the water was boiling hot. As the snuffling youth was coming too near she threw the scalding water between his legs, and he ran out of the house roaring and yelling with pain.[365]

THE WATER-HORSE AT LOCH BASIBOL, TIREE

On the north side of this loch, which has been already mentioned as a haunt of the water-horse, there was a farm where there are now only blowing sandbanks, called *Baile nan Cràganach* ('the Town of the Clumsy Ones') from five men who resided there having each six fingers on every hand. They were brothers, and it was said the water-horse came every night in the shape of a young man to see a sister who staid with them.[366]

With the tendency of popular tales to attach themselves to known persons, this incident is related of Calum Mòr Clark and his family. Calum had three sons, *Iain Bàn Mòr* ('Big Fair John'), *Iain Bàn Òg* ('Young Fair John') and *Iain Bàn Meadhonach* ('Middle Fair John').[367]

The four conspired to beguile the young man from the loch – who came to see the daughter – into the house, and got him to sit between two of them on the front of the bed. On a given signal these two clasped their hands round him and laid him on his back in the bed. The other two rushed to their assistance; the young man assumed his proper shape of a water-horse, and a fearful struggle ensued. The conspirators cut the horse in pieces with their dirks, and put it out of the house dead.

Not far from the south end of the same loch there is a place called *Fhaire na h-Aon Oidhch'* ('the One Night's Watch'), said to derive its name from an incident of which the water-horse was the hero, similar to that told of the urisk of Gleann Màili (see page 106).[368]

A water-horse was killed in Skye, where the stream from Eisgeadal falls into Loch Fada at the foot of Storr, by sticking a knife into it. It had previously killed a man.[369]

THE KELPIE

The kelpie that swells torrents and devours women and children has no representative in Gaelic superstition. Some writers speak as if the water-horse were to be identified with it, but the two animals are distinctly separate. The water-horse haunts lochs, the kelpie streams and torrents. The former is never accused of swelling torrents any more than of causing any other natural phenomenon, nor of taking away children, unless perhaps when wanted to silence a refractory child.[370] A Shetland friend writes: "Kelpies, I cannot remember of ever hearing what shape they were of. They generally did their mischief in a quiet way, such as being seen splashing the water about the burns, and taking hold of the water-wheel of mills and holding them still. I have heard a man declare that his mill was stopped one night for half an hour and the full power of water on the wheel, and he was frightened himself to go out and see what was wrong. And he not only said but maintained that it was a kelpie or something of that kind that did it."

THE WATER-BULL (*TARBH UISGE*)

This animal, unlike the water-horse, was of harmless character, and did no mischief to those who came near its haunts. It staid in little lonely moorland lochs, whence it issued only at night. It was then heard lowing near the loch, and came among the farmers' cattle, but was seldom seen. Calves having short ears, as if the upper part had been cut off with a knife – or, as it is termed in Gaelic, *corc-chluasach*, i.e. knife-eared – were said to be its offspring. It had no ears itself and hence its calves had only half ears.

Corc-chluasach is also applied to calves the ears of which are in any way naturally marked as if with a knife, slit in the points, serrated in the upper part, or with a piece out of the back.

In the district of Lorn, a dairymaid and herd, before leaving in the evening the fold in which the cows had been gathered to be milked and left for the night, saw a small ugly very black animal, bull-shaped, soft and slippery, coming among the herd. It had an unnatural bellow, something like the crowing of a cock. The man and woman fled in terror, but, on coming back in the morning, found the cattle lying in the fold as though nothing had occurred.[371]

THE KING OTTER

The water-dog (*dobhar-chù*), called also the king otter (*rìgh nan dòbhran*), is a formidable animal, seldom seen, having a skin of magic power, worth as many guineas as are required to cover it. It goes at the head of every band of seven (some say nine) otters, and is never killed without the death of a man, woman or dog. It has a white spot below the chin, on which alone it is vulnerable. A piece of its skin keeps misfortune away from the house in which it is kept, renders the soldier invulnerable in battle by arrow or sword or bullet, and – placed in the banner – makes the enemy turn and fly. "An inch of it placed on the soldier's eye," as a Lochaber informant said, "kept him from harm or hurt or wound though bullets flew about him like hailstones and naked swords clashed at his breast. When a direct aim was taken, the gun refused fire."

Others say the vulnerable white spot was under the king otter's arm, and of no larger size than a sixpence. When the hunter took aim he required to hit this precise spot, or he fell a prey to the animal's dreadful jaws. In Raasa and the opposite mainland the magic power was said to be in a jewel in its head, which made its possessor invulnerable and secured him good fortune; but in other respects the belief regarding the king otter is the same as elsewhere.

The word *dobhar* (pronounced **dooar, dour**), signifying water, is obsolete in Gaelic except in the name of this animal.[372]

BIAST NA SROGAIG

This mythical animal, 'the beast of the lowering horn', seems to have been peculiar to Skye. It had but one horn on its forehead, and, like the water-bull, staid in lochs. It was a large animal with long legs, of a clumsy and inelegant make, not heavy and thick but tall and awkward. Its principal use seems to have been to keep children quiet, and it is little to be wondered at if, in the majority of cases, the terrors of childhood became a creed in maturer years. *Scrogag*, from which it derives its name, is a ludicrous name given to a snuff-horn and refers to the solitary horn on its forehead.[373]

THE BIG BEAST OF LOCH AWE

This animal (*Beathach Mòr Loch Odha*) had twelve legs and was to be heard in wintertime breaking the ice. Some say it was like a horse, others like a large eel.[374]

7

SUPERSTITIONS ABOUT ANIMALS

BUARACH BHAOI, LAMPREY

The *buarach bhaoi*, literally 'wild (or 'wizard') shackle', called also *buarach na baoi* ('the shackle of the furious one'), was believed to be a leech- or eel-like animal, to be found at certain fords and in dark waters, that twisted itself like a shackle round the feet of passing horses so that they fell and were drowned. It then sucked their blood. It had nine eyes or holes in its head and back at which the blood it sucked came out. Hence it was called *buarach bhaoi nan sùilean claon* ('the furious shackle of the squinting eyes').[375]

In Skye it was believed the animal was to be found in Badenoch. It was said to haunt the dark waters of Loch Tummel (*Tethuil* 'Hot Flood', from the impetuosity of the river) in Perthshire, and was also known on the west coast of Argyllshire.[376] The word is translated 'lamprey' in dictionaries, but the description suggests the tradition of some species of gymnotus or electric eel.[377]

CÌREIN CRÒIN, SEA SERPENT

This was the largest animal in the world, as may be inferred from a popular Caithness rhyme:

> *Seachd sgadain sàth bradain,*
> *Seachd bradain sàth ròin,*
> *Seachd ròin sàth muice-mara,*
> *Seachd mucan-mara sàth Cìrein Cròin.*[378]

("Seven herring are a salmon's fill, / Seven salmon are a seal's fill, / Seven seals are a whale's fill, / And seven whales the fill of a Cìrein Cròin.") To this is sometimes added 'seven Cìrein Cròin are the fill of the big devil himself'.[379] This immense sea-animal is also called *mial mhòr a' chuain* 'the great beast of the ocean', *cuartag mhòr a' chuain* 'the great whirlpool of the ocean', and *uilebheist a' chuain* 'the monster of the ocean'. It was originally a whirlpool, or the sea-snake of the Edda that encircled the whole world.[380]

GIGELORUM

The *giolcam-daoram*, or gigelorum, is the smallest of all animals. It makes its nest in the mite's ear and that is all that is known about it.[381]

LAVELLAN

This animal is peculiar to the north, where it is said to be able to hurt cattle from a distance of forty yards: "Lavellan, Animal in Cathanesiâ frequens, in Aquis degit, capite Mustelæ sylvestri simile, ejusdemque coloris Bestia est. Halitu Bestiis nocet. Remedium autem est, si de aquâ bibant, in quâ ejus caput coctum sit." (Sibbald's *Scot. Ill.*, lib. 3, fol. 11.)[382]

Pennant, when at Ausdale, Langwell, Caithness-shire, says: "I enquired here after the Lavellan, which, from description, I suspect to be the water shrew-mouse. The country people have a notion that it is noxious to cattle: they preserve the skin, and, as a cure for their sick beasts, give them the water in which it has been dipt. I believe it to be the same animal which in Sutherland is called the water-mole."[383]

It is also mentioned by Rob Donn, the Sutherland bard, in his satirical song on 'Mac Rorie's Breeches':

> *Na leigibh o bhail' e*
> *Do mhòinteach no coille*
> *Mun tig an labhallan*
> *'S gum buail i e.*

"Let him not go away from the houses / To moss or wood / Lest the lavellan come / And smite him."[384]

BERNICLE GOOSE, *CADHAN*

In the Hebrides, as in England, the bernicle goose was believed to grow from the thoracic worm, attaching itself to floating wood that has been some time in the water, often so closely as to hide the surface of the log.[385]

Calum na Cròige, a native of Croig in Mull, who went about the country some thirty or forty years ago – the delight of youngsters by his extraordinary tales of personal adventures and of wonders he had seen, and the energy with which, sitting astride on a stool, he raised with their assistance the anchor, hoisted sail, and performed other nautical feats – told that in the Indian seas he and a comrade jumped overboard to swim to land. They swam for a week before reaching shore, but the water was so warm they felt no inconvenience. The loveliest music Calum ever heard was that made by bernicle geese as they emerged from barnacles that grew on the soles of his feet![386]

EEL (*EASGANN*)

It is still a very common belief in the Highlands that eels grow from horse hairs. In a village of advanced opinions in Argyllshire, the following story was heard from a person who evidently believed it: "In the island of Harris, in a time of scarcity, a person went out for fish and succeeded only in getting eels. These animals are not eaten in the Highlands and his wife would not taste them. The man himself ate several.

"By and by he went mad, and his wife had to go for succour to a party of English-men who had a shooting lodge near. On arriving with loaded guns, the sportsmen found the eel-eater in the fields fighting a horse. He was so violent that they had to shoot him. On inquiry it turned out that the cause of his madness and fighting the horse was that the eels he had eaten had grown from horse hairs!"[387]

WHALE

The round-headed porpoises or caaing whales (*mucun bearraich*, literally 'dogfish pigs') derive their Gaelic name from being supposed to grow from dogfish. An overgrown dogfish still retaining its own shape is called *burraghlas*.[388]

HERRING

The food of the herring is said to consist of crustacea and small fishes, but there is ordinarily so little appearance of food in their stomach that an easier explanation has been found in saying they live on the foam they make with their own tails!

A doorkeeper at Dowart Castle is said to have successfully warned a MacKinnon from Skye of the dangers awaiting him at the banquet to which he had been invited, by asking him if they were getting any herring in the north at present, and then praising the herring as a royal fish (*iasg rìgh*) that never was caught 'by its mouthful of food or drink' (*air a bhalgam no air a ghreim*).

On hearing this remark MacKinnon turned on his heel and made his escape.[389]

FLOUNDER

According to Sutherland tradition, the wry mouth of the flounder (*leòbag*, as it is called in the north) arose from its making faces at the rock-cod. A judgment (which children, who make faces, are liable to) came upon it, and its mouth remains as it then twisted it.[390] In Tiree and Iona the distortion is said to have been caused by St Columba. Colum-Kil met a shoal of flounders and asked: "Is this a removal, flounder?"

"Yes it is, Colum-Kil crooked legs," said the flounder.

"If I have crooked legs," said St Columba, "may you have a crooked mouth."

And so the flounder has a wry mouth to this day.[391]

LOBSTER

The three animals that dart quickest and farthest in the sea, according to a popular and perhaps truthful rhyme, are the lobster, mackerel, and seal. "The dart of lobster, the dart of mackerel, and the dart of seal; and though far the lobster's dart, farther is the mackerel's dart, and though far the mackerel's dart, farther is the seal's dart."[392]

SERPENTS

A serpent, whenever encountered, ought to be killed. Otherwise, the encounter will prove an omen of evil.

The head should be completely smashed (*air a spleatradh*) and removed to a distance from the rest of the body. Unless this is done the serpent will again come alive. The tail, unless deprived of animation, will join the body, and the head becomes a *beithir*, the largest and most deadly kind of serpent. The big beast of Scanlastle in Islay was one of this kind. It devoured seven horses on its way to Loch-in-Daal. A ship was lying at anchor in the loch at the time, and a line of barrels filled with deadly spikes, and with pieces of flesh laid upon them, was placed from the shore to the ship. Tempted by the flesh, the 'loathly worm' made its way out on the barrels and was killed by the spikes and cannon.[393]

A person stung by a serpent should rush to the nearest water. Unless he reaches it before the serpent, which also makes straight for it, he will die from the wound.[394] Another cure for the sting is water in which the head of another serpent has been put.

There was a man in Applecross who cured epilepsy by water in which he kept a living serpent. The patient was not to see the water.

Farquhar the Physician obtained his skill in the healing art from being the first to taste the juice of a white serpent. He was a native of Tongue in Sutherlandshire, and on one occasion was met by a stranger who asked him where he got the walking-stick he held in his hand. The stranger further got him to go to the root of the tree from which the stick had been cut, take a white serpent from a hole at its foot, and boil it. He was to give the juice without touching it to the stranger.

Farquhar happened to touch the mess with his finger, and it being very hot, he thrust his finger in his mouth. From that moment he acquired his unrivalled skill as a physician, and the juice lost its virtue.[395]

A week previous to St Bridget's day (1st February OS) the serpents are obliged to leave their holes under ground, and if the ground is then covered with snow they perish. In the popular rhyme relating to the subject the serpent in Argyllshire and Perthshire is called the 'daughter of Edward', but in Skye *an rìbhinn*, the damsel. In both cases the name is probably a mere euphemism suggested by the rhyme to avoid giving unnecessary offence to the venomous creature.[396]

RATS AND MICE

When a place is infested to a troublesome extent with rats or mice, and all other means of getting rid of the pests have failed, the object can be accomplished by composing a song – advising them to go away, telling them where to go and what road to take, the danger awaiting them where they are, and the plenty awaiting them in their new quarters. This song is called the rat (or mouse) satire, and if well composed the vermin forthwith take their departure.

When the islet of Calv (*an Calbh* 'the Inner Door'), which lies across the mouth of Tobermory harbour, was let in small holdings, the rats at one time became so numerous that the tenants subscribed sixpence apiece and sent for *Iain Pholchrain* to Morvern to come and satirise the rats away. He came and made a long ode in which he told the rats to go away peaceably and take care not to lose themselves in the wood. He told them what houses to call at, and what houses (those of the bard's own friends) to avoid, and the plenty and welcome stores – butter and cheese and meal – to be got at their destination. It is said that after this there was an observable decrease in the number of rats in the island![397]

An Ardnamurchan man, pestered with mice, in strong language tried to get them away, and all who have had experience of the annoyance will heartily join him in his wishes. The poet, with whips and switches, gathers the mice in a meadow near a stream, and sends a number of the drollest characters in the district to herd them, and 'old men, strong men, striplings, and honest matronly women, with potato beetles', to chase them. At last he gets them on board a boat at *Eabar an Ròin*, and sends them to sea.

> *The sea roaring boisterously,*
> *The ocean heaving and weltering,*
> *The tearing sound of sails splitting,*
> *The creaking of the keel breaking,*

> *The bilge water through the hull splashing*
> *Like an old horse neighing.*

And leaving them in this evil plight, the song ceases.[398]

CORMORANT

This bird passes through three stages of existence. It is

> *Seachd bliadhna 'na sgarbh,*
> *Seachd bliadhna 'na learg*
> *'S seachd bliadhna 'na bhallaire bodhain.*

"Seven years a scart (*pelecanus cristatus*), / Seven years a speckled loon (*colymbus arcticus*) / And seven years a cormorant (*pelecanus carbo*)."[399]

MAGPIE

The pyet (*piaghaid*) is called *gille ruith nan Caimbeulach*, 'the messenger of the Campbells', a name also given (for what reason the writer has not been able to ascertain) to a person who is 'garrulous, lying, interfering with everybody' (*gobach, briagach, 'g obair air na h-uile duine*). It is said of a meddling chatterbox, "What a messenger of the Campbells you have become!"

It is 'little happiness' (*beagan sonais*) for any one to kill a magpie.[400]

BEETLES

The *ceardalan* or dung-beetle is spared by boys when met with, but the *daolag* or clock is mercilessly killed. The reason assigned is that when the former met those who came to seize the person of our Saviour, and was asked how long since he had passed, it said,

> *Fhichead latha gus an-dé*
> *Chaidh Mac Dhé seachad.*

("Twenty days ago yesterday / The Son of God passed.") But the latter said,

> *An-dé, an-dé*
> *Chaidh Mac Dhé seachad.*

("Yesterday, yesterday / The Son of God passed.") Hence when boys hammer the life out of a 'clock' they keep repeating with savage unction, *Air a bhòn-dé, bhradag* ("The day before yesterday, wretch") or a rhyme:

> *Cuimhnich an-dé, an-dé,*
> *Cuimhnich an-dé, a bhradag,*
> *Cuimhnich an-dé, an-dé,*
> *Nach do leig Mac Dhé seachad.*

("Remember yesterday, yesterday, / Remember yesterday, wretch, / Remember yesterday, yesterday, / That let not the Son of God pass.")[401]

EMMET (*CAORA-CHÒSAG*)

This animal is shaken between the palms of the hand and laid upon the table. It is believed by boys to indicate the weather of the following day (by lighting on its back or belly, and the alacrity with which it moves away).[402]

SKIP-JACK

This insect – *gobhachan*, i.e. 'little smith', or *buail a' chnag* 'give a knock' – when laid on its back emits a loud crack in springing to its proper position. It is a favourite amusement of boys when they get hold of one to make it go through this performance. In Skye, when watching it preparing to skip, they say,

> *Buail an t-òrd, a ghobhachain,*
> *No buailidh mi sa cheann thu.*

("Strike with your hammer, little smith, / Or I will strike your head.")

8

MISCELLANEOUS SUPERSTITIONS

GISREAGUN, EAPAGUN, UPAGUN

Of the same class with magical charms and incantations, that is, of no avail to produce the results with which they are credited, were various minor observances and practices to which importance was attached as lucky or unlucky, and ominous of – if not conducive to – future good or ill.[403]

In some cases these observances became mere customs, followed without heed to their significance or efficacy; and many were known to (and believed in only by) the very superstitious. So far as causing or leading to the result ascribed to them was concerned, they were, 'like the Sunday plant', without good or harm, but a mind swayed by trifling erroneous beliefs of the kind is like a room filled with cobwebs. Superstition shuts out the light, makes the mind unhealthy, and fills it with groundless anxieties.[404]

THE RIGHT-HAND TURN (DEISEAL)

This was the most important of all the observances. The rule is 'deiseal (i.e. the right-hand turn) for everything', and consists in doing all things with a motion corresponding to the course of the sun, or from left to right. This is the manner in which screwnails are driven, and is common with many for no reason but its convenience. Old men in the Highlands were very particular about it. The coffin was taken deiseal about the grave when about to be lowered, boats were turned to sea, and drams are given to the present day to a company according to it.

When putting a straw rope on a house or corn-stack, if the assistant went tuaitheal (i.e. against the course of the sun) the old man was ready to come down and thrash him. On coming to a house the visitor should go round it deiseal to secure luck in the object of his visit. After milking a cow the dairymaid should strike it deiseal with the shackle, saying mach is dachaigh ('out and home'). This secures its safe return. The word is from deas, right-hand, and iul, direction, and of itself contains no allusion to the sun.[405]

Rising and Dressing

It is unfortunate to rise out of bed on one's left side. It is a common saying when evil befalls a person who seems to himself to have rushed to meet it, *Is mise nach d'éirich air mo làimh dheis an-diugh.* "I did not rise on my right hand today."

Water in which eggs have been boiled or washed should not be used for washing the hands or face. It is also a common saying when mischance befalls a person through his own stupidity, "I believe egg-water was put over me."[406]

When done washing himself a person should spit in the water, otherwise if the same water should be used by another for a like purpose, there will be danger of quarrelling with him before long.

Clothes

When a person puts on a new suit it is customary to wish him luck of it: "May you enjoy and wear it."

A man should be always the first to do this – the tailor, if he has the good sense. It is unlucky if a woman be the first to say it, and prudent women delay their congratulations and good wishes till they are satisfied some male friend has spoken first. It is less unfortunate if the woman has had a male child.[407]

If a person wearing a dress dyed with *crotal* – a species of lichen – be drowned, his body will never be found. This belief prevails in the north, and there the home-made dress indicated (which is of a reddish-brown colour) is frequently seen.[408]

Houses and Lands

There should be placed below the foundation of every house a cat's claws, a man's nails and a cow's hoofs, and silver under the door-post.

These will prove omens of the luck to attend the house. If an outgoing tenant leaves the two former below the door it is unfortunate for the incoming tenant, as his cattle will die.

An expectant occupier, or claimant, will secure to himself possession of land by burning upon it a little straw. This straw was called *sop seilbhe* 'a possession wisp'. If, for instance, there were two claimants to land and one of them burnt a 'possession wisp' on it, he might go about his business with his mind easy as to the result of the lawsuit. Or if a tenant ran in debt and had to leave his farm, and another who had a promise of the holding came and burnt a 'possession wisp', no evil or debt of those formerly attaching to it would then follow the holding.[409]

BAKING

In baking oatmeal cakes there is a little meal left on the table after the last cake is sprinkled previous to being fired. This remnant should not be thrown away or returned to the meal chest, but be kneaded between the palms into a little cake, to be given to one of the children. This little bannock was the *bonnach fallaid* – called also *siantachan a' chlàir*, 'the charmer of the board' – to which in olden times housewives attached so much importance. Unless it was made the meal lost its substance, and the bread of that baking would not be lasting (*bàn*).[410] On putting a hole through it with the forefinger, as already explained, it was given to children, and placed beside women in childbed to keep the Fairies away.[411] It mightily pleased little children, and was given to them as a reward for making themselves useful.

> *A little cake to Finlay,*
> *For going to the well.*

Its origin is said to have been as follows. A man fell in with a skull in a graveyard and took it to a tailor's house, where bread was being baked. The tailor gave it a kick, saying, "There was one period of the world when your gabful of dough was not small, and if I had you on a New Year's day I would give you your fill."[412]

When the New Year came round, a stranger came to the tailor's house asking for a mouthful of dough. The tailor set his wife to bake, and whatever she baked the stranger ate, and then asked for more. The tailor's stock of meal (and that of his neighbours) was devoured, and still the stranger asked for more. An old man of the neighbourhood was consulted, and he advised that the remnants – or dry meal used for sprinkling the cakes – should also be baked for the voracious guest. On this *fallaid* cake being given, the stranger declared himself satisfied and went away.[413]

If bread, when being baked, breaks frequently, a hungry stranger will come to eat it. Many cakes breaking are a sign of misfortune, by which the housewife is warned that 'something is making for her'.

If the cake for breakfast falls backwards, the person for whom it is intended should not be allowed to go on a journey that day: his journey will not be prosperous.[414] The evil can, however, be remedied by giving plenty of butter 'without asking' with the cake. To avert this omen, cakes should not be placed to harden at the fire on their points, but on either of the two sides or on their round edge. An old woman in Islay got into a great rage at a wake on seeing the cakes (that is, quarters of a 'farl' or large round bannock) placed on their points.

It is not good to count the cakes when done baking. They will not in that case last any time.[415]

REMOVAL CHEESE (*MULCHAG IMRICH*)

When leaving the summer pastures in the hills on Lammas day and returning with the cattle to the strath, a small cheese made of curds was made from that day's milk to be given to the children (and all who were at the *àirigh*) for luck and goodwill.

The cows were milked early in the morning, and curds were made and put in the cheese vat (*fioghan*). This hastily-prepared cheese was the *mulchag imrich*, and was taken home with the rest of the furniture for the purpose mentioned.[416]

LEG CAKE (*BONNACH LURGAINN*)

This was a cake given to the herd when he came with news that a mare had foaled, or to the dairymaid when she brought word that a cow had calved.[417]

GIVING FIRE OUT OF THE HOUSE

On the first day of every quarter of the year – New Year day, St Bride's day, Beltane and Lammas – no fire should be given out of the house. On the two last days especially it should not be given, even to a neighbour whose fire had gone out. It would give him the means of taking the substance or benefit (*toradh*) from the cows. If given, after the person who had come for it left, a piece of burning peat (*ceann fòid*) should be thrown into a tub of water to keep him from doing harm. It will also prevent his coming again.[418]

On New Year's day fire should not be given out of the house on any consideration to a doubtful person. If he is evil-disposed, not a beast will be alive next New Year. A suspected witch came on this day to a neighbour's house for fire, her own having gone out, and got it. When she went away a burning peat was thrown into a tub of water.

She came a second time, and the precaution was again taken. The mistress of the house came in, and on looking in the tub found it full of butter.

THUNDER

In a storm of thunder and lightning, iron (for instance the poker and tongs), put in the fire, averts all danger from the house. This curious belief seems to have been widespread at one time throughout the western Highlands, though now its memory barely survives. Its rationale seems to have been in some way to propitiate the fire, of which lightning is the most powerful exhibition. A woman in Cnoydart (a Roman Catholic district), alarmed by the peals of a thunderstorm, threw holy water on herself, put the tongs in the fire, and, on being asked the reason, said, "The cross of Christ be upon us! The fire will not harm us."

Perhaps the practice had some connection with the belief that the *beithir*, or thunderbolt, was of iron, a sharp-pointed mass. It seems one of the most irrational practices possible, but was probably of remote origin. In Kent and Herefordshire a cold iron bar was put on the barrels to keep the beer from being soured by thunder.[419]

THEFT

The stealing of salt, seed of plants, and lint make the thief liable to judgment without mercy. He may escape punishment from men but he will never attain to rest, as the rhyme says:

> *Mèirleach salainn 's mèirleach frois,*
> *Dà mhèirleach nach fhaigh fois;*
> *Ge b'e có thig no nach d'thig a-nìos,*
> *Cha d'thig mèirleach an lìn ghlais.*

"The stealer of salt and the stealer of seeds, / Two thieves that get no rest; / Whoever may or may not escape, / The stealer of grey lint will not." Another version of the rhyme is:

> *Mèirle salainn 's mèirle frois,*
> *Mèirl' o nach fhaigh anam clos;*
> *Gus an téid an t-iasg air tìr*
> *Chan fhaigh mèirleach an lìn clos.*

"Thief of salt and thief of seeds, / Two thefts from which the soul gets no repose; / Till the fish comes on land / The thief of lint gets never rest."[420]

SALT

In addition to the testimony this rhyme bears to the value of salt, there was a saying that a loan of salt should be returned as soon as possible; if the borrower dies in the meantime and without restitution being made, his ghost will revisit the earth. No fish should be given out of the house without being first sprinkled with salt. Meal taken out of the house in the evening was sprinkled with salt to prevent the Fairies getting its benefit.[421]

COMBING THE HAIR

A person should not comb his hair at night, or if he does, every hair that comes out should be put in the fire. Otherwise they will meet his feet in the dark and make him stumble. No sister should comb her hair at night if she have a brother at sea.

If the hair is allowed to go with the wind and it passes over an empty nest, or a bird takes it to its nest, the head from which it came will ache. No person should cut his own hair, as he will by doing so become an unlucky person to meet. If the hair, when thrown on the fire, will not burn, it is a sign the person will be drowned.[422]

BIRD NESTS

On falling in with a nest for the first time that year, if there be only one egg in it, or if there be an odd egg in it, that egg should be broken.

Any one finding a cuckoo's nest will live to be widowed.

HEN'S FIRST EGG

A young hen's first egg should be tapped on the hearth, saying, "One, two, three," etc. As many numbers as were repeated before the egg broke (or the youngster who was persuaded to try the experiment got tired), so many eggs would that hen lay.[423]

EUPHEMISMS

By giving diseases and other evils a good name when speaking of them, the danger of bringing them upon oneself by his words is turned away. It will be remembered that for a similar reason the ancients called the Fairies 'Eumenides', and the Celt called the Fairies 'good people'. The smallpox was called 'the good woman', epilepsy 'the outside disease'.[424]

In telling a tale of any one being taken away by the Fairies, the ill-will of the 'people' was averted by prefixing the narrative with the words, "A blessing on their journeying and travelling! This is Friday and they will not hear us."[425]

When a person sneezes it is customary for the bystander to say 'thank you', to which is sometimes added, "We will not take his name in vain." Some say 'God be with you', others 'God and Mary be with you', and others 'St Columba be with you'. By saying 'The hand of your father and grandfather be over you' the Fairies are kept away.[426] Any words would seem to have been deemed availing, and some of the phrases used were not choice. If the bystander should say 'Your brains the next time!' the person sneezing should answer, 'The bowl of your head intercept them!'[427]

When a child yawns, the nurse should say, "Your weariness and heaviness be on yonder grey stone!"[428]

When the story of a house having taken fire is told, the narrative should be prefixed by saying, "St Mary's Well be in the top of every house! The cross of Christ be upon us!" This averts a similar calamity from the house in which the tale is told.

In some places old people are to be found who, when a person comes in with any tale of misfortune (of the death of one of the cattle, a neighbour's house taking fire, etc.), pull threads from their clothes and throw them in the fire, saying 'Out with the evil tale!' or 'To tell it to themselves'.

In speaking of the dead, it is proper to speak of them only in commendatory terms – *de mortuis nihil nisi bonum*. Hence *moladh mairbh* ('praise of the dead') denotes faint praise, not always deserved. In speaking of the dead, old people always added *chuid a fhlaitheanas da* ('his share of paradise be his') or *chuid a thròcair da* ('his portion of mercy be his'). If their tale was not to the credit of the deceased or they were obliged to make any statement unfavourable to him, they said, "It is not to send it after him."

BOAT LANGUAGE

When in a boat at sea, sailing or fishing, it was forbidden to call things by the names by which they were known on land. The boat-hook should not be called *croman* but *a' chliob*, a knife not *sgian* but *a' ghiar* ('the sharp one'), the baling dish not *taoman* but *spùidseir*, a seal not *ròn* but *béist mhaol* (the 'bald beast'), a fox not *sionnach* but *madadh ruadh* (the 'red dog'); the stone for anchoring the boat was not *clach* but *cruaidh* ('hardness'). This practice prevails much more on the east coast than on the west, where it may be said to be generally extinct. It is said to be carefully observed among the fishermen about the Cromarty Firth.[429]

It was deemed unlucky by east coast fishermen coming to Tiree (as several boats used to do annually to prosecute the cod and ling fishing) to speak in a boat of a minister or a rat. Everywhere it was deemed unlucky among seafaring men to whistle in case a storm should arise. In Tiree, Heynish Hill (the highest in the island) was known at sea as *a' Bhraonach*, Hogh Hill (the next highest) as *a' Bheinn Bheàrnach no Sgoilte* (the Notched or Cloven Hill), and a species of whale as *cas na poite* (the leg of a pot). It should not be said *bhàthadh e* 'he was drowned' but *shiubhail e* 'he journeyed', not *ceangail ròp* 'tie a rope' but *dèan e* 'make it'. In the north it was held that an otter, while in its den, should not be called *béist dubh* (the 'black beast', its common name), but *càrnag*. It would otherwise be impossible for the terriers to drive it from its refuge.[430]

FRESH MEAT

When fresh meat of the year's growth is tasted for the first time a person should say,

> *A death-shroud on the grey, better grey, old woman*
> *Who said she would not taste the fresh meat,*

I will taste the fresh meat
And will be alive for it next year.

This ensures another year's lease of life.[431]

KILLING THOSE TOO LONG ALIVE

If a person is thought to be too long alive, and it becomes desirable to get rid of him, his death can he ensured by bawling to him thrice through the keyhole of the room in which he is bedrid,

Will you come, or will you go?
Or will you eat the flesh of cranes?[432]

FUNERALS

It was customary to place a plate of salt, the smoothing iron, or a clod of green grass on the breast of a corpse while laid out previous to being coffined. This, it was believed, kept it from swelling. A candle was left burning beside it all night. When it was placed in the coffin and taken away on the day of the funeral, the boards on which it had been lying were left for the night as they were, with a drink of water on them in case the dead should return and be thirsty. Some put the drink of water or of milk outside the door, and, as in Mull and Tiree, put a sprig of pearlwort above the lintel to prevent the dead from entering the house.[433]

When coffining the corpse every string in the shroud was cut with the scissors;[434] and in defence of the practice there was a story that, after burial, a woman's shade came to her friends to say that all the strings in her shroud had not been cut. Her grave was opened, and this was found to be the case.

The only instance the writer has heard of 'cere-cloth' (that is, cloth dipped in wax in which dead bodies were wrapped) being used in the Highlands is that the Nicholsons of Scorrybreck in Skye (a family said to be of Russian descent through *Neacal Mòr* who was in Mungastadt) had a wax shirt (*léine chéir*) which, from the friendship between themselves and the chief of the MacLeods, was sent for from Dunvegan on every occasion of a death.[435]

THE WATCH OF THE GRAVEYARD (*FAIRE CHLAIDH*)

The person last buried had to keep watch over the graveyard till the next funeral came. This was called *faire chlaidh*, the graveyard watch, kept by the spirits of the departed.[436]

At Kiel (*Cill Chaluim Chille*) in Morvern the body of the Spanish princess said to have been on board one of the Armada blown up in Tobermory Bay was buried. Two young men of the district made a paction that whoever died first, the other would watch the churchyard for him. The survivor, when keeping the promised watch, had the sight of his dead friend as well as his own. He saw both the material world and spirits. Each night he saw ghosts leaving the churchyard and returning before morning. He observed that one of the ghosts was always behind the rest when returning. He spoke to it, and ascertained it to be the ghost of the Spanish princess. Her body had been removed to Spain, but one of her little fingers had been left behind, and she had to come back to where it was.[437]

When two funeral parties met at the churchyard, a fight frequently ensued to determine who should get their friend first buried.

SUICIDES

The bodies of suicides were not taken out of the house for burial by the doors, but through an opening made between the wall and the thatch. They were buried, along with unbaptised children, outside the common churchyard.

It was believed in the north, as in Skye and about Applecross (*a' Chomrach*) in Ross-shire, no herring would be caught in any part of the sea which could be seen from the grave of a suicide.[438]

MURDER

It was believed in Sutherlandshire that a murdered body remained undecayed till touched.

THE HARVEST OLD WIFE (*A' CHAILLEACH*)

In harvest there was a struggle to escape being the last done with the shearing, and when tillage in common existed, instances were known of a ridge being left unshorn (no person would claim it) because of it being behind the rest. The fear entertained was that of having the 'famine of the farm' (*gort a' bhaile*), in the shape of an imaginary old woman (*cailleach*), to feed till next harvest.[439]

Much emulation and amusement arose from the fear of this old woman; and from it arose the expression, *Is feàrr leum-iochd as t-fhoghradh na sguab a bharrachd.* "Better is a mercy-leap in harvest than a sheaf additional." The *leum-iochd*, or mercy-leap, is where a rocky mound or a soft spot where no corn grows occurs in a ridge. Its occurrence was a great help to the shearing being done.[440]

The first done made a doll of some blades of corn, which was called the *cailleach* ('old wife'), and sent it to his nearest neighbour. He in turn, when ready, passed it to another still less expeditious, and the person it last remained with had the 'old woman' to keep for that year. The old wife was known in Skye as *a' ghobhar bhacach* ('the cripple goat').[441]

The fear of the cailleach in harvest made a man in *Saor-bheinn*, in the Ross of Mull, who farmed his land in common with another, rise and shear his corn by moonlight. In the morning he found it was his neighbour's corn he had cut.[442]

BIG PORRIDGE DAY (*LÀ A' BHROCHAIN MHÒIR*)

In the Western Islands, in olden times (for the practice does not now exist anywhere), when there was a winter during which little seaware came ashore, and full time for spring work had come without relief, a large dish of porridge, made with butter and other good ingredients, was poured into the sea on every headland where wrack used to come. Next day the harbours were full.

This device was to be resorted to only late in the spring – the Iona people say the Thursday before Easter – and in stormy weather. The meaning of the ceremony seems to have been that by sending the fruit of the land into the sea, the fruit of the sea would come to land.[443]

FIRES ON HEADLANDS

In Skye, fires were lighted on headlands at the beginning of winter to bring in herrings.

STANCES

Particular stances, or sites of buildings, were accounted unlucky, such for instance as the site of a byre in which the death of several cattle had occurred; and it was recommended, to prevent the recurrence of such misfortunes, that the site should be altered.

NAMES

So with regard to names. If the children of a family were dying in infancy, one after the other, it was thought that, by changing the name, the evil would be counter-acted.[444] The new name was called an *ainm rathaid* ('road name'), being that of the first person encountered on the road when going with the child to be baptised. It was given 'upon the luck' (*air sealbhaich*) of the person met.

The MacRories, a sept of the MacLarens in Perthshire, were descendants of one who thus received his name. His parents, having lost a previous child before its baptism, were advised to change the name. They were on their way through the pass called *Làirig Isle*, between Loch Erne and Glen Dochart, to have their second child baptised, when they were met by one Rory MacPherson.[445] He was an entire stranger to them, but turned back with them, as a stranger ought to do to avoid being unlucky, and the child was called after him. *Clann 'ic Shimigeir*, a sept of the MacNeills, have also a road name.[446]

Delivery of Cattle and Horses

Before delivering a cow to the buyer at a market, the seller should pass the end of the rope by which she is led three times round his body. When taking delivery of a horse from one of whom you are not sure, you should come *deiseal* between him and the horse, and take hold of the halter inside his hand, that is, between him and the horse. Otherwise, the seller's eye will be after the beast.

Trades

Masons were said to be able to raise the devil, or, as the Gaelic expression more forcibly describes it, *mac mollachd thoirt ás a fhriamhaichean* – 'to take the son of cursing from his roots'.

Smiths, being people who work among iron, were deemed of more virtue against the powers of evil than any other tradesmen.

Tailors were looked upon with a feeling akin to that entertained in the south, where 'nine tailors made a man'. The reason probably was that in olden times every man fit to bear arms thought it beneath him to follow a peaceful occupation, and only the lame and cripple were brought up as tailors.

Tinkers are known as *luchd ceàird*, that is literally 'tradesmen', and the name is a memory of days when they held the first rank as hand-craftsmen.[447]

Saor, a joiner, means literally 'a freeman', whence it would appear that from the earliest times the trade was highly esteemed.

Iron

An oath on cold iron was deemed the most binding oath of any; when people swore on their dirks it was only because it was at the time the cold iron readiest to hand. A man who secreted iron, and died without telling where, could not rest in his grave.

At Meigh, in Lochaber, a ghost for a long time met people who were out late. An old man, having taken with him a Bible and made a circle round himself on the road with a dirk, encountered it, and, in reply to his inquiries, the ghost confessed to having stolen *soc a' chroinn*, a ploughshare, and told where the secreted iron was to be found. After this the ghost discontinued its visits to the earth.

Cold iron, e.g. the keys passed round the body of a cow after her return from the bull, keeps her from *ath-dàir*, that is, seeking to go on the same journey again.[448]

Empty Shells

Empty whelk shells (*faochagun failmhe*) should not be allowed to remain in the house for the night. Something is sure to come after them. Similarly, water in which feet have been washed (i.e. out of which the use or benefit has been taken) should not be left in the house for fear the noiseless people come and plunge about in it all night.[449]

Protection against Evil Spirits

On every occasion of danger and anxiety, the Highlander of former days commended himself to the protection of the cross. In a storm of thunder he blessed himself saying, "The cross of Christ be upon us." When he encountered a ghost or evil spirit at night, he drew a circle round himself on the road with the point of his dirk or a sapling in the name of Christ, saying "The cross of Christ be upon me", and while he remained in the circle no evil could come near him.

A person was also safe while below high water mark. Fairies and evil spirits had no power below the roll of seaweed.

When walking the high road at night, it is recommended to keep to the side paths in case of meeting the wraiths of funerals. The ghostly train may throw a person down, or compel him to carry the bier to the churchyard.[450]

Misnaming a Person

If a person be accidentally misnamed, as e.g. being called John when his name is Donald, he who made the mistake, on observing it, instantly exclaimed, "The cross of Christ be upon us."

Saining Straw (*Sop Seile*)

At certain seasons of the year, principally at Beltane and Lammas, a wisp of straw, called *sop seile* (literally 'a spittle wisp'), was taken to sprinkle the door-posts and houses all round sunwise (*deiseal*) to preserve them from harm. When a new cow came home it was also sprinkled to preserve it from the evil eye. The liquid used was menstruum.

In spring the horses, harness, plough, etc. were similarly sprinkled before beginning to plough.[451]

PROPITIOUS TIMES

A great number of the observances of superstition were regulated by days of the week or year. There were certain days on which alone certain works could be commenced under favourable auspices and with any chance of being successfully done.[452]

UNLUCKY ACTIONS

It is unlucky to wind black thread at night. A vicious wish made to one another by women quarrelling in olden times was, "The disease of women who wind black thread at night be upon you!" Some say the reason of the evil omen is that black thread is apt to disappear at night, or be taken by the Fairies, and be found through the house next morning. Superstition probably assigned some more occult reason.

It is 'little happiness' for anyone to kill a magpie or a bat.[453]

It is unlucky for a person on a journey to return the way he went. This belief had its origin in the instructions given to the 'man of God' who rebuked the idolatry of Jeroboam. "Eat no bread, nor drink water, nor turn again by the same way that thou camest" (1 Kings 13: 9).

9

AUGURY, PREMONITIONS AND DIVINATION

AUGURY (*MANADAIREACHD*)

The anxiety of men to know the future – the issue of their labours, and the destinies awaiting them – makes them ready listeners to the suggestions of fancy, and an easy prey to deception. The mind eagerly lays hold on anything that professes to throw light on the subject of its anxiety, and men are willing victims to their own hopes and fears. Where all is dark and inscrutable, deception and delusion are easy, and hence augury of all kinds, omens, premonitions, divinations, have ever exercised a noticeable power over the human mind.

The ordinary manner which superstition takes to forecast the future is to look upon chance natural appearances under certain circumstances as indications of the character, favourable or unfavourable, of the event about which the mind is anxious. Any appearance in nature, animate or inanimate, can thus be made an omen of, and an inference be drawn from it of impending good or bad fortune. If it be gloomy, forbidding, awkward or unpleasant, it is an unlucky omen, and the subsequent event with which the mind associates it will be unfavourable; but if pleasant, then it is a good omen and prognosticates pleasant occurrences.

Omens which proceed upon a similarity of character between the prognostic and its fulfilment are easy of interpretation. There are other omens which have no connection – natural, possible, or conceivable – with the impending event, and of which consequently the meaning is occult, known only to people of skill instructed in their interpretation.

These probably had their origin in one or two accidental coincidences. For instance, if the appearance of a fox is to be taken as an omen, it will naturally be taken as a bad sign, the stinking brute can indicate nothing favourable; but no amount of sagacity will teach a person that an itching in the point of his nose prognosticates the receipt of important news, or the cuckoo calling on the house-top the death of one of the inmates within the year. His utmost acuteness will fail to find in a shoulder-blade any indication of destiny, or any prophetic meaning in the sediment of a cup of tea. The meaning of these is a mystery to the uninitiated, and it is easy to see how they might be reduced to a system and lead to the wildest delusions of fortune-telling.

Everything a Highlander of the old school set about, from the most trifling to the most important, was under the influence of omens. When he went to fish, to catch his horse in the hill, to sell or buy at the market, to ask a loan from his neighbour, or whatever else he left home to do, he looked about for a sign of the success of his undertaking, and, if the omen were unpropitious, returned home. He knew his journey would be of no avail. He consulted mystagogues as to his fate, and at the proper seasons looked anxiously for the signs of his luck. Like the rest of mankind, he was, by means of these, pleased or depressed in anticipation of events that were never to occur. Hence the saying, "Take a good omen as your omen, and you will be happy."

Probably the Greek μαντεία, prediction by an oracle, is cognate to the Gaelic *manadh*, a foretoken, anything from which a prediction can be drawn. Both among Greeks and Celts a great number of omens were taken from birds.

As already mentioned, it is a bad sign of a person's luck during the day that he should rise from bed on his left hand or wash himself with water in which eggs have been boiled, or that the cakes for his breakfast should frequently break in the baking or fall backwards.[454] The coming evil can be averted in the latter case by giving plenty of *ìm gun iarraidh* ('butter without asking') with the cakes.

Indeed, 'butter unasked for' is of sovereign value as an omen of luck. A cake spread with it, given to fishermen, secures a good day's fishing. It is reckoned good in diseases, particularly measles, and a most excellent omen for people going on a journey. Its not being given to Hugh of the Little Head on the morning of his last battle was followed by his losing the battle and his life.[455]

Omens are particularly to be looked for at the outset of a journey. If the first animal seen by the traveller have its back towards him, or he meet a sheep or a pig, or any unclean animal, or hear the shrill cry of the curlew, or see a heron, or he himself fall backward, or his walking-stick fall on the road, or he have to turn back for anything he has forgot, he may as well stay at home that day: his journey will not prosper. A serpent, a rat or a mouse is unlucky unless killed, but if killed becomes a good omen. If the face of the animal be towards one, even in the case of unlucky animals, the omen becomes less inauspicious.

It is of great importance what person is first met. Women are unlucky, and some men are the most unfortunate omen that can be encountered. These are called *droch còmhalaichean*, i.e. bad people to meet, and it was told of a man in Skye that to avoid the mischance of encountering one of them when setting out on a journey, he sent one of his own family to meet him. If he met any other he returned home. In a village in Ayrshire there are three persons noted for being inauspicious to meet, and fishermen (upon whom as a class this superstition has a strong hold) are much dissatisfied at meeting any of them. One of them is not so bad if he puts his hand to his face in a manner peculiar to him.[456]

It is inauspicious to meet a person from the same village as oneself, or a man with his head bare, or a man going to pay rent. Old people going to pay rent, therefore, took care to go away unobserved. A plain-soled person is unlucky, but the evil omen in his case is averted by rolling up the tongue against the roof of the mouth. The Stewarts were said to have insteps; water flowed below their foot; it was, therefore, fortunate to meet any of them. All risk of a stranger proving a bad *còmhalaiche* is avoided by his returning a few steps with the traveller.[457]

A hare crossing one's path is unlucky, and old people, when they saw one before them, made considerable detours to avoid such a calamity. The disfavour with which this harmless animal and the pig were regarded no doubt arose from their being unclean under the Levitical Law. The hare chews the cud, but divides not the hoof; the pig divides the hoof, but does not chew the cud.[458]

The fox is unlucky to meet, a superstition that prevails also in East Africa. The king of Karague told Captain Speke that 'if a fox barked when he was leading an army to battle, he would retire at once, knowing that this prognosticated evil' (*Journal*, p. 241).[459]

It is unlucky to look back after setting out. Old people, if they had to turn to a person coming after them, covered their face. This superstition probably had its origin in the story of Lot's wife.[460] Fin mac Coul, according to a popular tale, never looked back after setting out on a journey. When he went on the expedition that terminated in his being 'in the house of the Yellow Forehead without liberty to sit down or power to stand up', he laid spells on his companions that no man born in Ireland should follow him. Fergus, who was born in Scotland, followed, and Fin, hearing footsteps behind him, called out without turning his head, in a phrase now obsolete, *Co sid a propadh mo cheaplaich?* – i.e., it is supposed, "Who is that following my footsteps?"[461]

To be called after is a sure omen that a person will not get what he is going in search of. This belief gave great powers of annoyance to people of a waggish humour. When everything prognosticated success, and the fishing boat had left the shore, or the old man, staff in hand, had set out on his journey, some onlooker cried out, "There is the fox before you and after you"; or, "Have you got the fish-hooks?" or, "Have you taken the bait-stone?" (The bait-stone, *clach shuill*, was a stone on which to break shellfish, potatoes, etc., to be thrown into the water to attract fish. The broken bait was called *soll, faoire*.) Immediately a damp was thrown on the expedition, a return home was made for that day, and the wag might be glad if the party called after did not make him rue his impertinence.[462]

Of omens referring to other events in the life of man than the success of particular expeditions may be mentioned the following. A *feadag* or golden plover (*charadrius pluvialis*), heard at night, portends the near approach of death or other evil. The cry of the bird is a melancholy wailing note. A *breac an t-sìl* or pied wagtail (*motacilla alba*), seen between them and the house, was a sign of being turned out of the house that year and 'losing the site' (*call na làraich*). The mole burrowing below a house is a sign the tenants will not stay long on that site. If the cuckoo calls on the house-top or on the chimney (*luidheir*), death will occur in the house that year.

In spring and early summer the omens of happiness and prosperity, or misery and adversity, for the year are particularly looked for. It is most unfortunate if the first foal or lamb seen that season have its tail toward the beholder, or the first snail (some say stonechat) be seen on the road or on a bare stone, and a most unmistakable sign of misfortune to hear the cuckoo for the first time before tasting food in the morning – 'on the first appetite' (*air a' chiad lomaidh*), as it is called.[463] In the latter case, the cuckoo is said to 'soil upon a person' (*chac a' chuthag air*),[464] and to avoid such an indignity people have been known, at the time of the cuckoo's visit, to put a piece of bread below their pillow to be eaten the first thing in the morning.

Cock-crowing before midnight is an indication of coming news. Old people said the bird had 'a tale' to tell, and, when they heard it, went to see if its legs were cold or not. If cold, the tale will be one of death; if hot, a good tale. The direction in which the bird's head is turned indicates the direction in which the tale is to come.

In visiting the sick, it is a sign of the termination of the illness whether it be the right or the left foot that touches the threshold first. Women pretended to know when they laid their hand on a sick person whether he would recover.

It is a good sign if the face of the chimney-crook (*aghaidh na slabhraidh*) be toward the visitor, but an evil omen if its back be toward him.[465]

Premonitions

These are bodily sensations by which future events may be foreknown. An itching in the nose foretells that a letter is coming, and this in olden times was a matter of no small consequence. There is an itching of the mouth that indicates a kiss, and another indicating a dram. A singing or tingling in the ears denotes death (a friend at the moment of its occurrence has expired and news of his death will be heard before long); an itching of the cheek or eyes, weeping; itching of the left hand, money; of the right, that one is soon to meet a stranger with whom he will shake hands; of the elbow, that he will soon change beds or sleep with a stranger; of the brow, that some person will make you angry before long.[466]

Hot ears denote that some person is speaking about your character. If the heat be in the right ear, he is supporting or praising you; if in the left, he is speaking ill of you (*chluas dheas, gam thoirt a-nuas; 's a' chluas chlì, gam shìor chàineadh*).[467] In the latter case persons of a vindictive nature repeated the following words:

141

An neach tha gam iomradh,
Mur h-ann air mo leas e
Esan bhith ga iomluain
Air sgeanaibh geura glasa,
Cadal an tom seangain da
'S na na cadal fallain da,
Ach baobh eadar e 's an doras
'S mis' eadar e 's a chuid 's a chadal.

"He who speaks of me, / If it be not to my advantage / May he be tossed / On sharp grey knives, / May he sleep in an ant-hill / And may it be no healthy sleep to him, / But a furious woman between him and the door / And I between him and his property and sleep."[468]

The evil wish went on – *cliath-chliat iarainn a sgrìobadh a mhionaich* ('that an iron harrow might scrape his guts') and something about *cailleach mharbh* ('a dead old woman') that my informant could not remember.[469]

TRIAL (*DEUCHAINN*)

The *deuchainn* (also *diachainn*), sometimes called *frìth*, omen, was a 'cast' or 'trial' made by lots or other appeal to chance to find out the issue of undertakings – whether an absent friend was on his way home or would arrive safe; whether a sick man will recover; whether good or bad fortune awaits one during the year; what the future husband or wife is to be; the road stolen goods have taken; etc. This 'cast' may be either for oneself or for another, *air a shon 's air a shealbhaich* ('for him and for his luck').[470]

On New Year day people are more disposed to wonder and speculate as to their fortunes during the year upon which they have entered than to reflect upon the occurrences of the past. Hence these 'casts' were most frequently made on that day. Another favourite time was Hallowmas night. Most of them might be made at any time of the year, and the difficulty was not in making them but in interpreting them.

In making a 'cast' for one's future partner, the approved plan is for him to go at night to the top of a cairn or other eminence where no four-footed beast can go, and whatever animal is thence seen or met on the way home is an omen of the future husband or wife. It requires great shrewdness to read the omen aright.

Another way is to shut the eyes, make one's way to the end of the house, and then (and not till then) open the eyes and look around. Whatever is then seen is an indication of fortune during the year. It is unlucky to see a woman, particularly an old woman bent with age and hobbling past. A man is lucky, particularly a young man riding gaily on a mettlesome horse. A man delving or turning up the earth forebodes death: he is making your grave, and you may as well prepare. A duck or a hen with its head below its wing is just as bad, and the more that are seen in that attitude the speedier or more certain the death.

A man who had the second sight once made a 'trial' for a sick person at the request of an anxious friend. He went out next morning to the end of the house in the approved manner. He saw six ducks with their heads under their wings, and the sick man was dead in less than two days.

Other seers who made 'trials' for reward made the person who consulted them burn straw in front of a sieve and then look through to see 'what they should see'. From the objects seen the seer foretold what was to befall.

When a trial was made to ascertain whether an absent friend would return, if on going out to the end of the house a man is seen coming, or a duck running towards the seer, his safe arrival will soon be; but if the object be moving away, the indication is unfavourable. By this trial it may also be known whether the absent one will return empty-handed or not.

Another mode of *deuchainn*, for the same purpose, is to take a chance stick and measure it in thumb-breadths, beginning at its thick or lower end and saying – when the thumb is laid on the stick – 'no' or 'yes' as the opinion of the person consulting the oracle may incline, and repeating 'yes', 'no' alternately till the other end is reached. According to the position of the last thumb will the answer be affirmative or negative or doubtful.

When a young woman wants to ascertain whether a young man in whom she feels an interest loves her, let her look between her fingers at him and say the following charm. If his first motion is to raise his right arm she is secure of his affections.

Tha deuchainn agam dhuit,
Tha sealltainn agam ort
Eadar còig aisnean cléibh Chrìost;
Ma tha 'n dàn no 'n ceadachadh dhuit
Feum dheanadh dhiom,
Tog do làmh dheas a-suas
'S na luaith i nìos.

"I have a trial upon you, / I have a looking at you / Between the five ribs of Christ's body; / If it be fated or permitted you / To make use of me, / Lift your right hand / And let it not quickly down."[471]

In the detection of theft the diviner's utmost skill could only determine the direction the stolen goods had taken.

DIVINATION (*FIOSACHD*)

The same causes which in other countries led to oracles, astrology, necromancy, card-reading and other forms of divination, in the Scottish Highlands led to the reading of shoulder-blades and teacups, palmistry, and the artless spinning of teetotums (*dòduman*).[472] In a simple state of society mummeries and ceremonies, dark caves, darkened rooms and other aids to mystification are not required to bring custom to the soothsayer. The desire of mankind (particularly the young) to have pleasant anticipations of the future supplies all deficiencies in his artifices. One or two shrewd guesses establish a reputation, and ordinarily there is no scepticism or inquiry as to the sources of information. It is noticeable that the chief articles from which the Highland soothsayer drew his predictions supplied him with a luxury.

SHOULDER-BLADE READING (*SLINNEINEACHD*)

This mode of divination was practised, like the augury of the ancients, as a profession or trade.[473] It consisted in foretelling important events in the life of the owner of a slaughtered animal from the marks on the shoulder-blade, speal or blade-bone.[474] Professors of this difficult art deemed the right speal-bone of a black sheep or a black pig the best for this purpose. This was to be boiled thoroughly so that the flesh might be stripped clean from it, untouched by nail or knife or tooth.[475] The slightest scratch destroyed its value.

The bone, being duly prepared, was divided into upper and lower parts corresponding to the natural features of the district in which the divination was made. Certain marks indicated a crowd of people – met, according to the skill of the diviner, at a funeral, fight, sale, etc. The largest hole or indentation was the grave of the beast's owner (*uaigh an t-sealbhadair*), and from its position his living or dying that year was prognosticated. When to the side of the bone, it presaged death; when in its centre, much worldly prosperity (*gum biodh an saoghal aige*).[476]

Mac a' Chreachaire, a native of Barra, was a celebrated shoulder-blade reader in his day.[477] According to popular tradition he was present at the festivities held on the occasion of the castle at *Bàgh Chìosamuil* (the seat of the MacNeills, then chiefs of the island) being finished. A shoulder-blade was handed to him, and he was pressed again and again to divine from it the fate of the castle. He was very reluctant, but at last, on being promised that no harm would be done him, he said the castle would become a cairn for thrushes (*càrn dhruideachun*), and this would happen when the Rattle Stone (*Clach a' Ghlagain*) was found, when people worked at seaweed in *Baile na Creige* (Rock-Town, a village far from the sea), and when deer swam across from Uist and were to be found on every dung-hill in Barra.[478]

All this has happened, and the castle is now in ruins. Others say the omens were the arrival of a ship with blue wool, a blind man coming ashore unaided, and that when a ground officer with big fingers (*maor nam miar mòra*) came, Barra would be measured with an iron string. A ship laden with blue cloth was wrecked on the island, and a blind man miraculously escaped; every finger of the ground officer proved to be as big as a bottle (!), and Barra was surveyed and sold.[479]

When *Murchadh Geàrr* (Murdoch the Short), heir to the lordship of Lochbuy in the island of Mull *c.* AD 1400, was sent in his childhood for protection from the ambitious designs of his uncle (the laird of Dowart) to Ireland, he remained there till eighteen years of age. In the meantime his sister (or half-sister) became widowed and, dependant on the charity and hospitality of others, wandered about the Ross of Mull from house to house with her family. It was always 'in the prophecy' (*san tairgneachd*) that Murdoch would return.

One evening, in a house to which his sister came, a wedder sheep was killed. After the meal was over, her oldest boy asked the farmer for the shoulder-blade. He examined it intently for some time in silence, and then, exclaiming that Murdoch was on the soil of Mull (*air grunnd Mhuile*), rushed out of the house and made for Lochbuy, to find his uncle in possession of his rightful inheritance.[480]

On the night of the massacre of Glencoe, a party of the ill-fated clansmen were poring over the shoulder-blade of an animal slain for the hospitable entertainment of the soldiers. One of them said, *Tha dòrtadh fuil sa ghleann.* ("There is a shedding of blood in the glen.") Another said there was only the stream at the end of the house between them and it. The whole party rushed to the door, and were among the few that escaped the butchery of that dreadful night.

It is a common story that a shoulder-blade seer once saved the lives of a company – of whom he himself was one – who had 'lifted' a cattle spoil (*creach*), by divining that there was only the stream at the end of the house between them and their pursuers.

A shoulder-blade sage in Tiree sat down to a substantial feast, to which he had been specially invited, that he might divine whether a certain friend was on his way home or not. He examined the shoulder-bone of the wedder killed on the occasion critically, unable to make up his mind. "Perhaps," he said, "he will come, perhaps he will not." A boy, who had hid himself on the top of a bed in the room that he might see the fun, could not help exclaiming, "They cannot find you untrue." The bed broke, and the diviner and his companions, thinking the voice came from the skies, fled. When the boy recovered he got the dinner all to himself.

PALMISTRY (*DEÀRNADAIREACHD*)

Of this mode of divination, as practised in the Highlands, nothing seems now to be known beyond the name. Probably from the first the knowledge of it was confined to gipsies and suchlike stray characters.

Divination by Tea, or Cup-Reading (*Leughadh Chupaichean*)

When tea was a luxury, dear and difficult to get, the 'spaeing' of fortunes from tea-cups was in great repute. Even yet, young women resort in numbers to fortune-tellers of the class, who for the reward of the tea spell out to them most excellent matches.

After drinking the tea, the person for whom the cup is to be read – turning the cup *deiseal* or with the right-hand turn – is to make a small drop left in it wash its sides all round, and then pour it out. The fortune is then read from the arrangement of the sediments or tea-leaves left in the cup.

A large quantity of black tea grounds (*smùrach dubh*) denotes substance and worldly gear. The person consulting the oracle is a stray leaf standing to the one side of it. If the *face* of the leaf is towards the grounds, that person is to come to a great fortune; if very positively its *back*, then farewell even to the hope 'that keeps alive despair'. A small speck by itself is a letter, and other specks are envious people struggling to get to the top, followers, etc.

Good diviners can even tell to their youthful and confiding friends when the letter is likely to arrive, what trade their admirer follows, the colour of his hair, etc.[481]

10

DREAMS AND PROPHECIES

DREAMS

Dreams (*bruadar*, plural *bruadaran*) have everywhere been laid hold of by superstition as indications of what is passing at a distance or of what is to occur, and, considering the vast numbers of dreams there are, it would be matter of surprise if a sufficient number did not prove so like some remote or subsequent event, interesting to the dreamer, as to keep the belief alive.[482] On a low calculation, a fourth of the population dream every night, and in the course of a year the number of dreams in a district must be incredible. They are generally about things that have been, or are, causes of anxiety, or otherwise occupied men's waking thoughts. "A dream cometh through the multitude of business," Solomon says, and a Gaelic proverb says with equal truth, *Aisling caillich mar a dùrachd*. "An old wife's dream is according to her inclination."[483]

Its character can sometimes be traced directly to the health or position of the body, but in other cases it seems to depend on the uncontrolled association of ideas. Out of the numberless phantasies that arise, there must surely be many that the imagination can without violence convert into forebodings and premonitions.

To dream of raw meat indicates impending trouble; eggs mean gossip and scandal; herring, snow; meal, earth; a grey horse, the sea. To dream of women is unlucky; and of the dead, that they are not at rest.[484] In the Hebrides, a horse is supposed to have reference to the Clan MacLeod. The surname of horses is MacLeod, as the Coll bard said to the Skye bard:

> *Is tric a mharcaich mi le m' shréin*
> *An dream dh'am bheil thu fhéin 's do bhean.*

"Often rode I with my bridle / The race you and your wife belong to."[485] In some districts horses meant the Macgnanean, and a white horse, a letter.[486]

PROPHECIES (*FÀISNEACHD*): THOMAS THE RHYMER

In Argyllshire and Perthshire the celebrated Thomas the Rhymer (*Tòmas Reuvair, Tòmas Réim*) is as well known as in the Lowlands of Scotland.[487] He is commonly called *mac na mnà mairbh* ('the son of the dead woman'), but the accounts vary as to the cause of this name. One account says he was, like Julius Caesar, taken out through his mother's side immediately after her death; another, that the cry of the child was heard in the mother's tomb after her burial, and on the grave being opened Thomas was found in the coffin.[488]

A third account says that a woman whose husband had been cut in four pieces engaged a tailor, at the price of the surrender of her person, to sew the pieces together again. He did so in two hours' time. Some time after, the woman died and was buried. Subsequently she met the tailor at night, and, leading him to her tomb, the child was found there.[489]

Both the Highland and Lowland accounts agree that Thomas's gift of prophecy was given him by a Fairy sweetheart, that he is at present among the Fairies, and will yet come back.[490] The Highland tradition is that Thomas is in Dunbuck hill (*Dùn Buic*) near Dunbarton. The last person that entered that hill found him resting on his elbow, with his hand below his head. He asked, "Is it time?" And the man fled.[491]

In the Outer Hebrides he is said to be in Tomnaheurich hill near Inverness. Hence MacCodrum, the Uist bard, says:

> *Dar thigeadh sluagh Tom na h-Iùbhraich*
> *Có dh'éireadh air tùs ach Tòmas?*[492]

("When the hosts of Tomnaheurich come / Who should rise first but Thomas?") *Tom na h-Iùbhraich*, the Boat Mound, probably derives its name from its resemblance to a boat, bottom upwards.[493] Another popular account makes it the abode of the Féinne, or Fin mac Coul and his men. There is a huge chain suspended from the roof, and if any mortal has the courage to strike it three times with his fist, the heroes will rise again. A person struck it twice, and was so terrified by the howling of the big dogs (*donnal nan con mòra*) that he fled. A voice called after him, *Dhuine dhona dhòlaich, as miosa dh'fhàg na fhuair.* "Wretched mischief-making man, that worse hast left than found."[494]

Thomas attends every market on the lookout for suitable horses, as the Fairies in the north of Ireland attend to steal linen and other goods exposed for sale. It is only horses with certain characteristics that he will take. At present he wants but two, some say only one – a yellow foal with a white forehead (*searrach blàr buidhe*). The other is to be a white horse that has got *trì Màirt, trì Màigh, agus trì Iuchara 'bhainne mhàthar* ('three March, three May, and three August months of its mother's milk'),[495] and in Mull they say one of the horses is to be from the meadow of Kengharair in that island.[496] When his complement is made up he will become visible, and a great battle will be fought on the Clyde.

> *Nuair thig Tòmas le chuid each*
> *Bidh latha nan creach air Cluaidh,*

Millear naoi mìle fear maith
'S théid rìgh òg air a' chrùn.

"When Thomas comes with his horses / The day of spoils will be on the Clyde, / Nine thousand good men will be slain / And a new king will be set on the throne."[497] You may walk across the Clyde, the prophecy goes on to relate, on men's bodies, and the miller of Partick Mill (*Muileann Phearaig*), who is to be a man with seven fingers, will grind for two hours with blood instead of water.[498] After that, *bidh sia baintighearnun diag as déidh an aon tàilleir chrùbaich* ('sixteen ladies will follow after one lame tailor'), a prophecy copied from Isaiah 4: 1.[499] A stone in the Clyde was pointed out as one on which a bird (*bigein*) would perch and drink its full of blood without bending its head, but the River Trustees have blasted it out of the way that the prophecy may not come true.[500]

The same prophecy, with slight variation, has been transferred to Blair Athole in Perthshire. *Nuair thig an crodh bàn do Bhlàr, cuirear seachd cuir de chuibhle-mhuilinn Bhlàir le fuil sluaigh.* "When the white cows come to Blair, the wheel of Blair Mill will turn round seven times with people's blood." The writer was told that the duke of Atnole brought white cattle to Blair more than fifteen years ago, but nothing extraordinary happened.[501]

Other prophecies ascribed to the Rhymer are *Cuiridh claigeann na caorach an crann o fheum* ('The sheep's skull will make the plough useless') or *Cuiridh claigeann na caorach an crann àraidh air an fharadh* ('The sheep's skull will put the plough on the hen-roost'); *Thig a' mhuir deas air a' mhuir tuath* ('The south sea will come upon the north sea'); and

Bidh Albainn 'na criosun geala
'S meall òir ann am bun gach glinne.

"Scotland will be in white bands / And a lump of gold will be at the bottom of every glen." The former has received its fulfilment in the desolation caused by the extension of sheep farms, the second in the making of the Caledonian Canal, and the last in the increase of highroads and houses.[502]

COINNEACH ODHAR

In the north Highlands prophecies of this kind are ascribed to *Coinneach Odhar* (i.e. Dun Kenneth), a native of Ross-shire, whose name is hardly known in Argyllshire.[503] He acquired his prophetic gift from the possession of a stone which he found in a raven's nest.

He first found a raven's nest with eggs in it. These he took home and boiled. He then took them back to the nest with a view to finding out how long the bird would sit before it despaired of hatching them. He found a stone in the nest before him, and its possession was the secret of his oracular gifts. When this became known, an attempt was made to take the stone from him, but he threw it out in a loch, where it still lies.[504]

He prophesied that

Òlaidh am fitheach a shàth far an làir
Air mullach Clach Àrd an Ùig.

"The raven will drink its fill of men's blood from off the ground / On the top of the High Stone in Uig" (a place in Skye). The High Stone is on a mountain's brow, and it is ominous of the fulfilment of the prophecy that it has fallen on its side.[505] Of the Well of Ta at *Cill' a' Chrò* in Strath, in the same island, he said:

Tobar Tà sin, 's tobar Tà,
Tobar aig an cuirear blàr,
'S bidh cnàimhean nam fear fàs
Air tràigh bhàn Laorais,
'S marbhar Lachann nan trì Lachann
Gu moch, moch, aig tobar Tà.

"Thou well of Ta, and well of Ta, / Well where battle shall be fought, / And the bones of growing men / Will strew the white beach of Laoras, / And Lachlan of the three Lachlans be slain / Early, early, at the well of Ta."[506]

In Harris a cock will crow on the very day on which it is hatched, and a white calf without a single black hair will be born – both which remarkable events have, it is said, occurred. A certain large stone will roll up the hill, turning over three times, and the marks of it having done so (and the proof of the prophecy) are still to be seen. On the top of a high stone in Scaristavor parks the raven will drink its fill of men's blood,[507] and the tide of battle will be turned back by Norman of the three Normans (*Tormod nan trì Tormoidean*) at *Càthaichean an Tairbeirt*, the Steps of Tarbert.[508] *Càth* is probably a step path in a rock.[509]

The Scaristavor stone is about ten feet high, and is one of the three fragments into which a larger stone, used by an old woman of former days as a hammer to knock limpets off the rocks (*òrd bhàirneach*), was broken.[510] Of the other two, one is in *Uidh an Taoibh Tuath* and one in Tarnsa islet.[511] At a spot from which these three fragments can be seen there is hidden an urn of silver and an urn of gold (*crogan òir 's crogan airgid*). It is easy to find a place whence one can see two, but when about to see the third, one of the first two disappears. Five or six yards make all the difference. A herdsman once found the spot, but when digging for the treasure he happened to see a heifer that had fallen on its back in a stream. He ran to its rescue, and never could find the place again.[512]

THE LADY OF LAWERS

Of similar fame for her prophetic gifts was the Lady of Lawers (*Bantighearna Lathair*), one of the Breadalbane family, married to Campbell of Lawers.[513] Her prophecies relate to the house and lands of Breadalbane, and are written, it is believed, in a book shaped like a barrel and secured with twelve iron hoops or clasps in the charter room of Taymouth Castle. This book is called 'The Red Book of Balloch'.[514]

An old white horse will yet take the lineal heirs of Taymouth (or, according to another version, the last Breadalbane Campbells) across Tyndrum Cairn. When she said this there were thirty sons in the family, but soon after twenty-five of them were slain in the battle at *Sròn a' Chlachair* near Killin (*Cill Fhinn*).[515]

If the top stone were ever put on Lawers Church no word uttered by her would ever come true, and when the red cairn on Ben Lawers fell the church would split. In the same year that the cairn (built by the sappers and miners on Ben Lawers) fell, the Disruption in the Church of Scotland took place.

> *Bidh muileann air gach sruthan,*
> *Crann an làimh gach giullain,*
> *Dà thaobh Loch Tatha 'na ghàracha-càil;*
> *Cuiridh claigeann na caorach an crann o fheum*
> *'S cuiridh ite geòidh an cuimhn' á duine.*

"A mill will be on every streamlet, / A plough in every boy's hand, / The two sides of Loch Tay in kail gardens; / The sheep's skull will make the plough useless / And the goose's feathers drive their memories from men."[516] This was to happen in the time of 'John of the three Johns, the worst John that ever was, and there will be no good till Duncan comes'.[517]

A stone called the 'Boar Stone' (*Clach an Tuirc*), a boulder of some two or three hundred tons in a meadow near Loch Tay, will topple over when a strange heir comes to Taymouth, and the house will be at its height of honour when the face of a certain rock is concealed by wood.[518]

The Féinn in the cave (see p. 148)

Ernest Griset (from *The Fians*)

11

IMPRECATIONS, SPELLS, AND THE BLACK ART

IMPRECATION (*GUIDHE*)

The imprecations which form so important a part of the vocabulary of thoughtless and profane swearing are in Gaelic corruptions of English expressions. Thus one of the commonest, *diabhal MacEadhar*, is a corruption of 'devil may care', and though no language has a monopoly of oaths and curses, and English is not always to blame, it is some satisfaction that needless profanity is not entirely of native growth.[519]

Most Gaelic imprecations are mere exclamations, condemnatory not so much of the person himself as of what he is saying or doing. Of these the following are of common use:

Droch còmh'l ort! 'A bad meeting to you!'[520]

Droch fàs ort! 'A bad growth to you!'

Droch ciall ort! 'Bad understanding to you!'

Droch sgiorram ort! 'Bad accident to you!'

Gum bu droch drùileach (or *drùthalach*) *dhuit!* 'Bad ———? to you!'[521]

Bùrn dubh ort! 'Black water upon you!' Does this refer to excommunication? A candle was then extinguished in water.

Beul sìos ort! 'A down mouth be yours!' Perhaps this means burial with the face downwards. The mother of an illegitimate child which died in infancy, and the paternity of which was denied, declared if she had known that would be the case, she would have buried the child with its face downward. This was said to be in Tiree, but all the writer's inquiries failed to find any one who had ever heard of such a thing being done. It is a saying, *Beul sìos air na mnathan mur faighear 's gach àit' iad.* "A down mouth to women if they are not to be found everywhere."[522]

Beul seachad ort! 'A wry mouth be yours!'[523]

Taigh do sheanar dhuit! 'Go to your grandfather's house!'

An dunaidh ad' chliathaich! 'The mischief be in your side!'

Losgadh do chridhe ort! 'The burning of your heart to you!'

Beagan piseach ort! 'Little increase to you!'

Beagan àigh ort! 'Little prosperity to you!'

153

Sian do ghonaidh ort! 'The spell of your death-stroke be yours!'[524]

Bàs gun sagart ort! 'Death without a priest to you!'

Gaoth gun dìreadh ort! 'Wind without rising be yours!' i.e. a wind that will throw you on your beam-ends, and not allow you to right.[525]

Sàr dubh do ghonaidh ort! 'Your black certain death-stroke to you!'[526]

Marasg (i.e. *marbh-thasg*) *ort!* 'The place of the dead be yours!'[527]

Àireamh na h-Aoine ort! 'The number of Friday be yours!'

Mollachd na h-Aoine ort! 'The curse of Friday be yours!'

Deireadh nan seachd Satharna dhuit! 'The end of the seven Saturdays to you!'[528]

Guma h-anamoch dhuit! 'May you be late!'

An taobh bheir thusa cùl do chinn, gar an d'thig an t-aon latha bheir thu t' aghaidh! 'The direction in which you turn the back of your head, may you never turn your face!'

When a curse proceeds from rage or malevolence, it is at the same time a confession of impotence. The party uttering it is unable at the moment to indulge his rancour in any other way. If he had the power he would bring all the woes he threatens or imprecates there and then on his enemy's devoted head. Patience is no element of wrath and rarely enters the house of malevolence, and if the man who curses his enemy had the artillery of heaven at command, he would at that moment devote his enemy to unspeakable misery. This impotence of rage is the reason why curses are so frequently ascribed to angry old women.

Those who have seen old women of the Madge Wildfire school cursing and banning say their manner is well calculated to inspire terror. Some fifteen or twenty years ago a party of tinkers quarrelled and fought, first among themselves, and then with some Tiree villagers. In the excitement a tinker wife threw off her cap and allowed her hair to fall over her shoulders in wild disorder. She then bared her knees, and falling on them to the ground, in a praying attitude, poured forth a torrent of wishes that struck awe into all who heard her. She imprecated: "Drowning by sea and conflagration by land; may you never see a son to follow your body to the graveyard, or a daughter to mourn your death. I have made my wish before this, and I will make it now, and there was not yet a day I did not see my wish fulfilled," etc., etc.[529]

"Once," says one who is now an old man, "when a boy I roused the anger of an old woman by calling her names. She went on her knees and cursed me, and I thought I was going to die suddenly every day for a week after."

The curse causeless will not come, but a curse deserved is the foreshadowing of the ultimate issue of events. The curse of the oppressed who have no man to deliver them is at times but the presage of the retribution which the operation of the laws of the moral world will some day bring about. Hence we find such expressions as: "She cursed him and obtained her wish." The curse came upon the oppressor not because of the malediction, but because what was asked for was part of the natural sequence of events in the moral government of the world.

For this reason, the curse of the poor is undesirable. There is something wrong in the relation between superior and inferior when it is uttered; authority has been misused, and wisdom and patience have been awanting, selfishness has overstepped its due limit, and the just influence of the superior has degenerated into wantonness of power. In the expatriations from the Highlands there was much in this respect to be reprobated, and it is most creditable to Highlanders, and is greatly to be ascribed to the influence of religion over them, that in the songs made at the time of the Clearances there are no curses against the oppressor.[530]

A common expression in the imprecations used by old women was: *Nach faicear toradh ad' im, no im ann ad' bhainne.* "May no benefit be in your cheese, and no cheese in your milk."[531]

There is said to be a curse on an estate in Argyllshire that a lineal descendant will never succeed to it, and on one of the principal castles in Perthshire that no legitimate heir (*oighre dligheach*) will own it till the third generation (*gus an treasa linn*). This latter curse was caused by the haughtiness of an old woman, a former mistress of the castle, who lived entirely on marrow.[532]

All evil wishes can be counteracted by the bystander saying, after each curse, "The fruit of your wish be on your own body" (*Toradh do ghuidhe far*, etc.).[533] On the occasion above referred to, of the banning by the tinker wife, her frightful tirade became ludicrous from the earnestness with which this was done by one of the native women who was listening.

Spells (Geasan, Geasaibh)

A person under spells is believed to become powerless over his own volition, is alive and awake, but moves and acts as if asleep. He is like St John's father, not able or not allowed to speak.[534] He is compelled to go to certain places at certain hours or seasons, is sent wandering, or is driven from his kindred and changed to other shapes.

In nursery and winter evening tales (*sgialachdun is uirsgeulun*) the machinery of spells is largely made use of. In the former class of tales they are usually imposed on king's children by an old woman dwelling near the palace, called *Eachrais Ùrlair* ('Trouble-the-House', literally 'Confusion of the Floor'). Her house is the favourite place for the king's children to meet their lovers. She has a divining rod (*slacan druidheachd*), by a blow from which she can convert people into rocks, seals, swans, wolves, etc., and this shape they must keep till they are freed by the same rod. Nothing else can deliver them from the spell.[535]

The story usually runs that the king is married a second time. His daughter by the first marriage is very handsome, and has a smooth comb (*cìr mhìn*) which makes her hair, when combed by it, shed gold and precious gems. The daughters by the second marriage are ugly and ill-natured. When they comb their hair there is a shower of fleas and frogs. Their mother bribes Trouble-the-House to lay spells on the daughter of the first marriage. Unless the princess enters the house the old woman is powerless to do this. One day the beautiful princess passes near the house, and is kindly and civilly asked to enter. "Come you in," says the designing hag. *Is tric a bha mise 'g imlich nam mias agus a' lomadh nan cnàmh an taigh t' athar.* "Often did I lick the platters and pick the bones in your father's house."[536] Misled by this artful talk, the princess enters, is struck with the magic rod, and converted into a swan.

It is a popular saying that seals and swans are 'king's children under enchantments' (*clann rìgh fo gheasaibh*). On lonely mountain meres, where the presence of man is seldom seen, swans have been observed putting off their coverings (*cochall*) and assuming their proper shape of beautiful princesses in their endeavours to free themselves from the spells. This, however, is impossible till the magician who imposed them takes them away, and the princesses are obliged to resume their coverings again.[537]

The expressive countenance and great intelligence of the seal, the readiness with which it can be domesticated, and the attachment which, as a pet, it shows to man, have not unnaturally led to stories of its being a form assumed by (or assigned to) some higher intelligence, from choice or by compulsion. In Caithness seals are deemed to be the fallen angels, and the Celtic belief that they are 'king's children under spells' is paralleled in the Shetland tales of the Norway Finns. These are persons, a native of these northern islands writes (in a private letter), who come across from Norway to Shetland in the shape of large seals.

A Shetlander on his way to the fishing, early in the morning, came across a large seal lying asleep on a rock. Creeping quietly up he managed to stab it with his knife. The animal was only slightly wounded, and floundered into the water, taking the knife along with it. Some time afterwards the fisherman went, with others, to Norway to buy wood. In the first house he entered he saw his own big knife stuck up under a beam. He gave himself up for lost, but the Norwegian took down the knife and gave it back to him, telling him never again to disturb a poor sea-animal taking its rest.

There is a sept in North Uist known as *Clann 'ic Codrum nan ròn*, 'the MacCodrums of the seals', from being said to be descendants of these enchanted seals. The progenitor of the family, being down about the shore, saw the seals putting off their coverings and washing themselves. He fled home with one of the skins and hid it above the lintel of the door (*arabocan*, as it is called in that part of the country). The owner of the covering followed him. He clad her with human garments, married her, and had a family by her. She managed ultimately to regain possession of her lost covering and disappeared.[538]

West of Uist there is a rock called *Connsmun* to which the neighbouring islanders are in the habit of going yearly to kill seals. On one of these expeditions, a young man named Egan son of Egan killed a large seal in the usual manner by a knock on the head, and put a withe through its paw to secure it, while he himself went to attend to other matters. When he came back, however, the seal was gone.

Some time after he was driven away in a storm, and landed in a district he did not recognise. He made his way to one of the houses, and was very hospitably entertained. His host, who had been surveying him intently, when the meal was over asked his name. He told, and his host said, *Ìogain 'ic Ìogain, ged thug mi biadh is càise 's uibhean duit, air do dhà làimh, Ìogain 'ic Ìogain, chuir thu 'n gad roimh mo dhòrn.* "Egan son of Egan, though I have given you meat and cheese and eggs, upon your two hands be it, Egan son of Egan, you put the withe through my fist."[539]

THE BLACK ART

Nothing was known in the Highlands of the dark science beyond what is conveyed in the name given to it, *sgoil dhubh Shàtain* ('Satan's black school'), and a few anecdotes of its more illustrious students. All accounts agree that Michael Scott was an advanced scholar. He, by his skill in it, made a brazen man, whom he compelled to do all his work for him. By means of him he brought *Mhòinteach Fhlansrach* (the Flanders Moss in the Carse of Stirling) across from the continent on bearers (*lunnun*). The moss is twenty-three miles long, and lies north of Stirling, where, unfortunately, the bearers broke.[540]

An t-Ollamh Muileach (the Mull Doctor) and *an t-Ollamh Ìleach* (the Islay Doctor) also attended the school, and adventures are assigned to them as to the other scholars. The Mull doctor passed a house from which loud sounds of talking proceeded. He remarked that in that house were either twenty men or three women.[541]

Cameron of Locheil (*Mac Dhòmhnaill Duibh*, the Son of Black Donald, is the Highland patronymic of the chiefs of this house), MacDonald of Keppoch (*Mac 'ic Rao'aill*), and MacKenzie of Brahan were at the school together, and when their education was finished the devil was to get as his fee whoever of them was hindmost. The three young men made a plan to chase each other round and round in a circle so that none of them should be hindmost. At last the devil was for clutching someone, but the young man pointed to his shadow, which was behind. The devil in his hurry caught at it, and the young man never had a shadow from that day.[542]

Locheil hired a servant maid to attend to a set of valuable china dishes of which he was the possessor. Her post was onerous, and she had another waiting-maid under her. Her life was to be the forfeit of any of the dishes being broken. One night when ascending the stairs with the dishes on a tray, the under-servant leading the way with a light, she noticed that the sugar bowl was in two and began to weep. A gentleman whom she had not till then observed was walking backwards and forwards on the stairhead. He asked her why she wept, and she told. He asked what she would give to have the bowl made whole as it was before. Would she give herself? She thoughtlessly said she would give anything. The bargain was struck, and on drying her tears and looking up, the maid found the bowl whole.

She told all this to her master, and when the devil came that same night to claim her Locheil gave his former teacher a hospitable reception. When it waxed late, the devil, afraid of the cock-crowing, was preparing to go away. Cameron coaxed him to remain till the inch still remaining of the candle on the table should burn down. Whenever he gave his consent Cameron blew out the candle and gave it to the servant, telling her her life depended on its safe custody. In this manner the devil was cheated by his own scholar.

A drover bought a flock of goats from MacDonald of Keppoch, who himself accompanied the drove to Locheil-side. Here, in crossing a ford, the goats were taken away by the stream, and went past the drover as red stalks of fern (*'nan cuiseagun ruadha rainich*), all except one dun hornless goat (*gobhar mhaol odhar*). The drover returned in search of MacDonald and found him lying on the heather, seemingly asleep. He pulled his hand to awaken him, but the hand came away with him. In the end, however, the hand was put right, and the goats were restored to the astonished drover.

Another time Keppoch and his dairymaid had a trial of skill in sorcery. While she was milking a cow in the cattle-fold, MacDonald, who was looking on, by his charms prevented the cow from yielding her milk. The dairymaid removed to the other side of the cow and defeated his conjurations. He then removed the hoop on the milk-pail. This also she counteracted.

MacDonald is said to have put a stop in his own country to the women winding black thread at night, but how or why does not appear.[543]

The mighty magician Michael Scott had a narrow escape from becoming the prey of the arch-fiend. On his death-bed he told his friends to place his body on a hillock. Three ravens and three doves would be seen flying towards it; if the ravens were first, the body was to be burned, but if the doves were first it was to receive Christian burial. The ravens were foremost, but in their hurry flew beyond their mark. So the devil, who had long been preparing a bed for Michael, was disappointed.[544]

12

THE DEVIL

The Devil and his Names

Superstition, in assigning to the devil a bodily shape and presence, endeavoured to make him horrible, and instead made him ridiculous. For this no doubt the monkish ceremonies of the middle ages are, as is commonly alleged, much to blame. The fiend was introduced into shows and dramatic representations with horns, tail, and the hoof of one of the lower animals; the representation was seized upon by the popular fancy, and exaggerated till it became a caricature.

The human mind takes pleasure in mixing the ludicrous with the terrible, and in seeing that of which it is afraid made contemptible. There is, as is well known, but one step from the sublime to the ridiculous, and, in being reduced to a bugbear, the impersonation of evil has only come under the operation of a common law. One bad effect to be traced to the travesty is that men's attention is diverted from the power of evil as the spirit that now worketh strife, lying, dishonesty, and the countless forms of vice, and the foul fiend is become a sort of goblin to frighten children and lonely travellers.

In Gaelic the exaggeration is not carried to the same lengths as in English. There is nothing said about the fiend's having horns or tail. He has made his appearance in shape of a he-goat, but his horns have not attracted so much attention (or inspired such terror) as his voice, which bears a horrible resemblance to the bleating of a goat. A native of the island of Coll – *Niall na Buaile*, who lived in a house alone several miles from any other house – is said to have got a good view of him in a hollow called *Sloc an Tàilisg*, and was positive that he was *corc-chluasach* (crop-eared, see pp. 115–16). He has often a chain clanking after him.[545]

In Celtic (as in German) superstition he has usually a horse's hoof, but also sometimes a pig's foot. This latter peculiarity – which evidently had its origin in the incident of the Gadarean swine, and in the pig being unclean under the ceremonial law – explains the cloven hoof always ascribed to him in English popular tales. In Scripture the goat, as pointed out by Sir Thomas More, formed the sin offering, and is an emblem of bad men.[546]

The reason why a horse's hoof has been assigned to him is not so apparent. In the Book of Job Satan is described as 'going to and fro in the earth'; and the red horses, speckled and white, which the prophet Zechariah (1: 8) saw among the myrtle trees were explained to him to be those whom 'the Lord hath sent to walk to and fro through the earth'. The similarity of description may be casual, but it is on grounds equally incidental and slight that many of the inferences of superstition are based.[547]

In addition to his Scripture names, the arch-fiend is known in Gaelic by the following titles:[548]

Am fear nach fhiach 'the worthless one'.
Am fear nach abair mi 'the one whom I will not mention'.
Am fear ud 'yon one'.
An aon fhear mòr 'the one big one'.
An t-aibhisteir 'the one from the abyss' (from *aibheis* 'an abyss, a depth').
An rosad 'the mean mischievous one'.
An dòlas mòr 'the big sorrow'.
Mac mollachd 'the son of cursing'.[549]
An riabhach mòr 'the big grizzled one'.
An donas 'the bad one'.
An t-ainspiorad, an droch spiorad 'the bad spirit'.
Dòmhnall Dubh 'Black Donald'.

In the north Highlands he is also known as *Bìdein, Dìthean, Bradaidh*.[550] It is said that *Connan* was a name given to him, and that *aisling connain*, a libidinous dream, means literally 'a devil's dream'.[551] The name must have been very local. There is a fable about Connan and his twelve sons pulling a plant in the peat moss, in which the name denoted the wren, and there was a St Connan, whose memory is preserved in *Cill Chonnain*, a burying-ground in Rannoch, and *Féill Connain*, the autumn market at Dalmally in Glenorchy.[552]

The occasions on which the devil has appeared in a bodily shape have been at meetings of witches; at card-playing, which is the reading of his books; when he comes to claim his prey; and when summoned by masons or magicians. He is apt to appear to persons ready to abandon their integrity, and to haunt premises which are soon to be the scene of signal calamities. He sometimes comes in unaccountable shapes and in lonely places for no conceivable purpose but to frighten people.

The following tales will illustrate the character of his appearances and the notions popularly entertained regarding him.

Card-Playing

A party of young people were playing cards; a stranger joined them and took a hand. A card fell below the table, and the youth who stooped to lift it observed the stranger to have a horse's hoof. The devil, on being thus detected, went up the chimney in smoke.

This story is universal over the Highlands. Cards are notoriously known as the devil's books.[553] When boys play them, the fiend has been known to come down the chimney feet foremost, the horse's or pig's foot appearing first. When going away he disappears in smoke, and neighs horribly in the chimney.

THE RED BOOK OF APPIN

This celebrated book contained charms for the cure of cattle, and was so powerful that its owner had to place an iron hoop about his head every time he opened it. All accounts agree that it was got from the devil, but they differ as to how this was done. Very likely the book was a treatise on the treatment and diseases of cattle, and the origin of the stories of its magic virtue lay in the fact that the Stewarts who owned it had a magnificent fold of Highland cattle.[554]

The first who got the book rode an entire horse (an animal that no evil power can touch) to a meeting of witches.[555] The devil wrote in a red book the names of the assembled company. The man, instead of letting the devil write his name, asked to be allowed to do so himself. On getting the book for that purpose he made off with it.

By another account (and the person from whom it was heard was positive as to its being the only correct account) it was got by a young lad under the following circumstances. The youth was apprenticed to the miller at Bearachan on Loch Awe-side. His master was unkind, and made him work more than he was fit for. One night he was up late finishing a piece of work. About midnight a gentleman, whom he did not recognise, entered the mill and accosted him kindly. Turning the conversation that ensued on the harsh conduct of the miller, the stranger promised to better the unhappy prentice's condition if they met at the *Cama-Linn* ('Crooked Pool') in the *Monadh Meadhonach* ('Middle Mountain') on a certain night.[556]

An assignation to that effect was made, but after the strange gentleman went away the lad got frightened, and next day told about the visitor he had. A conclave of sixteen ministers was called, and the matter was deliberated upon. As the youth had given his promise it was deemed necessary he should keep it, but he was advised to take a wand with him and at the place appointed trace a circle with it round himself, out of which he was not to move, whatever temptation or terrors the stranger might bring to bear upon him. A committee of the clergy went to watch on a neighbouring eminence the result of the interview.

The strange gentleman came at the appointed hour, and before giving the money promised, civilly asked the lad to write his name in a book. For this purpose the book was not handed but thrown to the youth, and he, on getting it into his possession, refused to give it up again.

The strange gentleman now showed himself in his true colours. Finding remonstrances and coaxing of no avail to get the book or the lad out of the circle, he got wild, and tried the effects of terror. First he became a grizzled greyhound (*mial-chù riabhach*) and came wildly dashing against the circle; then a roaring bull; then a flock of crows (*sgaoth ròcais*) sweeping above the youth, so near that the wind caused by their wings would have carried him out of the circle if he had not clung to the heather.

When cock-crowing time came the devil abandoned his attempts and disappeared. The book became the 'Red Book of Appin', and was last in possession of the Stewarts of Invernahyle (*Inbhir na h-Aoile*).[557]

COMING FOR THE DYING

A native of the neighbourhood of Oban, on his way home from Loch Awe-side, after crossing the hills and coming in above Kilmore, was joined by three strangers. He spoke to them, but received no answer.

At a small public-house on the roadside he asked them in for a refreshment. They then told him they had business to attend to, and that after entering the house he was not on any account to come out or attempt to go home that night. On parting, the strangers turned off the high road by a private road leading to a neighbouring gentleman's house.

The night proved unusually stormy, and the man did not move from the inn till morning. He then heard that the gentleman towards whose house the three mysterious strangers had gone had died the previous evening, just about the time they would have arrived there. No person in the house or neighbourhood saw anything of them.

It has been already mentioned that the devil (or his emissaries, in the shape of three ravens) waited to catch the soul of Michael Scott as soon as it left the body. A freebooter of former days, who first made a house underground for his wife in Loch Con in Lower Rannoch (*Bun Raineach*) that he and his men might swear he had 'no wife above ground', and then married another, was at his death carried away by twelve ravens.[558]

MICHAEL SCOTT: MAKING THE DEVIL YOUR SLAVE

Those who had the courage to perform the awful *taghairm* (see pp. 167–70) called up the devil to grant any worldly wish they might prefer; the disciples of the black art made him their obedient servant. Michael Scott, whose reputation as a magician is as great in the Highlands as in the Lowlands, made him his slave. He could call him up at any time.

In Michael's time the people of Scotland were much confused as to the day on which Shrovetide was to be kept. One year it was early and another it was late, and they had to send every year to Rome to ascertain the time (*dh'fhaotainn fios na h-Inid*).[559] It was determined to send Michael Scott to get 'word without a second telling' (*fios gun ath-fhios*). Michael called up the devil, converted him into a black ambling horse (*fàlaire dhubh*), and rode away on the journey.

The devil was reluctant to go on such an expedition, and was tired by the long distance. He asked Michael what the women in Scotland said when they put their children to sleep or 'raked' the fire (*smàladh an teine*) for the night.[560] He wanted the other to mention the name of the Deity, when the charm that made himself an unwilling horse would be broken. Michael told him to ride on. *Marcaich thusa, bhiast, romhad . . .* "Ride you before you, you worthless wretch, and never mind what the women said."

They went at such a height that there was snow on Michael's hat when he disturbed the Pope in the early morning. In the hurry the Pope came in with a lady's slipper on his left foot. *Is àrd mharcaich thu a-raoir, a Mhìcheil*, said the Pope. "You rode high last night, Michael."

Michael's reply called attention to the Pope's left foot. *Seall air do chois chlì!*[561]

Ceil orm 's ceilidh mi ort, said the Pope. "Conceal my secret and I will conceal yours." And to avoid the chance of being again caught in a similar intrigue he gave Michael 'the knowledge of Shrovetide', viz., that it is always 'the first Tuesday of the spring light', i.e., of the new moon in spring.[562]

In Skye this adventure is ascribed to 'Parson Sir Andro of Ruig' in that island. He is said to have started on his terrible journey from the top of the Storr Rock, a scene the wildness of which is singularly appropriate to the legend. The Storr is a hill upwards of 2,000 feet high, and on its eastern side (from which the parson must have set out for Rome) is precipitous, as if the hill were half eaten away; and the weird appearance of the scene is much increased by the isolated and lofty pillars from which the hill derives its name, standing in front – *fiacaill stòrach* means a buck tooth. Not unfrequently banks of mist come rolling up against the face of the cliffs, concealing the lower grounds and giving a person standing at the top of the precipices one of the most magnificent views it is possible to conceive. He seems to look down into bottomless space, and where the mist in its motions becomes thin and the ground appears dark through it, there is the appearance of a profounder depth, a more awful abyss. The scene gives a wildly poetical character to the legend of the redoubtable parson and his unearthly steed.[563]

Coming Misfortune

A part of the parish of the Ross of Mull is known ecclesiastically as Kilviceuen (*Cill Mhic Eoghain* 'the Burying Place of the Son of Hugh'). Its ancient church was of unhewn stone, and its last minister previous to its being united to Kilfinichen was named Kennedy – a native of Cantyre, an Episcopalian in the reign of Charles II.[564]

Tradition records that he came to his death in the following manner. His parishioners, about the end of spring, were taking a new millstone from Port Bheathain on Sgurra-side to the mill by means of a pole run through its eye.[565] The parson threw off his cassock and assisted them. The cassock was left where it was thrown off. In the evening his wife sent a servant-maid for it. The maid found, lying on the cassock, a large black dog, which would not allow her to touch the garment. She came home without it, and refused to return. The wife herself and another servant then went, were bitten by the dog, and ultimately twelve persons, including the minister, died of hydrophobia.

So shocking an event could not take place without superstition busying itself about it. On Beltane night shortly before the event, the minister's servant-man had gone early to bed while it was yet day. There was 'a large blazing fire of green oak' (*beòlach mhòr dhearg de ghlas dharach*) on the floor of the room, and he closed and locked the door before going to bed. Through the night he heard a noise, as of some one feeling for the lock and trying to open the door. He remained quiet, thinking the noise was made by young men who came courting and had mistaken the door.

Soon, however, the door opened, and a person whom he did not recognise entered. The stranger, without saying a word, went and stood at the fire. When he turned his back the servant observed that his feet were horse's feet (*spògun eich*). In a short time the apparition went away, locking the door after it.

The man rose and went to an old man, in great estimation for his piety, who lived alone at *Creag nan Con* ('the Dog Rock'). The old man's hut was a poor one, its door being made of wicker work and of the form called *sgiathalan*. No remonstrances could induce him to stay another night in the minister's house, and it was arranged that he should sleep at the hut, and in the daytime go to his work at the manse. He told the sight he had seen, and the good man inferred from the time of night at which the devil had been seen that evil was near the house.

It was shortly after this that the dog went mad, and the frightened servant was the only one of the minister's household that escaped.

THE GAÏCK CATASTROPHE (*MORT GHÀTHAIG*)

> *An Nollaig mu dheireadh den cheud*
> *Cha chuir mi an àireamh nam mias.*

"The last Hogmanay of the century / I'll not include in the count of the months."[566]

On the last night of last century a disastrous casualty, in which six persons lost their lives, occurred in the deer forest of Gaïck in Badenoch. The wild tract of mountain land to which the name is given was not formally made into a deer-forest till 1814, but its loneliness made it a favourite haunt of wild game at all times. There was not a house in the large extent of near thirty square miles beyond a hut for the shelter of hunters.

Captain MacPherson of Ballychroän, an officer in the army, with some friends and gillies, were passing the night of the 31st December 1800 in this hut when an avalanche or whirlwind or some unusual and destructive agency came upon them and swept before it the building and all its inmates. When people came to look for the missing hunters they found the hut levelled to the ground and its fragments scattered far and wide.

The men's bodies were scattered over distances of half a mile from the hut; the barrels of their guns were twisted, and over all there was a deep covering of snow, with here and there a man's hand protruding through it. The whole Highlands rang with the catastrophe, and it is still to be heard of in the Hebrides as well as in the district in which it occurred. Popular superstition constructed upon it a wild tale of diabolical agency.[567]

Captain MacPherson was popularly known as *Ofhaicheir Dubh Bhaile Chrodhain* ('the Black Officer of Ballychroän'). He is accused of being a man who was 'dark, savage' (*dorcha doirbh*), who had forsaken his wife and children, and had rooms below his house whence the cries of people being tortured were heard by those who passed the neighbourhood at night.

About the end of 1800 he was out among the Gaïck hills with a party of hunters, and passed the night in the hut mentioned. Late at night strange noises were heard about the house, and the roof was like to be knocked in about the ears of the inmates. First came an unearthly slashing sound, and then a noise as if the roof were being violently struck with a fishing-rod. The dogs cowered in terror about the men's feet. The captain rose and went out, and one of his attendants overheard him speaking to something, or someone, that answered with the voice of a he-goat. This 'being' reproached him with the fewness of the men he had brought with him, and the Black Officer promised to come next time with a greater number.

Of the party who went on the next hunting expedition not one returned alive. The servant who said he had heard his master speaking to the devil refused positively to be one of the party; neither threats nor promises moved him, and others followed his example. Only one of the previous party – a MacFarlane from Rannoch, a good and pious man it is said – went. It was observed that this day the officer left his watch and keys at home, a thing he had never been known to do before.

MacFarlane's body was not found on the same day with the rest. It was carried further from the hut than the searchers thought of looking, and a person who had found before the body of one lost among the hills was got to look for his remains. There is a saying that if a person finds a body once he is more apt to find another.

When the melancholy procession with the dead bodies was on the way from the forest even the elements were not at peace, but indicated the agency that had been at work. The day became exceedingly boisterous with wind and rain – so much so, when the Black Officer's body was foremost, that the party was unable to move on, and the order had to be changed.

Two songs at least were composed on the occasion. One, strong in its praises of Captain MacPherson, will be found in *Duanaire*, p. 13; the other, among other things, says of him:

> *Ofhaicheir Dubh Bhaile Chrodhain a bh' ann,*
> *Thréig e a bhean 's a chlann;*
> *Nan do thuit e 'n cath na Fraing*
> *Cha bhiodh an call cho farranach.*

"The Black Officer of Ballychroän it was, / He turned his back on wife and children; / Had he fallen in the wars in France / The loss was not so lamentable."[568]

The Bundle of Fern

A shepherd in Benderloch saw a large bundle of ferns rolling down the hillside, and, in addition to the downward motion given by the incline, it seemed to have a motion of its own. It disappeared down a waterfall. Of course this was Black Donald; what else could it be?[569]

The Pig in the Indigo Pot

A former tenant of the farm of Holm (in Skye) and his wife had gone to bed, leaving a large pot full of indigo dye on the floor. The pig came in and fell into the pot. The wife got up to see what the noise was, and on looking into the pot saw the green snout of a pig jerking out of the troubled water. She roared out that the devil was in the pot. Her husband shouted in return to put on the lid, and jumping in great excitement out of bed, he threw his weight on the lid to keep it down till the devil was drowned. His wife was remarkable for always commending what her husband did, and kept repeating, *Is iomadh duine d'an dèan thusa feum a-nochd, a Mhurchaidh!* "Many a person you will confer a favour on this night, Murdoch!"

At last the noise in the pot subsided, and Murdoch nearly called up the party he had sought to drown on finding it was his own pig he had been so zealously destroying.[570]

AMONG THE TAILORS

It is a saying that the only trade that the devil has been unable to learn is that of tailoring. The reason is that when he went to try, every tailor left the room, and having no one to instruct him, he omitted to put a knot on the thread he began to sew with. In consequence the thread always came away with him, and he gave up the trade in despair. It is presumed that he wanted to learn the trade to make clothes for himself, as no one would undertake the making of them.

TAGHAIRM

The awful ceremony to which this name was given was also known among old men as 'giving his supper to the devil'.[571] It consisted in roasting cats alive on spits till the arch-fiend himself appeared in bodily shape. He was compelled then to grant whatever wish the persons who had the courage to perform the ceremony preferred, or, if that was the object of the magic rite, to explain and answer whatever question was put to him.

Tradition in the West Highlands makes mention of three instances of its performance, and it is a sort of tribute to the fearless character of the actors that such a rite should be ascribed to them. It was performed by *Ailein nan Creach* (Allan the Cattle-Lifter) at *Dail a' Chait* ('the Cats' Field'), as it has since been called, in Lochaber, and by *Lachann Odhar* (Dun Lachlan) in *sabhal mòr Peighinn a' Ghobhann*, the big barn at Pennygown in Mull. Allan was a native of Lochaber, the most notorious district in the Highlands for cattle-lifters, and derived his name from having lifted a *creach* 'for every year of his life, and one for every quarter he was in his mother's womb'. He died at the age of 34.[572]

The details of these two ceremonies are so exactly the same that there is reason to think they must both be versions of an older legend. Nothing appears to create a suspicion that the one account was borrowed from the other.[573]

The third instance of its performance was by some of *Clann 'ic Cuithein*, 'the Children of Quithen', a small sept in Skye now absorbed (as so many minor septs have been) into the great family of the MacDonalds. The scene was a natural cavity called *an Eaglais Bhréige*, 'the Make-Believe Cave', on East Side, Skye. There is the appearance of an altar beside this church, and the locality accords well with the alleged rite.[574]

The following is the Mull legend. Lachlan Oär and a companion *Ailein mac Eachainn*, Allan the son of Hector (some say he had two companions), shut themselves up in the barn at Pennygown on the Sound of Mull, and putting cats on spits roasted them alive at a blazing fire. By-and-by other cats came in and joined in the horrible howling of those being roasted, till at last the beams (*sparrun an taighe*) were crowded with cats, and a concert of caterwauling filled the house. The infernal noise almost daunted Lachlan Oär, especially when the biggest of the cats said, "When my brother the Ear of Melting comes — "

Allan the son of Hector did not allow the sentence to be finished. "Away, cat," he cried, and then added to his companion, in an expression which has become proverbial in the Highlands when telling a person to attend to the work he has in hand, and never mind what discouragements or temptations may come in his way, *Dé sam bith a chì no chluinneas tu, cum an cat mun cuairt.* "Whatever you see or hear, keep the cat turning."

Dun Lachlan, recovering courage, said, "I will wait for him yet, and his son too."

At last the Ear of Melting came among the other cats on the beams, and said, while all the other cats kept silence, *Lachainn Uidhir 'ic Dhòmhnaill 'ic Néill, is olc an càramh cait sin.* "Dun Lachlan son of Donald son of Neil, that is bad treatment of a cat."

Allan to this called out as before, "Whatever you see or hear, keep the cat turning." And the fearful rite was proceeded with.

At last the Ear of Melting sprang to the floor and said, *Ge b'e có air am mùin Cluas an Leoghaidh chan fhaic e gnùis na Trianaid.* "Whomsoever the Ear of Melting makes water upon will not see the face of the Trinity."

Crois a' chlaidhimh ad' cheann, a bhiast, 's tu mùn fallais! answered Dun Lachlan. "The cross of the sword in your head, wretch, your water is sweat!" And he struck the cat on the head with the hilt of his two-handed sword.

Immediately the devil, under the potent spell, assumed his proper shape and asked his wild summoners what they wanted with him. One asked *conach is clann* ('prosperity and children'), and Dun Lachlan asked: *Cuid is conach, is saoghal fada 'na cheann.* "Property and prosperity, and a long life to enjoy it."

The devil rushed out through the door crying, *Conach! Conach! Conach!* "Prosperity! Prosperity! Prosperity!"

The two men obtained their desires, but were obliged (some say) to repeat the *taghairm* every year to keep the devil to the mark.[575]

When Dun Lachlan was on his death-bed his nephew came to see him, and in the hope of frightening the old fellow into repentance, went through a stream near the house and came in with his shoes full of water. *A mhic mo pheathar*, said Lachlan, *car son tha bogan ad' bhròig?* "My sister's son, why is there water in your shoe?"

The nephew then told that the two companions who had been along with Lachlan in the performance of the *taghairm*, and who were both by this time long dead, had met him near the house, and to escape from them he had several times to cross the running stream; that they told him their position was now in the 'bad place', and that they were waiting for his uncle, who (if he did not repent) would have to go along with them.

The old man, on hearing this melancholy message, said, *Nam bithinn fhìn 's mo dhà chompanach ann, 's trì groilleinean againn nach lùbadh 's nach briseadh, cha bhiodh deamhan a-staigh nach cuireamaid an làimh.* "If I and my two companions were there, and we had three short swords that would neither bend nor break, there is not a devil in the place but we would make a prisoner of." After this the nephew gave up all hopes of leading him to repentance.[576]

A native of the island of Coll and his wife came to see him. Lachlan asked them what brought them. *Dh'iarraidh,* said the Coll man, *seisreach each fhuair thu fhéin on donas.* "To ask a yoke of horses you yourself got from the devil."

Lachlan refused this and sent the man away, but he sent a person to overhear what remarks the man and his wife might make after leaving. The wife said, *Nach b' fhiadhaich an t-sùil bh' aig an duin' ud!* "What a wild eye the man had!"

Her husband replied, *Saoil am b'i sùil an t-slauchdain, ach sùil an t-saighdeir, mar bu chòir?* "Do you suppose it would be an eye of softness and not a soldier's eye, as should be?"

On this being reported to Lachlan, he called the Coll man back and gave him what he wanted.[577]

Martin, in his *Description of the Western Islands*, p. 110, quoted by Scott (*Lady of the Lake*, note 2T), after describing a mode of *taghairm* by taking a man by the feet and arms to a boundary stream and bumping him against the bank till little creatures came from the sea to answer the question of which the solution was sought, says: "I had an account from the most intelligent and judicious men in the Isle of Skie, that about sixty-two years ago the oracle was thus consulted only once, and that was in the parish of Kilmartin, on the east side, by a wicked and mischievous set of people, who are now extinguished, both root and branch."[578]

The *taghairm* here referred to seems to be that above-mentioned as having been performed by the MacQuithens in the Make-Believe or False Cave on East Side, Skye. The race have not borne a good reputation, if any value is to be attached to a rhyme concerning them and other minor septs in Skye. There is a venom and an emphasis in the original impossible to convey in a translation:

> *Clann 'ic Cuthain chur nam briag,*
> *Clann 'ic Cuithein chur an t-sodail,*
> *Clann 'ic Mhannain chur na braide*
> *Ged nach b' fhaid' iad na cas biodaig.*

"The MacCuthan, expert in lies, / The MacQuithens, expert in base flattery, / The MacVannins, expert as thieves / Though no bigger than a dagger handle."[579]

Another method of *taghairm* described by Martin was by wrapping a person in a cow-hide, all but his head, and leaving him all night in a remote and lonely spot. Before morning his 'invisible friends' gave him a proper answer to the question in hand, or, as Scott explains it: "Whatever was impressed upon him by his exalted imagination, passed for the inspiration of the disembodied spirits, who haunt the desolate recesses."[580] This method of divination cannot have been common; at least the writer has been able to find no trace of it.

As a third mode of *taghairm* Martin briefly describes that above detailed, viz., the roasting of a live cat on a spit till at last a very large cat, attended by a number of lesser cats, comes and answers the question put to him.[581]

Both Martin and Scott fall into the error of supposing that the object of the *taghairm* was solely divination, to ascertain the future, the issue of battles, the fate of families, etc. The mode by roasting live cats was too fearful a ceremony to be resorted to except for adequate reasons, and the obtaining of worldly prosperity, which was the object of the Mull *taghairm*, is a more likely reason than curiosity or anxiety as to a future event.

The naming of the word *taghairm* is not at first sight obvious. There is no doubt about the last syllable being *gairm*, a call. *Ta* is probably the same root that appears in so many words, as *tannasg*, *taibhse*, etc., denoting spectres, spirits, wraiths, etc., and *taghairm* means nothing else than the 'spirit-call', in fact 'the calling of spirits from the vasty deep'.[582]

GLAS-GHAIRM – THE POWER OF OPENING LOCKS

This was a rhyme or incantation by which the person possessing the knowledge of it could shut the mouths of dogs and open locks. It was reckoned a very useful gift for young men who went a-wooing. *Gilleasbaig Mhurchaidh* (Archibald son of Murdoch), or, as he was also popularly known, *Gilleasbaig Eutrom* (Archibald the Light-Headed), who was about twenty years ago a well-known character in Skye and its neighbourhood, knew the charm, but when he repeated it he spoke so fast that no one was able to learn it from him, and as to his teaching of it to any one, that was out of the question.[583]

Poor Archibald was mad, and when roused was furiously so. He went about the country attending markets and wherever there was a gathering of people, and found everywhere open quarters throughout that hospitable island. Indeed it was not wise to contradict him. He had a keen and ready wit, as numerous sayings ascribed to him testify, and composed several songs of considerable merit. The fear which dogs had of him, and which made them crouch into corners on seeing him, was commonly ascribed to his having the *glas-ghairm*, but no doubt was owing to the latent madness which his eyes betrayed, and of which dogs have an instinctive and quicker perception than men. On their offering the slightest sign of hostility, Archibald would knock out their brains without as much as looking at their masters.[584]

The *glas-ghairm* was supposed to be in some way connected with the safety of Israel on the night before the Exodus – Ex. 11: 7, 'against any of the children of Israel shall not a dog move his tongue, against man or beast'.

13

BLACK WITCHCRAFT

WITCHES

Witchcraft introduces us to a class of popular superstitions entirely different from those connected with Fairies. Fairies, water-horses and kindred supernatural beings were distinct from the evil spirits that gave to witches their unhallowed powers. They could not be compelled or conjured by mortals to appear when wanted, or enter into contracts of service. The powers of darkness, on the other hand, were always at the service of their votaries, and, by means of charms and incantations known to the initiated, were made to lend their aid in any scheme of malevolence.

A belief in magic widely – almost universally – prevails among the tribes of mankind, and the witchcraft of the Christian era, while it undoubtedly gained strength and character from mistaken interpretations of scripture, owes many characteristics to the delusions of pagan times.

The Highland witches have of course many points in common with their sisters of the south, but comparatively there is little repulsive or horrible in their character. Tales regarding them make no mention of incubus and succubus, midnight meetings and dances with the devil, dead men's fingers, and more of the horrible and awful, the ravings of poor women driven crazy by persecution and torture.[585] Neither is there mention of their riding through the air on broomsticks, nor, like the witch of Endor, raising the dead.[586] Their art was forbidden, and their powers came from the devil, but it does not appear under what paction – or that there was any paction under which this power was to be got. It was in the name of the devil, and against the name of the Trinity, they set about their cantrips, but a knowledge of the necessary charms, and the courage to use them, seem to have been all that was requisite.

Those having the reputation of being witches were (and are, for a few still survive) usually old women, destitute of friends and means of support, and naturally ready to eke out a miserable livelihood by working on the fears or the simplicity of their more prosperous neighbours.

There are instances in which a farmer has bribed a witch by yearly presents not to do harm to his cattle; and we must remember that in days of scarcity and famine, poverty with icy hand and slow-consuming age will make people resort to shifts of which they would never dream when food was abundant. In most cases the reputed witch was merely a superstitious and perhaps ill-favoured old woman, possessing a knowledge of rhymes and charms for the healing of disease in man and beast, and taking pains to 'sain' her own cattle, if she had any, from harm. Sometimes she was also dishonest, desirous of being looked upon with awe, and taking advantage of nightfall to steal milk from her neighbours' byres and corn from their stackyards.

Her powers of witchcraft satisfactorily accounted to the popular mind for her butter and cheese – even if she had no cows – being abundant when the stores of others failed. In dark uncultured times a claim to influence over the unseen powers of nature, and to intercourse with spirits, had only to be made to be allowed, and the mere pretension too readily invests the claimant with awe to make it safe for anyone to denounce the imposture. Many believed in the efficacy of the arts they practised, and in their own possession of the power with which the credulity of mankind was willing to accredit them. Unusual natural events and phenomena can easily be turned into proofs of a witch's claim; imposture readily leads to delusion, and hence among the poor and uneducated it is no wonder to find witchcraft practised and believed in.

The power of witches was always at the disposal of those who were willing to pay for it, and the fact that the rewards of witchcraft did not sometimes exceed a pound of tobacco alone shows how much the urgencies of want had to do with the pretence to supernatural powers. Unless payment was given the witch could do nothing: her spells were then of no avail. To explain the anomaly that witches possessed such tremendous powers and yet remained always in indigent circumstances, it was said the poor wretches could not benefit themselves; their power – as might be expected, considering the source from which it was derived – was only one of mischief and doing harm to others. Much of the superstition is at variance with this popular explanation, as, for instance, the taking of milk from the neighbours' cows and the substance from their butter and cheese, but contradictions and absurdities never stand in the way of credulity and superstitious fears.

The Gaelic name *buidseach* is identical in meaning with the English *witch*, a word it also somewhat resembles in form. The term *bao'* is sometimes translated wizard, but is properly only a careless conversational form of *baobh*, a wild furious woman, a wicked mischievous female who scolds and storms and curses, caring neither what she says nor what she does, praying the houses may be razed (*làrach lom*) and the property destroyed (*sgrios an codach*) of those who have offended her.[587] This is a word used in proverbs. *Gheibh baobh 'guidhe, ach chan fhaigh a h-anam tròcair.* "A raging woman obtains her imprecation, but her soul obtains no mercy." *Baoth* 'weak, foolish' is often confounded with it. Mackintosh (*Prov.*, p. 143) makes the expression *mac a bao* 'a wizard's son' instead of *macan baoth* 'a weak or little child':

Is mairg as màthair do mhacan baoth
Dar as ann air Diar-Daoin bhios a' Bhealltainn.

"Pity of her who is the mother of a helpless child / When May-Day falls on a Thursday" – i.e. owing to the infant mortality of the season.[588]

A common answer to the question 'What could witches do?' is 'What could they not do?' The classes of actions, however, ascribed to them are not numerous. They could take the milk from their neighbours' cattle, bring fish to their own coasts, make fishermen successful, go to sea for fish themselves and bring home creelfuls, raise storms, sink ships, drown those who offended them; give strings to sailors with knots on them, the unloosening of which raised the wind; they could go to wine-cellars in London or Ireland, and drink wine till morning; fly through the air with magic quickness, and cross the seas in the most unlikely vessels – sieves, eggshells, or dry cow-sherds; produce a wasting disease in an enemy, waylay and endanger the belated traveller, and by their cursed tricks keep a child in its mother's womb past its proper time; suck cows, and assume various shapes. They could benefit – or at least ward away evil from – a favourite, but their power of doing so seems to have been much feebler than their powers of mischief.

In carrying out their unhallowed cantrips, witches assumed various shapes. They became gulls, cormorants, ravens, rats, mice, black sheep, swelling waves, whales, and very frequently cats and hares. The shape was not always well chosen for the object to be attained – a hare, for instance, being but ill-formed for sucking cows, or a cat for drinking wine; neither was a sieve or an eggshell a likely vessel to go to sea in, nor a piece of tangle for carrying milk in, nor the chimney-crook a probable substitute for the cow's udder.

This, however, is of no consequence. It is only part of the witch's diabolical mode of going to work. The truth is that these harmless animals whose shapes witches were said to assume, being seen in unusual places at unusual times, or conducting themselves in an unusual manner, were converted by the terrified imagination into witches pursuing their unlawful practices. Many tales seem to have their origin in vain attempts to stagger credulity, and in that delight which people of lively imaginations sometimes take in 'cramming' their more stupid fellows.[589]

In addition to change of shape, witches had a machinery of charms, incantations, red, black, and blue threads, magic caps, and particularly a magic staff called *an luirgean, an lorg ohn*.[590]

There were certain nights of the year on which they were unusually busy. These were particularly the last night of every quarter. On Beltane night they were awake all night. (In Germany it was a common belief that witches met on the night before first May, i.e. Beltane night, on the mountain called the Blockberg to dance and feast with devils.)[591] Their object seems to have been to 'sain' – i.e. keep evil away from – their own cattle or those of the farmers who employed them for the purpose. Others were no doubt taking advantage of any neglect in this respect to secure to themselves the butter and cheese for the next three months. No one, however, knows what they were after; as a woman who believed in their being awake on Beltane night piously said, "God and themselves know what they are doing."

Many tales relating to witchcraft, as has been already remarked, must have had their origin in attempts to ridicule people out of their belief and in an unbridled exercise of imagination. They only furnished a proof that men will believe the incredible.

WITCHES AND MILK

To the poor a cow is invaluable, and its ailments are naturally a source of anxiety. Hence the poor man has been most frequently the victim of imposture, and his cow has the most frequently lost its milk through the machinations of witches. The folds of the affluent were seldom attacked, or those byres in which regard was paid to cleanliness and tidiness.

The stories of witches assuming the shape of hares and sucking cows are number-less. A boy who saw one described the hare as sitting on its hind legs with its fore paws resting on the cow's udder. Some people profess to have come upon the witch through the night while thus engaged, and caught her. The hare then became a woman.

When a witch assumes this shape it is dangerous to fire at her without putting silver – a sixpence, or a button of that metal – in the gun. If the hare fired at was (as indeed it often was) a witch in disguise, the gun burst, and the shot came back and killed the party firing, or some mischance followed. Old women used, therefore, to recommend that a sixpence be put in the gun when firing at a hare.

Parties who entered the house of a reputed witch in Cornaig, Tiree, found two churns full of water on the floor and a shallow milk-dish (*measair*) full of butter on the table.

In olden times the master of a ship, dining with the laird of Coll, was asked if the butter on the table was not very fine. He said it was, for pig's butter. The dairymaid was called up and questioned. She confessed that seeing a whale (*muc-mhara*, literally a sea-pig) passing, and hearing its bellow (*geumraich*), she had taken the substance (*toradh*) of its milk from it. If the laird believed her, he was an honest, unsuspicious man, who never dreamt of any collusion between her and his guest.

A Tiree witch once took all their milk from the laird of Coll's cows, and was on her way home with it in a *duitheaman*, a black seaweed not unlike a tangle, wrapped round her body. A man met her, cut the black tangle with his knife, and all the milk flowed out on the ground.[592]

Witches also carried away milk in needles, dung-forks, etc., and have been detected taking it in a stream from the chimney-crook. A sailor whose ship was on her way through the Kyles of Bute (*na Caoil Bhòdach*), hearing a bull roaring on the Cowal coast, took the milk from the herd of which it was lord by cutting the cable with an axe. The milk came streaming from the cable.

It is related of 'Mr Lachlan', a former minister of Kintail, that going one day to the house of a reputed witch without telling who he was, he induced her, as a specimen of her power, to milk the chimney-crook. The cow from which the milk was to be taken was the minister's own. The witch went to work till all the milk was extracted, and then asked the minister if he was satisfied. He told her to go on, and she milked the iron till blood came. When the minister went home he found his cow dead.[593]

The crook or pot-hanger seems to have been an important article of the witch's paraphernalia. A shepherd in Mull, coming in late from the hill with his feet wet, placed his stockings to dry on the pot-hanger. An old woman present pulled the stockings down again, saying to the shepherd, "Don't do that. *Cuimhnich gur duin' thus' tha siubhal a' mhonaidh latha 's a dh'oidhche*. Remember you are a person that travels the hill night and day." He never could ascertain what she meant.[594]

A witch in Lochaber had a little pet sheep, by milking which she gathered to herself the milk from the flocks of all the neighbouring farmers.

Dòmhnall Molach ('Hairy Donald'), a Morvern celebrity of last century, professing great skill in healing or hurting cattle by means of magic charms, was laughed at for his pretensions by the parish minister, and his powers were made game of. Donald, at his own request, was shut up in a room, and a particular cow was named by the minister for him to exercise his talents upon. Before he finished his incantations the cow fell over the rocks.[595]

A man bought at a market from a stranger a mart or winter cow. When killing it, the blows of the axe made no impression. An old man who came the way, when told of this, examined the cow's tail and found a red string tied round it. On this being taken away, the cow fell at the first blow.[596]

Counter-Charms

Of course the spells of witches could be counteracted. It would not be right that such dangerous powers should be unchecked. Some of the counter-charms were good disinfectants, but in general the efficacy of the remedy was as imaginary as the enemy whose machinations were to be defeated.

It was to prevent the taking of milk from cows that nearly all the counter-charms were used. Anything in which people believed would be sufficient, but the antidotes in ordinary use were these.

Juniper (*iubhar-beinne, aiteal*), pulled in a particular manner, was burned before the cattle and put in cows' tails.[597]

A ball of hair (*gaoisid*), called a *ronag*, was put in the milk-pail on Lammas day (or on the Thursday after) to keep its substance in the milk during the rest of the year.[598] MacSymon (*Mac Shìomoin*, a sept of MacArthurs), a native of Balemartin, Tiree, was much resorted to in former times for these constitution balls. On Lammas day (*Lùnastal*) he gave to all who came to him a little bag of plants, sewn up, to be placed in the cream jug (*crogan uachdair*) for the ensuing year, that the cattle and the milk might retain their virtue or substance (*toradh*).[599]

Stale urine (*maistir*) should be sprinkled on the doorposts and about the byre. It keeps away the evil eye. There was an old woman in Coll who was taken notice of by her neighbours for sprinkling cows and doorposts every night. Her intention no doubt was to make assurance doubly sure.[600]

The mountain ash (*caorann*) was the most powerful charm of any:

> A rowan-tree and a red thread
> Gars a' the witches dance to dead.[601]

Its efficacy was known in England as well as in the Highlands.[602] The peg of the cow-shackle (*cnag chaorainn sa bhuaraich*) should be made of it, as well as the handle and cross of the churn-staff (*crois na loinid*).[603] The ancient churn was broader at one end than the other, and its narrow end, or mouth, was secured with a prepared sheep-skin covering (called *fùileach* in Mull, *iomaideil* in Morvern and on the mainland generally). The cross or hoop that secured this covering in its place should also be of mountain ash. The churn was worked by the small end being lifted up and let down repeatedly.

In Islay, not twenty years ago, a man had a rowan-tree collar for securing his cow at night, and every time the animal visited the bull he passed this collar thrice through the chimney-crook.[604] On Beltane day annually he dressed all the houses with rowan. It was said of the man in Craignish who gathered potent herbs on St Swithin's day and studied magic with one foot in the chimney-crook:

> *Badan de nì 'chaorainn*
> *Thig o aodann Ealasaid,*
> *Cuir snàithn' dearg is sreang ás,*
> *Cuir siud an ceann a' chrathadair,*
> *'S ged thigeadh buidseach Endor*
> *Gun ceannsaicheadh Ailein i.*

"A tuft of rowan twigs / From the face of Ailsa Craig, / Put a red thread and a knot on it, / And place it on the end of the sprinkler, / And though the witch of Endor came / Allan could manage her." The rhyme was composed by the bard Ailein Dall.[605]

A horseshoe was of great power for the protection of cattle against witchcraft. As in England, it must be found by accident. It was put above the byre door, and a nail from it, driven into the lowest hoop (*cearcall*) of the milk-dish (*mias*), kept its substance in the milk. It preserved horses when put above the stable door, and ships when nailed to the mast.[606]

An entire horse could not be touched by evil spirits, and its rider was safe from the attacks of witchcraft. A person in the neighbourhood of Luing, Argyllshire, returning from a funeral, found himself unable to make any progress on his road home, though he did his utmost all night to get on. He was retarded by some unseen influence. He rode an entire horse, and found himself safe at daybreak. His safety lay in the horse he rode.[607]

The famed 'Red Book of Appin', according to one version of the tale, was got by one who rode an entire horse to a meeting of witches, and having got hold of the book, made off with it in despite of the devil and all his servants. In a West Highland tale (ii., 87), the owner of the 'Red Book' advises the shoe of an entire horse to be nailed on the byre door to counteract the witches who were taking the milk from the cows.[608] The shoes of entire horses probably are the proper kind to use, though others came into use from being found equally efficacious.

Tar put on the door kept witches away, and, put on the cow's ear, was believed to prevent *ceathramh gorm* or 'quarter ill'.[609]

If, notwithstanding all these safeguards, or through neglect of them, a cow lost its milk, or the milk ceased to yield butter or cream, there were several methods by which the witchcraft (which was undoubtedly the cause) might be counteracted. Some of these remedies appear more like the inventions of practical jokers than ceremonies from which any rational meaning can be taken.

When a cow ceases unaccountably to give milk, and witchcraft is suspected, its owner is to take some of the animal's urine (*maistir*), put it in a bottle and cork it well. The witch who has taken the milk cannot make a drop of water till the milk is allowed to come back. It is a common story that the owner of bewitched cows, under the advice of 'wise' people of his neighbourhood, put a potful of the cows' dung on the fire and boiled it. He then put in half an ounce of pins and stirred the compost, till at last the witch appeared at the hole which formed the window and entreated him to 'stop tormenting her and all would be well'. He stopped, and next morning his cows had milk as usual.

It was also said that by putting pins in the cow's milk and boiling till the dish is dry, the witch is made to appear and confess. A woman once did this in Tiree, and found her own brother was the guilty party.

Old people in the East Side of Skye remember the bull being put on the top of a suspected witch's house to bring back their milk to a farmer's cows. The more brutal method of 'scoring', or drawing blood from, the witch above her breath – the object of which could only be to make clowns strike poor old women on the face with their fists – was unknown in the Highlands. The plant *mòthan*, pearlwort, put in the milk-pail, was a more gentle but quite as sure a method of restoring its virtue to the milk. If a piece of it was in the bull's hoof at the time of pairing, no witch could touch the offspring's milk.[610]

In Tiree a person lost several stirks by the stakes falling and strangling them in the byre. A 'wise' woman, reputed a witch, advised (though her advice was not taken) that the right-hand part of a fore horseshoe with three nails in it should be put below the threshold (*stairsneach*) of the byre along with a silver coin, and that the hindquarter of one of the beasts should be taken west and buried beyond the limits of the farm. This was to prevent a similar calamity in future.

GOING TO SEA

The Lewis witches were accounted the best for raising wind. A large number of them were at one time destroyed in the following manner. A tailor, working in a farmer's house where there happened at the time to be a scarcity of seasoning for dinner (*gann de dh'annlan*),[611] was told by the farmer's wife this would not be the case tomorrow if he could get breakfast past without the goodman saying grace. The tailor managed this, and his curiosity being roused, remained awake the following night to see what the wife would do. He saw a number of women, among whom he recognised his own wife, assembling in the farmhouse and, accompanied by the farmer's wife, disappearing up the chimney, each in a wicker creel. In the morning the farmer's wife came back with her creel full of fresh herring.

The tailor, when he went home, strongly represented to his wife the propriety of allowing him to accompany the witches in their future fishing expeditions. Two shares of the fish would then fall to them instead of one. The proposal was laid before a meeting of the witches, and in the circumstances they consented. To the number of eighteen the witches went to sea on a line of worsted thread, the tailor's wife being left ashore to hold the ball, or end of the line, in her hand. The tailor persuaded her to go with the rest, and leave him in charge of the line. She went, and the tailor paid out more line till he thought the witches far enough out at sea. He then cut the thread and allowed the whole lot to drown.[612]

Similarly, somewhere in the north (all marvels of this kind are said in the south Highlands to have occurred in the north),[613] a tailor was working in the house of an old woman who knew the forbidden arts but at the time was short of 'kitchen' for dinner. She took a creel, sat in it, and having muttered some mystic words, disappeared through a hole in the roof that formed the chimney. In a while she came back with the creel full of herring.

The tailor kept the spell in remembrance, and the first day he got the old woman out of the way, sat in the creel and repeated it. He does not seem, however, to have learned the words quite correctly, for the creel, instead of making for the hole in the roof, rose straight up and hit his head violently against the rafters. It then floated along against the roof, as if in search of an outlet. It bumped his head a second time against the rafters and he roared out, "Where in the curse of God are you going now?"

Instantly, at the name of the Deity, the creel fell down, and the tailor dislocated his hips (*chaidh e ás a ghobhal*). He never again dabbled in the dark science.[614]

In Skye one of a party of women, assembled at an old woman's house to full cloth, went by accident into the barn and found it full of fish suspended from the roof. "There are many herrings here," she said; and there being no way by which the old woman could have got them but by witchcraft, she taxed her with unholy practices. The old woman got very angry at the exposure.

A Barra and a Uist witch one year tried each other's powers in drawing the fish to their respective islands. The Barra witch proved the stronger, and took the fish to Castlebay (*Bàgh Chìosamuil*).[615] Another year the Uist and Tiree witches had a similar contest. The latter prevailed, and the men of a bygone generation believed that every flounder caught that year on the Tiree shores had a hole in its tail, made by the witches in the struggle.

On the shallows (*oitir*) between Tiree and Coll the witches of the two islands were often seen fighting for the flounders that abound in the locality. The appearance that suggested the fancy was no doubt the same as is still to be seen on these banks in stormy weather.

A witch who left home every night was followed by her husband, who wondered what she could be about. She became a cat, and went in the name of the devil to sea in a sieve with seven other cats. The husband upset the sieve by naming the Trinity, and the witches were drowned. So the Skye story runs.[616] In the Sound of Mull the witches went on board the sieve 'against the name of the Father and the Son and the Holy Ghost', and the husband upset the concern by putting his foot on board in the name of the Father and the Son and the Holy Ghost.

In Tiree the unfortunate women were passing Kennavara Hill in eggshells on their way to Ireland when the husband of one of them, seeing the fleet, wished them God-speed. Instantly the eggshells sank, and the women were drowned.

Raising Storms and Drowning People

The belief that witches can trouble the sea and raise the wind is widespread, reaching even to the native Africans. It is part of the regular traffic of Finland witches to sell wind to mariners – as in the case of their Celtic sisters, tied in knots upon a thread.[617]

The following story is common to many places. A boatman from one of the southern islands was long detained in Lewis by adverse winds. He was courting a witch's daughter, and applied to her mother for a favourable wind. He gave her a pound of tobacco, and (assisted by neighbouring witches) after three days' exertion she produced a string with three knots upon it. The first knot was called *Thig gu fòill* ('Come gently'), and when he loosened it as he left the shore, a gentle breeze sprang up. The second knot was called *Teann nas fheàrr* ('Come better'), and on its being untied the breeze came stiffer. As he neared the harbour he out of curiosity loosened the last knot, the name of which was *Cruaidh-chàs* ('Hardship'). A wind came to 'blow the hillocks (*séideadh nan cnoc*) out of their places' and sent the thatch of the houses into the furrows of the plough-land, and the boatman was drowned. In Harris they say the boat was drawn up on land and secured before the last knot was untied. She was capsized and smashed to pieces.

The following, known as *Achanaich Mhic Mhuirich Mhòir*, 'Big MacVuirich's Supplication', is another form of the Celtic belief. *Mac Mhuirich nam buadh* ('MacPherson of power'), a noted wizard in South Uist, was on a passage by sea on a calm day.[618] The skipper said to him, *Iarr gaoth, a Mhic Mhuirich.* "Ask for a wind, MacVuirich." He did so, saying:

Gaoth an-ear on ailbhinn chiùin	An east wind from the calm aether
Mar a dh'òrdaich Rìgh nan Dùl,	As the Lord of the elements has ordained,
Soirbheas gun iomram gun abhsadh	A wind that needs not rowing nor reefing,
Nach dèanadh gnìomh fallsail dhuinn.	That will do nought deceitful to us.

Is lag leibideach a dh'iarr thu i, said the skipper, *'s mi fhìn air an stiùir.* "Weak and trifling you have asked it, when I myself am at the helm." MacVuirich answered:

Gaoth tuath cho cruaidh ri slait	A north wind hard as a rod
Ag oinealadh aig bial ar stuic	Struggling above our gunwale
Mar earba ruadh is i 'na h-airc	Like a red roe sore pressed
A' teàrnadh le ceann caol cruaidh cnuic.	Descending a hillock's narrow hard head.

Cha ruig moladh oirre fhathast, said the skipper. "It does not attain to praise yet." And MacVuirich went on:

Ma tha gaoth an ifrinn fhuar,	If there be a wind in cold hell,
A Chonnain, cuir 'nar deaghaidh i	Devil, send it after us
'Na tonnaibh 's 'na taosgaibh;	In waves and surges;
'S ma théid aon air tìr aiste, gur mis' e,	And if one go ashore, let it be I,
'S masa dithis, mis' agus mo chù.	And if two, I and my dog.

A sea came that rolled the boat's stern over her bows, and all were drowned but MacVuirich and his dog.[619]

The power of this wizard over the elements was also shown on another occasion. The MacRanalds were coming to attack the MacNeills of Barra, to whom MacVuirich was favourable.[620] Their boat was seen coming along the wild and rocky coast on the west of Skye, and was sunk by the mighty wizard uttering the following words:

> *A south-west wind toward Eiste point,*
> *Mist and rain,*
> *Clan Ranald on a breaking board —*
> *I reck it not;*
> *A narrow unsteady vessel,*
> *A lofty pointed sail,*
> *A lading of empty barrels*
> *And bilge-water to the thwarts;*
> *A weak irascible crew*
> *Having no respect one for another.* [621]

As might be expected, such a boat did not go far before sinking.

The usual way witches took to shipwreck a vessel was to put a small round dish (*cuach*) floating in a milk-pan (*measair*) placed on the floor full of water. They then began their incantations, and when the dish upset, the ship sank.

On one occasion three witches from Harris left home at night after placing the milk-pan thus on the floor in charge of a servant-maid, who was straitly enjoined not to let anything come near it. The girl's attention was, however, called away for a short time, and a duck came in and took to squattering about in the water on the floor. The witches, on their return in the morning, asked if anything had come near the milk-pan. The girl said no, and one of them said, "What a heavy sea we had last night coming round Càbag Head!"[622]

A few years ago a boat was lost coming from Raasa to Skye. The witches who caused the calamity were seen at work in the Braes of Portree, beside a stream. Three of them were engaged in the evil task, and a man was present along with them. Jobs of the kind require the presence of a man. A cockleshell (*slige coilleig*) was placed floating in a pool, and a number of black stones were ranged round the edge of the pool. When the incantation was at its height, the black stones barked like dogs and the cockleshell disappeared.

A farmer in Mull and his little daughter were walking along an eminence that overlooked the Sound, through which a number of ships were passing at the time. The little girl asked, "What will you give me, father, if I sink all these ships?"

Thinking she was in fun, he asked her how she would do it. She stooped down and looked backwards between her legs at one of the vessels. The ship whirled round and sank. In this expeditious manner all the ships in sight were sunk but one. The man asked why this one did not sink. The girl said it was because there was rowan-tree wood on board, and she could not touch it. He then asked who had taught her all this? She said it was her mother. The man, who was a good man, and before ignorant of his wife's dabbling in witchcraft, gathered his neighbours and burned herself and daughter.[623]

A witch was engaged to destroy a boat coming to Tiree. Another witch, however, wished its safety. The former came in shape of a gull that hovered about the boat and kept it back – a head wind? The other came as a cormorant (*sgarbh*), followed in the wake of the boat (*an uisge na stiùireach*, literally 'the waters of the rudder'), and saved it – favourable tide?[624]

A former Lord Macdonald (*Mà-Cònuill*) was on his way by boat to Uist, and experienced very unfavourable weather.[625] When near his destination, a towering wave – or, as it is called in Gaelic, *muir bhàite* 'a drowning sea' – nearly overwhelmed the boat, and two birds, a skua (*croma-ritheachar*) and an ordinary gull, were observed fighting in the air. The one was *Spòga Buidhe nighean Dòmhnaill 'ic Cormaig* ('Yellow Claws daughter of Donald son of Cormac'), the other *Gorm-Shùil Chrotach á Cràcaig* ('Hump-Backed Blue-Eye from Cràcaig'), both celebrated witches.[626] The former was for sinking the boat, the latter for saving it. Some time after, Blue-Eye met Lord Macdonald in Edinburgh, and reminded him of the incident and her own services on the occasion. He just remarked, "There was indeed such a circumstance."

A ship, sailing from Greenock, was to be destroyed by the captain's wife and two other witches. An apprentice overheard them planning this, and saying that they would come upon the ship on a certain day as three rolling waves, and the ship would be sunk unless the waves were cut with a sword. At the time said, the apprentice was allowed the command of the vessel, and standing in the bow with a drawn sword, cleft the waves and defeated the witches.

A boat from Hianish, Tiree, went out fishing on the day before the New Year. The morning was calm, but when the boat was returning the wind rose and the sea became very heavy. The best steersman in the boat took the helm. Another, sitting on the hindmost thwart (*tobhta shilidh*),[627] after looking for a while towards the stern, asked the helm from him, and being again and again refused, at last took it by force. When he got the rudder below his arm he said, "Now, come on!" And the boat reached shore in safety. He then explained that he had been seeing a gull – unseen by the first steersman – following the boat, and had recognised her as a woman of the neighbourhood. This woman had an illegitimate child by the first steersman, and it was thought her object in raising the storm and following so close in the wake of the boat was to snatch her seducer with her and drown him.

Ian Garve ('Stout John'), laird of Raasa (*Iain Garbh Mac 'Ille Chaluim Ratharsa*), a man celebrated in Highland song and legend for his great personal strength, was drowned by a witch who had this mysterious power of raising storms. The event occurred on Easter Monday (*Di-Luain Càisge*) in the great 'Storm of the Borrowing Days' of which a contemporary historian says 'the like of this tempest was not seen in our time, nor the like of it heard in this country in any age preceding', AD 1625; yet the traditions of the event are still fresh in popular memory.[628]

The witch was Ian Garve's own foster-mother (*muime*), and resided on the islet of Trodda (*Trodaigh*) on the east of Skye. She overheard a friend of hers say he wished Ian Garve, who was known to have gone to the Lewis, was drowned, and took up seriously words spoken only in jest. Others say she was bribed by an enemy to effect the hero's destruction.

He left Loch Sealg in Lewis to proceed home on a calm day. The witch was dairy-maid (*banachag*) in Trodda, and, seeing the boat coming, put milk in a large dish, and a small empty dish floating in it. A boy was placed standing in the doorway where he could see both the milk-pan and Ian Garve's boat. She herself stood with her foot in the 'swey' or chimney-crook, and began her unholy incantations.

Soon the dish in the milk-pail began to be violently agitated. The boy reported it first as going round sunwise (*deiseal*), then as going round against the sun and striking the sides of the basin, and finally as being capsized and floating bottom upwards (*air a bial foidhpe*).

The storm had been all this time increasing, till at last it blew a perfect hurricane. That night the heap of shingle on East Side (*'n Taobh Sear*) called *Mol Stabhan* was washed ashore.[629] Ian Garve's boat disappeared simultaneously with the capsizing of the bowl, and all on board perished.

Three ravens hovered about the boat as the storm was rising, and it became after-wards known that these three were *Spòga Buidhe* ('Yellow Claws') from Màiligeir on East Side, *Gorm-Shùil Chrotach* ('Hump-Backed Blue-Eye') from Cràcaig near Portree, and Doideag from Mull. When the boat was between *Sgeire Maola* ('Bare Skerries') and Trodda twenty birds flew about, and some of them assumed the shape of frogs (*muileacha màg*) on the deck. All the witches in Scotland were there, but were unable to sink the boat till Ian Garve said to the frogs, *Dé 'n riabhach thug an-seo sibh?* "What the brindled one has brought you here?"[630]

After that he became distracted from the number of birds and frogs coming upon him. A raven lighted on the gunwale of the boat, and Ian Garve, striking at it with his sword, cleft the boat to the water's edge. The first news of the drowning was heard on Minigeig Hill (*Monadh Mhinigeig*) in Badenoch, and the particulars became known by the telling of other witches. Another account says the hero appeared that night to his wife in her dreams, and said:

Di-Luain a dh'éirich a' ghaoth
'S thog i oirre fraoch is fearg;
Is innis do mhàthair mo chuirp
Gur h-e na h-uilc a rinn an t-sealg.

"On Monday the wind arose / And gathered its fury and rage; / Tell the mother of my body / 'Twas the evils made the hunt."

The shade came thrice and repeated this. Next day the wife told the dream to her mother-in-law, who exclaimed, *Tha mo laogh-sa caillte.* "Then my beloved is lost."

By far the most celebrated tale of this class is that of the destruction of Captain Forrest's ship by witches in the Sound of Mull. Viola (*Bheòla*), daughter of the king of Spain, dreamt of a remarkably handsome man, and made a vow not to rest till she found him. She fitted out a boat, and in the course of her wanderings came to Tobermory Bay. Here she saw MacLean of Dowart, who proved to be the man she was in search of, and, though he was a married man, became too intimate with him. MacLean's wife in her jealousy caused her servant Smollett, a south country man, to blow up the ship with all on board. After setting fire to a fuse leading to the magazine, Smollett made his escape, and by the time the explosion took place reached Penny-gown, a distance of ten or twelve miles. The cook was blown to Srongarve (*Sròn Gharbh* 'Rough Nose'), near Tobermory, where there is a cleft still bearing the name of *Uamh Chòcaire*, 'the Cook's Cave'. The princess herself fell somewhere in the sound, and was buried at *Cill*, the Loch Aline burying-ground in Morvern.[631]

The tale has this much truth in it, that one of the ill-fated Spanish Armada was blown up in Tobermory Harbour, AD 1589. The wonder would be, in those days when public news travelled slowly or not at all, if the history or object of the Spanish fleet should be known in the Highlands, or that it should be known to the Mull people that there was any ship in the fleet but the one that came to their own coasts.

Upon the news of the dreadful event reaching Spain, Captain Forrest (whose name is not very Spanish) was sent with a ship to take vengeance upon the Mull people by taking off the right breast of every Mull woman.[632] When the ship came the lady of Dowart sent for Doideag, the Mull witch, and by her means, with assistance procured from neighbouring witches, Captain Forrest's ship was sunk before next morning. Doideag shut herself up in a house alone at *Rubha Ghuirmein* (Guirman Point near Dowart) and there made her incantations. A rope was put through a hole in a rafter, and all night long the hand-mill (*brà*) was hoisted up to the beam, lowered, and hoisted again. A native of Tiree reported that, having come that evening to Doideag's house, he was compelled by her to hoist and lower and hoist the millstone all night without rest or refreshment, while the witch herself went away to Tiree and elsewhere for help. On her return she said that when in Tiree she had been detained a little in extinguishing a fire which had been caused by a spark falling among the fodder in the stirk-house belonging to the man who was her unwilling assistant.

As the quern was raised a gale sprang up, and increased in fury as the operation went on. At the same time gulls (others say hooded-crows, others black cats) appeared on the yard-arms of the devoted ship. Captain Forrest knew the black art himself, and went below. As word was brought him that another gull had appeared in the rigging, he said, *Fòghnaidh mi fhìn dhi seo fhathast.* "I will suffice for this one yet."

He could keep the ship against some say eight, others nine, witches, but "ere a' the play was play'd" there were sixteen, some say eighteen, on the yards.[633] Their names depend on the fancy of the narrator. All the Mull witches (*na doideagun Muileach*) were there, and the most powerful of the sisterhood from the surrounding districts. *Nic 'Ill' Dòmhnaich* from Tiree is commonly mentioned. A family of this name has had down to the present day a reputation for witchcraft. The last of them was known to the writer as a poor woman of much shrewdness and inoffensive character. She professed great skill in healing cattle by means of charms and suchlike *white* witchcraft.[634]

All accounts agree that when *Gorm-Shùil Mhòr bha sa Mheigh* ('Big Blue-Eye from Mey', the powerful Lochaber witch) came, the ship sank.[635] Shortly before this Captain Forrest told a sailor to look up and see how many gulls were on the yards: *Seall suas co miad faoileann air an t-slait.* On being told eighteen, he said, "We are lost."

In the morning Doideag was told her house had been unroofed in the gale, but she was comforted by being told the dreaded ship had gone down opposite Coire-na-theanchoir Bay.[636] *Ma tha thusa gun taigh, tha Captain Forrest gun long.* "If you are without a house, Captain Forrest is without a ship."[637]

WITCHES AS SHEEP

A native of Tiree was on his way home to the west end of the island in the evening with a new gun in his hand. When above the beach called Travay, he observed a black sheep running towards him from across the plain of Reef. Alarmed by the animal's motions, he put a silver sixpence in the gun, and on its coming near enough, took aim. The black sheep instantly became a woman (whom he recognised) with a drugget coat wrapped about her head.

The same woman had often persecuted him before, particularly in shape of a cat. She asked him to keep her secret, and he promised to do so, but one day, when drunk in the village to which the woman belonged, he told his adventure and the name of the woman. In less than a fortnight after, he was drowned, and the witch (for such the woman was universally reputed to be) was blamed as the cause.

Hector MacLean in Coll, according to his own account, was coming in the evening from Arinagour to Breacacha, a distance of four miles along what was then throughout the greater part a mountain track. When halfway, at Àirigh mhic Mharoich, a black sheep came about his feet, and several times threw him down.[638] At last he took out a clasp-knife (*sgian-lughaidh*) and threatened the sheep, if it came near him again, to stick it with the knife. It, however, again and again came and threw him down. In endeavouring to stab it, the knife closed upon his own hand between the finger and thumb, and cut him severely.

On coming to the large open drain or stream below Breacacha Garden, he stood afraid to jump across in case the black sheep should come about his legs and make him fall in the drain. He was now, however, within hail of his own house, and whistled loudly for his dog. It came, and was fiercely hounded by him at the sheep. Every time the dog made a rush and came too near, the sheep became an old woman (whom Hector recognised as one of his acquaintances) and jumped in the air. She asked him to call off his dog, and he refused. She asked him again, and promised, if he would do so, to befriend him in right and wrong (*an còir 's an eucoir*).

At last he did call the dog, but it would not obey. He caught it by the back of the neck, and it tried to turn upon himself. He promised to keep his hold till the woman made her escape. The witch became a hare, and Hector called out to her, as she seemed to have such wonderful power, to 'add another leg to her stern, to make her escape the faster'. When she was some distance away he let go the dog and went home.

The dog did not come home till the following afternoon; it followed the hare, compelled it to take refuge on a shelf of rock (*uirigh creige*), and lay below on the watch till forced by hunger to go home. The woman upbraided Hector, the first time she met him, for letting go the dog. Afterwards, when he went as servant-man to Arileod farm (*Àirigh Leòid*) in the neighbourhood, the same woman was often seen by him in the shape of a hare, sucking the cows. His dog, whenever it caught sight of her, gave chase, and compelled her to resume her proper shape.

When he left the farm, she was not seen there for some days. He went in search of her, and accused her to her face of having been the party that troubled the farm. She got into a rage, and said she would punish him for raising such a story about her. He answered that the proprietor of the island had offered a reward for the discovery of the guilty person, and if all the women in Coll were gathered on one hillock his speckled dog (*cù breac*) would pick her out as the offender. To this she made no reply. He asked her to go to Arileod dairy that night so that people would not have it to say it was for him the evil had arisen. She said this was Wednesday night, and it was out of her power to do anything, but the following night she would go, and he would hear of it.[639] On Thursday night she loosened the cows in Arileod byre, let in the calves, and did much mischief.

WITCHES AS HARES

In addition to the above tales in which this transformation has been mentioned, the following may be given as further illustrations of the superstition. A young man in the island of Lismore was out shooting. When near Balnagown Loch he started a hare and fired at it. The animal gave an unearthly scream, and it then for the first time occurred to the young man that there were no hares in Lismore. He threw away his gun in terror and fled home.

Next day he came back for the gun, and heard that a reputed witch of the neighbourhood was laid up with a broken leg. Ever after the figure of this woman encountered him and gave him severe thrashings. This preyed on his mind, and he never came to any good. He proved brooding, idle, and useless.

A Manxman who was in Tiree a few years ago told the following story. A party of sportsmen, engaged in coursing, were at a loss for a hare. An old woman told her grandson to go to them, tell them they would get a hare at a certain spot, and get half-a-crown for himself. The boy went, got his half-crown, and guided the sportsmen to the spot his grandmother had indicated. When the hare started he cried, "Run, granny, run!"

The hare made straight for the old woman's house, the dogs lost sight of it at the back of the house, and the old woman was found sitting at the fireside.

In Wigtonshire a hare ran up the chimney, and a suspected witch near hand was found with burnt feet.

WITCHES AS CATS

The association of witches with cats is of great antiquity. In the legends of Greece and Rome we are told of a woman who had been changed into a cat being chosen as priestess by Hecate (the goddess of sorcery and magic power) and of Hecate herself, when the gods were forced to hide themselves in animals, taking refuge in the shape of a cat. The association probably arose not so much from cats being the frequent, almost invariable, companions of the poor old women accused of witchcraft, as from the savage character of the animal itself. Its noiseless and stealthy motions, its persevering watchfulness, its extraordinary agility and tenacity of life, its diabolical caterwauling, prowling habits, deceitful spring, and the luminous appearance of its eyes in the dark, would alone suffice to procure it the name of unearthly; but when infuriated, glaring, bristling and spitting, it forms a vivid representation of a perfect demon. In the Highlands it was not, as in the witchcraft of the sixteenth and seventeenth centuries, looked upon as the familiar or attendant imp of the witch, but merely as an animal whose form witches frequently assumed.

There were other superstitions connected with the animal. Were it not the fear of being swallowed by the ground, a cat would run much faster than it does. When people have a cat along with them in a boat, they cannot – or will not – be drowned by witches. By burying a cat alive, people waiting for a favourable wind get a breeze from the direction in which its head is put; and a witch – that is, a young one – who is courted by a sailor can detain him with contrary winds as long as she likes by shutting up the cat in the cupboard.[640]

A cat scraping is a sign that some beast – horse, cow, pig, or dog – will be found dead on the farm before long. A cat washing its face portends rain next day, and turning its back to the fire storm and rain. When removing from one house to another (*imrich*) it is unlucky to take a cat. The animal was disliked by the MacGregors, and the Camerons of Glenevis could not tolerate it at all.[641]

A shepherd in Kintail, living alone in a bothy far from other houses, after kindling in the evening a bright cheerful fire, threw himself on a heather bed on the opposite side of the house. About twenty cats entered and sat round the fire, holding up their paws and warming themselves. One went to the window, put a black cap on its head, cried "Hurrah for London!" and vanished.

The other cats, one by one, did the same. The cap of the last fell off, and the shepherd caught it, put it on his own head, cried "Hurrah for London!" and followed.

He reached London in a twinkling, and with his companions went to drink wine in a cellar. He got drunk and fell asleep. In the morning he was caught, taken before a judge, and sentenced to be hanged. At the gallows he entreated to be allowed to wear the cap he had on in the cellar; it was a present from his mother, and he would like to die with it on. When it came the rope was round his neck. He clapped the cap on his head, and cried: "Hurrah for Kintail!"

He disappeared with the gallows about his neck, and his friends in Kintail, having by this time missed him and being assembled in the bothy prior to searching the hills, were much surprised at his strange appearance.

This is a fair specimen of the popular tale. It forms the foundation of the Ettrick Shepherd's 'Witch of Fife'. In Skye the adventure was claimed by a man nicknamed *But-ar-Scionn* ('Topsy-Turvy') as having occurred to himself. After coming home he made the gallows into a weaver's loom. The hero in Argyllshire made it the stern and keel of a boat which may be seen in Lorn to this day. In Harris the hero is a tailor; and the tale has been even found in the Monach Isles, west of Uist.[642]

Captain Burt (1730) tells a story of a similar kind which he had heard from a minister. A laird whose wine was disappearing mysteriously, suspecting witches, one night when he thought the plunderers were at work entered the cellar, closed the door, and laid about him with a broadsword. When light was brought, the cats, whose eyes he had seen glaring at him in the dark, disappeared, and only some blood was found on the floor. An old woman in the neighbourhood, suspected of being a witch, was found (on her house being entered) in bed with her leg cut off and lying below the bed.[643] The same story is told of the witches of Thurso (*Inbhir Eòrsa*).

A tailor named Macilduinn was left in a house alone on Hallowe'en night while the rest of the household went to a neighbour's house to hold the festivities of the evening. As he sat on a bed working at his trade, a great many cats came in, and attacking a bag of flesh at the end of the bed soon tore it up and devoured it. They then gathered round the tailor. One said, *Cùl mo spòige ri Macillduinn!* "The back of my paw to Macilduinn!" Another said, *Aghaidh mo spòige ri Macillduinn!* "The front of my paw to Macilduinn!"

These threats were repeated by all the rest, while they held out their horrid claws, some derisively, some menacingly, to the poor tailor. Frightened from his wits, he blew out the light, sprung to the door, and took to his heels. The cats gave chase, and by the time he reached a neighbour's house his back was scratched into shreds and thongs (*'na iallun*) by the claws of the infernal cats.

Cameron of Doïni, or Glenevis, was out hunting, and killed a wildcat. The animal, when expiring, asked him to tell, when he went home, that *Rìgh nan Cat* ('the King of the Cats') was dead, or according to others, *an Iuchair Chath* ('the Key of Battle') or *a' Bhruchail Bhreac* ('the Streaked Brindled One').[644] As he told his story, the little black kitten in the ash-hole (*an toll na luath*) bristled up and swelled till it was as large as a dog. Cameron said, "You are swelling, cat."

The cat answered, *Tha m' iteagun 's m' atagun ag atadh ris na h-éibhleagun!* "My feathers and my swellings are growing bigger with the heat!" And, springing at the chieftain's throat, killed him.[645]

The scions of this family (*Teaghlach Dhomhainnidh no Ghlinn Ibheis*) till quite recent times would not tolerate a cat in the house, from the memory of this tradition.[646]

The same story is told in the following manner, without any locality being assigned for the incident. A hunter killed a wildcat, and when he came home told his adventure. He said,

> *Sann a-nochd a thorchanaich leinn —*
> *Mharbhadh an urchaill earchaill mhòr.*

"Tonight has well prospered with us, / The big urchal-erchal has been slain."[647] A kitten that was listening rose and said, *An do mharbhadh Maol Meanachan nan Cat? Mur bhith na h-uile oidhche fhuair mi biadh is bainne 'nad theaghlach, bhiodh do sgòrnan fada riabhach ann am' ìnein. Innis do Bhruchd Riabhach gun d'eug Bladrum.* "Has Bald Entrails of the Cats been killed? If it were not the many nights I have got meat and milk in your family, I would have your long brindled weasand in my claws.

Tell Streaked Foul-Face that Bladrum is dead." And saying this the kitten went away, and was never seen afterwards.[648]

Near Vaul in Tiree, a man riding home at night with his son (a young boy) seated behind him was met by a number of cats. The boy had his hands clasped round his father, and the man, pressing them to his sides to make surer of the boy's hold, urged his horse to its speed. The cats sprang, and, fastening on the boy, literally devoured him. When the man reached home with his horse at full gallop, he had only the boy's arms left. A Wexford legend of the same kind (the two stories might have been originally identical), said to be at least as old as 1584, will be found in the *Dublin University Magazine* for September 1869.[649]

A woman detected a strange cat drinking the milk in her kirn, caught it by the back of the neck, and rapped its nose against the floor. It went about mewing in a melancholy manner till the woman took pity on it and called it, saying, *Puis, puis, gus am faigheadh tu diar*. "Puss, puss, till you get a drop."

The cat answered, *Chan e diar tha mi 'g iarraidh ach mar tha mo bhial, a Mhàiri*. "It is not a drop I want but the way my mouth is, Mary."

It then went away, but came back through the night with two other cats. One said they would take the back of their paws to the woman, but the second said the front of their paws. This resolution was carried by the casting vote of the injured cat, and the woman was torn in shreds.

A man, going in the evening to see a girl he was courting, was met at a lonely part of the road (near the end of Balefetrish Hill in Tiree) by seven cats, and was so terrified that he turned back and thereby lost his sweetheart. She married an old man from the village of Hianish, where a noted witch dwelt. The old man got the blame of bribing the witch to send the cats.

In olden times a cat belonging to the tenant of Heynish in Tiree was much addicted, like the rest of its kind, to stealing cheese. It was caught in the act, and, as a punishment for the past and a lesson for the future, its ears were taken off. The tenant had occasion to go from home, and on his return found the cat lying dead, having been hung for theft in his absence. He took it in his lap, and thus addressed it:

Nach tuirt mi riut, a Dhonnchaidh,	*Did I not tell you, little Duncan,*
Gum feumadh tu bhith falchaidh;	*You had needs of being wary;*
Nuair a reachadh tu gan ionnsaigh,	*When you went where the cheeses were,*
Gun ionnsaicheadh a' chroich dhut dannsa?	*The gallows would teach you how to dance.*
Is dona sin, a chait gun chluasan,	*Evil is it, earless cat,*
Mharbh iad thus' an geall a' chàise —	*They you have killed because of cheese;*
Dh'ìoc do mhuineal an smuais sin	*Your neck has paid for that refreshment,*
An uair sa an déidh do bhàis.	*At this time, after your death.*

On hearing these expressions of sympathy the cat began to revive, and the man went on:

> *A hundred welcomes wait you, cat,*
> *Since in my lap you've chanced to be;*
> *And though I do not much liberty allow,*
> *Many have you greatly loved.*
> *Are you the untamed cat that Fionn had*
> *That hunted wild from glen to glen?*
> *Had Oscar you at the battle of Bla-sguinn,*
> *And left you heroes wounded there?*
> *You drank the milk Catherine had*
> *For entertaining minstrel and meeting,*
> *And why should I praise you?*
> *You ought to be like any kitten,*
> *On the hillside seeking mice*
> *'Neath greyish grassy stems and bramble bushes.*

On hearing this the cat ran away and was never again seen.[650]

A Tiree boat was tacking out of a loch in the north. A man met it at a point of land near which it came, and asked to be taken to the other side. One of the boatmen was willing, but the rest were not, as they would thereby lose time. Next tack back, the man met the boat again, with the same result. "Well, then," he said, "perhaps you will repent it."

At the mouth of the loch the boatmen heard a howling as of innumerable cats. A storm arose, and with difficulty they reached shelter at the island of Eigg.

WITCHES AS RATS

A Tiree boatman, bringing a load of peats from the Ross of Mull, was met at the Treshinish Isles by two rats sailing along on dry cow-sherds. As good luck did not direct him, he threw a piece of peat at the rats and upset their frail barks.[651] A storm sprang up, and with difficulty he got to land. The rats were witches, and he should not have meddled with them.

WITCHES AS GULLS

A witch assumed the shape of a gull, delighting in storms – not only to bring danger or safety to a boat, as already told, but also for payment to bring back news of fishing boats driven away in a storm.

A boat from Tiree, going for a cargo of wood, was caught in a violent gale and driven north past Ardnamurchan Point. With difficulty the boatmen, four in number, secured her in a creek. They remained in a cave for four days till the storm abated. The suddenness and violence of the gale caused much anxiety to their friends, and two women (one of whom had two sons and a son-in-law in the boat, and the other, a widow, her youngest and only surviving son) consulted a famous witch, *Nic-ill'-Dòmhnaich*, in Caolas, as to their fate. The witch told them to come next day, and she would tell them.

Early next morning the widow went. "Yea," said the witch, "they live, and they had no little amusement last night fighting for the *fallaid* bannock, and your son had his own share of it."[652]

When the young men came home, they were questioned as to their seeing anything the night the witch was sent for news. They said a grey gull was seen by them sitting on the edge of the rocks that overhang their place of shelter and peering down at them. One was for throwing stones at it, but the rest dissuaded him. It was only seen that night and next morning.[653]

Witch as Cormorant

A man named Campbell in the Long Island (as the Outer Hebrides are called) had two sweethearts, for one of whom he did not very much care. They were both to be present at a gathering of women for fulling cloth, and he resolved to go and see them.[654] When he arrived he found only the one he least liked. He left shortly, and set off to where the other was.

On the way he had to cross a ford on large stepping-stones. As he was doing so a cormorant (*sgarbh*) came and splashed him fiercely with water. He had a cudgel in his hand, and gave the strange bird a whack on the back. He then passed on, and the distance being considerable did not return till next day.

When returning he had to pass the house of the slighted damsel. Her mother met him at the door and said she could not understand what was wrong with her daughter: she had got suddenly ill last night, and was very bad with a sore back. Campbell said he knew the reason, and would have nothing further to say to her daughter. The woman then threatened him, but no evil ever came of her threat.

Witches as Whales

A Skye fisherman gave the following narrative of witchcraft to which he himself was a witness. He and his brother were at the herring fishing in Portree in his native isle, and during that season out of all the herring boats one only was successful. It had only a crew of two, and every night caught from eight to ten crans of fish. The other boats were empty or nearly so.

One night when the nets were set, the boat in which he and his brother were sprang a leak, and was taken back to the harbour and beached. The rest of the crew went away to the village, but he remained till the boat was left dry by the receding tide. In a while he also left, and as he did so, saw a young girl coming out of a house and tapping at a neighbour's window. Another girl came out of that house, and wondering what the two could be about at that hour of the night, he followed them from the village. On reaching the green, the two girls began to disport themselves (*braise*), then of a sudden became hares, and chased each other round and round. After this they made their way to the shore, and at the edge of the water (*gob na tuinne*) leapt into the sea and became whales. They went out from land spouting the water as high as a ship's mast.[655]

Next morning the boats came in empty. The fishermen said they had seen during the night two whales throwing up the sea in a dreadful manner (*smùideadh na fairge gu h-eagallach*), which made them think there was fish in the neighbourhood. The lucky boat was full as usual.

The meaning of this tale seems to be that the man had been listening the night before to tales of witchcraft, had fallen asleep in the boat on the beach, and had a troublous dream.

Delaying the Birth of a Child

This infernal cantrip was played by means of a ball of black worsted thread in a black bag, kept at the foot of the witch's weaving loom where it might not be detected.[656] If the ball was taken away the plot fell through. In proof of this, there is a story told that a child was once kept twenty-two years in its mother's womb by means of witches, and when born it had hair, beard and teeth, like a person of that age.

The mother of a celebrated West Highland freebooter, *Ailein nan Sop* ('Allan of the Faggots'), was a servant-maid who became pregnant by a married man. The man's wife, when she heard of the scandal, got a bone from a witch which she was assured would (as long as it was kept) delay the birth of the child. Allan of the Faggots was thus kept in his mother's womb for fifteen months beyond the usual time.

The husband got word of his wife's doings, and took a plan to defeat her. He made his fool one day come home pretending to be very drunk, staggering about and smashing the furniture. On being called to task, the fool said he had been in a house down yonder (that of the servant-maid), where a child had at last been born, and had got a dram which went into his head. The wife, on hearing this, thought the witch had deceived her, and threw the bone into the fire. It disappeared in blue smoke and knocked down the chimney! Allan was then born, with large teeth.[657]

In other tales to the same effect, the trick usually is played on a married woman by the mother of a maid who had been slighted on her account.

CLAY CORPSE

The greatest evil that witches can do is to make, for a person whose death they desire, a clay body or image (*corp crèadha*) into which pins are stuck to produce a slow and painful disease, terminating in dissolution. Waxen figures for the same purpose, and melted by exposure to a slow fire, were known to Lowland superstition. In the Highlands wax was not accessible to poor bodies, and they had to make clay serve the turn. It is said that when a person wants a limb he cannot be destroyed by witches in this manner.[658]

Mac Iain Ghiorr, the Ardnamurchan thief, stole so many cattle from MacLean of Dowart that he made that chief his deadly enemy. On one of his roving expeditions he was passing at midnight the chapel or burying-ground of Pennygown (*caibeal Peighinn a' Ghobhann*) on the Sound of Mull. Seeing a light in the chapel, he entered and found three witches sticking pins in a clay body (*corp crèadha*) intended to represent MacLean of Dowart. As each pin was stuck in, MacLean was seized with a stitch in the corresponding part of his body. Only the last pin remained to be stuck in. It was to be in the heart, and to cause death. *Mac Iain Ghiorr* scattered the witches, took with him the clay corpse, and made his way to MacLean, whom he found at death's door. He took out in his presence the pins one by one, and when the last was taken out MacLean jumped up a hale man, and remained ever after the warm friend of *Mac Iain Ghiorr*.[659]

MacGilvray, a former minister of Strathfillan in Perthshire, was seized with burning pains all over his body, and was slowly wasting away by some malady of which the nature could not be understood. He lived at Clachan in that strath, and one morning early a woman from the opposite side of the river, on her way to call and ask for him, saw another woman going along before her, who had the reputation of being a witch. Wondering what her neighbour was about at that early hour, she kept well behind and watched. The foremost woman, on coming to a hollow, stooped down, buried something in the ground, and then walked on towards the minister's house. The other came and dug up what had been buried. It proved to be a piece of wood stuck all over with pins. She took it with her to the manse and produced it, to the confusion of the witch. On the pins being withdrawn the minister was freed from his pains and got quite well again.[660]

Ross-shire witches could not destroy *Dòmhnall na Cluaise* ('Donald of the Ear'), of whom they had made a clay figure, from being unable to put on the ear. Donald had lost the ear in battle. Similarly a *corp crèadha* made for Lord Macdonald by *Raonaid a' Chreagain* failed, because the witches never could put the arm on.[661]

Witches could also produce disease in other ways. Thus a young man in Perthshire – the tailor Cumming in Drimachastle, Rannoch – fell into a decline. He accounted himself for the loss of health, decay, and sweats at night by witches coming at night when he was in Badenoch (a district at the time celebrated for witchcraft) and converting him into a horse, on which they rode through the air to Edinburgh and other places to spend the night carousing in well-stored cellars. He now saw them often passing in different shapes and in eggshells, etc. The poor young man did not understand the sweats of consumption, and his imagination was disordered by the many tales of witchcraft he had heard.

The same tale, of converting men into horses, is with slight variations common. In Lorn, a woman came night after night and shook a bridle at the son of a neighbouring farmer. He immediately became a horse, on which she rode to London, etc. A younger brother exchanged beds with him, and when the witches were carousing, secured the magic bridle, converted the witch herself into a horse, rode home, and before taking off the bridle took his horse to a smithy and put on four shoes. Next day an old woman of the neighbourhood was found with her feet and hands horribly mangled.[662]

SILVER SIXPENCE

As already said, silver fired from a gun will wound a witch and force her to assume her proper shape. An English sportsman, according to a Perthshire version of an old story, was sitting surrounded by his dogs in a mountain bothy at the dead hour of night. A cat came in, but the dogs did not move. It sat with its back to the fire and swelled till it was as large as a yearling calf. The Englishman took a silver button off his clothes, and, putting it in the gun, fired at the cat. The brute scampered out at the door.

On going to the strath next day the sportsman, being a doctor, was sent for to see a farmer's wife who had got suddenly ill. He went, and extracted his own silver button from her right breast.

SAVING HORSES

In Uist, a band of horses wandered on to a ledge in the face of a steep precipice. It was impossible to take them from their dangerous position to the top of the cliff by ropes, and to force them from the ledge to the sea, which washed the base of the precipice, seemed (from the height of the fall) inevitable destruction. An old man who was reputed to know more than his paternoster advised, however, they should be driven over, and himself began an incantation beginning *Casa Gurra, Casa Gurra*, whatever that may mean. The horses of their own accord went over the ledge, and swam safely to land.[663]

TAILOR AND WITCHES

A Glen Quoich tailor, detected among a company of witches, was asked what had brought him into such society. He said it was 'for the pleasure of the company' (*mar shodan ris a' chuideachd*).[664]

CELEBRATED WITCHES

The best-known names seem to have been merely nicknames, given perhaps to more than one old woman. *Gorm-Shùil* ('Blue-Eye') is said to originate from the witch having one eye black or brown and the other blue. It is, however, a corruption of *Gormla*, an ancient and pretty Gaelic name, usually rendered Dorothy.[665] *Gormla Mhòr* from Meigh, Lochaber, was stronger than all the witches of Mull, and gave the finishing stroke, as already detailed, to Captain Forrest's ship.[666] She met her death when astraddle on a mountain stream to intercept a salmon that had made its way up to spawn. A large fish made a rush, knocked her backwards in the water, and drowned her. There was a Gormshuil in the village of Hianish, Tiree, a most notorious local witch, and one in Cràcaig in Skye, equally notorious.[667]

Cas a' Mhogain Riabhaich ('Brindled-Headless-Stocking Foot') and *Caiseart Gharbh nighean an Aodhair* ('Rough Footgear the Herdsman's daughter') were anywhere but where the person who is telling about them comes from himself. Shaw, the Lochnell bard, makes them sisters dwelling in Glenforsa in Mull when Ossian was a little boy, and contemporaries of Mac Rùslain.[668] *Ball Odhar* ('Sallow Spot') was from Kintra (*Ceann Trà*) in Ardnamurchan; *Spòga Buidhe* ('Yellow Claws') from Màiligeir on the East Side of Skye; *Doideagun* is the well-known name of the Mull witches, and is given by children to the falling snowflakes, which they are informed are the Mull witches on their journey through the air. Big Kate Macintyre in Fort William was extensively known some forty years ago as a person skilled in divinations and possessing mysterious powers.[669]

WIZARD RISING AFTER DEATH

People who practised forbidden arts, as may readily be supposed, did not rest after death. When buried they remained quiet like other people, but till then might be troublesome.

Among the hills of Ross-shire, an old man who in his time was not 'canny' died in his son's house, a lonely hut in the hills remote from other houses. He was stretched and adjusted (*air a ruidheadh 's air a chàradh*) on a board in a closet, and the shepherd, leaving his wife and children in the house, went to the strath for people to come to the wake and funeral.[670] At midnight, one of the children, playing through the house, peeped in at the keyhole of the closet and cried out, *Mhamaidh, mhamaidh, tha mo sheanair ag éirigh!* "Mother, mother, my grandfather is rising!"

The door of the closet was fast locked, and the dead man, finding he could not open it, began to scrape and dig the earth below it to make a passage for himself. The children gathered round their mother, and in extremity of terror all listened to the scraping of the unhallowed corpse. At last the head appeared below the door, the corpse increased its exertions, and the terror of the mother and children became intense. The body was halfway through below the door when the cock crew and it fell powerless in the pit it had dug. That pit could never afterwards be kept filled up to the level of the rest of the floor.[671]

In Tiree a headstone, placed at the grave of a man whom report accused of dabbling in the dark science, would not remain in its place till secured by a chain. It fell every now and then out of its position, but after the chain was fastened to it it remained firm, and is so now without the chain.

How to Detect Witches

Early in the morning on the first Monday of each of the four quarters of the year, the smoke from a witch's house goes against the wind. This may be seen by any one who takes the trouble of rising early and going to an eminence whence the witch's house can be seen.[672]

14

WHITE WITCHCRAFT

WISE PEOPLE

In English a distinction is recognised between black and white witches. The former could hurt but not help; their power was only one of mischief. White witches were honest, harmless practitioners of sorcery 'whom our custome and country doth call wise men and wise women' (Cotta, *Short Discovery of Unobserved Dangers*, 1612, quoted by Brand, iii. 3).[673]

In Gaelic there are no names corresponding to black and white witches, but the distinction indicated is well known. Those to whom the name *buidseach* (witch) properly applies could only do harm. They raised storms, drowned people, took the milk from cows, etc., etc. There were others who by magic charms cured disease in man and beast, bestowed luck, warded off dangers (real and imaginary), and secured various benefits to those who resorted to them.

One or more such wise people were to be found in every district, and any accusation of witchcraft, of dabbling in forbidden arts, or of being in league with the devil would be indignantly resented by them. On the contrary, as in the case of a shepherd in upper Argyllshire who was much resorted to for the magic cure of cattle, they claimed that their powers were given for a good purpose, and to counteract the powers of evil.

The machinery by which they secured these blessings to humanity consisted of rhymes or incantations, rites and ceremonies, plants and stones of virtue, observance of propitious seasons, etc. The use of these could only lead indirectly to harm by fostering a spirit of credulity and preventing inquiry into natural causes. Of themselves, the charms were like the Sunday plant, according to a common Gaelic saying, 'without benefit or harm'.[674] Any other rhyme or ceremony, plant or stone, would do equally well, if its use commanded the same amount of belief. The words or rhymes were praiseworthy commendations addressed to various saints, and the rites were harmless and merely trifling.

This kind of superstition still prevails among the lower ranks of society to an almost incredible extent in the south as well as in the Highlands, and 'wise people' are resorted to for the cure of obscure ailments by many of whom such folly might be little suspected. Not above five years ago[675] the daughter of a dairy farmer in Cowal came to Ardnamurchan, a distance of above 100 miles, to obtain from a man of reputed skill a charm to turn aside the misfortunes and maladies by which her father's dairy was afflicted. She went home happy in the possession of a bottle of water over which some magic words had been muttered. Occasional newspaper paragraphs show the practice is not extinct in England or the south of Scotland.

In the case of sick beasts, when e.g. a horse lies down and refuses to rise, or a cow ceases to give milk, or gives only milk mingled with blood, the usual mode of procedure to effect a magic cure is to go to a person of skill (i.e. a white witch), get a bottle of water prepared by whispering certain words over it, and sprinkle this on the sick beast, or perhaps put a few drops in its ear. Immediately the beast rises without anything being the matter with it. Other rhymes and ceremonies are ready for other occasions, and it would be possible to fill a book with a collection of incantations in use for various diseases or in different localities.[676]

The general name for trifling superstitious observances of the kind is *gisreag, eapag, upag*.[677] The different kinds are known as *eòlas* (knowledge) for the cure of disease; *òradh* (gilding) for securing gifts and graces; *sïan* or *seun* for protection from danger; and *soisgeul* (gospel) for weak minds.[678]

The rhymes contain internal evidence of having come from Roman Catholic times. The invocation of the Trinity and the saints, particularly St Bride and St Columba, St Michael and St Peter, is common to them all, and whatever be their merit as expressions of piety, they certainly convey no idea of traffic with the powers of evil. The utmost that truth can urge against those who use them is that they are ignorant, facile and credulous. The opprobrious name of *buidseachas* is in every case sincerely and piously repudiated by themselves, and in reality is unjust.

These charms are not readily accessible. The following have been collected from many different persons, and are of interest, some as illustrative of the antiquities of the Scottish Highlands and some for their poetical merits. Much of the chosen poetry consists in felicity of expression, and this is a merit next to impossible to infuse into a translation. No attempt is here made to do more than give the exact meaning of the original.

EÒLAS

The *eòlas* (knowledge), called also *teagasg* (teaching), was a charm for the cure of sickness in man or beast. It consisted of a rhyme, muttered over the sick person and over water to be drunk by (or sprinkled over) the sick animal. To render it more impressive, its use was accompanied by trifling little ceremonies, such as making the sign of the cross, yawning, making up mysterious particoloured strings, getting particular kinds of water on particular days, dipping stones of virtue in water, and similar mummeries. Its object was a good one, and this much can be said in its favour, that if it did not cure, it did not kill.

The ills for which the *eòlas* was used are generally transitory in their nature, as toothache, bruises, sprains, etc., and improvement or cure, following soon after its performance, kept alive a belief in the efficacy of the incantation. The rhymes are usually found in the possession of old women of the humblest class, to whom a meal or small present from a more affluent neighbour, for a bottle of water and a harmless rhyme, is a welcome gift.

These old women, it may be said in every case, believe in the efficacy of the charm as much as those who resort to them; but (while the whole company and its proceedings afford good grounds for ridicule) indignation or reprobation fairly attach themselves only to those who go to seek such foolish cures for sickness. The excuse of the poor white witch is to be found in the pressure of want and the relief which the Gaelic saying truthfully but coarsely embodies: *Is math an spòrs a lìonas brù.* "It is good fun that fills the belly."

Not a word of any kind was to be spoken by the person going for an *eòlas* (till he came home again) to any one but the 'wise' person. This was because Elisha, when he sent his servant before him to the Shunammite woman (2 Kings 4: 29), commanded him not to speak on the way. "If thou meet any man, salute him not; and if any salute thee, answer him not again."

On the way, the messenger must take up his quarters for the night before the sun goes down; and no spinning or reading is allowed. There is more probability of the charm becoming efficacious if he enter no house and take no meat.

CURE FOR THE EVIL EYE (*EÒLAS A' CHRONACHAIDH*)

An evil eye, according to the Highland belief, is one animated by a discontented and unhappy mind full of envy (*farmad*), covetousness (*sanntachadh*) and suchlike mean feelings, and looking repiningly on the good of others, and it may be too earnestly and anxiously on what belongs to oneself. It injures the object on which it falls, and animals or persons struck by it are seized with mysterious ailments, dwindle, and perhaps die.

The believers in the gift assert that the evil eye may exist in man or woman, in friend or foe, and that it is prudent not to give causes for the feelings which give rise to it. Thus, for instance, it is advisable not to allow a cow to go out with a full udder.[679] An evil eye may rest upon it, and the animal be lost. The practice is commendable, though the reason assigned may not be the correct one.

From a similar fear, a pedlar has been known to go about with his goods only at night. A mother can hurt her own child, and some have been said to hurt their own cattle. The traditions of various localities, in the islands and on the mainland, tell of a man who was not allowed to see his own cattle, from his possession of the unhappy gift. If he did see them, one of the best cows was found dead next day.

When a healthy and thriving child is seized with unaccountable illness, and becomes uneasy and sickly, it is suspected of being struck with the evil eye, and a 'wise' woman of the neighbourhood is sent for. She fills a bowl with clean water, into which she puts a silver sixpence. The bowl is then quickly and dexterously turned upside down. If the sixpence stick to its bottom, the child is the victim of an evil eye (*air a chronachadh*), and the usual remedy is adopted.

An elder of the church who was witness to the ceremony, some fifty years ago, thus describes it (and he is a person very likely to have been observant even in his boyhood).[680] "When a little boy, I wandered into a neighbour's house, very likely with a piece of seaweed in my hand, and chewing away at it, as the manner of boys is. There was a child in the house very ill, but I did not think or know of this when I entered. I suppose the little thing had not sucked its mother's breast, or taken any nourishment, for some days previously.

"An old woman who came to inquire for it, on learning its condition, took a bowl half full of water from a large tub (*farmail*) that was in the house and, putting it on her knees, began to mutter over it. I was too young at the time to be heeded, and was not put out of the house.

"After muttering for a while the old woman began to yawn, and such yawning I have never seen in all my days. She yawned and yawned and yawned again till I thought she was going to die. The cat's paws were dipped in the bowl on her knee, and a red thread, brought by a girl belonging to the house, on being also dipped in the water, was put round the child's neck."

The water used must be that in which the 'hunter's feet' have been dipped (*uisge casan an t-sealgair*), and the cat is the hunter most readily available. The muttered words are the charm, which gives the whole ceremony its efficacy, and the yawning commences when the child's illness is being transferred to the person who performs the ceremony.

The evil eye is deadly to all animals to which the person having it takes a fancy. In the present day it is said of a man in Tiree who is accused by common report of having the gift that when he comes to buy a beast it is better to give it to him at his own price than keep it. If he does not get it, the beast is taken ill and perhaps dies soon after. This is said, but the maligned man never gets better bargains than his neighbours.

When a stranger having an evil eye meets a rider or person leading a horse, and praises the animal's points, the effects of his looks are soon evident. Before he is out of sight the horse is suddenly taken ill and falls down. The rider should immediately return after the evil-eyed stranger and boldly accuse him of having done the mischief. The more 'bitterly and abusively' (*gu searbh salach*) he does so, the better. On coming back he will find the horse all right.

If on his guard at the first meeting, when the stranger praises the horse he will praise it a great deal more. When the stranger says, "That is a good animal," the prudent owner will say, "It is better than that," and however high the stranger's praises are, the owner's should be higher. This will lessen, perhaps prevent, the power of the evil eye to do mischief.

In the prose part of a Gaelic poem published in Mackenzie's *Beauties*, Gilbride Macintyre from Ruaig in Tiree is said to have killed eighty hens with one glance of his evil eye, and to have wrecked a big ship of five cross-trees, notwithstanding her cables and anchors.[681] A man in *Cnoc Creagach* ('Rocky Mound') in Coll killed a mare and foal with it.[682]

It is said the wife of a former tenant of Heynish in Tiree (and the story is localised in several other places) would not allow her husband to look at his own fold of cattle. As sure as he did so, one of his best cows was found dead next day. The fear of this calamity made her put a very pretty cow, to which she herself took a great fancy, in an out-of-the-way place, near which her husband had never been observed to go. On returning one day from a stroll in the hill, he asked who put the cow where he had seen it. The wife's worst fears were realised. The cow was dead in a few days.

The credulous (of whom there is a large number everywhere) were assured that, when any beast belonging to them was praised, all evil consequences were averted by their saying:

> *Dia bheannachadh do shùil,*
> *Deur mùin mu d' chridhe,*
> *An luchaidh san tom*
> *'S an tom ri theine.*

"God bless your eye, / A drop of wine about your heart, / The mouse is in the bush / And the bush is on fire."[683]

There is a Gaelic saying that 'envy splits the rocks' (*sgoiltidh farmad na creagan*), and in proof of this the following story is told. An industrious, careful man sold more cheese than his neighbours, and was much envied when seen – as he frequently was – on his way to market with a cheese in a bag on his back. One day, instead of a cheese, he put a small millstone in the bag. His neighbours, filled with envy, saw him jogging along as usual to market, and stood in their doors looking after him and making remarks. On reaching the market and opening the bag he found the millstone broken in two, a certain proof of the power of envy and of the truth embodied in the proverb.

The charm for curing the evil eye, like many other similar mummeries, must be made on Thursday or Sunday.[684] The rhyme used varies with different localities. The following, with slight variations on the part of different individuals, is the one used in Tiree. The words within brackets are omitted when the charm is for a sick beast.[685]

Cuiridh mi an iob air a shùil,	*I will put salve on eye,*
An aon iob as fheàrr fon ghréin	*The best salve beneath the sun*
[Rinn Mac Dhé do dh'aingeal neòil]	*[The Son of God made for an angel of heaven]*
Air feadh a' bhlàir	*Throughout the world*
Air sùil bhig,	*For small eye,*
Air sùil mhòir,	*For big eye,*
Air mo shùil fhèin,	*For my own eye,*
Air sùil fir léith,	*For the grey man's eye,*
Air sùil nan naoi mnà seanga sìth	*For the eye of the nine slim Fairy women*
Nach do dh'ith air am beul,	*Who never ate*
Nach do chaill air am màs	*Or digested aught*
Sa bheinn ud thall.	*In yonder hill.*
Ge b'e có aig am bheil thu air ghlais	*Whoever has thee under lock*
Air sùil, air tnù no am farmad,	*Of eye or malice or envy,*
Gum b'ann air fhéin a laigheas i —	*On themselves may it fall —*
Air an cuid 's air an cloinn,	*On their goods and on their children,*
Air an sult 's air an saill,	*On their juice and on their fatness,*
Air an talamh fada bàn,	*On their long white ground,*
Air an taghadh buaile,	*On their choicest herd,*
Air an crodh druimfhionn,	*Their white-backed cows,*
Air an gabhraibh binneach	*Their sheep*
Agus air an caoraich:	*And pointed goats:*
Gach sùil 's gach farmad	*Each eye and each envy*
Ortsa	*That lies on thee, A. B.,*
Ann am fìor chridhe na h-àirde an-ear.	*In the very centre of the east.*
Is labhar sluagh farad,	*Talkative are folk over thee,*
Dhìth Crìost an coltas,	*Christ has taken away their likeness,*
Dà shùil dheug roimh gach sùil,	*Twelve eyes before every eye,*
Làidir sùil Mhic Dhé,	*Strong is the eye of the Son of God,*
Is lag sùil an eucoraich.	*Weak is the eye of the unjust.*

The five last lines probably mean that the Fairies or Elves, whom God has rendered invisible, are speaking among themselves over the sick person, and the succour of the twelve apostles and of Christ is more powerful than the injustice of man. Others for these lines substitute the following:

An t-sùil a chaidh a-null	*The eye that went over*
'S a thàinig a-nall,	*And came back,*
A ràinig an cnàimh	*That reached the bone*
'S a ràinig an smior,	*And reached the marrow,*
Togaidh mise dhiots' an t-sùil	*I will lift from off thee*
'S togaidh Rìgh nan Dùl leam.	*And the King of the Elements will aid me.*

A woman in Islay worked wonderful cures with the following. It is a wretched specimen of superstition, but is given to show how ancient creeds accommodate themselves to modern modes of thought. The ancient charm, instead of being entirely abandoned, became a sort of prayer.

Ma chronaich sùil,	*If eye has blighted,*
Bheannaich Triùir;	*Three have blessed;*
Is treas' an Triùir a bheannaich	*Stronger are the Three that blessed*
Na 'n t-sùil a chronaich —	*Than the eye that blighted —*
An t-Athair, am Mac, 's an Spiorad Naomh.	*The Father, Son, and Holy Ghost.*
Ma rinn nì sìth no saoghalt' coire dha	*If aught Elfin or worldly has harmed it*
San talamh a-bhos	*On earth above*
No an ifrinn shìos,	*Or in hell beneath,*
Gun till thus' e, a Dhé nan Gràs.	*Do Thou, God of Grace, turn it aside.*[686]

This was to be said thrice.

Charm for Sprains (Eòlas an t-Sìochaidh)

This charm also to be efficacious must be thrice repeated. The variations in the versions met with have been almost entirely in the omission of lines in some that are found in others:[687]

Eapa gu beachd	*A charm in sooth*
An eapa chuir Calum Cille	*The charm that Colum-Kil applied*
Ri glùn gille	*To a young man's knee*
Sa bheinn	*In the hill*
Air iodha, air at,	*For pang, for swelling,*
Air lian, air lot,	*For hurt, for wound,*
Air bhruthadh, air shìochadh,	*For abrasion, for sprain,*
Air ghreimeannan, air earrannun,	*For portions, for divisions,*
Air sgeith-féithe, air snuim cnàimhe.	*For varicose vein, for dislocated bone.*
Chaidh Crìost a-mach	*Christ went out*
Anns a' ghealbhain ud mhoich,	*At early morn,*[688]
Fhuair e casan nan each	*He found the legs of horses*

Briste mu seach;	*Broken by turns;*
Nuair thùirling e air làr	*When He alighted on the ground*
Gun shlànaich e cas eich —	*He healed a horse's leg —*
Chuir e smior ri smior	*He put marrow to marrow*
'S chuir e cnàimh ri cnàimh,	*And bone to bone,*
Chuir e fuil ri fuil,	*He put blood to blood*
Smuais ri smuais,	*And flesh to flesh,*
Feòil ri feòil, agus féith ri féith.	*Juice to juice, and vein to vein.*
Mar a shlànaich e sin	*As He healed that*
Gun slànaich e seo	*May He heal this*
Ás leth Chrìost 's a chumhachdan còmhla:	*Because of Christ and His powers together:*
Aon trian an-diugh,	*One third today,*
Dà thrian a-màireach	*Two thirds tomorrow*
'S e uile gu léir an-earar	*And the whole the day after*
Ortsa, Mhoire gheal	*Upon you, fair Mary*
Bh' aig sgàth na craoibhe —	*Who was at the shade of the cross —*
Masa h-euslainteach an-diugh	*If a patient today*
Guma slàn a-màireach.	*Be you whole tomorrow.*[689]

Part of the charm consisted of a handful of earth from a grey mound (*làn an dùirn an ùir á cnoc glas*) applied to the foot.[690] The sufferer must go three times *deiseal* (southwardly) round the mound on Sunday. In the extreme west of Tiree there is a hillock called *Cnocan an t-Sìochaidh* ('the Hillock of the Sprain'), but the practice of using it for cures of this kind has become obsolete.[691]

CHARM FOR BRUISES (*EÒLAS BRUTHAIDH*)

> *Patera Mary one, Patera Mary two*, etc., down to *Patera Mary nine,*
> Thou wilt flow like woman,
> Thou wilt flow like man,
> Thou wilt flow like royal fish;
> And the nine veins of thy body
> In one stream together.[692]

CHARM FOR RHEUMATIC PAINS: *EÒLAS GALAR THOLL* (LITERALLY 'PERFORATING DISEASE')

Dùin Dia umad / De	*Close God about thee,*
Seall sluagh farad	*Look people over thee,*
Do Chriosd, air neo	*To Christ, or else —*

Tog dhinn a chroich	*Lift from us the gallows,*
Fàl fàl fàl	*Away, away,*
Do nimh 's an lar	*Thy poison in the ground*
'S do chradh 's a chloich.	*And thy pain in the stone.*[693]

Otherwise:

> *An arrow thrown with sudden terror,*
> *Salt to cure the wound,*
> *Jesus Christ to keep the Elfin arrow quiet,*
> *The charm of God about thee,*
> *Blind are people over thee,*
> *Thy covering about Colum-Kil*
> *And the covering of Colum-Kil about thee*
> *To protect thee and watch over thee*
> *Against the people of this world*
> *And of the next.*[694]

CHARM FOR CONSUMPTION (*EÒLAS NA CAITHIMH*)

This was to be said on a Thursday and on two Sundays.[695] As in the case of other charms, some days of the year were more favourable than others, and the top of the ninth wave should be used in sprinkling the patient.[696]

Saltram ort, a ghlac,	*Let me tread on thee, tightness,*
Mar a shaltras an eal' air an tràigh,	*As the swan treads on the shore,*
A ghlac chùil, a ghlac chléibh,	*Tightness of the back, tightness of the chest,*
A ghlac bhràghadh,	*Tightness of the throat,*[697]
A sgrios dhiot a' ghalair mhosaich	*To strip from thee the foul disease*
O mhullach do chinn gu do bhonn	*From the top of thy head to thy sole*[698]
Gu d' dhà leis a-null	*To thy two thighs beyond*
Le neart Dhé 's a chumhachdan.	*By the might of God and His powers together.*[699]

FOR AFFECTIONS OF THE CHEST (*AIR SON IOMAIRT CLÉIBH*)

> *I will trample on thee, tightness,*
> *As on mountain dust tonight;*
> *On thyself be thy blackening, dwarfing power —*
> *Evil and painful is that.*[700]
> *The charm which Patrick put*

On the mother of the son of the King of Iver
To kill the worms
Round the veins of her heart[701]
For the four and twenty afflictions
In her constitution — [702]
For the water of the running stream of her boundary,
For the stones of the earth's waves,
For the weakness of her heart,[703]
For jaundice and distemper,
For withering and for asthma.[704]

CHARM FOR TOOTHACHE (*EÒLAS AN DÉIDE*)

It is not difficult to persuade a man distracted with toothache to try any remedy in reason that offers any hope of relief. It would be curious if a charm were not forthcoming. The writer has recovered only a portion of the Gaelic version.

The following English charm was obtained ten years ago in Tiree, and probably came originally from the isle of Man. It was to be sewn up in the clothes and worn about the person, and was given to those who applied for it for a small consideration. This was to be on Sunday, and payment was not to be asked for. If that had to be done, the charm was useless. The copy is word for word: "In the name of lord petter sat on a marble stone aweeping Christ came by and said what else you petter petter said o lord my god my dok toockage[705] christ said o lord petter be whole and not thou only but all that carry these lines in my name shall never have the toock Christ cure the toockaig. MADE FOR MERRION MACFADYN."[706]

In a small tract called Peacock's *Guide to the Isle of Man* (p. 66), the following version is given as in use in that island:[707]

Peter was ordained a saint;
Standing on a marble stone.
Jesus came to him alone
And said unto him, "Peter!
What is it makes thee shake?"
Peter replied, "My Lord and Master,
It is the toothache!"
Jesus saith unto him,
"Rise up and be healed!
Keep these words for my sake
And thou shalt nevermore be troubled with toothache!"

The Gaelic is to the same effect:[708]

> *The charm Colum-Kil applied*
> *To Mal-ii's right knee*
> *For gnawing and lancinating pain and toothache,*
> *Toothache and disease of the head.*[709]
>
> . . . . . .
>
> *Then said Peter to James,*
> *"I can get no peace or rest with the toothache."*[710]
>
> . . . . . .
>
> *Christ said, "Answer the question*
> *And the toothache and the verse*
> *Will never be in the same head together."*[711]

CHARMS FOR CATTLE

These were even more numerous than those for the distempers of men. Cattle are nowadays better housed, fed and attended to, and hence are not so liable to ill-understood ailments that gave persons of 'skill' employment. In the case of any beast being seized with distemper, this short charm might prove of use:

Ge b'e có rinn ort an tnù,	*Whoever has done you this deed of malice,*
Fear donn no té fhionn,	*A brown man or white woman,*
Cuiridh mis' an Triùir gan casg —	*I send these Three to check them —*
An t-Athair, am Mac, 's an Spiorad Naomh.	*The Father, Son, and Holy Ghost.*[712]

A more obstinate case demanded the charm for the evil eye, water in which stones of virtue were dipped etc. When a newly purchased animal is brought home, its return to its former home is prevented and its allurement to its new haunts is secured by blowing into its ear and saying:

Siop ga chur air a chluas dheas	*A blowing into your right ear*
Air do leas 's chan ann air t' aimhleas,	*For your benefit and not your hurt,*
Gaol an fhearainn tha fo d' chois	*Love of the land under your foot*
'S fuath an fhearainn air an d'fhalbh thu,	*And dislike to the land you left,*
Do cheangal am' làimh	*Your fastening in my hand*
'S glas iarainn ort, etc. etc.	*And an iron lock is on thee, etc.*[713]

When a cow loses its milk, as is sometimes the case, whatever be the cause (perhaps the eating of a noxious weed), it is necessary to procure the pearlwort and two other plants known to people of skill to bring back the milk. The following words are to be said when pulling the plants:[714]

Buainidh mis' am mòthan,	*I will pull the pearlwort,*
Liath-lus a bh' aig Fionn:	*The plant that Fionn had:*
Thàinig Mac nan Aingeal	*The Son of the Angels came*
'S mi crom os a cionn.	*When it was bending above it.*[715]
Thàinig Brighid dhachaigh thugad	*Bridget came home to thee*
Le d' ghruth 's le d' ìm,	*With thy curds and thy butter,*
A' Mhoire mhìn a thaisg e	*Smooth Mary that hoarded it*
Fo naoi glasa cruinn.	*Under her nine round locks.*[716]
Luibh bainne i, luibh saille i	*A plant of milk it is, a plant of fat*
'S luibh dàir —	*And a plant of pairing —*
Luibh sonais is àigh	*A plant of happiness and joy*
'S gach àit' am bi i.	*Wherever it is.*
Buainidh mis' an tom sona	*I will pull the joyful clump*
'S mi am' shuidhe air taobh bearraidh;	*Sitting by the top of an eminence;*
Cha tugainn do dhuin' e	*I would give it to no man*
Gun tuille 's mo bheannachd.	*Without more than my blessing.*
Buainidh mis' an t-seirc ghràdhach,	*I will pull the loving charity,*
Si 'n togh ghràdhach i,	*'Tis a loving delicacy, (?)*
Si 'churrasglach i,	*It is a crowding together, (?)*
Is math an ceann seud is siubhail i.	*It is a good object of travel and journey.*
'S dh'iarr Dia mar a h-aon i	*And God asked it as one*
'S bhuain e mar a dhà i;	*And pulled it as two;*
Gléidhidh i sonas is àgh	*It will give happiness and joy*
Anns gach àit' am bi i.	*Wherever it is.*
Buainidh mise luibh a' bhainne	*I will pull the milk-producing plant*
Mar a bhuain Màiri nighean Mhoire	*As smooth St Mary pulled it*
Air bhliochd, air thoradh, air dhàir,	*For produce, for fruit, for pairing,*
Air bhleoghann trom, air cheatha tiugh;	*For milking plentifully, for thick cream;*
Math do nì gun robh dhuit,	*The benefit of your herd may you have,*
Gach aon 'na shùil, 'na thnù, 'na fharmad —	*Each for his eye or malice or envy —*
A shùil san tom chonchas	*May his eye be in the bush of whins*
'S an tom ri theine.	*And the bush be on fire.*[717]

SIAN (CHARM AGAINST DANGER)

The *seun* or *sian*, Scots 'sain', was used for the protection of both man and beast from particular dangers, such as being taken away by an enemy, being drowned, or struck by sword, or arrow, or bullet in battle. It consisted of rhymes, or parti-coloured strings, or plants, and in many cases its nature remained a mystery. It was said over cows and sheep when leaving them for the night; it was put round the necks of infants; given by the Fairy mistress (*leannan sìth*) to her earthly lover; sewn by the foster-mother (*muime*) in the clothes of a beloved foster-son (*dalta*) about to leave her; etc.

After it was once given or said, the two – the giver and the recipient – must not see each other again. If they did, the charm lost its power. Usually there was some unforeseen danger of the class which the charm was intended to provide against that proved fatal. Thus, it is said, a young woman gave a *sian* to her soldier lover who was leaving for foreign wars, telling him the only thing he had to guard against was his own arms. He went scatheless through a protracted war, but after his return scratched his forehead with a pin which he carried in his clothes, and died from the effects.

THE OLD WIFE'S CHARM FOR HER COW (SIAN NA CAILLICH MU BÒ)

Tha mis' a' cur na h-aire mach a-nochd	*I set the watch tonight*
Air bharraibh boc,	*Against horns of he-goat*
Air ghuth tairbh,	*And voice of bull,*
Air ghuth mairbh,	*The voice of the dead*
Air an aon bhò bhioraiche,	*And each horned, fierce,*
Rusaiche, cluasaiche, màsaiche —	*Large-eared, large-buttocked cow —*
Clach muile donain	*The Evil One's millstone*
Bhith slaodadh ri d' sgonnan	*Be trailing at thy rump*
Gu madainn a-màireach.	*Till tomorrow morning.*[718]

When a stone was tied to the cow's tail and these mystic words were uttered, the animal was safe to be found in the same spot in the morning. This was believed to be as much owing to the words as to the anchor astern.

CHARM FOR A SHEEP IN ITS COT (SIAN NA CAORA MUN CHRÒ)

An t-sian chuir Moire	*The charm that Mary set*
Mu chrò chaorach	*About a sheep-cot*
Roimh na sgèanaibh, roimh na conaibh	*Against knives, against dogs*
'S roimh na daoinibh,	*And against men,*

Roimh chù, roimh mhadadh,	*Against hound and wild dog*
Roimh mhèirleach —	*And thief —*
An cnoc air an laigh,	*On the hillock where they lie down*
Guma slàn a dh'éireas.	*May they safely rise.*[719]

Against Drowning and in War (*Sian roimh Bhàthadh 's an Cogadh*)

A native of the island of Coll who served in the British army from the taking of Copenhagen, throughout the Peninsular and continental wars, and only died this year (1874), a most kind-hearted and powerfully built man, attributed his safe return from the wars in some measure to having learned this charm in his youth:[720]

> *The charm Mary put round her Son*
> *And Bridget put in her banners*
> *And Michael put in his shield*
> *And the Son of God before His throne of clouds,*
> *A charm art thou against arrow,*
> *A charm art thou against sword,*
> *A charm against the red-tracked bullet;*[721]
> *An island art thou in the sea,*
> *A rock art thou on land,*[722]
> *And greater be the fear these have*
> *Of the body round which the charm goes*
> *In presence of Colum-Kil*
> *With his mantle round thee.*[723]

Charm against Dangers in War

The following is taken from the Gaelic periodical *Cuairtear nam Beann* for January 1842.[724] It is said to have been got about the year 1800 from an old man in Glenforsa, in Mull.[725]

Air a shon 's air a shealbhadh	*For himself and for his goods*[726]
An seun a chuir Brìde mu nighean Dhordheal,	*The charm Bridget put round Dorgill's daughter,*[727]
An seun a chuir Muire mu 'Mac,	*The charm Mary put round her Son,*
Eadar a buinn 's a bràghad,	*Between her soles and her neck,*
Eadar a cìoch 's a glùn,	*Between her breast and her knee,*
Eadar a sùil 's a falt:	*Between her eye and her hair:*[728]

Claidheamh Mhìcheil air a thaobh,	*The sword of Michael be on thy side,*[729]
Sgiath Mhìcheil air a shlinnean —	*The shield of Michael on thy shoulder —*
Chan eil eadar nèamh a's làr	*There is none between sky and earth*
Na bheir buaidh air Rìgh nan Gràs.	*Can overcome the King of Grace.*
Cha sgoilt ruinn thu	*Edge will not cleave thee,*
'S cha bhàth muir thu,	*Sea will not drown thee,*
Bratach Chrìost umad,	*Christ's banners round thee,*[730]
Sgàil Chrìost tharad —	*Christ's shadow over thee —*
O mhullach do chinn gu bonn do choise	*From thy crown to thy sole*
Tha seun an àigh ortsa nis.	*The charm of virtue covers thee.*
Falbhaidh tu an ainm an Rìgh	*You will go in the King's name*
'S thig thu 'n ainm do Cheannaird:	*And come in your Commander's name:*[731]
Is le Dia 's na cumhachdan còmhla thu.	*Thou belongest to God and all His powers.*
Cuiridh mi an seun Di-Luain	*I will make the charm on Monday*
An astar cumhann biorach droighinn;	*In a narrow, sharp, thorny space;*[732]
Falbh a-mach 's an seun mu d' chom	*Go with the charm about thee*
'S na biodh bonn de dh'eagal ort!	*And let no fear be on thee!*
Dìridh tu mullach nan siùchd[733]	*Thou wilt ascend the tops of cliffs*
'S cha leagar thu taobh do chùil;	*And not be thrown backwards;*[734]
Is tu mac Eala chiùin sa bhlàr,	*Thou art the calm Swan's son in battle,*[735]
Seasaidh tusa 'measg an àir,	*Thou wilt stand amid the slaughter,*
Ruithidh tusa troimh chóig ceud	*Thou wilt run through five hundred*
'S bidh fear t' eucorach an sàs.	*And thy oppressor will be caught.*
Seun Dhé umad!	*God's charm be about thee!*
Sluagh dol far riut!	*People go with thee!*[736]

A smith in Torosa, Mull, was said to have got a charm of this kind from his father. He afterwards enlisted, and was in thirty battles. On coming home without a wound, he said he had often wished he was dead, rather than be bruised as he was by bullets. They struck him, but could not pierce him because of the charm.

Eachann Ruadh nan Cath ('Red Hector of the Battles'), a celebrated chief of the MacLeans of Dowart, had a *sian* which made him invulnerable in the many conflicts from which he derived his designation. It failed him at the battle of Inverkeithing in 1652, when he fell with 1,500 of his clan. Surrounded by overwhelming numbers and sorely wounded, he maintained a hopeless struggle, his gallant clansmen defending him to the last, 'each stepping where his comrade stood the instant that he fell', and calling out – in an expression which has been since proverbial in his native island – *Fear eile air son Eachainn!* "Another for Hector!"[737]

The charm which his Fairy mistress gave to *Caoilte* ('Thinman'), the fastest hero of the Fians, has been already referred to. When washing new-born babes wise women made use of these words:

Slàn fionn failce dhuit,	*Hale fair washing to thee,*
Slàn failce na Féinne dhuit,	*Hale washing of the Fians be thine,*
Slàn dhutsa, slàn dhàsan —	*Health to thee, health to him —*
'S na na slàn da d' bhan-nàmhaid.	*But not to thy female enemy.*[738]

Charm for Cloth

After being fulled, new cloth was folded and placed on a table. The women who had been engaged in the fulling then gathered round it and sang the following charm seven times. During the singing they kept time to the music by raising their hands simultaneously and beating the cloth with the tips of their fingers. After each repetition of the charm the cloth was turned over end.[739]

> *Well do I say my verse*
> *As I descend the glen,*
> *One verse, two verses, etc., down to seven-and-a-half verses.*
> *Let not the wearer of the cloth be wounded*
> *And may he never be torn,*
> *And when he goes to battle or conflict*
> *The full succour of the Lord be his.*[740]
> *[The little seagull yonder swimming*
> *And the white wave that she loves,*
> *She swims pleasantly*
> *And I swim cheerfully spinning;*
> *When I sow my flax*
> *And spin my lint*
> *I will make linen from the awns*
> *And get seven marks for the yard.]*[741]
> *Watercress pulled through flagstone*
> *And given to wife unawares,*
> *Deer's shank in the herring's head*
> *And in the slender body of the speckled salmon.*[742]

Then, striking the cloth faster, the singers say:

> *Let this be second cloth, and not enemy's spoil*
> *Nor property of clerk or priest*
> *But his own property, and may he enjoy and wear it.*

It is said there is a bone in the herring's head that resembles a deer's foot. Some say the word should not be 'deer's shank' (*lurg an fhéidh*) but 'deer's antlers' (*cuibhn' an fhéidh*). The part of the song within brackets seems to belong to the music more than to the meaning.

The final wish is that the cloth when turned, or made into a second suit, may prove as good as new, and not – like cloth found on dead bodies – a perquisite of the priest's. In olden times the seventh yard (*slat*) of chequered cloth (*clò breac*) was given to the factor and priest, as well as the seventh lamb from the fold.[743]

CHARM FOR GENERAL USE

Thou wilt be the friend of God
And God will be thy friend;
Iron will be your two soles
And twelve hands shall clasp thy head.
Thy afflictions be in tree or holly
Or rock at sea
Or earth on land;
A protecting shield be about thee,
Michael's shield be about thee;
Colum-Kil's close-fitting coat of mail
Protect thee from Elfin bolts
And from the enclosures of pain, (?)
From the trouble of this world
And the other world.
The woman on her knee
And on her eye,
On her choicest flesh
And on the veins of her heart
Till it reach the place whence it came,
Every jealous envious woman
That propagates her flesh and blood —
On herself be her desire and envy and malice.[744]

'THE GOSPEL OF CHRIST'

Of the same class was the charm to which this name was given. It consisted of a green string, which was kept in the mouth while the charm was muttered, and then secured to the charmed person's right shoulder. The ceremony must be performed on Thursday or Sunday.[745]

May God bless your cross
Before you go to any garden —
Any disease that is in it
May He take from it.
May God bless your crucifying cross
On the top of a house, the house of Christ,
From drowning, from danger and from fever.
When the King was stretched on high,
The King of the Three Hills
And a brown branch top
. . . (unintelligible) . . .
May God bless what is before thee.
When thou goest at their head
Success at meeting and in battle;
The grace of God and courteous look of all men be yours,
The banners of Christ be over thee
To protect thee from thy crown to thy sole.
Fire will not burn thee,
Seas will not drown thee,
A rock at sea art thou,
A man on land art thou,
Fairer than the swan on Loch Lathaich
And the seagull on the white stream;
You will rise above them
As the wave rises,
On the side of God and His powers.
Thou art the red rowan tree
To cause the wrath of men to ebb
Like a wave from the sea to flood-tide
And a wave from flood-tide to ebb.[746]

CHARM FOR CONFERRING GRACES (ÒRADH NAM BUADH)

I will wash thy palms
In showers of wine,
In the juice of rasps
And in honied milk.
I will put the nine graces
In thy white cheeks,

Grace of form and grace of good fortune,
Grace at meetings and of manners
And of goodly speech.
Black is yonder house
And black are its inmates;
Thou art the brown swan
Going in among them.
Their heart is in thy chest,
Their tongue under thy foot,
And they will not say to thee
Word to despite thee.
An island at sea art thou
And a castle on land,
The Lord's form is in thy face,
The loveliest form in the universe
In the name of the Father, Son, and Holy Spirit,
The best day in the week
And the best week in the year
Peter came, Paul came,
Michael came, John came,
The King of Virtues came as guide
To give to thee his regard and love.[747]

CHARM FOR THE FACES OF YOUNG WOMEN

Tha 'n fhéill air t' aghaidh,	Bounty is in thy countenance,
Mac Dhé gad chobhair	The Son of God succour thee
O dhroch dhaoin' an domhan,	From the evil men of the world,
Fhéille Moire is troma ghràdh,	The vigil of loving St Mary keep thee,
Teanga mhodhail mhìn ad' cheann,	A smooth modest tongue be in thy head,
Fionna fionn ad' dhà mhalai,	Fair hair in thy two eyebrows,
Fionn mac Cumhaill eatarra sin;	Fin, the son of Cuäl, between these;
On as e Moire agus a Mac	Since it be Mary and her Son
Chuir an tlachd sin orra(?),	That gave them that charm,
Gun robh blas na meala	May the taste of honey be
Air gach facal a their sibh	On every word you say
Ri mithibh agus ri maithibh	To commons and to nobles
Air an latha 'n-diugh	Upon this and each day
Gu ceann na bliadhna.	To the end of the year.[748]

LOVE CHARM

The knowledge of this rhyme is very widespread. It is ascribed by some to Duncan Ban Macintyre, the greatest of the Gaelic lyrical poets, and is printed in some editions of his poems as his composition, but others with more probability ascribe it to Blind Allan, the Glengarry bard. Allan eked out a livelihood by the practice of charms of the kind.[749]

Chan eòlas gràdhaich leam	*That is not a love-charm*
Uisge shràbh no shop	*Which is a charm of wisps and straws*
Ach gràdh an fhir thig riut	*But one to draw with warmth*
Le bhlàths a tharraing ort.	*The love of the man you like.*
Èirich moch Di-Ciadaoin	*Rise early on Wednesday*
Gu lic phliataich chòmhnaird,	*And go to a broad level flagstone,*[750]
Thoir leat beannachd pobaill	*Take with you the people's blessing*
'S currachd sagairt,	*And the priest's cowl,*[751]
Tog siud air do ghualainn	*Lift then upon your shoulders*
Ann an sluasaid mhaide.	*A wooden shovel.*[752]
Faigh naoi gasan ranaich	*Get nine stalks of fern*
Air an gearradh le tuaigh	*Cut with an axe*
Agus trì cnàimhean seannduine	*And three bones of an old man*
Air an tarraing ás an uaigh;	*Taken from a grave;*
Loisg sin ann an teine crìonaich	*Burn that in a fire of brushwood*
Gus am bi e gu léir 'na luath,	*Till you reduce it all to ashes,*
Crath an gealabhroilleach do leannain	*And shake it in your lover's fair bosom*[753]
An aghaidh na gaoith tuath e,	*Against a north wind,*
'S théid mi an dà urras	*And I will go twice security*
Nach fhalbh an duin' ud bhuat.	*That man will not leave you.*
Tha e sàs an-sin agad.	*You have a hold of him now.*

CHARM TO KEEP AWAY HARM IN A LAWSUIT

When a person is pulled up at law for abusive language, let him when entering the court-house spit in his fist, grasp his staff firmly, and say the following words. There is then no danger of being found guilty. The charm was originally got from *Ailein Mòr Cheannacoille*, Big Allan of Wood-End in Kingairloch, who had been a soldier at the time of the Irish Rebellion, and had himself learned it in his youth.[754] The names of the saints show the charm to be very ancient.

Dùinidh mis' an dòrn,	*I will close my fist,*
Is dìleas leam am fiodh;	*Faithful to me is the wood;*
Sann a shaoradh m' anacainnt	*It is to protect my abusive words*
Tha mi dol a-staigh.	*I enter in.*
Triùir Mac Cluannaidh a shaoras mi	*The three sons of Clooney will save me*
'S Manannan mac Leth	*And Manaman MacLeth*
'S Gille Caluim caomh cléireach	*And St Columba, gentle cleric,*
'S Alastair air neif.	*And Alexander in heaven.*[755]

The name 'Manaman MacLeth' is probably a corruption of 'Manannan MacLeirr', the Manx magician, who is said to have covered that island with a mist which was dispelled by St Patrick. *Ni-Mhanainnein* (i.e. the daughter of Manannain) is mentioned in a Gaelic tale as having remarkably beautiful music in her house, and *Bhanachag ni Mhannainein* ('the Dairymaid, the daughter of Manannan') is mentioned in another tale as a midwife whose residence was somewhere near the moon.[756]

SERPENT STONE

In addition to magic cures by means of rhymes, many were effected – and much security was obtained – by means of beads, stones and plants. A collection of these formed a considerable part of the armoury of witches, black and white.[757]

Of all the means of which superstition laid hold for the cure of disease in man or beast, the foremost place is to be assigned to the serpent stone (*clach nathrach*), also called the serpent bead or glass (*glaine nathair*). It is an undoubted relique of druidism, and as such worthy of particular attention.

Pliny (29 C. 3) tells us that the Emperor Claudius put to death a knight of the Vocontian Gauls for carrying a serpent-egg (*ovum anguinum*) about him while engaged in a lawsuit. He also gives a description of the manner in which the egg or bead is manufactured by the serpents. In summer innumerable serpents enwrap one another and generate the egg from the slaver of their jaws and bodies. They then, according to the druids, cast it up into the air by their hissings, when it must be caught in a garment lest it touch the ground. The person who is bold enough to intercept it must fly away on a horse, for the serpents follow till a river intercepts them. The test of a true egg is that it swims against the stream, even if bound in gold (*si contra aquas fluitet, vel auro vinctum*). The druids further say it must be got at a particular season of the moon. The one Pliny saw was about the size of a round apple. It procures victory in lawsuits and entrance to kings.[758]

The tales told in modern times of the serpent stone, its manufacture and wonderful properties, are of a similar class, and leave no doubt that in these beads and the use made of them we have the remains of an imposture, if not instituted, at least practised by the druids.

The ordinary *glaine nathair* (serpent glass) is of smaller size than is indicated by Pliny. The one which the writer saw was about the size of a gun bullet, and about 1¼ inches long. There was a hole through from end to end, and depressions on its sides, as if it had once been soft and had been taken up gently between the finger and thumb. It is of transparent glass, but glass unlike that of the present day. There are extremely brilliant and curious streaks of colour in it. It is now merely a family heirloom, but in olden times was in great demand for dipping in water to be given to bewitched persons or beasts. (The sloughed skin – *cochall* – of the serpent itself was used for the same purpose.) Water in which it was dipped was given to sick beasts. The tale as to the manner in which it was originally got is the same as is told of other beads of the same kind. The serpents are assembled in a coiling mass, with their heads in the air hissing horribly, slavering, and out of their slaver making the serpent stone. The spittle, in course of becoming solid, was known as *meall càchd*.[759] That the story was not implicitly believed is shown by the addition that when the bead is finished one of the serpents puts its tail through it. Thus the hole by which it is perforated is made.

In the case of the bead which the writer saw, the person who came upon the serpents at their work is said to have waited till the reptiles slept. He then worked the bead out of their circle with a straw or twig of heather. As he took it up between his finger and thumb and made off with it, he observed that the pressure of his fingers marked it, it being still soft, and this made him put a straw through it to carry it home. This story fairly accounts for the shape of the bead and the marks upon it. The marks look as if they were so made when the stone was soft.

Another account says that the finder came on a rock above where the serpents were at work, and, rolling his plaid into a ball, threw it down the rock near them. Instantly the serpents made a dash at the plaid, and while they were reducing it to shreds he made off with the adder stone. By means of a sharp-pointed stick, prepared for the purpose and thrust through the soft bead, he raised it to the top of the rock, and, taking it between his finger and thumb, ran home.

Similar legends of the adder stone were current in the Lowlands. Scott says the name is applied 'to celts and other perforated stones'.[760] In the Highlands the name is not applied to stones. In Wales and Ireland the bead is known as 'druid's glass'. A more than historical interest attaches to it from the means it gives of tracing, beyond the possibility of mistake, the use of amulets and superstitious charms to the times and teaching of the much-lauded druids, and raises – if it does not throw light upon – questions as to the early intercourse of nations.

The manufacture of serpent beads is involved in obscurity. There is nothing known to create a probability that they are of Celtic workmanship. The Phœnicians from a very early date knew the art of glass-making, and their commerce extended far and wide, and as far as the shores of the British Isles, then the remotest part of the known world. It is, therefore, possible these beads came from Phœnician sources. They are, it is said, found on the coasts of the Baltic and Mediterranean, in England and France, as well as in Ireland and Scotland, and it is possible enough their diffusion was owing to traders from Phœnicia and her colonies in Gaul and at Massilia. Similarly, idols are exported at the present day from England to India.[761]

Fully as much, however, can be urged in behalf of a supposition that the beads are of Egyptian origin, and were obtained by the Celtic priests from the ancient Egyptian enchanters. The Egyptians from the earliest times used glass extensively, and could cut, grind and engrave it, inlay it with gold, imitate precious stones in it, and colour it with great brilliancy. A bead found at Thebes is ascribed to 1500 BC, and relics of a similar class are not unfrequently found in the Egyptian catacombs. If they could be said to be of exactly the same manufacture with the Celtic beads the question is nearly set at rest.

Meyer gives it as his view that the first westward stream of Celtic immigration passed through Egypt, along the north coast of Africa, and entered Europe by the Straits of Gibraltar. Ancient Irish history, if there be any truth in its fables, points to a similar conclusion. The subject is one of which nothing certain is known, and its decision is of value in showing whether the Celtic priests got their aids to superstition from their Egyptian brethren.[762]

Snail Beads (*Cnaipein Seilcheig*)

Snails also are said to form themselves into a mass and manufacture a stone of great virtue as a charm (*clach shianaidh*). It protects its lucky possessor against all danger. Its name is 'a snail bead' (*cnaipein seilcheig*) or a 'snail stone' (*clach na seilcheig*). Four or five snails are engaged in the manufacture of each stone. Water in which it is dipped is good for sore eyes and for mouths broken out with tetter.[763]

Frog Stone

The king frog has in its head a stone of immense value. The 'frog stone' (*clach nan gilleadha cràigein*) is said by Pennant to be merely a kind of fossil tooth known as bufonite.[764] It has been made the best known of this class of physical charms from Shakespeare's comparison of adversity to the toad, which, though 'ugly and venomous', yet 'wears a precious jewel in its head'.[765]

The swamp at Achagaval in Morvern was tenanted by a king frog or toad, the reputation of which was widespread. It was called *Seid*, a word of which the usual meaning is 'a truss of hay or straw'.

One who stayed in the neighbourhood of the fen said he heard, not once but scores of times, the cry of the animal from as great a distance as the top of a neighbouring hill, *Beinn nam Bearrach*, and he could compare it to nothing so much as the yelping of 'a soft mastiff whelp' (*bog chuilein tòdhlair*).

The part of the fen which the king frog most frequented was called *Lòn na Seid*, and in winter, when it was frozen over, a tame otter was let down through a hole in the ice in the hope of driving the frog to the opening. Otters must come occasionally to the surface to breathe, and the one in question having come for that purpose, its owner, in his eagerness to secure the jewel, mistook it for the king frog, and gave it a rap on the head that killed it on the spot.[766]

STONES

In addition to jewels found in animals, superstition made use of stones of various forms, spherical and pointed, plain and ornamented, of unknown origin, but bearing evidence of having been reduced to form by human art. These were carefully preserved in families as heirlooms, and are found in tumuli, graves and road-cuttings, dredged from rivers, and turned up by the plough. They are undoubted relics of a remote past, and have been referred by antiquaries to a prehistoric age and savages who lived before iron was invented.

The ingenuity of those who advocate this view of their origin is sufficiently tested in finding a practical use for the stones as weapons of war or the chase, as employed in games of chance, or as articles of domestic use, corn-crushers, hatchets or personal ornaments. No doubt many of them were originally intended for such purposes; but the uselessness of others, and the absence of fitness for any known or conceivable purpose of utility, indicate a different origin. It is not easy, for instance, to assign any ordinary use to such a stone ball as that pictured in Wilson's *Prehistoric Annals of Scotland*, i., 195, and to many others of still more curious appearance and with more elaborate ornaments.[767] The incised ornaments forbid the idea of their being of ordinary service, and the prevalence of witchcraft – with its armoury of curiously-shaped stones and mysterious natural productions – among all savage tribes makes it highly probable they were the implements of the prehistoric conjurer's craft, and were from the first associated with strange virtues. As a lethal weapon the first stone picked up from the ground was as serviceable. They have been associated with the popular superstitions of very modern times. It is not unlikely that from the beginning they were so associated.

FAIRY ARROW

The most common of these primitive relics was the Fairy arrow or Elf-bolt (*saighead shìth*, pronounced **saït hee**), which was believed to be thrown by the Fairies at cattle and men. It was said in the Highlands the Elves could not throw it themselves, but compelled some mortal who was at that time being carried in their company to do so. When friendly, he missed his aim, and so disappointed his instigators.

A person struck instantaneously lost the power of his limbs and was taken to the Fairy dwelling. Only his semblance remained. He appeared to die, or an old Elf was substituted for him, to animate the powerless frame and receive the kindness bestowed by mortals on what they thought was their afflicted friend. Similarly Elf-struck cattle devoured all the food and gave all the trouble of healthy cattle, but yielded no return; they neither gave milk nor grew fat.

The Elf-bolt is a flint flake reduced with patient ingenuity to the form of an arrow-head, and is in length from one to six inches. Archaeologists say these flints formed the arrow- and the lance-heads of a primitive stone race, but their unsuitableness for being firmly secured to a proper shaft alone makes this supposition not always likely.

An arrow with a flint for a head must have been too weighty at one end, and the Allophylian (if there was such a person) must have been very destitute of ingenuity if he could not make a more serviceable arrow-head from bone splinters or hardened wood.[768]

When men believed in Fairies these flint heads made their appearance as readily as images do under a system of idolatry.

Whoever had one of these arrows in his possession was safe from Fairy attacks, and water in which it was dipped restored to health man or beast struck with sudden illness. Similar virtues were ascribed to the Fairy spade (*caibe sìth*), a stone that was smooth, slippery and black (*mìn sleamhainn dubh*), supposed to resemble a spade. It was also put in water to be given to sick people and cattle.[769]

CRUBAN STONE

The cruban stone (*clach a' chrùbain*) cured diseases in the joints. It is said by Pennant to have been that species of fossil-shell called gryphite.[770] Its name is from *crùban*, a sitting or squatting or crouching attitude in man or beast, the result of a disease in the feet that makes them unable to stand. A stone of this kind in Breadalbane was lent only 'under a pledge of two cows' (*an geall càraid cruidh*). If the stone was not returned the cows were to be forfeited.

VARIOUS

A round stone, exactly resembling the one above referred to as pictured by Wilson, with six regularly arranged circles carved upon it, was long in the possession of a family in Knapdale, and is now in Tiree. It was used for the relief of colic pains and other internal gripings, and was believed to cast a skin (*tilg rùsg*) when put in the water to be used. It was called *clach a' ghreimich* ('the gripe stone').[771] There was a companion stone of the same size for the cure of the evil eye.

Mary Macintyre, the noted Fort William witch, a native of Barra, had a stone called *Clach na Léig* ('the Pebble of Healing Virtues') with a hole in it through which she thrust her tongue previous to making divinations. It was of a blue colour, and by means of it Mary could give young women accounts of their sweethearts, secure for seamen and others who came to Fort William with flesh and other commodities a sale for their goods, etc.[772]

There is a stone in Caolas, Tiree, called *Clach na Stoirm* ('the Storm Stone'), almost entirely buried in the ground. If taken out of the ground, cleaned and set upright, it will cause a storm to arise.[773]

The Ardvoirlich Stone (in Perthshire) was used for the cure of murrain in cattle. A person going for it must not speak, or sit, or enter a house, or be found outside a house after sunset. He must take up his quarters for the night before the sun sets.[774]

SOISGEUL, GOSPEL

A 'gospel' consisted of a verse of Scripture, or a hymn, or some good words, usually got from the priest, and sewn in the clothes to keep the wearer from weakness of mind and as a protection from spite (*air son inntinn lag 's droch rùn*). When going for it a person must not speak to anyone on the way, and must take up his lodgings for the night before the sun goes down.[775]

MISCELLANEOUS CURES

Besides all these magic cures, there were others practised by boys and resorted to by the superstitious, without much thought as to there being magic in them or not. The cure in many cases was supposed to be effected or the desired gift conferred by natural means.

WARTS (*FOINEACHUN*)

These were cured by putting in a bag as many knots or joints of straw or grass (*glùinean shop*) as there were warts to be banished, and leaving them on the public road. The first person who lifted the bag was to have the warts in future. Another equally efficacious plan was to take a grain of barley (*spilgein eòrna*) for every wart and bury it in some retired spot, where it was never to be disturbed.[776]

Should both these simple cures fail, pig's blood was applied to the warts and rubbed off with a clout. This cloth was made up into a parcel and left on the road. The warts were removed to the hands of the first person who opened it.[777]

Stye (*Neònagan*)

A stye on the eye (pronounced *sleònachan*)[778] was cured by putting one end of a stick in the fire, pointing the burning end towards the sore eye, and whirling it round rapidly in a circle, saying, "A stye one, a stye two, a stye three," etc., down to "a stye nine," and then adding, "take yourself off, stye." The charm was also performed by repeating (while the stick was being whirled), "Go back, go back, go back, stye" (*air ais, air ais*, etc.). Others placed great faith in rubbing the eye with gold.[779]

Tetter (*Teine-Dé*, Herpes Labialis)

Boys troubled with eruptions on the mouth were infuriated by a rhyme:

> *Teine-dé air do bhus —*
> *Rug do mhàthair-chéil' ubh*
> *'S thug thu fhéin mach an gur.*

"A tetter on your mouth – / Your stepmother laid an egg / And you hatched the brood." The first part of the name is *teine*, a fire, and a curious question arises as to what *dé* is. It occurs also in *dearbadan dé*, a butterfly. It looks like the genitive of *dia*, god.[780]

Hiccup (*An Aileag*)

Hiccup was cured by accusing the person who had it of theft. This stands somewhat to reason in the case of children. If they be ingenuous, such an accusation, skilfully made, rouses their nature to such an extent that the hiccup disappears.[781]

Hooping-Cough (*An Trigh, an Triugh*)

It was a saying: *Fear sam bith dh'òlas bainne capaill le spàin chrithinn, cha ghabh e 'n trigh ach aotrom.* "Whoever drinks mare's milk with an aspen spoon will have hooping-cough but slightly."[782]

STIFF NECK

Stiff neck such as may be got from sleeping with too high a pillow, or the head awry, was cured by squeezing the neck between the legs of the tongs.[783]

TOOTHACHE (*DÉIDE*)

This excruciating disease was supposed to be capable of cure by putting a dead man's finger or a coffin nail in the mouth, and people have been known in their agony to try both expedients. The person resorting to this cure must go for the nail or dead man's finger to the graveyard (*roluig*), though very likely this part of the experiment was rarely tried. As in the case of those who go to have a tooth pulled, the pain disappeared on the way.[784]

FALLING SICKNESS (*AN TUITEAMAS*)

When a new-born child is being washed, a straw rope (*sìoman*) twined round it, and then cut in pieces, is a safeguard during life against epilepsy, falling sickness (*tinneas tuiteamas*), or as it was euphemistically called, *an tinneas a-muigh* ('the out sickness').[785] In Sutherlandshire a second attack was supposed to be prevented by burying a cock alive when the first occurred.[786]

MADNESS

In the Highlands, as elsewhere, rough usage (often amounting to brutality) was believed to be the most suitable treatment for those suffering under this, the greatest of human misfortunes, mental aberration.

On a Thursday (it should be no other day), a person was to take the lunatic behind him on a grey horse and gallop at the horse's utmost speed three times round a boundary mark (*comharra crìche*), and then to an immovable stone. On making the madman speak to this stone the cure was complete.[787]

A plan (of which there are traditions in the Hebrides) was to put a rope round the madman's waist and drag him after a boat till he was nearly dead.[788]

In Strathfillan (*Srath Fhaolain*, of which the common name is *Sraithibh*, the Straths) in Perthshire is a pool in the river which winds through the strath, and the ruins of a chapel (at Clachan, about half a mile distant) which at one time enjoyed a wide reputation for the cure of this affliction. One who was alive a few years ago, and used to assist at the ceremonies to be observed in the chapel, remembered as many as twelve madmen being left tied there at a time.[789]

Tradition says St Fillan had in his possession a stone of marvellous virtue. Some people were taking it from him by violence when he threw it in a deep pool in the river, and from this the pool derived its miraculous virtue. Mad people were made to go three times *deiseal* (i.e. keeping the pool on their right hand) round the linn and then were plunged headlong in. On being taken out, three stones were lifted from the pool and placed in a cairn (which may still be seen). A stone bowl was filled with water to be consecrated and poured on the patient's head. The madman was taken to the chapel and placed on his back on the ground, stretched between two sticks, and laced round with ropes in a very simple manner. If he succeeded in extricating himself before morning good hopes were entertained of his recovery. The ropes were so arranged that he could do so easily. He had only to push them from him towards his feet, but if he was outrageous he was hopelessly entangled.

The pool lost its virtue in consequence of a mad bull having been thrown into it. It is now known as *Linne 'n Tairbh* ('the Bull's Pool').[790]

MÀM, AXILLARY SWELLING

A swelling of the axillary glands (*fàireagun na h-achlais*) is an ailment that soon subsides or breaks into an ulcer. The 'skilful' professed to cure it in the following manner, and no doubt when the swelling subsided, as in most cases it did, the whole credit was given to their magic ceremony.

On Friday (on which day alone the ceremony was efficacious) certain magic words were muttered to the blade of a knife or axe (the more steel the better), which was held for the purpose close to the mouth, and then, the blade being applied to the sore place, the swelling was crossed and parted into nine, or other odd numbers or imaginary divisions.[791]

After each crossing, the axe was pointed towards a hill the name of which commences not with *beinn*, a lofty hill, but *màm*, a round mountain. For instance, in Mull and neighbourhood the malady was transferred – *do chuid-s' air* 'your portion's on', *tha siud air* 'that's on', *do roinn-sa air* 'your bit's on' etc.[792] – to *Màm Lìrein*, *Màm an t-Snòid*, *Màm Doire Dhubhaig*, *Màm Chlachaig*, *Màm Bhrathadail*, etc., all hills in that island. When the swelling was 'counted' (*air àireamh*) the axe was pointed to the ground, saying, *A ghoimh san làr 's a chràdh san talamh*. "The pain be in the ground and the affliction in the earth."

LUMBAGO (*LEUM DROMA*)

When the back is strained and its nerves are affected so that motion is painful, the afflicted person is to lie down on his face, and one who was born feet foremost is to step thrice across him, each time laying his full weight on the foot that treads on the patient's back. There is no cure unless the person stepping across has been born feet foremost.[793]

CONSUMPTION (CAITHEAMH)

On the farm of Crossapol in Coll there is a stone called *Clach Thuill*, i.e. the Hole Stone, through which persons suffering from consumption were made to pass three times in the name of the Father, Son, and Holy Ghost. They took meat with them each time, and left some on the stone. The bird that took the food away had the consumption laid upon it. Similar stones, under which the patient can creep, were made use of in other islands.[794]

LEPROSY (MÙR)

The waterfall at Scorrybreck, near Portree in Skye, called *Easa suc Con*, forms in the rock a natural trough or basin about the length and breadth of a man. A daughter of Lochlin, suffering from an incurable skin disease (*mùr*, leprosy?), in the course of her journeys in search of a cure (there being a prophecy that her cure was to be found in a northern island), came to this waterfall. The trough was emptied, and she was placed lying in it. She lay there till it again filled, and her cure was effected.[795]

LOCH MA NÀR

Loch ma Nàr in Sutherlandshire, if entered on the first Monday of August, was believed to cure any and every disease or sickness.[796]

WELLS

Throughout the Highlands there are wells to which wonderful powers in the healing of disease were ascribed in olden times. They were generally, but not always, called after some saint, and their waters were drunk on certain days (or at a particular hour of the day) and with certain ceremonies and offerings. The importance of these wells and the pilgrimages to them disappeared with the Roman Catholic religion, and hardly a trace now remains of their former honours beyond the name.[797]

Tobar Leac nam Fiann ('The Well of the Fian Flagstone') in Jura cured every disease. When the sick person went to it he had to leave in it a pin, a needle, a button, or other article, and if this was afterwards taken away there was no cure.[798]

In a cave beyond Sanna in Ardnamurchan, and near the village of Plòcaig, there

exil_ine

was about thirty years ago a hole, holding about a bowlful, made in the floor of the cave by water dripping from the roof. The waters of this receptacle were decreed of great efficacy in making those who drank it gay and strong. It was in request by young men of a lively disposition, women rising from childbed, etc. When entering, a copper coin, a metal button or a nail was placed somewhere near the door, and unless this was done it was not safe to enter. At the time mentioned the shelves of the cave were full of these offerings.[799]

In North Uist, between Loch Maddy and Dïusa in Merivale, there is a well that cures the toothache.[800] In the islet of St Cormick, on the east of Cantyre, there was a well that cured the jaundice till an old wife from Breadalbane asked the saint in rude or uncivil terms to cure her distemper (*vide* Old Statistical Account).[801]

In Coll, near the *tung* or family burying-ground of the MacLeans of Coll, there is a well called *Tobar nan Clach* ('the Well of Stones'), and not far from it a sunken rock in the sea called *Cairgein*. It was a saying that as long as a person got water from the one and dulse from the other he need never die of want.[802]

At the back of Hough Hill in Tiree there is a well called *Tobar nan Naoi Beò* ('the Well of the Nine Living') which in a season of great scarcity supported a widow and her eight children without any nourishment but itself and shellfish. Hence its name.[803]

PLANTS AND TREES: MOUNTAIN ASH

The efficacy of the wicken tree against witches, already described, was a widespread belief found in England as well as in the Highlands, where it was also said to make the best rod for a fisherman. If he takes with him

> *Beairt ribeach,*
> *Dubhan bradach,*
> *Slat cham chaorainn*

('Ragged tackle, / A stolen hook, / And a crooked wicken rod') he is most likely to be in luck. The reason is that no evil or envious eye will rest upon himself or his equipments (*cha laigh sùil orra*).[804]

PEARLWORT (*MÒTHAN*)

The trailing pearlwort (*sagina procumbens*), which grows in very dry places and on old walls, was one of the most efficacious plants against the powers of darkness. This efficacy was attributed to its being the first plant trodden on by Christ when He came on earth. Placed on the lintel of the door (*san àrd-doras*), it kept the spirits of the dead, if they returned, from entering the house.[805] If in the bull's hoof at the time of being with the cow, the offspring's milk could not be taken away by witches. When placed below the right knee of a woman in labour, it defeated the machinations of the Fairy women. It must be pulled with certain words:

> *Buainidh mise am mòthan,*
> *An luibh a dh'òrdaich Crìost —*
> *Chan eil eagal losgadh teine dhuit*
> *No cogadh nam ban shìth.*

"I will pull the pearlwort, / The plant that Christ ordained – / No fear has it of fire-burning / Or wars of Fairy women."[806]

St John's Wort (*Achlasan Chaluim Chille*)

The Gaelic name of the Upright St John's Wort (*hypericum pulchrum*) means literally 'St Columba's axillary one'. Why so called does not appear.[807] To be of use it must be found when neither sought for nor wanted. If sought for, it has no efficacy more than another plant, but if accidentally fallen in with and preserved, it wards off fever and keeps its owner from being taken away in his sleep by the Fairies. One version of the rhyme to be said in pulling it is in these words:

> *Achlasan Chaluim Chille*
> *Gun sireadh gun iarraidh,*
> *Cha toir iad ás do chadal thu*
> *'S cha ghabh thu fiabhras.*
> *Buainidh mis' an donn duilleach,*
> *Luibh a fhuaradh an taobh bearraidh;*
> *Cha tugainn e do dhuine*
> *Gun tuilleadh air mo bheannachd.*[808]

"The axillary plant of Colum-Cill / Unsought for, unwanted, / They will not take you from your sleep / Nor will you take fever. / I will pull the brown-leaved one, / A plant found beside a cleft; / No man will have it from me / Without more than my blessing." Another version runs:

> *Buainidh mis' an t-achlasan,*
> *Se luibh nam ban fionn e,*
> *Se 'chuirm eireachdail e*
> *'S a' chùirt shòghail;*
> *Luibh fhireann e, luibh bhoireann e,*

Luibh bh' aig eòin nan allt e,
Luibh bh' aig Nì Math 'na éiginn
'S aig Crìost air aineol,
'S b' fheàrr a dhuais don làimh dheas
Am bitheadh e.

"I will pull the axillary one, / 'Tis the plant of fair women, / 'Tis the graceful feast / And the luxurious court; / A male plant, a female plant, / A plant the birds of the streams had, / A plant the Good Being had in His need / And Christ had among strangers, / So better be its reward to the right hand / That holds it."[809]

Juniper (*Iubhar-Beinne*, literally Mountain Yew)

This plant is a protection by sea and land, and no house in which it is will take fire. It must be pulled by the roots, with its branches made into four bunches, and taken between the five fingers, saying:

Buainidh mis' an t-iubhar àigh
Roimh chòig aisnean croma Chrìost
An ainm an Athar, a' Mhic, 's an Spioraid Naoimh
Air bhàthadh, air ghàbhadh 's air ghriobhadh.

("I will pull the bounteous yew / Through the five bent ribs of Christ / In the name of the Father, Son, and Holy Ghost / Against drowning, danger and confusion.") The plant is also called *aiteal* in Gaelic.[810]

Yarrow (*Chathair Làir*)

This plant of power was also pulled with mystic words, of which but four lines have been recovered.

Buainidh mis' a' chathair làir
Mar bhuain Moire le dà làimh,
Buainidh mi le m' neart i,
'S buainidh mi le m' ghlaic i, etc.

("I will pull the yarrow / As Mary pulled it with her two hands, / I will pull it with my strength, / I will pull it with the hollow of my hand," etc.) In many parts of the Highlands the yarrow is called *cathair-thalanda*, which means the same as *cathair làir*, literally 'the ground chair'.[811]

'The Enticing Plant' (Lus an Tàlaidh)

This plant grows in soft places among heather, and has a purple flower. From the descriptions given of it, it seems to be the purple orchis or wild hyacinth. It has two roots, one larger than the other, and it is in these its magic power consists. The largest represents the man, the lesser a woman, whose affections are to be gained. The plant is to be pulled by the roots before sunrise, with the face directed to the south.

Whichever root is used is to be immediately placed in spring water, taking care that no part of the sun's surface is above the horizon. If it sinks, the person whose love is sought will prove the future husband or wife. If the charm is made for no one in particular, the root reduced to powder and put below the pillow causes dreams of the person to be married.[812]

The Daughter of the King of Enchantments (Nighean Rìgh Sionnach)

The daughter of *Rìgh Sionnach* was found in the hunting hill by a party of hunters, as the writer heard the story, and they took her home with them. The chief married her, and she lived with his mother in the same house, and had three children before she was heard to utter a word. Afterwards, on the occasion of a feast being prepared, they gave her a candle to hold, when she said:

> *A'r a chùis,*[813] *a choinneal*
> *Fhuair mi ann am' làimh ga cumail,*
> *Am' sheasamh a's an deathaich —*
> *'S cha b'e sin m' àbhaist*
> *An taigh mo mhàthar 's m' athar.*

("On thine account, candle / Put in my hand to hold, / Standing in the smoke – / That was not my customary wont / In my father's house.")[814] Her mother-in-law answered:

> *A'r a shocair, a bhuinneag,*
> *Is math a b' aithne dhòmhsa 'chuideachd —*
> *Aona mhart air thrì sinean*
> *'S naoinear de mhuinntir.*

("At your leisure, my good woman, / Well I knew the company – / One cow with three teats / And nine people.") She replied:

> *Cha b'e sin an gnathas*
> *Bha 'n taigh m' athar no mo mhàthar —*

Cha robh aona mhart air thrì sinean
No naoinear a mhuinntir,
Ach naoi slabhrainnean òir
An crocha' 'n taigh Rìgh Sionnach.

"That was not the custom / In my father and mother's house – / There was not one cow three-teated / Nor a company of nine in number, / But nine chains of pure gold / Hung in the house of the King of Enchantments." By her words it was found out whose daughter she was, and whence she had come.[815]

Stone ball referred to at pp. 222, 224

15

DEATH WARNINGS

INTRODUCTORY

Death has always been deemed the greatest evil that afflicts humanity, and the terrors and awe which its advent inspires have given superstition its amplest scope. The 'king of terrors' no doubt throws its shadows before it, but that foreshadowing belongs to medical diagnosis. The superstition connected with it consists in making unusual appearances and natural phenomena (having no relation to it beyond an accidental proximity in time) forerunners of its dread approach.

The mind loves to dwell on the circumstances connected with the death of a departed and dear friend, and amid a sparse population, death is not an event of that frequency and daily occurrence which make it to the townsman little heeded till it affects himself and his friends. Besides, doubt and scepticism are not spontaneous in the human mind, and whenever anyone states positively that he saw supernatural indications connected with the death or spirit of one departed, he naturally and readily finds credence. By being frequently told, the tale becomes more and more certain, and traditions – once they have attained the rank of beliefs – are very slow in dying out. That the excitable and imaginative mind of the Celt should, therefore, have a firm belief in supernatural forewarnings of death is not at all surprising.

Certain families and septs had death warnings peculiar to themselves, and whenever any of them was on his death-bed, particularly when the death of a chief was at hand, someone about the house was sure to see or hear the warning. Before the death of any of the Breadalbane family (the descendants of *Donnchadh Dubh a' Churraichd*, 'Black Duncan of the Cowl'), a bull was heard at night roaring up the hillside. The bellowing grew fainter as it ascended the mountain, and died away as it reached the top. The origin of this superstition probably is that Black Duncan is accused of having once had a bull's head brought in at a feast as a signal for the massacre of a number of the MacGregors whom he had invited in a friendly manner to the castle.[816]

The Clan MacLachlan were warned of death by the appearance of a little bird; a sept of the MacGregors known as *Clann Dhonnchaidh Dhuibh* ('the Children or Descendants of Black Duncan') by a whistle; another family of the same clan, *Clann*

Dhonnchaidh Bhig ('the Children of Little Duncan') by a light like that of a candle. Other signals were shouting (*sgairt*), cries of distress, screaming (*sgriachail*), sounds of weeping, etc. When any of them foreboded death, it was heard where no human being could be, and there was an unearthly tone about it that struck a chill into the hearer's heart.[817]

Before the death of a *duin' uasal* (duine wassal, a gentleman), a light or meteor called *dreag*, or rather *driug*, was seen in the sky proceeding from the house to the grave in the direction in which the funeral procession was to go. It was only for 'big men' (people of station and affluence) that these lights appeared, and an irreverent tailor once expressed a wish that the whole sky were full of them.

HUGH OF THE LITTLE HEAD (*EOGHAN A' CHINN BHIG*)

This was the best known and most dreadful spectre in the West Highlands, the phantom of a headless horseman which made its appearance whenever any of the MacLaines of Lochbuy in Mull were near their dissolution. The spectral horseman is mounted on a small black steed, having a white spot on its forehead, and the marks of the hoofs of which are not like those of other horses, but round indentations as if it had wooden legs. Whenever any of the sept which he follows are on their death-bed Hugh is heard riding past the house, and sometimes even shows himself at the door. He does not sit straight on his horse's back, but somewhat to one side, and the appearance of the almost headless body is that of a water-stoup tied on the horse's back.

The history of the man who is thus doomed to attend at the death of any of his clan is curious. Tradition is not always uniform on the subject, but the following statement reconciles most of the accounts and substantially agrees with them all.

Hugh was the only son of *Eachann Reuganach* ('Hector the Stubborn'), first chief of Lochbuy, in the fourteenth century, and brother of *Lachann Lùbanach* ('Lachlan the Wily'), first chief of Dowart.[818] He got the name of 'Hugh of the Little Head' in his lifetime, and from the actions ascribed to him fully bears his own testimony to the truth of the adage, *Ceann mòr air duine glic 's ceann circ air amadan.* "A big head on a wise man and a hen's head on a fool."[819]

Sayings of his which tradition has preserved illustrate the curious shrewdness sometimes found in connection with limited intellect. Thus, when his mother was being carried for burial, he thought the pall-bearers were carrying the body too high, and he told them not to raise her so high 'in case she should seek to make a habit of it' (*mum bi i 'g iarraidh a chleachdaidh*), and the phrase has since continued – 'to seek to make a habit of anything, like Hugh of the Little Head's mother'.

He was married to a daughter of the house of MacDougall of Lorn, and she proved but a very indifferent wife. Tradition ascribes to her several nicknames, all of them extremely opprobrious: *Chorra Thòn Dubh* ('the Black-Bottomed Heron'), *Gortag an Droch Chorra Dhubh* ('Stingy the Bad Black Heron'), *Curra Dhùghaill* ('the MacDougall Heron') and *Dubhag Tòn ri Teallaich*.[820] He was a fearless soldier, and altogether a very likely person to have been made a wandering spectre of after his death.

Lochbuy first belonged to the MacFadyens. MacLaine (so the family spell the name), having obtained a grant of the place from the Lord of the Isles, deceitfully asked MacFadyen for a site for a sheepfold (*crò chaorach*), and having obtained a hillock for the purpose, proceeded to build a castle. When the place was sufficiently fortified he shot an arrow from it at MacFadyen, who sat at some distance picking bones (*spioladh chnàmh*) at his dinner. In the end MacFadyen had to leave his own land and go to Garmony (*Gar'moin' an Fhraoich*), where he supported himself by coining gold gathered in *Beinn an Aoinidh*, Mull, whence his descendants became known as *Sìolachadh nan Òr-Cheàrd* ('the Seed of the Goldsmiths').[821]

After this Lochbuy and Dowart quarrelled. The properties of the two brothers adjoined, and between them lay a piece of ground the ownership of which they disputed. A ploughman belonging to Lochbuy was ploughing on the debateable ground when a friend of Dowart, who was out hunting, shot him. Some time after this Dowart's two boys were on a visit to Lochbuy, whose wife, being a relative of the murdered ploughman, went a piece of the way home with the children, and at a well since called *Tobar nan Ceann* ('The Well of the Heads') took off their heads and threw them into the well, leaving the bodies on the bank. For this foul deed a deadly feud sprang up between the two houses, and Hugh's wife, being a foster-sister (*codhalta*) of Dowart's wife, did not care though her husband and the house of Lochbuy should be worsted. This feud, joined to the other grievances of the 'Crane', led to there being so little peace at Lochbuy that the old chief gave Hugh a separate establishment and allotted to him the lands of Morinish.[822]

Hugh built himself a castle on an islet in Loch Sguabain, a small lake between Lochbuy and Dowart. His wife urged him to go and get the rights (*còirichean*, i.e. the title deeds) of the lands of Lochbuy – or perhaps to go and get more – from his father, and at last he went. It was explained to him that on his father's death he would have a right to the whole property, and he went away pacified. His wife, however, urged that it would be a small thing for Lachlan the Wily, his father's brother, to come and take from him everything he had. He went again, an altercation ensued, and he struck his aged father a violent blow on the side of the head. This came to the ears of the old man's brother, the chief of Dowart. Glad of an excuse to cut off the heir presumptive and make himself master of Lochbuy, and gratify his desire for revenge, Dowart collected his men and marched to take Hugh to some place of confinement or kill him. Hugh collected his own men and prepared to give battle.

Early on the morning of the fight, others say the evening before, Hugh was out walking, and at the boundary stream (*allt crìche*) saw an Elfin woman rinsing clothes and singing the 'Song of the MacLeans'.[823] (Others say his servant-man saw her first, a tradition which finds a ready explanation for the whole account, in an attempt to discourage Hugh by means of a prevailing superstition.) Her long breasts, after the manner of her kind (according to the Mull belief regarding these weird women), hung down and interfered with her washing, and she now and then flung them over her shoulders to keep them out of the way. Hugh crept up silently behind her, and catching one of the breasts, as is recommended in such cases, put the nipple in his mouth, saying, "Yourself and I be witness you are my first nursing mother."[824]

She answered, "The hand of your father and grandfather be upon you! You had need that it is so."[825]

He then asked her what she was doing. She said, *Nigheadh léintean nam fir ghointe agadsa* – "Washing the shirts of *your* mortally-wounded men," or, as others say, *aodach nam fear théid air na h-eich a-màireach 's nach till*, "the clothes of those who will mount the horses tomorrow and will not return."

He asked her, "Will I win the fight?"

She answered that if he and his men got 'butter without asking' (*ìm gun iarraidh*) to their breakfast he would win; if not, he would lose.[826]

He asked if he himself would return alive from the battle – *An tig mise ás beò?* And she either answered ambiguously or not at all; and when going away left him as her parting gift (*fàgail*) that he should go about to give warning of approaching death to all his race.

The same morning he put on a new suit, and a servant woman, coming in just as he had donned it, praised it and said, *Meal is caith e.* "May you enjoy and wear it."

It was deemed unlucky that a woman should be the first to say this, and Hugh replied to the evil omen by saying, *Na na meal thusa do shlàinte.* "May you not enjoy your health."[827]

For breakfast 'Stingy the Black Heron' sent in curds and milk in broad dishes. She did not even give spoons, but told Hugh and his men to put on hen's bills (*gobun chearc*) and take their food. Hugh waited long to see if any butter would come, rubbing his shoes together impatiently, saying now and then it was time to go, and giving every hint he could that the butter might be sent in. At last he threw his shoe down the house, exclaiming, *Cha ghluais bròg no bruidhinn droch bhean taighe* ("Neither shoes nor speech will move a bad housewife") and demanding the butter. *Cuir a-nuas an t-ìm, 's feudaidh tu fhéin itheadh a-màireach!* "Send down the butter, and you may eat it yourself tomorrow!"

Chan fhàg breabadair na seana bhròig craiceann air deàrnaidh, she retorted. "The kicker of old shoes will not leave skin upon palm."[828]

When the butter came, Hugh said he did not want her curds or cheese to be coming in white masses through his men's sides (*tighinn 'nan staoigean geala roimh chliathach nam fear aige*), kicked open the milk-house door and let in the dogs, and went away, leaving the breakfast untouched.

The fight took place at *Cnoc nan Sgolb*, at the back of Innsri (*cùl na h-Innsribh*) near *Ceann a' Chnocain*, and not far from Torness in Glenmore. As might be expected of fasting men, Hugh and his followers lost the fight. The sweep of a broadsword took off the upper part of his head (*copan a chinn*). Instead of falling dead, he jumped on the top of his horse, a small black steed with a white spot on its forehead, and ever since is 'dreeing his weird' by going about to give warning when any of his race are about to die.[829]

After his victory Dowart made prisoner of his brother, Lochbuy, and sent him to Kerneburg (a stronghold of which the Dowarts became heritable keepers) on one of the Treshinish Islands near Staffa, west of Mull. He sent *Mòr Dhubh Nic-a-Phì*, Black Sarah MacPhie from Suidhe in the Ross of Mull – the most ungainly woman he could get, so ugly that she was nicknamed *an t-Srathair*, 'the Pack-Saddle' – to take care of him. Black Sarah, however, became the mother of *Murchadh Geàrr*, who ultimately made himself master of his paternal acres.[830]

The ghostly 'rider of the black horse' (*marcaich an eich dhuibh*) crosses the seas in discharging his task. When coming to Tiree (where there are now but two or three persons claiming to be of the sept of the Lochbuy MacLaines) he takes his passage from Port na h-Amhn near Rubh' an t-Sléibh in Treshinish, Mull. About fifty years ago a Mull woman living there insisted that she had often, when a young woman, heard him galloping past the house in the evening and had seen the sparks from his horse's hoofs as he rode down to the shore on his way to Tiree.[831]

It is told of an old man of the Lochbuy MacLeans in Tiree that on his death-bed the noise of a horse clanking a chain after it was heard coming to the house. Thinking it was Hugh of the Little Head, he said, "The rider of the black horse is clanking on his own errand (*straighlich air ceann a ghnothaich fhéin*)." On looking out, the awe-struck company found the noise was caused by a farm-horse dragging a chain tether (*langasaid*) after it.

On the high road between Calachyle and Salen in Mull, a strong man of the name of MacLean was met at night by Hugh. The horseman spake never a word, but caught MacLean to take him away. MacLean resisted, and in the struggle caught hold of a birch sapling and succeeded in holding it till the cock crew. The birch tree was twisted in the struggle, and one after another of its roots gave way. As the last was yielding the cock crew. The twisted tree may still be seen. The same story is told of a twisted tree near Tobermory, and a similar one is localised between Lochaber and Badenoch. (Campbell of Islay's *West Highland Tales*, ii. 83.)[832]

Other premonitions of death were the howling of dogs, the appearance of lights, loud outcries and sounds of weeping, apparitions of the doomed person's 'fetch' or coffin or funeral procession, etc.[833] These sounds and appearances were more apt to precede an accidental and premature death, such as drowning, and to understand them properly it will be necessary to enter into an examination of the doctrine of the second sight.

16

SECOND SIGHT (*AN DÀ SHEALLADH*)

INTRODUCTORY

Freed from a good deal of mystery in which an imperfect understanding of its character has involved it, the gift of second sight may be briefly explained to be the same as being 'spectre-haunted', or liable to 'spectre illusions', when that condition occurs – as it often does – in persons of sound mind. The phenomena in both cases are the same; the difference is in the explanation given of them. In the one case the vision is looked on as unreal and imaginary, arising from some bodily or mental derangement, and having no foundation in fact, while the other proceeds on a belief that the object seen is really there and has an existence independent of the seer – is a revelation, in fact, to certain gifted individuals of a world different from, and beyond, the world of sense.

Science has accepted the former as the true and rational explanation, and traces spectral illusions to an abnormal state of the nervous system, exhaustion of mind or body, strong emotions, temperament, and others of the countless (and at times obscure) causes that lead to hallucination and delusion.[834] But before optical and nervous delusions were recognised by science, while the spectres were believed to be external realities having an existence of their own, the visions were necessarily invested with an awe approaching to terror, and the gift or faculty of seeing them could not but be referred to some such explanation as the doctrine of the second sight offers.

'The shepherds of the Hebrid Isles' are usually credited with the largest possession of the gift, but the doctrine was well known over the whole Highlands, and as firmly believed in Ross-shire and the Highlands of Perthshire as in the remotest Hebrides. Waldron describes it as existing in his time in the isle of Man.[835] It is a Celtic belief, and the suggestion that it is the remains of the magic of the druids is not unreasonable. In every age there are individuals who are spectre-haunted, and it is probable enough that the sage Celtic priests, assuming the spectres to be external, reduced the gift of seeing them to a system, a belief in which formed part of their teaching. This accounts for the circumstance that the second sight has flourished more among the Celts than any other race.

Second Sight (an Dà Shealladh)

The Gaelic name *dà shealladh* does not literally mean the 'second sight' but the 'two sights'. The vision of the world of sense is one sight, ordinarily possessed by all, but the world of spirits is visible only to certain persons, and the possession of this additional vision gives them 'the two sights', or what comes to the same thing, 'a second sight'. Through this faculty they see the ghosts of the dead revisiting the earth, and the fetches, doubles or apparitions of the living.[836]

The world to which apparitions belong is called by writers on the second sight 'the world of spirits', but the expression does not convey correctly the idea attached to visions of the kind. The object seen, usually that of a friend or acquaintance (the phantasm, phantom, apparition, or whatever else we choose to call it), was recognised to be as independent of the person whose semblance it bore as it was of the person seeing it. He knew nothing of the phantom's appearance; it was not his spirit, and played its part without his knowledge or his wish. The seer, again, could not, or did not, trace it to anything in himself; it did not arise from any suggestion of his hopes or fears, and was not a reproduction of any former state of his mind or thought. As to its owing its origin to anything abnormal in himself, he was (as far as he could judge) as healthy in mind and body as other people. As long, therefore, as men believed the phantasm to be an external reality, they were compelled to believe in doubles, or semblances, that move in a world which is neither that of sense nor that of spirits. The actions and appearances of these doubles have no counterpart in any past or present event, and naturally are referred to the future and the distant.[837]

The object seen, or phantasm, is called *taibhs* (pronounced **taïsh**), the person seeing it *taibhsear* (pronounced **taïsher**), and the gift of vision, in addition to its name of second sight, is known as *taibhsearachd*. It is noticeable that many words referring to spirits and ghosts begin with this syllable *ta*. The following are worth noticing.

Tannas, or *tannasg*, a spectre, generally of the dead, and (in the idea attached to it) more shadowy, unsubstantial and spiritual than a *bòcan*.

Tamhasg (pronounced **taüsg**), the shade or double of a living person, is the common name for apparitions by which men are haunted, and with which (according to the doctrine of the second sight) they have to hold assignations.

Tàchar, a rare and almost obsolete word, but the derivatives of which, *tacharan* and *tachradh*, are still in common use. The only instances known to the writer of its occurrence are in the names of places. *Sròn an Tàchair* ('the Ghost-Haunted Nose') is a rock between Kinloch Rannoch and Druim a' Chastail in Perthshire where faint mysterious noises were heard, and on passing which the wayfarer was left by the mysterious sprite which joined him in the hollow below. *Imire Tàchair*, in the island of Iona, is a ridge leading from near the ecclesiastical buildings to the hill, and, till the moor through which it runs was drained in recent years, formed an elevation above a sheet of water – a very likely place to have been haunted by goblins.[838] The natives of the island have no tradition or explanation of the name. The derivatives *tachradh* and *tacharan* are applied to a weak and helpless person: when the first syllable is long, in pity; when short, contemptuously, as e.g. *an tăchradh grànda* 'the ugly wretch'.[839]

Tàslaich, a supernatural premonition felt or heard but not seen, also applied to the ghosts of the living: for instance, a native of Skye being asked the reason why dogs were barking at night near a churchyard, said it was because they saw *tàslaich nan daoine beò*, the ghosts of the living, the premonition of a funeral.

Tàradh, noises (*straighlich*) heard at night through the house, indicating a change of tenants, a premonition by mysterious sounds of a coming event.

Taran, the ghost of an unbaptised child (Dr Macpherson, p. 307), not now a common word.[840]

Tàsg, perhaps a contraction of *tamhasg*, used commonly in the expression *éigheach tàisg*, the cry or wail of a fetch. Cf. *taghairm*, the spirit-call.[841]

The whole doctrine of these apparitions of the living (or as they are called in Cumberland, 'swarths') and premonitions of coming events proceeds on the supposition that people have a counterpart or other self, an *alter ego*, which goes about unknown to themselves, with their voices, features, form and dress, even to their shoes, and is visible to those who have the unhappy gift of the second sight.[842] This phantasm, or other self, is not the life or the spirit of the person whom it represents. He has nothing to do with it; he may, at the time it is seen, be sunk in unconscious sleep, or his attention and wishes may be otherwise taken up, and death may not be at all in his thoughts. At the same time, it is not without some connection with him. Strongly wishing is apt to make one's *tàradh* be heard at the place where he wishes to be, and if the person whose spectre is seen be spoken to the apparition disappears; but in general the *taibhs* is independent of all thought or action or emotion of the person whom it represents.[843]

The doctrine does not assert that all men have got such a double, much less that those who are most largely gifted with the second sight see it always, or even frequently. The spectres are visible to the seer only under exceptional circumstances, in certain situations, and at certain times. The most usual of these are after dusk and across a fire, when a sudden or violent death has occurred or is to occur, when a friend is ill, when strangers are to come, or any event is impending calculated to make a deep impression on the mind.

Spectres are often seen with as much distinctness as external objects, and it would be a great injustice to the poor man who claims to have visions of things that are not there at all to say he is telling an untruth. To him the vision is really there, and it is but natural for him to think it has an existence separate from himself, instead of referring it to an abnormal state of his mind and nervous system. Some spectres 'move with the moving eye', being what the poet calls 'hard mechanic ghosts'; others have their own proper motion, and probably arise in the brain. The former are the most common, and it was a test among **taïshers**, whether the figure seen was a wraith or not, to stoop down and raise themselves up again suddenly. If the figure did the same, it was an apparition, a *tamhasg*.

The gift of second sight was not in any case looked upon as enviable or desirable. Seers frequently expressed a wish that they had no such gift. In some instances it ran in the family; in others, but rarer cases, the seer was the only one of his kindred who 'saw sights' (*chì sealladh*).[844] Some had it early in life, upon others it did not come till they were advanced in life.

These characteristics alone show it to be in its origin the same as spectral illusions. It arose from hereditary disease, malformation or weakness of the visual organs, and derangements of mind or bodily health. It was not voluntary; the visions went and came without the option of the seer, and his being visited by them was deemed by himself and others a misfortune rather than a gift. A difference was also recognised in the kinds of apparitions visible to different individuals.

When the figure of an acquaintance was seen, the manner in which the *taibhs* was clothed afforded an indication to the skilful seer of the fate then befalling, or about to befall, the person whose *taibhs* it was. If the apparition was dressed in the dead-clothes, the person was to die soon; but if in everyday clothes, his death would not occur for some time. If the clothes covered the entire face, his death would be very soon; if the face was uncovered, or partly covered, death was proportionately more remote. Others saw the dead-clothes first about the head, and lower down at each succeeding vision. When the feet were covered death was imminent. There were, however, grave-clothes of good fortune (*lìon-aodach àigh*) as well as grave-clothes indicative of death (*lìon-aodach bàis*), and it was considered extremely difficult for the most skilful seer to distinguish between them. He required, he said, a close view of the spectre to tell which it had on.

The time of day at which the vision was seen was also an indication. The later in the day, the sooner the death. If as late as 5 p.m., soon; but if as early as 2 a.m., the man might live for years.

If the person seen was to be drowned at sea, phosphorescent gleams (*teine-sionnachain*), such as are common in the Hebridean seas on summer nights, appeared round the figure, or its clothes seemed to drip, or there was water in its shoes.

The swarths, or doubles, were believed to go through all the actions and occupy the places which the originals would afterwards perform or occupy. This was particularly the case with regard to funerals. They went for the glasses to be used on the occasion, for the coffin, and even for the wood to make it, and marched in melancholy procession to the churchyard.

When the funeral procession was seen, the seer was unable to say (except by inference) whose funeral it was. For anything he could directly tell, it might be (as it sometimes was) his own. He could only tell the dress, position in the procession, and appearance of those performing the sad duty.

It is dangerous to walk in the middle of the road at night, in case of meeting one of these processions and being thrown down or forced to become one of the coffin-bearers to the graveyard. Persons in the latter predicament have experienced great difficulty in keeping on the road, the whole weight of the coffin seeming to be laid upon them and pushing them off the path. If the seer goes among the swarths he will likely be knocked down, but in some districts (as Moidart) he is said to have one of the staves or bearers (*lunn*) of the coffin thrust into his hand, and to be compelled to take his part in the procession till relieved in due time. In Durness, in Sutherlandshire, the cry of "Relief!" (there used at every change of coffin-bearers) has been heard at night by persons whose houses were near the high road, called out by the phantasms in their ghostly procession.

Persons have been caught hold of by those reputed to have the second sight, and pulled to a side to allow a spectral funeral to pass; and it was universally believed that when the seer saw a procession of the kind – or indeed any of his supernatural visions – he could make others see the same sight by putting his foot on theirs and a hand on their shoulder.[845] He should, therefore, never walk in the middle of the road at night. **Taïshers** never did so. At any moment the traveller may fall in with a spectral funeral, and be thrown down or seized with the oppression of an unearthly weight.

The visions of the seer did not always relate to melancholy events, impending death, funerals and misfortunes. At times he had visions of pleasant events, and saw his future wife before he ever thought of her (at least so he said), sitting by the fireside in the seat she was afterwards to occupy. He could tell whether an absent friend was on his way home, and whether he was to have anything in his hands when coming. He could not tell what the thing was to be, but merely the general appearance of the absent man when returning, and whether he was to come full- or empty-handed.

It has been said that the phantasm (*taibhs* or *tamhasg*) was independent of all thought and volition on the part of those whom it represented, as well as on the part of the seer himself. At the same time, it was part of the creed that if the person whose double was seen was spoken to and told to cease his persecutions, the annoyance came to an end. The person spoken to, being utterly unconscious that his phantasm was wandering about and annoying any one, got very angry, but somehow the spectre ceased to appear. Before taking a final leave, however, it gave the person whom it had haunted (as an informant described it) 'one thundering lashing'. After that it was no more seen.[846]

When a double is first met, if it be taken to be the man himself whose semblance it bears, and be spoken to, it acquires the power of compelling the person who has accosted it to hold nightly assignations with it in future. The man, in fact, from that hour becomes 'spectre-haunted'. Hence it was a tenet of the second sight never to be the first to speak on meeting an acquaintance at night till satisfied that the figure seen was of this world. The seer did not like, indeed did not dare, to tell to others whose figure it was that haunted him. If he did so, the anger of the spectre was roused, and on the following evening it gave him a dreadful thrashing. When he resisted, he grasped but a shadow, was thrown down repeatedly in the struggle, and bruised severely.

This form of the disease was well known in the Western Islands. The haunted person, as in the case of those who had Fairy sweethearts, had to leave home at a certain hour in the evening to meet the spectre, and if he dared for one night to neglect the assignation, he received in due course a sound thrashing. Sometimes at these meetings the spectre spoke and gave items of information about the death of the seer and others. Ordinarily, however, it had merely an indistinct murmuring kind of speech (*tormanaich bruidhinn*).

People noted for the second sight have been observed to have a peculiar look about the eyes. One of them for instance, in Harris, was described as 'always looking up and never looking you straight in the face'. Those who are of a brooding, melancholy disposition are most liable to spectral illusions, and it is only to be expected that the gloom of their character should appear in their looks, and that many of their visions should relate to deaths and funerals.

Among a superstitious and credulous people the second sight, or a pretence to it, must have furnished a powerful weapon of annoyance, and there is reason to believe that, in addition to cases of nervous delusion and of men being duped by their own fancies, there were many instances of imposture and design. So much, indeed, was this the case, that a person of undoubted good character, born and brought up among believers in the second sight (and himself not incredulous on the subject), said: "I never knew a truthful, trustworthy man (*duine firinneach creideasach*) who was a **taïsher**."

While being spectre-haunted was honoured by the name of a second sight, and was invested with mystery and awe, no doubt many laid claim to it for the sake of the awe with which it invested them to annoy those whom they disliked, or to make capital out of it with those anxious about the future or the absent.

Spectres of the Living (*Tamhasg*)

Some thirty years ago a man in Tiree nicknamed the Poult (*am Bigein*) was haunted for several months by the spectre of the person with whom he was at the time at service. The phantom came regularly every evening for him, and if its call was disregarded it gave him next evening a severe thrashing. According to the man's own account, the spectre sometimes spoke, and, when he understood what it said, gave good advice. Its speech was generally indistinct and unintelligible. The person whose spectre it was, on being spoken to on the subject, got very angry, but the visits of the spectre ceased.[847]

Only a few years ago a young man, also in Tiree, was on his way home about midnight from the parish mill, where he had been kiln-drying corn. He had to go against a strong gale of north-west wind, and, having his head bent down and not looking well before him, ran up against a figure which he took to be that of a young man of his acquaintance. He spoke to it, and the figure answered in broken, inarticulate speech (*tormanaich bruidhinn*). Every evening afterwards during that half-year he had to leave the house in which he was at service to meet (he himself said) the spectre that had thus met him. A person who doubted this followed one evening, and saw him, immediately on leaving the house, squaring out in boxing style to some invisible opponent, and falling at every round.

The haunted youth said the apparition gave him much information. It said the person whose semblance it itself bore was to die of fever, that the coffin was to be taken out of the house by certain individuals – whom it named – and was to be placed on two creels outside the door. On speaking to the lad whose apparition haunted him, the persecution ceased. The common opinion was that this was a case of imposture and design.

Near Salen, in Mull, a workman, when going home from his employment in the evening, forgot to take his coat with him. He returned for it, and the apparition (*tamhasg*) of a woman met him and gave him a squeezing (*plùchadh*) that made him keep his bed for several days. In the same island a man was said to have been knocked off his horse by an apparition.

A crofter (or tenant of a small piece of land of which he has no lease) in Caolas, Tiree, went out at night to see that his neighbour's horses were not trespassing on some clover he had in his croft. He was a man who had confessedly the second sight. He observed on this occasion a man going in a parallel direction to himself, and but a short distance off. At first he thought it was only a neighbour, Black Allan, trying to frighten him, but, struck by the motion and silence of the figure, he stooped down and then raised himself suddenly. The figure did the same, proof of its being a *tamhasg* or phantasm. The seer reached home, pale and ready to faint, but nothing further came of his vision.

Three years ago a man who claims to have the second sight was on his way home at night to Barrapol, in the west end of Tiree, from the mill (which is in the centre of the island) with a sack of meal on his back. He laid down the sack and rested by the wayside. When swinging the burden again on his shoulder he observed a figure standing beside him, and then springing on the top of the sack on his back. It remained there, rendering the sack very oppressive, till he reached home, some miles further on.[848]

The son of a seer in Coll was away in the south country. The seer when delving saw his son several times lending assistance, and on two occasions when coming home with a creelful of peats, after taking a rest by the way, saw him helping to lift the creel again on his back. Before long word came of his son's death.

Alexander Sinclair, from Erray in Mull, was grieve at Funery in Morvern. Two, if not three, of the servant women fell in love with him. He had to cross one night a bridge in the neighbourhood, between Savory and Salachan, and was met by the apparitions of two women, whom he recognised as his fellow-servants. One, he said, was the figure of a dark little woman, and lifted him over the parapet. The other was that of the dairymaid in the house in which he was, and it rescued him. The adventure ended by his marrying the dairymaid.[849]

A man, going home at night to Ledmore (*Leudmòr*) near Loch Frisa in Mull, saw the kitchen-maid of the house in which he was at service waiting for him on the other side of a ford that lay in his way. Suspecting the appearance, he went further up the stream to avoid it, but it was waiting for him at every ford. At last he crossed and held on his way, the apparition accompanying him. At the top of the first incline the apparition threw him down. He rose, but was again thrown. He struggled, but the figure, he said, had no weight, and he grasped nothing but wind. On the highest part of the ascent (called *Guala Spinne*) the apparition left him.

After going home, the man spoke to the woman whose spectre had met him. "The next time," he said, "you meet me, I will stab you."

This made the woman cry, but he was never again troubled by her apparition.[850]

A native of Glenbeg in Ardnamurchan, Henderson by name, was at service in Kilfinichen in Mull. One of the servant-maids there made him a present of a pair of worsted gloves. After returning home from service, he had, one evening towards dusk (*am bial an anmuich*, literally 'in the mouth of lateness'), to go from Glenbeg to Kilchoan by a path across a steep incline on the side of the lofty Ben Shianta, towards the projection known as *Sròin Chloinn Illeathain* ('the Nose of the MacLeans'). Steep mountain paths of this kind are called *cadha*, and this particular *cadha* is called *Cadha na Muice* ('the Pig's Pass').

Near the top of the ascent (*aonaich*) and where the difficult path ceases (*bràighe na Cadha*), there is a narrow step (*aisre*) which only one person at a time can cross, leading towards another ascent (*aonaich*). When going up the first ascent, or *cadha*, Henderson was joined by the apparition of the woman who had made him the gloves in Kilfinichen. She was on the up side of him, and he saw when he came to the *aisre*, if she chose to give him a push, he would be precipitated into the black shore (*dubh-*

chladach) which the rocks there overhang, and become a shapeless bundle (*seirgein cuagach*). He blessed himself and, taking courage, crossed in safety. When he got on more level ground over towards Corrie-Vulin, he took the gloves she had given him and threw them at her, saying, "That is all the business you have with me."[851]

He stayed that night in *Laga Fliuch*, and next day went to Kilchoan. On his return he looked for the gloves, and saw them where he had thrown them. He had no return of the vision.

APPARITIONS OF THE DEAD

A **taïsher** in Tiree came upon a dead body washed ashore by the sea. The corpse had nothing on in the way of clothing but a pair of sea-boots. Old people considered it a duty, when they fell in with a drowned body, to turn it over or move it in some way. In this case the seer was so horrified that instead of doing this he ran away. Other people, however, came, and the body was duly buried.

Afterwards the dead man haunted the seer, and now and then appeared and terrified him exceedingly. One night on his way home he saw the corpse before him wherever he turned, and on reaching the house it stood between him and the door. He walked on till close to the house, and then called to his wife to take the broomstick and sprinkle the doorposts with urine. When this was done, he boldly walked forward. The spectre, on his approach, leapt from the ground and stood above the door with a foot resting on each side on the double walls. The seer entered between its legs, and never saw the horrible apparition again.[852]

A **taïsher** in Coll had no second sight till some time after his marriage. Working one day with a companion near the shore, he left for a short time, but stayed away so long that, on his return, he was asked what kept him. He said he had been looking at the body of a drowned man, which the waves were swaying backwards and forwards near the rocks. Others, however, were of opinion he had found the body on the shore, ransacked its clothes, and then thrown it again into the sea, and that the second sight was a curse sent upon him for the deed. Certain it is that from that day he had the second sight. His friends at first doubted him when he said he saw visions, till he one day told his sister a certain rope in the house would be sent for before morning to be used about a body lying on the 'straight-board'. This proved to be the case, and his reputation as a **taïsher** was established.

A noted seer named *Mac Dhòmhnaill Òig* in Kilmoluag, Tiree, was sitting one day at home when his brother entered and, opening a chest in the room, took out some money. In reply to the seer's inquiries, the brother said he was going to pay such-and-such a shoemaker for a pair of shoes recently got from him. The brother died soon after, and the shoemaker claimed the price of the shoes. The seer warmly resisted the claim, as he himself had seen his brother taking the money expressly to pay them. That same night, however, he saw the shade of his deceased brother crossing the room, and, as it were, fumbling in a particular place on the top of the inner wall of the house. Next day the seer himself searched in the same spot, and found there the money that had been taken out of the chest to pay the shoes. He could only think it had been placed there by his brother when alive, and had been forgotten.[853]

A **taïsher** whose house was at Crossapol, where the burying-ground of the island of Coll is, on his way home from the harbour of Arinagour about six miles away, experienced many mischances (*driod-fhortain*) such as falling, etc. He arrived at home to find his only child, a boy about twelve years of age, dead in the burying-ground where he had gone to play and fallen asleep. Its entrails (*màthair a mhionaich*) were protruding. The seer, in his distraction, belaboured the surrounding graves with his stick, accusing their tenants in his outcries of indifference to him and his, and saying he had many of his kindred among them, though they had allowed this evil to befall his child.

That night a voice came to him in his sleep, saying he should not be angry with them (shades of the dead), seeing they were away that day in Islay keeping 'strange blood' from the grave of Lachlan Mor (*cumail na fuil choimhich á uaigh Lachainn Mhòir*) and were not present to have rescued the child. This Lachlan Mor was a man of great stature and bodily strength – chief of the MacLeans of Dowart, and therefore related to the MacLeans of Coll – who had been killed at the bloody clan battle of Gruinard Beach in Islay, and was buried at Kilchoman churchyard.[854]

On hearing of the seer's vision the laird of Coll dispatched a boat to Islay, and it was found that on the day the child was murdered an attempt had been made to lift the chief's gravestone for the burial of a sailor whose body had been cast ashore on a neighbouring beach. The attempt had failed, and the stone was left partly on its edge (*air a leth-bhile*). The shades had laid their weight up it, so that it could not be moved further. This story the writer has heard more than once adduced as positive proof of the reality of the second sight (*taibhsearachd*), that is, of the capacity of some men to see and hear spirits, or whatever else the spectres are.

The power of the dead to lay a heavy weight upon persons as well as things, and even to punish the living, is shown by the following stories.

In the same island of Coll the wife of *Dòmhnall Bàn* ('Donald the Fair-Haired') was lying ill. She had strange feelings of oppression and sickness (*tinneas is slachdadh*). Donald's father was a **taïsher**, and came to see her. After sitting and watching for some time he told her she had herself to blame for her sickness, that she must have done some act of unkindness or wrong to her mother, and that her feelings of oppression were caused by the spirit of her dead father coming and laying its weight upon her. The seer professed to see the spirit of the dead leaning its weight upon the sick person.

A woman (the tale, which comes from Perthshire, does not say where), being ill-treated by her husband, wished – too strongly and unduly – her brother, who had some time previously died in Edinburgh, were with her to take her part. Soon after, when she was alone, her brother's shade appeared, and in a tone of displeasure asked her what was wrong, and what she wanted him for. She told.

Her husband was at the time ploughing in a field in front of the house. The woman saw the shade going towards him, and when it reached, her husband fell dead.

Strong and Undue Wishes

It is in fact part of the creed in the second sight that a person should never indulge in strong wishes, lest he overstep proper bounds and wish what providence has not designed to be. Such wishes affect others, especially if these others have anything of the second sight.

A woman in the island of Harris, known as *Fionnaghal a' Mhòir*, was celebrated for her gift of second sight. A young man related to her went to Appin in Argyleshire with a boat. One day, when taking a smoke, he expressed a wish that *Fionnaghal a' Mhòir* had a draw of his pipe. Next day, and long before it could be known in Harris the youth had expressed such a wish, Flora daughter of the Big Man (for that is the meaning of her name) told her friends that a pipe was being offered her all night by the young man, and that she was anxious enough to have a smoke from it, but could not.[855]

A young girl in Kennovay, Tiree, holding a bowl of milk in her hands, expressed a wish a certain woman (naming one, who was a *taibhsear*) had the bowl to drink. Next day the woman indicated in the wish told the girl she had a sore time of it all night keeping the bowl away from her lips.

In very recent times, not above four years ago, as the driver of the mail-gig was going through *Coill an Eannd* (the Wood of Nant between Bonawe and Loch Awe) at night, he was met by the figure of his sweetheart, and received from it such a severe thrashing that he had to turn back. On telling this to herself afterwards, she acknowledged that on the night referred to she was very anxious about him, and wished she could intercept him in case at his journey's end he should go to a house where fever had broken out.[856]

A woman in Lismore, making a bowl of gruel (*brochan blàth*) in the evening, expressed a wish her husband (who was then away at the fishing at Corpach, near the entrance to the Caledonian Canal) had the drink she was making.[857] When her husband came home he said to her, "I tell you what it is, you are not to come again with porridge to me at Corpach."

He said he had seen her all night at his bedside offering him his gruel.

The power ascribed to strong wishes, or rather the evil consequences by which they may be followed, is still more forcibly illustrated by the following tale. A young woman at Barr, Morvern, beautiful and much esteemed in her own neighbourhood, was about to be married. Other maidens were in the house with her, sewing the dresses for the marriage. As they sat at work, she sighed and said she wished her intended was come.

At that moment he was on his way coming over the shoulder of Ben Iadain, a lofty mountain near hand, of weird appearance and having the reputation of being much frequented by the Fairies. He observed his sweetheart walking beside him, and as the shadowy presence threw him down, he struck at it repeatedly with his dirk. The bride got unwell, and, before the bridegroom reached the house, died. The 'fetch' left him shortly before his arrival, and her death was simultaneous with its disappearance.[858]

It has been said that the appearance of the spectre was considered entirely independent of the thoughts or volition of the person whose image it bears. Yet the tales of the second sight indicate some mysterious connection between men and their doubles. Strongly wishing, as in the above instances, causes at times a person's likeness to be seen or heard at the place where he wishes to be, and the original (so to call him) may be affected through his double.

A man in Islay encountered a ghost and threw his open penknife at it. The weapon struck the phantom in the eye, and at that moment a woman whose likeness it bore, though several miles away, was struck blind of an eye.

A young woman residing in Skye had a lover, a sailor, who was away in the East Indies. On Hallowe'en night she went – as is customary in country frolics – to pull a kail plant that she might know, from its being crooked or straight or laden with earth, what the character or appearance or wealth of her future husband might be. As she grasped a stock to pull it, a knife dropped from the sky and stuck in the plant.

When her lover came home she learned from him that on that very night and about the same hour, he was standing near the ship's bulwark, looking over the side, with a knife in his hand. He was thinking of her, and in his reverie the knife fell out of his hand and over the side. The young woman produced the knife she found in the kail-stock, and it proved to be the very knife her sailor lover had lost.

Tàradh

When a person strongly wishes to be anywhere (as for instance when a person on a journey at night wishes to be at home), his footsteps coming to the house or the sounds of his lifting the door-latch are heard, or a glimpse of his appearance is seen, at the time of his conceiving or expressing the wish; and even without any wish being present to the absent person's mind, sights or sounds indicative of his coming may be seen or heard. This previous intimation is called his *tàradh*, and his double or shade, which is the cause of it, his *tàslach*.

These mysterious intelligences are also called *manadh nan daoine beò*, 'the omens of living men'. The family, sitting round the evening fire, hear a footstep approaching the house, and even a tapping at the door. The sounds are so lifelike that someone goes to open the door, but there is no-one there. The sound is only the *tàradh* of an absent friend, storm-tossed or wayworn and wishing he were at home.

The *tàradh* may be that of a complete stranger who is not thinking of (and perhaps does not even know) the place to which his *tàradh* has come. When there is to be a change of tenants the advent of the stranger is heralded, it may be years beforehand, by his double. It is said: *Thàinig a thàradh*, i.e. "His wraith or forewarning has come."

When a shepherd, for instance, from another part of the country, is to come to a place, his likeness, phantom or *tàradh* is seen perhaps years beforehand on the hills he is afterwards so frequently to traverse. It is not every kind of men who have this phantom or double, neither does it appear wherein those who have it differ from other men. At all events if all men have it, it is not always to be seen.

A feeling of oppression at night, and the sound of footsteps through the house and the noise of furniture being moved about, is the omen of a change of tenants, and the *tàradh* of the incoming tenant.

In the island of Coll, the chiefs of which in former times were among the most celebrated in the West Highlands, and where the return of the former lairds is talked about and believed in and prayed for among the few of the native population left, the figure of the laird who is to come is said to have been seen by the castle servants sitting in an empty chair with a long beard flowing down to his breast.

A young man, sleeping alone in a house in which a shop was kept by his father at Scarinish, Tiree, one night felt such an oppression on his chest that he could not sleep, and heard noises as if there were people in the house. He got up and made a thorough search, but found no-one. Before long there was a change in the occupancy of the house.

On the uninhabited and lonely islet of Fladda-Chuain, to the east of Skye, some storm-stayed fishermen were boiling potatoes in a deserted bothy, and heard the noise of voices outside. On going out they could find no-one. This occurred thrice. Some days after, and before the fishermen got away, a boat passing to the Outer Hebrides was forced by stress of weather to take refuge in the same islet. The voices of its crew were exactly those previously heard. Nothing further occurred in connection with the sounds.[859]

The spirit, thus coming in a visible or audible form about a treasure by which the thoughts are too much occupied, or where a person wishes too much to be, is also denominated *falbh air fàrsaing*, i.e. 'going uncontrolled (?)'.[860]

Second Sight (an Dà Shealladh)

MARRIAGE

Those gifted with the second sight were sometimes able to tell the appearance of a person's future wife. They saw her **taïsh**, or appearance, sitting beside her husband, and this long before the event occurred or was spoken of. For instance, a seer has been known to remark to a young man who did not dream of marrying at the time, "I think your wife must belong to a big house, for she has a white apron on," etc.

The event has proved the vision to be real. The woman was housemaid in a gentleman's house. Seers also said they saw their own future wives sitting opposite to them at the fireside.

A native of Coll, *Eoghan mac Dhòmhnaill Ruaidh* ('Hugh son of Donald the Red'), while serving with his regiment in Africa, said he saw, almost every evening for a period of five years, glimpses of the woman whom he afterwards married, and whom he never saw in reality till his return from the wars. Wherever he sat after the day's march, the figure of a woman came beside him, and sometimes seemed to him to touch him lightly on the shoulders. On each occasion he merely caught a glimpse of her.

When he left the army and was on his way home, he came to the village at Dervaig in Mull, from the neighbourhood of which the ferry across to Coll lay. He entered by chance a house in the village, and his attention was unexpectedly attracted by the sound of a weaver's loom at work in the house. On looking up he saw sitting at the loom the identical woman whose figure had for five years haunted him in Africa. He married her.

COMING MISFORTUNE

A **taïsher** in Caolas, Tiree, was observed to have great objections to going home to take his meals. Being questioned on the subject, he said that at home he saw a horrible-looking black woman with her head 'as black as a pot', and if he chanced to catch a glimpse of her at meal-times, her hideous appearance made him rise from his food. He said he did not recognise the woman, and was unable to say who or what she was.

This was continued for three months, when the place was visited with smallpox, and the seer's own sister took the disease very badly. Her head became hideous and literally 'as black as a pot', and the people understood the meaning of the vision.

A celebrated seer in the same village, *Dòmhnall Mac an Duibh* (Donald Black), was married for the fourth time. In his day lucifer matches were unknown, and when corn was kiln-dried a person had to sit up all night to keep the fire alive. As Donald sat at this work in a solitary hut – such as small kilns are still kept in – the figure of his first wife appeared and told him to beware, for 'the terror' (*an t-eagal*) was coming: it was at *Crudh an Eich*, 'the Horse-Shoe', a spot on the public road leading to Caolas, about a mile and a half distant, deriving its name from the plain likeness of a horse-shoe indented in the rock.

He, however, was dozing over into sleep again when his second wife, in more distressed tones, warned him the 'terror' was nearer hand – at *Cachlaidh na Cùil Connaidh*, 'the Gateway of the Fuel Enclosure'. He neglected this warning also, and was dozing again when his third wife warned him the 'terror' was at the *Bail' Uachdrach* (Upper Village).

He immediately went home, and had hardly got into bed when a sound like the rushing of a violent blast of wind passed, and the whole house was shaken so that the walls were like to fall. If this was not 'the terror' of which he had been so strangely warned, Donald could give no other explanation.[861]

EVENTS AT A DISTANCE

Some sixty years ago a seer in Ruaig, Tiree (the neighbouring village to the preceding), was one day employed in the harvest-field tying sheaves after the reapers, a work assigned to old people. One of his sons was away in the Ross of Mull for a cargo of peats. All of a sudden the old man cried out: *Och! Och! Mo chreach!* "Alas! Alas! My loss!"

His children gathered round him in great anxiety as to the cause of his distress. He told them to wait a minute, and in a short time said it was all right – his son was safe. It turned out that at the very time of his exclamation the boat in which his son was, on its way from the Ross of Mull, was run into by another boat at *am Bac Mòr* (the Dutchman's Cap, a peculiarly shaped island on the way), and his son was thrown overboard but was rescued in time. The view of this incident which his mystic gift gave the seer was the cause of his exclamation.[862]

DEATH

Visionary delusions are so frequently to be traced to a brooding, gloomy disposition that it is no wonder sorrowful sights were those usually seen by persons having the second sight, or that death was an event of which **taïshers** had particular cognisance. The doctrine is that the whole ceremony connected with a funeral is gone through in rehearsal by spectres which are the shades, phantoms, appearances, **taïshs**, doubles, swarths – or whatever else we choose to call them – of living men, not merely by the shade of the person who is to die, but by the shades of all who are to be concerned in the ceremony. The phantoms go for the wood that is to make the coffin, the nails, the dead-clothes, and whatever else may be required on the occasion; the sounds of the coffin being made are heard, of presses being opened, of glasses rattling; and the melancholy procession has been met in the dead of night wending its way to the churchyard.

These weird sights and sounds have been seen and heard by others as well as **taïshers**. The only difference is that he who has the second sight is more apt to see them.

COFFIN

The shades that go for a coffin are called *tathaich air ciste*, i.e. frequenters for a chest.[863] They are heard at night long after the joiner has ceased his day's labour. The workshop is closed, and the wright has retired to rest, when the sound of a hammer, a shuffling for nails, and the working of a plane are heard as if someone were at work. If anyone has the courage to enter the workshop, nothing is to be seen, and no answer is given though he speak.

Some fifty years ago there was a wright in Kinloch Rannoch in Perthshire who complained of having the second sight, and who, in emigrating to Australia, assigned as his chief reason for leaving his native land the frequency with which he saw or heard people coming beforehand for coffins. The tools of his trade, plane, hammers, saw, etc., were heard by him at work as distinctly as though he himself were working, and the frequency of the omen preyed so much on his mind that he left the country in the hope of relief. The shades were not those of the people whose death was imminent, but those of their friends and acquaintances, who afterwards proved actually to be the parties who came for the coffin.

A few years ago a medical student, in the west of Inverness-shire, sat up late on a summer night 'grinding' for his examination. A joiner's workshop adjoined the house in which he was. About two o'clock in the morning he heard the sound of hammers, plane, etc., as though someone were at work in the shop. The sounds continued till about three. The evening was calm. Next day when he told what he had heard his friends laughed at him.

Next night again, however, the noises were resumed and continued till he fell asleep. They were this night heard also by the other inmates; and as they were repeated every night for a week, every person in the house – including the joiner himself, who was brought in for the purpose – heard them.

Shortly after a woman in the neighbourhood died in childbed, and the joiner in whose workshop the noises were heard made her coffin. The mysterious hammering only discontinued when the coffin was finished. The persons who heard the noises were neither **taïshers** nor sons of **taïshers**.

A Tiree man assured the writer that he and a brother of his heard most distinctly (*gu faramach*) the sound of a hammer all night till morning on a chest in an empty room near which they slept. A woman next door died suddenly on the following day, and it was on that chest another brother of his made her coffin. The truthfulness of the persons who told this can be assured, whatever be the explanation given of the noise.

A very intelligent informant says that the only thing of the kind he himself was personally witness to occurred above fifty years ago, when he was a young lad.[864] An old woman of the neighbourhood lay on her death-bed, and while the rest of the household of which he was a member sat up, he was – on account of his youth – packed off to bed. Through the night he heard what he took to be the trampling of dogs on a loft above his sleeping place, and this he heard so distinctly that he asked his father next day what made him put the dogs there. He also heard a plank sliding down from the loft and striking on end in the passage between the doors.

The following night the old woman died, and the lad himself was sent up to the loft to bring down planks to make her coffin. A plank slipped from his hands, and, falling on end in the passage, made exactly the same noise as he had before heard.

Some forty or fifty years ago the trampling of horses and the rattling of a conveyance (*stararaich agus gliongarsaich*) were heard after dark coming to the farmhouse of Liaran in Rannoch. Every person in the house thought a conveyance was really there. The horses were distinctly heard turning round in the courtyard. On looking out nothing was to be seen or heard. In four or five days after, a hearse (a kind of conveyance till then unknown in the country) came from Appin of Menzies (*Apainn nam Meinearach*) with the remains of a cousin of the family who had been suddenly killed by a kick from a horse.[865]

As late as 1867 a coach was seen proceeding silently through the streets of a village in Ayrshire to the burying-ground, and was believed by the common people to be that of a rich lady in the neighbourhood known as Brimstone Betty, who died shortly after, not in the odour of sanctity.[866]

Noise of Glasses to be Used at Funerals

Some thirty years ago in Appin, Argyleshire, noises were heard in a cupboard upstairs (above a room which formed part of a neighbour's house) as if some one were fumbling among bottles.[867] The noises were heard by the inmates of both houses for several nights previous to a somewhat sudden death occurring in the house below. It turned out that bottles from that cupboard were used at the funeral.

It was also a belief in Tiree that glasses to be used before long for refreshments at a funeral were heard rattling as if being moved. Not many years ago there was an instance of this in the village of Kilmoluag. Skilful women professed to be able to tell by the baking board and the 'griddle' whether the bread of that baking would be used at a funeral.

FUNERAL PROCESSION

A boy in Rannoch was playing with his companions in sight of the public road when all of a sudden he exclaimed, *Dhia! Nach fhaic sibh tòrradh mo sheanamhair?* "Lord! Will you not look at my grandmother's funeral?"

His grandmother was ill at the time, but was not thought near her dissolution. In a few days after, her funeral took place as the boy described it, with a red-haired character of the neighbourhood dancing at its head.

The following incident is told by a person whose truthfulness is beyond question. He is a person of talents and education, and a clergyman of the Church of Scotland.[868] "A young lad, herd-boy in the village in the Western Islands to which I belong, was one day with me on the moors (*sliabh*) above the cultivated land when he said he saw two men carrying a coffin between them from a wright's workshop – then in sight – to the door of a house which he mentioned.

"He called my attention to the vision, but I could see nothing of the kind. He described the dress the two men had on, particularly grey trousers such as seafaring people of the place then wore. In about ten days after an event exactly corresponding occurred."

A Tiree **taïsher** told how he had seen a funeral procession leave a certain house, and persons (whom he named) acting as coffin-bearers when leaving the house. This was at Beltane, the first day of summer. Next Christmas a death occurred in that house, and one of those to whom the seer had told his vision took a good look at the funeral to see if matters would prove as the seer had said. They did so exactly.

"On one occasion," said a native of Harris, "I was out fishing till twelve or one o'clock in the morning with several others, of whom one – a man about 35 – was reputed to have the second sight. As we were coming home I kept the middle of the road, thinking it was the safest place, and that no evil could come near me there.

"Suddenly the man who had the second sight caught me by the shoulder and pulled me to the side of the road. As he laid his hand on my shoulder I saw a funeral procession – a coffin and men carrying it. I was afterwards at that funeral myself, and at the place where I met the **taïsh**, the men were in the same order in which I had seen them."

A young man going home at night along the south side of Loch Rannoch was joined by a funeral procession. One of the poles of the bier was thrust into his hands, and he had to march in the procession above a mile. He was on the loch side of the coffin, and had great difficulty in keeping on the road. The other bearers of the ghostly coffin were laying the weight to push him off the road.

A woman near Loch Scavaig (*Scathabhaig*) in Skye saw a funeral procession with the coffins passing along a hillside where no road lay and no one was ever observed to pass. After the woman's death, and two years after her vision, a boat was lost in Loch Scavaig, and the bodies of three persons lost in her were buried near the shepherd's house at the loch-side. They were afterwards raised and carried along in the direction the woman had pointed out as that taken by her vision.

One of these mystic processions was seen in Strathaird, in the same neighbour-hood, carrying something in a grey plaid. A man was drowned in a river there, and his body was not recovered for a week. It was then carried in a grey plaid in the same direction the spectral procession had taken.

A man in Skye met at night a funeral procession, and some occult influence made him walk along with it till he came to Portree churchyard. He then for the first time asked whose funeral it was. He received for answer, "Your own."

A man living in the Braes of Portree went daily to Portree, four miles away, to work. A neighbour whose house was a little further away was engaged in the same work, and was in the habit of calling him as he passed in the morning. The two then walked together to the scene of their labour.

One clear moonlight night he was awakened by what he took to be his companion's call. He hastily threw on his clothes and followed. Every now and then he heard a call before him on the road telling him to make haste. He followed, without thought, till he came to Portree churchyard. It did not strike him till then that the call was from no earthly voice.

WRAITHS SEEN BEFORE DEATH

When a person was about to die, especially if his death was to be by violence or drowning, his wraith or phantom was seen by those who had the second sight (or it might be by those who had no such gift).

In the island of Lismore, in the beginning of the nineteenth century, the minister was said to have seen the fetch of the man at whose funeral the custom was intro-duced of having the refreshments (*costas*) after the funeral.[869] In former times it was the practice in the Highlands to have the refreshments before starting, and consequently the funeral party were sometimes far advanced in drink before starting on their melancholy journey. There are even stories of their having forgot the coffin.

On the farm of Kirkapol in Tiree, where the burying-place of the east end of the island is, the figure of a man in a dress not belonging to the island – light trousers and blue jacket with white buttons – was seen about forty years ago by several people in the evenings going in the direction of the kirkyard. A celebrated seer in the neighbouring village saw it, and said it was not the **taïsh** of any man or any man's son in Tiree.[870]

Some time after, a ship was wrecked in the east end of Tiree and one of the sailors, whose dress when his body was found corresponded to that of the **taïsh**, was taken and buried in Kirkapol. After that the apparition was no more seen.

The body of a young man drowned in the same neighbourhood, before being coffined, was laid first on a rock and then on the greensward. A person who came to the scene after the body was laid on the grass asked if the body had been laid on the rock mentioned. He was told it had, and was asked why he enquired. He said his uncle had told him that his grandfather, who was a **taïsher**, had said a dead body would yet be laid on that rock. This shows that the fulfilment of the seer's vision does not necessarily take place soon after, or even within a number of years.

The **taïsher** in Caolas, Tiree, already mentioned as having seen the fetch of his sister in the smallpox, on a New Year night accompanied his brother-in-law, who had spent the evening with him (and from whom the story has been got), a piece of the way home.[871] When his brother-in-law urged him to return, as he had come far enough, he asked to be allowed, as this was the last New Year he would be with his friends. He was asked what made him think so gloomily of the future. He said the matter was to be so, and there was no chance of its being otherwise, for he had seen his own phantom three or four times. In March following the man was drowned.

A Tiree **taïsher** was going out to Tobermory, and taking his passage along with him was a neighbour going to consult the doctor. There was no medical officer in those days resident in Tiree. The seer said to one of the boatmen he wished he had not the sight he had, for he saw his fellow-passenger with the dead-clothes up to his eyes. "You may," he said, "take off my ear if the man's death is not near hand."

The event proved the correctness of his vision, and the right to take off his ear did not arise.

Drowning

It is a common story that a **taïsher** saw the figure of an acquaintance passing with dripping clothes and water in its shoes (*aodach fliuch agus bogan 'na bhròig*). Soon after, word was received of the drowning of the person whose resemblance it was, at the time the figure was seen.

The seeing of spectres about boats in which people are to be drowned is also common. When the superstition was in full force, a sure way of making a boat useless was to say that voices had been heard about it when it was drawn upon the beach, or that figures had been seen which disappeared mysteriously, 'whether the earth swallowed them, or the sky lifted them'. After that no one having a regard for his own life would put his foot in that boat.

A person from Tiree went for wood to Loch Creran, and at Tobermory forgot the parcel in which he had a change of clothes. One day he got wet – soaked through to the skin – and had to sit all evening in his wet clothes. On his return home to Tiree a woman who was reputed to have the gift of second sight asked him if, on a certain day of the week (mentioning the one on which this accident occurred), he had got himself wetted, that she had seen him, and thought he had been drowned. The man himself tells the story, and says he cannot conceive of any ordinary channel of information by which the woman could have become aware of his condition.

A man named Conn was drowned at Sorisdal in Coll. A seer who had been at daily work with him had long seen his boots full of water (*bogan uisge*) when there was no water in them in reality, and, for twelve months after the event, was haunted wherever he went by the vision of Conn's drowning.[872]

A seer in Skye saw, when in reality there was no such object, a woman sitting in the stern of a boat which afterwards drowned people in Portree Bay.

A fishing boat or skiff belonging to the people of Gortendonald, in the west end of Tiree, was sold because 'things' were said to have been seen about it till no one belonging to the village would venture to sea in it. It was bought by some persons in Scarinish (in the east end of the island) who professed not to believe in *taibhsearachd*, or second sight. They gave the loan of it to people in Vaul, on the north side of the island. Here sights began again to be seen about it, and it was even said that at a time when it was hauled up on dry land, six men were seen rowing in it and one steering.

At last no one at all would venture to sea in the boat, and it was sent back to Scarinish. So strong was the feeling that the Vaul men would not venture with it through the Black Water (*am Bun Dubh*), as the sound between Coll and Tiree is called, but drew it across the land to Gott Loch, whence the Scarinish people took it home. After this its odour in the east end of Tiree became so bad that it was sold again to villagers in the west end, at some distance from the place it originally came from. Here it terminated its career in Tiree by drowning six men.[873]

Sights were similarly seen about a boat in Iona, and it had to be sold. It went to Islay, and the visions were believed to have received their fulfilment from the boat being employed to convey dead bodies from a ship wrecked on the Rhinns of Islay (*an Roinn Ìleach*, literally 'the Sharp Edge of Islay').[874]

Not many years ago, a man told about a boat on the south side of Tiree that he had heard voices about it like those of people talking, but on going near found no person there. He did not know, he said, whether the air had lifted the people whom he thought were there, or the earth had swallowed them – but he had heard voices, and no person was there. The boat became worthless; it would drown some one some day, and no one would go out to fish in it. The owner, therefore, summoned the seer before the Sheriff and got him fined.

Horses and Dogs

These animals were deemed to have the gift of seeing spectres in a larger measure than the best seers. They are observed to be frightened, or to have their fury raised, without any visible or intelligible cause; they show signs of terror and distress when human eyes can see no cause, and it is part of the Celtic belief in the second sight that this excitement is caused by seeing the **taïsh** or shades of the living in those circumstances – and engaged in those services – in which the persons whose similitude they are will afterwards be.[875]

Dogs bark at night, and when this occurs on clear moonlight nights they are said in English to 'bay the moon'. The Celtic belief does not deny that they often bark at the moon, but it asserts further their clamour arises, as the event afterwards proves, from their seeing the forms of that world in which fetches and doubles move – the omens of an impending death.

Horses are better spectre-seers than even dogs. At places where a violent or sudden death is to occur they take fright, and no effort of the rider can get them to pass the spot, till at last he has to dismount and lead them past. This is caused by their seeing the 'fetch' of the subsequent event, but ordinary people pass it over merely as an 'unaccountable fright'.

"I have heard," said a Skyeman, "scores of times the dogs howling before a funeral was to take place in Kilmuir churchyard. It was because they saw the wraiths of the living (*tàslaich nan daoine beò*)."

It is a universal Highland belief that certain dogs cry at night when any one in the house is to die. In Lorn, a woman going with leather to a neighbouring shoemaker had on her way to cross a wooden bridge thrown over a mountain stream. She was accompanied by a young child, whom she left while she herself crossed the bridge to leave the parcel of leather on the other side. As she was crossing a second time, leading the child, the stream came down in flood – as mountain streams do – and carried away the bridge. The woman and child were drowned, and their bodies were found further down the stream at a place where, for fourteen days previously, a grey tailless bitch (*galla chutach ghlas*) belonging to a neighbour used to go and howl piteously.

The fierce growling of a dog at night, when nothing is known to be in the house to excite its fury, is also supposed to arise from its seeing spirits – or the spectres, it is not known which – of the living or of the dead. Stories of this class usually run in the same groove. A shepherd or servant-man has a very good dog, which is in the habit of sleeping in the same room with himself. One night it suddenly gets up growling, and is heard making its way to the other end of the room. It returns howling faintly, springs into bed, and, lying with its forepaws resting on its master, snarls fiercely at something invisible. The occupant of the bed, not seeing anything to account for the dog's fury, puts his head below the bedclothes and quakes with fear till daylight.[876]

A horse in Vaul (Tiree), ordinarily a quiet beast, used when carting to be most unaccountably startled, especially when passing a certain boat drawn up on the beach. This same boat has been mentioned already as having, in consequence of being spectre-haunted, been sold by people in the west end of Tiree to some villagers in the east end, who gave the loan of it to Vaul people. Sights began also to be seen about it, and it was ultimately sent back to the lenders, who again sold it to people in the west end.[877]

Here a melancholy loss of life occurred in it. A gale off the land suddenly sprang up when the boat, with its six of a crew, was within a few hundred yards of the shore. The men were seen rowing hard to bring the boat to land, but they had at last to give up the attempt. Some days after, the boat came ashore in Coll with only one of the crew in it. He was reclining on one of the thwarts, dead. It was the horse and cart mentioned that took home his body. After that day the horse was never known to be unaccountably startled or frightened. Its former fits entirely forsook it.

CRYING HEARD BEFORE DEATH

A wailing or unusual cry heard at night where no one is known to be (or can be) is an indication that at that place some one will break into lamentation for the death of a friend – of which he will there first receive intimation – or will have otherwise cause to cry. The voice heard is not that of the 'fetch' of the man who is to be killed or drowned, but that of some mourner – a wife or sister or near relation. In these cries before a sudden death, the voices of women are the most frequently recognised.

A cry or scream, indicative of death and believed to be uttered by a wraith, was called *tàsg* and *éigheach taisg* (or *éigheach tàsg*), i.e. 'the cry of a wraith'.[878]

In the case of a man accidentally drowned on Trabay Beach in Tiree, a cry described as 'a healthy cry' (*glaodh fallain*) was heard at night in the west end of the island several days previous to the disaster, and four miles from the scene of the accident, at the spot where the man's brother first received the melancholy intelligence. The cry consisted of "òh" said thrice, and each time at the full length of a man's breath (*fad analach*).

At the old quay in Port Appin, Argyleshire, the wailing of a woman was heard at night. Some days after, the mother of a young man who had been accidentally killed in Glasgow there met the remains (which came by steamer), and she broke into loud lamentation.

At *an Drochaid Mhòr*, the Big Bridge above Portree Manse on the road to Braes in the isle of Skye, strange sounds are heard by people passing there at night, such as the moaning of a dying person, sounds of throttling, etc. Mysterious objects, dogs, and indistinct moving objects are also seen at the haunted spot. These are supposed to denote that a murder will some time be committed here.[879]

Weeping and crying were heard at midnight near the mill-dam in Tiree, on a dark and rainy night, by a young man going for a midwife for his brother's wife. He heard the same sounds on his return.

The woman died in that childbed, and it was observed that at the very spot where the young man said he heard the sounds of lamentation, her two sisters first met after her death and burst into tears and outcries. The person to whom this incident occurred is now past forty years of age, is intelligent, and to be relied on as a person who would not tell a lie. There can be no doubt he heard the lamentation, whatever may have been the cause of his impression.

Strange noises of which the natural cause is not known are readily associated with the first incident that offers any explanation. In the island of Mull, lamentation (*tuireadh*) was recollected to have been heard where a young man was accidentally killed ten years after.

Thirty years ago horrible screaming and shouting – *sgiamhail oillteil agus glaodhaich* – were heard about eight o'clock on a summer evening across Loch Corry in Kingairloch.[880] In a line with the shouting lay a ship at anchor and the burying-ground on the other side of the loch. The cry was like that of a goat or buck being killed, a bleating which bears a horrible resemblance to the human voice. Next night the master of the ship was drowned, no one knew how. The man on the watch said that when sitting in the stern of the ship he saw the skipper go below, and then a clanking as if the chain were being paid out. He heard and saw nothing further. The night was fine.

In July 1870 a ship struck on a sunken rock in the passages between the Skerryvore lighthouse and Tiree, and sprang a leak. The shore was made for at once, but when within 150 yards of it the ship sank.

The crew betook themselves to the rigging and were ultimately rescued; but the skipper, in trying to swim ashore, was caught by the current that sweeps round Kennavara Hill, and drowned. The crying heard in Kennavara Hill four years previous was deemed to have portended this event.[881]

Crying was heard several times on the reefs to the east end of Coll, and to the best of the hearer's belief, it was in English. In the same year (1870) a boat or skiff with two east coast fishermen, following their calling in that neighbourhood, went amissing and was never heard of. Many were of opinion it must have been lost on the reefs where the cries had long previously been heard.[882]

LIGHTS

It was deemed a good sign when lights were seen previous to a person's death. The *dreag* was a light seen in the sky, leaving a tail (*dreallsach*) behind it, and, according to some, stopping above the house where the death was to occur; according to others, proceeding from above the house to the churchyard along the line the funeral was to take. The *dreag* was seen only when a person of consequence was near his dissolution. Hence an irreverent tailor in East Side, Skye, said he wished the sky was full of dreags.[883]

It was also a belief that the death-light went along the road a funeral was to take. An old man in Druim a' Chaoin, in Lower Rannoch, being sceptical on this point, was one night called to the door to believe his own eyes. His house overlooked the public road, and stepping boldly down he stood in the middle of the road awaiting the approach of the death-light. When it reached him it also stood right before him. The old man gazed fixedly at the unearthly light, and at last an indistinct and shadowy form became visible in the middle of it. The form slowly placed the palms of its two hands together and extended them towards him. With a startling suddenness it said "Whish!" and passed over his head. That old man never afterwards said a word against death-lights.[884]

In another instance of the death-light proceeding along the highway in the same district, a hare-brained young man went to meet it and stood waiting it behind his dirk, which he stuck in the middle of the road. When the light came to the dirk it stopped, and the young man, gazing at it, at last saw a child's face in its feeble glare. He then stooped down and drew his dirk from the ground. As he did so the light passed over his head.

Lights were also seen where a violent or accidental death was to occur, and might be seen by the person whose death they foretokened. Thus at Brae-Glen (*Bràighe Ghlinne*) in Glen Iuchar (where a river falls into Loch Sgamadail) in Lorn lights were seen two years previous to the drowning of a man of the name of MacLachlan in the stream when drunk. MacLachlan had seen these lights himself.[885]

Lights to which these mysterious meanings are attached are generally mere *ignes fatui*. They have of late years become prevalent in the Hebrides, and various explanations are given of them. In Tiree they are called *teine sìth* ('Fairy light') and are said to be produced by a bird. In Skye and the northern islands they are called *solas Uibhist*, 'the Uist light', and the following extraordinary account is given of their origin.

A young girl one Sunday night insisted, in spite of her mother's remonstrances, on starting with a hook and creel to gather plants in the field for some species of dye before the Sabbath was expired. Finding her counsels of no avail, the mother in a rage told her to go then and never return: the young girl never returned, but her hook and creel were found in the fields, and marks of fighting at the spot.[886]

When encountered, the light jumps three times, and its appearance is that of human ribs with a light inside of them.[887] It is only an odd number that can see this light. Two will not see it, but three can. Like other supernatural appearances it could only speak when spoken to. A young lad once had the courage to speak to it. The light answered that it was the young girl whom the above fate befell: that she had done wrong in disobeying her mother, and breaking the Sabbath day; that it was her mother's prayer that was the cause of her unrest; and that she was now doomed to wander about in the shape of this light till the end of the world.

Spirits Seen before Death

Shortly before death greenish bright lights were seen moving from one place to another when no other light was in the room. These were said to be spirits awaiting the soul of the dying person. When the body lay stretched out, previous to being coffined, these lights were seen hovering near, and perhaps seven or eight butterflies (*dealan-dé*) fluttered through the room. They moved about the chest in which were the bannocks to be used at the funeral, or the winding-sheet (*blà-lin*), and about the cupboard in which the glasses were. The belief in these appearances was not commonly entertained.

A belief in the occurrence of something supernatural at the moment of death seems to have been not altogether uncommon. On an occasion already mentioned of a sudden death at Port Appin, Argyleshire, which was preceded by the noise of bottles rattling, a girl opened the door of a side room at the moment of the sick man's dissolution. She returned in a state bordering on hysteria, cursing and swearing that she would not take the world and go in.[888] She said every article in the room seemed to meet her at the door.

Return of the Dead

The plant *mòthan* (trailing pearlwort or *sagina procumbens*) was placed by old women in Tiree above the door, on the lintel (*san àrd-doras*), to prevent the spirits of the dead – when they revisited their former haunts – from entering the house, and it was customary in many places to place a drink of water beside the corpse previous to the funeral in case the dead should return.[889]

There is a sept of MacDonalds called MacCannel of whom it is said in Tiree that when one dies and the body is laid out to be waked, all the dead of the race enter the room, go round the body – upon which each lays his hand – and then in solemn procession march out again. This is the case at every death of one of the sept, but only those who have the second sight can see the shades. A man married to one of the MacCannels whose father had been long dead enraged her beyond measure, on the occasion of the death of one of the sept, by asking her why she had not gone to Balevullin (where the death had occurred) last night to see her father.[890]

The spirits of the dead came back to reveal secrets and give good advice. Those who hid iron during their lifetime, and died without telling where, could not rest till they had told their secret. Notoriously bad men, misers, oppressors of the poor, and all whose affections were set too much on the things of this world, were believed after death to wander about their former haunts. They seek to be where they left their treasure. They do not speak till they are spoken to, and it requires great courage in a living person to address the spirits of the dead. The last buried had to watch the churchyard till the next funeral; and if the strings of the winding-sheet were not untied, it was also a belief that the spirit could not rest.[891]

It is very imprudent to enter into a compact with another that whoever dies first will come back to tell his fate to the survivor. The agreement is unholy, and will entail sorrow whether the dead man's position is in weal or woe. Two herdsmen at the summer pastures for the cattle (*bothan àirigh*) in 'the wilds of far Kintail' entered into a compact of this kind. One of them died, and a substitute came in his place.

The newcomer observed that his companion was anxious not to be alone for any time, however short, but one day he had to go to the strath for yeast (*deasgainn*), the two being engaged in brewing spirits, and did not return till far on in the night. The survivor of the two who had made the paction, being thus left alone, when night came on took to mending his shoes and singing at his work to keep his courage up. His thoughts constantly reverted to his dead companion and the bargain made with him – and the more he thought, the more uneasy he became.

At midnight a scraping noise began on the top of the house, as if someone were trying to make an entrance. The scraping became louder and louder, and the shoemaker in the agony of terror – but pretending to think the noise was made by his comrade who had gone to the strath – called out, "I know it is you trying to frighten me (*cuir eagal orm*)."[892]

As soon as he spoke, a man whom he recognised as his dead companion entered the hut, wrapped in the grave-clothes, but after saying it was a good thing for him where he (the dead man) had gone, went away and left him unharmed.

In another case of a similar agreement between two youths in the same district, the survivor forgot all about the paction till one night he was met on the public road by the figure of his departed friend, which told him to meet it alone at a certain place (which it named) at a certain hour, otherwise it would be worse for himself.

The man, terrified beyond measure, consulted the parish minister as to what he ought to do, but the minister merely advised him to pray that no evil would come of his rash and unguarded compact. He consulted an old man, who told him to go to the place appointed and take a ball of iron in his hand, and hold it out to the ghost when shaking hands. The man went, the ghost crushed the ball of iron and the man escaped, otherwise the spirit – which could only have come from a bad place – would have crushed his hand into atoms.

A woman in Flodigarry in Skye whose husband had been killed by witchcraft (*buidseachd*) saw him after his death sitting by the fireside. On being spoken to, the ghost asked why they had not shaved him before putting his body in a coffin.

An old man in Aharacle, in the north of Argyleshire, was shaved, his face was washed, his hair combed, and his personal appearance attended to in anticipation of his speedy dissolution. When an attempt was made to cut his nails, he told his friends to let them alone: *Is beag an t-armachd dhomh fhìn iad*, he exclaimed, *'s gun fhios 'am cean' tha mi dol.*[893] "They are but slight weapons for myself, seeing I don't know where I am going to."

Bones of the Dead and Place of Burial

It was part of the lesson impressed on the young Highlander to treat that which belonged to the dead with reverence. The unnecessary or contemptuous disturbing of graves, bones, or other relics of humanity was reprobated, and sometimes warmly resented. This praiseworthy feeling towards the dead was strengthened by the pride of race and ancestry which formed so prominent a feature of the Highland character, and by sundry tales of wide circulation.

The story has been already told of the tailor who irreverently gave a kick to a skull, and was ever after haunted by the man to whom it had belonged.[894] It is told of one who disturbed a grave at night that, on his taking up a skull in his hand, a feeble voice – that of the disturbed spirit – said, "That's mine."

He dropped that skull and took up another, when a like voice said, "That's mine."

The man cried out, "Had you two skulls?"

Tradition says the island of Islay derives its name from Ìle, a Scandinavian princess who went to bathe in a loch there and, sticking in the soft mud, was drowned. The head- and foot-stones of her grave are some distance from each other, and of three persons who successively attempted to open the grave to see what the bones were like, each died mad! Very likely this was the fate awaiting them at any rate. Their action in opening a grave to satisfy an idle curiosity was in keeping with a morbid character, and they only died as they lived.[895]

Stones from a disused burying-ground called 'the Burial-Place of the Big Women' on the farm of Heynish in Tiree were used for building one of the farm outhouses.

In this house a servant-man from Mull was sent to sleep. Through the night he was disturbed by his dog jumping into bed between him and the wall and, with its fore-feet resting upon his body, snarling fiercely at something he could not see. He heard feeble voices through the house saying, "This is the stone that was at my head."

Nothing more came of this visit of the spirits than that the Mull man (who was likely the victim of a hoax) positively refused to sleep in that house again.[896]

The manner in which shades haunt the places where their bodies are is very clearly shown in the following tale. The body of a woman was cast ashore by the sea on the North Beach, called *Tràigh Feall*, the Beach of Fell, in the island of Coll, and was buried in the neighbouring sandbanks.

After this the semblance of a woman was seen in the evenings on the beach, close to the tide. MacLean, the then tenant of Caolas, a farm near hand, ridiculed the belief. One evening, however, when going home across the North Beach at the *Sruth Bàn* ('White Stream') he thought of the numerous stories he had heard of the apparition, and, looking seaward, saw a woman sitting by the tide, rocking herself (*ga turraman fhéin*) and apparently in the utmost distress. He went where she was, and asked her what she was doing. "Hand of cleverness (*Làmh thapaidh*)," she answered, "I have been long here; I try to go home, but I cannot. I was a poor woman belonging to Uist; I was lost on a rock; my body came ashore here, and I try to go home, but cannot; my body keeps me."

MacLean asked what reward she would give if he took her body home. She promised to be with him in every quarrel or fight in which he might be involved. This offer he declined, saying his own hand was strong enough to extricate him in any difficulty of that kind. She then offered him the gift of knowing the thief if anything should be stolen in Coll. This gift he accepted, and the stones that marked the grave being told him, he sent for the woman's brothers, the body was taken home, and the spectre was no more seen on the North Beach.[897]

Spirits Appearing in Dreams

A deceased sister's ghost appeared to a woman in a dream and told her their brother had been buried the day before in Ireland. She also told the signs by which next day the truth of the dream was to be proved. The words of the ghost form in Gaelic a singularly beautiful and plaintive song. Each line is repeated twice in singing, first with one and then another of those meaningless choruses to be found in Gaelic melody, and suiting well with the genius of the language.[898]

E hà na hù rù,
Phiuthar chridhe, bheil thu 'd chadal?

E ha na hoo-roo,
Loving sister, are you sleeping?

Second Sight (an Dà Shealladh)

Ho lo bha, hù rù,	Ho lo va, hoo-roo,
E hà na hao-lo-ro ì.	E ha na hao-lo-ro hee.
Phiuthar chridhe, bheil thu 'd chadal?	Loving sister, are you sleeping?
Am bràthair bh' ann an Éirinn againn,	The brother whom we had in Erin
Gun d'fhalbh e 'n-dé air na maidean.	Went yesterday away on bearers.
Bha mis' ann, 's gun neach gam fhaicinn.	I was there, but no one saw me.
Treis air chois dhomh, 's treis air each dhomh,	A while on foot, a while on horseback,
Treis eile bualadh mo bhas dhomh.	Another while my hands wringing.
Bheir mi comharra dhuit air t' aisling:	I will give proofs of thy vision:
Bhàthach mhòr tha fo na martun,	The big byre where the kine are
Gum bi i màireach 'na lasair	Will be wrapped in flames tomorrow
'S an leanabh beag tha ann ad' asgaill,	And the infant in your bosom
Gheobh thu marbh e 'n calp do leapach.	You'll find dead on your bedside.

It is told of a widower who was unkind to his children that the ghost of his deceased wife in a similar manner appeared to him and said:

> Man, who hast shut the door upon me
> And left me lying here,
> Before the Christmas comes
> A greater loss will befall you.
> Man who hast the children,
> Rearing them unpeaceably,
> If oft your hand be raised
> I will not be long at peace with you.[899]

To Get Rid of the Second Sight

It was a belief in the island of Coll that a person afflicted with the second sight might get rid of his unhappy gift and – as it were – bind it away (*nasg*) from himself by giving alms (*déirc*) and praying the gift may depart. A seer living near Arinagour in that island had two sons in the army, then engaged in foreign wars, and in his visions saw what was happening to them. The visions preyed so much on his mind that, to rid himself of them, he gave half-a-crown to an old woman and prayed his second sight might be taken away.

After this he saw nothing of his sons, and, anxious to know their fate, he went to Tiree for a celebrated **taïsher** and brought him to Coll with him. He placed him beside the fire, which was on the middle of the floor. It was held by the best seers that visions are best seen through the fire (*roimhn teine*). Before long the Tiree seer began to sweat, and the other, who knew that this was caused by a painful vision, begged him to tell what he saw and hide nothing. He told that both the sons were killed – the one by a bullet through the head, the other shot through the heart and through the neck. Soon after a letter came to the laird of Coll corroborating the seer's vision.

17

HOBGOBLINS

INTRODUCTORY

The term *bòcan* (pronounced **baucan**) is a general name for terrifying objects seen at night and taken to be supernatural – bugbears, ghosts, apparitions, goblins, etc., in all their variety. The word conveys as much the idea of fright in the observer as of anything hurtful or violent in the object itself. It is derived from *bòc*, to come in a swelling and resistless flood, not an unapt description of the manner in which fear takes possession of its victims.[900]

Any object indistinctly seen may prove a hobgoblin of this kind. It may be merely a neighbour playing pranks by going about in a white sheet, a stray dog, a bush waving and sighing in the night wind, or even a peat-stack looming large in the imperfect light. There is a story of a man on Loch Rannoch-side who fought a bush in mistake for a ghost in a hollow which had an evil name for being haunted. The conflict continued till dawn, when he was found exhausted, scratched and bleeding.

Sometimes the **baucan**, or terrifying object, causes fright by its mere appearance, sometimes by the noises it makes, and sometimes by its silence. In appearance it is commonly a man or woman moving silently past, and not speaking till spoken to, if even then; but it has also been encountered as a black dog that accompanies the traveller part of his way, as a headless body (a particularly dangerous form of ghost), as a he-goat, or simply a dark moving object. At other times it is terrific from having a chain clanking after it, from its whistling with unearthly loudness, by horrible and blood-freezing cries and sounds of throttling; and sometimes it makes its presence known only by faint and hardly audible sounds. In fact the number and variety of things by which superstitious terror may be awakened at night are countless.

In most cases the **baucan** is deemed the precursor of a sudden or violent death to occur at the place where it is seen or heard. It is remembered after the event that an unaccountable light was seen there at night, or a horse had become uneasy and could not be induced by its rider to pass, or something extraordinary had been observed which the popular imagination connects with the subsequent event. At other times the **baucan** is the spirit of the dead revisiting the earth, that it may be spoken to and unburden itself of some secret that disturbs its rest. Sometimes it is an evil spirit on some message of darkness, and sometimes merely a sound or indistinct object by which the wayfarer is frightened, but of which he is unable to give any lucid description. Fright is destructive of curiosity, and a person ready to faint with terror cannot be expected to be critical in his observations, nor afterwards coherent in his statements. Besides, vagueness or indistinctness as to the cause – an element to which the obscurity of night lends a ready aid – tends to render fear more frantic. If the observer had a distinct view of the object of his alarm, and knew exactly what it was, even though it were a spirit of darkness, his terror would be less. *Omne ignotum pro magnifico* is an axiom that holds especially true in such cases,[901] and it is ignorance of its own cause that gives terror its wildest forms. A ghost or apparition seen in the daytime, if that were possible, would not be at all so dreadful.

It may be said that every Highland village has near it a locality where a ghost or **baucan** is (or was) to be seen. A favourite haunt for these unearthly visitants is by the fords of rivers (*beul àth na h-aibhne*) where generally bridges have been built in modern times, near churchyards, on dark moors, and in hollows (or rather at the top of the ascent from hollows) traversed by the public road.[902] Not unfrequently there is a projecting rock (*sròin creige*) near the spot, and this may have its own share in producing that sense of loneliness and awe which makes the belated peasant prone to convert stray animals and unusual appearances into ghosts and spirits.

It is a noticeable feature in ghost stories that it is principally to those travelling alone, and not accustomed to walk the night, that ghosts are visible. They have been seen in houses and even in towns, but ordinarily they affect lonely places where naturally men are more apt to be timorous.

The *dubh-chladach* ('black shore'), as it is called, i.e. the shore below the line or roll of seaweed thrown up by the tide (*ròlag ròid*), is according to Highland belief an asylum from all kinds of supernatural beings that haunt the night – Fairies, ghosts or evil spirits. No being 'at all, at all' of the kind (*seòrsa sam bith, sam bith*) can go below the tide-mark. The confidence of the timorous in this place of refuge is confirmed by the assurance that they are not exposed to a similar danger from the sea. It is a saying, *Cha d'thig olc sam bith on fhairge.* "Evil comes not from the sea."[903]

Ghosts and evil spirits cannot cross a running stream, a belief which had its origin before the days of bridges. The shock given to the nerves by the cold water, when it was of any depth, served to dispel the optical delusion caused by unfounded terror.

When about to encounter a **baucan** the dirk should be partly drawn from its sheath, otherwise it will prove impossible during the encounter to draw the weapon. In the event of the evil spirit asking its name it should not be called by its proper name, *biodag* ('a dirk'), but *piuthar m' athar* ('my father's sister'), *piuthar mo sheanamhair* ('my grandmother's sister'), or by some similar title.[904] This prevents enchantments being laid upon it to render it useless. The effect of these is that instead of giving the ghost its *quietus*, the weapon merely makes a tinkling noise (*gliong*) against it.[905] Evil spirits cannot bear the touch of cold steel. Iron, or preferably steel, in any form is a protection, though it is not obvious how or why, against the Fairies – an iron ring on the point of a staff is as good as a sword – but evil spirits are subdued by it only when made into a lethal weapon.

In the struggle the ghost is, in the hands of its opponent, soft as a bag of wool or impalpable as air. At every tussle, therefore, the unfortunate man is thrown down and injured.

In the presence of an evil spirit, a dog defends its master or crouches in terror about his feet, but a bitch jumps at his throat, and if it can will tear him. It is, however, rendered harmless by taking blood from its ear, or tying a collar (*conghal* i.e. *ceangal*, usually its master's garter) about its neck.[906]

Similarly, an entire horse was said to defend its master, but a mare attacked him. It was also a belief that an entire horse could not be injured by witches or evil spirits.[907]

The best protection is a circle drawn round one's self on the ground with the point of a sapling or dirk, saying, *Crois Chrìost oirnn!* ("The cross of Christ be upon us!") All the spirits that infest the night may dash in fury against this circle, but they can no more pass it than the most threatening waves of the sea the rocks that form their appointed bounds.

As already suggested, this circle is the superstitious representative of a person's own integrity, within which he is safe from the attacks and wiles of the devil. It is known also in Ireland, as the following story told in Arisaig (Inverness-shire) by an Irish packman shows.

A priest's brother having died, a young man who had been a bosom friend of his expressed an ardent wish some weeks after to see him again. That same evening he was met by the shade of his dead companion, and the two had a long talk together. They spoke of the pleasure they had in each other's society, and the dead man got the other to promise to meet him at the same spot the following evening. It added, "To make you sure it is indeed I, you will tell my brother the priest of such-and-such an occurrence [describing it], which nobody knows but he and I."

On his way home, the young man called upon the priest, and told what he had seen. "It is not my brother's ghost at all," said the priest, "but the devil, who is trying to decoy you into his power; I will go with you tomorrow night to meet him."

The two went together to the place of appointment, the priest taking with him a dirk, with which he traced a circle round them, and an iron hoop, inside of which also they stood. A figure in face and form like the priest's brother, 'most like, yet not the same', came, but on finding itself outwitted, and a Bible being opened before it, went away in a flame of fire.

THE *BODACH* OR CARLE

The *bodach* (literally a carle, an old man) is perhaps the commonest form of **baucan**, so common that in some districts – e.g. the Lord Reay country, *Dùthaich Mhic Aoidh*, as the seven parishes nearest to Cape Wrath are called – they have no other name for apparitions or terrifying objects seen at night. It is the figure of a man who is no 'living wight' seen at night, and as may readily be imagined, this kind of apparition is frequently seen when children are obstreperous, querulous, or crying without cause, as their manner is. *Bodach an Sméididh* ('the Beckoning Old Man') appears about the corners of houses, making signs with his hand for people to come to him. The *Corra-lòigein*, whatever his name may mean, stands in places which it is desirable to keep children from wandering to after dark, and will ill-treat any of whom it gets a hold.[908]

The principal of these *Lemures* is 'the Son of Platter-Pool', whose full title is 'the Son of Platter-Pool from grey spike, silken spike, great caterpillar' – *MacGlumag na mias, o liath tarrang shìoda, burrach mòr*.[909] This, as his name indicates, is really a frightful bugbear: he looks in at windows, flattens his face against the panes, sharpens his teeth with much noise, and takes away children in a twinkling unless they keep quiet. Neither he, however (nor any of his brother bugbears), enter a house unless called in. The threat of doing so is generally quite sufficient to silence the most ill-grained child.

FUATH

This word means literally 'aversion', 'hatred', but in Ross-shire is a common word to denote an apparition, ghost, spectre. In this latter sense it is rare in Argyleshire. In the poem of the *Muireartach* or *Muileartach* (which may be translated 'Western Sea', foster-mother of Manus king of Lochlin), describing her attack upon Fin mac Coul and his men it is said:

> 'S gum b' ainm don fhuath nach robh tìom
> A' Mhuireartach mhaol, ruadh, mhuing-fhionn;
> Bha aodann dubh-ghlas, air dhreach guail,
> Bha deud a carbaid claon-ruadh.
>
> Bha aon sùil ghlogach 'na ceann
> 'S gum bu luaith' i na rionnach maghair;
> Bha greann glas-dhubh air a ceann
> Mar choille chrionaich roimh chrith-reothadh.   M. S.[910]

("The name of the daring spectre (*fuath*) / Was the bold, red, white-maned Westlin

Sea; / Her face was dusky, of the hue of coal, / The teeth of her jaws crooked red. / In her head there glared a single eye / That swifter moved than bait-pursuing mackerel; / And on her head there bristled dark-grey hair / Like brushwood covered with hoar-frost.")[911]

The attributes of the *fuath* are different in different tales, and Mr Campbell (*Tales of the West Highlands*, ii. 191) has fallen into the error of conjoining attributes ascribed in several stories and representing the *fuath* as a water spirit having web-feet, tail, mane, etc. The name of a desolate moor near Ullapool in Ross-shire, *Leathad Leacanta nam Fuath* ('the Flat-Stoned Declivity of Fuaths'), is alone convincing it was not deemed particularly a water spirit.[912]

The following tales will illustrate the character of Highland hobgoblins and suchlike objects of terror better than a lengthened disquisition.

CACHLAIDH NA FEUSAIG, ISLAY

At the bottom of a dell or hollow through which the public road lies, in the island of Islay, there was a gate across the road bearing the above name, which means 'the Beard Gateway'. At this place things unearthly were encountered after dark. One night a man saw an indistinct object coming towards him. He could give no account of it, but that its mouth was wide open as if to devour him, and that from the width of its gape he could see its lungs (*sgamhan*) down its throat. He was accompanied, fortunately, by a large Newfoundland dog, which rushed between his legs at the 'thing', and a terrific fight ensued. He ran away home, leaving them at it. In the morning the dog came without any hair on its body, and shortly after its return expired.[913]

About the middle of February a party was coming home from the market held on the *Imire Còmhnard* ('Level Ridge') at Ballygrant ('Ugly Town').[914] Before parting they entered a roadside inn. One of them, Ewen MacCorkindale, had, after leaving, to pass through the Beard Gateway and the haunted dell. His companions made fun of him, and asked him if he was not afraid of the *bodach* (the 'carle' or 'old man') who haunted the dell. Out of foolhardiness Ewen proposed 'the health of the *bodach* (the old man), and let the *cailleach* (the old wife) go to the dogs'.

When he reached the haunted spot, two apparitions – an old man and an old woman – met him. The old woman endeavoured to attack him, but the old man kept her off, and ever after, at every opportunity, the same scene was rehearsed – the old wife attacked him and the old man defended him. The latter also told him to go to a smithy in Ireland (others say to two brothers in Cantyre) and get a dirk made, and as long as he kept this on his person the old woman would not venture to attack him. The dirk bent three times in the making, and from its possession Ewen acquired the title of *Eoghan na Biodaig* ('Ewen of the Dirk').

As he was working one evening by moonlight in the harvest field, he left the dirk on a stook of corn along with his vest. The carlin wife got between him and the dirk, and gave him such a squeeze that he put out three mouthfuls of blood. The *bodach* came, but too late, to his rescue. It, however, told him that if he survived till cock-crowing five years would be added to his life. Ewen woke up now and then to ask if the cock crew yet, but when it did it was too late.

Very likely the poor man died of some rupture or heart disease. The dirk was preserved by his son.

THE HEADLESS BODY (*COLANN GUN CHEANN*)

At the shore and forming part of the boundary between North and South Morar, on the west coast of Inverness-shire, there is a large rocky mound (*cnoc mòr creige*) which was long the cause of terror in the district.[915] At the base of the mound a road can be taken along the shore when the tide is out. No-one, however, taking it alone after nightfall, lived to tell the tale. His remains were found next day among the large boulder stones (*càrnach mòr chlach*) of which the shore is full, mangled and bearing traces of a ghastly and unnatural death.[916] Persons who had the second sight, looking over the rocks that overhang the shore, said they saw a phantom or 'something' haunting the place, having the shape of a headless human figure.[917]

Macdonall (or **MacCuïl**, as he is styled) of South Morar, *Mac Dhùghaill Mhòrair*, whose house was not far from the scene of the Headless Body's violence, unexpectedly became the means of expelling it from its haunt. He was one winter evening unexpectedly visited by a friend. He had no-one to send to Bracara across the river – to invite some more friends to come and join in the entertainment of his guest – but his son and heir, then about eighteen years of age. He strictly enjoined the youth not to return that night unless men came with him, for fear of the Headless Body.

The young man did not find the friends he was sent for at home, and with the temerity natural to his years came back alone. The Body met him and killed him, and in the morning were found traces of a fearful struggle – large stones displaced, and clots of blood, as if the youth had put out his heart's blood.

MacCuïl made a solemn vow neither to eat nor drink till he avenged his son's death. All that evening his friends tried to persuade him to remain at home, but to no purpose. The Headless Body never appeared but to those who passed its way alone, and the chief's friends had to return while he went on unaccompanied to the haunted rocks. The Body came out and said, "You have come to take your son's ransom (*éirig*); take counsel, and go home."

To this the chief replied by clasping his arms round the hated apparition. A furious struggle commenced, and to this day the stones may be seen which were rolled out of their way in the dread encounter. At last the strong and fearless chief got the Headless Body under, and drew his dirk to stab it. The Body cried, "Hold your hand, **MacCuïl**, touch me not with the iron, and while there is one within the twentieth degree (*air an fhicheadamh miar*) related to you in Morar, I will not again be seen."

When this story was heard some years ago there were only two alive within this relationship to the ancient chief – one a harmless idiot, the other a poor woman in Fort William. One or other of them must be still alive, for the Headless Ghost has not yet made its reappearance. The person from whom it was heard was a firm believer in its truth, and in his youth (half a century ago) was well acquainted with the district in which the events were said to have occurred. He had learned and practised the tailoring trade there.[918]

Another, and somewhat different, version of the tale will be found in Campbell's *West Highland Tales*, ii. 89. In it the subduing of the ghost is ascribed to Stout John, laird of Raasay, a proof of the manner in which floating popular tales attach themselves to known characters. The words ascribed to the Body as it went away were composed in the East Indies by a piper of the name of Bruce from East Side, Skye. *Beinn Heidera* and *Bealach a' Bhorbhain* are both in East Side, Skye. The words are an adaptation of an old tune 'Thogainn Fonn air Gille an t-Sealgair'.[919]

The tale quoted by Scott (*Lay of the Last Minstrel* note Q) from Henry the Minstrel of Sir William Wallace's encounter with the Headless Body is also known in the Hebrides, and has been told to the writer by a native of the extreme west of Tiree. According to this version, MacFadyen's head was cut off by Wallace to avoid his falling alive into the hands of the English. MacFadyen was an old man and not able to keep up with the rest of the retreating company. When Wallace himself went to open the door, the Headless Body stood holding the head by the hair in its hand and threw it at Wallace. Wallace picked it up and flung it out at the door as far as he could. The Headless Body went in search of it, and Wallace made his escape by a window on the opposite side of the castle.[920]

There is a rhyme with which probably some legend was formerly connected:

> *Dar chaidh Fionn don bheinn*
> *Thachair ris Colann gun Cheann.*

("When Fionn went to the hill / He met Headless Body.")[921] It was deemed very foolhardy in a boy to go out after dark alone and say,

> *Colann gun Cheann,*
> *Thig a-nall 's thoir leat mi.*

("Headless Body, / Come and take me away.")

THE GREY PAW (*SPÒG LIATH*)

In the Big Church of Beauly (*Eaglais Mhòr na Manachain*, i.e. of the Monastery) mysterious and unearthly sights and sounds were seen and heard at night, and none who went to watch the churchyard or burial-places within the church ever came back alive. A courageous tailor made light of the matter and laid a wager that he would go any night and sew a pair of hose in the haunted church.

He went and began his task. The light of the full moon streamed in through the windows, and at first all was silent and natural. At the dead hour of midnight, however, a big ghastly head emerged from a tomb and said, *Fhaic thu 'n t-seann bhò liath 's i gun bhiadh, a thàilleir.* "Look at the old grey cow that is without food, tailor."

The tailor answered, "I see that and I sew this," and soon found that while he spoke the ghost was stationary, but when he drew breath it rose higher.

The neck emerged and said, *Sgòrnan fada riabhach 's e gun bhiadh, a thàilleir.* "A long grizzled weasand that is without food, tailor."[922]

The tailor went on with his work in fear, but answered, *Chì-sa, mhic, chì-sa, mhic, chì-sa siud 's fuaigheam seo an-dràsta.* "I see it, my son, I see it, my son, I see that and I sew this just now." This he said drawling out his words to their utmost length.

At last his voice failed and he inhaled a long breath. The ghost rose higher and said, *Gàirdean fada riabhach 's e gun fheòil gun bhiadh, a thàilleir.* "A long grey arm that is without flesh or food, tailor."[923]

The trembling tailor went on with his work and answered, "I see it, my son, I see it, my son; I see that and I sew this just now."

Next breath the thigh came up and the ghastly apparition said, "A long, crooked shank that is without food, tailor."

"I see it, my son, I see it, my son; I see that and I sew this just now."

The long foodless and fleshless arm was now stretched in the direction of the tailor. *Spòg mhòr liath gun fhuil gun fheòil gun fhéithean 's i gun bhiadh, a thàilleir.* "A long grey paw without blood or flesh or muscles or food, tailor."[924]

The tailor was near done with his work and answered, "I see it, my son, I see it, my son; I see that and I sew this just now," while with a trembling heart he proceeded with his work.

At last he had to draw breath, and the ghost, spreading out its long and bony fingers and clutching the air in front of him, said, *Spòg mhòr liath 's i gun bhiadh, a thàilleir.* "A big grey claw that is without food, tailor."

At that moment the last stitch was put in the hose, and the tailor gave one spring of horror to the door. The claw struck at him and the point of the fingers caught him by the bottom against the door-post and took away the piece. The mark of the hand remains on the door to this day. The tailor's flesh shook and quivered with terror, and he could cut grass with his haunches as he flew home.

This is perhaps the most widely known and most popular story in the Highlands. Its incidents can be reproduced on a winter evening with frightful distinctness by means of a shadow on the wall. This gives it a wonderful attraction for children, and if fear can under any circumstances be called into healthy action (and dread, like any other power or capacity of the mind, must have a proper and healthy action), it is in listening to this or similar stories. Their baneful effects, if such there be, soon disappear.

There is hardly an old church in the Highlands where the event has not been said to have occurred. A writer in the last *Statistical Account* (Argyleshire, p. 682 note) claims it for the old church of Glassary.[925] In Skye it is placed in the *Eaglais Uamhalta* in Conasta near Duntulm.[926] The old church of Beauly has the most popular claim, though to a youthful audience the truth of the story is much confirmed by putting the scene in some place that they know.

In the cathedral of Iona there is a small nook pointed out called *Toll an Tàilleir* ('the Tailor's Hole') where it is said the monks kept the tailor who made their clothes. They kept him too long and too busy at his work, and at last 'things' began to trouble him at night. The worst of these was a fleshless hand that used to show itself on the wall and say, "A great grey paw that is without food, tailor."[927]

Another form of the tale is that the tailor was at the *aire chlaidh* (i.e. 'watching the graveyard') of a friend in a chapel (*caibeal*) when the foodless figure began to emerge from a tomb. The tailor did not run away till the figure had got up as far as the knees, and said: *Sliasaid liath reamhar* ('Grizzled grey thigh'), etc.[928]

EWEN AND THE CARLIN WIFE

One of the commonest of Gaelic sayings is: *A dheòin no dh'aindeoin, mar thàinig a' chailleach air Eoghan* – to which is frequently added, *bean cho mòr ri mhàthair*. "Whether he would or not, as the old wife came upon Ewen – a wife as big as his mother."[929] There are various versions of the origin of this tale, but none of them is common.

The celebrated Ewen Cameron of Locheil (who is characterised by Macaulay in his *History of England* as the Ulysses of the Highlands, a gracious master, a trusty ally, and a terrible enemy) was on a journey, as the story goes, from Aberdeen to Inverness.[930] He was at the time a young man, and on entering the inn in which he stayed at Aberdeen the evening before starting, he found sitting before him an old woman he had never seen before. On seeing Ewen she wrinkled up her nose, tossed her head, and said, "Hïh."

Ewen, being of a witty humour, replied by wrinkling up his own nose, tossing his head, and saying, "Hŏh."

Next morning when starting, he found the hag waiting for him at the door. She said, *Ceum ann, Eoghain!* "Step it out, Ewen!"

He said nothing, but went on his way. All day the old woman walked alongside, and whenever his steps flagged, repeated her challenge to him to step it out. Ashamed to be beat by an old woman, and agile as a wildcat, Ewen held on at a headlong pace, and before nightfall the pair were in Inverness, 108 miles away.

Ewen was sadly fatigued, as may well be supposed from the distance and the pace. That night he consulted an old man, who advised him to answer the old wife's challenge also in words, and no evil would result from his walk. Next day the hag, as before, was waiting for him at the door, and said, *Ceum ann, Eoghain!* "Step it out, Ewen!"

He answered: *Ceum air do cheum, agus ceum a bharrachd, a chailleach!* "A step for your step, and a step additional, old woman!"

This day they walked to *Caolas 'ic Phàdraig* ('Patrickson Sound'), as the ferry across Loch Leven at Balachulish is called, a distance of seventy-five miles. Ewen got into the ferryboat first, and pushed off from the shore. When the hag saw herself about to lose him, she called out, *Mo dhùrachd dhut fhéin, Eoghain!* "My sincere wishes are yours, Ewen!"[931]

He replied: *Rùn do chridh' air do chliathaich 's air a' chloich ghlais ud thall, a chailleach!* "Your sincere wishes be upon your own sides and on yonder grey stone, old wife!"[932]

The old wife looked at the grey stone, and it split in two, as may still be seen by anyone passing that way.

Another version of the parting of Ewen and the old wife is that the pair came to Ewen's foster-mother's house. That night his foster-mother put him to sleep on a hard deal board and placed a crock of butter to his feet, while she put the old wife in a soft and luxurious bed. In the morning Ewen was as fresh as a lark – his feet had soaked in the whole of the butter during the night, but the carlin wife was dead![933]

Another (and probably older) tale of the origin of the saying is of a wilder cast. Ewen was a jolly young fellow (*òganach grinn*) who went to a wedding. He had a switch in his hand with which, when the ceremony was being performed in the church, he tapped a skull in the church window, saying to it every word the minister said to the couple marrying. That night on going to bed he was seized by a shivering cold, and an old woman (*cailleach*) came and claimed him as her husband. She said they were married as surely as the couple in church that day. She came night after night, and Ewen, whose thoughtless fun had turned to such terrible earnestness, could not get rid of her, do what he could. An old man whom he consulted said there was a bad chance of her going away while he lived, but that he ought to consult Michael Scott.[934] Michael said, "I will separate you from her, but perhaps you will not live after. Here is a book, which you are to take to bed with you, and when she goes away, open the book, and follow her wherever she goes. While the book is open, she cannot leave you by walking. Before you come back, you will see the bed prepared for me, and will be able to tell me what it is like."

The hag went to hell, and Ewen followed. This is the origin, at least an illustration, of the saying, *Thoir bean á ifrinn, 's bheir i gu 'taigh fhéin thu.* ("Take a wife from hell, and she will take you to her own house.")[935] Several subordinate demons came first to the door, but Ewen demanded an interview with their chief. He then requested that the old wife should be bound with chains to keep her always in her infernal abode. This was done, but when he offered to go away, she followed. She was then put below a cauldron (*fo bhial coire*) on the bed of brimstone prepared for Michael Scott, and she is probably there still. Ewen came back to tell Michael that his bed was ready, and did not live long after his terrible adventure.[936]

THE BLACK WALKER OF THE FORD

Rather more than a century ago there lived at Amhulaich (in Rannoch) a miller much addicted to the use of tobacco, who, when unable to get it, was – like most smokers – very short and quick in the temper. It was in the house of this man, tradition says, that Allan Breac (the true murderer of Colin Campbell of Glenure), when making his escape, stayed the night after the murder. James Stewart of Ardsheal was hung in chains for the murder in 1752.[937]

On one occasion the miller ran out of tobacco, and sent for a supply by some Lochabermen who were passing through Rannoch on their way to Perth. The mill-stream ran close to his house, and he had to cross it on stepping-stones in going to and from the mill. As he was returning home one evening in the dusk, and was about to enter the house, he heard the sound of footsteps coming to the ford. He called out, "Who is there?" – but received no answer.

Being crusty for want of tobacco, and thinking it might be the Lochabermen returning, he called out a second time, very peremptorily and impatiently. He still received no answer. He called out a third time, turning down to the ford, and saying aloud that whether it was man or devil, he would make it answer. The thing then spoke, and said it (or he) was *Coisiche Dubh Beul an Àth*, the Black Walker of the Ford.[938]

What further passed between the two never transpired, but every evening after that for a year or more the miller left home at dusk, crossed the stream, and went to a small clump of trees about half a mile away, whence loud cries and yells were heard during the night. Before daybreak he came home with his knife or dirk covered with blood. When examined by the light the blood proved to be merely earth. An attempt was made on one occasion by some young men to follow him to the rendezvous, but he became aware in some mysterious way of the attempt, and, turning back, warned them not to follow. It was enough, he said, for himself to go, without their perilling their souls.

On the last night of his going to meet the Black Walker, such terrific outcries were heard from the clump of trees that the people of the neighbouring villages, Amhulaich and Cragganoür, came to the doors to listen. It was a winter night, and next morning marks of a foot or knee were found in the snow along with the miller's own footsteps, as if something had been engaged in a struggle with him.

Some years after this a man who had been away in America entered Amhulaich mill. The miller at the time was dressing the millstone, and when he observed the American,[939] threw at him the pick he had in his hand, and nearly killed another who was standing near. He told him never to appear in his presence again, that he had had enough of him. Many surmised it was this man who had troubled him before, but whether it was or not never appeared.

STROWAN, ATHOLE

Within the present century a native of Glen Erochty – *Gleann Eireachdaidh*, the valley that leads from Athole to Rannoch – was similarly afflicted. Every evening he went to meet the evil spirit at a small circle of trees on the top of the hill above the clachan of Strowan. The last occasion of his doing so was after the shinty-playing on New Year's day. He took with him a large stick which had been cut that same day in the wood and had served one of the players for a shinty-stick.

Next day this stick was found at the scene of the nightly meetings, twisted like a withe, while all round within a circle the snow was trampled as if there had been a struggle. There were marks of a man's foot and of a knee.[940]

THE UNEARTHLY WHISTLE

About seventy years ago a young man, a native of the village of Cornaig in Tiree, went in the evening to another village, Cruaidh-Ghortain, about two miles distant. When he reached it, he reclined on a bed, and being tired fell fast asleep. He awoke with a start, and, thinking from the clearness of the night (it was full moon) daylight had come, hurried off home.

His way lay across a desolate moor called the *Druim Buidhe* ('Yellow Ridge'), and when halfway he heard a loud whistle behind him, but in a different direction from that in which he had come – at a distance, as he thought, of above a mile. The whistle was so unearthly loud he thought every person in the island must have heard it. He hurried on, and when opposite *an Carragh Biorach* ('the Sharp-Pointed Rock') he heard the whistle again, as if at the place where he himself had been when he heard it first. The whistle was so clear and loud that it sent a shiver through his very marrow.[941]

With a beating heart he quickened his pace, and when at the gateway adjoining the village he belonged to, he heard the whistle at the Pointed Rock. He here made off the road and managed to reach home before being overtaken. He rushed into the barn where he usually slept, and, after one look towards the door at his pursuer, buried himself below a pile of corn.

His brother was in a bed in the same barn asleep. His father was in the house, and three times, with an interval between each call, heard a voice at the door saying, "Are you asleep? Will you not go to look at your son? He is in danger of his life, and in risk of all he is worth (*an geall nas fhiach e*)."[942]

Each call became more importunate, and at last the old man rose and went to the barn. After a search he found his son below a pile of sheaves, and nearly dead. The only account the young man could give was that when he stood at the door he could see the sky between the legs of his pursuer, who came to the door and said it was fortunate for him he had reached shelter; and that he (the pursuer) was such a one who had been killed in *Blàr nam Bigein*, the 'Field of Birds' in the Moss, a part of Tiree near hand.[943]

In its main outline, this tale may be correct enough. A hideous nightmare or terror had made the fatigued young man hide himself under the corn, and things as strange have happened, in the history of nervous delusions, as that he should have gone himself to the door of the dwelling-house to call his father.

THE BATTLE OF GAURA

This was the battle in which Cairbre and Oscar the son of Ossian were killed. It was fought in Ireland about the fifth century, and from the poem or ballad in which Ossian describes the battle and the circumstances of his son's death – and which is still extant in popular tradition – has always been the most celebrated of Celtic battles. Macpherson has worked up the popular accounts in the first book of Temora, but not very successfully.[944]

One night a little man of the name of Campbell was going home from the smithy with the ploughshare and coulter on his shoulder, and in a narrow glen encountered a gigantic figure that stood with a foot resting on each side of the valley. This figure asked him, "What is your name?"

He answered boldly (as became one of the clan), "Campbell."

It then asked, "Were you at the Battle of Gaura?"

He answered, "Yes."

"Show me your hand, then, that I may know if you were at the Battle of Gaura."

Instead of his hand, Campbell held out the ploughshare and coulter, and the figure grasped them so tightly that they were welded together and had to be taken back to the smithy to be separated. "I see," said the apparition, "that you were at the Battle of Gaura, for your hand is pretty hard."

Two men were during the night on their way, it is said, to steal sheep. One beguiled the way by telling the other about the Battle of Gaura. Two figures of immense size appeared, one on the top of each of two high hills in the neighbourhood. The gigantic apparitions spoke to each other, and one said, "Do you hear these men down there? I was the second best hero (*ursainn chath*, literally 'doorpost of battle') at the Battle of Gaura, and that man down there knows all about it better than I do myself."[945]

THE BEAST OF ODAL PASS

From Kylerhea (*Caol Reidhinn*), the narrowest part of the Sound of Skye, the Pass of Odal stretches westward and forms one of the most striking pass views in the Highlands. It was through it that the first public road was made in Skye about sixty years ago. At the time it was being made, the pass was haunted by 'something' awful – the more awful that its character was not distinctly known – that enjoyed an evil reputation far and wide as *Biast Bealach Odail*, 'the Beast of Odal Pass'.[946]

This thing, whatever it was, did not always appear in the same shape. Sometimes it bore the form of a man, sometimes of a man with only one leg; at other times it appeared like a greyhound or beast prowling about; and sometimes it was heard uttering frightful shrieks and outcries which made the workmen leave their bothies in horror.

It was only during the night it was seen or heard. Travellers through the pass at night were often thrown down and hurt by it, and with difficulty made their way to a place of safety. It ceased when a man was found dead at the roadside, pierced with two wounds one on his side and one on his leg, with a hand pressed on each wound. It was considered impossible these wounds could have been inflicted by human agency.

LUIDEAG, 'THE RAG'

At a small loch between Broadford and Sleat in Skye called *Lochan nan Dubh-Bhreac* ('the Lakelet of Black Trout'), thirty or forty years ago, the figure of a young woman with a coat about her head was commonly to be seen at night in the neighbourhood of – and on – the public road that passes that way. She went by the name *Luideag*, i.e. the 'Rag' or 'Slovenly Female'. She did not answer when spoken to, and disappeared as silently and mysteriously as she made her appearance.[947]

The place is lonely and far from houses, and there was no conceivable reason why anyone, much less a female, should nightly frequent it. An exciseman passing the way once spoke to *Luideag*, first in English and then in Gaelic, but she answered not a word. A man was found lying dead on the road at the place, and she never appeared afterwards.[948]

LOCHAN DOIMEIG

On the skirts of Schiehallion, the steepest and one of the highest hills in the kingdom, there is a small loch or tarn, near Crossmount in Lower Rannoch, the vicinity of which about fifty years ago was the scene of strange terrors at night. The road leading over the shoulder of the hill to Weem lay along the shores of this lake, and, where it was crossed by a small stream that falls into the loch, those who passed the way after dark were scared by strange sights. After crossing the ford the traveller was accompanied for about twenty yards by a dog, a he-goat, a dark moving mass, or some other object which, from the unaccountable manner of its appearance and disappearance, could not be deemed earthly.

A native of Kilchonan in Rannoch who had been for some time in the south as a gardener came on a visit to his friends, and had to pass in the neighbourhood of the loch. It was ascertained that at Cashieville (*Cois a' Bhile*), where he left the strath of the Tay to cross the skirts of Schiehallion, he had taken a drink of porter. It was fourteen days after before it was ascertained he never reached Kilchonan. A search was instituted; men gathered from Appin and Athole and Rannoch, and the whole country round about, and continued the search for three or four days, even as far as Glenlyon, but without success.

One of the exploring parties when above Crossmount was met by a woman who advised them to search round *Lochan Doimeig*, for she had dreamt last night she was cutting rushes there. Soon after a man met them, who gave them the same advice, and said he had had the same dream. On going round the loch they found the dead gardener lying on a green mound on the brink of the stream, already mentioned as crossing the road, in the attitude in which he had stretched himself to take a drink.[949]

RETURN OF THE DEAD

A former minister of East Side, Skye, was in his lifetime addicted to visiting his cattle-fold. His whole heart was given to his herds, and after his death his ghost was to be seen revisiting his former haunts.[950]

An old man undertook to meet and lay the ghost. The two met and saluted each other in the usual manner. When shaking hands, however, the man, instead of his hand, offered the ploughshare. After that the ghost never came back.

In the same neighbourhood, about thirty years ago, a man died suddenly. His wife watched the cows in harvest soon after this lest they should leave the fank or enclosure in which they were put at nights to keep them from wandering into the crops. She had occasion one night to leave her charge and go to a shop two miles away. On her return she went to close a gap (*beàrn*) in the fold (*buaile*). She found there her late husband, who told her not to be anxious, as he was watching in her stead.

Every night after this he was visible to anyone who chose to go and look for him. He even came to the house to *céilidh*, i.e. to while away the time, a favourite recreation in the Highlands (λέσχη of the ancient Greeks) of spending the evening by gathering in a neighbour's house to listen to gossip and tales and idle talk.[951]

The dead man's attentions at last made the wife resolve to sell all she had and go to America. On the day of the sale the cattle could not be gathered; they seemed to be taken possession of by an undefinable terror, and the sale and projected emigration had to be abandoned. A little bird hovering about was evidently the cause of the wildness of the cattle.[952] After this day the visits of the dead man ceased.

DONALD GORM'S GHOST

In 1616 a batch of West Highland and Island chiefs were brought before the Privy Council in Edinburgh, and bound over in restrictions as to the quantity of wine they were respectively to use in their houses. The narrative upon which the Privy Council proceeded is quoted by Gregory, *History of the Western Highlands*, p. 395: "The great and extraordinary excesse in drinking of wyne, commonlie usit among the commonis and tenantis of the Yllis, is not only ane occasioun of the beastlie and barbarous cruelties and inhumanities that fallis oute amangis thame, to the offens and displeasour of God, and contempt of law and justice; but with that it drawis nomberis of thame to miserable necessitie and povartie, sua that they are constraynit, quhen thay want from their awne, to tak from thair nichtbours."[953] The excessive use of wine by the West Highland chiefs is borne witness to by the distich:

> *Niall mac Ruairidh 'n astair*
> *Bheireadh fìon d'a chuid eachaibh*
> *Air son bùrn an lòin a sheachnadh.*

("Neil son of Rory, fast travelling, / Who gave wine to his horses / That they might avoid the meadow waters.")[954] Among these lawless and reckless chiefs was Donald Gorm Mor ('Big Blue Donald') of Sleat in Skye, the then Lord Macdonald of the Isles. He was prevented from attending the Council by sickness, but ratified all their proceedings. "He named Duntulm, a castle of his family in Trouterness (in Skye), as his residence; and six household gentlemen and an annual consumption of four tun of wine was allowed him."[955]

He died that same year, and was succeeded by his nephew, Donald Gorm Og ('Young Blue Donald'). So far history; the following tradition is well known in Skye. Some family document went amissing, and its loss was likely to be of serious consequence to young Donald Gorm. At the same time the figures of Donald Gorm Mor and two companions were repeatedly seen on the road leading to Duntulm Castle. Efforts were made to accost them, but the three figures passed those who met them in some mysterious manner without being noticed, and without giving any opportunity of being accosted. They were then seen to enter the castle.

An old man of the neighbourhood advised that seven staves of pine, *gathannan caol giuthais* – according to others seven spindles of oak, *seachd dealgun daraich* – with fire at their points should be taken, and entry be made into the room in which the ghosts each day took up their quarters. This was done, and the phantoms (Donald Gorm Mor and his two companions) were found drinking. To give confidence to the intruders that they might hear his tale, Donald said:

> *Bha mi 'n Dùn Éideann a-raoir,*
> *Tha mi 'm thalla féin a-nochd;*
> *'S fiach an dadam ud sa ghréin*
> *Chan eil annam féin de neart.*

("I was in Edinburgh last night, / I am in my own mansion tonight; / And worth a mote in the sunbeam / I have not in me of strength.") He then told where the lost document was to be found, and disappeared, saying:

> *Mur bhith na gathannan caol giuthais*
> *Bhiodh seo gu d' phuthar-sa, Dhòmhnaill Ghuirm Òig.*

("If it were not the slender lances of pine / This would be to thy hurt, Young Donald Gorm.")[956]

Taibhse Choimhlig

Peter Brown at Dun Crosg in Glen Lochy hid a ploughshare (*coltair*) and died without telling where. In consequence his ghost long haunted *Eas Choimhlig*, a waterfall in the neighbourhood, but no one had the courage to speak to it and ascertain the cause of its unrest.[957]

In every settled community the ploughshare is of greater value – though less glory is attached to it – than the sword or any other weapon, and in the Highlands the same terrors were attached to the hiding of so useful an instrument which afterwards, and in a more commercial state of society, were believed to follow the secreting of gold. The unhappy man who hid it, and died without revealing his secret, could not rest in his grave.[958]

Peter Brown's ghost was commonly seen as a roebuck (*boc earba*) that followed people passing the ravine of Coilig after dark, but also as a horse, dog, man, etc., and disappeared only about forty years ago.[959] A weaver had the courage to meet it, and had a long talk with it. He was told what would happen to his family, and that his daughter (whose marriage was then spoken of) would never marry. When he returned home he took to his bed and never rose.

There is now a bridge where the ford was formerly, and it was at the top of the bank above the ford the ghost was seen. It once fought a strong man, and the marks of the conflict long remained on the ground and trees.

KINGAIRLOCH, ARGYLESHIRE

A skiff was upset at Maodlach, the most rugged part of the coast of this rugged district. Of the two men who formed its crew, one was saved by clinging to the boat, but the other, a powerful swimmer, in trying to swim ashore, was drowned close to land. He omitted to put off his shoes and got entangled in the seaweed.

Some time after, his brother was coming from the smithy late at night along the shore, carrying an iron bolt on his shoulder. When opposite the place where his brother's body had been found this man was joined by a figure which (it was said) resembled a he-goat. He had at the time two dogs along with him, one of which cowered about his feet, but the other – a bitch – leapt up at his throat, and he had again and again to strike it down with the bolt he carried on his shoulder.

The figure spoke, but it never clearly transpired what it said. It gave messages to deliver to former associates, especially to one thoughtless individual, warning him to amend in time. When the brother reached a house and came to the light, he fainted away.[960]

FLADDA-CHUAIN

In this islet, which lies on the east coast of Skye, there lived at one time a native of Mull and his wife. In the place there is a burying-ground called *Cladh a' Mhanaich* ('the Monk's Burial-Ground') the existence of which adds much to the feelings of awe natural to so lonely a place – a solitary islet several miles from land in a stormy sea.[961]

A dead body came on the shore and was buried after being stripped of its clothes. After this the dead man came to the hut in which the Mullman stayed – regularly, at midnight – and sat warming himself at the fire, which was left burning all night on the floor. As he bent over the fire and held his feet and his hands to it he said, *Nì mi mo theóghadh 's mo theóghadh* ("I will softly warm myself, I will softly warm myself"), and then added,

> *Bhean thug mo thriubhas dhiom*
> *'S mo bhrògan grinne dubha bhuam*
> *'S an léine thug mo phiuthar dhomh —*
> *Thuige, thuige, chasan fuara,*
> *Is ioma cuan a shiubhail sibh.*

("Wife who took my trousers off / And my nice black shoes from me / And the shirt my sister gave me – / To it, to it, cold feet of mine, / Many a sea you've traversed.")[962]

After the Mullman left the place a party of fishermen, being in the neighbourhood, sent one of their number ashore, *Dòmhnall Ruadh* ('Red-Headed Donald'), to prepare dinner for them in the bothy. As Donald was bending down to kindle a fire something struck him violently on the skull and knocked him flat. Every time he attempted to lift his head the thing knocked him on the skull again. He felt sure it must be the ghost which warmed itself at the Mullman's fire – the *Teóghan* – of which his companions had warned him.[963]

Finding it would not allow him to rise, he lay on his back as he had been knocked down, and, not daring to look at his assaulter, wriggled himself along the floor till he got hold of a post, up which he clambered to hide himself among the rafters. When his companions arrived the ghost was found to be a pet ram – addicted, like its kind, to butting.

HAUNTED HOUSES

Some half a century ago or more a native of Rannoch resided at Bonskeid (*Bonn Sgaod*) in the neighbouring parish of Blair Athole. He was married to a Badenoch woman, who had brought servants with her from her own country. In fact the only servants about the house were from Badenoch. In obedience to the law which ascribes that which is mysterious to that which is remote, Badenoch was at that time esteemed a great place for witchcraft and things 'uncanny'.[964]

A series of unaccountable noises and appearances began about the house in Bonskeid. Turnips and peats – thrown by unseen hands – flew about the house, lights were blown out, furniture was mysteriously moved, bedclothes were pulled off, and no one could be sure that an article would be found by him where he had left it. In all this there was no appearance of mortal agency, and the whole business was at once assumed to be the work of evil spirits. A friend from Rannoch who had been on a visit to the house declared solemnly (and he was a God-fearing, trustworthy man) that he himself heard the spinning-wheel coming downstairs, and saw it falling in pieces on the floor of the room in which he and the family were sitting, without any visible agency and without any part of it being broken or injured. He put it together again, and with his own hands carried it upstairs and left it in its original place. He had not sat long after coming down when the wheel again came in the same mysterious manner, and fell in pieces on the floor.

On another occasion, as he stood in the byre a turnip came and knocked the candle out of his hand. To his certain knowledge there was no-one in the byre who could have thrown it. These flying turnips came sometimes as if they had been hurled through the wall.

The unhappy man in whose house this occurred endured the persecution for more than a year, and was sadly broken in health and spirits by the trouble. One day as he stood on the hearth-stone, warming the back of his feet to the fire, the hearth-stone began to move. A Badenoch dark hussy (*caileag dhubh*) was at the time standing by, with her elbow rested on the kitchen 'dresser' and her chin on her hand. He observed her smiling, and it struck him she was at the bottom of all this bedevilment. He turned her and all the rest of the Badenoch servants away, and no further disturbance took place.

About twenty years ago a house in Kilmoluag, Tiree, was the scene of similar disturbances. With one or two exceptions, all the people of the island believed them to be produced by some supernatural evil agency, and all the superstition that with the spread of education had been quietly dying out was revived in renewed vigour.[965] No-one could deny the agency of spirits when the evidence was so clear. The annoyance began by the trickling of dirty water (mixed with sand) from the roof. Then burning peats were found among the bedclothes, and pebbles in bowls of milk, where no peats or pebbles ought to be; linen was lifted mysteriously from the washing and found in another room; articles of furniture were moved without being touched by visible hands; and stones flew about the house. The disturbances did not occur during the day, nor when a large company assembled at the house. Several went to lay the ghost, and a good deal of powder and shot was wasted by persons of undoubted courage in firing in the air about the house.

The annoyance became so bad, and the advice of 'wise people' so positive, that the family removed to another house in the hope the evil would not follow. The removal, however, had no effect, and it is privately rumoured the disturbances ceased only when some money that had gone amissing was restored. The cause was never clearly ascertained, but there is reason to suspect it was caused, as all similar disturbances are, by some one suborned for the purpose and shielded from suspicion by a pretended simplicity and terror.

Numerous similar cases which have occurred in the Highlands might be instanced. Instances occurring in England (from that of Woodstock downwards) and in the south of Scotland differ only as the circumstances of the countries do.[966] They all seem to have the same characteristic – the tricks are such as it is perfectly possible for human agency to perform, but it is believed there is no human being about the place who does them. Stones come flying through the windows as if they were thrown from the sky, and are found lying on the floor; the leg of a wheelbarrow startles two persons engaged within the house in earnest conversation by coming flying between them through the window, and striking the opposite wall with violence; a peat strikes the incredulous stranger between the shoulders, and he goes home a believer, etc.

These cantrips are exaggerated by fear and rumour, till at last the devil is believed to be unusually busy in the locality. Once this belief becomes popular, the delusion is easily carried on.

BÒCAIN, GOBLINS

The number of these (resembling *Luideag*) seen about fords or bridges and near the public road in lonely places, as has been already said, are numberless.[967] Every unusual sight and sound in the locality which has the name of being haunted becomes a goblin to the timorous, and one of the most tiresome forms of ghost stories is how the narrator was nearly frightened out of his wits – the quantity of which is not mentioned – by a horse (standing with outstretched neck, and its head towards him, which he mistook for a gigantic human figure), by a white he-goat in the face of a rock, the plaintive cries of an owl, etc., etc.

Most ghosts, however, are dependent not so much on the imagination of the individual spectator as on accumulated rumours, and their explanation is to be sought in men's love of the marvellous and tendency to exaggeration. On the high road leading from the Wood of Nant (*Coill' an Eannd*) to Kilchrenan on Lochaweside, two or three summers ago, the traveller was met by a dark shadow which passed him without his knowing how. On looking after him, he again saw the shadow, but this time moving away, and a little man in its centre, growing less as the shadow moved off. The little man was known as *Bodach Beag Chill a' Chreunain*.[968]

About the same time a ghost haunted the neighbourhood of Inveraray, and caused great annoyance to the post and others travelling late. A man had a tussle with a ghost at *Uchdan a' Bhiorain Duibh* in Appin, and said it felt in his arms like a bag of wool. Phantom men were to be seen at *Uchdan na Dubhaig* above Balachulish; at *Ath-Flèodair*, a ford near Loch Maddy in Uist, 'things' are perpetually seen, and it takes a very courageous man to go from Portree home to Braes in Skye after dark. A mile above the manse, where the road is most lonely, and near the top of a gradual ascent, sounds of throttling are heard and dark moving objects are seen.[969]

In the island of Coll, the top of the ascent above Grisipol had at one time an evil reputation as a haunted spot. At the summit of the pass there is a white round rock called *Cnoc Stoirr*. One night a man on his way to the west end of Coll reached the place about midnight, and was joined by a man on horseback. The rider said not a word, and accompanied him for near three miles to the 'Round House' (as a house built for the accommodation of the farm-servants of Breacacha Castle was called). Whenever he attempted to enter any of the houses on the way, the silent horseman came between him and the house and prevented him. When they came to the Round House the cock crew, and the horseman disappeared over the gate in a flame of fire. The man was lifted into the house, pouring with sweat and going off in fainting fits.[970]

In Glen Lyon in Perthshire there is a village called *Caisle*, and near it a ford (now a bridge) and ravine called *Easa Chaisle*. In the early part of the present century, clods and stones were thrown by unseen hands at parties crossing this ford at night. At last no-one would venture to cross. A harum-scarum gentleman of the neighbourhood, popularly looked upon as an unbeliever and a man without fear of God or man, crossed one night, and the clods as usual began to fly about him. He cried out, "In the name of God I defy all from the pit!" – and on his saying this a mysterious sound passed away up the ravine, and clod-throwing at the place was never afterwards heard of.[971]

The district now forming the parishes of Kilmartin and Kilmichael, at the west end of the Crinan Canal, is known in the neighbourhood as Argyle (*Earra-Ghaidheal*), probably from a Celtic colony from Ireland having settled there first. The people, for instance, of Loch Aweside say of a person going down past Ford that he is going down to Argyle.[972] In course of time the name has been extended to the county.

The public road leading through the district was once infested by a ghost which caused considerable terror to the inhabitants. A person was got to lay it. He met the ghost and exorcised it in the name of Peter and Paul and John and all the most powerful saints, but it never moved.[973] At last he called out peremptorily, "In the name of the duke of Argyle, I tell you to get out of there immediately!"

The ghost disappeared at once, and was never seen again.

COMMENTARY

1 JGC's 'shi' is a sort of pronunciation-spelling of Gaelic *sìth*. It provides the second element in his term 'banshi', now commonly spelt 'banshee'. For a classification of the widespread international motifs which concern Fairies and Elves (nos. F200–F399) see Thompson 1955–58, vol. 3, pp. 37–81, or Henderson and Cowan 2001, pp. 218–23.

2 As J. G. Mackay once pointed out (1927a, p. 64), this belief in the method of progression affected by supernaturals may be parallelled from classical sources. He cites Halliday (1926, p. 107): "Heliodorus (*Aethiopica*, III. 13) tells us that gods, if disguised as human beings, can always be recognized because their eyes do not wink and they walk without moving their feet." However, JGC appears to be taking his cue from Keightley, who defines what he calls the *Daoine Shi'* as '*Men of Peace*, perhaps the *Stille-folk*, Still-people, or rather, merely Fairy- or Spirit-people' (1850, p. 384). In Old Irish the Fairies were the *síde*, who took their name from their dwelling-place, the *síd* ('Fairy mound, otherworld'). Scholarly opinion on the derivation of *síd* has tended to oscillate between the concepts of 'seat, settlement' (cf. Latin *sedes* 'seat, abode') and of 'peace' (modern Gaelic *sìth*). It has been plausibly suggested that the latter is in origin a euphemism, designed to avoid speaking the real name of – and thus potentially summoning – the powers of the otherworld. The *daoine sìth* may thus be understood as either 'the settlement people', i.e. those who enjoyed a permanent residence when the Celtic tribes were yet migratory, or 'the peace people', i.e. those who enjoyed peace when the main activity of the Celtic tribes was war (Macbain 1896, p. 293; Vendryes 1959–96, s.v. *síd, sìth*). Tomás Ó Cathasaigh has shown, however, that in early Gaelic tradition the concept of peace was closely linked to the otherworld. He conjectures (1977–79, p. 150) that the meaning of *síd* narrowed from 'abode' to 'abode of the gods' to 'hollow hill', adding (*ibid.*): "The use of this word, or of one based on it, to denote peace could logically have arisen at any stage in this progression. For an unsettled or migrant people, the notion of abode or settlement might readily be linked with that of peace."

3 See MacPhail 1900, p. 444.

4 By 'Bernera' JGC means not Bernera Lewis (*Beàrnaraigh Leòdhais*) but Berneray Harris (*Beàrnaraigh na Hearadh*), now more commonly called Berneray Uist (*Beàrnaraigh Uibhist*), see p. 72. For *meillich* ('a kind of seaweed', *CG*6, p. 107) see also p. 72. Dwelly (1977, pp. 645, 679) does not give *meillich* but *meilearach, muirineach*, 'sea-maram, sea-matweed', a grass-like seaweed. In Harris *milearach* is the short green grass that grows in places subject to flooding by the tide, especially amongst the rocks of the Bays (Joina MacDonald, personal communication, 6 February 2004). Carmichael (*CG*2, p. 328) gives it as *mileur, milereach, mileurach, milseanach, misleanach, mineurach*, and adds: "Dried and cured, the grass is used in the Isles for bedding, and in the south for upholstery."

5 JGC has here provided a dossier of evidence (note in particular his own translation 'unearthly') which shows that *sìth* is best understood not in the narrow sense 'Fairy' but in the broad sense 'otherworld(ly), supernatural'.

6 According to I. F. Grant (1959, pp. 54–55, 70, 86, 138) it was unfurled at the battles of Glendale (*c.* 1490) and Trumpan in Waternish (*c.* 1535). One source (*ibid.*, pp. 53–54) maintains that

it was unfurled at Bloody Bay in the Sound of Mull *c.* 1485. Another tradition has it that 'it was unfurled in order to check a cattle plague' (*ibid.*, p. 86). The potato famine of 1847–48 hit MacLeod's Country very hard, and at one point the chief claimed to be feeding 6,000 to 7,000 people (*ibid.*, pp. 583–85).

The Fairy Flag was actually unfurled for JFC just a day or two before his meeting with JGC at Portree on 9 October 1871 (NLS Adv. MS 50.4.6, f. 160r): "It is made of yellow raw silk with figures and spots worked on in red . . . There is something odd and uncanny about the whole thing. By rights there ought to have been legions of imps about our ears when the flag was unfurled but none came that I saw or heard." See also Mackay 1919–22, pp. 128–33; MacLeod 1933b, pp. 128–38; Spence 1948, p. 212; Pennant 1998, pp. 295–97.

7 "Each woman and cow will cast her calf." This is clearly an aspect of the flag as a powerful fertility charm, and, as Grant points out (1959, p. 86), 'it must be remembered that the tale of a woman who has to be released from enchantment to enable her child to be born appears in several Highland folk-tales'. Only one 'English wife of a former chief' was widowed when still of child-bearing age – Sarah Stackhouse (1767–1822), who married General Norman MacLeod in 1784 when she was 17 and was widowed in 1801 at the age of 34 (Morrison 1986, p. 188).

8 What JGC means, I think, is that legends about the Fairy Flag divide into those in which the banner was the gift of a *leannan sìth* and those which stress its magical power irrespective of its origins. They are discussed in Grant 1959, pp. 85–86. The *leannan sìth* stories focus upon the idea that an otherworld woman was mother or foster-mother to a MacLeod heir: she sang the 'Fairy Song' discussed at pp. 641–43 and wrapped the child in what became the Fairy Flag. The others focus upon the foreign origins of silk. The Bannatyne MS has it that the flag was brought back from Palestine by a MacLeod who had gone on a crusade. On his way back he was warned by a hermit to beware of a 'she-devil' who killed all true believers. She is named as 'Nein a Phaipen, or Daughter of Thunder' (MacLeod 1933b, p. 132); perhaps this is in error for *Nighean a' Bheithir* ('the Serpent's Daughter', 'the Dragon's Daughter', 'the Thunderbolt's Daughter', see pp. 121, 129). The hermit gave him a piece of the True Cross and told him how to overcome her. He duly defeated her in combat. As she died, she asked him to give certain messages to her earthly friends. By way of reward she foretold the future of the MacLeods and gave him 'the banner that had been tied about her loins' along with her spear to act as a flagstaff. Grant also mentions 'a wild verbal tradition' that 'the flag was received by MacLeod from the Christian slave-girl of an Eastern magician'.

The implication of both types of legend appears to be that the flag originated as a girdle (cf. Dilling 1912–14, p. 423), and Grant offers some scientific corroboration for this (1959, p. 28): "The silk of which the Flag is made is, according to the expert opinion of Mr Wace of the Victoria and Albert Museum, of Syrian origin, and he thinks that it was probably a garment, a relic of a saint, before it was a flag."

A sacred girdle (*sian-chrios*) was sometimes worn in pregnancy, as explained by Henderson (1911, p. 335): "This is to 'sain' the expected child as well as the mother from all harm, and to attach all good spiritual powers on her side." Such girdles had a general amuletic function as well as an obstetric one, as demonstrated in the Ossianic ballad 'Teanntachd Mhór na Féinne' (Campbell 1872, pp. 97, 99; Cameron 1892–94, vol. 1, p. 297):

> Gheibheadh tusa sin 's ceud crios,
> An slios mu'm bi cha tuit am blàr;
> Chaisgeadh iad leum droma 's sgìths —
> Seud rìomhach nam bùcall bàn.

"You would get that and a hundred girdles, / The waist they encircle won't fall in battle; /

They'd cure lumbago and exhaustion – / The beautiful treasure with the white buckles." (For *leum droma* see pp. 227–28.) In 1765 this verse was reinterpreted by James Macpherson for his southern audience in 'The Battle of Lora' (1996b, p. 121): "An hundred girdles shall also be thine, to bind high-bosomed women; the friends of the births of heroes, and the cure of the sons of toil." He explains in a note (*ibid.*, p. 442): "Sanctified girdles, till very lately, were kept in many families in the north of Scotland; they were bound about women in labour, and were supposed to alleviate their pains, and to accelerate the birth. They were impressed with several mystical figures, and the ceremony of binding them about the woman's waist, was accompanied with words and gestures which shewed the custom to have come originally from the druids." Alexander Carmichael had a different version of the quatrain (*CG2*, p. 258):

> *Gheobhaidh tu siud is ceud crios,*
> *Cha téid slios mu'n téid iad aog;*
> *Leighisidh iad leatrom is sgìths —*
> *Seudan rìomhach nam ban saor.*

("You will get that and a hundred girdles, / No body which they surround will die; / They'll relieve pregnancy and exhaustion – / The beautiful jewels of the noble women.")

The 'jewels' may be understood as fine stones or pieces of coral, judging from Martin Martin's description (1716, p. 209): "The *Plad* being pleated all round, was tied with a Belt below the Breast; the Belt was of Leather, and several Pieces of Silver intermix'd with the Leather like a Chain. The lower end of the Belt has a Piece of Plate about eight Inches long, and three in breadth, curiously engraven; the end of which was adorned with fine Stones, or Pieces of Red Coral." See also Rorie 1912–14; Dilling 1912–14; Thomson 1951, pp. 45–46.

When on trial for witchcraft on 8 November 1576, Elizabeth or Bessie Dunlop, spouse to Andro Jak in Lyne, in the barony of Dalry in Ayrshire, spoke of an obstetric belt of green silk lace which she had been given by the ghost of Thom Reid, who had died in 1547 at the battle of Pinkie, and which she had lost (Pitcairn 1833, vol. 1, p. 54, cf. Scott 2001, p. 93). "Sche being demandit, Gif sche culd do onye gude to ony wemene that wer in travell of thair chyld bed-lare? Ansuerit, That sche culd do nathing, quhill sche had first spokin with Thom; quha layit doun to hir ane grene silkin laise, out of his awin hand, and baid hir tak it to thair wylie coittis [tack or attach it to their petticoats], and knit about thair left arme; and incontinent [immediately] the seik woman suld be deliuer. Bot the said laise being layit anis [once] doun be Thom, sche culd neuir apprehend it, and maid grit seking thairfoir."

Dr Joseph Flahive has pointed out to me that two magic girdles are mentioned in an Irish poem about the contents of Manannan's *Corrbholg* ('Crane-Bag'): *crios Goibhnionn* 'Goibhne's girdle' and *crios do dhruimnibh an mhíl mhóir* 'a girdle of the great whale's back' (MacNeill 1908, p. 119). Manannan and Goibhne or Goibhniu the smith are among the few pre-Christian figures invoked in extant Gaelic charms (see p. 219 and Stokes and Strachan 1901–03, vol. 2, p. 248); the other *crios* may be of seaweed or the like, if we take the plural of *druim* in the sense of 'wave-tops' rather than of 'back' (cf. Murphy 1953, p. 21). Manannan later became a Christian saint, see note 579; another *sian-chrios* has been ascribed (albeit doubtfully) to St Fillan, see p. 89. For the *crios Bríde* see Danaher 1972, pp. 34–36.

9 Strictly *teine sìth* is 'Fairy fire, otherworld fire'. See p. 264.

10 This is a verse of a song otherwise known simply as 'Calum Beag'. It is by John MacLean (*Bàrd Bhaile Mhàrtainn*, 1827–95), for whom see 'Life of John Gregorson Campbell', p. 654 below; Cameron 1932, pp. 142–43; Cregeen and MacKenzie 1978, pp. 19–22; Meek 2003, p. 479. As published by Cameron (1932, p. 147) and reprinted with translation by Meek (2003, pp. 156–57), it looks like this:

Mar fhiadh anns a' bhùireadh air chùl nam beann fuara
A' direadh ri uchd garbhlaich 's an sealgair ga ruagadh,
Bha ise 's siubhal sìth aic' is sìnteagan uallach,
A' gearradh nan tonn uaine 's i fuaradh air càch.

"Like a deer in the rutting-place behind the frozen mountains, / climbing up the rough slopes when pursued by hunters, / she was sailing splendidly with paces that were noble, / cutting the green combers, and going to windward of all." Later in the song the poet remarks: *Mac Shìomoin ort mar fharainm 's MacArtair anns an rìnndeal*, 'You're called Mac Shìomoin as a nickname and MacArthur in the rental' (Cameron 1932, p. 149; Meek 2003, pp. 158–59). This Malcolm MacArthur or *Calum mac Shìomain* is the subject of at least seven songs or poems by *Bàrd Bhaile Mhàrtainn* and *Bàrd Bhaile Phuill*: 'Calum Beag' itself, 'Calum Beag á Tìr a' Mhurain', 'Laoidh Chaluim' (also called 'Eachdraidh Chaluim'), 'Uidheamachadh Luinge Chloinn Artuir' (see note 281), 'Iubhrach Chaluim', 'Calum MacArtuir' and 'Calum á Lub a' Gheòidh'. Six of these are published in Cameron 1932, pp. 143–55, 171, 231–33, and Cameron says (*ibid.*, p. 143): "Calum Beag was the subject of innumerable comic ditties by John Maclean, the Balemartin Bard. Calum was a clever little boatman, and the Bard placed him in all kinds of novel situations, as fancy prompted him. Trips to Glasgow and the Clyde by the intrepid mariner were favourite topics. 'A Chaluim Bhig, a Chaluim Bhig' is a ballad of surpassing merit. For inoffensive humour and poetic talent the Calum Beag series are all outstanding."

Clearly Calum Beag was the perfect butt for gentle satire; Niall M. Brownlie tells me that he never in fact left the shores of Tiree. See also note 599; *Tocher* 32, p. 85; *Tocher* 34, p. 217.

11 When a giant comes with *siubhal sìth* in the tale 'An Crochaire Lom-Rùsgach' ('The Bare-Stripping Hangman', MacDougall 1891, pp. 95, 129), this is explained by the editor (*ibid.*, p. 282) as: "With great speed, but without any perceptible effort. He moves his hands and feet so rapidly that they become invisible, and that he seems to glide through the air without touching the ground." See also Bruford and MacDonald 1994, p. 474. *Siubhal-sìthe* is now used metaphorically in senses like 'poetic speech' and 'effortless superiority' (MacInnes 1994–96, p. 8).

12 The word is usually spelt *sìthiche*, plural *sìthichean*. It is grammatically masculine. By 'of common gender' JGC means that it is applied equally to male and female Fairies.

13 Graham 1810, pp. 110–24 (*passim*). I do not know why JGC calls the distinguished Dr Graham (who was minister of Aberfoyle from 1787 to 1835) an unreliable authority. It could hardly be because his *Essay on the Authenticity of the Poems of Ossian* (1807) displays the normal anxiety of his day to refute the attacks made upon the accuracy of Macpherson's 'translations'. With respect to folklore *Highlands of Perthshire* is a pioneering work, and Scott said (1893b, vol. 2, p. 181 note) that his 'urbanity in communicating information on the subject of national antiquities is scarce exceeded even by the stores of legendary lore which he has accumulated'. Shi'ich seems to me a very adequate anglicisation of the word *sìthiche* usually employed in Gaelic today, showing loss of final syllable as was normal in Perthshire. For an Ossianic poem noted by Graham in 1782 from a native of Cowal see NLS Adv. MS 73.2.13, f. 74.

14 *Sìthbheire*, plural *sìthbheirean*, is the usual word in Tiree Gaelic for a Fairy. It is, I think, the last of the four terms cited by the Rev. Robert Kirk (in Gaelic script) as equivalent to 'Elves, Fauns and Fairies' (EUL MS Laing III 551, p. 1, cf. Hunter 2001, p. 78): *hubhrisgeidh, caibe,n, lusbarta,n, 7, siotbrudh.* (He actually writes *hubhrirgeidh* and *siotbsudh*, having some difficulty with the difference between *r* and *s*.) For *hubhrisgeidh* see note 350, and for *caibe,n* see note 58. *Lusbarta,n* is the term spelt *luspardan* (plural *luspardain*) by Dwelly (1977, p. 618) and defined by him as 'pigmy, dwarf; sprite; term applied to a dwarfish

child or boy; contemptuous term for a puny man'. W. C. Mackenzie suggested (1905, p. 265) a derivation from *lugh-spiorad* 'little spirit', but it is safer to say that it appears to be a corruption of *lùchraban*, Irish *luchorpán*, 'little-bodied one, leprechaun'; for further discussion see Winberry 1976 and Henderson and Cowan 2001, p. 54.

Kirk's *siotbrudh* should perhaps be understood as an otherwise unattested plural (*sìthbhreadha*) of JGC's *sìthbheire*. This word is not well served by existing dictionaries: Dwelly (1977, pp. 838, 841) gives *sibhreach*, *sibhreag* and *siobhrag* for 'Fairy, Elf', and *siobhraich* 'Fairy work, magic, enchantment', but not *sìthbheire*. The spelling of *sibhreach* varies, e.g. in *Tocher* 14, pp. 216–19 (a story from Islay), we find *sìthfhearach* and its plural *sìthfhearaich* as well as *sìthein* (clearly meaning 'Fairies', not 'a Fairy hill') and *daoine sìth*! Equally then, it is possible that by writing *siotbrudh* Kirk was simply trying to represent *sibhrich*, plural of *sibhreach*, or *sìthfhearaich*, plural of *sìthfhearach*; it is worth noting that the Arran pronunciation of *sibhrich* is simply **shivri** (Mackenzie 1914, p. 261). He is unlikely to have meant *sìth-bhrugh* 'Fairy hill or mansion' – he knew well that this term did not denote the Fairies themselves, but chose to spell it *Sìth-bhruaich*, as if the word in question were *bruach* 'bank' rather than the less common *brugh* 'mansion' (EUL MS Laing III 551, p. 23, cf. Hunter 2001, p. 85).

15 Slink: 'a prematurely born calf or other animal: its flesh or hide: a bastard child: a slinking gait' (Chambers 1983, p. 1218).

16 The *OED* defines 'elle-maid(en)' as 'a half-adoption, half-translation of Danish *elle-pige* elf-girl'; for the Grimms' discussion of it see Croker 1825–28, vol. 3, p. 64. JGC took the term from Keightley (1850, pp. 81–93, 234), where 'Elle-maid', 'Elle-king', 'Elle-people', etc. are used freely in an account of Danish folklore. They are introduced in a passage at pp. 81–82 translated from Thiele 1818–22, vol. 4, p. 26: "The Elle-people live in the Elle-moors. The appearance of the man is that of an old man with a low-crowned hat on his head; the Elle-woman is young and of a fair and attractive countenance, but behind she is hollow like a dough-trough. Young men should be especially on their guard against her, for it is very difficult to resist her; and she has, moreover, a stringed instrument, which, when she plays on it, quite ravishes their hearts. The man may be often seen near the Elle-moors, bathing himself in the sunbeams, but if any one comes too near him, he opens his mouth wide and breathes upon them, and his breath produces sickness and pestilence. But the women are most frequently to be seen by moonshine; then they dance their rounds in the high grass so lightly and so gracefully, that they seldom meet a denial when they offer their hand to a rash young man. It is also necessary to watch cattle, that they may not graze in any place where the Elle-people have been; for if any animal come to a place where the Elle-people have spit, or done what is worse, it is attacked by some grievous disease, which can only be cured by giving it to eat a handful of St. John's wort, which had been pulled at twelve o'clock on St. John's night. It might also happen that they might sustain some injury by mixing with the Elle-people's cattle, which are very large, and of a blue colour, and which may sometimes be seen in the fields licking up the dew, on which they live. But the farmer has an easy remedy against this evil; for he has only to go to the Elle-hill when he is turning out his cattle and to say, 'Thou little Troll! may I graze my cows on thy hill?' And if he is not prohibited, he may set his mind at rest." Leigh Hunt put the concept to good use in his poem of 1858 'The Shewe of Fair Seeming' (Milford 1923, p. 136), in which Love turns into Loathednesse:

> *Pale snakes, entwined with strings of coin, alas!*
> *Writhed foul, though little felt, about its head;*
> *And for the ghastlier anti-life, instead*
> *Of back, and substance, and where heart should be,*
> *The trunk, like to a tray disfurnishéd,*

Was front alone, and hollow now to see,
Like trunk of dread Elle-Maiden, haunting Germany.

17 JGC's point was confirmed by my late friend the Rev. Norman MacDonald (1904–78) from
Staffin in Skye. The old folk he knew in his boyhood days believed firmly in Fairies, and
clinched their argument like this (1958b, p. 121): "A fairy sweetheart is mentioned in the
Bible, and the last person who saw them here was a worthy elder of the kirk!"
     The reference is to the fifteen occurrences of 'familiar spirit' in the King James Bible
and of 'python' (in the sense of 'a familiar or possessing spirit, one possessed by a spirit',
from *Pŷthô*, the oracle of Apollo at Delphi) in the Vulgate. These are: Lev. 19: 31; Lev. 20: 6,
27; Deut. 18: 11; 1 Sam. 28: 3, 7, 8, 9; 2 Ki. 21: 6; 2 Ki. 23: 24; 1 Chr. 10: 13; 2 Chr. 33: 6; Isa. 8: 19;
Isa. 19: 3; Isa. 29: 4. The translators of the Gaelic Bible employed the term *leannan sìth* in
all these cases except two, Isa. 8: 19 and 29: 4, where *fiosaiche* ('seer') is used instead. The
effect is often both peculiar and misleading, especially where the witch of Endor is given a
leannan sìth (1 Sam. 28: 7–9).
     Yeats saw the 'Leanhaun Shee' as a metaphor for the all-consuming nature of love
(Welch 1993, p. 23), and JGC interprets *leannan sìth* as 'familiar spirit' in order to offer some
support to the translators of the Bible, but 'Fairy sweetheart' is the straightforward literal
translation and the one that best fits the many stories of *leannain shìthe* told by the people,
see e.g. note 30 below and *CG*5, pp. 124–65. As these stories are about sexual relationships it
is, I think, the references to whoring in Lev. 20: 6 and to stoning (the penalty for adultery)
in Lev. 20: 27 that first set the translators' minds running on *leannain shìthe*.
     JGC's 'consulters of the spirits of the dead' may be found, more or less, in Deut. 18: 9–12,
"When thou art come into the land which the Lord thy God giveth thee, thou shalt not learn
to do after the abominations of those nations. There shall not be found among you any one
that maketh his son or his daughter to pass through the fire, or that useth divination, or
an observer of times, or an enchanter, or a witch, or a charmer, or a consulter with familiar
spirits, or a wizard, or a necromancer. For all that do these things are an abomination unto
the Lord . . ." *'N uair a thig thu do'n fhearann a tha 'n Tighearn do Dhia a' tabhairt duit,*
cha-n fhòghlum thu 'dheanamh a réir gràineileachd nan cinneach sin. Cha-n fhaighear
'n 'ur measg neach air bith a bheir air a mhac, no air a nighinn dol troimh 'n teine, no a
ghnàthaicheas fiosachd, no speuradair, no fear-fàistineachd, no a ghnàthaicheas droch
innleachdan, no seunadair, no neach a dh'fhiosraicheas de leannan-sìth, no druidh, no
neach a dh'iarras eòlas o na mairbh. Oir is gràineileachd do'n Tighearn iadsan uile a ni
na nithean sin . . .
     'Spirit possession' is shamanism; there are traces of shamanism in Gaelic folklore (see
p. lxxvii above and notes 67, 108, 571 and 578 below), but there is no Gaelic word for it.
'Shaman' itself has entered English from Russian. See also Spence 1948, pp. 200–06, and
MacilleDhuibh 18.10.02.
18 This has now been pretty comprehensively discussed by Spence (1948, pp. 132–36), Briggs
(1959, chapters 4–5 'Shakespeare's Fairies' and 'The Fashion for the Miniature'), and
Henderson and Cowan (2001, pp. 47–57). Of Shakespeare, who came from a county where
Fairies were small, Briggs says (1959, pp. 45, 56): "He drew straight from his native folk-lore
some elements that had hardly appeared in literature before his time. The innovation that
strikes us most is the fairy smallness, not new to folk-lore, but nearly new in literature . . .
In the beginning of the Jacobean times a little school of friends among the poets, Drayton,
Browne, Herrick and the almost unknown Simon Steward, caught by the deliciousness of
Shakespeare's fairies, and coming from counties where the small fairies belonged to the folk
tradition, amused themselves and each other by writing fantasies on littleness."
     For a fantasy of this kind in Gaelic see Black 2002, pp. 274–83. The *bean nighe* in

particular was noted for her smallness (p. 23; Sithiche 1912, pp. 344–47). For examples of Fairies above normal size see pp. 15, 42, and (from Ireland) Wentz 1911, p. 62.

19 Deut. 3: 11, "For only Og king of Bashan remained of the remnant of giants; behold, his bedstead was a bedstead of iron: is it not in Rabbath of the children of Ammon? Nine cubits was the length thereof, and four cubits the breadth of it, after the cubit of a man."

20 Fionn spent sixty years in hell (Murphy 1933, pp. xii, 168–73, and 1953, p. cii).

21 JGC takes these terms at random from Keightley and Grimm. See in particular Keightley 1850, pp. 64–66 (Alfs), 66–67 (Duergar), 79 (Huldrafolk), 94–139 (Trolls, Hill-folk), 217–19 (Hill-folk), 298–305 (Pixies). At p. 216, citing the Grimms' *Deutsche Sagen*, vol. 1, p. 38, Keightley speaks of 'Zwerge (*Dwarfs*), Berg- and Erd-mänlein (*Hill* and *Ground-mannikins*), the Stille Volk (*Still-people*), and the Kleine Volk (*Little-people*)', see Grimm 1816, pp. 34–38 (*Zwerge*), 38–39 (*stille Volk*), 39–40 (*kleine Volk*), 40–43, 45–46 (*Zwerge*), 48–50 (*Bergmännlein*), 56 (*Erdmännlein*), 57–58, 221–31, 389–92 (*Zwerge*). For Sir Walter Scott on the Duergar see Scott 2001, pp. 76–81.

22 *Òthan* as such is not in any dictionary known to me, but is given (with precisely the same spelling and definition) in *CG6*, p. 113. It may be assumed that Carmichael (1832–1912) got both the word and its definition from *SHIS*. Angus Matheson, as editor of *CG6*, points to a word in *DIL*: '*othan*, f., a word of obscure meaning, found in poetic and cryptic language, perh. stone (?clay, soil) or burial-chamber, grave?'

23 *Ùigh* in the sense of 'a small green knoll or hummock of earth' is completely unknown to me. Perhaps it is a dialectal pronunciation of *uaigh* 'grave' in unstressed position, e.g. *uaigh Fhinn* 'Fionn's grave'.

24 JGC's list is not exhaustive – it fails to include *toman*, a word with a curious historiography in his day. Mrs Grant of Laggan spelt it *tomhan* while defining it correctly as 'fairy hillock' (1811, vol. 1, pp. 278–88, *passim*). She was a newcomer to the Gaelic language, but Stewart, who had no such excuse, says (1823, p. 91) that 'within those "*Tomhans*," or, as others term them, "Shian," sociality and mirth are ever the inmates'. The spellings *Tomhan* and *Shian* were accorded folklore's equivalent of holy writ by being copied from Stewart by the Grimms (see Croker 1825–28, vol. 3, p. 15). It is hardly surprising, then, that Keightley should declare (1850, p. 384): "The Gael call the Fairies Daoine Shi', (*Dheenè Shee*) and their habitations Shians, or Tomhans."

I think it unlikely that *tomhan* is for *òthan*; for *brugh* see p. 7.

25 See p. 51.

26 See also pp. 33 and 51; MacRitchie 1907–08, pp. 319–22; 'The Fairy of Tigh-Meadhonach', Mackenzie 1914, pp. 270–71; McPherson 1929, p. 99. In Ireland clean water was kept in the house at night 'for the Fairies', and if dirty water were thrown out a shouted warning was given first in case they got their clothes wet (Wentz 1911, p. 70). For the motif see MacDonald 1994–95, p. 44: "Request to move site of house because it interferes with fairy dwelling: luck follows compliance: misfortune refusal."

27 According to John Mackenzie (Mac-Choinnich 1844, pp. 237–38), *sìth-bhruth* is the word used of Cluny's 'cage' on Ben Alder by its distinguished occupants (who included Prince Charles) in September 1746. See Macpherson 1893, p. 481. Niall M. Brownlie points out to me that the expression *brugh nan sìthbheirean* 'the Fairy dwelling' was still common when he was a boy in Tiree between the wars.

28 Strontium was discovered at Strontian in 1790. The village takes its name from the hill to the east called *Tom an t-Sìthein*, which descends to Loch Sunart in the form of a promontory (*sròn*).

29 JGC is here using the Gaelic spectrum. *Ruadh* embraces deep yellow, reddish yellow, orange, pale red, roan and russet. Generally translated 'red', it is the colour of the celandine (*ceann ruadh*), ragweed flowers (see note 62), sand, brown bread (*aran ruadh*), brown

sugar, brown paper, carrots, the roe deer, the fox (*madadh ruadh*), grouse (*coileach ruadh*), coppers (*airgead ruadh*) and red hair (e.g. *Rob Ruadh*, Rob Roy). For *crodh breac ruadh* 'red speckled cattle' see p. 15. In the English spectrum *crotal* is generally described as yellow; at p. 126 JGC calls it reddish-brown. Speaking of weddings in Wester Ross, 'Fear Bha Ann' says (1887–88, p. 510): "Green must on no account be worn by the bride, bridegroom, or guests, as it was the Fairies' favourite colour, and they would be highly offended if wedding parties dared to wear it." Cf. Introduction, p. lxix; notes 156, 570; Hutchings 1997.

30 This is very peculiar. JGC is referring to the song entitled 'Cumha le Té da Leannan Sìth' in MacCallum 1821, p. 69, 'An Toman Cuilinn' in MacPherson 1868, p. 93, 'Gilbhinn' in Campbell 1872, pp. 211–12, and 'An Leannan Sìdh' in CG5, p. 150. It tells how a girl who had an otherworld suitor was betrayed by her sister, and how her brothers sought out her Fairy lover and killed him; W. B. Yeats mischievously remarked of it (Welch 1993, p. 27) that no Fairy would ever have been so badly treated in Ireland. Mrs Grant of Laggan (1811, vol. 1, pp. 285–90) offers an interesting variation on the story, along with a few lines of translation. Mrs Mary Mackellar's version begins (1888–89, p. 156):

> Far am biodh mo leannan falaich,
> Cha b'ioghna mise a bhi ann,
> Fàile nan ùbhlan meala,
> Dhe 'n fhodar a bha fodh cheann.

("Where my secret love would be, / It's no surprise if I was there, / For the smell of honied apples / Was off the straw where his head lay.") It is clearly a reference to the lover's breath, for, as Mrs Mackellar says (*ibid.*), the girl's brothers 'found the lover resting on a bed of straw that the maiden had made for him at their trysting place'. However, MacPherson gives the verse as:

> 'S far am beil mo leannan-fallaich,
> 'N ioghnadh mis' a dhol ann?
> Tha fàileadh nan ùbhlan meala,
> 'Chrùn na h-aid' a tha' air a cheann!

("And where my secret lover is, / If I go there is it surprising? / For the smell of honied apples / Is off the crown of the hat on his head!") In my opinion this is so bizarre that it cannot be right. I do not think it is a deliberate bowdlerisation. A more likely explanation is provided by rhyme – *meala* provoked the change of *fhodar* into *aid*, then *ùbhlan* suggested the additional flourish *'Chrùn*. See 'The Lost Appendix', p. 702 below; *Tocher* 28, pp. 212–15; MacilleDhuibh 7.2.03; GUL MS Gen. 1090/29, pp. 203–06.

31 On Fairy dress in various European traditions see Croker's translation (1825–28, vol. 3, pp. 8, 10, 77–81) of Jakob and Wilhelm Grimm's introductory essay to *Irische Elfenmärchen*; on headgear see also Dieckhoff 1914–19, pp. 257–58. It will be obvious to anyone who has been a tourist in Ireland that Fairies do not have to be Teutonic to wear hats. Of Irish Fairies the Grimms say that 'a hat or cap is indispensable' (Croker 1825–28, vol. 3, p. 2). Behatted or behooded fairies are mentioned frequently in Croker's stories from the south of Ireland (e.g. vol. 1, pp. 38, 143, 200; vol. 2, pp. 13, 73, 125). Croker himself says (vol. 2, p. 162): "The fairies generally appear in *Hata dubh, culaigh ghlas, stocaigh bana, agus broga dearga*; a black hat, a green suit, white stockings, and red shoes." Keightley points out (1850, p. 363) that in Leinster the usual Fairy attire was 'green with red caps'. It is difficult but not impossible to find examples of Fairy headgear in Scottish Gaelic stories. A female Fairy at p. 55 wears 'a cap bearing the appearance of the king's-hood of a sheep'. In 'Croitean an Doire Sheilich' ('The Hunchback of the Willow Brake') the hunchback meets a female Fairy who has on her head *boineid uaine le dos iteag airgid a' dannsadh 'na mullach* ('a green cap with a tuft

of silver feathers waving from its crown'), MacDougall and Calder 1910, pp. 204–05. The Rev. Norman MacDonald claimed that 'at times' Fairy women wore 'a large red feather in their hat and a short blue skirt' (1958b, p. 119). Alexander Macdonald speaks of a man on Loch Ness-side who met 'about a dozen little women wearing green caps' (1982, p. 224). And Alexander Carmichael translated for Wentz (1911, p. 116) a description of Fairies – male as well as female, seemingly – which he claimed to have collected in Barra in 1865 and in Harris in 1877: "Bell-helmets of blue silk covered their heads, and garments of green satin covered their bodies, and sandals of yellow membrane covered their feet."

The way Fairies were visualised in Gaelic Scotland would have depended upon how the seer conceived their origins. Carmichael's Fairies sound like angels. Male Fairies who were thought to be spirits of the dead must surely have been clothed in tartan kilts and plaids and blue bonnets before 1746, and in hodden grey breeches and blue bonnets after that year, just like men. Fairies who were gods may have resembled angels. Kirk wrote (Hunter 2001, p. 82): "Their apparell and speech is like that of the people and countrey under which they live: so are they seen to wear plaids and variegated garments in the high-lands of Scotland and Suanochs [*suanach* 'a plaid'] heretofore in Ireland." Cf. Spence 1948, p. 137, and Bennett 1997, p. 107.

32 "One of their two nostrils closed." See Introduction, p. lv.

33 This is the smith Lon mac Lìomhainn in 'Duan na Ceàrdaich' ('the Song of the Smithy'), who has, as JGC says, *aon sùil mholach an clàr aodainn* ('one gloomy eye in his forehead'). The word *lon* means primarily an ousel or blackbird, secondarily a demon or gluttony; it appears moreover to have been in occasional use in medieval Irish verse as a kenning for a chief, and thus to have formed a component of personal names. Any or all of these four senses may serve to explain the name of the sword, but the first, 'blackbird', is a good candidate, not only because it is the primary sense but also because the makers of Ossianic tales and ballads were fond of irony; compare Iain Lom's use of *greidlean* 'a bread-stick' for a sword in 'Latha Inbhir Lòchaidh' (note 576 below). *Lon mac Lìomhainn* may therefore mean 'Blackbird son of Filing'. *Mac an Luin*, 'the Son of the *Lon*', is the sword which he made for Fionn (Campbell 1872, pp. 65–68, cf. Campbell 1890, vol. 3, pp. 396–420, Campbell 1891, pp. 21, 26, and Murphy 1933, pp. 14–15):

Mac an Luin aig Fionn mac Cumhaill
Nach d'fhàg fuigheall de dh'fheòil dhaoine.

("Fionn mac Cumhaill's Mac an Luin / Who left no remnant of men's flesh.")

34 See 'The *Bean Nighe* or Washing Woman', p. 22; Introduction, p. lv.

35 For examples of Fairy smiths see notes 122 and 142. It is not clear to me how this is to be reconciled with the talismanic use of iron by human beings as a defence against otherworld forces, see 'Protection against Fairies', p. 24.

36 See pp. 130, 568; Henderson 1911, p. 18; Nicolson 1951, p. 52. Frazer (1911a, pp. 384–86) cites examples from around the world of peoples who regarded it as unsafe to speak of their gods or spirits at specific times of day or seasons of the year. He also points out (*ibid.*, pp. 416–17) that 'the speaker imagines himself to be overheard and understood by spirits, or animals, or other beings whom his fancy endows with human intelligence; and hence he avoids certain words and substitutes others in their stead'.

37 See 'Calum Clark and his Sore Leg', p. 32.

38 'Little palm-cake', see p. 36.

39 See p. 127.

40 See pp. 39, 56, 83–84; Campbell 1889, pp. 64–69; Henderson 1911, p. 296; Gregory 1970, pp. 212, 224. *Smàladh* is 'smooring, raking'; *air a smàladh* 'smoored, raked'.

41 See Gregor 1883a, p. 57; Henderson 1911, p. 219; GUL MS Gen. 1090/29, p. 65. On no account should dirty water be thrown out after sunset; a girl who did so in Benbecula is said to have disappeared and to have been found murdered (Bruford and MacDonald 1994, pp. 315–16, 470). *Loir* or *loirc* means 'wallow, roll in the mud, drub' (Dwelly 1977, p. 596): *gu'n loireadh fhéin ann* 'to roll themselves in, to wallow in, splash about in'.

42 The *maighdeann* should not be confused with the *cailleach*, for which see pp. 133–34. The *maighdeann* was the last handful of corn cut by the first reaper (or team of reapers) to finish work on a particular farm, while the *cailleach* represented the last reaper (or team of reapers) to finish – in other words, she represented the performance of the farm as a whole. The *maighdeann* was bedecked with ribbons, formed into a cross, ornament or doll, hung in the house or byre, and fed to the animals on New Year's day or at the start of ploughing in spring, thus transferring her virtue to next year's crop. The *cailleach* was larger and less tastefully made, being adorned with items of cast-off clothing such as a married woman's *bréid* or mutch, and was thrown (or even erected in some way) on the territory of a neighbouring farm which had not yet completed its harvest, cf. Frazer 1913, p. 172: "In Munzerabad, a district of Mysore in Southern India, when cholera or smallpox has broken out in a parish, the inhabitants assemble and conjure the demon of the disease into a wooden image, which they carry, generally at midnight, into the next parish. The inhabitants of that parish in like manner pass the image on to their neighbours, and thus the demon is expelled from one village after another, until he comes to the bank of a river into which he is finally thrown." See also Campbell 1895, p. 99; Maclagan 1895, pp. 148–54; Maclagan 1895–96; MacPhail 1900, p. 441; Mackenzie 1914, pp. 253–54; Grant 1925, p. 38; Banks 1937–41, vol. 1, pp. 62–91; Maclean 1964; Ross 1964; *Tocher* 18, pp. 52–55; *Tocher* 19, p. 108; *Tocher* 54/55, pp. 323–25; *Tocher* 56, p. 412; Youngson 2001, p. 506.

43 See *CG4*, p. 118:

> *Brisgein beannaichte earraich,*
> *Seachdamh aran a' Ghàidheil.*

Carmichael translates: "The blest silverweed of spring, / One of the seven breads of the Gael." No doubt the identity of the other six was a topic of conversation in many a ceilidh-house, especially in times of hunger: *aran-coirce* ('oat-bread') and *aran-eòrna* ('barley-bread'), presumably, then the rarer *aran-seagail* ('rye-bread') and *aran-peasrach* ('pease-bread'), finally perhaps the luxuries *aran-cruithneachd* ('wheaten bread', which might appear on the laird's table) and *aran-milis* ('sweetbread', 'gingerbread', brought around by packmen and sold at fairs). See also McDonald 1958, p. 50; Beith 1995, p. 242; Cheape 2002, pp. 120–21; GUL MS Gen. 1090/28, pp. 77–78.

44 See note 16 above. On Fairy food generally see Spence 1948, pp. 186–89.

45 Strictly *ceàird-chomain* 'craft of mutual assistance', 'craft of obligation', 'quid-pro-quo craftsmanship', from *ceàird* 'trade, craft' and *comain* 'mutual assistance, obligation', see also p. 52. In early Irish the term was commonly used – in the plural – of magical practices (*DIL* s.v. *cerd*), e.g. of Úath mac Imomain in 'Fled Bricrend' it was said (Windisch 1880, p. 293; Henderson 1899, p. 96) that *no gniad druidechta ocus certa commain* ('he would perform druidries and crafts of mutual assistance').

There are grounds for suspecting the existence of a further term *ceàird-chomaineach* denoting the otherworld person with whom one has such a relationship. In 'The Secret Commonwealth' Kirk says (Hunter 2001, pp. 80–81): "They avouch that a Heluo or great eater hath a voracious Elve to be his attender called *ceart-coimithech*, a joynt-eater, or just-halver, feeding on the pith and quintessence of what the man eats, and that therefore he continues lean like a hauke or heron, notwithstanding his devouring appetite." Similarly, in the 'Highland Rites and Customes', probably co-authored by Kirk (see p. xxiv), we find: "When good eaters continue lean they say, they are attended with one *Ceart chomach* who takes away the Foyson of his meat betwixt his hand & his Mouth." In the manuscript *chomach* replaces *Connach*, which is deleted (Hunter 2001, pp. 59, 217). Kirk is clearly seeing *coimitheach* and *comach* as derivatives of *comaidh*, defined by Dwelly (1977, p. 235) as 'mess; eating together or promiscuously of the same food, particularly if out of the same vessel', but it is much easier to understand *ceart* as a corruption of *ceàird* (cf. notes 119 and 839) than as the prefix 'joint', which would be tautological as well as unusual. *Comaineach* might certainly be misheard as *comaidheach*, and I would conclude that Kirk (or his informant) misunderstood *ceàird-chomain* or that its meaning had extended to include the sharing of food as well as of technical services.

46 See p. 31.

47 Or perhaps more literally 'travelling upon tall guiding stems'? It is not clear to me whether the image is of long grass stems uprooted and flying through the air like slender magic carpets, or of surfboarding along the tops of long grass stems as they bend in the wind until they touch each other, but either way it is highly effective. *Oiteag sluaigh* is an alternative to the more everyday term *iomaghaoth*, plural *iomaghaothan*. For a list of references to Fairy winds see Ó Duilearga 1981, p. 400; for a circumstantial seventeenth-century account of an eddy wind in the town of Forres and the superstitious instincts which it opened up see Hunter 2001, p. 154.

48 *Toisgeal* or *toisgeil* 'left, unlucky, unpropitious', cf. Campbell 1996, p. 72. By spelling it *toisgeul* JGC demonstrates an awareness that this mysterious word, for which Macbain (1896, p. 334) can offer no etymology, is related to *soisgeul* 'gospel'. O'Rahilly points out (1927, p. 23) that *an làmh shoisgéla*, 'the gospel hand', was used in Middle Irish to mean 'the left hand' from the fact that during Mass the gospel is read from the left-hand side of the altar.

Mrs Hynes of Slieve Echtge told Lady Gregory (1970, p. 213): "When you see a blast of wind pass, pick a green rush and throw it after them, and say, 'God speed you.' There they all are, and maybe the *stroke lad* at the end of them." By 'stroke' she meant 'stricken, bewitched', and Lady Gregory clarified the point further in her preface (*ibid.*, p. 10): "When the Sidhe pass by in a blast of wind we should say some words of blessing, for there may be among them some of our own dead."

Seán Ó Conaill from Cillrialaig in Kerry (1853–1931) had an anecdote about this which reads beautifully, even in translation (Ó Duilearga 1981, p. 271). "One fine autumn day long ago, a gang of men were reaping oats, and three women were binding the oats after them. They heard a whirlwind coming into the field with force. The women stood looking at the whirlwind. It was lifting the oats, taking it up into the sky, and whirling and whirling all the time. One of the women stooped, and pulled a wisp of grass from the side of the ridge, and when the whirlwind was making for them: 'Here,' she said, on purpose, 'take that instead of me!' throwing the wisp at it.

"'Aw,' said the whirlwind, 'you grey goose's shit, it wasn't you I was after!'"

49 First mentioned by Stewart (1823, p. 117) and picked up from him by Keightley (1850, p. 391). See MacilleDhuibh 15.11.02 and Introduction, p. lxx above.

50 JFC describes how a doctor told him about a recent 'lifting' (Campbell 1890, vol. 4, pp. 310–11): "Do you see that kind of shoulder on the hill? Well, a man told me that he was walking along there with another who used to 'go with the fairies', and he said to him – 'I know that they are coming for me this night. If they come, I must go with them; and I shall see them come, and the first that come will make a bow to me, and pass on; and so I shall know that they are going to take me with them.' 'Well,' said the man, 'we had not gone far when the man called out, "'Tha iad so air tighin.' These are come. I see a number of 'sluagh' the people; and now they are making bows to me. And now they are gone." And then he was

quiet for a while. Then he began again; and at last he began to cry out to hold him, or that he would be off.'

"Well," said the doctor, "the man was a bold fellow, and he held on by the other, and he began to run, and leap, and at last (as the man told me) he was fairly lifted up by the 'sluagh', and taken away from him, and he found him about a couple of miles further on, laid on the ground. He told him that they had carried him through the air, and dropped him there. And," said the doctor, "that is a story that was told me as a fact, a very short time ago, by the man whom I was attending."

After telling how a Macdonald known as *Bodach a' Phuill* who lived at Polcriskaig in Sutherland was 'lifted' by the Fairies, Alexander Mackay points out (1883–84, p. 209) that 'ever after this incident he was somewhat facile, a common thing, it was said, with people that had been borne off in that manner'. See also pp. 21 ('The Men of Peace'), 37–39 ('Lifted by the Fairies'), 46 ('The Bridegroom's Burial'), 49 ('Taking Away Cows and Sheep'), 543 ('*Sguabag*, the Sweeper'); *CG2*, pp. 257, 357–58; MacGregor 1901, pp. 48–49; Freer 1902, p. 31; Watson 1908–09, pp. 59–60; Sutherland 1937, pp. 28–29; Spence 1948, pp. 60–65, 95; Maclean 1959, pp. 195–96; MacPherson 1960, pp. 178–79; *Tocher* 28, pp. 221–24; *Tocher* 39, pp. 146–49.

51 Also called cat's-tail, typha, *bodan dubh* ('little black penis').

52 The apparent equivalence of *sìth* and *marbh* is notable.

53 A 'belemnite' is a fossil pointed like a dart, being the internal shell of a cephalopod, formerly known as a thunderbolt, thunder-stone or elf-bolt, from Greek *belemnon*, a dart (Chambers 1983, p. 113); see notes 760 and 773. The statements about colepexies' fingers and Fairy butter appear to have been taken by both Keightley (1850, pp. 305, 309) and JGC from Brand (1849, vol. 2, pp. 492, 513). In Wales, Fairy butter (*menyn y Tylwyth Teg*) was a certain type of greasy rock petroleum, found especially on limestone (Gwyndaf 1997, p. 163).

54 Cf. Croker 1825–28, vol. 2, p. 275.

55 *Spor shìth* may be JGC's slip (or a typographical error) for *spor sìth*, as *spor* is masculine in all other sources known to me.

56 JGC's scientific view of Fairy arrows was anticipated by the Rev. George Hickes (1642–1715), who wrote in 1700 (Hunter 2001, p. 173): "They are of a triangular form somewhat like the beard or pile of our old English arrows of war, almost as thin, as one of our old groats, made of flint, or pebles, or such like stones, and these the country people in Scotland believe that evill spirits, which they call *Elves* . . . do shoot into the hearts of cattel, as cowes, <oxen &> horses, and as I remember, my Lord Tarbot or some other Lord did produce one of these elf-arrows which one of his tenants or neighbours took out of the heart of one his cattel, that died of an usual death. I have another strange story but very well atteste<d> of an elf-arrow that was shot at a venerable Irish bishop by an evill spirt in a terrible noise lowder than any thunder which shaked the house, where the bishop was."

Hickes's view may be contrasted with that of his contemporary Robert Kirk as expressed in 'The Secret Commonwealth' (Hunter 2001, p. 99): "I have had Barbed arrow-heads of yellow flint, that could not be cut so smal, and neat, of so britle a substance by all the art of man. It would seem therefor that these mentioned Works were don by certane spirits of pure Organs, and not by Devils, whose continual torments could not allow them so much leasure." In his earlier 'Highland Rites and Customes' Kirk(?) had written simply (Hunter 2001, p. 68): "The Elf Arrow is like a barbed Arrow of an Orange colour, which they hang about the neck."

That belief in Fairy arrows was still strong in JGC's day is confirmed by JFC (Campbell 1890, vol. 4, p. 310): "A worthy antiquary shewed me, amongst a lot of curious gear, a stone arrow head, and said – 'That is a fairy dart, which a man brought me a few days ago. He said he heard a whistling in the air, and that it fell at his feet in the road, and he picked it up, and brought it away with him.' A tinker assured me, with evident belief, that a man had taken such an arrow from an ash-tree, where he had heard it strike."

See also Stewart 1823, pp. 134–35; *CG2*, pp. 346–47; Scott 2001, pp. 97, 100, 101; Henderson and Cowan 2001, pp. 77–79, 94.

57 JGC refers variously to the arrow being 'shot' and 'thrown', and even to the 'thrower'. 'Throw' may be a translation of Gaelic *tilg* or *caith*, both of which are also used in traditional sources for firing an arrow from a bow or a bullet from a gun, cf. MacDougall and Calder 1910, pp. 202–03. The issue of whether or not the Fairies used bows to fire their arrows is thus steeped in ambiguity. According to Edward Lhuyd, it appears to have been believed that the Fairies could make both bows and arrows, but had little power to do physical harm to human beings or animals, and employed humans to do it for them. Writing from Linlithgow, 17 December 1699, to Dr Richard Richardson, M.D., North Bierly, Yorkshire, to inform him of some of the discoveries made during his travels 'in the High-Lands . . . through *Cantire, Argyle*, and *Lorn*, beside the Isles of *Mac y Chormic, Mul*, and *y Columb Kil*; and in the Low-Lands through *Glasgow, Sterling*, and *Edenbrough*', Lhuyd says (1713, pp. 99–100, cf. Britten 1881, pp. 168–69): "As to this *Elf-stricking*, their Opinion is, that the Fairies (having not much Power themselves to hurt Animal Bodies) do sometimes carry away Men in the Air, and furnishing them with Bows and Arrows, employ them to shoot Men, Cattle, *&c.* I doubt not but you have often seen of those Arrow-Heads they ascribe to Elfs or Fairies: They are just the same chip'd Flints the Natives of *New England* head their Arrows with at this Day; and there are also several Stone Hatchets found in this Kingdom, not unlike those of the *Americans*. I never heard of these Arrow-heads nor Hatchets in *Wales*; and therefore would gladly be informed whether you have ever heard of their being found in *England*. These Elf Arrow-heads have not been used as Amulets above thirty or forty Years; but the use of the rest is immemorial: Whence I gather they were not invented for Charms, but were once used in shooting here, as they are still in *America*. The most Curious, as well as the Vulgar throughout this Country, are satisfied they often drop out of the Air, being shot by Fairies, and relate many Instances of it; but for my part I must crave leave to suspend my Faith, until I see one of them descend."

In 'The Battle of Trai-Gruinard' (p. 53), which describes a historical event, Dubh-Sìth is called an Elf, and his weapon is an Elf-bolt. Isabel Gowdie was quite specific that 'we haw no bow to shoot with, but spang [jerk] them from of the naillis of our thowmbes' (Introduction, p. xxxviii). Sir John Rhŷs appears to have been told by Arthur W. Moore that Manx Fairies shot at mortals with bows and arrows; this may have been a misunderstanding, since the question as put to Moore was whether they shot with bows and arrows or guns (Rhŷs 1901, p. 293, cf. Dorson 1968, p. 426). Marian MacLean, *née* MacNeil, from Upper Borve in Barra, told Wentz (1911, p. 108) through his interpreter, Michael Buchanan, that the *sluaghan* or Fairy hosts 'need men to help in shooting their javelins from their bows against women in the action of milking cows, or against any person working at night in a house over which they pass'. Clearly Marian sensed that whatever the Fairies' weapon was, it was no ordinary bow and arrow – the word 'javelin' probably reflects *gath* 'a dart'. Alexander Carmichael explains the nature of the arrow (Wentz 1911, p. 88): "The flint arrow-heads so much prized by antiquarians are called in the Highlands *Saighead sith*, fairy arrows. They are said to have been thrown by the fairies at the sons and daughters of men. The writer possesses one which was thrown at his own maid-servant one night when she went to the peatstack for peats. She was aware of something whizzing through the silent air, passing through her hair, grazing her ear and falling at her feet. Stooping in the bright moonlight the girl picked up a fairy arrow!"

All in all, no bow is specifically mentioned in any Gaelic Fairy story that I can recall. Could it be because in an anecdote like 'Throwing the Arrow' (p. 47) the 'arrow' is actually a bullet from a gun? The issue brings us to the heart of the debate as to whether the Fairies are mythological survival or sociological construct, for it is possible to argue that their choice of weaponry recalls that of the earliest heroes of Gaelic story-telling. This case is made by Maclagan, who points to the use of stones as projectiles by Cú Chulainn, to terms in the sagas like 'sling-hatchet' and 'champion's hand stone' (*leacan laoich Mìlidh*), and to the continuing use of slings and associated Gaelic terminology in his own day (1901, pp. 229–30, and 1903, p. 299).

The Fairies' choice of weapon and of how to propel it thus takes some explaining. From the time of Bannockburn in 1314 to the time of Killiecrankie in 1689 they dwelt among a race of mortals whose historical tales were full of famous archers and their exploits, and whose songs were full of detailed descriptions of bows and arrows. On the one hand the Fairies were said to have had smithies and should therefore have been capable of turning out swords, spears and steel arrow-heads. On the other hand the only material (as opposed to foodstuff) against which they were said to have some sort of tabu was iron, so the making of yew bows should have caused them no difficulty. The conundrum is best resolved, I think, if we regard the Fairies' alleged choice of weapon *aetiologically* as an origin-legend explaining the flints shaped like arrow-heads which could be picked up here and there in the Highlands (see p. 223) and *functionally* as code for a weapon of stealth or surprise. Before 1600 this would usually have been the bow and arrow; after 1600 it would generally have been a gun.

58 This term appears unexpectedly in the introduction to Kirk's 'Secret Commonwealth' (EUL MS Laing III 551, p. 1, cf. Hunter 2001, p. 78): "AN ESSAY / off the Nature and actions of the Subterranean (and for the most part) Invisible people, heirtofor going under the names of ELVES. FAUNES. and FAIRIES: or the like, among the Low-Countrey Scots, and termed *hubhrisgeidh, caibe,n, lusbarta,n, 7, siotbrudh* among the Tramontaines or Scotish-Irish, as they are described by those who have the Second Sight: and now, to occasione further enquiry, collected & compared." Alan Bruford thought that *caibe,n* might be a misreading for *taibhsean* 'fetches', the population of second-sight visions whom Kirk identifies with the Fairies (*Tocher* 28, p. 216), but in my view it can only represent *caibe(an)* 'spade(s)'. What may have happened is that Kirk heard the word *caibe* used in the context described here of a cure for sick people and cattle, but – as a fluent learner rather than a full native speaker of Gaelic – misunderstood it as referring to the supernatural source rather than to the physical agent of the cure. This would make particular sense if, as appears to be the case, he is equating *caibe* with 'faun', a Roman rural deity, protector of shepherds. (Whether *caibean* was ever used for spades in card-playing is doubtful. In HSD, vol. 2, p. 778, 'spade' as a suit of cards is given as *spaid*, from English 'spade'. In Irish it is *spéireata*, from 'spearhead'.)

JGC's likening of the *caibe sìth* to the sole of a shoe is interesting in light of Maclagan's description of Fairy arrows (1903, p. 299): "In Eigg these seem to be called *Ceapa-Sithein*, as if they had been used for blocking something on, as a shoemaker's last is used." However, I assume the word he heard in Eigg Gaelic was not *ceapa-sìthein* 'otherworld last' but *caibe-sìthein* 'otherworld spade'. See also note 350 and 'Fairy Arrow', p. 223.

59 *Beinne Bhric* cannot mean 'of the Spotted Hill', which would be (in the genitive, as here) *na Beinne Brice*. The original name of the mountain in the nominative appears not to be *a' Bheinn Bhreac* 'the Speckled Hill' but *Beinn a' Bhric* 'Trout Hill' (Grant 1925, p. 10). In a story told by Donald C. MacPherson, the oldest creature known in Lochaber is stated by a stag to be a one-eyed trout (*breac cam*) living in *Lochan Choire na Ceanainn*, whom the stag had got to know when he was a young calf following his mother over the *Làirig Leacach* from *Beinn a' Bhric* (Abrach 1908, cf. MacilleDhuibh 3.5.02 and Ó Crualaoich 2003, pp. 101, 236). As for the rhyme, the original is cited by JGC himself in Campbell 1885b, p. 262: "'The Carline Wife of the Spotted Hill' (*Cailleach Beinne-bric ho-ro*), 'the old wife

Commentary

big, broad, and tall' (*Cailleach mhòr, leathann, àrd*), 'who had a fountain high in the hill'
(*Cailleach mhòr an fhuarain àird*), possessed a herd of deer which she would not allow 'to
go with the neighbouring chief,' or 'to seek shell-fish on the shore.' The refrain about her
was at one time in almost every youngster's mouth. This connection was also the cause of
the enmity of fairy women to deer hunters." I have been unable to identify a single refrain
containing these elements, but they are present in various sources, e.g. Campbell 1860–62,
vol. 2, p. 352 = 1890, vol. 2, p. 369

> *Caileach Bheinna Bhric horo*
> *Bhric horo Bhric horo*
> *Caileach Bheinna Bhric horo*
> > *Caileach mhor leathan ard*
> > *Cha deachaidh mo bhuidheann fhiadh*
> > *Bhuidheann fhiadh bhuidheann fhiadh*
> > *Cha deachaidh mo bhuidheann riamh*
> > > *A dh'iarraidh chlaba do 'n traigh.*

("The cailleach of Beinn a' Bhric horo, / Bhric horo, Bhric horo, / The cailleach of Beinn a'
Bhric horo / Cailleach large and broad and tall. / They have not gone, my herd of deer, /
My herd of deer, my herd of deer, / They've never gone, my herd of deer, / Seeking clabbies
on the strand.") JGC may have understood *claba* to be weeds, but they are more likely
to be mussels or large cockles, see Kennedy 1894–96, p. 130, s.v. *claba-dudaidh*, Dwelly
1977, s.v. *clab-dubh*, Robinson 1987, s.v. 'clabbydhu', and Neil Munro's story 'War' (1935,
p. 89) '. . . splashing in the pools in the sand for partans and clabbie-doos . . .' A version in
Macdonald 1982, p. 231, includes this stanza:

> *B' annsa leam a' bhiolair' uain',*
> *A' bhiolair' uain', a' bhiolair' uain';*
> *B' annsa leam a' bhiolair' uain'*
> > *Bhiodh am bruach an fhuarain àird.*

("My favourite's green watercress, / Green watercress, green watercress; / My favourite's
green watercress / That would be in the bank of the mountain spring.") MacDougall and
Calder (1910, pp. 240–41) cite a twelve-line version which includes both Campbell's and
Macdonald's elements, except that for *leathan ard* they have *an fhuarain àird* ('of the
mountain spring'), for *chlaba* they have *shlige duibh'* ('shellfish'), and for *am bruach* ('in
the bank of') they have *an cois* ('beside', literally 'in the foot of').

Donald MacPherson offers a version in thirteen quatrains (Abrach 1873–74b,
pp. 369–70) containing many of these elements. Again, they do not include *leathan ard*,
but MacPherson tells us: *Bha miadachd mhór 's a' chaillich – theirteadh gu 'm buaileadh a
glùn an t-àrd-dorus.* "The cailleach was of great size – it used to be said that her knee would
strike the lintel." Seeing her herding the deer down through Glen Nevis, the women there
accused her of stealing their dulse and kail, and she stoutly declared (*ibid.*, p. 370):

> *Cha leiginn mo bhuidheann fhiadh,*
> *Mo bhuidheann fhiadh, mo bhuidheann fhiadh,*
> *Cha leiginn mo bhuidheann fhiadh*
> > *Dh'imlich shligean dubh an tràigh.*

> *Cha do ghoid mi cliabhan duilisg,*
> *Cliabhan duilisg, cliabhan duilisg,*
> *Cha do ghoid mi cliabhan duilisg*
> > *'S cha mhó ghoid mi ribeag chàil.*

Is mór gum b' anns' a' bhiolair uain',
A' bhiolair uain', a' bhiolair uain',
Is mór gum b' anns' a' bhiolair uain'
   Bhios air bruaich an fhuarain àird.

("I'd not permit my herd of deer, / My herd of deer, my herd of deer, / I'd not permit my herd of deer / To lick black shells in ebbing shore. / I stole no little creel of dulse, / Creel of dulse, creel of dulse, / I stole no little creel of dulse / Nor did I steal one scrap of kail. / They'd much prefer green watercress, / Green watercress, green watercress, / They'd much prefer green watercress / That's on the bank of the mountain stream.") See also MacPherson 1868, p. 121; Campbell 1885b, p. 262; Macbean 1888, part 2, no. 11; Grant 1902–04a, pp. 135–37, and 1925, p. 10; *CG*5, p. 170; Maclean 1975, pp. 36–37.

60 Elsewhere, in a more extended discussion of the issue of deer as Fairy cattle, JGC refers to this man as follows (Campbell 1885b, p. 263): "An old man of nearly eighty years of age, a native of the island of Mull, examined by the writer ten years ago upon the subject of Highland superstitions, said, 'I have always heard that deer were fairy cattle, and I have never heard that the fairies had any other.'" As this article is dated 1 January 1883, it seems likely that the conversation took place in 1872 or 1873. For Ben-y-Ghloe see pp. 50 and 66.

61 Achnahannait and its hillock, for which see MacLean 1949, pp. 159–61, are between Camustianavaig and Lower Ollach in the Braes. Forbes says (1923, p. 26): "Six wells said to be here." The precise significance of the term *annaid* to the medieval church has been the subject of much scholarly discussion (e.g. Forbes 1923, pp. 44–49; Watson 1926a, pp. 250–54; MacDonald 1973; Clancy 1995; Watson 2002, pp. 221–22), but the fact that Achnahannait is associated with the Fairies shows that its religious origins were well forgotten.

Dun Gerashader (*Dùn Ghearra-Shiadair*, probably 'the Fort of the Short Out-Pasture') overlooks a bend in the River Cràcaig one mile north of Scorrybreck. After referring obliquely to JGC's rhyme as 'thought generally well known', Forbes says (1923, p. 165): "This dun was once large and imposing, but was demolished by some Goth of a lowlander for bigging dykes!" For cow-names see note 233.

62 Cf. *falbh air chuiseagan treòrach*, 'travelling on tall grass stems', p. 13, and see also 'Fairies and Horses', pp. 77–78. Mrs Sheridan, an old woman at Coole, Co. Galway, told Lady Gregory about the Fairies (1970, p. 58): "I never saw them on horses; but when I came to live at Peter Mahony's he used to bring in those red flowers [ragweed] that grow by the railway, when their stalks were withered, to make the fire. And one day I was out in the road, and two men came over to me and one was wearing a long grey dress. And he said to me, 'We have no horses to ride on and have to go on foot, because you have too much fire.' So then I knew it was their horses we were burning." In his note on this (*ibid.*, p. 356) Yeats seeks to account for it by pointing out that ragweed was once used to make medicine for horses. He also points out that ragweed flowers are yellow, not red; this however is an example of *ruadh* (Irish *rua*) in the Gaelic spectrum, see note 29. Perhaps the best Scottish description of travelling on ragweed stems comes from Mackenzie's tale from Arran of how a farmer called MacMurchie travelled through the sky to Ireland with the Fairies of Cnoc 'ic Eoghain in Druimaghineir (1914, pp. 259–60): *Spìon gach aon diùbh geodhasdan, agus air dhaibh facail dhìomhair aithris, chaidh iad casan-gòbhlach air a' gheodhasdan, agus an àird gabhar iad anns an adhar cho aotrom ri iteig. Rinn Macmhurchaidh an nì ceudna, spìon esan geodhasdan, chaidh e casan-gòbhlach air, agus ag aithris nam briathran-sìthe suas gabhar e as an déidh cho luath 's cho aotrom ri h-aon diubh fhéin.* "Each one of them pulled a ragwort, and having repeated some mystic words they went astride the ragwort, and up they went into the air as light as a feather. MacMurchie did the same thing, he pulled a ragwort, went astride on it, and having repeated the Fairy words up he goes after them as swiftly and lightly as any of themselves."

63 In *SHIS* 31 JGC gave English translation only. In *The Fians*, however (Campbell 1891, p. 202), he indicated clearly that his source was Stewart 1804, p. 560 (in a poem headed 'Corag Bhrain, a's a Choin duibh'). I have therefore supplied the original from that source, slightly edited. JGC's translation in *The Fians* is as follows: "Yellow paws Bran had, / Two black sides, and underneath white, / The back green (on which hunting would rest), / Erect ears strongly red." Clearly the third line is problematic. I would interpret *suidhe sealg* (literally 'seat of hunts') as the rock from which Fionn and his companions directed the chase, and the line as 'Light-green back around their hunting seat'. Bran being an otherworld dog, it is not surprising that his back should be of that colour. The rhyme also appears in MacLellan 1961, pp. 11 and 211, where the third line is simply '*S druim uaine chon na seilge* 'And a green back for the hunt'. See Gray 1987, pp. 98–102.

64 See pp. 56, 63, 64, 76–77 ('Dogs Chasing Fairies').

65 See 'Witches as Cats', pp. 188–92.

66 "That beast has been stabbed/bewitched." For other examples of *gonadh* see p. 154 and Maclagan 1902, pp. 17, 127, 146, 220–21.

67 Alder is brittle, the least useful of all woods. In certain *taghairm* rituals (see p. 167) the shaman, if he may be so described, was seen as being metamorphosed by violent trauma into a log of birchwood or stick of alder (Martin 1716, p. 110 = 1999, p. 76; Ramsay 1888, vol. 2, p. 460). There is a curious parallel with a tradition of the Sulka of New Britain, mentioned by Frazer (1911a, p. 331), that when near the territory of their enemies the Gaktei they spoke of them only as *o lapsiek* 'the rotten tree-trunks', imagining that in this way they made their limbs ponderous and clumsy like logs. See pp. 46 ('The Bridegroom's Burial') and 47 ('Throwing the Arrow'); Dalyell 1834, pp. 263–65; Gregory 1970, p. 114; and compare further this sixteenth-century evidence from Ireland (Malcomson 1868, pp. 191–92): "Witches used to send to ye markets many red swine fair and fat to see unto, as any mought [*sic*] be, and would in that forme continew long, but it chanced the buiers of them to bring them to any water; immediately they found them returned either into wisps of Haye, Straw, old rotten bords, or some other such like trumpery, by meanes whereof they have lost their money, or such other cattel as they gave in exchange for them."

68 By *air a thiomnadh* JGC seems to indicate some such usage as *Tha Iain air a thiomnadh nach eil an t-ìm aige*, "John has sworn that he does not have the butter." Note Dwelly's *tiomain* 'swear by heaven' (1977, p. 952), wrongly ascribed to Armstrong.

69 See p. 535 ('New Year's Day').

70 *Bonnach beag 's toll ann* is 'a little cake with a hole in it', see pp. 10, 19, 25, 127. For the nail motif see also 'Protection against Fairies' (p. 24) and 'Taking Away Cows and Sheep' (p. 49).

71 By *brathainn* JGC seems to be indicating the plural of *brà*, given by Dwelly (1977, p. 111) as *bràthntan*. For *deiseal* see p. 125.

72 For quern-songs see MacPherson 1868, pp. 115–17; *CG2*, p. 305; *Tocher* 13, pp. 174–76; Purser 1992, p. 34. My thanks to John Purser for references. For a quern blessing see *CG1*, pp. 252–57, and for a quern rhyme see GUL MS Gen. 1090/29, pp. 242–43.

73 'A wisp being rubbed against the hand-mill to repay it': JGC's *b(h)rài*, more conventionally *b(h)ràthaidh* or *b(h)rathaidh*, represents the dative case. Cf. 'Saining Straw (*Sop Seile*)', pp. 136–37. The hand-mill of Scripture is in Matt. 24: 41 (cf. Luke 17: 35), "Two women shall be grinding at the mill; the one shall be taken, and the other left." The Gaelic Bible does not handle this well, for it has the women *a' meileadh anns a' mhuilean* ('grinding in the mill').

74 For a graphic instance of how a band of Fairies in hot pursuit was trounced with the contents of the *cuman mùin* see Jackson 1959, pp. 76–77. Jackson translates it as 'chamber-pot', but perhaps 'urine bucket' would be more accurate. Urine was carefully kept for use in

the waulking process. JGC mentions the Fairies' dislike of strong smells at p. 20; see also *Tocher* 22, pp. 242–43, and Bourke 1999, pp. 80, 127.

75 This is a variant of the custom noted by Edward Lhuyd as *Gyrhain leabhair* (*gaoth throimhn leabhar*, 'wind through the book'). According to Kirk(?), Lhuyd, Martin Martin, Mrs Anne Grant and Fr Allan McDonald, the leaves of a Bible were used in various ways to aerate the face of a sick, pregnant or otherwise vulnerable person – 'they clap a Bible frequently on their Faces' (Campbell 1975, p. 66 = Hunter 2001, p. 67), 'they let the leavs fly with their thumb' (Lhuyd in Campbell 1975, pp. 66, 69 = Hunter 2001, p. 67), 'it was to fan the patient's face with the leaves of the book' (Martin 1999, p. 152), 'the bed, containing the mother and the infant, was drawn out on the floor, the attendant took a Bible, and went thrice round it, waving all the time the open leaves' (Grant 1811, vol. 1, p. 166), and 'Harriet MacAskill got a bible and closed it to Marion's face so that the wind might go in her eyes' (Fr Allan in Campbell and Hall 1968, p. 291). Fr Allan's variant is the only one which fully justifies the tag *gaoth throimhn leabhar*. See Opie and Tatem 1992, p. 23.

76 See p. 43 and note 150.

77 See 'Ready Wit Repulses the Fairies' (p. 45) and Campbell 1967–68, pp. 25–26. Exchanges of wit were much admired whether Fairies were involved or not – other good examples may be found in Mackay 1919–22, pp. 13–16, and *Tocher* 14, pp. 235–38. Wentz was given this testimony by a schoolmaster from the Ben Bulbin country in Co. Sligo (1911, p. 58): "The belief in changelings is not now generally prevalent; but in olden times a mother used to place a pair of iron tongs over the cradle before leaving the child alone, in order that the fairies should not change the child for a weakly one of their own. It was another custom to take a wisp of straw, and, lighting one end of it, make a fiery sign of the cross over a cradle before a babe could be placed in it."

78 See note 75.

79 In the general context of 'Knots and Rings Tabooed', Frazer (1911a, p. 296) cites this as one of many examples of its kind from different parts of the world – aiding childbirth by untying every knot in the house, lifting the lids of chests, boxes and pans, presenting the woman with a key, etc. See Dalyell 1834, pp. 302–03, 306–10; Henderson 1911, pp. 250–51; McPherson 1929, p. 216; MacilleDhuibh 13.6.03.

80 Although this couplet scans neatly in English, it also works well in Gaelic – I suspect that it is a translation of something like *Ceirsle ghlas lìn is cìr choilich, / Dà nì an aghaidh nan àithnean.*

81 See Introduction, pp. li–lxvi; MacPhail 1900, pp. 443–44; MacDonald 1994–95, pp. 51–52; note 67 above.

82 See Bruford and MacDonald 1994, pp. 350–51 (where the mode of treatment is to leave the changeling on a sea-rock by the shore as the tide comes in), 474–75. Yet another method is noted by the Rev. Dr Mackintosh MacKay (on paper watermarked 1826, NLS Adv. MS 73.1.14, f. 93v): "A blacksmith is sought for, whose father and grandfather have been of the same craft. He is summoned into his smithy – the infant is laid upon the anvil: – the smith brandishes his heaviest fore-hammer, at full arm-stretch above the infant, vociferating – 'Gobha mi fhéin, gobha m' athair, gobha mo sheanair, chugad an t-òrd mòr!' i.e. 'Smith (am I) myself, smith, my father, smith my grandfather; – flee the great hammer!' The fairies alarmed for the safety of their own real child, repair like lightning to the spot, and the proper child is restored. We need hardly say, that the process of transference is invisible as it is quick; but the parents return home, quite satisfied of its reality, and the child forthwith prospers to a wish, unless overtaken by some other casualty. – This must in justice be spoken of in the *past tense*, for I believe in no corner of the Highlands would it now be thought of, or at least performed; but it is not forty years since, that it was performed in Lochaber; and the sons of the blacksmith of the name of Boyd, who performed it, are still living, and not

old men." Long before, in 1691, a man in the Dumfriesshire parish of Irongray was rebuked by the kirk session 'for bringing his child to a smith to be charmed with ane forge hammer' (Cowan and Henderson 2002, p. 203); see also note 142 and Sutherland 1937, p. 26.

83 A version of this is told by Keightley (1850, p. 365): "The mother puts down eggshells to boil, and to the enquiry of the changeling she tells him that she is brewing them, and clapping his hands he says, 'Well! I'm fifteen hundred years in the world, and I never saw a brewery of eggshells before!'" Keightley calls the story the Brewery of Eggshells and says that it is found 'in many places, even in Brittany and Auvergne'. Indeed, the motif occurs twice in MacDougall and Calder 1910 – in 'Torr-a-Bhuilg', pp. 100–03, and in 'Sìthiche Choire Osbainn agus an Tàillear' ('The Fairy of Corrie Osben and the Tailor'), pp. 154–57. In 'Torr-a-Bhuilg' the woman brings in a basket of eggs and places them in a circle on the floor. "What are you doing in that manner?" says the changeling. "I am making a brewing cauldron (*coire-togalach*)," she replies. "A brewing cauldron? I am more than three hundred years old and I never yet saw a brewing cauldron like that!" In the Corrie Osben story the tailor fills an eggshell with water and places it by the fire; in answer to the changeling's inevitable question he replies, *Tha mi a' dol a theasachadh uisge a bhogadh bracha*. "I am going to heat water to steep malt in." See notes 142, 208; Croker 1825–28, vol. 1, pp. 65–71, and vol. 3, p. 296; Campbell 1890, vol. 2, p. 58; Wentz 1911, pp. 204, 212; Mac Philib 1991, pp. 128–29; Munro 1997, pp. 261–62, 273, 278; GUL MS Gen. 1090/28, p. 101.

84 See Introduction, p. xxxvii.

85 'Howdie' or 'howdy', the Scots word for a midwife, is thought to derive from Old English *hold* 'gracious'.

86 See for example Bruford and MacDonald 1994, pp. 359–61, 476.

87 'Sithiche' was critical of this passage, saying (1912, p. 335): "The identity of the Bean-Nighe with the Bean-Shìth here implied seems hardly tenable in view of the other beliefs about the Bean-Nighe and the highly specific characteristics attributed to her. It is like the confusion between the fairies on the one hand, and kelpies, glaistigs, spirits, witches, and other creatures on the other hand, of which J. G. Campbell himself complains in his *Superstitions*, 3, *et seq.*, 45, 49, *et seq.*"

Coming from a commentator who appears to confuse himself with a Fairy, this is remarkably unfair. A *bean shìth* is any otherworld woman; the *bean nighe* is a specific otherworld woman. For the record, the passages to which he refers may be found at pp. 2–4, 23 ('Glaistig') and 26–27 of the present edition. The *bean-nighe* is described by Carmichael (*CG*2, pp. 227–29), Mac Thomais (1937–41, pp. 183–85) and MacDonald (1958b, p. 125); for lists of references see Ó Duilearga 1981, p. 402 (no. 133), and Lysaght 1996, pp. 387–88.

88 This happens, for example, in the tale 'Gille nan Cochla-Craicinn' ('The Lad of the Skin Coverings'), MacDougall 1891, pp. 36–37, 50–51, 269. The motif, T671 Adoption by Suckling ('Ogress who suckles hero claims him as her son', Thompson 1955–58, vol. 5, p. 415), is internationally widespread, see Maier 1999. See also p. 237; MacInnes 1890, pp. 238–40, 50, 269; Sithiche 1912, pp. 206–18, 335, 356; O'Brien 1938, pp. 372–73; Campbell 1940–60, vol. 1, p. 501; Mackechnie 1964, pp. 309–10.

89 'Dreeing this weird' = 'enduring this fate'.

90 JGC is here referring to an incident that preceded Cath Gabhra, the last battle of the Féinn, for which see 'The Battle of Gaura', pp. 283–84. It is described in 'Cath Gabhra, no Laoidh Oscair', which JGC took down from the dictation of Roderick Macfadyen, Scarinish, Tiree, in October 1868.

> *A bhaobh a nigheas an t-eudach,*
> *Deansa dhuinne 'n fhaistneachd cheudna,*
> *An tuit aon duine dhiu leinn,*
> *No 'n d' theid sinn uile do neo-ni.*

> *Marbhar leats' (ars ise) caogad ceud,*
> *'S gonar leat an righ e fein,*
> > *'S a raogha nam fear a laigheas leat,*
> > *A shaoghal uile gu'n d' thainig.*

JGC translates: "Weird woman that washest the garments, / Make for us the self-same prophecy, / Will any one of them fall by us, / Or shall we all go to nothingness? / There will be slain by thee, she said, nine hundred, / And the King himself, be wounded to death by thee, / And the choicest man that falls on thy side / All his lifetime has come." *Caogad ceud* is not 'nine hundred' but 'fifty hundred'. See Campbell 1891, pp. 31, 33–34, 39–40, and Sithiche 1912, p. 199.

91 See 'Hugh of the Little Head (*Eoghan a' Chinn Bhig*)', pp. 235–39.

92 *The Lady of the Lake*, canto 3: "Late had he heard, in prophet's dream, / The fatal Ben-Shie's boding scream."

93 See pp. 82–98.

94 These lines appear to be from a version, not of the ballad 'Thomas the Rhymer', but of the Cambridge manuscript (University Library MS Ff.5.48) of the fifteenth-century English romance 'Thomas of Erceldoune' (see note 487 below), modernised from a rather defective text published by Jamieson (1806, vol. 2, p. 17):

> > *Hir hare that hong upon hir hed,*
> > *The tother was black, the tother gray.*

> > *And all hir clothis were away*
> > *That he before saw in that stede;*
> > *Hir een semyd out that were so gray,*
> > *And alle hyr body like the lede.*

This manuscript is almost illegible in places from damp, and Jamieson was heavily criticised by a later scholar, J. O. Halliwell (1845, p. 57), for further defacing it with 'an infusion of galls' in trying to read it. However, a definitive text has now been established by Nixon (1980–83, vol. 1, p. 37):

> > *hir here þat hong vpon hir hed,*
> > *hir een semyd out, þat were so gray,*
> > *And alle hir clothis were a way,*
> > *þat here before saw in þat stede,*
> > *þe too þe blak, þe toþer gray,*
> > *þe body bloo as beten leed.*

The lines occur at the point in the story where Thomas has encountered a 'lady gay' at the Eildon Tree. Ignoring her protests that this will spoil her beauty, he makes love to her seven times. He then stands up, looks down upon her, and this is what he sees. The mid-fifteenth-century Thornton MS from Yorkshire (Lincoln Cathedral MS 91), the best and probably the earliest of the five sources of the romance, has the passage as follows (Murray 1875, p. 8; Nixon 1980–83, vol. 1, p. 36):

> > *Hir hare it hange all ouer hir hede,*
> > *Hir eghne semede owte, þat are were graye,*
> > *and alle þe riche clothynge was a waye,*

> *þat he by fore sawe in þat stede,*
> *hir a schanke blake, hir oþer graye,*
> *And all hir body lyke the lede.*

It is possible that JGC got his version of the lines from one of the numerous chapbook texts of the prophecies of Thomas Rhymer which were published in Scotland and England during the seventeenth, eighteenth and nineteenth centuries. According to Murray (1875, p. xlii), by the early nineteenth century 'few farm-houses in Scotland were without a copy of the mystic predictions of the Rhymer and his associates'. Some of these included modernised versions of the romance itself. *Sundry Strange Prophecies of Merlin, Bede and Others* (London, 1652) has (Nixon 1980–83, vol. 2, p. 94):

> *Her haire hung about her head,*
> *Her eyes seemed out, that were so grey.*
> *All her clothing then was away,*
> *That he before saw in that stead,*
> *One leg was black, the other grey,*
> *And al her body like to lead.*

The precise relationship between the romance and the ballad has been the subject of much discussion. The most recent authority, Nixon, concludes simply (1980–83, vol. 2, p. 43): "It seems likely that the story of Thomas and the lady existed in some form before the romance as it stands was put together."

95   See 'Prophecies (*Fàisneachd*): Thomas the Rhymer', pp. 147–49.

96   Frazer (1911a, pp. 230–33) cites this paragraph, and most of the following one, as part of his discussion of the worldwide tabu against iron, which, he suggests, 'perhaps dates from that early time in the history of society when iron was still a novelty, and as such was viewed by many with suspicion and dislike'. I do not understand how it is to be reconciled with the Fairies' working with iron and having smithies, see 'Their Occupations', p. 8. The Fairy aversion to iron is also discussed by Spence (1948, pp. 181–82).

97   See 'Taking Away Cows and Sheep', p. 49.

98   When a sinister otherworld woman attempts to seduce him in a shieling bothy, a hunter first draws his dirk from its sheath and lays it across his knees, then takes two trumps (*dà thruimb*) out of his pocket and begins to play. The woman says:

> *Is math an ceòl a tha 'san truimb*
> *Mur bhi am pong a tha 'na déidh:—*
> *Is math le fear d' an cuid i bhi*
> *'Na ghob an àite té.*

This is the exact spelling used by MacDougall and Calder (1910, p. 258) in telling the tale, 'An Ceathrar Shealgair is an Ceathrar Ghlaistig' ('The Four Hunters and the Four Glastigs'). Their translation (p. 259) is: "Good is the music of the trump, / Saving the one note in its train. / Its owner likes it in his mouth / In preference to any maid." They do not attempt to offer an explanation for the second line, but JGC's reference to the tongue of the instrument provides one. If we emend *am pong* ('the note') to *a' phuing* ('the point, tongue'), which provides rhyme for *truimb*, we may translate: "The music in the trump is good / Save for the tongue in its behind – / Its owner much prefers to have / It in his mouth than any girl." The hunter ignores this highly provocative remark, and carries on playing. This story is a variant of 'MacPhie's Black Dog' (pp. 58–64). For the trump motif see p. 64; Lang 1891, pp. 58–59; SoSS Maclagan MSS vol. 22, pp. 3854–55.

99 See pp. 10, 19, 39, 136 ('Empty Shells'), 202, 562.

100 Martin 1716, p. 117 = 1999, p. 80.

101 See pp. 18, 19, 127; GUL MS Gen. 1090/28, p. 257. For oatmeal as a safeguard against Fairies see Mackenzie 1914, pp. 269, 270, e.g. a married man was having an affair with a Fairy; his wife consulted a wise woman, who told her 'to watch when her husband was preparing to visit the fairy, and, as he was leaving the house, to sprinkle oatmeal on his back, unknown to him; this would have the effect of making him see his second love to be very ugly, and he would at once leave her' – which is what happened.

102 Carleton 1854, pp. 73–74: "Wherever a meal is eaten upon the grass in the open field, and the crumbs are not shaken down upon the spot for their use, there they are sure to leave one of their curses, called the *fair gurtha*, or the hungry-grass; for whoever passes over that particular spot for ever afterwards is liable to be struck down with weakness and hunger, and unless he can taste a morsel of bread he neither will nor can recover. The weakness in this instance, however, is not natural; for if the person affected [*sic*] but tastes as much meal or flour as would lie on the point of a penknife, he will instantaneously break the spell of the fairies, and recover his former strength. Such spots are said to be generally known by their superior verdure; they are always round, and the diameter of these little circles is seldom more than a single step. The grass that grows upon them is called as we have said, *hungry-grass*, and is accounted for as we have already stated." See p. 637 below.

Lady Gregory was told by a gatekeeper of a man who came through the gate as it was getting dark, then came to his door, came in and fell down on a chair (1970, p. 205). "And when I saw him shaking and his face so white, I thought it was the *fear gortha* (the hungry grass) he had walked on, and I called to the wife to give him something to eat."

The man said no, that the fright he had got was from a man and a woman appearing as he passed the big tree and falling silently into step with him, one on either side; the woman seemed to go away, but 'the man's step was with him till he came in at the gate'. It is, then, a *cachaileith* story, see pp. 75, 254, 275.

103 See pp. lvii, 19, 177, 203, 248, 537, 553.

104 See pp. 42, 55, 179, 229–31, 265.

105 John Knox wrote in the 1540s of 'the Bible lying upon almost every gentleman's table', and during the seventeenth century the Geneva Bible and the Catechism became the most widely used school text-books in Scotland. These developments took about a century to affect the Highlands. Many Highland gentlemen obtained Bibles during the religious controversies of the 1640s, and the Scriptures in English began to become accessible to the poor from the time the Society in Scotland for the Propagation of Christian Knowledge established its first schools in the Highlands in 1709. The New Testament in Gaelic was printed in 1767, and the last of four volumes of the Old Testament in 1801. Even then, however, the Bible had still not become in the Highlands (as in the Lowlands) a book which ordinary people owned, read and brought to church, and the work of putting cheap English and Gaelic Bibles into the hands of the people remained to be completed by organisations such as the Edinburgh Bible Society during the years 1809–43. These Scriptures 'received an extraordinary welcome from the Highlanders', but JGC's point about 'blind, unmeaning reverence' serves as an antidote to those who assume that this welcome involved a perfect understanding (Cameron 1993, pp. 71–73). While classical Gaelic survived, the Scriptures were in Latin; while a perfect knowledge of Gaelic yet remained to a largely monoglot society, the Scriptures were in English; by the time they were available in Gaelic, that language was being whipped out of children's heads. It is no wonder if the Bible was seen at all times as mysterious and magical.

106 JGC's spelling of the name is *Luran Mac-ille-dhui*. Both parts are of interest. *Luran* looks less like a baptismal name than a nickname or 'semi-proper noun' of the same type as

feminine *Lurag*, for which see Black 2002, pp. 19–21 – 'Pretty Boy', perhaps. *Mac-ille-dhui* is either a surname or a patronymic, i.e. *An Gille Dubh* may have been not Luran's eponymous ancestor but his father, in which case a spelling like *Luran mac 'Ille Dhuibh* would have been appropriate. However, we must assume that as JGC offers a translation 'Luran Black' he had heard that it was a surname.

107 *An Cuilibheir* was a common term in seventeenth-century Gaelic for a gun – from French *couloevre* 'snake'. Perhaps, like such a gun, this knoll was very long and straight, and thicker at one end than the other. Due to the shortage of suitable roof-timbers the houses of the period were long and narrow, so it is not surprising if a long narrow hillock became known as a *sìthein*. Corryvulin (for which see also p. 248) was the home during 1739–45 of the poet Alastair mac Mhgr Alastair (Alexander MacDonald) and the stated location of his song 'Allt an t-Siùcair' ('The Sugar Burn'), see Black 1986a, p. 31.

108 Donald Mackinnon, a South Uist man in Barra, told Wentz (1911, p. 106): "I have heard that the fairies used to *take* cattle and leave their old men rolled up in the hides. One night an old witch was heard to say to the fairies outside the fold, 'We cannot get anything to-night.' The old men who were left behind in the hides of the animals *taken*, usually disappeared very suddenly." Although it sounds shamanic (cf. note 571), the purpose is to perform a rite not of divination but of metamorphosis – the old Elf is made into the changeling of a cow, and a dead one at that, cf. 'Taking Away Cows and Sheep', p. 49. The comic element, less obvious to us perhaps than to the original ceilidh-house audience, is intentional. Tailors were frequently the butt of jokes.

109 A *còrn* is a cup made from a horn.

110 This reflects a very strong tabu against counting people or property, more especially on a Friday or when, as here, the number three was involved. See pp. 127, 568; MacGregor 1901, p. 35; Mackechnie 1964, pp. 122, 309; GUL MS Gen. 1090/29, p. 88. In fishing communities the tabu extended to boats and fish (Cameron 1903, p. 303). The converse is that styes in the eye, for example, were 'counted out' in order to get rid of them, see p. 225. In an Islay story recorded in 1971 (*Tocher* 1, pp. 26–27), a man's field of oats was reaped by the Fairies (*na sìbhridh*) every year and left for him in stooks (*adagan*). One year he decided to stay up at night and watch what happened. Night after night he watched, and eventually they came and set to work. After a while he approached them and a Fairy (*sìbhreach*) said: *Bheil thu gar cunntas?* "Are you counting us?" *Tha*, he said. "Yes." *Well*, said the Fairy, *tha sinn ann*: "Well, there are of us," and he said this rhyme, designed no doubt to demonstrate that counting Fairies is impossible:

> *Ceithir sèithean, ceithir seachd,*
> *Ceithir fir dheug 's a h-ochd,*
> *Naoi ciad 's a cóig deug —*
> *Se sen a-mhàin na th' air a' ghart.*

("Four sixes, four sevens, / Fourteen men and eight, / Nine hundred and fifteen – / That's all that's in the field.") And, the storyteller (Calum MacLachlan, a native of Kilchoman, Islay) concludes, *cha daich a' phàirc a bhuain riamh tuilleadh, on a bha e cunntas nan daoine. Chan eil còir agad a bhith cunntas dhaoine ann.* "The field was never reaped again, as he was counting the people. You should never count people."

111 *An cupa cearrarach*, properly *ceathrarach*, is 'the foursome cup' – its brim is square so that four people may drink from it in turn, each using his own side, see MacDougall 1891, pp. 30, 44–45, 267, and Grant 1959, pp. 185, 261–63, plate 1a. The *cupa c(h)eatharnaich* ('soldier's cup') in a tale noted by JGC is probably a corruption of the term (Campbell 1909–10b, pp. 371–74); he translates it three times as 'the warrior's cup' and once as

simply 'the *ceatharnach* cup' (Campbell 1906–07, pp. 7–9). Such cups are generally called *meadaran* or 'methers'. The National Museums of Scotland have seventeen, all apparently Irish, and the National Museum of Ireland has a very large number indeed.

I. F. Grant (1959, p. 262) tells a Harris version of the story from the Bannatyne MS to explain the presence in Dunvegan of Rory Mor's mether, the inscription on which shows that it was made in Fermanagh in 1493. In this version Luran's mother is a witch, and after he has brought the cup back to the house, she casts protective spells over him whenever he goes out. "But one day he went out without this protection and he was killed by the fairies. Eventually his mother gave the fairy cup to her foster-son and it was seized by his brother Nial Glundubh when the latter, infuriated by continued losses among his cattle, killed his brother and took all his possessions. The witch thereupon complained to MacLeod, who came to Luskintyre, executed the murderer, confiscated his possessions and took the Cup back with him to Dunvegan."

See also Mackenzie 1897–98, pp. 49–53.

112 *Rubha a' Mhàil* (Rhuvaal, 'Rent Point') is the northern tip of Islay.

113 Auchnabobane (strictly *Achadh na Bà Bàine*) is two miles west of Spean Bridge on the A82 Fort William road. Brackletter (*Breacleitir*, 'Rough Broken-Up Slope') is a mile further north.

114 The original Gaelic words, or something very like them, feature in a Uist story which involves not only Luran (as a human being), but also a man who bore the ironic nickname *Niall na Fìrinn* ('Truthful Neil') and is almost certainly to be identified with *Niall Sgrob*, for whom see p. 37. In this version (Campbell 1967–68, p. 25) Luran – or Luthran, as the name is spelt in this source – is a weaver. Chased by Niall na Fìrinn with a band of Fairies, he outruns them all and takes refuge in a house. He hears his pursuers singing:

> *O nach luath Luthran,*
> *Mur b'e cruadhas arain —*
> *Nam b'e lite bu bhiadh do Luthran*
> *Cha bheireadh am fiadh air Luthran.*

("O how swift Luran is, / Had it not been the firmness of his bread – / Were porridge Luran's food / Not even the deer could overtake Luran.") After this he takes to eating porridge instead of hard oatcake, and gradually loses his strength, as the Fairies hoped. When they get the chance they chase him again and this time they catch him, but as they have found this so easy to do they simply chastise him and let him go. See also MacPhail 1897, p. 385. Curiously, a *Dòmhnall na Fìrinn* from Balephetrish in Tiree is listed in an account of the surrender of weapons at Scarinish on 23 April 1716 (Maclean-Bristol 1998, p. 119): "Donald na ffirine / has no arms."

115 The two types of Luran story are defined by MacDonald (1994–95, pp. 54, 57) as 'Cup Stolen from Fairies' (F96) and 'Malicious Advice from Fairy' (F128), see p. 732 below. See also *Tocher* 13, pp. 172–75, *Tocher* 28, pp. 218–19, and Bruford and MacDonald 1994, pp. 300–03, 467. For 'Drinking Cup Stolen from the Fairies' (ML 6045) see Almqvist 1991a, p. 15, and Ó Catháin 1991, pp. 149–50.

116 JGC tells us ('Dogs', p. 16 above) that Fionn's otherworld dog Bran had a venomous shoe (*bròg nimhe*) with which it killed whatever living creature it struck, so it may be speculated that *Farbhann* is *far-bhonn*, the fore-sole of a shoe.

117 JGC lists *bac* at p. 6 as the third of eight topographical terms which have otherworld associations. The name *Fionnlagh* (Finlay) also appears to have had a particular connection with the Fairies, as they were often called *muinntir Fhionnlaigh* ('Finlay's people') in Lewis, cf. MacPhail 1896, p. 402, and Anon 1908–09a, pp. 157–58, 170. The explanation may lie in

the notoriety of 'Finlay the Changeling' (Donald A. MacKenzie 1935, pp. 120–30), or in a story which tells how the Fairies helped a man with his spring labour, but took away his entire harvest as their reward, upon which he tells them in despair (MacPhail 1900, p. 442): *Is miosa dh'fhàg na fhuair, oir tha sibh cho lìonmhor ri muinntir Fhionnlaigh.* "You've left worse than you found, for you're as numerous as Finlay's people." *Muinntir* is not so much a clan or tribe as a gang or retinue, and will be a reference to the Norsemen, or perhaps to some piratical band of Norse blood. W. C. Mackenzie stretched the evidence much further (1905, p. 267), arguing that the Fairies, the Lapps and the 'pigmies' of Eilean nan Lùchraban in Ness are one and the same, i.e. that a Finnish or Lapponic race once existed in the British Isles and that *muinntir Fhionnlaigh* are 'the little Finn people'.

118   The evidence of other versions (for which see note 120) suggests that the second line should probably read *Gus iarann fuar a chur a-mach* 'For producing cold iron'.

119   Although its meaning is obscure as it stands, this verse clearly contains matter of great interest, so I have left JGC's original and translation entirely unedited in order to provide a 'neutral' text for discussion. With regard to the first line, the reference is to the smith's wife, indeed all other versions have not *Gheur* but *bhean*. JGC reads *Geur* as a semi-proper noun 'Sharp One'; if this is so, one wonders why it is not *Geurag*. The choice appears to be between *Gheur* ('Sharp One'), *bhean* ('woman, wife') and *gheàrr* ('hare'). For it to be *bhean* one would have to argue that JGC was unable to read his own field-notes. *Gheur* and *gheàrr*, on the other hand, are homophonous when the stress is on a following adjective, as here. There are three good reasons why the Fairy should call the woman a hare: she is running fast, it is not Fairies but mortal witches who have the reputation of turning into hares (see p. 188), and he is about to set the dog(s) on her. Further, as there is no reason why he should address her directly, I imagine that the phrase is in the nominative and not the vocative case, which would mean that in the second line we should probably read *Thàin' i* or *Thàinig i* ('She came').

Tìr na(m) marbh ('the land of the dead') is extremely interesting. It is also the reading of Anon., Fear nan Sgeul, Mackenzie and *Tocher*, while MacPhail's is *tìr nam fear màrbh* 'the land of the dead men', JFC's is *tìr nan sealg* ('the land of chase', literally 'the land of the hunts'), and Carmichael's is *tìr nan sgarbh* ('the land of the cormorants'), which makes little sense, I think, despite the predilection of witches for turning into that bird (pp. 174, 183, 193). Mac Gilleathain (1945, p. 244) gives *Thàinig bean o thìr nam marbh* 'A woman has come from the land of the dead'. We have to accept, then, that *tìr nam marbh* is the correct reading, and ask why the Fairy should use it of the land of mortals. The question is easily answered, for man is indeed mortal, while in the otherworld time does not exist, and its denizens live for ever (see MacInnes 1994–96, p. 7).

The third line varies considerably from version to version, and is missing altogether in MacPhail's, but here it is unproblematic, except that we should perhaps supply a subject for the verb – *dh'fhuadaich i* 'she drove, she kidnapped' (see p. lxvi). The fourth line is excellent in the original, but the translation is a little garbled; some versions turn *an dul* ('the noose, loop, catch') into a second dog called *an Dubh* 'the Black' or *an Guth* 'the Voice', while Fear nan Sgeul, Mac Gilleathain and MacPhail give: *Fosgail* [*or Fuasgail*] *an Dubh is leig an Dearg!* "Open [*or* Release] the Black and let go the Red!" All in all, then, I would present the verse as follows:

> *A' gheàrr bhalbh ud 's a' gheàrr bhalbh,*
> *Thàin' i oirnn á tìr nam marbh,*
> *Dh'fhuadaich i 'n coir' on bhrugh —*
> *Fuasgail an dul is leig an Garbh!*

("Yon dumb hare and the dumb hare, / She's come on us from the land of the dead, / She's kidnapped the kettle from the house – / Slip the catch and release Ferocious!")

120 Campbell 1860–62, vol. 2, pp. 42–45 = 1890, vol. 2, pp. 52–55. Other versions: Fear nan Sgeul 1896; MacPhail 1897, pp. 381–82; Anon. 1908–09a, pp. 155–56, 170–71; Mackay 1927a; Mac Gilleathain 1945, pp. 244, 246; *CG*5, pp. 240–43; *Tocher* 13, pp. 196–201 = Bruford and MacDonald 1994, pp. 339–41, 474; cf. also Campbell 1895, p. 84. William Mackenzie (1891–92, p. 176) cites our stanza as a charm against strangury in cattle. JFC's 'Sanntrai' is Sandray, *Sanndraigh*, south of Vatersay.

121 The name is strictly *Peighinn a' Ghobhainn* 'the Pennyland of the Smith'. For an account of the system of land measurement which underlies it see Dwelly 1977, s.v. *peighinn*. As elsewhere, JGC's reference here is to a *quoad sacra* parish, the civil parishes in Mull being Kilninian & Kilmore, Torosay, and Kilfinichen & Kilviceon.

122 There is no loch on Ben Lomond. There is, however, a pool of very clear water, still called the Fairy Loch, a short distance up the steep slope from the shore on the opposite side of Loch Lomond, a mile north of Inverbeg. It is marked on Charles Ross's 1777 map of Dunbartonshire as 'Lochuane'. Beside it was a mill. The people used to leave their new-spun wool there overnight, and would return in the morning to find the Fairies had dyed it the desired colour; this came to an end when a witch left black wool with instructions to dye it white (information from Luss Visitor Centre, with thanks to Sheila Henderson, Balmaha). A minister of Arrochar, Hugh Sinclair Winchester, explains (1916, p. 12) how the women brought their yarn to the Fairy Loch and, placing it in the water, told the colour they wanted, left a small gift for the Fairy and went away. "And next morning, as soon as the sun peeped over the shoulder of Ben Lomond there was the web perfectly dyed in the colour which was asked . . . One day an evil-minded shepherd resolved to play the fairy a trick. He came at evening carrying a black fleece, and throwing it into the water he asked that the black fleece might be dyed white." The Fairy fled, but first spilled her colours into the loch, where they may still be seen, as Winchester says (*ibid.*, p. 13), 'glittering on the surface of the quiet water on a summer evening'.

Over and over in *The Gaelic Otherworld* lochans covered in water-weeds are shown to have supernatural associations, see pp. 55, 109, 111, and note 796. In the story 'Gille nan Cochla-Craicinn' ('The Lad of the Skin Coverings') a *Lochan Uaine* at the foot of *Beinn Eudain* was used by the Féinn for long-jump contests (MacDougall 1891, pp. 32, 47). *Beinn Eudain* is in origin *Binn Éadair*, the Hill of Howth near Dublin, but no doubt it was understood in Argyll to be *Beinn Iadain* in Morvern, see pp. 43, 80, 251. See also Gray 1987, p. 163. Speaking of the name *Lochan Uaine* in general, MacDougall says (*ibid.*, p. 268): "A small pond overgrown with grass is so called . . . The leafy marsh (*boga duilich*) is the soft-bottomed margin of the lake with the leaves of water-plants floating on the surface."

For the motif of setting the Fairies an impossible or unreasonable task, compare William Mackay's story of the *Gobha Sìth* (Fairy Smith) of Tornashee (*Tòrr na Sìdhe* 'the Otherworld Hill') in Glenurquhart (1914, pp. 429–30). Anyone in the glen who wanted a reaping-hook, spade or other such implement only had to leave a piece of iron at a stone in Tornashee wood in the evening, along with an offering, and in the morning the required article would be awaiting him. At last, however, a certain person left a wooden lint-beater to be converted into an iron mallet. When he came back the beater was untouched, and as he picked it up an echo reached his ear:

> *Cha shimid e, cha shimid e*
> *Ach maide-buailidh lìn,*
> *'S buille cha dèan mise tuille*
> *An coille Thòrr na Sìdh'.*

("It's no mallet, it's no mallet / But a stick for beating lint, / And I'll not strike another blow / In the wood of Tornashee.") Needless to say, the services of the *Gobha Sìth* were lost for ever; note the similarity of *maide-buailidh lìn* to *mhaide bhola lìon* in the previous section.

123 See p. 10. Port Vista (from Norse *vist* 'west') is in Kilmoluag, north-west of Loch Bhasapol. The Léig drains through Kilmoluag into Loch Bhasapol from the south-west (see note 196). When east coast fishermen came to Port Vista (see 'Boat Language', p. 131, and Maclean 1843, p. 215) they called it 'The Green'. At p. 114 Calum Mòr is described as living in *Baile nan Cràganach*; this will be *Baile nan Crògan* in Cornaigmore. The house must have been somewhere between the two places, where there is only blown sand today. JGC's 'six generations ago' suggests that Calum Mòr lived in the period *c.* 1700, and this is precisely confirmed by the account of a surrender of weapons at Scarinish on 24 April 1716. Under the heading 'Beist' (*Bhiosta*) we find that he had taken part with the MacLeans in the rising of 1715 (Maclean-Bristol 1998, p. 150): "Malcolm Clerk / gave in two guns & a pistol / he is to give in a gun which he did thereafter."

Niall M. Brownlie tells me that the only Clarks in Tiree in more recent times were in Ruaig, six miles away in the east of the island. For full discussion of the name *Port Bhiosta(dh)* see MacDougall and Cameron n.d., pp. 93–94.

124 "It was painfully sore."

125 *Lochan Nighean Shomhairle* is 'the Lochan of Sorley's Daughter'. No doubt the name commemorates a drowning. The loch is not known to Niall M. Brownlie, and is not marked on the six-inch Ordnance Survey map of Tiree (1883). Probably, like Clark's own farm (see p. 114), it had disappeared by then under the 'Blown Sand & Bent' – JGC's 'blowing sandbanks' – marked as lying between Loch Bhasapol and the sea. Though unknown nowadays in Tiree, the name *Somhairle* ('Sorle') was widespread there in 1716, see Maclean-Bristol 1998, pp. 123, 127, 128, 145. At the south end of Tràigh nan Gillean on the western shore of Tiree there is a rock on the low tide line called *Eilean t-Somhairle*; 100 yards further out is a reef called *Bogha Eilean t-Somhairle*.

126 This is the Rip Van Winkle story (see Bruford 1980, p. 55). The motif is characterised by MacDonald (1994–95, p. 46): "Man goes into fairy dwelling and spends year or more there dancing with cask or basket on his back." It is clear from JGC's examples that 'cask or basket' should be defined more broadly. See also Macbain 1887–88, p. 243; MacPhail 1900, pp. 442–43; Anon. 1908–09a, p. 169; Mackenzie 1914, pp. 266–67; Sutherland 1937, pp. 24–25; MacDonald 1958b, p. 121; *Tocher* 9, pp. 20–23 (a Morvern version localised in *Beinn Fhiadain*, i.e. Beinn Iadain); Bruford and MacDonald 1994, pp. 327–30, 472; Bruford 1994–95. *Leathad nan Clacha Mòra* is, I understand, the steep slope negotiated by the Tarbert–Stornoway road where it descends to Scaladale in North Harris, and in fact *Lochan nan Clach Mòra* is marked on Ordnance Survey maps in that location (one mile south of Ardvourlie Bay on Loch Seaforth).

127 The spelling *Fhearchair 'ic Nèill* could be held to imply a patronymic ('Farquhar son of Neil') rather than a surname, but the translation 'Farquhar MacNeill' is JGC's, and we have to assume that it is correct.

128 For the tale (but not the incident) see Campbell 1881a; Mackay 1927–28, especially pp. 4–5, 34–35, 77; Campbell 1940–60, vol. 1, pp. 2–27; Bruford 1969, p. 158. For the incident (and further references) see Ó Duilearga 1981, pp. 113–14, 384.

129 Miss Joina MacDonald, Horgabost and Glasgow, tells me (personal communications, 1 December 2003 and 6 February 2004) that traditions about Fairies in Manish focus upon *a' Chreag Shianta* ('the Enchanted Rock'), the only stone of any note in the neighbourhood. It lies a few yards south of the Manish township road. She points out that it is likely to have been called *Creag Mhànais* ('Manish Rock') by outsiders. There are cracks in it which could be likened to a door. Curiously, Ordnance Survey maps show another name in the vicinity, *Cnoc na Brathan* ('Quern Hill'), which reflects the topic of JGC's story. Joina's father, Donald

MacDonald (*Dòmhnall Sham*, i.e. *Dòmhnall Shomhairle mhic Ruairidh mhic Dhòmhnaill mhic Eoghain mhic Dhòmhnaill*), who was born in Manish and spent much time there as a child, has not heard the name *Cnoc na Brathan*. He points out that the hill above *a' Chreag Shianta* is *an Cnoc Buidhe*, and tells a story about a dog the Fairies had – one of the Manish people saw it going back into the rock, then heard the dog yelping (*a' sgiamhail*) while the Fairies were giving it a leathering (*ga shlaiseadh*) for running away!

130   For the *fallaid* see note 413. By saying that the woman should not put it back 'among the baking', the old man appears to mean that instead of making a *bonnach boise* or *bonnach fallaid* with it (as was traditional), she should break the best-known rule of baking and put it back in the meal-kist. It would sour the meal supply and she would soon be finished. This is by no means clear in JGC's telling, but we may assume I think that his story is basically identical to 'An Nighean a dh' Fhalmhaich Ciste-Mhine Do-Thraoghadh nan Sìthichean' ('The Girl who Emptied the Inexhaustible Meal-Chest of the Fairies') in MacDougall and Calder 1910, pp. 158–61. In this, the girl meets 'an old woman who had been carried off by the fairies in her youth, and who had been so long there that she had lost all hope of ever getting out'. She advises: *Gach uair a tha thusa a' sgur a dheasachadh, tha thu a' deanamh arain de'n fhallaid mu dheireadh. Ach an déidh so cuir thusa an fhallaid air a h-ais anns a' chiste, agus chì thu gu'n teirig na tha innte de mhin ann an ùine ghoirid.* "Every time you cease baking, you are making bread of the remaining sprinkling of meal. But, after this, put the sprinkling of meal back into the chest, and you will see that it will be emptied of all the meal it contains in a short time." In the story as heard by Donald MacDonald, Horgabost (*Dòmhnall Sham*), it was the other way round: she must not put the *fallaid* back into the barrel, because then the meal would never run out (Joina MacDonald, personal communication, 6 February 2004; thus also MacDonald 1958b, pp. 121–22). See MacDonald 1994–95, p. 49.

131   Cf. p. 78 and Anon. 1908–09a, p. 169.

132   By 'smuggling' JGC means *cùl-mhùtaireachd*, the illicit distillation of whisky. On being lifted by the *sluagh* see Dalyell 1834, pp. 591–92; Bruford and MacDonald 1994, pp. 358–59, 476. Our sources seldom make a direct connection between 'lifting by the Fairies' and madness, but it can be traced in one of W. B. Yeats's essays (Welch 1993, p. 209): "A man whose son is believed to go out riding among them at night tells me that he is careless about everything, and lies in bed until it is late in the day. A doctor believes this boy to be mad."

133   This township is in Gaelic *Sathalum* or *Sathalam*, and is marked on maps as Salum. The final *-n* in SHIS 69 must be a misprint. It will be from Norse *sal* 'sea' and *holmr* 'island'. According to Fr Allan McDonald (GUL MS Gen. 1090/29, p. 244, cf. McDonald 1958, p. 222), Niall Sgrob is the name given to the person who went at the head of the procession of the *sluagh*. He adds: *Niall Sgrob air thoiseach an t-sluaigh.* ("Niall Sgrob at the front of the *sluagh*.") See also Black 1999, pp. 154–55.

134   The farm of Eileirig or Eillearaig, on the northernmost shore of Coll between Bousd and Sorisdale, was the birth-place of the writer, poet and folklorist Hector MacDougall, 1889–1954 (MacDougall and Cameron n.d., p. 55). The Ordnance Survey six-inch map of 1881 shows the bay filled at low tide by *Tràigh Eileraig*, with quite a substantial island called *Eilean Eileraig* half-filling its mouth. Ardlàraich or Ardlarich is near the west end of Loch Rannoch, on the north shore opposite Eilean nam Faoileag.

135   Achabeg is two miles west of Lochaline. The river will be the Savary, beyond which is the farm of Savary (misprinted Sasory, SHIS 72). We may assume that *Sìthein Luran na Leaghadh* was connected in some way with the shadowy figure of Luran, all the stories about whom (pp. 28–30) involve an encounter of some sort with the Fairies. Strictly *Luran na Leaghadh* means 'Luran of the Meltings', but it may be that, as at p. 168, we should read *Luran na Leoghadh* 'Luran of the Manglings', see note 575.

136 Inveresragan was misprinted Invererragan in *SHIS* 72. It is five miles east of Connel Ferry on the north shore of Loch Etive, and was once famous for its yew (Smith 1787, p. 8; Fergusson 1877–78, pp. 150–51; *CG2*, p. 359; Grant 1925, p. 57; Nicolson 1951, p. 69; Newton 1998–2000, p. 295). Fort William is twenty-five miles away as the crow flies, and was probably best reached by sea; 'last century' means the eighteenth, before steamships. *Aon tadhal air a' bhall* is literally 'one visit at the ball', but with respect to shinty *tadhal* is more closely defined as a 'goal' or 'hail'. Before the rules of the game were codified there was no fixed pitch or number of players – the young men of one community met those of another halfway, and the game ended when the ball was driven as far as one township or the other. It is for this reason that, following codification, a 'goal' or 'hail' of the modern type tended to be called *leth-tadhal* or *leth-bhàir* ('one of two goals'). See pp. 536–37.

137 The *anainn* is, in general terms, the flat top of the wall. As JGC describes it as 'double', the wall in question was presumably very broad, built of stone rather than turf and filled with rubble, but perhaps as little as three or four feet high. The roof-timbers were set upon it, leaving an interior and an exterior shelf. In the present instance it is clear, I think, that the *anainn* is specifically the exterior shelf – Ewen puts his supper 'out' to cool upon it, and it is only at a later point in the story that the Fairies 'became quite familiar with Ewen' and 'entered the hut'. The *anainn* mentioned at p. 562 below is a top sod from the outside of a turf wall, and following Armstrong 1825 ('the eaves of a house', s.v. *anuinn*), the HSD ('the top of a house-wall', vol. 1, p. 49), and other dictionaries, Dwelly (1977, p. 32) defines *anainn* as 'top of a house or wall' and 'eaves'. Similarly, in Glenurquhart the *anainn* was the place on a haystack where it begins to taper – the 'taking in' (Barron 1980–82, p. 126).

Other sources, however, are almost unanimous in locating the *anainn* on the inside (MacInnes 1893–94, p. 216; Sinclair 1953, pp. 65, 74; Slade 1995, p. 47). Boyd says of Tiree (1986, p. 28): *'S e an* anainn *a theireadh iad ri ceann shuas a' bhalla bhig far an glèidhichte rudan beaga bìodach, leithid phìoban, sgèanan is eile.* "The *anainn* was what they called the top of the little wall where small articles like pipes, knives and so on were kept." According to Fr Allan McDonald (1958, p. 129) the interior shelf was the *annainn* and the exterior one the *fraighean*, yet in one of his own poems (Black 2002, pp. 236–37, 402) he says:

> *Ach ghoid e bhuam bean an taighe*
> *'S dh'fhàg na fraighean sa gun dòigh orr'.*

("But he stole the woman out of my house / And left these pantries in disarray.")

It seems, then, that the precise meaning of the term was subject to fluctuation. I am grateful to Miss Catrìona Mackie for her help on this point.

138 *A bhuineagag* is properly *a bhuinneagag*, vocative of *buinneagag*, a hypocoristic derivative of *buinneag* 'a twig', 'a young maiden'. It is as if Ewen said: "Are you always like that, twiglet?"

139 See pp. xxxvi and 10. *Smàladh an teine* is more literally 'the smooring of the fire', that is, covering it up to keep it alive for the night. To judge from a story told at p. 56, by 'raking coal' JGC means the burning end of a peat placed outside when making up the fire for the night.

140 JGC points out in a footnote: "The man in Flodigarry got rid of his Fairy assistants by telling them to bale out the sea." This refers to a tale told in 'Fairy Assistance', p. 51.

141 Campbell 1860–62, vol. 2, pp. 52–55 = 1890, vol. 2, pp. 62–65; see also Anon. 1908–09a, pp. 165–66; Wentz 1911, p. 110; Campbell 1967–68, p. 18; *Tocher* 38, pp. 18–19; O'Neill 1991; MacDonald 1994–95, p. 59.

142 Why JGC spells the name *Tun Bhuirg* I am not quite sure. Perhaps he means it as a compromise between *Dùn Bhuirg* ('the Fort of Burg'), the form in which it appears on

maps, and the two old women's *Tòn Bhuirg* ('the Backside of Burg'); possibly he was thinking of Ardtun on the opposite shore. (As the stress is on *Bhuirg*, these nuances are irrelevant to pronunciation.) In the story as told in MacDougall and Calder 1910, pp. 100–03, the name is *Torr-a-Bhuilg* ('Bellows Hill'); on being told that Torr-a-Bhuilg is on fire, the Fairy rushes out, shouting: *M' ùird is m' innean 's mo bholg!* "My hammers and my anvil and my bellows!" A variant of this is in Nicolson 1951, p. 298: "'Làmh d' athar 's do sheanar ort!' is used as a threat; and a story is told of its application by a blacksmith, who strongly suspected that his wife's baby was a changeling, and satisfactorily proved it. He came in one day exclaiming, 'An sìthean ri 'theine!' – The Fairy [hill] is on fire! on which the little imp, thrown off his guard, cried out, 'O m' òrd 's m' innean!' – O my hammer and anvil! The smith now saw that the creature was not only a Fairy, but a fellow-craftsman; and taking him out to the smithy, placed him on the anvil, and swinging his big hammer, said, 'Gobha mi fhein, gobha m' athair, gobha mo sheanair; 's làmh d' athar 's do sheanar ort! an t-òrd mór!' – Smith am I, smith was my father, smith my grandfather; thy father's and grandfather's hand on thee! the big hammer! Before the hammer could descend the little sprite vanished, and when the smith returned home, he found his own true and pretty child sitting cosily at the fireside!" See also notes 82, 83, 180; Forbes 1923, p. 163; GUL MS Gen. 1090/29, pp. 213–15.

143 By 'Ross of Mull' JGC means the parish of Ross, officially Kilfinichen and Kilviceon. Tàpull or Tavool House is not in the Ross *per se* but on the opposite (Ardmeanach) shore of Loch Scridain on the road to Burg. It is only a mile from Dùn Bhuirg itself. The second element is clearly Norse *bolstaðr* 'farm, homestead'; MacQuarrie (1983, p. 98) takes the first from Gaelic *tàmh* 'rest, quiet', Maclean (1997, p. 34) from Norse *há* 'slope, high'.

144 Dùn Bhuirbh in Lyndale lies on the eastern shore of Loch Greshornish near Edinbane in the north-west of the island. Beinn an Ùine represents *Beinn an Dùine*, i.e. its name comes from the *dùn* itself, which commands the low-lying isthmus between Portree Harbour and Loch Snizort (Forbes 1923, p. 67). *Druim Uighe* or *Druim Uidhe* (Drumuie), which lies directly below it, is clearly 'Isthmus Ridge', cf. note 511.

145 *Bùrn luadh* (properly *bùrn luadha*, *bùrn luaidh* or *bùrn luadhaidh*), literally 'fulling water', will be the stale urine used as an ammoniac in the waulking process. No doubt in cold weather it would be warmed over the fire as a kindness to the women's hands. Presumably it is mentioned here to illustrate the Fairies' attention to detail. There is no trace of rhyme in the verse as JGC gives it, but see Campbell 1889, pp. 64–65, and 1890, vol. 2, pp. 62–64 (where the references, incidentally, are to *bùrn luaidh* and *uisge luaidh*).

146 JFC's introduction (1890, vol. 1, pp. i–cxxviii) is one of the most wide-ranging, penetrating and consistently entertaining essays ever written about the Gael, and is rivalled only by Carmichael's shorter, angrier effort in *CG1*. In the course of it JFC mentions many places, people and things, but Largs is not among them; indeed he has very little to say about Lowland Scotland at all. I think what JGC is referring to is this very characteristic remark at p. cxv: "There are plenty of lowlanders as well as 'ignorant' Highlanders who think that they are seers, without the aid of a deal board through which to look into futurity, by the help of a medium, and it is by no means uncommon, as I am told, for the Astronomer-Royal to receive English letters asking his advice, *ex officio*."

147 A 'kit' in Scots is normally a tub or container. Katherine Whyte Grant, who, like JGC, grew up in Appin, refers (1925, p. 38) to a 'kitful' of butter. Hattit kit, however, is 'a preparation of milk with a top layer of cream, variously flavoured' (Robinson 1987, *s.v.* hat). *DOST* offers two examples from the Treasurer's Accounts in which 'kit' appears to refer to a tubful of cream rather than to the cream itself: "To ane woman brocht kittis and cheis" (1507); "To the wif of Erncrag for mylk and kittis to the King" (1508). Mrs Marace Dareau of *DOST* suggests to me (personal communication, 6.12.02) that JGC's example represents a similar transfer

of use from container to sowen water. On the following two anecdotes see Introduction, pp. xxxiv and xxxix.

148 See 'Stealing Women and Children', p. 19, and 'Pearlwort (*Mòthan*)', pp. 229–30.

149 Rahoy is south of Loch Sunart, on the eastern shore of Loch Teacuis in Morvern, which is dominated by Beinn Iadain. Macbain (1896, p. 47) gives *bruchorcan* as 'stool bent' or 'heath rush' with the comment that it is said to be derived from obsolete *brú* 'hind' (cf. *brú* 'doe', *DIL*) and *corc-an* 'oats', hence 'deer's oats'. It appears in 'Moladh Beinn Dóbhrain' as *bruchorachd*, which would suggest 'deer's sowing' (MacLeod 1952, p. 204). I know of no other source which suggests that it has occult power. On the well-known power of the *buarach*, however, see e.g. Maclagan 1895, pp. 158–59; Maclagan 1902, p. 120; Henderson 1911, pp. 296–97.

The otherworld reputation of *Beinn Iadain* was enhanced, if not caused, by the correspondence of its name to *Beinn Eudainn* of Gaelic mythology, which was in turn derived from *Binn Éadair* – the Hill of Howth, Co. Dublin. The story 'Mar a Chaidh Fionn do Rìoghachd nam Fear Mòra', which JGC got from Donald Cameron, Ruaig, Tiree, begins: *Bha Fionn 's a chuid dhaoine ann an cala Beinn Eudainn air cnoc, air chùl gaoith' 's air eudain gréine, far am faiceadh iad a h-uile fear 's nach fhaiceadh duin' idir iad.* JGC translates (Campbell 1882, p. 178, and 1891, p. 176): "Fin and his men were in the Harbour of the Hill of Howth on a hillock, behind the wind and in front of the sun, where they could see every person, and nobody could see them." He points out in a footnote that 'the name of this hill is uniformly known in *Tales of the West Highlands* (in which it is frequently mentioned) as *Beinn Eudainn*, but in Irish it is called *Beinn Eadair* (the Hill of Howth, near Dublin)'.

The connection between *Beinn Eudainn* and *Beinn Iadain* appears to have been made by the people of Morvern, at least. In his description of that parish the Rev. Norman McLeod wrote (1793, p. 275 = new edn, p. 374): "*Kemin*, is steps in the form of a natural stair, pretty regular, in a rock, towards the top of a hill called *Bein-eiden*, mentioned in an old poem ascribed to Ossian; but whether this, or another of that name in Ireland, be the hill therein referred to, it is not pretended to say." By *Kemin* he may have meant either *Ceuman* 'Steps' or *Ceum Fhinn* 'Fin's Step', but fortunately his son the Rev. Dr John made the Fin connection explicit (McLeod 1843, p. 165): "Towards the summit it is accessible by a singular flight of steps formed by excavations in the rock, known to the inhabitants of the country, as Ceumanan-Fhin, or *Fingal's steps* or *stair*."

150 As marriage is a sacrament, the handkerchief was already a consecrated item; and no doubt the three knots were to be tied upon it in the name of the Father, the Son and the Holy Ghost. See pp. xxxiv and 19. In an Arran variant, 'The Fairies of Claoinead', the wife's instrument of redemption is the wedding-cloak – the husband is to leave the front and back doors of the house open on a certain night and throw it over her when the Fairies bring her careering through, but at the critical moment his courage fails him and she is snatched away again for ever (Mackenzie 1914, pp. 257–59). In a similar story from Skipness (very near Arran), the husband is to fetch his lost wife back by going to a particular place with her wedding gown and Bible. He fails to do so, as he is about to marry again. Soon afterwards he is working in the barn when a whiff of wind comes and gives him such a blow on the head that his mouth is twisted until the day of his death (*Tocher* 28, pp. 220–21). "Everybody believed it was his first wife that did it out of vengeance."

151 Presumably the word was *càc* 'shit'. Bourke points out (1999, p. 80) that among weapons against the Fairies, in addition to iron and fire, is 'human urine, often mixed with hen's droppings'. In a story told by Lady Gregory of a man whose wife was 'taken', the revenant instructs her husband (1970, p. 119): "Come tomorrow night to the gap up there beyond the hill, and you'll see the riders going through, and the one you'll see on the last horse will be

me. And bring with you some fowl droppings and urine, and throw them at me as I pass, and you'll get me again." In the event, as Yeats put it (Welch 1993, p. 177), although he saw her on the last horse, 'his courage failed him, and he let what he had in his hand drop, and he never got the chance to see her again'. JGC himself points out (p. xciii above): "The cause of Fairy aversion to ordure is that it is matter out of which the substance has been already taken. Hence also their objection to dirt of every kind, and the reward given by them, according to the Teutonic creed, to tidy servants."

The names Castle Lionnaig and Loch Aline call for comment. Firstly, JGC's explanation of Loch Aline as *Loch Àluinn*, 'the Pretty Loch', has the support of W. J. Watson (1926a, p. 46) but not of Iain Thornber, who lives on the shores of the loch at Knock and sees in it the element *linn* 'pool', relating the name to what is now the 'Big Pool' on the *Geàrr-Abhainn* ('Short River'), which is wrongly shown as the River Aline on modern maps. "The pool," he tells me (personal communication, 16 November 2003), "has a strong traditional link with Somerled and his extirpation of the Norsemen from the area." It is at Claggan, a mile north of the castle, a few yards downstream from a stone bridge built in 1821, at the foot of which the remains of a ford may be seen; the story tells how the MacInneses of Morvern made Somerled their leader after seeing him hook a prodigious salmon, and he led them to victory by a stratagem (Loudon 2001, pp. 64–65).

I believe that Iain Thornber is correct. Names carrying an unambiguously aesthetic rather than functional or narrative charge are hard to find. *Loch Bòidheach* ('Pretty Loch') in Coll and *a' Bheinn Bhòidheach* ('the Pretty Hill') in Skye (p. 73) will in fact be *Loch Buaidheach* ('Magic Loch') and *a' Bheinn Bhuaidheach* ('the Magic Hill'), see notes 195, 236. JGC's *Gleann Eireachdaidh* 'Shapely Glen' is 'Glen of Assembly' (note 175). The names of the larger lochs are generally taken from their rivers, no matter how short, and in several important instances there appears to be a third name, that of a female water-spirit: *Airceag, Loch Airceig, Airceag; Cuach, Loch Cuaich, Cuachag; Éire* (Findhorn), *Éireag; Éite, Loch Éite, Éiteag; Mórar, Loch Mórair, Mórag; Nis, Loch Nis, Niseag(?); Seile, Loch Seile, Seileag; Spé, Loch Spé, Speitheag* (Carmichael 1914, pp. 151–52; Watson 1914–16, p. 266; Baran 1942–50, p. 121; Black 2000, p. 51; EUL MS CW 503, ff. 195r, 271–72; cf. Mackinlay 1895–96, pp. 70–72, and Henderson 1911, pp. 150–51). Loch Sealg (?Seileig), the alternative name of Loch Shell in Lewis, is, I think, taken from that of the water-spirit, *Seileag* (J. M. 1908–09, p. 251); the case of Loch Arkaig, probably from *airc* 'a strait, a difficulty', will be similar (Watson 1926a, pp. 449–50). In the present instance there are two lochs of average size joined by a river: *Loch Àirigh Aonghais* ('the Loch of Angus's Shieling', Loch Arienas), the *Geàrr-Abhainn*, and Loch Aline. It is unusual for a sequence of three waters to bear unrelated names, and if *Àluinn* is reinterpreted as *Àth-Linn* 'Ford Pool', i.e. a pool where the *Geàrr-Abhainn* could be forded, an onomastic relationship can at least be established between the river and Loch Aline.

As it happens, the name 'Castle Lionnaig' appears, with minor orthographic adjustment, to offer us the name of the water-spirit, *Linneag* (perhaps the 'nn' as JGC heard it was neutral). Neither Iain Thornber nor Ian Fisher has heard this name, and JGC appears to be our only source for it. It is, I am sure, a traditional name for Kinlochaline Castle, a fifteenth-century tower-house otherwise known as *Caisteal an Ime*, 'the Castle of the Butter', for the following reason (McLeod 1843, p. 184): "The Castle of Kenlochaline, consisting of a square tower, and built on a very picturesque situation overhanging the estuary of Geur Abhain, is supposed to have been erected by Dubh-Chal, a lady of the McInnes tribe, who, according to tradition, paid her architect with the very extraordinary remuneration, a quantity equal to the full of the castle, of butter."

'Dubh-Chal', literally 'Black Girl', is, I suppose, a nickname, Dwelly's *dubh-chaile* 'scullion, trollop, girl of the lowest rank of peasantry' (1977, p. 368, cf. MacLeod and Dewar

1831, p. 258). It is much less likely to represent *dubh-chall* 'black loss, loss of cattle'. The story squares with the name 'Castle Lionnaig' to the extent that, unusually, the building of the tower is ascribed to a female. What is more, it offers a further explanation for the spelling 'Lionnaig', for it may well be that in an earlier version of the origin-legend the spirit of the river, or her MacInnes *alter ego*, paid her architect with the full of the castle of *lionn* – ale. A stone panel above the fireplace in the main chamber of Kinlochaline Castle depicts a naked woman in a kneeling position holding a plate or bowl, with a pitcher beside her head and an elongated object resembling a flask clutched under her arm (RCAHMS 1980, p. 207, see sketch); this is assumed to represent Dubh-Chal dispensing hospitality.

'Lionnag' or *Linneag*, 'Dubh-Chal' or *dubh-chaile*? Carving at Kinlochaline Castle, see above

It should also be noted that *linneag* is potentially the name for any well-defined stretch of water with an opening at both ends, whether in a river or in a sea-loch, e.g. the Linack in Loch Sunart between Salen and Laudale (see Loudon 2001, p. 42).

152 The *Léigich* or 'Marsh People' of Balemartin were the fishing community there. JGC's *air an léige deas*, better perhaps *air an Léig a-deas* ('on the southern Marsh'), is intended to distinguish the *Léig* of Balemartin from that of Kilmoluag to the north, see note 196 below and Campbell 1895, p. 44. *An Léigeach* 'the Balemartin man' is misinterpreted in *Tocher* 32, p. 84, as *a' Ghéigeach* 'a collective nickname for the people of Balemartin'.

153 *Bean mo choltais* in the fourth line is 'a wife like me' – she was a Fairy man's wife now. See Introduction, p. lxxix.

154 Down to this point the story resembles one sent to JGC by JFC on 10 October 1871 as the Barra tradition underlying the 'Fairy Song' (Campbell 1895, pp. 140–47, see pp. 641–42 below): 'There was a time, at first, when before children were christened they used to be taken by the fairies. A child was born and it was in a woman's lap. A fairy came to the *Bean-ghlùn* and she said to the midwife, "'S trom do leanabh." "'S trom gach torrach," said the other.

"'*S aotrom do leanabh*," said the fairy. "'*S aotrom gach soghalach*," said the midwife. "'*S glas do leanabh*," said the fairy. "'*S glas am fiar 's fàsaidh e*," said the other; and so she came day by day with words and with singing of verses to try if she could "word" him away with her – "*am briatharachadh i leatha è*." But the mother always had her answer ready. There was a lad recovering from a fever in the house and he heard all these words, and learned them, and he put the song together afterwards: after the child was christened the fairy came back no more.'

155 JGC points out in a footnote that the first two lines of this quatrain occur also in 'a song on the deceitfulness of women, by a young man, whose first love had forsaken him'. She 'killed him with a stony stare', and merely asked, *Co ás tha 'n corra-ghille glas?* ("Whence comes the sallow stripling?") There is in fact something wrong with the verse as it stands, as it has only one pair of rhyming words (*thalamh : ghlaise*). The difficulty is resolved by Lord Archibald Campbell, who prints the song in full (1885a, p. 237):

> *Se labhair i, le còmhradh borb,*
> *Gun robh mi 'm chorra-ghille glas.*
>
> *Is glas am fochann, is glas am feur,*
> *Is glas a' choill fo a duibhneul;*
> *Is glas an dos tha 'm bàrr a' chroinn,*
> *'S ar leam fhéin gur glas an cuileann.*
>
> *Is glas an claidheamh tha san truaill,*
> *Is glas an tuadh sa bheil a' chas,*
> *'S ma bhios a faobhar gu tana geur,*
> *Gu dé as misd' a mèinn a bhith glas?*
>
> *Is geal am bainne thig bhon bhuar,*
> *Is milis 's is buan a bhlas;*
> *'S nuair sgaras an gruth on mheadhg*
> *Tionndaidh e thaobh 's bidh e glas.*

("What she declared, with wild speech, / Was that I was a sallow stripling. / Sallow's the young corn, sallow's the grass, / Sallow's the forest beneath her black gloom; / Sallow's the tuft at the top of the tree, / And in my opinion sallow's the holly. / Sallow's the sword that's inside the scabbard, / Sallow's the axe in which is the handle, / And if its blade is shallow and sharp, / How is it worse if its ore is sallow? / White is the milk that comes from the cows, / Sweet and enduring is its taste; / And when the curds separate from the whey / They turn to one side and then they go sallow.") This shows that JGC's lines 1 and 2 do not belong together at all. See also EUL MS CW 503, ff. 906–07.

156 Down to this point JGC has translated *glas* as 'grey'. I would substitute 'pale, pallor' for 'grey, greyness' as being more appropriate to the segment of the spectrum which is in question here – yellow-grey shading into light green, the colour of new growth, metaphorically denoting innocence and inexperience. At p. 164 JGC translates *glas dharach* as 'green oak'; see also notes 29, 62, 431, 570 and 690. In the first line, *feur* means 'grass', not 'flowers' (it is the same word as *fiar* in the preceding conversation). For *gnè ghlaise* compare 'Òran na Comhachaig' by Dòmhnall mac Fhionnlaigh nan Dàn, *c*. 1590 (Watson 1959, p. 253):

> *B' annsa leam na dùrdan bodaich*
> *Os cionn lice ag eararadh sìl*

Commentary

Bùirein an daimh 'm bi gnè dhuinnid
Air leacainn beinne 's e ri sìn.

("I'd prefer to a peasant mumbling a charm / Over a flagstone while graddaning corn / The roar of the stag that is brownness epitomised / On the slope of a hill facing into a storm.") All in all, then, I would rephrase JGC's translation as follows: "Pale is the foliage, pale is the grass, / Pale is the axe in which is the handle, / And there is nothing that comes through the earth / That isn't essentially pale in its nature."

157   Soa is a large tidal island at the eastern approach to Gott Bay, Tiree's principal anchorage.

158   In *SHIS* 87 the English translation is footnoted *Ma tha tùr aig marbh, nach bi thu oidhche dhìth do leabaidh.* Clearly JGC omits the words *tha mi 'g òrdachadh* because his system is to provide the Gaelic for key words only. I emend *leabaidh* to *leapa* because the former is incorrect in the genitive. As *marbh* is singular, JGC's 'If the dead have feeling . . .' should strictly be 'If a dead person has feeling . . .'

159   See pp. xliii, lxvii; note 67 above. The threshold of Glenstockdale House in Appin was supposed to have been made from a block of wood which had been left in a bed there to simulate a young mother whom the Fairies had carried off (Grant 1925, p. 29). For the Green Island see note 479.

160   *Coileach dubh màirt* is cited by JGC as *coileach dubh màrt.* Calder glosses the expression as follows (MacDougall and Calder 1910, p. 328). "Curtin, *Tales of the Fairies*, p. 115, says – A cock hatched in March from a cock and hen hatched in March. MacD[ougall] has this note – Is e sin coileach-tighe, dubh 'san dath, agus a thugadh a mach am mìos a' Mhàirt. Cha 'n 'eil coileach eile a ghlaodhas cho fior. Goiridh e 's a' mhionaid a thionndaidheas an oidhche gu là.

Coileach dubh a' Mhàirt
Coileach is fìre 'tha.

That is, a domestic cock, hatched in March, and black in colour. No other cock crows so true. He crows at the very moment when night turns to day. 'The black cock of March, / The truest in existence.'" Curtin (1895, p. 115) is footnoting the expression 'March cock' used in a story. According to Ní Anluain (1991, p. 47) and Bruford and MacDonald (1994, p. 470) a cock from an egg laid and hatched in March was believed in Scotland and Ireland to have special powers. See also GUL MS Gen. 1090/29, pp. 2, 10; Gregory 1970, pp. 235, 279; Almqvist 1991a, p. 20. Ó Duilearga (1981, p. 399) gives a list of references.

161   JFC here cites 'the black cock of March' (Campbell 1860–62, vol. 2, p. 98 = 1890, vol. 2, p. 109). Niall M. Brownlie tells me that he remembers hearing this tale from his mother. He grew up in *Goirtean Dòmhnaill* (Barrapol), Tiree, between the wars. On *màrt* as 'a busy time of the year' see p. 545.

162   The River Awe, spelt *Abhainn Abha* by Watson (1926a, pp. 75, 477), has a different vowel from that in Loch Awe, *Loch Obha.* The underlying word is simply Old Irish *ab* 'a river'. Watson says (*ibid.*, p. 75): "What is the reason for the difference in vowel I cannot say, but it appears in other instances of *abh*." See p. 86 ('At Inverawe House') and Hamp 1988, p. 150.

163   Glen Cannel lies at the head of Loch Bà in the middle of the island.

164   It was said of a tailor whom the Fairies of *Sìthein na Caillich* had in their power (MacDougall and Calder 1910, pp. 122–23): *Cha b' urrainn iad coire a dheanamh air aon duine ach tre dhuine eile, agus le sin, bhitheadh iad 'ga thabhairt-san leò, agus bheireadh iad air na saighdean sìthe a thilgeil air an neach d' an robh iad an droch rùn.* "They could not hurt any human being except by means of another, and for that reason they used to take him with them, and make him throw the Fairy arrows at the person to whom they bore ill-will." We should understand from this that the prohibition was a *geas* or tabu imposed

in specific circumstances on a particular tribe of Fairies, in the same way that certain tabus were imposed from time to time upon Cú Chulainn and the Ulaidh, or upon Fionn and the Féinn. The motif is characterised by MacDonald (1994–95, p. 48): "Man taken by *sluagh* and made to wound someone (woman, animal) with elf-shot."

165 See Introduction, pp. lxxiii–lxxiv, and note 57 above. For an Arran version of this story as a whole, 'Sithichean Dhruim-a-Ghìneir', see Mackenzie 1914, pp. 259–61.

166 JGC's spelling is *Mac Challum a Chrònain*. We must take his word for it that *Mac Challum* is a surname and not a patronymic. It is not possible to be sure what the sobriquet means. *Crònan* may be intended in the sense of 'lullaby' (perhaps referring to an incident of childhood), or to a habit of humming, or to the noise made by his arrows – presumably the use of arrows is one of the things that JGC means by 'the habits of the Fairies and ancient hunters'. Mrs Grant of Laggan says (1811, vol. 2, pp. 237–38): "Before, and indeed for some time after the year 1745, there were here and there, in remote glens in the highlands, persons whose chief subsistence was derived from hunting, and a few solitary individuals who devoted themselves entirely to it . . . They shot with arrows, long after such weapons had fallen into general disuse; the report of a gun rendering it unsuitable to the privacy of their pursuits." Clearly MacCallum was one such. See Introduction, pp. lxxi–lxxiii.

167 The motif of this story is characterised by MacDonald (1994–95, p. 53) as 'loan of sieve (etc.) asked for in curious language'. For more examples see *Tocher* 28, pp. 195–96. The winnowing machine first appeared in Scotland, in imitation of a Dutch original, in the years after 1710. According to Fenton (1976, p. 91), "This was a simple device with four vanes of thin wood or metal revolving in a hollow drum and blowing a strong stream of air through an opening. The grain to be cleaned was allowed to trickle through this jet, which blew away the chaff and roughly separated the heavy and light grains of corn." The whooshing and rattling of the grain passing through the jet of air would have been amplified by the hollow drum, and no doubt the revolving vanes contributed to the noise.

168 See note 33. The *Druim Dearg* lies between Hianish (Heanish) and Baugh, the neighbouring township to the west. Sanndaig is far away on the west side.

169 *Thug e iasg-leum ás* 'he took a fish-jump out of it'.

170 Or more literally perhaps: "It having been fat or lean, damned be he who would not feed a calf for himself."

171 See p. 28.

172 See note 70. W. B. Yeats supplies an example of the frightful consequences that might ensue if the nail were not driven in (Welch 1993, pp. 185–86): "A man at Doneraile told me a story of a man who had a bullock that got sick, and that it might be of some use, he killed it and skinned it, and when it was in a trough being washed it got up and ran away. He ran after it and knocked it down and cut it up, and after he and his family had eaten it, a woman, that was passing by, said: 'You don't know what you have eaten. It is your own grandmother that you have eaten.'"

173 Schiehallion in Rannoch is 'the Otherworld of the Caledonians' or 'the Caledonian Otherworld'. For Ben-y-Ghloe see note 213. At 1,806 feet, *Sithein na Rapaich(e)* dominates the Morvern coast west of Loch Aline. Gaskell calls it Sithean na Raplaich (1968, p. 65). The word *rap(l)aich* 'tempestuous weather' is unknown to me. Dunniquoich at Inveraray is well known; the other two hills face each other across Loch Fyne a few miles south. *Dùn Deacainn* is in fact *Dùn Leacainn* ('Hillside Fort', 1,173 feet) at Furnace. In a poem by Donald MacPhedran in praise of the celebrated Inveraray novelist Neil Munro we find (Renton and Beaton 2000, p. 7):

> San t-samhradh, san earrach
> Bidh tu dìreadh Sròn Reithe,

A' tadhal Dùn Leacainn
'S àird na Cruaiche Mòire.

("In summer, in spring / You'll be climbing Stron Ray, / Visiting Dùn Leacainn / And the height of Cruach Mhòr.") My thanks to Ronald Renton and James Beaton for information.

174 The translation is mine, as JGC did not offer one. *As àirde slios* is an instance of 'the formula' (see Black 2002, pp. 27–28) and therefore tricky to translate. I am taking *slios* in the sense in which it is used in Morvern (see p. 93) and on Loch Rannoch-side (*an Slios Garbh* 'the Rough Shore', *an Slios Mìn* 'the Smooth Shore'). *Sìthein Sluaigh* and *Sìthein an t-Sluaigh* are the correct forms of the name which appears on modern maps as *Sith an t Sluain*; JGC refers to it again in Campbell 1889, p. 55. The Rev. Charles Stewart called it 'Sien-Slui, the fairy habitation of a multitude' (1791, p. 561 = new edn, p. 403), while George Langlands' 1801 map of Argyll gives it as Sheansluai. It is a conical hill of 1,428 feet, just south of Strachur and clearly visible from Inveraray (McLean n.d., pp. 120–21). John Mackenzie says (1841, p. 156): "There are several hills in the Highlands which still bear the name *Tom-na-h-Iubhraich*, all haunted by the fairies. One of them is near Strachur, Lochfine side . . ." My guess is that he misnames *Sìthein Sluaigh* because he associates it with Thomas Rhymer, see p. 148.

In an intriguing passage, Angela Bourke likens such hills to the police barracks of nineteenth-century Ireland (1999, p. 148): "The idea of surveillance, monopolized by the state from the nineteenth century, was a long-established part of fairy discourse too: the 'good people' were commonly spoken of as eavesdroppers; the hills typically said to belong to them . . . are isolated summits that command panoramic views." We need not doubt but that the Fairies also provided a code for spies and eavesdroppers of all kinds in the Highlands, such as those of whom Chambers speaks (1840, p. 81) in his description of the events of 15 April 1746. "The Duke of Cumberland having, like a prudent general, taken measures, ever since he approached the Highlanders, to watch their slightest motions, was by no means ignorant of their march towards his position, though he did not apprehend a nocturnal attack. He had commissioned various country people, and some of his own Highland militiamen, to mingle with their columns, and inform him from time to time of the progress they were making."

175 Glen Erochty or Erichdie is not 'Shapely Glen' but 'Glen of Assembly' – from *eireachd* 'a court of justice', not *eireachdail* 'lovely' (Watson 1926a, pp. 439, 491, cf. note 151 above). *Càrn na Sleabhach* will be for *Càrn nan Sleaghach* 'the Rock-Pile of the Gullies', cf. Watson 2002, pp. 150, 178, 188. No doubt the Fairies were thought to haunt the gullies.

176 As Loch Awe lies at the foot of Glenorchy, we may perhaps link this with JGC's discussion of Fenian tales in *The Fians* (Campbell 1891, pp. 3–4): "Tales of this kind are denominated, in popular lore, 'Tales of Fionn, Son of Cumhal, and the Fian Host' (*Naigheachdan air Fionn MacCumhail agus Feachd na Féinne*), and the matter to which they refer was so much the subject of talk that it became a saying, that if the Fians were twenty-four hours without anyone mentioning them they would rise again. They are lying, it is said, in the boat-shaped mound called Tom-na-h-iubhraich, which for some years past has been used by the town of Inverness as a burying-ground; others say they are lying in Glenorchy, Argyleshire; and there is a story that when they were last seen it was by a person who chanced to enter the place where they are lying. When he struck a chain that was suspended from the roof, the Fians rose upon their elbows, and their big dogs began to bark. The intruder was so much frightened that he ran away. As he was going out at the door he heard a voice calling —

Evil and ill-guided man,
Who leaves us worse than when found.

A dhuine dhona dholaich
'S miosa dh' fhag na fhuair."

The story is of course told of locations other than Tomnahurich and Glenorchy, see p. 148; notes 174, 494; Nicolson 1951, pp. 28–29; Scott 2001, p. 85; GUL MS Gen. 1090/29, p. 75. Donald A. MacKenzie put it like this (1911): "In the Highlands the Fians are giants about 60 feet high. In Tom-na-hurich, Inverness; Craig-a-howe, Black Isle; Ossian's Cave, Glencoe; and Smith's Rock, in Skye, they lie wrapped in dreams like 'The Seven Sleepers'."

177 Also quoted at p. 7.

178 *Eilean Fhlòdaigearraidh*, formerly *Eilean Altabhaig* – Martin's 'Altig' or 'Altvig' (1999, pp. 93, 106), see Robson 2003, p. 162. It is mentioned by Eoin Óg Ó Muirgheasáin in an elegy on Ruairi Mór MacLeod (d. 1626) as the site of a battle in his war with the MacDonalds of Sleat (Royal Irish Academy MS 23.N.12, cf. Macdonald 1955, p. 46):

> *D'fhoiléim a ghasraidh i ngliaidh*
> *Fá Oiléan Altabhaig uaidh,*
> *Do chuir mar tharadh i dtráigh*
> *Fuil cháigh fá chaladh an chuain.*

("By his warriors' onset in battle / Around Flodigarry Island for him, / He has put like seaweed on ebb-shore / Enemy blood round the sea-harbour.")

179 In addition to meaning the month of March (*am Màrt, am mìos-Màirt*) and Tuesday (*am Màrt, Di-Màirt*), *màrt* appears to have become a word for a suitable opportunity for agricultural labour, especially sowing, see note 495. In this sense I like to translate it as 'tuesdaytime'. This probably arose from the varied and concentrated nature of agricultural work in March; note also that Tuesday 'is a lucky day to begin cutting corn, or doing any work requiring a sharp instrument' (*CG2*, p. 271). The following saying (Smith 1964, p. 28) has many variations, one of which is given by JGC at p. 545 below.

> *Éist a' chiad Mhàrt*
> *'S an dara Màrt*
> *'S an treas Màrt mas fheudar*
> *Ach olc air mhaith gum bi an t-sìd'*
> *Cuir an sìol san fhìor mhàrt*
> *Gar rachadh tu do cheithir fhaid' fhéin*
> *An aghaidh na gaoithe tuath.*

("Listen the first Tuesday / And the second Tuesday / And the third Tuesday if you have to / But be the weather good or bad / Sow the seed in the true tuesdaytime / Even if you have to go on all fours / Against the north wind.") In my view, *Màrt* in each of the first three lines might equally be 'tuesdaytime'; conversely, *san fhìor mhàrt* in the fifth could be 'on the correct Tuesday'. The concept of 'listening' here is very interesting; other versions avoid it, beginning *A' chiad Mhàrt leig seachad* ('Let the first Tuesday pass'). The 'listening' will not be to the wind but to the soil. All in all, in deciding whether it was time to sow, it appears that the farmer would have taken into account the weather, the soil, the day of the week, and a fourth factor – whether or not it was a saint's day, of which there are a remarkable number in March. See MacDougall 1891, pp. 298–99; Camshron 1926, pp. 53–54, 58; MacDonald 1926, p. 104; Mac Iomhair 1927–28, p. 347; Mac a Phì 1938, p. 41; Nicolson 1951, pp. 26–27; *CG6*, p. 77; Dwelly 1977, s.v. *Màrt*; Meek 1978, p. 2; Macdonald 1982, p. 326; GUL MS Gen. 1090/29, pp. 47–48.

180 In Campbell 1895, pp. 25–26, JGC tells a story of a 'doughty little archer' called *Iain Beag a' Bhuilg Bhàin* who served the MacLachlans of Coruanan in Lochaber. Once when Coruanan was attacked by cattle-raiders Iain's adversary said to him, *Iain Bhig a' Bhuilg Bhàin, bheir mise am fireach dhiot.* ("Little John of the White Arrow-Bag, I will take the hillside from you.") JGC explains: "In a struggle it is always an advantage, even when other things are even, to have the higher position on a hill side."

Iain retorts: *Làmh d' athar 's do sheanar, a Ghamhainn Bhàin, cuiridh mise biorach ort.* ("The hand of your father and grandfather be over you, White Stirk, I will put the branks on you.") JGC explains: "The *biorach*, branker, was a spiked iron gag, or instrument set with pointed iron pins, fixed round the head of calves to keep them from sucking. The expression 'The hand, &c., be over you' was a common expression, meaning much the same as the English 'Look out,' or 'Take care of yourself.' Saying this, Little John let fly an arrow which struck the other in the forehead, toppled him over, and put an end to the discussion."

Martin Martin had written (1999, p. 81): "It has been an ancient custom amongst the natives, and now only used by some old people, to swear by their chief or laird's hand. When a debate arises between two persons, if one of them assert the matter by your father's hand they reckon it a great indignity; but if they go a degree higher, and out of spite say, by your father's and grandfather's hand, the next word is commonly accompanied with a blow." Although Martin says that *Làmh d' athar 's do sheanar* was considered very insulting, according to Alexander Nicolson (1951, p. 298) 'it would be more correct to say that it was an insult to be thought capable of disregarding it'. It is, in other words, provocative.

On invoking the dead see Introduction, p. xxxii. Nicolson points out that the expression is properly *Air làmh d' athar 's do sheanar* ('By the hand of your father and grandfather'); it is thus an invocation of certain deceased individuals being made by one who has less right to invoke them than the person addressed, and is intended as a challenge. Kirk(?) wrote in 'Highland Rites and Customes' (Campbell 1975, p. 90; Hunter 2001, p. 72): "They swear by their Fathers hand, which if another doe, it is the greatest provocation."

Carmichael draws attention (CG6, p. 93) to *Air làimh d' athar 's do sheanar 's do shinn-seanar* ('By the hand of your father and grandfather and great-grandfather') and adds: "This form of asseveration was formerly common in Uist, the oath becoming more emphatic with each additional -father. It is not wholly obsolete, but it gives great offence to the person addressed. In the Isles of old they used to kiss the ground in emphasising their word, as they do still in parts of Ireland."

In 'Teàrlach Mac Sheumais', one of his greatest propaganda songs, Alastair mac Mhgr Alastair thus addresses King George (Campbell 1984, p. 60):

> *Làmh th' athar, làmh th' athar, làmh th' athar, a Dheòrsa,*
> *Gum faigh sinne buaidh ort, 's bidh an tuagh air do sgòrnan.*

"Your father's hand, your father's hand, your father's hand, Geordie, / We will defeat you and the axe will be on your throat."

After telling the story reproduced in note 142 above Nicolson concludes (1951, p. 298): "Apparently another version of this saying is, 'Lamh a thart, tart do sheanar dhut!'" The best one can say about this is that it looks as if *th' athar* ort and *t' athar* ort have been corrupted into *thart* and *tart*, giving rise to a partially modernised insult: "Your father's hand upon you, may you have your grandfather's thirst!" The expression has been discussed at length by Matheson (1956–57, pp. 247–48). He cites numerous examples, but not JGC's. See also pp. 130 ('Euphemisms'), 237; CG2, p. 256; Henderson 1911, p. 77.

For more on *Iain Beag a' Bhuilg* (or *a' Bhuilgein*) *Bhàin* see note 208 below and Loudon 2001, p. 64.

181 "The earth was not 'in heat' (i.e. ready for the bull) yet." For the practice of inserting sticks into the ground to see if it is 'on heat' for ploughing see Maclagan 1912–14, p. 35; MacilleDhuibh 7.4.89 and 21.2.92. The correspondent *c.* 1898 who gave Maclagan the phrase *tha 'n talamh air dàir* ('the ground is in rut') got the information from a certain *Donnchadh Seann* (*Tocher* 32, p. 112), seemingly thus providing a valuable example of Carmichael's rare word *sionn* 'of the otherworld', e.g. *saighead sionn* 'an otherworld arrow, a Fairy arrow'. Could *sionn* be derived from the name of one of the kings of the Shannon, *Flann Sionna* (note 665) or *Tadhg Sionna* (see note 815)?

182 For the 'association-craft' see note 45 above. The story exists in many different versions, cf. MacDonald 1994–95, p. 56. They may be classified into those in which the rhyme refers to Tuesday and those in which it refers to Friday. 'Tuesday' versions include: MacDougall 1891, pp. 216–21, 'Tuathanach Lìodasdail' ('The Farmer of Liddesdale'), the most elaborate variant; Mac a Phì 1938, p. 41; Mac Gille Sheathanaich 1959, p. 222 (a Gaelic retelling of JGC's version); CG6, pp. 76–77; Meek 1978, p. 81 (rhyme only). 'Friday' versions include: Robertson 1904–07, pp. 272–75; Camshron 1926, pp. 51–52; MacDhòmhnaill 1981, pp. 40–41. On the 'three Tuesdays' see Dwelly 1977, p. 634, and note 495 below.

183 Comparing JGC's *plàdar* with the Skye word *plàt*, 'a corn bag made of plaits of straw', Charles Robertson queried in a paper published in 1902 (1898–99, p. 87) whether it might not be in error for *plàdan*. However, Niall M. Brownlie confirms to me that *plàdar* is a Tiree word for a circular dish made from straw, used for corn; it will be from English 'platter'. For further detail on the *plàt* or *plàd* see Campbell 1967–68, p. 9.

184 See also p. 286. Carmichael defines *torc-sona* as 'bird of luck' (CG6, p. 140), but its literal translation is 'lucky pig', 'boar of prosperity', or, as JGC suggests, 'happy hog'. The editor of CG6, Angus Matheson, cites the following as from Ness, Lewis: *Rud anns a robh cumail ris / seasamh fada, chante: 'A chiall, 's ann a bha 'n torc-sona.'* "Of something which was persistent or long-standing, people would say: 'My dear, the *torc-sona* was certainly in it.'"

Questions of why a little brown bird should reside in the seed at sowing-time, be responsible for its increase, and be called a pig, boar or hog can all be answered with reference to the work of Sir James Frazer, who demonstrates (1912, vol. 1, pp. 270, 304) that in the harvest customs of Europe and elsewhere the 'spirit of the corn' may be represented not merely in human form by the old wife and maiden but equally by an astonishing variety of creatures, including the wolf, dog, hare, fox, cat, goat, cow (ox, bull), pig and horse as well as the cock, goose, quail and bird generally; also, less commonly, the stag, roe, sheep, bear, ass, mouse, stork, swan and kite. As Frazer shows (*ibid.*, pp. 164, 197), the Highlands and Islands are unusual in offering simultaneous examples of both maiden (*maighdeann*) and old wife (*cailleach*) in addition to the goat (*gobhar bhacach*, 'lame goat'), and it would not be surprising to find other creatures appearing as well; nor, in my opinion, need we even be surprised at a bird being called a boar. We may assume that the *torc sona* was originally a boar.

Frazer cites examples (1912, vol. 1, pp. 298–99) of the harvest corn-spirit as pig, boar or sow from many different parts of Germany and also from Estonia; in all cases it is simply a word for the corn itself, for the last sheaf, for the man or woman who cuts, binds, carries or threshes it, or for the dumplings eaten by such a person at harvest home. Unusually, however, and of great interest from our point of view, the 'pig' thus harvested continues to feature through Christmas and New Year into seed-time (*ibid.*, pp. 300–03). "In Sweden and Denmark at Yule (Christmas) it is the custom to bake a loaf in the form of a boar-pig. This is called the Yule Boar. The corn of the last sheaf is often used to make it. All through Yule the Yule Boar stands on the table. Often it is kept till the sowing-time in spring, when part of it is mixed with the seed-corn and part given to the ploughmen and plough-horses or plough-oxen to eat, in the expectation of a good harvest . . . Formerly a real boar was sacrificed at Christmas, and apparently also a man in the character of the Yule Boar. This, at least, may perhaps be inferred from a Christmas custom still observed in Sweden. A man is wrapt up in a skin, and carries a wisp of straw in his mouth, so that the projecting straws look like the bristles of a boar. A knife is brought, and an old woman, with her face blackened, pretends to sacrifice him." At sowing-time in various parts of the area now covered by Belarus, the Baltic states, Poland and Germany, particular parts of a cooked pig are either mixed with the seed-corn or stuck into the field (*ibid.*, p. 300). "In the whole of Hesse, Meiningen, and other districts, people eat pea-soup with dried pig-ribs on Ash Wednesday or Candlemas. The ribs are then collected and hung in the room till sowing-time, when they are inserted in the sown field or in the seed-bag amongst the flax seed."

With regard to why the *torc sona* should have become a bird, we may look to the virtual tabu on pork that has prevailed in the Highlands and Islands in recent centuries (see p. 140, Grant 1792, p. 177 = new edn, p. 4, MacGregor 1901, p. 17, MacKenzie 1935, pp. 41–55, and Simmons 1998, pp. 65–66), but also of course to birds as corn-spirits. One instructive parallel is from far-off Indonesia (Frazer 1912, vol. 1, pp. 182, 295–96). "The Toradjas of Central Celebes think that the soul of the rice is embodied in a pretty little blue bird which builds its nest in the rice-field at the time when the rice is beginning to germinate, and which disappears again after the harvest. Thus both the place and the time of the appearance of the bird suggest to the natives the notion that the blue bird is the rice incarnate. And like the note of the quail in Europe the note of this little bird in Celebes is believed to prognosticate the state of the harvest, foretelling whether the rice will be abundant or scarce." It should also be noted that the soul has often been conceived as a bird, and that in primal belief-systems animals such as pigs are quite capable of having souls – thus as a bird the *torc sona* may be at one and the same time the spirit of the slaughtered corn and the soul of the slaughtered pig (Henderson 1911, pp. 88–98; Frazer 1911a, pp. 33–37).

In an elegy by Donald Chisholm (*Dòmhnall Gobha*) to Alexander, *An Siosal Bàn* (*c.*1750–1793), chief of the Chisholms, the *torc sona* symbolises the traditional route to prosperity approved by the people (Mackenzie 1891, p. 96, cf. Chisholm 1884–85, p. 220):

> *Cha b'e àrdachadh màil*
> *Dh'fhàg do bhancaichean làn*
>   *Ach torc-sona bhith ghnàth ad' chòir.*

("No increase of rent / Left your bank accounts full / But a *torc-sona* being always beside you.")

185   For full discussion of the Dubh-Sìth episode, and of the diminutive stature traditionally ascribed to archers, see MacInnes 1990–92, pp. 385–86, and cf. Gregory 1836, p. 285; Glenmore 1859, pp. 135–40; Chisholm 1883–84; Campbell 1895, pp. 5–6, 25–26, 28; Fergusson 1896–97, pp. 334–41; Lorne 1898, pp. 191–99; Sinclair 1899, pp. 157–58; Dieckhoff 1926, pp. 190–91; Budge 1960, p. 27; Mackechnie 1964, pp. 269–72; Barron 1976–78, pp. 429–31; Barron 1980–82, pp. 118–20; *Tocher* 35, pp. 323–24; *Tocher* 39, pp. 158–61; Gray 1987, pp. 225–27; *Tocher* 44, pp. 110–17; Bruford and MacDonald 1994, pp. 431–32, 483, 486; Maclean-Bristol 1999, pp. 241–43; Youngson n.d., p. 61; Youngson 2001, pp. 91, 94, 114–15.

186   Niall M. Brownlie does not know what village in Tiree JGC is referring to. *Sìthbheirean* is the word most commonly used in the island for 'Fairies'. *Clann Dubh-Shìth* could be MacPhies; Niall knows of only two families of MacPhies (MacPhees) who lived in the island, one in Balemartin and one in Scarinish.

Nor do I know who asserted that Dubh-Sìth was the ancient name of Duncan. 'Duncan' is from *Duncanus*, a Latinised form of Gaelic *Donnchadh*, which derives from the elements *donn* 'brown, noble' and *cath* 'battle' (Macbain 1896, p. 359). A *bodach* is a peasant (JGC's 'carle', see Black 2001, pp. 464–66), also a mutchkin, a liquid measure equivalent to three-fourths of an imperial pint, one-fourth of a Scots pint. *Ochdaran bodaich* thus appears to mean something like what would nowadays be called a dram.

187 I give the name as it stands in *SHIS* 102. As JGC says, it is difficult to translate. *Fasta* could be a genitive singular of *fasadh, fosadh* ('stance, encampment'). *Litheag* could represent *liobhag* ('broad-leaved pondweed') or possibly a derivative of *liath*, the colour of grey hair or mouldy bread. The best guess, then, is 'the Little Loch of the Pondweed Stance', especially if the weed provided good grazing for cattle, cf. p. 72 and note 122.

188 For *ailmeid* compare *almadh* 'tincture of alum' (Dwelly 1977, p. 26). A sheep's 'king's-hood' is its second stomach.

189 See 'St John's Wort (*Achlasan Chaluim Chille*)', pp. 230–31.

190 JGC wrote: "What could she want with snuff, when she had no nostril to put it in?" I have altered 'she' and 'she had' to 'you' and 'you have', which seemed more logical.

191 See note 913. 'Neither hair nor fur' will be alliterative: *cha robh falt no fionnadh air*.

192 The point, I take it, is that the stepmother is in league with the Fairies.

193 Niall M. Brownlie points out to me that *Cnoc Ghrianal*, properly *Cnoc Ghrianail* (Gaelic *cnoc* 'hillock', Norse *groene* 'green' and *vollr* 'field'), is very close to a flat grassy area which may be the site of a chapel dedicated to St Mo-Bhi. 'The Yellow Ridge', *an Druim Bhuidhe* nowadays, is a stretch of desolate moorland on the west side of the Cornaig road, see note 941.

194 This appears to be an extension of the principle that the Fairies may be let into the house 'by the fire, unless it be properly "raked" (*smàladh*), i.e. covered up to keep it alive for the night' (p. 10). See also p. 39.

195 Behind 'the pretty smooth-white' will be *am mìn-gheal bòidheach* or the like: *geal* is the colour of both silver and snow, and here it happens to denote silver. Is it possible that there is confusion between *bòidheach* 'pretty' and *buaidheach* 'magic, potent'? See notes 151, 236.

196 In a footnote, JGC explains Croy-Gortan as *Cruaidh-Ghortain* 'Stone-Field' and the *Léig* as 'a winter stream falling into Loch Vasipol'. *An Cruaidh Ghoirtean*, perhaps more literally 'the Hard Field' and pronounced *an Cruairtean* in the west of Tiree (cf. p. 282), is simply the Gaelic name for the township of Heylipol (which is from Norse *helgi* 'holy' and *ból* 'township'). The *Léig* ('Marsh') is a large ditch which flows through the middle of the township of Kilmoluag into the south-western corner of Loch Vasipol (*Loch Bhasapol*). JGC's *Léige* will be the genitive case – *thar na Léige* 'across the *Léig*'. See note 152.

197 JGC published the story in both Gaelic and English, with an introduction, in Campbell 1885b, dating his article 'Manse of Tiree, 1st Jany, 1883'. There are numerous differences between the two translations, however, the one written in 1883 being literal where ours (despite JGC's claim) is the more stylish. Two examples will suffice. The third sentence of our translation begins 'He levelled his gun at it'; in the original this is *Chuir e 'ghunna r' a shùil*, literally translated in the 1883 version 'He put his gun to his eye'. Similarly, the sixth sentence of our translation ends 'and walked up till he was close to the woman's breast'; in the original this is *agus dh'fhalbh e gus an robh e ri 'broilleach*, literally translated in the 1883 version 'and went until he was close to her breast'. This suggests that the 1883 translation (not necessarily made in 1883, of course) may have pre-dated ours, but we cannot be certain even of that. For Donald Cameron, Ruaig, see pp. 633, 654, 668. For the story see also Mackay 1927b, p. 62; MacFarlane 1927–28, pp. 149–50; Cameron 1937–41, pp. 209–11; Mac'illeathain 1942–50, p. 45; Macdonald 1982, pp. 227–28; Youngson n.d., pp. 43–44; MacDonald 1994–95, pp. 55–56. The dog became proverbial (*Tocher* 47, p. 297): *Tha 'latha fhéin a' feitheamh air cù dubh Mhic-a-Phì.* "MacPhee's black dog's own day is awaiting it." But more commonly (Nicolson 1951, p. 366): *Thig là a' choin duibh fhathast.* "The black dog's day will come yet."

198 This is how the passage is laid out in *SHIS* 111, suggesting that JGC regarded it as a 'run' (a passage containing obscure and often archaic diction which storytellers enjoyed repeating

for effect). In Campbell 1885b, pp. 266 (Gaelic) and 270 (English), however, JGC laid it out as ordinary prose, as follows: "'*D e do naigheachd, a Shianach?*' *ars' esan.* "*D e sin duitse, a Bhrian Brugh?*' *ars' ise.* "*Chunna' mis' thus', a Shianach,*" *ars' esan,* "*is tu gabhail coinne ris na Fiantaichean, 's tu falbh le Diarmad o Dhuibhne, 's tu falbh leis o phill gu pill.*" "*Chunna' mis' thusa,*" *ars' ise,* "*a Bhrian Brugh, is tu marcachd air seann each dubh, leannan na mnà seanga sìdh, is tu 'ga sìor-ruith o bhrugh gu brugh.*" "'What's your news to-day, Sianach?' said he. 'What's that to you, Brian Brugh?' said she. 'I saw you, Sianach,' said he, 'when you held meetings with the Fingalians, when you went away with Diarmid o Duibhne, and accompanied him from covert to covert.' 'I saw you,' said she, 'Brian Brugh, when you rode on an old black horse, the sweetheart of the slim fairy woman, and ever chasing her from brugh to brugh.'" In this passage, metaphorically and perhaps also physically, MacPhie speaks to the woman in the language of the otherworld, and receives a spirited response which proves her identity. He addresses her by name as Sianach, showing that he knows, or guesses, who she really is. In our version of the translation JGC loses the impact of this somewhat by generalising it into 'Elle-maid' (on the basis of *sian* 'a charm'), presumably after recalling that the name of Diarmad's celebrated lover was not Sianach but Gráinne; compare *Sianag*, p. 86. Sianach, in turn, identifies MacPhie as Brian Brugh – Brian Boru, no less – and takes pleasure in the little piece of racy word-play that his sobriquet allows. Thus does the passage put to comic use the single most important fact about the Gaelic otherworld – that time does not exist there, and its denizens live for ever.

199   Campbell 1860–62, vol. 2, p. 52 = 1890, vol. 2, p. 62: "A family who lived in Gaolin Castle, Kerrera, near Oban, had, as they supposed, a delicate child; it was advancing in years but not growing a bit; at length a visitor from Ireland came to the castle, and recognized her as the fairy sweetheart of an Irish gentleman of his acquaintance. He addressed her in Gaelic or Irish, saying, *Tha thusa sin(n) a shirach bheag leannan Brian MacBraodh.* 'There thou art, little fairy sweetheart of Brian MacBroadh.' So offended was the elf at being exposed, that she ran out of the castle and leaped into the sea from the point called *Ru(th)adh na Sirach*, the fairies' point, to this day." *Brian MacBraodh* is clearly another reflection of Brian Boru, victor of Clontarf (1014), and all in all it can clearly be seen that this Kerrera story has much in common with the 'run' discussed in note 198 – indeed *Rubha na Sìbhreach*, the southernmost point of the island, appears on modern maps as *Rubha nan Seanach*, forming a curious doublet with JGC's *Sianach* 'Elle-maid'. According to Mrs Morag Smith (*née* MacFadyen), Oban, who grew up in Kerrera, this is *Rubha nan Seunach* 'the point of the charms, luck, fortune, enchantments, etc.' (Angus Peter Campbell, personal communication, 21.8.03). Since JGC understood *Sianach* to mean 'Elle-maid', I think it is reasonable to infer that *Sianach/Seunach* is roughly synonymous with *Sìbhreach*, and may be understood as 'enchanted one', 'otherworld being', or indeed, as Alexander Forbes had it, 'monster' (Dwelly 1977, p. 837).

200   As a native of Colonsay himself, Professor Donald Mackinnon (1839–1914) had a particular interest in JGC's story, and commented upon it in a manuscript note in his interleaved copy of *The Scottish Celtic Review*, now EUL Mackinnon (1924) 2.3. "The story of McPhee & his black dog was repeated to me in 1881," he wrote ('1881' is uncertain, and seems to have been corrected from '1882'), "by Angus McMillan (Black Angus) Kilchattan, Colonsay. It differed considerably from this. According to McMillan, McPhee brought the dog as pup from Jura when he was in hiding during his boyhood & early manhood. The beast was lazy & ugly & was kicked & cuffed by all & sundry. McPhee took his side, always saying: 'Wait you: thig latha choin duibh fhathast.' He was married to a relative of McLean. One day while out on the green, his wife & he saw the McLeans aproaching. The wife's life, being a blood relation, was safe, but McPhee & his man, Mac-a-Bhàsdair, took to the hill. The black dog followed. Mac-a-Bhasdair swam out to the rock in Traigh Bàn still called after his name &

was drowned. McPhee & the dog betook themselves to 'Slochd dubh Mhic a-Phi' – at the time an 'uamha thuill' or toll ruith – & one stood at either entrance to guard it. Dog & man made good their defence till the MacLeans penetrated the roof of the cave, came down behind & killed both. In Oban Telegraph (20/8/86) some of the details of the story as given here are located at Rossnish in E. of Benbecula. McPhee & 12 men arrive to carry away spoil. They enter a shieling & the Colonsay men as they lie down say 'I wish I had a girl with me now'. Twelve beautiful women enter, seize the men & kill them. One stood without. McPhee asks her name. 'Marion.' 'Marion is not an admired name among women. It is not the name of my maid.' 'Let me see what you can do, you black useless dog,' says McPhee to his dog which had not barked for 5 yrs. previously. The dog fixed his teeth in the female, & only at cock crow did she & the twelve depart. McPhee remained some years in Uist, & became the progenitor of all the McPhees in S. Uist."

201 See Black 1972–74, pp. 219–21.

202 For the ballad – which is in the romantic taste of his day, and would nowadays not even be called 'beautiful' – see Leyden 1875, pp. 100–11. His lengthy introduction begins (p. 96): "The following poem is founded upon a Gaelic traditional ballad, called Macphail of Colonsay, and the Mermaid of Corrivrekin . . . The Gaelic story bears, that Macphail of Colonsay was carried off by a Mermaid, while passing the gulf above mentioned: that they resided together in a grotto beneath the sea for several years, during which time she bore him five children; but finally, he tired of her society, and having prevailed upon her to carry him near the shore of Colonsay, he escaped to land."

He tells in his *Journal* (Leyden 1903, pp. 48–50) how he 'fell in' with the story. He and his two companions had chartered a small boat, rowed by four fishermen, to bring them from Iona to Oban, and were spending the night in a hut at Carsaig on the coast of Mull. "During the night the fishermen amused us with singing concerning Oscar MacOshin, who, as they translated the stanza, was so dreadfully gashed at the battle of Ben Eden that the cranes might have flown through him, yet he was cured by Fingal . . . They likewise related the story of MacPhail of Colonsay, with whom the Mermaid of the gulf of Corrivrekin fell in love; and snatching him down to her palace in Davie's locker, detained him for a long period, during which she bore him several children, and generally appeared to him in the form of a beautiful woman, advising him, however, to keep his distance whenever she assumed her fishy tail, lest she should devour him. But carrying him one day near the land, he sprang suddenly ashore and deserted his sea-goddess. This last story, however, seemed to amuse us much more than the fishermen, who appeared to be dreadfully afraid of some sea-spirit's appearance from some of the stormy recesses of the dark shore of Mull. I know not how far they might be to the taste of a sea-nymph, but I apprehend there was little danger of their being ravished by a land one."

Leyden appears to have been strangely insensitive to the metaphorical dimension of the tale, for the six men, crossing the open sea as they were in a little coble with crude oars and scarce room to move, were in real danger of their lives. See also Henderson 1902, pp. 277–301.

203 Cf. *dùbhra, dùbhradh* 'shade, spectre' (Dwelly 1977, p. 370).

204 JGC here remarks in a footnote: "It is often observable in popular tales that articles of modern use are ascribed to those who lived before their invention. Anachronisms are not heeded in popular lore."

205 See also Cameron 1937–41, pp. 207–08, and *Tocher* 28, pp. 204–07. JGC says that *Sgrìob na Caillich* is in Islay, but the best-known feature of this name is a huge trail of scree at the back of Beinn an Òir in Jura, facing Rubha a' Mhàil across the mouth of the Sound of Islay (Youngson 2001, p. 21 and cf. p. 484): "Sgriob na Caillich . . . is interpreted as a medial moraine deposited between two streams of the ice-sheet as they converged after sweeping

around and through the Paps from the east. It is 3.5 km long and drops from 450 m OD to 30 m OD at which point the boulder belts are cut off by a low cliff and raised coastal platform . . . No other medial moraine in Scotland can compare with Sgriob na Caillich in either size or complexity.'

206 See note 98. In Scott's telling of the story (1806, pp. 1–2) there is no dog at all, but the Jew's harp figures prominently. Two hunters in a bothy are confronted by two beautiful young women dressed in green. One of the hunters is seduced, disappears, and is torn to pieces and devoured, but the other 'continued to play upon a trump, or Jew's harp, some strain, consecrated to the Virgin Mary', and when daylight comes his temptress vanishes. Scott used the story for his ballad 'Glenfinlas, or Lord Ronald's Coronach' (*ibid.*, p. 15):

> *And, bending o'er his harp, he flung*
> *His wildest witch-notes on the wind;*
> *And loud, and high, and strange, they rung,*
> *As many a magic change they find.*

A version in Anon. 1908–09a, pp. 164–65, apparently from Lewis, is very similar.

207 See for example p. 15 above; Abrach 1873–74b; Anon. 1908–09a, pp. 157–58; Grant 1925, pp. 10–11; MacKenzie 1935, p. 152.

208 JGC discusses historical aspects of this anecdote in a footnote. *Dòmhnall mac Iain*, he says, is probably to be identified with *Dòmhnall Dubh Beag Innse Ruithe*, a celebrated bowman and follower of Cameron of Locheil who, according to tradition, shot an arrow that nailed the hand of *Aonghas Mòr mac 'ic Eòin* of Ardnamurchan – one of the most stalwart men of his day – to his forehead in *Coir' Ospainn* in Morvern *c.* 1596. He adds that according to others the hunter whose arrow struck the hind was *Iain Dubh Beag*, and that another (perhaps the same) celebrated Lochaber archer was *Iain Beag a' Bhuilg Bhàin* from Coruanan, for whom see note 180 above. (He was presumably of the MacLachlans of Coruanan; the *balg bàn* or 'white bag' would have been his quiver.) For Coir' Ospainn see note 83, and for an Achintore cowherd called *Dòmhnall mac Iain* see note 211.

209 The motif of the hair out of the cailleach's head (*riobag as a falt*) appears in the story 'Sealgair Shrath Eirinn is a' Chailleach' ('The Strath Dearn Hunter and the Witch') in MacDougall and Calder 1910, pp. 230–33. The hunter pretends to tie his dogs with the hair, but uses one of his own garters instead. When the dogs leap at her she cries out: *Teannaich, a riobag!* "Tighten, hair!" And the hunter responds: *Lasaich, a ghartain!* "Slacken, garter!" It is in fact the central motif of a tale containing the four elements of deer-hunter, woman, hair and dog(s) which, remarkably, is well known in the Caucasus and Gaelic Scotland but nowhere else (Davidson and Chaudhri 1993). See also Mac Dhughaill 1913, p. 32; Grant 1925, pp. 1–2; MacDonald 1994–95, pp. 36–37; note 211 below.

210 This will mean *c.* 1854, I think.

211 This motif appears in MacDougall and Calder's tale (1910, pp. 236–37) of how an Achintore cowherd called *Dòmhnall mac Iain* (cf. note 208 above) meets a glaistig on Beinn Bhreac. *A Dhomhnuill MhicIain*, she says, *bha mi air an Uiriallaich an uair a chuir thu a' cheud srad 'san spong, agus an Coire na Snaige an uair a ghabh an sop teine, agus tha mi an so a nis an uair a tha an connadh a' tòiseachadh air gabhail.* "Donald MacIan, I was on the Uralich when you put the first spark in the tinder, and in the Woodpecker's Corrie when the wisp took fire; and here I am now as the fuel is beginning to kindle." *Is math a choisich thu, a bheathaich bhochd*, he replies fearlessly. "You have walked well, poor creature." There then follows the motif of the hair and the garter discussed in note 209. See p. 98, where *Coire na Snaige* has become the Coolin Hills, and the word *snag* ('woodpecker', 'clinking sound', 'nightjar', see CG2, p. 299) has taken the place of *srad* 'spark'. *Coire na Snaige* is also

mentioned in 'Òran na Comhachaig' by Dòmhnall mac Fhionnlaigh nan Dàn (Watson 1959, p. 253):

> *Nuair bhùireas damh Beinne Bige*
> *'S a bheucas damh Beinn na Craige,*
> *Freagraidh na daimh ud d'a chéile*
> *'S thig féidh á Coire na Snaige.*

("When the stag of Beinn Bheag bellows / And the Beinn na Craige stag roars, / Yon stags will answer each other / And deer will come from the Woodpecker's Corry.")

There is an *Allt an t-Snaige* in Glen Nevis south of *Màm Beag*. One informant told Professor Rankin that *Coire na Snaige* was on the *Garbh Bheinn* south of Kinlochleven, but he could not find it there on any map (1998, p. 116). I would add that if this were the case, it would be the only place-name in that entire poem in the *dùthchas* of the Glencoe MacDonalds. In any case, I think the context makes it clear that the three place-names in this stanza are to be found close to each other, and Rankin believed (*loc. cit.*) that *Beinn Bheag* and *Beinn na Craige* were to be identified with Meall Mór and Creag Uanach respectively, which puts them just east of the head of Glen Nevis.

It seems to me that if we can identify the *Uiriallach* (which I have so far failed to do), *Coire na Snaige* must lie approximately halfway between it and *Beinn Bhreac*. The only mountain-names I know which come slightly close are *Sgùrr Coire nan Eiricheallach* north of Loch Quoich, *Càrn na Fuaralaich* ('the Cairn of the Cold Place') behind the Cluanie Inn in the parish of Glenshiel (Watson 1904, p. 174; Mackay 1968, p. 10) and *An Cearcallach* ('The Circular One') above Moy at the head of Glen Spean, the last of which deserves to be mentioned only because it lies in an area steeped in occult associations, see note 635. In the meantime we have a working hypothesis that *Coire na Snaige* lies at the head of *Allt an t-Snaige* in a bend of the River Nevis, but the varying gender is a worry.

212 *Féith Chiarain* is the gloomy morass that lies trapped between the steep slopes of *Beinn a' Bhric* and *Meall a' Bhainne*. It is drained south-south-west by *Allt Féith Chiarain* into *Loch Chiarain*, then south by the Ciaran Water into what is now the Blackwater Reservoir.

213 Ben-y-Ghloe is given by JGC at p. 50 as *Beinn a' Ghlotha* and by Ó Murchú (1989, pp. 184–85, 291) as *Beann a' Ghlotha* (?), na Beinnichean Glotha 'the peaks of Beinn a' Ghlo'. It presumably reflects Dwelly's *glo* 'veil, covering, hood' (1977, p. 504). It lies north-east of Blair Atholl above Glen Tilt.

214 By 'wife' he means *cailleach*, not *bean*. The *cailleach* here is all the things she is elsewhere. For the 'witch' of Ben-y-Ghloe see Scrope 1894, pp. 160–66, and Gray 1987, pp. 13–14.

215 Ossian, Scottish Gaelic *Oisein*, Irish *Oisín*, means 'Little Deer', from *os* 'a deer'. For an intriguing story of a deer as *leannan sìth* see Henderson 1911, pp. 124–25.

216 'Oisein's Song to his Mother', Campbell 1872, pp. 198–99; 'Oisein's Warning to his Mother', *ibid.*, pp. 199–200. See also Campbell 1891, pp. 78–80, and Tolmie 1911, pp. 249–50.

217 Malcolm Sinclair, *Calum Bàn*, was father of the celebrated twentieth-century tradition-bearer Donald Sinclair, *Dòmhnall Chaluim Bàin*, who called himself *am Bàrd Tostach* ('the Silent Poet'), see *Tocher* 18, pp. 41–65, and Cregeen and MacKenzie 1978, pp. 16, 21, 22, 24, 25. Calum Bàn settled in Barra for a while, but returned, and worked for JGC for a time (see 'Life', p. 665 below). As JGC knew perfectly well (Campbell 1885b, p. 262), the tale he told is part of one usually called 'Leigheas Coise Céin', 'Sgeulachd Choise Chéin', 'The Healing of Keyne's Leg', etc. This version (original and translation) was read for JGC to the Gaelic Society of Inverness by Alexander Macbain on 14 December 1887 and published in 1889 (see Campbell 1887–88a). For other versions see MacInnes 1890, pp. 206–77; Henderson 1901–03; Campbell 1940–60, vol. 1, pp. 68–73; MacNeil 1987, pp. 56, 454–55. For discussion of

the tale see 'Life', pp. 635–39 below, and Bruford 1969, pp. 134–36; for a fuller source-list see *ibid.*, p. 262.

218 The original (Campbell 1887–88a, p. 79) has *b' e aite còmhnuidh a chòiruisg.* Loch Coruisg (*Loch Coir' Uisg'*) in Skye and Corsica (*Corsic*) in the Mediterranean would fit quite well (Hogan 1910, p. 298), but the locus is Ireland, and I know of no such place there. See p. 638 below.

219 JGC discusses the identity of these individuals in a note in Campbell 1887–88a, p. 99. They clearly represent Brian Boru or Boroime (victor of Clontarf 1014, slain in the battle) and his sons Murchadh (also slain at Clontarf), Donnchadh (d. 1064) and Tadhg (d. 1023), see Todd 1867, p. 247. JGC remarks: "MacCimi is a designation of the Lovat family. The writer can give no explanation of it . . ." Clearly however it represents not Lovat's patronymic *mac Shimidh* but Brian Boru's – *mac Cinnéidigh.* Brian Borr (Bòrr, Brugh, Braodh) and Murchadh mac Bhriain occur frequently in Gaelic verse and tales, see for example pp. 59, 98 ('The Gruagach'); Stewart 1804, pp. 549–53; Campbell 1872, pp. 22, 26, 209–10; Campbell 1890, vol. 2, pp. 209–31; Grant 1925, pp. 17–18; Bruford 1967–68; Bruford 1969, pp. 136–43; Ó Duilearga 1981, pp. 209–18 (further references p. 391); Bruford and MacDonald 1994, pp. 153–70, 454.

On 15 September 1871 JGC gave JFC a splendid 'arming run' about Eoghan O Neill which the latter printed in Campbell 1872, pp. 210–11, under the heading 'EOGHAN O NEILL A CHIUR AIR EACH'. Obtained 'from Harry . . . Beadle of the Strowan Church, Blair Atholl, Perthshire, 1859', it is described as 'a Caricature of Murcha Mac Brian, or of some other such person'. Elsewhere on the same page JFC describes it as "a parody which I got from a Gentleman, in Tiree, in 1871. He got it somewhere in the east of Scotland from a man who could say it by heart." See Mackechnie 1964, p. 279. It is certainly comical: of Eoghan's horse, for example, the beadle says: *Bha trì gnèithean de ghnè na mna ann an each Eoghain, tòn mhòr, meadhon seang, 's mairsinn buan air a mharcachd.* ("There were three aspects of a woman's nature in Eoghan's horse, a big backside, a slender waist, and lasting forever when ridden.") It also contains distinct traces of the *crosanachd* structure once widely used for satire (see Black 2001, p. 408). It is 'a Caricature of Murcha Mac Brian' in so far as it clearly bears some relationship to a more sober run on the same subject which JFC prints on the same page (Campbell 1872, p. 210) from the Rev. Donald McNicol's collection under the title 'MURCHADH MAC BRIAN', with this introduction: "As these old tales decay and the old language becomes difficult, it becomes a feat to be able to recite a particular passage. The man who can 'put Murdoch Mac Brian in his riding dress' is famed now . . . The Hero of the story was one of the Heroes of the Battle of Clontarff. The composition must therefore date between 1014 and 1750, when Mac Nicol flourished. An old weaver at Tobermory recited a version of this to me in 1870. John Dewar wrote a version in 1869; and generally this pervades Scotland." Murchadh is not named within the text, however, and it seems likely that runs of this kind might be applied to any great Gaelic warrior – there is one in the 'Little Book of Clanranald' (Cameron 1892–94, vol. 2, pp. 258–65) addressed to John, last Lord of the Isles. They seem to have come from the oral narrative tradition, see for example Mackay 1927–28, pp. 22–23, and the run beginning *A chòtan caomh cotain air uachdar na caomh chotaige* in 'Gaisgeach na Sgéithe Deirge' ('The Knight of the Red Shield'), Campbell 1890, vol. 2, pp. 458, 475; Macleod 1906–07, p. 264; Murchison 1988, p. 156.

220 In the original (Campbell 1887–88a, p. 81) this is *o cheann gu ceann do'n tur Bhaile-Chaisteil* – Ballycastle, Co. Antrim, a place very well known to the Islay folk, especially at the time of its celebrated Lammas Fair.

221 JGC's fellow minister in Tiree from 1879 to 1886, John MacRury, published a Gaelic translation of the Arabian Nights, *Sgeulachdan Arabianach,* in Inverness in 1897.

222 'An Gruagach Bàn, Mac Rìgh Eireann' ('The Fair Gruagach, Son of the King of Eirinn'), Campbell 1860–62, vol. 2, pp. 410–34 = 1890, vol. 2, pp. 424–49.

223 What JGC means is that JFC's version of the charm is the best that JGC has come across, but that JFC's *translation* leaves something to be desired, which is very true – e.g. for *buaraiche* ('cow-fetters, spancels') JFC gives 'herdsmen', which JGC alters to 'shackles'; for *caitheadh-beatha* ('livelihood') JFC gives 'wearing of life'; and, I would add, for *laogh* both JFC and JGC rightly give 'calf', but it deserves to be pointed out that this word can be a term of endearment for a child (see p. 185). JFC's original and translation are as follows (Campbell 1860–62, vol. 2, pp. 410–11, 425–26 = 1890, vol. 2, pp. 424–25, 440): *Tha mi 'ga d' chur fo gheasan agus fo chroisean, fo naoidh buaraiche mnatha sìthe, siùbhlaiche, seachranaiche; an laogh beag is meata 's is mi-threòraiche 'thoirt do chinn, 's do chluas, 's do chaitheadh-beatha dhìot; mu ni thu tamh oidhche na latha, far an gabh thu do bhraiceas nach gabh thu do dhinneir, agus far an gabh thu do dhinneir nach gabh thu do shuipeir, ge b'e àit 'am bi thu, gos am faigh thu 'mach ge b'e àit am bi mise fo cheithir ranna ruadha 'n t-saoghail.* "I am laying thee under spells, and under crosses, under holy herdsmen of quiet travelling, wandering woman, the little calf, most feeble and powerless, to take thy head and thine ear and thy wearing of life from off thee, if thou takest rest by night or day; where thou takest thy breakfast that thou take not thy dinner, and where thou takest thy dinner that thou take not thy supper, in whatsoever place thou be, until thou findest out in what place I may be under the four brown quarters of the world."

The beginning of the charm is repeated later in the story. With reference to his translation JFC remarks in a footnote (1st edn p. 411, 2nd edn p. 425): "This sort of incantation is common, and I am not certain that it is quite correctly rendered." For a version of the charm in the tale 'Gille nan Cochla-Craicinn' ('The Lad of the Skin Coverings') see MacDougall 1891, pp. 35, 49; cf. Campbell 1891, pp. 260–61, 268, 274; *CG*1, p. 285; MacLellan 1961, pp. 21, 212; Dorson 1968, p. 405; MacNeil 1987, pp. 50–57. See also Campbell 1881a, pp. 63, 71, and Nutt 1881, p. 138.

224 See Jackson 1962.

225 See pp. 15 and 24.

226 This belief that goats' milk was the food of the Fairies – and therefore, arguably, the secret of eternal life – probably lay behind the eighteenth-century fashion for retreating to a simple life in the country and drinking only the whey from goats' milk. According to Hamilton (1981, p. 101), "The resorts which provided this were at Callander and Luss and in 1740 it was recorded that in Glasgow in July, all the ministers were absent, being 'at the goat's whey'." See also Mackellar 1887–88, pp. 149–50, and Moodie 1902–04, p. 331.

227 See p. 148. The name Dunbuck – *Dùn Buic* 'He-Goat Fort', 'Buck Fort' – is itself relevant. Any distinctively rounded hill with a caprine name was likely to gain otherworld associations. Viewed from the Clyde or beyond, Dunbuck (now usually Dumbuck) is very prominent.

228 'Lying in the smallpox' represents Gaelic idiom, see also p. 259 and compare the lines

> *Is truagh nach robh m' athair an galar*
> *Agus Cailean Liath am plàigh.*

('It's a shame my father was not in a sickness / And Grey Colin was not in a plague', Watson 1959, p. 244.)

229 Milkmaids tended to contract cowpox, which prevented them catching smallpox.

230 By 'about the end of last century' JGC means *c*. 1790.

231 On *meillich* see note 4. Mary Mackellar was told by a man in Harris that his forefathers had such cows for generations (1888–89, p. 168). "One of his ancestors had been out hunting on the hill-side, and as he lay still he saw these creatures of the flood rushing past him. He had the presence of mind to know what they were and threw a handful of earth towards them. The one on whose back it fell stood spell-bound unable to follow the herd to the sea. He led

her home, and she seemed quite content with her new mode of life. She and her progeny were all good milchers."

JGC's *Losg an Tìr* deserves comment, as it sheds light on the pronunciation of the name if not its meaning. Loscantire, usually now spelt Luskentyre, is a point of land facing the isle of Taransay, and according to Donald MacIver (1934, p. 42) 'it was customary to kindle a fire here to draw the attention of the islanders to the urgency of crossing the sound in a boat'. The second element is not *an Tìr* but *Ceann Tìr(e)* 'Point of Land'. For the first element MacIver offers 'lios, leus, losg, G[aelic], burning heather'. Of these, only *leus* 'blaze, flame', having a long vowel, would remain semi-stressed when qualified, as in the pronunciation of the name (cf. *Laoisguitir, Laoisgiutar,* Mac a Phì 1938, p. 125). In origin, then, the name appears to be *Leus Ceann Tìr(e)* 'Headland Blaze', modified under semi-stress to *Luscantìr, Loscantìr.* Nisibost Beach, *Tràigh Niseabost*, lies to the south of the headland, just east of *Clach Mhic Leòid,* see note 510.

232   By 'Bernera in Uist' (or 'Bernera, in Uist', as it stands in *SHIS* 136) JGC means the island now indeed known as Berneray Uist (*Beàrnaraigh Uibhist*) but then more usually as 'Berneray Harris' (*Beàrnaraigh na Hearadh*). Once an important centre of the power of the MacLeods of Harris, it is now joined to North Uist by a causeway. The only other island of the name which is still inhabited is Bernera Lewis (*Beàrnaraigh Leòdhais*), which has been joined to Lewis by a bridge since 1953. Cf. note 4.

    Creag Mhòr Mhic Neacail, which guards the northern entrance to Loch Portree, is referred to by Forbes (1923, p. 145) as *Creag 'Ic Neacail*: "It is where Prince Charlie landed, a long scaur at Scorribreac, north of Portree harbour." The Prince landed there from Raasay about 11 p.m. on 3 July (some sources say 2 July) 1746. It is given by Chambers (1840, p. 107) as 'Nicholson's Great Rock' and by his translator John Mackenzie as *Creag mhòr Mhic-Neacail* (Mac-Choinnich 1844, p. 208). See Sellar and Maclean 1999, pp. 3–4, 18, 59.

233   JGC did not offer a translation, so I have supplied one. These are characteristic cow-names, with which we may compare Carmichael's list of over 100 cow- and bull-names from Vallay (North Uist) and Torrantuirc (Lorn) in *CG6*, p. 271 (= EUL MS CW 504B, ff. 132r–134r). Points of interest here are *cionnan* (*ceann* 'head' + *fionn* 'white'), otherwise *ceannann*, and the fact that, while they certainly denote cows, four of the five semi-proper names here are grammatically masculine – quite a high proportion. In his similar (but detailed) account of the Fairy cows that used to come ashore on the machair of North Uist and Benbecula (*Tocher* 16, pp. 308–11), Peter Morrison gave the Fairy herdsmen's call as

> *Donnach, Tromach, Sgiathan, Liathan!*
> *Thigeadh an crodh-laoigh*
> *Co-dhiùbh thig no dh'fhan na buachaillean.*

("Brownie, Preggie, Wingie, Grizzly! / Let the milch cows come / Whether the herdsmen come or have stayed.") See also Mackellar 1888–89, p. 168; MacPhail 1897, pp. 384–85; *CG2*, pp. 260–61; Mac Thomais 1937–41, p. 181; McDonald 1958, p. 257; Campbell 1969–81, vol. 2, p. 364; Ó Duilearga 1981, p. 278; Macdonald 1982, pp. 194–95; Black 2002, p. 19; EUL MS CW 504A, f. 40r.

234   Campbell 1860–62, vol. 2, pp. 68–69 = 1890, vol. 2, pp. 79–80. The story concerns a man in Berneray Harris, but was sent to JFC from North Uist, 11 August 1859, by 'Malcolm MacLean, who learnt it from his grandfather, Hugh MacLean'. The traveller's words when he heard the sound of churning were: *B' fheàrr leom gon robh mo phathadh air a' bhanachaig.* JFC translates: "I had rather that my thirst was on the herdswoman." I am not sure what JFC meant by 'herdswoman'; *banachag* is conventionally translated 'dairymaid'.

235   'Three generations ago' will mean *c.* 1780. It is hard to know what song is meant. Perhaps

it is the port-á-beul 'Cnoc Mhàrtainn' to which children used to dance (Mhàrtainn 2001, pp. 95, 124), and which was sung in the nursery at Bracadale manse in Skye in 1861 (Tolmie 1911, pp. 180–81):

> *Fac' thu na féidh gu léir, a Bhoireagain,*
> *Fac' thu na féidh, a Theàrlaich?*
> *Fac' thu na féidh gu léir, a Bhoireagain,*
> *Suas gu mullach Cnoc Mhàrtainn?*
> *Ruidhlidh Boireagan, dannsaidh Boireagan,*
> *Ruidhlidh Boireagan Theàrlaich.*
> *Aran is ìm dhomh fhìn 's do Bhoireagan,*
> *Suas gu mullach Cnoc Mhàrtainn.*

("Have you seen all the deer, Boireagan, / Have you seen the deer, Charlie? / Have you seen all the deer, Boireagan, / Going to the top of Cnoc Mhàrtainn? / Boireagan will twirl, Boireagan will dance, / Charlie's Boireagan will twirl. / Bread and butter for me and Boireagan, / Going to the top of Cnoc Mhàrtainn.")

236 See Forbes 1923, p. 331. This is at Gedintailor. In the words of Malcolm Nicolson (MacNeacail 1975, p. 39):

> *Rugadh mis' ann an Gead an Tàilleir,*
> *Baile beag a tha sa Bhràighe*
> *'S e fo shàilean na Beinn Bhòidheach —*
> *Sann a fhuaradh na h-àrmainn.*

("I was born in Gedintailor, / A small township in the Braes / Beneath the heels of the Pretty Hill – / That's where the warriors were found.") As Dr John MacInnes has pointed out to me, however, *bòidheach* 'pretty' is regularly pronounced *buaidheach*. The latter word means – or used to mean – 'magic, potent'; this will be the real meaning of the mountain's name. Note that *Bhuaidheach* gives *aicill* rhyme with *fhuaradh* (*aicill* is present in nearly every couplet of the poem). Nicolson makes clear in later stanzas that his *àrmainn* are those of the Battle of the Braes (1882), not sleeping warriors under the hill.

237 The motif is defined by MacDonald (1994–95, p. 55) as 'fairy song (a) or tune (b) overheard and learned'. *Cnoc na Clàrsaich*, 'Harp Hillock', is at Port Bàn on the eastern tip of Tiree. Fiona MacKinnon tells a story about it (1992, no. 2) which is not the one given here but strongly resembles one summarised by JGC at p. 51 as: "A man who avoided tethering horse or cow on a Fairy hillock . . . was rewarded by the Fairies driving his horse and cow to the lee of the hillock in stormy nights." See Spence 1948, pp. 182–84.

238 There are two possible derivations of the name MacCrimmon (*MacCruimein*), neither of which is the one given by JGC. The eponymous *Cruimean* may have been early Irish *Crimthann* or *Crumthann* – O'Brien (1962, pp. 569–72) lists fifty-eight separate individuals named *Crimthann* or *Crumthann* who are mentioned in Irish manuscripts, but only one named *Crommán* and one named *Crummín*. Ó Corráin and Maguire (1990, pp. 61–62) point out that Crimthann was one of the most popular names in early Ireland, that it was borne by ten warriors of the *Féinn*, and, most telling of all from our point of view, that it was said to have been the real name of Calum Cille. Alternatively, as pointed out by Black (1946, p. 480) and by Hanks and Hodges (1988, p. 357), the eponym may have borne the Old Norse name *Hroðmundr* (*hród* 'fame', *mundr* 'protection'). In view of the Norse origin of the MacLeods and of various associated kindreds (see note 435), the latter explanation probably has the edge.

The Cremona claim was first put into print by the Rev. Dr Norman MacLeod, *Caraid nan Gaidheal*, in an essay published in August 1840 (MacLeod 1840–41). Perhaps he had heard the pipe tune 'The Battle of Cremona' (Macaulay 1968), or perhaps he was influenced by some tradition similar to that of *Feadan Dubh nan Siosalach*, the Black Chanter of the Chisholms, said to have been brought from Italy by a Chisholm chief and his Cameron piper (Mackenzie 1891, p. 73; Campbell 1940–60, vol. 2, pp. 54–59). He may have regarded this as more rational than the widespread belief that the MacCrimmon chanter was a gift from the Fairies, but in fact Italy was regarded by the people as 'the country above all others in which the "Black art" was to be acquired' (Mackay 1876, p. 340, cf. McPherson 1929, p. 183, and MacInnes 1966, p. 107); this supernatural element is well to the fore in the story of the Chisholm chanter. Unfortunately he chose to write of the MacCrimmons (MacLeod 1840–41, p. 134): *Thainig a' cheud fhear do 'n ainm so maille ri Mac Leòid o bhaile anns an Eadailt d' am b' ainm* Cremona. *Bu chruitear a bha san duine so. Bha e 'na fhear-ciùil ainmeil 'na latha 's 'na linn féin. Ghabh e ainm an àit anns an d' rugadh e, agus na thainig uaithe dh' ainmich iad Clann-'ic-Chruimein.* "The first man of this name came with MacLeod from a town in Italy called *Cremona*. This person was a harpist. He was a famous musician in his own day and generation. He took the name of the place in which he was born, and his descendants they called the MacCrimmons."

The comments of Fred T. MacLeod on the alleged derivation are worth citing in full (1933b, pp. 5–6): "The oft-repeated statement that the first member of the MacCrimmon family was a native of Cremona in Italy, and that MacLeod of Dunvegan, when on a visit to that town, took this man into his service as a musician and brought him home to Dunvegan, giving to him the name 'Cremonach', is, in my view, erroneous. It has been suggested that this man became MacLeod's piper and that his descendants, following the usual highland custom, prefixed 'Mac' to their surname. So far as I have been able to ascertain, these statements first appeared in the short account of the MacCrimmons written in Gaelic by the Rev. Dr Norman MacLeod (Caraid nan Gaidheal). Dr MacLeod, unfortunately, throws no light on the source of his information. When in Skye over thirty years ago I conversed with my grandfather, who was then bordering on 100 years of age, and from him and other old people in the MacCrimmons' native parish I endeavoured to ascertain local knowledge as to the origin of the family, and I found the Cremona view strongly supported, which I at first regarded as important. It was, however, frankly admitted to me by the people who expressed that view that they were simply following the lead of Dr MacLeod, with whose Gaelic account of the MacCrimmon family they were familiar."

Norman MacLeod, the old man in question, was born in 1802 and died in 1901 (*ibid.*, pp. 18, 23). Fred T. MacLeod was quite impressed by reports of the Cremona tradition being heard in St Kilda (*ibid.*, pp. 6–7), but it has to be said that the essays of Caraid nan Gaidheal would have been read in the ceilidh-house – or indeed in the church – there as elsewhere. When Caraid nan Gaidheal's son-in-law reprinted the offending essay (Clerk 1867, p. 378) he quietly added some words at the beginning of the statement to absolve his father-in-law from blame: *Tha iad ag ràdh gu'n d'thàinig a' cheud fhear de 'n ainm so maille ri Mac Leòid o bhaile anns an Eadailt d' am b' ainm* Cremona . . . "They say that the first man of this name came with MacLeod from a town in Italy called *Cremona* . . ."

I recall that in the 1960s the deputy director of the College of Piping in Glasgow, Thomas Pearston, took advantage of a holiday in Italy to research the matter in Milan's Biblioteca Ambrosiana. Not surprisingly, he found nothing. See also Carmichael 1905–06, pp. 76–77.

239 This is a common story, characterised by MacDonald (1994–95, pp. 54–55) as 'Fairies teach piping', cf. Dixon 1886, p. 160; Carmichael 1905–06; Anon. 1908–09a, pp. 158–59; McDonald 1908–09; Wentz 1911, p. 40; *Tocher* 26, pp. 108–13. In 2003 my daughter, Catrìona Black, made a version from South Uist (SoSS SA 1975/32/A1) into an animated film called *Pìobairean Bhòrnais*.

240 We may assume from the stories told in 'Fairies and Horses' (p. 77) and note 250 that he was blinded because he was able to see these banshis, i.e. because he had the second sight. None of the MacCrimmons are on record as being blind, although Pàdraig Caogach, to judge from his cognomen, must have suffered from some kind of twitch or squint in the eye (Mackenzie 1841, p. 94; Maclean 1951–52, p. 285). The story here told by JGC almost certainly refers to the one man universally known as *Am Pìobaire Dall* – John MacKay, the Blind Piper of Gairloch (1656–1754), who may reasonably be described as the first of the MacKays to acquire fame as a piper outside his own district, having been sent to the MacCrimmons to complete his education by his father, Ruairidh (*c.* 1592–*c.* 1689), a native of Sutherland who had been piper to Lord Reay in his youth but who had served the Gairloch family from the age of seventeen (Maclean 1951–52, pp. 287–88; Black 2001, p. 423).

    Pace John Mackenzie, who states (1841, p. 94) that both Ruairidh and his son John were blind from birth, Ruairidh does not appear to have been blind at all, and Osgood Mackenzie says of the *Pìobaire Dall* (1980, p. 191): "He was not blind from birth, as has been erroneously stated, but was deprived of his sight by smallpox when about seven years old." It is a matter of great interest that this tragic case of a child being blinded by smallpox appears to have been interpreted by tradition as a deliberate act of blinding by a female Fairy.

241 The 'laird of Dungallon' will be Archibald Cameron, tacksman of Dungallon (son of John Cameron of Glendessary), d. 1719, or possibly one of his sons – John, d. 1739, or Alexander, d. 1759. Dungallon is a rocky islet near Camusinas at the mouth of Loch Sunart; the family did not live there but on the eastern edge of Sunart in Glenahurich, which opens on to the south shore of Loch Sheil (Stewart 1981, pp. 213–15). Callart, another Cameron stronghold, is far to the south on Loch Leven. For the Macintyre pipers of Rannoch see Stewart 1928, pp. 295–96; MacLeod 1933b, pp. 58–59; Scott 1968; MacLennan Nov. 1971, pp. 25–27.

242 For the MacGregor pipers known as *Clann an Sgialaiche*, whose college was at Drumcharry in Rannoch, see Stewart 1928, pp. 296–97, and MacLennan July 1971.

243 *Cladach a' Chrògain* is the shore of Balephetrish Bay (see note 366); JGC calls it 'Crogan beach' at p. 76. The 'extensive plain' to which he refers is *an Ruighe* ('the Common Shieling'), generally anglicised as 'the Reef'; it is now the location of Tiree Airport. JGC's *Cachla* (properly *Cachaileith*) *nam Fidean*, 'the Gate of the Raised Greenswards', appears to be in Balephetrish. A *fidean* is a grassy spot which remains uncovered even at high tide (Dwelly 1977, p. 434, cf. MacQuarrie 1983, p. 71), a reference presumably to the occasional flooding of the Reef.

244 The place is at the east end of Balephetrish Bay.

245 For the motif of the dog's hair being singed off see note 913.

246 By 'some sixty years ago' JGC means *c.* 1814. His predecessor, the Rev. Neil Maclean, wrote (1843, pp. 218–19): "Among the natural disadvantages under which Tiree labours, scarcity of fuel may be considered as one of the most considerable. The only peat-moss in the island, which is of very inferior quality, accommodates only a few families in its neighbourhood, and is now nearly exhausted. The people are consequently obliged to bring their fuel, with great labour and at a heavy expense, some from Mull and some from Coll. I scarcely conceive how poor families, who have no boats of their own, can afford the hiring of boats for this purpose, and other unavoidable expenses attending them. If any value is set on their own labour, as should reasonably be done, the average expense to each family cannot be reckoned less than L. 4 per annum. Supposing that, out of 768 families, 500 import their fuel in this manner, we have an annual expense of L. 2000 in the article of fuel alone."

    The main source of peat was the Ross of Mull, for the simple reason that it, too, belonged to the Argyll Estate, see 'Events at a Distance', p. 254. Forty years later the only fuel used in Tiree was coal (Napier 1884, vol. 3, p. 2165), supplied by the coasting trade. See also Mac a Phì 1938, p. 62; Cregeen 1964, pp. xx, 56; note 540 below.

247 These lochs are properly *an Loch a-Tuath* and *an Loch Cumhann*. The journey may have been from Torloisk or Kilninian on Loch Tuath to Dervaig or Penmore on Loch Cuan, or *vice versa* – JGC's 'from . . . and' should read 'between . . . and' or 'from . . . to', an easy mistake to make.

248 See Introduction, p. xlv. The seduction motif is the same as that used by Scott (1806, p. 11) in 'Glenfinlas, or Lord Ronald's Coronach', where the plot is that of 'MacPhie's Black Dog' without the dog:

> *All dropping wet her garments seem;*
> *Chilled was her cheek, her bosom bare,*
> *As, bending o'er the dying gleam,*
> *She wrung the moisture from her hair.*

249 The *Féill Fhaolain* was held in Killin on St Fillan's Day, 9 January OS, 20 January NS. It survived on the third Tuesday of January 'for general business' until at least 1912 (Stewart 1845, p. 1094; Fionn 1912a, p. 34).

250 The Rev. Dr Patrick Graham, minister of Aberfoyle, tells a similar story (1810, pp. 116–18, also in Robertson 1904, p. 302). A woman is captured by Fairies with her baby. In the *sìthein* she sees them mixing ingredients in a cauldron and anointing their eyes with the resulting 'composition'. While the Fairies are out of the room, she attempts to anoint her own eyes with 'the precious drug' but has only applied it to one eye when they come back. With this eye she sees everything as it really is: "Not . . . in deceptive splendor and elegance, but in its genuine colours and form. The gaudy ornaments of the apartment were reduced to the naked walls of a gloomy cavern." When her baby is weaned she is sent home. One day she sees the Fairy in whose possession she had left her child 'though to every eye invisible'. As is very natural, she asks how her child is. The Fairy is astonished and demands to know how she has seen him. "Awed by the terrible frown of his countenance, she acknowledged what she had done. He spat in her eye, and extinguished it for ever."

  The principal motif of these stories is characterised by MacDonald (1994–95, p. 47): "Woman enlisted to serve as (a) midwife: (b) nurse to fairies." See also note 496 below. On the putting out of the eye (whether by blowing, spitting, pulling, or with the point of a stick) see Wentz 1911, pp. 50, 54, 131, 136, 140, 205; cf. Dorson 1968, p. 104.

251 See p. 36, where the original is given.

252 Compare the refrain cited at p. 44.

253 See Introduction, p. xxxiv.

254 A more accurate rendering of the last phrase would be 'the quern of songs', 'the song-quern'.

255 In Balephetrish. *Cnocana* will be a plural form of either *cnoc* 'a hillock' or *cnocan* 'a little hillock'. Niall M. Brownlie has the name as *na Cnocan Ruadh* 'the Red Hillocks', where *cnocan* is clearly plural of *cnoc*.

256 There were not many MacMillans in Morvern, and it seems distinctly possible that the couple in question is one listed by Iain Thornber as living at Kinlochteacuis in 1841 (MacLeod 2002, p. 253): Allan MacMillan, 75, agricultural labourer, and his wife Janet, 60.

257 For *crògan*, an open claw, presumably here denoting the shape of the bush or of the gully in which it grew, see note 366. *Sgitheach* (whitethorn, hawthorn) marks the entrance to the otherworld, see MacilleDhuibh 20.4.01. JGC is here describing a spot on his two-mile walk to school from Port Appin to Tynribbie. I have discussed the locations he mentions with a number of Appin people, all of whom are thanked in my preface. His route from Port Appin took him through *Bealach nam Marbh*, at the top of what is now known as 'The Avenue' (which leads from Airds House on Airds Bay to Airds Lodge at *Ceann t-Sàilein*, the

southern extremity of Loch Laich), then around the shore of Loch Laich at the base of Airds Hill, passing *an t-Sròn Dubh* and *Uchdan a' Bhiorain Duibh* (see p. 291) where the road turns eastwards at Berandhu; the hawthorn bush must have been somewhere above Airds Lodge. This, in reverse, was the route taken by funeral processions from the Strath of Appin on the way west to Port Appin for burial in Lismore, hence *Bealach nam Marbh* (which is pronounced *Bealach na Mar'á* locally, cf. Grant 1925, p. 20). See 'Life of John Gregorson Campbell', p. 609 below.

258 See pp. 19, 24, 42, 44.

259 At p. 38 'Calum Clever' is associated with Inveresragan in lower Benderloch. JGC's Gortan Dubh will be the 'Goirtean-dubh' marked on the Ordnance Survey six-inch map of 1974 as halfway down the Abhainn Dalach, which rises in the Braes of Appin and flows south and east to enter upper Loch Etive opposite Glen Kinglas. This district would usually be described as upper Benderloch, but as Alastair Campbell of Airds has pointed out to me, the entire north Argyll mainland as far as Loch Leven, including Appin and Glencoe, was once known – at least to Campbells – as Lorn. In referring to upper Benderloch as part of Lorn JGC probably reflects Appin usage. A similar story was heard by R. C. Maclagan from John Gillespie, Conispie, Islay (SoSS Maclagan MSS vol. 22, pp. 4988–89): "The reciter tells a story which he says was at one time currently reported, and accepted as true, of a man who was in Conispie at one time, who had offended the fairies that were living there some way, and one day they came upon him when he was out dibbling potatoes, and shoot [*sic*] an arrow at him. It did not strike him fortunately: If it had he would have been killed, for it struck the shaft of the spade he had in his hands with such force that it sunk into it. He got it out and kept it, and many a person saw it after that."

260 JGC's *tana* 'thin, shallow' is usually used of liquids; like the description 'a lath of a body' at p. 83, it suggests a woman who is not so much slim as ethereal. His 'wan looks' is probably a reference to *glas* rather than to *uaine*, see note 431. For an excellent collection of glaistig stories from Lorn, Appin, Lochaber and Ardnamurchan see MacDougall and Calder 1910, pp. 216–69; see also Dieckhoff 1914–19, pp. 241–42; MacKenzie 1935, pp. 176–85; Spence 1948, pp. 50–54; MacDonald 1958b, p. 128; EUL MS CW 504C, ff. 16r–33r.

261 JGC means lath in the sense of a thin slip of wood.

262 Presumably JGC's *stig* is Macbain's *stig* 'a skulking or abject look or attitude; from Norse *styggr*, shy' (1896, p. 313), MacAlpine's *stic* 'a bad pet of a person, blackguard' (1929, p. 247), Carmichael's *stic* 'imp, demon' – *droch stic* 'evil imp', *stic an donais* 'imp of the devil', *stic an deamhain mhoir* 'imp of the great demon', *stic taighe* 'house imp', *stic starsaich* 'doorstep imp, generally applied to a quarrelsome woman, occasionally to a quarrelsome man' (*CG*2, p. 364). Charles Robertson says that in Wester Ross *stic* is synonymous with *stèic* 'a fellow, imp': *Nach b'e an droch stèic e!* "What a bad boy he is!" He adds that in Gairloch it has a broad *t* and the further meaning 'severe blow', and conjectures that it is from English 'stick', as in a 'bad stick' (1899–1901, p. 364). The eponymous haunted house of John MacRury's brilliant short story 'Taillear Ghearraidh-bo-Stig' (1893–94a) is I suppose intended to be *Gearraidh Both Stig* – 'the Field of the House of *Stig*, Stighousefield'. *Stic* found its way from *CG* into Thompson 1997, p. 133; on the other hand, to the best of my knowledge *stìg* and *stig* bear no relation to the eponymous caveman in Clive King's best-selling children's novel *Stig of the Dump*, which was made into a BBC TV series in 2002.

   One source (Anon. 1902–03, p. 196) alleges that the Gaelic term was *stig* or *glas-stig*. However, the second element is subject to considerable variation: *glaisrig*, p. 85; *glaslich*, Pennant 1998, p. 344; *glaisnig, glaislig, glaislid*, Chisholm 1884–85, p. 222, *CG*2, p. 302, and Watson 1908–09, pp. 60–62; *glaisirig* in *Tocher* 28, pp. 198–99; Manx *glashtin, glashtyn*, Wentz 1911, p. 131, and MacKenzie 1935, p. 176; cf. Manx *glashan*, Campbell 1890, vol. 1, pp. xlvi–xlviii, and p. 102 below. This raises the possibility that it does not represent the

Norse word but a suffix. I have seen *glaisteag* in writing more than once (e.g. Mac Dhughaill 1911), but in each case it seems merely to be a pedantic hyper-correction of *glaistig*. Since *glaistig* (with one important exception) is unknown in Ireland, the possibility of a P-Celtic derivation is worth considering. The feminine suffix *-ig* is well known in Welsh, e.g. *afonig* 'a little stream' from *afon* 'river', *oenig* 'a little ewe-lamb' from *oen* 'lamb'. The first element presents little difficulty – *glas* in Welsh has a virtually identical set of meanings to *glas* in Gaelic and Irish, i.e. 'stream' (obsolete) and 'blue, pale, grey, green, young, raw' (surviving). It may be argued, then, that *glaistig* is in origin a Pictish word meaning simply 'female stream-dweller' – a *bùrnag* or burnie, if I may coin Gaelic and Scots equivalents. With the disappearance from the lexicon of *glas* in the meaning 'stream', the identity of the *glaistig* may subsequently have been shaped by the perception that she was a grey creature of no particular habitat.

The sole Irish instance occurs in the Fionn literature, *Glasdic* or *Glasdíc* being the boyhood name of Fionn himself. The earliest recorded spelling is in these lines from the Book of Leinster by the twelfth-century poet Gilla in Choimdhedh (Meyer 1910, pp. 46–47):

> *Glasdíc ainm dó ar tús tind,*
> *Meic Morna tucsat fair Find;*
>   *Secht mbliadna dó i ndeilb doraid —*
>   *Fo Loch Ríach fúair findchobair.*

("*Glasdíc* was his name in the hard beginning, / The sons of Morna renamed him Fionn; / Seven years he was in hard plight – / Under Loch Ree he found fair help.") Immediately after his birth Fionn was 'maliciously thrown or accidentally dropped into a body of water', but survives to emerge 'with a salmon, an eel, or both of these creatures in his hands'; indeed, in a modern telling of the story, the name becomes Glaisdigheadh, which is explained by the storyteller to mean 'eel' (Nagy 1985, pp. 111, 115). Eoin MacNeill explained it as *Glais Díge* 'Stream of the Dyke' (1908, pp. 33, 133); Nagy is sceptical, but puts forward the even more doubtful suggestion that 'we should perhaps look to Irish *deog* (gen. *dige*) "drink" or *dígu* "refuse"' (1985, p. 272, note 56). Ó hÓgáin is less precise, seeing it as 'meaning "backwash" or the like' (1988, p. 99).

Whether basically Norse or Pictish, there need be no doubt, I think, but that *glasdíc* or *glaisdic* was borrowed from our *glaistig* as a suitably exotic and otherworldly name for an amphibious baby of prodigious size and strength. Stories of the glaistig will have travelled to Ireland just as they clearly did to the isle of Man, where, as we have seen, the term became gaelicised as *glashtin, glashtyn, glashan*.

263 HSD, vol. 1, p. 487; MacLeod and Dewar 1831, p. 326 ('a supposed she-devil or hag in the shape of a goat'). The latter is repeated by Dwelly (1977, p. 498), who adds a further definition, attributed to Alexander Henderson, Ardnamurchan: "Beautiful female fairy, usually attired in a green robe, seldom seen except at the bank of a stream, and engaged in washing, also known as maighdean uaine."

264 See p. 10. A spinning-wheel can revolve unaided. "An old friend of the writer," said the Rev. Norman MacDonald (1958a, p. 142), "remembered having seen a spinning wheel working in this inexplicable manner, all through the Sabbath, although no one was near it." For another instance see Cowan and Henderson 2002, p. 204.

265 Thus also the brownie, see pp. 101–02.

266 See note 45 above.

267 By 'plug' JGC appears to mean the word in its primary English sense of 'a peg stopping, or for stopping, a hole: a bung: a stopper' (Chambers 1983, p. 987). He seems to have in mind

the primary Gaelic sense of *goc* 'a wooden pipe, or faucet, put into a cask, to give passage to the liquor' (HSD, vol. 1, p. 500). However, Gaelic dictionaries list *gocan* quite separately with the meaning 'little attendant', and it seems in fact to derive ultimately from Scots *gowk* 'a cuckoo, a fool'. *Gocan* is a common word in Tiree: *gocan de dhuine*, 'a perky little fellow', to use JGC's own expression ('On Baugh, Tiree', p. 94). As for the *méilleachain*, Mackenzie tells several stories from Arran about such creatures (1914, pp. 276–80, 284), spelling their name *mèileachan*, plural *mèileachain*, 'bleaters' – 'from the bleating sound which they uttered'.

268 See the following item. The story is related in full in MacDougall and Calder 1910, pp. 222–25, 'Maighdean Ghlinn-Faochain' ('The Glen-Faochain Maiden'). The servant is warned by her master to take in the water before dark in case NicilleMhìcheil is displeased with her, and she retorts: *Ma thig i tarsuinn ormsa, cuiridh mi car 'na h-amhaich dhi.* "If she comes across me, I'll twist her neck for her." The result is as aforesaid. When her master finds out what has happened he leads the girl out by the hand and brings her around the house saying, *A Nic Gille Mhìcheil, a thruaghain, nach cuir thu, air mo bhuidheachas féin, ceann na searbhanta mar bha e roimhe?* "Nic Gilmichael, poor body, will you not, to oblige me, put the servant's head as it was before?" The second slap then puts things right.

269 Sròn Chormaig, now known as Glenfeochan, is marked on the six-inch Ordnance Survey map of 1883 as standing on Eas a' Bhrochain about half a mile east of the head of Loch Feochan. The name of the neighbouring stream to the west is given as the *Eas Raineach* ('Bracken Ravine'), properly no doubt *Eas Rainich*; this will be JGC's *Eas Ronaich*.

270 Glen Iuchair (anglicised Euchar) lies over the hill to the south of Glenfeochan, only a mile from the source of the Eas Raineach.

271 This is probably the ghost called 'Green Jean' said to have been seen at Inverawe over a long period. The last sighting is described by Diarmid Campbell (1998a, p. 63): "The Captain of Dunstaffnage who was living when the original version of these Notes was written, told the writer that once, when he was standing in the hall at Inverawe putting up a fishing rod, he glanced upwards at the tip of the rod and, to his astonishment, saw a girl in a green dress walking along the gallery that overlooked the hall. The girl had beautiful fair hair, and looked to be about sixteen years of age. Having reached the end of the passage, she passed into what is known as the Ticonderoga room, and was not seen again." Alastair Campbell of Airds, who lives at Inverawe House, tells me (personal communication, 13 October 2003): "Popular superstition is that she appeared no more after the sale of Inverawe by the Campbells of Dunstaffnage around 1913."

272 *Sianag* is probably a variant of *Sianach*, for which see note 198. It may, however, have been understood by some to represent 'screaming woman', from *sian* 'shriek, scream'. For 'Elle-maid' see note 16 above. *Mulad* means 'sorrow', *aighear* 'joy'. One wonders what connection exists, if any, between the *Sianag* and the *Bodach Glas* described by Lord Archibald Campbell (1885a, p. 90): "There is said to be a small old man in Truish, with a grey plaid and Lowland bonnet, called the Bodach Glas (old grey man), who appears on the death of any of the Dunstaffnage family (or on the death of the head of the family – all do not agree on this point)." For an example of a brownie of variable sex see note 549.

273 That is, the nineteenth; the story of the *gruagach* of Island House is well known in Tiree to this day. The house appears to have been variously joined to the mainland by a drawbridge, stepping-stones or a causeway, but in the eighteenth century the intervening space was filled up with stones and soil (McColl 1792, p. 402 = new edn, p. 264; Campbell 1895, p. 14; Beveridge 1903, p. 117; MacDougall and Cameron n.d., pp. 116–18; Mac a Phì 1938, p. 60; RCAHMS 1980, pp. 208–09). The original castle was demolished in 1748 to make room for the factor's house; no doubt this led to much talk of the *gruagach*, and to an increase in sightings of her. Brownlie tells a story (1995, pp. 104–05, cf. MacDougall and Cameron n.d., p. 117, and Mac a Phì 1938, pp. 60–61) of how the factor, Malcolm MacLaren or MacLaurine

(for whom see Cregeen 1998, pp. 22–23), unjustly ordered a poor man to fetch an extra load of stone for the masons, to be met with the reply: *Mar as àill leat, uasail, ach cùm cluas rium. Cha chuir thusa seachad aon oidhche ded bheatha an Taigh an Eilein.* "I'll do as you command, but you will never pass a night under the roof of Island House." The factor took ill, and in order to give the lie to the prophecy had himself carried on a blanket to the house; before they could get him over the threshold, he breathed his last.

274 Breacachadh Castle was restored in the 1960s and 1970s by the historian Nicholas Maclean-Bristol and is still his residence. He tells me that he has never seen the glaistig. It is 'old' in comparison with the eighteenth-century house at Breacachadh, which was virtually demolished in the 1860s and replaced with a Gothic castle by John Lorne Stewart; abandoned in the 1940s, it is now being restored by Mr Nigel Kennedy-Cochrane-Patrick. See RCAHMS 1980, pp. 177–84, 228–29.

275 The keeping of fools appears to have been a normal practice for Highland chiefs, see for example p. 194; Mackenzie 1841, p. 93; Campbell 1890, vol. 1, p. xxvii; Carmichael 1912–13, pp. 323–24; Mackay 1919–22, pp. 6–7; Nicolson 1951, pp. 30, 57; *Tocher* 22, pp. 240–43; Shaw 2002, pp. 100, 106–09, 117–19, 125. In 1808 Sir Walter Scott wrote (1832, p. 92): "Fifty years ago there was hardly a great house in Scotland where there was not an *all-licensed* fool – half crazy and half knavish – many of whose *bon mots* are still recited and preserved. The late Duke of Argyle had a jester of this description, who stood at the sideboard among the servants, and was a great favourite, until he got into disgrace by rising up in the kirk before sermon, and proclaiming the banns of marriage between himself and my friend Lady Charlotte Campbell."

Even in Scott's own time, according to Isabel Anderson (1885, pp. 184–85), 'old County families' in the Highlands still liked to maintain such a person among their dependents, giving them regular wages, cast-off livery and plentiful meals in exchange for the entertainment afforded to master and servants alike. "To have a regular 'Fool' in the kitchen," she noted, "was always a mark of aristocracy."

276 I assumed at first that this referred to the celebrated Alasdair Ranaldson MacDonell (1773–1828), chief of Glengarry 1788–1828, who hunted much and went about on foot with his 'tail' of retainers. However, Mr Norman H. MacDonald, Edinburgh, author of *The Clan Ranald of Knoydart and Glengarry*, tells me (letter dated 25 October 2002): "I have not come across any references to Alasdair Ranaldson MacDonell having had a residence in Strathglass. As far as I know his deer stalking expeditions took place from Invergarry House . . . I would have thought it unlikely that Alasdair Ranaldson or any other Glengarry chief had a house in Strathglass." It would appear, then, that the *Mac 'ic Alastair* who owned the house was not a MacDonell but a Chisholm.

277 'Forty years ago' will mean *c.* 1834. *Staing* is a peg for hanging clothes, sometimes called a *clìc*, cf. *Gur lìonmhor bonaid ghorm air staing ann* ('Many a blue bonnet hangs on a peg there', Watson 1959, p. 248). Why JGC calls it 'paling', as if it were a fence, I do not know. 'Amry', more usually 'aumry', Gaelic *àmraidh*, Latin *armarium*, is a cupboard or press.

278 JGC here says in a footnote: "Both names have the same meaning, being derived from a kind of head-dress (*ceann-eididh, cuaraig*) peculiar to the clan." This cannot be allowed to stand. The progenitor of the Carrick Kennedys was *Ceinneideach*, early Irish *Cennétech*, *Cinnéideach* ('Chief Protector'?); it was also the name of Brian Boru's father, see note 219. The modern Gaelic surname is *Ceanadach*, used among others by the singer Calum Kennedy. The progenitor of the Lochaber Kennedys, on the other hand, was *Ualgharg* ('Proud Fierce'?), giving the modern surname *MacUalraig*, which is regarded as a more genuine alternative to *Ceanadach* (Macbain 1896, p. 362). The name *MacUalraig* 'is said to be derived from one Ulrick or Walrick Kennedy, a scion of the Kennedys of Dunure, Ayrshire, who fled to Lochaber early in the sixteenth century and founded the sept of

M'Walrick of Leaneachen' (Black 1946, p. 569). In Galloway and Carrick Gaelic *Ualgharg* was equated with Anglian *Ulrick*, which survives today in German as *Ulrich*.

279 "He locked her hands."

280 On the curse of the glaistig of Lianachan see pp. 611 and 681 below; Macdonald 1897–99, p. 341; *CG2*, p. 303; Fionn 1900–01a; Anon. 1902–03; Mac Dhughaill 1911; Fionn 1912b and 1913; Maclean 1975, pp. 20, 26–27; MacDonald 1994–95, p. 58; Cheape 1999, pp. 76, 81. The central part of the story, the 'task' motif, is not present in all versions, and may be a secondary element tacked on to provide an origin legend for Foich House, see notes 281, 287 and 289. On the Lochaber Kennedys see Macdonald 1897–99, pp. 340–43; Fionn 1900–01b; Carn Dearg 1913; J. McG. 1913; D. M. R. 1913.

281 MacPherson 1868, pp. 123–26. JGC chose not to give the original, saying: "The Gaelic is not given as the volume is easily accessible." *An Duanaire* is now out of print, so I have supplied the original text. I think there can be little doubt but that the 'collector' himself, Donald Campbell MacPherson (1838–80), was the author. Note the start of his introduction (*ibid.*, p. vii): "Most of the pieces contained in the following collection were taken down some time ago in the Braes of Lochaber. Several of them are of a pretty old date, and a few are illustrative of manners and customs, and are couched in pure, idiomatic language, without a single expression calculated to offend the most delicate ear."

Our poem is clearly 'illustrative of manners and customs', but equally clearly it was not 'taken down some time ago in the Braes of Lochaber'. From a literary point of view it is highly innovative. It contains echoes of rhythm, *aicill*, end-rhyme and verse-structure, but applies none of these consistently, and should therefore be seen as an attempt to mould folk narrative into a new creative medium for the language on the model of the kind of verses cited elsewhere in *The Gaelic Otherworld* – most of these are remarkably loose in their structure, and provide a clear stepping-stone between traditional metres and free verse, see notes 807 and 809. In this respect 'Glaistig Lianachain' is by no means unique, however. There are other examples of the mode in *An Duanaire*, nor was MacPherson its first practitioner. 'Uidheamachadh Luinge Chloinn Artuir', one of the 'Calum Beag' series by John MacLean (*Bàrd Bhaile Mhàrtainn*, 1827–95), is structurally experimental, taking the *snéadhbhairdne* of 'Birlinn Chlann Raghnaill' as a loose and whimsical starting-point (Cameron 1932, pp. 153–55; see above, note 10, and below, notes 302, 621, and p. 579). Exactly the same may be said of 'Cath Mhonadh Bhraca', published in 1858 by the Islay poet William Livingston (1808–70). Three other poems published by Livingston in 1858 are in free verse, all on historical subjects: 'Cath Allt a' Bhannaich', 'Comhradh mar gu'm biodh e eadar Bantighearn' Ellerslie agus Thomas Learmont', and 'Cath Thom Ealachaidh' (Mac Dhun-Leibhe 1858, pp. 1–12, 26–33, 84–89, 95–99). His 'Blàr Thràigh Ghruineart', which appeared later, is in a mixture of rhyming couplets and free verse (Livingston 1882, pp. 101–12; Meek 2003, pp. 318–37).

'Glaistig Lianachain' contains several names of places in the middle part of Brae Lochaber, and appears to suggest that what the glaistig built for Kennedy was not a barn in the hills at Lianachan but a dwelling-house surrounded by a defensive ditch down at Foich in Keppoch's 'metropolis' of Inverroy. That the structure was a house is confirmed by Mac Dhughaill 1911.

The poem has also inspired a rendering into English verse, see MacKenzie 1908–09. For a biography of Donald Campbell MacPherson see Mackenzie 1879–80, p. 38.

282 JGC's translation is misleading. As is clear from other sources, *an Gille Dubh* was Kennedy's Christian name (it is the eponym of *MacilleDhuibh* 'Black'). Perhaps the best translation here would be 'big Gille Dubh MacCuaraig' and in the first line of the poem 'Hail to thee, big Gille Dubh'.

283 This is the Cour, which flows north from the mountains through Coille Lianachain as

Allt Choire an Eòin and, much swollen by tributaries, enters the Spean opposite Inverroy, halfway between Bunroy and Spean Bridge. The farm of Lianachan lies on one of its tributaries, Allt an Lòin. Lachlan MacKinnon refers (1973, p. 11) to the following traditional wisdom about one of these tributaries, the Fionnasgag, which in wet weather produces as many as three distributaries: *An uair tha aon laogh aig Fionnasgag théid duine Cùrr; an uair tha dà laogh aig Fionnasgag théid duine air each Cùrr; ach nuair tha trì laoigh aig Fionnasgag cha téid Fionn no a chinneadh Cùrr.* "When Fionnasgag has one calf a man may cross the Cour; when Fionnasgag has two calves a man on horseback may cross the Cour; but when Fionnasgag has three calves neither Fionn nor his clan can cross the Cour." MacPherson gives the same name as 'Finisgeig'; according to Calum Maclean (1975, p. 27), Finisgeig is not a tributary but a fall on the Cour, and its 'three calves' are 'three rivulets tumbling over the edge of the waterfall as well as the main stream'.

I do not understand the relationship of the river-name Cour (genitive *Cùrr*) to the nearby farm-name Cour (genitive *na Cùir*), which MacKinnon (1973, p. 22) calls 'the only place name in Lochaber with an article' – it features in the expression *Mionnan Dhòmhnaill na Cùir 's e 'na sheasamh air ùir Challaird* ('Donald of Coor's oaths while standing on Callart soil', Campbell 1967–68, p. 23, and Meek 1978, p. 135). MacKinnon takes the name from 'Cour, edge, boundary', by which he will mean *cùrr*, feminine, usual genitive *na curra*, 'edge, inner corner, end', etc., as in Iain Lom's *ite e á cùrr na sgéithe* 'a feather is he from the inner corner of the wing' (MacKenzie 1964, pp. 24–25, 243). As another example of the word MacKinnon cites 'Coire Chùr above Kinlocheil'. As if to confuse things still further, MacMillan (1971, p. 275) explains the river-name as *a' Chaoir* 'the rapid torrent', which makes excellent sense but is out of line with our evidence that the river-name is *Cùrr*.

284 This is a *crios sianta* or 'charmed girdle', for which see note 8 above, Dalyell 1834, pp. 135–36, and CG6, p. 53. It is implied that as Fillan was a Christian saint, a belt or girdle charmed (*air a shianadh*) with an incantation that invoked his name would have the power to restrain an otherworld creature. Whether *sian-chrios Fhaolain* was an object known to tradition or a figment of MacPherson's imagination I have no idea. Henderson (1911, pp. 320, 335–36) read the poem uncritically as a *bona fide* piece of folklore, but was at least able to point to another saint's girdle, that of Brigid.

Either way, *sian-chrios Fhaolain* was presumably inspired by a memory of the 'five relics of St Fillan' known to documentary sources: the Quigrich (*coigreach* 'stranger', a crozier), the Bernane (*beàrnan* 'gapped one', a bell), the Fergy (*fairge*, perhaps from *airce*, a shrine), the Mayne (*mionn* 'diadem') and the Meser (presumably *measair* 'dish'). The first two may be seen today in the Museum of Scotland in Edinburgh; the third, the *fairge*, is given by Henderson (1911, p. 320) as *fairche* 'originally, the mallet for bruising barley, but in later ages used for stirring the pool'. To them we may add the reliquary of St Fillan (a silver case believed to contain his left arm-bone) carried to the field of Bannockburn by the Abbot of Inchaffray and venerated by King Robert on the eve of battle, if Boece may be believed (Batho and Husbands 1941, pp. 273–74, cf. Scott 1806, pp. 19–20, and Dorson 1968, p. 113), and the healing stones of St Fillan preserved in the old mill (now a visitor centre) in Killin, cf. Maclagan 1902, p. 171. The arm-bone has been identified with the Mayne, wrongly I would have thought. See p. 227; Lindsay, Dowden and Thomson 1908, p. xlv; Gillies 1938, pp. 64–82; Barrow 1976, p. 226; Watson 2002, pp. 167, 177, 183.

285 MacPherson's spellings. *Bailgionn = balg + fionn*; *cean-fhionn = ceann + fionn*.

286 *Buaidh cnuic* 'success on hill' is success in councils, law-making, lawsuits and the conclusion of treaties, i.e. in meetings by appointment. *Buaidh c(h)òmhlach* 'success in company' is success in accidental meetings, see note 719 and pp. 139–40, 536.

287 As MacPherson spells *Foich* with a capital letter both here and below, he must have had a specific location in mind. Thanks to a collection of Lochaber place-names obtained by

Andrew Wiseman from the late Ann MacDonell, Achluachrach, I have been able to identify it as Foich or Foichs (Gaelic usually *faiche* or *faithche*, 'parade-ground') at Inverroy in Brae Lochaber.

288 *Còrn na Fiùbh* 'the Horn of Worth' is, I believe, in error for *Còrn na Fiodhbhaidhe, Còrn na Fiùbhaidh, Còrn na Fiùthaidh*, 'the Horn of Wood', 'the Horn of Timber'. Corrupted into *an Gurra-Fiodha* but very reasonably translated 'the Wooden-Crier', this formidable clarion appears in a tale entitled 'Creag a' Ghobha 's an Eilean Sgitheanach' ('The Smith's Rock in the Isle of Skye') in MacDougall 1891, pp. 73–75. It is the story of Fionn as the sleeping messiah – for which see p. 148 – transferred from *Creag a' Chobh* (Craigiehow, 'the Rock of the Cave') in the Black Isle (Cameron 1892–94, vol. 2, p. 492; Watson 1904, p. 140; McPherson 1929, p. 85; Meek 1978, p. 98; MacKenzie 2002, p. 202; note 797 below) to *Creag a' Ghobha* in Skye, while the hero is cleverly given a trade appropriate to the change of name. He has heard that the Fianntan are sleeping in the rock and that three blasts of the *Gurra-Fiodha* which lies beside Fionn will make them arise as hale and hearty as ever, so he makes a suitable key and lets himself in. *Chunnaic e àite ro mhòr agus ro fharsainn air thoiseach air, agus daoine anabarrach mòr 'n an laidhe air an ùrlar. Bha aon fhear 'bu mhò na càch 'n a laidhe 'n am meadhon, agus cleith mhòr de mhaide agus e fosgailte troimhe 'n a laidhe laimh ris. Smaointich e gu 'm b' e so an Gurra-fiodha. Ach bha e cho mòr agus gu 'n robh eagal air nach b' urrainn e a thogail, no idir a shéideadh. Sheas e 'g amharc air car ùine, ach mu dheireadh thubhairt e ris fhéin gu 'm feuchadh e co dhiù bho 'n thàinig e cho fada. Rug e air a' Ghurra-fiodha, agus thog e air éiginn a cheann an àird r' a bhéul. Shéid e le uile neart e; agus, leis an fhuaim a rinn e, shaoil e gu 'n do thuit a' Chreag agus na bha os a ceann a nuas air a mhuin. Chrith na slaoid mhòra 'bh' air an ùrlar o mhullach an cinn gu bonnaibh an cas. Thug e 'n ath shéideag air a' Ghurra-fiodha, agus a dh' aon léum thionndaidh iad air an uilnibh. Bha 'm meòir mar mheòir gobhlaige, agus an gàirdeinnean mar shailean daragan-daraich. Chuir am mèud agus an coltas uamhasach a bh' orra a leithid do dh' eagal air 'us gu 'n do thilg e uaith' an Gurra-fiodha, agus gu 'n do léum e 'mach. Bha iad an sin a' glaodhaich as a dhéigh, 'Is miosa dh' fhàg no mar fhuair, is miosa dh' fhàg no mar fhuair.'* "He saw a very great and wide place before him, and exceedingly big men lying on the floor. One man, bigger than the rest, was lying in their midst, having a large hollow baton of wood lying beside him. He thought that this was the Wooden-Crier (Whistle). But it was so large that he was afraid that he could not lift it, much less blow it. He stood for a time looking at it, but he at last said to himself that, as he came so far, he would try at any rate. He laid hold of the Wooden-Crier, and with difficulty raised its end up to his mouth. He blew it with all his might, and so loud was the sound it produced that he thought the Rock and all that was over it came down on the top of him. The huge unwieldy men who lay on the floor shook from the tops of their heads to the soles of their feet. He gave another blast on the Wooden-Crier, and with one spring they turned on their elbows. Their fingers were like the prongs of wooden graips, and their arms like beams of bog-oak. Their size and the terrible appearance they had put him in such fear that he threw the Wooden-Crier from him, and sprang out. They were then crying after him, 'Worse have you left us than as you found us, worse have you left us than as you found us.'"

The *Gurra-Fiodha* also appears in 'Mar bha Fionn 'an Tigh a' Bhlàir-Bhuidhe' ('How Finn was in the House of Blar-Buie', MacDougall 1891, pp. 56–72) as a horn which Fionn sounds *in extremis* – 'when he would play on it, its sound would pass through the seven borders of the world (*troimh sheachd iomaill an domhain*)'. In the version of the tale which Donald C. MacPherson got from his grandmother he spells the term *còrn-nam-fiùth* and translates it 'the horn of the worthies' (Campbell 1870–72, pp. 196, 199). See also MacLauchlan 1882, pp. 98–99, where *Còrn na Fiùbh* has become a mere *fìdeag* ('whistle'); Campbell 1940–60, vol. 1, p. 513; and *Tocher* 18, pp. 62–65, a tale told by Dòmhnall Chaluim Bàin from Tiree in which, again, *An Gurra Fiugha* appears as a *fideag* or whistle. In a parallel development, the term *dord Fianna* 'Fenian chant', broadly understood by tradition-bearers as some kind of bell, came to be rendered *òrd* as if it meant 'hammer' (Matheson 1956–57, pp. 257–58, cf. GUL MS Gen. 1090/29, p. 18; Carmichael n.d., p. 13; MacLellan 1961, pp. 12, 211).

289 Ann MacDonell's place-names collection (see note 287) gives *Lón Mór* as 'opposite Foich house on upper side of road'. Cf. *Fearann an Lòin* later in the poem.

290 Presumably the falls of the Spean at Clinaig, halfway between Achluachrach and Bunroy, although these are given by MacMillan (1971, p. 276) as *Eas Chlaoinaig*, while Clinaig itself is given by MacMillan (*ibid.*, p. 155) and MacKinnon (1973, p. 22) as *Claonaig* 'a little slope, a small declivity'.

291 This will be on the riverside meadows of the Spean at Insh (*an Innis*) below Bunroy.

292 Ann MacDonell's place-names collection (see note 287) shows *Coille Chaorainn* 'Ash Tree Wood' at 321.803, i.e. in the triangle between the Spean and Allt nam Bruach on the southern slope of Brae Lochaber. This is probably what MacPherson means by *a' Chaor'naich'*. Mac Dhughaill confirms (1911) that *a' Chaornach* is a wood about five miles east of the house built by the glaistig (*coille a tha tuaiream air cóig mìle 'n ear air an aitreabh*).

293 Cf. *CG2*, p. 290, *Gach fiodh 's a choill ach fiodhagach* 'Any tree in the forest save the wild fig-tree'. The context is suggestive of the present one: MacMhuirich Mór has seized *isean na béist*, the young of the beast, and obliges her to build him a house of nine couples, thatched with the down and feathers of birds; this is part of the song she sings while doing it. See also Mackay 1914, p. 425, MacDonald 1963, pp. 212–14, and Gillies 2000, pp. 16, 18.

294 As Macbain points out (1896, p. 318) this word is 'doubtful Gaelic'. Its only authentic source appears to be the ballad 'Bàs Dhiarmaid' (Gillies 1786, p. 287, cf. Campbell 1872, p. 163, Campbell 1890, vol. 3, p. 85, and Campbell 1891, p. 62):

> *Cumhachdach gu mealladh bhan*
> *Mac o Duimhne bu mhor buaidh;*
> *An t suireadh cha do thog a suil*
> *O chaidh an uir [air] do ghruaidh.*

("Powerful at beguiling women / Was Ó Duibhne's charming son; / The maiden has not raised her eye / Since the soil went on your cheek.")

295 JGC reduces these two lines to one: "The skin of her palm stuck to it (the coulter)."

296 Dwelly (1977, p. 988) simply gives 'monster' for this word. It will be a derivative of early Irish *omun, ómun, uamun* 'fear, dread': *mollachd nan uamhlach* 'the curse of the dreaded'.

297 Cf. note 289 above.

298 For no obvious reason, JGC's translation of the last five lines parts company from the original, which means literally: "I built a big house on the Field; / I will put out my heart's blood / High on the peak of Finisgeig, / Upon three rush-covered hillocks / Which will be red for evermore." For Finisgeig see note 283 above.

299 JGC was correct in diagnosing the poem as modern (see note 281 above), but wrong (and surprisingly so) in basing his diagnosis upon the ethnological evidence of the final couplet. For a supernatural hound that breathes green flame see p. 63; for a person being devoured by green flames in revenge for the death of a Fairy see Grant 1811, vol. 1, pp. 287, 290; for a ghost whose breast is aglow with red flame see note 887; and for supernatural beings going away in flames see MacDiarmid 1904–07, p. 39 (where the flames are blue), MacDougall and Calder 1910, pp. 172–73, and – most tellingly of all – pp. 273 and 292 of the present work, where a dead man's ghost and a supernatural horseman both disappear 'in a flame of fire'.

300 More literally the Gaelic phrase means that no Campbell 'would be conceived and cry out'. Bochyle (*Both Chaoil*, 'the Bothy of Wattles', see p. 571) was halfway down the glen on the

left bank of the Orchy. The name is given as Bochyles (i.e. two farms) on Langlands' 1801 map of Argyll.

301 Alternatively perhaps 'MacMillan has the right to Knap / As long as wave is striking rock'. JGC gives the impression that *an Cnap* ('the Knap') is a single location, whereas in fact it is three – not surprisingly, given that, as he says, it simply means 'the Lump'. The Ballachulish Hotel is several miles from Shuna Island and stands on its own lump, and both of these places are very far indeed from the third *Cnap*, the point of land which juts into the sea between lochs Sween and Caolisport, forming the symbolic heart and religious centre of Knapdale. Kilmory with its chapel and cross lies close to the point, with Castle Sween a couple of miles further north, and the holy 'islet of St Cormick' (p. 229) two miles offshore.

According to the Rev. Somerled MacMillan (1952, p. 29), the charter of the first chief of the MacMillans (Malcolm Mor of Knap) is believed to have been engraved on a rock at the bounds of his estate. Tradition alludes, he says, to one boulder about a gunshot away from Knap Point, only visible at low tide, and another on the Eiteag, not far from Tiretigan Farm in the parish of Kilberry. Both stones were known as *Còir MhicMhaolain* ('MacMillan's Right'). He then cites JGC's couplet and the following variation:

> *Fhads a ruitheas sruth is gaoth*
> *Bidh còir MhicMhaolain air a' Chnap.*

("As long as wind and current run / MacMillan's right will be to Knap.") He discusses whether the 'charter' thus inscribed took the form of these Gaelic couplets themselves, or of a footmark similar to those at Keil and Dunadd, and says: "Tradition affirms that John Campbell of Calder, under Argyll's instructions, defaced the rock-charter off Knap Point in 1615, and the boulder on which it was inscribed he hurled into the sea. It is believed Colin Campbell of Kilberry, better known as 'Mad Colin', destroyed the MacMillan rock-charter on 'the Eiteag' in 1767, because it hurt his vanity to be continually reminded that he was not the original owner of his proud and ancient estate."

The *Éiteag* charter was in fact that of the MacMurchies (who came to be regarded by many as MacMillans), as is made clear by the anonymous gentlemen of South Knapdale who communicated an account of their parish to Sir John Sinclair in 1796. After pointing out that the MacMillans were anciently proprietors of Kilchamaig (in Kintyre) as well as of Knap, they speak of the last MacMillan to hold both titles (Anon. 1796, pp. 310–11 = new edn, pp. 310–11): "The last of the name, to prevent the prostitution of his wife, butchered her admirer, and was himself obliged to abscond. His charter was inscribed in the Gaelic language and character upon a rock at the extremity of his estate. It proved but a feeble security against the rapacity of a barbarous age. The property was contested for by the Campbells and Macneils, the latter of whom were a powerful clan in North Knapdale, and decided in favour of the former by compromise. It continued in the same family till the year 1775, when, after the death of the tenth possessor, the estate was purchased by the late Lieutenant-General Sir Archibald Campbell of Inverneil. The sword of Macmillan is said to be still in preservation. But it is sincerely to be regretted, that the inscription was defaced by a collateral of the Knap family about 30 years ago. Unless prompted by the vanity of having his ancestors considered in future as the aborigines of their property, it is difficult to assign a probable motive to an action so gothic.

"Macmillan's mode of investment, in heritable right, is not without precedent. The Macmurachies, of old, were proprietors of Terdigan and Kilberrie, lying in that part of Knapdale annexed to Kilcolmonel. Their charter is also engraved, in the same language and character, upon a rock near the shore of these lands."

One wonders whether, as a Campbell himself, JGC's avoidance of this entire issue is deliberate. The same proverb is given by Anon. 1911 with one slight variation (*ri creag* for *air creig*) and the translation: "MacMillan's right to Knapdale – so long as wave beats on the rock." See also Gillies 2000, p. 56.

302 *Hùg* and *hùgan* appear to be onomatopoeic – 'whooch' and 'whoochie' or the like, cf. Mac Mhgr Alastair's 'Birlinn Chlann Raghnaill' (MacLeod 1933a, p. 41):

> *Hùgan le cuan, nuallan gàireach,*
> *Héig air chnagaibh.*

("Whoochie from ocean, a roaring howl, / Wheech upon thole-pins.") MacLeod's own draft translation of the couplet (Edinburgh University Dept of Celtic MS 28, f. 13r) was: "'Swish' from the ocean, a roaring howl, / Crash on tholepins." He subsequently deleted 'Crash' and substituted 'Straining'.

303 According to the story 'Glaisrig Bhaile Bheòlain agus Sealbhach Mac Shealbhaich' ('The Balieveolan Glasrig and Selvach Mac Kelvie') in MacDougall and Calder 1910, pp. 216–21, the glaistig lived at Balieveolan in Lismore and was known as *Maighdeann Bhaile Bheòlain*. Her cry was *Buille air, a Shealbhaich* ("A stroke on it, Selvach"), and his reply was: *Buille eile oirre, a chailleach.* "Another stroke on her, old woman." See also Watson 1908–09, p. 62, and Grant 1925, pp. 2–3. *Allt Aogainn* rises in the centre of Lismore and flows west through a ravine (partly underground) into the bay called *an Sàilean*. It appears to bear a man's name, *Aogan*, Irish *Aodhagán*, in the Western Isles *Ìogan*, better *Iagan*, see p. 157.

304 *Galghad* 'darling' is only used in the vocative, as here: 'My dear!' It derives from Old Irish *galgat* 'a champion'. In Uist, where it is common, it is still used of both boys and girls, elsewhere now of girls only. It may well have given rise to the English word 'galoot', for which the *OED* offers two meanings – an English seaman's term for an awkward soldier or marine (on record 1812–67) and US slang for a generally awkward or uncouth fellow, often used as a term of good-natured depreciation (on record from 1866). It is, or was, found in Australia too (Sydney *Bulletin*, 6 August 1898): "'Who's that galoot 'as lost his 'orse, Sirs?' Bendigo was asking."

305 Ardnadrochit is on the south side of Loch Don. In 1845 the parish of Torosay was divided into three parts – from north to south, Salen, Craignure and Kinlochspelvie (Scott 1915–50, vol. 4, pp. 115, 118, 123). For Lamonts in Torosay see Currie 1998, p. 23.

306 For *gocan* see note 267. Baugh (*am Bàgh*, 'the Bay') is on the south shore of the island; the precise location of 'the Glaistig's Bed', presumably *Leabaidh na Glaistig*, is unknown.

307 Bantling 'a child'.

308 That is, *c.* 1834.

309 JGC means 'suspicious' in its old sense 'doubtful, uncertain'.

310 Perhaps the moral of the story is that he did not jump upon the black horse soon enough. The glaistig's second instruction appears to mean that the 'wife who owned the white-faced yellow cow' was a witch who would remove the *toradh* of his own cows and bring it to him in his hideout.

311 Despite the fondness of the Gael for irony, it is more likely that *maol* is intended in the sense 'foolish, silly, easily deceived'. For Ardnacallich (*Àird na Caillich* 'the Height of the Cailleach') see MacKenzie 2000, pp. 166–67.

312 For Staon(n)aig see MacArthur 2002, pp. 6–7, 12, 14.

313 Saorbheinn (*Saor-Pheighinn*, 'Rent-Free Pennyland'), also mentioned at p. 134, is two miles south-east of Bunessan, while *Cnoc na Feannaig* (on maps as Knocknafenaig) is two miles south-west (MacQuarrie 1983, pp. 57, 94; Maclean 1997, pp. 30, 33, 154). As MacQuarrie points out, the latter also means 'hill of the arable rig', an appropriate origin for a settlement-name.

314 This name appears in a bewildering variety of spellings: Corry-na-Henchor and *Coire na Sheanchrach* as here, Coire-na-Theanchoir at p. 186, *Coire nan Eunachair* and Corrynachenchy on maps, Corenahenachair in Loudon 2001, p. 90, and *Coire na h-Eunachair* 'Corrie of the fowler' in MacQuarrie 1983, p. 62 – followed by Maclean (1997, p. 23), who supplies the historical forms Korinahaenach (1654), Corry na henich (1801, 1824) and Corinahanocha (1852). Maclean adds (p. 158): "I have also seen this called 'Coire-na-theanchoir Bay', which would give 'corry of the tongs' and indicate that a blacksmith worked here." JGC's forms suggest to me that all of these must be attempts at representing *Coire na h-Anshocrach* or its likely variant *Coire na h-Anshocair* – 'the Corry of Sickness'. Presumably there is, or was, a story behind the name. *Anshocair*, whose usual pronunciation is better represented by *anacair*, is given by Dwelly (1977, p. 36) as 'pain, distress, trouble; uneasiness, restlessness; affliction, sickness', but by Fr Allan McDonald (1958, p. 27) as 'illness'. It is still in general use. See notes 700 and 702.

315 All sources agree that his name was Archibald MacDonald. Mrs Mackellar says of him (1888–89, p. 162): "He was of good family, being of the Macdonalds of Mingarry in Ardnamurchan. His mother had been early left a widow, and she married a farmer in Mull." In his historical poem 'Blàr Shùnadail', William Livingston (1882, pp. 74–100) made him a native of Sunart and a contemporary of Ailean nan Sop (for whom see 'Delaying the Birth of a Child', pp. 194–95), but about 1870 an old man claimed that his own grandfather had once been in a band of men pursuing Mac Iain Ghiorr across Mull after he had stolen their horses, and that would appear to place him at the beginning of the eighteenth century (MacFadyen 1902, pp. 19–20). Anon. 1835–36, followed by Anon. 1906–07, claimed that he was a native of Appin who inherited a small farm, lost it when young, took instead a tack of a much more substantial one in Ardnamurchan, and, after many adventures, deceptions and narrow escapes, died *c.* 1650. This information was picked up by M. E. M. Donaldson (1923, pp. 405–06, 409), who stated that his new property was Girgadale near Ardnamurchan Point and that he was believed to have brought two sculptured slabs from Iona to mark his parents' grave at Kilchoan.

In Anon. 1835–36, p. 55, and Anon. 1906–07, p. 234, is the story of his last raid – he landed with his men upon one of the smaller islands off the coast and quietly gathered its cattle, but their owner defended his property with vigour and one of the raiders foolishly shot him dead. Maclean Sinclair (1899, p. 404) identifies the murdered man as Hector MacLean of Muck, second son of Lachlan MacLean of Coll (*c.*1582–1642) and a hero of Kilsyth (1645). Mac Ian Year is said to have been tried for the crime at Inveraray but acquitted. In later life he was personally known to a divinity student from Strathspey who wrote at some point during 1692–94 to James Garden, professor of theology at Aberdeen, on the subject of the second sight (Hunter 2001, pp. 148–50). Referring to seers the student says: "The most remarkable of this sort that I hear off now is one Archibald Mackeanyere alias Mackdonald living in Ardinmurch within 10 or 12 miles or therby of Glencoe, and I was present myselfe where he foretold somthing which accordingly fell out." He recounts in detail how Archibald foretold Argyll's rebellion of 1685, certain events in Dundee's campaign of 1689, and (three months before it happened) the murder of his (Archibald's) friend John MacDonald of Glencoe in 1692. "What became of Archibald himselfe, I am not sure; I have not seen him since nor can I gett a true account of him. Only I know he is yet alive . . . Arch. Mackeanyere will not deny himselfe, but once he was on of the most notorious theives in all the highlands: but I am informed since he came to this knowledge which was by an accident too longsome here to sett down here, that he is turned honester-like than befor." All in all then we may assign him a *floruit* of 1624–94.

See also p. 195; *CG2*, p. 300; Kennedy-Fraser 1909, pp. 72–73; Campbell 1940–60, vol. 2, pp. 2–10; Cameron 1954, p. 8; *Tocher* 52, pp. 156–57; Loudon 2001, p. 64; MacKenzie 2002,

p. 138; MacilleDhuibh 7.3.03, 21.3.03, 4.4.03, 18.4.03; GUL MS Gen. 1090/28, pp. 6–7; EUL MS
CW 504C, ff. 34r–38r.

316 The reason for confusion between white and grey may be that both *geal* and *glas* rhyme
on short *a*, or it may be that JGC is using 'grey' for *bàn*. As given by Nicolson (1951, p. 362)
the proverb is: *Tha taobh dubh 's taobh geal air, mar bha air bàta Mhic Iain Ghearr.* ("He
has a white side and a black side, like the boat of Short John's Son.") However, only *bàn* for
white or *liath* for grey would give acceptable *aicill* rhyme (with *bàta* and *Iain* respectively),
and only *liath* would give acceptable end-rhyme with the correct genitive form *Ghiorr*. Mrs
Mackellar (1888–89, p. 162) gives it as *Taobh dubh us taobh bàn a bh' air bàta mhic Iain
Ghiarr*, and so, more or less, does 'North Argyll' (Cameron 1954, p. 8), while it is as follows
in Anon. 1906–07, p. 233:

> *Taobh dhi dubh is taobh dhi bán,*
> *Mar a bha báta Mhic Iain Ghìorr.*

I have found no instances containing *liath*.

317 Carmichael (*CG6*, p. 122) gives *sall(t)* 'a paw' without further explanation.

318 *Du* is sometimes written *dubh* in this common expression, but it is far from certain that it
represents *dubh* 'black'. Dwelly gives (1977, p. 367): *Cha robh a dhubh no a dhath ri fhaicinn.*
"He was not to be seen anywhere (alive or dead)."

319 See notes 211 and 469; MacDonald 1994–95, p. 48.

320 Indeed, it corresponds in many respects to the story 'An Dà Bhràthair a bha an Odhanaich
agus Glaistig na Beinne Brice' ('The Onich Brothers and the Glastig of Ben Breck'),
MacDougall and Calder 1910, pp. 242–47; see also Watson 1908–09, pp. 62–63, and *Tocher*
28, p. 199. Mac Ian Year's connection with the glaistig has been explained like this (Anon.
1835–36, p. 55): *Chum giorag a chur air a luchd-dùthcha, bha e gabhail os làimh gu'n
robh co' chomunn tric aige ri Glaistig a bha fo ainm a bhi san tìr, m'an robh a luchd-
leanmhainn-san ag aithris a choimhlion seanchas m'an cheannas a bh' aige oirre, 's gu'n
robh iad fo na h-uiread eagail roimhe, 's nach robh chridh' aca faire 'chumail air an cuid
spréidhe, leis an d' fhuair an cealgair carach so gu furasda greim orra.* "To frighten his
countrymen, he took care to have frequent intercourse with a Glaistig who was reputed to
be in the district, about whom his own followers told so many tales of the authority he had
over her, that they [his countrymen] were so frightened of him, that they did not have the
nerve to keep watch upon their cattle, by which means this wily trickster was able to get
hold of them with ease."

321 JGC explains the name in a footnote: "In olden times a wall (of turf) was commonly built to
separate the crop land from the hill ground, and was known as *Gàradh bràgh'd*, or Upper
Wall. The ground above the *Gàradh bràgh'd* was known as the *Eirbhe*." See Watson 2002,
pp. 16, 45.

322 Fernach (Fernoch) is on the western shore of Loch Awe, a few miles south of Kilchrenan.

323 Murchadh mac Brian died at Clontarf in 1014, see note 219. With regard to tales see e.g.
'O'Cronicert's Fairy Wife', pp. 67–70 above. With regard to poems see e.g. Mac-an-Tuairneir
1813, pp. 342–49, Campbell 1872, pp. 61–63, 203–10, and Campbell 1890, vol. 3, pp. 168–91.

324 From a poem entitled 'CORADH tiamhaidh eadar Inghean oighre Bhailacliath, agus Murcha
Mac Brian, Righ Eirin' ('An emotional conversation between the Daughter of the heir of
Dublin, and Murchadh mac Briain, King of Ireland') in Stewart 1804, pp. 549–53, reprinted
in Campbell 1872, pp. 209–10; cf. *CG2*, p. 308, and Bruford 1969, p. 161. For Fionn's encounter
with an 'Inchanter' called the Gruagach see Campbell 1872, pp. 61–63, and Cameron
1892–94, vol. 1, pp. 363–65 (from GUL MacLagan MS 166). For the gruagach in general see
EUL MS CW 504C, ff. 11r–12r; Dalyell 1834, pp. 531–32; Macbain 1887–88, pp. 245–47; *CG2*,

pp. 306–08; MacGregor 1901, p. 34; Watson 1908–09, p. 64; Dieckhoff 1914–19, pp. 236–38; Mackay 1926; Mackay 1927–28, pp. 24–25; MacDonald 1934–36a, pp. 198–99; Mac Thomais 1937–41, pp. 180–83; Spence 1948, pp. 55–58, 101–04; MacDonald 1958b, pp. 125–26; Ballard 1997, pp. 77–78; Pennant 1998, pp. 757–59; and the tale 'Fear na h-Eabaid', for which see Bruford and MacDonald 1994, pp. 153–70, 453–54, and the other references given in note 815. In GUL MacLagan MSS 35 and 85 is a poem of twenty-two quatrains from east Perthshire headed (in MS 35) 'Comhradh eadar an Gruagach Soluis & Roibeart Gabha 'n (Glean-briathrachan)' – 'A Dialogue between the Gruagach of Light and Robert Gow in (Glen Brerachan)'. It begins, intriguingly, with Robert's greeting to the gruagach:

> *Umh amh, umh amh!*
> *Chan eil do Ghàidhlig ach leamh —*
> *Is maith a dh'aithn'inn air do chraos*
> *Gun itheadh tu staoig amh.*

("Raw egg, raw egg! / Your Gaelic is just daft – / I can easily tell from the size of your mouth / That you'd eat raw steak.") See note 949.

325 A head of long hair, in Gaelic *leadan*, is suggestive of the wealth required to have servants look after it, and the relaxation that allows plenty of time to have it washed, combed and deloused. It is therefore characteristic of warrior aristocracies such as those of the *Féinn*, of medieval Ireland, and of the post-medieval Highlands. A MacGregor chief is mightily praised *c.* 1604 for having *luchd leadan ann ri ceàrrachas*, 'long-haired people there gambling' (Watson 1959, p. 241), and during the course of that century the ministers of the Reformed religion tried to maintain their dignity by conforming to this fashion, appearing even in Church courts 'in kilt and bonnet, and wearing their hair long like the ordinary Celt of the time'. The mainly Lowland Synod of Moray disapproved of the habits of the members of the Presbytery of Inverness within its bounds, ordaining in 1640 'that all ministers be grave and decent in their apparell, in their carriage and behaviour; that none weare long hair, but that bothe in lyfe and habite they may be knowne by their men [mien?] to be the ministers of Jesus Chryst' (Mackay 1896, pp. xix, xx). There were no prejudices against women of any sort having long hair; it was never cut, and down to the early twentieth century 'anyone doing so was looked upon as being common' (Macdonald 2003, p. 37).

326 This is not entirely accurate. Dr Johnson wrote (1775, p. 247): "In *Troda*, within these three-and-thirty years, milk was put every Saturday for *Greogach*, or *the Old Man with the Long Beard*. Whether *Greogach* was courted as kind, or dreaded as terrible, whether they meant, by giving him the milk, to obtain good, or avert evil, I was not informed. The Minister is now living by whom the practice was abolished." JGC's spelling 'Greogaca' is the result of a misprint in JFC's influential introduction to the *Popular Tales of the West Highlands*: 'the other, who in the days of Johnson, haunted the island of Troda as "Greogaca," ...' (Campbell 1860–62, vol. 1, p. xciii). For Trod(d)a see also p. 184.

327 'The Glaistig's Little Rock in MacQueen's Big Rock.' The location of this is uncertain. Peadar Ó Donnghaile, Camustianavaig, tells me (personal communication, 10 November 2003) that when the Braes were surveyed in 1877 for the six-inch map published in 1882, the name 'McQueen's Rock' was wrongly given to Creag na Sgaillin, a long scree slope above the eastern spur of Beinn Tianabhaig. On the pouring of libations see Henderson 1911, pp. 252–54.

328 The quotation is from Burns's 'On the Late Captain Grose's Peregrinations thro Scotland' (Burns 1993, p. 373):

> *If in your bounds ye chance to light*
> *Upon a fine, fat, fodgel wight,*

O stature short but genius bright,
That's he, mark weel:
And wow! he has an unco sleight
O cauk and keel.

(Fodgel = dumpy; cauk = chalk; keel = pencil.) On the brownie see also Stewart 1823, pp. 137–44; Dalyell 1834, pp. 530–31, 533; Macbain 1887–88, p. 247; Mackenzie 1914, p. 275; Dieckhoff 1914–19, pp. 238–40; Spence 1948, pp. 34–46; Macdonald 1982, pp. 226–27.

329 That is, the west coast of Kintyre, facing Gigha and Cara.

330 As so often, JGC's English reflects Gaelic idiom: 'stark naked' is in Gaelic *lomnochd*, literally 'bare-naked', see p. xii above. For a full and detailed account of the brownie of Cara see Macdonald 1894–96, pp. 61–63. Brownies appear to have been particularly associated with the smaller islands of Argyll, and to have been thought capable of a fair degree of violence. Liusaidh NicCoinnich speaks of the brownie in Shuna, between Luing and Craignish (Mac a Phì 1938, p. 141): "He would announce his arrival with a shrill whistle (*fead chruaidh*). Heaven help those who neglected to fill his grinding mortar (*a chnotag bhleith*) full of milk and leave him a substantial sandwich (*ceapaire somalta*). Seemingly he would go howling (*nuallanaich*) around the house and every article of furniture (*gach ball airneis*) dancing and brawling, and usually one of the cows (*feudail*) would be lying in a pit with a broken leg in the morning."

331 Hilton Hall had a brownie called the Cauld Lad (Keightley 1850, p. 296). "Every night the servants who slept in the great hall heard him at work in the kitchen, knocking the things about if they had been set in order, arranging them if otherwise, which was more frequently the case. They . . . resorted to the usual mode of banishing a Brownie: they left a green cloke and hood for him by the kitchen fire, and remained on the watch. They saw him come in, gaze at the new clothes, try them on, and, apparently in great delight, go jumping and frisking about the kitchen. But at the first crow of the cock he vanished, crying

Here's a cloak, and here's a hood!
The Cauld Lad of Hilton will do no more good;

and he never again returned to the kitchen; yet it was said that he might still be heard at midnight singing those lines in a tone of melancholy."

332 "A good woman had just made a web of linsey-woolsey, and, prompted by her good nature, had manufactured from it a snug mantle and hood for her little Brownie. Not content with laying the gift in one of his favourite spots, she indiscreetly called to tell him it was there. This was too direct, and Brownie quitted the place, crying,

A new mantle and a new hood;
Poor Brownie! ye 'll ne'er do mair gude!

Another version of this legend says, that the gudeman of a farm-house in the parish of Glendevon having left out some clothes one night for Brownie, he was heard to depart, saying,

Gie Brownie coat, gie Brownie sark,
Ye 'se get nae mair o' Brownie's wark!"

The second version (Keightley 1850, p. 358) is from Chambers 1826, p. 267 = 1841 and 1847, p. 108.

333 The source used by Keightley (1850, pp. 384, 395) is Stewart (1823, pp. 137, 143), who gives the verse as *Huar Prownie coad agus curochd / Agus cha dian Prownie opar tullidh*: "Brownie has got a cowl and coat, / And never more will work a jot." See Almqvist 1991a, p. 35, and MacDonald 1994–95, p. 57.

334 Why Gunna should be so called is not stated. The obvious explanation appears to be that Gunna is the name of the island (identical in size to Cara) that lies between Tiree and Coll (see pp. liv–lv above). Another interpretation is possible, however, if we take Alexander Carmichael's version into account. I give it exactly as it stands in EUL MS CW 504C, f. 4r, under the heading 'Crodh Mara (sea-cattle)': "The people were fishing at Sathalum Tiree and they fished up a man upon their hooks. The man was alive but he had no speech – *guth cainnt cha robh aige.* They put him to herd the *crodh mara*. They made trews for him and they prevailed upon him to put them on. Sheall an duine a sios air fhein agus thubhairt e

> *Triubhas air a ghunna dhuibh*
> *'S an gunna dubh ri buachailleachd*
> *'S na na mheal mi*
> *Mu ni mi tuilleadh buachailleach*

Dh fhalbh an duine 's chan fhacas riamh tuilleadh e." ("The man looked down at himself and said: 'Trews upon the black gun / And the black gun tending cattle / And may I not enjoy —— / If I tend cattle any more.' The man went away and was never seen again.")

335 This will be the joint-tenancy farm of Unimore (*an t-Aoineadh Mòr* 'the Great Headland', the name of the mountain which rises behind) at Loch Doire nam Mart in the interior of Morvern. In 1779 it had a population of 45; in 1824, by which time the population had risen to about 75 (in ten houses), it was ruthlessly cleared by its new proprietor, a Miss Christina Stewart of Edinburgh (Gaskell 1968, pp. 33–34, 155).

This clearance was the subject of an important essay by the Rev. Dr Norman MacLeod (*Caraid nan Gaidheal*, 1783–1862), one of the greatest of all Gaelic writers. MacLeod published it anonymously in his own periodical *An Teachdaire Gaelach* in September 1829 under the title 'Sgeul' mu Mhàiri nighean Eoghainn bhàin; air aithris leatha fein' ('A story about Mary daughter of fair-haired Hugh; told by herself' (MacLeod 1829–30, p. 97), indexing it as 'Highland Family removed to Glasgow, account of'. Five years after his death it was reprinted by his son-in-law, the Rev. Dr Archibald Clerk of Kilmallie (1867, pp. 319–28), and a number of things were clarified or otherwise altered: (1) its authorship was unequivocally ascribed to *Caraid nan Gaidheal*; (2) its title was changed to 'Sgeul air Màiri an Aoinidh-Mhòir, air 'aithris leatha fhéin' ('The story of Mary of Unimore, told by herself'); (3) the names of Mary's husband and sons were changed – *Iain* to *Seumas*, *Aonghas* to *Iain*, *Alastoir* to *Dòmhnull*; (4) toponyms were changed or firmed up – *an Doire-mòr* to *an t-Aoineadh-mòr*, *cnochd na'n càrn* to *Cnoc-nan-càrn*. The key passage, as edited by Clerk (1867, pp. 319–20), is as follows: *An latha 'fhuair sinne bàirlinn gu falbh, shaoil sinn nach robh ann ach maoidheadh chum am barrachd màil 'fhaotainn, agus thairg sinn sin gu toileach; ach cead fuireach cha d'fhuair sinn. Reiceadh am meanbh-chrodh, agus mu dheireadh b' éigin dealachadh ris an aona mhart. C'uin a dhì-chuimhnicheas mise ciùcharan bochd nam pàisdean, ag ionndrainn a' bhainne nach robh na b' fhaide r'a thoirt doibh? C'uin a dhì-chuimhnicheas mi 'n sealladh mu dheireadh a fhuair mi de m' bhadan bòidheach ghabhar, a' miogadaich air bile nan creag, mar gu-m biodh iad g'am fhuran gu dol g'am bleodhan? – ach cuach cha do leigeadh dhomh a chur fòpa. Thàinig latha na h-imrich; bha na maoir 'n a chois, agus fiù aon oidhche na b' fhaide cha robh ri 'fhaotainn de dh'fhasgadh tighe. B' éigin falbh. Ràinig e mo chridhe a' ghaoir a thug an teine as air lic an teintein 'n uair a bha iad 'g a bhàthadh. O'n a dh'fhairtlich oirnn bothan 'fhaotainn 's an dùthaich, cha robh againn ach a' Ghalldachd a thoirt f'ar ceann. Bha 'n t-seana bhean, mo mhàthair-chéile, 's an àm sin beò, 'n a cripleach lag, aosda; thog Seumas i ann an cliabh air a dhruim; lean mis' e, le Iain beag 'n a naoidhein air mo chìch, agus thusa nach maireann, a Dhòmhnuill ghaolaich, 'ad loireanach beag a' coiseachd le d' phiuthair ri m' thaobh. Ghiùlain ar coimhearsnaich leo am beagan àirneis a bh' againn, agus thaisbein iad gach caoimhneas a b' urrainn caomh chàirdeas a nochdadh. An latha 'dh' fhàg sinn an t-Aoineadh-mòr shaoil mi gu-n sgàineadh mo chridhe; bhithinn ceart, ar leam, na-m faigheadh mo dheòir sileadh, ach faochadh air an dòigh so cha d' fhuair mi. Shuidh sinn greis air Cnoc-nan-càrn, a' gabhail an t-seallaidh mu dheireadh de 'n àite 's an d' fhuair sinn ar n-àrach. Bha na tighean cheana 'g an rùsgadh; bha mèilich nan caorach-mòr' air a' bheinn – fead a' bhuachaille Ghallda, agus tathunn a chuid con air an uchdaich. Bha sinn brònach, ach, taing Dha-san a thug dhuinn an comas, cha chualas guidhe, no droch rùn o aon againn. 'Cha-n eagal duinn,' arsa Seumas; 'tha 'n saoghal farsuing, agus seasaidh Dia sinn; tha mis' ann an so, a' giùlan mo mhàthar, agus thusa, a Mhàiri, agus mo phàisdean, ag imeachd maille rium, air an imrich bhochd so, 'chearta cho sona, agus ma dh' fhaoidte 'm chulaidh fharmaid cho mòr ri oighre 'n fhearainn, a chuir air an allaban sinn.'* "The day we received the summons to leave, we thought it was only a threat in order to get more rent, and we offered that gladly; but permission to remain we did not get. The sheep and goats were sold, and eventually the only cow had to be parted with. When will I forget the wretched whimpering of the children, missing the milk which they could no longer be given? When will I forget the last sight I got of my beautiful herd of goats, bleating on the edge of the rocks as if inviting me to go and milk them? But not a cup was I allowed to put under them. The day of the flitting came; the ground officers came with it, and not even one night longer of a house's shelter was to be had. There was no choice but to go. What reached my heart was the scream emitted by the fire on the hearthstone as they were drowning it. Since we had been unable to find a bothy in the district, the only thing we could do was head for the Lowlands. The old woman, my mother-in-law, was alive at that time, a weak, aged cripple; James lifted her in a creel on his back; I followed him, with little John a baby at my breast, and you who live no longer, my darling Donald, a little toddler walking with your sister at my side. Our neighbours carried the small amount of furniture we had, and demonstrated every kindness that loving kinship could show. The day we left Unimore I thought my heart would burst; I would be all right, I felt, if I could cry, but I could get no relief of that kind. We sat for a while on Cnoc nan Càrn, gazing for the last time on the place where we had been brought up. The houses were already being stripped; the bleating of the great sheep was on the hill – the whistle of the Lowland shepherd, and the barking of his dogs on the slope. We were sad, but, thanks to Him who empowered us, not one oath or word of ill-will was heard from any of us. 'We need not be afraid,' said James; 'the world is wide, and God will defend us; I here, carrying my mother, and accompanied by you, Mary, and my children, on this wretched flitting, am just as happy, and perhaps as much to be envied, as the proprietor who has sent us wandering.'"

As in all MacLeod's writings, a doctrine of political, social and moral compromise is being preached, but no doubt it contains a kernel of fact, and Gaskell's comment is worth noting (1968, p. 34): "The party apparently took the extremely steep path leading up through the Bealach na Sgairn, an extraordinary feat in view of James's burden. The 'Knock-nan-Càrn' is probably the hill-top immediately to the east of the Bealach which has some large boulders perched on its south face."

336 *Recte* Keightley 1850, p. 403, condensed from Train 1845, vol. 2, pp. 149–51. The story is worth retelling from its original source. "A gentleman having resolved to build a large house and offices on his property, a little above the base of Snafield mountain, at a place called *Sholt-e-will*, caused the requisite quantity of stones to be quarried on the beach, but one

immense block of white stone, which he was very desirous to have for a particular part of the intended building could not be moved from the spot, resisting the united strength of all the men in the parish. To the utter astonishment, however, of all, not only this rock, but likewise the whole of the quarried stones, consisting of more than an hundred cart-loads, were in one night conveyed from the shore to the site of the intended onstead [*sic*] by the indefatigable *phynnodderee*, and in confirmation of this wonderful feat, the *white stone* is yet pointed out to the curious visitor.

"The gentleman for whom this very acceptable piece of work was performed, wishing to remunerate the naked *phynnodderee*, caused a few articles of clothing to be laid down for him in his usual haunt. The hairy one on perceiving the habiliments lifted them up one by one, thus expressing his feelings in Manks:

> *Bayrn da'n choine, dy doogh da'n choine,*
> *Cooat da'n dreeym, dy doogh da'n dreeym,*
> *Breechyn da'n toyn, dy doogh da'n toyn,*
> *Agh my she lhiat ooiley, shoh cha nee lhiat Glen reagh Rushen.*

> Cap for the head, alas, poor head.
> Coat for the back, alas, poor back.
> Breeches for the breech, alas, poor breech.
> If these be all thine, thine cannot be the merry Glen of Rushen.

Having repeated these words, he departed with a melancholy wail ... Many of the old people lament the disappearance of the *phynnodderee*, for they say, 'There has not been a merry world since he lost his ground.'" See also Henderson 1911, p. 178; Wentz 1911, pp. 120, 129; Dorson 1968, p. 422.

337 Keightley 1850, p. 261: "Though his clothes were old and worn, he steadily refused to let the people get him new ones. But when at last they would do so, and one evening the lake-man was presented with a new coat, he said, 'When one is paid off, one must go away. After this day I'll come no more to you.' And, unmoved by the excuses of the people, he never let himself be seen again." Keightley's source is Jacob Grimm's *Deutsche Mythologie*, p. 453 (see Grimm 1875, p. 401, note 1).

338 Campbell 1860–62, vol. 1, pp. liii–lv = 1890, vol. 1, pp. xlvi–xlviii; the Manx spelling is *glashan*, see note 262 above.

339 See Keightley 1850, pp. 139 (Nis), 163 (Niägruisar), 239 (Kobold, Hobgoblin), 317 (Hobgoblin).

340 The highly circumstantial account of Hinzelmann (a Kobold or house-spirit said to have haunted the castle of Hudemühlen in Lüneburg from 1584 to 1588) was taken by Keightley (1850, pp. 240–54) from Grimm (1816, pp. 103–28). The Grimms had abridged it from a 379-page work in duodecimo by a clergyman at Eickelohe called Feldmann. It includes (Keightley 1850, p. 253) the following description alluded to by JGC: "When children were collected about Hudemühlen house, and were playing with one another, he used to get among them and play with them in the shape of a pretty little child, so that all the other children saw him plainly, and when they went home told their parents how, while they were engaged in play, a strange child came to them and amused himself with them. This was confirmed by a maid, who went one time into a room in which four or six children were playing together, and among them she saw a strange little boy of a beautiful countenance, with curled yellow hair hanging down his shoulders, and dressed in a red silk coat; and while she wanted to observe him more closely, he got out of the party, and disappeared."

341 Pinkerton 1809, pp. 330–31 = Pennant 1998, pp. 312–13.

342 Campbell 1860–62, vol. 1, p. xciii, and vol. 2, p. 101 = 1890, vol. 1, p. lxxxvii, and vol. 2, p. 112.

343 The classic account in Gaelic of the Breadalbane urisks is MacDiarmid 1901–03, pp. 133–42. It is summarised in English in Gillies 1938, pp. 340–46, and partly retold in Wheater 1980, *passim*. See also Macbain 1887–88, pp. 247–48; Mackenzie 1914, p. 284; Dieckhoff 1914–19, pp. 249–51; MacKenzie 1935, pp. 185–87; Spence 1948, pp. 41–43; MacDonald 1958b, pp. 128–29; Watson 2002, pp. 178, 204.

344 Ben Loy or Lui is on the Argyll–Perthshire border between Glen Lochy and Glen Falloch. Strictly Sococh (*an Socach*) lies in lower Glen Lochy, but the neighbouring Glen Orchy gave its name in medieval times to the estate and to the parish. In Gaelic the River Lochy is *Lòchá Urchaidh* ('Lochy of Orchy') to distinguish it from the Perthshire Lochay, *Lòchá Albannach* ('Lochay of Alba', that is, I suppose, of the kingdom of the Scots and not of the Isles), for which see note 957; Glen Lochy is *Gleann Lòchá Latharna* 'Glen Lochy of Lorn', and *an Socach*, Succoth, 'the Snouted Place', is a common name for the spit of land between two burns (Watson 2002, pp. 164, 186, 188). The form 'Succoth' is biblical, e.g. Ps. 60: 6 and 108: 7, "I will divide Shechem, and mete out the valley of Succoth."

  'Easmurag' is marked on George Langlands' 1801 map of Argyll as a township lying where a stream joins the Lochy from the south. This will be the *Eas Daimh* ('Stag Waterfall'), which rises on Beinn Laoigh. On the six-inch Ordnance Survey map of 1883 'Easmurag' (*Eas Mòraig* 'Morag's Waterfall') has become 'Airidh-nan-cìoch' (*Àirigh nan Cìoch* 'the Shieling of the Paps'), and a waterfall and footbridge are shown 100 yards up the Eas Daimh. By 1880 a viaduct had in fact been built over the Eas Daimh to carry the Oban railway, still in use; the area is now under forestry.

345 For another story about Srath Dubh-Uisge see Mackechnie 1964, pp. 102–06, 305. 'Kick-frost' is a splendidly onomatopoeic translation of *ceige-reoth*, but I imagine *ceige* means here 'a mass of matted hair' and denotes *Géigean*, the 'wild man' figure who presided over 'death revels' at the beginning of winter (see note 700). By this analysis *Reoth* and *Ceige-Reoth* are the actual names of the urisks – 'Frost' and 'Jack Frost', as it were. See note 351.

346 Glen Mallie opens off the south shore of Loch Arkaig. The story 'Uruisg an Easa Bhuidhe' ('The Urisk of Eas Buidhe', MacDougall and Calder 1910, pp. 298–99) begins: *Ann an Gleann-Màilidh an Lochabar, tha eas ùigeil ris an abrar an t-Eas Buidhe. Anns an eas so bha e air a ràdh gu 'n robh na h-Uruisgean ag gabhail fasgaidh.* MacDougall and Calder translate: "In Glen Mallie, in Lochaber, there is an eerie ravine called Eas Buidhe. In this ravine it was said that the Urisks took refuge." They cite a little *rann* –

  Ùruisg an Eas Bhuidhe
  'Na shuidhe 'n Gleann-Màilidh.

("The Urisk of Eas Buidhe, / Sitting in Glen Mallie.") The story is as told in note 365 below and not as cited here by JGC.

347 Graham 1810, p.19; Robertson 1904, p. 294. Graham was using 'stated' in its old-fashioned sense 'scheduled, regular'.

348 For *Strathaibh* (*Sraithibh, Sraitheo*) see Watson 2002, pp. 165–66.

349 This would appear to place *Slochd an Aoirisg* between Hynish in the west and Scarinish in the east, but I have no information as to its exact location. Niall M. Brownlie has not heard the name.

350 HSD, vol. 2, p. 246. The concentration of urisk stories in the central Highlands suggests Pictish origin, but the term appears to derive ultimately from Norse *ófreskr*, a mythological term meaning 'endowed with second sight, able to see ghosts and apparitions hidden from the common eye' – hence objects so seen, which are differently imagined in different localities, and thus *ófreskja* 'monster' (Henderson 1910, p. 79). In the isles the term is by no

means unknown, but shows evidence of semantic and morphological development – in Ness, Lewis, it is applied to a huge uncouth female, while JGC's *Slochd an Aoirisg* in Tiree, being masculine, suggests a derivation from *ófreskr* rather than *ófreskja*, with assimilation to *aoir* 'satire'. Carmichael (*CG2*, p. 373) points to *Coire nan Ùraisg* and *Bealach Coire nan Ùraisg* in Skye as well as to *Gleann na h-Ùraisg* in Kilninver, Argyll.

It appears that the identity of the urisk on the mainland has been affected by the natural assumption that the final element represents *uisge* 'water' – an assumption encouraged by lexicographers, beginning with Armstrong (1825, p. 585), who chose to spell the word *ùruisg* in preference to *ùraisg*, proposing a tentative – and very wrong – derivation *urr(a) uisge* 'water person'. The earliest writer to mention the term, the Rev. Robert Kirk, made no such connection (EUL ms Laing III 551, p. 1, cf. Hunter 2001, p. 78): he spelled it (in the plural) *hubhrisgeidh* and equated it to 'Elf', see note 58.

On the mainland, urisk stories occur as far north as Poolewe, where, as so often elsewhere, the urisks are associated with a waterfall. Armstrong makes the word masculine, no doubt because the identity of the urisk, like that of the brownie, is fundamentally male, but most instances of the word are grammatically feminine. All in all it appears that the figure of the *ùraisg* drifted east as a female spirit with increasingly hydrophilous tendencies, gradually mingling with that of the brownie as it worked its way from the Lowlands. See Campbell 1890, vol. 1, pp. 244–45, 252–53; MacDougall 1891, pp. 296–97; MacDougall 1897; Henderson 1910, pp. 79–83; Bruford and MacDonald 1994, p. 470.

351 Presumably *B'e Donnchadh aonan* and *B'e Fearchar dithist*, or the like. This seems to belong to a tradition of supernatural creatures naming themselves, their cries being heard here amongst the wind and the waves. See note 345; Mac Calum 1913; MacKenzie 1935, pp. 85–98; Spence 1948, p. 58; MacLennan 1994–96, pp. 242–43; Thompson 1997, pp. 103–04. JGC's 'Shant Isles' is usually now 'Shiant Isles'.

352 See McDonald 1958, p. 126, and GUL ms Gen. 1090/29, pp. 215–16.

353 Cf. p. 156. The 'fishy covering of her lower limbs', elsewhere called *cochall*, will be a fertility symbol akin to the *crios* or *criosan*, see note 8. "'Well, my lady, I'm taking you home,'" says the lucky man in a version recorded in 1995 from Mrs Dolly Sutherland MacDonald, Hilton, Easter Ross (Ó Catháin and Watson 1996–97, p. 340), "and he took the . . . the skirt off her, her tail, and he said, 'As long as I have this, you must stay with me.'" On mermaids in general see Dixon 1886, pp. 162–63; Macbain 1887–88, pp. 249–50; Campbell 1890, vol. 1, pp. 72–104; MacDougall 1891, pp. 145–86; MacPhail 1897, pp. 384–86; *CG2*, pp. 324–26; Henderson 1902, pp. 277–301; Grant 1925, p. 1; Polson 1926, pp. 74–80; Sutherland 1937, pp. 96–98; Mac Thomais 1937–41, pp. 178–80; Campbell 1940–60, vol. 2, pp. 116–19; MacDonald 1958b, pp. 139–40; MacPherson 1960, pp. 186–87; MacLellan 1961, p. 122; Dorson 1968, p. 144; Temperley 1977, pp. 132–35; Ó Duilearga 1981, pp. 267–77, 402; Miller 1994, pp. 277–90; Bruford 1997, pp. 122–23; Thompson 1997, pp. 127–29; EUL ms CW 504C, ff. 1r–3r.

354 For the name *MacMhannain* see note 579. On egg-water see pp. 126 and 139. What the mermaid probably meant was that egg-water thrown upon a person had the effect of an aphrodisiac, as is explained in SoSS Maclagan mss vol. 22, p. 3867: "From Mary McLean, Port Charlotte, Islay. It is said that a woman can secure for herself a lad's attention and affection in spite of fate by throwing the water upon him in which an egg has been boiled; and there is a saying among people, which the reciter has often heard used as accounting for the fact of a lad being in love with an unprepossessing girl – 'Chuir i uisge nan ubha air.' (She has put the egg water upon him). Which means that the charm of the water has accomplished for her what she had not sufficient personal charms to procure."

W. M. Mackenzie tells a story from Arran (1914, pp. 279–80) of a farmer who became the unwilling host of a young *mèileachan* or 'bleater' (see p. 85 above). When its mother the *glaistig* came to fetch her, she embraced her offspring and said: *Tha mi an dòchas nach do leig thu ris dhaibh éifeachd uisge uibhe no bun na feanndaig.* "I hope you haven't revealed to them the effect of egg water or nettle root."

355 Eilein Anabaich is on the shore of Loch Seaforth at Maaruig. The name refers to a shoal off the mouth of the river there (Lawson 2002, p. 166).

356 This chapter is fundamental to our understanding of the Highland water-horse. See also Stewart 1823, pp. 145–57; Dalyell 1834, pp. 543–44; Anon. 1886–87c; Macbain 1887–88, pp. 248–49; Campbell 1890, vol. 4, pp. 300–12; MacDougall 1891, pp. 294–95; Black 1892–93, p. 500; Mackinlay 1895–96, pp. 72–73; MacPhail 1896, p. 400, and 1897, pp. 383–84; Watson 1908–09, pp. 52–54; Anon. 1908–09a, pp. 166–68; Henderson 1911, pp. 137–43, 161–65; Dieckhoff 1914–19, p. 243; Grant 1925, p. 1; Polson 1926, pp. 81–87; MacDhùghaill 1929–30, pp. 124–28; MacDonald 1934–36a, pp. 189–91; Sutherland 1937, pp. 98–99; Mac Thomais 1937–41, pp. 185–86; MacLean 1942–50, pp. 150–52; MacDonald 1958b, pp. 129–30; MacPherson 1960, pp. 190–91; Macdonald 1982, pp. 237–40; Almqvist 1991b; Almqvist 1991c, pp. 236–39; Bruford and MacDonald 1994, pp. 322–24, 471–72; MacDonald 1994–95, pp. 50–51; EUL MS CW 504C, ff. 9r–10r.

357 'Mac Fir Àrois' was excluded from *WSS*, but fortunately it was transcribed from JGC's lost appendix by Alexander Carmichael into EUL MS CW 241, ff. 13–16, and by George Henderson into GUL MS Gen. 1090/77, ff. [5–7], see pp. 701–04. In twenty-five couplets, the words are those of a young woman who laments the death of her beloved fair-haired Roderick, *Mac Fir Àrois na Leitreach* ('the son of the tacksman of Aros upon the Slope').

Sann Di-Sathairne bhàthadh
Mac Fir Àrois nan ròiseal.

Sann a-mach air Loch Frìosa
Chaidh an dìobhail, 's bu mhòr i.

Gur h-ann an deaghaidh mhic Làire
Ghlac thu 'n t-àrdan ad' phòraibh

'S bha na h-easganna sàthach
Le fuil an àilleagain bhòidhich.

("On Saturday there was drowned / Aros's son of the great sails. / When going out on Loch Frisa / Disaster hit, and it was big. / In pursuit of *mac Làire* / You struck pride in your pores / And the eels filled their wames / With the gorgeous man's blood.") Henderson writes *mhic Làire* ('Mare's son'), Carmichael *mhic làire* ('a mare's son'), so the animal was clearly a stallion, and the line about pride suggests that he may have followed it willingly rather than being dragged into the loch. (For this expression *mac làire* cf. also p. 94 'On Baugh, Tiree'.) The singer is under no illusions about the creatures which attacked the corpse. She reaches the house of mourning to find it stretched out on a deal board under the window while the women sew the shroud. He is lamented throughout Mull that evening, she says, for although this mere puddle (*lòn*) has done for him, he was a good sailor. She regrets that she did not become pregnant by him to allow her to 'lift the collar of his coat' (*a thogail colair do chòta*), that is, to identify him as the father, and she ends in true pop-song fashion by challenging a young girl's worst nightmares, facing the kirk session (*mòd*) and enduring its sentence of ritual humiliation.

Is truagh nach robh mi uait dìolain
Ged a sgrìobht' aig a' mhòd e

No ged chuirt' mi 'm sheasamh
Anns an eaglais Di-Dòmhnaich

Ann an làthair nan ceudan
Ás mo léine gun chòmhdach.

("Too bad you didn't make me pregnant / Even if it were written at the *mòd* / Or even if I had to stand / In the church on Sunday / In the presence of hundreds / Wearing nothing but my shirt.")

This then is a summary of the song sung in Mull about the event. Elsewhere the story appears to have been remembered in the song generally known as 'Cumha Mhic an Tòisich' ('Mackintosh's Lament'), or, in the islands, 'Cumha Mhic a h-Àrasaig' or the like. Unlike 'Mac Fir Àrois' it has been published many times. It has become a pipe tune, and the same names are found in the piping literature. 'Cumha Mhic a h-Àrasaig' appears, on the face of it, to mean 'The Lament for the Lad from Arisaig', but the name is peculiar and appears to be a corruption. A hymn by Fr Ranald Rankin was stated by Colin Chisholm (1888–89, p. 239) to have been composed to the air 'Cumha Mhic Arois'. An obvious title for a lament for *Mac Fir Àrois* would be 'Cumha Mhic Fhir Àrois', and this is probably what underlies both 'Cumha Mhic a h-Àrasaig' and 'Cumha Mhic Arois'. Donald C. MacPherson called it 'Cumha Mhic a Arois' (Abrach 1873–74a, p. 168).

Under the title 'Cumha Mhic-an-Tòisich' the Revs A. and A. MacDonald say (1911, pp. lvi–lvii): "We have given this composition the name by which it is best known, but in the Western Isles, where the version given here was obtained, it is called 'Cumha Mhic a Arisaig', or 'Bealach a Ghàraidh'. Our version seems to have no connection with the air given in Campbell's Anthology, and one or two other publications. The very name of the hero of the Lament is against the assertion that he was a Mackintosh chief. Eoghann Og was not the name of any of the chiefs of that family. The title, 'Cumha Mhic a Arisaig', would seem to identify him with the Clanranald country. Evidently two compositions originally distinct, but bearing a resemblance to one another, have been amalgamated and now form one song. There are several traditions, differing very materially, in regard to its Mackintosh origin. The present Mackintosh believes it to have been composed by the family bard, MacIntyre, in the year 1550, on the death of William, who was murdered by the Countess of Huntly that year."

There is, I think, much to commend this idea that the Mackintosh connection comes from a different song which has become conflated with it. The internal evidence of island versions (such as the MacDonald ministers') supports JGC's description of *Mac Fir Àrois*. He was clearly a man 'of great personal activity', being described as a courtier, a dancer, a hunter of deer and of capercailzie, and a fisher of trout. He is praised for his horsemanship, being *marcraich ùr nan steud àlainn* 'the gallant rider of comely steeds' and *marcraich an eich leumraich dhuibh* 'the rider of the prancing black steed'. He is killed by being thrown, dragged and trampled by a horse: *reub an t-each bàn thu* 'the white horse mangled you', and:

Leag an t-each ceannfhionn thu,
Thog an t-each ceannfhionn thu,
Leag an t-each ceannfhionn thu
An ionad a' ghàrraidh.

("The white-faced horse threw you, / The white-faced horse raised you, / The white-faced horse threw you / In the place where the wall was.") There is a repeated reference to *bealach a' ghàrraidh*, translated by Carmichael 'the breach of the wall' (*CG5*, pp. 346–53), just like the place (p. 110, 'Farmers and Water-Horses') where the rider 'plants a foot against each pillar and throws himself off its back': *Eoghain òig, leagadh tu / Am bealach a' ghàrraidh . . . / Och nan och, leagadh tu / Am bealach a' ghàrraidh . . . / Eoghain òig, leagadh tu / Am bealach a' ghàrraidh.* "Young Ewen, you were thrown / In the breach of the wall . . . / Horror of horrors, you were thrown / In the breach of the wall . . . / Young Ewen, you were thrown / In the breach of the wall." No loch is mentioned at all, but it is clear that the body was recovered, and that this happened 'between his espousal and marriage', a point not mentioned at all in the Mull song.

> Am fìon bha gu d' bhanais,
> Sann chaidh e gu t' fhalair:
> Rìgh, gur mì a bha galach
> An àm nan galan a thràghadh.

("The wine for your wedding, / It served for your wake: / O King, how I wept / As the gallons were drained.") So the girl who laments him is caught forever between maidenhood and marriage, with his favour in her bonnet, his ring on her finger, a wife's kertch on her head *gach féill agus Sàbaid* ('each feast-day and Sabbath'), but no husband or child to show for it: her confusion is vividly portrayed. As further confirmation, the two outstanding features of the Aros district were its medieval castle (uninhabited by 1680, see Currie 2000, p. 8) and its fair (*An Fhaidhir Mhuileach*, see note 496); both a castle and a fair are mentioned in 'Mackintosh's Lament' (*tùr nan clach àrda* 'the tower of high stones', *gu féill no gu faidhir* 'to feast or to fair', *aig féill agus faidhir* 'at feast and at fair').

It may be argued that the story of the young man's death is a floating one, ready to attach itself to the son of any local grandee. In Wester Ross and west Inverness-shire the song appears to have been much as in the islands despite being called 'Cumha Mhic an Tòisich' – with the further complication that in Ross-shire 'Eoghan Òg' was understood to be a Mackenzie of Gairloch who was accidentally killed while going to be married to a daughter of MacLeod of Cadboll; the air, a favourite lullaby, was quite distinct from that of the pipe tune (Mackenzie 1876–77). What is more, I have been unable to identify a historical *Eoghan Òg Mac Fir Àrois*. A Malcolm MacLean, son of the captain of Aros, is on record in 1592 (RCAHMS 1980, p. 177). He may possibly be the 'Gillicalum McNeill VcRorie' who is captain of Aros in 1651–52 (Anderson 1931–33, p. 123); this at least gives us a Roderick, *c.* 1550–92. The title *Fear Àrois* fits Donald MacLean (*c.* 1650–1700), fourth son of Charles MacLean of Ardnacross and Drimnin, but he is not known to have had sons called Eoghan or Roderick – 'he married Catherine, second daughter of Donald Macquarrie of Ulva, by whom he had Alexander, Angus, Charles, and others' (Sinclair 1899, p. 452).

Carmichael was told of a prediction that Mackintosh would die through the instrumentality of his glossy black steed (C.M.P. 1894–95). Mackintosh continued to ride it, but it was so fractious on his wedding day that he drew his pistol and shot it dead. He was given another mount, a roan or piebald, but on his way from the church it shied at the black horse's body, and he was thrown and killed. Charles Stewart, Killin, understood that this happened in 1526 to Lachlan, fourteenth laird of Mackintosh, or to William, who was murdered in 1550 as stated above; the Rev. Alexander MacGregor, Inverness, had a circumstantial account of how Mackintosh's widow composed the lament as the funeral procession moved 'from the family castle at Dalcross to the burying-ground at Petty' (Stewart 1884, p. 46).

See also Gillies 1786, pp. 204–05; Abrach 1873–74a, pp. 168–69; Carmichael 1876; Brown 1884, p. 185; Macbean 1888, part 2, no. 25; Fionn 1889b; MacDonald 1911, pp. 336–38; *CG5*, pp. 346–59; Maclean 1975, p. 68; GUL Gen. 1042 (MacLagan) MS 61; GUL MS Gen. 1090/28, pp. 256–57; EUL MS CW 503, ff. 628–34.

358 This little round loch in the hills above Loch Spelve in east Mull (688.302) is more usually known as *Crùn-Lochan*, seemingly from its resemblance to a crown or five-shilling piece (MacQuarrie 1983, p. 66; Maclean 1997, p. 75). It may be compared to *Lochan a' Bhuinn-a-Sè* 'the Sixpenny Lochan' in the hills west of Lochaline in Morvern. Maclean (1997, pp. 75, 78) mentions two other lochs in Mull bearing the same name: a small one in the hills east of Torloisk (442.446) and a much larger one in the mountains south of Glen More which is marked on maps as *Loch an Eilein* or Loch an Ellen (623.295). In a story recorded in 1953 (SoSS SA 1953/49/B5) and published by Ó Crualaoich (2003, pp. 115–18, 241–44), *Crùlachan* is described as 'not far from Glen More in Mull' (*chan eil i fada on Ghleann Mhór ann am Muile*) and the *Cailleach Bheurr* complains wrily of its depth.

> *Crùlachan dubh domhainn,*
> *An loch as doimhne san domhan —*
> *Ruigeadh Caol Muile mo ghlùinean*
> *Ach ruigeadh Crùlachan mo shléistean.*

("Deep dark Crùlachan / Is the deepest loch in the world – / The Sound of Mull would reach my knees / But Crùlachan would reach my thighs.") Since Crùlachan behind Glen More is the only one of the three which she would be obliged to wade through on a journey, it may be the one meant in the rhyme. On the other hand, JGC himself tells us of the *Cailleach Bheurr* that 'in Ardiura, in the parish of Torosay in Mull, there is a small tarn or mountain loch called *Crù-lochan* (*i.e.* the Horse-shoe Lakelet), which she said (and her long life must have made her a good authority) was the deepest loch in the world' (Campbell 1914–15, p. 414). Not only does this offer a derivation from *crudha* 'a horseshoe', but it brings us back to the hills above Loch Spelve. JGC then quotes a variant of the rhyme (his Gaelic original was excluded by the publisher, but I give it from EUL MS CW 241, f. 67, see p. 703 below):

> *Crùlochan beag dorcha domhainn,*
> *An aon loch as doimhne air domhan —*
> *Ràinig a' mhuir mhòr an glùn domh*
> *'S rainig Crùlochan an tòn domh.*

He translates: "The Horse-shoe tarn, little, dark, and deep, / The deepest lake in all the world; / The great sea reached my knee, / And the Horse-shoe Tarn reached my haunch." See also Gray 1987, pp. 160–61.

359 Loch Annla, Amhla, Anlaimh or Amhlaidh – Olaf's Loch, see Campbell 1895, p. 7, and MacEchern 1914–19, p. 320 – is in the centre of the island. Amhlaidh Mór, who lived in the stone-built fort in the loch and gave it its name, is thought to be the progenitor of the MacAulays of North Uist (Matheson 1980–82, pp. 337–38). See Introduction, p. xl.

360 James Boswell was told a version of this story in 1773 by 62-year-old Malcolm MacLeod of the Raasay family as they approached Dun Can (Levi 1984, p. 256). "Before we reached this mountain, we passed by two lakes. Of the first, Malcolm told me a strange fabulous tradition. He said, there was a wild beast in it, a sea-horse, which came and devoured a man's daughter; upon which the man lighted a great fire, and had a sow roasted at it, the smell of which attracted the monster. In the fire was put a spit. The man lay concealed behind a low wall of loose stones, and he had an avenue formed for the monster, with two rows of large flat stones, which extended from the fire over the summit of the hill, till it reached the side of the loch. The monster came, and the man with the red-hot spit destroyed it. Malcolm

shewed me the little hiding-place, and the rows of stones. He did not laugh when he told me this story."

In 1859 JFC got a version of the tale which was published with translation and notes in Campbell 1940–60, vol. 2, pp. 12–14; see also MacInnes 1988–90, pp. 9–10. Another version was noted for JFC in 1861 by Donald Kenneth Torrie (NLS Adv. MS 50.1.11, ff. 292r–293r). Lachlan Robertson, son of the innkeeper at Lussa near Kyleakin, told Torrie that *nighean Gobha Rhasay* had borne a child to a young man, only to find that he was a water-horse from *Loch Leointe* ('the Loch of Wounding'). She fled, leaving the child behind. *Bha eagail air a ghobha gum faigheadh e groim a rithist orra, agus se am plan a rinn e, thog e ceartach ri taobh an Loch, agus mharbh e mart, agus thoisich e air rosladh a mhairt. Thoisich easan air tighinn air sailbh a rosla. Bha an gobha deanaimh boutaichean iaruinn dearg agus gan cuir anns' an fheoil, agus gan tilgidh sios am bheul, agus e fosgailte aige agus coltas anabarrach fiadhaich air. Mar so chuir e crioch air an each. Nuair a thoisich easan air spreätaich chuir an gobha gata mor iarruinn thro chorp. Shin an gobha dhachaidh cho luath 's a burrain dha. Nuair a thanaig e latha-r-n-mhaireach, cha robh ann ach na h-iarruinn am measg tor rhonn.* ("The smith was afraid it would get hold of her again, and the plan he devised was, he built a smithy beside the Loch, and slaughtered a cow, and began to roast the cow. It started to come on account of the roast. The smith was making red iron bolts and putting them in the flesh, and throwing them down its mouth, which it had open, looking extremely fierce. In this way he finished off the horse. When it started to burst the smith put a big iron spear through its body. The smith raced home as quickly as he could. When he came next day, nothing was left but the irons amidst a heap of slavers.") Torrie concludes: "This one is very common about Broadford. I have heard pieces of it from a great many but none of them as complete as the above. All the reciters believe it to be true, and say that where the smithy stood is still to be seen. Their versions don't agree upon many points. According to some the horse never came to the Smithy but that the meat was roasted in the smithy and that the juice mixed with melted iron was conveyed to the horse by means of pipes laid under the ground and communicating with the Loch. That the horse attracted by the smell, came to the pipe and having drank of this stuff was instantaneously killed, and that nothing of the child was ever seen, nor of the horse either but their livers."

Torrie (1832–78), then a divinity student at Glasgow, was a son of Alexander Torrie, a farmer in South Uist; he spent four years, 1871–75, as minister of Glencoe, a detached part of the parish of Lismore and Appin, and died at Kyleakin aged only 46 (Scott 1915–50, vol. 4, p. 85).

As told by Sorley MacLean, JGC's 'hut', MacLeod's 'low wall' and Robertson's 'smithy' become 'a kind of cavern at the north-east end of the loch'. MacLean goes on (1974–76, pp. 382–83 = Mac Gill-Eain 1985, pp. 300–01): "He then roasted a sheep to entice with its smell the water-horse, which ate and slept until the Smith transfixed him with a red-hot coulter. Whether a water-horse could be killed or not is not clear but, at any rate, he could be hurt and discouraged from further abductions. The Gobha Mór is not given a name, but I know a Raasay MacKenzie genealogy which goes back for eleven generations and ends with an unnamed Gobha Mór. The cairn just on the east side of the north end of Loch na Mnatha is still called 'Obair a' Ghobha Mhóir', the Work of the Big Smith." Taking this evidence with JGC's, it appears that the smith may have been an Alexander MacKenzie who lived *c.* 1550.

361 See Introduction, pp. lxxiv–lxxv above. There is an account of Ewen MacPhie or Macphee (*c.*1784–1850) in Ellice 1931, pp. 97–99. Following his desertion he was captured while living with his sister at Feddan in Glengarry. He escaped from a steamer at Corpach by snapping his handcuffs against an iron bar on the deck. After two years on Loch Arkaig-side he moved north to the island in Loch Quoich (Cuaich). "His bothy built, he must needs have

a wife; so one fine morning he stepped across the hill to Glen Dulochan, where he had previously made the acquaintance of a girl, and, without much more courting, popped her on his back, and returned to his island, where they were duly married."

Ellice also tells how he was looked up to as a seer, a curer of cows and a 'weaver of charms'; how he was pursued by sheriff's officers for sheep-stealing; how in his absence his wife once fired on two officers as they rowed towards the island; and how he 'was caught and taken to prison, where he eventually died'. MacPhie has been made the subject of a very readable 130-page work of fiction (Mitchell 2003), but arguably sufficient material exists in English and Gaelic for a factual study of similar length, see Anon. 1841–42a; McIan and Logan 1847, part 19, 'Clann Dhubhi – The Mac Phees', p. 3; McIan and Logan 1848, p. 19; Fraser-Mackintosh 1897, pp. 215–16; Macdonald 1897–99, p. 342; Logan 1900, pp. 212–22; MacKintosh 1902–03; Burn 1917, pp. 168–69; MacDonald 1982, pp. 158–59; Mitchell 1995; MacLeod 2002, p. 224; MacilleDhuibh 29.11.02.

362   *Loch an Àir* is in the south-eastern tip of Tiree near Rubha Nead Geòidh, Rubha a' Bhodaich and Port an Dùin. The name suggests 'the Loch of Slaughter' or 'of Ploughing'. There is nothing in oral tradition to suggest that it could have been the site of a battle, so the latter meaning is perhaps more likely, but the water-horse connection could well have given rise to either – or both. Niall M. Brownlie has drawn my attention to this verse in a song by Captain Alick MacDonald, Milton, Caolas (Brownlie 1991a, p. 23):

> *Aig Taigh Loch an Àir thogadh iomadh deagh bhàta,*
> *Ainmeil bhon làimh chluicheadh tàl agus tuagh;*
> *Am beagan th' air fhàgail den tobhta tha 'n làthair,*
> *Tha mo chridh' ann am bàidh rith' seach àite mun cuairt.*

("At Loch an Àir House were built many fine boats, / Made famous by the hand which would wield adze and axe; / My heart loves the little that's left of the ruins / More than anywhere else in the district around.")

By 'last century' JGC means the eighteenth.

363   Loch Assapol is a large loch above Bunessan. The shieling story is 'Àirigh na h-Aon Oidhche', see note 368.

364   Loch Meudaidh lies two miles due south of the village of Durness. On the maps it is Loch Meadaidh or Meadie. John Mackay's proposed derivation from *meud* 'size' (1889–90, p. 46) suggests that JGC's spelling is the correct one.

365   See note 346. The story is commonly told as a variant in which the creature is not a water-horse but an urisk. In MacGregor 1901, p. 63, the urisk's reply as he runs off is in verse.

> *Ochan! Loisg thu mi, chràidh thu mi*
> *Le d' bhrochan teth tana gun stàth,*
> *Ach fhads bhios uisg' ann an Lìobhain*
> *Cha chrìochnaich do pheanas gu bràth.*

> *A chailleach gun mhodh is gun nàir',*
> *Is tu chiùrr mi gu goirt 's gu searbh,*
> *Ach thig mi le armachd gun dàil*
> *Is cuiream gu bàs thu gu dearbh.*

"Ouch! You've burned me and tortured me / With your hot, thin and worthless gruel, / But as long as there's water in Lyon / Your punishment will never end. / Old woman without manners or shame, / You've injured me sorely and bitterly, / But I'll come right away bringing weapons / And put you to death for sure." Usually when the urisk appears he asks the woman's name, and she replies, as a girl might well do in such a situation, *Mi fhìn*. "Myself." After being scalded he runs off to the protection of his fellow urisks, who demand to know who has done this to him. *Mi fhìn*, he says. "Oh, in that case," they say, "there is nothing to be done. If it had been someone else, we would have killed them and burned their house around their ears" – or words to that effect. See for example 'Uruisg an Easa Bhuidhe' ('The Urisk of Eas Buidhe'), in MacDougall and Calder 1910, pp. 298–301; Campbell 1890, vol. 2, p. 206; Scott 2001, p. 73; note 468 below.

366 Niall M. Brownlie tells me that *Baile nan Cràganach* can only be today's *Baile nan Cògan*, a township in the village of Cornaigmore. If this is so, the name should also be linked with that of *Cladach a' Chrògain*, which is two miles east. MacLeod and Dewar (1831, p. 193) give *cràganach* as 'an in-footed, intoed, person', and no doubt that is the word JGC had in mind – the vowel will be subject to the same variation as in *cròg, cràg*, 'a large or clumsy hand'. *An Crògan* in south-east Mull, the birthplace of the poet *Lachann Dubh a' Chrògain* (for whom see MacDonald 1995, p. 67, and Lobban 2004), is said by Gillies to be from *cròg* 'a claw' (1906, p. 110), 'given as fancifully indicative of the shape of the place', and I believe that is roughly how we should understand *c` rogan* here – as a place nestling in the palm of an enormous *cròg* or hand. In this way we may see *Baile nan Cràganach* as 'the Township of the *Crògan*-Dwellers', and it is not surprising to find the name transferring itself to the alleged physical attributes of its inhabitants. Note also *Tràigh Chrògan* 'Crògan Beach' on the west side of Salum Bay in Tiree, and *an Crògan Sgithich* 'the Hawthorn Bush', p. 80, in both of which cases I believe a similar shape is indicated.

  Cladach a' Chrògain is explained by MacDougall and Cameron (n.d., p. 87) as 'the Graip Shore', referring presumably to the implement (usually *gràpa* or *crogan*) used for harvesting seaweed. I do not find this convincing.

367 See Introduction, p. xliii, and notes 123 and 444. An account of the surrender of weapons at Scarinish on 24 April 1716 lists three sons of this Malcolm Clerk or Clark, none of whom had taken part in the previous year's rising, and only one of whom was called John (Maclean-Bristol 1998, p. 151): "Donald Clerk his son / gave in his gun & sword & pistol / Lachlan Clerk his son / he has no arms / John Clerk his son / he has no arms." On the other hand, in an account of the feats of strength attributed to Malcolm Clerk of Kilmoluag, whom he calls 'one of the remarkable men of Tiree', Lord Archibald Campbell (1885a, pp. 254–55) mentions two sons, Donald Bane and Charles. In one of the tales MacInnes the factor brings his bully for a wrestling match; Malcolm refuses the challenge but puts forward his son Donald in his place. The two men prove equal, and swearing at his son, Malcolm tells him to stop fooling and throw the bully into 'the hottest place in the house', with the result that 'he pitched the bully to the fire, and scattered the embers, so that he nearly burned the bully, factor, and house'.

368 This is a curiosity. Since JGC describes the water-horse as the 'hero' of the incident, it must be a simple story of how it recognised a man dressed in woman's clothes, as at p. 106 above (*SHIS* 197). However, *Fhaire na h-Aon Oidhch'* is hard to dissociate from *Àirigh na h-Aon Oidhche* ('the One Night's Shieling'), the location of a vampire tale similar to 'MacPhie's Black Dog' (pp. 58–64 above); indeed a version from Benbecula published by Bruford and MacDonald (1994, pp. 318–19, 470) consists of the vampire story with the dog as an additional character, while JGC himself once remarked of 'MacPhie's Black Dog' (Campbell 1885b, p. 263): "It is known in the Western Islands as the 'One Night's Watch' (*Aire na h-aon oidhche*)."

  The place of the sixteen women in 'MacPhie's Black Dog' is usually taken in the *Àirigh na h-Aon Oidhche* stories by a water-horse or some other terrifying supernatural creature. JGC tells the story in a few words at p. 114 when he describes how the girl who encounters the water-horse is sometimes 'one of a band of women assembled at the summer shieling – the rest are killed and she makes her escape'. There are no shielings in Tiree, but the stress being on *aon* in any case, it is easy to see how *àirigh* might become subject to reinterpretation in that island as *aire* 'attention' and spuriously linked with *faire* 'watch'. The purpose, of course, is to explain why some isolated dwelling-place should have been abandoned after only one night of use. The Tiree *Àirigh na h-Aon Oidhche* is in Cornaigmore, south-east of Loch Bhasapol. See Robertson 1904–07, pp. 268–69; Mac Calum 1913; MacMillan 1968, p. 365; *Tocher* 27, pp. 182–83; Burnett 1986, pp. 131–32.

369 Loch Fada is not exactly at the foot of Storr, but is one of the so-called 'Storr Lochs', the other being Loch Leathann. The stream in question will be one of two which rise on Beinn Mheadhonach and enter Loch Fada from the west. The more southerly of these is given on Ordnance Survey maps as Lòn Coire na h-Airidh; the other is unnamed. Beinn Mheadhonach is also the source of the Eskidal Burn, whose valley is JGC's Eisgeadal (for which see also Campbell 1891, p. 76). It flows south to become the River Leasgeary which empties into Portree Harbour. In a clear echo of JGC's work, but without acknowledgement (see note 795), Alexander Forbes says of Eisgeadal (1923, p. 184): "Where the river or stream from here falls into Loch Fada, at the base of the Storr, a 'water-horse' is said to have been killed!"

370 The distinction drawn here between the *each-uisge* and kelpie is of fundamental importance. The apparent confusion between them in published accounts in English is simply due to the common practice of translating *each-uisge* as 'kelpie'. Thanks to JGC's rule of thumb, we may for example identify the topic of Gregor 1883b as the kelpie and that of Anon. 1886–87c as the *each-uisge*, even though the term employed in both articles is 'kelpie'. I have proposed for it a derivation from an assumed P-Celtic (Pictish and/or Cumbric) *ceffyl-pol* ('river-horse'), giving *celpow*, hence 'kelpie' (MacilleDhuibh 21.5.99). The kelpie is well described in McPherson 1929, pp. 61–67; for further references see Dorson 1968, p. 143.

371 For more on the water-bull see note 374; Dalyell 1834, pp. 544, 682; Dixon 1886, pp. 161–62 (the 'beast' of *Loch na Béiste* in Gairloch, for which see also Mackenzie 1980, pp. 187–89); Campbell 1891, p. 89; Mackinlay 1893, pp. 171–73; Mackinlay 1895–96, pp. 73–74; Sutherland 1937, pp. 99–100; MacDonald 1958b, pp. 133–35; Mackechnie 1964, pp. 125–27, 310. On the term *corc-chluasach* see *CG2*, p. 260.

372 On the king otter see Campbell 1940–60, vol. 2, pp. 4–5, 9–10. On *dobhar* see Watson 1926a, pp. 453–56.

373 Perhaps no item better illustrates the difficulty of editing JGC's work than this. It appears as 'Biasd na Srogaig' in the list of contents and sectional sub-title (*SHIS* xvii, 217) but as 'Biasd na Grogaig' in the index (*SHIS* 313), while JGC says here that it derives its name from *scrogag*. We should probably take 'Grogaig' as a typographical error for 'Srogaig' (cf. 'Gaining' in error for 'Saining', *SHIS* 248). As for 'Srogaig' itself, if not a ghost-word it can certainly be taken as a by-form of *scrogag*. That is still not the end of the story, however, for *scrogag* is (quite properly) spelt *sgrogag* by Dwelly (1977, p. 834) – following Robertson, who defines the word (1899–1901, p. 363) as 'crumpled horn', citing *béist na sgrogaig* 'the unicorn in armorial bearings; in Skye a mythical aquatic animal (Gregorson Campbell's Superstitions of the Highlands)'!

374 Sir John Graham Dalyell claimed (1834, p. 544) that 'the water bull is still believed to reside in Loch Awe and Loch Rannoch, nor are witnesses wanting to give testimony to the fact'. Over 300 years previously Hector Boece reported a conversation with Sir Duncan Campbell, who told him that in 1510 a terrible beast had come out of 'Garloll, ane loch of Argyle' (Brown 1893, p. 72). As big as a greyhound, with feet like a gander, it struck down great trees with a thump of its tail. It slew three hunters with three more strokes of its tail, and would have slain others had they not climbed into oak-trees; after that it fled back into

the loch. Wise men predicted that upheaval would follow in Scotland – it had been seen before, and trouble resulted on every occasion.

This is according to a pattern in which the appearance of a beast in one of the larger freshwater lochs presages the death of that loch's temporal guardian; and indeed Archibald, earl of Argyll, Chancellor of Scotland, was killed at Flodden, 9 September 1513. I have therefore argued (MacilleDhuibh 7.5.99) that 'Garloll' should be understood not as the Gareloch (a sea-loch in the Lennox) but as Loch Awe (the largest freshwater loch in Argyll, and the symbolic heart of the Campbell patrimony).

One wonders, also, what might be the connection between Dalyell's water-bull, Boece's gander-footed monster and JFC's 'boobrie' (Campbell 1890, vol. 1, p. xci): "There is a gigantic water bird, called the Boobrie, which is supposed to inhabit the fresh water and sea lochs of Argyllshire. I have heard of him nowhere else; but I have heard of him from several people. He is ravenous and gigantic, gobbles up sheep and cows, has webbed feet, a very loud hoarse voice, and is somewhat like a cormorant. He is reported to have terrified a minister out of his propriety, and it is therefore to be assumed that he is of the powers of evil."

The Rev. George Henderson (1911, p. 134) explained 'boobrie' as *boibhre* 'cow-giver, cow-bestowing', or as *DIL* has it (s.v. *boibre*), 'cow-behaviour, behaving like the cow, a kind of fool'. He says (Henderson 1911, pp. 134, 140): "It was conceived as a sort of hermaphrodite lusting to graze at a loch side along with cows. From recent tradition I know of the Tarbh Boibhre having been spoken of; the description given pointed to some mythic animal often emerging from deep inland lochs – for instance, Loch Bruiach in Inverness-shire – and capable of assuming the form of a bull or of a cow at pleasure, and of emitting a peculiar cry like to that of powerful birds in the night time ... Sometimes the tarbh boidhbhre has been thought of as asexual, and the phrase has been rendered 'the bull of lust'." The second element has been variously rendered *Baoighre* (Campbell 1891, p. 89), *baoidhre, boidhre* (*CG2*, pp. 241, 368), *fhaire, eithre, boidhre, bo'eithre, bo-oibhre* (Henderson 1911, pp. 134, 146), *aoidhre, boidhre* (Dwelly 1977, p. 934), *Oire* (Mackenzie 1980, p. 187), and *eighre* (in *Tocher* 39, pp. 148–50).

375 *Baoi* is clearly for *baoibh*, genitive singular of *baobh*, see note 468.

376 JGC's etymologies are not to be relied upon. Watson says (1926a, p. 451) that Tummel is *Abhainn Teimheil*, 'river of darkness', Old Irish *temel*, now *teimheal*, 'gloom, shade', adding that 'it was so called from its thickly wooded gorge'.

377 JGC's Linnæan term 'gymnotus electricus' for the electric eel has since given way to 'electrophorus electricus'. The lamprey is a genus of cyclostomes that fix themselves to stones by their mouths.

378 JGC did not give the original, but I have supplied it from Cameron 1892–94, vol. 2, p. 504; the first two lines are commonly found, being proverbial (Nicolson 1951, p. 345). Cameron's fourth line runs *Seachd mucan-mara sàth mial-mhòir (a' chuain)*, 'Seven whales the fill of the great beast (of the ocean)', but he footnotes it: ' "Cean-chrò" (?) or "an fhir nach còir." ' *Cean-chrò* clearly reflects JGC's *Cìrein Cròin*, the forms of which vary widely; for *an fhir nach còir* see next note. Forsyth's version (1999, p. 29) ends *seachd Mhuc-Mhara, sàth an Cinnlan Crò; seachd Cinnlan Crò, sàth an Fhir-nach-Còir*. The fullest of all is in *CG2*, p. 348, and Meek 1978, p. 149:

> *Seachd sgadain sàth bradain,*
> *Seachd bradain sàth ròin,*
> *Seachd ròin sàth muice mara bige,*
> *Seachd muca mara beaga sàth muice mara móire,*
> *Seachd muca mara móra sàth Cìrein Cròin,*
> *Seachd Cìreinean Cròin sàth mial mór a' chuain.*

("Seven herrings are a salmon's fill, / Seven salmon are a seal's fill, / Seven seals are a small whale's fill, / Seven small whales are a big whale's fill, / Seven big whales are a Cìrein Cròin's fill, / Seven Cìreinean Cròin are the fill of the great beast of the ocean." I have used JGC's *Cìrein Cròin* here, with nominative plural *Cìreinean Cròin*. The form in *CG2* (both genitive singular and nominative plural) is *cionarain-cro*; Carmichael gives *cionarain-crothain* as an alternative for both. Duncan Campbell's form in Meek 1978, p. 149 (again undifferentiated), is *cionnanain-crò*. These all look like plurals however, and if JGC's *Cìrein Cròin* is something like the base form, Carmichael's *cionarain* may be seen to have suffered metathesis (*cìrein > cìoran > cìoranan > cìonaran > cìonarain*). At C, Dwelly (1977, p. 196) gives another possible base form, *cionnan-crò*, defining it as 'the "leader" of a school of whales', with the example *seachd mucan-mara beaga, sàth cionnan-crò* 'seven small whales a full meal for a bull whale', thus demonstrating how folklore terminology could be recycled for use in twentieth-century whaling fleets. By the time he got to S (*sàth*) he had received a fuller version:

> *Seachd sgadain, sàth bradain;*
> *Seachd bradain, sàth ròin;*
> *Seachd ròin, seachd muice mara bhig;*
> *Seachd mucan-mara beaga, sàth cionnain crò;*
> *Seachd cionnain crò, sàth miol-mhóir a' chuain.*

This he translates: "Seven herrings, a full meal for a salmon; / Seven salmon, a full meal for a seal; / Seven seals a full meal for a small whale; / Seven small whales a full meal for a large whale; / Seven large whales, a full meal for a bull whale; / Seven bull whales, a full meal for the Leviathan of the sea." It may be seen from this that that the last two lines of his original should in fact consist of three:

> *Seachd mucan-mara beaga, sàth muice mara mhóir;*
> *Seachd mucan-mara móra, sàth cionnain crò;*
> *Seachd cionnain crò, sàth miol-mhóir a' chuain.*

Dwelly's version is thus shown to be identical to Carmichael's and Duncan Campbell's, if we except the base-form *cionnan-crò* (genitive singular and nominative plural now *cionnain crò*), some grammatical niceties, and his prescriptive – rather than purely descriptive – approach to interpretation. See also GUL MS Gen. 1090/28, p. 88.

Etymologically I can make nothing of *cionnan-crò*, but on the basis of JGC's *cìrein* 'a cock's comb, a crest', *crón* or *cróine* 'dark place, abyss, pit, hell' (*DIL*) and *eccla píasta na cróine* 'the fear of the beast of hell' (Meyer 1907, p. 216), I have suggested (MacilleDhuibh 12.3.99) that the term means 'Hell's Crest' (cf. also *d'fios na cróine* 'to hell', Murphy 1933, p. 168). It was used by the South Uist poet Donald Macintyre (1889–1964), see Black 1999, pp. 154–55:

> *Chuala mi mun Chìrean Chròin*
> *'S mun mheudachd a bhiodh anns an t-seòrsa —*
> *Nam biodh 'earball aig an Òban*
> *Bhiodh a shròn aig Loch a' Chàrnain.*

"I heard about the 'Crest from Hell' / And the size the species was – / If his tail were at Oban / His nose would be at Loch Carnan."

379 Probably *Seachd Cìreinean Cròine sàth an fhir mhòir fhéin*, cf. *seachd Cinnlan Crò, sàth an Fhir-nach-Còir*, literally 'Seven Cinnlan Crò are the fill of the unkind man' (see previous note), where the 'unkind man' will be the devil, see note 548.

380 JGC's phraseology reflects that of JFC, who, after telling a splendid story from Lorn about a man who saw an eel so long that it took an entire day to pass his fishing-rock, remarked (Campbell 1890, vol. 2, p. 386): "That eel was a bouncer, but not so big as the sea-serpent of the Edda, which went round the world." Of course both men knew Scott's 'Lay of the Last Minstrel', with its evocation

> *Of that Sea-Snake, tremendous curl'd,*
> *Whose monstrous circle girds the world*

(Robertson 1904, pp. 44, 86). JGC's use of the word 'whirlpool' leaves one doubting his grasp of the English language. *Cuartag* can indeed be a whirlpool, and that is the primary meaning given in the dictionaries of JGC's day, but in the present context it must be seen simply as a feminine derivative of *cuairt* 'circle' – 'encircler' or the like.

381 The HSD (vol. 1, p. 484) defines *giolcam-daobhram* as 'an animalcule, the smallest supposable living thing (common speech)'. A further explanation is provided by the Rev. John MacRury (1894–96, p. 149): *Is i an fhrìde creutair cho beag 's is urrainn sùil duine fhaicinn. Is iomadh duine aig nach 'eil fradharc cho geur 's gu faic e i. Is minic a chunnaic mi feadhain aig am biodh fradharc geur 'g an toirt a mach á craicionn nan làmh ri latha soilleir, grianach 's an t-samhradh. Dheanainn a mach i a cheart-air-eiginn air gob na snathaide-bige. Aig an àm bha mo fhradharc anabarrach geur. A nis, bha na Gàidheil a' creidsinn gu robh creutair ann a bha mìle uair ni bu lugha na frìde. B' e sin an Stiolcam-staodhram a bha ann am bacan na h-ioscaid aice. Mar a bha an fhrìde a' tighinn beò le bhith 'cnuasach ann an craicionn an duine, bha an Stiolcam-staodhram mar an ceudna a' tighinn beò le bhith 'cnuasach ann an craicionn na frìde.* ("The *frìde* is as tiny a creature as the human eye can see. Many people are not sharp-sighted enough to see it. I have often seen keen-sighted people taking them out of the skin of the hands on a bright, sunny day in summer. I could only just make it out on the point of the pin. At the time, my sight was extremely sharp. Now, the Gael believed there was a creature a thousand times smaller than a *frìde*. That was the *Stiolcam-staodhram* which was in its houghs. As the *frìde* lived by burrowing in the skin of a human being, so did the *Stiolcam-staodhram* live by burrowing in the skin of the *frìde*.") Donald Macintyre must have been familiar with JGC's work, for immediately following the stanza quoted in note 378 above he claims (Black 1999, pp. 154–55) to have heard:

> *Gun robh 'n giolcam-daobhram sìnte*
> *Ri bacan iosgaid na frìde . . .*

('That the animalcule reclined / In the curves of the fleshmite's houghs . . .') As for JGC's 'gigelorum', I can find no authority for it; he must have made it up himself on the model of *giolcam-daoram*. See also CG2, p. 295; Watson 1908–09, pp. 68–69; MacDonald 1958b, p. 130; EUL MS CW 504C, ff. 150r–154r.

382 "Lavellan, an animal common in Caithness, it lives in water, its head resembles that of a forest weasel, a beast whose colour it shares. Its breath is injurious to beasts. The cure, however, is for them to drink the water in which its head has been cooked." Sibbald 1684, book 3, p. 11. I have restored the words and spelling of his text, from which JGC strayed slightly. It appears in a list headed 'Inter Quadrupedes gloria prima Lepus'. JGC's attention appears to have been drawn to it by the footnote 'Sibbald's Hist. Scotland' in Pinkerton 1809, p. 86 = Pennant 1774, p. 175.

'Lavellan' may represent *labhalan* (HSD, vol. 1, p. 546) or *la-bhallan* (Dwelly 1977, p. 560), but Henderson (1911, p. 338) suggests a derivation *an fhadhbh-alan* ('the water-mole'), '*alan* being a Pictish word, root as in Alnwick, the river-name Alaunos of Ptolemy', while Dwelly (1977, p. 410) also cites *famhalan, famh-bhual, famh-fhual* 'water-vole', cf. CG2, pp. 286–87, and Campbell 1978–81, p. 206. With regard to its injuring of domestic animals compare Carmichael's comments on the *lucha shìth*, 'fairy mouse' or lesser shrew (*CG2*, p. 323): "The lesser shrew is much disliked, from a belief that it causes paralysis of the spine in sheep, cows, and horses, by running across the animal when lying down. This is called 'marcachd shìth' – fairy riding. To counteract its effects, a live common shrew if available, otherwise a dead one, is carried across the loin and spine of the animal affected, in name of Father, of Son, and of Spirit." See also Campbell 1967–68, pp. 28–29.

383 Pinkerton 1809, p. 86 = Pennant 1774, p. 175. Pennant thus describes the water shrew (1812, vol. 1, p. 155): "This species inhabits the banks of ditches, and other wet situations, and is in some places called the Blind Mouse, from the smallness of its eyes. The *Germans* call it *Græber* or digger. I imagine it to be the same which the inhabitants of *Sutherland* call the water mole, and those of *Cathness*, the *Lavellan*, which the last imagine poisons their cattle, and is held by them in great abhorrence."

384 JGC did not give the original, so I have supplied it. 'Briogais Mhic Ruairidh' is a humorous song about a man who loses his trousers at a wedding. JGC's translation would lead one to believe that the joke is the eighteenth-century equivalent of: "Never go out with holes in your underwear. You might be knocked down by a bus." However, that interpretation depends on the *labhallan* being very large – a 'leviathan'? The late Ian Grimble offered an interpretation (1979, p. 80) which identified the animal firmly as a shrew while taking a pardonable liberty with the verb *buail* ('smite, strike'): "Don't let him leave home / For the moors or the woods / Lest the water-shrew come / And nip him." See Morrison 1899, p. 154.

385 Also called the 'tree-goose', because as Pennant points out (1768, pp. 451–52), it was believed to be 'generated out of wood, or rather a species of shell that is often found sticking to the bottoms of ships, or fragments of them'. He goes on to explain (p. 452 note) that the animal which inhabits the barnacle shell (JGC's 'thoracic worm') is 'furnished with a feathered beard; which, in a credulous age, was believed to be part of the young bird'. Lord Reay, chief of the MacKays, writing to Samuel Pepys from Durness on 24 October 1699 about the 'claik' or barnacle goose, shows himself exquisitely poised between traditional belief and scientific scepticism (Hunter 2001, pp. 164–65). "I Cannot positivly tell you whether the Clay goose be Suppositious or not tho all this Countrey men afirm it for a trueth I have seen my selfe ane old maste of a ship come in one the shore full of larg holes As If made by wormes wherinto ther sticks a shell within which ther is a small thing Which resembles a foull in every thing <in a warm day the shell oppens and the fowl would seem to strech their wings.> But many of undoubted honestie assure me they have seen a foule with wings feathers feet and taill sticking to a tree by the bill but wanted lyfe the shell falls away when they com to perfectione as ane Egg braiks and they stick by the bill till they Get lyfe Those that were seen sticking to the tree wes as Larg as a small Chickine they engender only in firr trees . . ."

　　See also Pennant 1812, vol. 2, p. 238, and vol. 4, pp. 152–53; Brand 1849, vol. 3, pp. 361–62; Dorson 1968, pp. 164–65, 181. It was above all the astonishing biological complexity of the humble barnacle that led Charles Darwin to his theory of evolution (Stott 2003).

386 *Calum na Cròige* is simply 'Calum of Croig', a spot at the mouth of Loch Cuan in Mornish where cattle were landed from the isle of Coll (Maclean 1997, p. 24). 'Thirty or forty years ago' suggests *c.* 1834–44. See p. 609 below.

387 This belief was widespread in the Highlands and Islands, as is the general prejudice against eels, see Pennant 1774, p. 84; Macintyre 1792–93, p. 344 = new edn, p. 118; Freer 1902, p. 36; Cameron 1903, p. 303; MacKenzie 1935, pp. 46, 80–81; Nicolson 1951, p. 297; MacMillan 1968, pp. 235–36; MacKillop 1982–84, p. 117; Levi 1984, p. 76; Rea 1997, p. 79; Simmons 1998, p. 67; GUL MS Gen. 1090/28, pp. 73–74.

388 Citing Alexander Forbes, Dwelly gives this as *buraghlas* (1977, p. 142). *Burraghlas* he defines (*ibid.*, p. 143) as 'torrent of brutal rage', cf. Caimbeul 2003, p. 331. Probably the two meanings are connected. Forbes himself gives the fish's name as *buraghlas, borraghlas* (1905, pp. 40, 357); it is presumably a corruption of *biorach ghlas* 'grey dogfish'. A caaing whale, from Scots *caa* 'drive', is a species of dolphin often taken by driving ashore (Chambers 1983, p. 173).

389 Cf. Martin Martin (1999, p. 95): "There is a big herring almost double the size of any of its kind, which leads all that are in a bay, and the shoal follows it wherever it goes. This leader is by the fishers called the king of herring, and when they chance to catch it alive, they drop it carefully into the sea; for they judge it petty treason to destroy a fish of that name." Martin's evidence is cited by Frazer (1912, vol. 2, p. 252) in the general context of the propitiation of wild animals by hunters.

390 Compare the Manx story of the fluke and the herring told by JFC (Campbell 1890, vol. 1, p. xlviii).

391 Niall M. Brownlie has given me the exchange as follows. The flounder says: *'S tu seo a Chaluim Chille chamachasaich!* ("And you here, bandy-legged Calum Cille!") The saint replies: *Mas camachasach mise, is camabheulach thusa!* ("If I am bandy-legged, you are crooked-mouthed!")

Uist tradition as noted by Fr Allan McDonald in GUL MS Gen. 1090/29, pp. 221–22, has Calum Cille wading through a sea-ford when he meets a flounder resting upon the sand. She starts on hearing him come and Calum Cille says: *Imbrig á seo, a liabag!* "Shift out of here, flounder!" The flounder replies, *A Chaluim Chille léith, cuiridh mise car 'nam bheul a' magadh ort!* "Grey Calum Cille, I will put a twist in my mouth mocking you!" The saint responds: *Chan eil mise 'g iarraidh air Dia ach an car sin a bhith 'nad bhial-sa gun tighinn ás.* "I ask of God only that that twist be in your mouth never to come out." Another version (*CG4*, p. 10) has him treading upon the fish's tail, whereupon she exclaims:

> *A Chaluim mhóir mhosaich*
> *Le d' chasan croma crosgach,*
> *Is mór a rinn thu mo dhosgadh*
> *Nuair a sheas thu air m' earball.*

("Big nasty Calum / With your fat bandy legs, / Great mischief you did me / When you stood on my tail.") Stung by the insult, the holy man replies:

> *Ma tha mise croma-chasach*
> *Bitheadh tusa cearra-ghobach.*

("If I'm bandy-legged / Be you crooked-mouthed.") In Seán Ó Conaill's Irish version (Ó Duilearga 1981, p. 2) the saint is Patrick and the plaice, with a mocking twist in its mouth, is behind him. "St Patrick turned back when he heard it making fun of him, and saw the twist in its mouth. He said the mouth would remain that way, and so it has."

There is also a Tiree version in which Calum Cille slips and falls when he treads on a plaice lying in the shallows, and condemns the fish to have both eyes on the same side of its head in future to avoid a repetition of the accident. See Freer 1902, p. 37, and Mac a Phì 1938, pp. 78–79; for a list of references see Ó Duilearga 1981, p. 380 (no. 3); and for an entirely different account of why the flounder has a twist in its mouth see Macdonald 2003, pp. 112–13.

392 *Is luaithe ròn na rionnach, is luaithe giumach na ròn*, Nicolson 1951, p. 264: "Seal is swifter than mackerel, lobster is swifter than seal." *Giomach, rionnach agus ròn, trì seòid a' chuain*, Meek 1978, p. 100: "Lobster, mackerel and seal, the three heroes of the sea." *Sitheadh*

giumaich, sitheadh rionnaich, sitheadh ròin, na trì sithean as luaithe sa chuan mhór, Nicolson 1951, p. 264: "Dart of lobster, dart of mackerel, dart of seal, the three swiftest darts in the great sea." See also GUL MS Gen. 1090/29, p. 79.

393 Scanlastle, usually written Scanistle or Scan(t)listle, lies between Ballygrant (for which see p. 275) and Port Askaig in the east of the island, see Campbell 1890, vol. 3, pp. 407–08. Captain Thomas interpreted the name as *Scanlannsdalr* 'Scanlann's Dale' (1881–82, p. 259), pointing out that according to one source a Scanlann was king of Dalriada *c.* AD 612.

Much the same story is told with respect to Loch Leven at Ballachulish in 'Beithrichean Beinn Bheithir' ('The Ben Vehir Dragons'), in MacDougall and Calder 1910, pp. 96–99. The saviour was *Teàrlach Sgiobair* ('Charles the Skipper'). *Dh' acraich e 'n soitheach aige astar math a mach o'n àite 'sam bheil an ceidhe nis suidhichte; agus eadar an soitheach agus an cladach rinn e drochaid de bharaillean falamh, ceangailte r'a chéile le ròpaibh, agus làn de spéicean iaruinn. An uair a bha 'n drochaid crìochnaichte, las e teine mór air bòrd an t-soithich, agus chuir e pìosan feòla air na h-éibhlibh. Cho luath 's a ràinig fàileadh na feòla loisgte 'n Coire, theirinn a' bheithir 'na leumannan a dh' ionnsaidh a' chladaich, agus as a sin dh'fheuch i ri rathad a dheanamh air na baraillean a mach chum an t-soithich. Ach chaidh na spéicean 'na corp, agus reub iad i cho dona 's nach mór nach robh i marbh mu'n d'ràinig i ceann a mach na drochaide. Aig a' cheart àm bha 'n soitheach air a tharruing air falbh o'n drochaid gus an robh bealach mór eadar i féin agus am baraille mu dheireadh. Thar a' bhealaich so cha robh de neart air a fhàgail aig a' bheithir gu'm b'urrainn i leum thairis air gu ruig clàr-uachdair an t-soithich, agus do bhrìgh nach b'urrainn i pilleadh an rathad a thàinig i, fhuair i bàs d'a leòn far an robh i aig ceann na drochaide.* "He anchored his vessel a good distance out from the site of the present pier, and between the vessel and the shore formed a bridge of empty barrels, lashed together with ropes, and bristling with iron spikes. When the bridge was finished, he kindled a large fire on board the vessel, and placed pieces of flesh on the burning embers. As soon as the savour of the burning flesh reached the corrie, the dragon descended by a succession of leaps to the shore, and thence tried to make her way out on the barrels to the vessel. But the spikes entered her body, and tore her up so badly that she was nearly dead before she reached the outer end of the bridge. Meantime the vessel was moved from the bridge, until a wide interval was left between it and the last barrel. Over this interval the dragon had not sufficient strength left to leap to the deck of the vessel, and, as she could not return the way she came, she died of her wounds where she was, at the end of the bridge." Cf. also 'Killing the Raasay Water-Horse', p. 112; Mac a Phì 1974–76, pp. 281–82; Fleming 2002, pp. 166–67.

394 Thus also Stewart (1851, p. 54), who explains that an injured serpent, or even the head of one which has been chopped into pieces, will make for water, where it will be made whole.

395 Cf. Campbell 1890, vol. 2, pp. 377–78; Henderson 1910, pp. 90–93; Bruford and MacDonald 1994, pp. 288–91, 465–66; MacDonald 1994–95, p. 61; Beith 1995, pp. 51–52; Beith 2000, p. 102; Gillies 2000, pp. 45–46. The motif is ML 3030 / AT 673, see p. 732 below. As Henderson points out (1910, pp. 93–95), the tale has something in common with the way in which Fionn obtained the salmon's wisdom, see note 836 below. Equally, in this general context of what he calls 'the homoeopathic magic of a flesh diet', Frazer (1912, vol. 2, pp. 146–47) is able to cite specific parallels from other traditions. "Democritus is reported to have said that serpents were generated from the mixed blood of certain birds, and that therefore whoever ate a serpent would understand the bird language. The Arabs in antiquity were supposed to be able to draw omens from birds because they had gained a knowledge of bird language by eating either the heart or liver of a serpent; and the people of Paraka in India are said to have learned the language of animals in general by the same means. Saxo Grammaticus relates how Rollo acquired all knowledge, including an understanding of the speech of animals, both wild and tame, by eating of a black serpent. In Norway, Sweden, and

Jutland down to the nineteenth century the flesh of a white snake was thought to confer supernatural wisdom on the eater; it is a German and Bohemian superstition that whoever eats serpent's flesh understands the language of animals. Notions of the same sort, based no doubt on a belief in the extraordinary wisdom or subtlety of the serpent, often meet us in popular tales and traditions."

Among the authorities he cites from many countries are Campbell 1890 (as above) and Stewart (1851, pp. 53–56), who tells a tale of how Michael Scot or Scott (for whom see pp. 157–58) obtained his supernatural wisdom from a decoction of the flesh of a white serpent.

396 This paragraph reflects a complex of curious St Brigid's day rhymes about the serpent, the *rìbhinn* ('damsel') or *nighean Ìomhair* ('Edward's or Ivor's daughter'). These are widespread throughout the Highlands and Islands. JGC's 'week previous to St Bridget's day' is found along with *nighean Ìomhair* in the following (Nicolson 1951, p. 296):

> *Seachdain roimh Fhéill Brìghde*
> *Thig nighean Ìomhair ás an tom;*
> *Cha bhi mise ri nighean Ìomhair*
> *'S cha mhotha bhios nighean Ìomhair rium.*

("A week before St Brigid's / Ivor's daughter leaves the ground; / I won't be at Ivor's daughter / Nor will Ivor's daughter be at me.") JGC then says that 'if the ground is then covered with snow they perish'; this reflects something like the following (*CG1*, p. 169):

> *Thig an nathair ás an toll*
> *Latha donn Brìghde*
> *Ged robh trì traighean dhan t-sneachd*
> *Air leac an làir.*

("The snake will come out of the hole / On brown St Brigid's day / Were there even three feet of snow / On the slab of the ground.") The *rìbhinn* (*rìghinn, rìoghan*) variation is by no means restricted to Skye. Carmichael cites (*CG1*, p. 170):

> *An-diugh Là Brìde,*
> *Thig an rìghinn ás an tom,*
> *Cha bhean mise ris an rìghinn,*
> *Cha bhean an rìghinn rium.*

He translates: "This is the day of Bride, / The queen will come from the mound, / I will not touch the queen, / Nor will the queen touch me." When I quoted this verse in *The Scotsman*, 14 February 1981, using Carmichael's word 'queen', I received a letter from R. MacLennan, Stornoway, who remembered his grandmother saying that

> *Air latha Fhéill Brìghde*
> *Thig an rìoghann ás an toll.*

('On St Brigid's day / The *rìoghann* comes out of the hole.') He thought of the *rìoghann* (which may be understood as 'supple one') simply as the snake coming out of hibernation. See also Fergusson 1877–78, p. 133; Henderson 1911, pp. 53–54, 166–68; GUL MS Gen. 1090/29, p. 72.

It would be fair I think to see these rhymes in Frazerian terms as depicting the sterile, even poisonous, spirit of winter – the last vestige of the previous year's *cailleach* – which must leave the ground unmolested before any attempt can be made at ploughing. What they are essentially telling us is that once St Brigid's (1 February OS, 13 February NS) is over, it is safe to begin testing the ground to see if it is *air dàir* ('on heat') in the manner suggested at p. 52.

As to why the snake (or spirit of winter) should be called *nighean Ìomhair*, there may be a connection with Norse mythology, although not necessarily the one suggested by Henderson (1910, pp. 89–90). Following a four-month siege in AD 871, Ivar Beinlaus 'the Boneless', whose father Ragnar Lodbrok had been tortured in a snake-pit by King Ella of Northumbria, captured the Strathclyde capital Al Cluith (Dumbarton Rock) along with Olaf, king of Dublin. They seized such a quantity of slaves and booty that two hundred longships were required to carry everything home. Ivar reigned as king of Dublin for two years until his death in 873, and fathered a race of people called the *Clann Ìomhair*, apparently through a daughter. Why Ivor the Boneless? "Because he was a snake," the late Nora Chadwick is said to have remarked in answer to a student's question, although if we were to believe Reginald Scot we might wish to argue that it was because he became a ghost (Scott 2001, pp. 110–11); I believe her explanation lay in traditions about what happened in King Ella's pit, cf. note 701 below. Given his anguine associations, he may I think be assumed to be the Ivor referred to by Carmichael who says (*CG1*, p. 169): "It is said that the serpent will not sting a descendant of Ivor, he having made 'tabhar agus tuis', offering and incense, to it, thereby securing immunity from its sting for himself and his seed for ever."

Nighean Ìomhair thus became an appropriate nickname for a female poisoner. Says Nicolson (1951, p. 296): "A lady called 'Nighean Iomhair', wife of John McKenzie, constable of Eilean-Donnain Castle, was suspected of having poisoned there (1550) John Glassich of Gairloch, who claimed the Kintail estates." We do not know the precise identity of this lady, but it is safe to assume that the poisoning came first, and that the name followed. For snake-kings in general see Frazer 1911b, pp. 87, 133.

397 *An calbh*, more commonly *an cailbhe*, means in Gaelic 'the partition', referring to an interior room-divider of wattle or clay. There is no doubt but that this was what the people of Mull understood the name of the island to mean, and in that sense JGC's interpretation is both correct and logical – Calve divides Tobermory Bay from the Sound of Mull. However, in origin the name is Norse *Mylarkalvr* 'the Calf of Mull' (MacQuarrie 1983, p. 9, and Maclean 1997, p. 97).

The spelling *Iain Pholchrain* is as in *SHIS* 226. Seemingly a MacPherson, he was a well-known character in his day. Iain Thornber tells me (personal communication, 5 December 2002): "There was an old lady living in Lochaline until 10 years ago whose family originally hailed from the Drimnin 'end' of the Parish who often spoke about him."

Polchrain, near Drimnin, is properly *Poll Luachrain*; it had been cleared by 1841, so 'Iain Pholchrain' will have been born before then (Gaskell 1968, p. 158). Iain Thornber believes that the following inscription in the Drimnin graveyard at Cill Dhonnaig is his: "Sacred to the memory of John Macpherson, Polchurin, Morven and Ann MacDonald, his spouse, also eight of their children and their son in law, James Cameron, Scalasdale, beloved husband of their surviving daughter Marjory Cameron, Rhum who has erected this memorial in 1907. Also Marjory Cameron, wife of James Cameron, Scalasdale, who died 28 April 1921 at the Island of Shuna."

There was also an *Eoghan Mór Pholl Luachrain* (his father or brother, perhaps?) who composed two songs remembered only as 'Bha mi a-raoir an Glaschu, 's gum b'e siud diù nan cairtealan' ('I was in Glasgow last night, and it was the worst of accommodation') and 'Se uircean mo dhunach an t-uircean a bh' ann' ('Yon piglet was my downfall'). It seems that he had sold the beast to a man for what turned out to be a worthless piece of paper (Anon. 1941).

398 On Gaelic rat and mouse satires see Forbes 1905, pp. 206–09; Dorson 1968, p. 184; Thornber 1986–88; Morrison 1990–92; Black 2001, pp. 218–23. Frazer, clearly unaware of this very large body of evidence from his native land (he was a native of Glasgow, not a Gaelic speaker), nevertheless contextualises it historically and anthropologically in a chapter entitled 'The Propitiation of Vermin by Farmers' (1912, vol. 2, pp. 274–84). He speaks of rituals, idolatries, charms, incantations, chants, formulae and even written letters addressed in desperation to vermin of all kinds, but fails to mention poetry or songs other than by remarking of southern Africa that a plague of caterpillars can be removed by little girls 'singing through the fields' and that when brown beetles begin to swarm a number of them are picked off the bean-stalks and placed in a calabash, which is thrown by a little girl into a lake – whereupon 'the women bellow out obscene songs, which they never dare to utter except on this occasion and at the ceremony for making rain' (*ibid.*, p. 280).

It is clear from Frazer's many examples that, just as in the Gaelic satires cited by JGC, all over the world rats, mice and other pests have been politely cajoled to move on to some other field, village or tribe, or else symbolically dumped in the sea (*ibid.*, pp. 278–79): "In the Kangean archipelago, East Indies, when the mice prove very destructful to the rice-crop, the people rid themselves of the pest in the following manner. On a Friday, when the usual service in the mosque is over, four pairs of mice are solemnly united in marriage by the priest. Each pair is then shut up in a miniature canoe about a foot long. These canoes are filled with rice and other fruits of the earth, and the four pairs of mice are then escorted to the sea-shore just as if it were a real wedding. Wherever the procession passes the people beat with all their might on their rice-blocks. On reaching the shore, the canoes, with their little inmates, are launched and left to the mercy of the winds and waves."

Part of the Ardnamurchan man's song is given in EUL MS CW 241, ff. 19–20 (Alexander Carmichael's transcript of JGC's original, see p. 702 below), under the heading 'Aoir Nan Radan' ('The Satire of the Rats'):

> Dà dhroch còmhdhail dheug is coinneamh
> Air luchd nan casa caola croma,
> Nam beul braoisgeach bu gheur faobhar —
> Sgrios na h-aoir gun dèan bhur lomadh,
>
> Sgrios na h-Aoine air ur n-ògaibh
> 'S leònadh air bhur leanaibh:
> Sann san eucoir tha sibh eòlach,
> 'S théid ur fògradh air ur n-aineol.
>
> Treuda 's dì-moladh is càineadh,
> Mì-fhortan 's dosgainn 's cra-lighe —
> Bidh mnathan agus nigheanan
> Sa h-uile h-àit' am bì iad,
>
> A' guidheachadh 's ag òrdachadh
> A' chuid nach fhàg am baile dhiubh
> Gun ladhar iad sa mhòintich,
> 'S a chuid nach gabh an t-aithreachas
> Na mhill iad de ghnìomh banaraich,
> Gaoth 's teine 's dealanaich
> Gan gearradh ás am beòshlaint,

Dìol nan cnoca falaisge
Ga shéideadh ris na breamainean,
An sreud nach deach a bheannachadh
Làn galair agus fòtais . . .

A' mhuir a' beucadh nuallan
'S an cuan ag éirigh 'na sgideil,
Crònanaich a seòl a' sracadh
'S an ròmhanaich a droma briste
'S an taoim air a feadh a' glagraich
Coltach ri seann each a' sitrich.

("Twelve bad encounters and a meeting / Be on the tribe of slender bandy legs / And of grinning sharp-bladed mouths – / May satire's destruction strip you bare, / Friday's destruction be on your young ones / And wounding be upon your children: / You're no strangers to criminal behaviour, / And you'll be banished to lands unknown. / Triads(?) and dispraise and reproof, / Misfortune, disaster and sickness – / Women and girls / Will be in every place that they are, / Cursing and ordaining those of them / Who fail to leave the township / To be footless in the moor, / And those who fail to repent / Their damage to the work of a dairymaid, / May wind and fire and lightning / Cut them out of their livelihood, / May the yield of muirburn hillocks / Be blown around their buttocks, / And the tribe who've not been blessed / Be full of sickness and decay . . . / The sea roaring lamentations / And the ocean rising to a splash, / The hum of her sails tearing / And in the groan of her broken keel / As the bilge-water gurgles through her / Like an old horse neighing."

The translation is mine. It sounds as if JGC's summary of the song – the gathering with whips and switches, the droll characters, the potato beetles, the departure from *Eabar an Ròin* – represents what is lost in the elipsis.

399 Dwelly gives *learg* as 'rain-goose', of which Martin wrote (1716, p. 72): "The Rain-Goose, bigger than a Duck, makes a doleful Noise before a great Rain; it builds its Nest always upon the brink of fresh-water Lakes, so as it may reach the water." *Ballaire bòdhain* is literally a 'speckle-belly' – *ball* 'a spot', *bòdhan* 'belly'. Dwelly's *sgarbh a' bhothain* ('bothy cormorant', 1977, p. 816) should presumably read *sgarbh a' bhòdhain* ('belly cormorant'). For *ballaire* see also Watson 1911–12, pp. 369–70.

400 See 'Unlucky Actions', p. 137.

401 In this section JGC omitted the translation of the second line of each of the two couplets, and the original of the quatrain. As these can all be inferred without difficulty from his other remarks, I have supplied them. For other versions of the story see Macbain 1887–88, p. 266; *CG2*, pp. 188, 248, 267; 'Why the Beetle is Blind', *Tocher* 34, pp. 155–56; Ó Duilearga 1981, p. 2 (with further references at p. 380); Bruford and MacDonald 1994, pp. 273–75, 464; Forsyth 1999, p. 26; MacilleDhuibh 22.3.02; Black 2002, pp. 386–87; GUL MS Gen. 1090/29, pp. 53–54. JGC's *ceardalan* is usually *ceardubhan*, see Campbell 1978–81, pp. 204–05. In a North Uist version, ducks take the place of the dung-beetle and the *daolag* becomes hens, which is why hens are drenched by rain but showers simply slip off ducks' feathers to this day (*Tocher* 1, pp. 14–15).

402 I detect some uncertainty here. An 'emmet' is an ant; *caora-chòsag* is literally 'a sheep of little crevices', and JGC describes it as an 'animal'. I suspect that in using the word 'emmet' JGC was influenced by Brand (1849, vol. 3, p. 224), who quotes Alexander Ross's *Arcana Microcosmi* of 1652 on the subject of that insect. Elsewhere the creature in question is well known as *corra-chòsag* (literally perhaps 'lanky little crevice lady'), a slater, wood-louse or cheslip; the following rhyme is used in the course of inviting it to foretell the weather (Smith 1964, p. 16):

> *A chorra-chorra-chòsag,*
> *An innis thusa dhòmhsa*
> *Am bi latha math a-màireach ann*
> *'S nì mi paidhir bhròg dhut!*

("Lanky-little-crevice-lady, / Please will you tell me / If it'll be a fine day tomorrow / And I'll make you a pair of shoes!") In Uist Fr Allan McDonald heard it not as *corra-chòsag* but *cailleach-chòsag*, presumably by equivalence of *corra* 'crane, heron' and *cailleach* 'hag' as in note 432, see GUL MS Gen. 1090/29, pp. 241–42 (cf. McDonald 1958, p. 57):

> *Cailleach cailleach chòsag*
> *Mura dian thu latha briagh 'màireach*
> *Bogaidh mi ann an lòn thu.*

("Little crevice hag hag / If you don't make a fine day tomorrow / I'll duck you in a puddle.") But Fr Allan adds: "It was never killed." See also NLS MS 14990, f. 140r, and Grant 1925, p. 46. In Ireland the insect used was the droning-beetle, but the rhyme was similar (Ó Duilearga 1981, p. 356).

403 On the terms *gisreagun*, *eapagun* and *upagun* see p. 200, where JGC defines them collectively as a 'general name for trifling superstitious observances'. *Gisreagun* actually appears as *Gisvagun* in both text (*SHIS* 229) and list of contents (*SHIS* xviii), but since it reappears in the singular as *Gisreag* in WSS 56 (*gisreag*, p. 200 of *The Gaelic Otherworld*), I am confident that what JGC wrote was *Gisragun*, and that this may legitimately be further emended to *gisreagun* in line with the editorial principles laid out at p. xv above. Note the phrase used of a witch in a story from Islay in *Tocher* 14, p. 216, *thòisich i air na geasagain 's na h-oibeagain*, 'she started on her spells and incantations'.

404 On the Sunday plant see pp. 199 and 564.

405 See Dalyell 1834, pp. 455–60; MacGregor 1901, p. 35; Maclean 1975, pp. 62–63; *Tocher* 46, pp. 228–29. Macbain (1896, p. 116) derives *deiseal* from *deas* 'right, south' and *seal* 'while, space'. It is in origin a noun, and remains largely so in Irish. In Scottish Gaelic its use is principally adjectival and adverbial, and it is therefore now frequently spelt *deiseil* (as in Macbain), but JGC's presentation shows strong traces of its nominal beginnings. *Deiseal!* was said in Uist to a choking child (GUL MS Gen. 1090/29, p. 78); it was also a common response to a sneeze, cf. p. 130. The assistant who put the straw rope *tuaitheal* on the house or corn-stack was committing what is known as the 'left heresy'; the old man's prejudice against it has been shown to have had serious consequences for the development of machinery in the modern world, see Blake-Coleman 1982.

406 See p. 108 above and MacNeil 1987, pp. 386–87, 474.

407 The expression is a common one – *Meal 's caith e!* "Enjoy and wear it!" *Gum meal 's gun caith thu e!* "May you enjoy and wear it!" A traditional story published elsewhere by JGC hinges upon the misfortune that ensues when a woman says (Campbell 1891, pp. 263, 270): *Gu' m meal 's gu 'n caith thu do dheise; 's tu fear nan Cochulla Craicinn.* "May you enjoy and wear your dress: your name will be The One with the Skin Coverings." JGC explains (*ibid.*, p. 276): "In Tiree, even at the present day, when a person puts on a new suit for the first time, a woman meeting him says: 'Have they said it to you?' ('*An d' thuirt iad riut e?*') . . . It is said in some places that a married woman, whose firstborn is a son, can use the expression harmlessly with the addition of 'I may say it' ('*Faodaidh mise a ràdhain*')." Corroborating that it is unlucky if first said to the wearer by a female, Dwelly adds (1977, s.v. *meal*) what sounds like a curse: *Na 'n na mheal thu e!* "May you never enjoy it!" That is, "May you never live to wear it!" See p. 237.

408 See 'Fairy Dresses' (p. 7 above) and MacInnes 1994–96, p. 18. Neil Munro visited Eriskay in 1901 wearing a suit of *crotal* dye, and wrote of Fr Allan McDonald (Black 2002, p. 60): "Laughingly he professed astonishment that I had found boatmen in Barra willing to ferry me in such a garb, for Barra believes that the *crotal* ever hankers for the native rock, and whoso wears it in a boat courts sure destruction."

409 *Sop-seilbhe* is defined by the HSD (vol. 2, p. 134) as 'infeftment in house and land by the formal delivery of a wisp of straw to the entrant' – clearly not the custom described by JGC. The *sop-seilbhe* should be carefully distinguished from the *sop seile*, see p. 136.

410 JGC writes *baan*. *Bàn* means 'white' or 'fallow', 'unproductive', hence here 'not lasting'. 'White bread' is *aran geal*. See also Campbell 1895, p. 132.

411 Pp. 10, 18, 19, 25, 39.

412 See also 'Bones of the Dead and Place of Burial', p. 267.

413 The *fallaid* is defined as follows by MacRury (1896–97, pp. 372–73): *Is i an fhallaid, a' mhin a bhithear a' suathadh ris an uibe thaoise, an àm a bhith 'g a leanachadh, no 'g a thanachadh 'na bhreacaig. An uair a tha 'n taois air a taosnadh gu math, tha i air a deanamh 'na h-uibe. Tha 'n t-uibe coltach ri muillean-siucair – cruinn mu'n bhonn, agus a sìor fhàs biorach gu 'bharr. An uair a tha 'bhean-fhuinne 'tòiseachadh ri' leanachadh an uibe thaoise, tha i 'cur làn no dhà a dùirn de 'n mhin fodha air a' chlàr. Mar a tha i 'ga leanachadh, tha i an dràsta 's a rithist a' cur na mine air 'uachdar, agus 'g a suathadh ris, gus am bi aig a' bhreacaig na ghabhas i air gach taobh dhe 'n mhin. A nis, an uair a tha 'n fhuinne ullamh, tha faisg air na dheanadh breacag de mhin air a' chlàr-fhuinne. Tha mhin so tais; oir bha i 'tarruinn beagan de 'n uisge as an taois an àm a bhith 'deanamh na fuinne. A bharrachd air sin, tha beagan de 'n taois air a feadh. Nan cuirteadh a' mhin so – an fhallaid – air ais do 'n chiste-mhine bheireadh i air cuid de 'n mhin eile blas goirt a ghabhail, agus dh' fhàsadh na cnapan taoise cruaidh. An ath uair a theannteadh ri fuinne, bhiodh na cnapan cruaidhe taoise so anns an aran, agus, mar a tha furasda gu leòr dhuinn a thuigsinn, cha bhiodh blas no buantas air an aran. An àite a' mhin a chur air ais do 'n chiste, dheanadh a' bhean-fhuinne "bonnach-boise" de na bhiodh a dh' fhallaid air a' chlàr. Theirteadh "bonnach-boise" ris a chionn gu'n robh e air a leanachadh eadar a basan, an àite bhith air a leanachadh air a' chlàr. Cha bhiodh fallaid idir air. Tha againn an so eachdraidh an t-sean-fhacail, "Bonnach deireadh-fuinne nam ban, b' e sid an geinneanach tiugh."* ("The *fallaid* is the meal that is pressed into the lump of dough as it is being flattened out, i.e. thinned into a cake. When the dough has been well kneaded it is made into a lump. The lump is like a sugar-cone – round at the bottom and narrowing steadily up to a point. When the woman doing the baking starts to flatten the lump of dough she puts a fistful or two of the meal underneath it on the board. As she flattens it, she puts the meal on top of it now and again and presses it in until the cake has as much meal on each side as it can take. Now, when the baking is ready, there is nearly as much meal on the baking-board as would make a cake. This meal is damp, for during the course of preparation it has been drawing some of the moisture out of the dough. In addition to that, some of the dough is mixed in with it. If this meal – the *fallaid* – were put back into the meal-kist, it would impart a sour taste to some of the rest of the meal, and the lumps of dough would grow hard. The next time a baking was started, these hard lumps of dough would be in the bread, and, as is easy enough for us to understand, the bread would be neither tasty nor lasting. Instead of putting the meal back into the kist, the woman who was baking would make the *fallaid* left on the board into a 'palm-bannock'. It was called a 'palm-bannock' because it was pressed out between her palms instead of being pressed out on the board. There would be no *fallaid* on it at all. Here we have the origins of the proverb: 'The women's end-of-baking bannock, what a sturdy little chunk that was.'") MacRury's proverb is completed by Fr Allan McDonald, see GUL MS Gen. 1090/28, p. 88 (cf. McDonald 1958, p. 162):

Bonnach deireadh fuine nam ban,
B'e sin an gnagairneach tiugh —
Ged thigeadh cóig lethsgaran diag air fhichead ás
Sheasadh e rithist air oir.

("The women's end-of-baking bannock, / What a sturdy little chunk that was – / Should thirty-five slices come out of it / It would still stand up on its edge.") According to Carmichael (*CG2*, p. 226), if the *fallaid* is put back in the meal-chest, the *cailleach* 'will come and sit in the chest, eating up all the luck of the family, and will not leave till five o'clock in the morning'. See also Henderson 1911, p. 296; Campbell 1969–81, vol. 3, pp. 222–23; Bruford and MacDonald 1994, pp. 342–44, 474; GUL MS Gen. 1090/28, p. 257; GUL MS Gen. 1090/29, pp. 211–13.

414   According to MacRury (1896–97, pp. 373–74), the 'front' (*beulaobh*) of a traditional cake of bread is the side first baked – the heat of the fire produces a bulge (*copan*) on that side; even after it has been turned over to let the other side bake, part of the bulge remains, and it was forbidden (*air a thoirmeasg*) for a cake of bread to be placed upside-down on the plate. In their wisdom, therefore, the old men used to say that bad luck would befall the woman who placed the bread upside-down, whether carelessly or deliberately. On the other hand, if she knew that the person who was going to eat it was in danger, she was obliged to place it upside-down as a warning, and MacRury tells a long tale of a young man breakfasting in an inn who was warned in this way by a servant-woman who had heard the landlord plotting to rob him as he passed through a wood. *Cho luath 's a chaidh a maighstir am mach as an t-seòmar, thill i steach leis an nì a dh' fhàg i gun chur air a bheulaobh, agus thionndaidh i an t-aran a bh' air an trinnsear. Sheall an duine òg oirre gu dùr an clàr an aodainn. Sheall ise airsan. Agus an uair a thuig i gu'n robh e 'dol a chur ceisd oirre mu thimchioll an nì a rinn i, chrath i a ceann, agus chuir i a meòir air a beul, a' ciallachadh gu'm bu ghlice dhaibh le chéile gun aon fhacal a ràdh.* "As soon as her master had left the room, she went back in with what she had omitted to place in front of him, and turned over the bread that was on the plate. The young man glowered directly into her face. She looked at him. And when she realised that he was about to question her about what she had done, she shook her head, and put her fingers upon her mouth, meaning that it would be wiser for them both to say nothing."

415   This reflects the tabu on counting, see p. 29 above.

416   *Fioghan* is properly *fiodhan*, 'cheese-vat', 'cheese-press', from *fiodh*, 'wood'. The day on which people returned from the shielings was *Latha na h-Imrich*, the return itself was the *ath-thriall*. Lammas day (*latha Lùnastail*) was its theoretical date, but in practice it came to vary a good deal. The preparation of symbolic food was a normal quarter-day ritual designed to ensure the food supply during the next three months. I suspect therefore that what JGC describes here is essentially a quarter-day ritual named after the custom (*imrich*) with which it had formerly been associated. Mention of children suggests vestigial survival rather than dynamic reality. Fr Allan McDonald noted a variant of the custom in South Uist: *mulachag imprig* (GUL MS Gen. 1090/29, p. 154), *mulchag imbrig* (McDonald 1958, p. 185).

417   Since *lurgann* is a horse's or cow's hind leg as well as the human lower leg, it appears that the word is serving here as a code-word – not a euphemism but a noa-term – for foaling or calving in the same way that *glùn* ('knee') serves for childbirth, e.g. *bean-ghlùin* 'midwife'.

418   This is precisely the situation described in a tale from Vatersay, 'The Borrowed Peats' (Bruford and MacDonald 1994, pp. 403–04, 482), except that the day of the year is not mentioned. A similar story was recorded in Shetland (*ibid.*, pp. 401–02, 481–82). Compare the custom noted by Maclagan (1902, pp. 172–73) that if a person suspected of the evil eye

came into a house during churning, a live ember was taken from the fire and put into a dish of water to preserve the *toradh*, cf. *Tocher* 53, pp. 251–52.

419 On the cross of Christ see pp. 136 and 273; on beer being soured see e.g. Chaundler 1970, pp. 57–58.

420 JGC gave the second version in translation only. I have supplied the original from Nicolson 1951, p. 391. It is likely however that the second or fourth line ended *fois* to avoid repeating *clos* (same meaning). See also MacFarlane 1924–25, pp. 36–37, and note 471 below. For further versions of the rhyme see *CG2*, pp. 319–20; Nicolson 1951, p. 391; Campbell 1967–68, p. 22; Shaw 1977, p. 44; Meek 1978, p. 134; EUL MS CW 495, f. 1v.

Clearly lint and hemp-seed were regarded as being of unusual value. The strength of their fibres was seen as magical, and they were employed for occult as well as practical purposes (see p. 561). Carmichael explains (*CG2*, p. 319): "The people say that the hands and feet of Christ were bound with lint when He was taken down from the Cross, and before He was carried to the grave. In consequence of this the people speak of the lint with much reverence, and call it 'lìon beannaichte', blessed lint; 'lìon naomh', sacred lint; 'lìon Chrìosda chaoimh', the lint of Christ the kindly. They say that the person who would steal lint or lint-seed would be guilty of as heinous an offence as he who would sin against the Holy Ghost."

An excellent illustration of this is provided by Hugh Miller (1802–56) of Cromarty. A woman of Tarbat, he says (1994, pp. 59–60), was passing along the shore of Loch Slin – since drained – on her way to market at Tain with a large web of linen on her back, the lint for which she had stolen from her neighbours' fields. "She had nearly reached the western extremity of the lake, when, feeling fatigued, she seated herself by the water edge, and laid down the web beside her. But no sooner had it touched the earth than up it bounded three Scots ells into the air, and slowly unrolling fold after fold, until it had stretched itself out as when on the bleaching-green, it flew into the middle of the lake, and disappeared for ever."

421 For salt superstitions see e.g. Dalyell 1834, pp. 95–103; MacPhail 1900, p. 439; Maclagan 1902, pp. 136, 176–80; and the examples collected in Opie and Tatem 1992, pp. 338–44, especially those under the heads 'Salt as protection against witch or evil spirits / for luck' and 'Salt, borrowing or lending'. Fr Allan McDonald says that salt is put on a corpse to prevent it swelling (see p. 132, 'Funerals') and – in contrast to JGC – that a loan of salt should not be repaid, see GUL MS Gen. 1090/29, pp. 83, 165. One of Maclagan's Arran informants told an amusing story of a neighbouring woman who was so afraid of her cow being hurt by the evil eye that she always put salt in the milk (1902, p. 83, cf. Mackenzie 1914, p. 292). "For a while we were getting milk from her for a man staying with us who was seriously annoyed when the milk was more than ordinarily salt, giving vent to his discontent saying, 'Why the deuce does she not let us put saut in oor ain milk?'"

422 *Chan eil gas a dh'fhalbhas asaibh nach bi dol mu chasan duine bhuineas duibh anns an t-sathach*, Henderson was told (1911, p. 296): "Every hair you lose will entangle the feet of some one related to you in the vessel." In a paper given in 1686, Joshua Walker, a Fellow of Brasenose College and a member of the Oxford Philosophical Society, stated that 'Second Sighted men in Scotland' abhorred 'Women combing their heads' (Hunter 2001, p. 22), and it is notable that JGC twice portrays otherworld women combing their hair (pp. 77, 108), so it is no surprise if the combing of hair is a tabu-laden activity. In Ireland at least, the death-messenger is often seen to be combing her hair (Lysaght 1991, p. 68). Even so, such superstitions are but a pale reflection of the massive superstructure of tabu erected by traditional belief all over the world upon the cutting of hair. By way of explanation, Frazer points (1911a, p. 258) to the twin dangers of disturbing what he calls 'the spirit of the head' and enabling others to work magic against a person through 'the sympathetic connexion which exists between himself and every part of his body . . . even after the physical connexion has been broken'.

JGC's examples show that such magic can be performed accidentally; Frazer cites some of them (*ibid.*, p. 271) in support of his argument. As is so often the case, the Rev. George Sutherland's version of the tradition from Highland Caithness is tangentially different (1937, pp. 92–93): the reason why no woman who is in love should take down her hair and comb it at night, he says, is that if her sweetheart is out of doors he will be attacked by her double and given 'a severe handling'. In one case the double begins by lashing the man in the eyes and about his face with her hair, and after a struggle he flees to safety across a running stream. The young lady who is at home 'doing her toilet' is oblivious to the trouble she is causing. See also Freer 1902, p. 30; MacilleDhuibh 30.5.03; and the examples collected by Opie and Tatem (1992, pp. 184–86), especially those under the heads 'Hair: combing after sunset', 'Hair: disposing of combings/cuttings', and 'Hair thrown into fire: divination of life or death'. Finally, the idea that a headache can be caused by a bird eating one's hair is confirmed for Arran by Mackenzie (1914, p. 307).

423 A pullet's first egg: *ciad ugh eireig*, much in demand for divination at Hallowe'en, cf. *Tocher* 7, pp. 203–04.

424 'Eumenides' is Greek for 'gracious ones'. On epilepsy see 'Falling Sickness (*an Tuiteamas*)', p. 226.

425 See p. 10 above.

426 Cf. note 180.

427 See Opie and Tatem 1992, pp. 364–66, and MacilleDhuibh 1.8.97. Sir Walter Scott believed that the universal custom of 'saying God bless you, when a person in company sneezes' dated from a time of plague at Athens, sternutation marking the 'crisis' or turning point of the disease while the blessing expressed 'the hope that when it was attained the patient had a chance of recovery' (2001, p. 63).

428 Cf. p. 280 and Freer 1902, pp. 29–30.

429 For *a' chliob* see Dwelly 1977, s.v. *clip*. This paragraph is cited by Frazer (1911a, p. 394) in the general context of 'Common Words Tabooed'. Morag Cameron found that among Highland fishermen 'the words *minister, salmon, hare, rabbit, rat, pig*, and *porpoise* are all fraught with danger, and to mention any of them on board means failure to catch fish, or some disaster' (1903, p. 304). See Lockwood 1966–68.

430 *A' Bhraonach* is 'the showery/drizzly/dewy female' (because of the tendency of Heynish Hill to attract cloud). Beinn Hough, JGC's 'Hogh Hill', is from Norse *haugr* 'burial place' (there are viking graves there). Its cloven shape is explained by John MacLean, the Balemartin Bard, tongue firmly in cheek (Cameron 1932, p. 177):

> Nuair ràinig Teàrlach Mairearad —
> Is ainmeil e 's gach àit —
> Le eallach bhotal den deoch rìomhaich
> Chuir sa phrìosan càch,
> Leis a' bhuille fhuair Beinn Hogh san strì
> Bidh lag 'na druim gu bràth.

("When Charlie came home to Margaret – / It's well known everywhere – / With his burden of bottles of the lovely drink / Which put the rest in prison, / From the thump Beinn Hogh received in the strife / It will have a hollow in its ridge for ever.") In Tiree *cas poite* ('a pot leg') is a porpoise and *shiubhail e* is normal for 'he died'; *bhàsaich e* should only be used of animals ('it died'). *Béist dubh* should read *béist dhubh* as *béist* is feminine. *Càrnag* is a feminine derivative of *càrn* 'a rock-pile', 'a rocky or stony place'. JGC might well have extended his list to include noa-terms for islands such as *Eilein Tìr fo Thuinn* ('the Isle of the Land under Waves', Tiree), *Eilein Uaine an Fheòir* ('the Green Isle of Grass', Islay),

Eilein nam Ban Móra ('the Isle of the Big Women', Eigg), *Tìr an Eòrna* or *Tìr a' Mhurain* ('the Land of Barley' or 'the Land of the Bent Grass', Uist), and *Eilein na h-Òige* ('the Isle of Youth', Eriskay).

The terms for the smaller islands were clearly drawn by mariners from folklore and the literary tradition, for which see Robertson 1897–98b, pp. 200–01, and Murchison 1988, p. 20. *Eilein na h-Òige*, where Fionn could be found, was somewhere to the west of every other island (Campbell 1890, vol. 4, pp. 148, 150), JFC saying for example (*ibid.*, p. 295): "Beyond the Green Isle and the land of the dead was the Island of Youth, which was further off, and harder to get to, according to a story from Skye." See also Black 2002, p. 374. Those for the larger islands were clearly more practical. John Morison of Bragar wrote *c.* 1684 (Maciver 1989, p. 26): "The remotest of all the western isles of Scotland is commonlie called the Lews, by strangers the Nito." This I think can only represent *an Ì a-Tuath* 'the Northern Island'.

431   In the original the first line must have been *Marphaisg air a' chaillich ghlais* (or *léith*) *earraghlais*. JGC will have misinterpreted *earraghlais* 'grey-tailed' as its homophone *fhearraghlais* 'better grey'. The reference will be to the *cailleach* as winter deity, springtime wind and spirit of starvation. As pointed out in note 156, *glas* is not so much 'grey' as 'pale', 'wan', 'sallow', 'colourless'. The cailleach's 'tail' will thus be the drab mark left by her upon the land, similar in effect to *sgrìob liath an earraich* ('the grey track of spring'), for which see Gregory 1911, pp. 91–93, and Campbell 1940–60, vol. 1, pp. 104–13.

432   Full discussion of this practice will be found in Campbell and Thomson 1963, pp. 52–53, and McPherson 1929, pp. 128–29; see also Henderson 1911, p. 156. As we know that euthanasia was traditionally inflicted by suffocation in cases of rabies and syphilis (Mackenzie 1932–36), we need not be surprised to find that some form of it was also applied in cases of senile dementia; note also my discussion of infanticide, Introduction, pp. lxiii–lxiv. The Gaelic words were first recorded by Edward Lhuyd in Welsh orthography from the Rev. John Beaton in 1700, and transliterated thus by Campbell and Thomson (1963, p. 52):

> *An dig thu no an déid thu,*
> *No an d'ich thu feòil churra?*

("Will you come or will you go, / Or have you eaten heron's flesh?") Lhuyd does not say that the calling of the words hastens death – simply that when some one is on the point of death, all windows are opened, a man goes out, puts his head in through a hole, and speaks the words. It should be noted, however, that Beaton was a hereditary physician. A still earlier instance of the practice is on record from 1663 in the session minutes of Alves in Morayshire, in which the stated purpose was to hasten the death of 'ane aged and diseased poor woman called Margaret Anderson'. Andrew Angus and Agnes Rob were charged with 'the ringing of a millen bridle (as they call it)'; Agnes confessed to the session that she 'went and sought for and brought to the house the bridle at the diseased woman her own desyre', while Andrew 'confessed he rang the bridle', and on being asked 'what were the words he spake at the ringing of it', he answered (Cramond 1900, p. 44, cf. McPherson 1929, p. 128): "Cran's flesh or Wran's flesh come out thy way."

Alves, near Elgin, was a Gaelic-speaking parish throughout the Middle Ages, and it may be assumed that behind 'millen' lies a Gaelic word. The most likely candidate is *maoilean* 'friar' (as in *Mac a' Mhaoilein* 'MacMillan'), which would imply either that mendicant friars performed euthanasia with their bridles, or that the jingling of their harness was suggestive of their arrival to perform the last rites; for magic bridles see note 662. Citing parallels from England, South America and the Far East, McPherson concludes (1929, p. 129) that 'in exactly what manner Margaret Anderson met her end one cannot say without knowing something more of the instrument employed, but it was possibly by strangulation'. The evidence of the session minutes, however, is that the jangling of the bridle and the calling of the words were considered enough to make sufferers turn their faces to the wall. The flesh of cranes and wrens sounds like neither a normal diet nor an adequate one, and the opening of the windows suggests some idea akin to that of the soul departing the body in the form of a bird, cf. note 184; what is more, Carmichael points out (*CG6*, p. 49) that 'to see a heron is a bad omen, in some places an omen of death'. Carmichael collected two variants of JGC's couplet (*ibid.*):

> *An tig na 'n téid thu, chailleach,*
> *Na 'n ith thu feòil corra-ghritheach?*

("Will you come or will you go, old woman, / Or will you eat the flesh of herons?") And:

> *An tig thu na 'n téid thu, chailleach,*
> *Na 'n ith thu feòil curra?*

("Will you come or will you go, old woman, / Or will you eat the flesh of a crane?") Clearly kirk sessions such as that of Alves had made their point, however, because despite the revealing *chailleach* the real purpose of the words had been forgotten – Carmichael tells us of the first saying that it was 'used by a person when tugging at something difficult', and of the second: "This called out through the keyhole of the door cured the sick person within."

Cranes and herons were not well-respected birds. In St Kilda herons were thought to be witches from Stornoway (Harman 1997, p. 229). JGC points out (p. 139) that seeing a heron was a bad omen to the traveller; according to Sithiche (1912, p. 334) the crane 'personified a miserly parsimony that would starve another to death'. This is going a bit far, but Matheson (1938, p. 260) accepts that *còrr* 'was apparently used as a term of contempt', perhaps because 'the heron was regarded as an ungainly bird', and he cites (among other examples) a saying *aithris an darna curra air a' churra eile* 'one worthless woman's reproach of another', see also pp. 236–37; note 908; Campbell 1891, p. 47. In satirical verse (e.g. Gillies 1786, p. 292; MacDonald 1894, p. 155; Matheson 1938, pp. 72–73) *còrr* is used to describe the appearance of a bagpipe.

433 See 'Pearlwort (*Mòthan*)', pp. 229–30. Lewis Grant, Strathspey, told Neil MacGregor an amusing story about the practice of placing salt on the corpse (Bennett 1992, p. 239). A young lad is working at a farm. The pig dies, and the farmer says, "Go up to the grocer's and get a bag of salt." They are to salt down the pig for the winter. But they have an old cow, and she dies, and off the lad has to go again for the salt. Finally the old granny dies, and the farmer tells him to go up for salt. He goes, but he never comes back: "If they're going to start salting grannies I'm out of here!"

The usual explanation for the salt was that it was to prevent the corpse swelling (*ibid.*, pp. 234, 238–39), but Kenneth Macdonald (1891–1957) from Lewis wrote (2003, p. 132): "Once I saw a saucer of coarse salt lying on the abdomen of the dead one. I was told it was to keep away evil spirits, while another said it was to absorb any offensive odours from the body."

434 Cited by Frazer (1911a, p. 310) in the context of 'Knots and Rings Tabooed'. According to a similar belief from Switzerland (*ibid.*), if there are any knots in the thread with which the corpse is sewn into the shroud, these will hinder the soul of the deceased on its passage into eternity. Fr Allan McDonald noted that in South Uist and Eriskay the bands were loosened on the corpse before the coffin was closed (GUL MS Gen. 1090/29, pp. 32, 84, cf. Freer 1902, p. 60), and that, according to George Henderson, in north Inverness-shire 'at the time of childbirth and when a death occurs it is a custom to open every door & trunk and lockfast

place so that the child will obtain freedom from his confinement and that the departing soul may not be locked up & detained' (GUL MS Gen. 1090/28, pp. 262, 263). See also Anon. 1884–85 and p. 266 of the present work.

435 The Nicolsons, like the MacLeods, MacAskills, Lewis MacAulays and Skye MacSweens, are generally believed to be of Norse origin. There is no trace in Sellar and Maclean 1999 (the most comprehensive and reliable work on the family) of JGC's allegation that they were of Russian descent, and David Sellar tells me that he has never come across it (personal communication, 28 June 2004). Perhaps it has something to do with the very distinctive Nicolson forename Armchul, which is unknown in other Highland kindreds. Armchul is now understood to represent Old Norse *Arnketil* ('Eagle Kettle'), see Sellar and Maclean 1999, p. 14.

436 Norman MacLeod of the Barony (1882, pp. 241–42 = 2002, p. 114) discusses *faire a' chlaidh* as practised in north Argyll in a lengthy footnote which serves as a preamble to his highly romanticised version of the story of the Spanish princess. "It is not esteemed as an enviable position, but one to be escaped if possible; consequently, if two neighbours die on the same day, the surviving relatives make great efforts to be first in closing the grave over their friend. I remember an old nurse, who was mourning the death of a sweet girl whom she had reared, exclaiming with joy when she heard, on the day after her funeral, of the death of a parishioner, 'Thank God! My dear darling will have to watch the graves no longer!'

"A ludicrous but striking illustration of this strange notion occurred some years ago in the parish of A——. An old man and an old woman, dwelling in the same township, but not on terms of friendship – for the lady, *Kate Ruadh* (or red-headed Kate), was more noted for antipathies than attachments – were both at the point of death. The good man's friends began to clip his nails – an office always performed just as a person is dying. He knowing that his amiable neighbour was, like himself, on the verge of the grave, roused himself to a last effort, and exclaimed, 'Stop, stop; you know not what use I may have for all my nails, in compelling Kate Ruadh to keep *Faire 'Chlaidh* (to watch the churchyard), in place of doing it myself!'" See also Henderson 1911, p. 64; Maclean 1975, pp. 25, 62.

437 For other versions of this story see MacLeod 1882, pp. 241–46 = 2002, pp. 113–16, and Campbell 1885a, p. 331. For the story of the princess (who is sometimes from Spain, sometimes from *Lochlann*, Scandinavia) see McLeod 1843, pp. 182–83; MacLeod 1882, pp. 234–50 = 2002, pp. 111–18; Campbell 1885a, pp. 345–47; Ferguson 1894–95; Henderson 1911, p. 92; Mac Cormaic 1913; Bruford and MacDonald 1994, pp. 310–12, 469; MacDonald 1994–95, p. 65; MacKenzie 2002, pp. 130–34; SoSS Maclagan MSS vol. 22, pp. 3816–17, 3833–34.

438 See also Mitchell 1860–62, pp. 281–83; Ross 1886–87; Macdonald 1903, pp. 369, 374–75. *A' Chomrach* must be a typographic error: the name is universally *a' Chomraich* ('the Sanctuary'), see Watson 1904, p. 201. We should note the connection, pointed to by Bourke (1999, p. 144), between the changeling belief and a range of stigmatised human tragedies, including suicide: "It was sometimes used to rationalize the exposure, abandonment, and even the killing of children born with disabilities (and probably of some born to unmarried women), as well as death by sudden illness, suicide or other misadventure; it could be invoked to justify cruel punishment of children or adults; but it also contained that proviso of compassion for those who were temporarily 'not themselves'."

439 For full discussion of the *cailleach* of harvest and comparable customs see the chapter 'The Corn-Mother and the Corn-Maiden in Northern Europe' in Frazer 1912, vol. 1, pp. 131–70, particularly pp. 140–42, 164–67 (JGC's evidence is cited at p. 140). See also Banks 1937–41, vol. 1, pp. 62–84; Maclean 1964; Ross 1964; Ross 1976, pp. 142–45; Danaher 1972, pp. 190–99; Hutton 1996, pp. 332–47. For further references see note 42 and Ó Duilearga 1981, p. 411.

440 JGC adds in a footnote that *leagadh-iochd* is the remission of arrears of rent, literally 'a

merciful letting down'. Nicolson endorses JGC's explanation of the *leum-iochd* saying (1951, p. 248), but adds an alternative interpretation from Aberdeenshire (*ibid.*, p. 415): "In lands allotted on the 'run-rig' system, the crofter who got a 'balk' attached to his rig was considered luckier than his neighbour with a somewhat larger rig, but without the balk, the grass of which was of more than compensating value. The Rev. Mr Michie of Dinnet has heard the above saying used in the Highlands of Aberdeenshire in this sense." On the terms 'balk' and 'rig' ('ridge') see note 127 on p. 592.

441 See Tolmie 1876–77, p. 101, and Watson 1908–09, p. 67. In Frazer 1912, vol. 1, p. 284, the 'cripple goat' is discussed in the context of corn-spirits represented as animals (see note 184 above): "The corn-spirit was probably thus represented as lame because he had been crippled by the cutting of the corn."

442 See note 313.

443 See 'Shore or Maundy Thursday', pp. 548–49.

444 The traditional Gaelic method of naming children was: first boy after father's father, next boy mother's father, third boy father, subsequent boys named at will; first girl mother's mother, second girl father's mother, third girl mother, subsequent girls named at will (see also Nicolson 2004, p. 306). As a result, siblings often bore the same name and might have to be distinguished by the epithets *mòr* 'big', *meadhonach* 'middle' and *beag* 'little' or *òg* 'young' – irrespective of their height! For an example see p. 114 ('The Water-Horse at Loch Basibol, Tiree'). Conversely, when a child died in infancy it was normal to pass its name on to the next child of the same sex to be born, so what JGC is pointing out is that if two or three successive children of the same name were to die, the parents would not persist indefinitely with the name. See Mitchell 1860–62, p. 286.

445 By *Làirig Isle* and Loch Erne JGC means *Làirig Île* and Loch Earn (*Loch Éir*). His *Làirig Isle* probably indicates a local pronunciation in line with French *isle*, *île*. Confusingly, the place is marked on modern maps as 'Larig Eala'; this is not Gaelic *eala* 'a swan' but an anglicised spelling of *Île*. See Watson 1926a, p. 485; Morrison 1990–92, p. 340; Taylor 1996, p. 146; Black 2001, pp. 304–05.

446 I think what JGC means by this is that there is a sept of MacNeills called *Clann 'ic Shimigeir*; that they are descended from a person called Simigeir or Simigear; and that he received his name because the first person encountered by his parents on the road when bringing him for baptism was called Simigeir or Simigear. This is likely to have taken place in the general area of Knapdale, where MacNeills and Scrymgeours proliferated. Even allowing this to be the case, however, there remain more questions than answers. Is Simigeir or Simigear to be understood as a forename? Was Simigeir, Simigear or Scrymgeour a forename among the Scrymgeours or indeed among their neighbours – such as the MacNeills? Or should we disregard the 'road name' story and see *Clann 'ic Shimigeir* as simply a family of Scrymgeours who, being far outside their patrimony of Glassary – in Kintyre, perhaps – chose to identify themselves with their neighbours the MacNeills? For the Scrymgeours see Thomson 1912 and Moncreiffe 1967, pp. 95–98, and for the MacNeills see Sinclair 1909–10.

In Campbell 1895, p. 29, JGC cites an instance of the practice to explain the sudden appearance of the name Malise (*Maol Ìosa*, 'the Devotee of Jesus') amongst the MacLeans of Torloisk in Mull. Torloisk's children were dying young, one after another, when a 'promising healthy boy' was born. "The Chief was then advised by the sages of his race to give to his child the name of the first person whom he met on the way to have the child baptized. The first person encountered was a poor beggar man who had the name of Malise."

Describing a visit to a particular house in his parish, *c.* 1863, the Rev. Dr Archibald Clerk of Kilmallie recorded (Cheape 1999, p. 76): "I mentioned that I knew of people who were losing their children giving one of them the name of the first person they met on the road when going with the child to Baptism. [Isabella Kennedy] said her brother-in-law, Ewen, was so named – 'Se ainm an rathaid mhoir mar sin a tha air Eòghan againne' – the name of the *High-way* – a *High-way* name."

447 On *mac mollachd* (the devil) see p. 160. For stories about smiths countering the powers of evil see p. 112 and note 82; for tailors see Introduction, p. lxv. JGC speaks of the days when *luchd ceàird* 'held the first rank as hand-craftsmen', but even in the following lines showing how feathers were tied to arrows, probably dating from 1604, the term *fear-ceàird* (genitive *fir-cheàird*) is used pejoratively to mean 'jack of all trades, general craftsman' (Watson 1959, p. 240):

> Sìod' á h-Éirinn
> 'S meòir ga réiteach' —
> Cha tig bréin' fir-cheàird air sin

> Ach fleisteir fìnealt'
> O Ghleann Lìobhann
> Sìor chur sìod' air chalpannan.

("Silk thread from Ireland / With fingers arranging it – / No tinker's botched work will achieve that / But an elegant fletcher / From Glen Lyon / Putting silk all the time upon arrow-shafts.")

448 For Meigh see note 635; for stealing ploughshares see '*Taibhse Choimhlig*', pp. 287–88; *ath-dàir* is more literally 'second heat'.

449 See pp. 10, 25, 39.

450 On the cross of Christ see the next section ('Misnaming a Person'), also pp. 128 ('Thunder') and 273. On the roll of seaweed see p. 272, and on the wraiths of funerals see p. 244.

451 For *sop* see note 683. The sectional title in *SHIS* 248 (also in contents list, p. xix) is 'Gaining Straw'. This could have made sense as an alternative rendering of *sop seilbhe* 'possession wisp' (see 'Houses and Lands', p. 126) but does not do so here. I have therefore taken it to be a misreading of 'Saining Straw' in JGC's manuscript. For a clearer example of 'S' being misread as 'G' see note 373 above.

By 'menstruum' JGC does *not* mean menstrual fluid. This was universally regarded as unclean, would have been difficult if not impossible to collect, and does not resemble spittle. In any case, by JGC's day it was no longer called 'menstruum' – the last use of the word in the singular to mean menstrual blood is logged by the OED at 1677. Due to a fancy of the alchemists, the modern meaning of the term is 'solvent'. The OED explains: "In alchemy the base metal undergoing transmutation into gold was compared to the seed within the womb, undergoing development by the agency of the menstrual blood." By 'menstruum', therefore, JGC simply means water which has been in contact with gold or silver (*uisge òir, uisge airgid, uisge air airgead*), for which see Anon. 1883c; MacPhail 1898, pp. 86–87; Maclagan 1902, pp. 151–66; Mackenzie 1914, p. 300; McPherson 1929, p. 255 – best of all, 'water into which a piece of gold has been thrown', Sheila Macdonald says (1903, pp. 371–72), 'a wedding ring, for instance'. In addition, the practitioner might spit into the water, or pass it into the bottle via the mouth (Maclagan 1902, pp. 164–65), hence *sop seile*. See also note 463 below.

452 See pp. 563–69 below.

453 On black thread see pp. 158 and 194, and on magpies see 'Magpie', p. 123.

454 See pp. 126 ('Rising and Dressing') and 127 ('Baking').

455 See pp. 237–38 and *Tocher* 20, p. 152.

456 The village may be Largs, see 'The Lowland Fairies', pp. 40–41. On *droch còmhalaichean* see p. 153 and note 719. A man in South Uist, Hugh Nicolson, was known as *Ùistean Còmhdhalach* 'because he was thought a lucky person for fishermen and others to meet as they set out, a "guid fit" in Scots or *deagh-chòmhdhalach* in Gaelic' (*Tocher* 41, p. 331).

457 See p. 135.

458 Lev. 11: 4–8; Deut. 14: 6–8. On the pork tabu see note 184.

459 Speke 1863, p. 241, where the explorer reports his conversation with Rŭmanika, king of Karagŭé in East Africa.

460 Gen. 19: 26; Luke 17: 32.

461 This is an echo of material from two traditional stories published by JGC. The expedition that terminated in Fin's being 'in the house of the Yellow Forehead . . .' is described in 'Mar bha Fionn 'an Tigh 'Bhlàr Bhuidhe gun Chead Suidhe na Comas Éiridh' ('How Fionn was in the House of the Yellow Field, without Leave to Sit Down or Power to Stand Up', Campbell 1891, pp. 233–38). As a noun *blàr* means primarily a field, secondarily a white patch on an animal's face or forehead, while as an adjective it means (of an animal only) 'white-faced, having a white forehead'. It seems clear, then, that a mistake made *c.* 1874 in *SHIS* (and long forgotten?) was corrected in 1891 in *The Fians*, and that JGC decided between *c.* 1874 and 1891 that what seemed at first to be a single story was in fact two, for the laying of spells on his companions, and the resulting incident involving Fergus, are described in 'How Fionn Found His Missing Men', Campbell 1891, pp. 192–96.

I print the strange question *Co sid a propadh mo cheaplaich?* exactly as it stands in *SHIS* 255. The corresponding passage in Campbell 1891, p. 192, is as follows: "Fergus followed him; Fionn hearing the sounds behind him, and not caring to break his own custom or injunction, called out, 'Who is it that is following my footsteps?' (*Co sid propadh mo cheaplaich?*) The words used by him in this question are obsolete, but they are valuable as remains of expression that probably date far back in the history of the language. The answer he got was, 'I am here, one of your men and Fergus' (*Tha mise so, fear agus Fearghus*)."

For *propadh* 'supporting' see Matheson 1938, pp. 72–73, and Dwelly 1977, p. 739. I think, however, that the word may be *prabadh* or *pràbadh* 'disarranging', 'throwing into confusion' (*ibid.*, p. 733), and that *ceaplaich* can only be Watson's *caiplich* 'place of horses, i.e. horse pasture', from *capall* (2002, p. 157). It is quite common as a place-name, e.g. there is a Caiplich near Inverness and a Water of Caiplaich on the border of upper Banffshire and Inverness-shire, see also Chisholm 1885–86, p. 143; Mackay 1914, p. 430; MacKenzie 1964, pp. 4–5; EUL MS CW 502, ff. 149–50. If these surmises are correct, the question is: *Có siud a' prabadh mo chaiplich?* "Who's that disturbing my paddock?"

462 *Soll* is broken bait or, as Fr Allan expresses it, 'pounded shellfish' (McDonald 1958, p. 225, cf. *Tocher* 20, p. 159); *faoire* appears to be a misprint for *faoise* (see p. 685 below). The *clach-shuill* is the stone with which the whelks, cockles, limpets, mussels etc. are pounded, and *solladh* is the process of throwing the *soll* into the sea. Carmichael says (*CG2*, p. 361): "The Lady Amie, wife of John, Lord of the Isles, sent men round the islands to make hollows in the rocks in which the people might break shell-fish and prepare bait. Such pits are called 'toll solaidh', bait holes. These mortars resemble cup cuttings, for which antiquarians have mistaken them."

463 JGC is referring to a well-known rhyme (Nicolson 1951, p. 144, cf. MacPhail 1898, p. 84, MacGregor 1901, p. 35, and Macdonald 1982, p. 173):

> *Chuala mi 'chuthag gun bhiadh am' bhroinn,*
> *Chunnaic mi 'n searrach 's a chùlaobh rium,*
> *Chunnaic mi 'n t-seilcheag air an lic luim*
> *'S dh'aithnich mi nach rachadh a' bhliadhn' ud leam.*

("I heard the cuckoo without food in my belly, / I saw the foal with its back to me, / I saw the snail on the bare stone slab / And I knew that that year would be bad for me.")

Air a' chiad lomaidh means more literally 'while before eating', i.e. fasting, Irish *ar 'on*, *céad* 'first', 'pre-', 'before', *longadh* 'eating'. It has been comprehensively discussed by Greene (1954, pp. 146–48) and Matheson (1956–57, pp. 250–51), citing examples (including the present one) from Irish and Scottish Gaelic, to which we may add, from John Mackenzie (Mac-Choinnich 1844, p. 92), *fhuair am Prionnsa e* [sic] *chiad-lungaidh (no* bhracbhaist*)* 'the Prince got his breakfast' and, from Fr Allan (McDonald 1958, pp. 68–69), *Tha mi air chialaidh fhathasd* 'I did not break my fast yet' and *Cha deach e far na ciadhlaidh* 'He did not break his fast'. When a man has been without food all day, Fr Allan points out, he is *air chialaidh mhainneadh* – literally 'on the morning's first eating'. His editor, J. L. Campbell, cites the Canna form as *air chialamaich* ('fasting'), which preserves a little more of the original structure. Not surprisingly perhaps, the expression is common in medieval medical texts. In NLS Adv. MS 72.1.2, f. 102v, lines 28–29, an anonymous (?)fifteenth-century hand writes: *Item isin geimrad ar cedlongad dlegar an tvisgi beatha dol roim loighi sa samrad roim biadh 7 na dhiaigh isin earrach 7 isin fogmar.* ("Whisky should be drunk fasting in winter, at bedtime in summer, and before and after meals in spring and autumn.") And in NLS Adv. MS 72.1.3, f. 80v, lines 18–20, James Beaton (for whom see note 554) writes: *Deoch is ferr fa neimh ar uichachar .i. gab clamhan lin 7 bruith ar lionn oir e 7 tabhair tri deaochanna da ol ar maidin ar chedloghadh 7 bu slan and.* ("The best drink in the world for jaundice is to take dodder and boil it in menstruum and give three drinks to be taken when fasting in the morning and it will be cured straight away.") For menstruum (*lionn óir* 'fluid of gold') see note 451 above.

464 "The cuckoo shat upon him."

465 This refers to the 'face' and 'back' of the hook; *aghaidh na slabhraidh* is literally 'the face of the chain'. The *slabhraidh* is the focus of a good deal of superstition, see p. 176, Freer 1899, p. 276, Henderson 1911, p. 294, and Black 2002, p. 17. It can be no coincidence that the devil 'has often a chain clanking after him' (p. 159).

466 See Kerr 1887–88, p. 103; Macdonald 1903, p. 379; Sutherland 1937, p. 104; Macdonald 1982, p. 174; Opie and Tatem 1992, pp. 130 ('Ear, ringing in: ill omen'), 136–37 ('Elbow itches'), 143 ('Eye itches'), 186 ('Hand itches = money'), 288 ('Nose itches'). The itch of the lip that foretells a dram is *sgrìob an drama*, and the itch of the palm that foretells money is *sgrìob an airgid* (MacPherson 1960, p. 151). On the night of 20–21 July 1746, when Donald Cameron of Glenpean was about to guide Prince Charles through the military cordon that had been strung across the mountains from Loch Hourn to Loch Sheil, he kept rubbing his nose and saying (Forbes 1895–96, vol. 2, p. 376, cf. Chambers 1840, p. 114), "O Sir, my nose is yuicking, which is a sign to me that we have great hazards and dangers to go through."

They waited until two sentinels had met, exchanged greetings and were returning to their respective fires; then they crept on all fours along a deep ravine whose stream had shrunk to a trickle in the dry weather. When they had reached a place where they were screened from enemy observation the Prince whispered: "Well, Donald, how does your nose now?"

"It is better now, but it still yuicks a little."

"Ay, Donald," said the Prince, "have we still more guards to go through?"

467 "The right ear, bringing me up; and the left ear, constantly criticising me." See also Opie and Tatem 1992, pp. 130–31 ('Ear or cheek tingles = someone talking about you').

468 *Baobh* or *badhbh*, here glossed as 'a furious woman', is defined by Dwelly (1977, p. 67) as (1) 'wizard', (2) 'wicked mischievous female, who invokes a curse or some evil on others', (3) 'foolish, disagreeable female', (4) 'she-spirit supposed to haunt rivers'. The word originates in medieval literature as the name of the war-goddess *Bodb*, a scaldcrow who seeks and devours corpses. In later Irish folklore, especially in Co. Waterford, it occurs as a term for the supernatural death-messenger (Lysaght 1996, pp. 28, 34–39, 126–33, 196–218). In the sense of a malicious water sprite or hag, it passed into the English of Easter Ross as 'vow'

(Watson 2002, p. 235). Speaking of Highland Caithness, the Rev. George Sutherland defines *baobh* as 'a big, clumsy, and somewhat silly water goblin' (1937, pp. 95–96), and places a young male of the species in the classic *Mi fhìn* story (note 365). See also pp. 118 and 173 of the present work.

469 *Cliath-chliat(a)* 'a harrow' appears to derive from *cliath* (any grid-shaped object – a harrow, grate, hurdle, etc.) and a genitive form (*cliathta*) of the verbal noun *cliathadh* 'harrowing' – thus 'a harrowing grid', 'a grid for harrowing'. In the Lochaber tale 'Dòmhnall Bàn 's am Bòcan' the hero is so pestered by the ghost of a man who stole and hid plough-irons when alive (cf. '*Taibhse Choimhlig*', pp. 287–88) that he leaves home altogether, but the *cliath-chliata* which has been lying beside the house proceeds to bump along behind him (Craigie 1895, p. 355). Compare JGC's story (p. 98 above) of how the glaistig pursues Mac Ian Year and his brother all the way to the Outer Isles with the amusing excuse that 'they had forgot the old harrow, but she had brought it'.

470 Or 'for you and for your luck', see notes 726 and 729; cf. p. 134 ('Names'). For the *frìth* see Mackenzie 1891–92, pp. 103–08; *CG*2, pp. 158–59; Freer 1902, pp. 47–52; Henderson 1910, pp. 72–74, and 1911, pp. 223–24; *CG*5, pp. 286–97; MacPherson 1960, pp. 183–85; MacInnes 1989, p. 17; Campbell 2000, pp. 56, 60. Freer's material is plagiarised from Fr Allan's notebooks: EUL Carmichael–Watson MS 58A, ff. 37r–37v, 77v (nos. 146, 350); GUL MS Gen. 1090/28, p. 104; GUL MS Gen. 1090/29, p. 74.

471 There is something wrong with JGC's rendering of the last line. *Nìos* or *a-nìos*, as Dwelly says (1977, p. 699), is not 'down' but 'up' – specifically 'from below, up (towards the speaker)', as at p. 129 above where it appears to mean 'up to heaven'. There is no verb *luaith*; it is conceivable that the verb is *luaidh* 'move' as in Irish, but the resulting meaning 'And don't move it up' would contradict the previous line. There is *aicill* rhyme *a-suas* : *luaith*, but *aicill* does not appear to be a structural requirement in charms such as these, and indeed the only clear prosodic feature of any kind in this one is the end-rhyme *Chrìost* : *dhìom* : *nìos*. The verb here will not be *luaith* or *luaidh* but *luth* or *lugh* 'bend, flex', as of a bow or an oar, cf. mac Mhgr Alastair's

> *Sìnibh, tàirnibh is luthaibh*
> *Na gallain liagh-leobhar ghiuthais*

('Stretch, pull and bend / The long-bladed saplings of pine', MacLeod 1933a, pp. 42, 78–80). By this argument the line means 'And don't flex it upwards' or 'Without flexing it upwards', referring to the arm as a whole rather than merely to the hand. The straighter the arm, the better the omen.

472 *Dòduman*, more commonly *dòtaman*, is the singular form; the plural is *dòdumain*, *dòtamain*. The teetotum is also called a *gille-mirein* or 'whirligig'. It was the focus of a popular New Year's game; for how it was played see Knockfin 1876, pp. 110–11, and Maclagan 1901, p. 125.

473 According to Burnett 1983, evidence of scapulimancy may be found all over the world – not merely in Scotland, Ireland and Europe, but also among Mongols, Chinese, Japanese, native Americans, and, most notably, Arabs. Arabic treatises on scapulimancy were being translated in the twelfth century by scholars such as Michael Scot or Scott (see pp. 162–63). The practice is described as occurring in Wales by Giraldus Cambrensis in 1188, is mentioned by Chaucer in the 'Parson's Tale', and, if we wish to believe JGC, had reached the Highlands by 1400, the year of Chaucer's death. For examples see Pennant 1774, p. 179; Dalyell 1834, pp. 515–19; Maclagan 1895, p. 157; MacPhail 1895, p. 167; Lorne 1898, pp. 185–86; Henderson 1911, pp. 230–31; Ó Cuív 1954; Matheson 1958, pp. 75, 92–93; Jackson 1959, pp. 84–85; Kirk 1976, pp. 67–68; MacInnes 1989, pp. 17–18; Stewart 1990b, p. 35;

MacilleDhuibh 14.12.90 and 28.12.90; Pennant 1998, p. 280; Hunter 2001, pp. 59, 88; NLS MS 14990, f. 14 (Rev. Neil Campbell); EUL MS CW 504C, ff. 50r–61r. The Chelsea bookseller Donald MacPherson (for whom see Mac a' pharsuinn 1977 and NLS MSS 14890–95) gave William J. Thoms, who coined the term 'folk-lore' in 1846, a 'manuscript account of the superstitions of his countrymen' which included a particularly interesting account of scapulimancy as practised by a man named MacTavish who had been *aireach* or cowherd to MacDonald of Gallovie in Laggan (Thoms 1878).

474   By 'speal' JGC means the Scots word for 'shoulder', not the Gaelic word for 'scythe'. Strictly he should have written 'speal-'.

475   In the context of 'Tabooed Things', Frazer points out (1911a, p. 229) that the forecasts will not be accurate unless the flesh has been removed from the bones without the use of iron. He cites JGC along with many other sources for the practice worldwide.

476   Literally 'that he would have the world'.

477   His name is confirmed as *Mac a' Chreachair(e)*, which would mean 'the Cattle-Lifter's Son', 'the Plunderer's Son', by Matheson 1969–70, p. 66, and Campbell 1990, p. 57, but Fr Allan McDonald heard it as *Mac a' Chreachainn* ('the Son of the Scallop-Shell'). In GUL MS Gen. 1090/28, p. 192, Fr Allan wrote: "The name of the fiosaiche or Wizard that the old McNeils of Barra had was 'Mac-a'-Chreachainn'. Can it have been Mac- Neachtain or Mac Neacail – the latter a common enough name in Barra to-day. 'The-son of-the scallop-shell' seems a strange name. He said. 'Bithidh Barraidh fhathasd fo rodain 's fo gheoidh ghlasa.' = 'Barra will yet be under rats & grey geese.' The prophecy is true as to Eoiligarry around which was the home of the people before they were evicted. Eoiligarry is proverbial for its rats today." Cf. Campbell and Hall 1968, p. 278, and Sutherland 1987, p. 129.

   A possible explanation for the name *Mac a' Chreachaire* is suggested by JGC's 'common story' (p. 145) of how a shoulder-blade seer saved the life of a party of *creachairean*.

478   *Baile na Creige* is now always Craigston in English. The prophecy runs (Macdonald 1904–05, pp. 266–67, cf. Macneil 1923, p. 192, and Campbell 1990, p. 57):

> *Ri linn Ruairidh an t-seachdamh Ruairidh*
> *Thig an cuaradh air gach neach:*
> *Mac na baintighearna caoile bàine,*
> *Is mairg a bhios ann ri linn,*
> *Is mì-niarach a bhios ann ri linn —*
> *Bidh Cìosamul 'na ghàrradh bhiastan-dubha*
> *'S 'na nead aig eunlaith nan speuran.*

("In the time of Rory of the seventh Rory / Misery will be everyone's lot: / The son of the slender fair-haired lady, / Pity those who will live in his time, / Unhappy those who will live in his time – / Kishmul will be an otters' enclosure / And a nest for the birds of the skies.")

   The reference to *Clach a' Ghlagain* is of great interest. It would be more accurately translated 'the Ringing Stone', and is clearly a reference to a 'rock gong' similar to *Clach a' Choire* ('the Kettle Stone') at Balephetrish in Tiree, listed by John Mackenzie (1845, p. 8) as one of the seven wonders of Scotland – a huge granite erratic covered with fifty-three cupmarks, the deepest of which are at the most resonant parts of the stone. 'Rock gongs' are found worldwide and have been defined by M. C. Fagg (1997, p. 2) as 'naturally situated and naturally tuned rocks, boulders, exfoliations, stalactites and stalagmites which resonate when struck and show evidence of human use as idiophones'. She points out that in Nigeria they have been used as playthings, as accompaniments for singing and dancing, and for signalling (1997, p. 3). "They have also been used as church bells, not only at Coptic churches in Ethiopia but in Brittany, where the Celtic missionary St Gildas reputedly called the faithful to prayer using a gong which is still extant in his grotto ... A rock gong on the Pacific island of Bora Bora, known as the Bell Stone of Hiro, the god of war, can be heard over the whole island and was used to call the people together ... Another gong on the summit of Mango Mountain in Fouta Djalon, Guinea, was used by villagers to announce deaths, public gatherings or the approach of enemies. It must have been regarded as a threat to authority, for after the establishment of a station nearby, the French had the stone removed to their Residence ... It is the attribute of a 'voice' which associates mystery with such rocks: the voice of the rock is believed to be the voice of an ancestor or other spirit with power to summon the supernatural."

It seems then that JGC is relaying a tradition of a rock gong in Barra which had been lost or destroyed. According to Fagg (1997, p. 86), *Clach a' Choire* was 'said to contain a crock of gold – but if it is ever split, Tiree will disappear beneath the waves'. If true (Mrs Fagg mistakenly attributes the statement to *SHIS*) the legend thus contains both a motive for destroying such stones and a warning against doing so; probably this applied to *Clach a' Ghlagain* as well. Compare Newton 1992, p. 145, where it is claimed that if *Clach a' Choire* 'ever shatters or falls off the pedestal of small stones on which it rests, Tiree will sink beneath the waves'.

There is also a type of *clach ghlagain* to which JGC's translation 'rattle stone' would be entirely appropriate but which is unlikely, I think, to be what is referred to in the prophecy. It is mentioned by Captain Thomas, R.N., in a note on crannogs (1879–80, p. 393): "The approach is by stepping stones, which I have never seen placed in a straight line, but always in a curve, an obvious advantage in defence. It is a general belief that one of the stones, *Clach Ghlagainn*, Gaelic = warning-stone, was balanced, so that it made a noise when trodden upon, and hence gave a warning at night, when any one was coming over the stepping-stones."

479 Kishmul was abandoned in 1748 when Roderick MacNeil took up residence elsewhere in Barra, but was restored by Robert Lister Macneil between 1938 and 1968 (Macneil 1975, pp. [7], 115, 162–66). Mackenzie gives the prediction as follows (1877, p. 20), attributing it by implication to Coinneach Odhar: *Nuair a bhios maor nan òrdagan móra agus dall nan ceithir meòiribh fichead còmhla ann am Barraigh, faodaidh MacNèill Bharraigh bhith dèanamh deiseil na h-imrich.* "When a sheriff's officer with big thumbs and a blind man with twenty-four fingers are together in Barra, MacNeil of Barra may get ready to flit." He explains (*ibid.*, pp. 20–21): "This prediction, which was known in Barra for generations, has been most literally fulfilled. On one occasion 'the blind of the twenty-four fingers', so called from having six fingers on each hand, and six toes on each foot, left Benbecula on a tour, to collect alms in South Uist. Being pretty successful there, he decided upon visiting Barra before returning home. On arriving at the Ferry ... he met *Maor nan Ordagan mora*, and they crossed the kyle in the same boat. It was afterwards found that the 'officer' was actually on his way to serve a summons of ejectment on the laird of Barra; and poor Macneil not only had to make ready for, but had indeed to make the flitting. The man who had acted as guide to the blind on the occasion is, we are informed, still living and in excellent health, although considerably over eighty years of age."

Barra was sold in 1838. Mackenzie's statement about the man over 80, who would have been born *c.* 1790, was left unchanged in all subsequent editions (1878, p. 51; 1882, 1899, 1945, p. 50; 1977, p. 83). In one of his posthumously-published articles (Campbell 1907–08, p. 192) JGC cites a related prophecy to the effect that a submerged island north-west of Barra will reappear *ri linn Ruairidh nan trì Ruairidhean*, 'in the time of Roderick of the three Rodericks'. Its name is usually spelt *Rocabarra* or *Ròcabarra*, cf. Rockall. "Others say, the man prophesying with a shoulder-blade said, that in the time of the last of seven Rodericks, every one of whom was to have a black spot on his shoulder (*ball dubh air a shlinnein*), and of the miller with three thumbs (muilleir nan trī ōrdag), *Rôca Barra* would appear, or (as the expression may also be explained) a heavy burden was to come on Barra (thig Rôc air Barra). The name of the imaginary island is *Roca Barra*, and it is alleged to be the property of the ancient family of the MacNeills of Barra. It was sunk by an earthquake at the time a great part of Tiree sank, and its inhabitants every year put past the rent in the eye of a lime-kiln (sūil āth) till a chief of the MacNeills comes to claim it. The Island is not large, but is very beautiful, and, according to the Barra people, is the real 'Green Island' of old tales. Barra itself has been sold by the McNeills, and the fourth Roderick in a direct line has been chief, but Roca Barra has not yet been seen."

For the 'Green Island' see p. 46 above.

480   JGC places Murchadh Geàrr too early. He is on historical record during the years 1534–79, and appears to have been a half-brother of Eoghan a' Chinn Bhig, see p. 238 (MacLean 1889, pp. 237–38; Sinclair 1899, pp. 257–59; MacLean 1923–25, vol. 1, pp. 201–02; *Tocher* 24, pp. 292–97; Bruford and MacDonald 1994, pp. 426–29, 485; Maclean-Bristol 1995, pp. 97, 102, 117, 143, 155, 181, 185).

481   On cup-reading see Opie and Tatem 1992, pp. 391–92.

482   See the examples collected by Opie and Tatem (1992, pp. 125–26) under the heads 'Dream, telling: before breakfast'; 'Dream, telling: Friday night's'; 'Dream, unseasonable'; 'Dreams by contraries'.

483   See Eccl. 5: 3 and Nicolson 1951, p. 7.

484   JGC presumably means that it is unlucky for men to dream of women, and one can imagine why this might be the case. For libidinous dreams see p. 160, and for dream signs generally see Macbain 1887–88, p. 259, Mackenzie 1914, pp. 289–90, and Macdonald 1982, p. 170. It would be interesting to know whether it is also unlucky for women to dream of women. As for the dead, JGC means that if a person dreams of them, they are not at rest.

485   I have been unable to identify the Coll bard or the poem. It is a distortion to say that 'the surname of horses is MacLeod', and the quotation is intended satirically, especially as the Skye poet's wife is dragged in. The matter is best stated in Dr John MacInnes's words (1989, p. 17): "In dream lore the MacLeods are represented by a horse. It is of great interest that in some Gaelic songs (the examples are seventeenth-century MacDonald compositions and hostile to the MacLeods) the MacLeods are referred to as the 'Seed of the Mare'. These references to the equine ancestry of the MacLeods were taken by themselves as highly insulting." The 'Seed of the Mare' is *Sìol na Làire* or, in a rhyme cited by Henderson (1911, p. 117), *Sìol a' Chapaill*. Similarly, to dream of a deer was, at least in Jura, to dream of a Buie (Youngson n.d., p. 13); the screech of an owl was said to portend the death of MacNab (SoSS Maclagan MSS vol. 22, p. 3859).

486   'Macgnanean' is a mystery. I can see how 'Macquarie' might have been misread by the printer of SHIS as 'Macgnane', but I cannot explain '-an'. Even when spelt in Gaelic, surnames do not have plurals in -an. Nor do I know whether or not the dream sign of the Macquaries (MacQuarries) is a horse. Other possibilities include (1) a surname ending '-an' such as MacLennan; (2) a surname of the *MacGill-* type such as *MacGill'Eain* 'MacLean'; (3) a plural word like *magairlean* 'testicles'.

487   There appear to have been two Thomas Rhymers, father and son. They were natives of Erceldoune, now Earlston in Berwickshire, where an alleged 'Rhymer's Tower' may still be seen behind the petrol station. Thomas the elder appears to have lived *c.* 1225–95, Thomas the younger *c.* 1270–1340. We may see Thomas the elder as poet, scholar and translator, a lay member of the educated middle class at a time of political, social and cultural ferment. Nowhere was that ferment greater than in the Borders, where a society in which Anglian-speaking peasants were kept in check by Gaelic-speaking warriors had just been swept aside, and the remnants of the Welsh language and its traditions of Myrddin (Merlin)

were disappearing in the west. Norman barons controlled the countryside and Flemish merchants the streets, while the great abbeys had amassed enormous economic power and war with England was an ever-present threat. The cultural phenomenon of the time was the huge success of Geoffrey of Monmouth and his imitators in breathing fresh life into old stories about King Arthur, Merlin and the knights of the Round Table.

Taken together, these facts explain why Thomas the elder, like Michael Scot, became associated with the occult, with prophecy (see Dalyell 1834, p. 618), and, in particular, with a journey to the otherworld which has so much in common with Celtic mythology. No doubt he put some old Welsh story of a visit to the Fairy world under the Eildon Hills into rhyme in some of the newer languages whose communities he served – and from being its translator, oral tradition made him its hero, with the result that Henderson and Cowan's description (2001, p. 172) of Robert Kirk might equally be applied to Thomas: "He . . . became personally entwined with the very traditions that he dedicated the latter part of his life to studying, a paradoxical situation in which the historical figure was absorbed as part of the folk tradition." The result was the fifteenth-century romance 'Thomas of Erceldoune' and the ballad 'Thomas the Rhymer' (see p. 24).

The prophecies in the romance speak of a bastard who will come out of the west, become leader of Britain, fight a last great battle at a place called Sandyford, and die in the Holy Land. Thomas Rhymer's identity in folklore is not merely as inspired prophet but also as warrior messiah, Gael, and wandering horse-dealer; the solution to this was first suggested by John Geddie, who pointed (1920, p. 30) to a Norman family who owned castles and land in the countryside around Erceldoune, and took what became their surname from a village five miles east – Gordon. "In Thomas's time, the head of the family, Sir Adam de Gordon, was Warden of the Marches, and these barons of the Merse, who dispensed justice at the 'Hanging Tree' at Gordon, had already begun to put down roots in Strathbogie and other lands north of the Mounth, their rise being on the ruin of the Comyns, the Cheynes, and other houses planted earlier in the region between Spey and Dee . . . It is hardly an extravagant conjecture that the neighbourhood of Gordon to the Rymour's Tower may explain the abundant traces of Thomas's fame and presence in the counties of Aberdeen and Banff."

The cult of Thomas Rhymer (in the shape of the ascription to him of many highly localised prophecies) is indeed very strong in those counties, which were then thoroughly Gaelic-speaking, but Gordon influence there began only after Bannockburn in 1314, when Sir Adam received Strathbogie from the king 'no doubt as part of the price of winning him over' after the battle (Barrow 1976, p. 387, cf. Gordon 1784, part 1, p. 7). Sir Adam, clearly a charismatic character, went on to serve Bruce well, being one of the two knights who carried the Declaration of Arbroath to the Pope at Avignon in 1320 (Barrow 1976, p. 426). His acquisition of Strathbogie had spectacular results, his descendants becoming earls, marquises and dukes of Huntly and Gordon, lords of Lochaber, and generally 'Cock o' the North'. The Gordons' early years in Aberdeenshire – e.g. an alleged handfast marriage of Adam's great-great-grandson Jock of Scurdargue to a daughter of MacLeod of Harris – have been discussed by John M. Bulloch (1931–33, pp. 323–26).

It may be assumed that Thomas the younger played a role in the development of the new Gordon territory, and that this role involved the acquisition of suitable horses. It would have brought him as far as Inverness; his association with Dumbuck can easily be explained by his Border roots, which place him firmly in the political and cultural milieu of the diocese of Glasgow and the former kingdom of Strathclyde. In oral tradition, the composite Thomas Rhymer was best remembered in the north of England as horse-dealer; in the Borders and Lowlands as horse-dealer and otherworld visitor; in the north-east as prophet and horse-dealer; in the Highlands as sleeping messiah, horse-dealer and prophet;

and in the Islands as sleeping messiah and horse-dealer (Stewart 1823, pp. 101, 131–32; Diarmad 1876; Mackay 1916; Bruford 1994–95, p. 2; Lindsay 1995; Scott 2001, pp. 82–87; Henderson and Cowan 2001, pp. 142–52).

For the sleeping messiah in Scottish tradition see MacDonald 1994–95, p. 63, and in Irish and other traditions Croker 1825–28, vol. 2, pp. 324–25, and vol. 3, pp. 266–72; Hartland 1891, pp. 207–21; Dorson 1968, p. 148; Ó Buachalla 1989; Ó hÓgáin 1991. It is a widespread motif (AT A151.1.1 etc., p. 731 below); for a large list of references see Ó Duilearga 1981, p. 395. Ó hÓgáin identifies four basic elements in the story as told in Ireland: the enchanted sleeping army; the fated hour of delivery; the near-awakening due to some act of the visitor; and the sale of a horse by the visitor to the hero or to one of his men (1977, p. 307). He adds (*ibid.*, p. 308): "The close parallel of the legend in Ireland with Arthurian tradition suggests that the Normans brought the legend to Ireland as they did also to Sicily."

488 In the manner of the 'heroic biography' (for which see Ó Cathasaigh 1977, p. 3), these accounts seek to ascribe supernatural features to Thomas's birth. Appropriately for a warrior messiah, they are tinged with violence. Similarly, in the eighteenth century Captain Burt noted Lord Lovat's claim 'that, at the instant he was born, a number of swords, that hung up in the hall of the Mansion House, leaped of themselves out of the scabbards, in token, I suppose, that he was to be a mighty man in arms' (Simmons 1998, p. 246).

489 This account makes Thomas a bastard in line with the romance. A version of it entitled 'Tòmas Reumhair, Mac na Mnatha Muirbhe' ('Thomas the Rhymer, Son of the Dead Woman') was published by J. L. Campbell (1939, pp. 10–11, 31–34). He had recorded it from Seonaidh Caimbeul, South Uist, for whom see Black 1999, pp. 717–18. A girl asks an itinerant tailor to make a dress for her, promising to sleep with him as payment. He makes the dress and leaves without keeping her to her bargain. Soon afterwards she dies. She subsequently appears before him and reminds him that the dress has not been paid for. "I was only joking," he says in effect, but she points out that if the debt is not paid she will have to follow him everywhere. They sleep together, and she says: *Nist, trì ràithean an déidh anochd thig thusa chon na liceadh agamsa, agus gheobh thu leanabh gille air a' lic agam, agus bidh an dala leath dheth fo'n talamh agus an leath eile an uachdar an talmhana, agus feir thu Tòmas a dh'ainm air; agus gheobh thu leabhar dearg comhla ris air a' lic, agus cha doir thu dha e gus am bi e ceithir bliadhn' diag a dh'aois.* ("Now, nine months from tonight you will come to my grave-slab, and you will find a baby boy on my grave-slab, and half of him will be under ground and the other half above ground, and you will call him Thomas; and you will find a red book along with him on the slab, and you will not give it to him until he is fourteen years old.")

It happens as she says. The tailor finds no one who can read the book, but he gives it to Thomas when he is fifteen and he reads it without difficulty. It becomes clear that he has the gift of second sight, and soon he leaves the tailor for ever. For red books see pp. 151, 161.

A converse motif, the impregnation of a woman by the dust of dead men's bones, appears in the origin-legend of the church of Kilmallie, no doubt to emphasise its sanctity. The story is told in the eighteenth century by Walter Macfarlane (1906–08, vol. 2, p. 162), in the nineteenth by Sir Walter Scott (1810, pp. liii–liv, a note on Canto Third of 'The Lady of the Lake') and the Rev. Dr Archibald Clerk (1858, p. 94), and in the twentieth by the Rev. Dr George Henderson (1911, pp. 64–65). Briefly, the young people of Corpach and Annat are herding cattle at *Cnoc nam Faobh* ('the Hill of the Spoils'), which is strewn with the bones of the slain, presumably following some battle between feuding kindreds. To keep warm they kindle a fire and feed it with bones. Towards morning, says Clerk, they return to their homes 'without the conduct of any of the party exciting remark'. One girl who is very cold stays a little longer. Macfarlane: "She being quyetlie her alone without anie other companie took up her cloaths above her knees or therby to warme her awhile, did come and caste the ashes below her cloaths, and some of the same entering into her privie member she was conceived of ane Manchild." Clerk: "The only cause she assigned for her being in such a condition was, that when sitting alone by the fire, and taking up her clothes to benefit by the warmth, a sudden gust of wind blew the ashes of the dead men's bones about her . . . Her son survived, and from the above probable story of his paternity given by his mother, was known as 'the Son of the Bones'."

Macfarlane mangles the name (*Gille dow Maghre-vollich*) but Clerk spells it out: *An Gille Dubh Mac 'Ille Chnàmhlaich*, 'The Black Lad, the Son of the Cadaverous Lad'. He was a good scholar, became a godly man, and built the church.

490 This is the element of 'Thomas of Erceldoune' which survived in the ballad which succeeded it. It is the grandest of all *sìthein* stories. See p. 24 above.

491 See 'Fairies and Goats', p. 71. Dumbuck is a volcanic plug on the north shore of the Clyde where the A82, squeezed between it and the shore, forks right for Loch Lomond and the north and left into Dumbarton. Regrettably, the hill is now being quarried away from behind. It was a place of enormous strategic importance. Dumbuck Shoal was the lowest point where the Clyde could be crossed by cavalry – or indeed forded by infantry, merchants and travellers in general – until a passage seven feet deep was made through it in 1775 (Riddell 1979, pp. 38–44).

The story of Dumbuck was noted by Alexander Carmichael in Gaelic from a sailor from the island of Coll named John MacKenzie at Carbost in Skye on 8 January 1861 (EUL Carmichael–Watson MS 470; MacilleDhuibh 16.11.01). Two farmers were once coming into Dumbarton, he said. They each had two carts of meal for sale. They were met by a man with the air of a gentleman who asked, "Where are you going with the meal?" "To sell it." "I'll buy it from you." They agreed on a price and the gentleman asked the farmers to follow him with their carts. Following him into *Dùn Buic*, they found themselves in a huge hall. It was amazingly beautiful, and they reckoned they had never seen nor heard of any place like it. After they had deposited the meal the gentleman offered to show them around. *Mo riar fhéin b'e sin an taigh!* What a house. They could not believe the number of men they were seeing. They were sleeping everywhere – countless numbers of them. Each had his hand under his cheek and his weapons beside him on the floor. Thomas Rhymer (for that is who it was) told the farmers that on no account (*air na chunn' iad riamh*) must they touch anything they saw. They wandered around in utter amazement. Seeing a chain coming down from the roof, one of the farmers put his finger on it, and it started clinking and clanking and filling the hall with sound – *thòisich an t-slabhraidh air glingaraich 's air glingaraich 's an taigh gu léir air fuaim*. All the multitudes around them woke up and every man jumped to his feet, grabbing his weapons and shouting: *Seo an t-àm! Seo an t-àm!!* ("The time has come! The time has come!!") *Chan e fhathast*, commanded Thomas. "Not yet. Lie down as you were." They lay down again.

Thomas was furious at the farmer who had touched the chain and said, "Why did you do that? Didn't I ask you not to touch anything you saw?" He escorted them out of the house and no one else has seen it since. See also Campbell 1890, vol. 3, p. 97, and vol. 4, p. 35.

492 From 'Moladh Chlann Dòmhnaill' ('The Praise of Clan Donald'), see Matheson 1938, pp. 130–31. This is the last example of the last recrudescence of the 'cult' of Thomas, 1647–1760: the sleeping Messiah as Jacobite icon in Gaelic verse. Reference was made in each case to an alleged prophecy which appeared to say that Scotland would be freed, and/or Britain united under Scottish kings, by a last great battle fought by the Gael on the Clyde. See Stewart 1885, p. 45; Ó Baoill 1972, p. 153; MacilleDhuibh 13.2.98.

493 *Tom na h-Iùbhraich* is primarily 'the Mound of the Yew Grove', however (Watson 2002, pp. 42, 162). Many yews still grow upon it. Pennant, who much enjoyed his walk there in 1769, remarked that it 'looks like a great ship with its keel upwards' and 'if it was not for its

great size, might pass for a work of art' (1774, p. 161). Since the 1860s it has formed part of the principal cemetery of Inverness (Mackenzie 1945, pp. 9–12). Many otherworld tales have become attached to the name, not all of them concerning Thomas or Fionn, see for example Stewart 1851, p. 68, MacRitchie 1890, pp. 147–49, Anon. 1891a, pp. 20–37, and 'Aonghas Mór Thom na h-Iùbhraich agus na Sìthichean' ('Angus Mor of Tomnahurich and the Fairies') in MacDougall and Calder 1910, pp. 132–41. John Mackenzie put it another way (1841, p. 156): "There are several hills in the Highlands which still bear the name *Tom-na-h-Iubhraich*, all haunted by the fairies. One of them is near Strachur, Lochfine side; another near Inverness. According to popular belief, Thomas the Rhymer was captain of the fairy troops."

494 See note 176. Lt. Donald Campbell gives a version which is worth citing in full (1862, p. 141). "Alexander Gillies, the great Glengarry tale-reciter, used to recite a touching romance of the Feinn; who, one day, when hunting on Meal-fuar-mhonaidh, had been enticed on an adventure of exploration into the Sith-bhrugh of Tom-na-hiuirich, near Inverness, by a sorceress of Lochlin [*Lochlann*, Scandinavia], and were there placed under enchantment. Here they were doomed to lie stretched around the cave, side by side, in a profound sleep, arrayed in their full costume and arms, with the hand of each warrior on the hilt of his sword, ready for action, the moment the charm should be terminated; which, however, it never would, until three blasts should be blown on a war-trumpet, suspended behind the gate of the cave.

"The legend gave an exceedingly graphic description of a chivalrous tailor who took upon himself, on a Halloween-night, when all fairy-knowes are open, to attempt the adventure of setting the Feinn free. He entered the brugh of Tom-na-hiuirich, in which darkness was made visible by a lurid glare of supernatural light, which exposed to the eyes of the startled tailor a row of warriors of a supernatural size, stretched prone on their shields, but in their complete war panoply, around the cave. Though staggered by their enormous size, and the fierce scowl which contracted their brows and compressed their lips (and he had some misgiving as to the fate of mankind should such savage-looking giants be set loose upon them), he screwed up his courage, and determined at least to sound one blast of the trumpet, and have a parley with them.

"He blew a blast, and so loud and terrific was the sound, that Tom-na-hiuirich shook to its base, and the distant mountains reverberated. The great warriors opened their eyes, and stared at the tailor with an incomprehensible look; but they did not move. He was greatly frightened, and had sad misgivings; but rallying his staggered senses by degrees, he blew a second blast. The great warriors rose slowly to their left knees, and leant forward in an incumbent position on their elbows, their hands grasping the hilts of their half-unsheathed swords, and cast eager but indefinable glances at the tailor, who felt himself impelled by a sudden panic, dashed the trumpet to the ground, and sprang out of the cave.

"Here he stood for a moment in compassion and doubt, hearing a moan spreading through the cave, while the following words were uttered in a voice in which scorn struggled with sorrow, 'A leabeadean 's mise dh-fhag na thuir;'—poltroon, worse you left than found (us.)"

See D.B. 1873–74; Grant 1925, p. 24; Dorson 1968, pp. 110, 148. Fionn and his men are also reputed to be in a cave under Craigiehow in the Black Isle, for which see notes 288, 797, and Watson (1904, p. 140): "In this cave lie the Feinn, awaiting the blowing of the horn which is to rouse them from their sleep. It is, or was, believed to extend to Loch Lundy. A dropping well at the mouth of the cave was resorted to until quite recently to cure deafness."

For a more detailed description of Craigiehow see MacilleDhuibh 30.4.93.

495 A saying provoked by the widespread idea of *trì Màirt* (three 'Marches', 'Tuesdays' or sowing-times), see note 179. It is the kind of *dubh-fhacal* or 'dark word' beloved of storytellers, i.e. it sounds at first as if an unweaned three-year-old is meant, but as the story

unfolded it probably emerged that there were three 'Mays' and three 'Augusts' in the year as well. I can guess how this might be. Not only was there a *céitein earraich* ('spring maytime', the two weeks before 1 May) and a *céitein samhraidh* ('summer maytime', the two weeks after 1 May), but Carmichael says (CG2, p. 248) that there was a *céitein geamhraidh* ('winter maytime') as well. There was a *iuchar samhraidh* ('summer bordertime', the two weeks before 1 August) and a *iuchar foghair* ('autumn bordertime', the two weeks after 1 August) as well as the *iuchar* ('bordertime') itself, which JGC calls August, but which is now the calendar month of July. There is also some evidence to suggest that the term *iuchar* might be associated with the period around 1 November (Black 1985, pp. 7–10).

496 Kengharair is in Glen Bellart south of Dervaig. The *Faidhir Mhuileach* or Mull Fair was held for centuries at *Druim Taigh Mhic Gille Chatain* at the head of Glen Bellart. Cattle were traded there in mid-May and mid-October, horses in mid-August. The August fair was singled out in the eighteenth century by Ramsay of Ochtertyre (1888, vol. 2, pp. 405–06): "The fair of Mull is the most considerable one in the West Highlands. It is held in August, upon the side of a high hill, four or five miles from any houses. Thither great numbers of persons resort from all the Western Isles and adjacent countries; and it is attended by pedlars from the Low country, and sometimes from Ireland. It lasts a week; and though it is now less frequented by the gentry, it is still a season of great festivity with the commons. People who come from a distance are obliged mostly to eat and sleep in tents or temporary huts, where droll adventures often occurred. In such a multitude of people quarrels were unavoidable, though since the Disarming Act less dangerous."

See RCAHMS 1980, pp. 240–42; MacKenzie 2002, pp. 23–29. Confirmation that Thomas was said to appear at the *Faidhir Mhuileach* is forthcoming from a story noted in Gaelic on 8 January 1861 by Alexander Carmichael from John MacKenzie, a native of the island of Coll (EUL Carmichael–Watson MS 470, MacilleDhuibh 16.11.01). There was once a man at the Mull Fair buying horses, MacKenzie told him, and he would only take those that were allowed to run at their mother's side. He needed six, and they all had to be *blàr buidhe* – that is, as Carmichael explains, 'with a white spot on the face and the rest dun'. He got one, the last one he is known to have bought. In due course he was noticed by a girl that used to work for him. "Oh!" she said, "there's my old employer Thomas Rhymer." She went over to talk to him. "What eye did you recognise me with?" he asked. "The right eye," she replied. So he put his finger on her right eye and she never saw as much as a gleam with that eye again. She had worked for him for three years and never till that day did she know that Thomas Rhymer was not of this world (*nach bu duine saoghalta e*). Although she had been seeing his court in all its splendour and beauty she had never given it a second thought (*cha do chuir i riamh umhail sam bith*). She lived for a long time afterwards in Mull and often spoke of Thomas Rhymer and his house.

One wonders if Thomas's 'court' was the farmhouse of Kengharair; for the motif of the finger in the eye see p. 77 ('Fairies and Horses'), and for the rest of John MacKenzie's story see note 491 above.

497 The fourth line means literally 'A young king will go upon the crown', i.e. will attain the crown. According to John MacKenzie from Coll (for whom see notes 491 and 496 above), Coinneach Odhar said:

> *Nuair dh'éireas Tòmas le chuid each*
> *Bidh glaodh nan creach mu Chluaidh.*

"When Thomas and his horses rise / Clyde will ring to cries of plunder." Or alternatively *eubh nan creach* (same meaning). On that day, said MacKenzie, five hundred freeholders (*coig ciad fear fearainn-shaoir*) will fall and a young king will be crowned (*théid rìgh òg a chrùnadh).* Happy is the man who lives after that. All will be well with Scotland from that day on. As a sign of the truth of this prediction, a woman will bear a son with seven thumbs. He will be a miller in *Fearaig* and will be called *muillear nan seachd òrdag,* 'the miller of the seven thumbs'. This miller, MacKenzie concluded, is there now and many people have seen him. *Tha am muillear seo ann gun teagamh. Agus is iomadh fear a chunnaic e.* See also Campbell 1890, vol. 4, pp. 34–35.

498 During 1508-24 a waulking mill appears to have been built on the Kelvin at Partick by a Donald Sym. In 1568 the Regent Moray granted the bakers of Glasgow, which was two miles to the east, permission to build a wheat-mill there, the 'gentlemen's corn-mills upon Kelvin' being unsuitable for grinding wheat. In 1577 Archibald Lyon's mills on the Kelvin were bought by the city council when their own mills on the Molendinar 'were found to be in a ruinous condition' (MacGregor 1881, pp. 72–73, 88, 121–22).

499 Describing the ruin of Jerusalem, the fall of Judah and the disappearance of luxury Isaiah declares: "And in that day seven women shall take hold of one man, saying, We will eat our own bread, and wear our own apparel; only let us be called by thy name, to take away our reproach." In NLS MS 14990, f. 140r, it is given by the Rev. Neil Campbell (1850–1904) as a prediction of Thomas Rhymer: *Theid sechd bantearnan deug suas Rannoch andeigh aon taillear crubaidh.* ("Seventeen ladies will go up Rannoch after one lame tailor.") He adds: "No sign of genitive in pronunciation, it is dying out in Perthshire."

500 The gradual process of deepening and straightening the Clyde from Dumbuck to Glasgow can be traced back to 1556, when the river was so clogged with fords and shoals as to be barely navigable for even the smallest craft. It began to be tackled in earnest in the eighteenth century (MacGregor 1881, pp. 79, 175, 315–16, 332, 346). In 1854, however, the liner *Glasgow* shuddered to a halt about a mile upstream of Renfrew ferry, that is, at Elderslie (Scotstoun), about two miles down from Partick. It was the site of the long-removed Blarthill Shoal. The Clyde Navigation Trust had become accustomed to removing stones by dredging, or even by hacking away from a diving bell, but this proved to be a seam of hard volcanic lava, and in 1860 the Trustees decided that it would have to be broken up by means of explosives. Underwater blasting was then in the earliest stages of development, but 'soon the channel at Elderslie was resounding to the muffled thump of the exploding powder'. The process was so successful that it was continued until the Clyde in 1907 was twenty-eight feet deep as far up as the Broomielaw (Riddell 1979, pp. 151–52, 240).

501 By 'more than fifteen years ago' JGC will mean prior to 1859. Compare the prophecy attributed to Coinneach Odhar concerning the Millburn near Inverness (Mackenzie 1878, p. 51 = 1882, 1899 and 1945, p. 50, and 1977, p. 83): "The day will come when thy wheel shall be turned for three successive days by water red with human blood; for on the banks of thy lade a fierce battle shall be fought, at which much blood shall be spilt."

502 JGC gives the second *Cuiridh claigeann . . .* saying in Gaelic only, so I have offered a translation. Nicolson (1951, p. 159) puts *peirceall* 'jaw' in place of *claigeann* 'skull'; Chambers cites it as 'the teeth of the sheep shall lay the plough on the shelf' (1841, p. 19). It is often attributed to Coinneach Odhar (Mackenzie 1977, pp. 48, 139); see also 'The Lady of Lawers', p. 151. *Meall òir* in the couplet is 'a lump of gold' or 'a shower of gold', and I am quite sure that the 'houses' JGC has in mind are inns (*taighean òsta, taighean seinnse*). These were, and are, typically located where a river is crossed by a trunk road at the debouchment of a valley. A better translation might be: "Scotland will be silver girdles / With a shower of gold at the foot of each glen." It appears to be prophetic of roads, railways, canals and trade, perhaps even tourism. For the Caledonian Canal see pp. 611 and 615 below.

503 Since JGC's time, due to the gradual shrinking of the area in which Gaelic is spoken and traditions are remembered, Coinneach Odhar has come to be regarded as the pre-eminent Highland seer. A native of Easter Ross, he is listed in a commission of justiciary dated 25

October 1577 as 'Keanoch Ower' among six men and twenty-six women charged with 'the diabolical practices of magic, enchantment, murder, homicide and other offences within the bounds of the Earldom of Ross, the lordship of Ardmanach (i.e. the Black Isle), and other parts of the Sheriffdom of Inverness', and in another commission dated 23 January 1578 as 'Kenneth alias Kennoch Owir, principal or leader of the art of magic' along with 'other men and women using and exercising the diabolical, iniquitous and odious crimes of the art of magic, sorcery and incantations'. The trial took place at Chanonry (Fortrose), and though there is no record of whether Coinneach Odhar was among those tried and sentenced, he is said in tradition to have been burnt on Chanonry Point in a barrel of tar (Mackenzie 1877, p. 34 = 1878, p. 81; 1882 and 1899, p. 80; 1945, pp. 79–80; 1977, p. 116), so it is probable that he was indeed among them, and that his date of death may be fixed at 1578 (Matheson 1969–70, pp. 68–72).

Like Thomas Rhymer, he became a figure of folklore upon whom many prophecies were fathered, especially during the seventeenth century and almost exclusively in the counties of Ross and Cromarty – including Lewis, where it came to be believed that he was a native of Uig in that island. He was first called 'the Brahan Seer' in a popular collection of his prophecies, many of them cited in English translation only, which has gone through at least six editions and innumerable reprints (Mackenzie 1877, 1878, 1882, 1899, 1945, 1977; Sutherland 1987, pp. 196–230, 314–51). See also MacRae 1908, pp. 147–202; Henderson 1911, pp. 232–42; MacDonald 1934–36a, pp. 186–89; Dorson 1968, p. 145.

504 Other traditions of how Coinneach received his gift have much to say about a stone (Mackenzie 1877, pp. vii, 3–4 = 1878, pp. 5–9; 1882, 1899, 1945, pp. 5–8; 1977, pp. 28–34), but none that I know of refer to a raven's nest. It should be remembered that JGC appears to have *written* these words before Mackenzie published his work on Coinneach's prophecies in 1877, but that they were not *printed* until after Mackenzie's death in 1898. See also MacDonald 1934–36a, pp. 187–88; Henderson and Cowan 2001, p. 93.

505 This is a variant of a tradition discussed by Mackenzie (1877, pp. 7–8 = 1878, pp. 13–15; 1882 and 1899, pp. 14–16; 1945, pp. 13–16; 1977, pp. 41–43) in relation to *Clach an t-Seasaidh* ('the Standing Stone') near the Muir of Ord, e.g. "The day will come when the ravens will, from the top of it, drink their three fulls, for three successive days, of the blood of the Mackenzies." It is also called the *Clach Mhór* and *Clach nam Fiann*, misspelt *Fionn* by Mackenzie (1877, pp. 7, 13 = 1878, pp. 13, 33; 1882, 1899, 1945, pp. 14, 34; 1977, pp. 41, 67):

> Is òlaidh am fitheach a thrì saitheachd
> De dh'fhuil nan Gaidheal bho Chlach nam Fiann.

"And the raven will drink his three fills / Of the blood of the Gael from the Stone of the Fiann."

506 I have translated this elsewhere (MacilleDhuibh 12.1.01): "That Well of Tà, and Well of Tà, / Well where battle will be fought, / And the hermits' bones will be / On the white beach of Liveras / And the third of three Lachlans will be slain / Early, early, at the Well of Tà." I take *fear fàs* to be Dwelly's *fear-fàsaich* 'ascetic', literally 'wilderness man', thus 'hermit'. Stone implements and human bones were found in a chambered cairn at Liveras near Broadford in 1832; a field there called *Pàirce nan Laogh* contained an ancient burial-ground, while a rock on the shore was known as *Creagan an Teampaill* (Lamont 1913, pp. 7–8, 38, 159–60; Nicolson 1994, p. 1). The penultimate line looks like a reference to Sir Lachlan MacKinnon of Strath, *mac Lachainn Òig mhic Lachainn Duibh*, fl. 1601–28 (Sinclair 1907–08, pp. 35–37); however, JGC adds in a footnote that it also exists as *'S marbhar Torcuil nan trì Torcuil* ('And Torquil of the three Torquils will be slain'). Such prophecies may be assumed to have been made after the event, and this will refer to the death of the third Torquil of the Lewis

line – his sister had married Lachlan MacKinnon of Strath, and he may have met his death in MacKinnon territory through having come to Skye for refuge or aid (Matheson 1978–80, p. 336).

Lamont (1913, p. 163) has the rhyme as:

Tobar sin is Tobar Tà,	*This same fountain Tobar Ta*
Tobar aig an cuirear blàr,	*A bloody battle yet shall stain,*
Marbhar Torcul nan trì Torcul	*When Torcul of the Torculs three*
Air là fliuch aig Tobar Tà.	*Shall on a rainy day be slain.*

I have argued (MacilleDhuibh 12.1.01) that Tà was in origin the name of either (a) a Gaelic saint, feast-day 13 January, 'whose dedications range widely from Loch Lomondside (in Strathclyde) through Argyll and Perthshire to Aberdeenshire and out to Skye', or (b) the spirit of the River Tay, personified as female, whose cult spread from Perthshire 'south to meet that of St Serf, west to Loch Lomond and Argyll, north to Aberdeenshire, and even out to Skye'. January 13 is also the feast-day of Kentigern, once an obscure Welsh-speaking saint, now the patron of Glasgow.

At some stage Tà took on Kentigern's nickname Mungo, which Jocelyn of Furness explains as *carissimus amicus* ('very dear friend'), apparently as if from Welsh *mwyn* 'kind, dear' and *cu* 'dear, amiable'. When the kingdom of Strathclyde became a diocese 'there was an urgent need to strengthen it by establishing a legend that would unite its cathedral at Glasgow with its remotest parts'; Jocelyn supplied that legend *c.* AD 1200 from the remotest part of all – Furness in modern Lancashire – by piecing together whatever stories came to hand, including those of Serf and Tà.

507 This is clearly a reference to *Clach Stèineagaidh* (Lawson 2002, pp. 19–20). In her charming song about it, Mrs Joan MacSween (1900–72) put to good effect the tradition mentioned at p. 148 that Fionn and his companions lie asleep, awaiting a final call to arms (Lawson 1996, p. 27; Black 1999, pp. 234–35, 753):

> *Their cuid anns a' bhaile*
> *(Mas e fìrinn neo breug e)*
> *Gur clach-chinn i bh' air ceannard*
> *Ann an cogadh na Féinne.*
>
> *Ma bhios armachd is eallach*
> *A-rithist ag éirigh*
> *Nach e gheibh an damaist*
> *Tighinn a-mach fo Chlach Stèineagaidh!*

("Some say in the township / (Be it truth or a lie) / She's the headstone of a chief / In the war of the Féinn. / If his arms and equipment / Are to rise up again / Won't he cause havoc / Coming out from Steinigie Stone!")

508 Mackenzie expresses this prophecy in the following words (1877, pp. 6–7 = 1878, p. 12; 1882, 1899, 1945, p. 13; 1977, p. 40): "However distant it may now appear, the Island of Lews will be laid waste by a destructive war, which will continue till the contending armies, slaughtering each other as they proceed, reach Tarbart in Harris. In the Càws of Tarbert, the retreating host will suddenly halt; an onslaught, led by a left-handed Macleod, called Donald, son of Donald, son of Donald, will then be made upon the pursuers. The only weapon in this champion's hands will be a black sooty *cabar*, taken off a neighbouring hut; but his intrepidity and courage will so inspirit the fugitives that they will fight like mighty men

and overpower their pursuers. The Lews will then enjoy a long period of repose." Matheson gives the original (1969–70, p. 77):

> *Dòmhnall nan trì Dòmhnall*
> *Chlann MhicLeòid, 's e air a' chearraig —*
> *Le cabar dubh á taigh a nàbaidh*
> *Tillidh e 'n nàmhaid sa Chadha.*

("Donald of the three Donalds / Of the MacLeods, a left-handed man – / With a black rafter from his neighbour's house / He will repulse the foe in the Cadha.") He points out that this will be an *ex post facto* prophecy referring to a battle between the Morrisons of Ness and the MacLeods of Harris that took place on the Cadha (the path leading to the Bays from the south shore of East Loch Tarbert) *c.* 1544–45. *Tormod nan trì Tormoidean* is a phrase taken from a well-known prophecy relating to the unfurling of the Fairy Flag, see Mackenzie 1877, pp. 19, 20 (= 1878, pp. 48, 49; 1882 and 1899, pp. 47, 49; 1945, pp. 47, 48; 1977, pp. 81, 82); MacLeod 1933b, p. 135; cf. note 6 above.

509   Perhaps by 'step path' JGC means 'steep path'. The singular form is properly *cadha*, which JGC defines at p. 247 as 'steep mountain path'.

510   *Clach Stèineagaidh* at Scaristavor is only about six feet high. JGC is clearly referring here to *Clach Mhic Leòid*, the gathering stone on the headland of Aird Nisabost two or three miles further north, which is about twelve feet high (Lawson 2002, pp. vii–viii). *Òrd bhàirneach* is a limpet hammer.

511   *Uidh an Taoibh Tuath* is strictly the isthmus beyond the present township of Northton in south Harris, but at one time the name appears to have been applied to the Northton–Scarista area in general – when the parish church of Harris was moved from the *Uidh* to Scarista it continued to be known as *Eaglais na h-Uidhe* and was marked on maps as 'Uig' (for Uiy) Church (Lawson 2002, p. 29). The stone in *Uidh an Taoibh Tuath* is therefore *Clach Stèineagaidh*.

      By 'Tarnsa islet' JGC means Taransay, which lies off the west coast of south Harris. The Taransay stone is at one end of the island's own *Uidh*; it is known as *Clach an Teampaill* ('the Stone of the Pre-Reformation Church') or *Clach an t-Sagairt* ('the Priest's Stone') and has a cross engraved on one side (Lawson 1997, pp. 6–7, and 2002, p. 40). In the story as told by Lawson (2002, p. xiii), the *cailleach* gives such a tremendous blow to a limpet on Aird Nisabost that her hammer breaks into three pieces. One flies across the sea to become *Clach an Teampaill* in Taransay, another flies along the shore to become *Clach Stèineagaidh* at Scarista, and the third lands on the hill behind her to become *Clach Mhic Leòid* itself – which, being the biggest, is often called the *Òrd Bhàirnich* (properly *Òrd Bhàirneach*) to this day.

512   Lawson makes the valid point (2002, pp. 28–29) that the story of hidden treasure may relate to plunder taken from the pre-1700 parish church of Harris. Its ruins stand upon a little point of land jutting into the sea, *Rubh' an Teampaill*, south of the hill called Ceapabhal at the western extremity of *Uidh an Taoibh Tuath*. "The old people used to say that there was treasure buried on Ceapabhal, on a spot where you can see the three uidhean, or sand-shores, of Huisinis, Tarasaigh and Taobh Tuath. Old traditions take a long time to die out altogether, and it could well be that this treasure came from the church. The old folk even knew who was going to find it – Amadan MhicCuthais: a simpleton by the name of MacCuish."

      Clearly there is disagreement as to whether the treasure story relates to three standing stones or to three *uidhean*; but then, this is in line with one of the ten most common types of 'buried treasure' legend, at least in Ireland – 'treasure marker confusion' (O'Reilly

1994–95, p. 200). According to Joina MacDonald, who got the story from her father, *Dòmhnall Sham*, the three markers are as in Lawson's version, but the treasure is a *seice òir* ('skin bag of gold') hidden in *beinn an Taoibh Tuath*, the hill at Northton (personal communication, 6 February 2004). *Tha e uabhasach doirbh na trì fhaicinn còmhla oir tha Thùisinis air cùlaibh Tharasaigh agus ma thèid thu ro fhada timcheall beinn an Taoibh Tuath tha thu a' call sealladh air Aoidh an Taoibh Tuath. Ach tha aon àite sònraichte ann far am faiciste na trì còmhla 's tha e coltach gun do lorg fear ás an Taobh Tuath an t-àite. Stob e a bhata dhan talamh agus chaidh e a dh'iarraidh spaid ach cha d'fhuair e riamh lorg air a' bhata an dèidh tilleadh!* ("It's very difficult to see the three together because Husinish is behind Taransay and if you go too far round the hill at Northton you lose sight of Northton Isthmus. But there's one particular place where the three may be seen together and seemingly a Northton man found the place. He stuck his stick into the ground and went to fetch a spade but he never could find the stick after he came back!")

For other stories of buried treasure see note 682 below; Dixon 1886, pp. 165–66; Craigie 1898, pp. 373, 377; Sutherland 1937, pp. 77, 99; Mac a Phì 1938, pp. 48, 79–80; Barron 1967–68, p. 213; Barron 1969–70, p. 238; Temperley 1977, pp. 34–37, 106–07; Macdonald 1982, pp. 75–77; Gray 1987, p. 243. This one from North Uist is particularly circumstantial (Morrison 1965, p. 72): "Kenneth MacQueen, who held the Cnogaire as tack in the 17th century, was a man of considerable wealth. On his death-bed he told his family that he had concealed his wealth at the base of Cnogaire Hill. It could be discovered, when the Pleiades (grioglachan) were right above Marradh hill at a time when the moon was a certain angle above the same hill. At the time of MacQueen's death, his two white horses, with their forelegs tied together, were within thirteen steps of the spot. The treasure has never yet been discovered."

513 The Lady of Lawers was believed to be a woman from Appin in Argyll, either a Stewart or a MacCombaich (Colquhoun); she appears to have married a younger son of Campbell of Lawers *c.* 1645. For her prophecies see MacMillan 1901, pp. 69–70; Gillies 1938, pp. 247–52; Sutherland 1987, pp. 263–66; McKerracher 1988, pp. 31, 78–88; MacilleDhuibh 19.5.00, 2.6.00, 16.6.00. It is difficult to find them in the original Gaelic, but one such source is NLS MS 14990, ff. 136r, 141r, 142r; see also Robertson 1897–98a, p. 37, s.v. *drèug*.

514 Balloch is *Bealach* or *Bealach nan Laogh* ('the Pass of the Calves'), the Gaelic name of Taymouth (Watson 2002, p. 179). There is in fact a 'Black Book of Taymouth'. Dated 1598, it contains no prophecies, and consists mainly of a record of successive acquisitions of property by the Campbells of Glenorchy. It was mainly compiled by Master James Bowie, 'who seems to have discharged the double duty of family notary and pedagogue to the grandsons of Sir Duncan Campbell, the seventh laird' (Innes 1855, p. i). It is now GD112/78/2 in the National Archives of Scotland.

515 The battle of *Sròn a' Chlachain* – not *Sròn a' Chlachair*, which is on Loch Katrine – appears to have taken place on 4 June 1646, although a date in 1640 has also been suggested. It represented an attempt by the Campbells to defend their territory against a raiding party of Keppoch and Glencoe MacDonalds (Gillies 1938, pp. 147–48; Watson 1959, p. 325; MacKenzie 1964, pp. 233–34; Mackechnie 1964, pp. 242–43, 360–62; Watson 2002, p. 188).

516 The third line should probably be translated 'Each side of Loch Tay will be a kail garden', and the fifth (assuming *daoine* for *duine*) 'And a goose feather will drive their memories from men'. See also p. 149.

517 'John of the three Johns' (*Iain Glas nan trì Iain*, or *Iain Glas mac 'Ain 'ic Iain*), the third consecutive John to hold the title of Campbell of Glenorchy, was universally disliked. "He was cunning as a fox, wise as a serpent, but as slippery as an eel," said one contemporary. When in 1677 he became the first earl of Breadalbane, he was allowed to nominate as his successor 'any one of his sons whom he should designate in writing'. Outside the Highlands the reason was alleged to be the feeble-mindedness of his eldest son Duncan, Lord Ormelie.

Inside the Highlands, where Duncan was better known (and better liked than his father), the real reason was believed to be that while Duncan and his sons were loyal Jacobites, his younger brother John was as willing as his father to bend with the wind. Iain Glas died in 1717 and was duly succeeded by his younger son; Duncan died in 1727. See Gillies 1938, pp. 163, 176, 221–27; Black 2001, pp. 492–93.

518 *Clach an Tuirc* is at Fearnan, and, as Gillies says (1938, p. 251), it is difficult to conceive of it toppling over.

519 We would express this differently nowadays by saying that whereas swearing in English tends to be sexual in nature, in Gaelic it is mostly religious. JGC's example *diabhal MacEadhar* (which personally I have never heard) illustrates this well, for 'devil-may-care' is a light-hearted, innocent expression, but in the Gaelic dialects with which I am familiar any mention of the evil one by his principal name *diabhal* 'devil' is potentially swearing. In GUL MS Gen. 1090/29, p. 5, Fr Allan McDonald wrote of the South Uist people (Black 2002, p. 48): "It would be considered dreadful & as grating on all their traditional feelings . . . if a priest in preaching were to say 'diabhol' = devil. It is not so much so on the mainland. I gave a copy of a hymn to an old man & 'diabhol' came into it, & he told me that he changed the word as he could not go to bed with 'diabhol' on his lips."

On the other hand, it is distinctly possible that *diabhal MacEadhar* is a corruption of the much more Gaelic-sounding *diob[h]adh air mac athar* ('death without issue upon the son of a father') noted by Kenneth Macleod as 'generally applied to a family' (Campbell 1996, p. 80).

520 From *còmh(dh)ail* 'meeting', cf. *còmhal(t)aich(e)* 'a person the meeting of whom is ominous of good or bad fortune', see pp. 139–40, 536; cf. MacNeil 1987, pp. 412–13, 475.

521 It is pretty clear from Dwelly 1977 s.v. *drùth* etc. that these words will be variations on (or corruptions of) *drùthaileachd* 'sex'. Probably JGC knew this well.

522 Cf. *Gun d' rug beul sìos oirnn* 'a black fate has overtaken us', Matheson 1938, pp. 134–35. It appears that women who indulged in improper or unnatural behaviour were buried face downwards, see Matheson 1951–52b, pp. 15–16, 24, and Black 2001, p. 389. The longer saying is intended ironically – pointing out that it means in effect 'women's work is never done', Nicolson translates (1951, p. 63): "Confound the women, if they are not found everywhere!"

523 Using a common dialectal variation of *beul*, Nicolson gives this (1951, p. 63) as: *Bial seachad ort!*

524 For *gonadh* 'stabbing, bewitching' see 'Fairy Theft', p. 17 above.

525 Frederick Rea describes the highlights of a windy day in January 1891 at Garrynamonie school in South Uist, where he was headmaster (1997, pp. 19–20). "By dint of holding on to the stones and pulling myself sideways, the wind pressing me tightly against the wall all the time, I managed to reach the opening into the playground where I was at once torn from my hold and whirled away right past the school door." When school is over for the day, he returns his charges to the arms of their parents. "I was alarmed as I took the first two children for, when we reached the opening through which I had passed in trying to get into school that morning, they were lifted right up in the air while I, hanging on grimly to their hands as they were blown out straight before me, only just managed to get them safely across to a sheltered part." Finally he returns home. "I do not remember exactly how I got back into my house, but I have a lingering impression of crawling on all fours."

526 *Sàr* is Dwelly's noun *sàr* 'oppression, violence; distress, difficulty; arrestment for debt, distraining; stoppage, hindrance, provention' (1977, p. 791). The expression thus means: "The black oppression/distress/arrestment/stoppage of your stabbing/bewitching upon you!" That is, "May you be bewitched to death!"

527 JGC gives the pronunciation familiar to him from north Argyll, and from it deduces an etymology based upon *marbh* 'dead' and *tasg* 'storage', i.e. 'place'. The word is normally spelt

marbhphaisg and understood to mean 'shroud', from *marbh* 'dead' and *paisg*, feminine, 'web or parcel of cloth, anything folded up' (Dwelly 1977, p. 716). That the latter is the correct understanding is sufficiently demonstrated by early Irish *marbfásc* 'swathings of a corpse' (*DIL* s.v. *marb*), modern Irish *marbh-fhásc* 'a binding for the hands or feet of a corpse', *marbh-fháisc ort* 'death take you' (Dinneen 1927, p. 715), although it has to be admitted that there is some confusion in Scottish Gaelic between *fàisg* 'squeeze, wring' and *paisg* 'wrap'.

528 JGC did not give the originals of the three Friday/Saturday sayings, so I have supplied them. See pp. 568–69.

529 JGC's 'fifteen or twenty years ago' suggests 1854–59, shortly before he arrived in Tiree. Madge Wildfire, in *Heart of Midlothian*, is the insane daughter of a gypsy thief; she was seduced when a girl, and this, with the murder of her infant, turned her brain. Coleridge called her 'the most original character ever created by Scott' (Benét 1948, p. 1211). For cursing on the knees cf. Cramond 1900, p. 24, and for the belief of such women in the efficacy of their words see Scott 2001, p. 201: "I kenna how it is, but something aye comes after my words when I am ill-guided and speak ower fast."

530 This is true in a general but not in a particular sense. It is indeed the case that the Highlanders accepted the Clearances with a degree of resignation, and this fact (now widely regarded as regrettable) is certainly ascribed to the influence of religion, see for example note 335 and Henderson 1982. The Rev. Donald MacCallum once said of those for whom he had tried to fight (MacInnes 1996–97, p. 417): *Phòg iad an t-slat leis an do sgiùrsadh iad.* "They kissed the rod with which they were scourged." On the other hand it is quite possible to find Clearance songs in which the oppressor is cursed, e.g. Meek 1995a, pp. 54–55.

531 For 'cheese' read 'butter' (twice). Strictly as direct speech *Nach faicear toradh . . .* ('That no benefit shall be seen . . .') should read *Na faicear toradh . . .* ('May no benefit be seen . . .')

532 Perhaps this is a version of 'the Curse of the Breadalbanes', said by McKerracher to have been uttered by the Lady of Lawers (for whom see p. 151) about 1681, and characterised by him (1988, p. 85) as: "The Earldom will not descend beyond a grandson in one line." If so, the castle in question is Taymouth.

533 Assuming that *far* represents *thar* 'over' rather than *bhàrr* 'off', *Toradh do ghuidhe far . . .* will mean literally 'The fruit of your wish be over . . .'

534 Luke 1: 20–22, 62–64.

535 *Sgialachdun is uirsgeulun* are literally 'tales and myths'. The term *eachrais ùrlair* is dealt with quite exhaustively in an appendix to Campbell 1940–60, vol. 1, pp. 492–99. Originally *eachlach urláir* 'a domestic servant', more literally a 'floor rider', male or female (cf. Black 1976–78, pp. 336–37, 363), it came to mean a witch or sorceress connected to a large house (cf. Watson 1937, pp. 152–53). It developed such by-forms as *eachlaraich(e)*, *each(a)lair ùlair*, *eachlais ùrlair*, *iorasglach ùrlair* and even *clàrsach ùrlair*; according to Mrs Wallace, who translates it as 'Cantrips' or 'Trouble the House', it was invariably *achlas urlair* in Tiree (1887–88b, p. 495), and MacDougall tells us (1891, p. 280) that an untidy person is, or was, still called *Iorasglach* in contempt. See Campbell 1881a, pp. 67, 74; Mackellar 1887–88, pp. 143–45; MacDonald 1893–94, p. 45; Campbell 1906–07 and 1909–10b; Bruford 1965, pp. 156–61, 168–71; *Tocher* 2, pp. 38–57; *Tocher* 13, pp. 184–85 (*Iochlach Ùrlair*); Campbell 1975, pp. 31–33; Bruford and MacDonald 1994, pp. 98, 448; Hunter 2001, p. 58.

536 According to a footnote in Campbell 1940–60, vol. 1, p. 496, JGC's words are those spoken by the witch in 'MS. Vol. x., No. 126' (the Cinderella story 'Clann an Righ air an Cuir fo Gheasaibh', NLS Adv. MS 50.1.10, ff. 508–31). This is not so. Her salutation, spoken on four separate occasions at ff. 512–14, is: *Mar mhi bior am chois, cnaimh am leis, s cath-chliar mo leanabh big [bige, beag] am uchd, dh'eirinn s ghabhainn duit le pogan.* "Were it not for a thorn in my foot, a bone in my hip, and the fretfulness(?) of my baby in my lap, I would get up and shower you with kisses."

537 JFC says (Campbell 1890, vol. 1, p. cx): "The enchanted king's sons, when they came home to their dwellings, put off cochal, the husk, and become men; and when they go out, they resume the cochal and become animals of various kinds." John G. Mackay adds (Campbell 1940–60, vol. 1, pp. 358–59): "Enchantment and disenchantment are sometimes plainly equivalent to donning and doffing the hide of some animal."

538 Cf. p. 108. On the MacCodrums' connection with the seals see Matheson 1938, pp. xxxiv–xliv; Campbell 1967–68, pp. 12–13; *Tocher* 8, pp. 258–63; Bruford and MacDonald 1994, pp. 365–67, 477; MacDonald 1994–95, p. 53; MacInnes 1994–96, pp. 10–14; Black 2002, p. 382; cf. also Croker 1825–28, vol. 2, pp. 13–20; Frazer 1911b, p. 125; and the Arran story 'Innis Eabhra', Mackenzie 1914, pp. 284–88. With JGC's *arabocan* 'lintel' we may compare Donald MacAulay's *arrasbacan* 'threshold' from Bernera, Lewis (presumably the same word), as in his poem 'An t-Sean-Bhean': *far an robh am maide-buinn air fàs 'na / arrasbacan*, 'where the threshold had grown / into an obstacle' (MacAmhlaigh 1967, pp. 61, 100). See 'Life of John Gregorson Campbell', p. 685 below.

539 Connsmun or Causamul lies two miles west of Àird an Runnair in North Uist, birthplace of the poet John MacCodrum (1693–1779). The story is also told by William Mackenzie (1892–93, pp. 471–73), Alexander Carmichael (*CG*2, pp. 333–34) and William Matheson (1938, p. xxxviii), and in an Irish variant by Lady Gregory (1970, pp. 293–94). According to Mackenzie, a hole was put in the seal's paw, a rope was passed through it, and it was taken in tow (*rinneadh toll 'na spòig, chuireadh ball ann, is cheangladh ris an sgoth e*), but the huge creature was only stunned and made its escape – *thug e na habh air*, it made out to sea. Not long afterwards fog descended and the hunters lost their bearings. After hours of rowing they heard the sound of the sea breaking on some shore, and the mist suddenly lifted (*chualas muir a' bualadh ri cladach, agus thog an ceò*). They landed on a strange island which contained a solitary house. According to one version, says Carmichael, they were in Lewis, and according to others, in Mull, Tiree or Scandinavia. In the house was a gigantic grey-headed old man and a family of sons and daughters, by whom they were hospitably received, and given food and drink. "Their host," says Carmichael, "was a big grizzly-bearded man, whose face, hands, and feet were full of scars and mended bones, as if he had fought his way through some desperate battle." Mackenzie, Carmichael and Matheson give his reply in the form of a rhyme. The three versions are very similar; these are Matheson's words, put back into eight lines like Mackenzie's:

> *Ìogain a thàinig a-nall*
> *Air bharraibh nan naoi caogada tonn,*
> *Fhir a bhrist fiaclan mo chinn,*
> *Is aognaidh leam t' fhaicinn mar rium;*
> *Ìogain MhicÌogain, ged a thug mi biadh dhuit —*
> *Aran is ìm is càis' is feòil —*
> *Air mo dhà làimh, Ìogain,*
> *Gun chuir thu 'n gath am' spòig.*

("O Egan who's come over / On the tips of nine fifties of waves, / O man who broke the teeth of my head, / I'm appalled to see you with me; / Egan Mackiegan, though I've fed you – / Bread and butter and cheese and flesh – / By my two hands, Egan, / You put the spear in my paw.") For a list of references to seal traditions, including this one, see Ó Duilearga 1981, pp. 400–01. See also Bruford 1997, p. 121.

540 'Flanders Moss' is usually given as *a' Mhòine Fhlànrasach*; JGC's *(a') Mhòinteach Fhlansrach* shows metathesis *ras > sr*. The name clearly derives from 'Flanders', because of its flatness, or because in the middle ages Flemish engineers were brought to drain it,

or both. This led to the association with the black arts and Michael Scott, for whom see pp. 162–63. As to why Michael should wish to do such a thing in the first place, we need look no further than the frightful dearth of peat that came to afflict Tiree by 1843, see note 246.

541 For generations, indeed centuries, the 'Mull Doctor' and 'Islay Doctor' were leading members of the pre-eminent family of hereditary physicians in the Highlands and islands, the Beatons or *Clann Mhic Bheatha*, for whom see Bannerman 1986 and Beith 1995, pp. 45–73. The story given here is a variant of one more commonly told of Gaelic physicians, that they could tell the disease that was in a house by observing the smoke rising from its smoke-hole.

542 The reader may perhaps assume that these Highland chiefs were believed to have studied the black arts because they were savages. The opposite is the case. What folklore regarded as uncanny was the ability to read and write; what it regarded as truly diabolical was attendance at a university. Michael Scott was a leading academic; the Gaelic physicians possessed manuscripts translated from Latin at Montpelier, and passed on higher education in their own schools in Ireland; even in the sixteenth century some Highland chiefs (e.g. Lachlan Mòr MacLean, for whom see pp. 53–54) were literate in several languages, and from the seventeenth most of them were sent to the Lowlands or England for their education. There are various social and cultural reasons for the association of universities with the black arts, one of them being the study of anatomy and the associated practice of dissection. What is perhaps of greater interest is that the captain of a Spanish warship 'knew the black art himself' (p. 186); perhaps this shows that he was seen as a technocrat rather than a warrior, or perhaps Spain partook of Italy's superior reputation in the black art (note 238). See also notes 554, 618 and 936.

543 The section 'Unlucky Actions' (p. 137) provides an adequate explanation, one would have thought.

544 For this story see also Stewart 1823, pp. 88–89, and MacDonald 1972, pp. 20–21. Cf. 'Michael Scott: Making the Devil your Slave', pp. 162–63.

545 *Sloc an Tàilisg* is 'the Pit of Backgammon' or 'the Gambling Pit'. *Tàileasg* is in origin simply 'tables' and may therefore refer to any table-game, but the numerous references to *tàileasg* in the Gaelic verse of the sixteenth and seventeenth centuries point to a form of backgammon in which money was wagered (MacWhite 1948, MacilleDhuibh 31.3.95, 14.4.95). Since the devil was strongly associated in Protestant Gaelic tradition with the playing of cards (see 'Card-Playing', pp. 160–61), one can see why an impressionable individual might have expected to see the devil in a place called *Sloc an Tàilisg*. Neil MacDonald (*Niall na Buaile*, d. 1872), a bachelor, lived at a place called *a' Bhuaile Bheag* on the south-east coast of Coll; Betty MacDougall (1978a, p. 24) calls him 'the last person to live in the rough bounds between Airigh Mhaoraich and Airigh Bhoidheach, Sorasdal' (see also Mac a Phì 1938, pp. 38–39, 62–63).

546 Lev. 11: 7; Num. 28: 22; Num. 29: 22–38; Deut. 14: 8; Mark 5: 13; Luke 8: 33. For 'More' read 'Browne'. JGC here misquotes Brand (1849, vol. 2, p. 517): "The learned Sir Thomas Browne is full on this subject of popular superstition in his Vulgar Errors: 'The ground of this opinion at first,' says he, 'might be his frequent appearing in the shape of *a Goat*,' (this accounts also for his *horns* and tail,) 'which answer this description. This was the opinion of the ancient Christians concerning the apparition of Panites, Fauns, and Satyrs; and of this form we read of one that appeared to Anthony in the Wilderness. The same is also confirmed from expositions of Holy Scripture. For whereas it is said, Thou shalt not offer unto devils: the original word is Seghuirim, that is, rough and hairy goats, because in that shape the devil most often appeared, as is expounded by the Rabins, as Tremellius hath also explained, and as the word Ascimah, the God of Emath, is by some conceived.' He observes, also, that the goat was the emblem of the sin-offering, and is the emblem of sinful men at the day of Judgment."

Sir Thomas Browne (1605–82) was an English physician, scholar and author, noted for his wide, eccentric learning and quaint, exotic prose style, see Anon. 1830, pp. 60–83. The work here quoted is his *Pseudodoxia Epidemica* of 1646, better known as *Vulgar Errors*. JGC is confusing him with the better-known Sir Thomas More (1478–1535), English statesman, humanist and poet, author of *Utopia* and Lord Chancellor to Henry VIII, by whom he was executed.

For the representation of the devil in folklore see Dalyell 1834, pp. 546–51; Macbain 1887–88, pp. 237–40; Mackay 1914, pp. 418–22; Polson 1926, pp. 156–62, and 1932, pp. 40–62; McPherson 1929, pp. 134–44; MacDonald 1958b, pp. 140–43; Macdonald 1982, pp. 218–19.

547 Job 1: 7 and 2: 2; Zechariah 1: 8–11; cf. MacilleDhuibh 8.3.02.

548 For a more complete listing (thirty-six names) see Black 2002, pp. 16–17 – to which we may add *am fear nach còir* 'the unkind man/one' (note 379 above), *am fear mosach* 'the meanie' (Maclagan 1902, p. 107), *an droch rud* (Mackay 1914, p. 418), *am fear as miosa* or *am fear a bu mhiosa* (Mac a Phì 1938, pp. 55, 77) and *an dubh-sgoileir* 'the black scholar' (Brownlie 1971, p. 21). That would make forty-one. In his song on the Rev. John MacLeod, M.D. (pp. 651–53), JGC himself uses *an nathair* 'the snake, serpent', for which see Black 2002, p. 17. Macbain points out (1897–98, p. 167) that *Iain Dubh* is 'a mild sobriquet for the Devil', and that *mac an riabhaich*, another of his names, should probably therefore be understood as *mac Iain Riabhaich*. Carmichael's *Saothair an Daobh* 'the Devil's Work' (*CG6*, p. 122), a common name for a trap-dyke or ditch dug as a pitfall – otherwise known as *Lorg an Fhir Mhillidh* 'the Track of the Destroyer', certainly one of the devil's names – should I think be understood as *Saothair Iain Duibh*. And when a man in a Benbecula story encounters the devil at a place called *Abhainn Muileann Iain Duibh* ('the River of Black John's Mill'), one cannot help wondering if there is a connection (*Tocher* 21, pp. 204–07).

549 This name appears to have undergone an unusual degree of corruption in the folklore record. The Islayman Thomas Pattison wrote in 1862 (NLS Adv. MS 50.1.13 (ii), f. 485r, cf. Henderson 1911, p. 269): "It seems if you make a 'Taghairm' the 'Mac-Mollach' will come and tell you anything you ask him." Much more curiously, it is hard not to see 'Meig Mullach', 'Meg Mulloch', 'Mag Moulach', 'Maug Vuluchd' or 'Meig Mallach', the brownie of Tullochgorum House in Strathspey, as a further development. He (or she) first appears on record *c.* 1693 in a letter about second sight from the 'gentleman's son in Strathspey being a student in divinity' quoted in note 315 above (Hunter 2001, pp. 150–51, cf. MacRae 1908, p. 53, and Gordon 1960, p. 48): "There was one James Mack-coil-vic-Alaster alias Grant in Glenbruin near Kirk-Michael in Strathawin that had this sight; who, I hear of severals that were well acquainted what him, was a very honest man & <of right> blameless conversation. he used ordinarily by looking to the fire, to foretell what strangers would come to his house, the next day or shortly thereafter; by their habit & arms; & sometimes also by their names; and if anie of his goods or cattell were amissing; he would direct his servants to the very place where to find them, whether in a mire or upon dry ground; he would also tell if the beast were already dead, or if it would die ere they could come to it: and in winter if they were thick about the fire-side; he would desire them to make room to some others that stood by tho they did not see them, else some of <you> would be quickly thrown into the midst of it. but whether this man saw anie more than Brownie and Meig Mullach, I am not very sure: some say he saw more continually, & would be often very angry like, & something troubled, nothing visibly moving him: others affirm, he saw those two continually & sometimes many more . . . Megg Mullach, & Brownie . . . are two ghosts, which (as it is constantly reported) of old haunted a family in Strathspey of the name of Grant. they appeared, the first in the likeness of a young lass the 2nd of <a> young lad."

The 'young lass' next appears *c.* 1707 in a manuscript 'Root, Rise, and Offspring of the name of Grant', one of various copies of which is cited by Sir John Graham Dalyell (1834, p. 541): "Meg Mullach seems to have been of diminutive size: something of the browny tribe. She was 'a little hary creatur, in shape of a famel child,' serving in the family of Grant of Tullochgorum, 'till, by the blessing of God the Lord, reformation from popery, and more pure preaching of the gospel, she is almost invisible.' *Mag Moulach* is said to signify; one with the left hand hairy."

A different view of the brownie's sex is presented by Walter Macfarlane (*c*.1699–1767) in his *Geographical Collections* (1906–08, vol. 3, p. 243): "Opposite to Kincharden, lyeth the Parish of Inver-Ellon belonging to the Laird of Grant. The Chief family here is that of the Clanphadrike, Tullachcorume being the Head of that Tribe of the name of Grant. In old there frequented this Family a Spirit called Meg Mulloch. It appeared like a little Boy, and in dark nights would hold a candle before the Goodman, and shew him the way home, and if the Goodwife would not come to bed, it would cast her in beyond him and if she refused to bring what he desired, it would cast it before him. Excellent corns here."

What appears to have happened is that *mac* of *mac mollachd* had become *màg* (genitive *méig*) in line with the devil's exalted status (see note 625), but that *màg mollachd* was no longer correctly understood in Strathspey, where *màg* was known only as a feminine noun meaning, as Dwelly says (1977, p. 622), 'paw', 'claw', 'ludicrous term for the hand'; when subsequently shortened to *mag* through loss of stress it was thought by some to be the Lowland forename Meg. Certain learned members of the Synod of Moray seem to have retained a better understanding, however, judging by Lachlan Shaw's history of Moray (1775, p. 306): "Apparitions were every where talked of and believed. Particular Families were said to be haunted by certain Demons, the good or bad Genius's of these Families: Such as; on Speyside, the Family of Rothemurchus, by *Bodach an Dun*, i.e. 'The Ghost of the Dune.' The Baron of Kinchardine's Family, by *Red Hand*, or 'A Ghost one of whose hands was blood-red.' Gartinbeg by *Bodach-Gartin*. Glenlochie, by *Brownie*. Tullochgorm, by *Maag Moulach*, i.e. 'One with the left hand all over hairy.' I find in the Synod Records of Moray, frequent orders to the Presbyteries of Aberlaure and Abernethie, to enquire into the truth of *Maag Moulach's* appearing: But they could make no discovery, only that one or two men declared, they once saw, in the evening, a Young Girl, whose left hand was all hairy, and who instantly disappeared."

A full text of the 'Root, Rise, and Offspring of the name of Grant' was printed privately for Sir Archibald Grant of Monymusk in 1876. It refers to two specific 'familiars' of the Grants (Chambers 1876, pp. 24–25, cf. Gordon 1960, p. 47): "The one following Clan Daunachy, called Protach Charter, and the little spirit following Tullochgorim, called Meg Mullach or Phronach, a little hairy creature in the shape of a female child – this little familiar spirit followed the family and served for great drudgery to them, till by the blessing of God since the more pure preaching of the Gospel and reformation from Popery, the same is altogether invisible and extinct."

'Protach Charter' will be a misreading of 'Protach Gharten', *Proitseach Ghartain*, 'the Boy of Garten', an alternative rendering of Shaw's *Bodach-Gartin* 'the Peasant of Garten' (see Gray 1987, pp. 206–08); 'Phronach' will be a feminine adjective, probably *bhronnach* 'big-bellied' rather than *bhrònach* 'sad'.

Thomas Pennant came across Shaw's book, and refers in later editions of his 1769 tour to 'Maug Moulach, or the girl with the hairy left hand' (Pinkerton 1809, p. 69). It looks as if *mollachd* 'cursing' was persistently misunderstood (and mispronounced) as *molach* 'hairy' (cf. *Dòmhnall Molach*, p. 176), no doubt because 'a curse' in Strathspey was *mallachd* (cf. note 569). Inevitably the next development was to *Màg Mholach*, and this is at least half reflected by W. Grant Stewart's 'Maug Vuluchd' (1823, p. 144, and 1860, vol. 2, pp. 140–45). After describing the male brownie he says (1823, pp. 143–44): "The female was more pawky in her ways; and, instead of being a laughing-stock to the female-servants with whom she wrought, she was a sort of a mistress over them. She was seldom on good terms with them, in consequence of the fidelity with which she reported their neglect of duty to their master or mistress. It was her custom to wear a super-abundance of hair, in consequence of which, she was commonly called '*Maug Vuluchd*,' or 'Hairy Mag.' Mag was an honest and excellent housekeeper, and had the service of the table generally assigned her, in which capacity she was extremely useful. The dexterity and care with which she covered the table, always invisible, was not less amusing to strangers than it was convenient to their host. Whatever was called for came as if it floated on the air, and lighted on the table with the utmost ease and celerity; and, for cleanliness and attention, she had not her equal in this land."

Sir Walter Scott had already come up (1803, p. cvi, cf. Dorson 1968, p. 109) with a further variation on the name, May, and in the introduction which he wrote for the Waverley edition of *The Monastery* in 1830 he suggested that 'May' and the tutelary spirits of the neighbouring families might be thought of as demons (Scott 1893a, vol. 1, pp. xxix–xxx): "These demons, if they are to be called so, announced good or evil fortune to the families connected with them; and though some only condescended to meddle with matters of importance, others, like the May Mollach, or Maid of the Hairy Arms, condescended to mingle in ordinary sports, and even to direct the Chief how to play at draughts." She subsequently becomes *May Moullach* ('a girl, who had her arm covered with hair') in note 2H (XXXIII) to 'The Lady of the Lake' (Lockhart 1869, p. 242; Robertson 1904, p. 291).

Even after Scott's time, in Gaelic-speaking Glenlivet *Meg Mholach* was believed to survive still as the last and best of the brownies. She made her home in the farmhouse of Achnarrow (Calder 1914–15, p. 13): "One day some unexpected visitors arrived at Achnarrow. The goodwife busied herself in preparing refreshment for them. With Highland hospitality, she gave the best that the house afforded. She lamented to the servant girl that she had no cheese. No sooner had she said so than two large 'kebbucks' came rolling to her feet, and a voice sung out, 'Anything more?' The servant got frightened, but her mistress simply remarked that they came from her friend Maggie. The mystery surrounding this strange being was never satisfactorily explained."

The identity of Mag, Meg or May with *mac mollachd* is brought full circle by Henderson (1911, p. 73 and cf. pp. 55, 177), who says of the Manx *phynnodder(r)ee* (for whom see p. 102 above) that 'he is the "Dun Haired One,"' and parallel to the *Mag Molach* (Hairy Paw or Hand) of the Highlands, where it is a synonym for the Devil'. Curiously, Robert Sim tells a story (1862, pp. 95–96) about 'Meg Mulloch' from Strathbogie in Highland Aberdeenshire which resembles that of the *phynnodder(r)ee*: when stones for building a new church at Hecklebirnie in the parish of Drumdalgie (now part of Cairnie) disappear in the night, the mystery is put down to the 'known or alleged good understanding' between the gudeman of Hecklebirnie (the one man who is against the building of the new church) and Meg Mulloch. Finally, writing in 1914, Alexander Macdonald from Glenmoriston, one of the Grant territories in the west, refers (1982, p. 227) to 'the "Mha'ag Mhullach," and others often mentioned in the fairy tales of Strathspey' – thus making it clear that, whatever the creature's name was, to him at least it was not Meg. See also MacRitchie 1890, p. 158; McPherson 1929, p. 107; Spence 1948, pp. 38–39, 234; Gray 1987, p. 196; and note 569 below.

550 'Biter' (i.e. the devil as serpent), 'Annihilator', 'Thief'. JGC's spellings are *Bidein, Dithean, Bradaidh*.

551 See p. 181, where JGC's *A Chonnain* ('Devil') is in fact St Connan. His *aisling connain* is correctly *aisling chonnain*; the term has nothing to do with the name Connan. It appears to be a corruption of *aisling chollainn* 'a sexual dream' (cf. Black 2001, pp. 419–20, 460) and is clearly related to Middle Irish *aislingi coildnidi* (Gwynn and Purton 1911–12, p. 155; DIL s.v. *colnaide*). For *connan* 'lust' see NLS MS 14990, f. 342r.

552 This matter is complex. On the one hand there is a clear connection between Conan Còrr the wren and Conan Maol the jester of the Féinn – both are impudent trouble-makers, cf.

Bruford and MacDonald 1994, pp. 215–19, 458. On the other hand there is a clear, albeit much more extraordinary, connection between St Connan and the devil. The amusing story of Conan Còrr the wren, told in one case by JGC himself (Campbell 1895, pp. 121–22, McDonald 1911–12, pp. 371–74, and *CG*4, p. 6), is simply a children's tug-o'-war game in which each of Conan's twelve sons, one after the other, joins the effort to pull a root out of the ground, and they all fall in a heap; his jester-like character is much to the fore in other stories, however (Campbell 1890, vol. 1, p. 285; Campbell 1895, pp. 120–22; cf. *Tocher* 4, pp. 108–16).

The confusion between St Connan of Dalmally and the devil appears to have resulted from stories in which the saint fights the devil in hell for the souls of the nearly-damned of his flock. In areas where Connan was unknown his place appears to have been taken by Conan the jester, and this is the tradition relayed by Nicolson (1951, p. 53) in presenting certain sayings. *Beatha Chonain am measg nan deamhan: "Mas olc dhomh, chan fheàrr dhaibh."* 'Conan's life among the demons: "If bad for me, for them no better."' *Is olc do bheatha, 'Chonain!* "Bad is your life, Conan!" Once, according to the Rev. Neil Campbell (NLS MSS 14989, f. 299, and 14990, f. 184r), when St Connan had been cutting wood he sat down with his bill-hook beside him, and the devil, accidentally walking into it, thought it was his nails and fled. It was stories like these, apparently, that were picked up by Sir Walter Scott and used in *Waverley* (1892, vol. 2, p. 103). "And will ye face thae tearing chields the dragoons, Ensign Maccombich?" "Claw for claw, as Conan said to Satan, Mrs Flockhart, and the deevil tak the shortest nails." See also Campbell 1891, pp. 73–74.

St Connan's cult was well known in north Skye, where we find *Cill Chonnain* at Trumpan Head in Waternish and *Abhainn Chonnain*, the River Conon at Uig, so it is highly significant that the witch from Trotternish who drowned Iain Garbh of Raasay is said to have capsized his boat with words such as those cited by the Rev. Donald MacQueen of Kilmuir (NLS Adv. MS 73.2.21, f. 30r, cf. MacLeod 1931–33, p. 392):

> Gaoth tuath bho ifrinn fhuair
> A thionnd'as am muir ri aon uair
> A Chonnain, cuir 'na deaghaidh
> 'Na sradan tein' on teinntean.

MacQueen translates: "A north wind from cold hell, that in one hour drives the sea upwards from the bottom, St Conan push it on in sparks of fire, as from the hearth." Since no witch would summon a saint, we may conclude that – thanks perhaps to the Reformation – St Connan and the devil had merged into one. See p. 181 and note 619.

JGC refers both here and at p. 563 to the *Féill Connain* as the autumn market in Glenorchy. The name properly belongs to the fair held there on 8 March OS, 19/20 March NS, latterly the third Wednesday of the month. A traditional saying fixes it at *còig seachdainean den earrach, air Di-Ciadain*, 'five weeks of spring, on a Wednesday' (NLS MS 14990, f. 185r, cf. 14989, f. 299v). This March fair is, I believe, the one so splendidly described by Alexander Carmichael in *CG*3, p. 141. However, by Acts of Parliament in 1669, 1672 and 1686 the Campbells of Glenorchy obtained authorisation to hold fairs in the parish in September and October as well. That in September will be the *Féill Ròid* or Rood Fair of Glenorchy, described by Carmichael (1905–06, p. 350) as 'no less famous' than the *Féill Chonnain*. By 1843 just two were held annually: St Connan's on the third Wednesday of March and St Andrew's on the fourth Tuesday of November (Maclean 1845, p. 103). By 1860 the latter had been discontinued, but its place was taken by a feeing and cattle market held on the Friday after the autumn fair at Kilmichael Glassary, which was on the Tuesday before the last Wednesday of October – in other words, the new Glenorchy fair was on the last Friday of October or the first Friday of November (Marwick 1890, pp. 38, 60, 73). Judging from JGC's evidence, it took the name of the old March fair; this was hardly surprising, given that Connan was the patron of the parish, and the site was at *Dìseart Chonnain*, 'St Connan's Hermitage' (the place known in English as Dalmally), right opposite the churchyard: *Ma bhios mi beò bidh mi air Féill Connain, agus mura bi bidh mi m'a coinneamh* (NLS MS 14990, f. 185r). "If I live I'll be at St Connan's Fair, and if I die I'll be opposite it."

553 For the same story in Ireland, Wales and northern Europe see Puhvel 1965; Gregory 1970, pp. 217–18; Ó Duilearga 1981, pp. 158, 389; Ní Anluain 1991. Highland examples include Macbain 1887–88, pp. 237–38, and Matheson 1891–92, p. 10. The motif is ML 3015 'The Card-Players and the Devil', see 'Index to Tales', p. 732 below. For 'devil's books' see for example the poem 'Cluich nan Cairtean' ('Card-Playing') by Lachlan MacLachlan (*c.*1729–1801), a godly schoolmaster of Abriachan (Rose 1851, p. 100, cf. Maclean 1914–15, p. 14). He tells of his disappointment at finding two men (of whom he had expected better things) playing cards, and ends:

> *Bha ann a-siud milleadh tìoma*
> *Is solas dìomhain ga chaitheamh*
> *Is paisg de leabhraichean Shàtain*
> *Eadar dà làimh fir an taighe.*

"What was there was a waste of time / With light being pointlessly consumed / And a pack of Satan's books / Between the two hands of the host."

554 See Cheape 1993. Quite a strong case can be made for identifying a manuscript now in the National Library of Scotland, Adv. MS 72.1.3, as the 'Red Book of Appin'. A substantial and very attractively illuminated vellum book of eighty-five folios written in Gaelic in the fifteenth or sixteenth century, it contains a tract on materia medica and a number of miscellaneous cures and charms, and has strong connections with Appin. During the sixteenth century it was in the possession of the Mull Beatons. It was brought to Appin *c.* 1620 by the *Ollamh Muileach* of the day, James Beaton from Dervaig (Bannerman 1986, pp. 49–54, 142; MacilleDhuibh 20.8.93). At f. 22r he prescribes an infusion of betony for Duncan Stewart of Appin's ailing wife: *A deoch so thabart ren ól do Chatlín nin Neil ben mheic Eoin.* "Give a drink of this to Kathleen daughter of Neil, the wife of *Mac Iain*." At f. 80v he jots down a record of his attendance on the Stewarts: *A ceann mhis domhar do chuiagh me asiunna agus a ceann mhis do gheamradh do theanic me ann agus da oidhce do bi mi ann agus risd a ceann .vi seachtmhuin agus iii oidhce do thanigh me risd go folbh.* ("At the end of a month of autumn I left Shuna, and at the end of a month of winter I came there and I was there for two nights. And again at the end of six weeks and three nights the time has come for me to leave.") One of Stewart of Appin's homes, *Caisteal Shiunna*, was on the island of Shuna, which lies in Loch Linnhe half a mile from what is now Appin House.

Further references to Stewarts of Appin have been jotted on what is now the inside back cover. The present cover is reddish-yellow but dates only from the nineteenth century, presumably replacing an earlier one of cowskin which may of course have been red or reddish in colour. *Leabhar dearg na fiosachd* appears to have been a generic term in popular tradition for a 'red book of supernatural knowledge' (MacDougall 1891, p. 302), see note 489 above. Adv. MS 72.1.3 has been described in detail by Mackinnon (1912, pp. 17–22) and Mackechnie (1973, pp. 129–34).

555 By 'an entire horse' JGC means an uncastrated stallion, see also pp. 178 and 273.

556 The area described is in the Braes of Lorn. *Abhainn Cam Linne*, a tributary of the Nant, lies halfway between Glen Lonan and Loch Awe. Its source is at Midmuir – *am Monadh Meadhonach.* The Berchan (or Bearachan) River flows south and east from the same area into Loch Awe at Fernoch (for which see 'At Erray, Mull', p. 98). The six-inch Ordnance Survey map published in 1875 shows 'Fernoch Mill (Corn)' on its left bank.

557 Watson (2002, p. 112) makes the name *Inbhir na h-Aidhle* – 'the Estuary of the Adze', referring to its shape. As for NLS Adv. MS 72.1.3, all we know is that it passed, directly or indirectly, from James Beaton, who had it *c.* 1621, to the Rev. John Beaton, who had it *c.* 1671, and that it was subsequently obtained by Robert Freebairn, bookseller, Edinburgh, who sold it to the Advocates' Library in 1736. On the mythical Red Book of Appin, whose pages were said to glow 'red hot like metal plates in a fire', see MacDonald n.d., p. 9.

558 Kilmore is at Sron-Charmaig on Loch Faochan (Feochan), see p. 85. For Michael Scot(t) and the ravens see p. 158. Loch Con lies two miles north of Loch Erochty on the march between Rannoch and the Braes of Atholl.

559 Literally 'to get the knowledge of Shrovetide'.

560 *Smàladh an teine*: 'smooring the fire' by placing damp peats upon it which will keep it alive through the night without flaring up, see pp. 10 and 39. Fires were only fully extinguished once a year at Beltane.

561 "Look at your left foot!"

562 For the story told in full in Gaelic see Campbell 1889, pp. 46–53. The motif is characterised by MacDonald (1994–95, p. 60) as 'carried by the devil or by evil spirits'. For other stories about Michael Scot(t) see Stewart 1823, pp. 77–89; MacInnes 1963; MacDonald 1972, pp. 17–18; *Tocher* 25, pp. 30–32; Gray 1987, pp. 16–17; Bruford and MacDonald 1994, pp. 465, 481; GUL MS Gen. 1090/28, pp. 65–72. He has been described as 'the leading intellectual in western Europe during the first third of the thirteenth century'; according to Lowland tradition his birthplace was Balwearie in Fife, his principal residence Aikwood Tower near Selkirk, and his last resting place Melrose Abbey, but he is known to have spent his life abroad (Thorndike 1965, pp. 1, 11). See also Brown 1897 and Ó Duilearga 1981, p. 386.

563 *Ruig* is Rigg, the township at the foot of the Storr. 'Parson Sir Andro' may be identified with some confidence as Gill-Anndrais Dubh (fl. 1600), one of the Beatons of Connista near Duntulm who served as physicians to the MacDonalds of Sleat. His identity as a member of two learned professions is underlined by the survival of his hand in various Gaelic manuscripts in the National Library of Scotland. In the margin of a collection of religious verse, Adv. MS 72.1.29, f. 7r, we come upon him writing . . . *a duillibh o Ghiollainndris mac Domhnaill mhic Eoin* ('. . . in leaves from Andrew son of Donald son of John'). On the final page (otherwise blank) of a medical manuscript, Adv. MS 72.1.27, f. 5v, we find . . . *le so an . . . og . . . o Gillanntris Mac an Ollamg ma(d) ail le Diagh curigh* . . . ('. . . with this the . . . young . . . from Andrew Son of the Doctor if God wishes will send . . .'). On the former cover of Adv. MS 72.1.27, now Adv. MS 84.1.16, which appears to have previously formed part of a commentary in Latin on a legal treatise, he humorously notes his ownership of Adv. MS 72.1.27 and his disapproval of its calligraphy: *Me fein leobhar Ghillanndrias duibh 7 ni maith an litir so agam.* "I am Black Andrew's book and this writing of mine is no good." See Bannerman 1986, pp. 23, 108.

564 It would be interesting to identify this individual. Kilfinichen and Kilviceon appear to have been united early in the seventeenth century, i.e. before the reign of Charles II. No other source that I have seen lists a minister of the parish named Kennedy (cf. Scott 1915–50, vol. 4, p. 112; MacLean 1923–25, vol. 2, p. 318). There is however a gap between 1643 and 1682 which is only partly filled by a James Fraser (some point before 1667) and a Duncan Bethune (in 1677). It appears that the history of the parish in the seventeenth century has yet to be written, and that Kennedy should figure in it.

565 The *caibeal* of Kilviceon lies halfway between Loch Assapol and the sea on the road south from Bunessan to the township of Sgurra (Scoor). A mile to the west of Sgurra lies the little harbour of Port Bheathain.

566 JGC did not offer a translation of the couplet, so I have provided one. It is the beginning of a poem on the Gaick disaster by Duncan MacKay or Davidson (*Donnchadh Gobha, c.*1730–

*c.*1825), see Sinton 1906, p. 282, and Black 2001, p. 512. The poet appears to be referring to the choice offered by the Julian and Gregorian calendars with regard to intercalation. In the Julian calendar 1800 was a leap year containing 366 days, the extra one being of course 29 February. In the Gregorian calendar it was not a leap year and contained the usual 365 days. As an old man and an elder of the church, Donnchadh Gobha was the kind of person who had little time for the Gregorian calendar, which had been introduced by Act of Parliament in 1751 but which was still not fully adhered to in the Highlands and Islands even as late as the first half of the twentieth century. We may assume that the poem was made in January 1800, and what he is saying, I think, is that when dating the accounts for his smithy he is proposing to eliminate 31 December 1799 in preference to 29 February 1800 – which means that come 1 March he will be back in line with the law.

567 All this is true, and one can go further – the story, usually called 'Call Ghàig', was carried to Cape Breton Island, and a quite extraordinary version of it, 'Caiptean Dubh Bhaile Chròic', which tells of the pact made by the Black Captain with the devil and the catastrophe that resulted when the devil returned to claim his own, was recorded there by Dr John Shaw on 22 March 1978 from Dan Angus Beaton, Blackstone, Inverness County (MacNeil 1987, p. xxvi). I am grateful to Dr Shaw for sending me a transcript of this many years ago. The extraordinary speed with which fact turned into fiction may in fact be tracked through a string of early published references to the incident, beginning with the deaths column of *The Scots Magazine*, January 1800, p. 71: "Major Macpherson of Lorick, and four other gentlemen, unfortunately perished in a storm of snow, when on a shooting party on the Duke of Gordon's grounds in Badenoch."

James Hogg had picked up the story by 1810. He tells of the Captain's altercation, when on a hunting party, with a stranger who disappears as mysteriously as he appears; of how he arranges a second hunting party, declaring 'that he *must* and *would* go'; of how 'one solitary dog only returned, and he was wounded and maimed'; of how the search party finds mangled corpses, 'one nearly severed in two'; of how the bothy has been torn from its foundations, and no one is able to account for what has happened, supernatural agency thus being implied but not stated; in other words, he presents all the elements of the story except the most salient one, the avalanche (Hogg 2000, pp. 135–38). He told it again as 'Dreadful Story of Macpherson' (Hogg 1821, vol. 1, pp. 190–94).

In NLS Adv. MS 73.1.14, pp. 129–32, is a detailed statement of what actually happened, regrettably incomplete, in the hand of the Rev. Dr Mackintosh MacKay (1793–1873), who was minister of Laggan, the parish in which the event took place, from 1825 to 1832. I have published an edited transcript of it (MacilleDhuibh 12.1.90). It was prepared for Sir Walter Scott (MacKay n.d., p. 9): "In producing his article for the *Foreign Quarterly Review*, Sir Walter did me the honour to ask my assistance in collecting for him the historical parts of the case, in the most *vraisemblable* shape I might be able to find him. This I had little difficulty in accomplishing."

Scott's article was about the supernatural in fiction, however, and placed rather more weight on an alleged letter from 'an amiable and accomplished nobleman some time deceased'. This was subsequently said by the editor, Robert Cadell, to be 'the late regretted and beloved Lord W—— S——r', but the nobleman was himself a fiction. In this version, as in Hogg's, the bothy is destroyed by a storm, and snow is not mentioned; supernatural forces are implied; the Captain is 'popularly reported to be a man of no principles, rapacious, and cruel', and devious tricks are mentioned by which he obtained recruits. The nobleman's source is stated to be 'a schoolmaster in the neighbourhood of Rannoch', and Scott points out that 'the feeling of superstitious awe annexed to the catastrophe contained in this interesting narrative, could not have been improved by any circumstances of additional horror which a poet could have invented' (Scott 1827, pp. 68–70 = 1835, pp. 284–86).

This got Scott into a great deal of trouble. He received an angry letter from the Captain's daughter, Mrs Helen MacBarnet, Cluny, Grantown, 23 January 1828, demanding satisfaction for herself and her sister in the form of a public apology, and hinting darkly that, were their brother not in Mauritius, Scott could have laid himself open to a duel (NLS MS 869, f. 83r, cf. MacKay n.d., p. 10): "Neither she or I (in the absence of our only brother Captn. Macpherson of the 99th Regt now in the Isle of France) wish to push the matter so far as we know we might do."

Scott admitted to his diary (Anderson 1972, p. 451) that what he had published was 'a rawhead and bloody bones story'. He replied to Mrs MacBarnet, and a friend of MacKay's sallied forth as an intermediary to reason with her. MacKay himself drafted an apology, which duly appeared, as Scott pointed out to him afterwards, 'nearly in your own words' (MacKay n.d., p. 10). In this apology, Cadell (or rather MacKay?) begins by admitting that his own doubts about the veracity of the story were correct. After providing a detailed account of the Captain's recruiting activities he says that 'he was, in all his dealings, a man of strict honour and unblemished reputation', but that in Rannoch he was unpopular, if not feared, 'from his having been more than once engaged there, in the apprehending of deserters from the army; a species of service for which his great bodily strength, his activity, and hardiness of habits peculiarly fitted him'. On one occasion he arrested a deserter but the man escaped from his party at Dalnacardoch inn, with the result that 'the poetic talents of the districts of Rannoch and Athol, (never very celebrated,) were put in requisition to ridicule his prowess, and the military character of his clan' (Anon. 1828, pp. 352–53). In Rannoch, Badenoch had a great reputation for witchcraft (see pp. 196, 289).

Cadell (or rather MacKay?) explains that the Captain had been a keen sportsman in his youth. In 1799, when he was in the midst of 'severe pecuniary losses', his wife had died; 'both together preyed not a little on his mind, and did certainly produce a degree of change in his manners and wonted habits, at which his acquaintances could not wonder', so he returned to field sports with a passion which 'had made him obnoxious to his grace the Duke of Gordon's forester at Gaik'. Not six weeks before his death he pledged to the duke in person 'that he should never be found to contravene his grace's pleasure', upon which the duke 'allowed, or rather requested him to take a deer or two more, as he might wish, from the forest of Gaik, during that winter' (Anon. 1828, pp. 353–54). The disaster is then described in detail. Cadell(?) points to the likelihood that 'a catastrophe so fatal, and of such rare occurrence . . . would awaken into activity all the superstitious feelings of the country', and ends (*ibid.*, p. 354): "But unusual as such an event was, no one who sees the spot, and who recollects the quantity of snow then on the ground, can for a moment doubt, that the whole mystery might be readily explained by the single term of an avalanche."

No apology which used words like 'unpopular' and 'obnoxious' and revealed that the Captain had been ridiculed in a Gaelic satire (sadly no longer extant, to my knowledge) was likely to please Helen MacBarnet. She wrote again to Sir Walter saying that it was 'so far short of what I expected that my sister and myself are anything but satisfied with it' (NLS MS 869, f. 85v, cf. Anderson 1972, p. 451). MacKay confessed himself more to blame than Sir Walter, because, he said, 'the article written by *him* was throughout a dealing with the superstitions of the country, and never touching upon the deceased gentleman's character' (MacKay n.d., p. 10). His account of how fact turned into folklore during the retrieval of the bodies is illuminating (*ibid.*, pp. 8–9): "The whole male population of the three parishes forming the district of Badenoch were roused, and summoned to march in one collected body upon Gaig, the weather still continuing tempestuous and snowy. This was readily, and most creditably to the people, accomplished. All the bodies of the lamented individuals were found. The task of having these conveyed homewards was both a hard and sad task. Tokens of sadness pursued them. They found there was ice more than sufficient for them to cross the lake, which shortened their journey homeward. But in crossing that lake, a fearful and sudden squall overtook the body of travellers, of such fierceness, as absolutely to appear to minds unwontedly disturbed, altogether preternatural; and this incident gave additional impetus to the terrors which had already infected the minds of the people. The catastrophe was certainly very unusual. The report was soon noised abroad throughout the whole Highlands; and it is to be feared there was not much hesitation in ascribing it, generally, to even *diabolical* agency. I have spoken to not a few individuals who formed a portion of the body of men who went to Gaig on the sad errand: and if I attempted to reason with them on natural causes, the most emphatic reply, with very exceptional cases [*sic*], which I ever received, was a sad shake of the head. But long after the catastrophe, intelligent men, especially such as had made acquaintance with the country of Switzerland, had no difficulty in concluding that a real *avalanche* had been the cause of the whole sad event."

See also Glenmore 1859, pp. 68–73; Stewart 1860, vol. 2, pp. 188–91; Macbain 1889–90, pp. 185–86; Macpherson 1889–90, pp. 213–15; Lang 1891, pp. 46–57; Macpherson 1893, pp. 149–50; Scrope 1894, p. 111; Macpherson 1900, pp. 10–12; Macpherson 1925, pp. 9–17, 20–21; Gordon 1949, pp. 211–12; Macdonald 1982, pp. 203–04; Gray 1987, pp. 68–79, 88–89; Leitch 1990; Fleming 1997, p. 70; Mitchell 2004, pp. 137–38. In his account of 'Call Ghàig' Calum Maclean points out (1975, p. 91) that 'there are two histories of every land and people, the written history that tells what it is considered politic to tell and the unwritten history that tells everything'. His 'unwritten history' clearly crosses the unmarked boundary between fact and folklore, presenting the Black Captain not only as an unscrupulous recruiting officer but also as enjoying a pact with the devil. It would be possible to misunderstand Maclean as claiming that all of this is literal truth; what he means however is that the story furnishes splendid materials for a study of the relationships between fact, rumour and folklore. He ends memorably (*ibid.*, p. 94): "Thus came home the soulless body of the Captain of Ballachroan, a faithful servant of two principalities, the British Empire and the Powers of Darkness."

568 Born at Glentruim in 1724, and known as *Iain Dubh mac Alastair* from his dark complexion, he was second son of Alexander MacPherson of Phoness. As a young man he fought for the Jacobites under Cluny, distinguishing himself at Clifton, 18 December 1745 (Craigie 1905–06). He later obtained a commission in the 82nd Regiment and acted for some years as recruiting officer for the district, which made him unpopular (see Alexander 1917, p. 184, and Baran 1986–88, pp. 189–90); his passions were agricultural improvement and deer-hunting (Macpherson 1900, pp. 8–10, cf. Macpherson 1996a, p. 299). It has been alleged that his experiments with new methods of tillage were so successful that the more unsophisticated of his neighbours attributed them to supernatural agency (Macpherson 1893, p. 149, cf. *Tocher* 50, p. 57). This is exactly what happened to Caius Furius Cresinus, according to Pliny, and Sir Walter Scott refers in addition to an old woman somewhere in Lothian or the Borders *c.* 1800 whose successful rearing of chickens left her open to accusations of witchcraft (2001, pp. 61–62, 200); in the same way, JGC points out at p. 72 that the superiority of the Luskentyre cattle will have given rise to the belief that they were of Fairy stock, while W. B. Yeats remarked more than once (Welch 1993, pp. 208–09, 310–11) that in rural Ireland almost any exceptional cleverness, even the way a dog was trained, might be thought to be a gift from 'the others'. He told a story of a young man who did not go to church and shunned company, but worked hard and grew splendid crops, so that people said: "You may know well he has some that help him."

Equally, the Black Captain's otherworldly reputation – and the widely varying estimates of his character, see Barron 1953–59, p. 81 – may be explained by these words of Lachlan Macpherson of Biallid, written in 1847 (Macpherson 1900, p. 18): "In his latter days his liberality in assisting others embarrassed his own affairs; but in every trial, his conduct was distinguished by honour and integrity. Amidst his misfortunes he was deprived of his wife, after which he went little into society, but in his old age spent many of his days, like the ancient hunters, alone on the hills of Gaick or the corries of Beann-Aller with no other companion than his *cuilbheir* and his grey dogs!"

Save for the fact that Captain MacPherson's alleged associations were with what I have called the third otherworld and not the first, his biography thus fits the paradigm outlined by Bourke (1999, p. 59): "Eccentric, deviant, or reclusive individuals – or people with mental or physical disabilities – were often said to be 'in the fairies', or to have spent time 'away' among them; people who acquired unexplained wealth were similarly suspect, while women said to have been taken by the fairies, even if they later returned, were often infertile afterwards. These people's association with fairies might be simply a convenient metaphor, or it might be taken literally, but in either case it drew on a vast oral literature whose imagery and concepts were densely inscribed on the landscape – with fairy-forts as major reference points – and the individuals concerned were treated with caution, if not always with respect."

The song in praise of Captain MacPherson is, as JGC indicates, in MacPherson 1868, pp. 13–17. There is also a version in Sinton 1898–99, pp. 248–51, and 1906, pp. 277–81. It is by Malcolm Macintyre, otherwise known as *Calum Dubh nam Protaigean* ('Black-Haired Malcolm of the Practical Jokes'), and begins *Is beag iongnadh mi bhith dubhach*. The other song is the one by Duncan MacKay or Davidson whose first couplet is quoted at p. 164. Sinton's version of the stanza quoted here (1906, p. 283) is:

> Bha 'n t-Othaichear Dubh air an ceann,
> Chuir e cùl r'a thigh 's r'a chlann;
> Nan tuiteadh e 'n cath na Fràing,
> Cha bhiodh a chall cho farranach.

("The Black-Haired Officer was at their head, / He turned his back on his house and bairns; / Had he fallen in the battle of France / His loss would not have been so regrettable.") It sounds uncomplimentary, but was not intended to be. Sinton points out that if the Black Officer 'forsook his wife and children' – this should read 'his house and children', his wife having just died – it was only to go hunting in Gaick and lay in a store of meat for the festive season. And while the loss of his life would not have seemed so tragic had he died fighting the French, there is no evidence that he had had any part in the war against Napoleon. JGC was right in thinking that more than two songs were composed on the occasion: Sinton (1906, pp. 286–89) prints an elegy by Calum Dubh on one of the younger men killed in the tragedy, another John MacPherson, *Iain òg mac Alastair 'ic Uilleim*.

569 In Lady Gregory's stories at least, the Irish equivalent of JGC's bundle of fern appears to be 'a wool-pack coming riding down the road of itself' (Gregory 1970, p. 276). A girl called Feeney told her of a particular hollow (*ibid.*, p. 164): "Old Tom Stafford was led astray there by something like a flock of wool that went rolling before him, and he had no power to turn but should follow it."

Sim cites a variant of this from the eastern edge of the Highlands (1862, p. 94) in which the devil as *mac mollachd* has passed into Scots as Meg Mulloch, feminising himself in the process in the way shown in note 549 above: 'At a place in Ruthven, on the Isla side, called Littlemill, Meg used to appear occasionally, but only to Littlemill himself, assuming, when pleased, the semblance of a young child, and when angry, that of an old woman. She was said also to have appeared at times in the likeness of things inanimate. For instance, on the very occasion mentioned in the Legend, some had it that she was seen rolling down the "Gaet o' Couper-hill" (*i. e.*, towards Soutercroft), in the likeness of a wisp of "Pease-strae", from which a voice was heard to proceed to the effect that "a" was lost". On another occasion, it has been said, that she rolled into a company of her *proteges* (how happy they must have been in having such a protectoress!) in the shape of a "Highland Kebbuck".'

A kebbuck is a cheese, Gaelic *ceapag* 'a little block, a wheelbarrow wheel'. Sim's 'Legend' (*ibid.*, p. 7) concerns a freebooter called Peter Roy who descended on Keith with about forty men in 1667. "On their way from the upper districts, as the story runs, they received rather a strange addition to their party, in the person of a Highland prophetess, called Meg Mulloch, or Meg with the hairy hand . . . Having arrived at Keith, they took possession of the house of public entertainment at Cooperhill; and as they were regaling themselves there, Meg, from below the table, where she had, strangely enough, esconced herself, began to groan, when Roy struck at her with his foot, and cursed her to give over her groaning, as he neither wanted it nor any renewal of her predictions."

This may refer, says Sim, to a saying that if Peter Roy 'would save his neck from the "wuddie", he must keep his eyes from seeing the Pier of Leith'. His band is set upon by the townsfolk; he is wounded in the affray, captured, and sent to Leith where he is executed on the sands (*ibid.*, p. 10). Donald Shaw places the attack on Keith in 1666 and the hanging at Leith in 1667 (Glenmore 1859, pp. 140–47). He also gives Peter Roy's song, beginning *Mìle mallachd don òl . . .* ('A thousand curses on the drink . . .'); further west this was understood to have been composed by another captured freebooter of the same period, Dòmhnall Donn of Bohuntin in Lochaber (Macdonald 1982, pp. 87–88).

570   Holm is on the coast six miles north of Portree. In referring to the pig's indigo snout as 'green', JGC is using the Gaelic spectrum, whereby pale grey shading into pale green is *glas*, silvery grey shading into light blue is *liath*, and rich green shading into dark blue and shiny black is *gorm*. At p. 164 *glas dharach* is called 'green oak'. See also notes 29, 62, 156 and 431.

571   *Toirt a shuipearach dhan droch fhear* or the like, no doubt. The *taghairm* represents a substantial subject which received a great deal of attention from writers in the period 1810–30 due to the interest taken in it by Sir Walter Scott. Because of this, it enjoys unusual status as a Gaelic word which is to be found in English dictionaries. It is currently the object of research by Andrew Wiseman, a native of Lochaber who is a PhD student in the Department of Celtic, Aberdeen University. I am grateful to him for sending me a draft of his paper 'Caterwauling and Demon Raising: The Ancient Rite of the Taghairm' (*Scottish Studies*, forthcoming), the publication of which will shed some light on the possible origins of the practice and provide further references.

Though by no means the oldest, JGC's account of the *taghairm* constitutes one of the most important primary sources. As he points out (pp. 169–70), the rituals may be categorised according to whether the central role is played by cats, water, or wrapping in animal hide. Referring presumably to the judgement of folklorists such as von Sydow that 'The King of the Cats' is an exclusively Celtic development of the Pan Legend (see Ó Néill 1991, pp. 169–70), Alan Bruford has described the gathering of cats (as opposed to demons or a variety of animals) as 'a peculiarly Gaelic feature' (Bruford and MacDonald 1994, p. 450). In anthropological terms the pre-eminent part played by a gathering of cats in the surviving record of *taghairm* is certainly unusual, perhaps unique, though of course it will be connected with the role of the cat in supernatural beliefs and occult practices worldwide, and its antecedents in classical mythology remain to be fully explored.

There is, I think, evidence in the surviving record – particularly noticeable in JGC's account – that the *taghairm* story contained performance elements and was developing into pantomime. This helps to explain the prominent role given to talking cats. It also explains why the 'cat' category is last and least in Martin's account, as JGC makes clear (p. 170). It appears to have been regarded as secondary in Glenmoriston also, judging from William Mackay's account (1914, pp. 432–33), in which pride of place is given to a version of the shamanic 'hide' type in which the seer places himself in a cauldron. Mackay refers to this type as *Taghairm nan Daoine*, which we may translate 'the Summons of Men', and to the 'cat' type as *Taghairm nan Cat*, which we may translate 'the Summons of Cats'. Elements of both ancient shamanism and modern pantomime may be detected in JGC's account – the tale is also told in two languages by J. G. Mackay, 1919–22, pp. 19–24 – of a 'gifted woman' at Duntulm in Skye, Iseabail nic Raghnaill, who was asked to 'see' the whereabouts of a missing horse and cow (Campbell 1895, pp. 88–89): "Isabel said that she was not well prepared to go that day. The men asked what preparation she lacked (*'dé an cion dòigh a bh' oirre*). She then asked for one of the men's broad bonnets, and when she got it, rose, and leaving her hair, which was becoming grey, streaming over her shoulders, she put it on, and tying a goatskin round her, tying her shoes and making garters with stripes of the same fur, she put a rope of straw round her waist and took a large staff in her hand. 'She is prepared at last, and come now,' the men said. When she came in sight, the factor looked at her in amazement, for he had never before seen a creature of her appearance."

See also Armstrong 1825, pp. 535–36; Dalyell 1834, pp. 495–97, 500; C. C. 1835–36 = Henderson 1901, pp. 32–35; Maclean 1840, pp. 264–66; Cameron 1845, p. 426, followed by Macpherson 1893, pp. 94–95; NLS Adv. MS 50.1.13 (ii), f. 485r (Thomas Pattison, 1862); MacLean 1889, pp. 333–34; Sinclair 1899, pp. 349–51; Kilgour 1908, pp. 158–59; Henderson 1911, pp. 229–30, 267–69; Stewart 1928, p. 333; *Tocher* 36/37, pp. 436–37; Macdonald 1982, p. 183; McKerracher 1994, pp. 378–79; Gray 1997, pp. 30–31; Maclean-Bristol 1999, pp. 257–58; Hunter 2001, p. 60. In GUL Gen. 1042, MS 64, the Rev. James MacLagan noted simply: "Tagh-ghairm, a way of Extorting Responses by beating a man or Roasting a living Cat." For shamanism in Celtic culture see Trevarthen 2003 – she refers to the *taghairm* at p. 142 in the context of 'Burial and Sensory Deprivation' (pp. 137–39) and 'Binding' (pp. 139–43).

572 JGC may be quoting from Drummond 1842, p. 24: "This Allan McCoilduy had the charracter of one of the bravest captains in his time, which was chiefly the reason of his being so great a favourite of the great Lord I have just now mentioned. He is said to have made 32 expeaditions into his enemy's countrey for the 32 years that he lived, and three more, for the three-fourths of a year that he was in his mother's womb: whatever trewth may be in this, it is certain that his good fortune failed him in the end." It is also possible that JGC, like Drummond, had a traditional saying in mind, e.g. *creach mu choinneamh gach bliadhna d'a shaoghal, agus creach mu choinneamh gach ràidhe a bha e am broinn a mhàthar.*

The symbolism and purpose of a pantomime in Lochaber about roasting cats alive would have been clear, for the Camerons and Keppoch MacDonalds were at deadly feud with the Mackintoshes, whose claim to lands in Lochaber was bitterly contested and whose totem animal was the cat; according to Anon. 1915, when the feud came to a head at the battle of Mulroy in 1688 the Mackintosh piper played: *Thàinig na cait! Thàinig na cait!* "The cats have come! The cats have come!"

Dislike of cats was nowhere greater than in Glen Nevis, the very heart of Lochaber (though JGC offers a different explanation, see p. 190). MacCulloch rightly pointed out (1996, p. 118) that 'the Taghairm rite is said to have been performed, with its associated cats, in places distant from Lochaber where there were no Mackintoshes'; cats are a multi-purpose symbol, however, and there would be few communities where they did not have both local and global meaning, see notes 485 and 575.

573 This is not true of the Lochaber version told by Clerk (1858, pp. 94–95), MacMillan (1971, p. 193) and MacCulloch (1996, p. 113), in which Allan's demand of the King of the Cats is that he be told how to atone for his misdeeds. "You must build seven churches – one for each of the seven forays." The cat disappears into what becomes known as *Poll a' Chait* ('the Cat's Pool') in the Lochy, and Allan proceeds to build the churches. The location of these was a

topic keenly debated in the ceilidh-houses of Lochaber. Kilmallie, Kildonan (Kilmonivaig), Cill Choireil, Kilchoan (Knoydart), Arisaig, Morvern and Kilkillen (Loch Laggan) were popular candidates; see also the list in NLS MS 14990, f. 146r.

574   See p. 169. *Eaglais* means 'Church', not 'Cave'. Given by Forbes (1923, p. 178) as the *Eaglais Bhreugach* 'false or lying church', the name being 'from a rock, like a church, on East-side, Kilmuir'. Forbes goes on: "This rock, also known as *An Eaglais Bhréige*, the church of the lie or falsehood, has been described as a cave called 'the make-believe cave church,' from what was termed an altar beside it in the shape of a huge boulder whereon Clann 'Ic Cuithen performed an awful pagan ceremony of *Taghairm*, gathering summons." See MacKenzie 1995, p. 16.

575   JGC renders *Cluas an Leoghaidh* as 'the Ear of Melting' (*leaghadh* 'melting'). This makes no sense to me. In the earlier language *leoghadh* or *leodhadh* was 'cutting, hacking, mangling' (Dinneen 1927, p. 658). As I have pointed out elsewhere (MacilleDhuibh 29.6.01), *Cluas an Leoghaidh* may therefore be neatly rendered 'String Lug' on the model of David Stephen's classic children's novel *String Lug the Fox*. It is very possible, however, that *Cluas an Leoghaidh* is merely a corruption of *Cluasa-leabhra* ('Long Ears', 'Floppy Ears'), the form cited by Clerk (1858, pp. 94–95), see Dinneen 1927 s.v. *leabhar*, Dwelly 1977 s.v. *leobhar*. Elsewhere the cat is called *Cluas Mhór* 'Big Ear' (Maclean 1840, p. 266; Mac a Phì 1938, p. 55) or *Cam Dubh* 'Black Crook', 'Black One-Eye' (Stewart 1981, pp. 25–26); as 'Big Ears' Donald A. MacKenzie placed him centre-stage in a retelling which he entitled 'A Tale of Big Ears' (1931, pp. 44–46). In Stewart's satirical-sounding Lochaber version *Cam Dubh* appears to represent the Catholic church in the shape of Cardinal Beaton or the Pope, what would nowadays be called a 'Fat Cat' (MacilleDhuibh 13.7.01). In the Rev. Donald Cameron's version (1845, p. 426), later embroidered by Drummond-Norie (1898, p. 248), *Camdubh*, 'a black cat with one eye', tells Allan to atone for his guilt by building seven churches, and threatens to summon his brother, *Cluosa leabhra mo bhrathair* ('the cat with the long hanging ears, his brother'), also called *Cluasan leabhra*, who 'would take such summary vengeance, that Allan would never see his Maker's face in mercy'.

The following story told by Drummond of Balhaldy (1842, p. 29, cf. Drummond-Norie 1898, p. 249) of Allan's son Ewen, who followed him in the chiefship, provides a hint as to the real identity of *Camdubh* and *Cluasan leabhra*. "The death of his eldest sone Donald, which happned about this time, plunged him into so deep a melancholey, that he, on a sudden, resolved to give up the world, and apply himself to the works of religion and peace. To expiat for former crims, he sett out on a pilgramage to Rome; but arriving in Holland, he found himself unable to bear up against the fatigue of so long a journey, and, therefore, sent one McPhaill, a priest, who was his chaplain and confessor, to doe that job for him with the Pope. One part of the penance enjoyned him by his Holiness was to build six chappells to as many saints, which he performed. Some of them are still extant, and the ruins of the rest are yet to be seen in Lochaber and the bordering countreys."

On *Dé sam bith* . . . see Nicolson 1951, pp. 192–93. In MacilleDhuibh 29.6.01 I translated *Crois a' chlaidhimh* . . . as: "The cross of the sword be on your head, you brute – you're the pee of sweat." It looks like a combination of sanctification and of reversing an insult to turn threat into satire – any liquid coming out of String Lug can only be sweat, thanks to the heat of the fire beneath him. "This is pure pantomime, and it will have gone down a treat in the ceilidh house, especially one with a leaky roof. 'Oh yes I will!' 'Oh no you won't!' "

Equally, the men's requests make best sense in the context of a children's pantomime. Allan asks for prosperity and children, Lachlan for property, prosperity and long life. Elsewhere we are told that Allan 'made use of two words meaning wealth' while Lachlan asked for 'progeny and wealth' (Maclean 1840, p. 266). According to 'C. C.' (1835–36, p. 53 = Henderson 1901, p. 34) Allan asks for *beairteas* 'wealth', Lachlan for *beairteas agus clann* 'wealth and progeny'; elsewhere (Mac a Phì 1938, p. 55) the requests are *cuid agus clann* ('property and progeny') and *cuid agus saoghal fada 'na cheann* ('property and long life as well'). Nothing, however, produces quite the same comic reaction as *conach*, a less than ubiquitous word which is potentially a pun meaning 'doggy, canine'. JGC's reference to annual repetition of the *taghairm* suggests that the story was performed as part of one of the calendar festivals. This will be the sort of thing which, according to Skye tradition, was put a stop to by the Rev. Donald MacQueen when he walked all the way from Kilmuir to 'the Borreraig waterfall on the Scoribreck coast', a distance of over twenty miles, 'to censure the querent and his companions' (MacDonald n.d., pp. 19–20).

In presenting an account of one re-enactment Neil Morrison becomes tongue-tied with embarrassment, but says enough for us to understand that the highlight of the pantomime involved throwing cats into the fire, concluding (Mac a Phì 1938, p. 56): *Mo làmh-sa dhuibh-se ma bha am pronnusg dlùth air Lachuinn Odhar is Ailein MacEachainn nach robh tigh Iain chòir saor is am fàileadh aige gu ceann iomadh là an déidh sin.* "I guarantee you that if brimstone was close to Lachuinn Odhar and Ailein MacEachainn, good old John's house was not free of the smell of it for several days after."

This will be the sort of thing the late W. Macdonald Robertson was referring to when, introducing an account shamelessly plagiarised (as was a great deal of his material) from JGC, he remarked (1995, p. 119): "This Ceremony may be still held in certain parts of Argyll and the Inner Hebrides, including the isles of Mull and Islay. The late Mr. James MacKillop, Factor, Islay House, told me how he had witnessed 'Taghairm' with disgust."

576 A *groillein* or *greidlean* is a wooden girdle-stick or griddle-stick employed in baking oatcakes on the fire, and thus a comical word for a sword, to be used in satire – that is, when the intention is to making fighting sound easy. Iain Lom said of the MacDonald victory at Inverlochy (Watson 1959, p. 215, cf. MacKenzie 1964, pp. 22–23):

> *Sin nuair chruinnich mór dhragh na falachd*
> *An àm rùsgadh nan greidlean tana —*
> *Bha iongnan nan Duibhneach ri talamh*
> *An déidh an lùithean a ghearradh.*

("That's when the great pressure of bloodletting tightened its circle / In the time of unsheathing the slender girdle-sticks – / The Campbells' fingernails were stuck into the ground / After their sinews had been severed.") See also MacLeod 1952, pp. 6–7, and note 33.

577 Like much else in JGC's account of *taghairm*, this sounds like a satirical commentary on tradition rather than tradition itself, the target this time being the custom of *faoighe* 'thigging, genteel begging', see note 743. The husband's reply cannot be right – *ach* is surely *seach* 'rather than', but *sùil an t-slauchdain*, JGC's 'eye of softness', is a greater puzzle. The spelling *slauchdain* suggests a pronunciation roughly in line with *slabhcan, slòcan, slabhagan,* 'seaweed, called brown alva, boiled to a jelly', 'sea sloke, thin silklike seaweed growing on flattish rocks' (McDonald 1958, p. 222, cf. MacDonald 1934–36b, p. 45). The recipe is given from the Maclagan MSS in *Tocher* 27, p. 181: "After it has been well washed so as to remove all sand from it, it is boiled in a little water, and thickened to the consistency of porridge, by the addition of oat or barley meal. Salt, and a little butter are added. This is a well known dish in Lewis, and is called *Tobhtal*. It is eaten warm." Another possibility is Macbain's *slaucar* 'a slouching fellow (Suth.), a taunter; from Norse *slókr*, slouching fellow, whence Eng. *slouch*' (1896, p. 295), adopted by Dwelly (1977, p. 848) as *slabhcar* with the additional definition 'spiritless fellow'. My best guess is that JGC wrote *t-slauchdarseach* and that the printer read this as *t-slauchdain,ach* – naturally inserting a space after what looked like a comma. In MacilleDhuibh 29.6.01, I therefore put forward the translation:

"Do you suppose it was the eye of a miser rather than the eye of a soldier as should be?" See p. 685 below.

578 Martin 1716, pp. 110–11 = 1999, p. 77. Note 2T (Lockhart 1869, pp. 244–45) began life as note I on Canto Fourth (Scott 1810, pp. 360–61) and later became note XLIV (Robertson 1904, p. 295). This is the 'water' taghairm. Ramsay of Ochtertyre gives an account of what he calls *taghairm an uisge* ('summons by water') containing both 'water' and 'hide' elements (1888, vol. 2, p. 460). It is ascribed to 'McCurdhean' (a misprint for McCuidhean, i.e. MacQueen) and stated to have been performed at the waterfall of 'Eas-bhercraig' (a misprint for Eas-bhereraig, i.e. Eas Bhearraraig, six miles north of Portree). It is strongly shamanic (MacilleDhuibh 13.7.01). Pennant gives something similar (1998, p. 313). See also Henderson and Cowan 2001, p. 54.

579 By *chur* in lines 1–3 we should understand 'sowing' – 'for sowing the seeds of lies, flattery, theft'. William MacKenzie cites the same stanza in one of his two books (1930, p. 16), but offers a version with *dhubh* 'black' in the other (1995, p. 16):

> *Clann 'Ic Cuithein dhubh nam briag,*
> *Clann 'Ic Cuithein dhubh an t-sodail,*
> *Clann 'Ic Mhanainn dhubh na braide*
> *Ged nach b' fhaid' iad na cas biodaig.*

("The black MacQueens of the lies, / The black MacQueens of the flattery, / The black MacVannins of the theft / Though no bigger than a dagger handle.") This is not entirely convincing; perhaps what MacKenzie actually heard was *ghur* 'hatching' – 'for hatching lies, flattery, theft'.

By *Clann 'ic Cuthain* JGC will mean *Clann 'ic Còmhghain* or *Clann 'ic Gille Chòmhghain*, the MacCowans. By *Clann 'ic Cuithein* he means the MacQueens. *Clann 'ic Mhannain* bear an interesting name – that of Manannan mac Lir, euhemerised into St Mannan, hence Kildavannan in Bute, etc. In Uig, Lewis, the name has been anglicised as Buchanan, while in Skye it appears to have developed further into MacPherson by something like the following route (Forbes 1923, p. 179): *Mac Mhannain > Mac 'Annain > Cananaich* 'a canon's descendants' (> Buchanan) > *Pearsanaich* 'a parson's descendants' > MacPherson. Norman Macpherson, one of the 'Glendale Martyrs', was known as *Tarmad Cananach* (information from Allan Macdonald, Cromarty). See Black 2002, p. 418, and notes 8 and 354 above.

580 Robertson 1904, p. 294. This is the 'hide' *taghairm* proper, also described by Ramsay of Ochtertyre (1888, vol. 2, pp. 459–60), see MacilleDhuibh 27.7.01.

581 Martin 1716, pp. 110–12 = 1999, pp. 76–77.

582 As usual, JGC's etymologising is mostly wide of the mark. The root of the Classical Gaelic verb *toghairmim* 'I summon' is *do-gair* ('call'), in which *do* is a meaningless pre-verbal particle. *Taghairm* is thus simply 'a summons'. *Toghairmim* in the sense 'I induce' is particularly common in Gaelic medical manuscripts such as that described in note 554.

583 As JGC was therefore unable to cite the words of this unusually useful charm, I am pleased to be able to give them here exactly as they stand in an eighteenth-century manuscript, GUL Gen. 1042 (MacLagan) MS 64 (cf. Macbain 1890–91, p. 259, and Thomson 1992–94, pp. 420–21), where the title is: "Ubag a chasgadh coin o thabhan, no a ghlas ghairm." ("An incantation to prevent dogs barking, or the Lock-Cry.")

> *Co e 'm bailese Romhain?*
> *Ta Baile nan Gaimhne.*
> *Na gaireadh na coin no gu'n gaireadh na gaimhne*
> *Tri ceothan & ceothan crith,*

Bheir air a chrobh cothartaich & air an Talamh Crith.
Ugh pluib & cothart coin.
Ta mi guigheadh air Riogh nan Dul, na ta nad shuil a bhi air mo theanga.

I believe this means: "What's this farm before us? / It's the Farm of the Stirks. / May the dogs not cry till the stirks call up / Three mists and trembling mists / Which make the cattle bark and the earth shake. / A plopping egg and the bark of a dog: / I pray the King of the Elements for what's in your eye to be on my tongue." Macbain was unsure about *Ugh* and *shuil* but these readings are correct. The idea seems to be that the intruder seeks to anticipate everything that dog or man may see or hear and neutralise it with prayer, and that if things go wrong he wants glorious confusion in which to make his escape – drifting mists, earth tremors, cattle barking like dogs. As JGC says, it would make a good gift for a young man courting, but Macbain pointed out (*ibid.*, p. 258) that it was also useful to thieves and cattle-lifters. See Dalyell 1834, p. 270.

584 Gilleasbaig Aotrom (Archibald Matheson) possessed in abundance what JGC refers to at p. 235 as 'the curious shrewdness sometimes found in connection with limited intellect'. He flourished during the incumbency of the Rev. John MacGregor Souter as minister of Duirinish, 1814–39. A native of Aberdeen who appears to have first arrived in Duirinish as a factor on the MacLeod estate, Souter (who never married) had poor Gaelic and was the butt of many of Gilleasbaig's jokes (Domhnullach 1911; Scott 1915–50, vol. 7, p. 169; Mackay 1919–22, pp. 166–71; MacKenzie 1930, pp. 62–65; *Tocher* 5, pp. 152–55; MacLeòid 1975, pp. 229–39; Meek 1978, p. 33; MacLeod 1980–82, pp. 244, 257, 260, 262; MacNeil 1987, pp. 336–43; *Tocher* 45, pp. 163–68; Bruford and MacDonald 1994, pp. 229, 459; MacKenzie 1995, pp. 89–90; McKean 1997, pp. 99, 100, 149, 205–07; MacLeod 2002, pp. 146–49).

Gilleasbaig is said to have composed the song 'Fear a' Choire' to MacKinnon of Corriechatachan (MacDonald 1901, pp. 23–24; Mhàrtainn 2001, pp. 104, 125, 131). He is one of the last of the great Gaelic fools, and represents a tradition of being 'away' – with the Fairies, that is – that stretches back into antiquity, as pointed out by Yeats (Welch 1993, p. 209 and cf. p. 311): "A countryman at Kiltartan says, 'There was one of the Lydons – John – was away for seven years, lying in his bed, but brought away at nights, and he knew everything; and one, Kearney, up in the mountains, a cousin of his own, lost two hoggets, and came and told him, and he knew the very spot where they were, and told him, and he got them back again. But *they* were vexed at that, and took away the power, so that he never knew anything again, no more than another.' This wisdom is the wisdom of the fools of the Celtic stories, that was above all the wisdom of the wise. Lomna, the fool of Fionn, had so great wisdom that his head, cut from his body, was still able to sing and prophesy."

For fools in the older Gaelic tradition see Clancy 1992 and 1993; for fools kept for entertainment in great houses see note 275; for fools in more recent times see Macleod 1899–1901; Anon. 1908; Mackay 1914, pp. 562–64; cf. Macdonald 1982, pp. 120–27.

585 Succubus, a devil supposed to assume a female body and consort with men in their sleep (see notes 484, 859); incubus, a devil supposed to assume a male body and have sexual intercourse with women in their sleep, the most notable example being the conception of Merlin (Thorpe 1966, p. 168). The attention-seeking Robert Kirk alleged of the Highland Fairies that 'for the incontinence of their *leannain sith* or succubi who tryst with men, it is abominable' (Hunter 2001, p. 85 and cf. p. 106), but the sexual encounters described in the stories do not take place during sleep. 'Horrible and awful' is from Burns's 'Tam O' Shanter':

Wi mair o horrible and awful
Which e'en to name wad be unlawful.

See also Dalyell 1834, pp. 599–600, 682; Wentz 1911, p. 113.

586 1 Sam. 28: 7–25; cf. p. 177 and Scott 2001, pp. 40–42.

587 *Buidseach* is identical in meaning to English 'witch', and resembles it in form, for the simple reason that it is derived from it. *Làrach lom* is 'an empty plot', 'a bare house-site'; *sgrios an codach* is 'the destruction of their property'.

588 This was first recorded as *Is mairg a's mathair do-mhac a bao 'nuair is Diardaoin a Bhealltuinn*, with the very acceptable translation 'Woe is the mother of a son, when Beltein falls on Thursday' (Macintosh 1785, p. 71). Alexander Campbell, a notoriously bad editor, disimproved both (Macintosh 1819, pp. 142–43): *Is mairg a's mathair do mhac a bao 'nuair is Diardaoin a Bealtuinn*, "Woe to the mother of a wizard's son when Beltein falls on a Thursday."

     My understanding of the saying is as follows. *Bealltainn* is here I believe 3 May, *Latha Seachnaidh na Bliadhna* ('the Avoiding Day of the Year'), as opposed to 1 May, *Latha Buidhe Bealltainn* ('the Lucky Day of Beltane'). The day of the week upon which 3 May fell was regarded as being unlucky for the rest of the year, and it was particularly unlucky to begin any new work on that day. Thursday, Calum Cille's day, would normally have been regarded as extremely lucky, but it must be that *Latha Seachnaidh na Bliadhna* was felt to cancel this out. A child born when 3 May fell on a Thursday would thus be deprived of Calum Cille's patronage and would have to be strong to survive.

     All in all, the proverb may the better be understood if we translate: "Pity the woman whose child is sickly / When 3rd May falls on a Thursday." See '*Diar-Daoin*, Thursday', pp. 566–67.

589 Cram (slang) 'to make believe false or exaggerated tales' (Chambers 1983, p. 292).

590 *Luirgean* and *lorg* both mean 'staff'; *lorg ohn* will be a misprint for *lorgain* or *lurgain*. In what looks like a translation of this sentence, Niall M. Brownlie once wrote (1971, p. 22): *A thuilleadh air seo, bha innealan seuna agus gheasan aca, snàthainean de dheifir dhaithean agus cuaille daraich ris an canadh iad 'Lurgain.'* ("In addition to this, they had instruments of charming and superstition, threads of different colours and an oaken stick which they called 'Lurgain'.")

591 'Blocksberg', Brand 1849, vol. 1, p. 228. Writing in 1830, Scott referred to it by its modern name, the Brockenberg, and, from a Swedish source, as Blockula (2001, p. 131). This mountain near Hanover gave its name to the 'Brocken spectre', a gigantic shadow on cloud or mist (for which see Douglas 1891, Sharpe 1895, Omond 1895, and Gray 1997, p. 173). It enjoyed an honourable place in Cold War dialectic. After telling his readers that the witches hold their Sabbaths on the Brocken summit (3,750 feet), Fodor wrote in his guide to Germany (1964, p. 376): "By some miracle of surveying the witches have been left to the Russians, just across the border in the Soviet Zone, but in Bad Harzburg they will obligingly sell you Brocken Witch's Talismen to protect you, no doubt, from spells from across the border."

592 Niall M. Brownlie tells this story in greater detail (1971, pp. 22–23). A particular farmer in Tiree had a lot of cattle and carried on a brisk trade in milk with the islanders. He took on a female servant, but she proved to be 'as lazy as a pig' (*cho leisg ris a' mhuic*) and he had to let her go (*'cead a siubhail' a thoirt dhi*). His cows subsequently went dry for no obvious reason, but he had a young male employee who realised what was going on. Off he went herding (*Thog e air ris a' bhuachailleachd*), but he had not been long behind the cattle when he saw a big hare (*maigheach mór*) running back and forward and in and out under the cows' bodies. He kept his eye on it until it went out of sight behind a rock on the shore. He climbed on top of the rock, and instead of the hare he saw his master's former employee busy tying black sea-tangles (*trang a' ceangail dhuitheamain*) around her waist. *Thuig mo laochain ann an tiota gu dé a bha tachairt, tharraing e mach sgian, ghearr e na duitheaman, agus shil am bainne gu làr.* "Our hero understood immediately what was happening, pulled out a knife, cut the tangles, and the milk flowed to the ground."

In his supplement, Dwelly (1991, p. 73) gives: "duitheaman, *s.m. Laminaria digitata*, type of seaweed. *Tiree*." It is simply *dubh fheamainn* 'black seaweed', the kind with little swellings which emit a crack when pressed. In a variant recorded in Vatersay, a woman was said to have been caught on her way home from that island with a black tangle behind her back (*Tocher* 38, pp. 42–43 = Bruford and MacDonald 1994, pp. 404–05, 482). She had been noticed carefully holding it by both ends throughout her visit. When it was cut in two the milk of the Vatersay cows spilled out. Similarly, in Argyll it was said (Campbell 1885a, p. 97) that Campbell of Dunstaffnage once met an old woman on the moor between Lochawe and Glenfaochan dragging a heather rope after her. "What strange work the old woman is doing!" said his servant. "Though you would little suppose it," said Dunstaffnage, "she draws after her in that rope all the milk in Glenfaochan."

He cut the rope with his sword, and they were all nearly drowned in milk. She was a Lochaweside witch stealing the substance from the milk of Glenfaochan.

The Badenoch version adds a neat touch – the milk of all the cows in that country is carried away in a withe across the Monadh Liath as far as Killin in the heights of Stratherrick, where, in response to a counter-spell, it bursts (Macpherson 1893, p. 23). "This, so the tradition runs, has been the cause of the richness of the pasture of that plain, and of the superior quality and quantity of milk it produces. The good effects of this untoward accident were not, it is related, confined to the dell of Killin, for some of its streamlets glided down to Stratherrick, which is said to account for the excellence of the milk, cream, and butter in that district."

To this we may compare the comic realism of the Rev. George Sutherland's version from Highland Caithness, in which there is no sea-tangle or heather-rope, but instead the counter-charm causes milk to flow from every article of dress on the witch's body, from the mutch on her head downwards (1937, p. 56). "The inmates of each house that she passed were startled out of their beds with her cries, and on looking out they saw Betty rushing homewards for dear life followed by a train of dogs, cats, and pigs, all eager to get their full of the grateful fluid."

On witches as hares see p. 188 and cf. Ballard 1997, p. 75.

593   The *Fasti* give no minister of Kintail (or indeed of Lochalsh or Glenshiel) under this name, so JGC can only mean the celebrated Lachlan MacKenzie (1754–1819), *Mgr Lachlann*, who from 1782 to 1819 was minister of the only other contiguous parish, Lochcarron. This story adds a further dimension (though not a surprising one) to the many existing anecdotes of Mgr Lachlann. A passionate but wayward evangelical, an inspired preacher who used any means available to bring souls to salvation, he possessed the second sight and was renowned throughout the Highlands as a seer, see Murchison 1971–72, pp. 26–30; Murray 1979; Black 2001, pp. xxxvi–xxxix.

594   Cf. note 465.

595   This is Donald Livingstone (*Dòmhnall MacDhunlèibhe*, 1728–1816). He appears with his family (six males, four females) as a tenant at Savary in the Argyll Estate census of 1779 (Cregeen 1963, p. 69); see also Carmichael n.d., p. 177. According to K. W. Grant (1925, p. 66) the epithet *molach* appears to have been hereditary, and did not apply to him personally. Iain Thornber, Knock, Morvern, tells me (personal communication, 17 August 2003): "His main claim to fame was saving the Stewart of Appin Banner at Culloden and having a very fine armorial stone placed over the grave of his parents here at Kiel, Morvern. There are some original Gaelic stories told of him in the unpublished Samuel Cameron MS now in my possession." For the Samuel Cameron MS see Ó Baoill 1979, p. xxv. The minister mentioned by JGC was presumably the Rev. Norman MacLeod (1745–1824), for whom see MacLeod 2002, pp. xv–xvi, 9–17, 44–54; he came to Morvern in 1775.

Dòmhnall Molach's exploit at Culloden has been described in detail by Carmichael

(1909–10, pp. 340–45), Grant (1925, pp. 63–64, 66, 111), Thornber (1991) and Shackleton (1997). It was first placed on record, I think, by McIan and Logan (1847, p. 8 of 'Stewarts' section): "When the standard-bearer was slain, one of the corps called Mac an t-ledh from Morven, tore the banner from the staff, and wrapping it round his body carried it off." The standard-bearer's name was Dugald Stewart, according to Stewart and Stewart (1880, p. 209), who also describe the banner in detail (pp. 137–38): "The regimental colour borne by the Stewarts of Appin at Culloden is still in the possession of the head of the Ballachelish branch of the family. It is of light blue silk, with a yellow saltire, or cross of St Andrew, the dimensions being 5 feet hoist, with a fly of 6 feet 7 inches. Its gallant bearer, one of the Ardsheal family, was killed, and the banner is stained with his blood. It bears the marks of having been torn from the colour staff, which accords with McIan's account."

In 1931 the banner was presented to the National Military Museum, now the United Services Museum, in Edinburgh Castle. Calum Maclean found (1975, p. 156) that by the 1950s Dòmhnall Molach's feat was being ascribed in Appin to 'seven brothers named Livingstone, who rescued the banner of the Stewarts at Culloden and brought it safely back home to Castle Stalker'.

596 For the power of red thread (or string) see the next section.

597 See Maclagan 1902, p. 119, and 'Juniper (*Iubhar-Beinne*, literally Mountain Yew)', p. 231.

598 Thursday was a good day in the islands for the performance of protective magic, being sacred to Calum Cille. It is of great interest that Lammas day could be treated as a moveable feast, cf. note 166 on p. 600.

599 He lived at *Glac nan Smiar* ('Bramble Hollow'). Niall M. Brownlie gives this account of his 'constitution balls' (1971, p. 23): *Chuala mi m'athair ag ràdh gum faigheadh thu aige-san ronag-gaoiside agus nam biodh an ronag seo ceangailte mu làimh a' chumain-bhainne cha bhiodh e an comas na buitsich toradh a' bhainne a thoirt air falbh.* ("I heard my father saying that you could get from him a *ronag* of hair and that if this *ronag* were tied round the handle of the milk-pail no witch would be able to take away the produce of the milk.") He was father of the celebrated Calum Beag, for whom see note 10.

600 See note 683 and p. 687 below.

601 JGC's spelling is *caorrunn*, see p. xiv above. In classical Gaelic it is *caorthann*, in Dwelly (1977, p. 166) *caorunn*, in modern Gaelic *caorann*. Stewart explains (1823, p. 54) that to guard against ghosts a piece of rowan-tree was shaped into a cross with red thread. "This cross you will insert between the lining and cloth of your garment, and, so long as it lasts, neither ghost nor witch shall ever interfere with you." See also *ibid.*, p. 95. Chambers (1870, p. 328) gives the rhyme as

> Rowan-tree and red thread
> Make the witches tyne their speed

(tyne = lose). This, he says, is 'prevalent over all Scotland'. He also cites a Borders variant:

> Black luggie, lammer bead,
> Rowan-tree and red thread,
> Put the witches to their speed!

The 'proper antidote' to the theft of milk by witches, he explains (*ibid.*, p. 330), is 'to lay a twig of rowan-tree, bound with a scarlet thread, across the threshold of the byre, or fix a stalk of clover, having four leaves, to the stall'. See also Dalyell 1834, pp. 401–02, 681; *CG2*, p. 246; Maclagan 1902, pp. 114, 119, 133 (rowans), 102, 143–47 (red thread); Henderson 1911, pp. 180–81; McPherson 1929, pp. 219–21; Davidson 1949, pp. 59, 77; Scott 2001, p. 192; Henderson and Cowan 2001, p. 89.

602 Also in Norway and Germany (Frazer 1913, p. 267).

603 *Cnag chaorainn sa bhuaraich* is literally 'a rowan peg in the cow-shackle'.

604 By 'not twenty years ago' JGC means *c.* 1855.

605 See p. 172. Judging by the need for *aicill* rhyme, the first syllable of *Endor* is pronounced long – *Eanndor*. By 'Ailein Dall' JGC must mean the celebrated Blind Allan MacDougall (*c.*1750–1828), for whom see Black 2001, pp. 517–18, since he tells us elsewhere (p. 218) that he 'eked out a livelihood by the practice of charms'. There is no trace of this kind of verse in MacDougall's published poems (Dughallach 1798), presumably because he considered it beneath his dignity, especially following his appointment as bard to Alasdair Ranaldson MacDonell of Glengarry, for whom see note 276.

Dr Maclagan got another version of the rhyme from 'a simple-minded man of about seven-and-thirty', a tailor who belonged to 'one of the inner islands' (1902, pp. 94–96):

> *Nuair a nì thu tòiseachadh*
> *Cuir dòrlach math salainn ann,*
> *Cuir bun is bàrr an neònain ann,*
> *Cuir mionach ròin is gearr-fhéidh ann;*
> *Buain slat den chaorann*
> *A-nall o aodann Eallasaid,*
> *Snàthain dearg le snaoim teann*
> *Air a chur mu cheann a' chratachain,*
> *'S ged a thigeadh buidseach Hendry*
> *Cheannsaicheadh am balach i.*

("When you make a beginning / Put a good handful of salt in it, / Put the root and flower of the daisy in it, / Put the guts of a seal and of a hare in it; / Cut a twig of the rowan / Brought across from the face of Ailsa Craig, / A red thread with a tight knot / Placed round the end of the sprinkler, / And should the witch Hendry come / The boy could manage her.") The tailor explained: *Tha sibh a' faicinn, bha 'm buidseach Hendry anns a' Bhìoball. B'ise 'm buidseach bu làidire bha beò riamh; ach nam faigheadh neach sam bith na nithe sin uile, agus an cuir gu feum, cha b' urrainn dhise neo do bhuidseach sam bith eile a chron a dheanadh. Chunnaic mi fhìn an snàthain dearg air clann, gus olc a chumail bhuapa.* ("You see, the witch Hendry was in the Bible. She was the strongest witch that ever lived; but if any person could get all those things, and use them, neither she nor any other witch could harm him. I myself have seen the red thread on children, to keep evil from them.")

It is curious to note how 'Endor' has turned into the Arran surname Hendry (for which see Black 1993, p. 63) while retaining its rhyme with the long first syllable in *ceannsaicheadh*. There is a further development, however, from another informant (Maclagan 1902, p. 142):

> *Snàthainn dearg is snaoim air —*
> *Bidh siud air ceann a' chrandachain;*
> *Ged thigeadh Buidseach Henderson,*
> *Cheannsaicheadh Ailean e.*

("A red thread with a knot in it – / That will be on the top of the churn-staff; / Should Henderson the Witch come, / Allan would manage him.") Maclagan is silent as to Allan's identity, but these rhymes all sound like advertising slogans for Blind Allan's trade in charms, and the name Henderson is strongly connected with his native Glencoe.

Finally a word is required about the implements depicted in these rhymes, the *crathadair*, *cratachan* and *crandachan*. All are types of wooden churn. The names of the first two are based on *crath* 'shake', hence the erroneous translation 'sprinkler' as if they were salt-cellars or pepper-pots. Carmichael points out (*CG4*, p. 82) that 'the cream having been put in, the mouth of the vessel was covered with the dressed skin of lamb, sheep, kid, goat, or calf, and tightly bound with a cord of linen or leather' and that 'the process of churning consisted in agitating it rapidly to and fro' – in JGC's words, 'the small end being lifted up and let down repeatedly'. The rhymes describe a churn whose cover was bound with red thread; a twig of rowan, JGC's 'cross or hoop that secured this covering', was used to twist it tight. This is the 'ancient churn' described by JGC at p. 177; JGC gives *fùileach* and *iomaideil* for the cover, while Carmichael offers *bùilig, bùilich* and *bùileach*.

By contrast, Carmichael points out that the *crandachan, crannachan,* 'staff-churn' (based on *crann* 'staff, pole'), was 'felt to be an innovation'. It was operated by means of a plunger or churn-staff called a *loinid*, also called by Carmichael *simid, ceann-simid* and *maide-maistridh*. It had a removable wooden lid with a hole in it through which the *loinid* passed. JGC tells us that the handle and *crois* (the cross-shaped business end) of the *loinid* itself were made of rowan wood. Maclagan's second informant appears to say that the red thread is 'on the top of the churn' (*air ceann a' chrandachain*), but Maclagan makes this 'on the top of the churn-staff', presumably meaning that the thread is tied to that end of the *loinid* which projects from the hole. No thread could be used to form the *crois* as it must be kept sterile; this was not the case, however, with the disposable type of *loinid* used for whisking milk or whey, round the cross-piece of which was wound a circle of twisted hair from a cow's tail (Grant 1961, pp. 196, 213, 298). This could get very messy (Black 2001, pp. 14–15, 370).

See also Mackellar 1887–88, p. 139, and Mackenzie 1914, p. 302.

606 On horse nails and shoes see also Maclagan 1902, p. 121, and Opie and Tatem's entries 'Horseshoe at threshold', 'Horseshoe: how hung or placed', 'Horseshoe lucky to find', 'Horseshoe on ship', 'Horseshoe nail' and 'Horseshoe nail points towards one' (1992, pp. 202–04).

607 By an 'entire horse' JGC means an uncastrated stallion, see also pp. 161 and 273.

608 See pp. 161–62; Campbell 1860–62, vol. 2, p. 87 = 1890, vol. 2, p. 99. The advice was given to the elder brother of Campbell's informant, who said: "I do not know how he managed to get hold of the laird's stallion, but the shoe was nailed on our byre door before sunrise next morning, so our cows had plenty milk from that day forth."

609 In the context of the periodic expulsion of evils, Frazer (1913, p. 153) compares this with how Greeks smeared pitch on their houses to keep out demons who attacked women in childbirth, how Bulgarians tried to keep wandering ghosts from their houses by painting crosses with tar on the outside of their doors, and how Serbs painted crosses with tar on the doors of houses and barns to keep out vampires. The Athenians 'smeared the doors of their houses with pitch, apparently thinking that any rash spirits who might attempt to enter would stick fast in the pitch and be glued, like so many flies, to the door'.

Ceathramh here refers to a part of the animal, not of the year (that would be *ràidhe*), cf. Dwelly 1977, p. 213. Presumably *ceathramh gorm* is a famine-related condition in which some part of the beast's lower quarters appears dark-blue or shiny.

610 See 'Pearlwort (*Mòthan*)', pp. 229–30.

611 'Short of *annlan*'. *Annlan*, which JGC calls here 'seasoning' and subsequently 'kitchen', is anything taken with bread, such as butter, cheese, crowdie, fish or meat – the 'filling' of a modern sandwich.

612 See 'Man Drowns Witches', Bruford 1967, p. 21.

613 Note the Rannoch people's view of Badenoch (pp. 196, 289), and compare Douglas's words in the ballad of Otterbourne:

But I hae dream'd a dreary dream
Beyond the Isle of Sky —
I saw a dead man win a fight,
And I think that man was I.

The same is true of Ireland, of which W. B. Yeats wrote in 1902 (Welch 1993, p. 312): "The people of the North are thought to know more about the supernatural than anybody else, and one remembers that the good gods of the Celts, the children of Danu, and the evil gods of the Celts the Fomor, came from the North in certain legends. The North does not mean Ulster, but any place to the north, for the people talk of the people of Cruachmaa, which is but a little north of Galway, as knowing much because they are from the North."

614 *Chaidh e ás a ghobhal* 'he went out of his fork', i.e. ruptured himself. The tale-type is Bruford's W20 'Man Tries to Fly' (1967, p. 27), see p. 732 below. Its function in this case, like the story told at p. 695, note 64, is to explain the tailor's lameness, see Introduction, p. lxv.

615 Cf. note 478.

616 'The Witches who Went Fishing with a Sieve' (MacPherson 1960, pp. 203–04) is the same story, except that the witches turn into rats, not cats. See Bruford 1967, p. 21; *Tocher* 16, pp. 312–17; Bruford and MacDonald 1994, pp. 387–90, 479; MacDonald 1994–95, pp. 37–38. The motif is W5 (p. 732 below).

617 Kirk(?) wrote *c.* 1685 (Hunter 2001, p. 66): "In the Western Isles they sel a Gale of Wind ordinarly." See also Dalyell 1834, pp. 250–51; Dixon 1886, pp. 168–69; Anon. 1887–88, pp. 93–94 (a curious variant); Maclagan 1902, pp. 201–02; Cameron 1903, pp. 301–02; McPherson 1929, pp. 237–41; Polson 1932, p. 151; Sutherland 1937, pp. 60–62; MacPherson 1960, p. 209; Bruford 1967, pp. 31–33; *Tocher* 34, pp. 273–74; Gray 1987, p. 13; MacNeil 1987, pp. 162–67; Almqvist 1991a, p. 34; Mac Cárthaigh 1992–93; Miller 1994, pp. 267–76; Bruford and MacDonald 1994, pp. 391–95, 480; MacDonald 1994–95, p. 41; Robertson 1995, pp. 97–99; Ballard 1997, pp. 73–74. The motif is 'The Ship-Sinking Witch', see Almqvist 1991a, p. 30, and p. 732 below ('Index to Tales', W40A).

618 Far from being fictional wizards, the MacMhuirichs or MacVuirichs represent solid historical and literary fact. The longest-surviving family of hereditary poets and historians in Gaelic Scotland, they were descended from Muireadhach Albanach Ó Dálaigh (fl. 1220) and served a succession of magnates – notably the earls of Lennox, the kings of the Isles and the chiefs of Clanranald – for five hundred years, see Thomson 1960–63. As learned men possessing books (cf. note 542), it was perhaps inevitable that tradition would represent them as wizards like Michael Scot(t). For expressions of the type *MacMhuirich nam buadh* see Black 2002, p. 26. The MacMhuirichs had no connection with the Clan MacPherson, but *MacMhuirich* happens to be the correct Gaelic form of the surname used by both, for the simple reason that both kindreds are descended from an individual named *Muireadhach* (Scottish *Muireach*). In South Uist, therefore, the name *MacMhuirich* was often anglicised as MacPherson, see MacPherson 1960, pp. 14–15, and Black 1999, p. 763.

619 This is a well-known story with numerous variants, see MacPherson 1868, p. 97; Sinclair 1877, pp. 51–52; Macleod 1908, p. 253; Camshron 1915; MacLeod 1931–33, p. 392; *CG*5, pp. 306–13; MacLellan 1961, pp. 94–95, 223; Mackechnie 1973, p. 326 (a missing MacNicol manuscript); MacDhòmhnaill 1981, p. 42; Gillies 2000, pp. 28–31, 33–34. Gillies (2000, p. 7) also cites eleven recordings of it – including one from Tiree, SA1968/31/B5 – made between 1959 and 1972 and now in the archives of the School of Scottish Studies, Edinburgh. The original Gaelic words were excluded from *WSS*, but they were transcribed from JGC's appendix by Alexander Carmichael into EUL MS CW 241, ff. 21–22, and by George Henderson into GUL MS Gen. 1090/77, f. [3], see pp. 701–04 below. JGC's introduction is also traditional: *Turas dha'n robh Mac Mhuirich nam Buadh air taisteal fairge ri latha fiathail, thuirt an sgiobair ris: "Iarr gaoth, a Mhic Mhuirich." Fhreagair e agus thubhairt e ...*

Curiously, given that they share a common exemplar, Carmichael's and Henderson's transcripts do not always agree. I have preferred Henderson's, as it corresponds better to JGC's translation. At 'weak and trifling' Henderson has *lag leibideach*, Carmichael *beag leibideach*; at 'let it be I' Henderson has *gur mis' e*, Carmichael *Gur a mis an ti*; at 'surges' Henderson has *taosgaibh*, Carmichael *taosgadh/aibh*. JGC arranges the third verse in five lines, and Henderson follows suit, but Carmichael rearranges it into seven, ending *S mu theid aon air tir aisde / Gur a mis an ti / S ma theid dithis / Gur mi fhi s mo chu*. It is clear that Carmichael is pushing JGC's text towards conformity with what was ultimately published in *CG5*. The principal crux is in line 2 of the second verse, where at JGC's 'Struggling' our different sources give *'G ainealadh* (MacPherson), *'G a gann-shioladh* (Sinclair), *Ag oinealadh* (Henderson), *Ag sineagadh* (Carmichael), *A' sineagaich* (*CG5*, p. 308), and *A dh'fhuirealadh* (MacLellan, MacDhòmhnaill). The otherwise unattested *sineagaich* ('bounding') has duly found its way into the *Carmina* glossary (*CG6*, p. 260), but one cannot help suspecting that it developed in Carmichael's mind out of his misreading of JGC's *ainealadh* or *oinealadh* as *sineagadh*. As *ainealadh*, *gann-shioladh*, *oinealadh* and *fhuirealadh* look like different attempts to spell the same word, I would suggest that they are related to *anail* 'breath' – 'panting above our gunwale'.

JGC's translation 'Devil' for *A Chonnain* should read 'St Connan', see notes 551 and 552.

620 This is an inversion of historical fact. The MacMhuirichs were servitors to Clanranald.

621 There are various versions of this rhyme. In *CG4*, pp. 356–59, Alexander Carmichael published thirty-four lines (for his drafts see EUL CW MS 495, ff. 1–4, 11–14), while Nicolson (1882, p. 390), followed by Mackay (1914–19, p. 336), gives eight; the Rev. Archibald MacDonald published six (1934–36a, p. 202), and in Mac a Phì 1938, p. 69, the Rev. Dr Neil Ross cited four. Nicolson and Carmichael understood it to be a piece of MacLeod satire in mockery of the Sleat MacDonalds, indeed Carmichael heads it 'Guidhe nan Leòdach: The MacLeods' Petition'. Neither of these editors associated it with MacMhuirichs. Ross associated it with the battle popularly known as Blàr Milleadh Gàraidh and the pipe-tune 'Blàr Bhatarnais' by Iain Odhar MacCruimein. JGC's Gaelic original was excluded from *WSS*, but fortunately Carmichael transcribed it into EUL MS CW 241, f. 23, and George Henderson into GUL MS Gen. 1090/77, f. [18], see pp. 701–04 below. Henderson's transcript, which is untitled, corresponds perfectly with JGC's translation; here it is exactly as it stands in the manuscript.

> *Gaoth 'n ìar-'eas thun na h-'Eiste*
> *Ceò is uisge*
> *Clann Raonuill air bord a' bristeadh*
> *Leam cha mhiste*
> *Eathar caol corrach*
> *Seòl àrd biorach*
> *'S lùchd de bharaillean failmhe*
> *'S taoim gu totachan*
> *Sgioba fann frithire*
> *Gun urram fir d'a chéile.*

Carmichael's transcript is headed 'Guidhe Nan Leodach', as in *CG*, and is arranged in eleven lines beginning *Gaoth an iar eas / Thun na Feiste / Ceo is uisge / Clann Domhnull / Air bhorda briste / Eathar caol corrach*, i.e. *h-'Eiste* becomes *Feiste*, *Clann Raonuill* becomes *Clann Domhnull*, and *Leam cha mhiste* is omitted altogether, probably by mistake. Since the readings in *CG* are *Feiste* and *Clann Domhnaill*, I can only assume that Carmichael chose on this occasion to edit as well as transcribe. At any rate several things emerge clearly – the poem is in *snéadhbhairdne* metre (see note 25 on p. 579), lines 9–10 should be rearranged accordingly (*Sgioba fann frithire gun urram / Fir d'a chéile*), line 5 lacks three syllables, *biorach* : *totachan* is a poor rhyme, and *chéile* has no rhyme at all. The use of *snéadhbhairdne* points to the probability that these verses were formerly interspersed with even more highly satirical prose, which suggests a reason why they should have been attributed to a MacMhuirich, and provides a link with mac Mhgr Alastair's 'Birlinn Chlann Raghnaill' – we must, I think, now add this to the list of items which inspired that great poem (MacLeod 1933a, pp. 118–25; Thomson 1996, pp. 135–37; Ó Baoill 1997, p. 49; Black 2001, pp. 471–72).

622 The most easterly point of Lochs, Lewis. According to MacIver (1934, p. 60) the stressed vowel is short (*Cabag*) and the meaning, therefore, is 'cap' or 'cape' from Latin *caput* 'head, headland'. JGC makes the vowel long – *càbag* 'a kebbock, a cheese' – and this appears to be confirmed by Dwelly's *Ceann na càbaig* (1977, p. 1017). No doubt the former pronunciation is the local one, while the latter was used by mariners, cf. note 430 and note also the two names of Tiree (*Tiriodh, Tiridhe*), Raasay (*Ratharsair, Ratharsaigh*), etc.

623 See 'Duart's Daughter', Bruford and MacDonald 1994, pp. 390–91, 479–80. The tale-type is 'The Witch's Daughter and her Father', Bruford 1967, p. 22 – ML 3035 'The Daughter of the Witch', see McPherson 1929, p. 183, MacPherson 1960, pp. 204–05, and Mac Cárthaigh 1992–93, p. 278.

624 *An uisge na stiùireach* is literally 'in the water of the rudder'. It is a common idiom, e.g. *cha tigeadh e an uisge na stiùireach dha* 'he couldn't hold a candle to him', 'he wasn't fit to lick his boots', literally 'he wouldn't come in his rudder wake'. See Introduction, p. xxvii.

625 *Mà-Cònuill*, the name as it stands in *WSS* 23, is, as MacInnes explains (1990–92, p. 386), the title of the head of all Clan Donald. "In tradition this is not MacDhomhnaill but *Màg' ònaill*. The voicing of the *c* of *mac* is not uncommon (cf. *MagUidhir, MagAoidh*; and in English forms such as Maguinness; or, in pronunciation, Magloud). It may have been a high register pronunciation and had an honorific force. Some of the storytellers who used it did not realise it was 'MacDonald' at all; and neither did some eighteenth century writers, who reproduced it as *Matha Conail[l]*, which represents the pronunciation – *th* being merely a syllable divider – accurately enough."

On the issue of lengthening, *DIL* points out (s.v. 1 *mac*) that, after the introduction of surnames in the tenth and eleventh centuries, *mac* followed by the genitive of a masculine proper name 'becomes a common form of surname and often changes to Mág (*gen.* Méig); the usage is extended to foreign names'. In linguistic terms it is an extraordinary change. It may have something to do with the way in which names were 'cried' at banquets etc. Names in Ó predominated (the MacDonalds' original surname was Ó Colla, the Campbells' Ó Duibhne, the latter preserved in the Islay place-names *Àirigh O Dhùin* and *Maol Àirigh O Dhùin*); perhaps a long first vowel was essential to the crier's art. See note 549 and *CG2*, p. 292.

At p. 286 JGC explicitly uses the term 'Lord Macdonald of the Isles' of Dòmhnall Gorm Mór of Sleat, and it is very likely that he or his equally celebrated successor Dòmhnall Gorm Òg is meant here. See also p. 195.

626 *Cràcaig* is at Portree, see pp. 184, 197. The skua is given as *croma-ritheachan* in *CG6*, p. 53, so -*ar* may be a typographic error, cf. note 577 above. Either way, the name appears to mean 'curved racer'. Indeed the two spellings are so close – why not *croma-ruitheachain*, for example? – that I feel sure that JGC's manuscript was the source for Carmichael's word. See p. 685 below.

627 The spelling in *WSS* 24 is *tota shílidh*, but Niall M. Brownlie confirms to me that all the vowels are short. The latter word is given in the nominative case by Armstrong (1825, p. 552) as *tileadh* 'a ship's poop' and by Fr Allan McDonald (1958, p. 217) as *sileadh* 'little floor or platform at the stern of a boat'.

628 The 'contemporary historian' was the Rev. David Calderwood (1575–1651) in his *History of the Kirk of Scotland* (1845, p. 632): "The like of this tempest was not seene in our time, nor the like of it heard in this countrie in anie age preceiding." JGC took the quotation from Chambers 1859, vol. 1, p. 553, but he was wrong about the date. The Rev. James Fraser (1634–1709) makes it clear that Iain Garbh was drowned in 1671, when Easter Monday fell on 24 April, and thus not in the 'Borrowing Days' (the last three days of March) at all. Fraser is also very clear about the cause of the drowning, and makes no mention of witchcraft. After a christening in Lewis, he says (1905, pp. 498–99), "Rarsay takes leave to goe home, and, after a rant of drinking uppon the shoare, went aboord off his birling and sailed away with a strong north gale off wind; and whither by giveing too much saile and no ballast, or the unskillfullness of the seamen, or that they could not mannage the strong Dut[ch] canvas saile, the boat whelmd, and all the men dround in view of the cost . . . This account I had from Alexander his brother the summer after. Drunkness did the [mischeife]." See also Stewart 1823, pp. 184–96; Sinclair 1881, pp. 262–63; Macbean 1888, part 2, no. 6; Sinclair 1890, pp. 95–97; Kennedy 1899–1901, p. 166; Mackay 1914–19, pp. 270–72; MacLeod 1931–33, p. 392; *CG*5, pp. 300–04; Watson 1965, pp. 26–31, 100–01, 114–15; Bruford 1967, p. 38; MacLean 1974–76, pp. 384–88 = Mac Gill-Eain 1985, pp. 302–05; Maclean 1975, p. 127; Macdonald 1982, pp. 289–90; MacilleDhuibh 22.4.88; MacInnes 1988–90, pp. 10–11; Bruford and MacDonald 1994, p. 480. For the motif 'Witches Sink a Ship' see MacDonald 1994–95, p. 42.

629 JGC's spellings here (*WSS* 26) were *Du-sear* and *Moll-stabhan*. On the former see p. xiv above. On the latter, it is curious that in referring to the same cataclysm in *Dàin do Eimhir*, Sorley MacLean made the same error (Mac Ghill Eathain 1943, p. 35):

> 'S nan robh sinn air Moll Steinnseil Stamhain
> 's an fhairge neo-aoibhneach a' tarruing
> nan ulbhag is 'gan tilgeil tharainn,
> thogainn-sa am balla daingeann
> roimh shìorruidheachd choimhich 's i framhach.

He translates (*ibid.*, p. 99): "And were we on Moll Stenscholl Staffin, when the unhappy surge dragged its boulders and threw them over us, I would raise a rampart wall against a hostile crunching eternity." He corrected *Moll* ('Chaff') to *Mol* ('Shingle') in subsequent editions.

630 The *Sgeire Maola* lie between Fladda-Chuain and Trodda and are now marked by a beacon. They are mapped as *Sgeir nam Maol* ('the Skerry of the Bald Ones'); if this name is correct, it presumably refers to the religious who were buried in *Cladh a' Mhanaich*, the 'Monk's Graveyard' in Fladda-Chuain, for which see Robson 2003, pp. 167–68. *An riabhach* 'the brindled one', 'the grizzled one', is the devil, see p. 160; the speaking of his name proved fatal.

631 See 'The Watch of the Graveyard (*Faire Chlaidh*)', pp. 132–33, and *CG*2, p. 342. Smollett's name had been connected with the incident by the Rev. Dr Norman MacLeod, who wrote (Tormod Og 1830–31b, p. 136 = Henderson 1901, pp. 22–23): *Ghabh Albannach d'am b'ainm Smollet duais-bhratha chum an Soitheach a chur r'a theine.* ("A Scotsman called Smollett was bribed to set the vessel on fire.") Spanish sources confirm that John Smollett, a Dumbarton merchant, was among those provisioning the *San Juan de Sicilia* (McCaughey 1996, p. 220): "He gained easy access to the ship and the confidence of the crew. It seems that as 'the Spaniards were drying out some of their remaining powder on the forward deck . . . Smollett was able to drop a piece of smouldering lint nearby before departing'."

632 The captain of the ship which foundered in Tobermory Bay was understood to be named Don Farëia (MacLeod 1841–42a, p. 222 = Henderson 1901, p. 109), Don Fareija or Feraiya

(MacLean 1889, pp. 106–09), Pereira (Lorne 1898, p. 190, and McLeay 1986, p. 102) or Pottinger (MacLeod 2002, pp. 116–18). Tradition at Inveraray spoke of a Lieutenant Pereira who survived the wreck and later disclosed to the earl of Argyll in Spain that 'the vessel had carried a colossal treasure' (McLeay 1986, pp. 36, 46, 175). This would explain the name Forrest. He is called Forester by Lord Archibald Campbell (1885a, pp. 345–47) and Forast by the Marquis of Lorne (1898, pp. 188–90). The ship's name is generally cited as the *Florencia*, but recent research (McLeay 1986, pp. 149–87) suggests that she was in fact the *San Juan de Sicilia*, commanded by Don Diego Tellez Enriquez. Terence McCaughey has pointed out (1996, p. 215) that the story of the Spanish princess conflates the events of 1588–89 with those of July 1653, when a Colonel Ralph Cobbett landed in Mull to enforce the rule of the Commonwealth, Duart Castle was garrisoned by a company successively commanded by Captain John Hargrave and Captain James Emerson, and three ships – the *Swan*, the *Martha and Margaret* and the *Speedwell* – sank during an eighteen-hour storm. What is more, when told further south in Argyll the location of the princess's burial shifts from Morvern to Kintyre, and MacLean of Duart turns into MacDougall of Dunollie (*ibid.*, pp. 213, 217–19).

633 The quotation is from the ballad of Sir Patrick Spens – appropriately, since it is about a ship going down.

> *O laith, laith were our gude Scots lords*
> *To wet their cork-heel'd shoon;*
> *But lang ere a' the play were play'd*
> *They wat their hats aboon.*

634 *Nic 'Ill' Dòmhnaich* will be for *Nic Mhaol Dòmhnaich*. As far as I know there is no name *Gille Dòmhnaich*. The 'poor woman' referred to gave Alexander Carmichael the original of the 'envy spell' which JGC translates under 'Charms for Cattle' at p. 209. Carmichael describes her (*CG2*, p. 379) as Nic-al-domhnaich, cottar, Bail-a-phuill, commenting (*CG2*, p. 74): "This woman had known many such runes, but was forgetting them." She is probably to be identified with Mairead (*Mairead Dhubh*), the Balephuil witch who figures in the story of *Fuadach Bhaile Phuill*, the drowning tragedy of 1856, see note 653. For a witch of the same name in Caolas see p. 193.

635 Literally 'Big Blue-Eye who was in the Plain'. This is *a' Mhoigh*, anglicised as Moy or Mey, see Dwelly 1977, s.v. *magh*. There are two places of the name in Lochaber. One, usually Moy, is in the Great Glen just south of Loch Lochy, and may be the one referred to by JGC as Meigh ('Iron', p. 135). The other, also usually Moy, overlooks the dreary wastelands between the head of Glen Spean and Loch Laggan which have now largely been drowned by the damming of the Spean above Tulloch Station. This, I understand, is Gorm-Shùil's home. It is the marchland between Lochaber and Badenoch, between MacDonalds and MacPhersons, and in the hills behind it are *Lochan na Cailliche*, *Creag na Cailliche* and *An Cearcallach*, for which see note 211. For *Bean an Lagain*, Gorm-Shùil's *alter ego*, see note 669.

636 In the Sound of Mull, see 'In Corry-na-Henchor', p. 97.

637 For another version of this story see MacKenzie 2002, pp. 148–51.

638 The spelling of this name in *WSS* 31 is Airidh-mhic-mharoich. MacDougall and Cameron pinpoint its location in their *Handbook* (n.d., p. 30): "Rounding the bend in the road at Airigh Mhic Mhairich, we see Cille Bhrighde Farm on the left of the road." It suggests the existence at one time of a personal name *Maireach*; compare the Moidart surname MacVarish, presumably derived from Mauritius, Maurice.

'Morrison's Shieling', if I may so translate it, may be considered along with other toponyms in the vicinity. 'Faygaravick', which suggests a first element *féidh* 'bog', appears to be the name of which MacEchern says (1914–19, p. 329): "Lochgualabrick of Langland's [*sic*] map is pronounced Loch airigh Meall(a) bhride, and is not very far from Kilbride. Loch of the shieling of Bridget's Hill." Setting aside the first elements *féidh, loch, loch àirigh*, we thus have a name variously rendered as *garavick, gualabrick* and *Meall(a) bhrìde*. Giving due weight to MacEchern's evidence, these forms may be rationalised as *(Mhic) M(h)aol Bhrìghd(e)*, i.e. the principal element designates an individual baptised in the name of St Brigid who may have had some hereditary responsibility for the nearby church dedicated to that saint; Maurice may have been another. For the curious -*ick* ending we may compare the rendering of the Inverness fair called *Lagaidh Bhrìghde* ('St Brigid's Hollow') in sixteenth- and seventeenth-century documents as *Legavrick, Legrievrike, Legraweik* (Black 2000, p. 32).

639 Perhaps what prevented her on Wednesday was the fear of sterility. MacPhail tells a story (1897, p. 380) about a woman who is passing between the two knolls of Caipighill at Shawbost in Lewis when she hears the glugging sound of butter being churned in the Fairy mound (*fuaim maistridh anns an t-sìthein*). She says quietly to herself, *Is truagh nach robh mo phathadh air bean a' ghlugain.* "It's a pity the glugging woman didn't have my thirst."

No sooner has she said this but a *bean shìth* or Fairy woman dressed in green comes out of the *sìthein* with a drinking-cup (*cuach*) of buttermilk and offers it to her to drink. Taken aback, she declines, saying she is not thirsty. *Car son ma-tà a dh'iarr thu i?* says the Fairy. *A bheil eagal ort gun dian i cron dhuit?* "Why did you ask for it then? Are you afraid it will harm you?"

Tha, she says. "Yes."

The Fairy woman replies: *Galar na té a chuir a' chiad chìr Chiadaoin 'na ceann armsa ma nì i cron ort.* "May the affliction of the woman who put the first Wednesday comb in her hair be upon me if it does you any harm."

Ciod an galar a tha sin? "What affliction is that?"

Tha, says the Fairy woman, *galar a bhith gun mhac, gun nighean, gun ogha, gun iarogha.* "The affliction of being without son, without daughter, without grandchild, without great-grandchild."

See pp. 386–87, 602–04 (notes 422, 185, 189). On women as hares see Ó Duilearga 1981, p. 270 (with valuable list of references at pp. 399–400); Ní Dhuibhne 1993.

640 Opie and Tatem provide examples (1992, pp. 57–64) of an extraordinary range of cat superstitions, ranging from 'Cat = witch' to 'Cat or dog passes over corpse'.

641 JGC explains the reason for this in the case of the Camerons of Glen Nevis at p. 190; perhaps a similar story was told of some MacGregor chief. There is no shortage of models, e.g. the story 'MacMhuirich and the Kitten' (Gillies 2000, pp. 25–26, cf. *CG2*, p. 263), which tells how MacMhuirich came home from the hunt and told the kitten that the dogs had killed Cugrabhat, the king of the wild cats, whereupon the kitten 'leapt and took a grip on his steel helmet, and did not let him go until its head was cut off by the sword'. Sir Walter Scott wrote in 1830 of how 'a late gallant Highland chieftain', presumably Glengarry who died in 1828, 'has been seen to change to all the colours of his own plaid if a cat by accident happened to be in the room with him, even though he did not see it', but we may put this down to allergy (2001, p. 25).

642 In the last thirty comic verses of 'The Witch of Fife', an old man is enabled by hearing the witches' magic word (we are not told what it is) to fly to Carlisle and drink the Bishop's wine. He is caught, and is being burnt at the stake when his wife (one of the witches) flies down in the form of a bird, puts a red cap on his head, 'then whisperit ane word intil his lug'. The old man's shackles fall off, he says the word (whatever it is) and flies home through the air to Fife. Hogg explains in a footnote that the 'catastrophe of this tale' is founded on popular tradition (Thomson 1874, pp. 13–16, cf. Mack 1970, pp. 18–30). See MacLellan 1961,

pp. 101–04; Bruford and MacDonald 1994, pp. 383–86, 479; MacDonald 1994–95, p. 40; SoSS Maclagan MSS vol. 22, section paginated 4905. We may compare the adventure that allegedly befell an ancestor of Lord Duffus, said to have been walking in a field in Morayshire when he heard the noise of a whirlwind and voices crying: "Horse and hattock!" He repeated the cry and was found next day in the king's cellar in Paris with a silver cup in his hand (Pitcairn 1833, vol. 3, p. 604; Hunter 2001, p. 153; Henderson and Cowan 2001, p. 38). Bruford points out (1967, p. 27) that although the story is very popular in Gaelic, the witches' spell is usually in English, so it is 'probably an import to the Highlands from further south'. As remembered by Donald MacDonald, *Dòmhnall Sham*, from Manish, Harris, the cries were 'Off to London!' and 'Off to Manish!' (Joina MacDonald, personal communication, 6 February 2004).

643 Simmons 1998, p. 150. Captain Burt was told the story in the presence of Simon, Lord Lovat. He follows it with an interesting account of the ensuing discussion. The minister claimed that the truth of it was proven by a certificate signed by four of his fellow-clergymen; Lovat silenced Burt's sceptical reaction by saying to the minister: "Sir, you must not mind Mr —, for he is an atheist."

644 Cf. *Bruchd Riabhach* three paragraphs later. For the wonderful names given to the King of the Cats cf. 'Old Calgravatus' which became in Gaelic *Curra Mhàgais* (*Tocher* 13, pp. 186–87), *Cugar, Cugarbhad* (*CG2*, p. 263), *Cugrabhat, Gugtrabhad* (*Tocher* 7, pp. 222–29; Shaw 1991, pp. 99–100; Bruford and MacDonald 1994, pp. 2–3, 107, 450), *Tucrabhat* (*Meall Thucrabhat* in South Uist, Caimbeul 2003, p. 372). For the motif 'The King of the Cats is Dead' see Almqvist 1991a, pp. 20, 22.

645 Ó Néill remarks (1991, p. 186) that the changes in shape and character undergone by the domestic cat in this tale-type 'are stamped with such realism that one is tempted to suppose their ultimate background to be factual observation of the real wild cat (*Felix sylvestris grampia*), which is so much bigger and more robust than its domestic relative and when threatened and in a fighting mood arches its back and raises its fur, so that it seems to grow to twice its normal size'. In a story told by Donald Macdonald, Bunacaimb, Arisaig, a cat 'grows and grows until it assumes the form of a woman' (Maclean 1975, p. 59). It should be pointed out however that the swelling of an innocent creature into a monster also features in stories unconnected with cats such as 'Gillecriosd Tàillear, agus a' Chailleach' ('Gilchrist, the Tailor, and the Hag') and 'Sealgair Shrath Eirinn is a' Chailleach' ('The Strath Dearn Hunter and the Witch') in MacDougall and Calder 1910, pp. 226–33. In the former an old woman comes to a shieling bothy at night, and as she dries out by the fire she swells and swells. Eventually she tries to murder the inhabitants. Foiled by the tailor, she calls upon *Gormla Mhór o'n Mhaigh an Lochabar* (for whom see p. 186) and *Nighean Fhir Leirg na h-Uinnsinn an Cnapadal* ('the daughter of the Laird of Ashfield, in Knapdale'). Fortunately at that point the black-cock crows on the brae above, and she is obliged to take the road. In the latter story, also located in a shieling bothy, the innocent creature is a hen which, again, swells into a ferocious woman. The hunter sets his dogs upon her, and next day in the village he comes across a woman whose breasts have been ripped off. She is clearly the culprit, and he puts her to death as a witch. See MacDonald 1994–95, pp. 36–37.

646 See note 572.

647 *Earchall* is loss or misfortune, usually by the death of cattle in spring. *Urchaill earchaill* (spelt *urchuill earchaill* by JGC) seems to be modelled upon it, perhaps echoing *urchoid* 'hurt, harm, calamity, loss' and semantic pairs like *ullamh/eallamh, ultach/eallach, urlainn/earrlann*. A comparable English expression is 'rack and ruin'.

648 Cf. Grant 1925, p. 2. This is reminiscent of a feature noticed by Ó Néill in Irish 'King of the Cats' stories (1991, p. 178), in which the message "contains a short rhyme, the rhyming words being the name of the dead cat and that of the cat which is to receive the message. In some

instances an even more striking effect is achieved through the outlandish and whimsical character of these names."

649 This refers, under the sub-title 'The Wexford Legend of the Cat' (Anon. 1869, pp. 324–26), to Malcomson 1868, a report of a book called *Beware the Cat* by William Baldwin (London, 1584), which includes a tall story told by an Englishman who had heard it in Ireland, cf. Opie and Tatem 1992, p. 57. It concerns a 'kern' or brigand (what Scott would have called a cateran) named Patrik Apore – presumably Pádraig de Paor or Power. After lifting a cow and a sheep from a farmstead in Co. Wexford and murdering the inhabitants, Pádraig and his horse-keeper take sanctuary in a church, 'thinking to lurk ther til midnight was past'. Having had little to eat all day, they build a fire in the church, kill the sheep and roast it. When it is ready, however, a cat comes in, sits down beside Pádraig, and says in Irish: *Shane foel*. Since this is translated 'Give me some meat' by the author, it may represent *Sín chugham feoil*, though Ó Néill (1991, p. 185) prefers to see *shane* as *'seáin*, i.e. *teaspáin* 'show' in the sense 'give', 'hand over to me'. The rest may be told in Baldwin's words. "He amased at this gave her the quarter that was in his hand, whiche immediately she did eat up, and asked more, till she had consumed all the sheep, and like a cormorant not satisfied therwith, asked stil for more, wherfore they supposed it were the Devil, and therefore thinking it wisdome to please him, killed the Cow which they had stolen, and when they had flaid it, gave the Cat a quarter, which she immediatlye devoured; then they gave her two other quarters, and in the mean while, after the contrie fashion, they did cut a peece of the hide, and pricked it upon fower stakes which they set about the fire, and therein they set a peece of the Cow for themselves, and with the rest of the hide they made eche of them laps to were about their feet like broges, bothe to keep theire feet from hurt all the next day, and also to serve for meat the next night if they could get none other, by broyling them upon coles. By this time the Cat had eaten three quarters, and called for more, wherfor they gave her that which was a seething, and douting lest when she had eaten that she would eat them to, because they had no more for her, they got then out of the Church, and the *Kern* tooke his horse, and away he rode as fast as he could hie.

"When he was a mile or two from the Church, the moone began to shine, and his boy espied the cat upon his master's horse behinde him; tolde him, wherupon the Kern took his dart, and turning his face toward her, flang it, and stroke her thorough with it; but immediatly there came to her such a sight of Cats that after long fight with them his boy was killed, and eaten up, and he him self, as good and as swift as his horse was, had much to do to scape. When he was come home, and had put of his harnes (which was a Corslet of maile, made like a Shirt, and his Scul covered over with gilt lether, and crested with Otterskin), all weary and hungry, set him down by his wife, and tolde her his adventure, which when a kitling which his wife kept, scarce half a yeere, had heard, up she started, and said, hast thou killed *Grimmalkin?* and therwith she plunged in his face, and with her teeth took him by the throte, and ere that shee could be taken away she had strangled him."

650 JGC's Gaelic originals of these verses were excluded from *WSS*, but Alexander Carmichael transcribed them from the lost appendix into what is now EUL MS CW 241, ff. 24–25, under the title 'An Cat Thainig Beo' ('The Cat that Came Alive'), see p. 702 below. What is now the penultimate line on p. 191 appears in CW 241 as *Dh-iòcaich iad do mhuinneal an smuais sin*; as this makes no sense to me, I have adjusted it in line with JGC's translation. Carmichael also appears to have collected the poem himself, noting it under the heading 'An Cat A Bha Marbh Agus A Thainig Beo' ('The Cat that was Dead and Came Alive') in what is now EUL MS CW 503, ff. 851v and 853v, with some alternative readings. In line 2 he offers both *falachaidh* ('wary') and *iomachaidh* ('circumspect, well-behaved'). In line three he gives not *gan ionnsaigh* but *dhan Mheanachain* with three question-marks – 'to the Monastery' or, more probably, 'to Beauly'. For lines 5–8 he has (his spelling):

> *Is dona dhuits a chait chluasaich*
> *Bhuaileadh thu an geall a chaise*
> *Dh iochd do mhuinneal min an smuaich*
> *An uair seo an deigh do bhaise*

I translate: "It's tough for you, you big-eared cat, / That you've been struck because of cheese – / Your smooth neck's paid for the refreshment / At this time following your death."

Following the cat's revival, the poet's words are as follows (edited from CW 241):

> *Ciad fàilte romhad, a chait,*
> *On thàrladh dhuit a bhith am' uchd;*
> *'S ged nach leig mi mòran leat,*
> *Is iomadh neach thug ròghradh dhut.*
> *An tu 'n cat fiadht' a bh' aig Fionn*
> *Bha fiadhach o ghleann gu gleann?*
> *No 'n tu bh' aig Osgar là bhlàr sguinn,*
> *No 'n tu dh'fhàg suinn fo dhochair ann?*
> *Dh'òl thu àis Catrìona 's am bainne*
> *Bha ri dìoladh cléir is coinneamh,*
> *'S dé 'm fàth dhòmhsa bhith gad mholadh?*
> *Mharbh thu, chait ghrànda dhona!*
> *Bu chòir dhuit bhith mar phiseag,*
> *Bhith san t-sliabh ag iarraidh luchag*
> *Fo chuiseig riabhaich 's fo dhriseig.*

It will be seen from this that a line is missing from JGC's translation: "You have killed, you ugly evil cat!" should appear after "And why should I praise you?" In fact, as the rhyme structure reveals, the poem is in quatrains, and the first line of the last quatrain is lacking in JGC's Gaelic as well as his English. Carmichael's version in CW 503 is helpful, however:

> *Dh ol thu bainne Cairistine*
> *Bha gu dioladh cleir us crabhaich*
> *De am fath dhomh bhi dha/ga innseadh*
> *Mharbhadh thu chait mhiogaich mhagaich.*

> *Is am bu choir dhuit bhi mar phiseig*
> *An tir/taigh a phoir ag iarraidh luchag*
> *fo mheoir na driseig*
> *An aite corcaich bhi mu d ruchaig.*

"You drank the milk that Catherine had / To entertain the clergy and the pious – / What's the point of my relating it? / You've been killed, you smirky creepy cat. / And should you be like any kitten / Seeking mice in land/house of grain / —— under boughs of bramble bushes / Instead of hemp being round your little neck." Probably *Is am bu choir* 'And should you be' ought to read *Is ann bu chòir* 'You should be'.

Some other points are worth making. JGC's line *Is iomadh neach thug ròghradh dhut* is stuffed full of alternatives in CW 503: *Is iomadh 'ad/laoch/bard* ('Many are they / the heroes / the poets') *a thug gradh/failte dhut* ('who welcomed/loved you'). *Là bhlàr sguinn* appears in CW 241 as *la bhlar sguinn* and in CW 503 as *la blar Sguinn*, but JGC's translation 'battle of Bla-sguinn' is also helpful. For 'skull' Lhuyd (1707, pp. [327], 427) first gives *blaosgaoin*, *blasgaoin*, then, when he has consulted further, *blaosc a chinn*, i.e. *plaosg a' chinn* ('the husk of the head'); the original of the line was probably *No 'n tu bh' aig Osgar là bhlasgaoin* (or *là phlaosg-cinn*)? "Or did Oscar have you at the battle of head-husks?" It will be a reference to Cath Gabhra, in which Oscar was killed, see pp. 283–84 'The Battle of Gaura'. *Blaosg a chinn* and *blasgaoin* were picked up from Lhuyd by the HSD (vol. 1, pp. 123–24) and found their way into Dwelly (1977, pp. 99–100) as *blaosg, blasgaoin.*

Finally, JGC's *cléir is coinneamh* 'minstrel and meeting' is of interest. His *coinneamh : dhona* is excellent rhyme, as is Carmichael's *cràbhaich : mhàgaich*. No doubt *cléir* still existed as a plural or genitive singular of *cliar* 'poet band', hence 'minstrel(s)', but by JGC's time its primary meanings were 'clergy' and 'presbytery'. Perhaps the *àis* 'milk preparation' and *bainne* 'milk' were intended for himself!

For another version of the poem see Mackenzie 1879–80, pp. 38–39.

651 See note 246. JGC's 'as good luck did not direct him' reflects the Gaelic idiom *mar nach d'òrdaich sealbh e*.

652 See notes 413 and 634. It looks as if we should distinguish between this semi-mythical *Nic Mhaol Dòmhnaich* in Caolas and the historical *Nic Mhaol Dòmhnaich* in Balephuil, at the opposite end of Tiree. Brownlie (1971, p. 21) adds 'Maol Nic Domhnuich á Tiridhe' to the black litany which includes the Doideag, Gorm-Shùil, Ball Odhar, etc., as given at p. 197 ('Celebrated Witches'). For what it is worth, we may note that among those from Caolas who appeared at the surrender of weapons at Scarinish on 23 April 1716 was 'Mildonich McIlchallum in taur', i.e. *Maol Dòmhnaich mac Gille Chaluim an t-Saoir*, a carpenter's grandson (Maclean-Bristol 1998, p. 114). Probably the solution to the *Nic Mhaol Dòmhnaich* problem lies in JGC's words at p. 197: "The best-known names seem to have been merely nicknames, given perhaps to more than one old woman."

653 This story is remarkably similar to that of a tragedy of 8 July 1856 – in which at least nine, perhaps twelve or more, of forty fishermen on seven Balephuil boats were drowned – as told in Gaelic and English by Niall M. Brownlie (1995, pp. 85–87). "At the time there was a famous witch in Balephuil by the name of Mairead . . . On the evening of the storm, an exhausted seagull (*faoileann chlaoidhte*) alighted on the gunwale (*stoc*) of Calum Bàn's boat. One of the crew wanted it killed, as he considered it to be a bird of ill-omen (*gum b' e droch chomharradh a bha innte*). But Calum told him to let it be, as it was only a bird of passage (*eun siubhail*). That night Mairead informed the villagers that Calum Bàn's boat and all on board were safe and nearing Islay." It appears that a migratory legend has attached itself to Calum Bàn as one of the best known sons of Balephuil, even though he was only a boy at the time and was not on any of the boats that day; it is, however, true that two of the boats reached safety in Islay, one of them carrying a Malcolm Macdonald, who was rescued when his own boat sank (Cameron 1932, pp. 125–26; *Tocher* 18, p. 59; cf. MacDougall and Cameron n.d., p. 106). Interestingly, Calum Bàn's son Donald also attributed the disaster to witchcraft, but the women he blamed were Mary Campbell and Isabella Maclean, *née* Black (his own great-aunt), both of whose husbands perished (*Tocher* 18, pp. 56–58, and Cregeen 1998, pp. 27–31). It is curious that JGC nowhere mentions the tragedy, which is well remembered in Tiree to this day. See also *Tocher* 32, pp. 90–91, and note 634 above.

654 A 'gathering of women for fulling cloth' is generally known as a *luadh, luadhadh* or 'waulking', see p. 214, also Martin 1716, p. 57; Mackellar 1886–87; Grant 1925, p. 44; Campbell 1969–81, vol. 1, pp. 3–16, and vol. 3, pp. 2–5; *Tocher* 24, pp. 308–11; *Tocher* 41, pp. 262–63; *Tocher* 50, pp. 5–25; Pennant 1998, pp. 284–85; Simmons 1998, p. 213; Shaw 2000, pp. 16–17, 72–76, 80–83, 369–70; Black 2002, pp. 377–78. For another version of the story see Introduction, p. lxiv.

655 *Braise* is 'brashness, boldness, wantonness, excitability', etc., e.g. *theann iad ri braise* 'they became excited', 'started carrying on', or, as JGC puts it, 'began to disport themselves'; *gob na tuinne* is literally 'the beak of the waves'.

656 For the tale-type 'Witch Delays Birth of Child' see Bruford 1967, p. 24; Maclean 1975, p. 43; Bruford and MacDonald 1994, p. 476; MacDonald 1994–95, p. 39. On black thread see pp. 137, 158.

657 Much has been written on Ailein nan Sop, see e.g. Anon. 1841–42b = Henderson 1901, pp. 87–92; Abrach 1875; Thomson 1994, p. 3; Maclean-Bristol 1995, pp. 94–103, 117–18, 128–31, 176; Ó Baoill 1996; Ó Baoill 1997, pp. 1–2, 47–49; Ó Baoill 1998; Pennant 1998, p. 241. JGC's 'Allan of the Faggots' is a little tiresome, but has some justification: John Mackechnie says (1964, p. 308) that he got the nickname from his skill and ability in smoking his enemies out of their hiding-places. Perhaps a more likely explanation, however, is that a remarkable number of urine-laden wisps were aimed in his direction around the time of his birth, which was obviously a difficult one – see 'Saining Straw (*Sop Seile*)', pp. 136–37. On the keeping of fools see note 275.

658 On the *corp crèadha* see also Stewart 1823, pp. 183–84; Dalyell 1834, pp. 328–71; Anon. 1884a; Anon. 1886–87a, p. 41; Macdonald 1893–94, p. 274–75; Maclagan 1895, pp. 144–48; Maclagan 1902, p. 9; Macdonald 1903, pp. 373–74; Henderson 1911, p. 15; Mackay 1914, p. 431; McPherson 1929, pp. 198–209; *Tocher* 18, pp. 56–58; *Tocher* 54/55, pp. 331–34; Scott 2001, pp. 188, 193, 196; Youngson 2001, pp. 493–94; SoSS Maclagan MSS vol. 22, pp. 3875–3983 (*sic*, error in pagination).

659 See 'Mac Ian Year', pp. 97–98 above.

660 Donald MacGillivray (1777–1835) was born in Inverness-shire. He served as missionary in Strathfillan 1813–16 and 1819–20, and was minister of Kilmallie from 1831 to 1835. In 1817 he published a Gaelic translation of *An Authentic Narrative of the Life of John Newton, late Rector of St Mary, Woolnoth, London* (see MacLean 1915, pp. 301–02, and Scott 1915–50, vol. 4, p. 135).

661 The implication is that he had only one arm. At p. 286 JGC uses the term 'Lord Macdonald' of Dòmhnall Gorm Mór of Sleat, but I am not aware that he or any other Sleat chief lost an arm. It would help if *Raonaid a' Chreagain* could be identified. The only other *Creagan* mentioned by JGC is *Creagan na Glaistig an Creag Mhòr Mhic Cuinn* in the Braes of Portree (p. 100), which is indeed MacDonald of Sleat territory.

662 For Badenoch's reputation for witchcraft see p. 289 ('Haunted Houses'), and for turning a person into a horse by shaking a bridle at him see Scott 2001, p. 150. The magic bridle as an international folklore motif is discussed by Oates (2003, pp. 210–13). For an alleged magic bridle belonging to Gregor Willox, Kirkmichael, Banffshire (c.1755–1833), see Stewart 1860, vol. 1, pp. 116–27; Maclagan 1902, p. 149; Henderson 1911, pp. 116, 306; Mackay 1914, p. 432; MacFarlane 1927–28, pp. 148–49; McPherson 1929, pp. 164, 260–61, 265; Macdonald 1982, pp. 142–43; Gray 1987, pp. 228–33; McGregor 1994; Sutherland 1997; MacilleDhuibh 10.9.99. In Lauder 1837 is a frontispiece showing Willox apparently holding the bridle. This sketch also appears on the front cover of one of the latest editions of JGC's work (Campbell 2003a).

663 The phrase is not *casa gurra* but *casa curra* 'stilts', 'heron legs'. Carmichael gives the incantation as follows (CG2, pp. 132–35):

Feith Mhoire,	*Ditch of Mary,*
Feith Mhoire;	*Ditch of Mary;*
Casa curra,	*Heron legs,*
Casa curra;	*Heron legs;*
Feith Mhoire,	*Ditch of Mary,*
Feith Mhoire;	*Ditch of Mary;*
Casa curra fothaibh,	*Heron legs under you,*
Drochaid urra romhaibh.	*Bridge of warranty before you.*

Chuir Moire gas ann,	*Mary placed a wand in it,*
Chuir Bride bas ann,	*Bride placed a hand in it,*
Chuir Calum cas ann,	*Columba placed a foot in it,*
Chuir Padra clach fhuar.	*Patrick placed a cold stone.*
Feith Mhoire . . .	*Ditch of Mary . . .*
Chuir Muiril mirr ann,	*Muirel placed myrrh in it,*
Chuir Uiril mil ann,	*Uriel placed honey in it,*
Chuir Muirinn fion ann,	*Muirinn placed wine in it,*
'S chuir Micheal ann buadh.	*And Michael placed in it power.*
Feith Mhoire . . .	*Ditch of Mary . . .*

He got it from John Macinnes, crofter, Staoligearry, South Uist, of whom he says (*CG*2, p. 375), "Several volumes of old lore, mostly heroic tales, died with this nice, intelligent man." He explains: "Flat moorland is generally intersected with innumerable veins, channels, and ditches. Sometimes these are serious obstacles to cattle, more especially to cows, which are accurate judges. When a cow hesitates to cross, the person driving her throws a stalk or a twig into the ditch before the unwilling animal and sings the 'Feith Mhoire', Vein of Mary, to encourage her to cross, and to assure her that a safe bridge is before her . . . The practice of throwing down the wand and repeating the hymn gave rise to a proverb among the more sceptical of the people:—'Cha dean thu feith Mhoire orm-s' idir a mhicean'—Thou wilt not make a 'vein of Mary' upon me at all, sonnie." It is curious how little Carmichael has to say about horses. See also GUL MS Gen. 1090/29, p. 47.

664 It is impossible to know for certain whether JGC means Glen Quoich in west Inverness-shire or Glen Quaich in south Perthshire. Both are *Gleann Chuaich*. The latter is better known in Gaelic tradition, however (from the song 'Iain Ghlinne Chuaich'), and is perhaps marginally more likely.

665 This is correct. *Gormla* is in origin *Gorm(fh)laith* 'Blue Aristocrat'. The most celebrated possessor of the name was daughter of the high-king *Flann Sionna*, who died AD 916. She was married to three kings in a row: Cormac, king-bishop of Cashel (d. 916), his conqueror Cerball mac Muirecáin (d. 909), and Niall Glúndub, who fell in battle against the vikings in 919, after which she is said to have died in poverty. A sequence of poems is attributed to her, for which see Bergin 1970, pp. 202–15, 308–15; I have argued (MacilleDhuibh 26.7.02) that this led to her name being used (as 'Goneril') by Geoffrey of Monmouth in *Historia Regum Britanniae* (Thorpe 1966, pp. 81–83) and by Shakespeare in *King Lear*. Anglicised 'Gormelia' rather than 'Dorothy', the name remained popular in Lewis until the early twentieth century. See Derick Thomson's long poem 'Gormshuil' (MacThòmais 1991, pp. 126–39).

666 See p. 186 above; Kilgour 1908, pp. 181–82, 158; Mackechnie 1964, pp. 89–91; McKerracher 1994, p. 381. For other traditions about Gormshuil see Livingstone 1886–87, p. 264, and Mackellar 1889–90, pp. 272–76.

667 See pp. 183 and 184. Niall M. Brownlie tells me he has not heard of Gormshuil in Hianish.

668 JGC cites this stanza in the context of a discussion of the name Mac an Uidhir, which is probably for *Mac 'Ain Uidhir* 'the Son of Tawny-Faced John', though JGC makes it simply 'the son of Euar' (Campbell 1895, p. 18, cf. Henderson 1908–11, p. 389, and Matheson 1951–52a, p. 327):

An cuala sibhse riamh iomradh
Mu Chaiseart Gharbh, Nic an Uidhir?

Bha i òg an Gleann Forsa
Nar bha Oisean 'na ghiullan;
Bha i falbh 's i 'na proitseach
Le Cas a' Mhogain a piuthar —
Is mis' an truaghan 'nan déidh
'S gun fhios gu dé thàinig riutha.

JGC offers this translation: "Did ever you hear mention / Of Rough Foot-gear daughter of Euar? / She was young in Glenforse / When Ossian was a young boy; / She was going about as a slip of a girl / With Headless Stocking her sister. / I am a wretched creature after them / Not knowing what became of them." A *mogan*, as JGC says, is a footless stocking (a common article of clothing in boggy country), *cas* is the foot and lower leg, and *riabhach* is 'brindled', 'streaky brown' (usually used of hide or rocks, here of undyed wool), so *Cas a' Mhogain Riabhaich* could alternatively be translated 'the Leg with the Undyed Footless Stocking'. In more modern terms she would be 'that woman who wears undyed footless stockings on her legs', not exactly a fashion icon.

For Mac Rùslain (Mac-a-Rusgaich, MacCrùislig, MacRùsgail), the Tyll Eulenspiegel of Gaelic tradition, see Campbell 1890, vol. 2, pp. 318–43; Watson 1926b, pp. 210–11; Nicolson 1951, pp. 138, 209, 340; Ó Duilearga 1981, p. 403; Bruford and MacDonald 1994, p. 456. He is the subject of the first Gaelic traditional tale ever published (Mackenzie 1836), and belongs to every age and none – he appears as a stealer of pigs in the children's game 'MacCrùslaig 's na Mucan' (Morrison 1907–08, pp. 362, 369), and the drunkard in a version of the bacchanalian song 'Cuach MhicillAnndrais' ends up lying on his back looking at the stars and *choltaich mi iad uile / Ri Cuchulainn 's Dòmhnall MacCrùislig* ('I likened them all / to Cuchulainn and Donald MacCrùislig', Mac-na-Ceàrdadh 1879, p. 479, cf. Shaw 2000, pp. 298–99). However, he appears to have originated as a historical character, Crítán mac Rustaing, who lived in Armagh in the early seventh century AD and enjoyed a reputation as a trickster and comedian. His grave in Ross Ech is described in the notes to the 'Félire Óengusso' (Clancy 1992, p. 87): "No woman can see it without farting or without a loud foolish laugh afterwards."

James Shaw (Seumas MacGilleSheathanaich, *c.*1758–*c.*1828) was a native of Mull, but lived latterly in the mainland parish of Ardchattan, where he was known as *Bàrd Loch nan Eala* 'the Lochnell Bard'. According to John Mackenzie (1841, p. 311), 'he lived in a state of idleness and dissipation; praising those who paid him well for it, and composing satires on those who refused him money or liquor'. His work may be found in Mac-an-Tuairneir 1813, pp. 247–64; Mackenzie 1841, pp. 311–15; Mac-na-Ceàrdadh 1879, pp. 161–62, 243–44; Sinclair 1891–92, p. 293; Henderson 1908–11, pp. 385–93; Cameron 1932, pp. 134–35; Matheson 1951–52a, pp. 326–29; Cregeen and MacKenzie 1978, p. 18.

669 For *Spòga Buidhe* see also pp. 183 and 184 above. The nickname *Spòg Bhuidhe* ('Yellow Claw') was given to a mysterious highwayman who robbed travellers crossing a bridge near Perth, and turned out to be the local innkeeper (*Tocher* 7, pp. 210–15 = Bruford and MacDonald 1994, pp. 412–14); I am tempted to wonder if he was the parsimonious Dunkeld innkeeper called Johnstone who was satirised *c.* 1760 by Lachlan MacPherson of Strathmashie (Black 2001, pp. 220–23). *Doideagun* is JGC's spelling of *doideagan*, plural of *doideag*, see Bruford and MacDonald 1994, p. 430. There was a *Doideag Chanach* (Doideag from Canna) as well as the *Doideagan Muileach* (Mac a Phì 1938, pp. 80–81). 'Forty years ago' means *c.* 1834; at p. 224 JGC refers to a witch in Fort William called *Mary* Macintyre.

Bean an Lagain (for whom see Stewart 1823, pp. 189–98; Stewart 1860, vol. 2, pp. 191–200; Macpherson 1893, pp. 23–26; Macpherson 1925, pp. 7–9; Bruford 1967, pp. 37–39; Gray 1987, pp. 33–36) is missing from the list for the simple reason that she and *Gormshuil na*

Moighe appear to have been regarded as one and the same – the former being her name in Badenoch and the east, the latter in Lochaber and the west (see note 635). Her name refers to a little-known Laggan a mile east of Kingussie (Macbain 1889–90, p. 191, and Baran 1986–88, p. 187), but this nuance was presumably lost upon natives of the West Highlands, who would have linked her with Gormshuil's native parish of Laggan. Eachann Mac Dhughaill says of her (1913, p. 31): *'S an àm anns* [sic] *robh i beò – suas mu dheireadh na sèathamh linn deug – bha, co dhiùbh, seachd de na buidsichean a b' ainmeile a bha riamh an Albainn beò; agus b' iomadh sin cron is call mu 'n robh iad. Bha an Doideag Mhuileach, Cré Inbhirnis, Nighean Dualachain as an Eilean Sgitheanach, Cailleach a' Mhogain Riabhaich á Loch Aillse, agus té a bha, cha mhór, co-ionann ri Bean an Lagain fhéin, a' Bhuidseach Mhór Abarach: Gorm-shuil Bhàrr-na-Maighe.* "In her day – up around the end of the sixteenth century – there lived at least seven of the most famous witches Scotland has ever known; and many indeed were the tragedies and disasters they perpetrated. There were the Doideag of Mull, Cré of Inverness, Dualachan's Daughter from Skye, the Hag of the Undyed Footless Stocking from Lochalsh, and one who was more or less the same as the Wife of Laggan herself, the Great Lochaber Witch: Gormshuil from Moy." Mac Dhughaill footnotes *Cré Inbhirnis* as follows:

> *Dìol na Cré Mhóir a bha 'n Inbhirnis dhuit;*
> *Dh' fhuiling ise dòrainn 's bu mhòr a tiodal;*
> *Bhiodh i 'cur na dìollaid air fear a tighe;*
> *Làraichean nan cruidhean a chaidh 'na làmhan*
> *'S àileachan nan srein air a bheul air caitheamh.*
>
> Sean Oran.

("Be you treated like a victim of Big Cré in Inverness; / What agony she suffered, she richly deserved it; / She would put the saddle on the man of her house; / The marks of the hooves that turned back into hands / And the bit of the reins ground down on his mouth. / *Old Song*.") W. Grant Stewart, who calls her *Crea Mhoir cun Drochdair*, says she was 'burnt and worried at a stake at Inverness, about two centuries ago, for bewitching and keeping in torment the body of the provost's son' (1823, p. 183, and 1851, p. 127); *cun Drochdair* will be for *cù 'n droch fhir* 'the devil's hound', cf. Stewart's spelling *Maug Vuluchd* for 'Hairy Mag', p. 414 above.

Some circumstantial detail is supplied by John Maclean, 'the Clachnacuddin Centenarian', in an account first published in 1842. Cré, or Creibh, lived with her sister in a bothy in the Millburn valley (a mile east of Inverness), a sinister spectre-haunted place which was still notorious for witchcraft as late as 1745. Some children found a *corp crèadha* in the burn 'stuck all over with pins' (see pp. 195–96 above). "One of the children said she often saw her grandmother, 'Creibh Mhor', make the like of that." Gossip led to a judicial enquiry. Creibh was arrested and tortured, but denied practising witchcraft. Her sister was then tortured. She 'acknowledged their mutual guilt' and stated that the effigy was meant to represent Cuthbert of Castle Hill, a prominent merchant in the town. Both sisters were condemned and a stake was prepared for them on the Barn Hill opposite the Castle (Maclean 1886, pp. 93–94).

According to a separate tradition (Barron 1971–72, p. 240, and 1986–88, pp. 201–02, cf. Anon. 1891a, pp. 6–7), Creibh fled to Flichity in Strathnairn, where she was caught in Pairc Druim a' Chal. She asked for two plates; they gave her one and she made a wing of it; she asked for another, and when it was refused she said: *Mur toirt sibhs' an truinnsear eil' dhomhs' cha chum sibh fad' so mi.* ("If you don't give me the other plate you won't keep me here for long.") They brought her to the Longmans (*chon na Longmans*) and before they had burned her she cursed Flichity. *Fhid' 's (fhad' 's) a bhith an allt aig Flichtidh ruith dha an taobh tuath bithidh mollachd air Flichtidh. Ma gheobh an tuathanach math cha gheibhinn an tighearna agus ma gheibhinn an tighearna math cha gheibhinn an tuathanach.* "As long as the burn at Flichity runs north, Flichity will be cursed. If the farmer prospers the laird will not, and if the laird prospers the farmer will not."

Creibh was burned first. According to Alexander Polson (1932, p. 131) she cried out for water. An onlooker went to get some, but when 'a so-called wise man' was told it was for her he emptied the vessel upon the earth. Seeing this, Creibh cursed them but also said, "If only I had got a mouthful of that water I would have turned Inverness into a peat bog."

Anon. (1887–88, p. 92) ascribes this story not to Creibh but to 'a contemporary of hers – one of the last witches burnt in the town'. Having betrayed her, her sibling also considered escaping, but was brought to watch her burn, and the chief constable 'commenced unfastening the massive Highland brooch which confined the plaid of the weird sister'. "Well, well," she said, "if I had thought it would have come to this, there would have been many who wear scarlet cloaks here today!" And she denounced the Cuthberts. The scarlet cloak was a sign of gentility, and what she meant was that many of the ladies of Inverness were as much involved in the black art as *purchasers* of charms, spells and fortunes as she and Creibh had been as *purveyors* of them, which was self-evidently true (Maclean 1886, pp. 94–95, 101). Creibh and her sister may probably be identified as two married women named McQuicken and McRorie who were tried and executed for witchcraft in Inverness in 1695 by commission from the Privy Council. No more women were ever tried for witchcraft in the town, but two men, George and Lachlan Rattray, were tried and burnt there in 1706 (Black 1938, pp. 80, 82; Larner, Lee and McLachlan 1977, pp. 148, 150).

Another witch-name not mentioned by JGC is *Nic Neamhain, Nic Creamhain* (presumably in origin *Nic Naomhain, Nic Naoimhein*, see Macbain 1897–98, p. 166), referred to in Lowland sources as 'Nicneven' (Hanham 1969). In Arran *MacCreamhain* has been anglicised as Crawford, hence Carmichael's reference to *bana-bhuidseach mhòr Nic Creafain* as 'the great arch witch daughter Crauford, Mac Creafain, now Crawford' (*CG2*, p. 370). There was a story that the MacNivens are descended from a child who was called *Craoibhean* ('Little Tree-Man') because he was found at the root of a tree (*Tocher* 25, p. 49).

670 *Air a ruidheadh* is properly *air a righeadh*, 'stretched out'.

671 See also Campbell and Hall 1968, p. 250, and *Tocher* 8, pp. 240–41 = Bruford and MacDonald 1994, pp. 309–10, 469. MacDonald (1994–95, p. 66) calls this story-type 'The Cannibal Corpse'.

672 A new quarter was regularly celebrated on the first Monday, being the appropriate day of the week for beginnings, and clearly this applied to superstitious beliefs of all kinds, see *CG4*, pp. 150–51.

673 Brand 1849, vol. 3, p. 3. In Brand's source (Cotta 1612, pp. 71–72) the terms are repeatedly written as one word: 'wisemen', 'wisewoman', 'wisewomen'. This is also the origin of 'wizard', Cotta's 'wisard'.

674 On the Sunday plant see pp. 125 and 564.

675 This was footnoted in *WSS* 55: "The author wrote this chapter in 1874. – ED." The editor had simply noticed JGC's mention of this date at *WSS* 74 (now p. 212 above). See 'Life', pp. 643–44 below.

676 This had already been fulfilled by the time JGC's words were published in 1902, the book being *CG2*. Smaller collections include Mackenzie's (1878–79, pp. 123–28, and 1891–92), Macbain's (1890–91 and 1891–92) and Macdonald's (1982, pp. 175–82, first published in 1914). For an excellent general introduction to the subject see Maclean 1959, pp. 191–94, and for some further notes see Ross 1957, pp. 138–40.

677 For discussion of these and similar terms see *CG2*, p. 337, Campbell 1978–81, p. 198, and Black 2001, p. 374; cf. also '*Gisreagun, Eapagun, Upagun*' (p. 125 above) and Norman MacLeod's remark, first published in 1867 (1882, p. 248): "What *ùbag, obag*, and *gisreag* (charm, incantation, and canting) they used I know not . . ."

678 See '*Eòlas*', pp. 200–01, 'Charm for Conferring Graces (*Òradh nam Buadh*)', pp. 216–17, and '*Soisgeul*, Gospel', p. 224. *Òradh nam Buadh* should read *Ortha nam Buadh*, because JGC is quite wrong in imagining that *ortha* 'charm, incantation' is to be explained as *òradh* 'gilding' – it is, as Macbain points out (1896, p. 243), from *orationem*, accusative of Latin *oratio* 'speech'. JGC's spelling in *WSS* 56 is '*Oradh* (Gilding)'. See Campbell 1978–81, pp. 214–15.

679 The words as they stand in *WSS* 59 are 'to go without a full udder', but this makes no sense, so I have guessed that JGC intended 'to go out with a full udder'. For the evil eye in Scotland see Dalyell 1834, pp. 3–18; Mitchell 1860–62, pp. 285–86; Anon. 1886–87b; Maclagan 1895, pp. 154–56; MacGregor 1901, pp. 34–35; Maclagan 1902; Macdonald 1903, pp. 379–80; Henderson 1911, pp. 25–29; Mackenzie 1914, pp. 291–94; Polson 1926, pp. 112–17; McPherson 1929, pp. 191–93; Polson 1932, pp. 173–80; Sutherland 1937, pp. 105–06; Macdonald 1982, pp. 140–42; Davidson 1992; *Tocher* 47, pp. 328–30; Youngson 2001, pp. 501–03. For collections of essays relating to the evil eye world-wide see Maloney 1976 and Dundes 1992. Maloney says (1976, p. xiv): "There are so many aspects of the evil eye belief found contiguously from Scotland at one extreme of its main area of distribution to Sri Lanka at the other, that we must rely heavily on a diffusionist explanation. In Scotland, for example, where this belief was described by Maclagan at the turn of this century, cattle and milk products and the churning process were especially susceptible to evil eye attack; the eye could make a cow's udder or a woman's breasts dry up, or cause milk to be devoid of butterfat. All this is true at the other geographical extreme, in India. A charm of a knotted red thread, or of hair, may be tied on children or on a pregnant cow both in Scotland and in South Asia. A fragment of the Bible may be sewn in the clothes as a preventative in Scotland, while in South Asia a fragment of the Koran or a Hindu incantation may be put in a receptacle and tied on children . . . In the two regions the belief serves similar functions in the folk etiology, is popularly regarded as preventing too much self-praise, and is explained as suppressing envy . . . It must have been spread in large measure by the expansion of Indo-European- and Semitic-speaking peoples (in contrast with speakers of Sinitic, Malay, or Bantu languages, for example), and the early dairying and herding traditions of those peoples may account for the statistical association of the belief with those features."

680 By 'some fifty years ago' JGC means *c*. 1824. The elder in question is probably Neil MacLean, Cornaig, for whom see pp. 654 and 660 below.

681 The reference is to 'Crosanachd Fhir nan Druimnean' ('The Laird of Drimnin's Crosanachd') by the Mull poet John MacLean (*Iain mac Ailein, c.* 1660–1741), published in Mackenzie 1841, pp. 74–75, and Black 2001, pp. 104–11. A *crosanachd* is a mode of composition in which verse alternates with prose. The remark about Macintyre arises from a bawdy incident in which a woman sees a man's genitals and expresses the wish that her own husband's were as large. *Se adhbhar thug don mhnaoi bheusaich, cheart, chòir, seo a ràdh, a rùn deagh-chneasta, chum gum biodh aig a fear fhéin a leithid 's a bhiodh aig a nàbaidhean; 's nach sùil ghointe no lombais a bh' aic' air cuid a coimhearsnaich, mar bh' aig Gillebrìde Mac an t-Saoir ann an Ruthaig an Tiridhe, a mhort an ceithir fichead cearc le aon bheum-sùla 's a bhris long mhòr nan cùig crannag, a dh'ainneoin a càblaichean 's a h-acraichean. Uaithe sin a dubhradh: 'Sann den cheàird a' chungaidh.'* ("What made the virtuous, proper, decent woman say this was her perfectly kind wish that her own husband should have the same as her neighbours; and not any evil eye or covetousness that she had for what belonged to her neighbour, as had Gilbert Macintyre in Ruaig in Tiree, who murdered eighty hens with one look and destroyed a great five-masted ship, despite her cables and her anchors. That's why it has been said: 'The tools are part of the trade.'")

Perhaps Gillebrìde Mac an t-Saoir may be identified with the 'Gilbreid McIntyre' from Salum (a neighbouring township to Ruaig), listed in an account of the surrender of weapons at Scarinish on 23 April 1716 (Maclean-Bristol 1998, p. 115). He 'has no arms', while 'Callum McIlbreid McIntyre his son / has no arms but a durk which he give in'. One individual of the surname is listed as from Ruaig itself – 'Callum McIntyre / has no arms'. Niall M. Brownlie tells me that in more recent times there have been Macintyres in Kilkenneth, Balemartin and Gott, but not in Ruaig.

682   The location of *Cnoc Creagach* is pinpointed for us by MacDougall and Cameron (n.d., p. 52). After passing (or passing through) Torathastan, Triadhlan and Bealach na Gaoithe on the road north from Gallanach to Cornaigbeg, "At the side of Cnoc Creagach we see a tiny cairn of loose stones at the road-side. This marks the spot where the old Postman, Alasdair Fowler fell dead when engaged at his duties in the year 1893 . . . Somewhere on the hill on the other side of the boglach to the right of the road is a 'crogan òir' (hidden treasure), and at a spot 'on which the sun rises and sets on mid-summer day'."

We then go on to Uchd nan Càrn, Lochan a' Chnuic and Cornaigbeg.

683   See p. 210. *Mùin* is not wine but urine – clearly a typographical error, especially as *mùin* is fixed by rhyme with *shùil*. Maclagan got the same two lines from the neighbourhood of Ardrishaig (1902, pp. 222–23, cf. *Tocher* 22, p. 242):

> *Beannachd Dhia air do shùil,*
> *Sop mùin mu do chridhe.*

("God's blessing on your eye, / A splash of urine round your heart.") Maclagan's informant explained, "This is a good protection against injury by an Evil Eye. I used it always with reference to the young chickens, and found it kept them from being hurt by any greedy person." For the sprinkling of urine in general see pp. lvii, 19, 25–26, 177, 248, 553; also Maclagan 1902, pp. 135–39, 177–78; McPherson 1929, pp. 236–37; Hunter 2001, p. 64. The second couplet looks like a 'mouse satire' in miniature (see p. 122) and surely expresses a wish rather than a fact: "The mouse be in the bush / And the bush be on fire."

684   The two luckiest days – Thursdays being sacred to Calum Cille, and Sundays to the Trinity. Bede speaks of a monk at Coldingham in the seventh century AD, a Gael called Adamnan, 'who led a life so devoted to God in prayer and austerity that he took no food or drink except on Sundays and Thursdays' (Farmer 1990, pp. 251–52). See 'Charm for Consumption (*Eòlas na Caithimh*)', p. 207; Dalyell 1834, p. 70; Maclagan 1902, pp. 92, 209.

685   JGC's Gaelic original of this charm was excluded from *WSS*, but I have supplied it from CW MS 241, ff. 26–27 (see p. 703 below). One or two points have to be made. *Iob* is not 'salve' in the physical sense but a charm – also *eab, ob, ub*, etc. *Air a shùil* is for *air do shùil* 'on your eye', see note 729. The words *nèamh* 'heaven' and *neul*, genitive *neòil*, 'cloud' are confused in these texts (cf. pp. 206, 212, 213 and 219), so JGC is right to translate *neòil* as 'of heaven'. Lines 10–11 present a revealing picture of Fairy biology: JGC bowdlerises, but their real meaning is 'Who never ate by their mouths / Or expelled by their buttocks'. This picture is amplified in line 27, which JGC explains very satisfactorily.

For charms against the evil eye see Mackenzie 1841, p. 268; Macbain 1890–91, pp. 239–41 = 1891–92, pp. 179–81; Mackenzie 1891–92, pp. 130–37; CG2, pp. 42–71; *Tocher* 11, p. 120. Some echoes of JGC's Tiree charm appear in those sources, e.g. *Air suil bhig, air suil mhoir* ('On small eye, on large eye', CG2, pp. 70–71), *'S air naoi bean seang sìthe* ('And against nine slender fairy women', Mackenzie 1841, p. 268, and Mackenzie 1891–92, pp. 135–36), *Ge be co rinn dut an t-suil, / Gun laigh i air fein, / Gun laigh i air a thur, / Gun laigh i air a spreidh, / Gun laigh i air a shult, / Gun laigh i air a shaill, / Gun laigh i air a chuid, / Gun laigh i air a chlainn* ('Whoso made to thee the eye, / May it lie upon himself, / May it lie upon his house, / May it lie upon his flocks, / May it lie upon his substance, / May it lie upon his fatness, /

May it lie upon his means, / May it lie upon his children', *CG2*, pp. 52–53), *Aon eud 's an ath eud is euchd, euchd, / Air do shlàinte-sa A. B.* ('One envy, the next envy, and feats, feats, / For your health A. B.', *Tocher* 11, p. 120). The following text in an unknown (?)fifteenth-century hand in a Beaton manuscript (NLS Adv. MS 72.1.2, f. 117v, lines 7–8) illustrates an earlier and more literate phase of the tradition: *Ar bheim sula elabia diabalo oit.asmino in misericordia tra cantar so a cluais an duine no an ainmithi fris am bi pater prae pater post.* "Against the evil eye: *elabia diabalo oit.asmino in misericordia* – when this is spoken in the ear of the person or animal affected, it is preceded and followed by a paternoster."

686 Again, JGC's Gaelic original was excluded from *WSS*, and I have supplied it from CW MS 241, f. 28 (see p. 703 below).

687 The Gaelic original was excluded from *WSS*, but was transcribed from JGC's lost appendix by Alexander Carmichael into what is now EUL MS CW 241, ff. 29–30, see p. 703 below. It was subsequently given by James Maclehose to the editor of *Am Bolg Solair*, where it appears (Story 1907, pp. 99–100) under the heading: "EOLAS AN T-SIOCHAIDH. From the Collection of the late Rev. J. Gregorson Campbell, of Tiree." I have edited it from these sources, and also provided a translation of the last four lines, which JGC omitted. The charm begins *Eapag a beachd. / An eapag chuir Calumcille* in CW MS 241 and *Espag a beachd. An eipa chuir Callum Cille* in Story. Most of it is familiar from other sources in any case. Lines 1–9 and 24–26 resemble the conclusion of a 'charm for a bursting vein' given to Carmichael by Donald Macpherson, shoemaker, Griminish, Benbecula (*CG2*, pp. 14–15): *An t-eolas a rinn Calum-cille, / Air eorlain a ghlinne, / Do sgocha feithe, do leum cnamha – / Tha thu tinn an diugh, bithidh thu slan am maireach.* "The charm made by Columba, / On the bottom of the glen, / For bursting of vein, for dislocation of bone – / Thou art ill to-day, thou shalt be well to-morrow." (For *leum cnàmha* 'dislocation of bone' cf. *leum droma* 'slipped disc', note 793.) The central part (from 'Christ went out' to 'May He heal this', lines 10–22) is not only the best known of all Gaelic incantations, but is also demonstrably ancient and internationally widespread, crossing cultural and linguistic boundaries, see for example Dalyell 1834, p. 27; Anon. 1842–43; Chambers 1870, p. 349; Mackenzie 1878–79, p. 125; Macbain 1890–91, pp. 223–24, 230, 246–48 = 1891–92, pp. 119, 226–28; Mackenzie 1891–92, pp. 166–68; MacDonald 1893–94, p. 46; MacPhail 1900, p. 449; *CG2*, pp. 14–21; Frazer 1911a, p. 305; McPherson 1929, p. 249; *CG4*, pp. 214–15; Davidson 1949, p. 53; Macdonald 1982, p. 179; Larner 1983, p. 140. JGC's translation is slightly misleading – *smuais* is the juice or marrow of the bones, *feòil* is flesh.

688 I am at a loss to understand *ghealbhain* (Carmichael's spelling; Story's is *ghealbhin*). The usual reading at this point is *Anns a' mhadainn mhoich* 'In the early morning', which corresponds to JGC's translation. Assuming that the word is feminine (thus justifying *mhoich*), perhaps it represents *gealdhain* 'lull or intermission in a rain-storm', attributed by Dwelly (1977, p. 483) to Alexander Henderson, Ardnamurchan. In Breadalbane *gealbhan* took the place of *dreag* in the sense of a meteor, a moving light or fireball which presaged a funeral (Henderson 1911, pp. 225–26). For *geilbhinn* in the sense of a beautiful and charming woman, possibly a temptress or seductress, see Mac-Choinnich 1844, p. 122.

689 The last four lines are problematic in various ways, which is presumably why JGC omitted them from his translation (see note 687). I hope I have understood them correctly as describing how Christ's agony was reduced through being shared by Mary. *Aig sgàth na craoibhe* is simultaneously 'at the shade of the cross' and 'in thrall to the horror of the cross'; for *craobh* 'cross' see Black 2002, p. 19. In Story the penultimate line begins *Mar a h-euslainteach*, which makes no sense, even if emended to *Mura h-euslainteach* 'If not sick'. Carmichael has the solution, however, reading *Mas a h-euslainteach*. It is impossible to know whether this is an imaginative reinterpretation or merely a better reading of JGC's handwriting.

It is common to evoke the Trinity, usually at the end of a charm as here, either directly (e.g. *CG2*, pp. 18–21, 54–55, and *CG4*, pp. 216–17) or by suggesting the number three (e.g. *CG2*, pp. 52–53, 60–61) or both, as in this classic example, which I have tentatively re-edited from a counter-charm against the evil eye (*CG2*, pp. 44–47).

> *Trian air na clacha glasa dheth,*
> *Trian air na beanna casa dheth,*
> *Trian air na h-easa brasa dheth,*
> *Trian air na liana maiseach dheth*
> *'S trian air a' mhuir mhóir shàlaich —*
> *Si féin aisir as fheàrr gu ghiùlan,*
> > *A' mhuir mhór shàlach,*
> > *Aisir as fheàrr gu ghiùlan.*

> *An ainm Trì nan Dùl,*
> *An ainm nan Trì Naomh,*
> *An ainm nan uile rùn*
> *Agus nan cùrsa còmhla.*

"A third of it upon the grey stones, / A third of it upon the steep hills, / A third of it on the hurtling waterfalls, / A third of it on the beautiful meadows / And a third upon the great salt sea – / She herself being the best path to carry it, / The great salt sea, / The best path to carry it. / In the name of the Three of the Elements, / In the name of the Holy Three, / In the name of all the mysteries / And curses put together." Cf. *CG2*, p. 118.

690 To give the meaning indicated, the Gaelic should read *làn an dùirn a dh'ùir á cnoc glas*. As pointed out in notes 156 and 431, *glas* is not exactly 'grey' but the colour of new growth. I assume the point is that the soil of such a mound is *air dàr, air dàir* (at its most potent), see p. 52.

Niall M. Brownlie informs me that there is in fact a particular Fairy knoll in Tiree called *an Cnoc Glas*. It is close to Travee Bridge on the march burn between Barrapol and Balephuil in the south-west of the island. He says (personal communication, 22 October 2003): "There was a man from Balephuil who, if alone, would not use this right of way under any circumstances."

691 Niall M. Brownlie has been unable to trace the location of this hillock for me. Perhaps it is the one now called *an Cnoc Glas*, see previous note.

692 JGC's Gaelic original was excluded from *WSS*, but was transcribed by Carmichael into what is now CW MS 241, f. 31 (see p. 703 below):

> *Paidire Mhoire h-aon, Paidire Mhoire dhà, gu naoi Paidire Moire,*
> *Sruthaidh tu mar bhoireannach,*
> *Sruthaidh tu mar fhireannach,*
> *Sruthaidh tu mar iasg rìgh;*
> *'S naoi féithean do chuirp*
> *Air an aon sruth còmhla.*

It is hard to see how this can be a 'charm for bruises'. *Bruthadh* or *brùthadh* (for which see p. 205, 'Charm for Sprains') means 'bruising, contusion, crush; act of bruising, pounding, squeezing, or crushing' (Dwelly 1977, p. 132); it is commonest nowadays in the simple senses 'pushing, pressure'. It appears from *CG4*, p. 300, that there was indeed a term *eòlas bruthaidh* meaning 'a charm for bruise', 'a charm against bruising' (*Ta eòlas agam air bruthadh …*

'I have a charm for bruising . . .'), but the content of the charm cited here by JGC suggests some other context. Obviously pressure may be applied to staunch the flow of blood, but none of the charms cited by Carmichael for *casgadh fala* (*CG4*, pp. 280–85) involve personal contact. It is, I am sure, a charm to induce bleeding, and the connection with *brùthadh* is explained by an anecdote told by William Mackenzie (1891–92, p. 158 note) of Donald MacDonald (*am Bàrd Conanach*, 1780–1832) from Strathconon in Ross-shire, for whom see John Mackenzie 1841, pp. 347–51, Macbain 1890–91, pp. 253, 256 (= 1891–92, pp. 293, 295), and MacDonald 1900, pp. 48–49. "In local tradition he is represented as having been particularly successful both in letting and in staunching blood. On one occasion, while at the harvest in the Lothians, he lodged with a weaver, who was also a noted phlebotomist. A full-blooded damsel of the district called on the weaver in order that he might let her blood. He tried all his skill, but the blood would not come. Whereupon the Bard took the damsel in hand, and, taking her by the small of the wrist, squeezed an artery, with the result that blood squirted in the weaver's face." William Mackenzie goes on to say that the weaver asked the poet to tell him his method, and that the latter replied in verse.

> *Cha tugainn eòlas mo làmh fhìn*
> *Dh'fhear bhuaileadh slinn no chuireadh i.*

> *Lot thu gàirdean na nighean duinn*
> *'S chan fhac' thu steall den fhuil aice.*

> *'S an uair a theannaich mi caol a dùirn*
> *Mu 'dhà shùil bha 'n fhuil aice.*

("I wouldn't give the skill of my own two hands / To a man who'd be striking or setting a sley. / You injured the arm of the brown-haired girl / And not one squirt of her blood did you see. / And when I tightened the small of her wrist / All about his two eyes was her blood.") Curiously, the poet had a version of JGC's 'Patera Mary one' which he used to staunch blood (Mackenzie 1891–92, p. 158); it had the same structure as JGC's, beginning *Paidir Mhoire, h-aon* ('The Pater of Mary, one'), going on to *Paidir Mhoire, seachd* ('The Pater of Mary, seven'), and containing five further lines that describe the purpose of the charm, but these five lines are entirely different from JGC's. See also Macbain 1890–91, pp. 241, 248, 265 = 1891–92, pp. 181, 228, 347; Anon. 1908–09b, p. 344; *CG4*, pp. 164–65.

693 Again, JGC's Gaelic original was excluded from *WSS*, but fortunately it was transcribed by Carmichael into what is now CW MS 241, f. 32 (see p. 703 below). In this case I have supplied it unedited, exactly as it stands in the manuscript. The presence of accents is notable, as Carmichael only uses them when particularly anxious to indicate that a vowel is long.

An galar tholl, literally as JGC says 'the perforating disease' (*tholl* 'of holes' functioning adjectivally), appears to denote what Carmichael (*CG4*, p. 307) calls 'chest disease' or, as JGC says, 'rheumatic pains'. Dwelly (1977, p. 473) gives *galar tholl* only as diarrhœa, on what authority I do not know – it sounds unlikely. Carmichael says (*CG4*, pp. 306–07): "For a cure, they first blew on the finger-tips and then rubbed with the points of the five fingers the front of the shoulder; the 'galar toll' [*sic*] was before and behind the shoulder, 'air chùl agus air bhial na gualainn.'" Like JGC, Carmichael offers two *eòlais* under this rubric. The first is:

Dùirn Dé umad,	*The hands of God be round thee,*
Sùil Dhé tharad,	*The eye of God be over thee,*
Rùn Rìgh nan neof	*The love of the King of the heavens*
Sùigh dhìot do chnoidh.	*Drain from thee thy pang.*

Falbh! falbh! falbh!	*Away! away! away!*
Balbh! balbh! balbh!	*Dumbly! dumbly! dumbly!*
Do nimh a bhith san làr,	*Thy venom be in the ground,*
Do chràdh a bhith sa chloich!	*Thy pain be in the stone!*

This sheds much light on JGC's version, which makes sense as it stands, but only just: "Enclose God around you, / Show any Fairy host above you / To Christ, or else . . ." Clearly Carmichael adds *De* to the first line because he is uncomfortable with JGC's version and prefers his own. Indeed, if we read the second line as *Sùil sluagh farad* 'The eye of hosts be over you', the first word of the *eòlas* falls into place analogically as *dùirn* 'fists, hands'. Similarly *air neo* 'or else' may be seen to be a misunderstanding of *air nèamh* (with vocalised *mh*) 'in heaven'. Again, Carmichael's 'from thee thy pang', *dhìot do chnoidh*, would be identical to the Tiree pronunciation of *dhìot a' chroich* 'from you the gallows' or *dhinn do chroich* 'from us your gallows', so we should probably reject JGC's 'gallows' altogether in favour of something closer to Carmichael's version. Being helpfully marked long, *fàl* can only be for *falbh*, cf. the pronunciation of *ortha* 'charm' as *òr*. After this, the only puzzle is Carmichael's own *balbh* 'dumb(ly)', which seems out of place. All in all a fully edited version of JGC's charm would be as follows:

Dùirn Dé umad,	*The hands of God be round you,*
Sùil sluagh farad —	*The eye of hosts be over you —*
A Chrìost air nèamh,	*O Christ in heaven,*
Tog dhìot do chnoidh,	*Lift from you your pang,*
Falbh, falbh, falbh,	*Away, away, away,*
Do nimh san làr	*Your sting be in the ground*
'S do chràdh sa chloich.	*And your pain be in the stone.*

694 Carmichael's second 'charm for chest disease' (*CG*4, pp. 306–07) has four lines only, and these correspond quite closely to the first four lines here:

An t-saighead a thàine le sgaoim,
Salann a leigheas cnoidh,
An achan a rinn Ìosda Crìosda,
An t-saighead shìth a chur 'na tosd.

("The arrow which came with fright, / Salt which heals pain, / The prayer prayed by Jesus Christ, / To still the fairy arrow.") He also transcribed JGC's original Gaelic into what is now EUL MS CW 241, f. 32, heading it in line 1 as an afterthought 'Doigh eile' ('Otherwise'). This is the text as it stands in the manuscript:

Saighead a thainig le sgoim/Doigh eile
Salann a leaghadh air lot
Iosa Criosda tha na boinn
An t-saighead shith a chur na tosd
Sian Dhia umad
'S dall sluagh farad
Do chochull mu Chalum-cille
'S cochull Chalum chille umad/tharad
Ga d dhion 's ga d choimhead
O shluagh an t-saoghail seo
'S an t- saoghail eile

Line 2 means 'Salt to melt upon wound', but as this would disinfect it we may accept JGC's word 'cure'. Line 3 of the translation corresponds to lines 3 and 4 of the original; this may be because JGC wrote only 'Iosa Criosda'. Carmichael left the rest of the line blank save for a short horizontal stroke, then inserted what looks like *tha na boinn* or *tha na broinn* later. Either these words were so uncertain in JGC's text that he ignored them in his translation, or Carmichael got them from another source. If we read *tha na bhroinn*, the meaning of the couplet is: "May Jesus Christ who is inside it (the salt) / Keep the Elfin arrow quiet." In lines 5, 6 and 8, *umad* means 'around you', *farad* and *tharad* mean 'over you'.

It is of great interest to find chest pains regarded as an assault by Fairy arrows, especially in light of William Mackenzie's remark (1891–92, pp. 147–48, cf. Ó Madagáin 1989, p. 30): "People blessed themselves, and prayed the Almighty to protect them from Fairies, but I have not come across any Anti-Fairy charms in the Highlands." Instead he cites two charms from the west of Ireland and one from the isle of Man, but these are strikingly ambiguous in their language, and their precise purpose is described only in their titles, the nearest thing to a reference to the Fairies themselves being the line *Go m-budh sluagh dall an sluagh seo chugainn*, 'A blind host be this host that approaches us'. We may compare this to *CG1*, pp. 174–75, to the charm for protection from the Fairies in *CG5*, pp. 250–51, to Carmichael's *saighead shiodhach* in note 721, to JGC's *saighead shìth* 'Elfin arrow' and *sluagh an t-saoghail seo / 'S an t-saoghail eile* 'people of this world / And of the next' in this charm, to his *nì sìth* 'aught Elfin' (p. 205), to his *saighde sìth* 'Elfin bolts' (p. 215 and note 744), etc. I know of no direct parallels to the last six lines here, but they read like the kind of incantation which might be described as *seun* or *sian* ('a saining'), *ortha dìona* ('a charm for protection'), *caim* ('an encircling') or *fàth fithe*, which was designed to render the subject invisible (Mackenzie 1878–79, p. 127; Dixon 1886, pp. 165–68; Anon. 1886–87a, pp. 37–38; Macbain 1887–88, pp. 251–52; Macbain 1890–91, pp. 225–26, 234–39, 265 = 1891–92, pp. 121, 174–79, 347; Mackenzie 1891–92, pp. 139–47; *CG2*, pp. 22–37, 240–41; *CG3*, pp. 64–109; Campbell 1940–60, vol. 1, p. 460; MacDonald 1958b, pp. 132–33). For the practice of the *caim* see pp. xlviii, 136 ('Iron', 'Protection against Evil Spirits'), 161, 273; note 744; Sutherland 1937, pp. 40, 94; *CG3*, pp. 102–07.

The above citations suggest that mankind required protection from the otherworld, but – as we have repeatedly noted – there were good Fairies as well as bad ones. A hint of benign intervention appears in a charm recorded by the kirk session of Kingarth in Bute in 1650, employed by a man called Archibald MacNeill to heal sprains in horses' legs (Paton 1932, p. 20): *Eolus chuir shiag obi er bhrissadh er chliseadh er shiachadh er att er ith er anibhais nach deachie fomo dhume no mo bheach acht fo leadhas dhia nan dule.* A reconstruction in standard orthography might look like this: *Eòlas. Chuir sìtheag oba air bhriseadh, air chliseadh, air shiachadh, air at, air ith', air anabhàs nach deachaidh fo mo ghoimh no mo bheachd acht fo leigheas Dhia nan Dùl.* "A charm. A female Fairy placed a charm upon fracture, upon dislocation, upon sprain, upon tumour, upon decay, upon sudden death that have not been subject to my malice nor to my sight but to the healing of God of the Elements."

I am grateful to Professor William Gillies for drawing my attention to the Kingarth charm.

695 Cf. note 684.

696 This is clearly related to two charms given by Carmichael in *CG4*, pp. 262–65, under the titles 'Eòlas na Glacaich' ('Charm for Seizure') and 'Eòlas na Caitheimh' ('Charm for Consumption'). Only the second (pp. 264–65) is attributed – *O Chalum Mac na Cearda, coitear, Baile Phuill, Tiriodh*: 'From Malcolm Sinclair, cottar, Baile Phuill, Tiree'. Not surprisingly, it is the closer of the two to JGC's. It consists of four quatrains; these are compared to JGC's text in the following notes. For water from the ninth wave cf. p. 655 below.

JGC's Gaelic original was excluded from *WSS*, but I supply it here from Carmichael's transcript in EUL ms CW 241, f. 33 (see p. 703 below). In line 2, Carmichael wrote *shaltras eal* 'swan treads' then emended this for some reason to *shaltradh an eal* 'the swan would tread'. In line 4 he wrote *bhragha-dh*, presumably to indicate alternative genitive singular endings. These are not strictly in line with the demands of either Irish (*brágha*, gs. *brághad*, f.) or Scottish Gaelic (*bràghad*, gs. *bràghaid*, m.), but they sound authentic.

697 It appears that part of the cure required the practitioner to stand on the patient's chest – compare 'Lumbago (*Leum Droma*)', pp. 227–28, where the cure involves treading on the patient's back. Sinclair's first two quatrains (see note 696) are:

> *Saltraim ort, a ghlac dhona,*
> *Mar a shaltras eal air sàl,*
> *A ghlac chùil, a ghlac chléibh,*
> *A ghlac bhreun bhràgh.*

> *Soisgeul Chrìosda féin*
> *Dha do dhèanamh slàn,*
> *Soisgeul Léigh nan léigh,*
> *Soisgeul Dhé nan gràs.*

("I trample on thee, evil wasting, / As tramples swan on brine, / Thou wasting of back, thou wasting of body, / Thou foul wasting of chest. / May Christ's own Gospel / Be to make thee whole, / The Gospel of the Healer of healers, / The Gospel of the God of grace.") For *glac chléibh* see Masson and Aitken 1887–88, p. 301. The second quatrain is omitted from JGC's version, resulting in a non sequitur; see 'The Gospel of Christ', pp. 215–16.

698 Sinclair's third quatrain (see note 696) is:

> *A sgrios dhìot do thinn*
> *Ann an linn na slàint*
> *O chìrein do chinn*
> *Gu bonn do dhà shàil.*

("To remove from thee thy sickness / In the pool of health / From the crown of thy head / To the base of thy two heels.") The second line appears to relate to a cure which involves bathing or immersion, and it is therefore not surprising that it is omitted from JGC's version. In Sinclair's version the Gospel has been invoked to bring about this effect; the thrust of JGC's lines 5–6 is more reminiscent of the second verse at *CG4*, p. 262: *Triath treun nan dùl / Sgrios do ghalair chuim / Bho mhullach do chinn / Gu ìochdar do shàil*. "May the strong Lord of life / Destroy thy disease of body / From the crown of thine head / To the base of thy heel."

699 Sinclair's fourth verse (see note 696) is:

> *O do dhà leis a null,*
> *Gu do dhà leis a nall,*
> *A uchd Dhé nan rùn*
> *Agus nan cumhachdan slàn,—*
> *Rùn nan gràs!*

("From thy two loins thither / To thy two loins hither, / In reliance on the might of the God of love / And of the whole Powers together,— / The love of grace!") Once again, JGC's text sounds like a reduced version of Sinclair's.

700 JGC's Gaelic original of this charm was excluded from *WSS*, but Carmichael transcribed it into what is now EUL MS CW 241, f. 34 (see p. 703 below). Here is the text exactly as it stands in the manuscript.

> *Saltraidh mis' ort a ghlac,*
> *Mar thalamh sleibh a nochd*
> *Ort fhein do dhubhadh a ghisgein*
> *Don agus doruinneach sin*
> *An eapa chuir Pàdruig*
> *Air mathair mhic Righ an Ibhir*
> *Mharbhadh nam beisdean*
> *Bha mu fheithean a cridhe*
> *Air na ceithir anshocraibh fichead*
> *Bha na h- aoraibh*   _
> *Aig uisge ruith uillt criche*
> *Air clacha tuinne na talmhuinn*
> *Air amhuinn a cridhe*
> *Air bhuidhich 's air a mhioghladh*
> *S air a chrionaich s air a' chneadhaich.*

The charm as a whole is a version of one printed in *CG4*, pp. 266–69, under the heading 'Iomairt Cléibhe' ('Chest Conflict'), consisting of four long-lined quatrains followed by four short-lined ones. It is unattributed. It begins as follows:

> *Saltraim ort, a ghlac ghlongach,*
> *Mar air thalamh sléibh a nochd;*
> *Ort fhéin do shaighead, a Ghéigein!*
> *Is déin agus is déistinneach do lot.*

("I trample on thee, thou slimy chest seizure, / As upon mountain land this night; / On thyself be thine arrow, O Géigean! / Intense and horrible is thy wounding.") Carmichael's version of these lines has retained its prosodic structure, whereas JGC's has not. Line 3 is of great interest – as in 'Charm for Rheumatic Pains' (pp. 206–07), chest pains appear to be rationalised in Carmichael's version as Fairy arrows, and it is not going too far to say that the otherworld creature is here named as Géigean. This name is quite common in traditional rhymes and tales, and takes various forms (e.g. Géig, Géige, Gìgean, Guaigean, Céigean, Cìogan, Cìgean, Cuaigean), but it is significant I think that *Rìgh Géigean* ('King Géigean') was the name given to the 'wild man' figure who presided over 'death revels' at the beginning of winter (Macleod 1887–88; *CG2*, pp. 300–01, 306; *CG3*, p. 72; *CG4*, pp. 92, 122; *CG5*, pp. 68, 356; MacAonghais 1955; Meek 1978, pp. 162–63; cf. Grimble 1979, p. 101, and note 345 above). In *a ghisgein* JGC offers a further variant, a vocative noun whose nominative will be *Gìsgean*. His translation of it as 'dwarfing power' raises the issue of its relationship to Dwelly's *ceigean* 'diminutive and unhandsome person', 'corpulent man, clumsily formed and of low stature' (1977, p. 185), the problem being the difference in vowel quantity.

701 The second quatrain in *CG4*, pp. 266–67, is:

> *An eab a chuir Pàdraig féile*
> *Ri màthair rìgh an Ibhir*
> *A mharbhadh nam béistean*
> *Bha ri féithean a cridhe.*

("The charm placed of Patrick the generous / On the mother of the king of Ibhir / To kill the beasts that fastened / Upon the veins of her heart.") Again this is very close to JGC's version (see note 700); again the most interesting line is the third. Carmichael's *màthair rìgh an Ibhir* is a corruption of *màthair inghean Ìomhair*, 'the mother of Ivar's daughter', while JGC's *mathair mhic Righ an Ibhir* is *màthair mhic nighean Ìomhair*, not 'the mother of the son of the King of Iver' but 'the mother of the son of Ivar's daughter'. There need be little doubt but that the reference is to Ivar Beinlaus (king of Dublin AD 871–73), whose mother, as pointed out in note 396 above, is reputed to have been a snake. The association with St Patrick (*c.* AD 385–461) is an anachronism, but makers of charms were not interested in historical niceties. The implication is that the charm will relieve the kind of crushing chest-pains suffered by a woman who had been impregnated by the son of a snake, or is herself the granddaughter of a snake.

702 The third quatrain in *CG4*, pp. 266–67, is:

> *Air na ceithir gaoda fichead*
> *A bha an aorabh dhaoin is bhrùid,*
> *A bha an aorabh fir is mnatha,*
> *A bha an aorabh mic is muirn.*

"Upon the four and twenty diseases / That were inherent in men and in beasts, / That were inherent in man and in woman, / That were inherent in son and in daughter." Carmichael's *muirn* 'daughter' is very doubtful. JGC's version (note 700) reduces the last three lines here to one, with a short horizontal line to indicate missing text. For *anshocair* 'illness, affliction' see note 314.

703 The fourth quatrain in *CG4*, pp. 266–67, is:

> *Air uisge ruith uillt sléibhe,*
> *Air uisge ruith uillt crìche,*
> *Air clacha teinne na talmhainn*
> *Agus air anbhainneachd cridhe.*

("Upon the running water of the mountain stream, / Upon the running water of the boundary stream, / Upon the rigid stones of the earth, / And upon the weakness of the heart.") This seems to develop the image introduced in the first two lines of the charm, that of walking upon the human body as upon a landscape; JGC's choice of 'for' for *air* is not, I think, helpful. *Aig* (note 700) is probably a transcription error; *tuinne* 'waves' will be a mishearing or misunderstanding of *teinne* 'rigid', and *amhuinn a cridhe* of *anbhainneachd cridhe* 'weakness of heart'.

704 The last four quatrains of the charm in *CG4*, pp. 266–69, consist of alliterative lists of diseases, or words resembling diseases – *Air a' bhiolgach / bholgach / bhorgach / bhuidheach*; *Air a' mhioglach / mhoglach / mhuglach / mhaglach*; *Air a' chritheach / chruthach* or *dhruthach / chruadhach* or *chuartach / chnàmhach*; *Air a' ghlucach / ghlacach / ghlupach / ghruthach* or *ghriuthach* or *ghrapach* or *ghranrach*. JGC's *bhuidhich, mhioghladh, chrionaich* and *chneadhaich* (note 700) appear to represent one word from each group. Carmichael makes no attempt to translate the second group, so JGC's 'distemper' stands on its own. Given Carmichael's *mioglach* etc., JGC's *mhìoghladh* (rhyming with *chrìonaich* 'decay') may represent *mì* + *glac* – 'severe seizure'? The Gaelic for 'asthma' will be *cneadaich*, not *cneadhaich* – *cnead* is a harsh breathing sound, but *cneadh* is simply a wound.

705 St Peter's curious utterance 'o lord my god my dok toockage' is explained, I think, by another English version, copied in South Uist by William Mackenzie (1891–92, p. 152): "Peter sat

upon a marble stone weeping. Christ came by and asked, 'What ails thee.' Peter answered and said, 'My Lord and my God, my tooth toothache;' and the Lord said unto him, 'Rise up, Peter – not for you alone, but all who will carry these lines in my name shall never feel what is the toothache. In the name of the Father and the Son and the Holy Ghost.' Mackenzie glosses 'my tooth toothache' as 'my tooth is aching', and 'my dok toockage' will be a further corruption of the same phrase. It has been described as 'perhaps the commonest of all written charms found in the United Kingdom' (Bower 1904, cf. Masson and Aitken 1887–88, pp. 310–11, McPherson 1929, p. 247, and Macdonald 1982, p. 181).

706 MacFady(e)n is a Tiree name, not a Manx one. Presumably JGC says that the charm 'probably came originally from the isle of Man' because that is what he was told. Clearly it was 'given to those who applied for it for a small consideration' by writing it out and adding the customer's name. It is the first written charm to be mentioned in this chapter. The charming of toothache by means of a 'letter' in this way was a well-known practice; usually the 'letter' was in English or Latin for the simple reason that the writing of Gaelic was a rare accomplishment, but Mackenzie (1891–92, p. 152) prints a Gaelic version from Barra. "The following very common English charm was lately caught going its round," says Macbain (1890–91, p. 252 = 1891–92, p. 291), and it resembles JGC's two 'Manx' ones very closely: "St Peter sat on a new-rolled stone / Weeping and wailing; / Jesus came by, and said – / What ails you, Peter? / Oh, Lord, my God, the toothache. / Jesus said, Be healed; / And whoever will carry / These few lines for My name's sake / Will never feel the toothache."

GUL Gen. 1042 (MacLagan) MS 134 consists of a 'letter' of this kind; originally folded to *c.* 3 cms square, it is in bad Latin, but follows the usual lines: *Petrus sedit ex marmorum Lapis Dominus Noster venit eo et Dixit petrus quid te gravit, petrus respondit Dominus Meus et Deus meus Caput et Dentes meos vexant me Dominus Noster Dicat surge petrus salva tu non solum tu sed etiam omnia qui teneant haec mea Dicta per virtutem De haec verbis Dominus Noster et in ejus Nomine Dice tuus pestis non moleste te Detri*[hole in paper] *Minius Pratrus.* On the outside, presumably written by the Rev. James MacLagan, is: *Eolusan ciallach Cumhachdacha!!!* ("Sensible powerful charms!!!") One assumes that the 'marble' or 'new-rolled' stone on which St Peter invariably sits is a dental metaphor.

Macbain (1890–91, p. 251 = 1891–92, p. 291) explains how the letter was used – the sufferer, he was told, must on no account open it. "If he does," wrote his informant, "the worse for himself, for the toothache will at once come back. I know a young woman who once got this line. She placed it carefully in the lining of her corset. One day, however, she happened to be washing, and, having neglected to remove the line, she destroyed it in the process of washing this particular article of attire. She told me that the toothache came back like a shot, and she had to give up her washing that day. A second line, she said, would do her no good, and so the toothache ever since has been paying her an unwelcome visit now and then."

See also SoSS Maclagan MSS vol. 22, pp. 3868–69, and Sutherland 1937, pp. 107–08.

707 Peacock 1863, p. 66. I am grateful to John Bowring of Douglas Public Library for sending me a copy of the relevant pages of this eccentric-looking 72-page work. I have re-edited the charm back into line with Peacock's spelling and punctuation. It is the last item in a chapter on superstitions, and Peacock introduces it like this (p. 66): "Let me conclude this chapter with an original and poetical charm against the toothache, recommending the same to all professors of dental surgery as an invaluable means of making their fortune." He concludes (p. 67) with reference to the penultimate line of the charm: "'These words!' *What* words? The omission is curious, and shows the simplicity of the isolated agricultural population. I vouch for the accuracy of the above, and there are now living both old men and women in the north of the Island who will not only repeat this 'poetical' charm, but testify to its success."

Peacock's question "*What* words?" is a valid one, I think, and he does not mean to be insulting. The most obvious retort is: "These three lines." But other answers are possible. It may be a subtle reference to 'keeping' the charm about the body in the form of writing. Equally, the Gaelic charms found in manuscripts such as Adv. MS 72.1.2 frequently include a little piece of mumbo-jumbo in a mixture of Latin and Gaelic (see note 685 for an example), and since Peacock collected this one in English it is not surprising if such an incantation was lost. Assuming that his informants were bilingual and Peacock a monoglot, one wonders on which side 'simplicity' lay.

708 JGC does not mean that what follows is a Manx charm from Peacock's book, but that it is a translation of a Scottish Gaelic one heard by himself in Tiree or elsewhere. His Gaelic original was excluded from *WSS*, but Carmichael transcribed it into what is now EUL MS CW 241, f. 35 (see p. 703 below). I give it as it stands in the manuscript:

> An t- eolas a chuir Calum-cille
> Ri glun deas Mal- idhe/Idhe
> Air ghuin air ghoin air dheide
> Air dheide air ghalar chinn
>
> Sin thuirt Peadair ri Seumas
> Cha'n fhaigh mi fois no clos leis an deide
>
> Thuirt Criosta freagair a cheist
> 'S cha bhi an deide s an rann
> 'S an aon cheann am feasd

This is closely related to a version published in *CG4*, pp. 198–99 (unattributed), under the title 'Eab an Déididh' ('The Charm of the Toothache') and also to one obtained from an Eigg crofter by William Mackenzie (1891–92, p. 154). Together, these three bear a distant relationship to one got by Carmichael from Mairiread Macdonald, cottar, Hougearry, North Uist, and published in *CG2*, pp. 10–11, under the title 'Eolas an Deididh' ('Toothache Charm'). These versions are compared in the following notes. (See also *Tocher* 35, pp. 311–12, for an oral toothache charm from Lewis invoking SS Peter, Paul, James and John.)

709 The first verse in *CG4*, pp. 198–99, reads:

> An eab a chuir Calum Cille
> Ma ghlùn deas Mhaol Iodha,
> Air ghuin, air ghoin, air ghuim,
> Air ghalar dheud, air ghalar ghuim.

("The charm placed of Columba / About the right knee of Maol Iodha, / Against pain, against sting, against venom, / Against tooth disease, against virulent disease.") Carmichael notes *chuim* 'bodily' as an alternative reading to *ghuim* 'virulent'; for *ghuim* 'venom' cf. *dhume* = *ghoimh*, note 694. The Eigg version is worth quoting as well, with Mackenzie's translation:

> Labhair Calum-Cille nan Orth'
> Ann an ordag dheas mo Righ —
> Air chnuimh, air dheidh, air dheideadh —
> Air dheideadh a' ghalar-chinn.

"Columba of the Incantations / Spoke in the right thumb of my King – / On worm, on ache, on toothache – / On toothache, the head-disease." This has credibility for the good reason that it contains a full set of *aicill*- and end-rhymes, marred only by the repetition of *dheideadh*. The relevance of knees and thumbs must be that the incantation was said while tying a thread around the part in question. The North Uist version, which is different in all other respects, concerns St Brigid and the thumb of the Virgin Mary. That is credible, since tradition portrays Brigid as the midwife who brought Christ into the world, but we have to ask how likely it is that Calum Cille would perform a similar service for Christ himself (*mo Righ*, 'my King'). A possible answer is that Calum Cille is said to have visited heaven 'when he wished, every Thursday while he was alive' (Grosjean 1927, pp. 162–63), hence the sanctity of that day in Scottish Gaelic tradition, and no doubt that is how the Eigg crofter would have explained it. Both JGC and Carmichael heard -*l*- in the name, however, and I think we must take it that the -*l*- is correct, and that *mo Righ* was a later development (confusion between palatal *l* and *r* is common, cf. *Peadail* for St Peter).

Who then is Mal-ii (*Maol Iodha, Mal- idhe/Idhe*)? My best guess is that these spellings represent a pronunciation of *Mo-Liba*. This saint gave his name to Kilmalieu (*Cill mo Liubha*) at Inveraray, to another *Cill mo Liubha* on the west side of Loch Linnhe in JGC's native Kingairloch, to 'Kilmalew in the lordship of Morvern', to *Achadh da-Liubha* (Achdaliew, Do-Liba's or Mo-Liba's Field) on the north side of Loch Eil, and to a 'Killmalive' in Skye (Watson 1926a, pp. 304–05).

710   The Eigg version of these lines is incomplete and unsatisfactory. Judging from his rows of dots JGC appears to have felt the same. The second verse in *CG4*, pp. 198–99, reads:

> *Thubhairt Peadair ri Seumas,*
> *"Nar faigh mi fois o'n déideadh,*
> *Ach a' laighe agus ag éirigh*
> *Agus a' leum thar mo bhuinn."*

"Said Peter unto James, / 'I get no respite from toothache, / But (it is with me) lying down and rising / And leaping on my soles.'"

711   The rhyme-scheme of JGC's original (note 708) suggests that these are lines 2–4 of a quatrain, and it may be conjectured that the missing first line took the form of a question posed to Christ, e.g. *"Dé nì sibh dhomh?" arsa Peadar.* "'What can you do for me?' said Peter." The third verse in *CG4*, pp. 198–99, is very similar:

> *Thubhairt Crìosd a' freagar na ceist,*
> *"Cha bhi an déideadh agus an rann*
> *Anns an aon cheann am feasd."*

"Said Christ answering the problem, / 'The toothache and the rune / Shall not henceforth abide in the same head.'" I think this makes more sense than JGC's version, in which Christ merely passes the buck. We may therefore reinterpret JGC's third-last line as *Thuirt Crìost, a' freagairt a cheist* . . . "Christ said, answering his question . . ."

The Eigg version also has three lines: *Labhair Criosda ris na h-Ostail* 'Jesus said to the Apostles' is followed by a similar answer.

712   JGC's Gaelic original was excluded from *WSS*, but fortunately it was transcribed by Carmichael into what is now EUL MS CW 241, f. 36 (see p. 703 below), and I supply it from there. It was headed 'Eolas Airson Cnuidh (Cnoimh)', best translated 'A Charm For Pain (Worm)', which implies especially toothache, but clearly JGC chose to reinterpret *cnuidh* 'pain' as *cruidh* 'cattle'. In Tiree these words would be hard to tell apart, nasalisation being present in *cruidh* as well as in *cnuidh*.

In *CG2*, pp. 74–75, Carmichael printed an almost identical charm (with a more helpful translation) under the heading 'Eolas Tnu' ('Envy Spell'):

> Ge be co rinn duit an tnu,
> Fear dubh, no bean fionn,
> Triuir cuirim riu ga chasg —
> Spiorad Numh, Athair, Mac.

"Whoso made to thee the envy, / Swarthy man or woman fair, / Three I will send to thwart it – / Holy Spirit, Father, Son." He had got it from a woman called Nic 'Al Dòmhnaich in Baile Phuill whom JGC describes at p. 186 above (*CG2*, p. 379).

713   Again, I have supplied JGC's Gaelic original from Carmichael's transcript in EUL MS CW 241, f. 36 (see p. 703 below), where it is headed 'Eolas Airson Beathach Ealadh (Thaladh)'. It is laid out there in five lines, line 5 being broken into two in JGC's translation. Perhaps *Thaladh* ('Lullaby, Coax') is Carmichael's gloss on *Ealadh*, which makes no sense to me: 'A Charm to Coax a Beast'. This is a version of lines 1–4 and 7–8 of a charm published as two quatrains in *CG4*, pp. 68–69, under the title 'Tatan Beothaich' ('Attracting an Animal'):

> Ioba 'ga chur ad chluais dheis
>   Gu do leas is chan ann gu t'aimhleas;
> Gaol na fearainn tha fo d' chois,
>   Is fuath na fuinn bho'n d'fhalbh thu.
>
> Tha fois aig mo ghaol a nochd
>   Am fochara nam farrabheann;
> Do cheangal teann am làimh nochd,
>   Tha glas iarainn ort, a Tharragheal.

"The spell is placed in thy right ear / For thy good and not for thy harm; / Love of the land that is under thy foot, / And dislike of the land thou hast left. / My love has rest this night / Hard by the mountain ridges; / Thy fast binding in my bare hand, / An iron lock is upon thee, 'Breast-white'." *Ioba* is the same as *eab*, *eaba*, etc., see note 709. I do not think there is such a word as *siop* 'a blowing', and I suspect that what JGC heard began *Seo iop* . . . or *Seo iob* . . . 'This is a charm . . .' His *air a chluas* is for *air do chluas*, see note 729. For *farrabheann* see p. xv above; strictly, *Tarragheal* is not 'Breast-white' but 'Belly-white'.

714   What follows is best regarded as three separate charms. JGC's Gaelic originals were excluded from *WSS*, but I have been able to supply them from Carmichael's transcript in EUL MS CW 241, ff. 37–38 (see p. 703), where they are headed 'Luibhean A Thoirt A Bhainn Air Ais' ('Plants To Bring Back The Milk'). For the *mòthan* see Stewart 1823, p. 136; Mackenzie 1891–92, pp. 128–29; *CG2*, pp. 110–15; *CG4*, pp. 78–81, 132–35. JGC calls it the pearlwort, but other sources suggest that it is the bog violet, and in line 2 it is called a *liath-lus* ('hoary plant', 'frost-coloured plant'), which is given by Dwelly (1977, p. 589) as the mugwort.

The second of the three charms is perfectly clear in the manuscript, but contains a remarkable concentration of words of doubtful significance. This may result from JGC's determination to set down what he heard rather than attempt to rationalise it. *Tom sona*, *seirc ghràdhach*, *togh ghràdhach* and *currasglach* may all be plant-names, but if so they are not listed as such in the available literature. The question-marks are JGC's. Perhaps *'n togh ghràdhach* is for *'n t-so-ghràdhach* 'the much-loved female'; *a' churrasglach* may I think be explained as *a' charr asgailleach* 'the axillary root', cf. 'St John's Wort (*Achlasan Chaluim Chille*)', p. 230. *Carr* 'crust, root' is misinterpreted by Carmichael as *cathair* 'chair', cf. his names for yarrow, *a' chathair aigh* 'the joyful chair', 'the gracious chair', *mo charr àigh* 'my joyful crust', 'my gracious root' (*CG2*, pp. 70–71, and *CG4*, pp. 122–23).

By 'the milk-producing plant' JGC almost certainly means the *torranan* or figwort, which is strongly associated with milk in the traditions and charms concerning it which Carmichael collected (Macbain 1890–91, pp. 238–39 = 1891–92, pp. 178–79; Mackenzie 1891–92, pp. 129–30; *CG2*, pp. 78–91). Curiously, I find no textual connections between these charms and others for the same plants in different sources (but see note 716).

715 The Gaelic means 'When I was bending over it', so the first 'it' in this line must be a printing error. *Mac nan Aingeal* (*Mac nan aingeal* in the manuscript) will be Christ.

716 Lines 5–8 correspond loosely to the following in Carmichael's charm 'A' Charr Àigh' ('The Gracious Root'), for which see note 714 (*CG4*, pp. 124–25):

> *Thàinig Brighde dhachaidh*
> *Le ìm, le gruth, le càis,*
> *Is chuir i fo na naoi glasa glinn*
> *Na naoi mill an sàs.*

"Brigit came homeward / With butter, curd and cheese, / And she laid under the nine firm locks / The nine stocks securely." With his 'nine stocks' Carmichael is drawing upon the lore which he had collected about the *mòthan* (*CG2*, p. 110): "When the 'mothan' is used as a love-philtre, the woman who gives it goes upon her left knee and plucks nine roots of the plant and knots them together, forming them into a 'cuach' – ring." This suggests that these lines are in the correct place when cited by JGC, and in the wrong place when cited by Carmichael. In EUL MS CW 241, f. 37, Carmichael gives the line as *Fo naoi glasa cruinn/ croinn?*); *glasa cruinne* would be 'round locks', *glasa croinn* could be 'bolted locks' (*crann* 'a bolt'). Probably *glasa glinn*, Carmichael's 'firm locks', is a mistake for one of these, or for *glasa grinn(e)* 'fine locks'.

717 Cf. the rhyme cited at p. 203. Presumably *conchas* is a variant of *conasg* 'furze, whin, gorse'. *Màiri nighean Mhoire*, which JGC translates 'smooth St Mary', is rather 'Mary the daughter of St Mary'. Secular *Màiri* is distinguished from sacred *Moire*, just as *Pàdraig* is distinguished from *Peadar*, *Iain* from *Eòin*, *Pàl* from *Pòl*, and *Calum* from *Calum Cille*. *Màiri nighean Mhoire* is truly a 'Child of Mary' in the sense intended by the Jesuit-inspired devotion of that name, a 'daughter of Mary' who chooses a neglected tabernacle and remains always in spirit before it. However, JGC's 'smooth St Mary' suggests that what lay before him was not *Màiri nighean Mhoire* at all but something like *Mìn Mhoire*, and that Carmichael took this to be an abbreviation.

718 JGC's Gaelic original was excluded from *WSS*, but I supply it from Carmichael's transcript in EUL MS CW 241, f. 39 (see p. 703). This charm may be compared in general terms with those for cattle protection in *CG4*, pp. 40–87. The dangers to grazing cattle – from each other's horns, for example – are well enumerated in 'Sian Seilbh' ('Charm for Stock'), *CG4*, pp. 50–53. Some specific points may be noted. In line 2 *boc* will be genitive plural – 'of he-goats'. In line 4 *mairbh* will be genitive singular – 'of a corpse'. Lines 5–6 are extraordinary. The basic adjectives are *biorach* 'pointed, horned', *rusach*, which JGC says means 'fierce', *cluasach* 'eary, big-eared' and *màsach* 'buttocky, fat-buttocked'. We might expect *Air an aon bhò as bioraiche, / (As) rusaiche, (as) cluasaiche, (as) màsaiche*, 'Against the one cow that's the sharpest, / Fiercest, biggest-eared, fattest-buttocked'. What we get however is a scarcely credible syntax in which each epithet appears to become an abstract noun: "Against the one cow of pointedness, / Of fierceness, big-earedness, fat-buttockedness."

Finally, JGC's 'Evil One's millstone' must be rejected. He is assuming that *donain* (nominative *donan*) is a kenning for the devil on the lines of *an donas*, cf. p. 160. There is no authority for this, and an appeal to the devil for protection would be highly unusual. Most charmers would have considered it counter-productive. It is the saint's name Donnan – Donnan of Eigg, for whom see Watson 1926a, p. 283.

719 JGC's Gaelic original was excluded from *WSS*, but again I supply it from EUL MS CW 241, f. 40 (see p. 703). It corresponds to lines 1–6 and 11–12 of a charm in twelve lines published under the title 'Sian Chaorach' ('Sain for Sheep') in *CG4*, pp. 48–49:

> Sian a chuir Moire
> M'a comhail chaorach,
> Romh ianaibh, romh chonaibh,
> Romh bhiastaibh, romh dhaoinibh,
> Romh mhadaidh, romh mhèirlich,
> Romh fheòcaill, romh thaghain . . .
> An cnoc bhur laighe,
> Slàn dhuibh éirigh.

"The sain placed by Mary / Upon her flock of sheep, / Against birds, against dogs, / Against beasts, against men, / Against hounds, against thieves, / Against polecats, against marten-cats . . . / On the hillock of your lying, / Whole be your rising." *An t-sian* shows that *seun* or *sian* 'a protective charm' can be feminine as well as masculine; this is because it is an old neuter, from Latin *signum* 'a sign (of the cross)'. JGC's *crò chaorach* 'sheepfold' is surely preferable to Carmichael's *comhail chaorach*, from *còmh(dh)ail* 'a gathering, a meeting' – cf. *droch còmhalaichean* 'bad people to meet', p. 139. Line 5 of the manuscript offers *mhadra* as well as *mhadadh* for 'wild dog'; both are acceptable.

720 John MacLean, *am Peinnseanair Mór*, 1780–1874 (MacDougall 1978a, p. 35). For items of this kind see Macbain 1890–91, pp. 235–37 = 1891–92, pp. 175–77; Mackenzie 1891–92, pp. 139–42; *CG2*, pp. 26–37. At *CG3*, pp. 94–97, under the heading 'Seun Sàbhalaidh' ('Charm of Protection'), are thirty-six surviving lines of an incantation got by Carmichael from Catherine MacNeill, Ceann Tangabhall, Barra, along with a very good description of how it should be placed by a woman upon a man in a 'hidden glen' in the presence of God alone. Our Coll charm represents lines 1–7, 27–28 and 31–34 of the Barra one, but it should be noted that at *CG3*, pp. 96–97, a row of asterisks indicates a lacuna between lines 32 and 33. JGC's Gaelic original was excluded from *WSS*, but fortunately Carmichael transcribed it into what is now EUL MS CW 241, f. 41 (see p. 703 below):

> An t-sian chuir Moire mu Mac
> 'S a chuir Brithid 'na brat
> 'S a chuir Mìcheal 'na sgéith
> 'S a chuir Mac Dhé roimh chathair neòil,
> Sian thu roimh shaighead,
> Sian thu roimh chlaidheamh,
> Sian thu roimh pheileir na sgrìoba ruaidhe;
> Eilean thu air muir,
> Carraig thu air tìr —
> Guma motha eagal gach codach dhiubh sin
> Roimhn chorp mu'n téid an t-sian
> Ann am fochair Chaluim Chille
> 'S a chochall fhéin umad.

For *sian* as a feminine noun see note 719, and for JGC's spelling *Brithid* see p. 541. 'In her banners' should read 'in her mantle', implying the covering in which St Brigid wrapped the infant Jesus at birth, cf. *CG1*, p. 165, and notes 8, 730 and 746. For confusion between *nèamh* 'heaven' and *neul* 'cloud' see notes 685 and 693; *roimh chathair neòil* thus means in effect 'before the throne of heaven', cf. *CG3*, pp. 94–95:

> *Seun a chuir Brighid m'a Dalt,*
> *Seun a chuir Moire m'a Mac,*
> *Seun a chuir Mìcheal m'a sgéith,*
> *Seun a chuir Mac Dhé mu chathair neof.*

"The charm placed of Brigit about her Fosterson, / The charm placed of Mary about her Son, / The charm placed of Michael militant about his shield, / The charm placed of God's Son about the city of heaven."

721 For these three lines the Barra version has (*CG3*, pp. 94–95):

> *Seun romh shaighead,*
> *Seun romh chlaidhe,*
> *Seun romh shleagha . . .*

"Charm against arrow, / Charm against sword, / Charm against spears . . ." It can be seen that Carmichael's 'spears' (*shleagha*) have been updated into JGC's 'red-tracked bullet' (*pheileir na sgrìoba ruaidhe*). This appearance in a charm of the late medieval loanword *peileir* 'a bullet' is, I think, unique – *luaidh* 'lead' would be more usual, cf. Mackenzie 1891–92, pp. 141–42. Elsewhere Carmichael cites a five-line charm from South Uist which seems, like JGC's, to offer protection against arrow, sword and bullet, in that order, except that the arrow is an Elf-bolt, the sword is a *gath* ('sting', 'dart', hence usually 'spear'), and the bullet appears as *luaidh shaoghlach*, literally 'worldly lead'. Here it is, original and translation exactly as given by Carmichael (1909–10, p. 282):

> *Sian romh shaighead shiodhach*
> *Sian romh ghath shluaghach*
> *Sian romh luaidh shaoghlach*
> *Sian a bheatha bhorcach bhuan*
> *Romh shluagh agus romh bhaogha.*

"Charm against dart of fairies, / Charm against spear of hosts, / Charm against lead of men, / The charm of the sprouting lasting life / Against men, against mishap." Carmichael was clearly surprised to meet *pheileir*, for at this line in EUL MS CW 241, f. 41, he jotted *pheithir/* in the left margin. This would give us *Sian thu roimh pheithir na sgrìoba ruaidhe* 'You are a charm against the red-tracked beast'. Against it however is the fact that *ruadh* is the red of rust and not of blood.

722 Cf. *CG3*, pp. 96–97, *Is eilean thu am muir, / Is tulach thu air tìr* . . . "An isle art thou in the sea, / A hill art thou on land . . ."

723 Cf. *CG3*, pp. 96–97:

> *Is mór eagal am beatha dhàibh-san*
> *A chì a' cholann mu'n téid an t-sian.*
> *   *   *   *   *   *
> *Tha cobhair Chaluim Chille mar riut,*
> *Agus a chochall féin umad.*

"Great fear have they for their lives / Who see the person around whom shall go the charm. / The succour of Columba is with thee, / And his own cowl around thee." *Cochall* can be much more than a monk's cowl, however, see p. 156.

724 MacLeod 1841–42b, p. 312 (JGC's *Cuairtear nam Beann* should read *Cuairtear nan Gleann*). The article was published anonymously, but was subsequently revealed as the work of the Rev. Dr Norman MacLeod, *Caraid nan Gaidheal*, through being included in his collected works by his son-in-law Archibald Clerk (1867, pp. 338–43). The charm is given in both sources in Gaelic only, headed *Seun / A fhuaradh o chionn da-fhichead bliadhna bho sheann duine ann an Gleannforsa, ann an Eilean Mhuile* – 'A Charm / Which was got forty years ago from an old man in Glenforsa, in the Island of Mull'. JGC gives it in English only. MacLeod's original and JGC's translation are here brought together in print for the first time. The Gaelic text is MacLeod's from 1842, lightly edited by myself for spelling and punctuation. Clerk, an intrusive editor, made many unnecessary changes (e.g. *shealbhadh* to *shealbhaich* in the first line) and one or two helpful ones. Another translation was published by John Abercromby in *The Folk-Lore Journal*, vol. 1, 1883, p. 192; it begins 'For thee and for thy heirs' and ends 'A host going over thee!'

725 It corresponds closely to an incantation printed in *CG2*, pp. 26–31, under the title 'Sian a Bheatha Bhuan' ('Charm of the Lasting Life'). Carmichael had got it from a policeman called Duncan Cameron at Lochaline in Morvern, of whom he remarks (*CG2*, p. 379): "Much traditional lore of great excellence died with this highly intelligent lorist." It has forty-two lines, of which our text corresponds to lines 1–2, 5–9, 12–18, 21–25, 27–28 and 30–42 – that is to say, both texts are in the same order, our text occasionally prints two of Carmichael's lines as one, and all but eight lines of Carmichael's forty-two are represented here. For Cameron see note 743 and pp. 634, 638, 641, 654.

726 Clerk corrected this line (1867, p. 343) to *Air do shon, 's air do shealbhaich*, cf. p. 142 and note 729. Carmichael (*CG2*, pp. 28–29) has it as *Cuirim an seun air do chom, / Agus air do shealbhachd*: "I place the charm on thy body, / And on thy prosperity." Perhaps, therefore, the correct reading of the first three words of our charm is *Air do chom*, and the translation should read 'On your body and on your goods'. On the other hand, Dr R. C. Maclagan got this charm, beginning *Air do shon, 's air do shealbhaich*, from Hugh MacLellan, Port Charlotte, Islay, who told him (SoSS Maclagan MSS vol. 22, p. 4974): "Soldiers used to get *seuns* put on them. I told you about the old woman who told me that she could put a *seun* on any one. I learned the words of the *Seun* from 'Caraid nan Gaidheal'."

727 Carmichael (*CG2*, pp. 28–29) has this as *Mu mhuineal min Dhornghil* 'round the fair neck of Dornghil', probably the same as *ighinn Dorail* 'the daughter of Dorail' (*ò* long), *CG2*, pp. 66–67. These will be variations on *nighean Taoi(dh)g, nighean Torgill*, see pp. 67–69 and note 815. Referring to the arming run discussed in note 219 above, Carmichael says (*CG2*, p. 275) that Dorn-gheal or Dor-gheal was the name of the man who clothed Murchadh mac Brian in his war vestments and equipped him with his weapons. Torgill (Tadhg) was Murchadh's brother.

728 In *CG2*, pp. 28–29, *a* 'her' is omitted: "Between sole and throat, / Between pap and knee . . . / Between eye and hair."

729 Here and in the following line JGC appears at first sight to depart from the literal meaning of the original – 'his side', 'his shoulder', presumably referring to Christ. It is very likely however that for *air a* we should read *air do*, as *air a, ar a*, or *a, orra* are common in speech for *air do* (cf. MacLeod 1952, p. 554, and McDonald 1958, p. 192). This was Clerk's opinion also – he altered the phrases to *air do thaobh, air do shlinnein* (1867, p. 343). Likewise, *CG2*, pp. 28–29, has *air do thaobh, air do shlinnean*. See notes 685, 726, 752 and 813.

730 This will be for *Brata Chrìost umad* 'Christ's coverings round thee'. *CG2*, pp. 28–29, has *Brat Chriosda fein umad* 'The mantle of Christ Himself about thee'. See note 721 above.

731 Like the devil (p. 160), God enjoyed numerous kennings. These are two of them.

732 This is the key couplet with respect to the performance of the charm. *Astar* should be understood in the sense of 'path', corresponding to *ceum* in *CG2*, p. 30. The charm is spoken

on a Monday (a suitable day for commencing a journey, see p. 565) on a narrow path which symbolises danger, no doubt while tying coloured threads to a thorn-bush – *droigheann*, blackthorn, the Easter thorn (MacilleDhuibh 6.4.01, 20.4.01; Black 2002, p. 484).

733 This will be a typographical error – Clerk emends to *stùchd* (1867, p. 343), while the reading in *CG2*, p. 30, is *stuc* (for *stùc*).

734 Or 'And you will not be laid low from behind'; *CG2*, pp. 30–31, has *Dionar tu a thaobh do chuil* 'Protected thou shalt be behind thee'.

735 Following MacLeod's original, JGC capitalises Swan as if it were a name or nickname; Clerk (1867, p. 343) follows suit. The solution, however, lies in *CG2*, pp. 30–31: *Is tu an eala chiuin 's a bhlar* 'Thou art the calm swan in battle'. The swan was much admired, and much hunted and killed, as Ailein Dall makes clear (Dughallach 1798, *passim*, cf. Ballard 1997, p. 72). No doubt people liked to think that in eating it they were ingesting its qualities of calmness and graceful beauty, but there was also a more overtly superstitious custom of vowing upon roast swan (Dughallach 1798, p. 57; Campbell 1862, p. 204; *CG2*, p. 278). It may perhaps be worth noting that a sanctuary stone in a field below the parish church in Lismore is called *an Eala*, misunderstood to mean 'the Swan'; those who touched it were safe from prosecution for a year and a day (Campbell 1885a, p. 323, see also *CG2*, pp. 278–79, and Black 2001, p. 393).

736 JGC translates *far riut* as if it were *mar riut*, which is plausible. In such a context one would understand *sluagh* as otherworld people. However, Clerk emends *far riut* to *tharad* (1867, p. 343), and this is in line with *CG2*, pp. 30–31, where the reading is *Feun De tharad!* "The arm of God above thee!" (Carmichael glosses *feun* at *CG2*, p. 290, as 'the arm, the hand, the hollow of the palm'.) It seems likely, then, that the correct reading in our text is *Sluagh dol tharad!* "May the host go over you!" Again, this probably refers to the Fairy host (cf. note 694), but given the purpose of the charm, it may also denote a worldly army.

737 See Nicolson 1951, p. 385, and Ó Baoill 1979, pp. 197–98. The battle was fought on 20 July 1651, not in 1652; of 700 MacLeans who took part, only forty are said to have survived. The lines 'Each stepping where his comrade stood, / The instant that he fell' are from Scott's 'Marmion', Canto Sixth, verse 34 (Lockhart 1869, p. 141).

738 JGC's Gaelic original was excluded from *WSS*, but I have supplied it from EUL MS CW 241, f. 42 (see p. 703 below).

739 That is, turned upside-down like a mattress, Scots 'owerend', 'over-end'. JGC's Gaelic original of this charm was excluded from *WSS*, but fortunately it was transcribed by Carmichael into what is now EUL MS CW 241, ff. 43–44 (see p. 703 below):

> *Is math a ghabhas mi mo rann*
> *'S mi teàrnadh leis a' ghlean,*
> *Aon rann, dà rann, sìos gu seachd gu leth rann.*
> *Na na gonar fear an éididh*
> *'S na na reubar e gu bràth,*
> *'S nuair théid e 'n cath no 'n còmhrag*
> *Làn chomaraich an Dòmhnach da.*
> *[An fhaoileann bheag ud air an t-snàmh*
> *'S an tonn geal ga bheil a miann,*
> *Ise gu subhach a' snàmh*
> *'S mise snàmh gu subhach snìomh;*
> *Nuair a chuireas mi mo chuid lìn*
> *'S a shnìomhas mi mo chuid frois*
> *Nì mi anart air a' chalg*
> *'S gheibh mi seachd marg air an t-slait.]*
> *Biolair air a buain roimh lic*

> *'S air a toirt do mhnaoi gun fhios,*
> *Lurg an fhéidh an ceann an sgadain*
> *'S an caol chalp' a' bhradain bhric.*

> *Ath-aodach seo, 's na na faoibh e,*
> *Cha chuid cléir no sagairt e*
> *Ach a chuid fhéin, 's gum meal 's gun caith e e.*

In line 5, I emend *reubas* (which makes no sense) to *reubar*. Probably Carmichael misread JGC's *r* as *s*, see p. xvii. For non-declension of *Dòmhnach* (line 7) cf. p. 564. Carmichael placed a horizontal stroke above *ub* in line 11; this indicates that in line 10 JGC's writing was hard to read, and that Carmichael checked the translation in *WSS* before going back to complete the line.

In 1888 JGC made a fresh translation and sent it to Alexander Carmichael with some notes (see below, p. 668). Here it is, exactly as written out by his sister Jessy (EUL MS CW 359, f. 39r). The reorganisation of line structure (and the comma after 'Well' in line 1) must be due to the hazards of the dictation process.

> *Well, I can say my verse*
> *As I descend the glen*
> *First verse, second verse, third verse,*
> *Fourth verse, fifth verse, sixth verse,*
> *Seven and a half verses.*
> *May the wearer of the cloth,*
> *Never be wounded to death,*
> *Or torn to pieces.*
> *When he goes into fight or combat*
> *The full succour of the Lord be his*
> *Cress gathered through slate*
> *And given to a woman unawares*
> *The shank of Deer*
> *In the head of the Herring*
> *And in the slender part*
> *Of the calf of the salmon*
> *This will form a second dress*
> *And not booty*
> *Or the property of cleric or priest*

This is followed, also in Jessy's hand, by the following 'Note' (EUL MS CW 359, ff. 39r–40r). "The meaning of the expressions in this Incantation is very difficult to get at. Evidently the watercress, the Herring in the stomach of which no food has ever been found, the deer which is a model of activity and elegance, and its fondness for feeding on watercresses, would indicate a deep knowledge of natural history. Cloth that would possess the properties ascribed to these articles would be of extra quality and merit. The watercress *Biolar uaine an fhuarain àrd* is only to be found in very gently moving water, so that to get it from under a *leac* which would be apt to make water stagnate, the difficulty of dissecting either fish, or deer and giving an article so pungent as watercress to any one unawares imply greater skill than is ordinarily possessed. If the rhyme was part of the machinery of the skilful wizard any failure, in the cloth, could be readily ascribed to a failure in any of the requisites mentioned." For *Biolar uaine an fhuarain àrd* see note 59 above.

740 Ada Goodrich Freer wrote (1903, pp. 261–62, cited in Campbell 1969–81, vol. 1, pp. 10–11), no doubt with a good deal of help from Fr Allan McDonald, that after the women had waulked the cloth, they would roll it up from both ends to the middle of the table and pat it to straighten out the creases, a song being sung meanwhile to a different metre. "This finished, one standing up calls out, 'The rhymes, the rhymes!' And those who have been working reply: 'Three rhymes, four rhymes, five and a half rhymes.' This is very mysterious – probably the last remains of some forgotten ceremony. Then the cloth is unwound, and again very carefully rolled up, this time into one firm bale, and then all rise and stand in reverent silence while the leader of the fulling-women pronounces the quaint, old-world grace with which their work concludes. Laying one hand on the cloth, she says:

> Let not the Evil Eye afflict, let not be mangled
> The man about whom thou goest, for ever.
>
> When he goes into battle or combat
> The protection of the Lord be with him.

And then some man of the party – it would not be etiquette for a woman – turns to the owner and says with emphasis: 'May you possess it and wear it.'" There are clear echoes in this of lines 3–7 of JGC's charm, and no doubt the remark about these being 'the last remains of some forgotten ceremony' comes from Fr Allan. A fellow native of Lochaber, Mrs Mary Mackellar, whom he must have known, had in fact described this ceremony in print some years before (1886–87, p. 215, cited in Campbell 1969–81, vol. 1, pp. 13–14). "During the foot-waulking, the web was rolled different ways three times, so that all parts would get the benefit, and after it was done they beat it with the open hands for some time. Then some old woman shook it out of the roll, and with a charm put all the witches from having any power over it, saying – 'Roinn a h-aon, roinn a dhà, roinn a trì, roinn a ceithir, roinn a còig, roinn a sia, roinn a seachd, chan aodach so a shagart no chléir,' &c. Then the girls took it to the river or burn, where they tramped all the soapy suds out of it, and all the part of the dye that might be loosened in the course of the day's work."

The meaning of Mrs Mackellar's charm appears to be: "Part one, part two, part three, part four, part five, part six, part seven, this is no cloth for priest or clergy." *Roinn* 'part' is translated 'division' by Carmichael (*CG1*, p. 307) and Campbell (1969–81, vol. 1, p. 13). Campbell adds: "*Roinn* seems to be the word Miss Goodrich Freer rendered as 'rhyme'." That is going a little far, as JGC makes the same word 'verse(s)', and at *CG1*, pp. 308–09, Carmichael cites a very full version of the charm in which the word used throughout is *rann*, which he translates by one of his favourite words, 'rune(s)'. Whether in the form *rann* or *roinn*, and whether translated as 'part', 'division', 'rhyme', 'verse' or 'rune', this is one and the same word (see note 874). The key to its meaning here is, I think, provided by JGC when he says that the charm is sung seven times: the *rann* or *roinn* will be the incantation itself, which will in origin have been incremental in the same way as 'On the First Day of Christmas' and other traditional rhymes. *Aon rann* or *Roinn a h-aon* will be sung the first time round, *Aon rann, dà rann* or *Roinn a h-aon, roinn a dhà* the second time round, and so on. I imagine dual and plural forms were once used: *Aon rann, dà roinn, trì ranna, ceithir ranna, còig ranna, sé* (or *sia*) *ranna, seachd ranna*. This was fun, and the women would have enjoyed it.

We should, I think, see line 2 as a simple metaphor for coming to the end of the work. Carmichael has it as *A teurnadh le gleann*, which he translates 'Descending with the glen', but 'Coming downhill' might be more accurate. His version of these first seven lines is almost identical to JGC's (*CG1*, pp. 308–09):

Is math a ghabhas mi mo rann,
A teurnadh le gleann;
Aon rann, da rann, tri rann, ceithir rann, coig rann, sia rann, seachd rann, seachd gu leth rann.
Nar a gonar fear an eididh,
Nar a reubar e gu brath,
Cian theid e 'n cath no 'n comhrag,
Sgiath chomarach an Domhnach da.

Carmichael repeats *seachd gu leth rann* and lines 6–7; this suggests that the performance may have been incremental in a different way, i.e. that each of the above seven lines was a *rann*, and that the double *seachd gu leth rann* was provided by the repetition of lines 6–7. Carmichael's translation of line 7 is 'May the sanctuary shield of the Lord be his'; at p. 564 below JGC cites the line as *slàn chomraich an Dòmhnach da*, with the translation 'the full succour of our Lord be his'. This suggests that he originally understood *chom(a)ra(i)ch* as *chobhrach* (genitive of *cobhair* 'succour').

741 JGC points out a few lines later that 'the part of the song within brackets seems to belong to the music more than to the meaning'. It looks like a spinning song, but I have failed to identify it. The swimming gull is, I think, an introductory metaphor for the task of spinning, just as the act of coming downhill was an introductory metaphor for the task of consecrating the cloth. For the sacred nature of flax, lint and linen, and the use of linen thread in the making of charms, see *CG*2, pp. 319–20, 331–32, 353, and *CG*3, pp. 182–83. 'Awns' are the beard-like bristles of flax; the word is more usually used of barley and oats. The references to flax and a cash economy have a late seventeenth- or early eighteenth-century ring. In the Treaty of Union, 1707, the value of the mark or merk (13s 4d Scots) was fixed at 13⅓d sterling, or, as Pennant expressed it (1998, p. 277), 'little more than thirteen pence farthing'. It may be that, embedded as it is in the charm for cloth, JGC has preserved for us a spinning song older than any which survive in the original.

742 These four lines (written as a separate quatrain in MS 241) appear to be riddles, but they demand to be taken seriously as part of the charm, I think, as they also form the conclusion of Carmichael's own version (*CG*1, pp. 308–09):

> *Biolair uaine ga buain fo lic,*
> *'S air a toir do mhnai gun fhiosd;*
> > *Lurg an fheidh an ceann an sgadain,*
> > *'S an caol chalp a bhradain bhric.*

His translation is: "Cresses green culled beneath a stone, / And given to a woman in secret. / The shank of the deer in the head of the herring, / And in the slender tail of the speckled salmon." Perhaps *fo lic* should read *bho lic* 'from a flagstone'. Probably in any case the reference is to watercress growing around a well covered by a flagstone: *biolair* 'was much prized, and was used as food, as medicine, and as an occult agent' (*CG*2, p. 231). Line 2 of the quatrain appears to show it being used as an aphrodisiac. In line 4 *calpa* is neither 'body' nor 'tail' but the calf of the leg; both JGC and Carmichael err in interpreting it as part of the fish. The line derives from the panegyric verse tradition: it means 'And in the slender calf like the speckled salmon', referring to the shape of a man's lower leg and to its colour (*breac*, tartan) when clothed in well-fitting trews or hose. This makes good sense out of *lurg an fhéidh*, the only disagreement about which is that introduced by JGC himself a few lines later (p. 215), where he gives *cuibhn' an fhéidh* 'deer's antlers' as an alternative. His remark about the bone in the herring's head is unhelpful, as *ceann an sgadain* appears to be a part of the male anatomy.

If I have read the riddles correctly, then, they can be seen to mix the arts of love, of magic, and of cloth-making. When watercress (the favourite food of the deer, see note 59) is plucked by a man 'through a flagstone' and eaten by his sweetheart without her knowledge, her waulking will give him the virility and swiftness of a stag.

743 All other sources for the 'final wish' (*CG1*, pp. 307, 308–09; *CG4*, pp. 98–99) begin *Chan ath-aodach seo* 'This cloth is not second-hand'. That is not to say that JGC's text is incorrect, however, because Carmichael himself pointed out (*CG2*, p. 225) that to some people *ath-aodach* meant 'new cloth', the explanation being that wool is *aodach na caora*, sheep's clothing, before being made into men's clothing. However, JGC's point about 'the cloth when turned, or made into a second suit' may be disregarded. The same sources also show that the penultimate word in that line is not *faoibh* (JGC's 'enemy's spoil') but *faoigh* 'thigging, genteel begging', see Henderson 1911, pp. 246–47, and Black 2001, pp. xxix–xxxii, and cf. note 577 above. For *gum meal 's gun caith e e*, 'may he enjoy and wear it', see 'Clothes', p. 126, and Freer's 'May you possess and wear it', p. 469.

The first two lines of the three form the middle section of Carmichael's 'Coisrigeadh an Aodaich' ('The Consecration of the Cloth', *CG1*, pp. 308–09). As the rest of JGC's charm (other than the part which he places in square brackets) also appears there, albeit in a different order and with one or two textual variations, it is clear that JGC's version and Carmichael's are closely related. This is not surprising, as Carmichael got his from Duncan Cameron, the policeman at Lochaline in Morvern, whom JGC is likely to have known (see note 725).

According to Carmichael (*CG1*, p. 307), 'when the women have waulked the cloth, they roll up the web and place it on end in the centre of the frame'. This appears to be another variation on JGC's 'turning the cloth over end', Freer's 'rolling it up from both ends to the middle' and Mrs Mackellar's 'shaking it out of the roll'. Carmichael says that 'they then turn it slowly and deliberately sunwise along the frame', accompanying each turn of the web with a recital of *Chan ath-aodach seo . . .* or of *Roinn a h-aon, roinn a dhà . . .* followed by:

> Chan aodach seo do shagairt no chleir,
> Ach 's aodach e do mo Dhomh'lan caomhach fein,
> Do m' chombanach graidh 's do Iain an aigh,
> 'S do Mhuiril is aillidh sgeimh.

He translates: "This is not cloth for priest or cleric, / But it is cloth for my own little Donald of love, / For my companion beloved, for John of joy, / And for Muriel of loveliest hue." Unusually for *CG*, Muriel (*Muireall, Muireann*) is clearly a mortal and not an angel. The explanation continues: "Each member of the household for whom the cloth is intended is mentioned by name in the consecration. The cloth is then spat upon, and slowly reversed end by end in the name of Father and of Son and of Spirit till it stands again in the centre of the frame. The ceremony of consecrating the cloth is usually intoned, the women, hitherto gay and vivacious, now solemn and subdued, singing in unison. The woman who leads in the consecration is called 'coisreagan,' consecrator or celebrant. After the cloth is waulked and washed it is rolled up. This is called 'coilleachadh'—stretching,—'coilleachadh an aodaich'—stretching the cloth,—a process done with great care in order to secure equal tension throughout the web."

In *CG4*, p. 88, Carmichael describes the conclusion of the process; in the *làn luathadh* or 'full waulking' it appears to have involved a separate ceremony of consecration. Following the folding or *coilleachadh*, spelt more correctly *coinnleachadh* in *CG4*, the cloth is 'rolled upon a piece of wood, round or flat as may be most conveniently got'. This is the *còrnadh*. "The cloth is rolled slowly and carefully, bit by bit, hard and firm as the strong arms of the women can make it, in order that the tension may be evenly distributed. When the 'cornadh' is completed and the end secured, the web of cloth is laid across the waulking frame. The ceremony of consecration is now performed, the first part solemnly, the second jubilantly. There are three celebrants, the oldest of them leading, the others following according to age. The first celebrant seizes the cloth and moves round about half a turn. Freeing her hands, she seizes it again and brings it round to complete the turn. With the first move the woman says, 'Cuirim car deiseal,' 'I give a turn sunwise'; and with the second move, completing the circle, she completes the sentence, 'am freasdal an Athar,' 'dependent on the Father.' The other two women turn the web similarly in name of Son and in name of Spirit."

At pp. 96–97 Carmichael gives the words of this second consecration in full, obtained 'from Duncan Cameron, police constable, Morvern, a man who was full of valuable old lore', and at pp. 98–99 he offers an 18-line version of *Chan ath-aodach seo . . .*

The importance of these rituals is well underlined, I think, by the conversation of Eoghan a' Chinn Bhig and the washer-woman of the ford (*CG5*, p. 283). *Agus an tig mi fhéin beò ás a' chath, a mhuimeag?* says Eoghan. "And will I escape alive from the battle, little foster-mother?"

Thig, replies the prophetess, *ma bheannaicheas do bhean dha do dheise chlò.* "Yes, if your wife blesses your suit of cloth."

As may be seen at pp. 237–38 of the present work, however, his suit was praised by a servant woman, and it was as a living corpse that he left the battlefield.

744 JGC's Gaelic original was excluded from *WSS*, but fortunately it was transcribed by Carmichael into what is now EUL ms CW 241, ff. 45–46 (see p. 703 below). It corresponds pretty closely to the 'Sian Sàbhalaidh' ('Charm for Protection') obtained by Carmichael from an unknown informant and printed at *CG3*, pp. 196–99. JGC's version has twenty-three lines (arranged in his translation as twenty-two); Carmichael's has thirty-two, arranged – with some justification – in quatrains, of which lines 5, 26 and 27 consist of rows of asterisks. As none of these three missing lines are present in JGC's version, it is possible that they never existed. However, our line 8, which is not present in *CG*, appears to represent the completion of the second quatrain, so it may be that Carmichael's first row of asterisks is simply in the wrong place. For the sake of comparison, in what follows I place the *CG* text on the left and JGC's on the right, followed in each case by Carmichael's translation and some notes.

Gabhaidh tu ri Dia,	*Gabhaidh tu le Dia*
Gabhaidh Dia riut,	*'S gabhaidh Dia leat;*
'G iadhadh do dhà bhonn,	*Iarann do dhà bhuinn*
'S a dhà làimh mu d' cheann.	*'S do dhà làimh dheug mu d' cheann.*

("Thou shalt take to God, / God shall take to thee, / Surrounding thy two feet, / His two hands about thy head.") JGC's third line means 'The iron of your two soles', which makes no sense to me, and I think it should read *'G iadhadh do dhà bhuinn* 'Surrounding your two soles'. It describes the *caim* or 'encompassing', by which a circle is drawn around the feet and the ground within it is blessed, see note 694. JGC's fourth line means 'And your twelve hands around your head'; we should replace *do* 'your' with *a* 'His' as in *CG*. Why God should have twelve hands (*dhà làimh dheug*) I am not sure, unless it refers to the laying on of hands by the apostles.

* * * * * *	*Do dhris an crann no an cuileann*
Do dhrisean crann no cuileann;	*No 'n carraig air muir*
Is carraig thu air muir,	*No 'n talamh air tìr;*
Is daingneach thu air tìr.	*Sgiath dhìdein umad,*

("To thorns of trees or hollies; / A rock thou art at sea, / A fortress thou art on land.") Here it is JGC's text which supplies the deficiencies in Carmichael's. There is acceptable rhyme throughout (*cuileann : carraig; muir : umad; tìr : dhìdein*). *Do dhris*, 'Thy afflictions', is literally 'Your thorn'.

Tha sgiath Mhìcheil umad,	*Sgiath Mhìcheil umad;*
Tha sgàth Chrìosda tharad,	
Tha lùireach chaol Chaluim Chille	*Lùireach chaol Chaluim Chille*
Dha do dhìon o na saigheada sìth.	*Roimh na saighde sìth*

("Michael's shield is about thee, / Christ's shelter is over thee, / The fine-wrought breastplate of Columba / Preserves thee from the fairy shafts.") The first line here is given in the manuscript as *Sgiath Mhicheil umad/tharad*. As in the previous quatrain, JGC's text expresses a wish, Carmichael's a statement of fact.

Roimh na corracha-cri,	
Roimh na corracha-cnàmh,	*'S roimh na gara cràidh,*
Roimh bhuaireadh an t-saoghail a bhos,	*Roimh bhuaireadh an t-saoghail sa*
Roimh olcas an t-saoghail thall.	*No 'n t-saoghail eile.*

("Against the screeching cranes (?), / Against the gnawing cranes (?), / Against the troubling of the world here, / Against the evil of the world beyond." Carmichael offers *rosad* 'mischief' as an alternative to *olcas* 'evil'.) JGC's *gara cràidh* is enormously helpful in unlocking the mysteries of *CG*. 'Screeching cranes' and 'gnawing cranes' make no sense. *Corracha cri(th)* and/or *corracha cnamh* occur in three other charms collected by Carmichael; they are left untranslated in *CG2*, pp. 8–9, and rendered as 'crooked cranes' and 'crooked bones' in *CG2*, pp. 52–53. In *CG4*, pp. 190–91, *corracha cnàmha* is rendered as 'gnawing cranes (?)', and it may well be that Carmichael's informant thought of them as monsters. The usual plural of *coire* 'fault, offence, sin, crime' is *coireannan* (Dwelly 1977, p. 231), but *coireacha(n)* is also possible. In all cases *coireacha cridhe* or *coireacha cràidh* would account satisfactorily for the origin of the term, yielding the following fresh translation of the *CG* text: "Against the crimes of passion, / Against the crimes of pain, / Against the trouble of this world / And of the world over there."

A' bhean air a glùn,	*A' bhean air a glùn,*
A' bhean air a sùil,	*A' bhean air a sùil,*
A' bhean air a gnù,	
A' bhean air a farmad;	

("The woman on her knee, / The woman at her (evil) eye, / The woman with her spleen, / The woman with her envy.") This shows that the charm is intended to counteract the evil eye, assumed to have been cast by a woman in a kneeling position, cf. p. 154 above.

A' bhean air tànach a tréid,	*Air a raghainn tànach*
A' bhean air àlach a spréidh,	
A' bhean air àrach a greigh,	
Guna ruig i féithean a cridh.	*'S air féithean a cridhe*
A' bhean mhùgach bhreun,	*Gus an ruig e 'n t-àite*
Gun ruig i an t-àit as an tàinig i.	*'S an t-ionad ás an tàinig e,*

("The woman at the cattle of her herd, / The woman at the young of her cows, / The woman at the rearing of her flocks, / Until it reach the fibres of her heart. / The woman frowning and foul, / Until she reach the place whence she came.") For *A' bhean mhùgadh bhreun* Carmichael might well have said 'The snotty toffee-nosed woman'. His 'Until she reach the place whence she came' (*Gun ruig i an t-àit as an tàinig i*) is clearly at variance with JGC's 'Till it reach the place whence it came' (*Gus an ruig e 'n t-àite / 'S an t-ionad ás an tàinig e*, literally 'Till it reach the place / And the spot whence it came'). Carmichael is wrong. This is the spell, incantation or 'eye' (*ortha, eab, sùil*) being turned back by the charm (*sian, seun*) upon (*air*) its originator and all that she owns – which is why *air* has been repeated so often. In MS 241 the last line is written *S an t ionad as an tainig e/ise*, literally 'And the spot whence he/she came', i.e. the preposition depends on the reciter's opinion of whether the word referred to is *ortha, eab, sùil*, etc. One or two other points are worth making. *Raghainn tànach* is 'the choicest of herd', the woman's best cow or cows. Carmichael renders *air àrach a greigh* as 'at the rearing of her flocks', but it will refer to horses: 'upon the breeding of her stud'. The last line describes well the reflection of the evil eye into the heart from which it came – this charm is a defensive mirror.

Gach bean gnùthach farmadach,	*Gach bean thnùthach fharmadach*
A sgaoileas a fuil, a feòil, is a gaorr,	*Sgaoileas a fuil 's a feòil —*
Oirre féin bitheadh a gnù agus tearbadh,	*Orra fhéin a rùn 's a tnù 's a farmad.*
O'n là an diugh gu là deireannach an t-saoghail.	

("Each woman who is full of spleen and envy, / Who sunders her blood, her flesh and gore, / On herself be her spleen and her severing, / From this day to the final day of the world.") For Carmichael's 'sunders' we should substitute JGC's 'propagates', which is very helpful. 'Severing' is an odd word; perhaps 'sundering' would be better. The references are of course to fertility and sterility. Finally, *orra* should strictly be *oirre*.

745 On the importance of Thursday and Sunday see note 684. JGC fails to touch upon the relationship between this oral charm known as *Soisgeul Chrìost* ('the Gospel of Christ') and the written one called simply a *soisgeul* ('gospel', p. 224). Judging from its content, the purpose of the former was to sanctify a crucifix; according to Carmichael, however, its purpose was to sanctify a *soisgeul*. Introducing 'Soisgeul Chrìosd' Carmichael says (*CG*3, p. 182): "This was the name of a charm worn upon the person to safeguard the wearer against drowning at sea, against disaster on land, against evil eye, evil wish, evil influences, against the wrongs and oppressions of man and the wiles and witcheries of woman, against being lifted by the hosts of the air, and against being waylaid by the fairies of the mound. Such a charm might consist of a word, a phrase, a saying, or a verse from one of the Gospels, and from this came the name, 'Gospel of Christ'. The words were written upon paper or parchment, and were often illuminated and ornamented in Celtic design, the script being thus rendered more precious by the beauty of its work and the beauty of its words. The script was placed in a small bag of linen and sewn into the waistcoat of a man and the bodice of a woman, under the left arm. In the case of a child the bag was suspended from the neck by a linen cord."

From JGC's description it appears that the cord had survived but that the *soisgeul* itself was redundant.

746 Once again, JGC's Gaelic original was excluded from *WSS*, but we have it as transcribed by Carmichael into what is now EUL MS CW 241, ff. 47–48 (see p. 703 below). When this is compared to 'Soisgeul Chrìosd' ('The Gospel of Christ', *CG*3, pp. 184–89) it seems vestigial and rather confused. That is not to say that it is unimportant, however. Carmichael is known to have 'improved' his materials, and it is possible that 'Soisgeul Chrìosd' as published in *CG*3 (the source for which is given as Malcolm Sinclair, fisherman, Baile Phuill, Tiree) is a

conflated version employing ingredients from a variety of texts, including JGC's original or something like it. JGC's version has thirty lines, while Carmichael's has seventy-seven.

Systematic comparison reveals that the manuscript version is very close to the *CG* text at first but gradually diverges from it. The manuscript version begins:

> *Gum beannaicheadh Dia do chrois*
> *Mun téid thusa air lios —*
> *Aon ghalar gam biodh ann,*
> *Cha toir thu e ás.*

> *Gum beannaicheadh Dia do chrois cheusta*
> *Air druim taighe taighe Chrìosta*
> *Roimh bhàthadh, roimh ghàbhadh*
> *'S roimh ghrìsinn.*

This corresponds to lines 1–7 of JGC's translation and to Carmichael's first two verses:

> *Gum beannaicheadh Dia do chrois*
> *Mun téid thu thar lear;*
> *Aon ghalar dh'am bi ad chois,*
> *Cha tobhair e thu leis.*

> *Gum beannaicheadh Dia do chrois cheusda*
> *Air druim-taighe Chrìosda,*
> *Romh bhàthadh, romh ghàbhadh, romh ghéisne,*
> *Romh gheur-ghuin, romh ghrìsne.*

Carmichael: "May God bless thy cross / Before thou go over the sea; / Any illness that thou mayest have, / It shall not take thee hence. / May God bless thy crucifying cross / In the house-shelter of Christ, / Against drowning, against peril, against spells, / Against sore wounding, against grisly fright." This provides a satisfactory revision of line 2 – *air lios* 'to any garden' surely comes of JGC misreading his own field-notes. In line 3, JGC's 'that is in it' is excessively literal – he means 'that may exist'. His line 4 is very confused: *Cha toir thu e ás* means 'You won't take it out', not 'May he take from it'. Again Carmichael solves the problem: we should emend JGC's text to *Cha toir e thu ás* 'It won't take you out'.

The image in line 6 is of the crucifix being blessed upon the ridge of Christ's roof. In the manuscript this is expressed as 'On the house-ridge of Christ's house' and in *CG* as 'On Christ's house-ridge'. This will mean that the charm should be performed on a church roof or on a high mountain. In line 8 Carmichael offered *mhìorun* 'malice' as an alternative to *ghrìsne* 'grisly fright', but both *ghrìsne* and JGC's *ghrìsinn* look like dative forms of *grìs*, *grìsionn* 'a shiver of cold', 'a shivering cold' (MacDonald 1934–36b, p. 45, and *CG*6, p. 88); *ghrìsne* may be for dative plural *ghrìsnibh*.

JGC's next eight lines correspond to lines 8–13 of his translation. This is exactly how they stand in the manuscript:

> *Mar a bha Righ sìnte suas*
> *Righ nan trì bean/brì*
> *'S barr dosrach donn*
> *Mar thogadh corp Dhe gun gheall (fheall?)*
> *Mar fhear nan sach*

> *Nach teid a mach air an ceann*
> *Gum beannaicheadh Dia na bheil romhad*
> *'S tusa dol nan ceann*

The second line certainly means 'The King of the Three Hills' – either *Rìgh nan Trì Beann*, rhyming with *gheall* or *fheall*, or *Rìgh nan Trì Brì* (an Irish word). The fourth, fifth and sixth lines are described by JGC in his translation as 'unintelligible'. Can *CG* help?

> *Mar bha Rìgh nan rìgh sìnte suas*
> *Gun iochd gun truas ri crann,*
> *Am Barr dosrach donn dual,*
> *Mar bhuadhaich corp Chrìosd gun fheall,*
>
> *'S mar bhean nan seachdamh beannachd*
> *Tha dol a steach 'nan ceann,*
> *Gum beannaicheadh Dia na bheil romhad*
> *Agus thus tha triall 'nan teann.*

Carmichael: "As the King of kings was stretched up / Without pity, without compassion, to the tree, / The leafy, brown, wreathed topmost Bough, / As the body of the sinless Christ triumphed. / And as the woman of the seven blessings, / Who is going in at their head, / May God bless all that are before thee / And thee who art moving anear them." If we can understand this, we can understand JGC's version too. Fundamental to it is the image of the warrior as a tree in the third line – provoked by *crann* ('tree, cross') in the previous line, but enhancing the image of Christ's victory in the fourth (cf. MacAonghuis n.d. and Black 2001, pp. xxiii–xxiv, 527). We may retranslate: "As the King of Kings was stretched up / Without pity or compassion on the cross, / As Christ's guileless body triumphed, / The leafy, noble, curly-haired treetop, / And like the woman of the seven blessings / Who goes in to meet them – / So may God bless all who are before you / And you who travel near them." Presumably 'the woman of the seven blessings' (*seachda*, not *seachdamh*) is a seventh daughter of a seventh daughter. Turning now to JGC's text, clearly his fourth line should read *Mar thogadh corp Dhé gun fheall*: "As Christ's guileless body was raised." His fifth line is incomplete and should presumably read *Mar fhear nan seachda beannachd* or similar – "Like the man of the seven blessings." Although the next line makes sense within itself ('Who does not go out at their head'), I do not see how it fits in with the rest. JGC's last line means: "And you who go to meet them."

The two texts now begin to diverge. JGC's next two lines correspond to his translation 'Success at meeting and in battle; / The grace of God and courteous look of all men be yours':

> *Buaidh chnoc is buaidh làrach,*
> *Aoibh Dhé is aghaidh gach duine chì thu.*

The 'courteous look' is thus cast not by the traveller but upon him. Carmichael's fifth verse, on the other hand, consists of a 24-line formulaic sequence beginning *Buadh cruth, / Buadh guth dhut* ('Grace of form, / Grace of voice be thine') and ending *Buadh réidh, Buadh Dhé dhut* ('Grace of peace, / Grace of God be thine').

JGC's two lines beginning 'The banners of Christ' are as follows:

> *'S brat Chrìost air a chàradh umad*
> *Gu d' dhìon o mhullach gu d' bhonn.*

Brat Chrìost is not 'the banners of Christ' but 'Christ's mantle', see note 720. These lines correspond to the first couplet of Carmichael's eleventh verse:

> *Brat Chrìosda dh'a chàramh umad,*
> > *Dha do sgàth bho do mhullach gu d' bhonn;*
> *Brat Dhé nan dùl dha do chumail,*
> > *Dha do churadh agus dha do chonn.*

("The mantle of Christ be placed upon thee, / To shade thee from thy crown to thy sole; / The mantle of the God of life be keeping thee, / To be thy champion and thy leader.") Carmichael's twelfth and thirteenth verses, totalling thirteen lines, are not represented in JGC's text at all. JGC concludes as follows:

> *Cha loisg aingeal thu,*
> *Cha bhàth marannan thu,*
> *Carra air muir thu*
> *'S duin' air tìr thu,*
> *Is gil' thu na 'n eal' air Loch Làthaich*
> *Agus faoileann air an t-sruth bhàn;*
> *Éiridh tus' os an cionn*
> *Mar a dh'éireas an tonn*
> *Ás leth Dhia 's nan cumhachdan.*
> *Is tus' an caorann dearg*
> *A thraoghadh fearg gach duine*
> *Mar thonn o mhara gu lìonadh*
> *'S mar thonn o lìonadh gu tràghadh.*

With *Carra air muir thu* ('A rock at sea art thou') we may compare 'An island at sea art thou' (*Eilean thu air muir*) on p. 217. These thirteen lines correspond fairly closely to Carmichael's eighth, ninth and tenth verses:

> *Cha ghearr claidheamh thu,*
> *Cha loisg athain thu,*
> *Cha reub saighead thu,*
> *Cha bhàth maranna thu.*
>
> *Is gil thu na 'n eal air loch làthaich,*
> *Is gil thu na faoileag bhàn an t-sruth,*
> *Is gil thu na sneachd nam beann arda,*
> *Is gil thu na gràdh ainglean nan nimh.*
>
> *Is tus an caorrann caon dearg*
> *A thraothas fraoch is fearg gach duine,*
> *Mar thonn mhara bho lìonadh gu tràghadh,*
> *Mar thonn mhara bho thràghadh gu lìonadh.*

("Nor sword shall wound thee, / Nor brand shall burn thee, / Nor arrow shall rend thee, / Nor seas shall drown thee. / Thou art whiter than the swan on miry lake, / Thou art whiter than the white gull of the current, / Thou art whiter than the snow of the high mountains, / Thou art whiter than the love of the angels of heaven. / Thou art the gracious red rowan /

That subdues the ire and anger of all men, / As a sea-wave from flow to ebb, / As a sea-wave from ebb to flow.") Thus, we are told, the 'Gospel' endows the wayfarer with the protective qualities of the rowan (for which see pp. 177 and 229). *Fraoch* and *fearg* represent not simple anger but passion, which explains I think why the tide is described as flowing as well as ebbing. There are two sea-lochs called *Loch Làthaich*, Loch Laich, 'the Muddy Loch', or, as Carmichael would have it, 'the Miry Lake', one in Appin and one in the Ross of Mull, but it is not necessary to regard it as a specific place-name.

747 This is the celebrated 'Ortha nam Buadh' ('the Charm of the Graces'), for which see *CG*1, pp. 6–11, and Black 1999, pp. 2–7. After explaining that he got it from Duncan Maclellan, crofter, Carnan, South Uist, who had it from Catherine Macaulay, Mol-a-deas, Corradale (who saw Prince Charles several times when he was in hiding there in 1746), Carmichael says (*CG*1, p. 7): "I heard versions of this poem in other islands and in districts of the mainland, and in November 1888 John Gregorson Campbell, minister of Tiree, sent me a fragment taken down from Margaret Macdonald, Tiree. The poem must therefore have been widely known. In Tiree the poem was addressed to boys and girls, in Uist to young men and maidens. Probably it was composed to a maiden on her marriage. The phrase 'eala dhonn,' brown swan, would indicate that the girl was young – not yet a white swan."

Uniquely, in this case we have two manuscript versions of JGC's Gaelic original and also a second translation, although none is in his hand. The earlier of the two originals, along with his second translation, is in his sister Jessy's hand in EUL MS CW 425, ff. 174–77 (versos blank). These were sent to Carmichael in 1888 (see p. 674 below). The later of the two originals is in Carmichael's own hand, copied *c.* 1905 into EUL MS CW 241, ff. 49–50, presumably from a version written *c.* 1874 by JGC. The two originals are almost identical, except that Jessy puts in accents, but Carmichael leaves them out. The two translations are by no means identical, which suggests that the one written out by Jessy in 1888 may have been made from scratch by herself.

The following is the Gaelic text exactly as written by Jessy. It is clear that Carmichael made some use of it for *CG*, as additions and figures appear here and there in his hand, e.g. where Jessy writes *Latha 's fhearr san t-seachdainn / 'S an t-seachdain is fhearr sa bhliadhna*, Carmichael writes *dhuit* at the end of each line then scores it out and writes the more archaic *duit* instead; these lines duly appear in *CG*1, p. 10, as *An la is fearr 's an t-seachdain duit, / An t-seachdain is fearr 's a bhliadhna duit.*

> Ionnlaidh mi do bhasan
> Anns' na frasan fiona
> Anns' an t-sugh-chraobh
> 'S anns' a bhainne mheala
> Cuiridh mi na naoi buaidhean
> Ann ad ghruaidhean geala
> Buaidh cruth as buaidh rath
> Buaidh chnoc is eireachdais
> 'S deagh labhradh.
> Is dubh an tigh ud thall,
> Is dubh gach duine th' ann
> Is tusa 'n eala dhonn,
> Dol a stigh nan ceann;
> Tha 'n cridhe fo d' chom
> 'S an teanga fo d' bhonn
> 'S cha'n abair iad riut
> Facal is oil leat,

> *Eilein air muir thu,*
> *'S caisteal air tìr thu,*
> *Cruth an Dòmhnach ad aghaidh,*
> *Cruth is àill air an domhan,*
> *'N ainm an Athar, a Mhic 's an*
> *Spioraid Naoimh.*
> *Latha 's fhearr san t-seachdainn*
> *'S an t-seachdain is fhearr sa bhliadhna,*
> *Thàinig Peadar, thàinig Pòl,*
> *Thàinig Mìcheil, thàinig Eòin*
> *Thàinig Righ nam feart air stiùir*
> *Nochda dhuit a rùin 's a ghràidh.*

The only substantial differences in Carmichael's MS 241 transcript are: line 3 *craobh* (same meaning, more archaic); line 17 *Facal is ail leat / oil* (i.e. *as àill leat* 'that you like'); line 18 *Eilean thu air muir* (same meaning); line 19 *'S caisteal thu air tir thu* (first *thu* scored through); line 20 *Domhnaich* (same meaning, more grammatically correct); lines 22–23 written as one line as at p. 217; line 29 *Thoirt* ('To give') in place of *Nochda* ('To reveal'), and *duil* in place of *dhuit*; *duil* will simply be a misreading of JGC's *duit*.

The more substantial departures in Jessy's translation (if I may call it that) from the one on pp. 216–17 are: line 1 'I will bathe your hands'; line 6 'In your fair face'; lines 8–9 'Grace at meetings, and gatherings / Of good looks, and goodly speech'; line 12 'You are the auburn Swan'; line 14 'Their heart is under thy chest'; line 17 'A word that will offend you'; line 19 'And a fort on land'; lines 20–21 'The form of the *Deity* be in thy face ['(Our Lord)' in margin] / The fairest form on Earth'; last two lines 'The King of Might is come to be your guide, / And to shew you his good will, and Love.' Certain phrases in Carmichael's translation in *CG*1, e.g. 'In the juice of the rasps' and 'goodly speech', appear to owe something to Jessy's.

Carmichael's 'Ora nam Buadh' has seventy lines; JGC's has twenty-eight, of which only line 22 ('In the name of the Father, Son, and Holy Spirit') fails to correspond with anything in Carmichael's. JGC's lines 1–21 correspond more or less exactly to Carmichael's 1–2, 5–9, 11, 13, 17–25, 30–31 and 50–53, while JGC's lines 23–28 correspond more or less exactly to Carmichael's 55–56, 58–59 and 68–69.

It is clear from the beginning of the charm that it is addressed to a young person; Carmichael's version adds little at this point to JGC's. Following the ritual washing of hands comes bestowal of the graces. *Is cuirime na naoi buaidhean glana caon*, says Carmichael, *Ann do ghruaidhean caomha geala*: "And I place the nine pure choice graces / In thy fair fond face." JGC goes on to mention five graces, while it is characteristic of Carmichael that he is able to supply them all. *Buaidh cruth, / Buaidh guth, / Buaidh rath, / Buaidh math, / Buaidh chnoc, / Buaidh bhochd, / Buaidh na rogha finne, / Buaidh na fior eireachdais, / Buaidh an deagh labhraidh*: "The grace of form, / The grace of voice, / The grace of fortune, / The grace of goodness, / The grace of wisdom, / The grace of charity, / The grace of choice maidenliness, / The grace of whole-souled loveliness, / The grace of goodly speech." A *cnoc* is, by definition almost, a suitable spot for a *mòd* ('court') or township meeting of any kind, hence *Buaidh chnoc* 'The grace of hillocks' becomes Carmichael's 'The grace of wisdom', JGC's 'Grace at meetings'.

JGC's lines 10–17, the 'yonder house' passage, are repeated almost exactly in *CG*, save that *an tigh ud thall* becomes *am bail ud thall*, meaning a farm township, a rural community. To the young person who has never been away from home unaccompanied, the short journey to take up employment is the first fearful step into manhood or womanhood, and we may compare the sinister use of *am bail ud thall* to that in 'Fairy Raids' (p. 10 above). The use of *dubh* is a clear warning. Carmichael's *fo do chonn*, literally 'under your sense', is unlikely to be correct; JGC's *fo do chom* 'in thy chest' sounds right, but no doubt Carmichael's 'under thy control' is the correct interpretation. What gives the young person this much-needed sense of control is, of course, the charm itself.

Carmichael's third verse consists of an eight-line series of formulaic statements of the type represented by JGC's *Eilein air muir thu, / 'S caisteal air tìr thu*, 'An island at sea art thou / And a castle on land' – Carmichael's *Is eilean thu air muir, / Is cuisil thu air tir (cuisil, properly caiseal*, is strictly a bulwark, *caisteal* a castle). In all of these the charmed person is represented as being helpful or protective to those in need, the blind, the thirsty and so on – a fundamental principle in Gaelic society. Carmichael's fourth and fifth verses, each eight lines long, are equally formulaic, invoking upon the charmed person the attributes of named religious and mythological figures, and of natural objects and creatures. None of this appears in JGC's text; Carmichael's sixth verse, on the other hand, is very fully reflected in JGC's two lines beginning *Cruth*:

> *Cruth aluinn an Domhnuich*
> *Ann do ghnuis ghlain,*
> *An cruth is ailinde*
> *Bha air talamh.*

("The lovely likeness of the Lord / Is in thy pure face, / The loveliest likeness that / Was upon earth.") JGC's two lines beginning *Latha 's fhearr* 'The best day' are unclear as they stand, but are explained (as shown above) by Carmichael's seventh verse:

> *An trath is fearr 's an latha duit,*
> *An la is fearr 's an t-seachdain duit,*
> *An t-seachdain is fearr 's a bhliadhna duit,*
> *A bhliadhn is fearr an domhan Mhic De duit.*

("The best hour of the day be thine, / The best day of the week be thine, / The best week of the year be thine, / The best year in the Son of God's domain be thine.") At the close of Carmichael's version the saints, the angels and the Trinity are comprehensively invoked in a verse of thirteen lines as having come 'To bestow on thee their affection and their love' (*A bhaireadh duit-se graidh is ruin*); in JGC's text this is disposed of in four lines. See also note 973.

748 JGC's Gaelic original of this charm was excluded from *WSS*, but fortunately it was transcribed by Carmichael into what is now EUL MS CW 241, f. 51 (see p. 703 below), headed 'Oradh Airson Aodan Nigheanan' ('Charm For Girls' Faces'), and I supply it from there. In line 2 Carmichael gave both *ga d* and *dha'd* (same meaning). His last word in line 9 looks like *air* ('on him = on it'), but could conceivably be *oirr* (*oirre* 'on her = on it'), while JGC's translation suggests *orra* ('on them'), which tends to be indistinguishable in sound from *oirre* (see note 744). His word 'charm' in the same line is ill chosen in this context: *tlachd* means 'pleasantness'.

These fourteen lines correspond fairly closely to the eighteen-line 'Òra Aodann Nighinn' ('Charm for the Face of a Maiden') in *CG3*, pp. 226–27, which Carmichael received from an unknown informant. The concentration on eyebrows is remarkable, and, as always, a comparison of the two versions sheds extra light on both. Carmichael's first verse is:

> *Tha féil Dhé air th'aghaidh,*
> *Tha Mac Dhé dha d' chomairc*

Commentary

O dhroch dhaoin an domhain,
Tha Rìgh nan reul ma d' choinneimh.

He translates: "The beauty of God is in thy face, / The Son of God is protecting thee / From the wicked ones of the world, / The King of the stars is before thee.") *Féil(e)* is not beauty but bounty, generosity, the 'giving' quality. Perhaps what Carmichael heard was *féile*, not *Féil Dhé*. JGC does not have Carmichael's fourth line at all; the rules of prosody suggest that he should. Carmichael's second verse is:

Tha féil Mhoire an troma gràidh,
Teanga mhodhail mhìn mhàld,
Fionna fionn eadar do dhà mhalaigh,—
Fionn mac Cumhaill eatorra sin.

He translates: "The beauty of Mary of the deep love, / A tongue mannerly, mild, modest, / Fair hair between thy two eyebrows,— / Fionn son of Cumhall between these." This coaxes some sense out of the first line by ignoring the first word, but cannot be allowed to stand. JGC's 'vigil' (*féill*, from Latin *vigilia*) is clever, his informant having been influenced by the common calendar term *Féill Mhoire* (Marymas, see p. 558 below and Black 2000, pp. 40–41). As it stands, *Fhéille Moire is troma ghràdh* means 'The vigil of the Virgin Mary and very great love'.

A footnote in *CG* by Carmichael or his editor says: "Fionn means 'Fair'." Like the English word, *fionn* means 'beautiful' when it does not mean 'blonde'. One can imagine a young girl working on her eyebrows using a little mirror got from a packman and muttering these punning words about her 'beautiful beauty' and the 'beautiful man' who would kiss her between the eyes. Fionn mac Cumhaill is often invoked in charms when the non-Christian virtues of strength, power and virility are sought. Carmichael's next verse is:

O's i Moire agus Ìos a Mac
A chuir an tlachd sin féin ad ghnùis,
Gun robh blas na meala mìn ort
Agus air gach facal mar a their thu.

He translates: "Since it is Mary and Jesus her Son / Who set this pleasantness in thy face, / May the taste of mild honey be upon thee / And upon every word thou speakest." The prosody here could be improved, and JGC's version appears to do just that: *ad ghnùis* shows that the eyebrows are meant, and *orra : their thu* is acceptable rhyme. Carmichael's final verse is:

Ri mithibh agus ri maithibh,
Ri fearaibh agus ri beanaibh maoth,
O'n là an diugh a th'againn ann
Gu là ceann crìch do shaoghail,
A uchd nan cùmh agus nan cumhachdan sìorraidh,
A uchd Dhé nan dùl agus a uchd cluthadh a Mhic.

His translation: "To simple and to noble, / To men and to tender women, / From this day that we have here / Till the day of the ending of thy life, / In reliance on the beloved and the powers eternal, / In reliance on the God of life and the shielding of His Son." JGC's conclusion contains elements from three of these lines.

481

749 As a native of Glencoe, Blind Allan was from the same parish as JGC (see notes 605 and 735). The Gaelic original of this charm was excluded from *WSS*, but Alexander Carmichael transcribed it from JGC's lost appendix into what is now EUL MS CW 241, f. 52 (see p. 703 below), and I give it from there. A version of it has also appeared in every edition of Macintyre's work except the first (1768), and may conveniently be consulted in the most recent, MacLeod 1952, p. 418. In his notes (p. 554) MacLeod refers to JGC's comment and adds: "There is no attempt to explain how Allan MacDougall's verses came to be included in Macintyre's second edition without reference or acknowledgment." The second and third editions were both prepared under Macintyre's personal supervision (1790, 1804). Two further versions were obtained by Alexander Carmichael from Aonas Macvuirich, crofter, South Lochboisdale, South Uist, and John Pearson, a US Army veteran, Ceanntangaval, Barra (*CG2*, pp. 38–41, 376, 378).

750 JGC says in a footnote that other texts have 'early on Sunday, to a level stone on the shore'. MacLeod gives *Eirich moch Di-dòmhnaich / Gu lic chòmhnaird phlataich* 'On Sunday rise thou early / to a level, broad flagstone' (1952, pp. 418–19), while 'to a level stone on the shore' reflects *lic chomhnard chladaich*, the reading in *CG2*, p. 40.

751 The 'people's blessing' and 'priest's cowl' are plants – seemingly the butter-bur and monkshood. As MacLeod points out (1952, p. 554), the former occurs variously in different editions of the poem as *beannachd pobuill* 'folk's boon', *puball beannach* 'pinnacled canopy' and *beannach pubaill* 'pointed canopy'. *Beannach(d) pubaill* gives *aicill* rhyme with *currachd* and is probably therefore to be preferred to *puball beannach*. However, Henderson comments very plausibly (1911, p. 335): "Things connected with or named after a priest's belongings, such as a biretta (*currachd sagairt*) or a processional canopy (*puball beannach*), are used in love-charms." See also *CG2*, p. 343, and Campbell 1978–81, p. 200.

752 JGC's translation shows that (like some of Duncan Ban's later editors, who substituted *Agus* for *Ann an*) he did not understand that the items in the previous couplet were plants. *Ann an sluasaid mhaide* is very clear in Carmichael's transcript, and the correct translation is: "Lift them on your shoulder / In a wooden shovel." Carmichael wrote *air a ghualainn* then corrected *a* to *do*, see note 729.

753 For this line MacLeod has *Suath sin r' a ghealbhroilleach* 'Rub this on his white breast' (1952, pp. 418–19). JGC's version resembles *Crath an dearbh bhrollach do leannain* 'Shake it in the very breast of thy lover' and *Crath am brollach broth do leannain* 'Sprinkle in the fleshy breast of thy lover', *CG2*, pp. 38, 40.

754 If a soldier in 1798, Allan must have been born by 1780, and if JGC means that he got the charm from him in person, this could not have been earlier than the 1850s. We may therefore tentatively place Allan's dates at *c*.1780–*c*.1860. Perhaps he was a son of Allan MacLean of Ceann na Coille (1740–1806), for whom see Thornber 2000, p. 8.

755 JGC's Gaelic original of this charm was excluded from *WSS*, but fortunately it was transcribed by Alexander Carmichael into what is now EUL MS CW 241, f. 53 (see p. 703 below), headed 'Airson Ana-cainnt' ('For Ill Report'), and I have supplied it from there. It corresponds to lines 1–6 and 15–16 of the 24-line 'Òr Anacainnt' ('Prayer against Ill Report') got by Carmichael from Una MacDonald, crofter, Buail Uachdrach, Ìochdar, South Uist (*CG4*, pp. 140–43). It was designed not to keep away harm in a lawsuit but simply to counteract ill-will, bad report and evil speaking, the curse of many Highland communities to this day. "The man suffering from these," says Carmichael, "went to the 'mòd' or court held on the hill or knoll without or in the house within. He held his staff in his grasp and his wit upon his tongue, and looking round defiantly upon those present, he said his rune in the full assurance that it would obtain a hearing and be efficacious." The *mòd* in question might be a baron court, presided over in later times by the baron baillie or factor (see e.g. Forsyth 1999, pp. 105–13); after 1747, although such courts technically survived the abolition

of heritable jurisdictions, it was more likely to be a kirk session (*seisean*), see pp. 365–66 and 631–32. Here are the eight lines as they stand in *CG4*, pp. 140–41, with the translation there given.

> *Dùinidh mi mo dhorn,*
> *Is dùthaidh domhs am fiodh;*
> *Is ann a shaoradh dòchainn*
> *A thàinig mi staigh.*
>
> *Triùir mac Rìgh Cluainnidh,*
> *Is Manann mac Rìgh Lir,*
> *Is Calum Cille Cléireach,*
> *Is Alasdair air neif.*

"I will close my fist, / Fitly I hold the staff; / 'Tis to efface evil speaking / That I have come within. / The three sons of King Cluainnidh, / And Manann son of King Lear, / And Columba, the Cleric, / And Alexander, against venom."

Clearly this raises a number of questions about JGC's translation. *Dùthaidh* is connected with *dual* 'tradition', *dùthaich* 'homeland, countryside', *dùthchas* 'patrimony, inheritance', and asserts the plaintiff's hereditary rights through his staff; JGC's *dìleas* serves the same function. Carmichael's *dòchainn* is not *docha(i)nn* 'harm' but an otherwise unattested compound of *do-* 'evil' and *cainnt* 'speech'; *m' anacainnt* is not to be understood literally as 'my abusive words' but as 'abusive words concerning me', 'ill report of me'. For *a shaoradh*, therefore, Carmichael's 'to efface' must be preferred to JGC's 'to protect'. It is the key to the the poem; logic is in Carmichael's favour; the *CG* heading stands, JGC's 'Charm to Keep Away Harm in a Lawsuit' falls away.

We now come to the mythological allusions. The 'three sons of Clooney' or of 'King Cluainnidh' will be the three sons of Brian Boru, king of Ireland and victor of Clontarf (*Cluain Tarbh*), who are so prominent in Scottish Gaelic tradition, see note 219; no doubt the Highland *Cluainidh*, which is both a place and a person, has affected the form and function of the name. In MS 241 Carmichael writes it *Cluañaidh*, i.e. *Cluannaidh*. In the next line it may be that Ailein Mòr was uncomfortable with *Lir* and substituted a familiar word with the appropriate short vowel, *leth* 'half'. It is more likely, however, that *mac Leth* is for *MacLéigh*, *MacLéith* (MacLeay), a common corruption of *MacDhunshléibhe* ('Livingstone'), given that it is supposed to rhyme with the last word, which Carmichael correctly makes short (*neif*, i.e. *nimh* 'venom'), but which Ailein Mòr clearly lengthened into *nèamh* 'heaven'. *Alastair*, finally, is Alexander the Great, who is as well known in Gaelic as in any other European literary tradition, cf. Nicolson 1951, p. 165.

756 See Bruford 1969, p. 164. JFC's fieldnotes of a tale 'Curachag Ni Mhananain', difficult to read, are in NLS Adv. MS 50.2.2, ff. 195–202. For Manannan see notes 8 and 579 above.

757 For amulets see Dalyell 1834, pp. 130–32, 135, 138–60, 186, 679–80; Simpson 1860–62; Campbell 1885a, pp. 425–26; Paton 1886–87; Black 1892–93; Maclagan 1903; Henderson 1911, pp. 147, 200–02, 227–29, 300, 308–16; McPherson 1929, pp. 259–62; McNeill 1957–68, vol. 1, pp. 90–96; Davidson 1960, pp. 140–45; Henderson and Cowan 2001, p. 93.

758 Curiously, the term used by Pliny does not appear to have been *ovum anguinum*. The sources for his text employ a number of variants, of which Jones (1963, p. 217) regards *urinum* ('wind egg') as 'the best stop-gap'. He adds: "The vulgate *anguinum* (serpent's egg) is so obvious and easy that it is most unlikely to have been corrupted into the variants of our MSS." Here is his translation of Pliny's account in full (1963, pp. 217, 219): "There is, moreover, a kind of egg which is very famous in [*sic*] the Gauls, but not mentioned by the Greeks. Snakes intertwined in great numbers in a studied embrace make these round

objects with the saliva from their jaws and the foam from their bodies. It is called a 'wind egg'. The Druids say that it is tossed aloft by the snakes' hisses, and that it ought to be caught in a military cloak before it can touch the earth. The catcher, they say, must flee on horseback, for the serpents chase him until they are separated by some intervening river. A test of a genuine egg is that it floats against the current, even if it is set in gold. Such is the clever cunning of the Magi in wrapping up their frauds that they give out as their opinion that it must be caught at a fixed period of the moon, as if agreement between snakes and moon for this act depended upon the will of man. I indeed have seen this egg, which was like a round apple of medium size, and remarkable for its hard covering pitted with many gristly cup-hollows, as it were, like those on the tentacles of an octopus. The Druids praise it highly as the giver of victory in the law-courts and of easy access to potentates. Herein they are guilty of such lying fraud that a Roman knight of the Vocontii, for keeping one in his bosom during a lawsuit, was executed by the late Emperor Claudius, and for no other reason. However, this embrace and fertile union of snakes seem to be the reason why foreign nations, when discussing peace terms, have made the herald's staff surrounded with figures of snakes; and it is not the custom for the snakes on a herald's staff to have a crest."

In 1772 Allan MacDonald of Kingsburgh, husband of the celebrated Flora, gave a *glaine nathair* to Thomas Pennant, who wrote (1998, pp. 299–300): "The *glain naidr*, or Druidical bead, as it is vulgarly called, is an unique in its kind, being of a triangular shape; but, as usual, made of glass, marked with figures of serpents coiled up. The common people in Wales and in Scotland retain the same superstitions relating to it as the ancients, and call it by the name of serpent-stone. The Gauls, taught by their priests, believed the strangest tales of their serpents . . . The ancients and moderns agree in their belief of its powers; that good fortune attends the possessor wherever he goes. The stupid Claudius, that *Ludibrium aulae Augusti*, put to death a Gaulish knight, a serpent-stone about him. The vulgar of the present age attribute to it other virtues; such as its curing the bite of the adder, and giving ease to women in childbirth, if tied about the knee. So difficult is it to root out follies that have the sanction of antiquity."

759 As printed in *WSS* 86 this term is *meall èochd*. There is no such word as *èochd*. However, at *WSS* 191 is *eòmach mòr chlach* 'the large boulder stones' which is clearly for *càrnach mòr chlach*, see p. 276. It appears, therefore, that JGC's *cà* was capable of being misread as *eò*, and on this basis I have emended *meall èochd* to *meall càchd* ('a heap of shit'). In his description of how serpent-stones are made (*CG4*, pp. 204–05) Carmichael says: *Dar a tha na ronnan a chuir an nathair air a' chraobh fhraoich a' fuarachadh agus a' tiormachadh, tha an stuth a' fàs co cruaidh ri cloich ach co eutrom ri spuing.* "When the spittle emitted by the serpent on the heather plant cools and dries, the stuff grows as hard as a stone but as light as tinder."

760 We must take JGC's word for it that Scott (by whom I assume he means Sir Walter) said this, as I have been unable to identify the source. In 'Marmion' he says (Robertson 1904, p. 107):

> They told how in their convent-cell
> A Saxon princess once did dwell,
>   The lovely Edelfled;
> And how, of thousand snakes, each one
> Was chang'd into a coil of stone,
>   When holy Hilda pray'd.

On this Scott remarks in a note (*ibid.*, p. 185): "The relics of the snakes which infested the precincts of the convent, and were, at the abbess's prayer, not only beheaded, but petrified, are still found about the rocks, and are termed by Protestant fossilists, *Ammonitae*." It is remarkable if Scott's alleged use of the rare archaeological term 'celt' went unnoticed by the *OED*, which places its first use in English at 1715 and defines it as: "An implement with chisel-shaped edge, of bronze or stone (but sometimes of iron), found among the remains of prehistoric man. It appears to have served for a variety of purposes, as a hoe, chisel, or axe, and perhaps as a weapon of war. Some specimens in bronze are flat, others flanged, others winged, others have sockets to receive a handle, and one, or two, ear-like *ansæ* or loops." See Wilson 1863, vol. 1, pp. 197–98, and vol. 2, p. 126; Logan 1976, vol. 1, pp. 309–11. For the belief that celts were thunderbolts see Peacock 1883, and cf. notes 53 and 773. The best nineteenth-century account of snake-stones is Black 1892–93, pp. 468–74, and for a comprehensive twentieth-century one see Morgan 1983. See also Pennant 1812, vol. 3, pp. 41–42, plate VI; Shaw 1827, p. 286; Dalyell 1834, pp. 140–41, 151–52, 157; *CG2*, p. 335; MacGregor 1901, p. 9; Maclagan 1902, pp. 170–71; SoSS Maclagan MSS vol. 22, pp. 3869–71; Henderson 1911, p. 339; MacDonald 1934–36b, p. 10; Macdonald 2000, pp. 166–67.

761 Edward Lhuyd found no evidence for snake-stones in Ireland. He says (1713, p. 98, cf. Britten 1881, p. 167): "The *Snake-button* is the same described in the Notes on *Denbighshire* in *Camden*, by the Name of Adder-Beads: But there are of these great Variety, as to Colour and Ornament; insomuch, that betwixt *Wales* and the High-Lands, I have seen at least fifty differences of them. In *Ireland*, though they are tenacious enough of all old Customs, I could hear nothing of them: So I conclude, that either the *Irish* had no *Druids*, or that their want of Snakes frustrated their advancing that Imposture amongst the People: But there were but a few Places where we inquired; and perhaps we may hereafter hear of them in other Parts of that Kingdom. Not only the Vulgar, but even Gentlemen of good Education throughout all *Scotland*, are fully perswaded the Snakes make them, though they are as plain Glass as any in a Bottle."

762 The reference to Professor Kuno Meyer (1858–1919) is helpful with regard to dating the text of WSS. Meyer obtained a lectureship in Teutonic Languages in University College Liverpool in 1884, at the age of 26, and launched himself into the distinguished career of research and teaching in Celtic Studies which led to his appointment as Reader in Celtic there in 1902. His interest had been aroused as a teenager during 1874–76, when he enjoyed a two-month holiday lodging in a house in Arran where the farmer and his family were Gaelic speakers (Ó Lúing 1991, pp. 1–4, 20, 22). His name became known to the public in Scotland through his magisterial *Cath Finntrága* (Oxford, 1885), the introduction to which makes good use of *Popular Tales of the West Highlands*, and this reference to him will therefore have been inserted between 1885 and 1891, the year of JGC's death. I suspect that JGC misrepresents his views, however. 'Lebor Gabála' ('The Book of Invasions') represents a determined attempt by the medieval Irish to construct a mythology that brings the Gael from the Holy Land via Egypt and the Straits of Gibraltar, 'Cath Finntrága' itself tells how Ireland was attacked by a force that included the kings of India, Greece and Spain, among others, and in *The Celtic Magazine* – which JGC would certainly have read – Meyer quotes the boast of the giant Curoí mac Dáire in 'Fled Bricrend' (1886–87, p. 216): "What I have come to seek, I have not found in Erinn, nor in Alba, nor in Europe, nor in Africa, nor in Asia, as far as Greece and Scythia, and the Orkneys, and the Pillars of Hercules . . ." But I know of no work in which Meyer endorses anything like this as historical fact, and I suspect that JGC's source is an inaccurate newspaper report.

763 Edward Lhuyd says (1713, p. 99, cf. Britten 1881, p. 168): "The *Snail-stone* is a small hollow Cilinder of blue Glass, composed of four or five Annulets: So that as to Form and Size it resembles a midling *Entrochus*. This, amongst others of its mysterious Virtues, cures Sore Eyes." See Dalyell 1834, pp. 141–42, 411; Black 1892–93, p. 503.

764 Writing of the mouth of the common wolf fish, Pennant says (1812, vol. 3, p. 204): "In the centre are two rows of flat strong teeth, fixed on an oblong basis upon the bones of the palate and nose. These and the other grinding teeth are often found fossil, and in that state

called *Bufonites*, or *Toad-stones*: they were formerly much esteemed for their imaginary virtues, and were set in gold, and worn as rings."

Bufonites take their name from the zoologist Georges-Louis Leclerc, Comte de Buffon (1707–88). Of the toad Pennant comments (*ibid.*, pp. 20–21): "It was believed by some old writers to have a stone in its head, fraught with great virtues medical and magical: it was distinguished by the name of the reptile, and called the *Toad-Stone, Bufonites, Crapaudine, Krottenstein*; but all its fancied powers vanished on the discovery of its being nothing but the fossil tooth of the sea-wolf, or of some flat-toothed fish." See also Dalyell 1834, pp. 142, 406–09; Black 1892–93, pp. 506–09.

765 *As You Like It*, Act 2, Scene 1. Edward Lhuyd says (1713, p. 99, cf. Britten 1881, p. 168): "The *Toad-stone* is some Peble, remarkable for its Shape and sometimes variety of Colours. This is presumed to prevent the burning of a House, and the sinking of a Boat: And if a Commander in the Field has one of them about him, he will either be sure to win the Day, or all his Men shall fairly dye on the spot."

766 Achagavel (*Ach' a' Ghobhail* 'the Field of the Fork'?) lies at the head of the Gleann Dubh deep in the interior of Morvern, about five miles from JGC's native Kingairloch. Beinn nam Bearrach is shown on maps as Beinn nam Beathrach, which suggests *Beinn na Beithreach* 'Dragon Mountain' or the like – for the *beithir* (a colossal worm, dragon, serpent or similar monster) see notes 8 and 393.

No doubt the monster in question was the king frog himself. His name *Seid* means, as JGC says, 'truss of hay', but also 'belly-full', 'flatulent swelling' (Macbain 1896, p. 277), 'tympany, swelling of the body from flatulence', 'swelling in a person from luxurious living and deep potations' (Dwelly 1977, p. 804). Not a bad name for a toad – especially one who symbolised the dangers of a swamp.

767 Wilson's illustration (1863, vol. 1, p. 195) is reproduced at p. 233 of the present work. The object was 'found near the line of the old Roman way which runs through Dumfriesshire on its northern course from Carlisle'. See also 'Various', p. 224.

768 The term 'Allophylian', literally 'of a different tribe', was used in the mid-nineteenth century to designate any non-Aryan, non-Semitic 'other' linguistic survival in Europe (*OED*). JGC thus evokes one of the theories which have been advanced to explain the origin of the Fairies, that of the conquered aboriginal race living in primitive conditions underground. See pp. lxxxix–xci above.

769 See note 58; Dalyell 1834, pp. 157, 351–59, 371, 539–40; Black 1892–93, pp. 462–68; Maclagan 1902, p. 180; Maclagan 1903, p. 299 (two 'celts', Fairy arrows from Islay, are shown); Spence 1948, pp. 172–73; Bruford and MacDonald 1994, p. 476.

770 Pinkerton 1809, p. 289 = Pennant 1998, pp. 219–20: "A present was made me of a clach clun ceilach, or cock-knee stone, believed to be obtained out of that part of the bird; but I have unluckily forgotten its virtues. Not so with the clach crubain, which is to cure all pains in the joints. It is to be presumed both these amulets have been enchanted; for the first very much resembles a common pebble, the other is that species of fossil shell called Gryphites."

771 Judging from this, 'gripe' in the nominative will be Dwelly's *gramaiche* 'one that keeps a good hold, flesh-hook, smith's vice, etc.', or *greimeadh* 'grasping, biting' (1977, pp. 521, 524).

772 *Clach na Léig* is more literally 'the Stone of the Jewel'; *léig* is the genitive of *leug*, often used specifically of a stone 'to which healing virtues are ascribed', as Dwelly puts it (1977, p. 586).

773 It is at Croish in Caolas. Professor Donald Meek, a native of Caolas, gives me the name as *Clach na Stoirmeadh*. MacDougall and Cameron say (n.d., pp. 128–29): "Only the faintest traces remain of the ancient burial-ground of Crois a' Chaolais. These are in a small enclosure by the roadside, half a mile from the ferry which formerly existed between Tiree and Coll . . . But on the other side of the road, opposite the burial-ground, there are two large stones embedded in the soil, and between these the Cross is said to have stood. There

is a tradition that if ever the larger of these stones be removed a hurricane will sweep the island with devastating violence."

This may be related to the belief, found almost everywhere in the world, that imperforate Stone Age axes are thunderbolts which have fallen from the clouds during thunderstorms (Black 1892–93, pp. 459–60, cf. notes 53 and 760 above). The German tradition, for example, was as follows (Grimm 1880–88, vol. 1, p. 179): "In popular belief, there darts out of the cloud together with the flash a *black wedge*, which buries itself *in the earth* as deep as the highest church-tower is high. (This *depth* is variously expressed in curses, &c. *e.g.* May the thunder strike you into the earth as far as a hare can run in a hundred years!) But every time it thunders again, it begins to rise nearer to the surface, and after *seven years* you may find it above ground. Any house in which it is preserved, is proof against damage by lightning; when a thunder-storm is coming on, it begins to sweat."

774 For the Ardvoirlich Stone see Simpson 1860–62, pp. 220–21; Black 1892–93, pp. 438–39; McNeill 1957–68, vol. 1, p. 92; Davidson 1960, p. 143. As far as I know it is still in Ardvorlich House on Loch Earn.

775 See p. 200; notes 745, 746; Masson and Aitken 1887–88, p. 309; Black 1892–93, pp. 492–94; Gregory 1970, p. 99; Campbell 1975, pp. 66–68; Shaw 1977, p. 248; Higgitt 2000, p. 344; Hunter 2001, p. 67; GUL MS 1090/29, p. 3.

776 As pointed out by Frazer (1913, p. 48) in the context of what he called 'the transference of evil', these are variations upon a very ancient and widespread remedy: "In the fourth century of our era Marcellus of Bordeaux prescribed a cure for warts, which has still a great vogue among the superstitious in various parts of Europe. Doubtless it was an old traditional remedy in the fourth, and will long survive the expiry of the twentieth, century. You are to touch your warts with as many little stones as you have warts; then wrap the stones in an ivy leaf, and throw them away in a thoroughfare. Whoever picks them up will get the warts, and you will be rid of them." Indeed, a variant of the barley cure was still remembered in the islands at the end of the twentieth century (Parman 1977, p. 109): "A person could cure his own warts by taking 81 stems of oats (which are bumpy, like warts), binding them into nine branches of nine each and secreting them under a stone; as the stems rotted, the warts were expected to disappear."

Carmichael offers a number of variations on the theme (*CG2*, p. 334; *CG4*, p. 221), remarking in *CG4*: "If the little bag containing the nine nine joints were thrown away, and another person took it up, the warts would be transferred to the finder. This, however, is not considered honourable, and is rarely done by the most careless boy or girl."

See also GUL MS Gen. 1090/29, pp. 87, 244; Hardy 1878; Macbain 1887–88, p. 257; MacDonald 1961, p. 191; Walters 1992.

777 Blending this with French, Belgian and German evidence from as far back as the seventeenth century, Frazer says (1913, p. 49) that among cures for warts are: "To rub the troublesome excrescences with down or fat, or to bleed them on a rag, and then throw away the down, the fat, or the bloody rag. The person who picks up one or other of these things will be sure to release you from your warts by involuntarily transferring them to himself." Again Carmichael offers variations (*CG4*, p. 221): instead of blood he mentions rust (dry or moist), a poultice of broad-leaved tangle, water found lying on a gravestone, and – rather surprisingly – rubbing the wart 'against the clothes of one who has committed fornication'.

778 What JGC appears to mean is that although a stye is *neònagan* according to the dictionaries, the form with which he was familiar was *sleònachan*. The word varies enormously from dialect to dialect: *sleamh, sleamhnan, sleamhnagan, sleamhran, sleamhragan, sleòn, sleònan, sleònagan; leamhnan, leamhran, leamhnadan, leamhnagan, leamhranan, leònad; neamhnad, neamhnan, neamhnagan, neòn, neònad, neònan, neònagan;* etc. See *CG2*, p. 356, and *CG6*, p. 260.

779 Carmichael has a good deal to say on the cure of styes, and cites the charms in full (*CG2*, pp. 72–73; *CG4*, pp. 218–20). His material comes close to JGC's where he speaks of rubbing a finger-ring around the stye and of twirling a glowing splinter of wood in front of the eye (*CG4*, pp. 219, 220). JGC's 'stye one' will be *neònagan a h-aon* or the like, and 'take yourself off' will be *thoir do chasan leat*. Carmichael's material in *CG2* is supplemented by MacPhail (1900, pp. 449–50); see also Freer 1902, p. 58; Mackenzie 1914, p. 307; *Tocher* 9, pp. 24–25; Macdonald 2003, p. 115. The gold cure was still remembered in the islands in the late twentieth century (Parman 1977, p. 109, cf. *Tocher* 45, p. 196): "A stye could be cured by rubbing a wedding ring around the eye, or tapping the stye with a copper penny while saying, 'Why one if not two, why two if not three . . .' all the way up to ten and backwards in one breath."

780 Other names for this condition are erysipelas and St Anthony's fire (because St Anthony is believed to have stayed an epidemic of it in 1089). When Carmichael, or rather his grandson J. C. Watson, published a version of the rhyme in *CG4*, p. 207, he translated *teine-dé* as 'ringworm', but had no hesitation about its derivation – he called it 'God's fire', perhaps recalling Macbain on *dealan-dé* 'butterfly' (1896, p. 112): "The G[aelic] also means the phenomenon observed by whirling a stick lighted at the end. Apparently the meaning is 'God's fire.'" Macbain could offer no explanation of *dearbadan-dé*, however (*ibid.*, p. 113). Carmichael's rhyme is:

> *Teine Dé da do bhus!*
> *Rug do mhàthair chéile luch;*
> *Thug thu féin a mach an gur,*
> > *Busan dubh an dranndain!*

He translates: "Ringworm be upon thy snout! / Thy mother-in-law brought forth a mouse; / Thou thyself broughtest forth the hatching, / Black snoutie of the growling!" *Màthair-chéile* is certainly 'mother-in-law', not 'stepmother', and although Carmichael confirms that the rhyme was used by children when bandying words over ringworm, 'often in hot resentment', I suspect that – like many another children's rhyme – it had serious adult origins. It looks to me like a fragment of flyting in which a woman insults another woman's husband and wishes syphilis upon her. This is clearer in Carmichael's version than in JGC's, which is the more childish of the two.

781 This unusual solution to the problem is not listed in Opie and Tatem 1992 ('Hiccup, cures for', pp. 198–99).

782 Using *triuthach* for (w)hooping-cough, Nicolson gives the same proverb (1951, p. 183) and comments: "The first part of this prescription is rational; the virtue of the spoon was supposed to be derived from the sacred character of the aspen tree." Aspen may be sacred in the sense that it has a connection with Scripture, but it is cursed (*CG1*, p. 201; *CG2*, pp. 104–05). It is said that the cross upon which Christ was crucified was of aspen (*CG5*, p. 317), as a result of which it was condemned to quiver in the lightest breeze (McDonald 1958, p. 85, cf. GUL MS Gen. 1090/29, pp. 191–92), and 'Highlanders will not use aspen in any form either on land or sea' (*CG2*, p. 259). I think therefore that this is another example of shock therapy.

In one of his journals (NLS Adv. MS 50.4.6, ff. 113v–114r) JFC sketches an oak-tree in which a thick branch appears to have departed the main stem and rejoined it. It was shown to him by Duncan MacArthur on Lochaweside, 19 August 1871. "Returning through a wood MacArthur shewd me an old oak growing in a loop as on the sketch. He has often within the last forty years helped to pass children through the loop thrice without touching the ground as a cure for whooping cough. Triugh."

783 Among 'iron cures' from Pliny onwards, Opie and Tatem (1992, p. 209) include an instance from the isle of Man (*c.* 1870) of treating a swelling in the neck by rubbing it with 'old pokers, old nails, and other odds and ends of the same metal, making in all nine pieces'.

784 By *roluig* JGC means the word more usually spelt *réilig* (Latin *reliquiæ* 'relics'). For more on toothache see pp. 208–09 and note 800.

785 See p. 130 ('Euphemisms').

786 By no means merely in Sutherlandshire – see also Dalyell 1834, p. 420; Simpson 1860–62, p. 216; Mitchell 1860–62, pp. 273–75; MacPhail 1895, pp. 167, 303–04; MacPhail 1900, p. 446; Macdonald 1903, pp. 370–71; Mackay 1914, p. 435; Mackenzie 1914, p. 308; McPherson 1929, pp. 230–31; Sutherland 1937, pp. 106–07; GUL MS Gen. 1090/29, p. 33. Frazer (1913, pp. 68–69) presents the burial of the cock as a variation upon a widespread custom of driving out disease by hammering a nail into the wall, or the ground, or a tree. "Pliny tells us that an alleged cure for epilepsy, or the falling sickness, was to drive an iron nail into the ground on the spot which was first struck by the patient's head as he fell . . . Probably the disease was supposed to be buried with the cock in the ground."

A medieval variation upon this principle may be found in a Gaelic text on epilepsy (*an galar tuitimach, epilennsia*) written somewhere in Scotland or Ireland by an anonymous (?)sixteenth-century hand in what is now NLS Adv. MS 72.1.2, f. 94v, following a number of herbal cures for the condition. I translate: "The patient is taken to the bank of a stream which has a strong current, preferably on a Thursday 'after kindling' (*iar n-adhnadh*), one woman with him if it is a man, and if it is a woman, a man should be with her. Let the patient lie down on the bank of the stream, and let the companion rise up and pick ten thorns of the whitethorn (*a x. neilgi sgiach*), saying an Our Father and a Hail Mary (*paidir 7 avia Mairia*) with every thorn picked.

"Let the companion bring the thorns where the patient is and set the patient on both knees there and take one of the thorns and say an Our Father into its point (.*p. na rinn*) and circle the patient. On coming round to the patient's face, let the companion go down on both knees and press the point of the thorn against the patient's mouth and say, *In ainm in athar 7 in mhic 7 in spiraid naem so* ('I do this in the name of the Father and of the Son and of the Holy Spirit'), thrusting the thorn all the way (*tara mheall*, 'over its pommel') into the ground. And let the companion do that with every other thorn as well, and pull the patient by the hair (*ar fholt*) and call out his or her correct name (*ainm diles*) and say: *Go tigedh na deilgi so ar fud domain a talamh na ti in galar cedna cugad.* 'Till these thorns come out of the earth through all the world, let not this disease come to you.'

"And let the patient stand up in the stream and take a mouthful (*bolgum*) from the surface of the stream and throw it against the stream, then take two other mouthfuls and do likewise. And let the companion say, 'Until those three mouthfuls come along the same path against the stream, let not this disease come to you' (*no gu tiged na tri bolguma sin a frithiug na conaire cedna anaigidh in tsrotha na ti in galar cedna cugadsa*), saying his or her correct name.

"And let them come then from there to the church, and let the patient bring three wax candles (*iii coinnle ciara*) and three pennies (*tri pinginni*) with a penny stuck in each candle, and let the patient give these into the priest's hand, and let the priest say a Mass to the Holy Spirit for possession of the sick person (*ar seilbh in duine ghalair*).

"And let the patient give the priest a kiss (*pacsa*) after the Mass and bring the priest three candles and three pennies on the anniversary of that day (*a comhainm in lae sin*) every year and take bread and water (*denadh aran 7 uisge*) on that day throughout his or her life; and let the patient never see that spot on the river again. And there is no one under heaven who would perform this cure in good faith and fulfil his tabus (*do dhenadh maille re dutracht an t-urchosg so 7 do choimheoladh a gheasa*) who would ever again be stricken by epilepsy."

787 The alleged importance of Thursday to the cure suggests that it was carried out in the name of Calum Cille, see note 709.

788 The best descriptions of this 'plan' are those concerning Eilean Ma-Ruibhe in Loch Maree. The patient was dipped three times, or even towed three times round the island (Godden 1893, p. 500; Scott 1908–09, p. 271; Beith 1995, p. 139). When an 'idiot daughter' received the latter treatment in 1852 it was reported by *The Inverness Courier* that 'the hitherto quiet imbecile has become a raving maniac' (Reeves 1857–60, p. 289). On Eilean Ma-Ruibhe see Mitchell 1860–62, pp. 251–64, 266; Dixon 1886, pp. 150–58; Hogg 1888, pp. 84–85; Mackinlay 1893, pp. 28–30; Campbell 1895, p. 75; MacGregor 1901, pp. 57–59; Henderson 1911, p. 323; McPherson 1929, pp. 75–76; Banks 1937–41, vol. 1, p. 167; MacNeill 1962, pp. 364–65; Willis 1989; Pennant 1998, p. 331.

789 For *Strathaibh* (*Sraithibh*, *Sraitheo*) see Watson 2002, pp. 165–66.

790 The rituals were described in still greater detail by an anonymous Englishman who visited the pool and chapel on 9 August 1798 (Gillies 1938, p. 76): "When mad people are bathed they throw them in with a rope tied about the middle, after which they are taken to St. Fillan's Church, about a mile distant, where there is a large stone with a nick carved in it just large enough to receive them. In this stone, which is in the open Churchyard, they are fastened down to a wooden frame-work, and there remain for the whole night with a covering of hay over them, and St. Fillan's Bell is put upon their heads. If in the morning the unhappy patient is found loose, the saint is supposed to be very propitious. If, on the other hand, he continues in bonds, he is supposed to be contrary." For the bell see note 284; see also Mitchell 1860–62, pp. 268–69.

791 The importance of performing the cure on a Friday characterises it as black magic. Those who based their superstitions on Christian observance preferred to avoid using iron on Fridays, see pp. 549, 567–68.

792 The translations are mine, as JGC did not offer any. On 'Eòlas nam Màm' ('The Charm of the Swellings') see Guraig 1889; Fionn 1889a; MacFadyen 1889; Mackenzie 1891–92, pp. 163–65; *CG4*, pp. 276–79; Macdonald 2003, p. 115.

793 Describing the same treatment, other tradition-bearers have defined *leum droma* (literally 'leap of back') as a slipped disc, see MacDonald 1961, p. 191, and *Tocher* 57, pp. 44–47.

794 This stone is a mystery, as it is not otherwise referred to in the literature on Coll. It is not mentioned by Muir, for example, who describes the graveyard at Crossapol as it was in the year that JGC became minister of Tiree and Coll (1861, p. 151). Nicholas Maclean-Bristol, Breacachadh, tells me that he has searched for it on numerous occasions without success. JGC's information appears to have been picked up by John Sands, who understood that the stone was on the west side of Tiree (p. 655 below). Again, however, the literature on Tiree contains no reference to it, and Niall M. Brownlie, a native of the west side of Tiree, tells me that he has never heard of such a stone in the island. Sands's report was picked up by George Henderson (1911, p. 338) from *The Folk-Lore Journal* and cited with source. There is a Crossapol in Tiree, but it could hardly be described as 'on the west side', as it faces east across Hynish Bay on the south shore; in any case, we should take JGC's evidence at face value. Probably the stone has long been buried under a sand-dune, of which the west end of Coll has a great many. See also Reeves 1854, p. 244, and RCAHMS 1980, p. 137; for the passing of patients through gapped stones see McPherson 1929, p. 80.

795 Macbain (1896, pp. 231–32) derives *mùire* 'leprosy' from *mùr* 'countless number (as of insects)'. Lochlin is *Lochlann*, Scandinavia.

Easa suc Con is the spelling exactly as it stands in *WSS* 100; Alexander Forbes describes it (1923, p. 317) as 'a waterfall near Scorribreac named Easa Sue Con, which is unexplained as given, only that beneath it the hollow or trough was the place into which leprous patients were placed for a cure'. Forbes's 'Sue' can only be a misprint. His source for the name, at least, will be *WSS* itself – it is clear from comments which he makes elsewhere, e.g. on Eisgeadal (*ibid.*, p. 184, cf. note 369 above), that he draws freely on JGC's work without acknowledgement.

Easa suc Con will be for *Easa Suic Con* 'the Dogs' Snout Falls'. It is possible to imagine reasons for such a name. The falls are on *Abhainn Chràcaig*, the 'Scorry River', a few yards before it enters Portree Bay. The singer Donnie Munro, who lives nearby at Scorrybreck House, has known them all his life, and though of Gaelic-speaking parents, has only ever heard them called 'the Scorry Falls'. I am grateful to him for the illustration below. The upper fall forms a narrow trough – clearly the Norsewoman's basin – from which the lower fall spills into a large pool, providing a curtain, as it were, for the cave in the rock which lies under the basin.

Easa(n) Suic Con, see note 795   Diagrammatic sketch by Donnie Munro

796　A beautiful little loch, this is at Chesthill in Strathnaver. Of the type described in note 122, until the early twentieth century it was one of the most popular resorts for healing in the north of Scotland. It is usually called Loch Mo Nàire; the name is, I think, that of St Mo Nàile, for whom see Martin 1716, p. 225 = 1999, p. 139; Plummer 1925, pp. 97–155; Pennant 1998, p. 175. Most commentators say that the night for the cure was the one preceding the first day (or Monday) of any of the quarters, but one of the earliest, the Rev. Donald Sage (1789–1869), says (1899, p. 180): "The method was to come there on the evening previous to a certain day of the year – I think the first day of February." This is close to St Nàile's feast-day, 27 January (Anon. 1873). See also Henderson 1911, pp. 310–20; Sutherland 1937, p. 107; Banks 1937–41, vol. 1, pp. 130–31; MacNeill 1962, pp. 367–68; Temperley 1977, pp. 70–72.

797　This is a surprising statement, though not without some validity. It may be contrasted with Katherine Whyte Grant's account of the wells of his native Appin (1925, p. 34), or with Macbain's view that 'nearly every district has a holy well and a rag bush near at hand' and that 'their number is almost countless' (1887–88, p. 268). The tenacity of the people in clinging to the rituals associated with healing wells has been well documented, notably perhaps in Dalyell 1834, pp. 79–95, 297; Mitchell 1860–62, pp. 269–72; Maclean 1886, pp. 105–10; Mackinlay 1893, pp. 86–127; Macdonald 1894–96, pp. 63–64; *CG2*, p. 286; MacPhail 1900, pp. 445–46; MacGregor 1901, pp. 54–61; Maclagan 1902, pp. 181–83; Grant 1902–04b, pp. 360–64; Macfarlane 1906–08, vol. 1, pp. xix–xxi, and vol. 2, pp. liii–lv; Henderson 1911, pp. 320–32; Polson 1926, pp. 137–44; McPherson 1929, pp. 37–60; Dingwall 1932–36; Banks 1937–41, vol. 1, pp. 125–70; Morris 1982; Willis 1995; Harman 1997, pp. 243–44; Forsyth 1999, pp. 44–46; MacLeòid 2000; MacLeod 2000. Most striking of all is the survival of three major clootie wells and a dropping well at Munlochy and Culloden, in the part of the Highlands most strongly associated with evangelical Protestantism from the seventeenth century to the twentieth (MacilleDhuibh 30.4.93). On the other hand, there appear to be few notable survivals in the area best known to JGC, north Argyll. It is symptomatic of this, perhaps, that a saying about the dropping well at Munlochy (*Ged as mór Creag a' Choth, is beag a math*, 'Though large is Craigiehow, small is its use') is attributed to a man from Mull when complimented on the size of his wife (Meek 1978, p. 98).

798　Remarking that Jura has 'several Fountains of excellent Water', Martin Martin says (1716, p. 234 = 1999, pp. 144–45): "The most celebrated of them is that of the Mountain *Beinbrek* in the *Tarbat*, called *Toubir ni Lechkin*, that is, the Well in a stony Descent; It runs Easterly, and they commonly reckon it to be lighter by one half than any other Water in this Isle: for tho one drink a great Quantity of it at a time, the Belly is not swell'd, or any ways burden'd by it. Natives and Strangers find it efficacious against Nauseousness of the Stomach, and the Stone. The River *Nissa* receives all the Water that issues from this Well, and this is the reason they give why Salmons here are in Goodness and Taste far above those of any other River whatever."

Tobar Leac nam Fiann is on Ben Garrisdale, not Beinn Bhreac, but its waters find their way into the Lussa, which is clearly Martin's 'Nissa', and Youngson confirms (2001, p. 422) that it may safely be identified with *Tobar na Leacainn*. John Mercer, who calls it 'the Fairies' Well', excavated it *c.* 1970. He says (1974, p. 191, cf. Youngson 2001, pp. 422–23): "The water, a few inches deep and upon glacial clay, is covered by a neat lichened cairn. In the earth in front were 20 Stone Age flints, either knapped by the well's first users or collected as charms by later people, this a well-known custom in the islands; 24 lumps of milky quartz, natural on Jura; 80 pieces of crystal, probably from one or more balls, used as important charms in the region up to at least the mid-nineteenth century; a small glass ball . . . an ersatz offering, it was in fact an ancient form of bottle-stopper; 5 clay pipe fragments; rivet, buckle, 4 buttons, all copper; 36 lead shot, and lumps of lead and iron; broken glass and china; a paste amethyst from a brooch. On the underside of the well's sill-stone had been cut eight sets of initials, with dates up to 1869. Actually in the water were half a dozen low value coins, the earliest an 1861 penny, the latest a 1926 sixpence."

799 By 'about thirty years ago' JGC means *c.* 1844. See pp. 643–44 below.

800 This is Tobar Chuidhearaidh, Carmichael's *Cuidh-airidh* 'Sheiling of the Enclosure', NF 809695, east of Rathad na Comataidh on the south slope of Maireabhal, JGC's 'Merivale'. On their journey to the well people did not speak until they had knelt and drunk three times from it. They left a coin or other gift on a stone slab. Each time they drank they said:

> *Tha mise a' fàgail déideadh,*
> *Léireadh agus cnàmh mo chinn*
> *Anns an tobair nach tràigh a-chaoidh*
> *An ainm an Athar, a' Mhic 's an Spioraid Naoimh.*

("I am leaving my head's / Toothache, pain and decay / In the well that will never ebb / In the name of the Father, Son and Holy Ghost.") The well was also known as *Tobar an Déididh* or *Tobar na Cnoidh* ('the Toothache Well') and *Tobar Cnuimh Fhiacaill* ('the Well of the Tooth Worm'), it being widely believed that tooth decay was caused by a worm – indeed in NLS Adv. MS 72.1.33, p. 36, the Rev. John Beaton tells us that one cure for toothache is to tempt the worm out and drown it quickly in a bowl of water: *Dean caoinnil do meacurrig eigin .7. cuir frass an luibhe renabrar an gaffin i.e* [he leaves a space, presumably having forgotten the English word 'henbane'] *annsin bhuacis no annsin easgirt a bhias annsin caoinnill 7 lass an chaoinnill 7 leig toit na caoinle trid fuinneall no intrumeint iomchubhaidh eigin eile a steach san mbeul chum na fiacaile ata (?)faniar 7 cum ort tammil mait fedfad uair na leathuar [ní is lú no is mó) 7 tuitidh cruimhega beaga amach asin mbeul sios san uisge.* "Make a candle of some soft substance and put henbane seed in the wick or tow of the candle and light the candle and by means of a funnel or other suitable instrument direct the smoke of the candle in through the mouth to the tooth in question. Continue for a good while, perhaps an hour or half an hour (more or less), and little worms will fall out of the mouth and down into the water." See Mac Intoisich 1831, p. 87; Black 1883, pp. 32–33; Black 1892–93, p. 493; *CG2*, pp. 10–11; MacLeod 2000, pp. 52–53; MacLeòid 2000, pp. 54–55.

I print JGC's 'between Loch Maddy and Dïusa in Merivale' exactly as it stands in *WSS* 102. It is rather poetic, but reflects a scribble in a notebook rather than knowledge gleaned from walking the ground. *Tobar Chuithairidh*, as it is marked on the six-inch Ordnance Survey map of 1881, lies right in the middle of North Uist on the south-easterly slope of Marrival, and is on a straight line between Alioter at the head of Loch Maddy (see note 969) and Dusary Mill at the foot of the 'Committee Road'. Dusary is *Dubhasairigh*, apparently *Dugfúss-erg* 'the shieling of Dugfus' (Beveridge 1911, pp. 60, 316), and must I think be JGC's 'Dïusa'. I am grateful for information on this point to Norman E. MacDonald, Motherwell, whose grandfather lived in Dusary House.

801 Either 'east' is a misprint for 'coast', or JGC's geography is worse than one would have thought. This island, now called simply Eilean Mór, is off the west coast of Knapdale, which is north of Kintyre, see note 301. The tradition to which JGC refers is in the Old Statistical Account of South Knapdale, written 'from Materials communicated by some Gentlemen in the Parish', and is worth repeating here, as it contains a Gaelic *rann* which deserves to be translated (Anon. 1796, p. 316 = new edn, also p. 316): "Miracles were performed by the saint for many ages after his death. At length a woman, labouring under a dysentry, addressed him from the opposite shore, in the following verses:

> *'S mise bean bhochd a' Braidealban*
> *A m' sheasamh air lic Mha' Charmaig*

So naomh ann an Eilean na fairge
Thig's tog a bhuineach o m' earbal.

It was an unlucky business for the invalids of those days. The saint granted her request; but was so scandalised by the indelicacy of her language, that he became deaf to the prayers of his votaries ever after." The *rann* means: "I'm a poor wife from Breadalbane / Standing on St Cormick's flagstone, / And, O saint in the ocean island, / Come and lift the runs from my tail."

802 The burial-ground is at the south end of Tràigh Sgaisteil, on the promontory between Crossapol Bay and Loch Bhreacachaidh. According to the Ordnance Survey 6 in. map of 1881, *An Carraigean* is a sunken rock east of the island of Soa, which is reached from Port na Luinge near the burial-ground.

803 Cf. *CG2*, p. 286. Niall M. Brownlie, who has not seen the well but gives the same tradition (1995, p. 52), has confirmed the name personally to me; thus also MacDougall and Cameron n.d., p. 96. The well enjoys, or enjoyed, a spectacular location at the north-western extremity not only of Tiree but of Argyll as a whole, looking out over Hough Bay to the open Atlantic. It is not clear to me whether it is to be identified as the well of the old township on the west side of Beinn Hough, which was choked following a sandstorm in the spring of the year of Waterloo, resulting in the removal of the people to Kilmoluag (Cregeen 1998, p. 20).

Its name deserves to be considered in the contexts of the sanctity in which the number nine was allegedly held in Tiree (see pp. lxxxvi, 207 and 655) and of novenary dedications elsewhere. The latter have been explored by Mackinlay (1905–06) and myself (MacilleDhuibh 27.7.90), and in much greater detail by Stuart McHardy (2003); for the significance of the number nine in Gaelic tradition generally see *CG2*, pp. 332–34. I found a series of wells, altars, chapels and fairs in Angus, east Perthshire and Aberdeenshire bearing names like the Nine Maiden Well, the Chapel of the Seven Maidens, Ninemadinchapell and the Nine Virgins Day, along with a story representing these women as daughters of a seventh- or eighth-century saint called Donald. Feeling that their cult smacked of river-worship, I concluded that it had become localised at the main junctions of the Tay.

McHardy throws his net much wider, pointing to various locations called Ninewells and claiming for the cult a dedication to St Fyndoca at Innishail in Loch Awe; he discusses islands of women, the magic use of nine (such as the ninth wave), and stories about nine women (including the Muses) in Celtic, Arthurian, Norse, Roman and Greek mythology, drawing attention to major figures like Apollo, Arthur, Brigid and Odin who dominate or oversee such groups. He does not mention *Tobar nan Naoi Beò* (or Tiree), but it fits his model of novenary sites on mountain-tops and islands, associated with Arthur, Brigid and oak-trees – MacArthurs are prominent in Tiree, there was a Kilbride at Lag nan Cruachan in Cornaigmore just two miles east, and only the oak-tree is lacking (though the presence of peat in Tiree until the nineteenth century shows that this may not always have been the case).

I know of no other novenary dedications in Gaelic. The island and fair of the Nine Virgins at Kenmore were simply *Eilean nam Bannaomh* (now Priory Island) and *Féill nam Bannaomh*, 'the Isle/Fair of the Female Saints'. We may therefore ask why *Tobar nan Naoi Beò* is so called. Is it because the widow and her eight children remained alive when most of the island's population had died? Is it because they were the largest surviving family? Is it because they were survivors of a shipwreck? Or is it because they live forever as saints in heaven?

804 *Cha laigh sùil orra*: 'no eye will rest upon them'. The three epithets in the rhyme are deliberately ambiguous, denoting purpose as well as origin: *ribeach* 'entangling, snaring' as well as 'ragged, hairy'; *bradach* 'thieving' as well as 'stolen'; *cam* 'bending' (with weight

of catch) as well as 'crooked'. For *caorann* (rowan, mountain ash, 'ash', quicken, wicken) see p. 177 above and Opie and Tatem's section 'rowan protects' (1992, pp. 333–34).

805 See p. 132 ('Funerals'). As Macbain points out (1896, pp. 18, 148), *àrd dorus* 'high door' is a piece of folk etymology: the word for 'lintel' is *fàrdorus* (now *fàrdoras*), from *for, far* 'over, upon' and *dorus* 'door'. See p. xv.

806 The *mòthan* was the magic plant *par excellence*. In *CG2*, pp. 110–15, 329–31, Carmichael describes its uses and offers different versions of the rhyme, all longer than JGC's. He identified it tentatively (*CG2*, p. 329) as 'either the thyme-leaved sandwort (*arenaria serpyllifolia*) or the bog-violet'; Fr Allan made it the pearlwort or sandwort (McDonald 1958, p. 184), and Mary Beith (1995, p. 207) the bog violet or butterwort (*pinguicula vulgaris*). The Rev. Duncan Campbell said that 'what the plant is or was has never been definitely expiscated' (1967–68, p. 14). See also Campbell 1978–81, pp. 185–86, and MacDonald 1994–95, p. 61.

Bruford and MacDonald (1994, p. 476) distinguish *mungan* 'pearlwort' from *mòthan* 'bog violet', cf. *Tocher* 28, pp. 206–13. Carmichael (*CG2*, pp. 331–32) gives *mungan* as 'fairy flax (*linum catharticum*)' and says that the common name for it in Gaelic is *lìon na mnatha sithe* ('the flax of the Fairy woman').

807 See Opie and Tatem's section 'St John's wort protects' (1992, pp. 336–37), Beith 1995, pp. 40, 122, 205, 220, and GUL MS Gen. 1090/29, p. 36. Carmichael quotes numerous rhymes about the plant in *CG2*, pp. 96–103, and *CG4*, pp. 116–17, explaining *achlasan* 'armpit package' as follows (*CG2*, p. 96): "The plant is secretly secured in the bodices of the women and in the vests of the men, under the left armpit." JGC's two rhymes offer a neat contrast in terms of structure – the first is in standard fixed metre, i.e. showing regular end-rhyme (e.g. *iarraidh* : *fiabhras*) and *aicill* or so-called 'internal rhyme' (e.g. *Chille* : *sireadh*); the second is in free verse, cf. note 281.

808 At *CG4*, pp. 116–17, Carmichael offers a version of this in twelve lines (three quatrains), of which JGC's represents the first eight. Carmichael's second couplet is: *Cha togar as mo chadal mi / 'S cha sparrar mi air iarann.* "I shall not be lifted away in my sleep / And I shall not be thrust upon iron." It can be seen from this that JGC's interpretation of his own second couplet ('it wards off fever and keeps its owner from being taken away in his sleep . . .') is correct. Carmichael's translation of *an donn duilleach*, 'the brown leafy one', is preferable to JGC's 'brown-leaved one'.

809 Again, Carmichael offers a version of this in twelve lines (*CG4*, pp. 116–17). This time, systematic comparison of the two versions can offer useful insights into the gradual decomposition of fixed metres into free verse – the fixed metres being Carmichael's, and the free verse being JGC's. Carmichael begins:

> *Buainidh mise m'achlasan,*
> *Luibh allail nam ban fionn,*
> *Luibh na cuirme shòlasaich*
> *Bha 'n cùirt shòghail Fhinn.*

This corresponds quite well to JGC's first four lines. Carmichael translates: "I will pluck my armpit-package, / Renowned plant of the fair women, / Plant of the joyful feast / That was in the delightful court of Fionn." In line 2, *sith* would have given better rhyme with *Fhinn*, but *fionn* is present in both versions, so we cannot assume that *sith* was the original reading. *Fionn* can mean 'holy' but not, as far as I know, 'otherworldly'. JGC's *fionn e* : *shòghail* is rhyme of a sort. Carmichael's second quatrain corresponds more loosely to JGC's next four lines:

Luibh fhireann i, luibh bhoireann i,
Luibh thogadh crodh is laogh,
Luibh Chaluim chaoimh chonnalaich,
Luibh loinneil nam ban caon.

"'Tis male plant, 'tis female plant, / Plant that would rear cattle and calf, / Plant of kindly wise Columba, / Lovely plant of the gentle women." *Chonnalaich* in the third line probably means 'from Donegal (*Tìr Chonaill*)' rather than 'wise'. Carmichael's version retains perfect *aicill* and end-rhyme, whereas JGC's offers no rhyme at all, though it has good rhythm. Carmichael's cattle, Columba and fair women have become JGC's birds, God and Christ. Finally, Carmichael's third quatrain corresponds to JGC's last two lines:

B'fhearr a duais fo m'achlais
Na prasgan do chrodh àil;
B'fhearr a duais bhuadha
Na cuallach do chrodh bàn.

"Better the reward of it under my arm / Than a crowd of calving kine; / Better the reward of its virtues / Than a herd of white cattle." These *crodh bàn* will be Fairy cattle (cf. Hemming 2002), the point being that small Christian graces are worth more than large otherworldly ones. By contrast, JGC's version simply peters out without rhyme, rhythm or sense – the comparative *b' fheàrr* has no comparator, but Carmichael provides it.

810 See p. 177 above; Maclagan 1902, pp. 119–20, 136, 175; GUL ms Gen. 1090/28, p. 257. Juniper was used for flavouring whisky, cf. Beith 1995, p. 60. Carmichael (*CG4*, pp. 128–29) gives a version of the charm in three quatrains, of which JGC's version resembles the first and last couplets, with two salient exceptions: (a) the second line of each quatrain cites the number of Christ's ribs through which the plant is pulled as one, three and nine respectively, contrasting with JGC's five; (b) JGC's last word *ghriobhadh*, which he appears to have understood as equivalent to *griobhag* 'confusion', fails to rhyme with *Chrìost*, so perhaps Carmichael's *gìomh* 'fear' is a better reading.

811 *Cathair* ('chair') in all these terms, as also Dwelly's *cathair-thalmhuinn* (1977, p. 174), appears to be a misunderstanding for *carr, càrr* 'anything hard, tough, and immovable; a strong root' (*CG6*, p. 34, cf. Campbell 1978–81, p. 200). Carmichael cites a 17-line rhyme which appears to be about yarrow in *CG2*, pp. 70–71 (*a chathair aigh*, i.e. *a' chathair àigh*, which he translates 'the gracious yarrow', more literally 'the glorious chair', perhaps a mishearing of *a' charr làir*); two shorter ones in *CG2*, pp. 94–95, in both of which the plant is *an earr reidh*, which he translates 'the yarrow fair', but which is more literally 'the smooth tail' – *earr, eàrr*, 'end, extremity, tail', *earr-thalmhainn* 'yarrow', literally 'earth-tail'; and finally a very long rhyme indeed (36 lines) in *CG4*, pp. 122–25, which he or his editor cautiously entitles 'A' Charr Àigh: The Gracious Root'. It begins similarly to JGC's:

Buainidh mi mo charr àigh
Mar bhuain Brighde le leth làimh.

("I will cull my gracious root / As Brigit culled it with her one hand.") Another beginning of this type may be found in Carmichael's 'An Eidheann-mu-Chrann: The Tree-Entwining Ivy', *CG2*, pp. 76–77:

Buainidh mis an eidheann-mu-chrann,
Mar a bhuain Moire le a leth-laimh.

"I will pluck the tree-entwining ivy, / As Mary plucked with her one hand." I can find no other source for JGC's second couplet, however. For superstitions regarding yarrow see MacFarlane 1924–25, pp. 37–38, and Opie and Tatem 1992, pp. 453–54.

812 JGC is coy, but clearly this plant was an aphrodisiac. It is given in *CG6*, p. 102, as 'the enticing plant, enchanter's nightshade', *lus an tàlaidh* from Glen Elg and *lus* (or *luibh*) *an tataidh* ('the caressing, cuddling, petting plant') from Skye: "Girls were wont to bribe old women to procure them this plant, which was administered to a lover without his knowledge, in order to entice him. When put in water it is said to make the water bubble."

813 The reading in *WSS* 108 is *A'v a chuis*. This will be a misprint for *A'r a chuis*, i.e. *Air do chùis*, see note 729 and *A'r a shocair* in the next *rann*.

814 Literally 'in my mother's and father's house'. It is hard to imagine anything more degrading than being forced to stand holding a tallow candle, the smell of which was very bad. Nor would the smoke have been that of the candle alone. In any ill-ventilated house with a fire in the middle of the floor a pall of smoke hung about the rafters. The only way to be sure of avoiding it was to sit down.

815 In origin at least, this is a story not of the otherworld and this world, but of rich and poor, abusers and abused, abductors and abducted (see Introduction, pp. lxviii–lxix). At a literal level the 'cow with three teats' is deformed or injured, a poor man's beast which gives little milk. It is notable that the animal in question is a *mart* (not a milch cow at all but one being fattened for slaughter). It seems likely, therefore, that *Aona mhart air thrì sinean / 'S naoinear de mhuinntir* is a riddle referring to the chief hunter, his genitals and the nine members of his gang. JGC translates *Rìgh Sionnach* as 'the King of Enchantments', presumably because that is how his informant understood it (cf. *CG2*, p. 352, and *CG6*, p. 127), but it is more likely to represent *Rìgh Sionna* 'the King of the River Shannon'. The Shannon is in Irish *Sionann*, genitive *Sionna, na Sionna, na Sionainne* (Hogan 1910, p. 603; Dinneen 1927, p. 1038) or *na Senoine* (Bruford 1967–68, p. 306). There is a very different version in *CG5*, pp. 388–91, under the title 'Rìgh Sionn' ('The King of Sionn'), in which the storyteller offers *Sionnaidh* and *Sionnachan* as variants, and links the name explicitly with *sionnach* 'a fox'. In this version when the dumb girl bears the hunter a son the priest is sent for to baptise the child, a great feast is arranged, and the hunter's mother 'set the brown-haired maid, daughter of the King of Sionn, standing on a pedestal (*cailbh*) at the head of the feast, and put a wick-candle (*coinneal bhuaice*) in her hand to make sure that the world's people should have sight of the russet-haired damsel (*air an rodaidh ruaidh*), daughter of the King of Sionn'. She finds her voice and addresses the smoky candle in four quatrains, but these are almost entirely different from JGC's fifteen lines. She speaks at length of the pleasure of hunting deer with her father and grandfather, and finishes:

> *Cha b'e tùrlach na deathcha*
> *An robh mi air thùs air mo chleachdadh,*
> *Ach teach gun smùrlach gun smalan,*
> *Dùn muirneach m'athar 's mo mhàthar.*

("It was not a smoky bonfire / To which I at first was used, / But a house without ashes or dust, / The blithe castle of my father and mother.") Tadhg Sionna ('Tadhg of the Shannon'), one of the sons of Brian Boru, appears in the tale usually called 'Fear na h-Eabaid' ('The Man in the Cassock'), see pp. 67–69 above (*Torgill mac Brian*), Craig 1944, p. 17 (*do Hig Sionna mac Brian*), MacDonald 1953, pp. [2]–[3] (*do Thig Sionna mac Brian* 'Tadhg of-the-Shannon son of Brian'), Bruford 1967–68, p. 305 (*Taodhg*), Bruford and MacDonald 1994, p. 153 (*Tig Sionna mac Brian*). See also notes 181, 665 and 727.

JGC returned to the topic in a paper written about 1887 (Campbell 1907–08, pp. 197–98).

Giving the girl's name as '*Screuchag* (*i.e.* a shrill-voiced female)', he says: "The Tiree story is, that a man found a young and beautiful woman sleeping on a hillock. When wakened she would not speak. He took her home, and, though apparently deaf and dumb, married her. He had three children by her. For seven years she never uttered a word. At the end of that time his mother said she would make her speak. On the occasion of a cow being killed, she put her on the other side of a fire placed on the floor, with a 'grey candle' (coinneal ghlas), *i.e.* a candle in which the cloth that serves for a wick is wrapped round the tallow. The house was filled with smoke, and the candle was dripping on her hands. At last she spoke, and her mother-in-law followed up the conversation."

JGC says that verses of the conversation have been got 'in Tiree, at Loch Awe side, and from a native of Morven'. He gives the following in translation, and although he calls them 'fragments' they represent a substantial advance on the text cited above. His Gaelic originals were excluded from the paper as published, but they had been transcribed by Carmichael from JGC's lost appendix into what is now EUL MS CW 241, ff. 65–66 (see p. 703 below); I give them from that source, edited slightly. Screuchag says:

> *Air mo chubhaidh-s', a dhubh-choinneal,*
> *Ged a dhubh mo làmh ad' dheathaich,*
> *Ar leam cha b'i 'n obair ghnàthaichte*
> *An taigh mo mhàthar no m' athar.*

"By my dignity, black candle, / Though my hand is black beneath thy smoke, / Methinks that was not my wonted work / In the great house of my father or mother." Her mother-in-law says:

> *Uiseag eutrom, eòin iongadaich*
> *Thàinig á tìr nan eun fiadhaich,*
> *Is ann a ghoir thu orm gu riochdail*
> *An ceann do sheachdamh bliadhna.*

> *Is aithne dhòmhsa mar bhiodh agad*
> *Nuair a thàrla tu 'n taigh d' athar:*
> *Aon bhò chaol cham air trì sinean,*
> *Dall ann is ceathrar muinntir.*

"Cheerful lark, wonderful bird / That came from the land of wild birds, / Thou hast called with stately cry / At the end of thy seventh year. / I know how it fared with you / When you chanced to be in your father's house: / A lean cow, blind of an eye and with three teats, / A blind man and four of a company." And Screuchag replies:

> *Is breugach dhut e,*
> *Is amhlaidh sin a bhiomaid ann:*
> *Brataichean sròil gan cur ri crann,*
> *Léine shìoda air gach neach ann*
> *S am fìon donn a' dùrdail ann.*

> *Bha ciad bean òg ann a b' àirde sealladh*
> *Le'n eachaibh donna 's le'n srianaibh;*
> *Bha seachd seisrichean ri àraidh,*
> *Dèanadh aran an taigh m' athar.*

Bha slat iubhair, bha slat bhràghad
Is usgraichean de dh'òr 's de dh'airgead
Is naoi slabhraidhean òir an snìomh
An taigh mòr nan turaid àrd,
al/An taigh mo rìgh mhiannaich mhòir,
An taigh Rìgh Sionnaich.

Air a dhrumag cha laigh sùith,
Cha b'e an cuileann,
'S cha b'e an eidheann,
'S cha b'e am feàrn
Air am bi faob,
Ach an fhiodhag sleaghach slioghach,
Sluagh mu timcheall, 's deathach àrd;
Macan nan steud as gile ball
'Na ruith roimh shléibhtibh 's roimh thuinn
'S aon mhaighdeann chaol mhailgheach dhonn
'S a ceòl binn an cnocan cruinn.

"That is a lie, / For like [the following] we were there: / Silken banners raised on high, / A silken shirt on every man / And the brown wine gurgling there. / A hundred young dames of loftiest looks / Were there with brown steeds and their bridles; / Seven teams were ploughing, / Making bread for my father's house. / There were yew wands and neck wands / And ornaments of gold and silver / And nine chains of twisted gold / In the house of my magnanimous big king, / In the house of King Sionnach, / In the big house of lofty battlements. / On its roof-tree lies no soot, / Not of holly is it, / Nor of ivy, / Nor the alder / Full of knobs, / But the wild fig, spear-like, full of sap, (?) / With hosts around, and lofty smoke; / A mounted youth of whitest limbs / At speed over land and over waves / And a brown maid with narrow eyebrows / Making sweet music in a rounded hillock."

In the first of these four sections we may note *sin* ('that') meaning 'the following', and *fion donn* 'noble wine', literally 'brown wine'. In the third section Carmichael's *al/* implies that the two lines that follow are alternatives to the previous one; in his translation he puts them in before it. In the fourth section 'soot' was misprinted 'root'. I print the words *an fhiodhag sleaghach slioghach* as Carmichael wrote them; if we wish to accept JGC's tentative translation we should emend to *an fhiodhag shleaghach shlìogach*, I think. There is no prosody to help us: as they stand, these sections are in free verse. The wild fig is the *fiodhag* or *fiodhagach* (see p. 90), a 'crossed' or banned wood and therefore a clear indication of supernatural origins.

For a second copy of JGC's 'Screuchag' material and a draft of his own 'Nighean Rìgh Sionn' (*CG5*, pp. 388–91), see Alexander Carmichael's transcripts in EUL MS CW 503, ff. 878–87.

Alexander Carmichael's own manuscript materials on this subject, full of alternative readings, are to be found in EUL MS CW 503. At ff. 878r–880r, headed 'Rìgh Sionn', is a rough draft of the Gaelic prose text eventually published in *CG5*, p. 388. At ff. 881r–884r, headed 'Sgreuchag', is a longer version (fifty lines as opposed to thirty-eight) of JGC's poem 'Screuchag', with Gaelic text in ink on left and gapped English translation in pencil on right. Finally, at ff. 885r–887r, headed 'Nighean Rìgh Sionn / Nighean Rìgh Nan Sionn', without translation, is a poem of nine-and-a-half quatrains, of which only qq. 1–4 appear in *CG5* (p. 390). At f. 878r one of Carmichael's editors has scribbled 'Poem rather difficult & not specially fine'; the material *is* difficult, but the context supplied by JGC shows it to be very fine indeed. Any future editor will find it rewarding.

816 The story is told (of the MacGregors of Dunan in Rannoch) in Newton 1998–2000, pp. 285–87. On their way to the feast at Taymouth they encounter an old man on Drummond Hill who is saying over and over to a large stone beside the road, *Sann ris a' chloich ghlais a their mi e.* "It's to the grey stone I tell it." (See pp. 130 and 280.) They ask him what he means and he replies to the stone, *Nuair a thig ceann an tairbh dhuibh air a' bhòrd is còir do chlanna Ghriogair a bhith 'nam faicill.* "When the head of the black bull comes upon the table the progenies of Gregor should take the alarm." Duly warned, they have their dirks ready, and when the bull's head arrives each captures the man beside him. They make their escape, releasing their hostages one at a time; Donnchadh Dubh is the last to be let go, at the top of Drummond Hill.

Equally, the death-warning and the bull's head story may both represent a survival of totemism, cf. note 485. For Donnchadh Dubh (Sir Duncan Campbell of Glenorchy, *c.*1553–1631) see Gillies 1938, pp. 135–42, and *Tocher* 47, pp. 321–27. According to Carmichael (*CG2*, p. 345) he got his sobriquet from being born with a caul on his head; or it may have been because he liked to cover his baldness with a cap (cf. *Tocher* 47, p. 321) as shown in the portrait of him painted by an unknown artist in 1619 (Thomson 1974, plate 14). Neil MacEwen described him (NAS RH13/40, cf. Watson 1916–17, p. 133) as:

> *Fear lér tughadh ardfhuil Ailpín*
> *'S nár umhlaidh d'aon a n-am chruaidh.*

("A man who challenged the high blood of Alpin / And yielded to no one in time of strife.") The 'high blood of Alpin' is the Clan Gregor.

817 The *Clann Dhonnchaidh Dhuibh* were MacGregors of Learagan, which is near the east end of Loch Rannoch, on the north shore. Amelia MacGregor explains (1898–1901, vol. 1, pp. 121–22): "Duncan Macgregor, younger son of Gregor MacGregor of Roro (No 4) commonly called Donnacha dubh Liomhanach, from his having come from Glenlyon, got possession of Learagan, in Rannoch, from a tribe called clann Tavish, that resided there about the year 1480. His Estate consisted of eleven merks of land, extending from Aldcheardie to the Clachghlas near the east end of Loch Rannoch . . . The descendants of Donnacha-dubh liomhanach, occupied Learagan either as Proprietors or as Tenants, from the above mentioned period till 1792 when the present system of sheep farming caused their removal." See also vol. 1, p. 118, and vol. 2, pp. 225, 236–49.

Duncan's brother Alexander was the first MacGregor of Dunan. He appears to have been called *Donnchadh Dubh Lìomhannach* to distinguish him from his celebrated seventeenth-century descendant *Donnchadh Dubh na Gealaiche* ('Black Duncan of the Moon'). Clearly the latter name reflects the cattle-raiding exploits for which the Rannochmen were notorious throughout Scotland, but the learned historian of the MacGregors goes to great lengths to avoid such a charge. He got the name, she says (vol. 2, p. 237), "because he often expressed a wish that he had the Michaelmas moon enclosed in a bag, in order to deprive the thieves of the advantage of its light which enabled them the more easily to discover and drive off his cattle. He was a rich man and those in his neighbourhood who lived on the public used always about that time to pay him an unwelcome visit."

The *Clann Dhonnchaidh Dhuibh* may have been JGC's mother's people, see p. 612 below. The *Clann Dhonnchaidh Bhig* were MacGregors of Morinch or Morenish, on the north shore of Loch Tay near Killin. They were descended from Donnchadh Beag of Roro, who died at Roro in 1477. Morinch previously belonged to the Menzieses, and was taken from the MacGregors by Sir Duncan Campbell of Glenorchy in 1602, see note 816 (MacGregor 1898–1901, vol. 1, pp. 42, 59, 87, 113, 118, 120, 328, 479).

818 Subsequent scholarship shows this judgement to be wide of the mark. J. P. MacLean

says (1889, pp. 332–33) that Eoghan a' Chinn Bhig was 'eldest son of John Og, fifth son of MacLean of Lochbuie, and fell with his father in a clan battle with Duard in 1538, and then taken to Iona for interment, where his tombstone is still to be seen'; he confirms however that Eoghan 'was married to a daughter of MacDougall of Lorn, an ill-tempered and penurious woman'. Following MacLean 1889, p. 237, Maclean-Bristol (1995, pp. 97, 181, 185) makes him second son of John MacLean of Lochbuie, who is on historical record during the years 1485–1534, and, confirming JGC's 'Pack-Saddle' story at p. 238, a half-brother of Murchadh Geàrr (for whom see also p. 145 above): Hugh 'quarrelled with his father and both were killed in the same battle at Glencannir in Mull in 1538'.

Hugh's death resulted in a struggle for the Lochbuie succession which was ultimately won by his legitimised half-brother Murchadh (Cregeen and MacKenzie 1976–77, p. 295). See also Tormod Og 1830–31a = Henderson 1901, pp. 28–32; Campbell 1895, pp. 65–66; Fionn 1907, pp. 250–53; Henderson 1911, pp. 297, 342; Sithiche 1912, pp. 212–21, 333–39, 344; MacLean 1923–25, vol. 1, pp. 202–05; Nicolson 1951, pp. 102, 410–11; *CG*5, pp. 282–84; MacNeil 1987, p. xxxix; Youngson n.d., p. 49; Youngson 2001, p. 501; GUL MS Gen. 1090/29, p. 231; SoSS Maclagan MSS vol. 22, pp. 3846–47.

819 See Nicolson 1951, p. 78.

820 *Chorra Thòn Dubh* (spelt *Chorra thòn du* in *WSS* 113) should probably be *Chorra Thòndubh*, i.e. the stress will be on *Thòn*. *Curra Dhùghaill* is more literally 'Dugald's Heron', presumably referring to her father. For the imagery of cranes and herons see note 432. *Dubhag Tòn ri Teallaich* would nowadays be translated 'Blackie whose Bum's to the Hearth' (presumably she liked to warm herself at the fire). *Teallaich* shows that *teallach* is dialectally feminine, cf. Dieckhoff 1932, p. 162, and Mac a Phì 1938, p. 136. For *Dubhag* cf. note 969.

821 On the MacFadyens see Anon. 1912; *Tocher* 24, p. 297; Maclean-Bristol 2002b. The principal Garmony is on the Sound of Mull opposite Ardtornish, but the one meant here is a much wilder place, Garmonyreoch or Garmony Reich on the south shore of Loch Spelve. It is given by Maclean (1997, p. 26) as *Garbh Monadh Riabhach* 'Rough Speckled Moor', but the earliest spelling appears to be Garmonroch (1801, 1824), and this could well support JGC's *Gar'moin' an Fhraoich*, i.e. *Garbh M[h]òine an Fhraoich* 'the Rough Mossland of the Heather'. MacFadyen still had a long way to go for his gold, as *Beinn an Aoinidh*, 'the Mountain of the Steep Promontory', is on the south shore of Brolas at Carsaig, twelve miles west of Garmonyreoch as the crow flies and half as much again by sea. However, in Campbell 1895, p. 41, JGC put the matter slightly differently: "MacFadyens were said by one of the clan, of whose judgment and intelligence the writer has cause to think very highly, to have been the first possessors of Lochbuie, and when expelled, that they became a race of wandering artificers, (*Sliochd nan òr-cheard* – the race of goldsmiths), in *Beinn-an-aoinidh* and other suitable localities in Mull. The race is a very ancient one, but it has often been noticed that they are without a chief."

822 *Tobar nan Ceann* in Lochbuie is given by Maclean (1997, p. 84) at grid ref. 683.299, i.e. a quarter of a mile west of the *Crùn-Lochan* on the Craignure–Lochbuie road (see 'The Talking Horse at Cru-Loch', p. 111). Fostership was traditionally the strongest of all ties – *comhdhaltas gu ceud, agus càirdeas gu fichead*, 'fostership to a hundred degrees, and blood-relationship to twenty' (Nicolson 1951, pp. 27, 155). Sithiche points out (1912, p. 334): "Two foster-sisters would be probably much more bound to each other . . . than to their respective husbands, and they may have collaborated for the downfall of Eòghann." Generally speaking, *corra* is a heron, *corra-ghritheach* a heron or crane, see notes 432, 908 and 947. Morinish or Mornish is in the north-western corner of Mull, as far from Lochbuie as it is possible to go without leaving the island.

823 Carmichael quotes two verses which the woman sang (*CG*5, p. 283). Perhaps this is what JGC means by the 'Song of the MacLeans'.

Tha mi nigheadh léinteag nam fear geala
  A théid a mach 's nach tig a steach gu bràth,
Crònan tuirim nam fear ullamh
  A théid a mach 's a thuiteas anns a' chàs.

Tha mi sluistreadh caimis nam fear geala
  A théid a mach air thùs a' mhoch-thràth
Air na h-eachaibh crùdhach glasa
  'S nach till a steach 'na thràth.

Carmichael translates: "I am washing the shrouds of the fair men / Who are going out but in shall never come, / The death-dirge of the ready-handed men / Who shall go out and fall in the peril. / I am lustring the linen of the fair men / Who shall go out in the morning early / Upon the well-shod grey steeds / And shall not come back in season due."

824 See p. 22 above. Carmichael remarks rather improbably (*CG*5, p. 282) that 'her breasts troubled her as she stooped to wash, and now and then she would throw them over her shoulder, as African and Indian women do when travelling'.

825 See note 180.

826 See p. 139.

827 See 'Clothes', p. 126 above.

828 This appears to be a proverb (otherwise unrecorded, I think) loaded with double meanings. *Breabadair* 'a kicker' is also a weaver. Weaving was regarded as the most contemptible of all occupations. The weaver who wore poorly-soled shoes when operating the pedals or treadles was likely to get his palms skinned by the quickly-moving shuttle (Macinnes 1893–94, p. 214; Dwelly 1977, pp. 84–85). In the present instance Hugh is *breabadair na seana bhròig*, literally 'the kicker of the old shoe'. In traditional Gaelic society *bualadh bhas* 'the striking of palms' (clapping) was an expression not of approbation but of grief. It was done by women at funerals until the blood flowed from their hands. Thus Hugh's wife is warning him that his tantrum with the shoe will lead to his death.

829 'Dreeing his weird' = 'enduring his fate'. The places mentioned are in and around the valley of the Lussa, which flows northwards from Eoghan's crannog in Loch Sguabain, then turns sharply eastwards below the head of Glen Cannel to flow into Loch Spelve. MacLean (1889, p. 333) refers to the fight as 'the battle of Glen Cainnir', i.e. Cannel, see Watson 1926a, p. 276, and Maclean 1997, p. 145. JGC's *cùl na h-Innsribh* 'the back of Innsri' provides valuable evidence for this name, which appears on maps as Ishriff; earlier forms are Israch 1801, Ishrof 1824, Ischduoff 1826, Fishriff 1876. *Pace* MacQuarrie (1983, p. 77) and Maclean (1997, p. 28), who suggest a baffling variety of underlying elements including Norse *fjós* 'cow-house', *iss* 'ice' and *riff* 'reef', Gaelic *riamh* 'beauty' and *reabh* 'wile, trick, cunning', it looks as if the name is formed from a simple or locative plural (*innseacha, innsibh*) of Gaelic *innis* 'river meadow' with intrusive -r- as in *rìghrean, rìghribh*.

830 See p. 145.

831 'About fifty years ago' will mean *c.* 1824. The precise spelling of the place-names in *WSS* 118 is '*Port-nan-amhn*' near *Ru-an-t-sléibh*, in Treshinish, Mull'. These are in the north-western part of the island, south of Calgary Bay. *Rubh' an t-Sléibh* 'Moorland Point' is the old name for what is now *Rubha Threisinis* or Treshnish Point (Maclean 1997, p. 113). Sailing north in 1772, Pennant notes (1998, p. 270): "Pass the point Ruth-an-i-sleith, in Mull, when Egg high and rounded, Muck small, and the exalted tops of the mountainous Rum, and lofty Skie, appear in view. Leave on the east, Calgara Bay, in Mull, with a few houses, and some signs of cultivation; the first marks of population that had shown themselves in this vast island." There is a tiny harbour at the westernmost extremity called *na Hann, Port na Hann*, Haun,

from Norse *hafn* 'harbour' (Maclean 1997, pp. 28, 82); *Port-nan-amhn'* will be a misprint for *Port-nah-amhn'*, i.e. *Port na h-Amhn'*, which is a good way to spell the name in Gaelic orthography, but makes it look as if it involves the genitive of *abhainn* 'a river', so I have removed the apostrophe from the text as well as altering *nan-amhn* to *na h-Amhn*.

832 'An Dà Chìobair' ('The Two Shepherds'), Campbell 1860–62, vol. 2, pp. 82–85 = 1890, vol. 2, pp. 94–97. Norman MacLeod, 'Caraid nan Gaidheal', offers a different version of the story which he places in Glen Forsa as recently as 1818 (Tormod Og 1830–31a, pp. 93–94). The tree was not birch but willow, and was 'twisted like a withie by the struggle' (*air a sniomh mar ghad leis an spàirn*). However, as Calachyle (Callachally) is in Glen Forsa, the two tellings probably relate to the same incident. See also SoSS Maclagan MSS vol. 22, pp. 3806–07, and Fionn 1907, p. 253. The legend survives in Cape Breton to this day (Rankin 2004, p. 63).

Sir Walter Scott speaks (2001, p. 206) of an appearance during the Peninsular War of 1808–14: "The spectre is said to have rode his rounds and uttered his death-cries within these few years in consequence of which the family and clan, though much shocked, were in no way surprised to hear by next accounts that their gallant chief was dead at Lisbon, where he served under Lord Wellington."

These rumours of the death of Lt. Murdoch MacLaine of Lochbuie (1791–1844) were much exaggerated. Although he fought with the 42nd Royal Highlanders – the Black Watch – in several of the battles of that war, he lived to tell the tale (Sinclair 1899, p. 270). It was for some of the MacLaines who were with him that the spectre made its ghastly appearance, as for example in 1812 (Fionn 1907, p. 253): *Bu shiùbhlach e air barr-bhalla Bhurgos, 'san Spainnt, an oidhche a chuireadh "Am Freiceadan Dubh" a ghlacadh an àite sin, agus Murchadh Og Locha-buidhe 's a dhaoine 'san iomairt.* ("It galloped along the top of the wall of Burgos in Spain on the night when the Black Watch was sent to take that place and young Murdoch of Lochbuie and his men were engaged.")

833 'Fetch' – the apparition, double, or wraith of a living person. JGC seems to be getting the word from Brand (1849, vol. 3, pp. 228, 238).

834 Compare the following conclusion based on detailed scientific examination of a series of well-documented case histories (Cohn 1996, pp. 294, 298, 300): "Second sight is experienced across a spectrum of states of mind, most occurred while in an awake state, some in a hypnagogic state, whilst others occurred in a dream state ... The phenomenology of second sight suggests that it is expressed as a form of eidetic-like imagery. In this regard, insights into the process of second sight may flow from a better understanding of the neurophysiological correlates of mental imagery derived from the application of sensitive non-invasive techniques for mapping brain activity ... Any theory of second sight must find a meeting point between the spiritual and genetic bases of mind."

There is a considerable literature on second sight. For a very useful bibliography see Cohn 2000, pp. 180–85 (note however that she confuses the Rev. Alexander MacGregor, author of MacGregor 1901, with his son Dr Alastair Macgregor, author of Macgregor 1897–99 and 1899–1901). She also offers an analysis and critique of JGC's presentation of second sight (Cohn 2000, pp. 162–64, 172).

835 See Waldron 1865, pp. 38–39, 110–11. JGC's 'shepherds of the Hebrid Isles' are a recollection of some lines from James Thomson's 'The Castle of Indolence' (1788, vol. 1, p. 197):

> *As when a shepherd of the Hebrid-Isles ...*
> *Sees on the naked hill, or valley low,*
> *The whilst in ocean Phœbus dips his wain,*
> *A vast assembly moving to and fro:*
> *Then all at once in air dissolves the wondrous show.*

836 According to 'Mac Lachainn agus a' Ghlaistig' ('MacLachlan and the Glastig', MacDougall and Calder 1910, pp. 250–53), the first of the MacLachlans of Ardnamurchan captured a glaistig who, from jealousy at his being an incomer, had murdered the offspring of his favourite grey mare three years in succession. As blood-price (*éirig*) for not putting her to death she promised him: *Sealladh an dà shaoghail dhuit féin, agus soirbheachadh dhuit féin agus do d' shliochd ad dhéidh.* "The vision of the two worlds to yourself, and prosperity to you and to your descendants after you." This 'vision' came to him in the same way in which it had come to Fin MacCoul (Campbell 1872, pp. 37–38). When fishing on the Spean he caught a salmon and cooked it. A blister (*bolgan*) arose on the fish and he thoughtlessly jabbed it. He then put his burnt finger in his mouth to cool it. *Cha bu luaithe a rinn e sin na fhuair e sealladh an dà shaoghail, no am briathraibh eile, an dara sealladh.* "No sooner had he done this than he obtained the vision of the two worlds, or, in other words, the second sight."

837 Kirk has much to say on doubles in 'The Secret Commonwealth' (Hunter 2001, p. 80). He begins by pointing out that second-sighted people often see otherworld beings at funeral banquets. "Some men of that exalted sight (whither by airt or nature) have told me they have seen at those meetings a double-man, or the shape of the same man in two places, that is, a Superterranean and a Subterranean Inhabitant perfectly resembling one another in all points, whom he notwithstanding could easily distinguish <one> from another by some <secret> tockens and operations, and so goe speake to the man his neighbour, and familiar, passing by the apparition or resemblance of him . . . They call this Reflex-man a *coimimechd* or Co-walker, every way like the man, as a Twin-brother and Companion, haunting him as his shadow and is oft seen and known among men (resembling the Originall) both befor and after the Originall is dead, and was els often seen of old to enter a house; by which the people knew that the person of that liknes was to visit them within a few dayes . . ."

One of the most circumstantial accounts of a double appears in a letter from George MacKenzie, Lord Tarbat, to Robert Boyle, seemingly written in 1699 (Hunter 2001, p. 168). Tarbat got it from the Rev. Daniel Morrison, Barvas, Lewis. "It was of a young woman in his parish, who wes mightilie frightened, by seeing her own Image still befor her alwayes when shee came unto the oppen air And the back of the Image being alwayes to her, So that it wes not a reflectione as in a mirrour But the species of such a body as her owne And in a very lyk habitte which appered to her self Continually befor here, The parsone keeped her a long tyme with him But had no remedie of her evill which troubled here exceedinglie I wes told afterwards that when shee wes 4 or 5 years older shee saw it not."

Discussing the *co-choisiche* or doppelgänger, MacInnes points out (1989, p. 20) that it is 'not so much a replica as an anarchic alternative personality'. Still more interesting are the personal experiences of the late Eilidh Watt, who wrote (1989, p. 32): "I believe that I have a co-walker, and am sometimes of the opinion that there may be more than one, each possibly with different functions." See also Dalyell 1834, p. 588.

838 Given JGC's description of the spot, his *Imire Tàchair* will almost certainly be for *Imire Tòchair* 'Causeway Ridge' – see Watson 1926a, p. 486, and RCAHMS 1982, pp. 35, 142; compare also Tauchers, a farm near Keith which gave its name to Glentauchers distillery and single malt. In its place however we may put *Carraig an Tàcharain* 'the Ghost's Rock' (in a stretch of shore called *Lag na Buidseachd*, 'the Hollow of Witchcraft'), half a mile north of Laggan Point in Lochindaal, Islay, and *Dail an Tàchrain* 'the Ghost's Meadow', between Conait and Ceannchnoc in Glen Lyon, of which Watson simply remarks (2002, p. 208): "Its story is unknown to me."

839 It thus becomes clear why JGC chooses to spell *tàcharan* and *tàchradh* without a lengthmark. His argument is not convincing. It is normal for a qualifying adjective, e.g. *grànda* in *an tàchradh grànda*, to attract stress and thus shorten any long syllable in the

noun. (*Tir-mór* 'mainland', from *tìr* 'land' and *mór* 'big', is an everyday example.) It seems that to express contempt *tàchradh* and *tàcharan* required a qualifying adjective, but to express pity they did not. Carmichael, who seldom marks vowel-length, has a good deal to say on *tàch(a)ran* in *CG2*, p. 367, and takes pains to show by means of a macron (*ā*) that the first syllable is long. It means 'a kelpie, a water-sprite, a dwarf', he says, and he cites *Clachan an Tàcharain* 'the Ford of the Kelpie' in Islay (*clachan*, 'stepping-stones') and *Poll an Tàcharain* 'the Pool of the Kelpie' in Perth – i.e. Perthshire? After quoting some verses in which *tàcharan* means roughly 'dwarf', 'pigmy' (in one of them it rhymes with *làidir*, demonstrating that the first syllable is long), he concludes: "'Tachran cuthaig', 'tachan cuthaig', the page of the cuckoo – generally the meadow-pipit. When the cuckoo sings, the pipit emits a hissing sound resembling 'tach! tach! tach!' This may have originated the name in this case."

For *tàcharan* 'changeling' see MacLeod 1952, pp. 180–81, and p. li above.

840 JGC has muddled his sources. The reference is not to Macpherson 1768 but to a much better work of the same period, Shaw 1775, pp. 307–08 (cf. Pinkerton 1809, p. 69, and Brand 1849, vol. 2, p. 73): "It was likewise believed . . . that Children dying unbaptized (called TARANS) wandered in woods and solitudes, lamenting their hard fate, and were often seen. It cannot be doubted, that many of these stories concerning Apparitions, Tarans, &c. came out of the Cloysters of Monks and Friars, or were the Invention of designing Priests, who deluded the World with their stories of *Purgatory* and *Limbus Infantum*."

It was of Macpherson 1768 that Boswell remarked, quite fairly in my opinion (Levi 1984, pp. 248–49), "After dinner I read some of Dr Macpherson's *Dissertations on the Ancient Caledonians*. I was disgusted by the unsatisfactory conjectures as to antiquity, before the days of record. I was happy when tea came."

The Rev. Dr John Macpherson (1713–65) was minister of Sleat from 1742 to his death; there is no mention of *taran* in his book, but there is one at p. 341 to '*Taranis* of the ancient Gauls'. See also McPherson 1929, pp. 113–14, and O'Connor 1991, p. 43. *Tàradh* (for which see pp. 251–52) is given by Brownlie (1995, p. 142) in the meaning 'premonitory noise, usually heard at night'.

841 Robertson showed phonologically that *tannasg* and *tamhasg* will be the same word (1908–09, p. 82), and Henderson saw *tàsg* as an abbreviation of *tannasg*, perhaps by confusion with Irish *tásc* 'report' etc. (1911, pp. 48, 184). See also Robertson 1899–1901, p. 365. For *taghairm* see pp. 167–70.

842 JGC takes 'swarths' from Brand (1849, vol. 3, p. 228).

843 See 'Strong and Undue Wishes', pp. 250–51.

844 Literally 'sees sights'. The poet referred to in the previous paragraph is Tennyson, and the quotations are from part 2 of 'Maud', published in 1855:

> *Plagued with a flitting to and fro,*
> *A disease, a hard mechanic ghost*
> *That never came from on high*
> *Nor ever arose from below,*
> *But only moves with the moving eye,*
> *Flying along the land and the main —*
> *Why should it look like Maud?*
> *Am I to be overawed*
> *By what I cannot but know*
> *Is a juggle born of the brain?*

See Tennyson 1913, p. 303.

845 The putting of one foot upon another is almost universally described as the way in which Gaelic seers passed on the second sight. The placing of the hand on the shoulder, or even the head, is simply the natural accompaniment of that action (Dalyell 1834, pp. 469, 481; Mackenzie 1914, p. 288; Gregory 1970, pp. 246, 262; *Tocher* 39, p. 138; Hunter 2001, pp. 60, 144, 147, 191; Henderson and Cowan 2001, pp. 183–84). In one instance the neophyte stands on *both* the seer's feet (Mackenzie 1914, p. 272), in another the vision is transmitted by putting the hand on the seer's left shoulder and looking over his right shoulder (*Tocher* 6, pp. 192–93). MacInnes points out that the essential element is simple touching (1989, p. 15): "When the contact is broken, participation in the vision ceases immediately. A more elaborate device requires the would-be participant to hold the seer's hand while placing a foot on his foot and looking over his shoulder. There are variants of this stance but in most of the descriptions the left hand or foot or shoulder is involved. In that sense alone, it is a 'sinister' ritual. In some instances this ritual confers only a temporary power, more or less brief; in other instances the faculty remains, although apparently only for the lifetime of the initiated person."

Wentz gives examples (1911, pp. 153, 215) of how a vision was communicated in Wales (by the putting of one foot upon another) and Brittany (by simple touching), but perhaps one of the most interesting recent cases comes from Gaelic Scotland. It was related to John MacInnes (1994–96, pp. 5, 19) by the Rev. Donald MacLeod (1872–1955), a United Free Church minister from Torrin in Skye. As children, he, his sister and another little boy all experienced the same vision of Fairies dancing in a ring around a fire. "They were accompanied by a certain Miss or Mrs MacAllister, who was reported to have Second Sight. This woman held the children by the hand and it was then they saw the fairies."

846 See p. 246.

847 'Some thirty years ago' will mean *c.* 1844. As JGC himself reveals in the last verse of 'Òran a' Ghunna' (p. 646 below), the *Bigein* lived in Earnal, which is west of Gott common grazing and is 'the most sterile piece of ground in Tiree' (Brownlie 1995, p. 26). His real name is not known. See also Introduction, p. xl.

848 Compare how the Fairies would increase the weight of a deer being carried off the hill until a knife was stuck into it, pp. 15, 24, 70–71. 'Three years ago' will mean *c.* 1871.

849 According to the 1841 census, an Archibald (not Alexander) Sinclair, 45, agricultural labourer, was living at Fiunary in that year, apparently with his wife Ann, 35, and six children aged 12 to 1 (MacLeod 2002, p. 247). The marriage must have taken place *c.* 1828. Perhaps Archibald was related to John Sinclair, the Tobermory merchant who had bought Fiunary and Savary in 1821 (Gaskell 1968, p. 30) and was described in 1844 as 'a clever clear headed old fellow, but damned sharp in his dealings with his poor Tenants' (Loudon 2001, p. 77). Savory lies a mile to the east of Fiunary, Salachan a mile to the west.

850 Loch Frisa, four miles long, is in the interior of north Mull. Ledmore (properly *an Leathad Mòr* 'the Big Slope') is at its foot. The stream appears to have been one of two which rise on *Guala Sp(e)inne* 'the Shoulder of Sp(e)inne' between the twin summits of Speinne Mòr and Speinne Beag to the north. The meaning of Speinne is unknown; 'Spine' and 'Hawthorn' have been suggested (see MacQuarrie 1983, p. 34, and Maclean 1997, pp. 58, 159). James Robertson, sheriff substitute at Tobermory 1842–46, spelt it Sbinne in his diary (Loudon 2001, pp. 54, 113).

851 For Corrie-Vulin (Corryvulin) see p. 28 above. Ben Shianta (Hiant) rears its bulk halfway between Kilchoan and Glenbeg, which lies three miles east of the mountain on the shore of Loch Sunart. The MacLeans' Nose (or Point), the southern flank of Ben Shianta, guards the entrance to the loch.

852 For sprinkling with urine see note 683 above.

853 Niall M. Brownlie has pointed out to me that there was a noted seer, poet and piper

in Kilmoluag called *Dòmhnall mac Iain Òig* ('Donald the son of Young John', Donald MacDonald, *c*.1773–1835). He died in Barra. He is described in Sinclair 1881, pp. 241–44, MacDonald 1900, pp. 45–46, and Cameron 1932, p. 28. Has JGC muddled his patronymic, or is *Mac Dhòmhnaill Òig* ('the Son of Young Donald') a different person?

854 See 'The Battle of Trai-Gruinard', pp. 53–54 above.

855 I have been unable to identify *Fionnaghal a' Mhòir*. As my Harris friends have pointed out, the name is more likely to represent *Fionnaghal 'Ain Mhòir* 'Flora, daughter of Big John', cf. note 861 below. On the other hand there is little doubt, I think, but that adjectives like *mòr*, *dubh* and *gorm* could serve as names, perhaps especially in Argyll, e.g. Carmichael tells of a Baron of Bachuill in Lismore called *An Gorm Mòr* which he translates 'the big blue' (1908–09, p. 373); cf. also the ballad 'Duan an Deirg'.

856 See Introduction, pp. xlvii and xlix.

857 *Brochan blàth* is 'warm porridge', really, although described as drunk rather than eaten.

858 Barr lies near the western shore of Loch Teacuis, looking across to Ben Iadain which dominates the loch on the other side.

859 Fladda-Chuain is north, not east, of Skye, see note 630. Commenting on the young man's sense of oppression on his chest, Niall M. Brownlie tells me (personal communication, 22 October 2003): "This is known in Gaelic as *trom-lighe*, 'a heavy load coming over a person when asleep'. I have personally experienced a *trom-lighe*." Indeed, the fact that the stress is on the second element shows that *trom-lighe* is literally 'lying weight', 'bedtime weight', 'weight experienced while lying down'. The history of the word is thus parallel to 'nightmare', the second element of which is Old English *mære*, 'a female spirit or monster supposed to beset people or animals by night, settling upon them when they are asleep and producing a feeling of suffocation by its weight' (*OED*): not then a horse but a succubus (see note 585); popular tradition, however, allows it to be both, see Davies 2003 and Oates 2003.

860 No, this will be *falbh air fàrsan* 'going on a journey', see Black 2002, p. 304. JGC was in good company here: Fr Allan McDonald had difficulty with the word too (Black 2002, p. 46).

861 As Professor Donald Meek has pointed out to me, *Mac an Duibh* is in error for *mac 'Ain Duibh* 'the son of Black John' (cf. notes 548, 855), and Donald was not a Black but a MacDonald. The patronymic of his great-grandson Malcolm, who served in the Peninsular War as a surgeon's valet and thus enjoyed the nickname *an Lannsair* ('the Lancer'), is given by Cregeen (1998, p. 24) as *Calum mac Iain 'ic Nèill 'ic Dhòmhnaill 'ic Iain Duibh*, 'Malcolm son of John son of Neil son of Donald son of Black John'. It is clear from this that Donald flourished *c*. 1700. The family were well known in Caolas as seers and were spoken of as *na Duibh* (pronounced na *Duich*), 'Black Ones', which would of course explain JGC's 'Donald Black'. Genuine Blacks are descended from an ancestor called *an Gille Dubh*; informally in Tiree (where they are descended from a minor estate official who came from Lismore *c*. 1800, see Cregeen 1998, pp. 24, 27, 33) they are *Blackaich*, formally *Clann Mhic Ghille Dhuibh* or *Clann MhicilleDhuibh*.

  Cruidh (not *Crudh*) *an Eich* is a well-known bend in the B8069 road west of Caolas, close to Salum and Ruaig. *Am Bail' Uachdrach*, Upper Caolas, is the central part of Caolas (around Croish) as opposed to *Am Bail' Ìochdrach*, Lower Caolas, on the shore to the south.

  Presumably *Cachlaidh na Cùil Connaidh* was the entrance to Caolas from the west. If so, it is now long gone. Professor Meek recalls other *cachlaidhean* however: *Cachlaidh Ruaig* 'the Ruaig Gateway', *Cachlaidh a' Chaolais* 'the Caolas Gateway', *Cachlaidh an t-Sléibhe* 'the Gateway to the Outrun'. (In Tiree *sliabh* is the outrun as distinct from the *monadh* or hill ground.)

862 'Some sixty years ago' will mean *c*. 1814. On the problems of fuel supply at that time see note 246 above.

863 'Visitors to a coffin' might be a more helpful translation. This is not the common verbal noun *tathaich* 'frequenting' but the plural of *tathach* 'guest, visitor, stranger'.

864 JGC's 'fifty years ago', both here and at p. 255, will mean *c.* 1824. 'A few years ago' at p. 255 will mean *c.* 1870.

865 'Some forty or fifty years ago' will mean 1824–34. Liaran (Learan, Leiran) is halfway along the north side of Loch Rannoch. The name is perhaps *Leathoirean* 'Twin Slopes', see Dwelly 1977, s.v. *leth-oir*. The story is retold in Cunningham 1989, p. 129. For Appin of Menzies see note 867.

866 I do not know what village is meant. JGC's information about Largs ('The Lowland Fairies', pp. 40–41) appears to have been gathered in 1859, although of course he may have holidayed there again in later years. It is more likely that he got the story from his Ayrshire brother-in-law James Wallace, who was part of the family from 1873 to 1876, precisely the period in which *The Gaelic Otherworld* was written (see pp. 643–44, 650). Wallace was from Irvine – emphatically not a village but a Royal Burgh, the port which provided much of the coal which had become the life's blood of Tiree, see note 246.

867 'Some thirty years ago' will mean *c.* 1844. See also 'Spirits Seen before Death', p. 265. The Argyll Appin is traditionally known as *Apainn Mhic Iain Stiùbhairt* ('the Appin of John Stewart's Son') or *Apainn nan Stiùbhartach* ('the Appin of the Stewarts') to distinguish it from the Perthshire one just mentioned, *Apainn nam Mèinnearach* ('the Appin of the Menzieses'). *Apainn* is in origin *apd(h)aine* 'abbacy, abbey land'. The Perthshire *apdaine* belonged to the abbey of Dull, the Argyll one presumably to Moluag's community in Lismore (Watson 1926a, p. 124). Lismore and Appin formed a single post-Reformation parish. See note 949.

868 It is not possible to know to whom this refers. Archibald MacDonald did not come to Heylipol till 1877, John MacRury till 1879 (see p. 647). With regard to the dancing referred to in the previous paragraph see Newton 2004. Dancing was once a normal part of funerals not only in the Highlands (see Bennett 1992, pp. 237–38, and Simmons 1998, p. 244) but throughout Europe (Ó Súilleabháin 1967, pp. 29–31, 155, 160, 172).

869 This will be the Rev. John Stewart (1757–1837), a Perthshire man who was minister of Lismore from 1802 to 1837. He is described on his tombstone as 'a primitive, kind, honest man' (Scott 1915–50, vol. 4, p. 99). For the custom of drinking at funerals see pp. 610–11 below.

870 JGC's own church was at Kirkapol (Norse *kirkja* 'church' and *ból* 'township'), overlooking Gott Bay; his 'about forty years ago' will mean *c.* 1834.

871 See p. 253. For the expression 'in the smallpox' see p. xii and note 228.

872 Sorisdal is at the eastern tip of Coll. *Bogan uisge* is a puddle of water, cf. p. 168.

873 Gortendonald, *Goirtean Dòmhnaill* ('Donald's Field') is the Gaelic name for Barrapol (Norse *bara* 'burial-ground', *ból* 'town') in the south-western part of Tiree. Vaul is in Gaelic *Bhalla*, from Norse *fjall* 'hill'. 'Gott Loch', *Loch Ghot*, is Gott Bay. See p. 262.

874 JGC's explanation of the name is confused, but there is no reason to believe that the fault is his. Although a 'sharp edge' is *rinn*, he correctly gives the Gaelic as *an Roinn Ìleach* 'the Islay Division'. As Watson says (1926a, p. 496), 'the Rinns formed one of the three divisions of Islay'. Being a by-form of *rann*, which now means a verse of poetry, *Roinn* becomes *Ranna* in the genitive, e.g. *MacAoidh na Ranna* 'MacKay of the Rinns'. Likewise, a Rinns-man is *Rannach*. The misleading English form 'R(h)inns' is presumably modelled on the R(h)inns of Galloway, whose Gaelic name *na Reanna*, plural of *rinn* 'a point, a sharp edge', brings us back to JGC's explanation (Watson 1926a, p. 165). Sailing clockwise, the principal 'sharp edges' of the R(h)inns of Galloway are Killiness Point, the Mull of Galloway and Laggantalluch Head in the south, and Corsewall Point and Milleur Point in the north, but there are many others in between.

875   See MacDhùghaill 1929–30, p. 106; MacInnes 1989, p. 14; Watt 1989, p. 34; Ballard 1997, p. 65.

876   For other stories of this kind see p. 268 and Watt 1989, pp. 34–35.

877   See p. 260 above. I have emended 'Lights' (*WSS* 165) to 'Sights' on the basis that (a) at p. 260 JGC refers twice in this context to 'sights' and (b) his 'S' could be misread as 'L'. When this happened in his lifetime (Campbell 1881a, p. 62) he had a correction printed (Campbell 1881c, p. 140): "In the first number of the *Review*, there is a misprint of Lamhanaich for *Samhanaich*, the giants who dwelt in caves by the sea."

 A similar tale concerning a boat owned by A. MacDonald, Balevullin, is told by Lord Archibald Campbell (1885a, pp. 252–53). Strangers appear and disappear around it and noises are heard. It is put on the market and bought by Neil MacDonald, Balemartin, for his sons. The strange occurrences continue, and they go back to Balevullin to have the deal made void. This is refused, and the unfortunate owners consult the Tobermory lawyer William Sproat (cf. 'Life of John Gregorson Campbell', p. 622 below), who says that their fears are superstitious. Unconvinced, they abandon it for a while, then use it for fishing in harvest. "This last harvest they launched her again; and while fishing for lobsters with two men in it, the purchaser's son being one, the boat got on a rock at Hynish, capsized, and MacDonald's son was drowned."

878   The Gaelic words are here printed exactly as in *WSS* 166. Probably they should read *tàsg*, *éigheach tamhaisg* and *éigheach tàisg*. Trabay Beach in Tiree, mentioned in the next paragraph, is *Tràigh a' Bhàigh* 'the Beach of the Bay', 'Baugh Beach', on the south shore.

879   See also pp. 258 and 291 ('*Bòcain*, Goblins'). The mill-dam in Tiree, mentioned in the next paragraph, was at Balevullin (*Baile a' Mhuilinn* 'the Township of the Mill').

880   'Thirty years ago' will mean *c.* 1844. Loch Corry is *Loch a' Choire*, the *Geàrrloch* ('Short Loch') of *Ceann Gheàrrloch*, Kingairloch. It is a broad inlet of Loch Linnhe, see p. 615.

881   The Skerryvore is eleven miles from the western end of Tiree; the lighthouse was completed in 1844. The tragedy was described in *The Oban Times*, 23 July 1870: "MASTER DROWNED.— The Dunvegan Castle (ss), Captain Macewen, arrived from the North and West Highlands at Glasgow on Wednesday evening. Captain Macewen reports that the schooner Favourite was wrecked last Monday night off the island of Tiree, when the captain was drowned. The schooner was bound for Peterhead with salt.—Mail." The same newspaper reported on 5 November: "REWARD FOR SAVING LIFE.—The Royal National Lifeboat Institution have, through Mr Maccallum, writer, Tobermory, honorary agent to the Shipwrecked Fishermen and Mariners' Royal Benevolent Society, paid Mr Alexander Sinclair, Balefuil, Tiree, and five others, the sum of £1 sterling each, as a grant or reward by the Institution in consideration of their praiseworthy services in putting off in a boat and saving the lives of four persons from the schooner Favorite, of Douglas, which was, during thick and showery weather, wrecked off Balefuil on the west coast of the island of Tiree on 19th July last."

882   Under the heading 'DROWNED', the *Oban Times* correspondent in Coll reported on 30 April 1870: "Two East-coast fishermen are supposed to have been drowned during the storm of last week on this coast. They left Cornaig Bay on Monday in a small sailing fishing boat, with the intention of procuring bait for the deep-sea fishing carried on regularly by five others of their party. Not returning on Wednesday, as was expected, a boat was despatched to Tyree on Friday in search of them, but had to return again without obtaining any information regarding them. Search was also made along the coast of this island, but up to Monday of this week, no trace was found of the missing boat and men. It is now presumed they must have perished in the gale of last week. Both men, one old and the other young, were most respectable."

883   A good joke, but JGC has used it already (p. 235). On spectral lights, etc., see for example Mackenzie 1914, pp. 288–89, and Campbell and Hall 1968, pp. 250–301.

884 Druim a' Chaoin or Drumachine is a short distance north of what is now the Dunalastair
Water, east of Kinloch Rannoch, see Mackenzie 1877–78, pp. 71–73; Black 1994–96, p. 352;
Rankin 1998, p. 121; Rankin 1999.

885 This is in Upper Lorn, between Loch Feochan and Loch Awe. The river in question is the
Allt Braglenmore. Brae-Glen or Braglen is not *Bràighe Ghlinne* ('the Brae of the Glen') but
Bràigh-Ghleann, Bràighleann ('the Glen of the Brae'), and the river is *Allt a' Bhràighlinne
Mhòir*, see Campbell 1885a, pp. 193, 196, 199, and Gillies 1906, p. 58.

886 *Teine sìth* is literally 'Fairy fire'; in Uist the term is *teine mór* 'big fire' or *teine biorach*
'pointed fire' (McDonald 1958, p. 240). In a Benbecula version of the story (MacRury
1893–94b, pp. 161–62) the girl is stated to have been careful to go out *air oidhche Luain-
Domhnaich, is e sin ri ràdh, an deigh dà uair dheug oidhche Dhomhnaich*: 'on Sunday-
Monday night, that is to say, after twelve o'clock on Sunday night'. See also GUL MS Gen.
1090/29, p. 66, and Freer 1902, p. 43.

887 Of *Taibhse Choimhlig* (see pp. 287–88) MacDiarmid says (1904–07, p. 52): *Sgioblaich i a
cleoc gu taobh, oir bha shamhuil sin de rud oirre. Ciod chunnaic am figheadair ach mar
gu 'm biodh broilleach an Taibhse 'na chaoir dhearg theine, no mar gu 'm biodh lanndair
laiste a dearsadh 'na com.* "It drew aside its cloak, for it was wearing some such thing. What
did the weaver see but that the Ghost's chest appeared to be glowing red with fire, or as if it
had a lighted lantern shining in its body."

888 That is to say, she would not go in for the world. For the story see 'Noise of Glasses to be
Used at Funerals', p. 256.

889 See 'Pearlwort (*Mòthan*)', pp. 229–30, and Henderson 1911, p. 219.

890 There were MacCannels in Tiree (Caolas) and Coll (Breacachadh) in 1716 (Maclean-Bristol
1998, pp. 113, 164). A tailor called Archibald McDonald is listed in a Tiree census of 1776;
he is given again amongst the cottars of Kilkennethmore as 'Archibald McCannol taylor' in
1779 (Cregeen 1963, pp. 30, 131). There were many McConnels among the tenants of Caolas
in 1779, and this will be the same name (*ibid.*, pp. 48–49). It is unknown in the island
today, having presumably given way to MacDonald. Not all Tiree MacDonalds will be
MacCannels, however. I do not know whether it is the name behind *Eilean Mhic Conaill*,
a fortified crannog referred to by MacDougall and Cameron (n.d., p. 80) as 'the island of
MacConall on Loch Bhasapol'.

  Although as MacCannel, Cannel, MacConnell or Connell the name seems to have
been widespread in the Argyll islands, Kintyre and Man, the Argyll Estate census of 1779
reveals no instances of it outside Tiree (Cregeen 1963, p. 131). It seems in many cases to
derive from *Mac Gille Chonaill*, which has been shown to have become 'MacWhannell' in
Perthshire and other mainland areas; Mac Gille Chonaill was boat-builder to the earls of
Argyll (McWhannell 1997 and 1999). The issue is complex, however. Many Islay and Jura
MacCannels are on record in spellings of the type Macilchonil, but it is hard to reconcile
this with the pronunciation *mac cainneil* or *mac aineoil* which is, or was, common in those
islands (Youngson n.d., p. 64, cf. *Tocher* 25, p. 49), and probably more than one eponym is
involved. I am grateful to Dr Donald McWhannell, Dundee, for extended discussion of this
mystifying name over a number of years.

891 See also 'Funerals', p. 132, and 'The Watch of the Graveyard (*Faire Chlaidh*)', pp. 132–33.

892 Or, more strictly, *eagal a chur orm*.

893 This shows (once again) JGC's poor grasp of the relationship between gender and
declension: *an t-armachd* should be *an armachd*.

894 See p. 127. For a tale about a minister who is transported to the otherworld after kicking a
skull see Maclean 1957. The sinister consequences of kicking and breaking a skull form the
central motif of John MacRury's superbly-constructed ghost-story 'Taillear Ghearraidh-
bo-Stig' (1893–94a).

895 *Ìle*, pronounced **eela**, is the Gaelic for Islay. Watson (1926a, p. 87) tentatively suggests a derivation from some protruding part of the body, e.g. flanks or buttocks, and compares Welsh *ilio* 'ferment' from a root meaning 'swell'. R. C. Maclagan received a version of the tale from Issabel MacCalman, Conispie, Islay (SoSS Maclagan MSS vol. 22, pp. 3828–29). It appears designed to explain one pair of stones in the bed of Loch Leodantais (the harbour at Port Ellen) and another on the shore nearby. *Is iomadh uair a chaidh mi seachad air uaimh Ile. So an doigh a tha iad ag innseadh san d'fhuair i a bais. Bha i air bord soitheach ann an Loch Leodantais, agus air dhi saoilsinn gu'n rachadh aice air an tir a ruigheachd, leum i amach as an soitheach agus bhathadh i. Chaidh a casan an sàs 'sa ghruinnd co domhainn, is Co daingeann 's nach b'urrainn iad a bhi air an tarruing as; agus b'fheudar a casan a shabhadh bho na gluinean: agus dh'fhag iad a casan ann sin, agus thug iad leothe an còrr, agus dh'adhlaiceadh i anns an uaimh so. Bha i co mhor 's nach robh uaimh eile air fhaicinn a riomh a bha co fada rithe.* Maclagan (or his informant) translates: "Many a time I passed Ile's grave. This is the way in which they say she came by her death. She was on board a vessel in Loch Leodantais, and thinking she could reach the land, she jumped out of the vessel and was drowned. Her feet stuck in the bottom so deep, and so firmly, that they could not be drawn out; and it was necessary to saw her feet off by the knees, and they left her feet there, and took what remained along with them, and she was buried in this grave. It was so large that there never was another grave seen so long as it."

896 The 'Burial-Place of the Big Women' is presumably *Cladh nam Ban Mòra*. It probably refers to nuns – 'great women' rather than 'big women'? Niall M. Brownlie has not heard the name, but tells me that he thinks it may be identified with the *Cladh Beag*, of which Sands says (1881–82, p. 463): "At Hynish there is a meadow still called the *Cladh beag*, or little burial-ground, where a chapel once stood; but the last farmer was a practical man, and used the church and tombstones to build stables and byres with. A stone with a cross on it is still to be seen forming part of the pavement at the farm-steading. On digging I discovered some of the mortar and stones of this ancient chapel." Convents usually had burial grounds of their own, which would naturally have been small. One wonders what connection there might be, if any, between this faint echo of monastic life in Hynish and the following rhyme relating to two other townships in south-western Tiree (Grant 1925, p. 12):

> *Mìosachan beag rìgh Lochlainn*
> *Fo chlachan ann am Baile Phuill*
> *Is Ulabhag nighean rìgh Lochlainn*
> *Fo chlachan an Crosapol ud thall.*

("The little calendar of the king of Norway / Underneath stones in Balephuil / And Ulabhag daughter of the king of Norway / Underneath stones in Crossapol yonder.") See also Beveridge 1903, p. 155; MacDougall and Cameron n.d., pp. 99, 109; RCAHMS 1980, pp. 135–36; Brownlie 1995, pp. 90–91.

897 *Tràigh Feall*, the north-facing Beach of Fell, is in Feall Bay on the western tip of Coll. The *Sruth Bàn* flows through it from the dunes which fill the entire neck of land between it and Crossapol Bay to the south. *Tràigh Feall* is locally the North Beach, *Tràigh Chrosapuil* the South Beach.

898 The Gaelic original was excluded from *WSS*, but fortunately it was transcribed from JGC's lost appendix by Alexander Carmichael into EUL MS CW 241, f. 54, and by George Henderson into GUL MS Gen. 1090/77, f. [4], see pp. 701–04 below. *Maidean* 'bearers' is literally 'sticks, staves'; *bualadh mo bhas* is 'striking my palms' (even till the blood flows), clapping in those days being a demonstration of grief, not of approval. The spelling *martun* (written *mart-un* by both Carmichael and Henderson) is characteristic of JGC, see p. xiv.

Ann ad' asgaill is 'in your oxter', indicating a child older than is suggested by JGC's 'in your bosom'. The last line is given by Carmichael as *Gheobh thu marbh e n calp do leapach*, and by Henderson (who liked to tidy up spelling and grammar while transcribing) as *Gheibh thu marbh air calp do leapach*. The *calp(a)* of the bed, as of the leg, will be its broad part – its middle, not its side, cf. *CG5*, pp. 54–55. The Rev. John MacRury knew two versions of the song (1889–90, pp. 105–07), one of which corresponds more or less to JGC's first ten lines.

> *Piuth'rag nam piuth'r, bheil thu d' chadal?*
> *Ill-i-rinn is hò-rò, ill-i-rinn is hò-rò,*
> *'M bràthair a bha 'n Éirinn againn,*
> *Hi-ibh-òho-hi, na-hi ùraibh ò-ro-hi.*

> *'M bràthair a bha 'n Éirinn againn,*
> *Hi-ibh-òho-hi, na-hi ùraibh ò-ro-hi,*
> *Bha e 'n-dé ac' air na maidean,*
> *Hi-ibh-òho-hi, na-hi ùraibh ò-ro-hi.*

> *Bha e 'n-dé ac' air na maidean,*
> *Ill-i-rinn is hò-rò, ill-i-rinn is hò-rò,*
> *Bha mis' ann 's cha robh fios ac' air,*
> *Hi-ibh-òho-hi, na-hi ùraibh ò-ro-hi.*

> *Bha mis' ann 's cha robh fios ac' air,*
> *Ill-i-rinn is hò-rò, ill-i-rinn is hò-rò,*
> *Greis air làr is greis air each dhiom,*
> *Hi-ibh-òho-hi, na-hi ùraibh ò-ro-hi.*

> *Greis air làr is greis air each dhiom,*
> *Ill-i-rinn is hò-rò, ill-i-rinn is hò-rò,*
> *Greis eil' anns an t-sròl am pasgadh,*
> *Hi-ibh-òho-hi, na-hi ùraibh ò-ro-hi.*

Frances Tolmie published the air (1911, p. 177), along with a few words of MacRury's original and this translation: "Little sister, dearest of sisters, art thou sleeping? The brother whom we had in Ireland they were bearing yesterday on staves. I was there unknown to them; now on the ground, then on horseback, and again for a while enfolded in silk." See also *CG5*, pp. 48–59, and GUL MS Gen. 1090/28, pp. 253–54. Tolmie calls it a lullaby, while Carmichael gives it as a waulking song.

899 I have been unable to trace this song. Presumably it begins *Fhir a dhùin a' chòmhl' orm* or the like. The 'door' is the coffin lid, the reference being to what the Rev. William Matheson once called 'the emotionally charged moment when friends took a last look at the deceased and the joiners stepped forward to nail down the boards that formed the coffin lid' (1983, p. 133). See pp. xxxvii above and 703 below.

900 *Bòcan* belongs to a complex group of 'spectre' words in western European languages which includes Irish *púca*, Welsh *bwg* 'ghost', *bwgan* 'scarer', *bwgwl* 'terror', Scots *bogle*, *tattie-bogle*, English *bogey*, *bogeyman*, *bugbear*, *bugaboo*, *puck*, *spook*, *pooka*; playing golf against a ghostly 'Colonel Bogey' came to mean 'one over par', i.e. playing one stroke too many (*OED*; Williams 1997, pp. 460–62). The precise form of *bòcan* may have been influenced by *bòc* 'swell', but that is not to say that it is derived from it.

901 From Tacitus, 'Agricola', §30, the celebrated speech by the Caledonian leader Calgacus:

'everything unknown (is taken to be) magnificent', or as Mattingly and Handford have it (1970, p. 80): "Now, the farthest bounds of Britain lie open to our enemies; and what men know nothing about they always assume to be a valuable prize. But there are no more nations beyond us; nothing is there but waves and rocks . . ."

902 *Beul àth na h-aibhne* is literally 'the ford of the river'.

903 In EUL MS CW 58A, f. 8rv, Fr Allan McDonald noted the following, got from a person named MacLeod in Eriskay in 1887: "The sea is considered much more blessed than the land. A man will stay all night alone in a boat a few yards from the shore without fear, yet he would not stay an hour in the darkness alone on the shore so near him. The boats of course are always blessed, and holy water is kept in each boat as a rule. On one occasion going to Eriskay after nightfall I was made aware of this idea of the sea's blessedness. I asked the man who came for me what place on shore would his companion be in, who was awaiting us. 'He won't be on the shore at all, by the book. He will be in the boat itself. The sea is holier to live on than the shore.' "

904 *Piuthar mo sheanamhair* is properly *piuthar mo sheanamhar*.

905 This passage is cited by Frazer (1911a, p. 396) in the context of 'Common Words Tabooed'.

906 Compare Dwelly's *coingheall* 'dog's collar' (1977, p. 227), attributed to J. G. Mackay, London. I assume that both *conghal* and *coingheall* are spellings of *coin-iall* 'dog-thong, dog-leash'. For an example of the different behaviour of dogs and bitches in the presence of an evil spirit see p. 288 ('Kingairloch, Argyleshire'). We may relate this tradition to one about a newly-married piper who fought with a demon, and whose wife joined in on the demon's side. The piper had no choice but to flee, leaving his wife with the monster; after a few days she returned to him, but her first child was born with a tail, and 'it is said that descendants of his live still not a hundred miles from Bonar-Bridge' (Macbain 1887–88, p. 267, cf. Sutherland 1937, pp. 91–92).

907 By an entire horse JGC means an ungelded stallion, see also pp. 161 and 178.

908 *Dùthaich Mhic Aoidh* is literally 'MacKay's Country'; Lord Reay was chief of the MacKays. The seven parishes of north and west Sutherland are, in sunwise order, Durness, Tongue, Farr, Lairg, Creich, Assynt and Eddrachillis. The expression 'living wight' is found in canto 1 of Scott's 'Lady of the Lake'. I suspect from the context that *Corra-lòigein* should be *Corra-léigein*, perhaps misheard or miswritten by JGC and not therefore understood when he returned to his field-notes. This would be 'a marsh crane', 'a drain crane', invented to keep children away from such places as the *Léig* in Kilmoluag, Tiree. Carmichael spells it *Corra-Liogan*: "Corra-Liogan," he says (EUL MS CW 503, f. 196r), "is an odious ogre standing motionless upon one leg like the corra-ghritheach keeping men and women and children from intruding upon its forbidden ground." For the use of *corr* as 'bogle' cf. Dwelly's *corracha-margaidh* 'market herons, birds or people, who haunt markets or places where they are likely to pick up something or find employment' (1977, p. 254) and Fr Allan's 'other night bogles were the *Corra-chagailtean* which equal in meaning the sulphurous green flames seen in embers' (McDonald 1958, p. 81).

909 *Lemures* is Latin for 'ghosts'. *Mac Glùmag na Mias* is mentioned in passing in a tale which JGC subsequently noted from John Brown, Kilmoluag, and others (Campbell 1890–91, p. 61). In a footnote he says (*ibid.*, p. 66): "The 'Son of Platter-Pool' is well known in the Island of Tiree as a hobgoblin or bugbear to frighten children when they make too much noise. He is said to be at the window, ready to come in and take them away. His full genealogy is, the Son of Platterpool, from Greyworm, Son of Silkworm, son of Caterpillar (Mac Glumag na Mias, o Liath-Dhurrag, 'o Dhurrag-Shiodhe, o Bhurrach-Mor)."

It looks from this as if *tarrang* 'spike' in *WSS* 187 is in error for *durrag* 'worm', the error being compounded by the fact that (as is clear from the translation 'grey spike, silken spike') *tarrang* was only printed once instead of twice (*liath tarrang, tarrang shìoda*). A *glumag* is a deep pool in running water, such as in the name of Scotland's highest waterfall, *Eas Glumaig* (the Falls of Glomach); *mias* is a dish, plate, or, as JGC has it, platter. Alexander Carmichael noted the genealogy as follows (EUL MS CW 495, f. 232r):

> *Glùmag nic Ghlumaig*
> *Bho Vic ic Ghlumaig*
> *Bho nic 'ic ic Ghlumaig*
> *Bho ghlun nam burrach mor.*

He translates: "Glùmag daughter of Glumag / From the daughter of the daughter of Glumag / From the daughter of the daughter / Of the daughter of Glumag / From the generation of the great caterpillar." He adds (*ibid.*, f. 233r): "This was composed when descent was counted from the mother and not from the father. There was much more of this and of a much more complex complicate [*sic*] character."

910 JGC tells us (Campbell 1891, p. 132) that he got the ballad as a whole from the dictation of Duncan Cameron, constable, Tiree, in 1871, but the letters 'M. S.' suggest that he also had these particular verses from Malcolm Sinclair, for whom see note 217 above. They are unlikely to stand for 'manuscript'. JFC provides five different versions of the two verses in Campbell 1872, pp. 68–71 and 80; see also Campbell 1890, vol. 3, pp. 136–60, 362.

911 JGC appears to mean that the Muireartach's name is derived from words meaning 'Western Sea', 'Westlin Sea'. By the time *The Fians* was published he had changed his mind (Campbell 1891, p. 131): "There is no difficulty in deriving it from Muireartach, the Eastern Sea." He must have been thinking of the elements *muir* 'sea', *iar* 'west' and *ear* 'east'. He was wrong both times, but where he describes the Muileartach as a personification of the sea (*ibid.*, p. 132) he is on surer ground. Commenting on this, Dr John MacInnes says (1987, p. 117): "Donald Sinclair, son of one of Campbell's informants, told me that his father, Calum Bàn, a fisherman, would glance out when the sea looked threatening and remark, *Tha droch coltas air a' Mhuilgheartaich an diugh*, 'The Muilgheartach has a bad appearance today.' This raises the interesting question: is the idea of the ocean personified a concept of native Gaelic tradition? Or did the learned minister of Tiree impart it to Calum Bàn?"

I would merely say by way of answer that the late Rev. Kenneth Macleod (1871–1955) had the same idea (Murchison 1988, p. 8): *Theagamh nach eileas fada clì san amharas gum b'i a' Mhuileartach an Cuan Siar fèin anns an fheòil.* "Perhaps one would not be far wrong in supposing that the Muileartach was the Atlantic Ocean in the flesh."

MacInnes points out that the Irish king Muircheartach, who was killed in 943 fighting against the Norsemen, had the nickname *na gcochull gcraiceann* 'of the skin coverings', and that this appellation is also given to characters of romance and folklore (cf. Bruford 1969, p. 124). This seems to have allowed his name to become contaminated by Norse traditions of the *margýgr* 'sea-ogress', who was of tremendous size, with webbed feet and thick heavy hair which fell all around her head and neck, and was seen before great storms on the Greenland coast. In the waulking-song 'An Spaidearachd Bharrach' the phrase *A Mhuilgheartach nan cochull craicinn* is used abusively, as MacInnes points out, and taken by singers to refer to the *Muilgheartach* of the ballad (Campbell 1969–81, vol. 2, pp. 128–29, 237). For the Muileartach as a man's nickname (a merchant in Leith!) see Mackechnie 1964, pp. 162, 170, 185–86. See also Campbell 1890, vol. 4, p. 42; Grant 1925, pp. 13–14; MacDonald 1994–95, p. 57; Gillies 2000, pp. 20, 57, 58; Black 2001, pp. 306–07.

Greann is a highly suitable word for use with a personification of the sea. It means simultaneously 'bristling of the hair, as on an enraged dog', 'ripple on the surface of water', 'uncombed hair', 'head having the hair standing on end', and 'a rippled, scowling aspect' as in *tha greann air an fhairge* 'there's a *greann* upon the sea' (Dwelly 1977, p. 523). But generally

Commentary

speaking the *Muireartach* appears to have lost her maritime attributes and to have become indistinguishable from the *Cailleach*, for whom see pp. 15, 66, 133–34, 279–80, 544.

For *mhaol* JGC almost certainly wrote not 'bold' but 'bald' (since that is what the word means), but as he also chose to describe the spectre as 'white-maned' with 'dark-grey hair', I have decided to leave well alone. When he republished the verses in Campbell 1891, p. 152, he treated *mhaol, ruadh* as a compound ('bald-red') and dispensed with 'hair' (*ibid.*, pp. 142–43): "The name of the dauntless spectre / Was the bald-red, white-maned *Muileartach*. / Her face was dark grey, of the hue of coals, / The teeth of her jaw were slanting red, / There was one flabby eye in her head, / That quicker moved than lure-pursuing mackerel. / Her head bristled dark and grey, / Like scrubwood before hoar frost."

912 JGC appears to mean that there is no reference to water in the name of the moor. The passage of which he is so critical is in Campbell 1860–62, vol. 2, p. 191 = 1890, vol. 2, p. 205: "From all these it appears that the Fuath in Sutherland is a water spirit; that there are males and females; that they have web-feet, yellow hair, green dresses, tails, manes, and no noses; that they marry men, and are killed by light, and hurt with steel weapons; that in crossing a stream they become restless. From the following stories it appears that they are hairy, have bare skin on their faces, and have two large round eyes." See Introduction, p. xx.

913 Cf. pp. 56, 63, 64, 76, 77. The motif of the dog returning from its encounter with the supernatural without any hair on its body also occurs in the widespread legend of 'Uamh an Òir' ('The Cave of Gold'), see for example Robertson 1904–07, pp. 289–90; Carmichael 1908–09, p. 357; Mackenzie 1914, pp. 272–73; Grant 1925, p. 1; Mac a Phì 1938, p. 41; MacDougall and Cameron n.d., p. 54; MacPherson 1960, p. 191; Buchan 1979, esp. p. 18; Bruford 1980; Bennett 1989, pp. 126–27; *Tocher* 47, pp. 280–84; MacDonald 1994–95, pp. 45–46, 59; Ballard 1997, p. 66. *Cachlaidh na Feusaig* was, I suspect, a mile south of Ballygrant at Cnoc na Cachlaidhe on the hill road to Port Ellen; there are standing stones nearby, just south of Knocklearoch Farm. Presumably the beard was the monster's distinguishing feature as it loomed out of the dark; indeed the word *feusag* may have had an otherworldly ring to it, as Duncan Ferguson (Portnahaven and Plockton) informs me that 'beard' in Islay Gaelic is not generally *feusag* at all but *ciabhag*.

For other examples of a haunted *cachlaidh* or *cachaileith* see p. 254 above and Robertson 1897–98b, p. 205. Where they marked the outer boundary of human settlement, such gates could have cosmic significance to the superstitious.

914 *Am Baile Grànda*, in the interior of Islay on the road from Bowmore to Port Askaig. The only fair cited by Marwick for Ballygrant was on the Tuesday after Bowmore in February, the Bowmore fair in question being 'on 12th February if Tuesday, if not, on Tuesday after' (1890, p. 68).

915 JGC points out in a footnote that North Morar is known as *Mòrair Mhic Shimidh* and South Morar as *Mòrair Mhic Dhùghaill*. These reflect suzerainty. *Mac Shimidh* is Fraser of Lovat, while *Mac Mhic Dhùghaill* is MacDonald of Morar, a cadet of the Clanranald family, see Fraser-Mackintosh 1888–89.

916 In *WSS* 191 the Gaelic words are *eòmach mòr chlach*. There is no such word as *eòmach*. Given JGC's definition 'large boulder stones', *eòmach* will be a misreading of *càrnach* 'stony ground, rocky place, cairn', giving *càrnach mòr chlach* 'a great welter of stones', and I have emended the text accordingly. See note 759.

917 For other modern traditions of headless beings see p. 41 above; Croker 1825–28, vol. 2, pp. 98–102; Mackenzie 1914, p. 290; McPherson 1929, p. 131; Gregory 1970, pp. 29, 234, 243; Ballard 1997, p. 66. Note also *Glac Gille Gun Cheann* 'the Hollow of the Headless Boy' on the north-eastern coast of Islay, presumably a memory of a corpse brought ashore by the sea. The medieval tradition is best represented by a poem in which Finn and his companions find themselves in a ghastly house occupied by a three-headed woman and a headless man

who has a single eye protruding from his breast, with nine bodies ranged along one side of the room and nine heads on the other (Stokes 1886, pp. 298–99).

> *Tócbait nói ngrécha garba,*
> *Nir chuibde ciar chomlabra;*
> *Frecraid in challech fósech*
> *Ocus frecraid in méidech.*

("They raise nine harsh shrieks, / Discordant though uttered together; / The hag replies separately / And the headless trunk answers.") With great difficulty, the Fianna fight their way out.

918 JGC's 'half a century ago' will mean *c.* 1824.
919 The ascription to Bruce is also given by William MacKenzie (1930, pp. 12–13, and 1995, p. 15), but JGC's reference to the East Indies is, I think, unique. By *Beinn Heidera* he means *Beinn Eadarainn*, which Watson (2002, p. 104) finds 'obscure as to meaning'; *Beinn eadar Dhà Abhainn* 'Mountain between Two Rivers' would describe it well, however, especially as viewed from the west. For Iain Garbh, JGC's 'Stout John', see p. 184 above.

The *West Highland Tales* reference is to Campbell 1860–62, vol. 2, pp. 89–91 = 1890, vol. 2, pp. 101–03. JFC says that the story is 'from the telling of a dancing master, a north country Highlander, and written by my friend Mr. John Campbell of Kilberry'. At the end 'the Coluinn flew off, singing the following doleful words – "S fada uam fein bonn beinn Hederin, s fada uam fein bealach a bhorbhan," which we can only translate by –

> "Far from me is the hill of Ben Hederin,
> Far from me is the pass of murmuring".'

He then gives the air in staff notation. It is a well-known song, especially in Skye (Tolmie 1911, p. 186; Mhàrtainn 2001, pp. 77, 123):

> *S fhada bhuam fhìn bonn Beinn Eadarra,*
> *S fhada bhuam fhìn bealach a' Mhorbhain,*
> *S fhada bhuam fhìn bonn Beinn Eadarra,*
> *S fhada gun teagamh bhuam bealach a' Mhorbhain.*
>
> *O bhonn gu bonn, bonn Beinn Eadarra,*
> *O bhonn gu bonn, bealach a' Mhorbhain,*
> *O bhonn gu bonn, bonn Beinn Eadarra,*
> *S fhada gun teagamh bhuam bealach a' Mhorbhain.*
>
> *Cùl am mullaichean, beul am bealaichean,*
> *Cùl am mullaichean, mullach Sròn Bhiornail,*
> *Dh'fhàg mi 'n crodh-laoigh am bonn Beinn Eadarra,*
> *Dh'fhàg mi 'n crodh-laoigh am bealach a' Mhorbhain.*

("Far from me is the base of Beinn Eadarra, / Far from me is the pass of Morven, / Far from me is the base of Beinn Eadarra, / Far indeed from me is the pass of Morven. / From base to base, the base of Beinn Eadarra, / From base to base, the pass of Morven, / From base to base, the base of Beinn Eadarra, / Far indeed from me is the pass of Morven. / The backs of their summits, the mouths of their passes, / The backs of their summits, the summit of Sròn Bhiornail, / I've left the cows and their calves at the base of Beinn Eadarra, / I've left the cows and their calves in the pass of Morven.")

Frances Tolmie links the story and the words like this (1911, p. 187): "Colann-gun-Cheann belonged originally to the district of Trotternish in Skye, whence, being a malignant being who hated mankind, he was banished for his wicked practices, and, after wandering about, took up his abode near Arisaig on the mainland. He had not long been there, when the inhabitants, discovering his evil character, condemned him to death, and cut off his head. But he nevertheless continued to be a cause of danger and consternation in that locality, for he was in the habit of amusing himself by floating in the air at a certain narrow pass, throwing his head down on people going that way, and killing them. A young man of courage went forth to have an encounter with him, and on reaching the pass caught the descending head on the point of a sword and refused to give it back to Colann (the body,) till he promised to return to his own country-side. It was then he sang the above lament in consideration of the distance there was to traverse ere he could reach Ben-Edar, and the pass of Morven, near Quiraing, in Trotternish. After that, he was never again seen near Arisaig."

In a further note Tolmie explains (1911, p. 271) that in Moidart and the Loch Arkaig district the song was sung by women only and the monster was understood to be female, having been expelled from 'Beinn Eadarrainn in Skye or Harris' for evil doings and exiled to Cross in Morar, where she killed the mother of a foster-brother of Raghnall mac Ailein Òig of Morar. The dead woman's son, the strongest man in Clan Donald, gave her a gun with which she shot off her own head, but her body was still able to fly, and she fought him all night. "In the version which I heard from an old man named Mac Varish, at the head of Loch Arkaig, the monster's habitat was at first at Trost, which the narrator believed to be somewhere in Skye."

See also Abrach 1874, p. 73; Fionn 1895–96; Fionn 1911, p. 168; Macdonald 1914–19, pp. 101–02; *CG5*, p. 318; Maclean 1975, p. 65; *Tocher* 34, pp. 226–27; *Tocher* 39, pp. 116–19; *Tocher* 42, p. 426; MacDonald 1994–95, p. 66; Gillies 2000, pp. 14–15, 19.

920 Note Q (Lockhart 1869, pp. 49–50) began life as note XVI of Canto First (Scott 1812, p. 238) and subsequently became note I. Henry's text is to be found in Moir 1889, pp. 80–81, and McDiarmid 1968–69, vol. 1, p. 79. It may be enjoyed as a fine story of Fawdoun's heroic self-sacrifice and Wallace's gnawing guilt. "The hero's little band had been joined by an Irishman, named Fawdoun, or Fadzean, a dark, savage, and suspicious character," says Scott. "After a sharp skirmish at Black-Erne Side, Wallace was forced to retreat with only sixteen followers. The English pursued with a Border *sleuth-bratch*, or blood-hound.

> *In Gelderland there was that bratchet bred,*
> *Siker of scent, to follow them that fled;*
> *So was he used in Eske and Liddesdail,*
> *While (i.e. till) she gat blood no fleeing might avail.*

In the retreat, Fawdoun, tired, or affecting to be so, would go no farther. Wallace, having in vain argued with him, in hasty anger, struck off his head, and continued the retreat. When the English came up, their hound stayed upon the dead body:—

> *The sleuth stopped at Fawdon, still she stood,*
> *Nor farther would fra time she fund the blood.*

The story concludes with a fine Gothic scene of terror. Wallace took refuge in the solitary tower of Gask. Here he was disturbed at midnight by the blast of a horn. He sent out his attendants by two and two, but no one returned with tidings. At length, when he was left alone, the sound was heard still louder. The champion descended, sword in hand; and, at the gate of the tower, was encountered by the headless spectre of Fawdoun, whom he had slain so rashly. Wallace, in great terror, fled up into the tower, tore open the boards of a window, leapt down fifteen feet in height, and continued his flight up the river. Looking back to Gask, he discovered the tower on fire, and the form of Fawdoun upon the battlements, dilated to an immense size, and holding in his hand a blazing rafter. The Minstrel concludes,

> *Trust ryght wele, that all this be sooth indeed,*
> *Supposing it be no point of the creed.*"

On the basis of a claimed resemblance of the story to that of Finn's struggle with the phantoms (see note 917), W. H. Schofield deduced (1920, p. 99) that 'the author here followed a Highland narrative'. In McDiarmid's view (1968–69, vol. 2, p. 168), 'no source for the tale of Fawdoun's ghost has been found, though William Schofield . . . tried to relate it to quite dissimilar Highland folk-tales'. It has to be said, however, that the *Colann gun Cheann* stories in general, and JGC's MacFadyen story in particular, show that Henry's tale does indeed have close connections in Gaelic folklore. Clearly the *Colann gun Cheann* motif lies first in the sequence, but what we cannot know is whether it inspired Henry to create a Celtic character called 'Fawdoun, or Fadzean' (as Scott put it) who subsequently found his way into Gaelic folk narrative as *Mac Phàidein* (MacFadyen), or whether the Gaelic story about Wallace and MacFadyen already existed in the fifteenth century and was incorporated lock, stock and barrel by Henry into his poem. JGC appears to imply that the story he heard in Tiree was derived from Scott, which is possible; the description of the encounter given by Lord Archibald Campbell from a Gaelic source is very different, but retains the central motif of decapitation. After Wallace had met and defeated an army led by MacFadyen and the MacDougalls in the Pass of Brander in 1300, says Campbell (1885a, pp. 175–76), MacFadyen hid in a cave in the face of a rock called Creag an Aoinidh. "Sir William sent the Knight of Lochow and a party of men in pursuit of the fugitives; and having found them in the cave, they cut off their heads, and placed them on stakes on the top of Creag-an-aoinidh. This cave is called MacFadyen's Cave to the present day."

The cave is marked on maps as high up on the hill on the southern side of the Pass of Brander, but the story of Wallace's expedition to Argyll is no longer accepted as historical (Maclean-Bristol 2002a, Fojut 2003). For more folklore on Wallace and the MacFadyens see Watson 1926b, pp. 80, 212, and for another splendid decapitation tale see Cameron 1845, pp. 426–27, followed by Macpherson 1893, pp. 95–96.

921 This appears to be an alternative beginning to that of the 22-line fragment printed in Campbell 1872, p. 212:

> *Là bha 'n Fhéinn ag òl,*
> *A' caitheamh 's ag iomairt lagha,*
> *Chunnaic iad colann gun cheann*
> *Dìreadh o ghleann an dà chlaidh . . .*

("One day when the Féinn were feasting, / Putting shot and bending the bow, / They saw a headless body / Climb from the glen of two graveyards . . .") The apparition demands of Fionn that he sleep with it, and Treun agrees to do so in his place. We may agree with JFC that the rest of the story, had it survived, probably had something in common with 'Nighean Rìgh fo Thuinn' ('The Daughter of King Under-Waves', Campbell 1890, vol. 3, pp. 421–40), in which a hideous creature approaches the Féinn on a wild night on the slope of Beinn Eudainn, and when Diarmaid allows her to sleep under the edge of his blanket she turns into a beautiful woman, after which they have many adventures together.

922 The weasand is the gullet, windpipe or throat.

923 In the rest of this section JGC uses 'meat' instead of 'food' to translate *biadh*. As the latter is more helpful to the modern reader, I alter 'meat' to 'food' throughout what follows.

924 Or alternatively: "A big grizzled bloodless fleshless sinewless claw that is without food, tailor."

925 Smith 1845, pp. 685–86 (not 682) note. By 'the old church of Glassary' JGC means the ruined church at Kil-neuair or Kilineuer on Loch Awe-side, which is probably *Cill Fhionnbhair* ('the Church of St Finnbarr') rather than *Cill an Iubhair* ('the Church of the Yew') as has been claimed. Smith tells the story well, describing it as one 'to which we have often listened with wonder and awe in childhood, and which has obtained a wide circulation'. The story was picked up from this source by Seton Gordon and used in his classic *Highways and Byways in the West Highlands* (1935), pp. 330–31 – by which time a much fuller version had appeared in MacDougall and Calder 1910, pp. 34–39, entitled 'An Tàillear agus Taibhse Chill-an-Iubhair' ('The Tailor and the Kilnure Animated Corpse'). The Rev. Malcolm MacPhail of Kilmartin remarks that the tale is associated with Chanonry (the cathedral at Fortrose) as well as Kil-Christ (Beauly) and, above all, Kil-Neuer (1898, p. 89): "The veritable finger-marks of the spectre are most assuredly to be seen on the door-post of the Kil-Neuer Church, even at the present day. The marks, however, are believed to be the result of an afterthought, and to have been made on purpose to substantiate the legend told in connection with the old chapel." See also Jacobs 1892, pp. 61–64, 249–50; MacDonald 1994–95, pp. 65–66; Watson 2001, p. 156.

　　The telling of stories by means of a shadow on the wall was known as *cròg-ri-fraigh* ('paw-against-wall', HSD, vol. 1, p. 295), *cròg-fraigh* ('wall-paw', CG2, p. 294), *crogada fraigh*, *crogaire fraigh* (McDonald 1958, p. 86, cf. Caimbeul 2003, p. 132).

926 See Forbes 1923, p. 136.

927 I asked Mr Ian Fisher, co-author of RCAHMS 1982, if he knew where *Toll an Tàilleir* was, and he responded (personal communication, 27 November 2003): "I have checked through the most likely visitors' accounts, and the only relevant mention is in Martin Martin (1934 ed., p. 289; Birlinn, p. 158): 'On the south side the gate, without the church, is the Tailor's House, for they only wrought in it.' The topography is rather uncertain and this sentence is followed immediately by a mention of 'the outer gate', of which nothing remains. There are no traces of any buildings south of the west door of the abbey, except on the south side of the nave. However, despite the lack of written sources, I am sure that I have heard oral accounts associating a tailor (only room for one!) with the little tower or lodge at the north end of the west wall of the nave, also said to be a place where 'Columbus' retreated for meditation. The tower has a window facing south to the abbey door, and its cusped outline is said to have been made by the tailor jumping through it to escape some danger. The setting would fit Campbell's description of a 'hole' better than Martin's 'house'."

928 The phrase *aire chlaidh* is more usually *faire chlaidh*, see p. 132. *Aire* and *faire* are basically the same word. By *caibeal* ('chapel') JGC means the roofless remains of a pre-Reformation church; he did not offer a translation of *Sliasaid liath reamhar*, so I have provided one.

929 A more modern way of expressing this might be: "With his consent or without it, as the old crone came upon Ewen – a woman as big as his mother." I suppose 'as big as his mother' means 'as big in relation to him as was his mother when she bore him', but this does not seem to apply to the story that follows.

930 Macaulay 1914, pp. 1597–98, cf. Pennant 1774, pp. 347–64, and Drummond 1842. The story is also told in CG2, pp. 142–43; Robertson 1904–07, p. 291; Mac a Phì 1974–76, pp. 283–84; McKerracher 1994, pp. 375–76.

931 Or: "My desire is for you, Ewen!" This was not charitably intended, see 'Strong and Undue Wishes', pp. 250–51.

932 Or: "Your heart's desire be on your side and on yon grey stone over there, old wife!" See p. 130 ('Euphemisms') and note 816.

933 JGC points out in a footnote that this may perhaps be connected with the saying, *Iarr gach nì air Camshronach, ach na iarr ìm air Camshronach*. "Ask everything of a Cameron, but ask no butter from a Cameron." The clan, he adds, are also called *Camshronaich bhog an ime* – 'the soft Camerons of the butter'. These are well-known proverbs. What he is implying, I think, is that the anecdote (which reflects little credit upon the Camerons) came first, and led to the sayings. See Nicolson 1951, pp. 75, 209. In fact the crock of butter motif appears in the same walking story as recorded at Carna in Co. Galway, Ireland (Ó Crualaoich 2003, pp. 106–07). In this version the man is unnamed, but the woman is the *Cailleach Bhéarthach*, for whom see Campbell 1914–15. See also p. ix above.

934 A 'poor chance' or 'little chance' would be better English, I think. See pp. xii and lxxviii above.

935 Cf. Nicolson 1951, p. 367.

936 For Michael Scott see pp. 157–58, 162–63, 546. The story shows how books were once seen by the illiterate as sources of magic power rather than of information or entertainment. If a book was not holy it was diabolical, if it had an author he must be a sorcerer. This may be described as a medieval view which survived in the Highlands and Islands until long after the Reformation. See note 542.

937 As JGC grew up in Appin, these words on the Appin Murder deserve especial respect. His contemporary the Rev. Alexander Stewart of Ballachulish was equally unambiguous (Nether-Lochaber 1883–84, pp. 352–53): "The assassin was Allan Breac Stewart, of the family of Invernahadden, in Rannoch."

After making a detailed study of the evidence, Seamus Carney concluded (1989, p. 167; 1994, pp. 493–94) that Allan Breac was indeed the murderer. However, circumstantial evidence gathered by John Dewar in the 1860s (Mackechnie 1964, pp. 201–03, 215–16, 354, cf. Gibson 2003, p. 112) points the finger firmly at a nephew of Alexander Stewart of Ballachulish (1684–1774) called Donald Stewart, the murder weapon being his gun, *an t-Slinneanach* or 'the Female Scapulimancer' (cf. note 473). Perhaps this is why recent Appin traditions about this weapon, as recorded by Dr John MacInnes, ascribe the murder to Stewart of Ballachulish himself (Black 2001, p. 453). The *Slinneanach* (for which see Matheson 1929–30, p. 404), or a gun very like it, may be seen today in the West Highland Museum, Fort William. Dewar was told of Allan Breac (Mackechnie 1964, p. 207): "He received a reward for fleeing and allowing the killing of Colin of Glenure to be imputed to him."

The condemned man, *Seumas a' Ghlinne*, is usually described not as of Ardsheal but as of Acharn. Stewart and Stewart say (1880, p. 140): "At the trial he was described as reputed to be a natural brother of Charles of Ardsheal, but this seems more than doubtful." They refer to the 'supposed' murderer not as Allan but as 'Donald Breck Stewart, who fled the country, after having at first sought shelter with his relatives near Invercomrie in Perthshire'. Invercomrie is at the west end of Loch Rannoch, two miles short of Ardlarich and eight short of Aulich. See also McOwan 2004.

For Amhulaich or Aulich on the north side of Loch Rannoch see Black 1994–96, pp. 392–95; for Allan Breac's visit see Mackechnie 1964, pp. 208, 346, and Carney 1989, p. 108. It is unlikely that Allan spent the night after the murder in Rannoch, as this involved a forty-mile walk across difficult country. The assassination took place in Appin on Thursday 14 May 1752. According to evidence brought forward at James Stewart's trial, Allan arrived at his uncle's house on Monday 18 May and stayed two days, still denying any part in the crime. The latest writer on the subject, Rosemary Gibson (2003, p. 64), points out that his uncle saw him again on Sunday 24 May, and that towards the end of the month he got provisions from the change-house at Innerhadden (at the east end of Loch Rannoch). Since he was 'on the run', it is hardly surprising if local tradition regarding his whereabouts is less than uniform. A Rannochman who lived one generation later than JGC, James Robertson, wrote (1978–80, p. 232): "Allan Breac . . . in the course of his flight from Appin, spent a night in his uncle's house at Airdlaraich. He left the next morning making towards Athole, and was accompanied, as far as Aulaich at any rate, by a packman who had also passed the night at Airdlaraich. He seems to have gone as far as Auchtarsin, whence the garrisons at Muileann a' Mhadaidh scared him back for he was seen that evening at 'Manach's' House at Inbhir Chadain, to which he must have crossed the river at Kinloch. After that, all trace of his itinerancy is lost until his arrival in France."

938 Amhulaich will, I think, be *Àth a' Mhullaich* 'the Ford of the Summit', or perhaps *Àth a' Mhuilich* 'the Mullman's Ford'.

939 JGC wrote 'whenever he observed the American'.

940 See note 175.

941 For *an Cruaidh-Ghortain*, better *an Cruaidh-Ghoirtean*, Heylipol, see note 196. The *Druim Buidhe* (nowadays *Druim Bhuidhe*, due to the decline of the case system) is on the west side of the Cornaig road, see note 193; *a' Charragh Bhiorach* (the word is feminine) is a pillar-stone on the east side of the Cornaig road.

942 *An geall nas fhiach e* is a characteristic Tiree expression for 'virtually at death's door'; 'in risk of all he is worth' is the more literal meaning.

943 As it stands in *WSS* 205 this phrase is 'the Field of Birds (*Blàr nam Big-ein*) in the Moas, a part of Tiree near hand'. I have prioritised the Gaelic name over JGC's English translation in line with our editorial policy. *Big-ein* I take to be JGC's way of showing that the word is made up of by-forms of *beag* 'little' and *eun* 'bird'; it is Dwelly's *bigein* 'rock-pipit, golden-crested wren, meadow pipit, any little bird' (1977, p. 93). 'Moas' will be a misprint, or a misreading of JGC's handwriting. According to oral tradition *Blàr nam Bigein* was the site of a battle which took place centuries ago in *Mòinteach nam Bigeanan* ('the Birds' Mossland') in Moss, in the west of Tiree; it is now part of the Barrapol common. The village of Moss is known as *a' Mhòinteach Ruadh* 'the Red Mossland'. The story is told, again in English (with a Gaelic translation, apparently not by a speaker of Tiree Gaelic), as MacKinnon 1992, no. 13. The man slain in the battle is there named as *Dòmhnall Mòr*.

944 For Cath Gabhra, the last great battle of the Féinn, see Campbell 1872, pp. 180–95; Murphy 1933, pp. viii, 32–57; Ross 1939, pp. 148–67, 237–38; Thomson 1951, p. 59; Murphy 1953, pp. 92–94. For the first book of Temora see Macpherson 1996b, pp. 225–34.

945 I suspect that JGC's phrase 'the second best hero' is meant as a translation of *an dara ursainn chath as fheàrr* or the like and not of *ursainn chath* alone; note that *an dara ursainn chath as fheàrr* would also mean 'one of the two best'.

946 JGC's 'about sixty years ago' will mean *c.* 1814, and indeed the Kylerhea–Sconser road was completed in 1813. It was not quite the first public road in Skye, the Dunvegan–Snizort section having been open since 1811 (Nicolson 1994, pp. 268–69). For the name *Caol Reidhinn* see Campbell 1890, vol. 3, pp. 120–25, and Carmichael 1904–05.

947 'Thirty or forty years ago' will mean *c.* 1834–44. Sithiche points out (1912, p. 343) that when JGC tells of a sheep changing into a woman she, also, has a coat wrapped about her head ('Witches as Sheep', p. 186), and that *Luideag* is the first of six witches named by one of the Rev. Dr Norman MacLeod's informants as responsible for sinking Captain Forrest's ship (MacLeod 1882, p. 249, cf. Nicolson 1951, p. 388): "*Luideag, Agus Doideag, Agus Corrag Nighin Iain Bhàin, Cas a' mhogain Riabhaich á Gleancomhain, Agus Gorm-shuil mhòr bhàrr na Maighe. Raggie* and *Frizzle, and the finger of White John's Daughter, Hogganfoot* from Glenco, and *Great Blue-Eye* from Moy, (in Lochaber.)" *Corrag Nighin Iain Bhàin* will not be 'the finger of White John's Daughter' but 'Little Heron (or Little Crane) the Daughter

of Fair-Haired John', see note 822; for *Gorm-shuil* see note 665. The *bean nighe* (for whom see pp. 22–23 above) is often called *Luideag na h-Aibhne* 'Raggie of the River' or *Luideag an Uillt* 'Raggie of the Burn' (Sithiche 1912, pp. 344–50).

948   I am tempted to wonder whether this has anything to do with the notorious prostitute *Màiri nighean Iain mhic Iain* (Mary MacDonald, known as *An Aigeannach*), a native of Moidart who is said (Mac-Dhonuill 1751, p. 154) to have plied her trade *da fhichid bliaghn' man heist* ('for forty years around Heist'), presumably referring to the anchorage at the head of Loch Eishort in Strath, Skye, less than two miles from *Lochan nan Dubh-Bhreac*. If to be taken literally, the forty years in question would have been *c.* 1705–45. See Ó Baoill 1978, pp. 103, 108–10; Black 2001, p. 397; Shaw 2002, p. 112. The names *An Aigeannach* and *Luideag* need not be seen as mutually exclusive – the former is glossed by the HSD (vol. 1, p. 19) as *une fille de joye*.

949   JGC's 'about fifty years ago' will mean *c.* 1824; Kilchonan, usually Killichonan, is near the west end of Loch Rannoch, on the north shore. The gardener's route home was by the military road from Weem through Appin to 'Cashieville' and across the hills. 'Appin' here refers to *Apainn nam Mèinnearach*, Appin of Menzies in Perthshire, not *Apainn nan Stiùbhartach*, Appin of the Stewarts in Argyll, see note 867. 'Cashieville', more usually spelt Coshieville, is presumably 'At the Foot of the Sacred Tree'. It is given by Paul Cameron (1890–91, p. 132) as *Cois-a-Bhileadh* and in *Tocher* 28, pp. 202, 222 (from Lady Evelyn Stewart-Murray's manuscripts), as *Cois-a'-bhil* and *Cois-a'-bhile*. Watson interpreted it as 'near the brae-edge' (2002, p. 194), but this fails to take account of the historical gender of *bile*. If 'Cashieville' is not a misprint, it reflects the nominative *cas* of which *cois* is the locative. For *bile* see Campbell 1885a, pp. 123–24; Henderson 1911, pp. 185–88; Kermack 1953, pp. 190–92; Mackechnie 1964, p. 290; cf. *faidhbhile* 'beech-tree'.

Lochan Doimeig is on the north side of Schiehallion, by the road down to Crossmount, which is on the south shore of what is now Dunalastair Water, a few miles east of Kinloch Rannoch. It takes its name from a woman or creature called *Doimeag* ('Slut', 'Slattern'). If we may judge from the retort to the verse quoted in note 324, *doimeag* must be synonymous with *gruagach* (GUL MacLagan MSS 35 and 85):

> *Cia dhèanadh am beannachadh soimeach*
> *A mhealladh nan doimeag?*
> *Cuim am biodh Bàrd nan Ullag*
> *Gun a bhalg air a dhronnaig?*

"Who would bestow such an affable greeting / To beguile the slatterns? / Why would the Bard of the Barley Gruel / Have no bag on his shoulder?" For *ul(l)ag* 'grain expeditiously dried for the quern' see MacPhail 1900, p. 440–41. In some places, like Lewis, it came to mean a mixture of oatmeal and cream (Macdonald 2003, pp. 25, 28).

950   'East Side' is the parish of Kilmuir, which includes what is now called Staffin. The reference must be to a minister of the parish who died in office at some point subsequent to the highly distinguished incumbency (1740–85) of the Rev. Donald MacQueen. The only one who fits that profile (at least until 1869, which is too late) is Robert MacGregor, a Moderate who was minister there from 1822 to 1846 and whose son and successor, the Rev. Alexander MacGregor, became the leading Gaelic writer of his time (Scott 1915–50, vol. 7, p. 172, and vol. 8, p. 684; MacLeod 1980–82, p. 246; cf. note 23 on p. 691). It was of the Rev. Robert that the very deferential William MacKenzie wrote (1930, p. 133): "Mr. MacGregor is said to have had an extensive knowledge of agriculture, and his help, guidance and example may have contributed not a little to the prominence of Kilmuir as the Granary of Skye."

951   JGC's 'about thirty years ago' will mean *c.* 1844. In common with many of his contemporaries,

he is rather dismissive of the *céilidh* and fails to represent it as the cultural and educational dynamo which (at its best) it undoubtedly was. No doubt this view was influenced by the unstructured, voluntary and wholly oral nature of its activities in comparison with the parish and charity schools which had proliferated in the Highlands since 1709. The Greek word to which JGC refers simply meant a 'lounging place', later a 'public building or hall', hence the talk or gossip that went on in such a place (Liddell and Scott 1996, p. 1040). For a more positive view of the *céilidh* see Campbell 1890, vol. 1, pp. xix–xx; *CG*1, pp. xxii–xxiii; Sutherland 1937, pp. 13–21; MacDonald 2000, pp. 68–73; Black 2001, pp. xii–xiv; and, above all, Macdonald 1982, pp. 207–10, 311–12.

952   See note 184.

953   I have restored the spelling of the statute as quoted by Gregory (1836, p. 395). The 'Statutes of Iona', of which this is one, have been receiving renewed (and richly deserved) attention from historians in recent years, see Lee 1980, pp. 75–82, 138–47; Macinnes 1996, pp. 65–81; Goodare 1998.

954   The first line should read *Niall mac Ruairidh 'n Tartair* 'Neil son of Rory the Tartar'. *Ruairidh an Tartair* (literally 'Rory of the Noise'), who died *c*. 1622, was chief of the MacNeils of Barra. He had two sons called Neil (by different women), one of whom succeeded to the chiefship. See Sinclair 1906–07, pp. 218–19, and MacPherson 1960, pp. 32–34. JGC's mistake is forgiveable – in Barra Gaelic *'n Tartair* sounds very like *'n astair*.

955   Gregory 1836, p. 396: "He named Duntullim, a castle of his family in Trouterness, as his residence; and six household gentlemen, and an annual consumption of four tun of wine, were allowed to him." *Gorm* 'blue' could be used of something black and shiny, e.g. a horse's coat or a person's hair; however, such epithets could become hereditary, so we cannot assume that every Dòmhnall Gorm was black-haired. For legends of Dòmhnall Gorm Mór see Mackay 1919–22, pp. 6–19.

956   The third line of the quatrain is perhaps rather 'And as much as yon mote in the sunbeam'. J. G. Mackay published a version (1919–22, pp. 18–19) in which there are nine torches of fir instead of seven torches of oak, and the couplet becomes:

> *Ach mur bitheadh na naoi gathan giuthais,*
> *A Dhòmhnaill Òig,*
> *Cha bhitheadh do chuid-sa cho ceart.*

("But were it not for the nine lances of pine, / Young Donald, / Your share would not be so right.") This provides good rhyme *ceart : neart*. Turning to leave the room, Mackay adds, the apparition raised his arms and exclaimed:

> *Se mo ghuidhe dhuts', a Dhòmhnaill Ghuirm Òig,*
> *Thu chumail a' chòir ris a' cheart,*
> *Bhith 'd ìochdar ris an t-sluagh, 's do làmh*
> *Bhith sìnte ris a' bhochd.*

("My prayer for you, Dòmhnall Gorm Òg, / Is that your dealings be just, / That you look up to the people, and that your hand / Be stretched out to the poor.")

957   Dun Crosg (*Dùn a' Chroisg*, Duncroisk) lies on the north side of Glen Lochay in Perthshire (north-west of Killin) where Allt Dhùn Croisg meets the Lochay (Watson 2002, pp. 183, 205). The story of *Taibhse Choimhlig*, or rather *Taibhse na Coimh-Sheilg*, is told by James MacDiarmid (1904–07, pp. 51–54) and Mairi B. Copland (1915). *Eas na Coimh-Sheilg* ('the Ravine of the Shared Hunting', JGC's 'ravine of Coilig') appears to be one of the streams that flow into the Lochay to the east of Allt Dhùn Croisg. According to MacDiarmid the ghost

was not that of Peter Brown but of *Iain Mac-ill'-Dhuinn* (John Brown), the weaver's name was MacPherson, and the event took place during the ministry of *Maighstir Eoghan*, who can only, I think, be the Rev. Hugh Macdougall, minister of Killin from 1795 to 1827 (Scott 1915–50, vol. 4, p. 185; Gillies 1938, p. 292).

Copland says that the guilty man's name was indeed Peter Brown (*Pàruig Mac-ill-bhriuthain*) but that he was usually called *Par Lonach*. She explains that he did not steal the ploughshare – he lived in times when it was customary for each joint-tenant of a runrig farm to own one important item required by all, which he duly lent to his neighbours as required. Par Lonach bought a new ploughshare but kept it to himself, deciding that the old one was good enough for lending. He buried the new one to hide it and promptly died; sometimes his ghost appeared as a big black dog, sometimes as a roebuck, sometimes as a man. In Copland's version the hero who meets the ghost is one *Alasdair Mór* who has been drinking in the Bridge of Lochay Inn (*Tigh-Osda Drochaid-Lòchaidh*) on St Fillan's eve (*oidhche Féille-Faolain*). See note 469 and MacilleDhuibh 21.2.03.

958 Cf. 'Iron', p. 135.

959 JGC's 'about forty years ago' suggests *c.* 1834, but as shown in note 957, the event seems to have taken place a little earlier than that. For other examples of *eas* in the sense of 'ravine' see pp. 70, 84, 85 ('The Glaistig at Sron-Charmaig'), 292. Watson wrote (1912–13, p. 244, cf. 2002, p. 131): "In Perthshire, at the present day *eas* means usually a steep, rough gully with water flowing through it."

960 Maodlach, *a' Mhaodalach* 'the Big-Bellied One', is the steep hill on the Loch Linnhe shore just north of Kingairloch. For the different behaviour of dogs and bitches in the presence of an evil spirit see p. 273.

961 See notes 630 and 859.

962 The wife will be that of the Mullman. She must have done the stripping. *Thuige* 'to it' appears simply to refer to the fire.

963 *Teóghan* might perhaps be translated 'Warming Ghost' or 'Heat-Generated Ghost'. It appears to be a nickname for the apparition coined from its favourite word *teóghadh*.

964 See p. 196. Bonskeid is at the lower end of Loch Tummel, a few miles west of Pitlochry.

965 This happened *c.* 1854, during the ministry of JGC's predecessor the Rev. Neil Maclean. Niall M. Brownlie tells me that the identity of the house is known to this day.

966 Woodstock Manor in Oxfordshire was allegedly haunted by a poltergeist in October–November 1649 while Cromwell's commissioners were attempting to remove all evidence of King Charles's occupancy of the building. His execution had taken place on 30 January that year. See Scott 2001, pp. 218–19.

967 See "*Luideag*, 'the Rag'", pp. 284–85 above.

968 JGC's 'two or three summers ago' suggests 1871 or 1872. The person referred to as 'the traveller' can hardly be himself, since he implicitly accuses him of credulity and exaggeration. Nor is it likely to be his fellow folklorist the Rev. Neil Campbell (1850–1904), for the simple reason that the latter was only 21–22 years old in 1871–72 and did not become minister of Kilchrenan until 1880 (Scott 1915–50, vol. 4, p. 93). *Cill a' Chreunain* is literally 'the Church of thy Little Deacon', possibly a reference to St Diún (Clancy 1995, pp. 112–13, see also Watson 1926a, p. 303, and 2002, p. 120, note 1).

969 An *uchdan* is a steep brae (*uchd* 'breast, bosom'). *Uchdan a' Bhiorain Duibh* will be what is now known as 'the Manse Brae' at Berandhu (*am Bioran Dubh*, 'the Black Spike', usually referring to a peaked hill, cf. Watson 1926a, p. 488), half a mile west of Tynribbie on the road to Port Appin (my thanks to Mrs Fiona Gunn and Paddy McNicol for information). *An Dubhag* 'the Kidney' or 'the Blackie' (cf. note 820) is a landmark on the shore half a mile east of Ballachulish Hotel; *Sgeir na Dubhaige* is a few yards offshore; *Uchdan na Dubhaig(e)* will be the hillside above the road.

Ath-Flèodair (Alioter) is a small promontory jutting into Lochmaddy Bay beside the A865 Trumisgarry–Lochmaddy road; there was a *sìthein* nearby where Fairies were seen, but recently it was pulled apart and the stones crushed for road-building. Beveridge describes it (1911, p. 274) as 'Sithean Dubh, a shapeless and very rocky hillock by the roadside at Alioter' and says that 'this is understood to be a fancy name recently invented for Cnoc Alioter'. If Beveridge is right (1911, p. 46) in explaining *àth-Leòdair* as 'Leod's ford' from the Norse personal name *Ljótr* ('Ugly'), the *F* in JGC's spelling is unhistorical. The place is mentioned twice by the poet Donald Maclean, Dòmhnall Bàn na Camairt. In his playful song 'Oran do Iain Ruadh Bhalegui' (MacDonald 1894, pp. 186–87, cf. 1889–90, p. 257) he says (MacDonald's spelling):

> *Ach tha mi 'n dùil 'nuair thig am Bàilidh*
> *Gur e fàbhar dhòmhs' e;*
> *'N uair gheibh Iain Ruadh Mac Eachain bàs,*
> *Bi Bhalegui fo m' spògan;*
> *'S leam an Ruchdi, 's leam a Phàirce,*
> *'S leam a machair mar a tha e;*
> *'S leam a h-uile dad a dh' fhàg e,*
> *'S geàrrachan Ath-leodair.*

("But I suppose when the Factor comes / That it will be in my favour; / When Iain Ruadh mac Eachainn dies / I'll have Vallaquie in my clutches; / I will have Ruchdi, I'll have the Park, / I'll have the machair just as it is; / I will get all that he's left behind / And the pastures of Alioter.") And in 'Òran Loireig' he meets what the editors call the 'wild wandering woman' of the title (MacDonald 1911, pp. xlix, 299):

> *Ghabh mi staigh gun fhiamh gun nàire*
> *Gus 'n do ràinig mi Àth-Leòdair;*
> *Có choinnich mi ach an Loireag,*
> *'S b'i ceann na mollachd air fògradh.*

("I walked inland without fear or shame / Until I arrived at Alioter; / Who was there to meet me but the Loireag, / And she was the banished head of cursing.") A *loireag*, as described by Carmichael, is a sort of female urisk of the Western Isles (*CG2*, pp. 320–22, cf. Watson 1908–09, pp. 54–55, and MacDonald 1958b, p. 126), but this particular Loireag appears to be a mortal woman who is 'away with the Fairies'. See also CCBG 2004, p. 127, where it is said that lights and other unnatural phenomena used to be seen at Alioter. My thanks to Norman E. MacDonald for information.

For the Portree story see also pp. 258 and 263 above.

970 The pass is on the road from Grisipol to Clabhach near the north shore of the island. *Cnoc Stoirr* will be 'Stake Hill', from Norse *staurr*, 'a stake, point', as in the Storr Rock in Skye, cf. Forbes 1923, p. 412. The Round House between Arileod and Breacachadh is still occupied; I recall it from the 1970s as being tenanted by a lady from South Uist who had originally come to Coll, like many others, to work as a dairymaid.

971 Caisle or Cashlie is near the top of the glen. *Easa Chaisle* is on *Allt Chaisle*, which flows south to Caisle from the peak called *Stùc an Lochain*. Watson points out (2002, p. 209) that the name is *Caislidh*, properly *Caislibh*, dative plural of *caiseal* 'a stone fort', four or five circular stone forts being concentrated here within a distance of about a mile.

972 The modern Mid Argyll, cf. Mackechnie 1964, p. 311. It would be more correct to say that the lower parts of Kilmartin and Kilmichael meet at the west end of the canal. Throughout its length the canal forms the boundary between Kilmichael and North Knapdale.

973 The invocation of 'Peter and Paul and John and all the most powerful saints' suggests a passing resemblance to the following charm from Arran, which contains a number of Irish features; I edit slightly from Mackenzie 1914, p. 295 (original readings on right).

> *Togaidh Crìost do chnàmhan*
> *Mar thog Muire a làmhan*
>   *Nar thuireadh a gcolann faoi neamh*   *[thuireadh golann*
>   *Mar chruinnich corp an choimdheadh;*   *[a chuimigh*
>   *Togaidh Peadar, togaidh Pòl,*
>   *Togaidh Mìcheal, togaidh Eòin,*
>   *Togaidh Mo-Lais is Mo-Linn*
>   *Cnàmhan do chinn suas ás an fheòil.*

"Christ will raise thy bones / As Mary raised her hands / When their body (?) was mourned under heaven / As they (?) gathered the corpse of the Lord; / Peter will raise, Paul will raise, / Michael will raise, John will raise, / Molaise and Moling will raise / The bones of thy head up out of the flesh." The 'bones of thy head' are basically the teeth, but the charm was used by a woman called Mary Stewart 'for healing the migrim and other distempers in the head'. She recited it to the kirk session of Kilbride on 3 June 1705 after being summoned on a charge of witchcraft. She was duly rebuked on the grounds that 'all charms proceeded from the Devil's invention, let the words be never so good', and ordered to 'make publick confession of her guilt before the congregation next Lord's Day'. See also *CG1*, pp. 10–11, and p. 479 above.

THE CELTIC YEAR

Bliadhna, a year, has been derived by writers on Celtic antiquities from *Bel-ain*, 'the ring or circle of Baal', but the derivation is at variance with etymological analogies, as well as inadmissible from there being no satisfactory evidence that Baalim worship ever extended to the Celtic tribes. It can only be regarded as part of that punning affectation with which Gaelic scholarship is disfigured. The initial *bl* occurs in many words which have in common the idea of separation; *bliadhna* is likely connected with such words as *bloigh* 'a fragment' and *ball* 'a spot', 'a limb', and denotes merely a division, or separate portion, of time.[1]

The notations of the Celtic year belong to the Christian period, old style. If there are any traces of pagan times they are only such as are to be gathered from a few names and ceremonies.

The four seasons are known as *earrach*, spring, *samhradh*, summer, *fogharadh*, harvest, and *geamhradh*, winter. The final syllable in each of these names is *ràidh*, a quarter or season of the year, a space of three months; and the student of Gaelic will note that the long and heavy vowel of which it consists is, contrary to the common rule affecting long vowels, shortened and made an apparently indifferent terminal syllable.[2]

It is still deemed, in many parts of the Highlands, unlucky to be proclaimed in one quarter of the year and married in the next, and the circumstance is called being *gobhlach mun ràidh* 'astride on the seasons'.[3] It is an old saying that the appearance of a season comes a month before its actual arrival: *mìos roimh gach ràidh a choltas*, i.e. 'a month before each season [is seen] its appearance'. The character of the seasons is described in an old riddle,

> *Thàinig ceathrar a-nall*
> *Gun bhàta, gun long —*
> *Fear buidhe fionn,*
> *Fear slatagach donn,*
> *Fear a bhualadh na sùiste*
> *'S fear a rùsgadh nan crann.*
> Tòimhseagan.[4]

527

("Four came over / Without boat or ship – / One yellow and white, / One brown, abounding in twigs, / One to handle the flail / And one to strip the trees.") There can be no doubt the origin of the names given to them belongs to a period anterior to Christianity.

Earrach, spring, is derived from *ear*, the head, the front, the east. In naming the four quarters of the heavens, the face, as in the case of the Hebrew names, is supposed to be toward the east. The right hand (*deas*) is the name given to the south, and the adjective *tuaitheal*, from *tuath*, the north, means 'wrong, to the left, against the sun'. Hence also *toirt fon ear*, literally to take a thing from the east, means to observe; *earalas*, foresight, i.e. the having a thing in view; *earar*, the day after tomorrow, i.e. the day in front of it. The Latin *bos*, and the Greek ἔαρ or ἦρ, would indicate that the ancient Celtic name of the season was *fearrach*, and if so it may be connected with *fear*, *vir* 'a man, the first *par excellence*', *for* 'before', *furasta* 'easy', etc. *Eàrr* means the tail, and the long syllable shows it to be only another form of *iar* 'west, behind, after', the opposite of *ear*.[5] Frequently these names for east and west are known as *sear* and *siar*, as e.g. *chan fheàrr an gille shiar na 'n gille shear*, 'the lad from the west is no better than the lad from the east', that is, it is but six of the one and half a dozen of the other.[6]

Samhradh 'summer', according to old glossaries, is from obsolete *samh* 'the sun', and means the sun season or quarter. This corresponds with the English name, which is evidently a softened form of *sun-mer*. *Samh* is now used to denote 'the suffocating smell produced by excessive heat' (Highland Society's Dictionary, *sub voce*). In Tiree it is the name given to the hazy heavy appearance of the western ocean, and few expressions are more common than *samh chuain t-siar*, the oppressive feeling of which the uneasy sea on the west side of the island is productive. In the north Hebrides *samh* means the ocean itself. A common description over the whole Highlands of an intolerable stench is *mharbhadh e na samhanaich*, i.e. it would kill the savage people living in caves near the ocean, as giants were fabled to do.[7]

Fogharadh, autumn, is likely connected with *fogh*, said to mean ease, hospitality, and *foghainn*, to suffice, with the same root idea of 'abundance'.[8]

Geamhradh, winter: Latin *hiems*, Greek χεῖμα. No doubt *geamh* is of the same origin as the Greek and Latin words, but it does not find its explanation in the Greek χέω, to pour.[9] From its being found in *gèamhlag*, a crow-bar, *gèimheal*, a chain, *geamhtach*, short, stiff and thick, there seems to have been a Gaelic root implying to bind, to be stiff, which gives a suitable derivation for the name of the season of frost and ice.

Mìos, a month, is supposed to be connected with *mias*, a round platter, from the moon's round orb completing its circle within the month. Greek μήν, Eolic μείς, a month; Latin *mensis*; Sanskrit *mâsas*, a month, *mâs*, the moon – these show that undoubtedly the origin of the word is connected with the moon. The names in the

Greek, Latin and Teutonic languages show that there was originally an *n* in the word, and the Gaelic (as well as Sanskrit) bears testimony to the same fact by the long vowel. It is a common thing in Hebrew for *n* at the end of a syllable and in the middle of a word to be assimilated to an immediately succeeding consonant, and it is more likely it so disappeared in some languages than that it was assumed by others. Another Gaelic name for the moon, *ré*, is also used to denote a portion of time: *ri mo ré*, during my lifetime.[10]

Computation of time, however, by months and days of the month as at present was entirely unknown to the Highlander of former days; and even yet, the native population do not say 'on such a day of such a month', but so many days before or after the beginning of summer or other season, or before and after certain well-known term days and festivals, as St Bride's day, St Patrick's day, Whitsunday (*Caingis*), Hallowtide (*Samhainn*), etc.

The time is always reckoned by the old style,[11] and this difference of notation is at first confusing to a stranger. For instance, when told that the ling fishing on the west coast lasts from the middle of spring till five weeks of summer, it will take a little thought on his part to realise that this means from the beginning of April to about the 18th of June. Names for the months are to be found in dictionaries, but they are obviously manufactured from the Latin names, and confined to modern printed Gaelic.[12]

A connected account of the festivals and days by which the year was marked must begin with the festivities by which its advent was celebrated.

NOLLAIG

The seven days from Christmas to the New Year were called *Nollaig*, and in the good easy-going olden times no work was done during them, but men gave themselves up to friendly festivities and expressions of goodwill. Hence the sayings

> *Am fear nach dèan an Nollaig sunndach,*
> *Nì e 'Chàisg gu tùrsach deurach*

('The man whom Christmas does not make cheerful, / Easter will leave sad and tearful') and *Chan eil Nollaig gun fheòil* ('There is no Christmas without flesh').[13] Christmas day was called *latha Nollaig Mhóir* ('the day of Big *Nollaig*') and the night before it *oidhche nam Bannagan* ('the night of Cakes'), while New Year day was known as *latha Nollaig Bhig* ('the day of Little *Nollaig*') and the night before it *oidhche nan Callainnean* ('the night of Blows').[14]

The name *Nollaig* is from the Latin *natalis*, as is made certain by the Welsh word being *Nadolig*, and therefore corresponds to the English 'Christmas'. Various explanations are given of the name of the night before it. Some say *bannag* means 'a feast of women' (from *bean*, a wife), a feast of rejoicing such as is customary when a child is born being prepared by women this evening in memory of the birth of Christ. Others say the *bannag* is the cake presented by them to everyone who entered the house that night. If the word means a cake, it is only applied to Christmas cakes or those used on this day. When there was a person of means, he took everyone he met that week – especially the poor – to his house and gave him his *bannag*, a large round cake (*bonnach mòr cruinn*).[15]

New Year's night, or Hogmanay, was variously known as *oidhche Choinnle* ('the night of the Candle') and *oidhche nan Callainnean, a' Challainn* ('the night of the Blows' or 'Pelting'). The former name may have been derived from some religious ceremonies being performed by candle-light, as is suggested to be the origin of the English name Candlemas (2nd February), or from a candle being kept lighted till the New Year came in.[16] The other name is said to be from the showers of rattling blows given to a dry cow's hide used in the ceremonies of the evening, *collainn* being also used to denote a thundering blow, or what is called in the Lowlands 'a loundering lick' (*stràic mhòr*). Thus *thug e aon chollainn air* 'he gave him one resounding blow'; *bidh tu air do dheagh chollainneachadh* 'you will be severely beaten'. The word, however, as was long ago pointed out by Lhuyd (*Archaeologia Britannica*, 1707), is from *Calendae*, the first day of every month, this being the beginning of the whole year, and the night being in the Highlands reckoned as preceding the day.[17]

CALLAINN

Towards evening men began to gather and boys ran about shouting and laughing, playing shinty, and rolling 'pigs of snow' (*mucan sneachda*), i.e. large snowballs. The hide of the mart or winter cow (*seiche a' mhairt gheamhraidh*) was wrapped round the head of one of the men, and he made off followed by the rest, belabouring the hide – which made a noise like a drum – with switches.[18] The disorderly procession went three times *deiseal*, according to the course of the sun (i.e. keeping the house on the right hand), round each house in the village, striking the walls and shouting on coming to a door:

> *A Challainn a' bhuilg bhuidhe bhoicinn,*
> *Buail an craiceann (air an tobhta) —*
> *Cailleach sa chill,*
> *Cailleach sa chùil,*
> *Cailleach eile 'n cùil an teine,*

Bior 'na dà shùil,
Bior 'na goile
A' Challainn seo:
Leig a-staigh mi.

"The *Callainn* of the yellow bag of hide, / Strike the skin (upon the wall) – / An old wife in the graveyard, / An old wife in the corner, / Another old wife beside the fire, / A pointed stick in her two eyes, / A pointed stick in her stomach / This *Callainn*: / Let me in, open this."[19]

Before this request was complied with, each of the revellers had to repeat a rhyme called *rann Callainn* (i.e. a Christmas rhyme), though – as might be expected when the door opened for one – several pushed their way in till it was ultimately left open for all.[20]

On entering, each of the party was offered refreshments, oatmeal bread, cheese, flesh, and a dram of whisky. Their leader gave to the goodman of the house that indispensable adjunct of the evening's mummeries, the *caisein uchd*, the breast-stripe of a sheep wrapped round the point of a shinty-stick. This was then singed in the fire (*teallach*), put three times with the right-hand turn (*deiseal*) round the family, and held to the noses of all. Not a drop of drink was given till this ceremony was performed. The *caisein uchd* was also made of the breast-stripe or tail of a deer, sheep, or goat, and as many as chose had one with them.[21]

The house was hung with holly to keep out the Fairies, and a boy, whipped with a branch of it, may be assured he will live a year for every drop of blood he loses. This scratching and assurance were bestowed by boys on one another, and was considered a good joke.

Cheese was an important part of the refreshments, and was known as the *càise Callainn* ('Christmas cheese'). A slice cut off at this feast, or a piece of the rind (*cùl na mulchaig*), if preserved and with a hole made through it, has strange virtues. It was called *laomachan*, and a person losing his way during the ensuing year, in a mist or otherwise, has only to look through the hole and he will see his way clearly. By scrambling to the top of the house and looking through it down the *fàr-lus* (the hole in the roof that served in olden times for chimney and window), a person can ascertain the name of his or her future husband or wife.[22] It will prove to be the same as that of the first person seen or heard named. A piece of *laomachan* is also valuable for putting under one's pillow to sleep over.

In this style the villagers, men and boys, went from house to house – preceded in many cases by a piper, and drowning the animosities of the past year in hilarity and merriment.

Christmas Rhymes (*Rannan Callainn*)

In general the rhymes used when seeking admittance varied but little in different districts. Sometimes an ingenious person made a rhyme suitable to the place and people, and containing allusions to incidents and character that increased the prevailing fun. The following is one of the most common of the class:[23]

Thainig mise seo air tùs	*I have come here first*
Dh'ùrachadh na Callainn;	*To renew the Hogmanay;*
Cha ruig mi leas a bhith ga innse,	*I need not tell about it,*
Bha i ann ri linn mo sheanar.	*It was kept in my grandfather's time.*
Caisein Callainn ann am' phòca,	*The* Callainn *breast-stripe is in my pocket,*
Is math an ceò thig ás an fhear ud;	*A goodly mist comes from it;*
Gheibh fear an taighe e air thòs	*The goodman will get it first*
'S cuiridh e shròn san teallach.	*And shove its nose into the fire upon the hearth.*
Théid e deiseil air na pàistean	*It will go sunwise round the children,*
'S gu h-àraid gheibh a bhean e;	*And particularly the wife will get it;*
Si bhean fhéin as fheàrr a thoill e,	*'Tis his own wife best deserves it,*
Làmh a riarachadh nam bannag.	*Hand to distribute the Christmas cakes.*
Éirich a-nuas, a bhean chòir,	*Rise down, young wife,*
'S a bhean òg a choisinn cliù;	*And young wife who hast earned praise;*
Éirich a-nìos, mar bu dual,	*Rise (and come) down, as you were wont,*
'S thoir a-nuas ar Callainn duinn.	*And bring down our* Callainn *to us.*
A' chàbag air am bheil an aghaidh réidh	*The cheese that has the smooth face*
'S an t-ìm nach do bheum sùil —	*And butter eye has not blinked —*
'S mur bheil sin agad air chòir,	*But if you have not that beside you,*
Fòghnaidh aran is feòil duinn.	*Bread and flesh will suffice.*
Tha bogan ann am' bhrògan	*There is water in my shoes*
'S tha mo mheòirean air an gearradh,	*And my fingers are cut,*
Is ann a-staigh taobh an teine	*There is in beside the fire*
Tha an rud a nì mo leigheas,	*What will cure my complaint,*
'S ma tha àit' agad gu gluasad,	*And if you have room to move,*
Éirich 's thoir a-nuas a' ghloine.	*Rise and bring down the glass.*

The following New Year's rhyme must have tried the breath of the speaker and the patience of his listeners considerably. It consists probably of several separate rhymes tagged together, and the allusions it contains to the 'big clerk of the street', etc., make it highly probable the ceremonies of the evening were remains of the Festival of Fools, and had their origin in the streets of Rome.[24] The rhyme is given as it came to hand.[25]

Beannaich am brugh fonn mhor	Bless this cheerful dwelling
Mar ghuth ceol-mhor	With a musical voice
Bhi coltach ri aros righill	That it be like a royal palace
Gun bhi stroghail	Without being wasteful.
Beannaich gach aon duine	Bless each man
Dh iadh mun choinneamh	Who surrounds this gathering
Eadar am fear a dh fhas liath le sinead	From the one grown grey with seniority
Gu aois leinibh.	To the one of infant's age.
Beannaich ar daoin-uaisle	Bless our gentle men
'S ar clann oga	And our young children,
Gach neach a tharlas an uair so	All who chance at this time
Teachd air Domhnull	To come to Donald's.
Fhearaibh se seo tus mo sgeula	Men! This begins my tale
'S fheudar innse	And I must tell it.
Ho gach du du fheile	Ho! Each black, black generous one!
Ho gu eile.	Hò-go! Each generous one!
Roinn mo chuidse	Divide this portion
Chliabh mo ghille	My servant harrowed!
Tuille toraidh	More produce!
Sin mar thuirt Mairearad	Then it was that Margaret said,
Fheudail uile tuille toraidh.	"O dear! More produce!"
Sin mar thuirt Mairi	Then said Mary,
Ghraidh mo cheile	"My dearest dear!
Tha Martuinn cul na comhla	Martin is behind the door,
'S e gar n eisdeachd.	Listening to us!"
So lethsgeul dha sinn ars ise	"That is his excuse," said she.
Hu fadar he feadar / fodar	Hu fudar! Hei fedar!
Suas a bhleidein	Up with you, you cajoler!
Dh eirich cuisnean garbh	Fierce icinesses rose
Air Domhnull	On Donald,
Bhuail e air Mairearad	He levelled at Margaret
Fior spreodadh	Fair abuse!
Bhuail e gnogag air a chlarsaich	He gave a tap to the harp
'S ghairm na teudan	And the strings sounded.
Thug e grad tharruing air crambail	He quickly drew a crambat[26]
'S theann ri gleusadh	And tried to tune it.
Rinn thu mistath ars an clarsair	"You have done a mischief," said the clerk,
Is liam nach misde	"That I don't regret!
Mo chreach leir a dh-eirich dhutsa	Utter ruin has come upon you

'S do chrann briste.	With your broken stick!"
Is ann agads tha m ballan ioclaint	"You have a healing vessel,"
Ars an clarsair	Said the harper.
Nuair a dh fhiachar riut a ris e	"When you are tried with it a second time,
Ni thu slan e	'Twill make the stick whole;
Do chuid dhuit de'n bhallan-ioclaint	So your share be yours of the healing cup.
Fheudail uile	O dearest sir!
Do chrann buadhor	May that stick of many virtues
S e lan toraidh.	Be full of produce!"
Chaidh mi Oidhche Choinlle/Choinnle	I went on Candle night to hold New Year revel
Thigh nam maragan reamhar	In the house of fat puddings,
Dh iarr mi fosgladh 's an dorus	I asked admittance at the door,
Gu brosnach teann	Coaxingly with fair words;
Labhair bleidire mor na sraide	The big clerk of the street spoke
Facal bruideil	A senseless word:
Nam biodh mo chaman oir am laimh	"If my gold crook were in my hand
Cha do leig mi do cheann slan o'n dorus	I would not let your head whole from the door."
Chaidh mi tuaitheal an doruis	I took the north turn to the door,
B'e sin tuaitheal mo chrochaidh	That was a north turn of mischief to me:
Bhuail mi ordag mo choise	I struck the big toe of my foot
Ann an aodan na cloiche	In the face of a stone,
Thuit am pinne thuit am painne	The pin fell, the pan fell,
Thuit a chliath chliata 's an dorus	The harrows in the door fell,
Rinn i gliong glang meanachan	They made a cling clang clattering!
Eirich a suas a bhean og	Rise down, young wife
'S a bhean choir a choisinn cliu	And honest dame, that hast carried praise,
Bi gu smearail mar bu dual/nos	Be womanly as thou wert wont
Eirich a suas a chailin duinn.	And bring our Christmas gifts to us —
Cabag an aghaidh reidh	The smoothed-faced cheese
'S pairt de mhionnach reidh gun sugh	And entrails prepared with juice;
Mar bheil sin agad ad choir	But if these are not convenient
Foghnaidh aran us feoil duinn	Bread and cheese will suffice.
Cha n e lon-craois	It was not greed with open mouth
Thug an bhaile mi	That brought me to the town
Ach maois air muin mo ghille sa	But a hamper on my servant's back!
Gille geal ga m' ghlacadh	A white servant catch me,
Saill ga m' losgadh	Fatness burns me!
Fosgail s leig a stigh mi.	Open and let me in!
Is fior sin arsa fear an tighe	"True for him," said the goodman,
Leigibh a stigh e.	"let him in."

The following rhyme was appointed for all who had nothing else to say:

Chan eil fuath agam air càise	*I do not dislike cheese*
'S chan eil gràin agam air ìm,	*And have no aversion to butter,*
Ach deuran beag de na tha sa bhuideal,	*But a little drop from the cask*
Tha mo shlugan air a thì.	*My throttle is in quest of.*[27]

NEW YEAR NIGHT

It was a practice not to be neglected to keep the fire alive in the house all night. No one was to come near it but a friend, and, as an additional security against its going out, candles were kept burning. Hence the other name given to the night, *oidhche Choinnle*, i.e. Candle night.[28] There was a rhyme (which the writer has not been able to recover) to be said when feeding the fire.[29] By this means evil was kept away from the house for the subsequent year.

If the fire went out no kindling could be got next day from any of the neighbours. The first day of the year was a quarter-day, on which it was unlucky to give fire out of the house.[30] It gave the means to witches and evilly-disposed people to do irreparable mischief to the cattle and their produce. The dying out of the fire was, therefore, a serious inconvenience in days when lucifer matches were unknown. The women made use of the occasion to bake bread for next day.

Old men, provident of the future, watched with interest the wind the old year left (*ghaoth dh'fhàgas a' Chollainn*). That would prove the prevailing wind during the ensuing year, and indicated its chief characteristics, as the rhyme says:

> *Gaoth deas, teas is toradh,*
> *Gaoth tuath, fuachd is gailleann,*
> *Gaoth 'n-iar, iasg is bainne,*
> *Gaoth 'n-ear, meas air chrannaibh.*

"South wind, heat and produce, / North wind, cold and tempest, / West wind, fish and milk, / East wind, fruit on trees."[31]

NEW YEAR'S DAY

New Year's day, *latha na Bliadhn' Ùir*, was also called *latha Nollaige Bige* 'the day of Little Christmas'.[32] On getting up in the morning the head of the family treated all the household to a dram.[33] After that a spoonful of half-boiled sowens (*cabhraich leth-bhruich*), the poorest food imaginable, was given for luck. Sometimes the sowens were whole boiled, and in some places the well-to-do farmer's wife left a little overnight at the house of every poor man on the farm.[34] The custom of having this dish of sowens was known in the central Highlands and in Lorn, but does not seem to have extended to Mull, Morvern, or the Western Islands. The salutations of the season were duly given by the household to one another, and to every person they met: *Bliadhna mhath Ùr dhuit*, "A good New Year to you."

Mar sin duit fhéin, is mòran diubh. "The same to you, and many of them."

The boys rushed away out to play at their everlasting game of shinty, and a more sumptuous breakfast than ordinary was prepared.

Nothing was allowed to be put out of the house this day, neither the ashes of the fire nor the sweepings of the house, nor dirty water, nor anything else, however useless or however much in the way. It was a very serious matter to give fire out of the house to a neighbour whose hearth had become cold, as the doing so (as already said) gave power to the evil-minded to take away the produce from the cattle. Indeed it was ominous that death would occur in the household within the year. Hospinian tells that at Rome on New Year's day no-one would allow a neighbour to take fire out of his house, or anything composed of iron (Ellis's *Brand's Antiquities*, i. 13).[35]

It was unlucky for a woman to be the first to enter the house, or if the person were empty-handed. A young man entering with an armful of corn was an excellent sign of the year's prosperity, but a decrepit old woman asking kindling for her fire was a most deplorable omen. The same belief that some people are lucky as first-foots led to the 'curious custom' in the isle of Man known as the *Quaaltagh* (Ellis's *Brand*, i. 538). That word differs only in spelling from the Gaelic *còmhalaich* or *còmhaltaich*, a person the meeting of whom is ominous of good or bad fortune. To ensure a good omen, a party of young men went in every parish in Man from house to house on New Year's day singing luck to the inmates. It was deemed an omen of good to see the sun this day.[36]

Towards midday the men gathered in some suitable place, the largest and most level field in the neighbourhood, for the great shinty match (*iomain mhòr*). A match was formed between adjoining districts and villages, or, if the village itself was populous, by two leaders, appointed for the purpose, choosing one alternately from those present till the whole gathering was gone through.[37] It was decided who was to choose first by the one leader holding his shinty-stick (*caman*) vertically, or up and down, and throwing it to the other, who caught it somewhere about the middle. The two then grasped the stick alternately, the hand of the one being close above that of the other, and the one who grasped the end so that he could swing the stick three times round his head had the first choice. Sometimes, to decide the point quickly, one asked the other which he would have, *chas no bhas* ('foot or palm'), meaning which end of the shinty-stick he made choice of, the 'foot' being that by which the stick is held, the 'palm' that with which the ball is struck. On a choice being made, the club was thrown into the air, and the matter was decided by the point of it that pointed southwardly more summarily than by the 'heads and tails' of a copper coin.[38]

In the game a wooden ball (*ball*) was used in the daytime, when men could guard themselves against being struck by it; but when the game was played at night, in the dusk or by moonlight, a ball of hair or thread called *crìod* was used. The object of the game was to drive this ball 'hail' (*thadhal*), that is, between and beyond certain marks at the two ends of the field. Of course the two parties had opposite 'hails'. The play commenced by setting the ball in a suitable place and giving the first blow, called *buille bhàraich,* to the chief, proprietor, priest, minister or other principal person present.[39]

A player stood opposite to him, and if the ball was missed at the first blow – as sometimes happened from excessive deliberation, want of skill and practice, etc. – whipped it away in the other direction; and, without further ceremony, every person ran after it as he chose, and hit it as he got opportunity. Two or three of the best players on each side were kept behind their party, 'behind hail' (*air chùl tadhail*), as in the game of football, to act as a guard when their adversaries too nearly sent the ball 'home'.[40]

Sometimes the company was so fairly matched that nightfall put an end to the sport without either party winning 'a hail'. Every player got as much exercise as he felt inclined for. Some did little more than walk about the field, others could hardly drag themselves home at night with fatigue. Much can be said on behalf of the game as the best of outdoor sports, combining healthy and (when the player chooses) strong exercise with freedom from horseplay.

A piper played before and after the game. The women, dressed in their best, stood looking on. At the end the chief (or laird) gave a dinner, or, failing him, a number were entertained in the house of a mutual friend. In the evening a ball was given, open to all.

New Year's day, like the first of every quarter of the year (*h-uile latha ceann ràidhe*), was a great 'saining' day, i.e. a day for taking precautions for keeping away evil from the cattle and houses. Certain ceremonies were carefully observed by the superstitious: juniper was burnt in the byre, the animals were marked with tar, the houses were decked with mountain ash, and the door-posts and walls, and even the cattle, were sprinkled with wine.[41]

By New Year's day the nights have begun to shorten considerably. It is a Gaelic saying that there is *uair ri latha Nollaige Bige* ('an hour of greater length to the day of Little Christmas') and this is explained to be *uair a' ghille chonnaidh* ('the hour of the fuel lad'). The word *uair* means 'a time' as well as an hour; and the meaning perhaps is that owing to the lengthening of the day the person bringing in firewood has to go one trip less frequently for fuel to make a light.[42]

Christmas day (*là Nollaige Mòire*) was said to lengthen *fad coisichean coilich*, a cock's stride or walk, and the expression was explained to mean that the bird had time to walk to a neighbour's dunghill, crow three times, and come back again.[43]

The same sayings are current in the Highlands as in the south. "A green Yule makes a fat kirkyard" has its literal counterpart in *Si Nollaig uaine nì an cladh miadh* (i.e. *reamhar*) and in *Is blianach Nollaig gun sneachda* (i.e. "Lean is Yule without snow").[44]

There is no reason to suppose that any pagan rites connected with the period of the winter solstice were incorporated with the Yule or *Nollaig* ceremonies. The various names connected with the season are of Christian origin; the superstitions, as that of refusing fire and allowing nothing out of the house, can be traced to Rome; the custom of a man dressing himself in a cow's hide, as suggested by Brand (i. 8), with every probability, is a vestige of the Festival of Fools, long held in Paris on New Year's day, and of which it was part that men clothed themselves in cowhide (*vestiuntur pellibus pecudum*).[45]

The holding of a singed piece of skin to the noses of the wassailers is more likely to have originated in the frolics of the same festival than in any pagan observance. The meaning of the custom is obscure, but its character is too whimsical to be associated with any pagan rite.[46]

THE TWELVE DAYS OF CHRISTMAS (*DÀ LATHA DHEUG NA NOLLAIG*)

These were the twelve days commencing from the Nativity or Big *Nollaig*, and were deemed to represent, in respect of weather, the twelve months of the year. Some say the days should be calculated from New Year's day.[47] "Whatever weather there is on the twelve days beginning with the last of December, the same will agree with the weather in the corresponding month" (Pennant).[48] In Ireland the twelve days were held to stand for the twelve Apostles, and 'on Twelve-Eve in Christmas, they use to set up as high as they can a sieve of oats, and in it a dozen of candles set round, and in the centre one larger, all lighted; this in memory of our saviour and his apostles, lights of the world' (Brand, i. 25).[49] The same, no doubt, was the origin of the Highland notation.

They are also looked upon as the twelve days between old and new style. There is evidence in the saying that 'an hour and a half is added to Candle day' (*uair gu leth ri latha Coinnle*) that some such custom was known of old in Scotland as in Ireland; and though Candle night (*oidhche Choinnle*) is now a name given to Christmas night, there is a probability it originally denoted Twelve Eve, or the Feast of the Epiphany.[50]

WINTER SEASON

The period during which the above festivities occurred, and some time before and after *Nollaig*, was popularly known as *Gearra Dubha na Nollaig*, 'the Black Cuttings of Christmas', from its liability to tempestuous weather. The sky is then lowering and dark, the 'level' sun gives little warmth, and high winds prevail.[51]

The *Dùlachd* of winter extended over the six weeks 'preceding the middle of spring' (*gu meadhon an earraich*). Some (e.g. Highland Society's Dictionary, *sub voce*) call it *Dùbhlachd*, and translate it simply 'wintry weather'. Others call it *Dùdlachd*, and denote by it 'the depth of winter'. The word is a contraction of *duaithealachd*, from *duaitheil*, extremely coarse and rough, an epithet applied to stormy weather. Thus, *Nach duaitheil an t-sìd'?* "Is it not desperately coarse weather?" *Ceann reamhar an duaithealais*, 'the thick end of coarseness', denotes extremely rough usage.[52]

Handsel Monday (*Di-Luain an t-Sainnseil*) was the first Monday after New Year's day, and was the principal day in the whole year for *deuchainn*, i.e. for making trials and forecasts of the future. It derives its name from *sainnseal*, Scots 'handsel', a present or gift in his hand given this day to every visitor to a house. *Sainnseal sona* is 'a happy or fortunate present'. In some districts cock-fighting was practised in the schools, and children brought a gratuity (in money) to the schoolmaster. In other districts this was not the case till Shrovetide (*Di-Màirt Inid*).[53]

In Skye the day is called *Di-Luain Traosta*; and it is from it the twelve days, corresponding in weather to the twelve months of the year, are computed.[54]

FEBRUARY (*FAOILLEACH*)

The name *faoilleach* is said to mean 'wolf-month', from *faol*, wild, whence also *faol-chu*, a wolf, literally a wild dog.[55] It embraces the last fourteen days of winter and the first fourteen days of spring, the former being called *am faoilleach geamhraidh* ('the winter *faoilleach*'), the latter *am faoilleach earraich* ('the spring *faoilleach*'). It is also known as *am marbh-mhìos* ('the dead month').[56] Winter is still ruling the inverted year, and all nature seems to be dead. The trees have long lost their foliage, the grass gives no sign as yet of returning growth, and fields and fallows are bare. When over all there is a coating of snow the name of 'dead month' appears peculiarly appropriate.

The time, being reckoned by old style, corresponds almost exactly to the present month of February, and the saying that 'every month in the year curses a fair February' is amply corroborated by the Gaelic sayings regarding it. Old men liked it to commence with a heavy storm and end with a calm, or (to use their own words) *tighinn a-staigh le ceann na nathrach, 's dol a-mach le earball peucaig* ('to come in with the head of a serpent, and go out with a peacock's tail').[57] There are to be three days of calm during it, according to the saying, *trì là Faoilleach san Iuchar, 's trì là Iuchar san Fhaoilleach.* "Three days of August in February, and three days of February in August."[58]

Both the February calm and the August storm, however, have become proverbial for their uncertainty and short duration. *Fiath Faoilleach is gaoth Iuchar* ('February calm and August wind') are the most fickle things in the world.[59] In the north it was said 'mist in February means snow next day' (*ceò san Fhaoilleach, sneachda màireach*). Old people said,

> *B' fheàrr leam a' chreach thigh'nn don tìr*
> *Na 'mhadainn chiùin san Fhaoilleach fhuar.*

"Better the land be plundered / Than a calm morning in February."[60] The most unreasonable of expectations is to expect 'black brambles in February' (*smeuran dubha san Fhaoilleach*).[61]

It is unfortunate if the heat of this season is such, as old men say they have seen it, that the cattle run with the heat; but it is a healthy sign of the season if men go about with their hands wrinkled with the cold till they resemble an animal's hoof, and kept in their pockets (anciently belts) for warmth.

> *Faoilleach, faoilleach, cruth an crios,*
> *Faoilte mhòr bu chòir bhith ris;*
> *Crodh is caoraich ruith air theas,*
> *Gul is caoidh bu chòir bhith ris.*

"Wild month, wild month, hoof in belt, / Much rejoicing should be held; / Cows and sheep running in heat, / Weeping and wailing then are meet."[62] It was said to be as unnatural to hear thunder at this time as to hear 'a calf lowing in its mother's womb' – *laogh a' geumraich am broinn a mhàthar.*

EARRACH BEAG NAM FAOCHAG

Earrach Beag nam Faochag, 'the Little Spring of Whelks', is the period from Christmas (*Nollaig*) to St Bride's day, or beginning of February. That species of shellfish is then at its best, and the soup made from it, called *siabh* or *brochan fhaochag,* was deemed as good as flesh.[63]

ST BRIDE'S DAY

St Bridget's or St Bride's day (*Féill Brìde, Brithid*) is the first day of spring, consequently the middle of the *faoilleach,* the 1st of February OS, but the 13th New

Style.[64] It is frequently confounded with Candlemas, but that day is the 2nd February, whereas St Bride's day is the 1st – this mistake is made by Martin (*Western Isl.*, 1716, p. 119). He says that on the 2nd of February 'the mistress and servants of each family take a sheaf of oats and dress it up in woman's apparel, put it in a large basket, and lay a wooden club by it, and this they call Briid's Bed; and then the mistress and servants cry three times, Briid is come, Briid is welcome' (Brand, i. 56).[65] The custom is long extinct in the parts of the Highlands with which the writer is acquainted, and the only particulars connected with it he has heard are that on St Bride's day a bed of birch twigs (*leaba bharraich*) was made by the women, and that they then cried at the door, *Bride, Bride, thig a-staigh, tha do leaba dèante.* "Bride, Bride, come in, your bed is ready."

As in the case of many Gaelic festivals, ceremonies, and other antiquities, the origin of St Bride's day is to be traced directly to Ireland. St Bridget, we are told, was the first nun in Ireland, and founded her first cell where the city of Kildare now stands, in 585. She was a native of Ulster, and, after building monasteries and performing miracles, became Patroness of Ireland. In 1185 her body was found in the same vault with those of St Patrick and St Columba. A well near her church in Fleet Street, London, gave its name, Bridewell, to a palace given by Edward VI to the city for a workhouse and a house of correction. The honoured name of St Bride, who during many ages was celebrated for her sanctity and piety, has thus by accident become associated with the criminal population.

It is a sign of the approaching spring that on this day the raven begins to build, and larks sing with a clearer voice. It has been explained in another part of this work that there was a belief the serpent had to come out of its hole seven days previous.[66] The rhyme regarding the raven ran:

> *Nead air Brithid, ubh air Inid*
> *'S eun air Càisg —*
> *'S mur bi sin aig an fhitheach*
> *Bithidh am bàs.*[67]

("A nest on St Bridget's Day, an egg at Shrovetide / And a bird at Easter – / If the raven have not these / Then it dies.") The correctness of the observations which it embodies is confirmed by White (*Nat. Hist. of Selborne*), who gives February 14–17 as the period at which the raven builds.[68]

In Tiree this was the day on which cock-fighting was practised and gratuities were given to the schoolmaster. In the evening it was customary to have a ball.[69]

The period from *Nollaig* to *Féill Brìde* was reckoned at one month and three days.[70]

Spring

The *faoilleach* introduces a series of names peculiarly Celtic and (so far as the writer is aware) having no equivalents in any other language. The divisions of time denoted by them extend to the beginning of summer; each name, in accordance with the genius of the Gaelic language as shown in names of places, nicknames, etc., is descriptive. Almanacs have long superseded the ancient notations, and it is not now an easy matter to arrange them in their proper order, or to reconcile the accounts retained by tradition with almanac notation. The length of time ascribed to each seems to have varied in different districts.[71]

Feadag, the Whistle

The *feadag* succeeds immediately to the wolf-month (*faoilleach*), though some place it before *cailleach* and about St Patrick's day. In MacLeod and Dewar's Dictionary it is said to be the third week in February, which reckoned by OS is from 1st to 8th March NS.[72] It is thus made to succeed the *faoilleach*, and the same seems the opinion of Hugh MacLachlan, of Aberdeen, a most learned and accomplished man. In a poem on spring he says:

> *Ràidhe 'n tig am faoilleach feannaidh,*
> *Fuar chloch-mheallain, stoirm nam peileir,*
> *Feadag, sguabag, gruaim a' ghearrain —*
> *Crainntidh 'chailleach as beurra friodhan.*[73]

("Season in which comes the flaying wolf-month, / Cold hailstones, a storm of bullets, / *Feadag, sguabag,* the *gearran*'s gloom / And shrivelling *cailleach*, sharp bristled.") It extends to three days, and its boisterous character is shewn in the rhyme:

> *Feadag, feadag, màthair faoilleach fuar,*[74]
> *Marbhaidh i caoraich is uain,*
> *Marbhaidh i 'n crodh mòr mu seach*
> *'S an t-each ris an aon uair.*

"*Feadag, feadag*, mother of the cold *faoilleach*, / It kills sheep and lambs, / It kills the big kine one by one / And horses at the same time."

Gobag, the Sharp-Billed One

This lasts for a week, others say three, four, and nine days.[75]

SGUABAG, THE SWEEPER

This seems the same as the three days called *ioma-sguaba na faoilleach*, 'the eddy winds of the storm month'. The appearance of spring is now to be seen, but the bad weather is not yet past. The worst weather comes back occasionally, and there are fewer gusts of wind, uncertain in their coming and duration, that well deserve the name of 'eddy winds from February'.[76]

GEARRAN, A GELDING, OR PERHAPS *GEARAN*, COMPLAINT

It is quite possible the latter may have been the original name, as there is always associated with it a period called *caoile*, leanness.[77] It extends over a month, and in Skye is made to succeed to the *faoilleach*. There was a rule known to old men that 'the first Tuesday of March (OS) is the last Tuesday of *gearran*' (*a' chiad Di-Màirt den Mhàrt an Di-Màirt mu dheire den ghearran*). In Tiree – from which the lofty hills of Rum form a conspicuous sight, and to the green appearance of which, in frosty weather, their snow-covered summits form a striking contrast – it is said that at this season 'the big mare of Rum turns three times to her colt', i.e. from cold and hunger. The expression refers to times when a little hardy breed of horses was found in the Western Islands – like Shetland ponies, and left to shift for themselves during winter. It was also said:

> *Thuirt an gearran ris an fhaoilleach,*
> *"Càit an d'fhàg thu 'n gamhainn bochd?"*
> *"Dh'fhàg mi e aig an Fhear rinn na dùilean*
> *'S a dhà shùil air an t-sop."*
> *"Ma bheireas mis'," thuirt am mìos-Màigh,*
> *"Air an anail am barraibh a chluas,*
> *Cuiridh mi ruideis air an tràigh e*
> *'S fheaman air a ghualainn."*

"Then said *gearran* to *faoilleach*, / 'Where left you the poor stirk?' / 'I left it with Him who made the elements, / Staring at a stack of fodder.' / 'If I catch it,' said the May month, / 'With the breath in the points of his ears, / I will send it racing to the hill / With its tail upon its shoulders.'"[78] The beast will pull through if it can 'lift its ear higher than its horn', which at that age (one year) it ought to do.

The high winds coming at this time, and well known in the south as the winds of March, were said in their violence to send seven bolls of driving snow through one auger-hole. *Chuireadh an gearran seachd bola catha staigh air aon toll tora, leis cho gailbheach 's a bha 'n t-sìd'.*[79]

The *gearran* is deemed the best time for sowing seeds. The high winds dry the ground, and all agricultural seeds are the better of being put in 'a dry bed' (*leaba thioram don t-sìol*).[80] It is a disputed point what precise date. The Perthshire rhyme also testifies to the still stormy character of the weather.[81] The calling the *gearran* short supports the opinion of many that it was properly only seven days:

> *Sin thuirt an gearran geàrr,*
> *"Ni mi farran ort nach fheàrr —*
> *Cuiridh mi bhò mhòr sa pholl*
> *Gus an d'thig an tonn far a ceann."*

"Then said the short *gearran*, / 'I will play you a trick that is no better – / I will put the big cow in the mud / Till the wave comes over its head.'" Some say the *gearran* is the month before St Patrick's day OS, others fourteen days before it and fourteen days after, i.e. before and after 29th March.

A' CHAILLEACH, THE OLD WIFE

This old wife is the same as the hag of whom people were afraid in harvest (the last done with the shearing had to feed her till next harvest) and to whom boys bid defiance in their New Year day rhyme, viz., 'the Famine, or Scarcity of the Farm'.[82] In spring she was engaged with a hammer in keeping the grass under.

> *Buailidh i thall, buailidh i bhos,*
> *Buailidh i eadar a dà chois*

("She strikes here, she strikes there, / She strikes between her legs"); but the grass grows too fast for her, and in despair she throws the hammer from her, and where it lighted no grass grows.[83]

> *Thilg i e fon chraoibh chruaidh chuilinn*
> *Air nach do chinn gas feur no fionnadh riamh.*[84]

("She threw it beneath the hard holly tree / Where grass or hair has never grown.")

TRÌ LÀITHEAN NAN ÒISGEAN, THREE HOG DAYS

In the rural lore of the south of Scotland the three hog days are held to be the last three days of March, and to have been borrowed by that month from April (Brand, ii. 42). Dr Jamieson (*Etym. Dict. of Scot. Lang.*) says, "Some of the vulgar imagine, that these days received their designation from the conduct of the Israelites in *borrowing* the property of the Egyptians."[85] There is a Highland explanation also connecting them with the departure from Egypt. They were days borrowed by the Israelites for the killing of the Paschal lamb. "Some went on this side of the hillock, some on that." (*Chàidh cuid an taobh sa 'n chnoc*, etc.)[86]

They are perhaps the days called in Tiree *trì latha na bò ruaidhe* i.e. 'the red cow's three days'.[87]

MÀRT, Seed-Time

This name is doubtlessly derived from the Latin *Mars*, in which case it ought to correspond to the month of March, OS. It does not commence till the 24th of that month.[88] The word has come to signify a busy time of the year, whether seed-time or harvest – usually, however, the former. *Saothair a' Mhàirt* is the 'busiest time of spring'; *a' ghaoth luath luimeineach Mhàirt* means 'the bare swift March wind', frequently mentioned in *Winter Evening Tales* to denote great speed,[89] and *am Màrt tioram blàth* means 'dry genial March'. It is a favourable sign of the season when the ground is saturated with wet at its beginning. Old men wished

> *An linge làn air chionn a' Mhàirt*[90]
> *'S tugha nan taighean an claisean nan iomairean*

('The full pool awaiting March / And house-thatch in the furrows of the ploughland') and deemed it a good sign if the violence of the wind stripped three layers of thatch (*trì breathan de thugha*) from the houses.[91] The advice for sowing seed now is:

> *Leig seachad a' chiad Mhàrt*
> *'S an dàrna Màrt mas fheudar e,*
> *Ach olc air mhath gun d'thig an t-sìd'*
> *Cuir do shìol san fhìor Mhàrt.*

("Let past the first March (i.e. Tuesday) / And second March if need be, / But be the weather good or bad / Sow thy seed in the true March.") Others say 'though you cannot send a pebble against the north wind' (*ged nach cuireadh tu dòirneag an aghaidh na gaoith tuath*) you are to sow.[92]

Is luaithe oidhche sa Mhàrt na dhà san fhogharadh. "A night in March is swifter than two in harvest."

INID, Shrovetide

The Gaelic name is from Latin *Initium*, this being the beginning of Lent. It was always reckoned as 'the first Tuesday of the spring light' (*chiad Di-Màirt den t-solas earraich*), i.e. of the new moon in spring. It is a moveable feast, and this is a simple way of calculating it. The plan adopted by the English church is more complicated – Shrovetide is always the seventh Tuesday before Easter, and Easter is 'the first Sunday after the first full moon, which happens on or after the 21st March; but if the full moon is on a Sunday, Easter day is the Sunday following'.[93]

Shrovetide was called *an Inid bheadaidh* ('shameless Shrovetide'), because the day of the festival was held to precede the night, while, in the case of all the other festivals, the night or vigil was held to precede the day. A good reason for this will be found in a natural aversion to beginning the austerities of Lent.[94]

It has been already told (art. Diabolus) how Michael Scott (or, according to Skye tradition, Parson Sir Andro of Rigg, near Storr in that island) went to Rome riding on the devil, and first ascertained from the Pope the rule for calculating the day.[95] In schools it was the day for cock-fighting and giving gratuities to the schoolmaster. The latter custom was observed with more correctness on the first Monday of the year, being the day allotted for presents.[96] The practice of cock-fighting is extinct in the Highlands, but presents to the schoolmaster are universally practised. The boy and girl who give the largest donation (and it seldom exceeds a shilling) are declared King and Queen of the school, and have the privilege of asking 'a play' (i.e. a holiday) for the school.[97]

The names connected with cock-fighting, still to be found in the Highlands, being Latin, shew the practice is not of native growth. Each boy came to the school with a dung-hill cock under his arm. The head of the bird was covered and its tail taken out to make it more ready to fight, and fight better when let loose opposite another bird. Runaway cocks were called *fuge*, and the name is still given to boys who shirk fighting. Shouts followed the defeated bird of *Fuge, fuge, coileach cam!* – "Run, run, cock with one eye!" – and its owner had to pay a penalty of some pence.[98]

Shrovetide was one of the great days for 'saining' cattle, juniper being burned before them, while other superstitious precautions were taken to keep them free from harm. Those curious or anxious about their future husbands or wives made a cake of soot (*bonnach sùith, bonnach Inid*) of which they partook, putting the rest below their pillows to dream over.[99] It was believed that if there was fair weather at *Inid* it would be foul weather at Easter, and vice versa, as the rhyme has it:

> *Thuirt an Inid ris a' Chàisg,*
> *"Càit am faigh mi àite cluich?*
> *Thoir thusa dhòmhsa pàilliun geamhraidh*
> *'S togaidh mi taigh samhraidh dhuit."*

("Shrovetide said to Easter, / 'Where will I get a place to play myself? / Give to me a winter palace / And I will build a summer house for you.'")[100]

Carghas, Lent

This is the period from Shrovetide to Easter. It extends to forty days, and refers to the miraculous fasts of Moses, Elias, and our Lord. The Gaelic mode of calculation was:

> *Seachd seachdainean geàrr goirid*
> *Eadar Inid is Càisg.*[101]

("Seven short weeks / From Shrovetide till Easter.") The name *Carghas* is a corruption of *Quadragesima*, Italian *Quaresimo*, 'Forty', just as *Inid* is from *Initium*. *Inid a' Charghais* is just 'the beginning of the forty days'. This derivation has been derived from – and others have been confirmed by – Lhuyd, *Archaeologia Britannica*, published at Oxford, 1707.[102] The work is folio size, and contains many curious and sensible philological observations. Its principal defect is that what is valuable is buried in pages of uninteresting glossaries.

St Kessock's Day (*Féill mo Cheasaig*)

This was March 10/22.[103] It is said, *Latha Féill mo Cheasaig bidh gach easgann torrach.* "On the Feast of St Kessock every eel is pregnant."[104]

The saint was bishop in Scotland in 560, and has given a name to Kessock Ferry (*Port a Cheasaig*), near Inverness, and to a market held at Callander, Perthshire, for hiring, on the 22nd March, or 10th old style. The fair is known as 'Tenth-Day', but among the Gaelic-speaking population as *Féill mo Cheasaig*.[105] A rock at the west end of the village is known as *Tom a Cheasaig*.[106]

St Patrick's Day (*Féill Pàraig*)

This is the middle day of spring and that on which the night and day are of equal length, March 17/29.

A certain sign of the day is held in the Hebrides to be a south wind in the morning and a north wind at night.[107] The saint comes from Ireland to see his parishioners in Barra and other places on the west of Scotland, and has a favourable wind coming and returning. He is in Highland lore described as *Pàdraig a bheannaich Éirinn* ('Patrick who blessed Ireland'), and is said to have been married to the daughter of Ossian, bard – and last – of the *Féinne*. He was born AD 373, but it is disputed whether his native place was Scotland, or Wales, or England, or France. There can be no question that in Ireland and the Highlands of Scotland the more lively and kindly recollections of him have been retained. Numerous places called after him are found scattered over Scotland, Wales, and Ireland.

After this day, *seach gun leum an Fhéill Pàraig* (literally 'once Patrick's Festival has jumped'), the limpet is better than the whelk, and is said in consequence to treat it with great indignity.

> *Latha Féill Pàraig*
> *Mùinidh bhàirneach air an fhaochaig.*[108]

Another piece of shore information connected with this season is that with the advance of spring 'as horses grow lean, crabs grow fat' – *mar as caoile 'n t-each, sann as reamhrad am partan.*[109] Others have it, *Nuair bhios an t-each caol, bidh 'n fhaochag reamhar.* "When the horse is lean, the whelk is fat."

The reviving influences of the spring are now making themselves visible, according to the saying,

> *Chan eil luibh san talamh*
> *Nach eil fad cluas luch dhith mach*
> *Latha Féill Pàraig.*

"There is not an herb in the ground / But the length of a mouse's ear of it is out / On St Patrick's day." Old men liked the days immediately preceding it to be stormy, and to see, as they said, *a chlaisich làn sneachda, làn uisge, 's tugha nan taighean* – 'the furrows full of snow, of rain, and the thatch of houses'.[110] There are particularly high tides on St Patrick's day and the Annunciation of the Virgin Mary, according to the saying

> *Reothairt na Féill Moire*
> *'S boilich na Féill Pàraig.*

("The spring tides of Lady day / And the mad tides of St Patrick's day.")[111] *Marbhladh na Féill Pàraig*, 'the deadening of St Patrick's day', means the quiet calm waters that sometimes occur at this season; others say *bog-mharbhlainn*, and say it means the swelling (*tòcadh*) observable at the time in the sea from the increasing heat.[112]

LADY DAY (*FÉILL MOIRE*)

This was known as *Féill Moire an t-Sanais* (St Mary's Vigil of Annunciation) to distinguish it from *Féill Moire Mòr* (the Big St Mary's day), the Assumption of the Virgin, which was the middle day of autumn.[113] It is March 25 / April 6.

SHORE OR MAUNDY THURSDAY

This was the Thursday before Easter, and was known in the Hebrides as *là Brochain Mhòir*, 'the day of the Big Porridge'. It was now getting late in the spring, and if the winter had failed to cast a sufficient supply of seaweed on the shores, it was time to resort to extraordinary measures to secure the necessary manure for the land. A large pot of porridge was prepared, with butter and other good ingredients, and taken to the headlands near creeks where seaweed rested. A quantity was poured into the sea from each headland, with certain incantations or rhymes, and in consequence, it was believed, the harbours were full of sea-ware. The ceremony should only be performed in stormy weather. Its object no doubt was, by throwing the produce of the land into the sea, to make the sea throw its produce on the land.[114]

GOOD FRIDAY (*DI-HAOINE NA CEUSA*)

The Gaelic name means literally Crucifixion Friday.[115] The day was the Friday before Easter, and was observed in memory of our Lord's passion. There was hardly any belief that had a stronger hold on the Highlander's mind than that on no account whatever should iron be put in the ground on this day.[116] So great was the aversion to doing so that the more superstitious extended the prohibition to every Friday. As a matter of course no ploughing was done, and if a burial was to take place, the grave was opened on the previous day and the earth was settled over the coffin with a wooden shovel. The origin of the observance perhaps was that our Saviour's sepulchre had been previously prepared, being a new tomb hewn out in the rock.[117]

It was said that if the day be cold, it is colder than any other, in fact the coldest day of the whole year.

EASTER (*CÀSG*)

The proper day for keeping this festival, the anniversary of our Lord's resurrection, was at one time the cause of bitter controversies in the Christian world. It was first a subject of keen dispute between the eastern and western churches, and again between the church of Rome and the Irish and British churches. The feast is moveable, and depends on the time of the first full moon after the vernal equinox. Owing to rectifications of the calendar introduced at Rome, but unknown to the British churches, two different days had come to be observed, and by the seventh century the discussion as to which day was the correct one had become so warm and the difference so scandalous that the civil powers interfered and the question was settled in favour of the church of Rome by Oswy, king of Northumbria, at Whitby in 664. The Celtic clergy were accused of being Quartodecimans (a very good word in a controversy), that is, of keeping the festival, according to the Jewish mode of calculation, on the fourteenth day of the month Nizan, whether that day fell on a Sunday or not. The accusation is now universally acknowledged to be ill-founded, but it is likely they followed the Alexandrian rule on the point, by which the Easter festival could not begin till the eighth of March, a rule which had been at one time observed by the church of Rome itself. Neither the cycle followed during the controversy by the Celtic church, nor that followed by the Romish church, is that now prevailing, so that if one day was of more value than another for the festival, both parties were in the wrong.[118]

The rule now observed in the Highlands is 'seven short weeks from Shrovetide to Easter' (Shrovetide being 'the first Tuesday of the new moon in spring'), or Easter is 'the first Sunday of the second wane of the moon in spring' (*chiad Di-Dòmhnaich den dara earra-dhubh san earrach*).[119]

The name *Càsg* is but the Gaelic form of the Hebrew *Pascha*.[120] The change of P into C, K or Q is well known in philology, and the most noticeable difference between the Welsh and Gaelic branches of the Celtic tongue is that the latter has an aversion which the former has not to *p* as an initial consonant, preferring *c* instead. Lhuyd (*Arch. Brit.*, p. 20) says, "It's very Remarkable, that there are scarce any words in the *Irish* (besides what are borrow'd from the *Latin* or some other Language) that begin with *P*. in so much that in an Ancient Alphabetical *Vocabulary*, I have by me, that Letter is omitted; and no less observable that a considerable number of those words whose *Initial Letter* it is, in the *British*; begin in that Language with a *K*. or (as they constantly write) *C*." He then quotes as illustrations Welsh *Pâsk* 'Easter', Irish *Kâsg*; Cornish *Pencas* 'Whitsuntide', Irish *Kinkis*; Welsh *pen* 'a head', Irish *keann*, etc. He quotes from Vossius instances of a similar change in the interrogatives and relatives of the Greek Ionic dialect. A readily recognised instance is the change of the Greek ἵππος into the Latin *equus*.[121]

On *Càisg* Sunday the sun was believed in the Highlands of Scotland, as in Ireland, to dance soon after rising, and many respectable people are to be found who say they saw the phenomenon. The alternate glancing and darkening of the sun on a fitful spring morning was no doubt often so construed by those who stared too long at a brilliant object.[122]

A liability to north wind has made *gaoth tuath na Càisg* ('the north wind of Easter') a proverbial expression. The most trying part of the spring is still to come, and it is an expression employed to moderate excessive joy, and to put people in mind that the cares of life are not all past yet, that there is *earrach fada 'n déidh Càisg* – 'a long spring after Easter'. Another expression, reminding men that it is not too late to acquit themselves of their duties or hold rejoicings, is: *Gléidhear cuirm an déidh Càisg*. "A feast can be kept after Easter."[123]

Easter was a particular holiday with the young, and preparations were made for it long beforehand. Every egg that a boy could steal, or lay his hands on unobserved, was hid by him in the thatch of an outhouse, or in a hole in the ground, under a turf, or wherever else he thought his treasure would remain undiscovered. When the great day came, he and his companions, each with his collection of eggs, went away to some retired spot at a distance from the houses and beyond the probability of being disturbed by their seniors. Here they had a grand feast of pancakes and enjoyed themselves uncontrolled. The eggs were deemed of no use unless they had been secreted or stolen, and this originated, perhaps, in a feeling that with honestly or openly got eggs the feast was not so entirely independent of the older people. The reason why eggs were used at all is supposed to be from an egg being emblematic of the Resurrection.[124]

Two Sundays were held as *Càisg*. The second was distinguished only by a better feast than usual in the houses. The first Sunday was called *Càisg Mhòr* ('Big Easter') and the Sunday after it *Càisg nam Bodach* ('Old Men's Easter'), corresponding to the English Low Sunday.[125]

ALL FOOLS' DAY

This is variously known in the Highlands as *latha na Gogaireachd* ('the day of going on Fools' Errands'), *latha na Cuthaig* ('Cuckoo day'), and *latha nan Car* ('the day of Tricks'). Its observance is on the first of April, NS, and this argues its very recent introduction into the Highlands. The tricks and practices of the day are the same as elsewhere, the sending of acquaintances on sleeveless errands.[126] Sometimes, but only rarely, there is some ingenuity displayed in taking advantage of local and passing events to throw the most suspicious off their guard and send them on fools' messages. It is not difficult to impose on men with a serious face and a plausible story when it entails but little trouble to see if so likely a story or so pressing a message is real.

BAILC NA BEALLTAINN

The fourteen days preceding May-Day were known as *Bailc na Bealltainn*, 'the Balk or Ridge of Beltane'. The sea is then as it were awakening, and is more obedient to the winds. *Balc* means a ridge, also swelling, strength, *onfhadh, foghail*. The weather threatens frequently without breaking.

> *Masa Bailc-Bhealltainn bhlàth,*
> *Masa turadh an treas là*
> *'S masa gaoth an-ear a-rithis,*
> *Is cinnteach gum bi meas air chrannaibh.*

("If warm May-Day be swollen [threatening], / And it be dry the third day / And it be an east wind after that, / There certainly will be fruit on trees.")[127]

BEALLTAINN, MAY-DAY

The advent of summer is everywhere hailed with joy, and the day recognised as the first of the season is naturally one of the most important days in the calendar. Another day of equal importance in the Celtic year was the first of winter, and the names of the two days, *Bealltainn* and *Samhainn*, cannot be traced, like so many other notations of the year, to ecclesiastical sources. Like the names *faoilleach* (the storm month) and *iuchar* (the hot month), they are best referred to pagan times.

Bealltainn is commonly derived from *Bel teine*, the fire of Baal or Belus, and is considered as sure evidence of the Phoenician origin of the sacred institutions of the Celts. It is a derivation, however, that wants all the elements of probability. There is a want of evidence that the Phoenician Baal, or any deity resembling him, was ever worshipped by the Celts, or that the fires kindled and observances practised on this day had any connection with the attributes ascribed to him; while the analogies of the Gaelic language prevent the supposition that 'the fire of Baal' could be rendered *Beall-tein*'. Besides, the word is not *Beall-teine*, but *Bealltainn*, a difference in the final syllable sufficiently noticeable to a Gaelic ear. It is the difference between the single and double sound of *n*.

Baal and Ashtoreth were the supreme male and female divinities of the Phoenician and Canaanitish nations, and are supposed to be personifications of the generative and receptive powers of nature, and to be identical with the sun and moon. In Hebrew and kindred languages *Baal* is a mere title of honour, signifying 'Lord or Possessor of', and in Gaelic the sun and moon are both feminine nouns, merely descriptive of the appearance of these planets. There is nothing that indicates their ever having been looked on as divinities, or ascribing to them any attribute such as belonged to Baal. In Gaelic the noun limited or possessed always precedes the qualifying noun, and it would require strong evidence to show that 'Baal's fire' could be 'Beltane' (i.e. Baal-fire), and not 'Tane-Bel' (*Teine-Bhàil*), i.e. fire of Baal. The contrast between English and Gaelic in this respect is often very striking, and a safe rule in etymology.

The final syllable is the same as in *Samhainn*, the end of summer, which is thought by Lhuyd to be from *fuinn* (connected with the Latin *finis*), an end.[128] In this case *t* is simply accresive. *L* has an attraction for *t* after it, as *m* has for *b*, and *n* for *d*. *Beall* is likely connected with the other words that have *bl* in their initial syllable, with a root idea of separating, parting, opening; and claims kindred with *blàth*, a blossom, *bial*, the mouth, *bealach*, a pass, more than with the title of a Semitic deity. It is the opening day of the year, when the rigours of winter are parted with, and the seasons, as it were, separate. Behind lay winter, cold, and unfruitfulness of the earth, but before was warmth and fertility and beauty. The final syllable has no more to do with fire than it has in *gamhainn*, a stirk, *calltainn*, a hazel tree.[129]

It was said, with truth, that whatever day New Year day fell upon, Beltane fell on the day following. *Nollaig an-diugh, Bealltainn a-màireach*: "New Year's day today, Beltane tomorrow."[130]

There is sometimes very cold weather at this time, and this was denoted by the expression *glaisein cumhach na Bealltainn*, 'the mournful linnet of Beltane'.[131] Snow at the time was known as *sneachda mu bhial na Bealltainn*, 'snow about the mouth of May-Day'.

On the night preceding it, i.e. Beltane eve, witches were awake, and went about as hares to take their *toradh*, produce (milk, butter and cheese), from the cows. People who believed in their existence were as earnest to counteract their machinations. Tar was put behind the ears of the cattle, and at the root of the tail; the animals were sprinkled with urine to keep them from fighting; the house was hung with rowan-tree, etc., etc. By having a churning past and a cheese made (*muidhe 's mulchag*) before sunrise, the Fairies were kept away from the farm for the rest of the year. If any came to ask for rennet (*deasgainn*), it should not on any account be given to them. It would be used for taking the substance out of the giver's own dairy produce.

When the day arrived, it was necessary, whatever the state of the weather, though people sank ankle deep in snow, or (as the Gaelic idiom has it) though snow came over the shoes, to get the cattle away to the summer pastures among the hills (*àirigh*). No fire on this or any other first day of a quarter of the year (*latha ceann ràidhe*) was given out of the house. It gave the borrower the power of taking the milk from the lender's cows.[132]

People had a feast in their houses with better food than ordinary. The arrival of the cuckoo was looked for, and boys shouted: *"Gug-ùg!" ars a' chuthag latha buidhe Bealltainn.* "'Cuckoo!' cried the 'gowk' on yellow Beltane day."[133]

In the *Statistical Account of Scotland*, 1794, XI. 620, there is a custom described as existing at Callander in Perthshire of boys going on this day to the moors and kneading a cake of oatmeal, one part of which was daubed black.[134] The bread was then put in a bonnet, from which each drew a piece. The boy to whose share the black piece falls is obliged to leap three times through the flames at which the repast was prepared. The minister of Logierait (V. 84) says the festivities of the day were chiefly observed by herdsmen,[135] and Pennant (*Tour*, p. 90) describes a similar feast of herdsmen in which pieces of the cake were offered to the fox, hoodie-crow, eagle, etc., with a request that they would avoid the cattle during the year.[136] In the south of Ireland, we are told (*vide* Brand on May-Day customs), cows were made to leap over lighted straw.[137] All this has been referred to Baal and human sacrifices, and the going through the fire and other observances have been assumed to be the remains of Syrian rites. They seem to be nothing but parts of the numerous superstitious observances for the 'saining' of cattle.

A *sop seilbhe* or 'possession wisp' was burned on land of which possession was to be taken at Whitsunday. The wisp was of fodder or heather. The burning of it on the land, as already explained, insured possession – *Bha e ceangailte aige tuille.*[138]

CÉITEIN, MONTH OF MAY

This is the month of which Beltane day, OS, forms the centre, and consists of the last fourteen days of spring and the first fourteen days of summer. Its derivation is from *ceud*, first, it being the beginning of the summer season.[139] It is identical with the present month of May. *Is fheàrr sneachda sa Chéitein na bhith gun uisge.* "Better is snow in May than to be without rain."

The month preceding Beltane was called *Céitein na h-Òinsich*, 'the May-Days of the Silly One', the word *òinseach* denoting both a silly woman and a cuckoo. The habits of the bird, which has no nest of its own and goes about all day aimlessly uttering its peculiar note, has earned for it the reputation of being silly (as is witnessed also by the Scotch word 'gowk'), and premature glimpses of fine weather are supposed to mislead it as to the advent of May.[140]

WHISTLING WEEK

Seachdain na feadaireachd, the whistling week, is the first week of summer, and the name is in allusion to the loud whistling winds that are apt to occur at the time. It is unlucky during it to proceed with field operations.

MÀIGH, MAY

The name *Màigh* for the first month of summer is quite common in the Highlands, and is to be found in songs and proverbs. This is mentioned as shewing incontestably that Roman (or rather ecclesiastical) notations of time were adopted into the ancient Celtic calendar.

THE AVOIDING DAY OF THE YEAR (*LATHA SEACHNACH NA BLIADHNA*)

This is the third day of summer, and its name is almost the only part of the beliefs concerning it that now survives. The writer searched far and wide for an explanation of the name, and only once heard one that was satisfactory. It was on this day that the fallen angels were expelled from Paradise, and on it people should avoid doing any kind of evil. If caught in the act they will be similarly expelled from the regions of forgiveness, and be visited with 'judgment without mercy'. If it falls on a Friday, it is unlucky to go on a journey. Pennant says about it, "The fourteenth May is unlucky, and the day on which it falls."[141]

CAINGIS, WHITSUNTIDE, PENTECOST

This and Martinmas are the two principal term days in Scotland, at which half-yearly servants enter on their duties, and at which removals take place. At Whitsunday term (old style) especially, the 25th of May, the towns of Scotland present an animated appearance from the number of removals or changes of residences. The streets are crowded with household goods being removed from one house to another. Tenants at will are removed and leases expire at this term.

In Lorn, and the districts to the south of it, along by Lochfyneside, the term is called *Féill Breunain*. St Brendan the Elder, from whom the name is derived, was abbot of Clonfert in Ireland AD 578.[142] His day is May 16/28. Kilbrandon parish (in Gaelic *Sgireachd a' Chuain*, 'the Parish of the Ocean') in the west of Argyllshire derives its name from him, and there is a farm in the island of Mull of the same name. History records that the saint with fourteen companions once made a voyage in search of Paradise, and in stormy weather, when the sea is rough and the sky inclement, and the earth is hid with driving showers (it excites a smile), that he came north in the hope of finding it. There are days indeed in summer in the Hebrides, when a glory covers the sea and sky and the hills 'that encircle the sea', when he might think that he was on the way.

In the Hebrides the name St Brendan's eve for the Whitsunday term is entirely unknown. It is told of a Tiree man of the last generation that he was promised a croft (or piece of land) by the then chamberlain of the island, who was a native of the mainland and said, "Your name will be put on the rent-roll on St Brendan's day." The Tiree man went home and consulted his godfather (*goistidh*) as to what day the factor meant. "I really don't know," said his godfather, "unless it be the day of judgment."[143]

In Sutherlandshire people reckon by the *Féill Chelzie*, a market held on Tuesday of the term, deriving its name from a wool manufactory (now discontinued) called New Kelso, near Loch Carron.[144]

The names *Caingis*, 'Whitsuntide' and 'Pentecost' are modifications of one and the same word. 'Pentecost' became *pencas* in Cornish, in Gaelic (which represents *p* of the Welsh dialects by *c*) *caingis* (**kinkis**), as *pascha* became Welsh *pâsk*, Gaelic *Càisg* (**kasg**).[145] The Gaelic *c* or *k* sound is represented in the Saxon tongue by *wh*. Thus we have *cuibhle* (**cuile**) 'wheel'; *cuip* 'whip'; *ciod* 'what?'; *cuilein* 'whelp'; *có* 'who?'; *cuist* 'wheesht!', 'be quiet!'; *caoin* 'whine'; etc. So *cencas* has become 'Whitsun'. The feast has no name in the languages of Western Europe but such as are derivations of the Greek word. The English name has been thought to be an exception, and to be, therefore, of modern origin. From the light thrown upon it by the Celtic languages, we infer that it is of the same origin as the rest.

Caingis is reckoned to be 'at the end of a fortnight of summer'.[146]

FÉILL SHEATHAIN, ST JOHN'S OR MIDSUMMER'S EVE (24TH JUNE / 6TH JULY)

On this day the cuckoo was said to enter its winter house: *Théid a' chuthag 'na taigh geamhraidh*.[147] It is not natural for its song to be heard after this. The bird may be seen, but it is not heard. It is – like the landrail, stonechat, or other birds that disappear in winter – one of the seven sleepers, who were believed to pass the winter underground.

Seathan, Swithin, is the old form of the name John, the common form being *Iain*, *Eòin*, and in Islay *Eathin*. It still survives in the name of the Clan MacLean, *Mac-ill'-sheathain*, also written *MacGhilleòin*. A former minister of Kilmore in Mull is still remembered as *Maighstir Seathain*, and an exceedingly plaintive song composed to her husband (who had been betrayed and executed for piracy) by his widow begins *Tha Seathan nochd 'na mharbhan* ('Swithin is tonight a dead one'), the names being those now denoted by John.[148]

MÌOS CROCHADH NAN CON, DOG-DAYS (LITERALLY 'MONTH FOR HANGING DOGS')

This is but a boyish and sportive name given to the month preceding *Lùnastal*, or first of August, the time of greatest scarcity with the poor. The stores of last harvest are exhausted, and the new supplies are not yet come in. If there is a scarcity of food for the dogs, it is recommended as the best thing that can be done, to hang them. Besides, the excessive heat makes it advisable to get rid of all superfluous dogs.[149]

LATHA MÀRTAINN BUILG, TRANSLATION OF MARTIN (LITERALLY MARTIN OF THE BAG'S DAY)

July 4/16 received its title of the Translation of Martin from being the day on which the remains of St Martin, bishop of Tours, 397, 'the apostle of the Gauls' (who also gives his name to the Martinmas term), were transferred to the cathedral of Tours. In Scotland the day is called St Martin of Bullion's day, and it was a proverb that if the deer rise dry and lie down dry on it, that is if the morning and evening be dry, it will be a dry season till harvest; and it was a general belief over Europe that rain on this day betokened wet weather for the next twenty days.[150] The day of St Martin of the Bag is commonly translated St Swithin's day, which is the 15th.[151] St Swithin was bishop of Winchester, and no name of an English bishop is found in the Gaelic calendar.

LÙNASTAL, LAMMAS, AUGUST 1/12TH

This, being a quarter-day, formed a great day with old women for 'saining' cattle and performing those ceremonies by which evil was to be kept away from them for the next three months. Tar was put on their tails and ears, charms (*òradh*) were said at their udders, red and blue threads were put on their tails, and various observances were gone through with balls of hair (*rolag*), plants, fire about the earthenware pipkins (*crogain*) in which milk or butter was to be put, etc. Curds and butter were specially prepared for a great feast held this day, at which it was highly important that everyone got as much as he cared for.

On Lammas day the gadfly 'loses one of its eyes' (*Latha Lùnastail caillidh chreithleag an leth-shùil*). The creature is not so vicious after this date.[152]

Lùnastal is not a word of Gaelic origin, at least no satisfactory Gaelic etymology can be given for it. It is perhaps a contraction of the Latin *luna augustalis*, the August moon.[153] The Roman month was lunar, and was reckoned from the first appearance of the moon's slender crescent in the sky. The moon in the harvest months is of more consequence to the husbandman than at any other season, and has always been taken notice of for its splendour. The temperature of the night air has much to do with this. The Gaelic bears its own testimony to it, in giving distinctive names to the autumn moon.

The corresponding English name, Lammas, had very likely the same origin, and it is a contraction of 'Lunamas'. The derivation of it from *Lamb-mas* is an 'affectation of punning', and that suggested by General Vallancey from *La-ith-mas*, 'a day of eating fruit', is extremely fanciful.[154] The omission of *n* in the middle of a word, for the sake of brevity or from inadvertence, frequently occurs. So *g* has been elided in *Lùnastal*. Augustus, which was adopted as the name of the sixth month in 6 BC, became *east* in Cornish and *eost* in Armoric.

IUCHAR, THE HOT MONTH (AUGUST)

The *iuchar* consists of fourteen days of summer and fourteen days of autumn, and (Lammas day, OS, being the first of autumn) corresponds to the present month of August. It is regarded, in point of weather, as the opposite of *faoilleach*, the 'storm month' of February.[155]

The name is derived from an obsolete verb *fiuchadh* 'to be hot'. Lhuyd (*Archæolog. Brit.*) renders *fiuchach* 'boiling' and *fiuchadh* 'a spring, *scatebra*'. In another place he gives *fiuchadh* as an equivalent of the Latin *æstus*.[156] In some districts of the north the name of the season is still called *fiuchar*. Linlithgow, celebrated for its wells, is known in the Highlands as *Gleann Iuch*, and the Linlithgow measures are called *tomhais Ghlinn Iuch*.[157] The dropping of *f* initial, as in the case of the Greek digamma, is too common to need illustration.

FÉILL MOIRE, ASSUMPTION DAY

This is the middle day of autumn (*latha meadhon an fhogharaidh*), August 15/27. It was counted a greater day than St Mary's day (*Féill Moire*) in spring, and was called 'the Big St Mary's day'. Harvest operations were now vigorously pushed forward, and hence the saying, *an Fhéill Moire mhòr as t-fhogharadh, sguab is ceangal 's daoin' ás an léintean*. "Big St Mary's Feast in harvest, sheaf and binding and men with their coats off."[158]

FÉILL RÒID, ROODMAS, SEPTEMBER 14/26TH

This day is the first of the rutting season among deer, and it was held that if the night before it (*oidhche na Féill Ròid*) be wet, or (as it was expressed) 'if the deer took his head wet into the rutting season' (*ma bheir e cheann fliuch san dàmhair*), there will be a month after it of dry weather, and the farmer need be under no apprehension as to securing his crops. The belling of red deer among the hills on this night is magnificent.[159]

The night succeeding Roodmas was called 'the night of the nut', 'the night of the Holy Nut' (*oidhche na cnò, na Cnò Naomh*), a name the reason of which is doubtful. Some say it arises from this night dividing harvest in unequal halves, as the kernel is divided in the nut.[160] Brand (i. 353) mentions a custom of going a nutting upon Rood day, and it seems to have been a popular belief that on this day the devil goes a nutting.[161] This does not explain why the nut is called the Holy Nut.

The Holy Rood is the same as the Cross.

MICHAELMAS (*FÉILL MÌCHEIL*)

This is also known in the Roman Catholic districts of the Highlands as 'the riding day' (*latha na marcachd*). On the level green of Borg (*machaire Bhorg*) in Barra a great race is held, the women bringing the horses and sitting behind the men on horseback. In the scamper that ensues, it is a lucky sign if the woman tumbles off. All the expenses of the festivity are borne by the women, each of whom takes with her to the racecourse a large thick bannock of oatmeal, made with treacle, butter, etc.[162]

SAMHAIN, HALLOWMAS

This is the first day of winter, and is also known as All Saints' day (*latha nan Uile Naomh*), November 1/13. It was a sign of a bad winter if it fell upon a Wednesday, according to the saying: *Nuair as Di-Ciadain an t-Samhainn is iargaineach 'na déidh.* "When Hallowmas is on Wednesday it is afflictive after it."[163]

The coming of winter was hailed with more fun and merriment than any other season of the year. The cold was now fairly set in, the fruits of the summer – down to the very nuts – were gathered, and the young became desirous of learning their fate with regard to that subject of anxiety in every age, their future husbands and wives. This natural welcoming of winter explains the ceremonies of the day and the games of the evening. Hardly any of them have reference to the practices or deities of the nations of antiquity or to Scripture, and this explanation must be sought for in pagan times.

On the last day of autumn children gathered ferns, tar-barrels, the long thin stalks called *gàinisg*, and everything suitable for a bonfire. These were placed in a heap on some eminence near the house, and in the evening set fire to. The fires were called *Samhnagan*. There was one for each house, and it was an object of ambition who should have the biggest. Whole districts were brilliant with bonfires, and their glare across a Highland loch, and from many eminences, formed an exceedingly picturesque scene. Some find in them traces of the worship of the invariable Baal, but there is no reason to look upon them otherwise than as the natural and defiant welcome of the season in which fires are most required, when the heat of the year is departed, and cold and frost and rushing winds cover all things with gloom. Bonfires are kindled on all occasions of public rejoicing or excitement, and Hallowmas fires are a natural expression of the change of season. It is possible a deity was originally associated with the practice, but there is now no trace of him in the name or practices of this day.[164]

As the evening wore on, the young people gathered to one house, and an almost endless variety of games (*cleasan*) were resorted to, with the object in every case of divining the future lot of the company. Were they to marry or not, was it to be that year or never, who was to be married first, what like the future husband or wife was to be, their names, trade, colour of hair, size, property, etc., were questions of great importance, and their answer was a source of never-failing entertainment. The modes of divination are of interest from the light they throw on the character of the people among whom they prevailed, and from an antiquarian point of view as remains of pagan times.

A shoe caught by the tip and thrown over the house fore-indicates the future by its position on the ground on the other side. In whatever direction the toe points, the thrower will go before long, and it is very unlucky if the shoe be found with the sole uppermost – misfortune is 'making for' him. A thin, fine shoe, used in this manner, led the man fished up from the Green Island to remark, after some years of silence:

> Bròg thana 's i gun mheas —
> Gun fhios có chaitheas i.

("A thin shoe little valued – / It is hard to say who will wear it.") He might well say so, for the owner of the shoe died in a few days.[165]

The white of eggs, dropped in a glass of pure water, indicates by certain marks how many children a person is to have. The impatience and clamour of the children often made the housewife perform this ceremony for them by daylight, and the kindly mother, standing with her face to the window, dropping the white of an egg into a crystal glass of clean water and surrounded by a group of children eagerly watching her proceedings, formed a pretty picture.

When the fun of the evening had fairly commenced, the names of eligible (or likely as possible) matches were written on the chimney place, and the young man who wished to essay his fortune was blindfolded and led up to the list. Whatever name he put his finger on would prove to be that of his future wife.

Two nuts were put on the fire beside each other, representing two individuals whose names were made known to the company. As they burned together, or flared up alone, or leaped away from each other, the future marriage of the pair – or haughty rejection of each other – was inferred.

A dish of milk and meal (*fuarag*, Scots 'crowdie') or of beat potatoes was made, and a ring was concealed in it. Spoons were given to the company, and a vigorous attack was made on the dish. Whoever got the ring would prove to be the first married. This was an excellent way of making the taking of food part of the evening's merriment.

Apples and a silver sixpence were put in a tub of water. The apples floated on the top, but the coin lay close to the bottom. Whoever was able to lift either in his mouth, and without using his teeth, was counted very lucky, and got the prize to himself.

By taking an apple and going to a room alone, dividing it there into nine pieces against the name of the Father and the Son, eating eight pieces with the back to a looking-glass and the face looking over the left shoulder, and then throwing the ninth piece over the same shoulder, the future husband or wife was seen in the glass coming and taking the piece of apple away.

A person going in the devil's name to winnow in a barn alone will see his future partner entering the door.

An unmarried woman, taking a ball of thread and crossing a wall on her way, went to a kiln or other outhouse. Here, holding one end of the thread, she threw the ball in the dark into the eye of the kiln (*sùil àth*), or over one of the rafters or a partition wall, in the name of a sweetheart whom she had before fixed on in her mind, and calling out *Có seo shìos air ceann mo ròpain?* ("Who is down there at the end of my little rope?"), at the same time she gave the thread a gentle pull. In reply, someone or something pulled the thread at the other end, and a voice called out the name of her future husband. There is a story of a tailor having hid himself in anticipation of this mode of divination being resorted to, and when the ball was thrown he caught it and gave the thread a tug. In answer to the question "Who is this at the end of my little rope?" he said, "I am, the devil" (*Tha mise, 'n deamhan*), and the woman to whom this frightful answer was given never tried divination again.

Young women sowed hemp seed (*fras lìn*) over nine ridges of ploughland, saying, *Tha mi cur fras lìn, 's am fear bhios 'na fhear dhomh, thigeadh e 's cliathadh e.* "I sow hemp seed, and he who is to be my husband, let him come and harrow it." On looking back they saw the figure of their future husband. Hallowe'en being the night preceding the first day of a lunar month[166] was always dark, and this ceremony was rendered more awful by a story that a woman once saw herself coming after her, and never recovered from the effects of the vision.

By dipping his shirt sleeve in 'a well to the south' (*tobar mu dheas*) and then pulling off the shirt and placing it to dry before the fire, the anxious youth, if he does not oversleep himself, will see his sweetheart entering through the night and turning the shirt.

On putting an odd number of keys in a sieve, going to a barn alone, and there riddling them well 'with the wrong hand turn' (*car tuaitheal*), the destined one will come and put the odd key right.

By holding a mouthful of water in the mouth and going to listen (*farcluais*) at a neighbour's window, the first name overheard will prove to be that of one's intended. The same knowledge was obtained by biting a piece of the last cart that sent in the corn, and with it in the mouth going, without speaking, to listen (*farcluais*) under a neighbour's window.

A common practice was to go and steal kail stocks. Unless the plants are pulled surreptitiously, without the knowledge or consent of their owner, they are of no use for the purpose of divination. A number of young people go together, and having cautiously and with difficulty made their way into a kailyard, pull each one the first stock that comes to hand after bending down. It must be the first that the hand meets. The plant is then taken home and examined by the light, and according to its height, straightness, colour, etc., will be the future husband or wife. A quantity of soil adhering to it signifies money and property. When put for the night above the lintel of the door, it affords indications by the first person entering below it in the morning; and, put below the pillow, it is excellent to dream over.

A straw, drawn at random from a stack, indicates by the number of grains upon it what family a person is to have. Three ears of corn similarly pulled and placed below the pillow for the night will cause dreams of the future husband reaping them.

A plate of clean water, one of dirty water, and one empty being placed on the floor, and a napkin thrown over the eyes, the dish in which the person blindfolded puts his forefinger indicated a maid, or widow, or none at all.[167]

A piece of flesh being buried this night, if any living creature was found in it in the morning, the person burying it would be married; but if not, he never would.

If water in which the feet had been washed were kept in the house this night (and the Fairies were apt to enter the house when that was the case), a person putting a burning peat in it will see the colour of his sweetheart's hair in it.[168]

If a mouthful of the top sod of the house wall (*fòid fàil na h-anainn*)[169] or a mouthful from the clod above the lintel of the door (*àrd-doras*) be taken into the house in one's teeth and any hair be found in it, it is of the same colour as that of the future wife of the person who performs the rite.

One of the chief performances of the evening was for young women to go to a boundary stream (*allt crìche*) – if between two neighbouring proprietors so much the better – and with closed eyes to lift from it three stones between the middle finger and thumb, saying these words:

> *Togaidh mise 'chlach*
> *Mar a thog Moire d'a Mac —*
> *Air bhrìgh, air bhuaidh 's air neart;*
> *Gun robh a' chlach sa am' dhòrn*
> *Gus an ruig mi mo cheann-uidhe.*

("I will lift the stone / As Mary lifted it for her Son – / For substance, virtue and strength; / May this stone be in my hand / Till I reach my journey's end.") The stones were for putting below the head when going to sleep.

Many other modes of divination were practised, too tedious to mention – by slices from the plough, different metals, eating a stolen raw salt herring, sprinkling corn in front of the bed, etc., etc. These observances can hardly be characterised as superstitions: they proceeded from a spirit of fun more than from any belief in their efficacy. There are in every community many weak and simple people who are easily imposed on, and made to believe almost anything; but the divinations of Hallowe'en left an abiding impression on few minds.[170]

FÉILL FIONNAIN

St Finan's eve is the longest night in the year, and hence it is said of a very stupid person, *Tha e cho dorcha ri oidhche Féill Fionnain, 's tha 'n oidhche sin glè dhorcha.*

"He is as dark as the night of St Finan, and that night is pretty dark." The shortest day is called in the MacKay country (the extreme north of Sutherlandshire) *latha nan Trì Suipeirean*, 'the day of the Three Suppers'. On this night it was said 'the rain is wine and the stones are cheese' (*Tha 'n t-uisge 'na fhìon 's na clachan 'nan càise*), and it was considered a joke to persuade boys to go out and see. "I remember," says one who is a shrewd intelligent man, "about fifty years ago, when I was a little boy, sitting quite contentedly on the eve of St Finan's day sipping with a spoon from a big tub of water, in the full hope that the next spoonful would prove to be wine."[171]

The name is derived from St Finan, confessor, bishop of Clonard in Ireland in the sixth century. This day is now fixed as the 12th December, but in the Highlands it is the shortest in the year, whatever day of the calendar that may fall upon. In olden times it was much esteemed, as the rhyme shows:

> *Féill Fionnain nam fleadh*
> *'S oidhche Nollaig na mòr bhladh.*[172]

("St Finan's night of festivities / And Christmas night of great cheer.")

Besides giving a name to the days of the calendar the saints were employed to designate local markets. St Kessock's day (*Féill mo Cheasaig*) at Callander has been already mentioned. St Connan's day (*Féill Connain*) is the autumn market in Glenorchy; *Féill Fhaolain* is held at Killin; *Féill Ceit* at Kenmore; and in other places we have *Féill Peadair*, *Féill Aindreis*, etc. Old men spoke of *Féill an Dìomhanais*, the Festival of St Idleness, a holiday frequently observed by a great many people. *Latha na sluasaid*, shovel day, means the day of one's burial. *Bliadhna na Braoisge*, Grinning Year, and *Là Luain*, Moon-Day (i.e. Monday Come-Never), mean the same thing, the Greek Kalends. *Bliadhna nam Brisgeinean*, the Year of Silverweed Roots, was shortly after Culloden, and is remembered in Tiree as a year of great scarcity. The land had been neglected in previous years from the disturbed state of the country, and in spring the furrows were white with roots (*brisgeinean*), and people made meal of them.[173]

DAYS OF THE WEEK

These play a more important part in Highland superstition than even the seasons of the year.[174] The names by which they are known are not Celtic: two, Wednesday and Thursday, are of Scandinavian or Teutonic origin, and the rest are from the Latin. The superstitions, as might be expected, can in most cases be traced directly to incidents in Scripture history. The division of time into weeks was introduced with the Christian religion from Ireland, and the Irish must be held responsible for the names adopted. Neither in the names nor in the superstitions is there any trace of an age anterior to Christianity.

Dĭ, which is prefixed to each name in the sense of 'day', is kindred with the Latin *dies*, and occurs in slightly modified forms in all the Celtic dialects.[175] It is curious that in Gaelic it occurs in no other form or combination in the sense of 'day', and a suspicion is thereby created that it is merely an adaptation of the Latin word – an easier adaptation because there are words of similar sound and kindred meaning in Gaelic.

DI-DÒMHNAICH, SUNDAY (*DIES DOMINI*)

The name *Dòmhnach* for our Lord is not common. It is evidently derived from the Latin *Dominus*. It occurs in the proper name *Maol Dòmhnaich* (Ludovic), literally 'the Bald One (i.e. the Shaven Priest) of Our Lord', a name still to be found in Skye, and formed like *Maol Mhoire*, Miles (literally 'the Priest of St Mary'), *Maol Ciaran*, *Maol Ruainidh*, etc. There is a streamlet near Strowan in Blair Athole called *Allt Dòmhnach*, the Streamlet of Our Lord, and a *Tobar an Dòmhnach*, the Well of Our Lord, in Balmeanach in the west of Tiree. In a charm for fulling cloth the expression occurs: "If he (the wearer of the cloth) enter field or fight, the full succour of our Lord be his" (*slàn chomraich an Dòmhnach da*).

The day is also known as *an Dòmhnach* without the prefix of *di*. Other names are those occurring in Scripture – Sabbath, etc.

The plant pulled on Sunday is, according to a proverbial expression, without good or harm (*luibh an Dòmhnach gun mhath gun chron*).[176]

DI-LUAIN, MONDAY

Luain is said in dictionaries to be a Gaelic name for the moon, agreeing in origin with the Latin *luna*.[177] It is used only in the name of this day and in the expression *Là Luain*, a poetic phrase for Monday Come-Never, i.e. 'nevermore'. The adjective *luaineach* 'restless' is supposed to be derived from it, but is a word never applied to the moon. It applies to whatever moves restlessly by fits and starts, from place to place, without staying long in one place, and never to anything on account of change of shape or form. Its derivation from *là uaine*, 'green day', is absurd, and there are grounds for suspicion that *luain* is a word manufactured by ancient Gaelic grammarians from the Latin.[178]

It was deemed unlucky to commence ploughing (stretching the team, as it was called, *sìneadh na seisrich*) or any kind of work on Monday. It will be proceeded with too quickly or too slowly, according to the adage,

> *Tinnste [Tionnsgnadh?] nìtear Di-Luain,*
> *Bidh e luath no bidh e mall.*[179]

"Work commenced on Monday / Will be (too) quick or will be (too) slow." It was deemed, however, a good day for removing or 'flitting' upon, just as Saturday was the reverse.

> *Imrich an t-Satharna mu thuath,*
> *Imrich an Luain mu dheas —*
> *Ged nach biodh agam ach an t-uan*
> *Sann Di-Luain a dh'fhalbhainn leis.*

("Saturday removal is to the north, / Monday removal to the south – / Though I had but a lamb / On Monday I would it remove.")[180] Old men called it *iuchair na seachdain* – 'the key of the week'.

DI-MÀIRT, TUESDAY

The name is obviously enough from *dies Martis*, the Latin name. This was a good day to begin ploughing upon, and it was ominous of good luck if any of the harness broke and the ploughing was stopped for the day. Such a belief could exist only in the easy-going olden days.

DI-CIADAIN, WEDNESDAY

Much ingenuity has been spent on the etymology of this word by those who delight in recondite meanings, and believe that every word in Gaelic must be traced to a Gaelic origin. What Lhuyd says of radicals and primitives is equally applicable to other words. It is a very common error in etymology to endeavour to derive all the radical words of our Western European languages from the Latin or Greek; or indeed to derive the primitives of any one language from any particular tongue. When we do this we seem to forget that all have been subject to alterations, and that the greater and more polite any nation is, the more subject they are (partly from improvement, and partly out of a luxurious wantonness) to remodel their language. Nearly all words connected with ecclesiastical affairs both in English and Gaelic have been imported from the Latin and Greek, undergoing only such changes as the difference of language requires.

When or why the name of a Scandinavian deity, and not a Roman name, was adopted by the British and Irish churches to designate this or any other day is a different question. We must seek (and this is a rule lamentably neglected by Gaelic etymologists) the true explanation of words in any language that offers one that is probable and rational; otherwise we make 'a useful art ridiculous', and the etymologist degenerates into 'a trifling conjecturer'.[181]

The Latin name of this day is *dies Mercurii*, which name was adopted in the Welsh, Cornish and Armoric, but the Teutonic names are derived from the Scandinavian deity *Odin* or *Woden*, who was supposed to correspond to Mercury. This was the designation adopted in Gaelic, both Irish and Scottish. Like the French the Gaelic has no *w*, and represents that sound by *g* or *c*. Thus, *gad*, withe; *gul*, wail; *cost*, waste; *clòimh*, wool; *cnuimh*, worm; *curaidh*, warrior, etc. Sometimes, as pointed out under Whitsuntide (*Caingis*), the corresponding English sound is *wh*.[182] So Woden's-Day, Wednesday, became *Di-Ceden*.

The derivation *ciad aoin'*, first fast, is open to the objection that there was no fast on Wednesday in the Celtic or any other church; that the use of the word *aoin'* to denote a fast is secondary and derived from Friday (*Di-Haoine*), the true fast day; and that the final syllable, being the essential one, would with such a derivation be heavily accented, instead of falling away into a mere terminal syllable. The grave *ia* in *Di-Ciadain* is accounted for by the *o* in *Woden* being long.[183]

There was a malediction used to young women, *Galar na tè chuir a' chiad chìr Chiadna 'na ceann*. "The disease of the woman be upon you who put the first Wednesday comb in her head." The disease was that she died childless.[184]

Many would not begin sowing seed in spring but on this day or Thursday. It was also counted a lucky day to begin ploughing upon.

A witch in the island of Coll, being asked by a person who had detected her in her unhallowed pranks to visit a farmhouse in shape of a hare, said that as the day was Wednesday she could do nothing. Why her power was limited on this day does not appear.[185]

DIAR-DAOIN, THURSDAY

The Latin name *dies Iovis* has been similarly followed, with slight alteration, by the Cymric branch of the Celts, while the Gaelic names are taken from *Thor, Tor*, and in some dialects *Thordan*, the Scandinavian deity, son of Odin.[186] This is a lucky day for a calf or lamb to be born upon, for beginning the weaving of cloth, and on which the hair should be cut, as the rhymes testify:

> *Diar-Daoin, latha Chaluim Chille chaoin —*
> *Latha chur chaorach air seilbh,*
> *A dheilbh, 's a chur bò air laogh.*

("Thursday, the day of benign Colum-Cill – / A day to take possession of sheep, / To put cloth in warp, and settle cow on calf.")[187]

> *T' fhalt 's t' fhionna Diar-Daoin*
> *'S t' ionga mhaol Di-Sathairne.*

("Cut your hair and beard on Thursday / And blunt the nail on Saturday.")[188] It is unlucky if Beltane day, the first of summer, falls upon a Thursday, according to the saying,

> *Is iomadh té bhios gun mhacan baoth*
> *Dar is ann air Diar-Daoin bhios a' Bhealltainn.*

("Many a woman will be without an infant son / When Beltane falls on Thursday.") McIntosh (*Gael. Prov.,* 146) has it, "Woe to the mother of a wizard's son, when Beltane falls on a Thursday." A similar prejudice existed against Hallowmas (*Samhain*), the first of winter, falling on a Wednesday.[189]

DI-HAOINE, FRIDAY, DIES VENERIS

Here the Gaelic names revert to the Latin. Venus is etymologically connected with the Gaelic *bean*, a wife, as *Friga* is with the German *frau*. In Armoric the name of the day is *dar guener*, and says Lhuyd (p. 9): "'Tis Observable that the Initial *Gu* is common to the *Britans*, with the *French, Spaniards* and *Italians*; and that the *Romans* frequently began such words with an *V*. Consonant."[190] The Gaelic word would be pronounced in the same manner, though spelled *Di-Fhaoine*, which probably is the more correct form. *Aoine* is said in dictionaries to mean a fast, but in that sense never came into popular use, and is not found in song or proverb.[191]

The number of superstitions attached to the day were very numerous, and this origin is to be traced to Friday, being the day of the Crucifixion. On Good Friday (*Di-Haoine na Ceusa*), the anniversary of our Lord's passion, the various beliefs had twofold force. So much was it a belief that the powers of evil have more power on this day than on any other that it was a common saying, *Tha Di-Haoine an aghaidh na seachdain.* "Friday is against the week."[192]

On Friday and on Sunday it was not deemed proper to go and see a sick person. Most took such a visit in anything but good part, and many would as soon see death coming to the house as a sympathising friend. In their opinion there was little difference.

The more superstitious would not allow iron to be put in the ground, and consequently no graves were dug and no ploughing was proceeded with. Commonly, however, ploughing was abstained from only on Good Friday.[193]

It was not lucky (*sealbhach*) on Friday to cut one's hair or nails, to sharpen knives, commence work, count animals, or go near the fire. In Argyllshire and the Highlands generally it is deemed unlucky for marriages, but in the south it is a favourite day, and in Appin, Perthshire, people did not care to be married on any other day. The aversion of seafaring men to leave on this day is well known.

On Fridays the Fairies visited men's houses, and people were careful not to say anything to give them offence. Friday was not called by its own name but *là bhaile ud thall* ('the day of yonder town'), and if anyone unfortunately mentioned the proper name, the evil was averted by the bystanders adding 'on the cattle of yonder town'.[194] Old women in Tiree averted the evil consequences of sharpening knives on Friday by saying 'on the farm of Clark', alluding to a big strong man of that name to whom a general dislike was entertained, and who was said to have entered a Fairy hillock and compelled the inmate to give him a cure for his sore leg.[195]

The aversion of the Elves to iron was a prominent feature in their character, and dislike to putting iron in the ground was perhaps aversion to disturb (especially with what the Elves disliked so much) the earth – under the surface of which that easily-offended race lives. The 'little folk' are quick to take offence, and dislike hearing the name of Friday, seeing iron sharpened, or the earth disturbed with it. When there was any occasion to mention the creatures, all danger of evil consequences is averted by saying, "A blessing on their journeying and travelling, this is Friday and they will not hear us."[196]

In the Western Islands it was a bitter curse to wish that 'the number of Friday' or 'the cross of the number of Friday' might come upon a person (*crois àireamh na h-Aoine dh'amas ort*).[197] To count three times cattle, chickens, men, etc., on this day was followed as a certain result by none of them being alive at the end of the year. Many in Tiree remember that in their youth a sure method of putting an old woman in a rage was to begin counting her chickens on a Friday. She seldom allowed them to get beyond three or four. The superstition probably arose from a belief that it was on Friday King David numbered the Children of Israel.[198]

People did not like to kill a cow, a sheep, or other beast, or cut or mark calves or lambs, on Friday, and there were many who would not allow their cattle to be shifted from one place to another. They would not alter their fold. If e.g. the day was come for removing cows to the summer hill pastures, the more superstitious would not allow it to be done if the day was Friday.

As work commenced on Monday proceeded too quickly or too slowly, work begun on Friday was said to be always hurriedly done – *Bidh i 'na ruith.* "It will be running." *Bidh neach a rugadh Di-Haoine driopail* ("A person born on Friday is always in a hurry"), hence the malediction, *Ruith na h-Aoine ort.* "The running (or hurry) of Friday be upon you."

Si 'n Aoine bhagarach nì 'n Satharna deurach ("A threatening Friday makes a tearful Saturday"), and if it came on to rain early on Friday, or (as the saying was) if Friday caught the rain 'in its mouth' (*nan glacadh an t-Aoine 'na bhial e*), it would be wet all day.[199]

DI-SATHAIRNE, SATURDAY (*DIES SATURNI*)

This, as might be expected, was not deemed a lucky day to begin work upon. It was not deemed of much consequence whether ploughing began or not, but the manufacture of cloth should on no account be begun. *An rud théid a dheilbh Di-Sathairne, bidh stad nan seachd Satharn' air.*[200] "The warp prepared on Saturday will have the delay of the seven Saturdays upon it." No spinning was to be done after sunset, but other work might proceed as usual. All work should stop at 9 p.m. It is still considered a bad thing among the old people in Kintail to work past that hour.

There is a man in Tiree who will not allow a newly-engaged servant to come home to enter on his service on Saturday. On one occasion, when the term-day happened to be Saturday, he persuaded the servant-man to come on Friday, though only to stand in the house for a few minutes, that the evil omen might be averted.

New moon on Saturday was deemed a presage of stormy weather. *Solas Satharna gabhaidh e na seachd cuthaich mun d'théid e mach.* "Saturday light goes seven times mad before it goes out."[201]

An evil wish is *Deire nan seachd Satharn' ort* ("The end of the seven Saturdays be upon you"), Macintosh's *Prov.*, p. 78; and in Cowal it is a vicious saying of one woman to another, *Thig nas miosa na sin ort, thig galar nan seachd Satharn' ort.* "Worse than that will come upon you, the disease of the seven Saturdays will come upon you."

The objection to removing on Saturday has been already mentioned under Monday. (*Vide* page 565.) The same objection is entertained in Ireland.

The end of the week is very grateful to the labouring man:

> *Och is och Di-Luain,*
> *Ach se mo luaidh Di-Sathairne.*

("Alas and alas is Monday, / But my love is Saturday.")[202]

WEATHER WISDOM, ETC.

Expressions denoting high wind are: 'the blowing of hillocks out of their places' (*séideadh nan cnoc*),[203] 'a wind to take the tails off horses' (*Bheireadh i na h-earbaill bhar nan each*),[204] and 'blow the barn over the house' (*chuir an t-sabhail thar an taighe*);[205] heavy rain takes 'pieces out of the ground' (*mìrean ás an talamh*) and gives 'milk to the whales' (*bainne do na muca mara*), it being supposed that in heavy rain whales lie on the surface to cool themselves; heavy snow 'confines the infirm to their cots' (*chròdhadh e na giùigirean*)[206] while strong robust men can go about their business. A dead calm is called 'the calm of birds' (*fiath nan ian*); on days when not a hair is moved by the wind, and the sea is unruffled, the young fry of fish come to the surface, and sea-birds, themselves also conspicuous in such weather, can look about them for their prey.

The first breath of wind after a calm comes from the south, hence: *Nuair a bhios gaoth air chall iarr á deas i.* "When the wind is lost look for it in the south." After a heavy fall of rain the wind comes west, as is told in the saying, *Gaoth 'n-iar 'n déidh uisge reamhar.* "West wind after fat rain." If frost comes on, when rivers and pools are swollen, and the ground is very wet, it does not last long; 'the freezing of the full pool does not rest long' (*reothadh an lodain làin, cha mhair e fada*). The heaviest rain comes from the north (or rather north-east), and the longest drought from the south: *Chan uisge ach on tuath, 's cha turadh buan ach on deas.* "There is no rain but from the north, or lasting dry weather but from the south."[207]

The frequency with which the violence of the wind moderates after a shower of rain has given rise to the proverb 'after wind comes rain' (*an déidh gaoth mhòr thig uisge*) to denote that after loud merriment and laughter come sorrow and the cares brought by reflection. "It is north wind that dissipates mist" (*Si gaoth tuath sgaoileas ceò*); "The first day of south wind, and the third day of north wind" (*Chiad latha den ghaoth deas 's an treas latha den ghaoth tuath*), i.e. they are moderate then, and are best for crossing ferries on. "A speckled chequered summer makes a white, sunny harvest" (*Nì samhradh breac riabhach fogharadh geal grianach*).[208] The south-west, being the direction from which rain commonly comes, is known in the Hebrides as *Cachlaidh na Buigeuisg*, 'the gateway of soft weather'.[209]

THE MOON

Both the sun (*a' ghrian*) and moon (*a' ghealach*) are feminine in Gaelic, and the names are simply descriptive of their appearance. There is no trace of a sun-god or moon-goddess. The root *gr* in *grian* denotes horrent or bristling, and alludes to the sun's rays. It is said by some writers that the name is connected with Apollo Grannua, but the connection is a mere accidental similarity in the initial letters. The root *gr*, denoting what is streaming or bristling, occurs in *gruag*, a wig, flowing hair; *greann*, a surly look, a bristling of the hair as on an enraged dog; *gràin*, aversion, from the turning up of nose and stomach and bristling appearance of one much disgusted, so ab*horrence*, etc.[210]

Gealach, the moon, is from *geal*, white. The names *luan*, *easga* or *easgann* are given in dictionaries, but have disappeared from common use. With the former is supposed to be connected *luaineach*, restless, and *luaisg*, to move. *Ré* denotes any planet.[211]

The moment the moon begins to increase is called *gob soillse* (literally 'the bill or beak of the light'). The height of the tide, which follows his changes, is *bolg reothairt* (literally 'the swollen womb of spring tide').[212] The moon's increase is *fàs*, and when waning she is *san earra-dhubh* (literally 'in her black boundaries'). When hid in her vacant interlunar cave, i.e. when she is waning and late of rising, the dark period of the night is called *rath dorcha* ('dark circle'). *Mhic an rath dorcha* ("Son of the moon's dark circle") is an expression of mild objurgation.[213]

At the instant the moon begins to increase (*air gob na gealaiche*) the horns of cows are loose on their pith (*slabhagan*) and may be pulled off and stuck on again.[214] It is told that a dispute having arisen on one occasion as to the correctness of an almanac about the moon's change, the old man who raised the question proved himself to be in the right by turning round and drawing the horn from one of his cows, as a sheath is taken from a knife, and sticking it on again. The story is told of a man who lived in Sconser, isle of Skye, of more than one person in Tiree, and was doubtless told of people in various places.

It was said that there is never any north wind at *gob gealaich*.

The first time an unmarried person sees the new moon, he should stoop down and lift whatever meets his hand. If, on taking it to the light, any hair be found among it, its colour will prove to be that of the future husband or wife. It is unlucky to see the new moon for the first time when washing one's hands, or with the hand on the face.[215]

In olden times great regard was paid to the increase and wane of the moon. Garden seeds, as onions, kail, etc., if sown in the increase, ran to seed, but if sown in the wane, grew as pot-herbs. Withies or slender twigs (*caol*) intended for creels and baskets were cut only in the wane.[216] Twigs cut in the increase proved brittle. Trees cut in the increase were believed to bud again, but not those cut in the wane. Eggs laid during the wane were preserved for hatching, rather than those laid during the increase. Hens came from the former; cocks from the latter. Birds hatched in the increase were deemed difficult to rear, and it was doubtful if any of them would ultimately survive. Hence *eòin an fhàs*, 'birds of the increase', is a name given to weakly pining children. They are worthless for hatching.[217]

Many would not cut (i.e. castrate) an animal – calf, or foal, or pig – during the increase of the moon, and it was a belief that cows seek the bull only in the first and third quarters of the moon, and never at neap tides.[218] A man in Islay pretended to tell, from the time the cow paid her visit to the bull, whether her offspring would prove a bull-calf or a cow-calf. If in the first quarter, the former; if in the wane, the latter.

The second moon in autumn, the harvest moon, or first after the autumnal equinox, was variously known as *gealach an abachaidh*, 'the ripening moon', from a belief that crops ripen as much by it as they do during the day; *gealach bhuidhe nam broc*, 'the badgers' yellow moon', these wary animals being engaged, it was said, in taking home their winter supplies; *gealach an t-sealgair*, 'the hunter's moon'; and the last moon in harvest, extending for a month before Hallowmas (*Samhain*).[219] The first of winter was known as *gealach an ruadhain*, 'the reddening moon', during which vegetation grew as much by night as in the day.

It was said there was no north wind at the exact period of the appearance of new moon (*gob gealaich*).[220]

THE CELTIC YEAR: COMMENTARY

1   As elsewhere in 'The Celtic Year', JGC comes close to perpetrating the very philological blunders which he so heavily criticises. The best one can say of his etymological excursi is that they are of their time, and that their time lay before the publication of Macbain's masterly *Etymological Dictionary of the Gaelic Language* (1896). *Bliadhna* derives from a root *bleid-* (with nasal suffix) of unknown origin (Macbain 1896, p. 35; Vendryes 1959–96, s.v. *bliadain*).

2   JGC's assessment that the final syllable of *samhradh, fogharadh* and *geamhradh* represents a reduced form of *ràidh* (earlier *ràith*) may well be correct, since *sam(h), fog(h)(a)m(h)ar, ga(i)m(h)* and *ge(a)m(h)* all existed independently of the suffix in early Irish, and indeed *foghar* is more usual than *fogharadh* in twenty-first-century Gaelic. He is clearly wrong about *earrach*, however, in which the final syllable is traceable to a reconstructed Celtic form *persâko-*, or perhaps simply represents an adjectival-type ending as in *tòs/toiseach* 'beginning', *eàrr/earrach* 'end, lower extremity' (Macbain 1896, p. 137).

3   Or more literally 'straddling the quarter'.

4   *Tòimhseagan*, more usually *tòimhseachan*, is the word for a riddle. Why it appears here I am not sure. Riddles were an intrinsic part of ceilidh-house fare, and perhaps it reflects a custom of saying *Tòimhseagan!* when one was posed. The answer is 'spring, summer, autumn, winter' (Mackay 1908, p. 345). For collections of Gaelic riddles see Campbell 1890, vol. 2, pp. 408–23; Nicolson 1938; Smith 1964, pp. 44–54 (includes the present one); Brownlie 1995, pp. 150–51.

5   The common expression *toirt fon ear*, now more usually spelt *toirt fa-near*, 'observing', 'noticing', has nothing to do with *ear* 'east', but JGC may be forgiven for guessing. It is an etymological curiosity, originating in an Old Irish verb *fo-fera* 'prepares, provides, brings about', later *fodera, fa deara* 'causes'. Its original function being lost, it came to be regarded as a prepositional phrase and used with a different verb, e.g. *cuiridh fo deara* 'orders (something to be done)', *do-bheir fa ndeara* 'causes (something to be done)', later 'observes, notices' (*DIL* s.v. *fo-fera*). JGC is right about *an-earar* 'the day after tomorrow', but wrong about *earalas*, which is from *áil* 'desire' with the intensive prefix *air-* (Macbain 1896, p. 136). For the derivation of *earrach* see note 2.

6   Nicolson agreed, remarking that *Chan fheàrr an gille siar na 'n gille sear* was 'much of the same import as Pope's now classic comparison " 'twixt Tweedledum and Tweedledee" ' (1951, p. 118). The Rev. Duncan Campbell, however, called it 'a Hebridean saying regarding the wind, which may bring dry or wet weather from either direction', and cited a few extra words to help prove his point (Meek 1978, p. 61): *Chan fheàrr an gille sear na 'n gille siar – is breac-riabhach le chéil' iad.* "The east lad is no better than the west lad – they are both drab and speckled."

7   JGC speaks of the *samhanaich* elsewhere as 'giants who dwelt in caves by the sea' and 'the strongest and coarsest of any' (Campbell 1881a, p. 62, and 1881c, p. 141, cf. *CG2*, p. 347, *CG6*, p. 122). With regard to 'the ocean itself' he is referring to *tabh*, from Norse *haf* 'the sea, the ocean', as in the celebrated song by the Harris poet Màiri nighean Alastair Ruaidh (Watson 1965, pp. 44–45):

Ri fuaim an taibh
Is uaigneach mo ghean —
Bha mis' uair nach b'e sean m' àbhaist.

("Listening to the sea / My mood is dejected – / There was a time when that wasn't my nature.") With regard to 'smell' he makes the same point in Campbell 1881c, p. 141: "*Samh* is a strong oppressive smell, and in the Western islands *Samh a' chuain t-shiar*, the strong smell of the western sea, is a common expression."

8 No. The elements are *fo* 'under' and *gamur*, from *gam* 'winter' – simply 'sub-winter' (Macbain 1896, p. 159; Stokes 1906, p. 89; *DIL* s.v. *fogamar*). See note 2.

9 JGC should have stopped here while he was doing well. Macbain (1896, p. 172) also compares Sanskrit *himá* 'cold'.

10 *Mìos* is indeed ultimately connected with the moon, as one would expect, and may certainly be compared with Latin *mensis*, a month. *Mias*, a dish or platter, is from Latin *mensa*, a table. *Ré* 'time, space' is thought to be in origin the same as *ré* 'moon', the moon being the measurer of weeks and months (*DIL* s.v. 2 *ré*); it also became the preposition *ré* 'during', sometimes assimilated to *ri* as in *ri mo ré*, which may thus be seen to be tautological (Macbain 1896, pp. 224, 225, 259, and note 213 below).

11 The Gregorian calendar was introduced for official purposes by Act of Parliament in 1751, resulting in the loss of eleven days, i.e. the day following 2 September 1752 was decreed to be the 14th (Duncan 1998, pp. 308–18). The old Julian style (OS) survived in popular usage in the Highlands and Islands until the early twentieth century, however, and after 1800 the difference between the calendars increased to twelve days, with the result that throughout JGC's lifetime New Year's day was widely celebrated on 13 January. His statement that 'time is always reckoned by the old style' is of no small interest, for by 1900 adherence to the Julian calendar had largely ceased to be a marker of communal identity and was instead a matter of individual preference, usually associated with the older generation; technically the gap between the calendars increased to thirteen days in 1900, but I have no evidence that this was acted upon.

No doubt the speed of change had been increased by the introduction of universal primary education in 1872, and indeed surviving school log-books from JGC's own county of Argyll suggest that the period of transition was roughly 1868–90. In 1868 an unsuccessful attempt was made at Newton of Kilmeny in Islay to change the New Year holiday in the school from 13 to 1 January; the last mention of the Old New Year there was in 1886. At Kilchoman, also in Islay, the final change took place in 1883. At Kilninver on the mainland it was in 1888, while in Lochdonhead in Mull the spirit of compromise survived in spectacular fashion, the teacher noting on 3 January 1890: "Holidays began on the First to continue till after the Old New Year's day." (I am grateful to Murdo MacDonald, archivist, Argyll and Bute Council, for this information, see MacilleDhuibh 10.1.03.)

12 Spring consists of the months of February, March and April. The middle day of spring is therefore 16 March NS, 28 March OS, roughly 'the beginning of April'. Summer begins 1 May, so strictly the fifth week of summer ends 4 June NS, 16 June OS. This useful example of JGC's illustrates two fundamental points: (1) the OS dating system used by the people lagged in theory twelve days behind NS, and in practice as much as two or three more; (2) it employed quarters, weeks and days but made sparing use of months, presumably because these were lunar. In the early example cited in note 554 (p. 417 above) the term 'month' appears solely in the contexts 'at the end of a month of autumn' and 'at the end of a month of winter'. The earliest Scottish Gaelic terms for calendar months were therefore of the type 'the first month of winter' (November) and 'the middle month of autumn' (September). The terms used in nineteenth-century periodicals were largely of the Latin kind described

by JGC – *Ianuari, Februari, Màrt, Giblin, Màigh*, etc. By the twentieth century, however, it had become possible to introduce to the canon a number of largely disused native terms for festivals and periods of weather, so the month-names in formal use today are a smooth blend of Latin and traditional influences: *am Faoilleach, an Gearran, am Màrt, an Giblin, an Céitein, an t-Ògmhios, an t-Iuchar, an Lùnastal, an t-Sultain, an Dàmhair, an t-Samhain, an Dùbhlachd* (Black 1985).

13   As given by Nicolson (1951, p. 21), the first of these sayings has *shunndach* for *sunndach* and therefore means 'He who hasn't a merry Christmas . . .' As the second line in both cases (JGC and Nicolson) suggests 'He will make Easter sad and tearful', it seems to me that JGC's first line should be given as 'The man who doesn't make Christmas cheerful'. None of this matters much; the point is simply that if there is not enough to eat at Christmas there will be still less at Easter. As for JGC's second saying, it appears to be taken from the following (Nicolson 1951, p. 126, cf. MacRury 1890–91, p. 26):

> Cha robh samhradh riamh gun ghrian,
>   Cha robh geamhradh riamh gun sneachd,
>   Cha robh Nollaig Mhór gun fheòil
>   No bean òg le deòin gun fhear.

("Summer has never lacked sun, / Winter has never lacked snow, / Christmas Day has never lacked flesh / Nor has willing young woman lacked a man.") For a story based on the rhyme see *Tocher* 4, pp. 128–31; for excellent lists of Scottish and Irish references to Christmas and Little Christmas eve see Ó Duilearga 1981, pp. 318–19, 407; and for Christmas more generally see Banks 1937–41, vol. 3, pp. 202–44; McNeill 1957–68, vol. 3, pp. 51–89; Danaher 1972, pp. 233–58; Hutton 1996, pp. 1–8, 25–41, 112–23.

14   In a literal sense it is 'the night of Blows', but as JGC shows at p. 530, the real meaning is 'the night of the Kalends'.

15   *Oidhche nam Bannag* is indeed 'the night of the Cakes' or 'of the Bannocks'.

16   *Coinnle* is the genitive case of *Callainn* 'Kalends' as well as of *coinneal* 'a candle', so 'Kalends' is the true derivation. 'Hogmanay' is French in origin. In northern French dialect it was *hoguinané*, going back to Old French *aguillaneuf*, meaning a gift given on New Year's eve or the word cried out in soliciting it. An account submitted to Sir Robert Waterton of Methley in Yorkshire for the period 1443–44 includes 'paid on 31st December (for) large *hagnonayse* (12d) and small *hagnonayse* (8d), 20d' – Waterton's grandfather had been put in charge of one of the most distinguished Frenchmen captured at Agincourt, the duc d'Orléans, who had presumably introduced the custom to his household (Yarwood 1984, p. 253). The earliest Scottish reference is in the kirk session records of Elgin for 1603, when a man was accused of 'singing and hagmonayis' at New Year (Hutton 1996, pp. 27, 33); probably the practice became widespread in Scotland *c.* 1540, when French influence was substantial at all levels of society in Lowland Scotland and large numbers of French troops were garrisoned here.

17   Lhuyd 1707, pp. 45, [332].

18   See also Dalyell 1834, pp. 110–11; *CG2*, pp. 304–05; Thomas 1906; N. M. 1908–09; Maclagan 1912–14; Dieckhoff 1914–19, pp. 244–48; *Tocher* 36/37, pp. 358–61; *Tocher* 41, pp. 288–89; Bennett 1989, p. 116; Macdonald 2003, p. 63. Dressing up a man in an animal skin at New Year, belabouring him with sticks and parading noisily through the community is characteristic of what Frazer called 'the periodic expulsion of evils'. He says (1913, p. 229): "Every year on the fourteenth of March a man clad in skins was led in procession through the streets of Rome, beaten with long white rods, and driven out of the city. He was called Mamurius Veturius, that is, 'the old Mars', and as the ceremony took place on the day preceding the first full moon of the old Roman year (which began on the first of March), the skin-clad

man must have represented the Mars of the past year, who was driven out at the beginning of a new one."

We may also recognise in this skin-clad man the scapegoat of Leviticus 16, although, as Frazer points out (*ibid.*, p. 210), 'the word translated "scapegoat" in the Authorised Version is Azazel, which appears rather to be the name of a bad angel or demon, to whom the goat was sent away'. Numerous more modern examples of the practice can be cited; for example in Poland a man was led about at Christmas with a wolf's skin over his head (Frazer 1912, vol. 1, p. 275). It is possible that in pre-Christian times the man was sacrificed; indeed, in comparable festivals in Mexico, the skins worn by Aztec priests were those of human victims (*ibid.*, pp. 288–305). In the eastern Highlands a dog seems to have been preferred (*ibid.*, p. 209): Ramsay of Ochtertyre tells us (1888, vol. 2, p. 439) that on the morning of New Year's day in the eighteenth century it was usual in some parts of Breadalbane 'to take a dog to the door, give him a bit of bread, and drive him out', saying: *Bis, a choin duibh! A h-uil' eug earchaill a bhiodh a-staigh gu ceann bliadhna gun robh ad' chreubhaig!* ("Get away, black dog! May every death from cattle-loss which could occur in this house till the year's end be in your body!")

In 1977 Mrs Peggy Morrison recalled her father, William MacDonald (*Uilleam Donn*) from Strond and Ardhasaig in Harris, saying that the year was, in a literal sense, buried (*Tocher* 41, pp. 290–91). She used to ask him: *Ciamar a dhei'adh ac' air a' bhliadhna thìodhlagadh?* "How did they manage to bury the year?"

"Oh," he would say, "they would take a cheese (*mulchag chàis*), a bottle of whisky (*botal uisge-bheatha*) and a barley bannock (*bonnach eòrna*), and go off with that and bury it in a hill above the village. And apparently they wept and wailed (*tha e collach gu robh iad a' caoineadh 's a' tuiream*) for the old year that had gone ... I don't know but that some people might go out after the bottle of whisky, but probably not (*is iongantach gun dei'adh*), because they believed so strongly in it (*bha iad a' creidsinn cho mór ann*), that it just needed to be buried exactly as a human corpse was buried (*mar gum biodhte tìodhlagadh dìreach corp duine*) and left there."

19 This is a particularly noteworthy version of a common Hogmanay rhyme, as it appears to portray the straw *cailleach* of harvest, which represents hunger (cf. p. 681), being found by the visitors in the house and ritually slaughtered. It thus seems to answer the twin questions of what the unfortunate recipient of a *cailleach* or last sheaf did with it at the end of harvest when no one remained to whom it could be passed on, and of how and when he was released from its spell. Crucially, it also provides a key to the symbolism of the *caisein uchd* (see next note), which may be seen as representing what was left of the animal (*boc* 'buck', *gobhar bhacach* 'lame goat') or human being (*cailleach*) slain on the harvest field, see 'The Harvest Old Wife (*a' Chailleach*)', pp. 133–34.

The first line consists I think of a vocative word and three genitive ones, and would be better translated 'O Hogmanay of the yellow (or lucky) buckskin bag', the bag probably being the one in which *bannagan* and other treats were carried away from the houses (Black 2001, pp. 501–02). The last line, *Leig a-staigh mi*, means simply 'Let me in'; JGC's 'open this' is superfluous. The conclusion of a version noted by Fr Dieckhoff (1914–19, p. 247) refers instead to the 'ritual slaughter' element:

> *Stob 'na goile*
> *'S i 'na teine dearg.*

("A stake in her stomach / As she goes up in red flames.") This shows the *gillean Callainn* throwing the straw *cailleach* into the fire, see also Barron 1969–70, p. 248.

20 Due to the change of calendar in 1752, 'Christmas rhyme' is indeed the traditional translation of *rann Callainn* and *duan Callainn*, both of which strictly mean 'Calendar

rhyme'. Some refer to Christmas, most to the New Year. For examples see MacPherson 1868, pp. 153–54; Mackenzie 1879–80, p. 29; Ramsay 1881–83, p. 200; Mackenzie 1885–86, p. 100; CG1, pp. 150–57; Mackenzie 1905–06, p. 329; Dieckhoff 1914–19, pp. 246–48; CG5, pp. 378–83; Barron 1969–70, p. 231; *Tocher* 4, p. 126; Buidse 1972–74, pp. 593–94; Barron 1974–76, pp. 149, 156; Shaw 1977, pp. 24–25; *Tocher* 36/37, pp. 360–65; Macdonald 1982, pp. 171, 362–63; *Tocher* 41, pp. 286–89; Bennett 1989, pp. 115–16; MacLennan 1994–96, pp. 224–27; Hutton 1996, pp. 65–67; Harman 1997, p. 242; Loudon 2001, p. 14; EUL MS CW 503, ff. 814–17. See also JGC's next section, 'Christmas Rhymes (*Rannan Callainn*)'.

21 The importance of the *caisein uchd* in traditional husbandry appears to have been that it could be kept as a memento of a particular beast, rather like a lock or curl of hair for a human being – indeed the term means literally 'breast lock', 'breast curl'. When *Mac Iain Ghiorr* ('Mac Ian Year', pp. 97–98 above) lifted a *creach* he 'only left the breast-bit, or *caisean-uchd*, of each cow to indicate that they need not look for them again upon the hill' (Mackellar 1888–89, p. 162). However, it is as the focus of New Year ritual that the *caisein uchd* is best remembered in Gaelic tradition to the present day, cf. *Tocher* 36/37, p. 364; *Tocher* 41, pp. 290–91; Black 1999, pp. 674–77, 813; Black 2001, pp. 369, 460; MacilleDhuibh 10.1.03. The evidence adduced by Frazer (1913, pp. 265–66) in the context of 'the Human Scapegoat in Ancient Greece' emphasises the purificatory nature of rituals of this kind. Everyone, it seems, should share in the blessings conveyed by the first animal sacrificed in the New Year, which is what the *caisein uchd* appears to represent. "Among the Arabs of Morocco the Great Feast, which is the annual sacrificial festival of Mohammedan peoples, is the occasion when men go about beating people with the kindly intention of healing or preventing sickness and benefiting the sufferers generally. In some tribes the operator is muffled in the bloody skins of sacrificed sheep, and he strikes everybody within reach of him with a flap of the skin or a foot of the sheep which dangles loose from his arm . . . the skin-clad mummer sometimes operates with sticks instead of a flap of the skin, and sometimes the skins in which he is muffled are those of goats instead of sheep, but in all cases the effect, or at least the intention, is probably the same."

In the yet more exalted context of 'processions with sacred animals', however, Frazer (1912, vol. 2, pp. 322–24) cites JGC's description of *Callainn* (to here) in full along with the very similar evidence provided by Johnson (Levi 1984, p. 129), Ramsay (1888, vol. 2, pp. 438–39) and Chambers (1847, p. 297), rightly comparing it to the 'hunting of the wren' which is (or was) ubiquitous at the same time of year in Ireland, Wales, Man and France, and by no means unknown in England (see Dalyell 1834, pp. 421–23, Danaher 1972, pp. 243–50, MacDonogh 1983, Hutton 1996, pp. 96–99, Muller 1996–97, and the excellent list of references in Ó Duilearga 1981, pp. 407–08). Like the *caisein uchd*, the captured wren was paraded from house to house, usually on the end of a pole. Frazer concludes (1912, vol. 2, pp. 324–25): "Formerly, perhaps, pieces of the cow-hide in which the man was clad were singed and put to the noses of the people, just as in the Isle of Man a feather of the wren used to be given to each household. Similarly, as we have seen, the human victim whom the Khonds slew as a divinity was taken from house to house, and every one strove to obtain a relic of his sacred person. Such customs are only another form of that communion with the deity which is attained most completely by eating the body and drinking the blood of the god."

The custom of dressing in animal skins at New Year was referred to in the ninth century by an unknown cleric, working somewhere in what is now France or Germany, who added it to the seventh-century 'Penitential of Theodore' (Kemble 1876, vol. 1, p. 525, cf. Elton 1882, p. 411; Frazer 1912, vol. 2, p. 323; Hutton 1994, p. 47, and 1996, p. 89). *Qui grana arserit ubi mortuus est homo, pro sanitate viventium et domus, etc. Si quis, pro sanitate filioli, per foramen terrae exierit, illudque spinis post se concludit, etc. Si quis ad arbores, vel ad fontes, vel ad lapides, sive ad cancellos, vel ubicunque, excepto in aecclesia Dei, votum voverit aut exsolverit, etc., et hoc sacrilegium est vel daemoniacum. Qui vero ibidem ederit aut biberit, etc. Si quis in Kalendas Januarii in cervulo aut vetula vadit, id est, in ferarum habitus se communicant* [i.e. *commutant?*], *et vestiuntur pellibus pecudum, et assumunt capita bestiarum; qui vero taliter in ferinas species se transformant, etc., quia hoc daemoniacum est.* ("Whoever burns grain when somebody dies, for the health of the living and the household, etc. Anyone who, for the health of a child, dies in a hole in the ground, and it closes up after him with thorns, etc. Anyone who makes a vow to trees, or to springs of water, or to stones, or to gates, or anywhere, except in God's church, and pays it off, etc., that too is sacrilege or demonic. Anyone who eats or drinks in that place, etc. Anyone who on the first of January goes about in a deer or a calf, that is, changes into the clothes of wild animals, and dresses in the skins of cattle, and puts on the heads of wild beasts; those who in that way really change into species of wild animal, etc., because that is demonic.") See also Dalyell 1834, pp. 499–500; CG2, p. 243; MacGregor 1901, p. 42; Henderson 1911, pp. 131–32, 263–66; Hutton 1996, pp. 7, 44–45. In recent times the beating of the skin and the *caisein uchd* were an exclusively Scottish custom, not an Irish one, but it was also practised in Rathlin (Danaher 1972, p. 262).

22 *Fàr-lus* is usually now spelt *fàrlas* – from *farleus*, early Irish *forlés*, an 'over-light', cf. p. xv above. For more on the *laomachan* see CG6, pp. 94–95.

23 This is a variant of a well-known Hogmanay rhyme. It appears to consist of six-and-a-half quatrains. Its closest recorded equivalents are, I think, the versions in CG1, pp. 150–51 (five-and-a-half quatrains) and 152–55 (seven quatrains). JGC's original was excluded from WSS, but I have supplied it from Carmichael's transcript in EUL MS CW 241, ff. 55–56 (see p. 703 below), where it is arranged as six quatrains + one couplet. The following points may be noted. End of line 4: /*thur* (*thar*) added to give alternative spelling *seanathar*. Line 5: *Caise Calluinn ann am phoca* /*Caisein* – Carmichael correcting JGC? Line 7 ends *tusa/thos* (i.e. *tùs* or *thòs*, same meaning); I adopt *thòs* for rhyme with *shròn*. End of line 13: /*suas* ('up') added as alternative to JGC's *a nuas* ('down'), but JGC has coped well with this in his translation: 'Rise down' i.e. 'Get up and come down' (from the box-bed, or from the upper end of a sloping floor). Line 15: after *a nios* Carmichael places an oblique then scores it out; it means 'up (towards the speaker)', presumably because the visitors arrive to find the wife seated or reclining, but whether JGC understands its function is uncertain, cf. note 471 above. End of line 20: /*ur* added, suggesting 'Bread and fresh meat (*feòil ùr*) will suffice' instead of 'Bread and meat will suffice for us', but JGC appears to be happy with rhyme *duinn* (*dùinn*?) : *sùil*, cf. *cliù* : *duinn* in fourth quatrain. End of line 21: /*mo* added in pencil ('*na mo bhrògan*, same meaning). End of line 23: *beola* added in pencil (*taobh na beòla* i.e. *beò-luath* 'beside the hot embers'). End of line 24: *bheo* added in place of *leigheas*, suggesting 'What will revive me'. No doubt these two changes reflect a version Carmichael has heard, but they alter the rhyme-scheme. End of line 25: /*aird* ('height') added as alternative to JGC's *ait-*, my *àit* ('room').

Quatrains 4 and 5 (*Éirich a-nuas* to *feòil duinn*) reappear, altered to some extent, at p. 534. JGC's *a bhean chòir* is not 'young wife' but 'dear wife'; his 'butter eye has not blinked' (*an t-ìm nach do bheum sùil*) is more literally 'butter that eye has not afflicted' in time of churning, cf. *beum sùla* 'the blow of eye', note 681 above. Probably therefore the face in *a' chàbag air am bheil an aghaidh réidh* (literally 'the cheese upon which is the even face') is not the 'smooth face' of the cheese but the 'friendly face' of the person who looks at it in time of making.

24 See note 46 below. In referring the 'big clerk of the street' to the Festival of Fools JGC is, in my opinion, stretching the 'comparative method' beloved of the anthropological folklorists a little too far. I see little difficulty in locating *sràid* in a Highland township, ironically or

otherwise. A row of houses in Balevullin in Tiree is known as *an t-Sràid Ruadh* 'the Red Street' (MacDougall and Cameron n.d., p. 94, and Brownlie 1995, p. 48). In any case 'clerk' is an odd word to use for *bleidire*, Dwelly's 'beggar, teazing petitioner' (1977, p. 101); probably JGC was thinking of the township clerk as a spokesman. Curiously, the duty of greeting King James IV with a New Year ballad appears to have fallen in 1491 to 'the Clerks to the Chapel' (McNeill 1957–68, vol. 3, p. 81, cf. Hutton 1996, p. 15).

25 JGC's original was excluded from *WSS*, but I have supplied it from Carmichael's transcript in EUL MS CW 241, ff. 57–61 (see p. 703 below). It is arranged there as two separate pieces: ff. 57–60, headed 'Rann Calluinn', grouped into lines 1–4, 5–8, 9–12, 13–16, 17–19, 20–21, 22–25, 26–30, 31–34, 35–36, 37–40, 41–44, 45–48, 49–52, 53–56, 57–60, 61–63; and f. 61, headed again 'Rann Calluinn', grouped into lines 64–67, 68–71, 72–74, 75–77, 78–79. I have chosen to present the Gaelic text unedited, exactly as it stands in the manuscript – it requires more detailed commentary than is possible here, and the text which gave rise to JGC's translation will be more helpful for present purposes than one which raises fresh questions (there are a number of things which I do not understand, e.g. the *gille geal* near the end, JGC's 'white servant'). Carmichael makes two additions in his left margin: *Choille/* as a further alternative to *Choinlle/Choinnle* at p. 534 line 10, and *nean/* (i.e. *neanachan*) as an alternative to *meanachan* at p. 534 line 24. Three lines later *dual* is preferable to *nòs* (similar meaning) as it rhymes with *suas*.

The structure of the piece is of great interest. Lines 1–16 (*Beannaich* to *Ho gu eile*) and 33–48 (*Bhuail e* to *S e lan toraidh*) are clearly in *snéadhbhairdne*, a verse-form which consists of alternating lines of eight and four syllables with end-rhyme linking the shorter lines, e.g. *ceòlmhor : stròdhail*. Lines 17–25 (*Roinn mo chuidse* to *gar n eisdeachd*) and 29–32 (*Dh eirich* to *spreodadh*) may originally have been in the same metre – *chéile : éisteachd* looks like a *snéadhbhairdne* rhyme. Lines 64–71 (*Eirich a suas* to *feoil duinn*), which are in an everyday metre with *aicill* and end-rhyme, correspond fairly closely to lines 13–20 of the *rann* on p. 532. The remainder exhibits no clear structure, but the 'hamper on my servant's back' is strongly reminiscent of 'thigging' or 'genteel begging' (Black 2001, pp. xxix–xxxii), while the words *Fosgail 's leig a-staigh mi*, 'Open and let me in', form a conclusion characteristic of many Hogmanay rhymes, cf. p. 531.

This certainly justifies JGC's comment that 'it consists probably of several separate rhymes tagged together', but we may go further. The use of *snéadhbhairdne* was largely restricted to a curious type of composition called *crosanachd* in which serious verse alternated with comic prose (Harrison 1989, pp. 55–70; Black 2001, pp. 408–09). Typically, an individual was praised in the verse while his enemies were satirised in the prose. It may well be, then, that the passages with no discernible structure are not poetry at all but prose; all of them are clearly intended to be comic.

The sixteen lines from *Bhuail e gnogag* to *S e lan toraidh* consist of comic verse on a sexual theme. The *crambail*, *crambaid* or 'stick' (harp-key, *crann*) is the male sexual organ, the harp the female one; the scenario is as in the Blind Harper's song 'Féill nan Crann' ('The Harp-Key Fair', Matheson 1970, pp. 12–19) except that here the key is broken, there it is lost. Indeed I think the bawdy section begins at line 13, *Fhearaibh*. I doubt very much whether *cuisnean* 'icinesses' (line 29) is a correct reading; I suspect the word is *cuislean* 'a little vein, pipe, etc.', but I have no evidence as yet for *cuislean* (or indeed *spreòdadh*, line 32) being used in a sexual context.

What JGC has preserved for us, then, is the 'script' of a light-hearted dramatic performance suitable for New Year's eve. We may note the comment of Dr P. D. Strachan, writing of Lewis in the 1880s (1932–36, p. 531): "Another objectionable feature in some of the less reputable *ceilidh* houses was the freedom with which adults discussed sexual relations in a ribald fashion before children."

26 A harp-key, presumably, cf. Dwelly's *crambaid* 'metal on the end of a sword-sheath or -stick, ferrule' (1977, p. 260). Carmichael's *crambail* may be a misreading of JGC's *crambait* or *crambaid*. Two lines later, JGC's 'clerk' is a mistranslation of *clàrsair* 'harper' – probably accidental, due to similarity of sound and semantic connections between *clàr* ('table, record') and 'clerk'.

27 JGC's original is not in *WSS*, but I have supplied it from EUL MS CW 241, f. 62 (see p. 703 below), where it is headed 'Rann Calluinn / Tha an rann so airson feadhain aig nach bheil rann eile' ('Hogmanay Rhyme / This rhyme is for those who have no other'), cf. *CG5*, pp. 378–79, where the same explanation is given: *Tha an rann a leanas air son clann-ghillean aig nach bheil rann eile.* "The rime that follows is for lads that have no other rime."

> *Nar bheil fuath agam air càise,*
> *Nar bheil gràin agam air ìm,*
> *Ach drùdhag bheag a shùgh an eòrna*
> *Tha mi deònach a chur sìos!*

("I have no dislike to cheese, / I have no disgust of butter, / But a little sip of barley bree / I am right willing to put down!")

28 This is a folk etymology for which JGC is by no means responsible, cf. pp. 530, 534, 538. The term is *oidhche Choilne* 'the eve of the Kalends', 'Calendar eve', *Coilne* being the genitive case of *Callainn*. Strictly *oidhche Choinnle* is the eve of Candlemas (2 February), the night following St Brigid's day, but no doubt many Protestants were more inclined to light candles on 31 December than on 1 February.

29 I take it that this is distinct from the various rhymes for smooring the fire at night (e.g. *CG1*, pp. 234–41, and *CG3*, pp. 324–27) or rekindling it in the morning (e.g. *CG1*, pp. 230–33); nor do I see any references to 'feeding the fire' in the Christmas and New Year rhymes in *CG1*, pp. 126–59.

30 It was not in itself a quarter-day, but was treated as a quarter-day.

31 Discussing this rhyme in 1890, the Rev. John MacRury remarked (1890–91, pp. 19–20): *Cha 'n eil mi 'gabhail orm fhein a radh co dhiu tha gus nach 'eil am beachd so fior, ach tha e comharraichte gur ann o 'n deas a bha a' ghaoth a' séideadh an uiridh agus am bliadhna an uair a thàinig a' bhliadhn' ùr a steach, agus gu robh a' ghaoth ni bu trice o 'n deas am bliadhna 's an uiridh anns a' Ghàidhealtachd na 's cuimhne le bheag a tha beò ... Bha teas is toradh gu leòr anns a' Ghaidhealtachd an uiridh, ach cha 'n urrainn duinn so a ràdh am bliadhna.* "I do not take it upon myself to say whether this idea is true or not, but it is remarkable that the wind was blowing from the south last year and this when the New Year came in, and that the wind was more often southerly this year and last in the Highlands and Islands than any living person can remember ... There was plenty of 'heat and produce' in the Highlands and Islands last year, but we cannot say the same for this year." A South Uist version (McDonald 1958, p. 136, cf. GUL MS Gen. 1090/29, pp. 78–79) has *Gaoth an-iar, uisge 's feamainn* ('West wind, rain and seaweed'), *Gaoth an-ear a dh'fhearaibh a' chuain* ('East wind for the men of the sea'), and *feannadh* 'flaying' for *gailleann*. Other variations (MacRury 1890–91, p. 19; *CG2*, p. 343; Dwelly 1907, p. 3; Fionn 1912a, p. 34; Camshron 1926, p. 46; Smith 1964, p. 26; *Tocher* 4, p. 123; Macdonald 1982, pp. 326, 427) include *mil* 'honey' instead of fruit, a west wind that brings *iasg gu caladh* ('fish to shore') or *iasg gu carraig* ('fish to fishing-rock'), and an east wind that brings *sneachd air beannaibh* ('snow on the hills') or *tart is crannadh* ('drought and parching').

JGC's version was first placed on record by the Rev. John Grant, minister of Kirkmichael in Highland Banffshire, who wrote of his congregation (1791, pp. 458–59 = new edn, pp. 297–98): "On the first night of January, they observe, with anxious attention, the disposition of the atmosphere. As it is calm or boisterous; as the wind blows from the S. or the N.; from the E. or the W., they prognosticate the nature of the weather, till the conclusion of the year. The first night of the New Year, when the wind blows from the W., they call dàr-na coille, the night of the fecundation of the trees; and from this circumstance has been derived the name of that night in the Gaelic language." Although his word 'call' is a little ambiguous, Grant thus shows some awareness that the real meaning of *dàir na coille* is not so much 'the fecundation of the trees' as 'the copulation of the Kalends', i.e. the ground will be ready for ploughing and sowing a month early, see p. 52.

32 JGC referred to this at p. 529, using a more informal variety of the genitive case, as *latha Nollaig Bhig*. For lists of references to Little Christmas eve and New Year's day in Ireland, Scotland and Man see Ó Duilearga 1981, p. 407. For New Year more generally see Banks 1937–41, vol. 2, pp. 75–118, and vol. 3, pp. 201–02; McNeill 1957–68, vol. 3, pp. 89–121; Danaher 1972, pp. 258–62; Hutton 1996, pp. 1–69.

33 Cf. Johnson: "A man of the Hebrides, for of the women's diet I can give no account, as soon as he appears in the morning, swallows a glass of whisky; yet they are not a drunken race, at least I never was present at much intemperance; but no man is so abstemious as to refuse the morning dram, which they call a *skalk*." And Boswell: "Some excellent brandy was served round immediately, according to the custom of the Highlands, where a dram is generally taken every day. They call it a *scatch*." Boswell may have written *scalck*; the word is *sgailc* 'a thump, bump, bumper' (Levi 1984, pp. 72, 253, 424 note 152). The contrast between Johnson's/Boswell's portrayal of the gentry and JGC's of the tenantry is instructive. To the gentry every day was Christmas.

34 I sense a symbolic contrast between noble and ignoble substances, whisky and sowens. A possible reason for the ritual consumption of the latter is that no-one need be excluded from the custom by poverty. It was a recognition that society depended as much upon the prosperity of the community as upon individual wealth. In Knockfin's account (1876, pp. 107, 111) ten bowls are filled with sowens. "In two of these a ring was placed, signifying, of course, speedy marriage; a shilling put into two others represented the old bachelor or old maid; and a half-crown in another represented riches."

35 Brand 1849, vol. 1, p. 13. In GUL MS Gen. 1090/29, p. 239, Fr Allan McDonald confirms that nothing was put out of the house on New Year's day.

36 Brand 1849, vol. 1, pp. 538–39. Ellis took the passage from Train 1845, vol. 2, pp. 114–16; see also Rhŷs 1901, pp. 336–38. On *còmhalaich* and *còmhaltaich* see above, pp. 139–40 and notes 286, 719.

37 These New Year shinty matches thus fit into a world-wide pattern in which ritual conflicts – be they tugs-of-war, ball-games or sword-fights – took place at an important juncture of the year, apparently in order to ensure prosperity in the coming season. After reviewing the evidence of tugs-of-war and Norman ball-games Frazer concludes (1913, p. 183): "The belief that the parish which succeeded in carrying the ball home would have a better crop of apples that year raises a presumption that these conflicts were originally practised as magical rites to ensure fertility. The local custom of Lande-Patry, which required that the ball should be provided and thrown by the last bride, points in the same direction. It is possible that the popular English, or rather Scotch, game of football had a similar origin: the winning side may have imagined that they secured good crops, good weather, or other substantial advantages to their village or ward. In like manner, wherever a sham or a real conflict takes place between two parties annually, above all at the New Year, we may suspect that the old intention was to ensure prosperity in some form for the people throughout the following year, whether by obtaining possession of a material object in which the luck of the year was supposed to be embodied, or by defeating and driving away a band of men who personated the powers of evil."

For traditional shinty matches see MacPherson 1868, pp. 190–91; Knockfin 1876, pp. 106–10; Maclagan 1901, pp. 24–36; Macdonald 1919–22; Nicolson 1963; *Tocher* 24, p. 327; Robertson 1978–80, pp. 263–65; *Tocher* 36/37, pp. 364–78; Macdonald 1982, pp. 196–97; Macdonald 1992, pp. 1–9; Hutchinson 1989; MacLennan 1994–96 and 1995; Black 2001, p. 501.

38 This description of shinty rituals should be read in conjunction with that of the Rev. Dr Norman MacLeod (Mac Aonghais 1830, p. 192 = Clerk 1867, p. 403, translated in McNeill 1957–68, vol. 3, p. 120). *Chomharaicheadh a mach an taodhall, agus thòisich iad air na daoin' a tharruing. "Buaileam ort, Alastair," arsa Domhnull, "leigeam leat," ars' Alastair. Is leamsa Domhnull bàn Chuilfhodair, an aon duine bu shine bh'air an fhaiche: thug Domhnull ceum gu taobh, agus shaoileadh tu gun leumadh an dà shùil as le h-aighear.* ("The goals were marked out, and they began to pick the men. 'I strike upon you, Alastair,' said Donald. 'I yield to you,' said Alastair. 'Dòmhnall Bàn of Culloden is mine' – the oldest man on the field. Dòmhnall Bàn stepped to one side, and you would have thought his two eyes were about to pop out of his head for joy.") *Buaileam ort* are the words spoken by the man who throws his shinty-stick to the other; *Leigeam leat* is said by the man who loses the contest of grasping the stick alternately (see also Mac a Phì 1938, p. 36, and *Tocher* 36/37, pp. 366–67). Honouring an old man who had fought at Culloden, rather than picking the best player, is a typical MacLeod touch.

MacLeod goes on: *'Nuair bha na daoin' air an roinn, dà fhichead air gach taobh, buideal aig gach ceann de'n taodhall, thilg Alastair ruadh an caman suas, Cas no Bas, a Dhomh'uill nan Gleann? Bas a chumas ri d' chois gu h-oidhche. 'Sann air Alastair a thainig an ceud bhuille bhualadh.* ("When the men had been divided, forty on each side with a cask at each end of the goal, Alastair Ruadh threw the stick in the air. 'Foot or palm, Donald of the Glens?' 'A palm that will keep up with your foot until nightfall,' [said Donald]. It fell to Alastair to strike the first blow.") This, then, is a way to decide who should begin the game in the absence of an officiating dignitary, not, as in JGC's account, an alternative way of picking sides. JGC's *chas no bhas* is for *a' chas no a' bhas* 'the foot or the palm'.

For other pre-shinty rituals see Maclagan 1901, pp. 30–35; Morrison 1907–08, pp. 369–70; McDonald 1912–13, pp. 166–67; Anon. 1959; *Tocher* 36/37, p. 438; MacNeil 1987, pp. 390–93; Hutchinson 1989, pp. 45–46; MacLennan 1994–96, pp. 186–89.

39 *Crìod* is otherwise spelt *cneut, cniad* (Dwelly 1977, p. 219), cf. *criatag* 'wooden football, cricket-ball' (Armstrong 1825, p. 152), *a' cluich air a' chneutaig* 'playing at cricket or shinty' (Dwelly 1991, p. 53). It seems to be from Norse *knǫttr*, from which also comes 'knotty', the word used in Shetland, Orkney, Caithness and Sutherland not merely for the ball but for the game of shinty itself. There is a particularly good account of how the wooden ball (*ball*) was shaped and hardened in *Tocher* 36/37, pp. 371–73; see also MacLennan 1994–96, p. 157. Nowadays to start the game the ball is simply thrown up by the referee.

40 'Hail' in this sense is found in all parts of Scotland. It is explained by the *OED*, which cites examples from 1673 onwards, as 'the act of saluting the dool or goal with the exclamation "hail!", when it is hit by the ball; hence, the act of hailing or driving the ball to the dool or goal'. It seems more likely, however, that the word derives from Gaelic *tadhal* 'visiting, calling' in the context (suggested by JGC) that the object of shinty was 'to drive the ball hail' (*am ball iomain a thadhal*). More precise terminology was available, however, usually based on *bàire*, cf. JGC's *buille bhàraich* (Macdonald 1919–22, p. 31; Campbell 1978–81, p. 213; *Tocher* 36/37, pp. 370–71; MacLennan 1994–96, p. 158, and 1995, p. 343). Kenneth Macleod says (1907–08, p. 315): "In Eigg *leth-chluich* means one 'hail', *cluich* two 'hails', *cluich gu leth* three 'hails'. In Morvern and Mull the words used are – *leth-bhair, bàire, bàire gu leth*. In many districts, however, *bàire* means one 'hail.'"

41 This will be a typographic error for urine – see pp. 25–26, 177, 248, 553.

42 This should be compared with: *Uair a' ghille-chonnaidh air an latha, là Fhéill Brìghde.* "The fuel-gatherer's hour is added to the day on St Brigid's day." The Rev. Duncan Campbell's explanation of this (Meek 1978, p. 171) is that 'because of the lengthening day, an extra hour can be used for gathering firewood'. This is the opposite of JGC's, but either solution might well apply to either proverb. Two further sayings are connected. One is: *Là Fhéill Brìghde gheibh an seirbheiseach tuarastal slàn* ('On St Brigid's day the farm-servant will receive full wages', Meek 1978, p. 125), which suggests that extra light means not less work but more. The other is:

> *Là Fhéill Pàdraig earraich*
> *Bheir na cait an connadh dhachaigh.*

"On St Patrick's day of spring / The cats will bring the firewood home." Taking a hint from Nicolson (1951, p. 296), I have preferred this reconstructed version to one beginning *Là Fhéill Brìghde bàine* ('On the day of fair St Brigid') on the grounds of rhyme *earraich : cait.* It means, I believe, that by St Patrick's day there is so much 'real' work to do that no one can be spared any longer for fuel-gathering. Curiously, by 1 May the idea has gone a step still further (Macdonald 1982, p. 202): *Air latha buidhe Bealltainn / Bheir an luchag dhachaigh cual chonnaidh.* "On yellow Beltane day / The little mouse will bring home a faggot of firewood." See note 50 below.

43 *Fad coisichean coilich* is 'the length of a cock's *coisichean*'. *Coisichean* in the sense of 'stride, walk' is otherwise unattested. The more usual form of the saying (Meek 1978, p. 42) was: *Ceum coise coilich air an latha, latha Nollaige.* "A cock's stride upon the day, Christmas day." That is to say, by Christmas day OS (6 January) the day is a little bit longer. If interpreted as meaning New Year's day OS (13 January), it is longer still. According to Neil MacLennan *coischeum coilich air sitig* ('a cock's strutting on the midden') was 'said of New Year's Day when the cock can walk an extra pace before going to roost' (Campbell 1963–65, p. 188). This is generally made explicit: *Tha coischeum coilich* (or *ceum cas coilich*) *air latha na Bliadhn' Ùir,* meaning in effect 'the cock goes one extra step on New Year's day', or as Carmichael puts it (*CG6*, p. 46), 'the cock took the hens a little farther afield that day'. Perhaps JGC's *coisichean* is in error for *coischeum.*

44 In other versions *dhubh* 'black' is substituted for *uaine* 'green'. These common sayings (for which see also Camshron 1926, p. 47; Banks 1937–41, vol. 3, p. 212; Nicolson 1951, p. 257; Dwelly 1977, s.v. *blianach*; Meek 1978, p. 106) are illustrations of a fundamental principle, *Is math gach aimsir 'na h-àm fhéin.* "All weather is good in its own time." If snow has not arrived by Christmas, when there is no outside work to be done, it is assumed that it will linger long into spring and delay the sowing and the harvest, with potentially fatal consequences. This is more true of the central Highlands than of the west coast and islands – which shows how the centre of gravity of the Gaelic-speaking area has drifted westwards since our traditional wisdom was created.

45 See note 21; Brand (1849, vol. 1, p. 8) takes the words from Du Cange's *Glossarium ad Scriptores Mediæ et Infimæ Latinitatis,* first published in Paris in 1678.

46 Frazer points out (1913, p. 334) that the Festival of Fools (*Fête des Fous*) fell in different places on Christmas Day, St Stephen's Day, New Year's Day or Twelfth Day. It appears, he says (*ibid.*, p. 336), to have been most popular in France, but was also celebrated in Germany, Bohemia and England. More recent approaches, notably the chapter 'Misrule' in Hutton 1996, pp. 95–111, portray the mock abbots of the Scottish burghs – the Abbot of Unreason in Inverness, for example, or the Abbot of Unrest in Peebles – as part of a universal custom of suspending or reversing normality during the midwinter festival (cf. McNeill 1957–68, vol. 2, pp. 11–18). Frazer explains (1913, p. 335): "The priests, wearing grotesque masks and

sometimes dressed as women, danced in the choir and sang obscene chants: laymen disguised as monks and nuns mingled with the clergy: the altar was transformed into a tavern, where the deacons and subdeacons ate sausages and black-puddings or played at dice and cards under the nose of the celebrant; and the censers smoked with bits of old shoes instead of incense, filling the church with a foul stench. After playing these pranks and running, leaping, and cutting capers through the whole church, they rode about the town in mean carts, exchanging scurrilities with the crowds of laughing and jeering spectators.

"Amongst the buffooneries of the Festival of Fools one of the most remarkable was the introduction of an ass into the church, where various pranks were played with the animal. At Autun the ass was led with great ceremony to the church under a cloth of gold, the corners of which were held by four canons; and on entering the sacred edifice the animal was wrapt in a rich cope, while a parody of the mass was performed. A regular Latin liturgy in glorification of the ass was chanted on these occasions, and the celebrant priest imitated the braying of an ass." See also Dalyell 1834, p. 446. JGC sees the *caisein uchd* as a comparable piece of buffoonery, but fails to explain why a custom should not be whimsical and 'pagan' at the same time. It is surely much safer to view the *caisein uchd* and the Festival of Fools as descendants of some common ethnological ancestor such as Frazer's intercalary period (see next note): cousins, perhaps, but not close relatives.

47 This is quoted by Frazer (1913, p. 324) in the course of an extended discussion of the Twelve Days in which he argues that, far from representing a Christian celebration of the time between Christmas and Epiphany, these may be in origin 'an intercalary period inserted annually at the end of a lunar year of three hundred and fifty-four days for the purpose of equating it to a solar year reckoned at three hundred and sixty-six days' (*ibid.*, p. 342). He justifies this thesis by pointing out that intercalary periods are typified by misrule, and that the Twelve Days, embracing as they did such extraordinary phenomena as the Scots 'Abbot of Unreason', the English 'Lord of Misrule' and the French 'Festival of Fools' (see previous note), conform to this pattern (*ibid.*, pp. 328–39). He also draws attention (*ibid.*, pp. 342–44) to the calendar of Coligny, which intercalates thirty days every two-and-a-half years instead of twelve days every year. "The thirty days of the intercalary month bear the names of the twelve months of the year repeated two and a half times. This seems to shew that, just as our modern peasants regard the Twelve Days as representing each a month of the year in their chronological order, so the old Celts of Gaul who drew up the Coligny calendar regarded the thirty days of the intercalary month as representing the thirty ordinary months which were to follow it till the next intercalation took place. And we may conjecture that just as our modern peasants still draw omens from the Twelve Days for the twelve succeeding months, so the old Celts drew omens from the thirty days of the intercalary month for the thirty months of the two and a half succeeding years." See also Lyle 1984; Bennett 1989, pp. 101–17; Hutton 1996, pp. 9–24.

48 Pennant 1998, p. 417: "The Highlanders form a sort of almanac or presage of the weather of the ensuing year in the following manner. They make observation on twelve days, beginning at the last of December, and hold as an infallible rule, that whatsoever weather happens on each of those days, the same will prove to agree in the correspondent months. Thus, January is to answer to the weather of December 31st; February to that of January 1st; and so with the rest. Old people still pay great attention to this augury."

49 Brand 1849, vol. 1, p. 8 (not 25), where the passage is sourced to p. 124 of an essay by Sir Henry Piers, Bt, of Tristernaght, 'A Chorographical Description of the County of Westmeath. Written A. D. 1682', published in Vallancey 1786, vol. 1, pp. 1–126. I have edited it back to that source.

50 The best comparator for this saying is, I think, *Uair a' ghille-chonnaidh air an latha, Là Fhéill*

Brìghde, for which see note 42. *Latha Coinnle* in the sense of 'Candle day' is Candlemas, 2 February, the day after St Brigid's, see note 28.

51 'Cuttings' would be *gearraidhean*. A more plausible translation of *Gearra Dubha na Nollaig* would be 'the Black Shorties of Christmas', referring to the shortness of the day at that time of year, cf. *làithean dubh geàrr na Samhna* 'the short black days of Hallowtide' (Black 1996, p. 50).

52 In Black 1985, pp. 10–11, I argued that the root of *Dù(bh)lachd, Dùldachd, Dùdlachd* is cognate with English *dull*, Old English *dold* ('stupid'), and that the term is therefore directly equivalent to 'doldrums'. *Dùbhlachd* is now 'December', see note 12 on pp. 574–75.

53 As I have pointed out elsewhere (Black 2002, p. 419), cock-fighting was engrained in the memories of those Gaelic speakers who received a school education during the years 1725–1825. A barbaric sport, it was introduced to the Highlands solely through the education system, and represented a traumatic experience for a young boy, see Sage 1899, pp. 118–19; Maclagan 1901, p. 87; Graham 1906, pp. 96, 122, 430–31; McNeill 1957–68, vol. 2, pp. 41–42; Hutton 1996, pp. 157–59; Forsyth 1999, pp. 238–39. For Handsel Monday see Banks 1937–41, vol. 2, pp. 118–23; Macdonald 1938, pp. 143–47; McNeill 1957–68, vol. 3, pp. 122–25; Danaher 1972, pp. 262–63; Simpson 1979; and p. 546 of the present work.

54 I imagine *traosta* is taken from the English word 'treats' (with metathesis), since that is the main feature of the day and is an effective translation of 'handsels'. It is otherwise on record as *Di-Luain Traoit, Traoight, Troight, Troit* or *Trait* – the same word, derived in each case from the singular (Black 2000, pp. 25–26). On the twelve days see the previous section.

55 *Faoilleach* or *faoilteach* is best understood as a calendar term meaning 'remainder, leavings', referring to its position at the juncture of winter and spring, but we cannot exclude the possibility of interference by a derivative of *fáel* (later *faol*) 'wolf' or some other word (*DIL* s.vv. *faílech, fuidlech*). I like to translate it as 'wolftime' because popular tradition is emphatic in deriving it from *faol* and in lining it up with the *gearran* and other zoomorphic wind-names that crowd into the Gaelic calendar after it (Black 1985, pp. 4–6). In the twentieth century, with the disappearance of the Julian calendar from the traditional memory, it came to be used for January. Kirk (?) says of the Highlanders that 'the most cold Season fourteen days before Candlmasse & 14 days after they terme by an irony Faoldach, the loving Season' (Campbell 1975, p. 17 = Hunter 2001, p. 54); what he means is that the normal meaning of the adjective *faoilteach* is 'happy at meeting, hospitable, generous, inviting, welcoming' (Dwelly 1977, p. 414), or, in a word, 'loving'. Kirk's oft-repeated personal motto was, it should be noted, "Love and live."

56 Or *am mìos marbh*, same meaning, see e.g. GUL MS Gen. 1090/29, p. 154.

57 A common saying, more usually applied to March, or to spring in general (Nicolson 1951, p. 78; MacKenzie 1964, pp. 194–95; Black 1996, p. 47).

58 I would prefer to translate the Gaelic saying more literally as 'three days of wolftime in bordertime, and three days of bordertime in wolftime'. Note the resistance of these terms to declension, at least as used by JGC – we would have expected *trì là Faoillich* and *trì là Iuchair*. See 'Iuchar, the Hot Month (August)', p. 557.

59 Again we would have expected to see some sign of the genitive case: *Fiath Faoillich is gaoth Iuchair.*

60 Strictly 'cold February'. For *aicill* rhyme one would expect *dùth'ich : chiùin* or, as elsewhere, *tìr : mhìn* (same meaning).

61 A popular story with very ancient roots, see Campbell 1940–60, vol. 1, pp. 410–36, and MacilleDhuibh 24.1.03.

62 The saying is cited elsewhere (e.g. MacRury 1890–91, p. 23) with *làmh* 'hand' in place of *cruth. Cruth* (i.e. *crùth*) appears to be *crubha* 'a hoof' in the special sense of 'uniting all the finger-tips of one hand together', inserted into the belt not against the cold but to indicate

idleness or, more probably, submission (Black 1996, p. 53). Thanks no doubt to being linked to the *faoilleach* in this well-known rhyme, however, it appears to have become closely associated with wintry weather (Campbell 1895, pp. 96–97):

> 'S na-na-rug ad bhothan smùid
> Ann an dùlachd crùth an crios.

JGC translates: "May no smoke rise from your dwelling, / In the depth of the hardest winter." The second line may be more literally rendered 'in the hoof-in-belt doldrums' – see note 52 on p. 585.

63 *Siabh* is given in various Gaelic dictionaries as 'a dish of stewed periwinkles' or the like. These entries stem ultimately from the HSD (vol. 2, p. 101): "A dish made of stewed periwinkles in the Hebrides." MacAlpine, an Islayman, called it a Skye word (1929, p. 231). *Brochan fhaochag* is simply 'whelk gruel'.

64 St Bridget's, Brigid's or Bride's is the *Féill Brì(gh)de*. The saint's name is in the nominative *Brighid*, in the genitive *Brìghde* or, for short, *Brìde*. JGC's *Brithid* appears to be his spelling of *Brighid*, taken from the rhyme quoted later in this section. On the festival generally see *CG*1, pp. 164–77; MacKenzie 1935, pp. 187–94; McNeill 1957–68, vol. 2, pp. 19–34; Danaher 1972, pp. 13–37; Ó Duilearga 1981, pp. 320–23 (with an excellent list of Irish, Scottish and Manx references at p. 408); Ó Catháin 1995; Hutton 1996, pp. 134–38.

65 Martin 1716, p. 119; Brand 1849, vol. 1, pp. 50–51 (not 56); Martin 1999, p. 81. I have edited the passage back to Martin.

66 See pp. 122 and 686.

67 Given by Nicolson (1951, p. 332) with *Brìghde* in place of *Brithid*. The use of *Brìghde* or *Brithid* as the full name of the festival is odd. Perhaps *air Fhéill Brìghde* was contracted to *air Brìghde* then 'corrected' to *air Brithid*, i.e. *air Brighid* 'on St Brigid', which assonates nicely with *air Inid*, see note 64.

68 White 1835, p. 339. This classic work was first published in 1789. Its editor, Thomas Brown, points out on the same page that during the same period in which White made his observations (1768–93), William Markwick of Battle in Sussex noted ravens building their nests on 1 April and having their young ones on 1 June.

69 Not merely in Tiree. Carmichael says (*CG*1, p. 168): "In the Highlands and Islands St Bride's Day was also called 'La Cath Choileach,' Day of Cock-fighting." See note 53 on p. 585.

70 Not counting Sundays.

71 See note 81 below. For an attempt to reduce the complexities of the Gaelic calendar to tabular form see Mackay 1908, pp. 348–49, 358–59, and 1909, p. 90.

72 MacLeod and Dewar 1831, p. 285. Kirk (?) says that 'Feadag id est the whistling week of cold winds' is the Highlanders' name for the eight days following the *faoilteach* (Campbell 1975, p. 17 = Hunter 2001, p. 54).

73 JGC did not include the original, so I have supplied it from Black 2001, pp. 348–49, where my translation is: "Quarter that brings the flaying wolftime, / Freezing hailstones, storms like bullets, / Whistler, sweeper, cutter's snarl – / Withering is the hag whose cutting edge is shrill." The poet, Eoghan MacLachlainn from Coruanan in Lochaber, is more generally known in English nowadays as Ewen MacLachlan. *Eoghan* tends to be 'Ewen' in the northern half of the Highlands (including Lochaber), 'Hugh' in the south.

74 Once again *faoilleach* proves resistent to declension: one would have expected *faoillich fhuair* (genitive case).

75 For the *gobag* or 'biter' see e.g. Watson 1908–09, p. 67; Mackenzie 1914, p. 311; Sutherland 1937, p. 102; Smith 1964, p. 27; Dwelly 1977, p. 511; GUL MS Gen. 1090/29, pp. 10–11.

76 For the *sguabag* or 'sweeper' see Camshron 1926, p. 50; Smith 1964, p. 28; MacMillan 1968,

p. 108. JGC's *ioma-sguaba na[m] faoilleach*, presumably 'the whirlwind of the wolftimes', appears to be a line from an oral calendar. Edward Lhuyd cited what appear to be precisely the same words in his notes on the 'Highland Rites & Customes' (Hunter 2001, p. 74, cf. Campbell 1975, p. 18): "The first three days of March Eym scobyg na Faoilach. because it's a severe tyme <then> with the Catle." In other versions of the calendar these appear as *Seachduin Ioma-sgobaidh / na Feadaig agus an Fhaoiltich* ('The whirlwind week / of the whistler and the wolftime', Fionn 1912a, p. 97) and *Thig a nis Seachdain iomadh-sgobach nam Feadag 's nam Faoilteach* ('There now comes the whirlwind week / of the whistlers and the wolftimes', Argathalian 1874, p. 56). A fragment of this calendar known to Ronald MacDonald, originally from Soay, Skye, was recorded in 2000 by Ann MacKenzie (2002, p. 193) from the late Peter MacLean, Dervaig, Mull. Another fragment, noted by Fr Allan McDonald, implies that the *sguabag* blows throughout the 120 days of December, January, February and March (GUL MS Gen. 1090/29, p. 11): *Sia latha faoillich, / Naoi latha gearrain, / Seachd seachdainean diag sguabaig – / Suas an t-Earrach!* "Six days of wolftime, / Nine days of cutter, / Seventeen weeks of sweeper – / Spring's up!"

77 The seasonal term *gearran* has nothing to do with *gearan* 'complaint'. It is basically a gelding or castrated horse, hence 'garron'. As a derivative of *geàrr* (the verb 'cut') it made an ideal wind-name ('cutter'), cf. ?Kirk's '*Gear[r]shion .i.* curt, inconstant tempests', glossed by Lhuyd 'Kyikiys Garrain <alias Garrain borb i.e. iumentum audax>, the next fortnight' ('a fortnight of *gearran*, <alias *gearran borb* i.e. an audacious beast of burden>, the next fortnight', see Campbell 1975, pp. 17–18, and Hunter 2001, pp. 54, 74. In JGC's time it had not yet taken on the formal meaning 'February'. This involves a second pun, and appears to have come about *c.* 1900 through the sense of humour of certain magazine editors. As an adjective *geàrr* means 'short', which made *gearran* ('short one') the ideal wind-name for February. The inspiration for this appears to lie in the rhyme about the *gearran geàrr* cited at p. 544 (Black 1985, p. 6).

78 Cf. Watson 1908–09, p. 67; Camshron 1926, p. 60; Smith 1964, p. 27; GUL MS Gen. 1090/29, pp. 20–21. JGC translates *air an tràigh* as 'to the hill', but it means 'on the beach'.

79 "The cutter would send seven bolls of blizzard into one wimble-hole, so stormy was the weather." For slight variations on the theme see Dwelly 1907, p. 8; Dwelly 1908, p. 18; Camshron 1926, p. 56.

80 "A dry bed for the seed."

81 JGC still falls a little short of reaching the obvious conclusion, that the reason the *gearran* is stormy but lacks a precise date is that, like the other names in the sequence (most of which, including the *cailleach*, are those of live creatures), the *gearran* is a wind. The Gaelic wind-names should be added to the extraordinary list of 434 wind-names from around the world, from the *aajej* of Morocco to the *zonda* of Argentina, cited in Watson 1985, pp. 330–44. That Watson lists none of the Gaelic names is the fault of scholars like JGC rather than his own. See Argathalian 1874; MacRury 1890–91, pp. 23–25; *CG2*, pp. 288–89; Grant 1902–04a, pp. 129–34; Maclagan 1907–09; Mackay 1908 and 1909; Watson 1908–09, pp. 65–67; Fionn 1912a, p. 53; Mackenzie 1914, p. 311; Grant 1925, p. 6; Nicolson 1951, pp. 411–14; MacilleDhuibh 13.3.87; Forsyth 1999, pp. 250–51; Cheape 1999, pp. 71–72; MacKenzie 2002, pp. 193–97.

82 Presumably *a' Ghort, no Gort a' Bhaile*, cf. p. 681 below. JGC does not exactly mean that this was the name of the rhyme, I think, but he indicates a popular awareness that the *cailleach* of harvest, the *cailleach* of the New Year rhyme and the *cailleach* who blows as a wind in spring – hell's breath, one might say – are one and the same, as indeed are *a' Chailleach Bheur, Cailleach Beinn a' Bhric* and the *Muilgheartach*. This is extremely helpful for the understanding of the concept, which is a cosmological one, see Stewart 1791, pp. 559–60 = new edn, pp. 401–02; Grant 1902–04a, pp. 122–37; Watson 1908–09, pp. 65–66; Mackay 1914, pp. 422–25; Campbell 1914–15; Grant 1925, pp. 4–19; Mackay 1929–31; MacKenzie

1935, pp. 136–75; Ó Duilearga 1981, pp. 219–21 (with a list of references, including many Scottish ones, at p. 392); Macdonald 1982, pp. 228–31; Miller 1994, p. 14; Ó Crualaoich 2003. The original meaning of *cailleach* was 'veiled woman', from Latin *pallium* 'a veil', see Ní Dhonnchadha 1994–95, p. 71.

83 Cf. *CG2*, pp. 239–40; Watson 1908–09, pp. 65–66; Grant 1925, p. 6; Cheape 1999, pp. 71–72.

84 *Gas feur* 'a blade of grass' is properly *gas feòir*.

85 Brand 1849, vol. 2, p. 42; Jamieson 1879, p. 254. I have edited the quotation to agree with Jamieson. See Exod. 3: 22; 12: 35–36.

86 What JGC appears to mean is that the Gaelic term *trì làithean nan òisgean*, 'the three days of the hog(g)s, ewes', connects the borrowing days with the three days' journey into the wilderness to sacrifice the Paschal lamb (Exod. 3: 18, 5: 3, 8: 27, 15: 22). The source of his 'hillock' quotation is unknown to me; it is not from the Bible, the Psalms, or the hymns of Dugald Buchanan or Peter Grant, all of which I have carefully searched. (Grant's hymns were very popular in Tiree.)

87 More correctly *trì latha na bà ruaidhe*. This is, I think, explained by the Irish story of the *riabhach* or *bó riabhach* ('brindled cow') who complained of March's harshness (Dinneen 1927, p. 893). March boasted that he would flay the skin off her, so she went into the woods and stayed there. March blew cold, wet and hard, and on the morning when it was over the *riabhach* came skipping into the open, saying: "Goodbye to you, little, ugly, biting, grey March!"

In Seán Ó Conaill's telling (Ó Duilearga 1981, p. 325), "March asked April for the loan of a day, and got it. That day blew hard with snow, rain and cold. The Brindle was too far from home, and had no shelter, and that day killed her. We don't know if April got the day back since. The last two days of March and the first day of April are called 'the Days of the Brindled Cow' since then."

Dinneen gives the three days as *laetheanta na riaibhche*, while Danaher points out (1972, p. 85) that in parts of the north of Ireland a more elaborate version of the story was told in which nine days were borrowed so that the blackbird and 'stone-chatter' (*claibhreán*) could be punished as well as the cow.

According to Dwelly (1908, p. 22) March in Scottish Gaelic is 'the month of the brindled cow' (*mìos na bà riabhaich*), meaning 'multicoloured weather', up-and-down weather (*don ciall 'sìde ioma-dathach,' sìde sìos 's suas*). For a valuable list of further references to the brindled cow and the borrowed days in Ireland, Scotland, Man, Spain and Corsica see Ó Duilearga 1981, p. 409.

88 It is certainly derived from Latin *Martius* 'March', but appears to have undergone a semantic shift in popular tradition. It is difficult to know what to make of JGC's categorical statement that *am Màrt* as 'seed-time' begins on 24 March, as this date bears no obvious relation to the beginning of March in either the Julian or the Gregorian calendar, and in any case popular tradition did not number the days of the month. What he probably means is that seed-time began at the equinox, marked in religious terms by the Annunciation – strictly 25 March.

89 Hogg 1821.

90 JGC's translation 'full pool' suggests that *linge làn*, which makes no sense to me, is for *linne làn*.

91 Dwelly's *tri breathan* 'three rows' (1977, p. 120) presumably derives from this saying. See also note 110 below.

92 Cf. Cheape 1999, p. 72, and note 179 on p. 330 above.

93 He appears to be quoting from the Book of Common Prayer (Blunt 1867, p. '26]', cf. Fionn 1912a, pp. 96–97): "EASTER DAY, on which the rest depend, is always the First *Sunday* after the Full Moon which happens upon, or next after the Twenty-first Day of *March*; and if the Full Moon happens upon a *Sunday*, *Easter Day* is the *Sunday* after."

94 *An Inid bheadaidh, thig an latha roimhn oidhche* (Nicolson 1951, p. 30): "The forward Shrovetide, the day comes before the night." It is certainly a little impudent for feast to precede vigil. For Shrovetide and Lent more generally see Danaher 1972, pp. 39–57, and Hutton 1996, pp. 151–78.

95 'Michael Scott: Making the Devil your Slave', pp. 162–63. See also p. 686 below.

96 See p. 539.

97 Cf. p. 541.

98 As always, JGC avoids using Gaelic orthography wherever possible, but his use of the Latin spelling *fuge* shows clearly the origin of Gaelic *fùidse* ('coward'), which is the same word in the same pronunciation; see for example Black 2002, p. 419. It is also noticeable that JGC gives the phrase *coileach cam* in the nominative although the vocative, *a choilich chaim*, would be expected.

99 For divination rites of this kind at Shrovetide see Banks 1937–41, vol. 1, pp. 4–8. In the Western Isles they were more strongly associated with Hallowe'en (*ibid.*, vol. 3, pp. 151–52).

100 This saying is otherwise unknown, I think.

101 *Geàrr* and *goirid* both mean 'short'. Cf. *Seachd seachdainean bho aois gu bàs eadar Càisg is Inid* (Nicolson 1951, p. 345): "Seven weeks from age to death between Easter and Shrovetide." Nicolson understood *bho aois gu bàs* 'from age to death' as meaning 'always'. It is explained by Carmichael's *o breith gu bas* 'from birth to death' (*CG2*, p. 311), i.e. the thirty-three weekdays of the Lenten fast stand for the thirty-three years of Christ's life on earth. Carmichael (*CG2*, p. 347) also heard *Seachd seachdaine gu brath* 'Seven weeks forever' (hardly 'till doom', as he put it), and Nicolson (1951, p. 345) also heard *eadar Càisg is Nollaig* 'between Easter and Christmas', which is just silly. Of the five versions, only JGC's makes good sense; in Nicolson's and Carmichael's, it appears as if the order of *Inid* and *Càisg* has been reversed in order to provide *aicill* rhyme *bàs : Càisg*. In JGC's, *aicill* is provided by *goirid : Inid*. All of this suggests the existence at one time of a version with end-rhyme:

> *Seachd seachdainean bho aois gu bàs*
> *Eadar Inid agus Càisg.*

It appears that *aicill* prevailed over end-rhyme, however, even at the expense of logic.

102 Lhuyd 1707, p. 133.

103 10 March OS, 22 March NS, see note 11 on p. 574 and MacilleDhuibh 25.2.00.

104 I have argued (MacilleDhuibh 9.3.01) that there may be a corruption here, and that for *easgann* 'eel' we should perhaps read *easan* 'little waterfall' or *easgan* 'a small natural ditch, a small fen, a small bog'. The proverb thus refers as much to the danger to travellers at this time of year as to the fecundity of nature.

105 Alternatively it was 'The Tenth of March Fair' (Black 2000, p. 19). It still bore this name in 1890 even though it was by then being held (principally for the hiring of farm servants) on the third Thursday of the month (Marwick 1890, p. 28).

106 I imagine the forms *Tom a Cheasaig* and *Port a Cheasaig* both contain a reduced form of the hypocoristic possessive pronoun *mo* 'my' or (at least in the latter case) *do* 'your'. See Watson 1926a, pp. 277–78.

107 This interesting comment reveals the need of the people for God-given signs to confirm even quite basic dates of the calendar. This may be seen in the light of the vacuum in religious teaching created by the Reformation, the Reformers' attempt to abolish saints' days, the lack of formal education prior to 1752, and the confusion caused by the belated introduction of the Gregorian Calendar in that year. We must see it as one type of ceilidh-house response to the need for an agreed calendar – the other being, of course, to seek scientifically accurate information from an authentic source. On the *céilidh* see note 951

above, and for St Patrick's day generally see Banks 1937–41, vol. 2, pp. 182–85, and Danaher 1972, pp. 58–66.

108 "On St Patrick's day / The limpet pees on the whelk." On *seach gun leum an Fhéill Pàraig* see p. xiii above.

109 More literally 'the leaner the horse, the fatter the crab'. *Reamhrad* (i.e. *reamhra* 'fatter' + *de* 'of it') is a rare example of the second comparative of *reamhar* 'fat', see Calder 1923, pp. 112–19.

110 JGC's *a chlaisich* for 'the furrows' makes little sense as it stands. The usual form of the saying is: *Cuiridh am faoilleach trì làin anns na claisean – làn sneachda, làn uisge, 's làn tugha nan taighean.* "The wolftime puts three fills in the furrows – a fill of snow, a fill of rain, and a fill of the thatch of the houses." I suspect that JGC heard *trì làin anns a' chlaisidh – làn sneachda, làn uisge, 's làn tugha nan taighean.* "Three fills in the furrow – a fill of snow, a fill of rain, and a fill of the thatch of the houses." Having somehow lost the first three words, he spelt *chlaisidh* as *chlaisich* to make it look a little more like a nominative case. (The sounds *-idh* and *-ich* are identical in Tiree.)

111 This saying commonly has *boile* 'madness' in place of *boilich* 'mad sound'. Both *boile* and *boilich* rhyme with *Moire*. JGC is, I am sure, quite right in suggesting that *boilich* refers to tides. Margaret Fay Shaw offers this version from South Uist (1977, p. 21):

> *Reothart mór na h-Éill Moire,*
> *'S bòlaich na h-Éill Pàdraig.*

She translates: "The big spring-tide of Mary's Day, / And the swell of the sea on St Patrick's Day."

112 It looks as if there may be confusion here between *bog* ('soft'), *bòc* ('swell') and *tòc* (also 'swell'). Further evidence is required from another source. Perhaps *marbhladh* and *marbhlainn* represent the singular and plural of Armstrong's *marbh-lath* 'a dull heavy day, a still cloudy day' (1825, p. 379). Niall M. Brownlie tells me (personal communication, 3 January 2004) that he has not heard *marbhladh* or *marbhlainn* in Tiree, and points instead to Kenneth Macleod's *marbh-shruth* 'dead current' (Murchison 1988, p. 21): *Theirteadh cuideachd gun d'rugadh Pilat ri marbh-shruth na contraigh – 's nach robh a bhuil air? Cha b'fhios da riamh dè an taobh a ghabhadh e, 's cha robh seasmhachd 'na ghnìomh no earbsa ri chur 'na fhacal.* "It used also to be said that Pilate was born during the dead current of the ebb-tide – and didn't he show it? He never knew which way to go, his behaviour lacked consistency and his word could not be trusted."

113 Strictly the term is either *Latha Fhéill Moire Mòr* (with masculine adjective) or *Féill Moire Mhòr* or *an Fhéill Moire Mhòr* (with feminine adjective). For Lady day see also Banks 1937–41, vol. 2, pp. 189–91, and Danaher 1972, p. 67.

114 See also p. 134. The porridge, gruel or ale was dedicated to a god or saint called Manannan (*Manntan, Bannan*) or Shony (*Seónaidh*). The ceremony is described in Tolmie 1876–77, p. 102; MacPhail 1895, p. 165, and 1900, p. 440; *CG1*, pp. 162–63; Banks 1937–41, vol. 1, pp. 32–33, and vol. 3, pp. 157–58; Mac a Phì 1938, p. 28; RCAHMS 1982, pp. 9, 265; Hutton 1996, p. 369; Martin 1999, p. 29; MacKenzie 2002, pp. 178–81. As it involved immersion and was usually performed on the night of Holy Thursday in Easter Week, it appears that *Seónaidh* is St John the Baptist, having undergone gradual Christianisation from Manannan mac Lir through St Bannan. Some writers, notably Banks and Hutton, have misunderstood Martin's 'Hallowtide' as meaning that the ceremony took place at Hallowe'en. In one recorded instance in Lewis (MacPhail 1895, p. 166) Manannan turned into St Brendan the Navigator (*Brianailt, Brianuilt*) instead, and the ritual took place on his feast-day, 15 May. For the traditional pronunciation *Seónaidh* I am indebted to Dr Finlay MacLeod, Shawbost.

Dr R. C. Maclagan was told of a development of the custom as practised in Lewis *c.* 1800.

Just as porridge, gruel or ale had formerly been given to the sea to stimulate a supply of seaweed to fertilise the fields, so was a living creature now given to it to encourage the fish (*Tocher* 20, p. 162): "A sheep or goat was offered as a sacrifice. The oldest man of the sea was expected to take the lead, assisted usually by the one who came second in respect of seniority and experience. The animal was brought down to the edge of the sea, and after a certain order of procedure was observed, the officiating person, who was a kind of priest for the occasion, in the midst of dead silence, and surrounded by the whole company of those interested, who stood looking on, went down on his knees, and proceeded to kill the victim, whose blood was carefully caught in a dish. This over, the officiating man waded out into the sea as far as he could, carrying the vessel in which the blood was, and scattered the blood as widely as he could on the water round about him. Then followed the disposing of the carcase, which was cut up into pieces corresponding to the number of poor persons in the district, and a piece was sent to each such person, to be eaten by them; but none else would touch it."

Maclagan's informant got the description from his father, who was present as a young boy when the ceremony was last performed in his part of Lewis. No time of year was mentioned, but Maclagan says that 'the fishing industry was thereby supposed to have been placed under good luck for what remained of that season'; we may guess that he meant the cod and ling fishery, which took place in summer (Macdonald 1978, pp. 95–97).

Assuming that 'Shore' in JGC's sectional title is not a misprint (it appears in the Contents and Index of *WSS* as well as the text), we may take it as an interesting reflex of the Scots name of the day, Skire or Skires Thursday, which means 'clear, bright, pure' Thursday and appears to be connected with Old Norse *Skíriþorsdagr*, Norwegian *Skirtorsdag*, *skjærtorsdag* 'Holy Thursday'. As I have pointed out (Black 2000, p. 27), the name has suffered infinite degrees of corruption in Scottish public records, e.g. 'Skyre', 'Sky', 'Skyries', 'Skeir' and 'Scarce' Thursday; English records yield in addition 'Sheer', 'Char', 'Shrift' and 'Sharp' Thursday (Hutton 1994, p. 22, and 1996, p. 187). I have come across no Gaelic term such as *Diar-Daoin a' Chladaich* from which it could have been translated, so I take it that 'Shore Thursday' represents a further attempt to make sense of the name, either by JGC or by his informant(s). The English name 'Maundy Thursday' derives from Christ's *mandé* or commandment to His disciples at the Last Supper to 'love one another' (John 13: 34).

115 'Crucifixion' is usually *ceusadh*, masculine, but in this phrase it is feminine *ceus*, genitive *ceusa*.

116 This is cited by Frazer (1911a, p. 229) in the general context of 'Tabooed Things'.

117 The tabu has entirely to do with the use of iron. The iron tabu is so strong and widespread that no other origin need be sought.

118 On the Easter controversy see Farmer 1990, pp. 27–28, 186–94, 308–22.

119 See '*Inid*, Shrovetide' and '*Carghas*, Lent' above, pp. 545–47.

120 *Càsg* is the historically correct form of the nominative. JGC subsequently uses the less formal *Càisg*.

121 Lhuyd 1707, p. 20. I have restored Lhuyd's spellings.

122 See CG2, pp. 274–75; Banks 1937–41, vol. 1, pp. 43–44.

123 *Earrach fad' an déidh Càsga, fàgaidh e na saibhlean fàs* (Nicolson 1951, p. 172): "A long spring after Easter will leave the barns empty." For *Gléidhear cuirm . . .* see *ibid.*, p. 205.

124 See Venetia Newall's chapter 'Resurrection' (1971, pp. 156–76), which she begins by pointing out that 'in early mythology the god who created the world egg often emerged from it himself in a different form'; note also 'Red Eggs of the Resurrection: The Easter Cycle', *ibid.*, pp. 220–31. For Easter in Gaelic Scotland see Macdonald 1982, p. 198, and for the festival more generally see Banks 1937–41, vol. 1, pp. 34–46; McNeill 1957–68, vol. 2, pp. 46–51; Danaher 1972, pp. 70–83; Hutton 1996, pp. 179–213.

125 'The Servants' Easter' would be a better translation, see Black 2002, p. 369.
126 A 'sleeveless errand' is a fool's errand, a futile journey. On the origins of All Fools' day see Mac an Toisich 1953–59, pp. 227–28. See also Banks 1937–41, vol. 2, pp. 195–97; McNeill 1957–68, vol. 2, pp. 52–54; Danaher 1972, p. 84; *Tocher* 21, p. 192; Hutton 1996, pp. 177–78.
127 The words 'swollen [threatening]' are JGC's. A more literal translation of the first line would be 'If it's warm Balk-Beltane'. I am not sure that it is helpful to translate *Bailc* as either 'swollen' or 'threatening'. *Bailc* is primarily the term for waste ground between runrig fields (see Dwelly 1977, p. 59, and Graham 1906, p. 157, cited in Black 2001, p. 520); as such it seems appropriate for a period of inbetweenness in the calendar (compare *iuchar*, note 157 below).

It is interesting that JGC interprets *Bailc-Bhealltainn* as May-Day even though he has defined *Bailc na Bealltainn* as the fourteen days preceding May-Day. It seems to me that the rhyme sets out the sequence of weather conditions for a good fruit harvest as follows: fourteen days warm weather (18–31 April, or perhaps 20 April – 2 May); dry on 3 May; east wind thereafter. Following the widespread introduction of enclosures (*c.* 1750–1850) and the switch from runrig to crofting, the primary meaning of *bailc* was lost to the language, and *Bailc-Bhealltainn* was understood by MacDonald (1888–89, p. 257) and Matheson (1938, pp. 24–25, 238) to mean 'dewy Beltane', but I am certain that JGC's basic explanation is the correct one.
128 Lhuyd 1707, p. [404]. JGC spells *Samhain(n)* sometimes with single and sometimes with double *n*, and at the phonological level it can certainly be argued that the final syllables of *Bealltainn* and *Samhain(n)* are the same. *Samhain(n)* may be derived, as Lhuyd noticed, from *sam* 'summer half' and *fuin* 'end', or (as now seems more likely) from a word *samain* cognate with Sanskrit *samana-* 'reunion, assembly, festival', Gothic *samana*, Old Icelandic *saman* 'get-together' (Vendryes 1959–96, s.v. *samain*). The origins of *Bealltainn* are very different, see next note.
129 This appears to be a refutation of Gen. Charles Vallancey's 'An Essay on the Antiquity of the Irish Language' (1786, vol. 2, pp. 251–336). JGC's strictures are unfortunate, as he is wrong on a number of basic points. In older Gaelic the qualifying noun frequently came first (e.g. *dobhar-chù* 'water-dog', an otter), and the final syllable of *Bealltainn* probably does have to do with *teine* 'fire'. No modern scholar is in a position to argue that the religion of the Phoenicians influenced that of the Celts, but that the Celts had a god Belenos, whose name may or may not be cognate in some way with that of Baal, is not in doubt. It still appears plausible, as argued by Macbain (1896, p. 27, cf. Henderson 1911, p. 260), that Scottish Gaelic *Bealltainn*, early Irish *beltene, belltaine*, is derived from words meaning 'bright fire', where the root *belo-* is allied to English 'bale' ('bale-fire'), Anglo-Saxon *bael*, Lithuanian *baltas*, 'white', and that the Gaulish god-names Belenos and Belisama, as Macbain says, come from the same root – thus also Shakespeare's Cymbeline, i.e. *Cunobelinos* 'Hound of Belenos'. Henri-Marie D'Arbois de Jubainville put forward an alternative suggestion, seeing *Beltaine* as derived from a possible verbal noun *beltu* (genitive *beltain*) 'dying', thus exactly cognate with Giltine, the name of a goddess of death. This does not, of course, preclude a connection with the god Belenos (Vendryes 1959–96, s.v. *Beltaine, Belltaine*). For Beltane and May-Day more generally see Mackay 1909, pp. 95–98; McPherson 1929, pp. 3–7; Banks 1937–41, vol. 2, pp. 215–44; McNeill 1957–68, vol. 2, pp. 55–82; Hutton 1996, pp. 218–43. For further references see Ó Duilearga 1981, p. 409.
130 "This is the result of an ingenious calculation," says Nicolson (1951, p. 334). "It is generally, but not absolutely, correct." There again, if Bealltainn is allowed to fall on the 2nd as well as the 1st of May, it will always be correct. See also McPherson 1929, p. 220, and GUL MS Gen. 1090/29, p. 154.
131 This will be a wind-name, see note 81 on p. 587.

132 This suggests the existence of an otherwise unrecorded saying along the lines of:

> *Ged thig sneachd thar nam bròg*
> *Is còir an crodh thoirt don àirigh*
> *Latha Buidhe Bealltainn.*

"Even if snow comes over the shoes / The cattle should be brought to the shieling / On the Yellow Day of Beltane." Both JGC (here) and Alexander Carmichael (*CG*1, p. 190) lay some stress on the move to the shieling taking place on 1 May, their accounts being based on the traditional wisdom of the people rather than on socio-economic fact. Many years ago I brought together as much evidence as I could find for the real start and finish of the shieling season (MacilleDhuibh 10.8.90). Among other things I pointed out that after publishing *CG*1 Carmichael appears to have shifted ground. In *CG*4, p. 38, he seems to recognise that *Bealltainn* may not be the time of departure, for he avoids mentioning it: "Throughout Lewis the crofters of the townland go to the shieling on the same date each year, and they return from it on the same date each year." I concluded that 'although a traditional shieling season of 1st May to 1st August was well remembered, in practice it might begin as early as March, it might last anything from six to fourteen weeks, and it might go on as late as September'. I have only two observations to add now. One is that in a paper written for Lord Napier in 1883–84 Carmichael said that the people go to the hill-grazing 'early in June' (1914–16, p. 364); the other is that the variability of *Bealltainn* – 1, 2 or 3 May – may perhaps be accounted for by the difficulty of setting out for the shieling on a day governed only by the calendar. On shielings and shieling traditions generally see Mackellar 1887–88 and 1888–89; D. M. 1908–09; T. M. 1908–09; Carmichael 1914–16, pp. 364–69; Grant 1925, pp. 45–46; Whitaker 1959, pp. 167–74; MacSween and Gailey 1961; Gaffney 1967; Miller 1967; Love 1981; Macdonald 1982, pp. 246–56; Macdonald 1984; Bil 1990; Stewart 1990a, pp. 106–14.
  On the tabu against giving anything out of the house see Bourke 1999, p. 101. Lady Gregory was given a powerful example (1970, p. 30) by a woman whom she calls Mary Moran – pure gossip, of course. "Up in the village beyond they think a great deal of these things and they won't part with a drop of milk on May Eve, and last Saturday week that was May Eve there was a poor woman dying up there, and she had no milk of her own, and as is the custom, she went out to get a drop from one or other of the neighbours. But not one would give it because it was May Eve. I declare I cried when I heard it, for the poor woman died on the second day after."
  There is a substantial chapter on May-Day in Ireland in Danaher 1972, pp. 86–127, convergence between Ireland and Gaelic Scotland being particularly apparent in the sections 'Charms and Counter-Charms' (pp. 109–19) and 'The Fairies at Maytime' (pp. 121–24).

133 See *CG*2, p. 350. Nicolson (1951, p. 207) translates *ars* as 'says' instead of 'cried', but comments: "The cuckoo is seldom heard so early now." It should be remembered however that until 1752 *latha buidhe Bealltainn* was a day now equivalent to 14 May.

134 Robertson 1791, pp. 620–21 = new edn, pp. 183–84; cf. MacGregor 1901, pp. 43–44.

135 Bisset 1791, p. 84 = new edn, p. 714.

136 Pennant 1774, pp. 97–98: "On the 1st of *May*, the herdsmen of every village hold their *Beltein*, a rural sacrifice. They cut a square trench on the ground, leaving the turf in the middle; on that they make a fire of wood, on which they dress a large caudle of eggs, butter, oatmeal and milk; and bring, besides the ingredients of the caudle, plenty of beer and whisky; for each of the company must contribute something. The rites begin with spilling some of the caudle on the ground, by way of libation: on that, every one takes a cake of oatmeal, upon which are raised nine square knobs, each dedicated to some particular being, the supposed

preserver of their flocks and herds, or to some particular animal, the real destroyer of them: each person then turns his face to the fire, breaks off a knob, and flinging it over his shoulders, says, *This I give to thee, preserve thou my horses; this to thee, preserve thou my sheep*; and so on. After that, they use the same ceremony to the noxious animals: *This I give to thee, O Fox! spare thou my lambs; this to thee, O hooded Crow! this to thee, O Eagle!*"

137 JGC is presumably referring to the section 'May-Day Customs' in Brand 1849, vol. 1, pp. 212–34. There is nothing there about cows being made to leap over lighted straw; there is, however, a reference to the 'Survey of the South of Ireland, p. 233' at p. 227.

138 "It was bound to him henceforth." See pp. 126 ('Houses and Lands'), 686.

139 This is correct. In early Irish it is *cétamain*, which may best be understood as *cét* 'first' + *samain* in the generalised sense of a major feast (Macbain 1896, pp. 70, 272, 373) or perhaps simply *sam* 'summer', the word then being assimilated to *samain*; cf. Irish *mithem*, Welsh *mehefin*, 'June', assumed to be from *me(dio)-samīno-* 'midsummer' (Vendryes 1959–96, s.v. *céitemain, cétamain*). For a poem in Old Irish on the delights of *Cétemain* see Murphy 1956, pp. 156–59. The Rev. Robert Kirk (?) appears to have heard a form of it which preserved the nasal – he declares that '14 days before Beltan or May & 14 days after they call Ceothom i.e. the soft misty moneth' (Hunter 2001, p. 54, cf. Campbell 1975, p. 17). My best guess is that he heard *Céiteam* and rationalised it as *ceathach* or *ceò* 'mist' combining with *tiom* 'soft' to give *ceò-thiom, ceothom*. See also Mackay 1909, p. 94.

140 Most of the earlier Gaelic almanacs (Anon. 1873, 1875, 1885–86a) place *Céitein na h-Òinsich* at 15 April, while Dwelly (1977, p. 187) places it at 19 April to 12 May. *Òinseach* is probably to be taken literally. Tasks to be performed at this time of year included stripping the thatch off the roof and spreading it on the fields, taking the cow out of the house (by lifting, if she were too weak to stand), removing the dung from the byre and spreading it, too, on the fields, scrubbing generally, washing blankets and spreading them out to dry; on 30 April the fire was extinguished and its debris removed from the house in preparation for ceremonial relighting on 1 May. Only an *òinseach* would start the work as early as 3 or 7 April OS, 15 or 19 April NS, when snow, frost and high winds were still likely.

Carmichael (*CG2*, p. 248) places what he calls *Ceitein Oinnsich*, 'Ceitein of the foolish woman', in autumn. He says that it is 'probably a mistake for "Ceitein Oinich," liberal Ceitein, the Ceitein of autumn, when Nature was generous and food abundant'. This is unlikely, but there may nevertheless have been a *céitein* in the year's end – at *CG2*, p. 300, he notes *an céitein geamhraidh* ('the winter *céitein*'), which he defines as 'the first day of winter' (1 November).

141 In his account of his tour of 1769 Pennant says (1774, p. 97): "A *Highlander* never begins any thing of consequence on the day of the week on which the 3d of *May* falls, which he styles *La Sheachanna na bleanagh*, or the dismal day." If 3 May is a Tuesday, for example, Tuesdays will remain unlucky for the rest of the quarter, the rest of the year, or even (to the ultra-superstitious) the rest of the next twelve months. In his account of his tour of 1772 he says (1998, p. 416): "The Scottish mountaineers esteem the May 14th unfortunate, and the day of the week that it has happened to fall on. Thus Thursday is a black day for the present year." Due to the Calendar Act of 1751, 14 May NS is 3 May OS. A more likely explanation for the 'avoiding day' is that it derives from Whit Sunday, the unluckiest day of the year in Ireland (Danaher 1972, p. 129). See also Banks 1937–41, vol. 2, pp. 246–49, and Mac an Toisich 1953–59, p. 227.

142 This was the year of his death. JGC calls him 'the Elder' to distinguish him from his younger contemporary St Brendan of Birr, who died in 565 or 573 (Watson 1926a, p. 274). On Scottish Gaelic traditions of St Brendan see *CG2*, pp. 235–38.

143 Niall M. Brownlie has pointed out to me that this does not mean that St Brendan (usually *Brèanainn, Brianainn, Brianailt, Brian* or the like) was unknown in Tiree, merely that his

feast-day (16 May) had slipped out of traditional memory. MacKinnon tells the story (1992, no. 11) of how St Brendan, when walking in Tiree, spotted what is now Balephetrish Hill and blessed it, so that it became known as St Brendan's Rock; her facing Gaelic translation (by a Lewiswoman, Mrs Margaret Mackay) gives this as *Creag an Naoimh Breanndan*, but Niall tells me that the correct name is *Creag Bhrinndein*. St Brendan and his feast-day are particularly well known in the Catholic island of Barra, where his memory is preserved in the name of a modern church and street as well as in traditional dedications. Of course JGC's story is also suggestive of the poor relationship that generally existed between tenant and factor in Tiree.

144   This resulted from an attempt by the Board of Manufactures to introduce the linen industry to Lochcarron in 1754. The mill was called New Kelso, and the Society in Scotland for the Propagation of Christian Knowledge paid the wages of a schoolmaster, mechanic, blacksmith and gardener, as well as supporting a number of apprentices (MacInnes 1951, p. 251). By 1760 it was clear that the scheme had failed, and support was withdrawn, but the market, called the *Féill Chealsaidh* after the mill, lasted rather longer. Originally held 'on Tuesday of the term' (otherwise known as Whitsuntuesday, Black 2000, p. 40) when founded as a cattle-market in the 1750s, by 1836 it had 'dwindled into an annual term for settling accounts and drinking whisky', and was in fact being held on the first Monday of June (Anon. 1836, p. 113).

I have to say that I think JGC is making a mistake however. I cannot see why the people of Sutherland should have been influenced in their habits by a failed industrial experiment on the far-off western seaboard of the neighbouring county, or the minor cattle-market which succeeded it. If, however, by *Féill Chelzie* we understand not *Féill Chealsaidh* but *Féill Choille* or *Choilne*, there is every reason why the year should be reckoned by it. I have already pointed out (Black 2000, p. 55) that 'Callons fair in January', which was still being held in Dornoch in the 1890s, will be a *Féill Challainn* or New Year's Fair, literally a 'Fair of the Kalends', leaving open the possibility that 'Sanct Callen his fayre', held in nearby Rogart at an unknown time of year (Gordon 1813, p. 7), referred not to a saint but to another *Féill Challainn*. JGC's evidence strengthens that possibility. There is no linguistic difficulty in seeing 'Callon', 'Callen' and 'Chelzie' all as reflexes of *Callainn* or its formal genitive case *Coilne*, and it is possible that a New Year Fair was held at one time in all eight parishes of the old earldom, the district traditionally referred to as Sutherlandshire – Kildonan, Loth, Clyne, Golspie, Rogart, Dornoch, Lairg and Creich.

145   On the assumption that JGC's 'Kinkis' and 'Kasg' (*WSS* 275) are an attempt to represent pronunciation, I have put them in bold with lower-case initial. 'Kankish' and 'Kaashk' might have been nearer the mark.

146   He is, I think, quoting in translation – *an ceann cealla-deug de shamhradh*? For Whitsuntide generally see Banks 1937–41, vol. 1, pp. 48–50, and vol. 2, p. 253; Danaher 1972, pp. 129–30; Hutton 1996, pp. 277–87. JGC's ingenious derivation of 'Whitsun' is incorrect: it is simply 'White Sunday', from a tradition of clothing newly baptized converts in white robes at Pentecost.

147   Cf. Nicolson 1951, p. 297:

Latha Fhéill Eòin as t-samhradh
Théid a' chuthag gu 'taigh geamhraidh.

("On St John's day in summer / The cuckoo goes to her winter house.") Carmichael gives the first line as *La leth an t-samhraidh* 'On Midsummer Day', *CG2*, p. 350.

For a useful list of references to St John's day see Ó Duilearga 1981, pp. 409–10. In Danaher 1972, pp. 134–53, there is a substantial chapter on Midsummer customs in

Ireland, mostly involving bonfires; see also McNeill 1957–68, vol. 2, pp. 86–93. The decline in the relative importance of the day in Gaelic Scotland will be due to the attraction of the quarter-days. Ronald Hutton says (1996, p. 320 and cf. p. 411) that 'the importance of the midsummer flames in Gaelic Irish tradition and their absence from Gaelic Scotland raises a further problem for those who would believe in a single "Celtic" cultural province of festivals'. I do not believe in provinces but in influences, and for Gaelic Scotland the model of cultural influence which I perceive is two-thirds Irish and one-third Brythonic, Anglo-Saxon and Norse. Hutton did not make his case well, however, given that the late Rev. William Matheson from North Uist told me that his mother's word for a bonfire was *tein' Fhéill Eathain* 'St John's fire' (it was only in adulthood that he realised its significance). A better example would have been skin-beating and dewlap-sniffing at New Year. These seem to have been ubiquitous in Gaelic Scotland, but stop dead at Rathlin (see note 21 on pp. 577–78).

148 This is an extraordinary farrago, though no doubt it bears some sort of traditional cachet. Iain, Eòin, Eathan and Seathan are certainly all derivatives of 'John' or 'Iohannes', and provide the MacLeans with their surname; by 'Eathin' JGC must mean Eathain. It is therefore unhelpful to translate Seathan as Swithin, since the latter is an entirely different name. Mgr Seathain (Rev. John MacLean of Kilninian and Kilmore, c. 1680–1756) is a well-documented minister and poet, see Ó Baoill 1979, pp. lxii–lxxxii. He may possibly have died of hydrophobia but he was not executed for piracy. The line *Tha Seathan a-nochd 'na mharbhan* occurs in the well-known waulking song 'Seathan Mac Rìgh Éirinn' and clearly has nothing to do with this or any other minister (*CG5*, p. 66; Campbell 1969–81, vol. 2, p. 42).

149 The 'dog-days' or *dies caniculares* are in origin the time when the dog-star Sirius rises and sets with the sun, about 3 July to 11 August. This dubious-sounding tradition was probably invented to explain the name.

150 The original of the proverb here cited appears to be something like: *Ma bheir am fiadh a cheann tioram gus an laigh a' ghrian air Latha Màrtainn Builg, bidh am foghar tioram.* ("If the deer keeps his head dry until the sun sets on Martin of Bullion's Day, the harvest will be dry.") I base this on the rather garbled version cited by James Macintyre, who connects it with *Féill Ròid* (Black 1996, p. 49), for which see p. 558.

151 'St Martin of the Bag' is JGC's translation of *Màrtainn Builg*, in which *Builg* is a gaelicisation of 'Bullion', no doubt influenced by the *A Challainn a' bhuilg* rhyme which so dominates the traditional calendar, see p. 530. St Martin of Bullion's legend has nothing to do with bags, but it provides him with an extra attribute, whatever that may be worth. See *CG2*, p. 326, and Ó Duilearga 1981, p. 233 (with references, p. 395).

152 It is possible that *creithleag* is not only a gadfly, horsefly or cleg but also a wind. *Creithleag* is the only Gaelic item cited by Watson (1985, p. 333) in his remarkable list of 434 wind-names from around the world (see note 81 on p. 587). He defines it simply: "Gentle breeze in Ireland." It is not an Irish word, however, but a Scottish Gaelic one. The Irish for a gadfly is *creabhar*.

153 *Lùnastal* (Irish *Lughnasa, Lúnasa*) is most certainly of Gaelic origin, being derived from *Lug*, the greatest of the pagan Irish gods, and *nasad* 'festival'. In function it is a harvest festival. See Macbain 1896, p. 212; Frazer 1911b, pp. 99–102; McNeill 1957–68, vol. 2, pp. 94–101; MacNeill 1962 (a magisterial work on the subject); Danaher 1972, pp. 167–77; and Hutton's stimulating little chapter 'First Fruits' (1996, pp. 327–31 and cf. p. 411), which uses evidence from Gaelic Scotland to respond to MacNeill's pan-Celtic model.

154 The reference is to p. 472 of Gen. (then Lt.-Col.) Charles Vallancey's essay 'Of the Gule of August; or, Lammas Day' (1786, vol. 3, pp. 468–511). On this occasion, JGC's opinion is entirely justified. However, it may be said on Vallancey's behalf that at least he acknowledges

the existence of the derivation of 'Lammas' now generally accepted as correct – Old English *hlāf-mæsse* ('loaf feast'). On the names of the moon in autumn see pp. 571–72.

155   What JGC means, although he expresses it badly, is that as the traditional *iuchar* lies fourteen days before *latha Lùnastail* (Lammas day, 1 August) and fourteen days after it, and as Lammas day OS is now 13 August, the traditional *iuchar* has become coterminous with the NS month of August. During the twentieth century, however, *an t-Iuchar* gradually came to be used in the formal Gaelic calendar for July, and *an Lùnastal* for August. In the same way, *am Faoilleach* is now January. See note 12 on pp. 574–75.

156   Lhuyd 1707, pp. 42, [365]; *æstus* is 'agitation, heat'. I have argued (Black 1985, pp. 7–10) that *iuchar* is the Scottish variant of a word for the 'border' (Irish *ochair*, Welsh *ochr*) between two quarters of the year, and that *an t-Iuchar* may thus be translated 'the Bordertime'. Compare *bailc*, note 127 on p. 592. Kirk(?) says that the season beginning fourteen days before Lammas is called by the Highlanders 'Eochar i.e. the Key of Harvest' (Campbell 1975, p. 17 = Hunter 2001, p. 54), and adds: "They have an other Key called Feil Hethan thereafter." Thus he interprets *iuchar* as *iuchair* 'key' – an appropriate term for a period of time which 'unlocks' a quarter – and hints at another one later in the year. The three best-known 'keys' are the *faoilteach* or *faoilleach* of spring, the *céitein* of summer and the *iuchar* of autumn; the name of the 'key' of winter, the period around *Samhain*, is one of the mysteries of the Gaelic calendar, even though the existence of such a period is not in doubt. It seems to me, therefore, that 'Feil Hethan' is a reference not to *Féill Sheathain* (St John's, 24 June) but to *Féill Shamhain*, more correctly *an t-Samhain* or *Féill na Samhna* (Hallowmas, 1 November), and that the original name of the period surrounding it may have been *iuchar na Samhna*, the first half being *an t-iuchar foghair* and the second half *an t-iuchar geamhraidh*. There is some confirmation for this in the medieval *dindshenchas* (place-lore) of the name Fornocht, which contains the story of a man who was called *Uince Ochurbel* ('Uinche Border-Mouth', translated by Stokes 'Uinche Keymouth') because he only spoke for three days and nights before and after *Samhain* (Stokes 1894, pp. 327–28; Black 1985, pp. 8–10).

157   Watson (1926a, pp. 384–85) explains 'Linlithgow' in terms of the Welsh words *llyn* 'lake', *llaith* 'damp' and *cau* 'hollow' – 'the Lake of Damp Hollow'. He surmises that it was correctly translated by Gaelic speakers into *Linn Fhliuch-Chua*, hence *Linn Liucha*; that *Linn* was subsequently misunderstood as *Ghlinn* (genitive of *gleann* 'glen') in expressions like *tobraichean Linn Fhliucha* 'the wells of Linlithgow'; and that the liquid *-l-* was absorbed into the preceding *-nn* (*Fh* being silent), hence *Gleann Iuch(a)*. There is thus no connection between *Iuchar*, *fiuchadh* and Linlithgow. John Mackenzie refers several times in his history of the '45 to *Gleann-Iuch*, genitive *G(h)linn-Iuch* (Mac-Choinnich 1844, pp. 49–50), and cites *Tobraichean Ghlinn-Iuch* as the first of the seven wonders of Scotland (1845, p. 8). From 1369 to 1707 the standard weights and measures of Scotland were superintended by four leading Royal Burghs (Mair 1988, pp. 120–23): Stirling for the pint or stoup (to regulate liquids), Lanark for the stone (which from 1567 was made of brass or lead), Edinburgh for the ell (by which the length of everything from cloth to land was measured), and Linlithgow for grain – the chalder, the boll, the firlot and the peck each being determined by a wooden vessel of a specific size, copies of which must be approved by the burgesses of the town.

158   The text in *WSS* 280 reads *an Fhéill Mhoire mòr*, which cannot be right. *Ás an léintean*, literally 'out of their shirts', corresponds in meaning to the English expression 'in their shirt-sleeves'. For the Assumption see *CG1*, pp. 194–97, Banks 1937–41, vol. 3, pp. 61–63, and Danaher 1972, p. 178.

159   *Dàmhair*, 'the rutting season', appears to be derived from *damh* 'stag' and *gaire, goire* 'calling' (*DIL* s.v. *dam-gaire*; Dinneen 1927, s.vv. *-ghaire, goire*; Watson 1959, p. 359; Vendryes 1959–96, s.v. *dam*). Surprisingly perhaps, the derivation given by Macbain (1896, p. 110) from *damh* 'stag' and *dàir* 'rutting' – for *dàir* see pp. 52 and 136 above – is thus superseded. *An Dàmhair*

is now the calendar month of October; for more on Roodmas see Banks 1937–41, vol. 3, pp. 76–78.

160 There is confusion here. JGC clearly means *oidhch' a' Chrò, oidhch' a' Chrò Naoimh*, 'the eve of the Holy Blood', cf. Carmichael's *caim na Cro-Naoimhe* 'the sanctuary of the Sacred Heart', *Cha tugainn dh' an Chro Naoimh thu* 'I would not give thee to the Holy Heart', *Tobar Cro Naomh* 'Well of the Holy Heart', *Teampull Cro Naomh* 'Temple of the Holy Heart' (*CG2*, pp. 259–60), Dwelly's *a Chriosda Chrò-naoimhe* 'O Christ of the Holy Blood' (1977, p. 274). *Cill a' Chrò* in Strath, Skye, now Kilchrist, is Corpus Christi Chapel, though believed by many to be 'the Church of the Cattle-Fold' (MacInnes 1994–96, p. 6). The differences between *cnò* 'nut' and *crò* 'blood' are of gender and nasalisation only. The term *Crò Naomh* is intrinsic to Roman Catholic ritual, but should not be confused with the doctrine of the Sacred Heart, which is relatively modern: it was only in 1856 that the Feast of the Sacred Heart was fixed on the day after Corpus Christi in June. It is not clear to me at present why the night following the Feast of the Exaltation of the Cross (Roodmas, as JGC calls it) should be dedicated to the Holy Blood; on the other hand JGC's statement that this festival, whatever it is, 'arises from this night dividing harvest in unequal halves, as the kernel is divided in the nut' has some authority, and may have led to the altering of *crò* to *cnò*, for James Macintyre wrote (Black 1996, p. 49): "They said again, *Leath an Fhaghari mar eitean na cnotha*, 'The half, or middle, of harvest as the nut's kernel'; that is, that the ripeness of the corn kept pace with that of the nuts." See also Campbell 1978–81, p. 207.

161 Brand 1849, vol. 1, p. 353: "It appears to have been the custom to go a nutting upon this day, from the following passage in the old play of Grim the Collier of Croydon:

> *This day, they say, is called Holy-rood Day,*
> *And all the youth are now a nutting gone.*

[The following occurs in Poor Robin, 1709:

> *The devil, as the common people say,*
> *Doth go a* nutting on Holy-rood *day;*
> *And sure such leachery in some doth lurk,*
> *Going a* nutting do the devil's work.]

It appears from the curious Ms. Status Scholæ Etonensis, 1560, that in the month of September, 'on a certain day,' most probably on the 14th, the boys of Eton school were to have a play-day, in order to go out and gather nuts, with a portion of which, when they returned, they were to make presents to the different masters of that seminary."

162 The place-name cited is in fact *Borgh*, genitive *Bhuirgh*, e.g. *machaire Bhuirgh*, anglicised not Borg but Borve. It derives from Old Norse *borg* 'castle, town' (Campbell 1998b, p. 231). The Michaelmas bannock is known as the *srùdhan*, see *CG1*, pp. 200–01, 212–15; Freer 1902, pp. 44–45; Macdonald 1903, pp. 381–82; Henderson 1911, pp. 255–58; Banks 1937–41, vol. 3, pp. 83–93; McDonald 1958, p. 232; *Tocher* 7, p. 232; *Tocher* 23, p. 282; Shaw 1977, p. 58; MacDhòmhnaill 1984; Pennant 1998, p. 272; GUL MS Gen. 1090/28, p. 88; EUL MS CW 504A, f. 1r. There is a general list of references to St Michael's day (mainly Scottish) in Ó Duilearga 1981, p. 410; see also *CG1*, pp. 198–215; Banks 1937–41, vol. 3, pp. 86–97; McNeill 1957–68, vol. 2, pp. 102–15; Danaher 1972, pp. 187–89.

163 See note 189 below.

164 See Ross 1965 and Ross 1976, pp. 152–54.

165 The Green Island 'submerged by enchantments, in which the inhabitants continue to live as formerly, and which will yet become visible and accessible' (Campbell 1907–08, p. 191)

is mentioned at p. 46 above, but JGC's reference to the man fished up from there has to do with a tale he tells elsewhere (Campbell 1907–08, pp. 194–95): "A native of Barra was one day fishing in the Western Ocean, and feeling a weight (trom) on his line, pulled it in and found a man entangled upon it. He took the strange fish home, and kept him for seven years. During that time his captive never said a word, but on three different occasions was heard to laugh. He ate whatever was set before him, but was never heard to speak. The occasions on which he laughed were, on hearing the servant man abusing a pair of new shoes, on seeing his host pulling some barley beards off his wife's clothes, and on seeing a young woman weeping bitterly.

"At the end of the seven years, a beautiful day occurred in the middle of tempestuous winter weather. Such days may be calculated on in the Hebrides, and are taken advantage of for thatching houses, straw being at the time in greatest abundance. The man from the submarine land remarked, that this was a very fine day for thatching the houses in the place he came from. The conversation being followed up, his host promised to let him down where he had been fished up and restore him to his own country, if he would tell the cause of his laughter on the three occasions mentioned. On the first occasion, when he heard the servant man abusing the new shoes for being too thin, he laughed to think that the man would never wear them. It was a case of 'New shoes little valued, / And no one knowing who was to wear them.'

> *Brōg thana 's i gun mheas*
> *Gun fhios co chaitheas i.*

The servant man died soon after, and another wore the shoes. On the second occasion he saw his host's wife coming in with barley beards on the back of her clothes. He laughed to see her husband pulling them off, as her too great intimacy with the servant-man in the barn was the cause of their being there. He laughed at the young woman weeping, because he knew she was weeping for her laughter of last year. Others say one of the occasions of the laughter was hearing people rating the two dogs belonging to the house, in ignorance that the animals were barking at robbers coming to plunder the house. Exactly the same story is told in Tiree of a man fished up near Biesta, on the north-west of the island."

With regard to the throwing of the shoe, John Shaw was told by Joe Neil MacNeil in Cape Breton (1987, pp. 400–01) that 'whatever direction the toe of the shoe was pointing when it landed was the direction in which one's lover was to be found' (*ge b'e gu dé an taobh a bha aghaidh na bròigeadh nuair a chaidh i a null dha 'n taobh eile, sin an taobh as an robh an leannan*). I take this to mean that, in line with other Hallowe'en pastimes, the throwing was usually done by young girls seeking information about their future spouses. On the other hand, Duncan Macdonald, Peninerine, South Uist (*Donnchadh Clachair*, 1882–1954), told Calum Maclean that the purpose was to discover if persons long absent were alive or dead (1953–59, p. 65). He cited this rhyme (I emend *bann* 'band' to *bonn* 'sole', which rhymes with *donn*):

> *Bròg far taigh tilgtear liom*
> *Fiach am maireann an deud-gheal donn,*
> *'S nuair a shiubhail bean a-null*
> *Fhuaras beul fo bonn.*

("Shoe over house is thrown by me / To see if the white-toothed warrior lives, / And when a woman has passed away / It has been found sole uppermost.") *An deud-gheal donn*, literally 'the brown tooth-white' (*donn* 'brown' in the generalised sense 'noble', hence referring to a warrior), is a common expression in classical verse. I assume that if the shoe pointed to the churchyard the person was dead, and that if a man were being sought and the shoe landed upside down, or if a woman were being sought and it landed the right way up, the throw could be retaken.

166 These are words of profound importance to the Gaelic calendar. I know of no other place where JGC or any other collector of traditions has explicitly stated that any of the Gaelic quarter-days fell other than on the first day, the first Sunday or the first Monday of the calendar months of February, May, August and November, either OS or NS. I have been arguing for some time that the Gaelic calendar has lunar origins (MacilleDhuibh 20.9.91, 4.10.91). The only other scholar who has made this case, to my knowledge, is Máire MacNeill (1962, pp. 16, 384–85, 419, 574); the contrary position is summarised in Danaher 1982, p. 222. See also note 598 on p. 431.

167 This is a very widespread and popular practice. The contents of the dishes – and their meanings – are capable of infinite variation. Frazer mentions a curious parallel (1912, vol. 1, p. 6): "On the first anniversary of a child's birthday the Chinese of Foo-Chow set the little one in a large bamboo sieve, such as farmers employ in winnowing grain, and in the sieve they place along with the child a variety of articles, such as fruits, gold or silver ornaments, a set of money-scales, books, a pencil, pen, ink, paper, and so on, and they draw omens of the child's future career from the object which it first handles and plays with. Thus, if the infant first grasps the money-scale, he will be wealthy; if he seizes on a book, he will be learned, and so forth."

168 The editor of *WSS* here inserted a cross-reference: "Campbell's *Superstitions of the Scottish Highlands*, p. 260." This appears to refer to a sentence now at p. 142 above: "Another favourite time was Hallowmas night." On water in which feet had been washed see pp. 10, 25, 39, 136.

169 On the *anainn* see note 137 on p. 321. Clearly a house built of turf is being described.

170 JGC concludes his excellent account of Hallowe'en customs with the kind of formal disclaimer required of a minister of religion. This is to be expected; what is of much greater interest is that Alexander Carmichael, who was not a minister of religion but whose purpose in writing *CG* was to display the Gael in the best possible light, omitted Hallowe'en entirely, while a Harriswoman of a much later generation, Christina Shaw from Ardhasaig, ended her oral account of the same customs (*Tocher* 41, pp. 272–77) in stammering embarrassment: *O well, nach robh iad neis iodhal-adhraidh an sen? Chan e iodhal-adhraidh ach black magic – buidseachd do black magic – chan eil fhiosam dé chanas mi – geasachd eile. Geasachd. Sè.* ("Oh well, were they not practising idolatry then? Not idolatry but black magic – witchcraft or black magic – I don't know what to call it – another form of superstition. Superstition. Yes.") For other good accounts see Dalyell 1834, p. 507; Mackay 1879–80; MacGregor 1901, pp. 44–54; Freer 1902, pp. 53–56; Wentz 1911, pp. 38–39; McPherson 1929, pp. 7–13, 166; Banks 1937–41, vol. 3, pp. 108–75; Maclean 1953–59; McNeill 1957–68, vol. 3, pp. 11–42; Ross 1965; McNeill 1970; Danaher 1972, pp. 200–27; *Tocher* 7, pp. 203–04; *Tocher* 15, p. 241; *Tocher* 19, pp. 106, 107, 119; Ross 1976, pp. 151–54; Macdonald 1982, pp. 184–90; MacNeil 1987, pp. 398–405; Bennett 1992, pp. 88–93; Miller 1994, pp. 61–68; Santino 1994; Hutton 1996, pp. 360–85; Macdonald 2003, pp. 60–63.

171 This tradition is clearly derived from the marriage feast of Cana (John 2: 1–11). As I have shown elsewhere (MacilleDhuibh 4.3.94), it appears to have been associated with Shrove Tuesday (*Oidhch' Inid*) and St Finnan's eve (*oidhch' Fhéill Fhinnein* or *Fhionnain*), but see also Ó Duilearga 1981, pp. 318, 407. Shrove Tuesday may fall on any date from 7 February to 6 March; there are two St Finnan's days, 21 January OS and 12 December OS. The January St Finnan's fell in the nineteenth century on 2 February NS, hence the link with Shrove Tuesday. The December St Finnan's fell strictly on 24 December, but, as JGC says, it became associated with the longest night of the year. JGC's story is paralleled, if not outdone, by

one recorded by Mairi MacArthur for the Mull Oral History Project on 10 February 1992 from Johnnie Campbell, 87, Taoslan, Bunessan, Mull. His grandmother, Kate MacDougall, who was married to a shepherd in Iona, was unwell at one time and asked her husband to fetch her some water. She tasted it and said, *Càit an d'fhuair thu 'm fìon?* "Where did you get the wine?" *Chan e fìon a tha sin*, he replied, *ach uisge an tobair.* "That's not wine, but water from the well." In the morning a neighbour came in to ask how she was, and was told what had happened. *O*, says he, *b'e sin Oidhche Cill Finnein, a chaidh an t-uisge a thionndaidh 'na fhìon, agus thachair gun do bhuail sibh air a bhlasad an uair sin.* "Oh, that was *Oidhche Cill Finnein*, when the water was turned into wine, and it so happened that you chanced to taste it at that point." *Oidhche Cill Finnein* was Johnnie Campbell's understanding of the term *oidhch' Fhéill F(h)innein*; he knew of the Biblical link, and from his tone and expression it was clear that he saw this as a remarkable thing which had actually happened to his grandmother. He died in 1999. My thanks for this to Mairi MacArthur, who has also published the story herself (1995, p. 76).

172 *Bladh* 'fame, etc.' is of varying gender: seemingly an old neuter (*DIL* s.v. *blad*), it is given as masculine by Dwelly (1977, p. 98) and other dictionaries, but as feminine by MacAlpine (1929, p. 37), so *na mòr bhladh* may be accepted as correctly expressing 'of great fame', if not quite JGC's 'of great cheer'.

173 For St Kessock's see p. 547, for St Connan's see note 552 on pp. 415–17, and for the *Féill Fhaolain* see note 249 on p. 345. For the *Feill Ceit* see Stewart 1928, pp. 187–88, and Black 2000, pp. 26, 50. For *brisgein* 'silverweed' see 'Food', p. 11. I discussed eighteenth-century famine years in MacilleDhuibh 28.3.97, but cannot put a precise date on *Bliadhna nam Brisgeinean*. For a story relating to the eating of *brisgein* in times of hardship in South Uist see Mac a Phì 1938, p. 132, MacLellan 1961, p. 221, and MacDhòmhnaill 1981, p. 35. In more recent times silverweed became a children's favourite, sometimes eaten after being singed over an ember of peat. By 1898 in Barra it was being stewed in a little water with sugar added and eaten as a sweetmeat (*Tocher* 25, p. 52). Professor Donald Meek has remarked to me more than once that he does not recall its being eaten in Tiree but that he has seen it being powdered, put into pipes and smoked. The 'flesh' is white, brittle (hence the name *brisgein* 'brittle one') and tasteless (Macdonald 2003, p. 35).

174 Carmichael provides a useful summary of traditions about the days of the week in *CG2*, pp. 271–74; see also Fionn 1908, pp. 192–96; Henderson 1911, pp. 293, 296; Mac an Toisich 1953–59, pp. 228–38; Ó Duilearga 1981, p. 407; Macdonald 1982, p. 172.

175 Scottish Gaelic *Di-*, Irish *Dé*, Manx *Je-*, Welsh *Dydd*, Cornish *dē-*, Breton *di-*; note also Catalan *di-*, French *-di*, Italian *-dì*.

176 *Dòmhnach* derives from *Dominicus*. A curious blindness to grammatical case is demonstrated here by JGC, or his source(s), or both. *Maol Ciaran* is properly *Maol Chiarain*, and we would expect *Allt Dòmhnaich, Tobar an Dòmhnaich, slàn chomraich an Dòmhnaich da.* It may be that *Dòmhnach* is unusually resistant to declension – Carmichael cites *Leanabh an Domhnach / Comhnartach ceum* 'The child of the Lord's Day / Even of step' (*CG2*, p. 273). For the charm for fulling cloth see p. 214.

177 *Luain* is the genitive case. The nominative is *Luan*.

178 There appears to be no connection between *Luan* and *luaineach*. *Luan* 'moon' can be derived from conjectural Indo-European *loukno-*, perhaps via Latin *luna*. *Luaineach*, Irish *luaimneach* 'volatile (as birds)' has been connected to Indo-European *ploug* 'fly', from which we also have English *fly*, German *fliegen*, Norse *fljúga* (Macbain 1896, p. 210).

179 JGC picks up an odd variant of the common saying (Nicolson 1951, p. 33, cf. *CG2*, p. 271):

An obair a thòisicheas Di-Luain,
Bidh i luath no bidh i mall.

("The work that begins on Monday, / It will be quick or it will be slow.") *Tionnsgnadh* 'beginning, devising' sounds like a correct interpretation of the unfamiliar *tinnste*, giving a first line that means literally 'A beginning that is made on Monday'. MacPhail puts it well (1900, p. 439): "What is begun on Monday will either be premature or late."

180 The implication of *mu thuath* and *mu dheas* is clearly 'unlucky' and 'lucky' respectively. They may be regarded as the kind of euphemisms necessary to a society in which people were expected to believe in predestination, not luck. There is a story of a woman who was sitting up late one night winding black thread (see p. 137, 'Unlucky Actions'), for she and her husband were moving house, perhaps due to eviction (MacDhomhnaill 1959). A voice said: *A bhoireannaich, gabh mu thàmh, agus na bi 'g obair air an t-snàth dhubh feadh na h-oidhche.* "Woman, go to bed, and don't be working at the black thread all night." She was dumbstruck, and the voice went on: *Na falbh a-màireach, se Di-Sathairne e.* "Don't go tomorrow, it's Saturday." Then it intoned:

> *Imich Di-Màirt mu thuath*
> *'S imich Di-Luain mu dheas —*
> *Ged nach biodh agad ach an t-uan*
> *Sann Di-Luain a dh'fhalbhadh tu leis.*

"Flit on Tuesday northwards / And flit on Monday southwards – / Though all you had were the lamb / It's on Monday you should go with it." They followed the advice.

181 JGC is paraphrasing Lhuyd 1707, pp. 35–36: "It's a very common Errour in Etymology, to endeavour the Deriving all the Radical words of our *Western European* Languages from the *Latin* or *Greek*; or indeed to Derive constantly the Primitives of any one Language, from any particular Tongue. When we doe this; we seem to forget that all have been subject to Alterations; and that the Greater and more Polite any Nation is, the more subject they are, (partly for Improvement, and partly out of a Luxurious Wantonness) to New model their Language . . . A Great number of words in the *Latin* tongue might better be Deriv'd from their Neighbouring Languages, than those Languages from it. A great many Etymologists, for want of making such Reflections, have fallen into so many Absurdities, that they had render'd a very usefull Art Ridiculous; till rescu'd by the Learned and Ingenious Observations of divers of our late Criticks . . . The Difference betwixt an *Etymologist* (notwithstanding his being sometimes mistaken) and a *Trifling Conjecturer*, will I presume appear from the following Comparison of *Derivations*, out of *Vossius's* Etymologicon, and *Joannes de Janua's Catholicon*, whose Etymons are commonly out of *Isidorus*."

182 See p. 555.

183 JGC is totally wrong about the derivation of *Di-Ciadaoin* 'Wednesday' and *Di-Haoine* 'Friday'. Wednesday and Friday fasts were well known to the early Christian Fathers, and became so popular in medieval Ireland that they developed into a three-day fast (*treadhan*) with the inclusion of Thursday as well (Heron 1888, pp. 23, 75, 185–86; MacPhail 1897, p. 381; O'Keefe 1905, pp. 204–05; Colson 1926, p. 27; Staniforth and Louth 1987, pp. 194–98; Farmer 1990, pp. 150, 228). *Aoine* is from Latin *jejunium* 'a fast', 'a fast-day', and the weakening or loss of its final syllable is entirely normal (Macbain 1896, pp. 17, 117–18; Vendryes 1959–96, s.v. *aín*).

184 See MacPhail 1897, p. 380, and note 189 below.

185 Presumably the invitation was designed to test whether the witch genuinely possessed the powers which she claimed to have. The association of Wednesday with sterility (for which see notes 639 above and 189 below) appears to have provided her with a convenient excuse.

186 No. *Diar-Daoin* is simply *Di-eadar-Dhà-Aoine* 'the Day between Two Fasts'.

187 Alexander Carmichael collected a version of this from Fionnladh Maccormaig, cowherd, Grogearry, South Uist, which extended to three quatrains. It begins (*CG1*, pp. 162–63):

> *Daorn Chalum-chille chaoimh*
> *La chur chaorach air seilbh,*
> *La chur ba air a laogh,*
> *La chur aodach an deilbh.*

Carmichael translates: "Thursday of Columba benign, / Day to send sheep on prosperity, / Day to send cow on calf, / Day to put the web in the warp." The other two quatrains portray Thursday as lucky for launching a boat, going to war, birth, death, hunting, harnessing horses, pasturing cattle (*chur feudail air raon*) and prayer. So far the meaning of *La(tha) chur chaorach air seilbh* is unclear, but the problem is solved by Nicolson, whose three-line version (1951, p. 168) is similar to JGC's:

> *Dirdaoin là Chaluim-Chille chaoimh,*
> *Là 'bu chòir a bhi deilbh,*
> *Là 'chur chaorach air seilbh.*

Nicolson translates: "When Thursday is dear Columba's day, the warp should be prepared, and sheep sent to pasture." See also GUL ms Gen. 1090/29, p. 66.

188 Or, more literally: "Your hair and your beard on Thursday / And your pared fingernail on Saturday."

189 Cf. note 588 on p. 429. JGC is referring to the very common saying (Nicolson 1951, p. 41, cf. p. 559 above):

> *Nuair as ciadaoineach an t-Samhain*
> *Is iargaineach fir an domhain.*

("When Hallowmas falls on a Wednesday / The men of the world are worried.") The tradition that Wednesday was the unluckiest day of the week, particularly with regard to fertility (see p. 566), is best recorded for Islay (Banks 1937–41, vol. 2, p. 80). One fanciful explanation given there was that Job was born on that day (*ibid.*, vol. 3, p. 109), but the real reasons are more likely to be the baleful influence of Mercury and the events of *Di-Ciadaoin a' Bhrath*, Spy Wednesday, when Christ was betrayed, tried and condemned to death. A manuscript life of Calum Cille in NLS Adv. ms 72.1.40, probably the one referred to by Martin Martin (1716, p. 264) as 'kept by *Mack-Donald* of *Benbecula*', cites the following verse (Grosjean 1927, pp. 166–67; Herbert 1988, pp. 212, 242, 264):

> *Cedain luid Iudass tar ord*
> *A lurg deman, dighal ngarg;*
> *Cedain ro gaib saint am saith —*
> *Cedain ro braith Isu ard.*

("On Wednesday Judas transgressed / Following demonic example, the vengeance of the fierce ones; / On Wednesday he grew greedy for wealth – / On Wednesday he betrayed noble Jesus.") As a quarter-day, *Samhain* ('Hallowmas') governed the events of the following three months – the winter quarter, when weddings took place, regarded as the most suitable time for conception in order that children might be born in the quarter which offered the best chance of both warmth and food (Black 1996, pp. 42, 52). The saying implies then that when 1 November is a Wednesday, married men face a winter of impotence and a childless autumn, leaving their wives open to the embraces of the *leannan sìth* – be he who he may!

190 Lhuyd 1707, p. 9. I have restored Lhuyd's spellings.

191 The name means simply 'Fast Day'. In the meaning 'fast' *aoine* is obsolete; the fact (which JGC chooses to deny) that it is present in the Gaelic names for Wednesday, Thursday and Friday shows that it must have been in popular use at one time.

192 This refers to the weather; perhaps JGC's 'powers of evil' argument helps explain why.

193 See 'Good Friday (*Di-Haoine na Ceusa*)', p. 549. A charm for gravel involving an otter's bladder failed 'owing to the fact that the cure was attempted on a Friday, which is well known to be an unlucky day on which to commence any undertaking or business' (Anon. 1881 and Anon. 1883a, p. 125, cf. SoSS Maclagan MSS vol. 22, pp. 3838, 4957).

194 *Air crodh a' bhail' ud thall.* See also Nicolson 1951, pp. 7, 407; GUL MS Gen. 1090/28, p. 240; GUL MS Gen. 1090/29, p. 66.

195 See 'Calum Clark and his Sore Leg', pp. 32–33.

196 See p. 10.

197 "To aim the cross of the number of Friday at you." Cf. McDonald 1958, pp. 29–30; GUL MS Gen. 1090/28, p. 290; GUL MS Gen. 1090/29, p. 33. As I understand it, the curse makes a direct connection between Christ's nakedness on that day and His death.

198 1 Chr. 21: 1–17. "And Satan stood up against Israel, and provoked David to number Israel . . . And David said unto God, Is it not I that commanded the people to be numbered? even I it is that have sinned, and done evil indeed; but as for these sheep, what have they done?"

199 There is confusion about gender in this paragraph. In the first phrase *Aoine* is correctly feminine and *Satharna* is logically masculine (it derives from Saturn, the Roman god of agriculture). In the second phrase *Aoine*, too, is masculine, which would be hard to justify from the recent history of the word, although it derives from an old neuter, *jejunium*, and could therefore in theory be of either gender (*DIL* s.v. 2 *aín*). It should read *nan glacadh an Aoine 'na bial e.* Cf. *Fhuair an Aoine 'na bial e / 'S faodaidh 'm fitheach a' bheinn a thoirt air* (GUL MS Gen. 1090/29, p. 33): "Friday has got it in its mouth / And the raven may go to the mountain."

Curiously, in *CG2*, first edition (1900), pp. 262–63, after giving *Aona* (= *Aoine*) four times as feminine ('*n Aona, an Aona, An Aona, An Aona*) and once questionably as masculine (*Aona bagarrach, / Sathurna deurach*), Carmichael cites *Ma gheobh an Aona na bhial e* (his spelling). In the second edition, p. 272, this was printed as *Ma gheobh 'n a Aona na bhial e.* Probably the editor, his daughter Ella (who died in the year of publication, on 30 November 1928), had intended this to read *Ma gheobh 'n t-Aona na bhial e.* It all leads one to wonder, not for the first time, if Alexander Carmichael had seen JGC's manuscript of *SHIS* and *WSS* during the 1890s. See p. 685 below.

200 *Sathairne* and *Satharna* are in free variation.

201 Carmichael cites the following version (*CG2*, p. 273):

> *Gealach Sathurna foghair*
> *Gabhaidh an caothach seachd uairean.*

He explains it thus: "An autumn Saturday moon / Will take (give?) madness seven times, *i.e.* madness will be seven times worse." This will not stand. JGC's interpretation of it as a weather prognostication is undoubtedly correct, and is supported by MacRury (1890–91, p. 30), who cites not only *solas na* [sic] *Satharna, gabhaidh e 'n cuthach seachd uairean*, meaning that the moon that comes in on a Saturday will usher in a week of stormy weather ('it will go mad seven times'), but also *solas earraich 's bean ga innseadh, gabhaidh e 'n cuthach trì uairean*, meaning that the spring moon whose first appearance is reported by a woman ('and a woman telling it') will bring three days of stormy weather ('it will go mad three times').

202 The 'end' or 'disease' of the seven Saturdays is suicide, referring to the seventh Saturday of Lent, when Judas hanged himself. The *och is och* couplet is part of a longer saying (*Tocher* 14, p. 234):

> Mo ghaol air Di-Haoine,
> Mo ghràdh air Di-Sathairn,
> Di-Dòmhnaich an cadal fad';
> Och! Och! Di-Luain!
> Tha 'n t-seachdain cho fhad 's bha i riamh.

("Friday I like, / Saturday I love, / A long sleep on Sunday; / Och! Och! Monday! / The week is as long as ever.")

203 "The blowing of the hillocks."

204 "It would take the tails off the horses."

205 JGC is presumably thinking of a context of the kind *gaoth a chur an t-sabhail thar an taighe* – 'a wind to put the barn over the house'.

206 Literally perhaps 'it would impound the cowards'.

207 For these four sayings see Nicolson 1951, pp. 38, 122, 191, 339. Probably Nicolson got the last from JGC himself, as he says (p. 122): "This saying, which comes from Tiree, is contrary to the experience of most other places." The first individual thanked in his preface, dated 1880, (*ibid.*, pp. xxxii–xxxiii) is JGC: "The largest and best collections were received from the Rev. J. G. Campbell of Tiree, and Mr. A. A. Carmichael, North Uist. Both came unasked, and were supplemented, as occasion required, by illustrations out of the rich stores of Gaelic Folk-lore, Poetry, and Tradition, which both these gentlemen are ever ready generously to communicate to those interested in them." See also pp. 644–45 below.

208 For the first two of these four sayings, with minor variations, see Nicolson 1951, pp. 28, 256. For the second see also MacRury 1890–91, p. 27. The third is a partial variant of the following (Smith 1964, p. 26):

> An treas latha den ghaoith an-iar,
>   An dàrna latha den ghaoith a-tuath,
> Maighdeanas na gaoith' a-deas,
>   A' ghaoth an-ear gach ial 's gach uair.

("The third day of the west wind, / The second day of the north wind, / The maidenliness of the south wind, / The east wind each moment and time.") MacRury (1890–91, p. 28, cf. Matheson 1951–52a, p. 379) cites it in a form which corresponds more closely to JGC's; it also has *aicill* rhyme in both couplets (*deas : treas; iar : ial*) as well as end-rhyme *tuath : uair*, and therefore sounds more authentic than Smith's, which has only one *aicill* rhyme, *deas : ear*.

> A' chiad latha den ghaoith a-deas,
>   An treas latha den ghaoith a-tuath,
> An dara latha den ghaoith an-iar
>   'S a' ghaoth an-ear gach ial 's gach uair.

("The first day of the south wind, / The third day of the north wind, / The second day of the west wind / And the east wind each moment and time.")

The fourth saying is also fragmentary. In its fullest form it is as follows (Camshron 1926, p. 49; Nicolson 1951, p. 198; Smith 1964, p. 20):

> *Geamhradh reòdhanach,*
> *Earrach ceòthanach,*
> *Samhradh breac riabhach*
> *Is foghar geal grianach*
> *Cha d'fhàg gort riamh an Alba.*

("A freezing winter, / A misty spring, / A chequered streaky summer / And a bright sunny autumn / Never left famine in Scotland.") See also MacRury 1890–91, p. 25, and Black 1996, p. 49.

209 I print *Cachlaidh na Buigeuisg* as it stands in *WSS* 304. *Buige* means 'softness', but *Buigeuisg* is an unlikely-sounding word, and may be the printer's misreading of JGC's handwriting. Carmichael gives *buigirisg* 'soft weather' (*CG*6, p. 25), and since his translation is identical to JGC's, I think he must have noted it from JGC's manuscript, cf. pp. 436 (note 626) and 685. Dwelly's *buigeasg*, genitive *buigeuisg*, 'soft weather' (1991, p. 36), may be disregarded, as the reference he cites is to *WSS* 304. It should be noted that JGC does not say that *Buigeuisg* is 'soft weather' but that *Cachlaidh na Buigeuisg* is 'the gateway of soft weather'. My best guess is that *buigirisg* is a flock of puffins – the Gaelic for 'puffin' is variously cited as *buigire*, *bùigire*, *budhaigir*, *buthaigre*, *budhaid*, *buthaid*. JGC explicitly links the expression with rain, so it is possible that he and Carmichael understood the term as *buigir-uisge* 'puffin-rain'.

210 Apollo Grannua is *recte* Apollo Grannus, a healing deity associated with therapeutic springs over a wide area from Brittany to the Danube. His name probably derives from what is now Grand in the Vosges and, as JGC says, is unconnected with *grian*, although he had a solar aspect (Green 1986, pp. 161–62, and 1992, p. 32). *Grian*, Old Irish *grían*, has been derived from conjectural Indo-European *greinâ*, from a root meaning 'warm' also seen in the Gaelic verb *gar* (Macbain 1896, p. 184).

211 *Geal* represents two qualities, whiteness and brightness. It is therefore the colour of the moon as well as of silver. Whiteness without brightness (e.g. of milk) is *bàn*. For *luaineach* see note 178 on p. 601. *Luaisg* appears to derive from an Indo-European root *ploud* or *plout*, *plou*, 'go, flow, move' as in *luath* 'quick' (Macbain 1896, p. 210). For *ré* see note 213 below.

212 The reference here to the moon as masculine may be a typographical error. The moon is universally conceived as feminine, and is grammatically so in Gaelic – *a' ghealach*. For customs connected with the rise and fall of the tide see MacPhail 1900, p. 440.

213 Cf. Nicolson 1951, p. 314. JGC appears to think that *rath* in *rath dorcha* 'interlunation' is *ràth* 'fortress, ring-fort'. It is in fact an unstressed form of *ré* which he has just defined as 'any planet'. This lack of stress has even led to a spelling *là dorcha* as if it meant 'dark day'. *Ré* is more usually regarded as meaning 'the moon', see p. 529; it appears to have been a word meaning 'time, season, duration, space of time', leading to the sense of 'lunar month, moon' and to the preposition *ré* 'during' (Dwelly 1977, p. 751, and note 10 on p. 574 above).

Another term for the interlunation is *earra-dhubh*, literally 'black tail', JGC's 'black boundaries', which he extends semantically to include the waning moon.

214 *Air gob na gealaiche* 'on the beak of the moon', cf. *gob gealaich* 'moon's beak'. *Slabhagan* appears to be the plural of Dwelly's *slabhag* 'horn-pith, socket of horn' (1977, p. 848), not the singular word *slabhagan* 'sea sloke' referred to in note 577 on p. 426 above. Macbain treated the two words as distinct (1896, p. 294); he traced the latter to English and Scots 'sloke' but could offer no explanation for the former.

215 See *CG*3, pp. 274–305; Opie and Tatem 1992, pp. 280–81, 'new moon: divination'.

216 See Dixon 1886, p. 161; Macbain 1887–88, pp. 271–72; MacGregor 1901, p. 40; MacDonald

1958a, pp. 147–48; note 300 above. *Caol* 'narrow, slender' functioned as a collective noun in the meaning 'wattles, osiers, withies', e.g. *caol* 'oziers', *caoldubh* 'black willow' (*CG2*, pp. 253, 259), *caoil dubh* 'black osier (?)' (Gillies 2000, pp. 24–25), *caol cuill no caol seilich* 'withes of hazel or willow' (*CG3*, p. 278), *grinne caoil* 'a bundle of osiers' (Dwelly 1977, p. 164), *taigh caoil* 'a very primitive dwelling of wattles and turf' (Macdonald 1982, p. 22).

217 Properly *eòin an fhàis*.

218 Perhaps there is a reflection here of the tradition mentioned by Frazer (1911b, p. 73) of marriages taking place in the interlunation. In any event, the subtlety of JGC's account of beliefs concerning the moon may be contrasted with Dalyell's (1834, pp. 285–86): "Good fortune depended so much on the encrease of that luminary, that nothing important was undertaken during its wane."

219 See note 166 on p. 600. Logically we would expect the last moon in harvest to be the third moon in autumn, but it may well be that in JGC's day the change in the calendar had caused confusion, the second moon in autumn occurring before Hallowmas NS (1 November), the third moon in autumn before Hallowmas OS (12/14 November). For moon-names see *CG2*, p. 366, and D. M. 1964, p. 124.

220 JGC has said this already (p. 571). It leaves the strong impression that his manuscript was unfinished.

FAMILY OF JOHN GREGORSON CAMPBELL

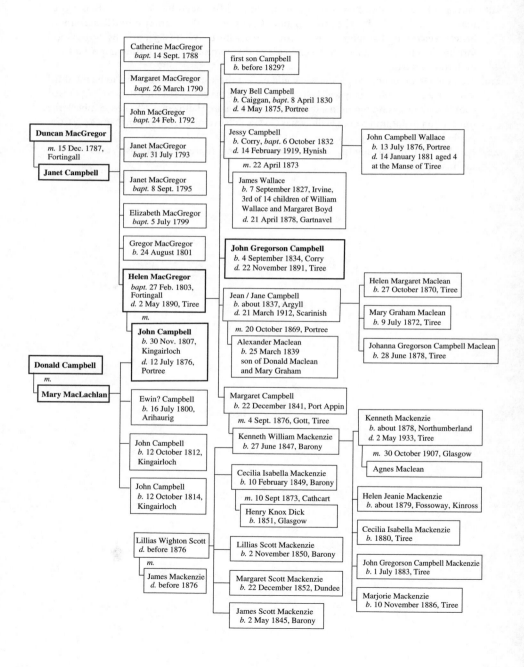

Duncan MacGregor
m. 15 Dec. 1787, Fortingall
Janet Campbell

- Catherine MacGregor
  bapt. 14 Sept. 1788
- Margaret MacGregor
  bapt. 26 March 1790
- John MacGregor
  bapt. 24 Feb. 1792
- Janet MacGregor
  bapt. 31 July 1793
- Janet MacGregor
  bapt. 8 Sept. 1795
- Elizabeth MacGregor
  bapt. 5 July 1799
- Gregor MacGregor
  b. 24 August 1801
- **Helen MacGregor**
  bapt. 27 Feb. 1803, Fortingall
  d. 2 May 1890, Tiree
  m.
  John Campbell
  b. 30 Nov. 1807, Kingairloch
  d. 12 July 1876, Portree

Donald Campbell
m.
Mary MacLachlan

- Ewin? Campbell
  b. 16 July 1800, Arihaurig
- John Campbell
  b. 12 October 1812, Kingairloch
- John Campbell
  b. 12 October 1814, Kingairloch

---

first son Campbell
b. before 1829?

Mary Bell Campbell
b. Caiggan, *bapt.* 8 April 1830
d. 4 May 1875, Portree

Jessy Campbell
b. Corry, *bapt.* 6 October 1832
d. 14 February 1919, Hynish
m. 22 April 1873
James Wallace
b. 7 September 1827, Irvine,
3rd of 14 children of William
Wallace and Margaret Boyd
d. 21 April 1878, Gartnavel

John Campbell Wallace
b. 13 July 1876, Portree
d. 14 January 1881 aged 4
at the Manse of Tiree

John Gregorson Campbell
b. 4 September 1834, Corry
d. 22 November 1891, Tiree

Jean / Jane Campbell
b. about 1837, Argyll
d. 21 March 1912, Scarinish
m. 20 October 1869, Portree
Alexander Maclean
b. 25 March 1839
son of Donald Maclean
and Mary Graham

Helen Margaret Maclean
b. 27 October 1870, Tiree

Mary Graham Maclean
b. 9 July 1872, Tiree

Johanna Gregorson Campbell Maclean
b. 28 June 1878, Tiree

Margaret Campbell
b. 22 December 1841, Port Appin
m. 4 Sept. 1876, Gott, Tiree
Kenneth William Mackenzie
b. 27 June 1847, Barony

Kenneth Mackenzie
b. about 1878, Northumberland
d. 2 May 1933, Tiree
m. 30 October 1907, Glasgow
Agnes Maclean

Cecilia Isabella Mackenzie
b. 10 February 1849, Barony
m. 10 Sept 1873, Cathcart
Henry Knox Dick
b. 1851, Glasgow

Helen Jeanie Mackenzie
b. about 1879, Fossoway, Kinross

Cecilia Isabella Mackenzie
b. 1880, Tiree

John Gregorson Campbell Mackenzie
b. 1 July 1883, Tiree

Lillias Wighton Scott
d. before 1876
m.
James Mackenzie
d. before 1876

Lillias Scott Mackenzie
b. 2 November 1850, Barony

Margaret Scott Mackenzie
b. 22 December 1852, Dundee

Marjorie Mackenzie
b. 10 November 1886, Tiree

James Scott Mackenzie
b. 2 May 1845, Barony

LIFE OF JOHN GREGORSON CAMPBELL

JGC was born at Kingairloch, a detached portion of the parish of Lismore and Appin in north Argyll, on 4 September 1834, son of John Campbell, who later became captain of the steamboat *Cygnet*, and of Helen MacGregor, a descendant of the MacGregors of Roro in Glenlyon. When he was between three and five years old the family moved across Loch Linnhe to live in Port Appin, from where he walked every day with his sisters to the Parish School in the Strath of Appin, a distance of about two miles (Campbell 1895, pp. ix–x).

JGC recalls this walk to school at p. 80 above. In Ireland every child was protected from Fairy interference by means of an old horse-nail hung around its neck with a bit of straw or string (Gregory 1970, p. 119; Welch 1993, p. 177); for precisely the same purpose JGC's friend had a nail, while he himself was the envied possessor of a knife. At pp. 119–20 he portrays a loveable teller of tall tales, *Calum na Cròige*, at whose feet he appears to have sat entranced as a boy, and at pp. 228–29 he describes a cave near Ardnamurchan Point which he seems to have visited when about ten years old. Other than this, although we are told that 'he loved to recall his early schooldays, and their memory was ever dear to him' (Campbell 1895, p. xi), we know nothing now about his childhood, but some idea of what it was like can be gleaned from the memoirs of his fellow-pupil Alexander Donald Mackenzie, which were printed for private circulation at the time of his death in 1915 but not published until 2003. Born in 1836, Mackenzie was a weaver's son from Blarchasgaig in the Strath of Appin who became a baillie of Edinburgh and chairman of the Leith Dock Commission. He says (2003, pp. 26–28):

> I remember quite well how things went on in our daily life. People lived upon oatmeal and potatoes; porridge for breakfast and supper, with milk most times, but not always; potatoes and herring for dinner, and, in winter, beef or mutton brochan – brochan in this case meaning soup. Sometimes it was braxy brochan, which was quite good and wholesome.
>
> Tea was never seen but on Sunday morning, but the young folks got none of it. Tea was about 4s to 4s 6d per pound, and brown sugar 6d per pound. Loaf bread was never seen in a crofter's house, and even flour was seldom used. An old woman, Mrs Cameron, carried on her back all the loaf bread used in the Strath of Appin and Glencreran every Saturday when she went her rounds.
>
> Workmen's wages varied from 1s to 1s 6d per day. At present three times as much is not considered a living wage; how men, women, and children lived in those days may seem a mystery, but they did live healthy and happy lives notwithstanding.
>
> There was far less grumbling and discontent than exists now. Of course the explanation is that the standard of living has changed. At that time small farmers and crofters grew their own corn, threshed it, and had it ground at the local mill, and then stored it up for the next year's consumption. Potatoes were grown and stored up for winter and spring. Poultry was kept, but though eggs sold for fourpence, even threepence, per dozen, they

were generally sold to the local dealer in exchange for the tea and sugar. A cow for killing for the winter's use could be bought for three or four pounds, and a sheep for six or seven shillings.

In regard to clothing, it was almost all home made, marriage suits being an exception. They either grew their wool or, when no sheep were kept, bought it; they carded and spun it, and had it woven into cloth of various kinds by the local weaver. The tailor was called in as required, and remained in the house as one of the family as long as his services were needed. Home-made shoes or brogans were just going out at the time I am writing of, but most men could do a little cobbling when it was needed. Boys and girls went barefooted and bareheaded nine or ten months in the year; full healthy and hardy they were. The houses were nearly all thatched, and not well thatched at that, nothing like as well done as thatched houses in the south. The floors were simply earth, or earth and clay. All this may look to us now like abject poverty, but it was not so looked upon then, and moreover, in general intelligence and intellectual capacity, the people were quite equal to those of the present day in the same station in life . . .

Among my earliest recollections is attending the Appin Parish School, which I understand was when I was only four years old, my lesson book being the alphabet pasted on a shaped little board, no doubt in order to prevent the paper being torn. I think I only attended school in summer, as I have a vivid recollection of getting my first pair of shoes, which event I looked forward to with great pleasure. Children went barefooted for at least nine months of the year, and although the feet suffered, probably it was better training than wearing tight shoes from infancy as is done now. I continued to attend the school (there was only one in that part of the parish) until I was thirteen, but not constantly, as I did a good deal of work on farms in the neighbourhood.

The subjects taught in the parish school of Appin were 'Gaelic and English reading, writing, arithmetic, and book-keeping, also English Grammar and Latin, and occasionally the elementary parts of mathematics' (McGregor 1841, p. 254). Gaelic was a normal part of the curriculum in Highland schools until swept away by the Education (Scotland) Act of 1872. Mackenzie continues (2003, pp. 28–30):

There were many books in English and Gaelic in our house, and I early acquired a great taste for reading, which has stuck to me all my life. In English, my favourites were a History of the Wars of the French Revolution, the 'Voyages of Captain Cook', etc. There was a book of physics called 'Matthew and Plilon', dealing with elementary science; this book I read more than once. 'Robinson Crusoe', which I was very fond of, and in Gaelic, 'The Highland Messenger' and 'Cuairtear Nan Gleann' were always a delight to me, as well as other publications from the pen of Norman McLeod (Old Norman), and, of course, the Old and New Testaments in both languages, as well as the Shorter Catechism and the 'Pilgrim's Progress'.

What a happy life it was roaming the woods and hills with no one to interfere, but a scolding from my mother when I stayed away too long or too late instead of attending to duties which she laid upon me in connection with our croft, or cutting peats, which, along with sticks, was our only fuel. Coals were never seen, except at the Laird's house.

I was for six months herding cattle at the farm of Elerig in Glencreran . . . Farm servants then lived a rough, hard life, never read anything as a rule, and their language was often of the roughest character, swearing and obscene conversation being the rule. They drank whisky whenever they could get it, always 'neat'. I never saw anyone diluting the spirits with water. Drinking to excess was the rule whenever there was an opportunity. The farmers themselves were not a whit better. Funerals, marriages, fairs, Christmas and

New Year holidays, nearly always finished up in wild drinking bouts and fighting. It was considered a deep disgrace not to have as much eating and drinking at all funerals as the relatives could afford. The beginning was generally three or four rounds of raw whisky, with oat bread and cheese, before the 'Body was lifted'. If the distance to the burying ground was considerable, another round or two on the way, finishing up by several rounds in the churchyard, then the quarrelling and fighting began.

I attended the funeral of one of the sheep farmers in the district of Kingairloch. They had the usual rounds before leaving the house, which was only a short distance from the burying place. After the burial the company of about two dozen adjourned to a boathouse in the vicinity. The Laird and his lady were toasted, then the son and ten daughters – thirteen rounds – by which time the whole company were quite drunk, and on the green sward fought like savages, as many as six or ten couples going at it all at one time. The very remembrance of it makes one shudder, but such scenes were the rule, not the exception.

When my brother Lachlan died I was about ten years of age. My father and mother broke through the horrid custom, and had no drink at the funeral. This was looked upon as a great scandal, but it was the beginning of a great reform.[1]

The work on the farm was never much to my liking, and I must confess I shirked it as much as possible. When 15 years of age I left my native place, the Strath of Appin, by a steamer from Port Appin to Glasgow. Those little steamers – there were two of them on the route – were named the 'Cygnet' and 'Plover'. They were of small size, in order to get through the Crinan Canal. Larger steamers went by the Mull of Kintyre, but this route was not fancied much if it could be avoided.

The small steamers generally passed Port Appin at about 10 to 12 p.m. There was no pier, the passengers and luggage being taken out by boat, and on dark and stormy nights it was not at all pleasant. I remember I was dreadfully sick nearly all the way to Greenock. The usual time taken on the way from Port Appin to Glasgow was about twenty four hours.

The *Cygnet* was launched by James and George Burns as the *Ben Nevis* in January 1848, but was renamed almost immediately. Being intended to ply between Glasgow and Inverness using the Crinan and Caledonian canals, she was only 77 feet 6 inches long and her paddle-boxes were flush with the bulwarks. Her sister-ships appear to have been the *Lapwing*, her twin, and the *Plover*, which some sources suggest was one of those larger vessels which plied between Fort William and Glasgow by the Mull of Kintyre. Since 1839 the Burns brothers had been involved with Samuel Cunard and Robert Napier in running the Cunard Shipping Company, and in 1851 they passed on their West Highland interests, including the *Cygnet*, to one of their own officials, David Hutcheson; in 1879 Hutcheson's company was taken over by his assistant David MacBrayne.[2]

The *Cygnet* was wrecked in Loch Ailort in 1882. Her skipper in better days, JGC's father, is described on the death certificate of his wife Helen as a steamer agent, and on those of his children JGC and Jessy as a Master Mariner. According to his own (which has him as a steamer agent), he was 73 years old when he died on 12 July 1876; he is described as a native of the parish of Lismore and Appin, son of Donald Campbell, a weaver, and his wife Mary MacLachlan. Perhaps the weaver's mother was a Kennedy (see p. 91), for JGC's biographer, Alfred Nutt, tells us (Campbell 1895, p. ix): "Through a paternal ancestor he traced back to a race that had had dealings with the 'good people', and on whom a *bean shith* had laid the spell 'they shall grow like the rush and wither like the fern' (*fàsaidh iad mar an luachair 's crìonaidh iad mar an raineach*)."

Parish registers fill in a little more detail. The Rev. Donald McNicol (and the Rev. John Stewart, who succeeded him in 1802) kept separate baptismal registers for the two main parts of the parish, Appin and Lismore. Kingairloch baptisms were sometimes recorded in the one, sometimes the other, perhaps because Kingairloch babies were often taken for baptism to Appin or Lismore. In the 'Lismore' register we find the baptism on 16 July 1800 of a 'son to Donald Campbell and Mary McLachlan in Arihaurig'. This is *Àirigh Shamhraidh* ('Summer Shieling'), a fertile spot on the Kingairloch shore halfway between Glensanda and Loch a' Choire; until that very year it was the site of the chief residence on the Kingairloch estate (Thornber 2000, pp. 30, 32). The name or word preceding 'son' is smudged and uncertain; it could be 'Eoin', 'Ewin' or even 'Twin'. If 'Eoin', it is – unusually for a parish register of the period – in correct Gaelic spelling; if 'Twin', it is odd; if 'Ewin', it approximates to 'Ewen', which may be found amongst the Appin christenings. *Eoghan* is normally rendered 'Hugh' in these registers, while another man in Appin insisted on 'Eugine'.

Stewart's baptismal register for Appin contains three relevant entries. These are, at 30 November 1807, 'John Son to Donald Campbell & Mary McLachlan Kingerloch was born & baptized Do.'; 12 October 1812, 'John son to Donald Campbell and Mary McLachlan Kingerloch was born and baptized 14th Instant'; 12 October 1814, 'John Son to Donald Campbell & Mary McLachlan Kingerloch was born & baptized 4th December'. As Captain Campbell was married about 1826–28, we may assume that he is the first of these. If taken at face value, it would appear that he had two brothers also called John. In terms of traditional naming practices this is not impossible (cf. p. 114 above), but as they also shared a birthday, one wonders if duplication has taken place – perhaps the minister jotted names and dates in a notebook when he visited Kingairloch, and made mistakes when transferring information to the parish register afterwards. All in all, however, it looks as if Captain John Campbell, *Iain Mòr Caimbeul*, was born in Kingairloch on 30 November 1807 and had three brothers: Ewen (*Eoghan Caimbeul*), born 16 July 1800; John (*Iain Meadhanach Caimbeul*), born 12 October 1812; and John (*Iain Beag Caimbeul*), born 12 October 1814. There may have been another brother, Duncan, born 1816, see opposite.

JGC's mother Helen MacGregor is described in the 1881 census for Tiree as a Gaelic speaker from Rannoch in Perthshire, aged 72. Her death certificate states that she was a daughter of Duncan MacGregor, tacksman, and his wife Jessy Campbell, and that she died on 2 May 1890 in the Manse of Tiree, aged 80. In both cases her age is understated. Duncan MacGregor and Janet Campbell were married in their native parish of Fortingall on 15 December 1787, and the parish register, now in the General Register Office for Scotland, lists the baptisms of eight children born to them at Aulich in Rannoch: Catherine, 14 September 1788; Margaret, 26 March 1790; John, 24 February 1792; Janet, 31 July 1793; another Janet, 8 September 1795; Elizabeth, 5 July 1799; Gregor, 24 August 1801; and finally (at f. 97v) Helen, 27 February 1803. This means that she was in fact 87 at her death. JGC's mention of the *Clann Dhonnchaidh Dhuibh* MacGregors at p. 234 leads me to speculate that her father Duncan MacGregor was the tacksman of Learagan on Loch Rannoch who was removed from his land in 1792 after more than three centuries of uninterrupted possession by his family (see note 817). Referring apparently to the same individual, Alfred Nutt says that JGC was descended on his mother's side 'from Duncan MacGregor, 13th in direct descent from the first MacGregor who settled at Roro' (Campbell 1895, p. ix). Less ambiguously, he calls JGC's maternal grandfather 'an ardent Gael, as may be judged by the letters that passed between him and Dr Mackintosh' (*ibid.*); this sounds like a reference to a published correspondence, and I can only assume that 'Dr Mackintosh' is an informal way of referring to the Rev. Dr Mackintosh MacKay (1793–1873), a Sutherlandshire man who edited the poems of Rob Donn and the Highland Society's Gaelic dictionary, advised Sir Walter Scott, spent a number of years as minister of Laggan in Badenoch, came out with the Free Church in 1843, and served as moderator of its General Assembly in 1849.[3] JGC records a number of traditions from Aulich and elsewhere on the north shore of Loch Rannoch, including one linked with the Appin Murder (p. 281), and this must be due to his family connection with the area.

In naming their son, Captain Campbell and his wife were paying a clear compliment to the MacGregor who owned the estates of Ardtornish, Eignaig, Tearnait, Liddesdale and Achagavel which marched with Kingairloch to the north and west – John Gregorson (*c*.1776–*c*.1845), the most prosperous as well as probably the best-liked proprietor in Morvern, who also served as sheriff for the district (Gaskell 1968, pp. 28–29). Presumably he was JGC's godfather.

The Lismore parish register lists Mary Bell, baptised 8 April 1830, daughter to John Campbell and Helen MacGregor, Caiggan (p. 90); Jessy, baptised 6 October 1832, daughter to John Campbell and Helen MacGregor, Corry (p. 98); John Gregorson, born 4 September 1834, son to John Campbell and Helen MacGregor, Corry (p. 104); and Margaret, born 22 December 1841, baptised 16 January 1842, daughter to John Campbell and Helen MacGregor, Port Appin (supplement, pp. 38, 100). The 1841 census records that the members of the household at Port Appin who were at home on the night of 6 June that year were Helen Campbell, 35, crofter, born outside Argyll, and Duncan, 25, Mary, 10, Jessy, 8, John, 6, and Jean, 4, all born in Argyll. In this census ages above 15 were supposed to be rounded down within five-year bands, so '35' may mean anything up to 39, and '25' anything up to 29; Captain Campbell was 33 years old and his wife was 38, so it is clear that Duncan, aged 25–29, was not their son. Perhaps he was a brother or cousin of the Captain's. However, Jessy told Nutt that JGC was 'the second son and fourth child of Captain Campbell of the *Cygnet* and of Helen MacGregor, his wife' (Campbell 1895, p. ix), and JGC was described at his death as 'the eldest son of Captain Campbell, of the *Cygnet*' (Anon. 1891b), so it looks as if he had at least one brother who died in infancy; all in all we may tentatively describe the family as consisting of a son (b. ?1828), Mary Bell (b. 1830), Jessy (b. 1832), John Gregorson (b. 1834), Jean (b. 1837), a son (b. ?1839), and Margaret (b. 1841). In due course Jean (Jane) married Alexander Maclean, who witnessed JGC's death in 1891, while Jessy married James Wallace, and Margaret married Kenneth William Mackenzie. Neither Mary Bell nor JGC ever married.

In April 1830, as we have seen, the family was at Caiggan. This will be *an Caigeann*, presumably meaning 'Rough Mountain Pass' (Dwelly 1977, p. 147), just south of the entrance to Loch a' Choire in Kingairloch, where modern maps show *Allt a' Chaiginn* (Caiggan Burn), *Rubha a' Chaiginn* (Caiggan Point) and *Camas a' Chaiginn* (Caiggan Bay). By October 1832 they had moved two miles west to Corry, the populous centre of

1834
104

July 22 Donald son to Duncan Black
& Mary Black Cregganich born

Sept. 2 Duncan son to Donald McColl
& Ann Carmichael Killean — Do

4 John son to Myles Kieth &
Chirsty McGlashen Achnard Do

" John Gregorson son to John Campbell
& Helen McGrigor Corry — Do

6 John son to Archd. Carmichael &
Mary McGlashen Cregganich Do

7 Duncan son to John Campbell &
Ann McColl Fiart — — Do

Oct. 5 Hugh son to Hugh McCorquodle
& Mary Black Portramsay Do

7 Archibald son to Neil Black &
Mary Black Point of Fiart Do

14 Dugald son to Hugh McKellaich &
Ann McCaig Kilcondrict Do

17 Janet daughter to Alex. McCorquodale
& Ann McColl Kilcondrist Do

Nov. 1 Mary daughter to Donald McInnes
& Mary McKillop Point Fiart Do

6 John son to Archd. McLachlen &
Chirsty McInnes Kilmalieu Do

16 Ann daughter to Alex. McCormick
& Catherine McGrigor Portramsay Do

17 Ronald son to Donald Mitchell &
Flora Cameron Glengalmadale Do

Lismore & Appin parish register showing JGC's birth   GROS

Kingairloch, at the head of Loch a' Choire. This was where JGC was born in 1834. Nutt tells us that 'when he was three years of age his parents removed to Appin' (Campbell 1895, p. ix), but as he (or rather Jessy) had wrongly placed JGC's birth at 1836, it is impossible to know whether the move across Loch Linnhe to Port Appin took place in 1837 or in 1839. Perhaps the omission of Jean's birth c. 1837 from the parish register has something to do with this. At any rate the family is well established in Port Appin by 1841, when the census is taken and Margaret is born.

Even if we assume that John Campbell was skipper of the *Cygnet* from the day she was launched in January 1848, we have to ask what he was doing in Kingairloch to c. 1837 and in Port Appin to c. 1847. Since the two places face each other across Loch Linnhe it would be logical to suggest that he ran a ferry service, but it is far from clear whether such a service existed in his day. McNicol speaks of ferries from Kingairloch to both Lismore and Appin (1790, p. 498 = 1983, p. 361), but no mention of these is made by McGregor, presumably because the steamers 'which pass twice a week through the parish during summer, and once a week during winter' (1841, p. 251) had by then taken their place. The nearest other ferry was, and is, ten miles north-east at the Corran of Ardgour. In all probability, then, Captain Campbell was in the coastal trade, supplying (among others) the builders of the Caledonian Canal, which was begun in 1803 and opened to traffic in 1822, but not completed until 1847.[4] There was plenty in Kingairloch to keep him. Loch a' Choire, the *geàrrloch* or 'short loch' which gives the district its name, is described by McGregor (1841, p. 229) as 'by far the most commodious harbour in the parish, being about a mile in length, and half that extent in breadth, being narrower still at the mouth; and, as the holding ground is exceedingly good, vessels of any burden may find in it a safe retreat from whatever quarter the wind may blow'. The landlords from 1800 to 1881, who were Forbeses of an old Aberdeenshire family, enlarged the mansion-house, built a church at Camusnacroise, opened a granite quarry on the north shore of Loch a' Choire – it employed twenty men and two boys – and reconstructed and remodelled many of the estate cottages and farm buildings; a post office opened there in the year of JGC's birth, and serious population decline did not set in until the 1850s (Thornber 2000, pp. 10, 16, 30, 33). The career of Alexander Cochran (1841–1900), a Helensburgh man who married Christina, daughter of William Blacklock, tenant of South Corry in Kingairloch, offers what may well be a mirror image to Captain Campbell's from later in the century (Thornber 2000, pp. 25–27):

At first Alexander and Christina Cochran lived with Robert Blacklock at South Corry which was probably a convenient arrangement as Alexander, by now a master mariner, was away at sea a great deal. However it was not long before it became apparent that the house was too small for both families so around 1877 the Cochrans moved to Oban. Their daughter Mary Jane was born on the 17th of January of that year but whether the event took place at South Corry or Oban I do not know. Apparently her father was taking his boat through one of the flights of locks on the Caledonian Canal when he received a telegram announcing the birth … As soon as an opportunity arose the family moved back, not to South Corry but to Camusnacroise … The base at Kingairloch/Camusnacroise would have been mutually beneficial as Alexander would have a pier from which to carry out his coastal trading and his wife could be with her brother and his family whenever her husband was away at sea. By now Alexander owned the 'Valentia', a seventy-eight foot long, eighty ton, steam vessel which he used for moving cargoes to and from numerous ports between the Clyde and Loch Linnhe including Belfast, Campbeltown, Glasgow, Crinan, Fort Augustus, Gigha and Fort William. One interesting activity the 'Valentia' was involved in was carrying loads of birch bark from Invergarry for use in iron works to prevent the molten metal from 'spitting' out. The Cochrans were able to bring to Kingairloch stores cheaper and more readily than they could be brought by road and as a result they ran a grocery business for the neighbourhood which was more likely done to render a service rather than to make money. It is incredible to think that such a wide-ranging enterprise could be efficiently and successfully conducted from a croft at Camusnacroise and a pier at Kingairloch without clerical assistance.

If we ask whether John Campbell had a pier at Kingairloch from which to carry out *his* coastal trading, I would point to the one on the south shore of Loch a' Choire, halfway between Caiggan and South Corry, which served the mill on Abhainn na Feàrna. "At one time," says Thornber (2000, p. 30), "the Kingairloch mill was used by people from the Island of Lismore and Appin who brought their sacks of grain by boat to a pier on the south side of Loch a' Choire and thence by horse and cart along a well made metalled road in front of South Corry House. The pier, at NGR NM 848518, has long since disappeared but the road to the mill can still be seen."

Nutt tells us that JGC was sent to Glasgow for further schooling at the age of ten (Campbell 1895, p. x). If he was really only ten this would have been in 1844 or 1845, but it may have been a couple of years later. His immediate destination was the 'Andersonian University' (Anderson's College or Institute) in George Street, which joins the north side of George Square to the High Street. A pioneering technical college, in 1887 it united with three other institutions to form the Glasgow and West of Scotland Technical College, 'The Tech', which evolved via the Royal College of Science and Technology into the University of Strathclyde, and we may be sure that Captain Campbell expected his clever young son to study navigation and engineering, then follow him to sea (Eyre-Todd 1934, pp. 377–78). JGC was here treading in the footsteps of the explorer David Livingstone (1813–73), whose grandfather had migrated to Blantyre from the north Argyll parish of Ulva in 1792 (cf. Carmichael 1908–09, pp. 371–72, and Grant 1925, pp. 64–68), and who attended the Greek and medical classes at Anderson's in 1836–38. The flavour of the college in those days is conveyed by Livingstone's biographer William Blaikie (1889, pp. 37–38); the medical classes included chemistry, taught by Professor Thomas Graham.

> While attending Dr Graham's class he was brought into frequent contact with the assistant to the Professor, Mr James Young. Originally bred to a mechanical employment, this young man had attended the evening course of Dr Graham, and having attracted his attention, and done various pieces of work for him, he became his assistant. The students used to gather round him, and several met in his room, where there was a bench, a turning-lathe, and other conveniences for mechanical work. Livingstone took an interest in the turning-lathe, and increased his knowledge of tools – a knowledge which proved of the highest service to him when – as he used to say all missionaries should be ready to do – he had to become a Jack-of-all-trades in Africa ... Dr Graham's assistant devoted himself to practical chemistry, and made for himself a brilliant name by the purification of petroleum, adapting it for use in private houses, and by the manufacture of paraffin and paraffin-oil. Few men have made the art to which they devoted themselves more subservient to the use of man than he whom Livingstone first knew as Graham's assistant, and afterwards used to call playfully 'Sir Paraffin'.

In 1847 or 1848 JGC left Anderson's for the last time and walked round the corner to the High School of Glasgow in John Street. When I attended the school in 1955–64, by then in Elmbank Street, it was regularly (if not monotonously) claimed to be eight hundred years old, and it can certainly claim to be the same Grammar School that is on record in 1460 (the name was changed in the year of JGC's birth). Frank Beaumont points out (1921, p. xiii) that by 1837 it offered an almost complete modern curriculum of seven departments, Classical, Mathematical, English, Modern Languages, Writing, Drawing and Chemistry. "Chemistry, however, was soon discarded: the time of science was not yet fully come."

This would have suited JGC perfectly well. The prospectus for 1838–39 reveals the following departments: Classical (the largest); Commercial (Arithmetic, Geography, Mathematics); English; Modern Languages; Writing; Drawing and Painting; and Philosophical. These operated independently, there being no rector, headmaster or overall structure. Masters collected their own fees and ruled supreme over their classes or departments. Some classes contained as many as 125 pupils. In JGC's day, Classics appears to have been good, English eccentric, Mathematics brilliant (Ashmall 1976, pp. 3, 5, 75–95, 188–89). Nutt describes JGC as 'the only Highlander in the school', which seems unlikely, but no doubt he had much to put up with. He later told how he suffered several hours' imprisonment for fighting another boy 'on account of my country'. He is described as quick-witted and hot-tempered, but also as a dreamy and somewhat indolent lad of whom his masters said (Campbell 1895, p. x): "If Campbell likes to work no one can beat him."

We have no way of knowing whether he made friends with a young fellow-clansman, Henry Campbell (1836–1908), who later became Sir Henry Campbell-Bannerman and served as Prime Minister from 1905 to 1908. As the son of a wholesale draper from Kelvinside, he was much more in his element than JGC (Wilson 1973, p. 32):

> In 1845 Henry went to Glasgow High School, where he was two years ahead of James Bryce, later a close friend and political colleague, whose father, Paddy Bryce, was the mathematics master. Another future Prime Minister, Bonar Law, followed him at the High School. Henry Campbell early formed the view that one man is as good as another. He went to school with the son of a miller, who was called a mealy boy because he brought a sack of meal with him which was his staple diet for the term. Henry thought the miller's son was as good a person as himself, and thought it wrong that he had no chance, as things were then, of going to a university.

Nutt remarks of JGC that 'like all who are steadily bilingual from early youth he recognised how powerful an intellectual instrument is the instinctive knowledge of two languages, and was wont to insist upon the aid he had derived from Gaelic in the study of Hebrew and Latin' (Campbell 1895, p. x). Despite the presence of Gaelic-speaking masters, not one word of Gaelic was taught in the High School of Glasgow in the 1950s or 1960s, and I have no reason to believe that the situation in the 1840s was any different. Why this should be so is a mystery far greater to me than the origin of the Fairies.

One day in 1850 JGC walked a short distance the other way, this time to the University of Glasgow in the High Street, where he matriculated in the Greek class presided over by Professor Edmund Law Lushington (Addison 1913, p. 488). Henry Campbell was taking a 'year out' to enjoy a Grand Tour of Europe with his brother, and would follow JGC into the same class in 1851, still only fourteen years old (Wilson 1973, p. 37). JGC was duly noted in the matriculation roll as *Joannes G. Campbell fil nat 2dus Joannis nautae Glasguensis*: 'John G. Campbell legitimate second son of John sailor of Glasgow' (Addison 1913, p. 488). Following the launch of the *Cygnet* in January 1848, Captain Campbell had brought the rest of his family to live in the city, and the 1851 census for the parish of Barony finds JGC with his father, mother and four sisters at 117 Cheapside Street, just round the corner from Steam Boat Quay. Since the *Cygnet* plied between there and Muirtown in Inverness (a minor port with few educational amenities), it was a logical choice. But in any case JGC was now surrounded by Gaelic-speaking students, and could begin to enjoy the educational experience once again. Like many others of his kind to this day, he served as secretary of the Ossianic Society, and indulged his interests. Says Nutt (Campbell 1895, pp. x–xi): "At this early date his love for the rich stores of oral tradition preserved by his countrymen manifested itself. He sought the acquaintance of good story-tellers, and began to store up in his keenly retentive memory the treasure he has been so largely instrumental in preserving and recording."

It would seem, then, that the genesis of the books published in 1900 and 1902 was JGC's notes from his fellow-students and others in Glasgow in the 1850s, when he was between sixteen and twenty-six years old. This fits well with James Maclehose's statement (p. 686 below) that 'much of the material was already collected before Mr J. F. Campbell of Islay published his *Popular Tales of the West Highlands* in 1860'. JFC began collecting in 1859 (Campbell 1890, vol. 1, p. iv), Carmichael in 1860 (Black 1999, p. 710). It appears that JGC was the greatest trail-blazer of the three.

Henry Campbell went on at eighteen to Trinity College in Cambridge; like him, JGC took no degree, and he, too, appears to have left at eighteen. Nutt tells us that 'after leaving college he read law for a while with Mr. Foulds' (Campbell 1895, p. xi). This would have been in 1854–56. Foulds was a solicitor who took apprentices to learn the work of preparing legal documents; he is to be found as Faulds or Foulds in Glasgow post office directories of the period, e.g. in 1860–61 'Faulds, W. B., writer and notary public, 112 West George street; house, 30 Parson street'. Nutt continues: "In his lonely island parish he later found his legal training of the utmost assistance. Many were the disputes he was called upon to settle, and, as he has recorded, few there were of his parishioners who needed to take the dangerous voyage to the Sheriff's court on a neighbouring island. At once judge and jury, his decisions commanded respect and acquiescence."

The 'neighbouring island' was Mull. And I would add that JGC must often have provided such legal services in exchange for traditions and superstitions, a part of the people's inner lives not normally revealed to a parish minister. W. B. Yeats wrote in 1890 of Sir William Wilde in his Dublin hospital that 'when grateful patients would offer to send him geese or eggs or butter, he would bargain for a fragment of folklore instead' (Welch 1993, p. 55). Indeed I suspect that JGC chose the ministry of the Established Church of Scotland in preference to the law for the simple reason that it offered greater opportunities for the pursuit of folklore. In 1854, at the age of twenty, he returned to Glasgow University to enrol as a divinity student, and for four years he attended the prescribed classes in Greek, Hebrew, Theology, Literature, Philosophy and Church History (NAS CH2/171/22, pp. 57–58, 76).

In May 1843 a third of the Church of Scotland had seceded over the issue of patronage (the right of lay patrons to 'intrude' a new minister into a parish against the congregation's will), leaving 451 vacancies to be filled.[5] The history of the Church of Scotland from 1843 to 1869 is told in a nutshell by J. H. S. Burleigh (1960, pp. 373–75), and this applies closely to JGC's experience, save for one point alone: the new Free Church was not strong in Tiree.

Ministers of proved ability and character were in great demand. One of them refused five offers of presentation to desirable vacant charges before he found one which he was willing to accept. Some sought a change for reasons of ambition, others in order to escape from the results of the schism in their parishes and the pain of broken pastoral relationships. But the dearth of ministers was a severe handicap to the Church. It could still call on a remarkable number of probationers mostly employed as schoolmasters, but some of these were 'stickit ministers' not likely in normal circumstances to have secured a presentation to any parish. Not all of them proved satisfactory and their weaknesses were exposed to the fiercest criticism when their predecessors continued, as they usually did, to minister in their parishes. There was a real danger that the Church might be unable to hold even those who had not been swept out of it by the wave of enthusiasm in 1843.

In the hope of preventing further secession Lord Aberdeen reintroduced in slightly modified form the Bill he had sponsored in 1840 and withdrawn when it was pronounced unacceptable by the non-intrusionists. At that time Dr Cook and his party had approved the Bill, but they disliked it and now only with hesitation acquiesced in a petition from the Church in favour of it. It proposed to give to the communicant members of a vacant parish the right to bring forward in writing objections of any kind whatever against a presentee, of which objections the presbytery should be sole judge with authority to decide whether or not to proceed to a settlement, subject to appeal to the superior courts of the Church. This well-intentioned Bill became law in the summer of 1843 and very soon it became apparent that Dr Cook's misgivings were not without justification. The right of objection was freely exercised. Complaints were expressed of the coldness, formality, incomprehensibility, and unedifying nature of the pulpit ministrations of presentees, their poor or unpleasing voices, their reputation for laziness; in the case of one of them his 'exuberance of animal spirits'!

It would be wrong to suppose that the objections offered were as frivolous as they may appear to us now. Some are obviously sincere and testify to a high ideal of the Christian ministry in the minds of simple people, but it must have been hard indeed to deal with them in such a way as to do justice to all parties and at the same time to give them satisfaction. The well-known essayist A. K. H. B. (A. K. H. Boyd, minister of St Andrews) wittily remarked that in contrast to 'the priest-ridden people' of Ireland, in Scotland there was a 'people-ridden clergy'. Between 1843 and 1869 there were no fewer than sixty-one cases of disputed settlements involving expense and consuming the time of the presbyteries and other church judicatories, and doing infinite harm to the peace of congregations.

It became obvious that something must be done to remedy this evil and many churchmen began to consider the possibility of having patronage abolished altogether. The matter came before the assembly of 1866 on an overture from the presbytery of Edinburgh, and a committee of inquiry was appointed, but not until 1869 was it resolved by majority to petition Parliament to end patronage.

In the first half of 1858, during his fourth and final session as a divinity student, JGC and a handful of others underwent trials for licence to preach. The professor of Divinity, the Very Rev. Dr Alexander Hill, certified to the Presbytery of Glasgow that they had delivered a homily, lecture, exegesis, 'exercise and addition', Hebrew exercise, and popular sermon. On 9 February they were examined by a committee of the Presbytery, who on 5 May allocated the scriptural texts on which the candidates were to base their *final* homily, lecture, exegesis, 'exercise and addition', and popular sermon. On 7–9 June the Presbytery itself met to hear the students deliver most of their pieces, and last but not least, at St Mungo's Church (now Glasgow Cathedral) on 24 June, the equivalent of a graduation ceremony took place. No doubt Captain Campbell and his wife and daughters were in the gallery along with the other families. The students delivered their remaining discourses and were examined in Church History, Greek and Hebrew, then the moderator read the relevant Acts and licensed them to preach (NAS CH2/171/22, pp. 57–58, 60, 68, 73, 75–76).

JGC now went to Blair Atholl (see p. 149 above) to serve as assistant to the Rev. Alexander Robertson Irvine (1806–67), whose father, the Rev. Dr Alexander Irvine of Little Dunkeld, had been a Gaelic scholar and collector of folklore (Scott 1915–50, vol. 4, p. 146; Black 1986b, pp. 27–29). While there he obtained a rare Gaelic 'arming run' about Eoghan O Neill from the beadle of the church at Strowan (Struan), a man in his late 40s called Harry who told him that he was one of only two people in the country who knew it.[6]

JGC was already suffering from a complaint that was to trouble him all his life, inflammation of the lungs. For six months he was forbidden to preach. We will find that on more than one occasion during his lifetime his congregations were unable to hear him properly; his chronic pulmonary condition must be the reason. It appears to have been at this point, probably the summer of 1859, that he enjoyed a holiday in Largs (see 'The Lowland Fairies', pp. 40–41), where his sister Jessy was working as a schoolteacher. He then went to help an old college friend, the Rev. John Alison (1835–1902), struggle with the grim social realities of his first charge, the Middle Parish in Paisley. Alison moved on in November 1861, and was later to spend many years as minister of Newington in Edinburgh. It was a formative experience for both men.[7]

At some point in the 1850s Captain Campbell ceased to be skipper of the *Cygnet* and took a job as Hutcheson's steamboat agent in Portree – the census of 7 April 1861 finds him, allegedly aged 56, living at no. 1 Quay Street in a four-roomed house with his wife Helen (now claiming to be only 48), along with JGC (aged 26 and described as 'Minister of Established Church'), Margaret (18 and unmarried) and a domestic servant, Marion Bruce from Kilmuir (26 and unmarried); Mary Bell was keeping house for Jessy in Largs. This means that for a period of about twenty years, down to the time he wrote up his notes on superstitions as what is now *The Gaelic Otherworld*, JGC's visits to his parents brought him to Skye. It explains why many traditions of the island are scattered around the book, relating especially to the town itself and adjacent districts: Scorrybreck and Staffin (*An Taobh Sear* 'the East Side') to the north, the Braes to the south.

April 1861 was an anxious time. In 1860 JGC had been presented by Argyll, as patron, to the parish of Tiree and Coll. George Douglas Campbell, the eighth duke (1823–1900), was deeply interested in both religious and agrarian issues, earning an accolade (from a radical opponent) as 'this elder of the Kirk, this sanctimonious prig, this pedantic priest of a played-out political gospel, who gloried in the policy of grab' (MacPhail 1989, p. 191) and another (from a later Presbyterian writer) as 'the most influential Scot of his day' (MacLean 1949, p. 146). The parish had been vacant since the death of the Rev. Neil Maclean on 26 August 1859, and was being looked after by two junior clerics, the Rev. James MacColl, minister of the parliamentary chapel in Coll, and the Rev. Hugh MacAlpine, missionary in Tiree, whose stipends were paid by the 'Royal Bounty' for Highland churches. MacColl, a Lismore man and a graduate of Aberdeen University, had been ordained to Coll on 25 August 1859 (Scott 1915–50, vol. 4, p. 74). MacAlpine appears in the *Fasti* only once, as Royal Bounty missionary at Ardrishaig in 1856–57 (*ibid.*, vol. 4, p. 1); like his namesake Neil MacAlpine from Islay (1786–1867), who was the author of a Gaelic dictionary, he was probably a schoolmaster with aspirations to a higher calling (MacAlpine 1929, pp. x–xii).

Clearances excepted, no event in the life of a nineteenth-century community was more passionately debated than the appointment of a new minister, and in this case the excitement reached the national stage. The duke's role as patron of the parish of Tiree and Coll was to find it a suitable pastor, but as he himself pointed out fourteen years later in the debate on the bill which finally abolished patronage through the Church Patronage Act of 1874, the people were much better qualified than he to select their ministers, and he could no more present any man he liked than he 'could fly to the moon' (Ansdell 1998, p. 165, cf. Macpherson 1901, p. 412). Before nominating JGC he would have received and read many letters of application and recommendation and would have consulted informally with the law officers of Argyll, the chamberlain of Tiree, and the Presbytery of Mull, in whose jurisdiction the parish lay.[8] It is clear from the diary of James Robertson, a Perthshire man who was sheriff substitute of Tobermory from 1842 to 1846, that district judges such as himself were heavily involved in the patronage process: when Alexander Robertson Irvine was translated to Blair Atholl in August 1843, for example, it was with Sheriff Robertson's active help, support and advice (Loudon 2001, p. 81, cf. pp. 62, 79).

JGC's letter of presentation was received by the Presbytery on 26 February 1860. They appointed him to preach at Kirkapol in Gaelic and English on Sunday 18 and Monday 19 March, and at Balinoe in the Moss on Sunday 25 March. They would then meet in the church at Balinoe on Thursday 5 April 'for the purpose of moderating a Call in favour of the Presentee, and receive objections to his settlement (if such shall be offered)'.

The process started badly and got worse. JGC was prevented by 'the unusual severity of the weather' from getting to Tiree in time to preach as required on 18 March, but preached – nervously, no doubt – at Kirkapol on 25 March, at Balinoe the next day, and at Balinoe again on 1 April. When the brethren duly arrived in the island on 5 April they found that thirty-five individuals had signed the call, but written objections were also handed in bearing thirty-nine signatures, along with a further 111 names on four separate pieces of paper, seemingly a list of those adhering to the objections (NAS CH2/273/7, pp. 4–5, 10, 12–15).

What was the problem? JGC's indifferent health? Perhaps. His preaching? Ten years later JFC found it a little strange. His bachelorhood? Surely not. A young man described as 'tall and fair, with deep blue eyes full of life and vivacity' (Campbell 1895, p. xiii) would surely get a wife. Actually he did not. Was it his interest in folklore, and especially superstitions? The church existed to eradicate superstition, not to encourage it.[9] Was there perhaps a preferred candidate? That view has been expressed to me by Dr John MacInnes, whose great-grandmother (*Mòr NicFhionghain*) was from Tiree.[10] Or was JGC, in his innocence, entangled in a net of island politics, and being rejected not for who he was, but for whom he represented? That is the view of Neil M. Brownlie, who says (personal communication, 22 April 2004): "I think the main reason for the Tiree people's objections to the appointment of JGC as parish minister may have been their strong dislike of the eighth duke and their hatred for his chamberlain, John Campbell."

At another time in history, superstitions might have seemed important. At *this* time, what mattered was that for fifteen years since the famine of 1846 the Argyll Estate (in the person of its chamberlain for Tiree, John Campbell of Ardmore) had been carrying out a ruthless policy of consolidation under which roughly one third of the island's sub-tenants and their families had been expelled while another third were reduced to the status of landless cottars.[11] There was a visceral loathing of Campbells in Tiree – a MacLean island until the 1670s – which was more than tribal and can best be likened to the Middle-Eastern view of Americans in the present day. At any rate the objections to JGC's appointment, as represented to the Presbytery, were:

1. Because to our experience his preaching is neither instructive nor impressive, and because his prayers are devoid of fervour.

2. That by all appearance, his constitution is not strong so as to enable him for the vigorous yet necessary, performance of his duties in such a large and populous Parish.

3. That his discourses are cold, dry, and unedifying, and not calculated to awaken the attention and impress the heart of his hearers.

These words were carefully recorded in the Presbytery minutes, followed in two columns by the long list of names of those unfavourable to the call (NAS CH2/273/7, pp. 12–15). Only one (Murdoch Campbell, Caolas Ardeas) was a Campbell, and along with others he later wrote to the Presbytery asking to be struck off the list. At their meeting in the church at Kirkapol on 6 April JGC found himself facing the principal objectors – Alexander MacLean, Balemeanach (elder), Alexander MacDonald, Allan MacFadyen, Hugh MacKinnon (church officer), Rory MacDonald and D. Brown. He had been instructed to submit (in a sealed envelope) the six sermons which he had preached, and this he did. Proceeding carefully in accordance with Church law, the Presbytery agreed that all objections were relevant if proven, and obtained the acquiescence of all parties to that decision. They found themselves unable to analyse the call and list of objectors for lack of a communion roll. At this point the names of forty-one adherents were added to the call, making a total of seventy-six signatures. Letters were subsequently received from four individuals – three Campbells and a Brown – seeking to be added to the call; unfortunately by then it was in Tobermory and they were obliged to come in person to sign it (NAS CH2/273/7, pp. 16, 18, 24–25).

The objections went to probation. At Tobermory on 1 May JGC appeared before the Presbytery and was told to submit a list of witnesses, as were MacLean, MacDonald and MacFadyen. JGC appeared before the brethren again on 13 June in the church at Kirkapol. By now he had obtained legal representation in the form of William Sproat, writer, Tobermory (for whom see also note 877 on p. 509), and Alexander MacPhie, writer, Glasgow – as did the objectors, in the form of John W. May, writer, Tobermory.

Malcolm Livingstone, session clerk of Tiree, now produced the communion roll.[12] On examination it was found that the call to JGC had been signed by twenty-three communicants and fifty-two other parishioners, while 'the residence of one Vizt. John Rankin is doubtful'. The objections had been signed by thirty-nine individuals, including fourteen communicants, two of whom had now withdrawn; the signatures on the detached papers consisted of 107 names, of which forty-three were communicants. Of these, six communicants and five others had now withdrawn. Even as the brethren deliberated, two more objectors appeared in person to withdraw their names, and four Campbells arrived (the three mentioned above, and one from Coll) to add their names to the call. Precognitions were taken from many individuals on both sides, but although the names of the witnesses are given in the minutes their evidence was always 'recorded separately' and may be assumed to have been destroyed. Among them was Hugh MacAlpine, who was 'interrogated for the Presentee, and examined for the Objectors' at Tobermory on 4 January 1861 (NAS CH2/273/7, pp. 23, 32, 34–35, 38–40, 115).

The formality of the minutes is designed to conceal the evidence, but where the clergy were themselves part of the story a little of the iceberg appears above the surface. This is particularly true of the Rev. Neil MacNeil, minister of Tobermory, who was moderator of the Presbytery until 6 November, when the Rev. Robert Stewart was elected in his place. During the meeting of 13 June Sproat attempted to have MacNeil removed from the chair on the grounds that 'before the objections were given in he Mr Mc Neill recommended or at least suggested that the parishioners should oppose Mr Campbell's settlement and has since advised and encouraged them in their opposition', and that 'he has already indicated an opinion that the Presentee is unsuitable and has thus prejudged the question remitted to probation'. This strategy was ultimately unsuccessful, and in due course Sproat withdrew his allegations, but the Presbytery refused to give its moderator their full backing (NAS CH2/273/7, pp. 43–44, 61–62, 93). Eight years later MacNeil was accused of 'very serious irregularities of life and conduct'; having failed to appear before the General Assembly of 1869 to answer the charges against him, he was deposed from the ministry. He died at Corra, Ardlamont, in 1881 (NAS CH2/273/8, p. 87; Scott 1915–50, vol. 4, p. 123).

JGC was present in person at the diets in Tobermory on 3 July and 2 October. His sermons were declared to be 'part of proof for objectors', and on 5 February 1861, in the course of the Presbytery's meeting in the courthouse at Tobermory, the sealed envelope was opened, and one of them – in English on Luke 3: 8 – was publicly read. The brethren reconvened in the Mull Hotel at 7 p.m. the same evening, where three more (in English on Col. 2: 10 and Job 28: 28, and in Gaelic on Rom. 10: 8–9) were read. The last two (in Gaelic on Acts 26: 8 and Luke 13: 24) were read the following day, and the sermons were 'received as part of Presentee's proof, having already been admitted as part of Objectors' proof' (NAS CH2/273/7, pp. 48, 59, 87, 118–20).

At the Presbytery's meeting in Tobermory on 27 February, JGC's agents 'tendered Certificates certifying the Ministerial gifts of the Presentee, and his fitness for the duties of a parish'. The names of the eight ministers who furnished these certificates are of great interest as reflecting the nature and spread of JGC's connections outwith the county of Argyll. The list is headed by the Rev. Norman MacLeod, D.D., Glasgow, followed by Donald MacKinnon of Strath, John Kinross of Largs, Hugh McArthur of Portree, John Alison of the Middle Church in Paisley, John Campbell of Killin, Donald McFarlane of Rannoch and James McGregor of Paisley.[13] The presentation of these certificates resulted in a brisk exchange during which it was pointed out that they were inadmissable as evidence on the grounds that 'it is not alleged that these parties are Members of the Congregation of Tyree' (NAS CH2/273/7, pp. 123–24).

The debate on the evidence took place at the Presbytery's meetings in Tobermory on 27 February and 1 March 1861. There was a lively discussion, and by Stewart's casting vote as moderator, the first and third objections were found proven, except for the words 'instructive' in the first and 'dry' in the third (NAS CH2/273/7, pp. 126–31).

Throughout the process JGC had had a powerful ally in the form of the clerk to the Presbytery, the Very Rev. Dr John MacLeod, the 'High Priest' of Morvern (1801–82), son of the Rev. Norman MacLeod of Morvern (1745–1824), youngest brother of the highly respected Rev. Dr Norman MacLeod, 'Caraid nan Gaidheal' (1783–1862), and uncle of the above-mentioned Rev. Dr Norman MacLeod of the Barony in Glasgow.[14] John MacLeod now 'protested for leave to complain to next ensuing General Assembly', and Sproat lodged a similar appeal. The six sermons were printed as part of the case for the defence, but for some reason only the three Gaelic ones appear to have survived.[15] Each is followed by the statement:

> That what is contained on this and the [. . .] preceding pages, is a true and correct copy lodged by Mr John Gregorson Campbell with the Presbytery of Mull, as one of the sermons preached by him at Tyree, as Presentee to that Parish, by appointment of Presbytery, is attested this 25th day of April, 1861, by

> (Signed)   JOHN MACLEOD, Presbytery Clerk.

Occasionally JGC's Gaelic raises an eyebrow, as where he writes *sibh-pe* for *sib' fhéin* ('yourselves', revealing his mother's Perthshire pronunciation) or *thairis agus thairis a rìs* ('over and over again' translated without heed to Gaelic idiom), but in the main his preaching is marked by good style, freedom and courageous orthodoxy.[16] In his sermon on Rom. 10: 8–9, for example, we find:

> Tha dream ann aig nach 'eil creideimh idir; tha dream eile ann aig am bheil seòrsa do chreidimh, ach cha 'n fheairrd' iad e a bheag. Is iad sin an dream tha cosmhuil ri Sìmon an Drùidh, cosmhuil ris an droch thalamh as am bheil sìol an fhocail air a thoirt air falbh le droch spiorad, a seargadh gu neo-bhrigh, no air a mhùchadh le luibheanaich, le droighionn is le cuilc; cosmhuil riusan ris nach d' earb' Criosd e fein; luchd aidmheil a chreidimh, nach 'eil fathast nam fior-chriosduighean. Tha 'n dream sin cosmhuil ri craoibh, air am bheil duilleach ach nach 'eil a giùlan toraidh; coltach ri solus nach 'eil a toirt seachad blàths'. Tha creidimh aca, ach tha e marbh, neo-thorrach; tha iad a faicinn Chriosd mar a chunnaic Balaam mac Bheòir e; tha iad ga fhaicinn ach is ann fada bh' uap'; tha iad ga fhaicinn ach is ann "o mhullach nan creag agus o na sleibhtean." Tha an creidimh diomhain, tha iad fathast ann nam peacannan.

> ("There are those who have no faith; there are others who have a kind of faith, but are little the better of it. These are the ones who are like Simon Magus, like the bad ground from which the seed of the word has been taken away by an evil spirit, withering to nought, or stifled by weeds, brambles and reeds; like those to whom Christ did not trust himself; confessors of the faith, who are still not true Christians. These are like a tree, which has foliage but bears no fruit; like a light that gives no warmth. They have faith, but it is dead, barren; they see Christ as Balaam son of Beor saw him; they see him but from afar; they see him but 'from the top of the rocks and from the hills'. Their faith is vain, they remain in sin.")

Likewise, in his sermon on Luke 13: 24 we find:

Feudaidh, cha 'n e mhàin moran eolais a bhi aig neach, ach mar an ceudna tiodhlaca spioradail, àrd agus urramach, agus gun e bhi 'na Chriosduidh. Feudaidh e ùrnuigh a dheanamh, feudaidh e searmonachadh, feudaidh e fàidheadaireachd a dheanamh gun ghràs Dhé a bhi 'na chridhe. Feudaidh talanndan ar deanamh saibhir a thaobh dhaoine, ach is e gràs a mhàin a ni sinn "saibhir a thaobh Dhé." Cha 'n urrainn iad an cridhe iompachadh, agus cha 'n urrainn esan a ta 'g earbsa asda dol a stigh do rioghachd neimh. Feudaidh iad duine a dheanamh fòghluimte, ach cha dean iad am feasd e na chreidmheach. Ann am briathran an neach sin mu'n do labhair mi cheana, "Feudaidh neach searmonachadh cosmhuil ri Abstol, ùrnuigh a dheanamh cosmhuil ri aingeal, agus gidheadh cridhe deamhain a bhi aige." Bha tiodhlaca mòr aig Iudas, oir bha e na dheisciobull, na Abstol a searmonachadh an t-soisgeil, gidheadh tha Iudas "air dol g'a àite féin;" bha tiodhlaca mòr aig na Sgriobhaichean agus aig na Phàirisich, gidheadh "c'àit' am bheil an duine glic? c'àit' am bheil an Sgriobhaiche?"

("A person may not merely have much knowledge, but also spiritual gifts that are great and honourable, without being a Christian. He may pray, he may preach, he may prophesy without having God's grace in his heart. Talents may make us rich toward men, but only grace makes us 'rich toward God'. They cannot convert the heart, and he who puts his trust in them cannot enter the kingdom of heaven. They may make a person learned, but they will never make him a believer. In the words of him of whom I have already spoken, 'A person may preach like an Apostle, pray like an angel, and yet have a demon's heart.' Judas had great gifts, for he was a disciple, an Apostle preaching the gospel, nevertheless Judas has 'gone to his own place'; the Scribes and Pharisees had great gifts, nevertheless 'where is the wise man? where is the Scribe?'")

JGC's fate may have been out of the hands of the Presbytery of Mull, but MacAlpine's was not, and the minute of its meeting at Acharacle on 2 May 1861 comes close to revealing what had been going on (NAS CH2/273/7, p. 140):

The Presbytery resumed consideration of the application on their table from the Revd. Hugh Mac Alpine, Missionary, Tyree, for a Presbyterial Certificate, when, after reasoning, it was unanimously agreed that, inasmuch as Mr. Mac Alpine's name is so much implicated in Tyree case, the Presbytery delay further procedure in this matter till said case, now under appeal to the General Assembly, is finally disposed of.

MacAlpine's reply was clearly intemperate, because at its meeting in Salen on 7 May the Presbytery 'without recording here, any remarks on the tenor of said letter appoint the same to be held in retentis and adhere to the finding already arrived at by them in the matter therein referred to' (NAS CH2/273/7, p. 144). MacAlpine's ecclesiastical career was nearing its end.

JGC's case came before the General Assembly in Edinburgh on Friday 31 May 1861. We may assume that he was in the gallery. He was represented by Adam Gifford and Henry Lancaster, advocates. John Burnet and Alexander Moncrieff, advocates, appeared for the objectors. The Presbytery of Mull was represented by the Revs William Fraser and Neil MacNeil; MacLeod, as Complainer, was heard for himself, and was first to speak.[17]

Dr MACLEOD, of Morven, addressed the Court at considerable length, and with great ability, in support of his complaint against the judgment of the Presbytery. He commenced by saying that if he had seen that the opposition to the settlement of the presentee in this case had arisen from integrity of purpose, or from other than causeless prejudice, he would not have appeared in the position of a complainer to that Assembly against the judgment of the Presbytery. The presentee, he maintained, spoke intelligibly, in an audible voice, and spoke pure Argyleshire Gaelic, so that there could be no objections to him upon these grounds. The Presbytery had found not proven the statement in the first objection that the preaching of the presentee was not instructive, although they had found that it was not impressive. Perhaps the Presbytery would explain how it could be instructive without being impressive, but it was sufficient for his purpose that the Presbytery had thus virtually admitted that the preaching of the presentee was instructive.

Dr Macleod proceeded to notice the evidence for the objectors, maintaining that all the witnesses reasoned in a circle, and that their evidence was neither more nor less than this, that the sermons were cold, dry, and unedifying, because they received no benefit, and they received no benefit from the sermons because they were cold, dry, and unedifying. That, with all respect, was the sum and substance of the whole evidence against the presentee in the case. In the course of his comments on the evidence, Dr Macleod said that one witness, William McKenzie, deponed – "I mean by a dead sermon, a sermon not lively or earnest enough to terrify us – (laughter) – and I apply this to the manner of delivery and to the sermons themselves. I attribute this partially to his holding by the sides of the pulpit." Well, admitting that the presentee held by the sides of the pulpit (said the rev. Doctor), we all know that the young sailor climbing up to the topmast is giddy enough when he first occupies that position, although he soon learns to go aloft nimbly and thoughtlessly; and so the pulpit is a giddy position to the young beginner, and when he sees on any of the faces before him indications of a coming storm, he may well "hold by the sides of the pulpit." (Laughter.)

MacLeod was clearly thinking of the word *crannag*, which in Argyll Gaelic means both 'pulpit' and 'crow's nest'. He continued:

Another witness, D. McKinnon, while stating that the sermons of the presentee were "low, cold, and slow," and that he derived no benefit from them, makes the following admission:—"I had no objections to the sermons, but only to the delivery. The sermon was the truth of God, so far as I heard him." And when he is interrogated whether he conceived that benefit was to be received from the mode of delivery or from the sermon itself, he depones, "I expected to receive benefit from the delivery only." (Laughter.)

In concluding his address, which he did amidst loud applause, Dr Macleod said that though he would be the last to withdraw any of the rights of the people, he maintained that they were not called upon to yield to popular desire farther than the law directed. He contended that the evidence in support of the objections was defective, and that there was abundant evidence to show that they originated in causeless prejudice, and it was the bounden duty of the Assembly, at all hazards, to reverse the judgment of the Presbytery. He scarcely required to assure the Assembly that this was no case of high-handed patronage, as no landed proprietor took a deeper interest in the people residing on his property than His Grace the Duke of Argyle did in the people of Tyree. (Applause.) He regretted that the majority of the Assembly could not judge of the merits of the Gaelic sermons, except through the English, but he would only say in regard to them that it would comfort his heart if in all the Highlands of Scotland such Gaelic sermons were preached. (Hear, hear.) If he could suppose it possible that the Assembly could return a judgment unfavourable to the presentee, he was confident, at least, of this, that in any event the presentee would remain untarnished in his character as a Christian man, and unblemished in his reputation as a gospel preacher. (Applause.)

The next speaker was JGC's counsel Henry Lancaster, who remarked that MacLeod's 'able and conclusive' address had made his duty an easy one, then went on to show 'that the objections were not personal to the presentee, but the result of causeless prejudice'. This oft-repeated phrase dated at least from 1841, when the seventh duke of Argyll had introduced a bill in the House of Lords giving all male communicants above the age of 21 the right to veto a presentation 'provided that the veto should be set aside in every case where it could be proved to have been due to factious and causeless prejudice' (Macpherson 1901, p. 389). It was due to the failure of this bill that the non-intrusionists had begun to give up hope of ever obtaining redress from the legislature, and to think instead of secession – the secession which split the Church so disastrously in 1843. It was now central to JGC's case to prove that there was indeed 'causeless prejudice' against him – to show, without going into detail, that the opposition to his appointment was really based on something which had nothing to do with incompetence, incapacity or immorality. If there had been slanderous gossip about his interest in superstitions, this was never going to be mentioned by either side: it was simply to be comprehended as part of the young man's scholarly bent. Following an adjournment, the case for those opposed to the call was opened by John Burnet.

> He began by referring to the number of objectors, contending that not only were they numerically superior to the callers, but that they included a larger number of communicants than there were among the callers. He was also, he thought, entitled to say, without casting any reflection upon the noble patron, the Duke of Argyle, that the fact that the parishioners were all tenants-at-will of his Grace had certainly not tended to diminish the number of the callers, as it had not tended to increase the number of the objectors. In fact, it was notorious that the feeling among the parishioners was very strong against the presentee. Mr Burnet proceeded to comment upon the evidence for the objectors, giving it as his opinion that, unless the Assembly were prepared to charge the witnesses with perjury, they could not possibly disregard and set it aside.

The issue of democracy was fundamental to the Church. In many Lowland parishes where patrons no longer exercised their rights, the minister was already chosen by communicant members. In this case, Burnet was alleging, opposition to the presentation would have been greater still were it not for fear and toadyism among the duke's tenants. Next to speak was JGC's counsel Adam Gifford.

> He said that the key to the whole case was to be found in the fact that eleven hundred people had petitioned the patron for Mr McAlpin, who had formerly been assistant in the parish. He submitted that it was clear from the evidence that it was not dislike to Mr Campbell, the presentee, but love for Mr McAlpin that had originated the objections in this case, and that he was, therefore, entitled confidently to ask the Assembly to dismiss the objections as founded on causeless prejudice.

After Moncrieff had replied for the objectors, the parties were removed and the debate began. JGC's former teacher, Alexander Hill, moved 'that the Complaint and the Appeal be sustained; that the sentence of the Presbytery of Mull be reversed; and that the Presbytery be enjoined to sustain the call, and to proceed to the settlement of the Presentee with all convenient speed, according to the rules of the Church'. The Rev. Samuel Cameron of Logierait moved to 'dismiss the Complaint and Appeal; affirm the judgment of the Presbytery of Mull refusing to proceed to Mr J. Gregorson Campbell's settlement in the parish of Tyree'. Hill's motion was seconded by Irvine of Blair Atholl and Cameron's by the Rev. Dr William Pirie, professor of Church History at the University of Aberdeen, whose opposition to JGC was firmly based on principle.

> He believed that the Act of Lord Aberdeen was to a certain extent on its trial, and he believed that on the decision the Assembly now gave in this and in future cases – for he feared they would have to carry on the struggle for a few years yet – would mainly depend whether he and a considerable number of members of this House, be not compelled to unite with Dr Lee in some such motion as he had brought forward. He believed the presentee in this case was a young man of no ordinary talent – a young man of high character and deserved reputation, and who, in the right place, would do honour to the Church of Scotland. But the question was whether, under Lord Aberdeen's Act, he was suited to the parish of Tyree. The question then involved was this, how far was the man suitable to the education, character, wants, and circumstances of the people of the parish? If they found a decided majority of the communicants coming forward solemnly to swear to objections peculiar to their own parish, which were applicable to their own feelings, they were entitled to be believed if they were honest and respectable men; and if these men said that the presentee was an inefficient or cold preacher to them, without spiritual fervour to them – it might be right or wrong on their part – still he held that the Assembly were bound to reject the presentee.

It was Pirie who went on in due course to secure the abolition of patronage by vote in the General Assembly of 1869 and by Act of Parliament in 1874; his caveat 'if they were honest and respectable men' was to prove the flaw in the objectors' case. The Rev. Dr James Bissett of Bourtie in Aberdeenshire spoke in support of Hill's motion, remarking 'that the sermons of the presentee were the best he had ever seen brought up to the Assembly under Lord Aberdeen's Act', and the Assembly then looked to the Rev. Dr Robert Lee – minister of Old Greyfriars, professor of Biblical Criticism at the University of Edinburgh, and a sworn opponent of patronage – to see whether or not he was willing to accept JGC's opponents as honest standard-bearers of democracy. Clearly he was not, for he opted instead to pick up Bissett's hint, turning a debate about democracy into one about preaching.

> He looked to the objections made to this rev. gentleman, and to the evidence thereof, and he found that all that was proved was this, that, in the opinion of certain people who had evidently been accustomed to a very vehement, boisterous, exciting style of preaching, his manner was too cold. He believed the presentee was a superior man, and he gathered so much from his sermons. He thought it, therefore, very likely that he should preach rather calmly, because he generally found that sound and sense were in the inverse ratio the one to the other. He thought that a man like this presentee required the protection of the General Assembly, and of all the Courts of the Church. There was too much demand among them, if he might speak without offence, for sound and fury, signifying nothing.

(Hear, hear.) Sober, vigorous, good sense was the thing that was needed, and if presentees were to be victimised because they could not roar so loud as some desired, and to be sent back to their studies in order to acquire that qualification, he, for one, thought they should teach the people a better lesson, and he had no fear that bad consequences would result to the Church. The settlement of a really good man never had done harm to the Church, but a blockhead settled in any parish, with whatever approbation, only became a nuisance and a running sore. (Applause.)

Lee was making the subtle point that democracy was not an end in itself but a means to an end – the end being to drive up standards and to avoid the imposition of blockheads on the Church by whatever mechanism. As principal of St Mary's theological college in St Andrews, the Rev. Dr John Tulloch was bound to agree with him:

He thought the presentee was in every sense a man of conspicuous talent. The English sermons, he thought, contained a clear, solid, vigorous statement of Christian truth, and judging merely from the words of the sermons, he should say they were impressive. Still, he admitted that these sermons might be excellent and yet not suited for the parish. Sermons might be thought warm in Greyfriars' perhaps, or in any other parish in Edinburgh, and yet be thought cold in the latitude of Tyree. (Laughter.) They were bound in that view, then, to take in the element of suitableness as to the character of the sermons. But looking to the sermons themselves, and to the evidence, it appeared to him that on this record that element of unsuitableness was not proved. In one word, he thought prejudice explained the whole case.

Pirie's words 'if they were honest and respectable men' must have been haunting him, for he threw in an afterthought.

It was not necessary to disbelieve these people; he believed them perfectly, but it was impossible to read the evidence without coming to the conclusion that prejudice was at the bottom of the whole case.

JGC's head must have been swimming by now at the compliments coming his way from the leaders of the Church. There was more discussion, but the die was cast, and the Assembly's official minute states (*Principal Acts*, 1861, p. 65):

A vote being called for, it was agreed that the state of the vote should be First or Second Motion; and the Roll being called, and votes marked, it carried First Motion by 182 to 18. Whereupon the First Motion became the judgment of the House. Parties were called in, and the judgment intimated; whereupon Dr John McLeod, for himself, and Mr Alex. Morison for the Presentee, took instruments and craved extracts, which were allowed. Messrs Cameron, Logierait, and McKenzie, Urquhart, dissented.

The young folklorist had won a spectacular victory. At Salen on 9 July he passed his trials for ordination with flying colours, and in the church at Balinoe on Thursday 22 August 1861 he was duly ordained as minister of Tiree and Coll.[18] It was a solemn occasion in more ways than one, for only three ministers attended, Donald MacFadyen (as moderator), John MacLeod and James MacColl. MacLeod's minutes, always meticulously kept, read here like a journal, and the tension is palpable.[19]

The Presbytery find that none of the brethren have come up, and that the extremely boisterous state of the weather this day renders a passage from Mull impracticable. They accordingly, under these circumstances, judge it best to proceed, more especially as the Revd. James McColl assistant Minister is present with them to take part in the solemn service of Ordination.

JGC went to live in the manse at Kirkapol on Gott Bay, where he remained for the rest of his life.[20] Only once, when offered the assistantship of St Columba's in Glasgow, did he consider leaving (Campbell 1895, p. xi). He did not attend Presbytery meetings for a while, and was absent when on 28 November 1861 at Salen the brethren took the step that effectively terminated MacAlpine's career in the ministry, instructing their clerk simply 'to grant Mr McAlpine an extract of his ordination, and to certify the time that he officiated as Missionary at Tyree' (NAS CH2/273/7, p. 164). JGC turned up at the Presbytery's meeting in the church of Kilmore in Mull on 6 May 1862, however, bringing with him a petition for a garden wall and 'offices' to be erected at the Manse of Tiree. The Presbytery threw themselves with remarkable gusto into the more agreeable challenge which he had now set them, obtaining a plan 'for the accommodation of six cows three horses with barn, cart shade & of corresponding dimensions' and filling many pages of minutes with deliberations about measurements, contractors and how to levy the heritors for the cost. Six years later, JGC came back looking for a loan to help him fence his glebe; this, too, they took in their stride.[21] In the meantime, on 29 November 1864, MacLeod informed his delighted brethren that Coll was to be made into a fully separate *quoad omnia* parish for the first time since 1618, the necessary funding having been made available by John Lorne Stewart of Coll and Colin Campbell of Caolas and augmented by a grant of £1,000 from the Endowment Committee of the Church. Disjunction was formalised on 11 March 1865, and on 13 March 1866 the trustees presented the Rev. Archibald Campbell, Ardrishaig, as first minister of the new parish; James MacColl promptly resigned and went to Canada.[22]

Clearly JGC had enemies in his own flock as well as in the Free Church and amongst Baptists and Congregationalists, but he had shown that he could stand up for himself. He was the epitome of the 'Moderate' – a man with a liberal education who took a broad view of the needs of his parishioners – and in a graphic little anecdote published after his death he makes clear his view of narrower forms of piety than his own: "On one occasion, the writer being himself ensconced under the side deck of a smack, then plying to the island, heard a Tiree boatman, who was conversing with a minister from the south of Argyleshire, and had no fancy for the overly pious talk of the too-zealous stranger, remarking that there was an old woman here and when she gave a snort, she could be heard over in Coll. ['*Tha Cailleach an so 's trà nì i sreothart cluinnidh iad 'an Cola i.*'] The minister said that that was most extraordinary, and as it now began to rain the boatman began to exhort him to go below, and professed much regard for the minister's health. At last he got rid of him."[23]

The Tireeman's *cailleach* was of the type described by JGC in 'A' *Chailleach*, the Old Wife' (p. 544 above), and in Campbell 1914–15. We should also note his brusque dismissal at p. 112 of the very common 'water-horse and children' tale as 'a pious fraud', and the relish with which he tells at p. 176 how one of the most revered evangelicals of the past, the Rev. Lachlan MacKenzie, took on a witch – and lost. Finally in *The Fians* he remarks (Campbell 1891, p. xi): "It cannot but be deplored that the 'rigid righteousness' and rigid wisdom have led to the loss of much valuable matter."

The best record of any Presbyterian minister's stewardship of his parish will normally be his kirk session minutes. The venerable minute book of Tiree, dating from 1775, is preserved in the National Archives of Scotland (NAS CH2/482/1). The minutes for 1861 and 1862 are in the hand of Malcolm Livingstone, the session clerk. Following JGC's induction (p. 429) we read of five meetings taking place at Moss, one nearby at Balinoe and one at Kirkapol (pp. 430–33, 436–41). In addition, at pp. 434–35, under the heading 'Population of Tirij at Census 1861', JGC jotted in the totals of houses and people for the various townships. At the end of 1862, however, a curious development took place, and it is difficult not to see it as an omen of his later stewardship of the parish. Livingstone writes:

> Kirkapol 15 Dec/62. This book with the Kirk-Session, Cash-Book Box and documents is this day delivered to The Rev J. G. Campbell per Alexr. McKinnon
>
> M. Livingston,
>
> his
> Alex ✗ McKinnon,
> mark.

From this point on the minutes are in JGC's hand. At pp. 442–50 he documents nine more meetings, five at Kirkapol and four at Moss. That of 4 October 1864 follows those of 21 and 29 December that year, which suggests that he mislaid some of his notes for a while. The one at Kirkapol on 23 May 1865 is the last to be documented. Following it, at the foot of p. 450, we find, in the hand of a man born in that very township, but not until the following year:

> The minutes of the Session do not seem to have been entered in this Book from 1865 until now and no record of the minutes during that period now remains.
>
> Hector MacKinnon
> Minister of Tiree
>
> Mar. 29. 1893.

JGC's sixteen recorded meetings are typical of their period in being almost entirely taken up by matters of discipline. At only three meetings out of the sixteen did discussion of anything else (e.g. money) take place. The discipline cases may be summarised as follows: alleged adultery (also referred to as 'criminal connection') 1; alleged assault 1; alleged fornication (also referred to as 'improper connection', 'improper intercourse', 'carnal knowledge') 8; alleged infanticide 1; paternity 3; total, 14. A case of alleged fornication which focuses upon certain Gaelic words is cited above, p. xlvi. As a social document, however, the most interesting minute by far is the following, which covers alleged cases of infanticide, assault, adultery and a request for baptism (pp. 438–40):

Moss Church
6th Aug. 1862.
Sedt. Revd. John G. Campbell, Moderator &
Messrs. Dond. McLean, Neil Brown,
Alex. McLean & Neil McLean, Elders.

Compeared Margt. Maclean, Balevullin, complaining that Hector Cameron, also in Balevullin, had called her a whore, & had accused her of having done away with an illegitimate child she had & buried it in the dunghill.

From the evidence of Mary Brown, Ballevullin, it appeared the parties had quarrelling when Kelp-making at Craginnis, behind Hough, Margt. Maclean having led to it by having accused the said Hector Cameron of stealing some of her sea-ware; that both parties were excited, and were using language merely to provoke each other.

Compeared also the said Hector Cameron, who admitted that he had never seen any reason for the accusation which he had made; that the language had been used by him when angry and excited, & he now expresses his sorrow for having lost his temper & given expression to such unbecoming language. In token of which he subscribed a declaration to that effect before the session; and as his conduct seemed to have been most culpable the session agreed that baptism should not be admitted to him for his child, (which he now asks) for some time, and both parties were admonished by the Moderator.

Compeared also Anne Cameron, dwarf, Balefuel, complaining of Allan Mackinnon & Archd. Macdonald, both residing at Balefuel, having entered her house through the night & taken hold of her in an unbecoming manner. On being further interrogated she confessed that she could not positively assert that it was these lads & could not be sure. The said Allan McKinnon & Archd. McDonald also compeared, & denied the accusation & expressed their willingness to make oath to that effect.[24] The case appeared to the session to be too trivial to call for their further steps in it, & the parties were dismissed with a caution.

At this point in the meeting JGC read out the judgement of the Presbytery of Mull in the case of alleged adultery. It had been dismissed by the session, but was referred to the higher court as a matter of routine – a relic of a Form of Process established by the General Assembly of 1707, which required kirk sessions to refer such serious sins as 'incest, adultery, relapse into fornication, murder, atheism, idolatry, witchcraft, charming, heresy and error' directly to the Presbytery (Cameron 1993, p. 245). The Presbytery approved the session's handling of the case, formally acquitting the three (!) accused and remitting to the session to deal with the complainant, 'whose conduct in the case has on his own admission been so very reprehensible according to the laws of the Church'. The meeting ended with the request for baptism:

Donald McKinnon, Crofter, Balemartin, appeared asking for baptism for an illegitimate child of John McKinnon, his son, & Mary McDonald, Moss, being their second lapse. On the said Donald McKinnon agreeing to hold the child himself for baptism, his request was allowed.

John G. Campbell, Modr.
Malcolm Livingston, Sess. Clk:

It will be clear by now that the fact that kirk session minutes disappear after May 1865 does *not* mean that JGC was not a good shepherd during the first half of his thirty-year ministry. He may have simply lost the taste for discipline cases, as had many of the more intelligent ministers of his generation. Indeed the Presbytery of Mull had faith enough in him to send him back to Edinburgh as one of their commissioners to the General Assembly in 1862, 1869, 1873 and 1876.[25] What it *does* mean is that, secure in his double mandate of ducal patronage and the Assembly's astonishing 182–18 vote in his favour, he felt free to do what he liked, and clearly his top priority was collecting folklore. We find him engaged in fieldwork as early as 19 February 1863, when he took down 'Sir Uallabh O'Corn' from Donald Cameron, Ruaig (Campbell 1886–87, p. 69). He got 'MacPhie's Black Dog' from Cameron in the same year (see p. 58 above); elsewhere, in a note subscribed 'Manse of Tiree, / 1st Jany, 1883' (Campbell 1885b, p. 273), he tells us that the tale was 'written down about twenty years ago from the dictation of Donald Cameron, Ruag, Tiree'. Of 'The Battle of the Sheaves' he says (Campbell 1891, p. 174): "This story was written as it was told by Donald Cameron, a native of Tiree, in the year 1865. Many other tales (*Sgeulachdan*) and songs (*orain*) were taken down from him at the time, and the writer cannot but express his admiration of Cameron, as the best reciter he has ever fallen in with."

Is it possible that this explains why 'Sir Uallabh' reads, in Bruford's words, 'like a complete repertoire of descriptive "runs" . . . linked by a few sentences of narrative'? Did Cameron himself make the selection, as Linda Gowans has suggested (p. xix above)? A year or two before his death in 1891 JGC wrote of a story about MacLaine of Lochbuie and his two herdsmen, alleged to date from 1602 (Campbell 1895, p. 32): "This tale was written down as it was told by Donald Cameron, Rùdhaig, Tiree, more than twenty-five years ago, and to whose happy and retentive gift of memory it is a pleasure to recur. He had a most extensive stock of old lore, and along with it much readiness and willingness to communicate what he knew."

JGC explains that Donald Cameron was 'in the lower rank of life; he had been at one time a crofter or small farmer, but was made a cotter, *i.e.* one without any land, not through any fault of his own, but from an idea that land would be better in larger holdings' (Campbell 1885b, p. 262). This was an example of the kind of tenurial reorganisation by the Argyll Estate in Tiree that eventually led to open rebellion (pp. 663–64 below), and these words of JGC's appear to me to encapsulate his view of the land question. Cameron was landless through no fault of his own; the amalgamation of holdings was 'an idea'. These sentiments do not seem remarkable nowadays, but during the early years of his ministry JGC was at the centre of a revolution imposed from the top by an opinionated duke. No doubt there is correspondence on the subject from JGC to the duke in the archives at Inveraray, but as these are currently closed to researchers, the nearest we can approach to their contents is, I think, the following words written to the duke on 4 June 1863 by Sir John McNeill of the Colonsay family (1795–1883). McNeill, the duke's brother-in-law, was the first chairman of the Board of Supervision of the Scottish Poor Law and a passionate believer in assisted emigration as a solution to Highland poverty.[26]

This afternoon's post brought me your letter of yesterday, inclosing one from The Revd. Mr. Campbell which I now return. It is a great pity that he is not more capable than he appears to be of giving the poor people of Tyree sound advise [*sic*] as to their worldly affairs &

prospects. If he were he might I think save them & their families much suffering. It appears to me to be so obvious that for them there is no other possible escape from misery than to leave the Island that cannot maintain them and Mr. Campbell's own statements point so distinctly to that conclusion that it is not easy to understand how he has managed to miss it or does not choose to see it. He does not expressly say so but I understand him to hint that further eleemosynary aid will be required and that the Proprietor is expected to furnish it. But the expectation of such aid is what prevents them from seeking what so far as I am able to see is the only permanent remedy that is practicable.

True to form, McNeill goes on to suggest that the duke provide assistance for emigration to those in Tiree who cannot afford to do it by themselves. It is a credit to JGC that in such a fundamental matter as the people's right to their land, he appears to have declined to toady to the magnate who had put him where he was, holding firm instead to a belief in the equitable distribution of wealth – and presumably of land – as the Christian solution to overpopulation in this most fertile of islands.

When JGC sat down one early winter's day to prepare 'Cath Gabhra' for publication, he subscribed his text 'Manse of Tiree, / 26th November, 1877' (Campbell 1887–88b, p. 211). Ten years later, when he had found a publisher, he added a prefatory note (*ibid.*, p. 167, cf. 1891, p. 31): "The following poem, or hymn (*Laoidh*) as it is called, was taken down word for word from the dictation of the late Roderick Macfadyen, Scarnish, Tiree, in October, 1868, now nearly twenty years ago. Macfadyen was then about eighty years of age.[27] He said he had learned it from his father, who died when he himself was only fifteen. He told the writer at the same time that old men, when they repeated these Ossianic hymns, put off their bonnets from a feeling of reverence, with which the sensitive reader will readily sympathise. One is, as it were, in the presence, not only of a master mind in the poem, but also in the presence of the deepest sorrow."[28]

The turn of the decade appears to have been a busy and happy time for JGC as he moved on to a variety of other informants in different parts of Tiree and elsewhere. The legend 'Mar a Chaidh Fionn do Rìoghachd nam Fear Mòra' is 'from very full notes taken of the tale as told by Murdoch McIntyre, Kilkenneth, Tiree, in January, 1869'.[29] The ballad of Manus 'was learned about forty-five years ago from a very old man in Balemeanach, Tiree, 1869, by Malcolm McDonald, Scarinish, from whose recitation it was taken down, 1869' (Campbell 1891, p. 113). Twenty-six lines of another ballad, the Muileartach, were 'written down in 1870, from the dictation of James Cameron, a native of Morven resident in Coll' (Campbell 1881b, p. 137 = 1891, p. 158); with regard to the rest of it, JGC explains: "Of the version here given, Part I has never appeared in print. It was written many years ago from the dictation of Duncan McFadyen, Caolas, Tiree, and has been compared with other oral versions; and part II from Duncan Cameron, constable, Tiree, in 1871."[30]

It is not clear to me whether this is the same Duncan Cameron who is mentioned in note 725 on p. 466 as the policeman at Lochaline in Morvern, but he is certainly the individual met by JFC when he visited the island that summer.[31] It was not JFC's first visit – he describes it as 'my return to Tiree' (Campbell 1895, p. 148). It was, however, the highlight of an enthusiastic correspondence between him and JGC which took place during the course of 1871. JFC had published his epoch-making four-volume work *Popular Tales of the West Highlands* in 1860–62, not an ideal time for JGC, who seems to have taken some time to catch up with it – at p. 31 above he speaks of hearing a particular story in Tiree several years before he saw JFC's book.[32]

The exchange of letters appears to have begun at the New Year when JFC wrote to JGC from London, asking to be put on the list of subscribers for the work on superstitions which he had heard he was writing. JGC replied on 10 January, seemingly confirming that he was planning such a book, and expressing the hope that JFC would visit Tiree in the near future. These first two letters have not survived, but the third, along with a number of others, was passed by JGC's sister Jessy to Lord Archibald Campbell (1846–1913), the eighth duke's second son, and found its way into print. In it JFC replies from his home at Niddry Lodge, Kensington, on 16 January (Campbell 1895, p. 148): "I shall be very glad to assist a namesake and a Highland minister who is engaged in literary work, in which I take a special interest myself. I now repeat my message, and ask you to place my name on the list of subscribers, if you have one. I shall be very glad to read your book.

"I am not publishing more Gaelic tales, but I am collecting, and I may some day publish a selection or an abstract or something from a great mass which I have got together. If you have anything to spare from your gatherings perhaps the best plan would be to employ some good scribe, etc. etc. etc. If you have any intention of publishing I beg that you will not think of sending me your gatherings. But anything sent will be carefully preserved. Superstitions are very interesting, but I should fear that the people will not confide their superstitions to the minister."

JFC then suggests that among superstitions particularly worth collecting are those about fowls, serpents, the sea, the connection between tree and well worship, and 'anything that is like the Vedic forms of religion'. He had clearly been reading Max Müller (see Dorson 1968, pp. 160–86). He ends: "All that is curious and very hard to get at. Even to me they will not confess their creed in the supernatural. I have a great lot of stuff that might be useful to you, and I shall be glad to serve you, because there is a certain narrow-minded spirit abroad . . . It is highly probable that I may be out in the west in spring or summer."

JGC appears to have replied that he intended publishing his superstitions but not his tales – the reverse of what actually happened. JFC's response has not survived, but under the heading '1871' we find the following memorandum amongst his papers (NLS Adv. MS 50.2.3, f. 176r): "Feby 8th sent the abstract from which this abstract was made and a letter as a sample of manuscript, to the Revd John Campbell Manse Tiree who has gathered stories, and who is about to publish a book on Fairy mythology and superstitions. He will set someone to copy some of his collection of popular tales, which he will not publish himself. So he says."

The abstract was of the tale 'O'Cian's Leg', a Tiree version of which appears as 'O'Cronicert's Fairy Wife' at pp. 67–70 above. JGC appears to have replied around mid-February, wondering if JFC would send him some books and asking why a man should sign himself *Sàil Dhiarmaid* ('Diarmad's Heel'). JFC wrote back on 27 February from the Travellers' Club in London, promising to get the books and responding phlegmatically to the other query, illustrating the point with a sketch of a foot (Campbell 1895, p. 138). "I know what the man meant who signed Sàil Dhiarmaid."

According to Lord Archibald's transcription, JFC then wrote (*ibid.*): "I have MacNicol, and know his remark about Ossian's leg." This should read 'O'Cian's Leg'. The reference is to McNicol 1779, pp. 321–22:

> In poetical compositions, it is well known that the memory is greatly assisted by the cadence and rhyme; and as to such pieces of any length as we have in prose, they are the more easily retained, as they generally consist of a variety of *episodes*, depending on each other, and highly adapted to captivate the fancy. Among the latter kind are our *Tales*, which are, for the most part, of considerable length, and bear a great resemblance to the *Arabian Nights Entertainments*. One of those, in particular, is long enough to furnish subject of amusement for several nights running. It is called *Scialachd Choise Ce*, or Cian O Cathan's Tale; and though *Scialachies*, or tellers of tales by profession, are not now retained by our great families, as formerly, there are many still living, who can repeat it from end to end, very accurately.

JFC proceeded to tell JGC that he had 'got the only copy of it that ever was written, so far as I know, and I shall be glad to get more'. This refers to one of the salient events in the history of folklore, the transcribing of 'O'Cian's Leg' by Hector MacLean from the dictation of an Islay-born shoemaker called Lachlan MacNeill in a Paisley public-house in August the previous year. It took them a week, for, as J. H. Delargy once pointed out, '*Sgeulachd Cois' O'Céin* is one of the longest folk-tales recorded in Europe'. JFC arrived in person and found them 'both rather screwed. Hector the worst.' He carried them off to a photographer and had a picture taken of the pair at work, with himself in the middle.[33] He goes on: "But we must all take what we can get. As far as fixing the king or the country and the date, that is perfectly hopeless. I have about 16 versions of one story in Gaelic, and no two have the same name. I suppose that there must be sixty versions of it known in other languages, and no two are alike. The oldest I know is scattered in ejaculations and separate lines through the Rigveda Sanhitâ, which is a collection of hymns in Sanscrit, and the oldest things known. St. George and the Dragon is a form of the story. Perseus and Andromeda is another. In Gaelic it is generally *Mac an Iasgair*, or *Iain Mac* somebody, or *Fionn Mac a' Bhradain*, a something to do with a mermaid or a dragon, the herding of cows and the slaying of giants."[34]

He concludes: "The stories to which I referred were told me by John Ardfenaig as facts (the Duke of Argyll's factor in the Ross of Mull). A man built a boat. Another, to spite him, said that the death of a man was in that boat – no one would go to sea in it, and at last the boat was sold by the builder to an unbeliever in ghosts and dreams. The other was how the turnips were protected in Tiree. If you know these you have got far, but if not you have a good deal to learn in Tiree. I wish you success anyhow."

John Campbell, 'Long John', a native of Ardmore in Islay, farmed at Ardfenaig in the Ross of Mull, and also served for some time as the duke's chamberlain in Tiree, where, as we have seen, he was hated. JGC certainly got both stories (see pp. 260, 262 and 663). Curiously, both are connected with Vaul, and the turnip tale is also attached to Long John by way of a complaint about his behaviour in having the turnips protected with rotten whale flesh. JGC's reply of 20 March has not survived, but JFC's of 28 March, again from Niddry Lodge, is one of those printed by Lord Archibald (Campbell 1895, p. 139) and quoted above, pp. xix–xx: "I have been too busy about festivities and work to be able to get the book which I promised to seek for you. I got your letter of the 20th, yesterday, and I am much obliged by your promise to put some one to write for me . . ."

He then continues the discussion about *Sàil Dhiarmaid* which, as Lord Archibald points out, presumably arose from the tradition that when Diarmad measured the boar which he had slain, he was fatally wounded in the heel by one of its bristles. In other words *Sàil Dhiarmaid*, addressed to a Campbell (a descendant of Diarmad Ó Duibhne), is a threat. The 'festivities' he mentions are the nuptials of Queen Victoria's fourth daughter Louise and his cousin Lord Lorne (the future ninth duke of Argyll), which took place at the Chapel Royal, Windsor, on 21 March 1871; JFC had had much to do with organising the ceremony, and describes it in his journal, NLS Adv. MS 50.4.6, ff. 5–11. Curiously, according to the NLS on-line catalogue, JGC was the author of a pamphlet entitled *The Princess' Welcome to Inveraray Castle / Failte na Bana-Phrionns' do Chaisteal Ionaraora*, consisting of a song composed on the occasion of the wedding and subscribed 'ISLAND OF TIREE, / MAY 2, 1871'. This is not so. The author was Archibald Farquharson (1800–78), minister of the Independent congregation, a prolific Gaelic author and poet who was described by Donald MacLean (1915, p. 119) as 'one of the greatest enthusiasts that ever lived for the fostering of a knowledge of the Gaelic language'.[35]

The census of 2 April 1871 finds JGC, aged 36, living in the sixteen-roomed Manse of Tiree at Gott. With him as housekeeper is his eldest sister Mary Bell, given as aged 39, unmarried, and born, like himself, in the parish of Appin. Also in the house are Archibald Kennedy, 20 (an unmarried farm servant), and Janet MacLean, 28 (an unmarried domestic servant), both natives of Tiree. JGC's parents are living prosperously in a six-roomed house at 2 Douglas Row in Portree. Captain Campbell, still working as a steamboat agent, gives his age as 63 and his wife's as 60. They have a domestic servant, Effy Nicolson, unmarried, aged 21, born in Portree. All their surviving offspring have left the nest – just eighteen months previously, on 20 October 1869, at Douglas Row, their daughter Jean (Jane) married Alexander Maclean, 30, tenant of Scarinish Farm in Tiree (son of Donald Maclean, farmer, and his wife Mary Graham), the ceremony being performed by JGC himself.

JGC replied to JFC from the Manse of Tiree the day after the census was taken (NLS Adv. MS 50.2.3, f. 181rv). "I return today per post Carleton's Fairy Legends, with many thanks.[36] The notes you have appended to each chapter are of more interest than the volume itself, in fact they are the only things in the book of any scientific value. I have put a few jottings of my own on a slip of paper inside.

"I also return the abstract of 'O Cein's Leg.' My pcl of paper has not yet come, but I expect it on Friday, & I will lose no time in then sending such fragments of the tale as I have. I have made a note of parts of which I may be able to find further traces."

One person not listed anywhere in the 1871 census is JFC. After the wedding he had taken himself off for a well-earned holiday in Paris. He found himself in the middle of a revolution, which he clearly enjoyed (NLS Adv. MS 50.4.6, ff. 12–59). Following his return to London on 14 April there is much in his journal (*ibid.*, ff. 59–97) on his work as secretary of the Coal Commission and on the development of the automobile. On 1 May JGC wrote to him at Niddry Lodge (NLS Adv. MS 50.2.3, ff. 194r–195v): "I send you today per Book Post a clean copy of the tale of Cian Mac an Luaimh, & a short outline of the Tale as known to Duncan Cameron, Constable, Tiree. The Tale is known in Tiree but in part, – that of which I send copy – to two persons, John McLean, Balemartin, & Malcolm Sinclair, Balefuil. Sinclair, from whom I wrote the version sent, learnt it from McLean.

"The copy was written out by Mr. Malcolm Livingstone, Parish Schoolmaster. I made no particular agreement with him as to the remuneration, but I said I thought 3d. or 4d. per sheet would not be grudged. His eyesight troubles him, & makes him unwilling to undertake any more, but he says there are several boys at the school who write a good hand and read Gaelic fluently, & he thinks they could copy out Tales of this kind if I asked them. I prefer to leave the question of remuneration to yourself. Good copying of Gaelic is a rare accomplishment, & its market value should be higher. On hearing from you I shall do all I can to meet your wishes.

"The first time I go to Glasgow, it will be easy for me to consult the Books I referred to in some public library; and I hope you will not be at any trouble about them."

JGC encloses (ff. 197r–215r, versos blank) the 'clean copy' referred to. In Livingstone's hand, it is headed 'Cian Mac an Luaimh'; it begins *Bha Fear bh' ann an Eirinn* and ends *ach innsidh mi ursgeul beag dhuit*. On the left margin of f. 215r JGC writes 'chorus got from an old man in Mull', and at the top of f. 216r he writes: "The foregoing version was taken down to the dictation of Malcolm Sinclair, Balefuil, Tiree 1869."[37]

He also encloses (ff. 217r–221r, versos blank) the 'short outline' referred to. It is in his own hand and is headed: "Cian Mac an Luaimh. / no Sgeulachd Cas Chian, according to Duncan Cameron, Constable, Tiree. 1871." It has been published by Henderson (1901–03, pp. 262–64). It begins *Bha Bodachan bochd ann an Eirinn d'am b' ainm O Crònaigil*. At ff. 218r–219r a passage in English explains how the king of Ireland must tell twenty-four true tales before Cian's leg can be healed. Following a passage of Gaelic at f. 219r, the tale ends in English at ff. 219r–220r. At f. 221r JGC notes that 'O Cròniceart' should be spelt as 'O Cròiniceart' and 'Còruisg' as 'Còrr-uisg' (see opposite and note 218 on p. 339), then he says: "In deciding which version is preferable that which assigns to the *Sith* wife the shape of a deer, or that of a hare, Gaelic superstition pronounces unmistakeably for the former. The form of a *hare* is ascribed to witches, but that of the deer to the Fairy (or Elle) women. When Thomas the Rhymer was taken away to Fairy Land, two *deer* (these were, two Fairy women) came for him, & there are many Gaelic tales of Fays encountered in the shape of Deer by the hunter. O Cronicert's Fay wife corresponds in every respect to the character assigned in similar tales to the *Bean shìth*. Cf. Gruagach Bàn (West Highl. Tales)."[38]

He then notes more changes of spelling – *cuaill* to *cual*, *aorachan* to *eighreachan* or *oighreachan*, *Torragheal* to *Torra-gheal* – then finally he writes: "Trosdan, a staff."

JFC received JGC's letter and enclosures on 3 May. He replied on the 4th to the effect that he had already sent him a *Times* review of the Rev. Archibald Clerk's *Poems of Ossian in the Original Gaelic* and 'a paper with an account of fighting in Paris, where I was at Easter'. He goes on to say of 'O'Cian's Leg', among much else, that 'between us we have already recovered something of a story 345 years old at least' (Campbell 1895, p. 149). Then in what is now NLS Adv. MS 50.2.3, f. 216r, following JGC's note referring to Malcolm Sinclair, JFC wrote this memorandum: "Read May 4. 1871. – This is manifestly

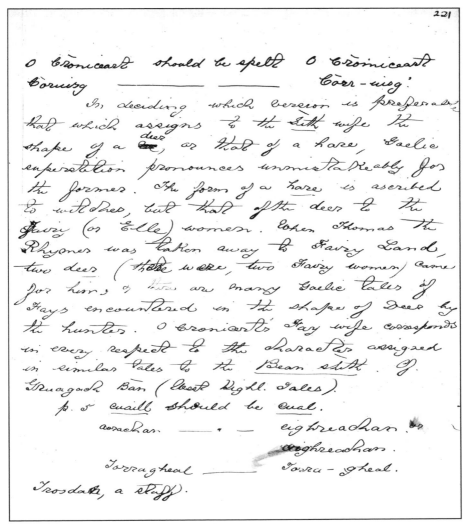

A specimen of JGC's hand: NLS Adv. MS 50.2.3, f. 221r

the same story which I have from Hector Mac Lean and the Islay man, but not nearly so much of it. The use of this version is to mend & amalgamate with the other, & so produce a reconstruction like that which I have made with the dragon story. This is well written and good vernacular local Gaelic, so far as I am able to judge. I have most of the runs &c. in many shapes from many sources some are printed in my book. & some of my stories there printed are here told. These are the same incidents, and this manifestly is a compound story going to bits. – J. F. Campbell."[39]

On 11 August JFC put his work in London behind him for the summer and took the night train north, determined to collect some heroic ballads in the field for his projected new book *Leabhar na Féinne*. He spent some weeks on the mainland, then left Inveraray on Monday 4 September to travel via Oban, Tobermory, Iona, the Ross of Mull (where he visited 'Long John' at Ardfenaig) and Iona (again), reaching Tiree on Friday evening. He wrote home to his mother: "When we got here at half-past ten it was pitch dark and we had to tumble over the side as best we could into a boat with fishermen and girls and boxes and gear. We landed on a rough pier and stumbled up somehow to the splendid Hotel where I am doing the usual thing waiting. I have fallen in with Geikie the Factor and MacQuarrie the Farmer and Brown a tenant at Campbell of Rudhe and the minister Campbell, and a man who works in the Light house boat every one has invited me to his house and I am going to visit MacQuarrie to begin with because he is a good Gaelic man and knows people who have stories, and will get them he says. But if I cared much about it I would try to do otherwise for I am amongst gentry the worst class for my purpose."[40]

This is an extraordinary vignette. First it places JGC in the Scarinish Hotel along with two of the island's most prominent – not to say notorious – characters, John Geikie and Lachlan MacQuarrie. Then it ignores JGC's credentials as a folklorist and all the two men's correspondence, awarding the palm to MacQuarrie instead!

John Geikie or Geekie, a non-Gaelic speaker from Lowland Perthshire, was a son of the factor to the earl of Mansfield. In 1864, when Geekie was a shy young man of 24, the duke had made him factor of Tiree as an 'experiment'. Until the same year MacQuarrie had been the Estate's ground officer in Tiree; now he was farming at Hynish and running a general store at Balemartin, but for the time being he continued to serve as the duke's eyes and ears in the island.[41] As early as May 1866 he observed Geekie turning to drink, and on 9 April 1867 the duke told Sir John McNeill that 'a report has reached me that the Factor in the Island of Tyree, Mr Geekie, whom I got when "John Ardmore" was removed, has become addicted to tippling, if not to drunkenness, and that the people consider him accessible to bribes in Whiskey &c'. Nevertheless, Geekie remained in post until 1876.[42] As for JGC, it is clear that he and JFC were not close, and he proceeded to make things worse. The renowned editor of *Popular Tales of the West Highlands* told his half-sister Castalia that his next encounter with him was on Sunday (NLS Adv. MS 50.4.6, f. 131r, cf. Mackay 1998, p. 121): "The Minister gave us a Gaelic Sermon and then seeing me said that he saw some one who did not understand Gaelic and took to English. His accent might have suited a Frenchman I never heard an accent quite like it."

The remark may have something to do with a tendency to turn final -*n* into a nasalised vowel. We have noticed it in JGC's spelling of *sib' fhéin* ('yourselves') as *sibh-pe*; Donald McNicol, minister of Lismore and a native of Glenorchy, had it too, judging from his spelling of *Céin* as *Ce* (p. 636 above). After this icy start things improved, and on the 15th JFC wrote from Scarinish (NLS Adv. MS 50.4.6, f. 132r, cf. Mackay 1998, pp. 121–22): "Next day. *13th. Wednesday.* I spent with the policeman who says Ossianic ballads very well. I got my own book from the Minister who is a learned man and found that with some variations I have all that the policeman could give and more. We walked up to the house [of] an old fellow here who can repeat the Lay of Osgur and found the same thing. I gave him my book to read when he had finished and he told me that I had misplaced the verses which he learned from his parents here long ago.[43]

"I have almost made up my mind to cease working at poetry for the mine seems to be nearly exhausted. My own story mines not nearly worked out. I get something new every day and if I could catch the people here I should have enough for a new book. I got this from the Minister just now. He got it in Coll. Three Giants lived in a Cave. On a day said one 'Chuala mi geam bo' I heard a Cows low. A year after the second said 'What was that you said a while ago?' But the first said 'nothing'. A year after the third said, 'If you do not cease your chatter I will leave you the Cave to yourselves'. As an illustration of the nature of Giants that little story is a Jewel."

Next day, Thursday 14 September, the weather was beautiful, and JFC took a walk from Scarinish to Caolas (which he calls 'the Sound of Coll'), speaking to people in their fields and houses. He met a man called MacLeod who gave him a drink of milk and challenged him to a wrestling match (NLS Adv. MS 50.4.6, ff. 133r–134r, cf. Mackay 1998, p. 122). "In MacLeod's house is a cripple idiot boy who is generally supposed to be a changeling. He is often quoted to the Minister as a proof of the fact in which all this Island most firmly believe. Coming back from the sound the Minister who had driven the Coll Minister to the ferry overtook me and told me of a stone which is good for raising a storm. A woman told him that she tried the spell for her brother who was a smuggler and chased by a revenue cruiser. According to the Instruction she dug up the stone with the tongs and turned the side to the [*blank*] that was needed but there was not a breath of wind."

This was *Clach na Stoirmeadh* in Caolas, see p. 224 and note 773. All in all it was a successful visit, and in his discussion of the ballads in *Leabhar na Féinne* JFC wrote (Campbell 1872, p. xxxiii): "In 1871 the Policeman in Tiree, who is a native of Ardnamurchan, sang and recited a considerable number of poems of this class to me, and gave me a list of 31 poems, which he could sing, or which he had heard sung, or which he knew about. The Rev. John Campbell, the Minister of Tiree, gave me a list of 8 Tiree men who were noted for reciting tales and poetry of various kinds. John Dewar made a collection of stories and ballads there for the Duke of Argyll; and I heard several men tell long stories and repeat fragments of Heroic verse in 1871."

On Friday 15 September, JGC gave him the splendid 'arming run' which he had obtained at Blair Atholl in 1859 (see pp. 339 and 620). It was his parting gift. JFC left the island that day and went on via Dunvegan to Harris, Barra, Mingulay, South Uist and North Uist, returning to Dunvegan on 5 October; regrettably the journal of his tour stops there.[44] In Uist and Barra he spent a great deal of time with Alexander Carmichael, travelling with him as far as Mingulay, where they were storm-stayed together (*CG2*, pp. 324, 352), and we may ask ourselves why it should be that he sought the company of the one folklorist but not of the other. At any rate, on 9 October, when JGC was on his annual holiday with his parents in Portree, the two men met once again, and the tone of the last two surviving letters which passed between them is fairly cordial. On 10 October JFC wrote to JGC in Portree from Conan House at Dingwall, the residence of his friend Sir Kenneth Mackenzie of Gairloch (Campbell 1895, p. 140): "I promised yesterday at Portree to send you my version of the fairy song, and asked you to return yours. You must remember that I never tried to write it from Gaelic, and that I never tried to write it from rapid dictation till last month. Correct my spelling, but mind that I took the *sounds* from ear, so preserve all that you can without reference to dictionary words. Don't be hard upon a clansman who is doing his best."

With the letter JFC enclosed his fair copy of 'The Fairy Song', along with notes on the reciter – 'John Cameron, a man about 60, who lives in the south end of Barra, about three miles from Castlebay' – and on the underlying tradition (Campbell 1895, pp. 140–44). He wrote (*ibid.*, p. 141): "I have given a rough copy to Miss MacLeod of MacLeod at Dunvegan, and I should like to have *this* or *a copy* back if it is not troublesome."[45]

When Lord Archibald published this material in 1895, ten years after JFC's death, he appended a transliteration and translation of the song which he had commissioned from Duncan MacIsaac of Oban (*ibid.*, pp. 144–47). What MacIsaac (who struggled to make sense of JFC's inadequate field-notes) and Lord Archibald did not know was that JGC had replied immediately with a transliteration and a much better version of his own, and that these were languishing amongst JFC's papers. On 11 October JGC wrote from Portree to JFC at Conan House (NLS Adv. MS 50.2.4, f. 138rv), thanking him for sending the Fairy song. "In return I send, as promised, the version I myself fell in with. You will observe that it is widely different . . ."

After remarking tactfully that neither version was satisfactory, JGC says that the song is probably one of the oldest in Celtic literature, and may throw light on the Picts. He compliments JFC on his Gaelic, then corrects him with regard to the spelling rule known as *leathann ri leathann*, and adds: "In taking down to dictation, the most troublesome sounds I have fallen in with are those of *l* and *ll*, & *n* & *nn*, & I am not sure that I am at all master of them."[46]

He goes on: "It will surely be well worth while getting Cameron's tales and lays taken down. The more versions the better chance of ascertaining the true reading. In Skye, the church has set its face so much against all such lore, that it has nearly disappeared. If I hear of any reciter of tales, I will let you know. I return also a copy of the version of the Fairy song, you have sent me."

To his improved version of JFC's 'Fairy Song' (ff. 139r–140r) JGC appended a note (f. 140rv): "I can make little out of the above in its present form. Is *mo mhilidh bhog* the '*mo bhile bhog*' of the following. J.G.C."

He continues: "The story connected with the Tiree Fairy song is this. A woman in Islay was taken away by the Fairies, but her child, the name of which was *Sìle* (Julia) was left. A nurse was got for it, & every night she heard the child's mother coming & singing to it the following lullaby. One night the husband remained on the watch, surprised his Elf-abducted wife, and, clasping his arms round her, refused to let her go. At last she told him, how he might get her back. On the first day of the following quarter of the year, he took with him a black cock born at a busy time of year (*coileach du màrt*, it is not known which, *màrt buain* or *mart cur an t-sìl*) and steel (*cruaidh*), and finding the brugh open, entered. Great festivities were going on within. The man hid himself in a corner. Near day break the cock crowed. The head fairy ordered a search. 'Big pitiless merciless Martin' (*Màrtuinn mòr gun iochd gun tròcair*) was found, & as he would not go away without his wife, she was sent off with him."[47]

JGC follows this with his Tiree version of the song (ff. 140v–141r). Headed 'Lullaby', it begins *Mo Shìle bhog bhinn thu* and ends *O mo leanabh 7c*. "The above," he explains (f. 141r), "was got from a young man, Walter Campbell, Gortendonald, Tiree, who learned it from his father. The song was much longer, but he does not think there is any one in Tiree who knows any of it. The following verses I quote from memory. I have heard them from Dr Maclachlan, Rahoy, and Hugh McDonald, Tiree."[48]

The verses that follow (f. 141rv) begin *Mo bhile bhog bhinn thu* and end *Mo bhìs òtach*. JGC concludes (f. 141v): "I am told a common Barra expression is ''s a bhi sàtach,' meaning 'my dear sir,' 'my good fellow,' as being originally 'a bhiadh 's eudach,' food & clothing."[49]

Whether the two men continued to correspond I do not know, but clearly JGC was encouraged by the interest taken in his work by the acknowledged pioneer of scientific folklore collection. He got some Ossianic fragments at some point in 1871 from 'a very estimable man' whom he does not name (Campbell 1891, p. 164), and in October that year he took down a version of 'Duan na Ceàrdaich', the so-called 'Lay of the Smithy', from Angus MacVurrich or MacPherson at Portree (*ibid.*, p. 159), but by about 1872, when JFC's new book appeared, he had turned his attention back to superstitions. In an article subscribed 'Manse of Tiree, 1st Jany, 1883' he tells us (Campbell 1885b, p. 263): "An old man of nearly eighty years of age, a native of the island of Mull, examined by the writer ten years ago upon the subject of Highland superstitions, said, 'I have always heard that deer were fairy cattle, and I have never heard that the fairies had any other.'"

JGC refers at p. 15 above to this interview as having taken place in Mull 'some years ago'. As Chapter 14 of *The Gaelic Otherworld* was written in 1874 (see p. 212 and note 675), it is difficult to know what biographical weight to put on this evidence. Is 'ten years ago' intended vaguely, leaving us to guess that the interview in Mull took place as early as 1870, when we found JGC in Coll? Is 'ten years ago' correct, pushing the interview forward again to 1872 or 1873 and the writing of Chapter 1 to the second half of the decade? If Chapter 1 was written in or shortly before 1874, it is unlikely that JGC would *subsequently* make an addition to it containing information obtained in 1870–73. All that can be said for certain is that, with one exception, there is a gap of nine years, 1871–80, in the sequence of JGC's dated fieldwork sessions relating to the collection of tales and ballads.

The exception concerns John Campbell, Hianish. Introducing 'Mar a Chaidh an Tuairisgeul Mòr a Chur gu Bàs', JGC wrote (Campbell 1881a, pp. 61–62): "The following tale was written down some years ago, in Gaelic, from the dictation of John Campbell, Hianish, Island of Tiree. It has the chief or necessary recommendation of whatever is gathered from oral sources, that it is given exactly as it came to hand, and that it is as free to the reader to draw his own conclusions from the language, or any other part of it, as to the person who committed it to writing . . . The translation is literal in the proper sense of the word – that is, each clause is rendered by the English expression which conveys to the English reader the same idea and the same phase of thought that the Gaelic conveys to the Gaelic reader. When there is anything noticeable in the difference of idiom, it is pointed out."

The phrase 'some years ago', probably written in 1880, suggests that the tale was taken down in the 1870s, but there is every indication that JGC's main academic activity during that decade was the writing-up of what is now *The Gaelic Otherworld*. He was a stranger as yet to academic publication – nothing survives in print from his early life except his three sermons – but the books to which he refers in his text (e.g. Peacock

1863, Anon. 1869, Campbell 1872, see pp. 67, 191 and 208 above) point to his reading and research having been done in the late 1860s and early 1870s, so I think it is reasonable to conclude that the work as a whole was put together around 1874. Other dating clues in the text are 'as late as 1867' (p. 256) and two recollections of events in 1870 (p. 263). Only one item, the mention of Kuno Meyer at p. 221 (see note 762), suggests a later date (1885–91); it is possible that JGC completed the text in the 1870s, but added to it from time to time. At any rate, in glossing his frequent datings of the type 'two or three summers ago', 'about twenty years ago', etc., I have chosen to assume in my notes that they were written *c.* 1874, and that 'about twenty years ago' therefore means '*c.* 1854'. Two small checks on this are available to us. Firstly, at p. 112 JGC says that the island in Loch Cuaich (Quoich) was tenanted by Ewen MacPhie 'some thirty years ago'; if we describe this as meaning '*c.* 1844' it is entirely accurate, as MacPhie lived on the island towards the end of his life and died in 1850. Secondly, at p. 149 JGC remarks that he 'was told that the duke of Athole brought white cattle to Blair more than fifteen years ago'; this would mean before 1859, precisely the year JGC spent at Blair Atholl.

By 1873 JGC's sister Jessy was working as a schoolmistress in Tiree, and on 22 April that year, in the Manse at Gott, JGC had the pleasure of marrying her to James Wallace. On the certificate Jessy gives her age as 36 (she was actually 40); James gives his as 45. He describes himself as 'Assistant Store Keeper General, Inland Revenue (Bachelor)' and gives his address as Osney Crescent, Camden Road, St Pancras, London. His parents are William Wallace ('Merchant Deceased') and Margaret Wallace, *née* Boyd. The witnesses, besides JGC himself, are Andrew Wallace and Jessy's brother-in-law Alexander Maclean. James and Andrew were respectively the third and thirteenth of the fourteen children of William Wallace and his wife Margaret Boyd of Irvine in Ayrshire – James born 7 September 1827, Andrew born 30 August 1848 (OPR Irvine).

They were presumably related in some way to the former Head Lightkeeper at Skerryvore, also James Wallace. Skerryvore is a sea-rock twelve miles west of Tiree (see p. 42 above). A lighthouse was built upon it in 1838–42, and during those years the shore base at Hynish expanded into a busy little colony of 150 souls. The 1861 census of Tiree lists James Wallace the lightkeeper, aged about 41 and understood to be a native of Leith, with his family at Hynish: his wife Marion, 40 (from Leith Walk in Edinburgh), and their children Janet, 18, James, 16, Marion, 14, Elizabeth, 10, and George, 8. Each of the four youngest – born at Dunnet Head lighthouse in Caithness or at Portpatrick in Wigtownshire – is described as 'scholar', and it is likely that one of their teachers during the 1860s was Jessy. She is not picked up, however, by the 1871 census.

Jessy's husband whisked her off to London, where they lived at 9 Busby Place, round the corner from his old lodgings at Osney Crescent. But the marriage was to be a short and tragic one, as we will see in due course.

It must have been around this time that JGC heard that Dr Alexander Nicolson from Skye (1827–93), the sheriff of Kirkcudbright, was preparing a new expanded edition of Donald Macintosh's *Gaelic Proverbs* of 1785. Apparently unsolicited, he sent Nicolson a large collection of material that he had gathered himself (see note 207 on p. 605). This appears to have led to an occasional correspondence that continued until the appearance in 1881 of the first edition of Nicolson's book, which remains the definitive collection of Gaelic proverbs to this day. When Nicolson (1951, p. 320) cites an item like *Mur b'e eagal an dà mhàil, bheireadh Tiridhe an dà bhàrr* ('But for fear of double rent, Tiree would yield a double crop') we may guess that he got it from JGC; when he then remarks that it is 'very suggestive, and not confined to Tiree', we cannot know whether the source of the additional information is JGC, Nicolson himself, or both, but the fact remains that any reference to Nicolson's book is always worth checking for its commentary.

When Nicolson visited the island in 1883 in his official capacity as a member of the Napier Commission, JGC was physically unable to meet him, but until 1877 he seems to have enjoyed robust health – he was able both to indulge in some strenuous duck-shooting and to make a cheerful song about it. Here, with my translation, is his 'Òran a' Ghunna' ('The Song of the Gun', Cameron 1932, pp. 139–41). He had borrowed the gun, and perhaps the song was by way of payment; its personification as a sweetheart is a well-established convention in Gaelic verse, and he handles it charmingly.

E horo mo ghunnachan,
    Gur mòr a thug mi spéis dhuit;
Nuair dh'fhalbhainn feadh nam munaidhean
Gun cuireadh e gach mulad dhiom,
'S gur sunndach mi a h-uile lath'
    On chaidh a cur gu feum leam.

An gunna fhuair mi iasad dhith,
B'e 'n diùthail i bhith dìomhanach —
Gur cuimseach, cinnteach, ciatach i
    Gu ianach feadh nan sléibhtean.

Gur mise ghabh an cùram dhith:
Nigh mi agus sgùr mi i
'S thug mi nial na sùithe dhith
    'S chaidh ùilleadh ri 'cuid ghleusan.

Chaidh fùdar cléibh is cluaise innt',
Chaidh làn a béil de luaidhe innt',
'S nuair fhuair mi air mo ghualainn i
    Bu luaineach bha mo cheuman!

Dh'fhiach mi 'n Druim a' Bhòrdain i,
Ri feadagan gun d' sheòl mi i;
Bha dithis marbh gun deò annta
    Is fras a beòil fo'n sgéithidh.

Thog mi leam do Chòrnaig i,
An t-àite 'n robh mi eòlach ann,
'S gur tric bha lacha leòinte leath'
    'S a bha na geòidh fo chreuchdan.

Aig eilean sin an Dùdaire
Is tric a chuir mi smùid aiste,
MacTall' is tric a dhùisg mi leath'
    Sna creagan cùl na cèardaich.

E horo my darling gun,
    How much I've come to love you;
When I'd go off around the hills
It would banish all my sorrow,
And I'm contented every day
    Since I began to use her.

It's a pity for the gun
I got a loan of to lie idle —
She's unerring, sure and lovely
    For shooting birds around the moors.

I've taken very great care of her:
I've washed her and I've scoured her
And removed the film of soot from her
    And kept her mechanism oiled.

She's had powder for chest and ears in her,
She's had a mouthful of lead in her,
And when I got her on my shoulder
    How frisky were my steps!

I tried her in Druim a' Bhòrdain,
I aimed her at some plovers;
Two were dead and lifeless
    From her barrel-blast under their wings.

I brought her with me to Cornaig,
The place I was acquainted with,
And she often left duck wounded
    And geese with injuries.

At that isle of the Dùdaire
I often banged away with her,
Often wakening Echo with her
    In the rocks behind the smithy.

Chaidh mi leath' don Bhriolcanaich	I brought her to the Briolcanach
'S gur iomadh ian chaidh spilgean ann,	And many birds got lead in them,
'S gun rinn i euchdan iomraiteach	And she performed famous deeds
Mu thimcheall Bhaile Pheutrais.	Round about Balephetrish.
Loisg mi 'm bun a' Chlachain leath'	I fired her in the Clachan braes
Air còmhlan de na lachaichean,	At a company of duckies,
'S a' chuid nach robh 'nan spaidein dhiubh	And those of them that weren't sluggards
Rinn cabhag gu ratreuta.	Hastily retreated.
Shiubhail mi gach àite leath'	I wandered everywhere with her
'S an Canradh Maol gun ràinig mi	And arrived in the Carragh Maol
Is sgrìob an Garadh-Phail bha mi	And took a jaunt to Gàrradh Fàil
Is bràigh na croit aig Teàrlach.	And the slope of Charles's croft.
Shiubhail mi na lòintean leath',	With her I've travelled the fields,
Na cladaichean 's na mòintichean,	The seashores and the moorlands,
'S na h-uile ian ri'n seòlainn i	And no bird I've ever aimed her at
Cha b' fhada beò 'na dhéidh e.	Was alive for long thereafter.
Nuair chluinneadh iad a h-urchairean	When they would hear her firing
Bhiodh gach ian is iomagain air;	Every bird would start to worry;
Bhiodh feadagan is guilbearnaich	Plovers, curlews and lapwings
Is gurracagan 'nan éiginn.	Would all be at risk.
Is iomadh geàrr a mharbh i dhomh	Many's the hare she's killed for me
Is gudaboc fhuair searbhag dhith	And woodcock's tasted her medicine
Nuair bhithinn-sa aig sealgaireachd	When I would be a-hunting
'S a dararaich as an déidhinn.	With her rat-tat on their tail.
Is shiùbhlainn feadh na liana leath'	I'd bring her all over the meadow
Ged bhiodh na frasan fiadhaich ann	Despite fierce showers of rain
'S mo bhròg cur sgideal siar aiste	With my boots splashing back
San lùb nach b' fhiach a dhreunadh.	Through puddles not worth draining.
Dh'éirinn anns a' ghlòmanaich	I'd get up at dawn of day
Is dh'fhalbhainn feadh nam mòintichean,	To set off around the boglands,
Is thillinn mu thràth neòin leatha	And bring her back about noon
Le eallach mòr de dh'eunlaith.	With a big load of birds.
Sann fhuair mi leath' na h-eallaichean	What burdens I've bagged with her
De shitheann far nam monaidhean —	Of tasty flesh from the moorlands —
Nam molainn i mar thoilleadh i	Were I to praise her as befits her
Se sgoilearachd a dh'fheumainn.	It's scholarship I'd need.
. . . .	. . . .
Ged mharbhadh tu na ficheadan	Should you even kill starlings
De dhruideachan 's de dhrilleachain,	And oyster-catchers in scores,
Bu mhòr am beud gum milleadh tu	It would be a shame if you injured
Am Bigean 'tha air Èarnal.	The Poult that lives in Earnal.

The row of dots before the last verse is as printed by Cameron to indicate missing text. For the *Bigean* or *Bigein* ('Poult') see p. 245 above; his home at Earnal was close to JGC's manse. What the song shows, however, is that JGC enjoyed shooting in the marshlands a little further west, especially perhaps in the district described in 'The Unearthly Whistle' (pp. 282–83). The *Briolcanach* is a bog in Balephetrish near the source of the river called *Abhainn na Fadhlach* or *an Fhadhail*, which drains the Reef into Baugh Bay (*Tràigh a' Bhàigh*). The *Dùdaire* or 'Trumpeter' is in Cornaigbeg. *An Clachan* or *an Clachan Mòr* is a piece of land on the shore at Cornaigmore which was, and is, rented by a family of MacPhails, originally from Mull, some of whom were poets, cf. Brownlie 1995, pp. 40–41. I give the names *an Canradh Maol* and *Garadh-Phail* on the left as they appear in the only source (Cameron 1932, p. 140) and on the right as emended in the light of discussion with Donald Meek and Niall M. Brownlie.[50] *An Carragh Maol* appears to be *A' Charragh Mhaol* 'the Bare Rock' (*carragh* is properly feminine) in Cornaigmore, also known as *Cnoc na Cuthaig* 'Cuckoo Hill', and the name that follows it seems more likely to represent 'Turf Dyke' (*Gàrradh Fàil*) than 'Paul's Enclosure' (*Gàrradh Phàil*), despite the presence of MacPhails in the district; it is on the boundary between Cornaigmore and Heylipol. Niall M. Brownlie thinks (personal communication, 22 November 2003) that *Teàrlach* may be *Teàrlach an Tuairneir* ('Charles the Turner', Charles MacLean) from Cornaigmore, who had a croft near *Gàrradh Fàil*. The whereabouts of *Druim a' Bhòrdain* appears to be unknown.

On 15 February 1875 the south-western half of Tiree, the district known in medieval times as Sorobie, was disjoined *quoad sacra* from JGC's parish to become the separate charge of Heylipol, the boundary running along by the *Gàrradh Fàil*. Thanks to the Church Patronage Act of the previous year the ministers of the new parish were chosen by the congregation from the beginning, and it is noticeable that the first three clerics to answer the call to this land of poets and storytellers had one thing in common – all went on to distinguish themselves in the field of Gaelic literature. The song-collector and historian Archibald MacDonald from South Uist (1853–1948), minister of Heylipol from 1877 to 1878 and of Kiltarlity from 1892 to 1929, was editor of *The Uist Collection* (1894), co-author of *The Clan Donald* (1896–1904), and co-editor of *The MacDonald Collection* (1911) and of *The Poems of Alexander MacDonald* (1924). John MacRury from Benbecula (1843–1907) came to Heylipol in 1879 from an assistantship in Islay and remained there until called to Snizort in Skye, his last parish, in 1886; an enthusiastic journalist, he contributed many articles to *Mac-Talla* and succeeded the Rev. Archibald Clerk of Kilmallie in 1887 as editor of the Gaelic supplement of the Church of Scotland magazine *Life and Work*.[51] He is our outstanding exponent of the folklore essay written in Gaelic, and his departure for Snizort was surely an immense loss to JGC, although, as we will see, the events of 1882–83 may have put a barrier between them.[52]

At p. 154 above JGC writes of 'the curse of the oppressed who have no man to deliver them'. The call to Heylipol received in 1887 by Donald MacCallum, a native of Craignish (1849–1929), was a deliberate act of defiance by a politicised congregation. The duke 'felt it his duty to tell them that in his opinion it would be injurious to the moral interests of the people that Mr MacCallum should take the position of pastor to them' (Meek 1977), and Niall M. Brownlie points out to me that both the duke and and his sub-factor Hugh MacDiarmid were totally opposed to the appointment.[53] The congregation rescinded the call and took legal advice. This was that the duke's powers as patron had lapsed with the Act of 1874 and that his powers as feudal superior did not apply to a *quoad sacra* parish, so the call was renewed and accepted, but the Argyll Estate denied MacCallum the use of the glebe and its contribution to his stipend.

While missionary at Arisaig (1882–84) MacCallum had published two little books of Gaelic songs written by himself. In the first we find poems of piety and of patriotism, of nature and of love. 'Tuireadh' ('Lament') to the Rev. Dr John MacLeod of Morvern, who died in 1882, begins (MacCallum 1883, p. 24):

Dèan tuireadh trom, mo chlàrsach,	*Mourn heavily, my harp,*
Cuir aighear 's àgh a thaobh —	*Put aside mirth and joy —*
Tha caraid 's rùn nan Gàidheal	*The friend and love of the Gael*
An-diugh aig tàmh le 'dheòin.	*Today lies willingly at rest.*

With the second, however, he stirs poems about clearances, emigration and landlordism into the mix. In 'Do na Gàidhil' ('To the Gael') he points out (MacCallum 1884, p. 8):

> *Thig fhathast an latha 's na dreisean nì fàs*
> *Air làrach Dhùn Éideann is Lunnainn na stàit,*
> *Is anns am bi 'Bheurla 'nis tha toirt buaidh*
> *Le Sas'naich is Goill gabhail cadal san uaigh.*

("The day will come yet when the briers will be growing / On the site of Auld Reekie and London of state, / And when the English language which now reigns supreme / With Englishmen and Lowlanders will sleep in the grave.") This sentiment had been applied by many poets to greedy landlords; by implication, the English tongue was the greediest landlord of all. Already in 1884 MacCallum showed that his sense of irony, which served him well later, was highly developed. 'Fios an Uachdarain' ('The Landlord's Message') begins with this address to the crofters (*ibid.*, p. 25):

Se leisg is lunndachd as adhbhar	*Sloth and idleness are the reason*
Sibh bhith gun chuid san t-saoghal	*Why you've no worldly goods*
'S ur sporan bhith cho aotrom	*And your purses are so light*
A dh'fhaodadh bhith làn —	*Which could be full —*
'S nach eil sibh gus na cluasan	*And aren't you up to the ears*
Am buachar gach là?	*In dung each day?*

While minister at Hallin-in-Waternish (1884–87) his oratory had inspired the crofters of Skye in their struggle against landlordism. His radicalism was unusual – and unique in its ferocity – for the Established Church ministry of his day. He was no folklorist, preferring to carry forward JGC's quiet sympathy with the people into a new era of direct action, but like JGC he was a difficult character. In 1889, driven from Tiree by his poverty, he went on to his last parish, Lochs in Lewis. Niall M. Brownlie points out to me that on his departure he was presented with a diamond ring and a printed scroll which declared among other things: *O eagal thrailleil smachd nan uachdaran, agus o shlat-sgiursaidh mhaor is mhinistearan, thug thu saorsa do mhoran.* ("From the slavish fear of landlords' jurisdiction, and from the scourging rod of officers and ministers, you released many.") A monument to his two years in Tiree stands on high ground in Kilkenneth; it bears the inscription *Bàs no Buaidh* ('Death or Victory'), and from this it is said in the island, *Sann le Dia tha 'n talamh air a bheil Tùr MhicCaluim.* "God owns the ground where MacCallum's Tower stands." After retiring in 1920 he published a good deal more original verse with his usual strong political slant. 'Domhnullan', for example, has verve, humour, variety, lyric power, and great philosophical integrity.[54]

We will perhaps never know whether JGC helped to bring these three talented young men to share his island with him, or how anxious they were to sit at his feet. But that they were kindred spirits is clear enough.

Two successive summers in the mid-1870s showed that bad news comes on a north wind. On 4 May 1875 JGC's eldest sister Mary Bell died aged 45 in their father's house in Portree. The cause of death was certified as paraplegia (three months), and the informant was her father. Later that year Jessy in London, two-and-a-half years into her marriage, found that she was pregnant, and in summer 1876, when preparations were being made for the wedding of her youngest sister Margaret, she made the long journey to her parents' house in Portree to prepare for the birth; then the unthinkable happened. On 7 July her father, still working as a steamer agent, sustained an injury to the spine – presumably the result of a fall – which led to general paralysis. At 3.45 p.m. on 12 July, he died. Jessy went into labour, and at 7 o'clock the following morning, 13 July, presumably in the house where her father's body lay, she gave birth to a son, who was of course named John Campbell Wallace.

It was the communion season, and it is unlikely that JGC reached Portree in time. The death and birth were registered together on 24 July; the informant was not JGC or any other relative, but John Nicolson, a steamer porter. He gave Captain Campbell's age on the death certificate as 73, but if born in November 1807 he was only 68.

It is possible that Margaret's wedding, like Jean's, was to have taken place in Portree. At any rate what happened was that the event – a high society one by Tiree standards – took place at Gott on 4 September. Margaret, described in the marriage certificate as 'Housekeeper (Spinster)' of Gott, aged 32, married Kenneth William Mackenzie, 29, of Gott, described – rather curiously for his age – as 'Merchant (retired) (Bachelor)'. Kenneth William's parents, both deceased, were James Mackenzie, merchant, and his wife Lillias Wighton Scott. The witnesses, in addition to JGC himself, were Glasgow merchant Henry Knox Dick (the groom's brother-in-law) and Tiree doctor Alexander Buchanan, both of whom, along with Kenneth William himself, were in due course to appear – and disappear – as executors in JGC's will.[55]

What appears to have happened was this. Gott Lodge was the former parish school of Tiree, where Malcolm Livingstone had officiated. When a new school was built following the Education (Scotland) Act of 1872 the old one was purchased by Kenneth William Mackenzie as a holiday home. He installed Margaret as housekeeper, and they fell in love.

Due to her husband's private means, Margaret's marriage was an unusually peripatetic one. Her first child, Kenneth, was born at Bamburgh in Northumberland, and her second, Helen Jeanie, at Fossoway in Kinross-shire; the next three (Cecilia Isabella, John Gregorson Campbell and Marjorie) were all born in Tiree. The children grew up bilingually, and Kenneth at least regarded the island as his home, but following the rebellion of 1886 the Mackenzies sold Gott Lodge to one of the eighth duke's daughters, Lady Victoria, who – like her brother Lord Archibald – was anxious to repair the damage done to her father's relationship with his tenants. She enlarged it and spent most of her time there.[56] By 1891 the Mackenzie family was living in Holland (Anon. 1891b), but the 1901 census finds Kenneth and Cecilia in the Macleans' home at Scarinish.

Margaret's marriage may have been a long and happy one, but Jessy's was not. On 21 April 1878, the eve of their fifth wedding anniversary, her husband James died in Gartnavel Royal Lunatic Asylum in Partick, Glasgow. The death certificate gives his age as 51, his occupation as Inland Revenue Officer, his parents' names as William Wallace and Margaret Boyd (both now deceased), and the cause of death as 'General Paralysis over two years'. Although he is stated to be married, the name of his spouse, unusually, is not given. In his will, dated London, 28 October 1875, he left to 'my dear wife Jessy' everything except his share of his father's estate, which 'at my Mothers death I bequeath equally amongst my Brothers and Sisters'; in a codicil, dated London, 14 April 1876, he revoked the gift to his relatives – Jessy was pregnant by then, and perhaps financial difficulties had set in (NAS SC70/4/174, pp. 1049–51).

On 9 August 1878 Jessy appeared before Dugald Campbell JP in Tobermory to obtain Confirmation of her husband's estate (NAS SC70/1/190, p. 6).

Appeared Jessy Campbell or Wallace residing at the Manse Tiree Executrix of the deceased James Wallace formerly of Nine Busby Place Camdentown in the County of Middlesex afterwards residing at Portree Isle of Skye but without any fixed or known domicile except that the same was in Scotland who being solemnly sworn and examined depones that the said James Wallace died at Gartnavel in the County of Lanark upon the Twenty first day of April Eighteen hundred and seventy eight domiciled in Scotland the domicile of his origin.

The most likely explanation, I think, is that following the birth of their son, Jessy had stayed on in Portree with her mother, leaving James to resign from his post in London and come back to Scotland to look for work as an Inland Revenue officer. It sounds as if the couple had drifted apart, but only the medical records at Gartnavel – if they exist – can tell us exactly what had happened to James.

By 9 August 1878, then, the house in Portree appears to have been sold, and three generations of Campbells – grandmother, mother and son – had come to live with JGC in the Manse of Tiree. The inventory of James Wallace's estate reveals that on 2 February 1877 he had loaned £100 to JGC at an annual rate of interest of 5 per cent, and that on 7 August 1877 he had loaned him another £20 at the same rate of interest. Clearly Jessy wished to pay for her keep and the child's, and this was the only way in which she could persuade JGC to accept the money. The value of James's estate at his death was £1,226 7s (NAS SC70/1/190, pp. 1–2, 5).

If he was balm to family and friends, JGC could be a dragon to his enemies, and soon after this we find him dealing in devastating manner with a new and dangerous opponent. There had been a small secessionist congregation in Tiree since the Disruption of 1843, numbering no more than a couple of hundred, but 1878 saw the arrival of an unusually gifted and well-travelled Free Church minister from Lewis in the form of the Rev. John MacLeod, M.D.[57] Born in 1844, he had studied initially in

Australia, where he attended the University of Melbourne and the Theological Hall of the Presbyterian Church of Victoria. Ordained by the Synod of East Australia at Grafton in 1869, he moved to Canada in 1872; after obtaining his medical degree at Montreal in 1876 he came to Scotland, joined the Free Church in 1878, and was promptly sent to Tiree, where he built a church – the first Free Church in Tiree – close to JGC's at Kirkapol.[58]

A minister with a degree in medicine was better positioned to win hearts and minds than one with a little legal knowledge. Fortunately for JGC, in his eagerness to improve the poor financial condition of his congregation MacLeod made the mistake of leaving himself open to ridicule. "He advised his people," says Cameron (1932, p. 136), "to sell all the eggs they had and give the proceeds to the church. They were also enjoined to give up tea, tobacco, &c., for the same laudable cause."

JGC responded as other traditionally-minded members of the Gaelic-speaking clergy appear to have done. In *An Lasair* I showed how a seventeenth-century Episcopalian minister, Alexander MacDonald of Islandfinnan, surreptitiously paid a poet to bring a sinner to heel by public ridicule, and how an eighteenth-century Presbyterian one, *Mgr Lachlann* (Lachlan MacKenzie of Lochcarron), quietly composed a satire himself for the same purpose and ensured that it was sung in the ceilidh-houses; then in *Eilein na h-Òige* I showed a Catholic priest, Allan McDonald of Eriskay, using poetic satire quite openly around the turn of the twentieth century as an instrument of social control.[59]

JGC took the MacKenzie route. His song 'An t-Ollamh Mòr Mòr' ('The Great Great Professor') is placed in the mouth of a wife and mother whose husband's name is Lachainn and who appears to have children called Iain and Anna and a neighbour called Màiri. She is a Tiree everywoman, the only truly identifiable characters being 'Professor' MacLeod and one of his elders, *Seumas beag Ruaig*, whose job it is to hold out the *ladar* or 'ladle', a collection box on a long pole, in front of each person in the pew. As for the word *ollamh*, it was most familiar to the Tiree people in the context of the leading Beaton physicians of the past, the *Ollamh Muileach* and *Ollamh Ìleach* (p. 157 above). In introducing the text, Cameron says (1932, p. 136) that there is 'no doubt at all' but that JGC was the author; he adds that 'the composition is dated, Tiree, November, 1879', so it would appear that he had it not from oral recitation but in manuscript. It is edited from Cameron in Meek 2003, pp. 178–83, 425–26; as there can never be enough renderings of a good poem, I translate it afresh below.

A Mhoire, is mis' tha fo mhulad,
   Sann a chaill mi na bh' annam de chlì:
Marbhaisg air ollamh na dubhaich
   Nach ceadaich dhomh cupan den tea.
Leigh'seadh i 'm pian ann am' mhaodal
   'S an soirbheas am' chaolain 'na mhill —
Ged dh'fhoghlaim esan mór oilean
   Gum fàg e ar goileachan tinn.

Am faca tu 'n t-ollamh mòr mòr
A thàinig g'ar leigheas á Leòdhas
   O dhrongaireachd, tea is tombaca?
'S a Rìgh gur h-e 'n gaisgeach MacLeòid!

My goodness, I'm feeling depressed,
   I've lost all my get up and go:
A plague on that wretched professor
   Who won't allow me a cup of the tea.
It would relieve the ache in my belly
   When the wind in my guts comes in squalls —
Although he's surpassingly learned
   He's going to leave all our stomachs ill.

Have you seen the great great professor
Who has come from Lewis to save us
   From drunkenness, tea and tobacco?
And O King he's the hero, MacLeod!

Gach nì chuireadh neart ann am' cholainn,	Every substance that strengthens my body,
Tea, siùcar, is cofaidh, is dram,	Tea, sugar, coffee, a dram,
A shàbhaileadh maoin 'dhol san ladar,	And might keep money out of the ladle,
Cha leig e aon bhlasad dhibh 'm cheann.	He'll let not one sip of you into my mouth.
Obh obh, ciamar a shluigeas mi 'n t-aran	Oh dear, how can I swallow my bread
Gun eanaraich gun bhainne gun ham?	Without broth, without milk, without ham?
Gheibh na coimhearsnaich latheigin tachdte	Some day Lachie and I and the children
Mi fhìn is Lachainn 's a' chlann.	Will be found by the neighbours choked.

Tha mi 'faicinn — se riaghladh an t-sagairt	I see — it's the sway of the priest
A ghabh e air mnathan na tìr';	That he's got on the local women;
B'e thus' agus mis' an dà dhallag,	How short-sighted we were, you and I,
A Lachainn, nuair thraisg sinn o thea.	When we fasted, Lachie, from tea.
Anna bheag, cuir an kettle air teine,	Little Anna, put on the kettle,
O eudail, ach staram mo chinn!	What a splitting headache I have, love!
Ruith, Iain, faigh cathair do d' athair —	Run, John, get a chair for your father —
Cha bhi sinn nas fhaide gun tea.	We'll not do without tea any more.

Shaoil e gum biodh e 'na Phàpa	He believed he could go like the Pope
A' marcachd air talamh Thirìth',	On his horse through the land of Tiree,
Gun riaghladh e 'n sporan 's an gluasad	That he'd rule their purse and behaviour
'S aig ainm gum biodh buaidh anns gach tìr.	And bring power to his name in each part.
Nach esan a nochd bhith gun eanchainn	Look how he's revealed to be brainless
Nuair chaidh e air iomrall cho claon!	When he has gone so completely wrong!
Sann dh'fheumadh e gliocas na nathrach	He must needs be as wise as the serpent
Mun seasadh e 'chasan ri 'taobh.	To remain on his feet by its side.

Mar as lugha th' aig duine de thuigse	The less sense a man possesses
Air tuigse sann as lugha 'chì feum,	The less sense he will see any need for,
Se fuaim soithich fhalaimh as àirde,	An empty vessel's the loudest,
Si 'n asal as àirde 'nì beuc;	The ass makes the biggest noise;
Ged nigheadh tu 'mhuc théid i 'n làthaich,	Wash the pig and she'll go into muck,
Se 'n dall air an t-sràid as àird' ceum,	The blind man on the street steps the highest,
'S am fear a chì smùirnein am' shùil-sa	And he who sees a mote in my eye
Tha sail anns an t-sùil aige fhéin.	Has a whole log of wood in his own.

Dh'ainneoin gach ollamh air thalamh	Despite all professors on earth
Si luibh tha ro-ghast' tha san tea:	Tea is a thoroughly excellent herb:
Bha mo cheann ré na seachdain gu sgaradh,	All week my head was near splitting,
Nis dhannsainn mar chaileag san tìr.	Now I could dance like any young girl.
Mealladh leis tuilleadh cha ghabh mi —	For no more of his tricks will I fall —
Cha traisg mi, bi'm fallain no tinn,	Be I well or ill, I won't fast
Air iarrtas luchd chòtaichean molach	By request of those who wear hairy coats
Le'n coingeas an Soisgeul no tea.	And treat the Gospel or tea much the same.

Biodh agads' deagh mhisneach, a Mhàiri,	Be of good courage, Mary,
Sgil fhuaradh, a ghràidh, aige fhéin:	A skill obtained, my love, from himself:
Cum thusa blàths ris na cearcan	Just keep the hens nice and warm
'S bidh dà ubh san là aig gach té.	And they'll each lay two eggs a day.

Bi ealamh, dèan nid dhaibh sa chlòsaid,
    Cuir brìg fòpa de dh'fhosradh an treud —
'S mas fheàirrd' an t-seann fheadhainn fallas
    Thoir sals dhaibh is faradh dhaib' fhéin.

Le uibhean ged lìonadh na taighean
    Cha togadh e 'n sac th' air mo chrìdh
'S mo ghùn lurach ùr anns an fhasan
    Nach faigh mi 'chur latha mu m' dhruim.
'N e plaide no clò 's e gun dath air
    An sgeadach as taitneach le mnaoi?
'S tha thu fhéin gun tombaca, a Lachainn,
    Tha seachdain on bhlaiseadh leat tea.

Se m' eagal gun dhealaich do chiall riut,
    Gabh comhairle rianail uam fhéin:
Leubh thu gur freumh uilc tha san airgead
    'S tha 'n t-ollamh seo 'sealg air a cheum.
Leis an sgil 'thug e dhuit ann a shearmon
    Air cearcan gu dearbh nì thu feum —
Dèan deas, rach g'a éisteachd Di-Dòmhnaich
    Is leth-gini 'd phòc 'dhèanadh réit'.

Thig Seumas beag Ruaig 's fiamh gàir' air
    Le 'bhoineid g'a càradh ri d' shròin:
"Thoir thusa gliog math air an ùrlar
    'N àm tilgidh a' chùinnidh o d' dhòrn!"
Ged chrochadh e cailleach gach Sàbaid
    Gheibh thusa do shàthachd tea òl,
'S mu d' chrostachd, mhionnan is bhriagan
    Chan fhosgail e 'bhial riut ri d' bheò.

Be clever, make them nests in the closet,
    Put a heap of dung underneath —
And if the old ones improve with sweat
    Give them salts and a roost to themselves.

Should the houses be filled with eggs
    It would still not relieve my heart's burden
If I may not one day put my lovely new gown
    Round my back while it's still in fashion.
Is a blanket or cloth without colour
    The clothing a woman enjoys?
And Lachie, you've got no tobacco,
    It's a week since you last tasted tea.

I'm afraid that you're out of your mind,
    Take some sensible advice from me:
You've read that money's the root of evil
    Yet this professor is hot on its trail.
With the skill that his sermon has given you
    You'll surely do well from the chickens —
Be prepared, go and hear him on Sunday
    With ten-and-six in your purse for atonement.

Little James of Ruaig will come smiling
    With his bonnet thrust into your nose:
"Just make a good clink on the floor
    When the coins are thrown out of your fist!"
Should he hang an old woman each Sabbath
    You'll get to drink all the tea you can take,
And of your ill nature, swearing and lies
    He'll say nothing to you all your days.

If, as I have suggested (Black 2001, p. xv), the measure of a traditional poem is how far it can be shown to have achieved the practical purpose for which it was intended, this is a very fine piece of work indeed, for in 1880, the year in which his church at Kirkapol opened its doors (Ewing 1914, vol. 2, p. 122), the Rev. John MacLeod, M.D., gave up the struggle and returned to Canada.

I pointed above (p. 643) to a nine-year gap in the sequence of JGC's datable fieldwork sessions relating to the collection of tales and ballads. They resume in 1880, when he heard the story of how the forests were burned by *an Dubh Ghiubhsach*, the daughter of the king of Norway.[60] His informant may have been a Lochaberman, for in two languages he says (Campbell 1895, pp. 103, 107): *Thiodhlaic iad i ann an Achanacairidh; 's am fear bho 'n deachaidh an naigheachd a chluinntinn an toiseach – anns a' bhliadhna 1880 – bha e 'g ràdhainn gu 'm b' urrainn dha a chas a chur air an uaigh anns an do chuireadh i.* "They buried her in Achnacarry; and the person from whom the story was first heard nine years ago [1880] said that he could put his foot on the place where she was buried."

This does not necessarily mean, however, that JGC spent every spare minute of the years 1871–80 writing up *The Gaelic Otherworld*. In *Clan Traditions and Popular Tales* (Campbell 1895, p. xx) Nutt provided a list of seventeen 'chief informants' from whom JGC had derived the material in that book and *The Fians* (Campbell 1891). No doubt some at least of JGC's undated interviews with them had taken place during the 1870s, for the list includes at least four individuals mentioned above (Donald Cameron, Ruaig, Malcolm MacDonald, Scarinish, Duncan Cameron, constable, Tiree, and Angus MacVurrich, Portree). Only one other informant – Hugh Macmillan, tailor, Tobermory – is from outside Tiree.[61] The remaining twelve, moving north-east to south-west, are: Duncan MacDonald, Caolas;[62] Neil MacLean (the elder), Cornaig (see pp. 202 and 660); Malcolm MacLean and Hugh MacDonald, Kilmoluag;[63] Donald Mackinnon and John Cameron (*Iain mac Fhearchair*), Balevullin; John MacArthur, tailor, Moss;[64] John MacLean, bard, Balemartin (one of whose verses is quoted by JGC at p. 3 above); Allan MacDonald and Donald Macdonald, both Mannal;[65] Malcolm Sinclair, Balephuil (*Calum Bàn*, for whom see p. 665 below); and Archibald Mackinnon (*Gilleasbaig Ruadh nan Sgeirean Dubha*).[66]

The beginning of 1881 brought tragedy to the Manse of Tiree. On 14 January – the day after Old New Year – Jessy's son John Campbell Wallace died there of peritonitis following five days of ileus. He was exactly four-and-a-half years old. His father is described on the death certificate as 'James Wallace, Assistant Storekeeper General, Somerset House, London (deceased)'. The death was certified by Alexander Buchanan and witnessed by one of the other uncles, Alexander Maclean.

When the census is taken on 3 April the manse household consists of JGC himself, now aged 46, along with his mother, whose age is given as 72, and Jessy, whose age is correctly given as 48. Neither lady is assigned a 'rank, profession or occupation'. There are three menials, all unmarried, all born in Tiree: Donald MacCallum, 21, farm servant; Christina MacDonald, 17, dairymaid; and Helen MacPhail, 17, table maid.[67] On this particular night there is also a young visitor, Hector MacFadyen, a fourteen-year-old schoolboy. All seven are given as Gaelic-speaking.

It was in 1881 that JGC's name first came before the public through his editions of three folktales and a ballad in *The Scottish Celtic Review*, edited by the Rev. Dr Alexander Cameron, minister of Brodick. It was a breakthrough, and collecting and writing for publication now became his abiding passion. That summer he took down the Lay of Diarmad 'from the recitation of John Sinclair, Barrapol, an old man of about eighty years of age, who said he learned it in his youth from Peter Carmichael, Tiree, who was at that time an old man'.[68]

Also in the island that year was the traveller John Sands, who described his archaeological findings there to the Society of Antiquaries in Edinburgh on 14 June 1882.[69] Less happily, perhaps, he appears to have been interviewed about a more sensational aspect of his visit by a reporter from the *North British Daily Mail* in Glasgow.[70]

Mr J. Sands, who has been spending some time in the Island of Tiree, says that certain houses are still believed to be haunted by fairies, although it is only gifted individuals who can see them. In one cabin they were wont to sit in swarms upon the rafters, and had the impudence even to drop down now and again and seize a potato out of the pot. Eventually they became such a nuisance that the tenant of the house determined to build a new dwelling and to abandon the old one. Unfortunately, when the new cabin was almost finished, he took a stone out of the haunted hut, with the result that all the fairies came along with it, so that his new home was as much infested as the old one had been.

This is only a sample of many ancient superstitions which, according to Mr Sands, still linger among the people of Tiree. Marriage parties, for example, still take care to turn to the right hand, and not to the left, when they enter the church; and the same rule is observed when a body is laid in the grave. When boats are launched from the shore the bow is brought round, although it may be a little inconvenient, agreeably to the apparent course of the sun.

Nine is regarded as a sacred number. Water taken from the crests of nine waves, and in which nine stones had been boiled, is an infallible cure for the jaundice. The shirt of the patient, after being dipped in this magic infusion, is put on wet. Mr Sands says he was personally acquainted with a man on whom this remedy was recently tried, but without effect, as he was on the brink of death. Water taken from nine springs or streams in which cresses grow is also believed to be an effectual cure for jaundice.

On the west side of the island there is a rock with a hole in it through which children are passed when suffering from whooping-cough or other complaints.

Sick cattle are treated in a curious way. The doctor being provided with a cog of cream and an oatcake, sits on the sick cow or other animal, and repeats a verse nine times, nine times taking a bit and a sup between each repetition of the rhyme. The cream and the bannock are the doctor's fee.

Mr Sands asserts that about five years ago a woman left her child, which she supposed to be a changeling, upon the shore, that it might be taken away by the fairies and her own infant restored; and he adds that at the present time a minister on the island has refused to baptise the children of a parishioner because he swears that a woman has bewitched his cows, and abstracted the virtue from the milk.

There need be little doubt but that the minister in question is JGC himself, not least because we know from Presbytery records and his own death certificate that the symptoms of the ataxia which eventually killed him made their first appearance in 1881. Indeed, although (or perhaps because?) Sands was an able and enterprising individual who had had ample opportunity to practise his Gaelic during a long winter in St Kilda, I would suggest that JGC is the principal source for most of his information. Material of this kind is not easily obtained by non-Gaelic speakers or learners other than from individuals who have spent a lifetime collecting it.[71] Nothing demonstrates this more clearly than the experience of Ada Goodrich Freer, who published substantial accounts of the superstitions of South Uist and Eriskay, all of which she had got at second hand from Fr Allan McDonald, expressing her debt to him in a variety of circuitous ways (Campbell and Hall 1968, pp. 61–62, 229–36). When she visited Tiree in 1896, five years after JGC's death, she was obliged to adopt the method of offering prizes of one pound, ten shillings, 7s 6d and five shillings for the four best essays written by the children of the island's schools on the topic 'A Winter Evening or Ceilidh in Tiree'; she followed this up with an offer of prizes to senior pupils for essays on ghosts and visitations, and one mother, at least, is on record as strongly disapproving of a competition on such a subject. Those essays which had been written in Gaelic were translated for her by an 'accomplished Gaelic scholar' (Campbell and Hall 1968, p. 86), and the results became the fourth chapter of her book *Outer Isles* (Freer 1903, pp. 61–81). She appears to have had no other information.

Sands's abilities should not be underestimated, but if we look at his revelations we find: (1) he begins with the Fairies, JGC's main interest; (2) the second paragraph consists of material which the parish minister was in a good position to observe, since his manse overlooked Gott Bay; (3) the third offers not an informant but an object of superstitious interest – probably JGC brought Sands with him on a pastoral visit to the sick man's bedside, just as I was myself cheerfully brought to a dying woman's bedside by the minister of Berneray in 1966; (4) JGC's own evidence reveals the fourth paragraph to be a half-truth, see 'Consumption (*Caitheamh*)', p. 228 above, and my note on that section; (5) the interest in cures reflects what we know of JGC in his latter years; (6) the second half of the final paragraph represents a serious indiscretion on Sands's part, given that it derives either from slanderous gossip or, as is more likely, from a joke made to him by JGC in private conversation. Unfortunately for both men, the *Mail* report was communicated to the Folk-Lore Society in London and reprinted in *The Folk-Lore Journal* with the heading 'Ancient Superstitions in Tiree' (Anon. 1883b).

At p. 195 above JGC tells of a minister of Strathfillan who 'was seized with burning pains all over his body, and was slowly wasting away by some malady of which the nature could not be understood' until a local witch was found to be sticking pins into a piece of wood; when the pins were taken out he recovered. Like Sands's revelations, it seems very close to the bone. In November 1881 JGC addressed a petition to the Presbytery of Mull, and it lay on their table through the darkness of winter; we do not know precisely what it said, but its contents may be guessed from the Presbytery's deliberations at Salen on 7 March 1882 (NAS CH2/273/10, pp. 63, 74):

> The Petition from the Revd. J. G. Campbell of Tiree of date 28th November 1881 was read and the Presbytery having expressed sympathy with him in his long-continued illness earnestly recommend him to procure the services of an Assistant without delay, and further the Presbytery request the said Mr Campbell to reply before next meeting.

JGC replied on 22 May, saying that he wanted to appoint an Arts student as his assistant. Meeting at Tobermory on 28 June, the Presbytery refused to sanction this.[72] They consulted with the convener of the Assembly's Commission as to how they should proceed, and in their meeting at Salen on 28 September 1882 the following motion was moved, seconded and unanimously agreed (NAS CH2/273/10, pp. 97, 187–88):

> That the Presbytery whilst deeply sympathizing with the prolonged illness of Mr Campbell Minister of Tiree which incapacitates him from discharging the functions of his office; resolve that it is indispensible that provision be at once made to maintain the ordinances of religion in that parish and enjoin the said Mr Campbell to provide a licentiate of the Church of Scotland to occupy his pulpit to the satisfaction of the Presbytery on or before October 26th next to come failing which, that he shall within the same date, come under an obligation to the presbytery to provide, so long as he is unable to discharge the duties of his office himself, the sum of £80 (Eighty Pounds Sterling) per annum payable quarterly to enable them to secure an assistant and the Presbytery appoint the following Committee namely Messrs Mac Dougall Coll, Mac Rury, Hylipol and Campbell Kilfinichen to convey and explain personally to him this finding.

This committee met JGC in the Manse of Tiree on 16 October 1882, in the second year of his illness. It was a difficult discussion. The minutes were read to the sick man, who proceeded to express 'his inability to obtemper [obey] the finding of the Presbytery for reasons which he was prepared at any time to state if called upon by the Presbytery' but also 'his desire that a Licentiate of the church should be procured if possible'. Clearly the main purpose of the delegation was to find out just how sick JGC was, while his aim was to maintain himself and his family in the Manse in the style to which they were accustomed, and to avoid the provision of an assistant becoming a permanent financial burden if he failed to recover his health. Four days later, on 20 October, JGC wrote the Presbytery a letter full of dark and meaningless insinuations about the Church's enemies. He avoids libel and does not so much as mention his illness, which no doubt by now he regretted having brought to the Presbytery's attention (NAS CH2/273/10, pp. 195–99).

I complain of this action of the Presbytery having been taken without inquiry into the state of the Parish of Tiree or of the possibility of the minister to obtemper the finding of the Presbytery. The resolution appears to me high handed and arbitrary calculated to place me at variance with my Presbytery and to injure the respect due to me as Parish Minister if not personally at least "for my office' sake". It implies if it does not actually state that the ordinances of Religion have been neglected in this Parish and that I have failed to use all the means at my disposal for the promotion of the interests of Religion within it. There has been no such neglect and the church of Scotland is not weaker within the parish and does not threaten to become weaker than at any time within my recollection: it offers no unfavourable contrast to other parishes within the Bounds of the Presbytery.

I can only infer that the Presbytery has been misinformed and that representations have been made to it inconsistent with truth. I should be sorry to think that agencies have been at work other than those that belong to Presbyterian discipline, and I regret if under the fair guise of Commissioners and Assessors the Presbytery is allowing underhand influences and personal representations to usurp its proper functions, to the imposition of impossible burdens upon any of its members.

I have all along in this matter been anxious that the Presbytery should make inquiries and being painfully aware that mis-representations are in circulation about Tiree, that it should interfere and so, if possible, save me from outside meddling as well as from having burdens laid upon me more than I am able to bear.

Will you kindly send me a copy of the remit of the General Assembly under which the Commissioners acted? I have no objection to a licentiate being provided but I am unable to contribute anything for that purpose myself.

Meeting at Salen on 31 October, the brethren decided to ask JGC to give any further reasons 'as to why he cannot obtemper the Presbytery's finding of date 28th September last', and to warn him 'that he is laying himself open to be proceeded against for dereliction of duty and contumacy'. On 7 November, having received no reply, they resolved (again meeting at Salen) that if JGC had not accepted the finding by 20 November, they would proceed against him on 28 November according to the law of the Church (NAS CH2/273/10, pp. 200–01, 205–06).

When they duly met at Salen on that day they had two letters from JGC before them. In one dated 13 November he described the Presbytery's injunction as 'unconstitutional and against the laws of the Church, as well as oppressive', and went on to plead (NAS CH2/273/10, pp. 209–14):

I would remind the Presbytery that at the beginning of summer, when a student came here and I found his services acceptable to the people, I sent word to the Presbytery before allowing the matter to go any further so that there might be no ground for faultfinding afterwards. In the absence of any Gaelic-speaking licentiate or any offer of assistance from the Presbytery this was the only help available to me and the Presbytery while properly enough not approving of such an appointment, gave no order to discontinue his services. He has now left for college and as my health still continues weak, tho' improving, I have to apply to the Presbytery to appoint supplies in usual course for the next three months.

In his other letter, dated 10 November, JGC said that he wanted the legal opinion of the Church's Procurator on whether a minister's salary, 'being a civil right', could be 'interfered with'. He added:

From the Assembly's Commissioners report to the Commission of Assembly as published in the Scotsman of 16th I infer that the state of church matters in the Parish of Tiree has been misrepresented and exaggerated. My state of health has prevented my preaching only for about a year past; the sacrament of the Lord's supper has been regularly administered every year since I came to the parish; Baptism has always been administered and I have always been accessible to those who wished my services and to whom by advice or direction I could be of use. Many of the Ministers of the church have helped me when able and I find myself, I am happy to say, on good terms with all classes in the parish. The injurious remarks made by the convener of the Assembly's Commissioners about the Tiree people have still more forcibly the excuse of the speaker's not knowing anything of what he was talking about.[73]

The Presbytery decided to submit the matter to the Procurator's arbitration, and appointed supply for the pulpit of Tiree on 10 December, 24 December and 14 January. JGC's response, dated 9 December, was to accuse the brethren of acting illegally (NAS CH2/273/10, pp. 214–16, 225–26).

What is wanted from the Procurator, is not his opinion of what the Presbytery ought to do – that opinion would be incompetent for him to give – but his opinion of the legal point, as to whether a Presbytery is entitled to lay an injunction upon one of its members, to set aside a part of his stipend to secure the services of an assistant, during his illness, whether long or short . . . In reply to your inquiry as to the stipend of Tiree, I would beg to observe that a Clerical Almanac is not a good authority for the Presbytery to proceed upon; £317 includes the manse and glebe, and the year when the return was made to Government was one of very high fiars prices, last year being £40 under it.

'Fiars' are defined by Chambers (1983, p. 466) as 'the prices of grain legally *struck* or fixed for the year at the *Fiars* Court'; Fiars Courts were constituted each year in February by a district judge – in JGC's case the sheriff substitute at Tobermory – acting with a jury to regulate the payment of stipend, rent and prices not expressly agreed upon (Loudon 2001, p. 72). The judgement of the Procurator, W. MacKintosh, was received from Edinburgh by both parties a week later. Dated 14 December, it was a complete vindication of the Presbytery's stance (NAS CH2/273/10, pp. 222–24).

He may perform his duties by an assistant, making arrangements for that purpose satisfactory to the Presbytery of the Bounds. The rule is, as I understand it, the same as that which holds e.g. in the case of Town Clerks and other public functionaries – and it has never, so far as I know, been doubted, that if any such functionary becomes disabled by bodily or mental illness, he is at least bound to make arrangements as suitable and sufficient as possible for the discharge of his duties. It follows that, in my opinion, Mr Campbell the Minister of Tiree is bound, being laid aside by illness, to provide an assistant to the satisfaction of the Presbytery and to assign a reasonable proportion of his stipend for that purpose. If he declines to do so, the Presbytery might I think proceed against him by action in the Civil Courts, but in any view they would, in my opinion, be entitled to proceed against him by libel for neglect of duty and contumacy.

The Presbytery forwarded JGC's letter of the 9th to the Procurator, provoking this illuminating addendum of 16 December (NAS CH2/273/10, pp. 229–30):

Assuming (as I have done) that Mr Campbell's illness is not a matter of days or weeks and that he is permanently disabled or likely to be so for a considerable or indefinite period I find nothing in Mr Campbell's letter to affect the opinion expressed in my former communication.

JGC had lost the battle, and after reading the Procurator's opinion he began to organise his retreat. On 18 December he informed the Presbytery (NAS CH2/273/10, pp. 228–29):

I do not think . . . that in the present scarcity of Gaelic preachers, it would be judicious to order a minister to get an assistant when such a one might be unpopular and have the effect of weakening the Church. I am, however, willing at whatever sacrifice of personal convenience to see the parish of Tiree supplied with an Assistant, but would deprecate the appointment of one who might injure the spiritual interests of the parish. I shall be glad to hear from the Presbytery the name of any licentiate who is likely to give satisfaction. This answer is not final till the supply appointed by the Presbytery is exhausted as my health is slowly improving.

On receiving this the Presbytery's patience ran out. They appointed a formal visitation of Tiree by three of their members (William MacKintosh, Donald MacFarlane and John MacRury) on Monday 12 February 1883 'that the heritors, elders, and communicants of said parish may be examined respecting the supply of ordinances therein'. The three men 'waited on Mr Campbell Minister of Tiree on the 10th current' and received a letter from him. Dated that day, it stated that he had agreed to pay John MacCowan £50 to serve as his assistant for six months. If he had not recovered by the close of five months from MacCowan's entry on duty, he undertook to make a more permanent arrangement with him or another individual at the rate of at least £80 per annum (NAS CH2/273/10, pp. 230–31, 235–37). JGC had found his assistant.

When MacKintosh, MacFarlane and MacRury met on Monday 12 February in the church at Kirkapol and duly constituted themselves the Presbytery of Mull, they declared that there was no longer a need for a formal visitation, but that instead they would 'hear objections or complaints, if there be such' to the new arrangement 'from the Parishioners who might come forward'. MacFarlane then preached, as previously intimated, taking as his text Isaiah 1: 18, "Come now, and let us reason together, saith the Lord: though your sins be as scarlet, they shall be as white as snow; though they be red like crimson, they shall be as wool."

Following the service the three men faced the congregation, announced the news of the settlement, and invited comments, which were not at all slow in coming (NAS CH2/273/10, pp. 237–42).

> Compeared Thomas Barr, Farmer, Ballefetrish, a Communicant, John Mac Gavin Farmer Gott, Hector Lamont Farmer Kirkapol, Neil Maclean Elder Cornaig Lachlan Mac Neil, Vaul, Communicant, Allan Mac Fadyen Farmer Scarinish, Neil Mac Fadyen Caolas Communicant and others who stated that there is no Kirksession in the Parish and no Session Clerk – and who agree to Mr Campbells arrangement for the supply of the pulpit but request that the same be under the sanction of the Presbytery . . . It was stated that the Sacrament of Baptism and the Lord's Supper were administered to a number of people who came to church only on Communion occasions as evidenced by a document which was at this stage of the proceedings handed in and the statements in which were corroborated by the testimony of Thomas Barr and Neil Mac Lean.
>
> Lachlan Mac Neil stated that he knew of twenty-nine (29) families in the East end of the Parish where he resides who have in whole or part left the church in Mr Campbell's time, and that he is prepared to give the names.
>
> Neil Mac Lean stated that Mr Campbell used to hold one Gaelic service only in the church on each Lord's day – that an English service was only occasionally conducted – that Mr Campbell has not preached for over a year and a half – that for about six months during that time an Arts' student officiated from the Precentor's desk – that he is of opinion the number of communicants in connection with the church at present is (47) forty seven or thereabouts – that no collections were made for the Schemes of the Church – that for six years or thereabouts there has virtually been no Divine service conducted by the Minister in the church of Tiree because though Mr Campbell till a year and a half ago or thereabouts did endeavour to conduct service, many of the congregation could not hear his voice and therefore stayed away – that Mr Campbell for a number of years has required more or less help in getting into and out of the pulpit – and that owing to bodily infirmity he was unable, though willing, to perform the duties expected of him as minister of the Parish.

Two important biographical facts emerge from Neil MacLean's statement. Since 1877, the year when the first minister of Heylipol, Archibald MacDonald, ascended his pulpit in the Moss, JGC's lungs had been so inflamed that the congregation were unable to hear him, and had simply left him to preach to his family and friends. And since 1881 his muscular disability had prevented him carrying out any duties at all.

The objectors of 1860 were vindicated. The Presbytery 'expressed their sincere sympathy with the congregation in their exceptionally unfortunate circumstances', and assured them that 'they would further impress on Mr Campbell the desirability, in the event of his not being able to resume duty at an early date, of his getting his assistant regularly ordained'.[74]

Six months later, on Tuesday 7 August 1883, a very different gathering took place in the church at Kirkapol. The members of the 'Commission of Inquiry into the Condition of the Crofters and Cottars in the Highlands and Islands of Scotland' – Lord Napier, Sir Kenneth Mackenzie of Gairloch, Donald Cameron of Lochiel, Charles Fraser Mackintosh, Professor Donald Mackinnon and JGC's erstwhile correspondent Sheriff Nicolson – landed at Scarinish that morning with their officials in bright sunshine. They had sailed overnight from Arisaig, where they had taken evidence the previous day. A large crowd was waiting to cheer them and accompany them to the church. JGC must have heard them pass from his bedroom in the Manse, where he was effectively a prisoner. Between seven and eight hundred of the island's remaining population of 2,700 crowded into the church to hear the proceedings. It was so warm that workmen had to be sent for to deal with the windows. They forced one open, and another had to be removed completely (Cameron 1986, p. 59).

During the day the commissioners examined seventeen witnesses, hearing of evictions, mass emigration and loss of common grazings. Since the famine of 1846 emigration had been encouraged and subsidised, and over two thousand people had left the island. Holdings were consolidated and sub-division prohibited, with the result that by now there were only 194 tenants and 300 cottars, but there was still a shortage of boats for fishing and no good harbour. One of the witnesses was the doctor, Alexander Buchanan; among a number of tense exchanges was this between Fraser Mackintosh and Hugh MacDiarmid, *am Bàillidh Dubh*, the duke's sub-factor (Napier 1884, vol. 3, pp. 2161–62): "Can you explain why it is there is such a large audience here today?"

"I suppose it is greatly out of curiosity."

"You won't attribute it to a deeper ground?"

"They will have an interest in the Commission coming here; it is very natural that they should come and see what is going on."

"Do you think they have any grievances?"

"I would not like to answer that question. I have found them always very nice people."

"You can give them a good character?"

"Yes, I can."

Niall M. Brownlie has pointed out to me that Hugh MacDiarmid (*Eoghan Dubh MacDhiarmaid*) and Tom Barr, tacksman of Balephetrish, had formed a cartel in Tiree to buy the island stock. "If a crofter refused MacDiarmid's offer, Tom Barr would not come near the crofter."[75]

Two weeks later, on 20 August, Barr wrote to the Presbytery of Mull urging them to appoint an 'Assistant & Successor or otherwise' to JGC. This was usual in the case of ministers who were aged and infirm. Doubtful of Barr's claim to represent the congregation, the Presbytery responded coolly: JGC had undertaken to make a more permanent arrangement by 5 October, they said, and they would take any further action necessary after that date.

In June they had awarded MacCowan a licence to preach. At Salen on 6 November they were confronted with a letter from JGC informing them that he was extending MacCowan's assistantship for six months – not the permanent arrangement which he had led them to expect – and a letter from Barr with a 'copy of Petition bearing 327 names as presented to the said Mr Campbell'.[76] Meeting at Salen on 4 March 1884, the Presbytery decided that if JGC did not implement his agreement of 10 February 1883 within a month they would submit the case to that year's General Assembly. JGC took them all the way, but it was no bluff, and at Tobermory on 6 May they duly prepared a petition to the Assembly. It began by pointing out 'that in the opinion of your petitioners, the state of the parish of Tiree calls for the special interference of the General Assembly' and 'that your Venerable House had this case before it, by report of your Commission, sent down to visit the Presbytery of Mull in 1882'. After referring to JGC's promise of 10 February 1883 it declared 'that the said Revd. John G. Campbell now declines to implement said promise, and has failed to give the Presbytery any guarantee whatsoever that the supply of ordinances shall be regularly maintained in the parish of Tiree' and 'that, in the opinion of your petitioners, it is now necessary that a regularly ordained assistant and successor be appointed in said parish, and that any other arrangement is not likely to prove satisfactory'. As in 1861, a dossier was printed for the Assembly at the Presbytery's expense, consisting this time of sixteen documents beginning with JGC's petition of 28 November 1881 and ending with his letter of 15 March 1884 (NAS CH2/273/11, pp. 3, 10, 14–17, 22–23).

The General Assembly heard the case on 27 May. Donald MacFarlane spoke for the Presbytery, but JGC's solicitors had instructed an advocate, Andrew Jameson, to appear for him, and they seem to have cancelled each other out. The Assembly told the Presbytery what it least wanted to hear, that an assistant and successor could not be unilaterally imposed, and that the only way to cast aside a recalcitrant parish minister was by long and expensive litigation. It enjoined JGC 'to make without delay adequate arrangements for the supply of religious ordinances in his parish, to the satisfaction of the Presbytery', but instructed the Presbytery 'in the event of Mr Campbell's failing to make such arrangements to proceed against him by libel for neglect of duty and contumacy according to the laws of the Church'.

On 11 June 1884, after receiving the Assembly's verdict, JGC wrote coolly to the Presbytery: "A fortnight after Mr MacCowan's departure, I engaged the Revd D. Mackay as assistant on the usual terms. He is ordained."[77]

Mackay appeared in person before the Presbytery of Mull in Tobermory on 18 June and presented his credentials. Licensed by the Presbytery of Lochcarron in 1852 and ordained by the Presbytery of Uist in 1854, he had a certificate from the Presbytery of Inverness for a ten-month assistantship in 1883–84. The brethren were suspicious. This man was older than JGC himself and had never settled. Why not? They questioned him about his engagement with JGC; he answered that it was for six months from 11 May, that he would stay no longer than that, and would leave sooner if the congregation did not want him. They were far from pleased, for before them lay another of Barr's petitions, 'purporting to be from members and adherents of the Church of Scotland in the parish of Tiree and signed by 215 persons', this time declaring *inter alia* 'that the appointment of an assistant and successor does not seem to the petitioners practicable; and that, in consequence of the petitioners' dissatisfaction with the present assistant, they have ceased to attend church'. The Presbytery wrote to JGC, enclosing the petition and urging him to consent to the appointment of an assistant and successor and to pay him £80 per annum; if he did not reply by 15 July, they added, he would be proceeded against 'in terms of the Deliverance of the General Assembly'.[78]

The answer, when it came, was from JGC's Edinburgh solicitors. He had rediscovered the benefits that legal representation could bring, and at their meeting in Tobermory on 30 July 1884 the Presbytery were confronted by James Reid, advocate. This gave them someone they could work with. All the resources of the Church were now brought to bear on the case – the Procurator, the Highland Committee, grant-awarding bodies – with the result that JGC agreed to appoint an assistant and pay him £80. His parish was by now so notorious, however, that an ordained assistant proved difficult to find.

In the winter of 1884–85 JGC appointed Duncan Clerk or Clarke, and when Peter MacLean, writer, Tobermory, appeared before the Presbytery on JGC's behalf at their meeting in Craignure on 31 March 1885 he told them that 'the difficulty in regard to the present assistant is obviated by the fact of his being on the point of leaving Tiree', but that, despite advertising, JGC had failed to find a successor. Help was, however, at hand, for the Presbytery had in their bounds a promising young student, Donald MacDonald from Knockintorran in North Uist (1855–1940), who was undergoing trials for his licence to preach. They appointed him as student missionary in Tiree and, following licence, as assistant, MacLean agreeing to this on his client's behalf. On 5 May 1885, following his trials at Tobermory, MacDonald was duly licensed, and for two years he brought peace to a troubled pulpit.[79]

It was just as well. In the second half of 1883 a branch of the Land League had been founded in Tiree, and on 15 May 1884 the duke of Argyll wrote from Argyll Lodge, Kensington, to his son John Campbell, marquis of Lorne:

> I have got a really incredible letter from Campbell minister of Tyree – enclosing a letter from a Vaull crofter stating his *"grievances"*. They all refer to cock-a bull stories about John Ardmore who has been in his grave some dozen years & whose alleged misdeeds refer to 1846–7–8. It is like a letter out of bedlam! One grievance is that people in the famine were fed on turnips & Indian meal – the great aggravation being that the turnip land had been manured with rotten whale flesh! Then stories about the fortune left by John Ardmore fill up the interstices of this idiotical composition. I have given evidence before the Commons Committee today about a fishing harbour. I *am* provoked by a man of education like Campbell sending me such trash, as showing the "tension" on the *land question*!! The Vaull crofter says he had a consultation about *you* & came to the conclusion that another such fine man as the Marquis was not alive! So you see you have at least done him good.[80]

Campbell of Ardmore, as we have seen, had been primarily responsible for carrying out the duke's policy of reducing the island's population and turning many of those who stayed – men like Donald Cameron, Ruaig – into landless 'cottars'. In Tiree as elsewhere the Crofters' Holdings (Scotland) Act, which became law on 25 June 1886, met with disapproval because although it addressed the specific grievances of existing crofters, it did nothing to restore land to the cottars. They now formed something like half the population, earning a precarious living from fishing, kelping and day labour on the farms.

By the time the Act was finally passed the Tiree cottars were incensed by land-hunger and pro-landlord in-fighting in the local branch of the Land League. When they discovered that the lease of the vacant farm of Greenhill (*Grianal*) in the west of the island had been granted to a prosperous crofter from Vaul, Lachlan MacNeill, they erupted (Meek 1977). This was the communicant who had told the Presbytery on 12 February 1883 that twenty-nine families in the east of the island had left the Church in JGC's time. He was the brother of Neil MacNeill, who had been president of the Tiree branch of the Land League 'until he betrayed his fellow members by carrying stories to the factor' (Niall M. Brownlie, personal communication, 22 July 2004). Not content with expelling both brothers, the cottars and their remaining friends among the crofters prevented Lachlan MacNeill from moving in and proceeded to stock the farm themselves. The duke complained about 'the gross act of illegal violence' and ordered that notices of interdict be served on fifty-one individuals. The procurator fiscal pointed out that if arrests were to be made a strong force of police would be required. Thirty-seven policemen and commissionaires landed at Scarinish on 21 July 1886, but were turned back by an angry crowd at Balephuil.

A military force was then sent. It consisted of 250 marines, 120 bluejackets and forty police, arriving in two naval vessels and a chartered steamer. They disembarked on Saturday 31 July and marched round the island (MacPhail 1989, p. 190):

> Although the Tiree people refused to co-operate with the police in identifying persons named in the notices of interdict, they kindly offered milk to the soldiers when they came to the doors of their cottages asking for a drink. The newspaper correspondents accompanying the expedition were faced with a serious problem in getting their stories to their newspaper offices not merely because of the lack of telegraph communication in the island but also because the march round the island took place on a Saturday. The *Scotsman* reporter suggested to his fellow newspapermen that they should all delay sending their reports until the Monday so as not to offend local feelings about the sanctity of the Sabbath. On the following day, which was the Sabbath, it was discovered that he had sent off a carrier pigeon to the mainland with a full account of the events of Saturday's march. The pigeon was mobbed by seagulls and returned to the hotel at Scarinish, the pages of the *Scotsman* dispatch being scattered through the island and giving cause for great amusement.

The marines marched around the island again on 7 August, this time with better intelligence. Six men were arrested and charged with trespassing on Greenhill farm and with the deforcement of the messenger-at-arms on 21 July. Five more were arrested in September.

At their trial in Edinburgh in October, the Tireemen were found guilty and given jail sentences of four to six months. Lachlan MacNeill was reinstated as tenant of Greenhill. When the new Crofters' Commission visited the island the following year (1887), the crofters' grievances as expressed to the Napier Commission were found entirely justified. On average, rents were reduced by a quarter and almost half of all arrears were cancelled. But nothing could be done for the cottars.[81]

The last piece of JGC's fieldwork (if that is still the right word) to which it is possible to attach a date is the noting of 'Eirig Fhinn' ('Fionn's Ransom'). When he wrote it up for the Gaelic Society of Inverness on 29 September 1888 he stated that it 'was told last spring by John Brown, Kilmoluag, and was written out from very full notes taken at the time' (Campbell 1888–89, p. 50). This will mean the spring of 1888. Presumably Brown and others visited him in the Manse to have their words taken down in the comfort of his study or of his bedroom, either by himself or by Jessy.

Clearly Brown was an important informant at this time; perhaps he was the 'native of the island, well acquainted with the traditions of his countrymen' who told JGC how the Browns first came to Tiree (Campbell 1895, p. 13). 'Na Amhuisgean', read to the Gaelic Society of Inverness on 19 February 1890, is 'from full notes taken of it as told by John Brown' (Campbell 1889–90, p. 112), and 'Sgoil nan Eun, no, Mac an Fhucadair', read to the Society on 4 February 1891, was 'heard principally from John Brown' (Campbell 1890–91, p. 64). He is, I suppose, the same John Brown from Kilmoluag who composed seven songs which have since been published,[82] by but if so he must be, at 34, one of the youngest individuals ever to have recited traditional tales of such substance into the Gaelic folklore record. At least this would explain why he appears so late in JGC's life. Says Cameron (1932, p. 246): "John Brown was born in Kilmoluag, Tiree, on the 4th May, 1854. He began his life as a herd-laddie, proceeded to be a ploughman, and afterwards followed the sea for a living. He was one of the quietest, most modest of men. Yet he was unsurpassed in wit, expressed in such soft and kindly tones that it often escaped many of his hearers, and the bard had his quiet chuckle all to himself. Besides being a poet of merit, he was also a good piper. His songs were mostly of a humorous order. He died on 21st August, 1906."

As a quiet, intelligent young man, John Brown must have been a particularly attentive listener in the ceilidh-house at Kilmoluag. Niall M. Brownlie tells me (personal communication, 22 April 2004) that he was piper to the Tiree Association, but grew over-fond of a dram, and was buried in a pauper's grave in Glasgow.

Part of 'Sgeulachd Casa Céin' was, says JGC (Campbell 1887–88a, p. 78), 'written from the dictation of Malcolm Sinclair, fisherman, Balephuill'. He does not say when, but it was read to the Gaelic Society of Inverness on 14 December 1887. In fact we know from Calum Bàn's son Donald Sinclair (DS), conversing in English with Eric Cregeen (EC) at Hynish on 6 May 1972 (School of Scottish Studies SA 1972.078), that at the end of JGC's life he employed Calum Bàn to work during the day in his garden – the very enclosure which he had persuaded the Presbytery to have built for him in 1862 – and tell him stories at night.

DS   My father died young. I was only a boy when my father died. But he was a storyteller. He knew a lot of things. He was a great friend, my father, with the Reverend John Campbell, that old minister that was in Tiree.

EC   The Reverend John Gregorson Campbell?

DS   Gregorson Campbell, aye. My father was a great friend of his. My father used to be over at the manse at Gott. He was looking after the garden there. Well, that was giving some work to my father. And at night he would be giving stories to old Mr Campbell who was on his death – on his bed. The Reverend John Campbell was for years on his bed. And there was no nurse in Tiree at that time. And my sister nursed him for two years. And there was all the relations. He had a sister called Mistress Wallace. She was staying at Hynish when [*i.e. after*] her brother, the Reverend John Campbell, died. For she was a great friend to us. She was very good to my father. She was a dear old lady. She would be giving him tobacco and pipes every time they would meet.

EC   So the Reverend John Campbell took down quite a lot of your father's stories?

DS   Yes, he did. That's right.

EC   Folklore.

DS   Folklore, yes.

EC   Did he write it down in a book?

DS   Aye. Aye. [*Long pause.*] I don't remember. I remember his sister well, Mistress Wallace. And another sister, she was married at Scarinish. A Mistress Maclean. We knew her well too. A nice lady too. But I have never seen Mr Campbell the brother.

EC   Was there not a minister once here called Neil Maclean, at one time?

DS   Yes. He was a Baile Phuill man.

EC   Oh was he?

DS   Aye.

EC   The minister.

DS   Aye, the minister, that's right. The minister of Tiree. Aye, he was a while in Islay. He was the minister in Islay too. Aye, and there was another minister Maclean in Tiree. His name was Dugald. Dugald Maclean. Och, I remember him well. As far as I know I think he was from Islay.

EC   Yes. Yes.

DS   Aye. He got good Gaelic anyway.

EC   There was the son of a minister that once was a doctor I believe. And he poisoned himself.

DS   Oh yes. That was Mr Neil, they used to call him.

EC   Oh was it?

DS   I don't know his second name, but the people in Tiree used to call him Mr Neil.

EC   I see.

DS   Yes, his son poisoned himself over at Gott Manse. Aye, at that room in the manse over at Gott. His father was a minister. And the room in which his son murdered himself, from then on it was not used.

EC   Was it not?

DS   No, because my sister, my late sister Marion, she was in the service of John Gregorson Campbell for years over at that manse, and she knew the house very well. And this room in which – Maclean was his name, as far as I know – murdered himself, was not opened any time. No.

EC   Why did he kill himself, I wonder?

DS   Well, he made a mistake. He was a doctor in Tiree. And his father was a minister over there at the east end. And he was a boozer. And he was on the booze. And he gave out the wrong medicine to a certain lady. And she was dead. And when he came to his senses he remembered what he had done. He went down to this room and poisoned himself. That's the true history about it.

EC   Yes, yes. Were there any others in the family? Any other brothers or sisters?

DS   As far as I know there were sisters, wherever they went. But he was the only son. *Mac Mhaighstir Nèill.*

In a footnote to the translation of a story collected by JGC which includes a Jonah motif (Campbell 1903–04, p. 300), the editor – James Maclehose, presumably – casts a little light on JGC's hopes and plans in the late 1880s. He had translated 'The Story of Conal Grund' into English, 'and intended that it should form the first of a volume of such Tales'. This probably means what would now be called non-Ossianic fortune, hero and trickster tales, an important category which is missing from his published books but is well represented in the papers published in journals – which by then included the *Celtic Magazine* as well as the *Scottish Celtic Review* and *TGSI*, see p. 708 below. JGC wrote in 1889, presumably by way of commentary on the motif (Campbell 1903–04, p. 300): "The occurrence of the whale in the western islands seems to have been quite common at one time, and there is a story of one having come ashore in the island of Tiree, of such dimensions that sixteen steps of a ladder were required to reach its top, *sia ceumannan deug faraidh*. In 1887, one came ashore in the same island, that was above 80 ft. in length."

It is ironic that by the time JGC had achieved fame as a scholar through the tales and ballads published in *The Scottish Celtic Review* between 1881 and 1885, his illness had advanced to such a point that he was unable to leave the island. Every one of the five sessions of the Gaelic Society of Inverness between 1886–87 and his death in 1891 was adorned by a story collected by the minister of Tiree. It was no small accolade, but JGC never delivered his papers in person. That of 26 January 1887 was read for him by the Librarian, John Whyte (Campbell 1886–87, p. 69). Those of 14 December 1887 and 19 December 1888 were read for him by Alexander Macbain (Campbell 1887–88a, p. 78, and 1888–89, p. 46). That of 4 February 1891 was read for him by the Secretary, Duncan Mackintosh (Campbell 1890–91, p. 58). Only once, on 19 February 1890, are we simply told that 'the paper for this evening was contributed by the Rev. J. Campbell, Tiree' (Campbell 1889–90, p. 110), but we know that by then he was bedridden.

We cannot know the precise nature of his disease, but clearly it involved loss of muscular control. His eldest sister Mary Bell had died of paraplegia in 1875, and a hereditary factor may have been at work. JGC would have been uncomfortably familiar with Sir Walter Scott's account of the German poet Ernst Hoffman (1776–1822), who suffered from a similar condition (Scott 1827, pp. 97–98 = 1835, pp. 331–32):

> The medical persons made the severe experiment whether by applying the actual cautery to his back by means of glowing iron, the activity of the nervous system might not be restored. He was so far from being cast down by the torture of this medical martyrdom, that he asked a friend who entered the apartment after he had undergone it, whether he did not smell the roasted meat. The same heroic spirit marked his expressions, that 'he would be perfectly contented to lose the use of his limbs, if he could but retain the power of working constantly by the help of an amanuensis'.

JGC had a superb amanuensis. By the late 1880s his sister Jessy had become a folklorist herself, earning a place in the bygoing as one of the few Scottish Gaelic scholars who have been women.[83] In 1887 she sent the tale 'Am Fomhair agus an Gille Ruadh' to Alexander Macbain, the editor of *The Celtic Magazine*, with a note stating (Wallace 1887–88a, p. 20): "The foregoing and similar tales were written from full notes taken during the recital of them by old and young people now living in Tiree, 'a chur seachad mo mhulaid' – to alleviate the deepest sorrow, as much as to gratify a taste acquired in childhood and the wish to do something to help those who have already done, with their great gifts and abilities, so much towards preserving what must be to every educated mind a charming national literature."

Jessy's analysis of her motives is obviously of great interest, and it is notable that catharsis stands at the top of the list. In August the following year *The Celtic Magazine* published another of her tales, 'An Iobhal Gheal' ('The Snow-White Maiden'), and it appears that her understanding of folklore methodology had improved in the interim, for this time it is made clear that she herself is the translator, she appends notes on the text, and – most importantly of all – she states her source (Wallace 1887–88b, p. 493): "This tale belongs to the Cinderella class of stories, and is the best Gaelic version of that class known to me. It was taken down in the early part of this year, from the recitation of M. Sinclair, Balephuill, Tiree, who said he heard it from the widow of Archibald Maclean (*Gilleasbuig Og*) in Kilmoluag and is given as nearly as possible in the words of the reciter. The comments and notes are drawn from the assistance within reach."[84]

Clearly it was Jessy herself who had taken down the tale from Calum Bàn.

During these last ten years of JGC's life the door of the Manse of Tiree may have been closed to ministers, except by warrant, but it was open to folklorists. One member of the latter species who would have received a warm welcome was Lord Archibald, whose inappropriately-named *Records of Argyll* – a collection of traditional stories, many of them from Tiree – was published in 1885. After 1886 his base in the island was nearby Gott Lodge, and we may assume that it was he who invited JGC to contribute a volume of Fenian lore to Nutt's 'Waifs and Strays of Celtic Tradition: Argyllshire Series', of which he was general editor. Another folklorist who knocked at the door was Alexander Carmichael, who recalled (CG2, p. 313): "In Tiree the people set small lines along the strand when the tide is out, to catch flounders and other flat fish. When the tide is in the long-tailed ducks dive for fry and sand-eels, and are caught on the hooks and drowned. During a visit to my friend and fellow-collector of folk-lore, the late Rev. Mr Campbell of Tiree, I saw at Hianaish, on the 23rd September 1887, seven of these graceful birds which had been drowned on one set of lines in one day."

This visit had lasting consequences in the shape of a series of manuscript texts given or sent by JGC to Carmichael, all of which are now in the Carmichael–Watson collection in Edinburgh University Library. The first dateable one is EUL MS CW 359, ff. 39–40, transcribed at p. 468 above. It is written in Jessy's very attractive hand and headed by Carmichael at f. 39r 'The Consecration of the Cloth – Translation by The Rev John Gregorson Campbell Minister of Tiree / Recvd 7 Nov. 1888. A.C.' and at f. 40r 'Coisrigeadh an Aodaich'.

It was probably during the visit itself, however, that JGC gave Carmichael a handwritten text of 'Sir Uallabh O Corn',[85] similar but not identical to the one which John Whyte had read for him to the Gaelic Society of Inverness eight months before and which duly appeared in the Society's *Transactions* in 1888 (Campbell 1886–87). It is in an unknown and rather unattractive hand – not Carmichael's, not JGC's, not Jessy's, not Malcolm Livingstone's. JGC had taken down the story from Donald Cameron, Ruaig, on 19 February 1863; assuming, as does Linda Gowans (1998, p. 24), that this manuscript represents a transcript of JGC's field-notes made for him by an amanuensis 'very soon after collection, before the text had received detailed editorial attention', it helps us understand JGC's collecting and editing methods. It begins *Bha Righ air Eirinn ris an abradh iad Arthuir Iuthair*: "There was a king over Ireland whom they called Arthur [son] of Uther." However, the text as published in 1888 begins *Bha Righ air Eirinn ris an abradh iad Ceann Artair Mac-Iuthair*, which JGC translates: "There was a King in Ireland called Kin [*sic*] Arthur Mac Ivar or Ewar." It appears that, following initial transcription, JGC elicited *Ceann Artair Mac-Iuthair*, an authentic-looking form, during one of his subsequent interviews with Cameron between 1863 and 1865 (see p. 633 above). This suggests a procedure consisting of immediate transcription of the full text followed by the checking of points of detail on later visits. Guided by Gowans's analysis, I will now compare three interrelated passages from different parts of the text (Campbell 1886–87, pp. 71, 73, 75, 77, 79, 81, cf. Gowans 1998, pp. 28, 30, 32):

(a) **Manuscript version:** *Dh'eirich e air mullach a chas 's bharraibh ordag, 's bhuail e mu mhullach na braghad e, agus dh'fhag e magairle air gach manachan aige.* "He rose on the points of his feet and the tips of his toes, and struck him at the top of the breast, and left a testicle on each of his groins." **JGC's published version:** *Dh' eirich e air mullach a chas 's air* *bharraibh òrdag, agus bhuail e mu cheann caol na braghad e, agus dh' fhag e leth-chollainn air gach manachan aige.* JGC's translation: "He rose on the points of his feet and the tips of his toes, struck him on the narrow part of his neck, and clave him to the ground." Comments: *mu cheann caol na braghad* sounds like an improvement on *mu mhullach na braghad*, perhaps made by Cameron when the latter was queried. *Leth-chollainn* is, I am sure, a synonym for 'testicle' (cf. Black 2001, p. 460), perhaps printed by JGC because it was a less well-known word than *magairle*; thus, either way, the last phrase means not 'clave him to the ground' but 'left a testicle on each of his groins'.

(b) Manuscript version: *Nochd iad na h'airm leadarra liobhaidh, etc., is dh'fhag Sir Uallabh O Corn magairl air gach manachan aige.* "They showed the sharp polished weapons, etc., and Sir Uallabh O Corn left a testicle on each of his groins." JGC's published version: *Nochd iad na h-airm leadarra liobha do chach a cheile. Tri dìthean a chuireadh iad diubh; dìth teine do'n armaibh, dith calcaidh do'n sgiathan, dìth fala da 'n cneasa 's dè'n collainn, iad a' bualadh 's a cruaidh leadairt a cheile.* JGC's translation: "They showed their sharp polished armour to each other, three blows they struck, a flash of fire from their armour, a flash of sound from their shields, and a flash of blood from their bodies, as they struck and hard smote one another." Comments: the manuscript version consists of (1) an introductory phrase, (2) 'etc.' and (3) the 'testicle' phrase. The published version consists only of (1) the introductory phrase and (2) an expansion of 'etc.' in the form of a battle run about the *tri dìthean*, a variant of the *trí ceatha* 'three showers' described by Bruford (1969, pp. 38, 186). *Dith calcaidh* is not 'a flash of sound' but 'a shower of chalk'.

(c) Manuscript version: *Nochd iad na h airm leadarra liomhaidh do chach a cheile, etc., etc., is dh'fhag e magairl air gach manachan aige.* "They showed the sharp polished weapons to each other, etc., etc., and he left a testicle on each of his groins." JGC's published version: *Nochd iad na h-armaibh leadarra liobha do chach-a-cheile. Tri dìthean a chuireadh iad diubh, dith teine do 'n armaibh, dith calcaidh do 'n sgiatha, dith fala da 'n cneasa 's de 'n collainn; iad a' bualadh 's a' cruaidh leadairt a cheile.* JGC's translation: "They showed their sharp polished armour to each other, three blows they struck, a flash of fire from their armour, a flash of sound from their shields, and a flash of blood from their bodies, as they struck and hard smote one another. Sir Olave O'Corn thought he was far from his friends and near his enemies; he rose on the points of his feet and the tips of his toes, struck him in the narrow part of his neck, and clove him to the groin." Comments: this time the manuscript version consists of (1) the introductory phrase, (2) 'etc.', (3) 'etc.' and (4) the 'testicle' phrase. The published version consists of (1) the introductory phrase, (2) the battle run, (3) a second run identical to one in passage (a), accidentally omitted in Gaelic but given in English, and (4) the 'testicle' phrase, omitted in Gaelic and bowdlerised in English.

It may be seen from this that JGC was in the habit of writing 'etc.' in his transcripts where a 'run' occurred which could be filled in at leisure, e.g. by copying from an earlier point in the text, and that he used a variety of techniques to avoid offending Victorian sensibilities – altering a Gaelic word to one less well known, bowdlerising the English translation, or omitting the phrase altogether. In this respect he was no different from JFC. The folklorist's mantra of 'writing without suppression, addition or alteration' fell silent at the portals of public performance and publication. We may note, however, that JGC was content to pass on his unexpurgated text to Carmichael.

In May 1885, as we have seen, the work of the parish of Tiree had been taken over by a young Uistman, Donald MacDonald. Meeting at Salen on 2 March 1887, the

Presbytery of Mull found before them a letter from Alexander MacLean, Thomas Barr, Lachlan MacPhail and John MacDonald, as representatives of the congregation, asking that Donald MacDonald be formally appointed as JGC's assistant and successor. Unfortunately, as it transpired, he was in the process of accepting a call to North Uist. The Presbytery expressed fulsome thanks to him for his work, and he went on to serve his native parish for fifty years until his retirement in 1937.[86]

JGC asked the brethren to find him a new assistant, and in July 1887 they appointed another young licentiate, Dugald Maclean (1861–1936), the Islayman mentioned above by Dòmhnall Chaluim Bàin. Maclean liked the Tiree people and the Tiree people liked him, but his ten months' tenure is punctuated in the Presbytery minutes by two unsettling truths – Maclean must leave the island to further his career, while in its anger over the land issue the congregation of Heylipol had called Donald MacCallum to be their minister. At Salen on 7 March 1888, with Maclean threatening to leave, Neil MacDougall of Coll and Donald MacCallum of Heylipol were appointed as assessors to help him form a kirk session of Tiree; meanwhile MacDougall and Robert Munro of Ardnamurchan were to speak to JGC 'with the view of inducing him to consent to the appointment of an assistant and successor'. If he did not agree, they would remit the case to the next General Assembly.[87]

MacDougall and Munro met JGC in the Manse of Tiree on 20 April, and reported back to the Presbytery at Tobermory on 2 May that they had been unable to persuade him either to retire from his benefice or to consent to the appointment of an assistant and successor. Worse, they had 'completely failed to induce Mr Campbell to consent to any arrangement other than the present mode of employing an unordained assistant'. The previous pattern was repeating itself, with one small adjustment: when Dugald Maclean was called in May to a parish of his own, his destination was Kinlochspelvie, which was within the Presbytery's bounds (NAS CH2/273/11, pp. 282–83, 295–98).

On 2 May 1888, then, the inevitable petition lay on the Presbytery's table – this time bearing 259 names and asking the brethren 'to bring about a more satisfactory arrangement as at present we feel that we have no minister' – along with a long letter from JGC pointing out that he was only 'about 53' (this at least was true), that he hoped to regain his health, that he was too young for an assistant and successor to be appointed, and that such an appointment, if made, would divide his congregation into 'two camps'. Noting drily that JGC had not discharged his duties for six-and-a-half years, the Presbytery once again referred the case to the General Assembly, appointing another young licentiate of their own, Donald MacLean, as assistant in the meantime.[88]

In its Deliverance of 1 June 1888 the General Assembly stated that 'adequate provision will in the circumstances be made when a duly qualified assistant with a competent salary is appointed and ordained by the Presbytery', but that 'the Assembly cannot legally insist on the appointment of an assistant and successor'. It also appointed two Edinburgh ministers as commissioners to visit Tiree, the Rev. Dr Archibald Scott of St George's and the Rev. Dr Norman MacLeod of St Stephen's.[89] Perhaps no one realised it at the time, but the key words in this judgement were 'and ordained'. The Assembly had just turned the parish of Tiree into a one-stop shop for Gaelic-speaking divinity students in search of speedy licence and ordination – a privilege that had not been accorded to Donald MacDonald, Dugald Maclean or Donald MacLean. Meeting with Scott and MacLeod at Tobermory on 10 July, the Presbytery agreed that JGC should be bound to provide at least £100 per annum from his stipend to pay for an assistant; the two commissioners went on to visit JGC, and reported back from Edinburgh on 28 July (NAS CH2/273/11, pp. 313–19).

> Though manifestly in a very infirm state of health he was able to see us on several occasions when we fully explained to him the views which are entertained by the Presbytery and by ourselves with regard to the present condition of the Parish. In particular we pointed out to him that as he will be required hereafter to pay £100 per annum for an ordained Assistant it would in our opinion be for his own advantage as well as for the advantage of the Parish that he should retire on condition that a suitable allowance could be provided. In this connection we expressed our belief that an allowance of not less than £120 a year should be secured to him for life, and we went the length of undertaking to use our best endeavour to provide £140 in the event of his agreeing to give up the whole emoluments with manse & glebe to his successor.
>
> Having considered this proposal for sometime he informed us that he could not accept it. We then submitted as an alternative proposal that he should acquiesce in the appointment of an Assistant and Successor, giving up the stipend but retaining the manse and glebe with an annual allowance of £50 or £60. This proposal he also declined to entertain. In these circumstances we regret that the only course open to the Presbytery meanwhile appears to be the appointment of an ordained assistant in terms of the General Assembly's Deliverance.

Meeting at Salen on 15 August, the brethren decided – on the advice of Scott and MacLeod – that a legal bond would be required to oblige JGC to pay £100 every year, and that they should themselves go to Tiree to consult the people. This provoked a sarcastic response from JGC, dated 20 August (NAS CH2/273/11, pp. 319–23, 326–28): "As you are soon to visit the Island and my word does not seem to be much esteemed by you; I hope when you do come it will be with unprejudiced minds and with a desire to act impartially and to give no credence to every or interested [*sic*] report."

He also demanded copies of relevant documents and refused to give a bond, but when the Presbytery – in the shape of MacDougall, MacFarlane, MacKintosh and Dugald Maclean – arrived in Tiree in time for public worship on Sunday 23 September, they had a draft bond with them. Scott and MacLeod were there before them, and were able to report to the meeting in the church at Kirkapol on the Monday that 'since our arrival at this Island on Friday last we have had two interviews with Mr Campbell, whom we regret still to find in a state of great bodily infirmity'. JGC again refused to retire, and pointed out that fiar's prices had had a deleterious effect on his income (NAS CH2/273/11, pp. 328–34). "We are sorry to have to inform you," wrote Scott and MacLeod, "that, on visiting him to-day he expressed himself as unwilling to give a guarantee for any amount and added that when he agreed to pay £80 the stipend was £70 better than last year. Thereupon we did our utmost to impress him with the very serious responsibilities under which he lies towards the parish and that it would be our duty to report both to the Presbytery and to the General Assembly that the present arrangements for the service of this parish were so unsatisfactory as to amount to a scandal."

JGC elaborated on his point about fiar's prices in a letter to MacLeod and Scott dated 24 September. Presumably he had it delivered to them at the Scarinish Hotel. In August 1884 when, through Reid, he had agreed to pay £80, the stipend was, he said, at £242; now although it stood at only £169 he was being asked to pay £100. His letter was laid on the church table along with the formal records of his stewardship of the parish.

> The Clerk intimated that he had called for the Minutes of session, the Baptismal Register and the Communion Roll. There were produced a book entitled Tiree Kirk-session Cash Book from 1793 to 31st December 1866, after which no proper entry appears and a Communion Roll for the years 1885 to 1888. No minutes of Kirksession nor Baptismal Register were produced, although it appears from entries in the Cash Book that a Baptismal Register was in existence in the years 1865 and 1866.

The Presbytery then met with the congregation, consisting that day of fifty-eight members and adherents. After prayer, MacFarlane (as moderator), MacLeod and Scott explained what had transpired (NAS CH2/273/11, pp. 335–38). "Thereupon, several members of the congregation expressed their sentiments all of them declaring their extreme dissatisfaction with the present condition of the parish."

It was agreed that an assistant should be ordained and have a competent salary. The Presbytery would select candidates, these would preach, the congregation would indicate their preference, and the Presbytery would 'give effect to the wishes of the congregation in the event of there being substantial unanimity'. The congregation also asked that elders be appointed, and that there be 'a meeting-house at Cornaig for the convenience of parishioners residing in that district' (NAS CH2/273/11, pp. 338–39).

The result of the meeting must have been duly reported to JGC, for by the time the brethren had reconvened in the Scarinish Hotel at 7 p.m. he had written to them, agreeing to a bond obliging himself to pay them £80 per annum for an assistant from March 1889. They agreed at once (NAS CH2/273/11, pp. 340–42). "The appointment as well as the supervision of the Assistant's work shall be entirely with the Presbytery inasmuch as in Mr Campbell's extreme state of infirmity, he having now been bed-ridden for several years, it is manifestly impossible for him properly to perform any of the duties of the pastoral office."

The Presbytery thought they had finally shaken free of the 'Tiree Case', as it was routinely called in their minutes. They had, however, underestimated the difficulties of dealing with a man whose body was deteriorating faster than his mind and of persuading capable young pastors that the assistantship of Tiree was a post worth having. On 18 October Donald MacLean left the island for Duirinish, while JGC moaned to the Presbytery that 'the whole proceeding which has been adopted with regard to this parish is illegal both ecclesiastically and civilly' and demanded the opinion of the Procurator in Edinburgh, Sir Colin Pearson. Pearson duly opined that 'Mr Campbell entirely misapprehends the present position' and that 'in the event of Mr Campbell's refusing to secure the extremely moderate provision now insisted on by the Presbytery their alternative is not to force him to do so but to proceed against him by libel as indicated in the Assembly's Deliverance of 1884' (NAS CH2/273/12, pp. 13–17, 29).

As always, JGC was sent the relevant papers and given a deadline for reply. Events now took a dramatic turn, however. Instead of the usual long letter from JGC, the clerk to the Presbytery received a brief note from the Tiree doctor.

> Manse, Tiree 13th. Novr. 1888
>
> Dear Sir,
> I am sorry to say that Mr Campbell is unable to sign any documents through a severe illness, and I have very little hope that he will recover from this illness.
>
> Yours faithfully
> (Signed) Alexr. Buchanan.
>
> The Revd. W. MacKintosh
> E.C. Manse, Craignure.

The next meeting of the Presbytery was at Salen on 30 November. When the brethren had begun to foregather and MacKintosh showed them the letter, several members suggested that this was an ideal occasion to make use of the telegraph line which had now been laid as far as Tiree. MacKintosh duly sent this message:

> Dr Buchanan, Tiree, Please wire immediately how Mr. Campbell is. Can he transact business? Moderator Presbytery Aros waiting reply.

Buchanan replied:

> Tiree Novr. 30th '88 3h18m received at 3h30m To Moderator Presbytery Aros. Campbell is no better. Cannot transact business especially writing.

On 6 December Jessy wrote to the Presbytery to thank them for their letters of 8 November and 1 December:

> I would have acknowledged receipt at the time but thought it best and more convincing that you should get word direct from Dr Buchanan of my brother's total inability to attend to business or writing. He still continues too ill to make any effort.

Two days later it was Buchanan's turn, but the line that he took was outwith the control of the invalid in the Manse bedroom.

> I am glad to inform you that Mr Campbell's health has greatly improved within the last ten days, and I am now of opinion that he is able to transact business as he is free from pain and his mind clear but at the same time he has not physical strength to sign documents (as he has yet to be fed) and I fear that it will take some time before he is able to sign his name. I would suggest to the Presbytery that any important papers requiring his signature and which cannot be deferred be witnessed by a notary.

MacLeod promptly sent from Edinburgh the form of docquet required to obtain JGC's assent to the bond as witnessed by a notary or Justice of the Peace. Determined to have a reply, the Presbytery appointed MacCallum and MacFarlane to visit JGC if necessary. Battling at this point on two other fronts, they were also desperate to obtain 'the help of either a licentiate or a lay-catechist or Bible-reader in attending to the spiritual wants of the sick and infirm in the parish of Tiree for the next two months or so', and to remedy the poverty into which MacCallum was sinking as a result of the obduracy of the duke of Argyll (NAS CH2/273/12, pp. 19–30).

They met with success on the first two fronts. The bond was duly signed with JGC's consent by Hugh MacDiarmid, acting in his capacity as a Justice of the Peace, on 28 January 1889, and an elder and catechist from Acharacle, Hugh Cameron, was persuaded to spend the period from 29 January to 13 March 1889 in the island (NAS CH2/273/12, pp. 31–35). It seems that JGC's relapse in December had allowed Jessy to inject a little sweetness into his affairs, and this may also be detected in a letter now received by Carmichael.

Manse of Tiree
17th Dec. '88

Dear Mr Carmichael,

To prevent your running the uncanny risk of a seaward voyage, at this time of year, I begged & have got permission from my brother to send you a copy of the very beautiful "Invocation to Saints", which I now enclose. He has his collection arranged in his large & most valuable work for publication, but the state of his health has been a grave hindrance & loss not only to Celtic but to other literatures. There is a very slight improvement in his health but not enough for any exertion or attention to business, & he requires constant watchings.

Your remembrances to both my mother & himself are most acceptable.

Thanks for sending me such a pretty hymn. I think some of the forms of words & expressions in Gaelic cannot be surpassed, nor can justice be done to them by any translation. You have our best wishes for your success with your publication, & if my brother gets better before then, he will do what he can for you. Have you one on 'Strangles' in horses? if not he may be able to send you one.

The *miorbhuilleach* word 'new' to you must I think be "Mìcheil" as in the manuscript from which I copied – English – "Michael" if not it will be a mis-spelt word on my part, a mistake very ready to occur in my Gaelic knowledge out of which many new, & incomprehensible words could be easily got. Mr John White Inverness knows about that! Will your oration!! before the Glasgow Gaelic Society be in any "paper" that we can see?

Our united kindest regards to you.

Yours truly
Jessy Wallace

Enclosed with Jessy's letter (EUL MS CW 487, ff. 183–85) were five sheets of paper, now EUL MS CW 425, ff. 174–77 and 197, on which she had written JGC's 28-line version of 'Oradh nam Buadh', along with an English translation (not the one which appears at pp. 216–17 above) and the following note:

This Invocation was taken down from an old woman in the east end of Tiree, who had learned it in her youth in Balephuill, in the extreme west end of the island. These Invocations seem to have been originally of pre-christian origin, and in their beginning were perhaps as much Druidic as *"Dàn an Deirg"* or *"Laoidh an Amadain Mhoir"* the names of Saints being substituted to give them a Christian character. The magic Invocations to which now the name of witchcraft is given were for the prevention and cure of diseases, for the warding off of danger, and for the bestowal of gifts, and must have formed part of the weapons of the Magician or Wise man, as they are called for in every age, and under every creed.

Manse of Tiree
17th Dec. 1888

As is pointed out at p. 478 above, the 'old woman in the east end of Tiree' was Margaret Macdonald; the reference to John 'White' must be to the work of preparing 'Sgeulachd air Sir Uallabh O'Corn' (Campbell 1886–87) for the press, I think, as it was not published until 1888. By the following spring JGC was well enough to work again, and he dictated to Jessy translations of two more hymns which Carmichael had sent. The first, now in CW MS 359, ff. 36–37, was 'Sloinntireachd Bhride' ('Genealogy of Bride'), which Carmichael had got from Donald Macdonald, a crofter at Griminish in Benbecula (*CG2*, p. 375). It was eventually published in *CG1*, pp. 174–75 – not, however, with the translation which JGC sent him, but with Carmichael's own. The text underlying JGC's translation appears to have been as published, except that there is no trace of the phrase *Lasair dhealrach oir* ('Radiant flame of gold'). JGC must have felt very much at home with Carmichael's line *Cha reub saighid sithich, no sibhich mi*, which he rendered: "Nor will I be hurt / by Fairy, or swift-speeding / Arrow." He dictated a note:

> The *Bride* or Bridget of this hymn is one of the famous Saints of Irish History, and her name is still used in many parts of the Highlands of Scotland to denote the first day of Spring O.S. The names of her progenitors have a meaning as most primitive names have.

(signed) John G. Campbell

Manse of Tiree
Mar. 1889

It may seem curious to us now that the revered author and collector of *Carmina Gadelica* should have been patronised in this way. The note tells us something about both individuals. Carmichael was not a scholar but a likeable man, enthusiastic and persuasive, with an open and enquiring mind. We may guess that when being told something for the umpteenth time he paid as much attention as if he had never heard it in his life. JGC, on the other hand, wore his scholarship upon his sleeve, talked as much as he listened, and had frightened even the great polymath, JFC: "Don't be hard upon a clansman who is doing his best." Now, to make things worse, he was living in the sealed-off twilight world of his bedroom, his books, and his admiring female relatives.

The other hymn which JGC translated for Carmichael in the spring of 1889 appears to have consisted of the material ultimately published in *CG2*, pp. 202–09, as two separate items: 'Ban-Tighearna Bhinn' ('The Melodious Lady-Lord') and 'Righinn nam Buadh' ('Queen of Grace'). Carmichael had got these from Malcolm Maclellan, a crofter at Griminish in Benbecula (*CG2*, p. 380). All that appears to survive of JGC's translation is the final page (EUL MS CW 359, f. 46r), representing the second half (lines 12–22) of 'Righinn nam Buadh'. It is in Jessy's hand. I give it here on the right; on the left I reprint the original as it stands in *CG2*, p. 208, breaking Carmichael's long lines to correspond with the translation.

Le maotharan og	As softly she hummed
am bonn nan stuc,	At the base of the knoll,
Gun lon dhaibh le cheil	Under the dew of Heaven,
fo chorr nan speur,	they were, without food,
Gon sgoth fo 'n ghrein	Or shelter, under the sun,
bho 'n namhaid.	From their foes.
Ta sgiath Mhic De	The Shield of the Son of God
da comhdach,	covers her.
Ta ciall Mhic De	The Blessing of the Son of God
da seoladh,	directs her.
Ta briathar Mhic De	The Word of the Son of God
mar bhiadh di fein,	is her sustenance.
Ta reul 'n a leirsinn mhoir	His Light is great insight
di.	to her.
Ta duibhre na h-oidhche dhi	The Darkness of night
mar shoillse an lo,	Is clearer than the day,
Ta an lo dhi a ghnath 'n a sholas,	Day is always a joy to her
Ta Moir oigh nan gras	Gracious Mary is in
's a h-uile h-ait,	every place.
Le na seachd graidh	With Charity,
'g a comhnadh.	ever, helping her.

This reveals that in the text sent to JGC the first line here ended not *og* 'young' but *bog* 'soft', and that the second-last line did not contain *seachd* 'seven'. Carmichael's translations of these lines in *CG* are 'With tenderest babe at the base of the bens' and 'With the seven beatitudes compassing her'.

The two following pages in CW MS 359, now incorrectly numbered as ff. 45 and 38, contain (again in Jessy's hand) JGC's commentary on the combined hymn, referring in particular to the words *lacha* and *lon(a)* which now appear in *CG2*, pp. 202 and 204. At the top of f. 45r Carmichael adds in pencil: "An Turaman-sleibhe = from tuiream and ian. from the doleful tone the bird assumes before a great snow storm." This refers to *Cha tarman tuirim / An t-sleibh i* 'Not the murmuring ptarmigan / Of the hill is she', *CG2*, pp. 204–05.

The *Lacha* translated 'singing duck' mentioned in the foregoing hymn is most probably the "Long-tailed Duck" which is called the musical duck, on account of the peculiarity of throat which the male bird possesses and its power to sing,

"When the storm is at its height, and the waves running mountains high, then their glee seems to reach its highest pitch, and they appear thoroughly to enjoy the confusion". (see) "Gray's Birds of the West of Scotland".

Lon commonly means blackbird, but here it represents a bird of melody.

Mermaids, if apocryphal, are yet believed in far, and wide. Among the Indians of Guiana, porpoises are said to be 'omars', or 'water-women', see, "Thurn's "Among the Indians of

Guiana", and the cry of the Mermaid has been immortalized by 'Leyden' the poet in his "Maid of Colonsay" where he speaks of "The mermaid's sweet sea-soothing lay"

The plaintive and human-like cry of the seal, for the loss of its young, is well known in the Western Islands.

How or why the 'singer' was called '*Uisneach*' is not known to the writer '*Uisneach*' being usually a masculine name, as *Clann Uisnich* nan each geala.

(Signed) John G. Campbell

Manse of Tiree
March 1889

For Leyden and 'The Mermaid', here misremembered as 'The Maid of Colonsay', see pp. 62–63 above. JGC now dictated a covering letter (EUL MS CW 487, ff. 195–96); it sheds some light on Carmichael's question about *Uisneach*.

Manse of Tiree
30th Mar. '89

My dear Sir,

I have had your letter of 14th inst. & in reply I send you translations of the Hymns, you sent, which seem to me very valuable & the translation is as literal & well done as I can.

I am familiar enough with the name of St. Bridget & other charms in which she figures but I never heard her descent, or that a prayer was offered to her. The incident connected with the '*Naomh Uisneach*' I never heard of & can offer no opinion regarding the event of her leaving Ireland.

Any assistance that I can offer will be gladly given & I will always be happy to hear from you. My health is continuing as it was. My mother is now better. All here join in kindest remembrances to you.

Yours truly
John G. Campbell
pr. J.W.

A Carmichael Esqr.

The 'incident' to which JGC refers is described in *CG2*, p. 202. Two nuns in Benbecula had been visiting the sick. On their way home they heard the shrill voice of a child and the soft voice of a woman coming from the foot of the cliffs. The woman was an Irish princess who had taken holy orders. The child was an Irish prince whose life had been threatened by a usurper to the throne, and who was being brought to safety in Scandinavia when the ship in which he was travelling was wrecked. JGC's reference to the 'singer' evokes the lullaby which the two nuns heard coming from the foot of the rocks. Carmichael says that the hymns were composed by the two nuns, that according to one version of the story the child grew up and succeeded to his throne in Ireland, and that according to another he died in the North Sea and was buried in North Ronaldsay in Orkney. Clearly in his letter of 14 March he had asked JGC if he knew of any historical evidence for the incident; he never did get the evidence he sought, but chose to follow the story with an account of the battle of Clontarf as an example of interaction between Norse and Gael.

The sick man's terseness in his letter of 30 March and his pedagogic tone in the next (a sign of improving health?) are mitigated by the overt femininity of his sister's hand (EUL MS CW 487, ff. 193–94).

Manse of Tiree
2d May '89

My dear Sir,

I have got your letter of 15th ult. with an enclosure of "old things" as you call them. My idea of these hymns or odes or invocations, is that they are simply the words used by those to whom the name of witches ['is commonly' *erased*] is very commonly given, professing to be for the cure of disease in man & beast, & said when pulling plants of magic power, & especially for the cure of the evil eye. No great efficacy is now popularly ascribed to them as remedial measures, but they are of interest as shewing a former state of belief. For me to enter into the subject at any length would would [*sic*] be to open up the whole of former beliefs.

I never heard of "*Sleamhnan*". The stye on the eye is elsewhere called *neōnagan* & was driven away by being counted, & a burning stick being whirled round in front of the eye, adding after the ninth time, "*Tàr as a neonagain*" (Fly away stye).

I have heard about the plant "*Foraman*" in Skye as being fennel where fresh water falls into the sea but I do not know its scientific name. But without entering into these subjects at any great length, I cannot but think that in point of value it is necessary, that the words of these rhymes are given by you exactly as they came to hand without addition, or suppression, or emendation. This will give them greater weight, & value as actually found in popular lore. I think therefore it would not be wise for me to interfere even if I could.

I send you copy of the *Eolas* for Strangles which I fell in with. My own health is no better than when you saw me.

Yours faithfully
John G. Campbell
pr. J.W.

A Carmichael Esqr.

P.S. I return the manuscript by this mail in case it may be required. JGC pr J.W.

This is of great interest with respect to Alexander Carmichael's work and the difference between the two men. JFC was now four years dead. JGC, being rather stiff, had not got on particularly well with the great man but believed implicitly in his dictum 'I would not give a snuff for "cooked" tradition'. Carmichael's personal warmth had allowed him to get on with JFC like a house on fire, but his instincts were those of the propagandist, and he was determined – like James Macpherson in the previous century – to write a book that would present the Gael to the Gall in such strong and glowing colours that his readers would cease to think of the Gael as illiterate peasants whose language should be swept aside. In a word, Carmichael was cooking.

JGC had clearly detected this in the questions posed to him, and his discomfort is evident. The problem does not lie with the cure for a stye (for which see p. 225) but with *foraman*. By the time Carmichael published his rambling account of this plant, which he had in three charms as *torranan* (*CG2*, pp. 78–91), he had forgotten – or cast aside – JGC's *foraman* 'fennel', deciding instead that it was the figwort and that its name was that of St Torranan of Uist, of St Ternan of Banchory, of the isle of Taransay, and of Taranis, the thunder god of the Gauls. There is no reason to doubt the overall authenticity of the three charms, but in his introduction to them Carmichael stirs such a spicy blend of speculation, history and topography into his basic ingredients (e.g. the streams in Benbecula called the *Gamhnach* and the *Deathachan*) that the unique flavour of genuine oral tradition is lost.

The charm to cure the strangles (*an stringlein*) in horses was duly sent, and Carmichael published it without comment in *CG2*, pp. 126–27, noting only at p. 349 that it was 'taken down from an old man, name omitted, by the Rev. John G. Campbell, Tiree'.

Meanwhile, the brethren of the Presbytery of Mull had found someone to shoulder the burden of JGC's parish – or so they thought. Neil Macleod from Strath, Skye, then a divinity student in Aberdeen, agreed to come to the island as student missionary and, following ordination, as assistant minister. Arriving in Tiree on 17 April, he was examined and licensed at Tobermory on 1 May, and duly ordained by the Presbytery in JGC's church at Kirkapol on 16 May. The terms of his contract were entered in the minutes: the Presbytery's agreement with Macleod is 'terminable by three months' notice on either side or by the decease, resignation or removal of the said Mr J. G. Campbell' (NAS CH2/273/12, pp. 49–53, 64–66).

These words were to appear several more times during the next two years. His ordination in the bag, Macleod waited just one month before giving notice. He withdrew it in July, but had to request payment of his salary in September, and was gone by 9 October, leaving behind him a paper-trail in the minutes as the Presbytery obtained a loan from the Clydesdale Bank in Tobermory (on the strength of JGC's bond) in order to pay him, then asked the duke of Argyll to remunerate them out of his contribution to the parish stipend of Tiree, shortly after which £20 arrived from JGC in any case – a process which was to be repeated (with slight variations) twice in the next two years.[90]

By the beginning of 1890 MacCallum had gone to Lochs, and neither half of Tiree now had a functioning Church of Scotland minister. The problem was solved however by the translation to Heylipol of Dugald Maclean, who had proved to be an extremely effective member of the Presbytery. Maclean was promptly authorised 'to administer the sacrament of baptism and to conduct Divine service within the bounds of the said parish of Tiree according to his discretion as occasion may permit or require until a regularly ordained assistant is appointed'. At the same time a divinity student called MacCallum was temporarily employed to serve as missionary in the parish of Tiree.[91]

Meeting at Tobermory on 2 April 1890, the Presbytery appointed James Mackinnon, M.A., from Killean, Kintyre, as student missionary with a view to being ordained as assistant. He was licensed at Tobermory on 7 May and it was decided that his ordination should take place at Kirkapol on 25 May. The people were not entirely satisfied with him; ordination was postponed, but on 8 June Dugald Maclean discussed the matter with the congregation and obtained their consent. Mackinnon was therefore ordained at Tobermory on 11 June before returning to the island as JGC's assistant. On 24 September his letter of resignation arrived; no doubt well aware of Neil Macleod's experience, he requested his salary at the same time.[92]

Ever since 24 September 1888 the name of Hector MacKinnon (1866–1913) had been making occasional appearances in the Presbytery minutes. This MacKinnon, at least, was no carpet-bagger. JGC had baptised him himself – a son of Donald MacKinnon, Kirkapol, he had grown up as *Eachann Dhòmhnaill 'ic Eachainn* under his very nose. Now, meeting at Salen on 4 March 1891, the Presbytery agreed to take him on trials for licence. They were also told that, after exhaustive advertising, a certain R. S. Macleod had applied for the assistantship. He was neither student nor ordained minister, and seemingly on the basis that they should only use a person like this if they could get him for nothing, they decided to ask the Highland Committee of the Church to fund him for eight weeks. Nothing more is recorded of Macleod, for on 6 May, at Tobermory, Hector MacKinnon passed his trials for licence, and by 24 May he had accepted the assistantship.[93]

On Wednesday 22 July 1891 the Presbytery gathered in the church at Kirkapol for MacKinnon's ordination. It was a day of hope for the congregation. At long last the pulpit was to be occupied by one of their own. Never one who enjoyed being ignored, however, and elated by the appearance that very summer of his first book, *The Fians*, JGC launched a missile in the brethren's direction. It was the last of many. For three decades now successive Presbytery clerks had preserved his missives for posterity in their minutes either by transcribing them in full or by briefly noting their subject-matter, the originals being either discarded immediately or preserved elsewhere and subsequently lost. All we know of JGC's last words to his colleagues is this: "The Clerk submitted a letter from the Rev J. G. Campbell (per J. W.) as to the dispensation of the Sacrament of the Supper in the parish of Tiree."

We may guess that JGC was demanding to know what arrangements had been made for that year's communion. His answer came swiftly. Hector MacKinnon, says the same minute, would celebrate Holy Communion the following Sabbath, 26 July. After JGC's death it was MacKinnon who succeeded him as parish minister of Tiree, and the schedule of debts annexed to JGC's will in 1892 by his executor, Duncan Cameron, includes a sum of £27 1s 10d 'assigned to the Presbytery of Mull, from stipend, towards salary of assistant minister'.[94]

On 17 February 1891 JGC had sent Carmichael two more translations written out for him by Jessy (EUL MS CW 359, ff. 41–44). The 'Invocation for Fishing' corresponds pretty closely to the text in *CG*1, pp. 318–20, except that where *CG* has *o'n Tri tha shuas* 'from the Three on high', JGC gives 'from Him on high', which suggests that the words Carmichael sent were *o'n Ti tha shuas*. Similarly, 'A Consecration at Seedsowing time' corresponds to the text in *CG*1, pp. 242–44, except that where *CG* has *Thig dealt a nuas a chur failt / Air gach por a bha 'n an suain* 'The dew will come down to welcome / Every seed that lay in sleep', JGC gives 'Wet will fall that will give growth / To every slumbering seed' – *a chur fais*, presumably. Less significantly perhaps, where *CG* mentions Ariel (*Airil*) and Gabriel (*Gabril*), JGC has Gabriel and Raphael. Carmichael's texts, unlike JGC's, were shifting sands. The 'Consecration' ends (*CG*1, p. 244):

Cha tig Cailleach ri an-uair
Dh' iarraidh bonnach boise bhuainn,
Duair thig gaillionn garbh na gruaim
Cha bhi gainne oirnn no cruas.

Carmichael: "No Carlin will come with bad times / To ask a palm bannock from us, / What time rough storms come with frowns / Nor stint nor hardship shall be on us." JGC: "No old woman (see footnote) will come unseasonably / To ask a handcake from me, / When winter comes with a frown / We will not have either want or hardship."

Clearly *bhuainn* was then *bhuam*, and *gaillionn* was *geamhradh*. JGC's footnote reads simply: "Old woman means want or scarcity."

By the time the census was taken on 5 April 1891 the Manse had been extended, and now boasted nineteen rooms. JGC's mother had died on 2 May of the previous year, but Jessy was still with him. She under-reported her age as 56 and kept her brother's in proportion at 55. Again she did not state her occupation. There were still three menials. The farm servant was now Allan MacFadyen, unmarried, aged 31, a native of Tiree. The housemaid was Christina Brown, married, also aged 31 and also a native of Tiree. Interestingly, the table-maid, now described as 'General Serv. (Domestic)', was from Harris: she is another Christina MacDonald, aged 22 and unmarried. Her presence in the house may be connected in some way with the fact that no other part of the Long Island is so well represented in *The Gaelic Otherworld* as Harris.[95] All members of the household spoke Gaelic and English except MacFadyen, who spoke Gaelic only.

The Fians, a substantial collection of Ossianic tales and ballads, was the only one of JGC's books published in his lifetime, and its impact on the world of folklore was considerable: Joseph Jacobs, a leading member of the Folk-Lore Society, included JGC's 'How Fin went to the Kingdom of the Big Men' in *More Celtic Fairy Tales*.[96] *The Fians* has two introductions, one by JGC and one by Nutt.[97] JGC's concludes (Campbell 1891, p. xiii): "The writer himself being unable to write, the work of transcribing this volume has been undertaken for him, in loving memory of one (his widowed mother's only child) who, though of tender years, and partly an alien, said of Gaelic, 'I love it best' (*Si Ghailig is docha leums*)."

These poignant words constitute almost all that can be said about the short and tragic life of Jessy's son John Campbell Wallace.

JGC died in the Manse of Tiree on Sunday 22 November 1891, aged 57. His age is given on the death certificate as 56. The condition that led to his death, certified by Buchanan, was a chronic degenerative disease of the nervous system (ten years) aggravated by congestion of the lungs (four days). *Crìonaidh iad*, as the glaistig said, *mar an raineach*, and perhaps Jessy truly believed in the curse, for she appears to have drawn it to Nutt's attention (Campbell 1895, p. ix). On 5 December the *Oban Times* ran two obituaries. The first was on JGC the man:

Although Mr Campbell has been long laid aside from duty through infirm health, still his death deserves more than a passing notice. He was a genial, kindly man, full of wit and humour; very fond of old Highland stories and folk-lore. In this field of study he was quite an authority, and the many stories and legends which he has collected, if ever given to the world, will form a series of volumes as interesting as those of the late J. F. Campbell of Islay. It is to be hoped that his talented sister, Mrs Wallace, will see her way to publish the rich stores of Celtic folk-lore which her brother collected.

Mr Campbell was never married. His mother, who has only recently passed away, lived with him, and also his widowed sister. Although for many years precluded from taking an active part either in ecclesiastical or social life, many in Tiree will miss his kindly greeting and his caustic wit, and not a few of his college friends and former associates will lovingly place a stone upon his cairn.

JGC's sense of humour, twice remarked upon here, bubbles to the surface occasionally in *The Gaelic Otherworld*, see for example 'Magpie', p. 123. The obituarist continues:

There was a large gathering at the funeral on Friday, the whole island being represented, and all seemed to feel the solemnity of the occasion. Rev. Mr MacLean, Moss, conducted a short service at the Manse, after which Rev. Hector MacKinnon engaged in prayer. Rev. Messrs Macfarlane and Mackay officiated at the grave. Among those present at the funeral were – chief mourner, Rev. Mr MacDougall, Coll; Mr MacDiarmid, factor; Mr Gunn, Ruaig; Mr MacKinnon, Cornaig; Mr Macfarlane, teacher, Moss; Mr Meechan, Scarinish; Mr MacLean, farmer, Scarinish; Mr MacLean, farmer, Caolis; Mr Macdonald, farmer, Heanish; Mr Oliver; Mr Barr, farmer; Mr Brown, farmer, Mannal; Mr Macfadyen, farmer, Coll; Mr MacPhail, poor inspector; Mr MacNeill, jun., of Greenhill, etc.[98]

This is basically a list of those to whom, just twenty years before, JFC had so succinctly referred as 'gentry the worst class for my purpose'; we have to assume that some at least of JGC's surviving informants, men like Calum Bàn, were also part of the gathering. Of the two ministers who officiated at the grave, Donald MacFarlane (1861–1923) was the successor of the 'High Priest' in Morvern; in 1907 he was to become minister of Gigha, where in due course he was succeeded by Kenneth Macleod, Marjory Kennedy-Fraser's collaborator in *The Songs of the Hebrides* (Scott 1915–50, vol. 4, pp. 55, 118, and vol. 8, p. 323). Donald Tulloch Mackay (*MacÀidh Thiridhe*, 1850–1932) was minister of the Free Church congregation in the island, but a very different kind of man from his predecessor John MacLeod, M.D. – a native of Lochalsh, he had an open heart full of evangelical love and generosity, and simply used Tiree as a base from which to spread the gospel throughout the islands and as far afield as Canada (Ewing 1914, vol. 1, p. 234, and vol. 2, p. 122; Dòmhnallach 1970). The chief mourner, the Rev. Neil MacDougall (1829–1906), was a much older man: ordained to Ardrishaig in 1863, he had been in Canada until 1877, when he became minister of Coll. He was deposed in 1895, reponed six years later, and spent the last year of his life as minister of the Gaelic Chapel in Rothesay (Scott 1915–50, vol. 4, pp. 1, 44, 109).

The second *Oban Times* obituary, by 'another correspondent', was on JGC the scholar; after enthusiastically describing *The Fians*, he (or she) says:

This work was prepared by Mr Campbell while lying on a sick bed, to which he had been confined for many years, weak in body but patient and vigorous in mind. He was earnestly engaged in preparing for the publication of another volume of Celtic lore when death put an end to his labours on Sunday last week, and deprived Scotland of an accomplished antiquarian, and his friends and parishioners of one of the kindest and best of friends.

The word 'antiquarian' reminds us that the terms 'folklore' and 'folklorist' had only been coined in 1846 (Dorson 1968, pp. 1, 75, 80–81). Presumably the volume he was working on at his death was the one mentioned above, p. 666.

The value of JGC's estate was £1,490 16s 7d, a substantial sum.[99] JGC's will, as confirmed at Inveraray on 24 March 1892 (NAS SC51/32/41, pp. 398–407), is a remarkable document. Drawn up by his Edinburgh solicitor, Francis John Martin WS, it was signed by JGC in Tiree on 24 April 1886 and witnessed by the Rev. Donald MacDonald ('my Assistant residing at Scarnish Tiree') and Hector MacKinnon ('Student in Arts at the University of Edinburgh presently residing at Kirkapol Tiree'). He begins, as we might have hoped, with his literary legacy.

> I The Reverend John Gregorson Campbell, Minister of the Parish of Tiree, residing at the Manse of Tiree, considering it to be a duty incumbent on me to settle my affairs in the event of my death, do hereby give and bequeath to my brother-in-law Kenneth William Mackenzie, residing at Kirkapol Cottage, Tiree and failing him to his two sons Kenneth Mackenzie and John Gregorson Campbell Mackenzie equally between them all my books and manuscripts with the exception aftermentioned with full power to him or them to publish the said manuscripts or to deal therewith as they may think proper;[100] but declaring that my three sisters Mrs Jessie Campbell or Wallace Mrs Jane Campbell or McLean, and Mrs Margaret Campbell or MacKenzie shall each be permitted to select any book they may respectively desire from my library to be retained as a memento of me; and having entire confidence in the integrity and ability of the persons afternamed for executing the Trust hereby reposed in them, I do hereby give grant assign and dispone to and in favor of Alexander Buchanan, Surgeon, Tiree, the Reverend Neil Macdougall Minister of the Parish of Coll, Henry Knox Dick Merchant in Glasgow, and residing at Homehill House Bridge of Allan, and the said Kenneth William Mackenzie or the acceptors or acceptor survivors or survivor of them as Trustees for the ends uses and purposes aftermentioned.

Briefly stated, the Trustees' duties are (1) to pay off all debts; (2) to convey the estate to JGC's mother; (3) in the event of her predeceasing him, to invest the estate and pay the annual interest equally to Jessy and Jean; (4) in the event of their death, to pay the interest equally to his nieces Helen Margaret Maclean and Johanna Gregorson Campbell Maclean until each is twenty-one; (5) after that, to share the capital equally between them; (6) 'failing both then the same shall be paid to my own next of kin according to the law of Scotland'.[101] Lengthy instructions follow with regard to the types of security in which the capital may be invested.

Three years later, in a substantial codicil dated 1 July 1889, JGC showed that, while his respect for his sisters and nieces was undimmed, he had found his 'entire confidence in the integrity and ability of the persons afternamed' to be misplaced.

> I give and bequeath to my sister Mrs Jessy Campbell or Wallace all books and manuscripts in my possession whether written by myself or by others to my dictation with full power and authority to arrange them for the press or to dispose of them in any way she may think fit and I accordingly recall any former bequeathing of the same to my brother-in-law my nephews or any one else. Further I nominate and appoint Duncan Cameron Merchant Kinloch Rannoch and his brother Ewen Cameron Merchant Valparaiso or the acceptors or acceptor, survivors or survivor of them, as sole and absolute Trustees for the purposes of the foregoing deed of settlement.

Thus did JGC sweep aside his entire nexus of friends in Tiree and Glasgow and turn instead to his cousins – for presumably such they were – from lonely Rannoch, one of whom now lived at the opposite end of the earth. The codicil concludes:

> By authority of the above named and designed John Gregorson Campbell, who declares that he cannot write on account of sickness and bodily weakness I Hugh Macdiarmid Justice of Peace for the County of Argyll, subscribe these presents for him, he having authorised me for that purpose and the same having been previously read over to him all in presence of the witnesses before named and designed who subscribe this document in testimony of their having heard authority given to me as aforesaid.

It was witnessed by MacDiarmid, John MacKinnon ('Ground Officer residing at Ballevulin Tiree') and Archie McCallum ('Man Servant at the Manse of Tiree').[102] The will as a whole was duly executed by the faithful Duncan Cameron, who appeared at Pitlochry on 15 February 1892 to be sworn to that effect by a Justice of the Peace, testifying among much else 'that Ewen Cameron, Merchant, residing in Valparaiso, Chili, was also nominated a trustee and executor ... but has not, as yet, intimated acceptance of said office, and is not expected to do so, being resident abroad'.

Following JGC's death his story becomes that of his collections. The first portion to be published consisted of some of the non-Ossianic tales, selected by Jessy and edited by her with the help of Duncan MacIsaac. *Clan Traditions and Popular Tales*, as it was called (Campbell 1895), is very much JGC's memorial volume. Thanks to an American publisher, Elibron Classics (www.elibron.com), it is once again in print today. It is described on the pre-title page as 'Remains of the Rev. John Gregorson Campbell', volume V of Lord Archibald's 'Waifs and Strays'. In addition to clan traditions and legendary history it includes two stories about Fairies, four folk-tales, seven beast fables, three boy's games, and an appendix containing (among other material) some letters to JGC from JFC, extracts from which are quoted above (pp. xix–xx and 635–42).

There is also (pp. ix–xvi) a memoir of JGC, compiled by Nutt chiefly from information provided by Jessy, who had now left the Manse to live at Hynish. I have made extensive use of it in this biography. It is silent however on the controversies which dogged him and the illness which led to his death. At pp. xiv–xv is a list of JGC's publications to date, two items in which are particularly worthy of note. One is 'The Good Housewife and her Night Labours', a splendid Tiree version of the Dùn Bhuilg story (pp. 39–40 above) which had appeared, without acknowledgement to JGC, in the first volume of 'Waifs and Strays' (Campbell 1889, pp. 54–70). The translation is subscribed 'J. W.' – Jessy Wallace, obviously. The other is an item in *The Highland Monthly* described as 'Vol. I. No. 10. p. 622, Introduction, &c.' This is 'The Highland Chieftain, and How he Won his Wife'. I give it in my bibliography (p. 726 below) as Wallace 1889–90, because it is bylined 'From Mrs Wallace, Manse of Tiree' and subscribed 'J. W. / 6th October, 1889', but clearly what we are to understand is that the transcription and translation of the story ('which was heard in the island of Tiree') are basically by Jessy, but that the three-page introduction and concluding note were dictated by JGC. They are in his characteristic anecdotal style, in English with key quotations in Gaelic.[103]

What happened to JGC's papers between 1895 and 1900? Did Nutt turn down the opportunity to publish what is now *The Gaelic Otherworld*? Did James Maclehose trump him with a better offer? And what was Lord Archibald's role, if any? He was, after all, surely the best person to take charge of JGC's legacy.[104] Dòmhnall Chaluim Bàin had a story about him (*Tocher* 18, p. 45):

> Lord Archibald Campbell . . . was coming this day to the township and he was calling at every house. He could talk the Gaelic too . . . And he happened to come into my uncle's house and my uncle was, he was at his dinner. It was potatoes and fish he had . . . Lord Archibald says . . . "Will I have a spit of potatoes?"
> "Yes, yes," says the old fellow, "yes and two of them. Take as many as you like."
> And he lifted two spits of potato and a bit of fish. And he ate it out of his hand. "No wonder," he says, "you're strong and healthy, the food you're taking."
> "I'm strong enough," he says. "There's not a Campbell in Argyll, I'll put the best Campbell in Argyll, I'll put him down wrestling."
> "Well," he says, "I'm very pleased to meet a man of your age, so hardy and healthy, in the Island of Tiree."

There was, however, a fourth individual with an interest in JGC's writings – Alexander Carmichael. Angus Matheson acknowledges using *SHIS* and *WSS* in the course of editing the fifth volume of *Carmina Gadelica*, which was published in 1954 (*CG*5, pp. 272, 306, etc.), and the two books are again specifically cited among the sources for the alphabetical list of 'Gaelic Words and Expressions Collected by Alexander Carmichael' that forms the main part of the sixth volume, which appeared in 1971 (*CG*6, pp. 1, 41, etc.). It is also clear that JGC is the main or unique source for various items in that list whose source is not stated, e.g. *arabocan* 'lintel of door (Uist)' (p. 156 above), *clach-shuill* 'bait-stone for breaking shells etc.' (p. 140 above) and *soll* 'broken bait' (*ibid.*). In three cases, however, words which appear to be otherwise unrecorded are given in *CG*6 in a spelling which suggests that what lay in front of Carmichael was not *SHIS* or *WSS*, where they were misprinted, but JGC's original manuscript. The words in question are *faoise* 'also means broken bait' (cf. *faoire*, p. 140 above), *croma-ritheachan* 'a skua' (cf. *croma-ritheachar*, p. 183 above), and *slabhdan, sùil an t-slabhdain* 'soft eyes' (*sùil an t-slauchdain*, best explained I think as *sùil an t-slabhcair*, p. 169 above). The table at p. xvii shows that 'r' and 's' are easily confused in JGC's hand (see also p. 639); this explains how *faoise* was misread as *faoire*. The other two examples both appear to result from confusion between 'r' and 'n', but as note 577 (pp. 426–27) shows, the matter is not quite so simple. What can safely be inferred, I think, is that Carmichael's *croma-ritheachan* is a correct reading of JGC's manuscript, and that his *sùil an t-slabhdain* is an attempt to improve the spelling of what looked to him – as to the printer of *SHIS* – like *sùil an t-slauchdain*.

At any rate Nutt and Lord Archibald fade out of the picture. It was Maclehose who took over the papers – publishing *SHIS* and *WSS*, lending material to the editor of *Am Bolg Solair*, and printing essays in his journal *The Scottish Historical Review*. I believe that what spurred him into action in 1900 was the publication of the first two volumes of *CG* by his Edinburgh rival Norman Macleod; no doubt Jessy felt strongly that materials which had been perused by Carmichael should be published in their own right as quickly as possible. Even so, Maclehose's approach was tentative. He did not accord JGC's manuscript the splendid presentation of *CG*, and though it was not excessively long, he divided it into two. Six different clues point to JGC's having conceived it as a single volume:

- There is no prefatory matter in *WSS*
- 'The Devil' (Chapter 12) and the closely-related material that follows it, 'Black Witchcraft' (now Chapter 13), are respectively the last chapter in *SHIS* and the first in *WSS*
- JGC says at *WSS* 176 (p. 267 above): "The story has been already told of the tailor who irreverently gave a kick to a skull . . ." The reference is not to *WSS* at all but to *SHIS* 233 (p. 127 above)
- Under 'St Bride's Day' JGC says at *WSS* 249 (p. 541 above): "It has been explained in another part of this work that there was a belief the serpent had to come out of its hole seven days previous." The reference is not to *WSS* but to *SHIS* 225 (p. 122 above)
- JGC wrote at *WSS* 256 (p. 546 above) that it 'has been already told (art. Diabolus) how Michael Scott . . . went to Rome'. This was now in the other book, and Maclehose found himself obliged to insert a footnote: "Campbell's *Superstitions of the Scottish Highlands*, p. 296."
- JGC says of the *sop seilbhe* at *WSS* 272 (p. 554 above) that 'the burning of it on the land, as already explained, insured possession'; it was not explained in *WSS* at all but at *SHIS* 231–32 (p. 126 above).

Yet Maclehose split it. In the unsigned 'Editor's Note' which appears at pp. v–vi of *SHIS* he declared:

> THIS volume is the result of many years' labour by the late Rev. JOHN GREGORSON CAMPBELL, while minister of Tiree during the years 1861— to 1891.
>
> Much of the material was already collected before Mr J. F. Campbell of Islay published his *Popular Tales of the West Highlands* in 1860, and readers of Lord Archibald Campbell's volumes on *Waifs and Strays of Celtic Tradition* are already acquainted with the valuable work contributed to that series by the Rev. J. Gregorson Campbell.
>
> It is hoped that this volume on the *Superstitions of the Scottish Highlands*, full as it is of racy stories, may throw fresh light on an extremely interesting subject.
>
> The MS. of a corresponding work by the same author on *Witchcraft and Second-Sight in the West Highlands*, is in the editor's hands, and in the event of the present work meeting with the reception which the editor thinks it deserves, the volume on Witchcraft will be published next year.
>
> Mrs Wallace, Hynish, Tiree, the author's sister, has kindly read the proofs.
>
> *August*, 1900

SHIS was well received, as we may judge from the folio of favourable press opinions on it from *The Antiquary*, *The Spectator*, *The Scottish Review*, *Folk-Lore*, *The Reliquary*, *Athenæum*, *Notes and Queries*, *The Scotsman*, *The Scottish Geographical Magazine*, *The Glasgow Herald*, *Man*, *The Northern Chronicle*, *The Bailie* and *The Oban Times* which was tipped into some copies, at least, of *WSS*. In his *Folk-Lore* review Nutt stated, rather pointedly perhaps, that *SHIS* had been edited by Mrs Wallace. He went on (1900): "The author has not essayed to harmonise the popular presentation of the fairy world, but has left it in all its striking and perplexing inconsistency. Thus, *e.g.*, on p. 23 we are told that '(fairy) gifts have evil influence connected with them, and however inviting at first, are productive of bad luck in the end,' whilst on p. 24 we learn that a fairy gift, or rather returned loan, of oatmeal 'proved inexhaustible,' provided certain conditions were complied with. This very inconsistency is a warrant of the faithfulness with which the lore has been recorded . . . Campbell of Tiree takes his place by the side of Kirk, and of Walter Gregor of Pitsligo, among those recorders of folklore to whom the student can always turn with increased confidence and admiration."[105]

By the time the 'volume on Witchcraft' appeared in 1902, JGC was acknowledged as the master of his subject, but *WSS* got no more attention than it deserved as an addendum to *SHIS*, and in a few brief words of his *Folk-Lore* review John Abercromby told his readers what they most needed to know (1903, p. 98): "The last chapter on the 'Celtic Year' contains many interesting items of folklore, though many of the derivations of Gaelic words must be rejected as erroneous. Though there are several misprints, only one need be mentioned. It occurs in a charm at p. 63; for 'drop of wine' read 'drop of urine (*muin*).'"[106]

Abercromby had revealed that the books were badly edited. Probably Jessy had left the task to Maclehose, who assumed that she had read over and corrected the materials. *CG* had been carefully typed by Carmichael's very able daughter Ella (see MacilleDhuibh 24.6.94), but JGC's copy was passed straight to the printers in handwritten form. Jessy had read a proof of *SHIS*, and we may assume that she read one of *WSS* too, but by 1902 she was seventy years old and may not have given the material the attention it deserved. The ticklish question of 'wine' and 'urine' was not always easily answered; perhaps she preferred to leave it be, for both liquids had traditional uses. There seems no good reason to suspect a misprint, for example, when the Rev. Malcolm MacPhail tells us (1900, p. 445): "If an infant was baptized with water in which a little wine had been mixed, instead of pure water, it was supposed to act as a protection against midge-bites ever after."

Curiously, as Angela Bourke points out (1999, p. 81), the press coverage of the Cleary case, for which see p. lxi above, reveals the same problem: "Some newspapers quoted witnesses as saying that 'wine and water' were thrown on Bridget Cleary as she lay in bed, but others mention 'a noxious fluid', and some specify urine. Urine is certainly what was meant."

In addition to the manuscript of what became *SHIS* and *WSS*, James Maclehose appears to have obtained a small collection of poetry, hymns and incantations, including the originals of a number of items translated or referred to in the books. Probably JGC intended them to be published as an appendix, so that is what I will call it. Following the publication of *WSS*, Maclehose had it bound in at the end of the manuscript of the book. He sent the volume to Alexander Carmichael, presumably in order to obtain his advice as to what might be done with it in future. Carmichael copied out the appendix (EUL MS CW 241, see p. 701–04 below), then appears to have forwarded the volume to the hyperactive George Henderson, who in 1906 became the first Lecturer in Celtic in Glasgow University. Henderson copied out some of the appendix (GUL MS Gen. 1090/77, see p. 704 below) before returning the volume to Maclehose. This will be why W. J. Watson, who can have had no knowledge of the volume, scribbled 'Items here seem copied from Henderson MSS in Glasgow' on Carmichael's transcript.

In 1907 Maclehose dipped into the appendix to provide three short contributions to a multi-authored publication in aid of Comunn Gaidhealach funds, *Am Bolg Solair: The Pedlar's Pack* (Story 1907, pp. 97–99). At p. 7 of that book we are told that JGC's manuscripts were 'kindly lent by Mr J. J. Maclehose'. The three items, each of which is separately described as 'from the Collection of the late Rev. J. Gregorson Campbell, of Tiree', are 'Altachadh an t-Sheann Ghaidheil' ('The Old Gael's Grace', see p. 701 below), 'Oran, le Bean Shith' ('A Song, by a Fairy Woman') and 'Eolas an t-Siochaidh' ('The Charm of the Sprain', see pp. 205–06 above). I have no further knowledge of Maclehose's volume, and the trail appears to have gone cold. Elaine Stanier of the Mitchell Library in Glasgow informs me that the large but uncatalogued MacLehose Collection in her care consists of about fifty boxes of proofs and does not appear to include correspondence or original documents of any kind. Peter Asplin of Glasgow University Library's Special Collections Department sums up the position (personal communication, 22 September 2004): "MacLehose went into liquidation in 1982. Michael Moss and I salvaged a few things as the factory was being cleared; these are now in Special Collections at MS Gen. 1594. See our Manuscripts Catalogue under Robert MacLehose & Co. Ltd for details. Nothing very exciting. Most of their records seem to have been destroyed during an earlier move to new premises. Our enquiries have failed to discover any other surviving material. We also have an archival collection of MacLehose publications, but there is no manuscript material with it."

Although not in JGC's hand, EUL MS CW 241 and GUL MS Gen. 1090/77 thus represent a priceless survival – the Gaelic originals of those longer items which appeared in *SHIS* and *WSS* in translation only. Of all JGC's *nachlass*, there is nothing we could have more fervently desired than this. Naturally I have incorporated their contents above, where appropriate, either in JGC's text or in my commentary.

To my knowledge the only manuscripts of JGC's which survive in his own hand are his entries in the kirk session records of Tiree and the letters and transcripts which he sent to JFC (pp. xlvi, 631, 637–43 above). GUL MS Gen. 1709/46/2, a two-page account of Cu Chulainn and Conlaoch headed 'Note by the Revd. John G. Campbell, Tiree', is a copy in an unknown hand; it looks like an early draft of some material which he published in Campbell 1891, pp. 6–8. In his *Descriptive Catalogue of Gaelic Manuscripts* Professor Donald Mackinnon – the same Professor Mackinnon who sat with his fellow commissioners in the heat of JGC's church on 7 August 1883 – concluded an appendix on 'Gaelic MSS. in Private Possession' with the following rather plaintive note (1912, p. 322): "There are several other literary remains of the nineteenth century that one meets with, or hears of, here and there. Conspicuous among recent collectors, not to speak of those still living, were Dr McLauchlan of Edinburgh, Rev. J. G. Campbell of Tiree, and the Rev. James Macdougall of Duror. But a considerable portion of presumably the most valuable part of the labours of these and other such men have been published at one time or other."

Maclehose launched *The Scottish Historical Review* (which continues today) in 1903. Between then and 1915 no less than five papers by JGC appeared between its covers. The first two, 'The Story of Conal Grund' (Campbell 1903–04) and 'Story of the King of Ireland and his Two Sons' (Campbell 1906–07), were tales of the type so enjoyed by the members of the Gaelic Society of Inverness, except that, true to form, Maclehose published them in JGC's English translation only; the Gaelic original of the latter was published in *The Celtic Review* a few years later (Campbell 1909–10b). In the last three JGC ranged discursively over topics which would not have been out of place in *SHIS* or *WSS*. 'The Green Island', written *c.* 1887 (Campbell 1907–08, p. 191), is about Gaelic traditions of a lost Atlantis. In 'The Origin of the Fairy Creed', written *c.* 1880 (Campbell 1909–10a, p. 364) and now reprinted at pp. lxxxv–xciii above, JGC discusses the evidence for the topic and presents his own considered views (see pp. xxvi–xxviii above). Finally, 'The Sharp-Witted Wife (*A' Chailleach Bheur*)', also written *c.* 1880 (Campbell 1914–15, p. 413), offers in five short but entertaining pages a variety of anecdotes about this *magna mater* of the Gael, for whom see note 82 on pp. 587–88.

The first of JGC's sisters after Mary Bell to pass away was Margaret Mackenzie, who was dead by October 1907 (see note 100 on p. 699). Next was Jean (Jane) Maclean, who died at Scarinish on 21 March 1912, aged 71, her death being witnessed by her daughter Nonnie. Finally, Jessy – 'Mistress Wallace', as she is remembered in Tiree – died at Hynish on 14 February 1919, aged 86. Her death was witnessed by Margaret's elder son Kenneth, the piermaster at Scarinish.

Such was the life of the man whom Dr John Lorne Campbell called 'a particularly able folklorist' (MacLellan 1961, p. xiv). I endorse this judgement wholeheartedly. John Gregorson Campbell began collecting folklore before JFC or Carmichael, found a parish that suited his self-imposed task down to the ground, and held on to it with ruthless tenacity. With Jessy's help, he pursued his aims in the face of debilitating illness and at the expense of what was left of his reputation as a churchman. Together they turned adversity into triumph.

NOTES

1   See p. 258 above, 'Wraiths Seen before Death'.

2   Mitchell 1883–84, vol. 1, p. 224; Haldane 1962, p. 207; Duckworth and Langmuir 1977, p. 8. Principal John Macleod recalled the *Cygnet* and *Plover* plying between the Broomielaw in Glasgow and Muirtown in Inverness (1990–92, p. 253).

3   See Black 1986b, pp. 29–32, and cf. notes 82 and 567 above (pp. 310–11, 419–21). Nutt's biographical information was supplied by JGC's elder sister Jessy (Campbell 1895, p. ix), and it could well be argued that if she referred informally to 'Dr Mackintosh', the letters in question are likely to be unpublished ones from him to her grandfather which survived in JGC's family and are now lost. Many of MacKay's letters to the Highland Society of Scotland are preserved in the Ingliston papers (Black 1988, p. 116), but there is little trace of correspondence among his publications.

     During 1845–50 he edited thirty-six numbers of a magazine called *An Fhianuis*. It contains occasional readers' letters, but none from Duncan MacGregor. In the last number (May 1850) a dialogue at pp. 648–55 'Beolaind Mhinsteirean na h-Eaglais Saoire. (Comhradh, eadar Callum Deacon, Seumas Gobha, Eoghan Tailleir, agus Fionnladh Grèasaiche)' is subscribed 'D. M.' – but then, these are very common initials! A work by MacKay called *Scots Worthies and Church History* (London, 1872) is mentioned in the *Fasti* (Scott 1915–50, vol. 4, p. 24), but this is merely his *Eachdraidh Eaglais na h-Alba . . . agus Eachdraidh na h-Eaglais Saoire*, published in *An Fhianuis* and reissued in London in 1872 under the same cover as *Eachdraidh nan Urramach ann an Alba*, a translation by Dr Charles R. Macgillivray of *The Scots Worthies* (MacLean 1915, pp. 222, 236–37).

4　The best accounts of the building of the canal are Haldane's (1962), especially the chapters 'In the Great Glen' and 'Nearing Completion', and Cameron's (2005); see also Ross 1886–87b.

5　On 17 December 1843 the sheriff substitute at Tobermory wrote in his diary about the Rev. John MacLeod of Morvern (Loudon 2001, p. 67): "The poor soft fellow had nine or ten good parishes in his offer, and incurred the expence of taking presentations to two of them; the Morven people object to his going away and he consents to remain among them to starve, and kill himself, in struggling with poverty and all its attendant evils. Verily there are but few parsons in the Church that would act as he has done."

6　Campbell 1872, pp. 210–11; see also pp. 339 and 641 of the present work.

7　Anon. 1891b; Campbell 1895, p. xi; Scott 1915–50, vol. 1, p. 86, and vol. 3, p. 180.

8　The members of the Presbytery at this time were the Rev. Mungo Campbell, Salen; the Rev. Duncan Clerk or Clark, Torosay; the Rev. William Fraser, Ulva; the Rev. Dr Donald MacArthur, Kilninian; the Rev. James MacColl, Coll; the Rev. Alexander MacGregor, Iona; the Rev. Angus Macintyre, Kinlochspelvie; the Very Rev. Dr John MacLeod, Morvern; the Rev. Neil MacNeil, Tobermory; the Rev. Robert Stewart, Kilfinichen; and the Rev. Donald MacFadyen. The last-named was translated from one parish in the Presbytery (Acharacle) to another (Ardnamurchan) on 13 September 1860 after the death of the Rev. David Stewart of Ardnamurchan on 8 May 1860, his place at Acharacle being filled on 14 May 1861 by the Rev. Donald Simpson (Scott 1915–50, vol. 4, pp. 104–25).

9　This is one of the 'contexts of ambivalence' described by Deborah Davis in an article whose thesis is unfortunately vitiated by ignorance of Scottish church history (1992). JGC himself, for example, she makes into a minister of the Free Church.

10　Dr MacInnes points out to me with pride that she was of the same family as that most celebrated of *Tiristich*, Captain Donald MacKinnon of the *Taeping*. Niall M. Brownlie adds (personal communication, 22 July 2004) that they were known as *Muinntir Iain Chola*.

11　*Tocher* 24, pp. 310–12; Meek 1980, p. 24; Brownlie 1995, pp. 18–19; Meek 2003, pp. 422–23. For a detailed account of this tenurial revolution and of how John Campbell carried it out see the chapter 'Emigration, Social Change and Economic Recovery: the Isle of Tiree, 1760–1890', in Devine 1988, pp. 226–44.

　　Tradition assigns 'Long John' of Ardmore, a big lanky man, a death appropriate to his sins. In one version (MacArthur 1990–92, p. 143) he 'came alive like a maggotty sheep', and hens were put under his arms to draw out the maggots. In another (*Tocher* 17, p. 27) he was eaten alive by lice while his ground officer, Lachlan MacQuarrie (for whom see p. 640), removed the insects with a brush and threw them into a big fire with a shovel.

12　Livingstone, a native of Kerrera, was the parish schoolmaster. At a later date his niece Mrs MacCulloch ran the Bayview Hotel in Oban (MacDougall and Cameron n.d., p. 123).

13　The minister of Kinloch Rannoch at this time was Duncan, not Donald, McFarlane (Scott 1915–50, vol. 4, p. 187, and vol. 8, p. 358).

14　John MacLeod was six feet seven inches tall (Murchison 1957, p. 67). For the life and work of 'Caraid nan Gaidheal' see Clerk 1867, pp. ix–xlviii; MacCurdy 1942–50; Macleod 1974–76; Ó Baoill 1981; Kidd 2000.

15　NLS Cam.2a1(16); GUL MS Gen. 1709/46/1 (pp. vi–vii missing); Newberry Library, Chicago, Bon. 7454. The attribution to JGC of two further printed Gaelic sermons in the Newberry, Bon. 7453, appears to be in error.

16　Vocalisation of the nasal when *fhéin, fhèin* or *fhìn* is followed by a consonant may be found in any dialect (e.g. CG2, p. 330, *Chan urra mi fhi g'a chur a dhi*), but only in Perthshire is it generalised to all situations (e.g. *Tocher* 27, p. 163, *i fhé agus a bana-chompanaichean*, and *Tocher* 28, p. 223, *bha 'bhean leath fhé' aig an tigh*). As Robertson puts it (1897–98a, p. 21), in that county *féin* is 'sometimes fhéin, but generally fhé'. For further examples see Bruford 1967, pp. 39–42, and Ó Murchú 1989, p. 343.

17　The case is minuted in *The Principal Acts of the General Assembly of the Church of Scotland* for 1861, pp. 64–65, and reported at length in *The Scotsman*, 1 June 1861. The quotations that follow are from the latter. For biographies of the main participants see Scott 1915–50, vol. 1, pp. 42–43 (Lee); vol. 4, pp. 118 (MacLeod), 146 (Irvine), 189 (Cameron); vol. 6, p. 150 (Bissett); vol. 7, pp. 48 (Rev. Peter McKenzie of Urquhart), 379–80 (Pirie), 402 (Hill), 423–24 (Tulloch).

18　NAS CH2/273/7, p. 152. In John MacLeod's Presbytery minutes (*ibid.*, p. 156) ordination is said to have taken place on 23 August. This is naturally the date published in the account of JGC's life in the *Fasti*

(Scott 1915–50, vol. 4, pp. 121–22). However, MacLeod's minute for 21 August says that ordination will take place 'to-morrow', and in the kirk session records for Tiree is the following entry in JGC's hand (CH2/482/1, p. 429): "The Revd. John Gregorson Campbell was admitted & ordained Minister of the Church & Parish of Tiree, on Thursday the twenty second day of August, eighteen hundred & sixty one years."

19 NAS CH2/273/7, p. 156. For a fine biographical tribute to MacFadyen see Macpherson 1888–89, pp. 235–37. He had an impetuous nature and a great sense of humour, and was 'a capital story-teller – of which he was himself frequently the hero'.

20 For his predecessor's description of the church, manse and glebe in Tiree, and of the legal provision made for his assistant in Coll, see Maclean 1843, p. 219. At JGC's death in 1891 the inventory of his estate included cattle, horses and farm implements to the value of £105 13s 6d. Among his outstanding debts was £16 5s 2d owed to the duke of Argyll, being a half year's rent of Scarinish farm (NAS SC51/32/41, pp. 398, 399).

21 NAS CH2/273/7, pp. 179–81, 188, 195–96, 199–200, 209–10, 213–14, 221, and CH2/273/8, pp. 41, 90.

22 MacColl became minister of De Sable and Orwell, Prince Edward Island, and of Earltown in Upper Canada. In 1877 he resigned and returned to Argyll, becoming successively minister of Cumlodden in 1879 and of Kilchoman in 1881. He was deposed in 1884 and went to Australia, where he died (NAS CH2/273/7, pp. 255–56; CH2/273/8, pp. 36–37, 40, 42–44; Scott 1915–50, vol. 4, pp. 74, 109, 119).

23 Campbell 1895, p. 67. For a lively little account of Moderatism in the presbyteries of Lewis, Uist and Skye during the period 1800–43 see MacLeod 1980–82. MacLeod points out (*ibid.*, p. 265) that after 1843 all who had remained loyal to the establishment were known colloquially in the Highlands as Moderates, despite the fact that some of them had sided with the Evangelical wing of the Church prior to the Disruption. We may recognise JGC in MacLeod's description of those Moderates who 'were concerned to maintain the culture and traditions of their parishioners' (*ibid.*, p. 249). The bitterness between followers of the two parties in the Disruption period is exemplified by the experience of the Rev. Donald MacFadyen of Ardnamurchan (Macpherson 1888–89, p. 236): "When a schoolmaster in Ross-shire, his sister was not allowed to take water from a public well, because her brother was a *Moderate*, and he himself was shunned as an outcast."

An anecdote told by William MacKenzie (1930, p. 133) clearly identifies the Rev. Robert MacGregor of Kilmuir in Skye (for whom see note 950 on p. 522) as a Moderate. On his rounds one day, MacGregor foregathered with the innkeeper at Camusmore, whose nickname was the Laird. *Car son a thug iad Laird ort?* enquired MacGregor in a jocular way. "Why did they call you Laird?"

Dìreach farainm, a mhinistir, came the reply, *mar a thug iad am Ministeir oirb' fhéin*. "Just a nickname, minister, in the same way they called you the Minister."

24 A specimen of the 'oath of purgation' is inscribed in the kirk session book for Kilmorie in Arran, 25 October 1705 (Mackenzie 1914, pp. 151–52). It is terrifying. "If I lye in this matter or do not speake truth, then I wish and pray with my whole soul that God may confound me with some visible judgement or other, that I may never prosper or thrive in this world, but that all my goods and geir may suddenly vanish and perish and that I may be a beggar and a vagabond & stricken with some loathsome distemper or disease till death seize me & that I may forever be banished from God and the society of the blessed and holy Angels and Saints, and shut up with Devils in the eternal torments of Hell for ever and ever."

25 See *The Principal Acts of the General Assembly of the Church of Scotland* for those years. Nor did Tiree go unrepresented during the second half of his ministry. Between 1876 and his death all four ministers of Heylipol attended the Assembly – MacDonald in 1878, MacRury in 1881, MacCallum in 1888 and Maclean in 1891.

26 NLS Acc. 8508 (Campbell papers) no. 44, bundle 7. For McNeill see Devine 1988, pp. 124–25, and Balfour 1990–92, especially pp. 431, 517.

27 According to Niall M. Brownlie (personal communication, 22 April 2004), Roderick Macfadyen was a relative of Allan Macfadyen, proprietor of the Scarinish Hotel. Allan was son of John Macfadyen and died in 1891, aged 90 (death certificate). Allan's son Charlie was the driver of the spring-cart which brought sheriff's officer George Nicholson to Balephuil at the time of the rebellion of 1886.

28 Similarly, the Rev. Dr Neil Ross (1871–1943), a native of Glendale in Skye, recalled that when *Iain Ruadh mac Dhòmhnaill 'ic Thormoid* sang 'Bàs Dhiarmaid' everyone present had to uncover their heads, and

that Iain's voice shook with emotion when he reached a verse that told how a hill that was green yesterday was red today with Diarmad's blood (Mac a Phì 1938, p. 68). And the Rev. Alexander Pope, minister of Reay, wrote of a man called Campbell *c.* 1739 (Campbell 1872, p. 218): "There is an old fellow in this parish that very gravely takes off his bonnet as often as he sings 'Duan Dearmot'. I was extremely fond to try if the case was so, and getting him to my house I gave him a bottle of ale, and begged the favour of him to sing 'Duan Dearmot'; after some nicety he told me that to oblige his parish minister he would do so, but to my surprise he took off his bonnet. I caused him stop, and would put on his bonnet; he made some excuses; however, as soon as he began, he took off his bonnet, I rose and put it on. At last he was like to swear most horribly, he would sing none, unless I allowed him to be uncovered; I gave him his freedom, and so he sung with great spirit. I then asked him his reason; he told me it was out of regard to the memory of that Hero. I asked him if he thought that the spirit of that Hero was present; he said not; but he thought it well became them who descended from him to honour his memory." For the Campbells' claim to be descended from Diarmad Ó Duibhne cf. p. 637.

29   Campbell 1882, p. 184 = 1891, p. 191. According to Niall M. Brownlie (personal communication, 22 April 2004), Murdoch McIntyre is probably the father of Colin and Donald Macintyre: "Colin (*Cailean Mhurchaidh*) had at least five of a family, three girls and two boys. I know very little about Donald's family, except that he had a daughter called Marion who married a Hector Kennedy from Balevullin. Their son Donald is still alive and lives in Balevullin. Colin's son Murdoch was in the Pioneer Corps and saw service on the Western Front. A daughter called Kate married a Hugh MacKinnon from Hough and they had two sons, and lived in Sandaig. John married Kate Kennedy, a cousin of mine, and they had a son Colin who lost his life at sea in 1943. Kate died when young. John then married Effie MacFadyen from Barrapol and they emigrated to Australia and raised a family there."

       The marriage certificate of Colin McIntyre, Kilkenneth, tells us that he wed Mary McKellaich, a maid at Island House, in Island House on 18 May 1881, JGC officiating; the sub-factor Hugh MacDiarmid was one of the witnesses. His parents are given as Murdoch McIntyre, crofter, deceased, and Flora McIntyre, *née* McArthur, also deceased. He appears to have had seven brothers and sisters in addition to Donald, but not all of them will have survived to maturity.

30   Campbell 1881b, p. 115 = 1891, p. 132. According to Niall M. Brownlie (personal communication, 22 April 2004), Duncan McFadyen appears to belong to a family who lived at Ardeas in Caolas: "One member of the family went to Mull, and his son Duncan was the father of the famous family of MacFadyen pipers."

       I remember the MacFadyen brothers well. John was headmaster of Busby primary school; Iain went to teach piping in schools in South-West Ross; I myself had many lessons from Duncan at the College of Piping in Otago Street, Glasgow. There was also a well-known cousin, Hector MacFadyen, Pennyghael. All four were superb players who competed at the highest level.

31   I have found only one Duncan Cameron, constable, in the public records. He died aged 85 on 7 March 1900, at Argyll Terrace, Tobermory, leaving a widow, Maryann Leonard, and a son Duncan. His parents were Alexander Cameron, crofter, and Catherine Cameron, *née* Cameron. According to Niall M. Brownlie (personal communication, 22 April 2004), he was from Lochaline, and had been stationed in Tiree for ten years. "Although he had left the island earlier, he was one of the 30 policemen who escorted George Nicholson to Balephuil to serve writs on some of the men who were involved in the 1886 rebellion. Nicholson and the police had to beat a hasty retreat when the crowd moved against them. But when 250 marines arrived, arrests were made and 8 appeared before Lord Mure in the High Court in Edinburgh. Duncan Cameron gave evidence at the trial."

32   For an assessment of the international importance of JFC's work see Dorson 1968, pp. 393–402.

33   Mackinnon 1892–93; Delargy 1960; Thompson 1984–86, pp. 55, 57; Maciver 1985, p. 30.

34   Campbell 1895, pp. 138–39. The manuscript of 'O Cian's Leg' as taken down by MacLean in Paisley is NLS Adv. MS 50.2.3. This also includes notes, letters, photographs and other relevant material brought together by JFC in his favourite 'scrapbook' style. At the end are letters and versions of the tale received from JGC. JFC awards them a rough title-page of their own (f. 193r): "Two Versions of the / story known as / O Ceins leg. / got from Tiree." Most of the material was published in Henderson 1901–03.

35   For Farquharson see Mackenzie 1877–78, pp. 57–60; MacLean 1915, p. 118; Ferguson and Matheson 1984, p. 62; McNaughton 1993, pp. 44, 481; Meek 1995b; McNaughton 2003, pp. 79–97.

36   Presumably a reference to Carleton 1854, which JGC quotes at p. 25 above.

37 See p. 67 above. For more on Sinclair (*Calum Bàn*) see pp. 654 and 665.

38 On the *Gruagach Bàn* see p. 70 above; on Fairies as deer see 'Cattle', pp. 14–16; on witches as hares see pp. 174–75, 188; and for Thomas Rhymer see pp. 24, 147–49. The following is Geddie's description (1920, p. 27) of Thomas's last departure from Ercildoune: "The story is that a mysterious Hart and Hind came slowly pacing through the village, and that, at the 'selcouth sight', the Prophet left the company with whom he was feasting:—

> *'True Thomas smiled above his harp,*
> *And turned his face to the naked sky,*
> *Where, blown before the wastrel wind,*
> *The thistle-down went floating by.*

> .   .   .   .

> *'Twas naked sky and nodding grass,*
> *'Twas running flood and wastrel wind,*
> *Where checked against the open pass*
> *The Red Hart turned to wait the Hind,'*

and to wait also for Thomas, who followed the mysterious visitors into the forest, and, beyond mortal sight, into Fairyland." See also Scott 2001, p. 85.

39 For the dragon story see Campbell 1911. NLS Adv. MS 50.2.3 was described by Nutt (1890, pp. 373–77) and published, almost in full, by Henderson (1901–03). Another Argyll version of the tale, 'Coise Céin', was published, with translation, by the Rev. Duncan MacInnes (1890, pp. 206–77, notes pp. 464–73). Two years later an Irish version ('Leighes coise Chéin mheic Mhaeilmuaid mheic Bhriain síosana') was published from manuscript by Standish Hayes O'Grady (1892, vol. 1, Irish Text, pp. 296–305, and vol. 2, Translation and Notes, 'How the Leg of Cian son of Maelmuaidh son of Brian was healed', pp. 332–42, 488, 536). Two years later again, JGC's and MacInnes's translations were combined by Joseph Jacobs to create a children's story called 'The Leeching of Kayn's Leg' (1894, pp. 169–93).

40 NLS Adv. MS 50.4.6, ff. 128r–129r, cf. Mackay 1998, p. 120. 'Campbell of Rudhe' is the tacksman of Reef (*an Ruighe*), probably the same individual who had testified to the Presbytery of Mull at Tobermory on JGC's behalf on 18 December 1861 (NAS CH2/273/7, p. 103): "Compeared Donald Campbell Esquire Tacksman of Reef Tyree, who, was solemnly sworn, and interrogated for the Presentee as his deposition is taken down in the separate Record." See also MacDougall and Cameron n.d., p. 85; Brownlie 1995, pp. 32–35.

41 According to Dòmhnall Chaluim Bàin the last *corp crèadha* ever made in Tiree (see p. 195 above) was for Lachlan MacQuarrie (*Tocher* 18, p. 57), but see note 68 below.

42 NLS Acc. 8508, no. 44, bundle 6 (I am grateful to Kirsteen Foster for this reference); Napier 1884, vol. 3, p. 2157. According to Dr Margaret Mackay, Geekie emigrated to the Strathclair / Shoal Lake area of Manitoba with many others from the island (1998, p. 120; personal communication, 29 July 2004). This outcome must have been very satisfactory to the duke, who went on to appoint his 'dream ticket' – a Gaelic-speaking sub-factor for Tiree (another Perthshire man, Hugh MacDiarmid), with a Lowlander, James Wyllie, to oversee the Argyll Estate as a whole (Napier 1884, vol. 3, pp. 2208–21).

43 See Campbell 1890, vol. 3, pp. 322–45.

44 NLS Adv. MS 50.4.6, ff. 135r–160r, cf. Thompson 1984–86, pp. 55–57, and Mackay 1998, p. 123.

45 The reason for Miss MacLeod's interest was that in Skye the song is associated with the 'Fairy Flag' – see note 8 on p. 294 above; MacDonald 1907, p. 5; MacDougall and Calder 1910, pp. 108–11; Tolmie 1911, pp. 174–77; MacDonald 1934–36a, p. 197; MacilleDhuibh 13.12.02. The Barra tradition cited by JFC is as in JGC's 'Ready Wit Repulses the Fairies', p. 45 above, see note 154 on pp. 325–26. For John Cameron see also CG1, pp. 42–43; CG2, pp. 374–75; CG5, p. 208.

46 See p. 552. It is hard to square JGC's strictures on *leathann ri leathann* with spellings like *Eathin* (*WSS* 276, p. 556 above).

47 See 'The Crowing of the Black Cock', pp. 46–47 above.

48 For Dr John MacLachlan of Rahoy in Morvern (1804–74) see Camshron 1942–50; Mac Gill-Eain 1985, pp. 56–65; Meek 2003, p. 481; EUL MS CW 58A, f. 29v. Sorley MacLean once said of him that 'many

reasons could be adduced for declaring him the best Gaelic poet of his century' (Mac Gill-Eain 1985, p. 57). Hugh McDonald is probably the Hugh MacDonald, Kilmoluag, referred to at p. 654.

49   Alexander Carmichael was fond, not to say over-fond, of this expression. See Bruford 1983, p. 9, and Campbell 1996, p. 73.

50   Compare the lines by Archibald MacPhail, Cornaigmore, *Gur e mise tha gu craiteach / Air an Chanradh 's i cho fuar* ('O what agony I am in / On the Canradh and it so cold', Cameron 1932, p. 205).

51   On his death in 1907 MacRury was succeeded in turn as editor of the supplement by a Tireeman, the Rev. Donald Lamont (1874–1958), minister of Blair Atholl, whom the current editor, the Rev. Roderick MacLeod, Cumlodden, calls 'arguably the greatest Gaelic prose writer of all time' (Thomson 1994, p. 146). In his brilliant short story 'Taghadh a' Mhinistear' ('The Choosing of the Minister'), Lamont wittily satirises the curiously oligarchic selection process that emerged from the Act of 1874 as applied in a fictitious mainland parish within the bounds of the Presbytery of Mull (Murchison 1960, pp. 88–94). There was a tradition behind it: Lamont's wry approach is foreshadowed by Fionn's essays 'Taghadh Ministear Sgireachd' and 'Mar a Thagh Sinn ar Ministear' (1907, pp. 106–24, 254–63).

52   The basic information in this paragraph comes from the *Fasti* (Scott 1915–50). For the disjunction of Heylipol see vol. 4, p. 119. For MacDonald see vol. 6, p. 471, and vol. 8, pp. 652–53. For MacRury see vol. 7, pp. 180–81. As Gaelic editor of *Am Pàipear*, the monthly newspaper published in Balivanich, Benbecula, I have been reprinting MacRury's writings in serial form for some years, and Calum Laing, Alness (a grandson of MacRury's brother), has contributed his biography (November/December 2002). Mr Laing has now (January 2004) read a paper on MacRury and his work to the Gaelic Society of Inverness, and I hope that this will appear in vol. 63 of their *Transactions*. See also MacLean 1949, pp. 151–53, and Matheson 1980–82, p. 332.

53   Personal communication, 22 April 2004, cf. Brownlie 1991b, p. 77.

54   Scott 1915–50, vol. 7, pp. 204–05; Meek 1977; Brownlie 1991b. In addition, for MacCallum the politician see MacPhail 1989, *passim*; for contrasting views of MacCallum the poet see Meek 1974–76, p. 313, and Black 1999, pp. xxvi–xxviii; and for a first-hand account of MacCallum the man see MacLean 1949, pp. 52–67, 69, 133. The translations of his verses are mine.

55   Dick had married Kenneth William's sister Cecilia Isabella. Buchanan had been the island's general practitioner since 1860 (see p. 666 and Napier 1884, vol. 3, p. 2148). The 1871 census of Tiree shows him aged 35, farming 125 acres at Baugh. A native of Callander in Perthshire, he had trained as a surgeon, and was a Member of the Royal College of Surgeons in Edinburgh. He was buried in Oran's Cemetery at Kirkapol, and a monument was erected to his memory at Cnoc Ibrig in Baugh (Brownlie 1995, pp. 26–28). There is a fine Gaelic elegy to him in Cameron 1932, pp. 297–99.

56   MacDougall and Cameron n.d., p. 123; Brownlie 1995, pp. 116–17.

57   His Lewis origins are indicated in the chorus of 'An t-Ollamh Mòr Mòr'. According to a manuscript note in the NLS copy of Ewing 1914, vol. 1, p. 248, he was from North Tolsta. On the size of the congregation see *ibid*., vol. 2, p. 122.

58   Ewing 1914, vol. 1, p. 248, cf. Meek 2003, p. 426.

59   Black 2001, pp. xxxv–xxxix, and 2002, pp. 39–41. For Mgr Lachlann see also p. 176 above. In *An Lasair* (p. xxxviii) I told the story of two brothers who used to pass his church on their way to the inn at Lochcarron. He brought them to heel with a piece of verse cited in English by Murray (1979, p. 19):

> John and Ewen do drink;
> They order half-mutchkin about;
> If both will go to glory
> Peter and Paul will go out.

Thanks to Ian Mackenzie, Pencaitland (personal communication, 12 January 2002), I now have the original of these lines. They were quoted on 9 December 1984 by the late John Mackenzie, Kishorn, then aged 90, in a taped interview with Alick John MacBeath, Kishorn, now also deceased.

> Théid Iain is Eoghan ag òl
> 'S òrdaich' iad stòp ma seach;
> Ma théid an dithis do ghlòir
> Théid Pòl is Peadair a-mach.

John Mackenzie went on to say that one of the brothers received grace and gave up drink, but the other 'died as a sinner'. For more satirical verse by Mgr Lachlann see Maclean 1912–13, p. 72.

60 Cf. Bruford 1967, pp. 25–26; *Tocher* 39, pp. 114–17; Gray 1987, pp. 250–52; Newton 2003, pp. 186–87.

61 In his diary for Friday 6 September 1844, James Robertson, sheriff substitute at Tobermory, noted drily (Loudon 2001, p. 110): "Met Sandy Macdougall the Flesher who gave a discourse on temperance and intemperance, instancing himself as a bright specimen of the sober class, and his brother Hector, MacMillan the tailor, and the poor fellow Hunter who drowned himself yesterday morning, as flagrant examples of inebriety."

62 According to Niall M. Brownlie (personal communication, 22 April 2004), this is probably *Donnchadh mac Ruairidh*, whose mother was Mary MacLean, a sister of *Iain mac Ailein*, 'the Laird of Coll's Poet' (1787–1848). For Iain mac Ailein see Sinclair 1881, pp. xiii–192; Sinclair 1898–1900, vol. 2, pp. 27–78; Cameron 1932, pp. 38–113; Thomson 1994, pp. 180–81.

63 The latter may be the Hugh McDonald mentioned above (p. 643) as knowing the 'Fairy Song'.

64 JFC met this man on 11 September 1871 (NLS Adv. MS 50.4.6, f. 131r, cf. Mackay 1998, p. 121): "Yesterday Monday was beautiful. I got a Tailor by name MacArthur and spent the whole day writing stories. I wrote 11 yesterday and the 12th this morning before breakfast." He is known to Niall M. Brownlie (personal communication, 22 April 2004) as *Iain Òg* who had a house on the march between Moss and Barrapol. "He had a daughter, Margaret, who was married to a Donald MacKinnon from Kilmoluag. I remember the couple." The following story connects him with the Fairies and seems designed to explain lameness, a handicap often associated with tailors (Brownlie 1995, pp. 74–75): "A man called John MacArthur, *Iain Òg* from Moss (*ás a' Mhòintich*), was courting a Fairy who lived in a Fairy knoll (*bean-shìth aig an robh brugh*) in Cromadh nan Creag. But he found a new love and forsook the Fairy. Two days after the parting, he was thatching the house (*a' tughadaireachd*) when the Fairy came up behind him and knocked him off the wall. He broke his leg in the fall and walked with a limp for the rest of his days. He never saw the Fairy again."

The public records reveal the tailor to be one of ten children of Neil MacArthur, crofter, and his wife Mary MacKinnon. The 1881 census finds him, aged 44 and unmarried, living at Moss with his brother, also John MacArthur, 57 (church officer, unmarried), their sisters Euphemia, 59 (spinner and knitter, unmarried), and Ann, 34 (grocer, unmarried), and their niece Maggie MacArthur, 13 (scholar). Maggie was the daughter of a third brother, Colin, born *c*. 1840, who had gone to Glasgow and married Catherine MacLeod in 1863; he died of a fracture of the skull when working as a surfaceman on the Caledonian Railway at Cook Street, 4 May 1883. It was quite common for children to be 'farmed out' in this way: by 1891, when Maggie is described by the census as the family's 'General Serv Domestic', a young nephew, John MacArthur, 12, has arrived in Moss to live with them. The tailor died on 3 September 1903, aged 74, still unmarried; Maggie signed the death certificate as the informant, and married Donald MacKinnon from Kilmoluag a few weeks later, on 18 November.

65 Allan MacDonald gave JGC the poem 'Oidhche Dhoirbh', see Campbell 1891, p. 101; according to Niall M. Brownlie (personal communication, 22 April 2004), Donald Macdonald may be a brother of Malcolm MacDonald, crofter, a close friend of the Rev. Donald MacCallum.

66 Niall M. Brownlie tells me (personal communication, 25 June 2004) that the *Sgeirean Dubha* ('Black Skerries') lie off Kirkapol, and that a *Gilleasbaig Ruadh* had a croft in the same township.

67 Niall M. Brownlie points out to me (personal communication, 22 April 2004) that all Tiree MacCallums are descended from one or other of two brothers, both millers, who came to the island in the mid-eighteenth century. See Brownlie 1995, pp. 38–40.

68 Campbell 1891, p. 57. According to Niall M. Brownlie (personal communication, 22 April 2004), John Sinclair will be the father of Donald Sinclair, *Dòmhnall mac Iain 'ic Chaluim*, president of the Tiree Branch of the Land League, who was arrested and incarcerated with five others in Inveraray following the rebellion of 1886. He was released when Lachlan MacQuarrie (for whom see p. 640 above) paid bail of £20 for each man. As John MacLean, *Bàrd Bhaile Mhàrtainn*, says (Cameron 1932, p. 169):

> An Inbhir Aora, toll dubh a' chruadail,
> Gun dhùineadh suas iad a Luan 's a Dhòmhnach,
> Ach bha de dh'uaisle an com MhicGuaire
> Nach biodh iad uair ann nam fuasg'leadh òr iad.

("In Inveraray, the black hole of hardship, / They were locked up, no days excepted, / But MacQuarrie had good enough blood in his veins / Not to leave them an hour there if gold could release them.") Donald Sinclair is even better remembered, however, as a spiritual poet – nineteen of his hymns were published in *Laoidhean Soisgeulach* (1913), see MacLeod 1980, p. 83; Ferguson and Matheson 1984, p. 34; Black 1999, p. 737.

As for Peter Carmichael, there was only one family of this surname in Tiree. They had a croft in Barrapol, but were evicted by John Campbell of Ardmore, *am Bàillidh Mòr*, who gave it to John MacNiven from Mull, and the Carmichaels settled as cottars on the 'Land' in Barrapol. Niall M. Brownlie has a distant recollection of the last of the family, *Dòmhnall Bàn Nèill*.

69 See Sands 1881–82. On 12 March 1883 he donated to the Society three bronze objects which he had found in Tiree: a pin, a needle and a 22-inch sword (*PSAS*, vol. 17, 1882–83, p. 285). In some ways Sands resembled Robert Louis Stevenson. He qualified as a lawyer but preferred a life of adventure, earning his living as a writer, journalist and illustrator; he was also a keen piper. He was a frequent contributor to *Punch* and *The Glasgow Herald*, and also tried his hand at juvenile fiction (Sands 1881b) and poetry (Sands 1888). He was born in Arbroath *c.* 1827, son of John Sim Sands, writer (solicitor) and poet, author of Sands 1832 and 1833. He lived mainly with his mother and two younger sisters at Tranent in East Lothian, but also spent long periods of time in South America, St Kilda, Tiree, Faroe and, from 1884, in Shetland, where he lived 'more or less as a recluse' in Vaila, Foula and Papa Stour (Sands 1888, p. 91). Of the six chapters in his book about Tranent, one is devoted to witchcraft and one to the battle of Prestonpans (Sands 1881a). He was in St Kilda twice, in 1875 and 1876–77, being marooned there throughout a very hungry winter; out of this experience came a learned paper, three magazine articles and a book (Sands 1876–78, 1877, 1878). He never married, although the St Kilda people thought that he was going to return to wed a young woman with whom he had become familiar. Wherever he went he took the side of the people against their oppressors either directly, such as by the gift of a boat, or indirectly, by taking up their case in the court of public opinion, such as the letters column of *The Shetland Times*, where he knew how to stop short of libel: "I sail close," he said, "but I never strike." Of Tiree he wrote (Sands 1888, p. 98):

> *Would any donor*
> *Make me the owner*
> *Of that flat isle, the farms I would divide;*
> *And inanition*
> *And all sedition*
> *Without coercion would at once subside.*

He left Shetland in the early 1890s, and died at Bowriefauld near Letham in Angus in 1900. See Nicolson 1937; Harman 1997, pp. 119, 280–81; Holbourn 2001, pp. 30, 92, 119–20, 272–78.

70 According to *The Folk-Lore Journal*, which reprinted it (Anon. 1883b, p. 168), the report first appeared in the newspaper on 20 March 1883. However, I cannot find it there on that or any other day in March 1882 *or* March 1883. Given the date of Sands's Society of Antiquaries paper, it struck me that he probably spoke to the reporter in the first half of 1882. We do not know exactly when he was in Tiree. The census of 3 April 1881 finds him in Tranent, but he tells us that he lived at Hynish for a year (Sands 1888, pp. 94–95):

> *A row of houses*
> *For the keepers' spouses*
> *And signal-tower appear on grassy heights;*
> *A dock and warerooms,*
> *And house with spare rooms,*
> *Belonging to the Board of Northern Lights . . .*

> *In this location*
> *A habitation*
> *Was vacant, and I took it for a year,*
> *With the intention,*
> *As I may mention,*
> *Of making antiquarian surveys here.*

In case the identity of the newspaper was mistaken, I also checked *The Glasgow Herald* and *The Scotsman* for 20 March 1882 and 1883, again with negative results. Perhaps the report was removed from later editions, cf. note 73 below.

71 For some discussion of this point by an experienced collector who is a fluent native speaker of Gaelic see MacInnes 1994–96, p. 2.

72 The other members of the Presbytery of Mull at this point were Archibald Campbell, Kilfinichen, formerly of Coll; John Campbell, Iona; Colin MacCallum, Salen; Alexander MacDougall, Ulva; Neil MacDougall, Coll; Angus Macintyre, Kinlochspelvie; William MacKintosh, Torosay; Duncan MacNaughton, Acharacle; John MacRury, Heylipol; Robert Munro, Ardnamurchan; and Duncan Turner, Kilninian. Of these, only Macintyre was a member at the time of the first 'Tiree Case' of 1860–61. Andrew MacPherson, Tobermory, left office on 18 May 1882 to be replaced by John Cameron on 25 September. The Very Rev. Dr John MacLeod, Morvern, died on 30 May 1882, and was replaced on 13 December that year by Donald MacFarlane.

73 NAS CH2/273/10, pp. 213–14. I have looked for the report to which JGC refers in *The Scotsman* of 16 August, September and October 1882, but cannot find it. Perhaps it was omitted from later editions, cf. note 70 above. For the Commissioners' visit to the Presbytery see p. 661.

74 NAS CH2/273/10, pp. 242–43. On 26 February 1883 JGC wrote to the Presbytery complaining 'against the Assessors sent down'. Presumably the Church was carrying out a valuation of its property in Tiree, including his manse and glebe. The complaint was rejected (*ibid.*, pp. 256, 279–80).

75 Personal communication, 22 April 2004; see also *Tocher* 32, pp. 98–101, and Brownlie 1995, pp. 28–31.

76 NAS CH2/273/10, pp. 258–59, 261, 267–73, 277–79, 287–88. MacCowan (1852–1909), a schoolmaster's son, went on the following year to become minister of the *quoad sacra* parish of Duncansburgh, Fort William, moving on to Cromdale in 1889 (Scott 1915–50, vol. 4, p. 131, and vol. 6, p. 359).

77 NAS CH2/273/11, pp. 24–27. The Rev. Donald Mackay (1829–1910) was born in Creich, Sutherland, and educated at the parish school of Creich and the University of St Andrews. He served as schoolmaster at Ullapool 1848–53 and as minister of Benbecula 1853–54. He became successively minister of Stoer in Sutherland in 1854, of Gareloch in Nova Scotia in 1876, and of St Columba's Gaelic Church in Paisley in 1880, from which he resigned on 18 October 1882 (Scott 1915–50, vol. 3, p. 182, and vol. 7, p. 187). On 29 August 1883 the Presbytery of Dornoch granted him a certificate to the effect that 'the Rev. D. Mackay was, on the 4th day of April last, received as an ordained Minister within the bounds of the Presbytery of Dornoch in consequence of a Communication from the Presbytery of Paisley, and that, so far as known, he has since the former date, until quite recently, resided within the bounds of this Presbytery' (NAS CH2/1290/8, p. 260). If this was an attempt to find a parish nearer home, it failed, and from July 1883 to April 1884 he served as assistant at Moy near Inverness (NAS CH2/553/15, pp. 625, 641–42).

78 NAS CH2/273/11, pp. 21–22, 27–30, 58. The statement in the minutes of the Presbytery of Mull that Mackay had been ordained by the Presbytery of Uist in 1854 contradicts the *Fasti*, according to which he was ordained to Stoer in the same year. Mackay simply disappears from these minutes, because at some point in 1884 he accepted a call from the congregation of Metiss in Quebec; he remained there till 1886, then returned to Scotland to serve as minister of Rothesay Gaelic Chapel from 1888 to 1897. Two things may be detected from the little we know of him: he was one of those ministers whose love for the Gaelic language exceeded his ability as a preacher, and he was a family man whose twelve children (several of whom were still quite young in 1884) went on to enjoy a variety of fulfilling lives and careers (Scott 1915–50, vol. 3, p. 182, and vol. 7, p. 100). His sixth, George William (1863–1931), spent some time as a student missionary at Kilninian and Kilmore in Mull, then went on to serve as minister of Killin (1888–1931) and president of An Comunn Gaidhealach (NAS CH2/273/10, p. 261; Scott 1915–50, vol. 4, p. 186, and vol. 8, p. 358; Gillies 1938, pp. 293–94).

79 NAS CH2/273/11, pp. 32–42, 48, 60, 70–79, 111, 115, 133–34, 138–39. 'Duncan Clerk or Clarke' will be the Rev. Duncan Clarke, minister of Benbecula from 1865. He was a son of Robert Clarke, medical practitioner, Harris. He appears to have left Benbecula by 1884, given that his successor, John Macphail, was appointed in that year but not ordained until 1889. He may therefore be identified with the Rev. Duncan Clark 'who has resided in the Parish of Inverness for some time' and who asked for and was granted a certificate from the Presbytery of Inverness on 3 July 1883 (NAS CH2/553/15, pp. 619–20). He will have been well known to John MacRury, who was born and brought up in Benbecula and was minister of Heylipol at that time. He died in Australia (Scott 1915–50, vol. 7, p. 187).

80 NLS MS Acc. 9209/1, letter 289. I am grateful to Dr Allan MacColl for drawing my attention to this.

81 For good summaries of the rebellion see MacPhail 1982–84, pp. 538–44; MacPhail 1989, pp. 186–92; MacKinnon 1992, section 16.

82 Cameron 1932, pp. 246–57; *Tocher* 32, pp. 94–95; Brownlie 1991a, p. 13.

83 The list consists principally of Mrs Anne MacVicar Grant of Laggan (1755–1838), Mrs Wallace (1832–1919), Mrs Mary Mackellar (1836–90), Frances Tolmie (1840–1926), Mrs Katherine Whyte Grant (1845–1928), Lady Evelyn Stewart-Murray (1868–1940), Mrs Ella Carmichael Watson (1870–1928), Rose Ethel Bassin (1889–1974), and, later in the twentieth century, Elizabeth Mackechnie, Dr Margaret Fay Shaw, Dr Annie M. MacKenzie, Morag MacLeod, Dr Ann Lorne Gillies, Dr Meg Bateman, Dr Sheila Kidd, Dr Anja Gunderloch and Dr Nancy McGuire. (For a fascinating new biography of Lady Evelyn see Robertson and Young 1997.) Even if we add to these seventeen the names of all other women whose work has ever been published in *Scottish Gaelic Studies* (founded 1926) or in Ó Baoill and McGuire 2002, the total still comes to only thirty-six, but the *proportion* of women to men is now growing at last.

84 *Gilleasbaig Òg* will be a son or grandson of the poet Archibald Maclean (*Gilleasbaig mac Lachlainn mhic Theàrlaich*, *c.*1765–*c.*1830) of Kilmoluag, also known as *Gilleasbaig Làidir* ('Archibald the Strong') and *Gilleasbaig Crosta* ('Archibald the Perverse'), a high-spirited man who often got into trouble; for a story about him see *Tocher* 32, pp. 71, 96–97. The Rev. A. Maclean Sinclair says (1898–1900, vol. 2, p. 1, cf. 1881, pp. 238–39) that Gilleasbaig Làidir had five sons, John, Archibald, Alexander, James and Hector, while Cameron says (1932, p. 16) that 'he was the great-grandfather of Seumas Mac Ghilleasbuig Oig, whom our own generation will easily remember'. My thanks to Niall M. Brownlie for information.

85 EUL MS CW 425, cf. Gowans 1992, p. 96, note 22, and Gowans 1998.

86 NAS CH2/273/11, pp. 181–82; Scott 1915–50, vol. 7, p. 192, and vol. 8, p. 689.

87 NAS CH2/273/11, pp. 189, 204, 211, 215–16, 220–23, 225–28, 240, 250–51, 254–55, 262–65, 270–71.

88 NAS CH2/273/11, pp. 283–91, 298–302. A Tireeman born in Greenock, Donald MacLean (1856–1917) was a product of Malcolm Livingstone's school and of Glasgow University. On 14 February 1889 he was ordained as minister of Duirinish in Skye. He lived at Dunvegan for the rest of his life, building up a substantial Gaelic library which was purchased in 1910 by the marquess of Bute (Scott 1915–50, vol. 7, pp. 169–70). MacLean's splendid *Typographia Scoto-Gadelica*, an annotated list of all Scottish Gaelic books published from 1567 to 1914, appeared in 1915 and is frequently cited in the present work. He includes in it only the three most Gaelic of JGC's works (Campbell 1861, 1891, 1895), remarking revealingly that 'another work of Mr Campbell deals with witches, fairies, etc.' – by which of course he means *SHIS* and *WSS*. Of Campbell 1861, 'Three Trial Sermons', he says: "The Rev. John Gregorson Campbell was presented to the Parish of Tiree, but his settlement was opposed by the Parishioners, and on appeal by the Presentee to the General Assembly, the appointment was sustained. Copy in The Bonaparte Collection now in Chicago."

If we ask how he knew that Lucien Bonaparte had acquired a copy of the sermons, the answer is on p. ix of his book: "I have searched the leading Libraries of Great Britain, and I have been in communication with Colonial and Continental Librarians and Booksellers. I have approached private collectors as far as I could go, and I have for many years scanned and noted the pages of booksellers' and auctioneers' catalogues."

Donald MacLean of Duirinish should not be confused with the Rev. Dr Donald Maclean from Lochcarron (1869–1943), professor of Church History in the Free Church College, Edinburgh, author of *The Spiritual Songs of Dugald Buchanan* (1913), *The Law of the Lord's Day in the Celtic Church* (1926), etc.

89 NAS CH2/273/11, pp. 304–07. Scott (1837–1909), like JGC, was an alumnus of Glasgow High School and Glasgow University and must have known him well. He obtained his licence to preach just one year after him, in 1859. MacLeod (1838–1911), another Glasgow University man, was eldest son of the late Rev. Dr John MacLeod of Morvern, and was therefore particularly embarrassed by the situation. A former minister of Blair Atholl, he moved on to Inverness in 1890 (Scott 1915–50, vol. 1, pp. 107, 116, and vol. 6, p. 459).

90 NAS CH2/273/12, pp. 80, 85, 91, 93, 98–99, 105–06, 113, 127. Neil Macleod (1861–1934), educated at Broadford School and the universities of Glasgow and Aberdeen, was minister of Edderton (1889–1901), missionary at Lochboisdale (1902), then successively minister of Lochranza (1907–10),

Kilcalmonell & Kilberry (1910–15) and Erchless (1915–23); he died at Connel (Scott 1915–50, vol. 6, pp. 452–53, and vol. 8, p. 651). One entry in the *Fasti* (*ibid.*, vol. 7, p. 55) says that he was ordained on 24 October 1889, but this was merely the date of his induction to Edderton.

91 NAS CH2/273/12, pp. 128–31, 144. Maclean remained at Heylipol until 1906, when he became minister of Gairloch (Scott 1915–50, vol. 6, p. 357, and vol. 8, p. 616). The divinity student will be John Stewart MacCallum (1867–1918) from Killean. Educated at Hutcheson's Academy and Glasgow University, he was licensed by the Presbytery of Kintyre in 1895; he served successively as assistant at Glenelg and, following ordination, minister of Kilchoman 1895–1904, Stornoway 1904–13 and the Gaelic Church in Greenock 1913–18 (*ibid.*, vol. 3, pp. 200–01).

92 NAS CH2/273/12, pp. 146–47, 151–55, 164–67, 193–94, 199. James Mackinnon (1865–1939) was educated at Glasgow High School and Glasgow University (M.A. 1887). He was successively missionary at Kilbride and minister of Strathfillan 1893–94 and Kildalton 1894–1938 (Scott 1915–50, vol. 8, p. 329). The statement in the *Fasti* (*ibid.*, vol. 4, p. 77) that he was ordained to Strathfillan on 1 June 1893 is incorrect. This misunderstanding shows how unusual it was in this period for a rural parish to have an ordained assistant.

93 NAS CH2/273/11, pp. 343–44; CH2/273/12, pp. 41–42, 49, 222–25, 233–36, 241, 249. I can find no trace of R. S. Macleod in the *Fasti*. Presumably he had gone through a divinity course and obtained licence to preach but was never ordained.

94 NAS CH2/273/12, pp. 251–56, 260–62; SC51/32/41, p. 399. MacKinnon moved on to Stornoway in 1894, Campbeltown in 1897, and finally Shettleston in 1905 (Scott 1915–50, vol. 3, p. 491, and vol. 4, p. 122). Niall M. Brownlie tells me (personal communication, 22 April 2004, cf. Brownlie 1995, pp. 118–21) that he was known as 'the Spurgeon of the North' from his eloquence as a preacher. He is interred in Shettleston, but a plaque to his memory hangs in the church at Kirkapol. Hundreds of people lined the route of the cortège to pay their tribute to him, not only as a pastor, but for his humanity. His son Robert S. MacKinnon was Niall's first doctor when he came from the island to Glasgow. See also MacLean 1949, pp. 68–75, 133–43, 210, 213.

95 See above, pp. 3, 33, 36, 72, 108, 120, 150, 181, 182, 189, 245, 250, 257, and note also 'Garlatha, a Tradition of Harris', Campbell 1895, pp. 80–82.

96 Jacobs 1894, pp. 194–203. For Jacobs's contribution to folklore see Dorson 1968, pp. 266–70, 436–39, and Fine 1987.

97 For biographies of Alfred Nutt (1856–1910) see Hull 1911–12 and Dorson 1968, pp. 229–39.

98 The farmer at Mannal was Murdoch Brown. One of his sons, also Murdoch, was a Surgeon Commander in the Royal Navy, and his daughter May became Medical Officer of Health for Argyll. 'Mr MacNeill, jun.' was John son of Lachlan (*Iain Mòr Ghrianail*), renowned in Tiree for his prowess with the hammer and putting the shot (Niall M. Brownlie, personal communication, 22 July 2004).

99 *Calendar of Confirmations and Inventories*, 1892, p. 145.

100 Kenneth Mackenzie was about five feet tall and deformed. At age 31, on 30 October 1907, in the Windsor Hotel, Glasgow, he married Agnes Maclean, 21, a master mariner's daughter residing at Nithsdale Place in Govan, the officiating minister being Hector MacKinnon. Kenneth's profession is given as 'Holder of Railway Stock' and his father's as 'Property Owner'; both his parents were deceased. He and Agnes had no family. In due course he became piermaster at Scarinish (where he had a very fine house) and a member of the Parish Council. He died on 2 May 1933 in the Cottage Hospital, Oban; Agnes survived him by many years (death certificate; Niall M. Brownlie, personal communication, 22 April 2004). His brother John Gregorson Campbell Mackenzie was born in Kirkapol Cottage on 1 July 1883, his father describing himself on the birth certificate as 'Kenneth William McKenzie, Retired Merchant'.

101 Helen Margaret Maclean was born on 27 October 1870 and Johanna Gregorson Campbell Maclean on 28 June 1878, both in the farmhouse at Scarinish; they had a sister Mary Graham Maclean, born 9 July 1872, who appears not to have survived. The byre at Scarinish called *Bàthach Nonaidh* was presumably named after Johanna, who was known to everyone as Nonnie.

102 Niall M. Brownlie points out to me (personal communication, 22 April 2004) that John MacKinnon, Balevullin (*Teonaidh Mòr*), was originally a member of the Land League, but that MacDiarmid had bought him over by making him Ground Officer. In the rebellion of 1886 he accompanied Nicholson to Balephuil, but fled back to Island House when the crowd charged the policemen. "He gave evidence at the crofters' trial at the High Court in Edinburgh. He was highly disliked by the Tiree crofters."

103 The items by JGC cited at p. 708 below are intended to represent as complete a bibliography of his work as I have been able to establish. In 2001 Elibron Classics issued a reprint of a book by John Lord Campbell, *Shakespeare's Legal Acquirements Considered* (London, 1859), giving the author's name on the cover as John Gregorson Campbell. JGC was not the author of this. Nor did he write *The Hittites: Their Inscriptions and their History* (2 vols, Toronto, 1890), although it, too, is ascribed to him by the Elibron website. Its author was the Rev. Dr John Campbell (1840–1904), a Canadian academic.

104 For his biography see Campbell 1913–14.

105 The material on gifts and loans now falls at pp. 12–13 above. For Kirk see pp. xxii–xxvi above, and for Walter Gregor see Dorson 1968, pp. 414–17.

106 *WSS* 63 now falls at p. 203 above. For *muin* read *mùin*.

THE LOST APPENDIX

EUL MS CW 241

This manuscript is referred to at pp. 687–88 above. It consists of seventy unbound single sheets of ruled paper, foliated 1–70 in pencil by Ann Frater. It has been catalogued in Mackechnie 1973, pp. 510–11. Except where stated, the writing is in ink by Alexander Carmichael and is on rectos only. 'Tyree M.S.' is pencilled on f. 70v. Carmichael's original foliation, now superseded, is 1–2, 9–70, revealing that six sheets are missing between what is now ff. 2 and 3. The genesis of the manuscript is explained by Carmichael in a note on f. 1 (see below). In so far as the contents relate to SHIS and WSS, they follow exactly the order of the two books. It seems likely that the missing six folios contained the three items which have been preserved in GUL MS Gen. 1090/77 (see below) but which do not appear here. All of them relate to items which have since been published in CG5. These are (1) Didi beag duitha (GUL MS Gen. 1090/77, item 1), 45 lines, a variant of the Fairy song of Dunvegan; (2) Till a Mhór is taobh ri d' mhacan (GUL MS Gen. 1090/77, item 2), 7 lines; (3) Mo bhile bhog bhinn thu (GUL MS Gen. 1090/77, item 10), 2 quatrains. The last of these is JGC's version of the Fairy song of Dunvegan which is referred to above (p. 642) by its first words as 'Mo Mhilidh Bhog', 'Mo Bhile Bhog', 'Mo Shìle Bhog', and at f. 1 of this manuscript as 'Mile Bhog'. The version noted by JGC in what is now NLS Adv. MS 50.2.4, ff. 140v–141r, has 29 lines + chorus, to which he added ten lines from memory at ff. 141rv. Although not directly mentioned in SHIS or WSS, it relates to the tradition of 'MacLeod's Fairy Banner' discussed at p. 3, right at the start of SHIS. If this is so, it may well be that JGC intended 'Altachadh' (f. 2) to stand as a prefatory prayer to the book as a whole, but that Maclehose swept it into the lost appendix along with the rest of JGC's longer Gaelic pieces. Here it is, slightly edited.

> Athair na fìrinn,
> Saor aig an àm seo 's aig gach àm sinn;
> Mhic Dhé, thoir maitheanas duinn
> 'Nar mionnan bréige 's 'nar cainnt dhìomhain;
> Seachain oirnn buaireadh is aibhistear,
> Teum sìth agus saoghalta;
> Mar a bha thu air thùs ar codach,
> Bi mu dheireadh ar saoghail —
> Na leig 'nar corp no 'nar colainn
> Nì nì lochd do'r n-anman.

I translate: "O Father of truth, / Free us at this time and at all times; / O Son of God, forgive us / Our false oaths and our idle talk; / Keep us away from temptation and demon, / From otherworldly and worldly snare; / As you were at the start of our portion, / Be at the end of our life – / Let not into our body or flesh / Any thing to harm our souls."

The presence at the end of this manuscript of four pieces of traditional verse whose translations appear in JGC's posthumously-published papers 'The Green Island' and 'The Sharp-Witted Wife (*A' Chailleach Bheur*)' suggests that he may have intended these papers to follow 'The Celtic Year' (pp. 527–72 above) as the last two chapters of his book. An argument in favour of this hypothesis is his failure to mention the *Cailleach Bheur* in either *SHIS* or *WSS*; against it is the fact that the 'Screuchag' story in 'The Green Island' is closely related to 'The Daughter of the King of Enchantments (*Nighean Rìgh Sionnach*)' at pp. 232–33 above. In any event, lack of space prevents the inclusion of these papers in the present volume.

Folio

1   Carmichael's hand: "*Versions* / The following versions are from a well bound manuscript sent to me by   Maclehouse, Glasgow. The manuscript is the manuscript of 'Witchcraft in the Highlands' by John Gregorson Campbell minister of Tiree. The following unpublished pieces are bound with the published." Unknown hand, pencil: "See Mile Bhog." Hand of W. J. Watson (?), pencil: "Items here seem copied from Henderson MSS in Glasgow."

2   'Altachadh', beg. *O Athair nan fìrinn*, 10 lines. Published from the lost appendix in an edited version entitled 'Altachadh an t-Sheann Ghaidheil', Story 1907, p. 97. See p. 701 above and MS Gen. 1090/77, item 5.

Fairy and water-horse songs (none of these were translated in *SHIS*, but one or two were mentioned):

3   'Oran A Bhodaich Shith', beg. *Is aithne dhomh Lite nan long*, 6 qq. + chorus. See MS Gen. 1090/77, item 6.

5   'Oran Do Leannan Sith', beg. *Far am bheil mo leannan falaich*, 12 qq. + 2 alternative couplets + chorus beg. *Ille bhig ille bhig shugraich*. Three of the twelve quatrains (beg. *Fhir ud thall an triubhais bhain*) are bracketed, presumably to indicate that they may not belong to this song. Cf. p. 7 and note 30 on p. 300; see MS Gen. 1090/77, item 11.

9   'Tuiream Te Da Leannan Sith / Mharbhadh a leannan siodha agus rinn i tuiream dha', beg. *S i mo ghaol do shuil bhoidheach*, 6 qq. See MS Gen. 1090/77, item 7.

11 'Oran Sith / Oran buana le bean shith', beg. *Tha mo lamh air a gearradh*, 8 lines + chorus beg. *O 's tha mo lamh air a gearradh*. Published from the lost appendix in an edited version entitled 'Oran, le Bean Shith', Story 1907, p. 98. See MS Gen. 1090/77, item 8.

12 'Oran Na Bean Shith Do'n t-Sealgair', beg. *O Chaluman na dean an cadalan*, 2 qq. See MS Gen. 1090/77, item 9.

13 'Mac Fir Arois', beg. *'S mi am shuidhe air Creagan na Sgurra*, 25 couplets. See note 357 and MS Gen. 1090/77, item 4.

17 'Comhradh Eadar Nighean Agus An t-Each-uisge', beg. *Horo leig dhachaidh gu m mhathair mi*, 18 lines. See MS Gen. 1090/77, item 12.

Originals of miscellaneous items translated in *SHIS*:

19 'Aoir Nan Radan', beg. *Da dhroch comhdhail dheug is coinneamh*, 28 lines. See pp. 122–23 and note 398.

21 'Achanaidh Mhic Mhuirich Mhoir', beg. *Gaoth an ear o'n eilbhinn chiuin*, 15 lines + prose. See pp. 181–82 and MS Gen. 1090/77, item 2.

23 'Guidhe Nan Leodach', beg. *Gaoth an iar eas*, 11 lines. See p. 182, note 621, and MS Gen. 1090/77, item 13.

24 'An Cat Thainig Beo', beg. *Nach tuirt mi riut a Dhonnachaidh*, 23 lines. See pp. 191–92 and note 650.

Originals of charms translated in *WSS*:

26 'Eolas A Chronachaidh', beg. *Cuiridh mi an iob air a shuil*, 35 lines. See p. 204.
28 'Eolas A Chronnachaidh' [*sic*], beg. *Ma chronaich suil*, 10 lines. See p. 205.
29 'Eolas An t-Seochaidh' [*sic*], beg. *Eapag a beachd*, 31 lines. Published from the lost appendix in Story 1907, p. 99; see pp. 205–06 above.
31 'Eolas Bruthaidh', beg. *Paidere Mhoire h-aon*, 8 lines. See p. 206 and note 692.
32 'Eolas Galar Tholl', beg. *Dùin Dia umad* (/*De* added in pencil), 7 lines. See pp. 206–07. 'Doigh eile', beg. *Saighead a thainig le sgoim*, 11 lines. See p. 207 and note 694.
33 'Eolas Na Caitheamh', beg. *Saltram ort a ghlac*, 8 lines. See p. 207.
34 'Airson Iomairt Cleibhe', beg. *Saltraigh mis ort a ghlac*, 15 lines. See pp. 207–08 and note 700.
35 'Eolas An Deide', beg. *An t-eolas a chuir Calum-cille*, 9 lines. See p. 209 and note 708.
36 'Eolas Airson Cnuidh/(Cnoimh)', beg. *Ge be co rinn ort an tnu*, 4 lines. See p. 209. 'Eolas Airson Beathach Ealadh (Thaladh)', beg. *Siop ga chur air a chluas dheas*, 5 lines. See p. 209.
37 'Luibhean A Thoirt A Bhainn Air Ais', beg. *Buainidh mis am mothan*, 32 lines. See p. 210.
39 'Seun Na Caillich Ma Bo', beg. *Tha mis a cur na h-aithre mach a nochd*, 9 lines. See p. 211.
40 'Sian Na Caora Mun Chro', beg. *An t-sian chuir Moire*, 9 lines. See pp. 211–12.
41 'Sian Roimh Bhathadh San Cogadh', beg. *An t sian chuir Moire mu mac*, 13 lines. See p. 212 and note 720.
42 'Failce Phaisdean', beg. *Slan fionn failce dhuit*, 4 lines. See p. 214.
43 'Aodach Ur', beg. *'S math a ghabhas mi mo rann*, 24 lines. See p. 214 and note 739.
45 'Seun', beg. *Gabhaidh tu le Dia*, 23 lines. See p. 215 and note 744.
47 'Soisgeul Chriosd', beg. *Gum beannaicheadh Dia do chrois*, 33 lines. See p. 216 and note 746.
49 'Oradh Nam Buadh', beg. *Ionnlaidh mi do bhasan*, 28 lines. See pp. 216–17 and note 747.
51 'Oradh Airson Aodan Nigheanan', beg. *Tha 'n fheill air t-aghaidh*, 14 lines. See p. 217.
52 'Oradh Gaoil', beg. *Chan eolas gradhaich leam*, 21 lines. See p. 218.
53 'Airson Ana-cainnt', beg. *Duinidh mis an dorn*, 2 qq. See p. 219.

Original of a song translated in *WSS*:

54 'Oran Na Taibhse', beg. *Phiuthar chridhe bheil thu d' chadal*, 11 lines + chorus. See pp. 268–69 and MS Gen. 1090/77, item 3. The original of *Man, who hast shut the door upon me*, p. 269 above, is conspicuous here by its absence.

Originals of New Year rhymes translated in *WSS*:

55 'Rann Calluinn', beg. *Thainig mise so air tus*, 26 lines. See p. 532.
57 'Rann Calluinn', beg. *Beannaich am brugh fonnmhor*, 63 lines. See pp. 533–34.
61 'Rann Calluinn', beg. *Eirich a suas a bhean og*, 16 lines. See p. 534.
62 'Rann Calluinn / Tha an rann so airson feadhain aig nach bheil rann eile', beg. *Chan eil fuath agam air caise*, 1 q. See p. 535.

Originals of verse translated by JGC in Campbell 1907–08 and 1914–15:

63 'Sir Uallaidh O Corn', beg. *Bhruadair Righ Bhreatunn na shuain*, 40 lines. This manuscript is one of the sources for the study of the text in Gowans 1992, see especially pp. 15–16. Cf. also *CG*5, pp. 85–105. JGC's translation is published in Campbell 1907–08, pp. 196–97.
65 'Sgreuchag', beg. *Uiseag eutrom eoin iongadaich*, 38 lines. See note 815. JGC's translation is published in Campbell 1907–08, p. 198.
67 'Chailleach Bheur', beg. *Cru-lochan beag dorcha domhain*, 22 lines. See note 858. JGC's translation is published in Campbell 1914–15, pp. 414–15.

69   'Comhradh / Eadar a Chailleach Bheur agus Uilleam Dean Suidhe', beg. *Ise – Co as a thainig fear a bhreacain chraobhaich*, 34 lines. JGC's translation is published in Campbell 1914–15, pp. 416–17; for other versions see Mackay 1929–31, pp. 36–45, and Mac Gilleathain 1958.

GUL MS GEN. 1090/77

This manuscript is referred to at pp. 687–88 above. It consists of eighteen unbound sheets of lined paper. The writing is in ink by George Henderson and is on rectos only. It has been catalogued in Mackechnie 1973, p. 401. The items are numbered but the folios are not. The contents may be described as tidied-up transcripts of fifteen items, mainly Fairy songs, from the lost appendix, including three Fairy songs missing from EUL MS CW 241 (see p. 701 above).

Item[folio]

1[1]   'Crònan na mnatha bha 'breugadh a leinibh leatha gu dol am measg nan sìthchean', 2 ff. beg. *Didi beag duitha*, 45 lines. A variant of the Fairy song of Dunvegan, see p. 701 above. Not in CW MS 241, but cf. *CG5*, pp. 188–94, 238–39.

2[3], line 1   'Oran An Eich-Uisge', beg. *Till a Mhór is taobh ri d' mhacan*, 7 lines. Not in CW MS 241, but cf. MacPherson 1868, pp. 95–96; Mackellar 1888–89, pp. 154–56; *CG5*, p. 146.

2[3], line 9   'Achanaich Mhic Mhuirich Mhóir', beg. *Gaoth 'n ear o'n ailbhinn chiùin*, 13 lines + prose. See pp. 181–82 and CW MS 241, f. 21.

3[4]   'Oran Na Taibhse', beg. *A phiuthar chridhe bheil thu ad chadal?* 11 lines + chorus. See pp. 268–69 and CW MS 241, f. 54.

4[5]   'Mac Fir-'Arois', beg. *'S mi m' shuidhe air creagan na Sgurra*, 25 couplets. See note 357 and CW MS 241, f. 13.

5[8]   'Altachadh an t-seann Ghàidheil', beg. *O Athair na Fìrinn*, 10 lines. Published from the lost appendix in an edited version entitled 'Altachadh an t-Sheann Ghaidheil', Story 1907, p. 97. See p. 701 above and CW MS 241, f. 2.

6[9]   'Oran A Bhodaich Shìth', beg. *Is aithne dhomh Lìte nan long*, 6 qq. + chorus. See CW MS 241, f. 3.

7[11]   'Oran eile le té chaidh a leannan sìth a mharbhadh', beg. *'S i mo ghaol do shùil bhòidheach*, 6 qq. See CW MS 241, f. 9.

8[12], line 6   'Oran Buain le Bean-Shìth', beg. *Tha mo lamh air a gearradh*, 8 lines + chorus beg. *O! s tha mo lamh air a gearradh*. Published from the lost appendix in an edited version entitled 'Oran, le Bean Shith', Story 1907, p. 98. See CW MS 241, f. 11.

9[13]   'Oran Na Bean-Shìth do'n t-Sealgair', beg. *O Chaluman na dean an cadalan*, 2 qq. See CW MS 241, f. 12.

10[13], line 11   'Crònan Sìth', beg. *Mo bhile bhog bhinn thu*, 2 qq. A fragment of the Fairy song of Dunvegan, see p. 701 above. Not in CW MS 241, but cf. *CG5*, pp. 198–200.

11[14]   'Oran do Leannan-Sìth', beg. *Far am bheil mo leannan-falaich*, 12 qq. + 2 alternative couplets + chorus beg. *'Ille bhig, 'ille bhig shùgaich*. Three of the twelve quatrains (beg. *Fhir ud thall an triuthais bhàin*) are given separately in brackets at f. [16], headed 'the follg three verses bracketed were given by the reciter before the stanza marked but seem wrongly interpolated GH.' Cf. p. 7 and note 30 on p. 300; see CW MS 241, f. 5.

12[17]   'Comhradh Eadar Nighean 'Og Agus Each-Uisge', beg. *Hòro! leig dhachaigh gu m' mhàthair mi*, 18 lines. Published from this manuscript, with translation, in Shaw 1977, pp. 171–72. See CW MS 241, f. 17.

13[18]   *Gaoth 'n iar-'eas thun na h-'Eiste*, 10 lines. See p. 182 and CW MS 241, f. 23.

BIBLIOGRAPHY & ABBREVIATIONS

The names and dates used for citations are printed below in bold. Entries for a given author (and for Anon.) are listed chronologically. Care has been taken throughout *The Gaelic Otherworld* to ensure that the last personal name before the date is the one used in the citation, e.g. the work referred to in the statement 'Principal John Macleod recalled the *Cygnet* and *Plover* plying between the Broomielaw in Glasgow and Muirtown in Inverness (1990–92, p. 253)' will be found below at **Macleod 1990–92**. Books or articles published in the same year by the same individual, or by individuals bearing the same surname, are distinguished by **a**, **b** or **c**, e.g. Lord Archibald Campbell's *Records of Argyll* is **Campbell 1885a** and JGC's 'Macphee's Black Dog' is **Campbell 1885b**. Articles in journals and other multi-authored publications are cited by author or editor, the only exception being items in the School of Scottish Studies' magazine *Tocher*, which are not normally bylined and are therefore cited in the style '*Tocher* 21, p. 192'. For general abbreviations see p. 726.

Abercromby, John, review of *WSS*, in *Folk-Lore*, vol. 14, **1903**, pp. 97–98

Abrach (Donald C. MacPherson), 'Ceol nan Gaidheal', *An Gaidheal*, vol. 2, **1873–74a**, pp. 166–69

——, 'Cailleach Beinn a' Bhric', *An Gaidheal*, vol. 2, **1873–74b**, pp. 369–71

——, 'Raonull Mac Ailein Oig', *An Gaidheal*, vol. 3, **1874**, pp. 72–75

——, 'Caismeachd Ailein-nan-Sop', *An Gaidheal*, vol. 4, **1875**, pp. 76–78

——, 'Iolaire Loch-Treig', *The Celtic Monthly*, vol. 16, **1908**, p. 96

——, see also **Diarmad** and **MacPherson**

Addison, W. I., *Matriculation Albums of the University of Glasgow from 1728 to 1858*, Glasgow, **1913**

Alexander, Henry, 'Gaick', *Scottish Mountaineering Club Journal*, vol. 14, **1917**, pp. 178–90

Almqvist, Bo, 'Irish Migratory Legends on the Supernatural', *Béaloideas*, vol. 59, **1991a**, pp. 1–43

——, 'Waterhorse Legends (MLSIT 4086 & 4086B)', *Béaloideas*, vol. 59, **1991b**, pp. 107–20

——, 'Crossing the Border', *Béaloideas*, vol. 59, **1991c**, pp. 209–78

Anderson, Rev. Adam E., 'Notes from the Presbytery Records of Lorne', *TGSI*, vol. 36, **1931–33**, pp. 112–38

Anderson, Isabel Harriet, *Inverness before Railways*, Inverness, **1885** [repr. Inverness 1984]

Anderson, W. E. K., ed., *The Journal of Sir Walter Scott*, Oxford, **1972**

Anon., 'Parish of South Knapdale', **1796**, in *The Statistical Account of Scotland*, ed. by Sir John Sinclair, vol. 19, Edinburgh, 1797, pp. 308–26 = new edn, vol. 8, Wakefield, 1983, also pp. 308–26

Anon., 'Notice to Correspondents', *The Foreign Quarterly Review*, vol. 2, **1828**, pp. 352–54

Anon., *Lives of British Physicians*, The Family Library, No. XIV, London, **1830**

Anon., 'Mac Iain Ghìorr', *An Teachdaire Ùr Gàidhealach*, vol. 3, **1835–36**, pp. 53–56

Anon., 'Parish of Lochcarron', **1836**, in *The New Statistical Account of Scotland*, vol. 14, Edinburgh, 1845, part 2, pp. 107–14

Anon., 'Ceatharnach-Coille Loch Cuaich', *Cuairtear nan Gleann*, vol. 2, **1841–42a**, pp. 73–75

Anon. (Rev. Dr Norman MacLeod, Campsie), 'Ailean nan Sop', *Cuairtear nan Gleann*, vol. 2, **1841–42b**, pp. 157–60

Anon., 'Saobh-Chràbhadh nan Gàidheal', *Cuairtear nan Gleann*, vol. 3, **1842–43**, p. 137

Anon., 'Old Irish Words and Deeds', *Dublin University Magazine*, vol. 74, July–December **1869**, pp. 324–41

Anon., *Am Feillire 1873*, Inverness

Anon., *Am Feillire: The Gael Almanac and Highland Directory, for 1875*, Edinburgh

Anon., 'Charms for Illness', *Folk-Lore Record*, vol. 4, **1881**, p. 183

Anon., 'Curious Superstition in Ross-shire', *The Folk-Lore Journal*, vol. 1, **1883a**, pp. 124–25

Anon., 'Ancient Superstitions in Tiree', *The Folk-Lore Journal*, vol. 1, **1883b**, pp. 167–68

Anon., 'Witchcraft in the Highlands', *The Folk-Lore Journal*, vol. 1, **1883c**, pp. 396–97

Anon., 'Witchcraft in the North', *The Folk-Lore Journal*, vol. 2, **1884a**, p. 121

Anon., 'Superstition in Ireland', *The Folk-Lore Journal*, vol. 2, **1884b**, pp. 190–91

Anon., 'Logierait Marriage Customs in the Olden Times', *Celtic Magazine*, vol. 10, **1884–85**, p. 542

Anon., 'Gaelic Almanack for April, 1886', *The Celtic Magazine*, vol. 11, **1885–86a**, p. 272

Anon., 'The Camerons of Rannoch', *Celtic Magazine*, vol. 11, **1885–86b**, pp. 285–88, 330–36

Anon., 'Spells and Charms', *The Celtic Magazine*, vol. 12, **1886–87a**, pp. 37–41

Anon., 'The Evil Eye', *The Celtic Magazine*, vol. 12, **1886–87b**, pp. 415–18

Anon., 'Tales of the Water-Kelpie', *Celtic Magazine*, vol. 12, **1886–87c**, pp. 511–15

Anon., 'Some Stories about Witches', *The Celtic Magazine*, vol. 13, **1887–88**, pp. 92–94

Anon., *The Witch of Inverness and the Fairies of Tomnahurich*, Inverness, **1891a**

Anon., 'Death of Rev. J. G. Campbell, Tiree', *The Oban Times*, 5 December **1891b**

Anon., 'The Legend of Lianachan', *The Celtic Monthly*, vol. 11, **1902–03**, pp. 196–97

Anon., 'Mac Iain Ghiorr', *The Celtic Monthly*, vol. 15, **1906–07**, pp. 233–35

Anon., *Fearchair-a-Ghunna, the Ross-shire Wanderer*, 3rd edn, Stirling, **1908**

Anon., 'Fairy Tales', *Celtic Review*, vol. 5, **1908–09a**, pp. 155–71

Anon., 'A Modern Instance of Evil-Eye', *The Celtic Review*, vol. 5, **1908–09b**, pp. 343–44

Anon., 'Clan Proverbs', *The Celtic Monthly*, vol. 19, **1911**, p. 113

Anon., 'The MacFadyens', *The Celtic Monthly*, vol. 20, **1912**, pp. 135–36

Anon., 'Latha na Maoile Ruaidhe', in Macleod **1915**, p. 65

Anon., 'Morvern Memories: Some Minor Poets', *The Oban Times*, 12 July **1941**

Anon., 'Camanachd', *An Gaidheal*, vol. 54, **1959**, p. 55

Ansdell, Douglas, *The People of the Great Faith: The Highland Church, 1690–1900*, Stornoway, **1998**

Argathalian, 'Aimsirean na Bliadhna', *An Gaidheal*, vol. 3, **1874**, pp. 55–56

Armstrong, Robert, *Gaelic Dictionary*, London, **1825**

Ashmall, Harry A., *The High School of Glasgow*, Edinburgh, **1976**

Balfour, Roderick, 'The Highland and Island Emigration Society', *TGSI*, vol. 57, **1990–92**, pp. 429–566

Ballard, Linda-May, 'Fairies and the Supernatural on Reachrai', in Narváez **1997**, pp. 47–93

Banks, Mary MacLeod, *British Calendar Customs: Scotland*, 3 vols, London, **1937–41**

Bannerman, John, *The Beatons*, Edinburgh, **1986**

Baran, Huisdean, 'Sgialachdan a Siorramachd Inbhirnis – Earrann II', *TGSI*, vol. 55, **1986–88**, pp. 187–202

——, see also **Barron**, Hugh

Baran, Ruaraidh, 'Baideanach', *TGSI*, vol. 39/40, **1942–50**, pp. 118–28

——, see also **Barron**, Roderick

Barron, Hugh, 'Notes on the Aird', *TGSI*, vol. 45, **1967–68**, pp. 196–231

——, 'Verse, Story and Fragments from Various Districts', *TGSI*, vol. 46, **1969–70**, pp. 217–49, and vol. 47, **1971–72**, pp. 218–44

——, 'Verse, Fragments and Words from Various Districts', *TGSI*, vol. 49, **1974–76**, pp. 135–58

——, 'Verse, Fragments, etc., from Various Districts', *TGSI*, vol. 50, **1976–78**, pp. 403–34, and vol. 52, **1980–82**, pp. 102–32

——, see also **Baran**, Huisdean

Barron, Roderick, 'A Highland Lady of Letters', *TGSI*, vol. 42, **1953–59**, pp. 68–90

——, see also **Baran**, Ruaraidh

Barrow, Geoffrey W. S., *Robert Bruce*, 2nd edn, Edinburgh, **1976**

Batho, Edith C., **and Husbands**, H. Winifred, eds, *The Chronicles of Scotland, Compiled by Hector Boece, Translated into Scots by John Bellenden 1531*, vol. 2, Scottish Text Society, Edinburgh, **1941**

Beaumont, Frank, *The Book of Service and Remembrance*, Glasgow, **1921**

Beith, Mary, *Healing Threads*, Edinburgh, **1995**

——, 'Fearchar Lighiche and the Traditional Medicines of the North', in *The Province of Strathnaver*, ed. by J. R. Baldwin, Edinburgh, **2000**, pp. 101–15

Benét, W. R., *Reader's Encyclopedia*, London, **1948**

Bennett, Margaret, *The Last Stronghold*, Edinburgh, **1989**

——, *Scottish Customs from the Cradle to the Grave*, Edinburgh, **1992**

——, 'Balquhidder Revisited: Fairylore in the Scottish Highlands', in Narváez **1997**, pp. 94–115

Bergin, Osborn, ed., *Irish Bardic Poetry*, Dublin, **1970**

Beveridge, Erskine, *Coll and Tiree*, Edinburgh, **1903** [repr. Edinburgh 2000]

——, *North Uist: Its Archæology and Topography*, Edinburgh, **1911** [repr. Edinburgh 2001]

Bil, Albert, *The Shieling 1600–1840*, Edinburgh, **1990**

Bisset, Rev. Dr Thomas, 'Parish of Logierait', **1791**, in *The Statistical Account of Scotland*, ed. by Sir John Sinclair, vol. 5, Edinburgh, 1793, pp. 75–87 = new edn, vol. 12, Wakefield, 1977, pp. 705–17

Black, George F., 'Scottish Charms and Amulets', *PSAS*, vol. 27, **1892–93**, pp. 433–526

——, *A Calendar of Cases of Witchcraft in Scotland 1510–1727*, New York, **1938**

——, *The Surnames of Scotland*, New York, **1946** [repr. New York 1986]

Black, Ronald, 'Colla Ciotach', *TGSI*, vol. 48, **1972–74**, pp. 201–43

——, 'The Genius of Cathal MacMhuirich', *TGSI*, vol. 50, **1976–78**, pp. 327–66

——, 'The Gaelic Calendar Months', *Shadow: The Newsletter of the Traditional Cosmology Society*, vol. 2, no. 1, June **1985**, pp. 3–13

——, *Mac Mhaighstir Alasdair: The Ardnamurchan Years*, SWHIHR, Coll, **1986a**

——, 'The Gaelic Academy', *Scottish Gaelic Studies*, vol. 14, part 2, **1986b**, pp. 1–38

——, 'The Gaelic Academy: Appendix: The Ingliston Papers', *SGS*, vol. 15, **1988**, pp. 103–21

——, 'An Emigrant's Letter in Arran Gaelic, 1834', *Scottish Studies*, vol. 31, **1993**, pp. 63–87

——, 'Mac Mhaighstir Alastair in Rannoch', *TGSI*, vol. 59, **1994–96**, pp. 341–419

——, 'James Macintyre's Calendar', *Scottish Gaelic Studies*, vol. 17, **1996**, pp. 36–60

——, ed., *An Tuil*, Edinburgh, **1999**

——, 'Scottish Fairs and Fair-Names', *Scottish Studies*, vol. 33, **2000**, pp. 1–75

——, ed., *An Lasair*, Edinburgh, **2001**

——, ed., *Eilein na h-Òige*, Glasgow, **2002**

——, see also **MacilleDhuibh**, Raghnall

Black, William George, *Folk-Medicine*, London, **1883**

Blaikie, William Garden, *The Personal Life of David Livingstone*, Philadelphia, **1889**

Blake-Coleman, B. C., 'The Left Heresy and Directional Preference in Early Science and Technology', *Folklore*, vol. 93, **1982**, pp. 151–63

Blunt, Rev. John Henry, ed., *The Annotated Book of Common Prayer*, 2nd edn, London, **1867**

Boog Watson, Charles B., ed., *Roll of Edinburgh Burgesses and Guild-Brethren, 1406–1700*, Scottish Record Society, Edinburgh, **1929**

Bord, Janet, *Fairies*, New York, **1997**

Bourke, Angela, *The Burning of Bridget Cleary: A True Story*, London, **1999**

Bower, Herbert M., 'Charm against Toothache', *Folk-Lore*, vol. 15, **1904**, p. 350

Boyd, Ailean, *Seann Taighean Tirisdeach*, Tiree, **1986**

Brand, John, *Observations on Popular Antiquities*, 2nd edn, ed. by Sir Henry Ellis, 2 vols, London, **1813**

——, *Observations on the Popular Antiquities of Great Britain*, 3rd edn, ed. by Sir Henry Ellis, 3 vols, London, **1849**

Briggs, Katharine, *The Anatomy of Puck*, London, **1959**

——, *A Dictionary of Fairies*, London, **1976**

Britten, James, 'Amulets in Scotland', *Folk-Lore Record*, vol. 4, **1881**, pp. 167–69

Brown, Colin, *The Thistle*, London, [**1884**]

Brown, Rev. J. Wood, *An Enquiry into the Life and Legend of Michael Scot*, Edinburgh, **1897**

Brown, P. Hume, *Scotland before 1700 from Contemporary Documents*, Edinburgh, **1893**

Brown, Terence, *The Life of W. B. Yeats*, Oxford, **1999**

Brownlie, Niall M., 'Beagan mu Bhuitseachd', *Gairm* 77, An Geamhradh **1971**, pp. 21–23

——, ed., *Na Cnuic 's na Glinn*, n.p., **1991a**

——, 'An t-Urramach Dòmhnall MacCaluim 1849–1929', in *Baragab: Bàrdachd agus Rosg an Gàidhlig agus Beurla*, An Comunn Gàidhealach, n.p., **1991b**, pp. 73–78

——, *Bailtean is Ath-Ghairmean a Tiriodh: Townships and Echoes from Tiree*, Glendaruel, **1995**

Bruford, Alan, 'A Scottish Gaelic Version of "Snow-White"', *Scottish Studies*, vol. 9, **1965**, pp. 153–74

——, 'Scottish Gaelic Witch Stories: A Provisional Type-List', *Scottish Studies*, vol. 11, **1967**, pp. 13–47

——, 'Murchadh Mac Briain agus an Díthreabhach', *Éigse*, vol. 12, **1967–68**, pp. 301–26

——, *Gaelic Folk-Tales and Mediæval Romances*, Dublin, **1969**

——, 'Legends Long Since Localised or Tales Still Travelling?', *Scottish Studies*, vol. 24, **1980**, pp. 43–62

——, '"Deirdre" and Alexander Carmichael's Treatment of Oral Sources', *SGS*, vol. 14, part 1, **1983**, pp. 1–24

——, 'Caught in the Fairy Dance', *Béaloideas*, vol. 62/63, **1994–95**, pp. 1–28

——, 'Trolls, Hillfolk, Finns, and Picts', in Narváez **1997**, pp. 116–41

——, **and MacDonald**, Donald Archie, eds, *Scottish Traditional Tales*, Edinburgh, **1994**

Buchan, David, 'The Legend of the Lughnasa Musician in Lowland Britain', *Scottish Studies*, vol. 23, **1979**, pp. 15–37

Buchanan, Dugald, *Diary*, Edinburgh, **1836**

Budge, Donald, *Jura*, Glasgow, **1960**

——, see also **Buidse**, Dòmhnall

Buidse, Dòmhnall, 'Baird an Eilean Sgiathanach', *TGSI*, vol. 48, **1972–74**, pp. 584–601

——, see also **Budge**, Donald

Bulloch, John M., 'The Gordons as Invaders', *TGSI*, vol. 36, **1931–33**, pp. 319–45

Burleigh, J. H. S., *A Church History of Scotland*, London, **1960**

Burn, Rev. A. Ronald G., 'Out of the Golden Remote Wild West', *The Scottish Mountaineering Club Journal*, vol. 14, **1917**, pp. 155–69, 207–23

Burnett, Charles S. F., 'Arabic Divinatory Texts and Celtic Folklore', *Cambridge Medieval Celtic Studies*, no. 6, winter **1983**, pp. 31–42

Burnett, Ray, *Benbecula*, Torlum, **1986**

Burns, Robert, *The Complete Poetical Works*, ed. by James A. Mackay, Darvel, **1993**

Burt, see **Simmons**

Caimbeul, Aonghas, *Suathadh ri Iomadh Rubha*, Glasgow, **1973**

Caimbeul, Aonghas Pàdraig, *An Oidhche mus do Sheòl Sinn*, Daviot, **2003**

Calder, George, *A Gaelic Grammar*, Glasgow, **1923**

Calder, Rev. R. H., Glenlivet, 'The Brownie', *Transactions of the Banffshire Field Club*, **1914–15**, pp. 9–13

Calderwood, David, *The History of the Kirk of Scotland*, ed. by Rev. Thomas Thomson, vol. 7, The Wodrow Society, Edinburgh, **1845**

Cameron, A. D., *Go Listen to the Crofters*, Stornoway, **1986**

——, *The Caledonian Canal*, Edinburgh, **2005** [1st edn Lavenham 1972]

Cameron, Alastair ('North Argyll'), 'The MacFies in Legend and Romance', *TGSI*, vol. 38, **1937–41**, pp. 206–16

——, *Loch Sunartside Memories*, Bunalteachan, **1954**

——, see also **Camshron**, Alasdair

Cameron, Alexander (Bàrd Thùrnaig), see **Camshron**, Alasdair

Cameron, Rev. Dr Alexander, *Reliquiæ Celticæ*, ed. by Alexander Macbain and Rev. John Kennedy, 2 vols, Inverness, **1892–94**

Cameron, Rev. Donald, 'Parish of Laggan', in *The New Statistical Account of Scotland*, vol. 14, Edinburgh, **1845**, part 1, pp. 417–31

Cameron, Rev. Hector, ed., *Na Bàird Thirisdeach*, Glasgow, **1932**

Cameron, Morag, Thurso, 'Highland Fisher-Folk and their Superstitions', *Folk-Lore*, vol. 14, **1903**, pp. 300–06

Cameron, Nigel, ed., *Dictionary of Scottish Church History & Theology*, Edinburgh, **1993**

Cameron, Paul, Blair Atholl, 'Perthshire Gaelic Songs', *TGSI*, vol. 17, **1890–91**, pp. 126–70

Cameron, R. W. D., 'The Macgregors of Rannoch',

Celtic Magazine, vol. 13, **1887–88**, pp. 175–84, 219–26

Campbell, Lord Archibald, *Records of Argyll*, Edinburgh, **1885a**

——, ed., *Craignish Tales* (Waifs and Strays of Celtic Tradition, Argyllshire Series, No. I), London, **1889**

Campbell, Diarmid A., *Some Notes on the Campbells of Inverawe*, 2nd edn, Lochgilphead, **1998a** [1st edn by Ian M. Campbell 1951]

Campbell, Donald, *Language, Poetry, and Music of the Highland Clans*, Edinburgh, **1862**

Campbell, Rev. Duncan, 'Gaelic Proverbs', *TGSI*, vol. 45, **1967–68**, pp. 1–32

Campbell, Rev. Gillespie, 'Lord Archibald Campbell', *The Celtic Review*, vol. 9, **1913–14**, pp. 65–70

Campbell, John Francis, *Popular Tales of the West Highlands*, 4 vols, 1st edn, Edinburgh, **1860–62**; 2nd edn, Paisley, **1890**, repr. Hounslow 1983–84

——, 'Fionn's Enchantment', *Revue Celtique*, vol. 1, **1870–72**, pp. 193–202

——, *Leabhar na Féinne*, London, **1872** [repr. Shannon 1972]

——, *The Celtic Dragon Myth*, ed. by George Henderson, Edinburgh, **1911**

——, *More West Highland Tales*, transcribed and translated by John G. Mackay, 2 vols, Edinburgh, **1940–60** [repr. Edinburgh 1994]

Campbell, Rev. John Gregorson, Tiree, *First Gaelic Sermon / Second Gaelic Sermon / Third Gaelic Sermon*, Mull, **1861**

——, 'Mar a Chaidh an Tuairisgeul Mor a Chur gu Bàs', *The Scottish Celtic Review*, no. 1, March **1881a**, pp. 61–77

——, 'The Muileartach', *The Scottish Celtic Review*, no. 2, November **1881b**, pp. 115–37

——, 'Note', *The Scottish Celtic Review*, no. 2, November **1881c**, pp. 140–41

——, 'Fin Mac Coul', *The Scottish Celtic Review*, no. 3, November **1882**, pp. 176–90

——, 'Macphee's Black Dog', *The Scottish Celtic Review*, no. 4, July **1885b**, pp. 262–73

——, 'Sgeulachd air Sir Uallabh O'Corn', *TGSI*, vol. 13, **1886–87**, pp. 69–83

——, 'Sgeulachd Casa Céin – The Healing of Keyn's Foot', *TGSI*, vol. 14, **1887–88a**, pp. 78–100

——, 'Cath Gabhra no Laoidh Oscair. (The Battle of Gavra or Oscar's Hymn.)', *The Celtic Magazine*, vol. 13, **1887–88b**, pp. 167–74, 202–11

——, 'Fionn's Ransom', *TGSI*, vol. 15, **1888–89**, pp. 46–62

——, 'The Good Housewife and her Night Labours', in Campbell 1889, pp. 54–70

——, 'Na Amhuisgean – The Dwarfs or Pigmies; or, The Three Soldiers', *TGSI*, vol. 16, **1889–90**, pp. 110–22

——, 'Sgoil nan Eun, no, Mac an Fhucadair', *TGSI*, vol. 17, **1890–91**, pp. 58–68

——, *The Fians; or, Stories, Poems and Traditions of Fionn and His Warrior Band* (Waifs and Strays of Celtic Tradition, Argyllshire Series, No. IV), London, **1891** [repr. by Elibron Classics, n.p., 2003?]

——, *Clan Traditions and Popular Tales of the Western Highlands and Islands* (Waifs and Strays of Celtic Tradition, Argyllshire Series, No. V), London, **1895** [repr. Elibron Classics, n.p., 2003]

——, *Superstitions of the Highlands & Islands of Scotland*, Glasgow, **1900** [*SHIS*]

——, *Witchcraft & Second Sight in the Highlands & Islands of Scotland*, Glasgow, **1902** [repr. Wakefield 1974] [*WSS*]

——, 'The Story of Conal Grund', *The Scottish Historical Review*, vol. 1, **1903–04**, pp. 300–05

——, 'Story of the King of Ireland and his Two Sons', *Scottish Historical Review*, vol. 4, **1906–07**, pp. 1–10

——, 'The Green Island', *The Scottish Historical Review*, vol. 5, **1907–08**, pp. 191–202

——, 'The Origin of the Fairy Creed', *The Scottish Historical Review*, vol. 7, **1909–10a**, pp. 364–76 [repr. pp. lxxxv–xciii above]

——, 'Righ Eirionn 's a Dha Mhac', *The Celtic Review*, vol. 6, **1909–10b**, pp. 364–74

——, 'The Sharp-Witted Wife (*A' Chailleach Bheur*)', *The Scottish Historical Review*, vol. 12, **1914–15**, pp. 413–17

——, *Second Sight in the Highlands of Scotland*, Dumfries, **2003a** [repr. from *WSS* 120–80, i.e. pp. 240–70 above]

——, *Scottish Hobgoblins*, Dumfries, **2003b** [repr. from *WSS* 181–223, i.e. pp. 271–92 above]

——, *The Celtic Year in Scotland*, Monmouth, **2003c** [repr. from *WSS* 224–307, i.e. pp. 527–72 above]

Campbell, Dr John Lorne, ed., *Sia Sgialachdan: Six Gaelic Stories*, Edinburgh, **1939**

——, 'Proverbs from Barra Collected by the Late Neil Sinclair', *SGS*, vol. 10, **1963–65**, pp. 178–208

——, *Hebridean Folksongs*, 3 vols, Oxford, **1969–81**

——, ed., *A Collection of Highland Rites and Customes*, The Folklore Society, Cambridge, **1975**

——, 'Notes on Hamish Robertson's "Studies in Carmichael's *Carmina Gadelica*"', *Scottish Gaelic Studies*, vol. 13, part 1, **1978**, pp. 1–17

——, '*Carmina Gadelica*: George Henderson's Corrections and Suggestions', *Scottish Gaelic Studies*, vol. 13, **1978–81**, pp. 183–218

——, ed., *Highland Songs of the Forty-Five*, 2nd edn, Scottish Gaelic Texts Society, Edinburgh, **1984** [1st edn Edinburgh 1933]

——, *Songs Remembered in Exile*, Aberdeen, **1990**

——, 'The Rev. Dr. Kenneth MacLeod's Collection of Gaelic Asseverations, Exclamations, and Imprecations', *SGS*, vol. 17, **1996**, pp. 71–81

——, ed., *The Book of Barra*, 2nd edn, Stornoway, **1998b** [1st edn London 1936]

——, *A Very Civil People*, ed. by Hugh Cheape, Edinburgh, **2000**

——, **and Hall**, Trevor, *Strange Things*, London, **1968**

——, **and Thomson**, Derick, *Edward Lhuyd in the Scottish Highlands 1699–1700*, Oxford, **1963**

Camshron, Alasdair (Bàrd Thùrnaig), 'A Bhana-Bhuidseach Leodhasach', in Macleod **1915**, p. 87

——, *Am Bard*, ed. by Iain Alasdair Moffatt-Pender, Edinburgh, **1926**

Camshron, Alasdair ('North Argyll'), 'Bard Rathuaidhe', *TGSI*, vol. 39/40, **1942–50**, pp. 20–35

Carleton, William, *Tales and Sketches* [or *Tales and Stories*] . . . *of the Irish Peasantry*, Dublin, **1854**

Carmichael, Alexander, 'Cumha Mhic-an-Toisich: Mackintosh's Lament', *The Highlander*, 5 Feb. **1876**

——, 'Caol Reathainn, Mar a Fhuair E an t-Ainm: Caol Reathainn (Kyle Rhea) – How It Got the Name', *Celtic Review*, vol. 1, **1904–05**, pp. 32–35

——, 'The Ruskins', *The Celtic Review*, vol. 2, **1905–06**, pp. 343–51

——, 'The Barons of Bachuill', *The Celtic Review*, vol. 5, **1908–09**, pp. 356–75

——, 'Some Unrecorded Incidents of the Jacobite Risings', *The Celtic Review*, vol. 6, **1909–10**, pp. 278–83, 334–48

——, 'Traditions of the Land of Lorne and the Highland Ancestry of Robert Burns', *The Celtic Review*, vol. 8, **1912–13**, pp. 314–33

——, *Deirdire and the Lay of the Children of Uisne*, 2nd edn, Paisley, **1914** [1st edn Edinburgh 1905]

——, 'Grazing and Agrestic Customs of the Outer Hebrides', *The Celtic Review*, vol. 10, **1914–16**, pp. 40–54, 144–48, 254–62, 358–75

——, *Carmina Gadelica*, abridged single-volume edn, ed. by C. J. Moore, Edinburgh, **1994** [1st edn Edinburgh 1992]

——, see also **CG**

Carmichael, E. C., ' "Never was Piping so Sad, and Never was Piping so Gay" ', *The Celtic Review*, vol. 2, **1905–06**, pp. 76–84

——, see also **Watson**, E. C.

Carmichael, Rev. Ian, *Lismore in Alba*, Perth, **n.d.**

Carn Dearg, 'Kennedys of Lianachan', *The Oban Times*, 4 January **1913**

Carney, Seamus, *The Killing of the Red Fox: An Investigation into the Appin Murder*, Moffat, **1989**

——, 'Was Allan Breck Guilty?', *The Scots Magazine*, May **1994**, pp. 490–94

Carroll, Michael P., 'Allomotifs and the Psychoanalytic Study of Folk Narratives', *Folklore*, vol. 103, **1992**, pp. 225–33

C. C. (Rev. Dr Norman MacLeod), 'An Taghairm', *An Teachdaire Ùr Gàidhealach*, vol. 3, **1835–36**, pp. 52–53

CCBG (Comataidh Coimhearsnachd Baile Ghrèinetobht), *1899, Bliadhn' a' Gheallaidh*, Grenitote, **2004**

CG1–6: Alexander Carmichael, *Carmina Gadelica*, 6 vols, Edinburgh, 1900–71: vols 1 and 2, 2nd edn, 1928 [1st edn Edinburgh 1900]; vols 3 and 4, ed. by James Carmichael Watson, 1940 and 1941; vols 5 and 6, ed. by Angus Matheson, 1954 and 1971

Chambers, Charles, ed., *Ane Account of the Rise and Offspring of the Name of Grant*, Monymusk, **1876**

Chambers, Robert, *The Popular Rhymes of Scotland*, Edinburgh, **1826**; 2nd edn, Edinburgh, **1841**; 3rd edn, Edinburgh, **1847**; 4th edn, London, **1870**

——, *History of the Rebellion in Scotland in 1745–6*, 5th edn, Edinburgh, **1840** [1st edn Edinburgh 1828]

——, *Domestic Annals of Scotland*, 2nd edn, 2 vols, Edinburgh, **1859** [1st edn Edinburgh 1858]

Chambers *20th Century Dictionary*, new edn, ed. by E. M. Kirkpatrick, Edinburgh, **1983**

Chapman, R. W., ed., *Johnson's Journey to the Western Islands of Scotland and Boswell's Journal of a Tour to the Hebrides*, Oxford, **1970**

Chaundler, Christine, *Every Man's Book of Superstitions*, London, **1970**

Cheape, Hugh, 'The Red Book of Appin', *Folklore*, vol. 104, **1993**, pp. 111–23

——, 'Etymologies and Traditions', *Scottish Gaelic Studies*, vol. 19, **1999**, pp. 66–82

Cheape, Jane, *Hand to Mouth*, Stornoway, **2002**

Chisholm, Colin, 'The Last of the MacMartin Camerons', *The Celtic Magazine*, vol. 9, **1883–84**, pp. 442–43

——, 'Old Gaelic Songs', *TGSI*, vol. 11, **1884–85**, pp. 216–40

——, 'Unpublished Old Gaelic Songs', *TGSI*, vol. 12, **1885–86**, pp. 118–66

——, 'A Collection of Unpublished Gaelic Songs, with Notes', *TGSI*, vol. 15, **1888–89**, pp. 238–55

Clancy, Thomas Owen, 'Mac Steléne and the Eight in Armagh', *Éigse*, vol. 26, **1992**, pp. 80–91

——, 'Fools and Adultery in some Early Irish Texts', *Ériu*, vol. 44, **1993**, pp. 105–24

——, 'Annat in Scotland and the Origins of the Parish', *The Innes Review*, vol. 46, no. 2, **1995**, pp. 91–115

Clerk, Rev. Dr Archibald, Kilmallie, *Memoir of Colonel John Cameron, Fassiefern, K.T.S.*, 1st edn, Fassiefern, **1858** [2nd edn also Fassiefern 1858]

——, ed., *Caraid nan Gaidheal: Aireamh Taghta de Sgriobhaidhnean an Ollaimh Urramaich Tormoid MacLeoid*, 1st edn, Glasgow, **1867**

C.M.P. (Calum MacPhàrlain), 'Cumha Mhic-an-Toisich. – Mackintosh's Lament', *The Celtic Monthly*, vol. 3, **1894–95**, pp. 137–38

Cohn, Shari Ann, 'The Scottish Tradition of Second Sight and Other Psychic Experiences in Families', unpublished PhD thesis, Edinburgh, **1996**

——, 'A Historical Review of Second Sight', *Scottish Studies*, vol. 33, **2000**, pp. 146–85

Colson, F. H., *The Week*, Cambridge, **1926**

Copland, Mairi B., 'Taibhse na Coimhlig', in Macleod **1915**, p. 86

Cotta, Iohn, Northampton, *A Short Discoverie of the Vnobserved Dangers of Seuerall Sorts of Ignorant and Vnconsiderate Practisers of Physicke in England*, London, **1612** [repr. Amsterdam 1972]

——, John, *The Triall of Witch-craft*, London, **1616** [repr. Amsterdam 1968]

Cowan, Edward J., **and Henderson**, Lizanne, 'The Last of the Witches? The Survival of Scottish Witch Belief', in Goodare **2002**, pp. 198–217

——, see also **Henderson and Cowan**

Craig, Kirkland Cameron, ed., *Sgialachdan Dhunnchaidh*, Glasgow, **1944**

Craigie, W. A., 'Donald Bàn and the Bócan', *Folk-Lore*, vol. 6, **1895**, pp. 353–58

——, 'Some Highland Folklore', *Folk-Lore*, vol. 9, **1898**, pp. 372–79

——, 'The Battle of Pìorait', *The Celtic Review*, vol. 2, **1905–06**, p. 121

Cramond, William, *The Church of Alves*, Elgin, **1900**

Cregeen, Eric R., ed., *Inhabitants of the Argyll Estate, 1779*, Scottish Record Society, Edinburgh, **1963**

——, *Argyll Estate Instructions*, Scottish History Society, Edinburgh, **1964**

——, 'Oral Tradition and History in a Hebridean Island', *Scottish Studies*, vol. 32, **1998**, pp. 12–37

——, and **MacKenzie**, Donald W., *Tiree Bards and their Bardachd*, SWHIHR, Coll, **1978**

Croker, T. Crofton, *Fairy Legends and Traditions of the South of Ireland*, 3 vols, London, **1825–28**

Cunningham, A. D., *Tales of Rannoch*, Perth, **1989**

Currie, Jo, *Mull Family Names*, Tobermory, **1998**

——, *Mull: The Island and its People*, Edinburgh, **2000**

Curtin, Jeremiah, *Tales of the Fairies and of the Ghost World*, London, **1895**

Dalyell, John Graham, *The Darker Superstitions of Scotland*, Edinburgh, **1834**

Danaher, Kevin, *The Year in Ireland*, Cork, **1972**

——, 'Irish Folk Tradition and the Celtic Calendar', in *The Celtic Consciousness*, ed. by R. O'Driscoll, Edinburgh, **1982**, pp. 217–42

Davidson, Hilda E., **and Chaudhri**, Anna, 'The Hair and the Dog', *Folklore*, vol. 104, **1993**, pp. 151–63

Davidson, Thomas, *Rowan Tree and Red Thread*, Edinburgh, **1949**

——, 'Animal Treatment in Eighteenth-Century Scotland', *Scottish Studies*, vol. 4, **1960**, pp. 134–49

——, 'Scoring Aboon the Breath: Defeating the Evil Eye', in Dundes **1992**, pp. 143–49 [first published in *Chambers' Journal* 1950]

Davies, Owen, 'The Nightmare Experience, Sleep Paralysis, and Witchcraft Accusations', *Folklore*, vol. 114, **2003**, pp. 181–203

Davis, Deborah, 'Contexts of Ambivalence', *Folklore*, vol. 103, **1992**, pp. 207–21

D.B., 'Facal as leth nan Gaidheal', *An Gaidheal*, vol. 2, 1873–74, p. 241

Deane, Tony, **and Shaw**, Tony, *The Folklore of Cornwall*, London, **1975**

Delargy, J. H., 'Three Men of Islay', *Scottish Studies*, vol. 4, **1960**, pp. 126–33

——, see also **Ó Duilearga**, Séamus

Devine, T. M., *The Great Highland Famine*, Edinburgh, **1988**

Diarmad (Donald Campbell MacPherson), 'Tòmas Reumair', *An Gaidheal*, vol. 5, **1876**, pp. 295–98

——, see also **Abrach** and **MacPherson**

Dieckhoff, Henry Cyril, 'Mythological Beings in Gaelic Folklore', *TGSI*, vol. 29, **1914–19**, pp. 235–58

——, 'Notes on Scottish Gaelic Dialects', *Scottish Gaelic Studies*, vol. 1, **1926**, pp. 188–94

——, *A Pronouncing Dictionary of Scottish Gaelic*, Edinburgh, **1932** [repr. Glasgow 1992]

DIL: *Dictionary of the Irish Language*, compact edn, Dublin, **1983**

Dilling, Walter J., 'Girdles', *The Caledonian Medical Journal*, vol. 9, **1912–14**, pp. 337–57, 403–25

Dingwall, Alexander, 'The Ancient Wells of Scotland and the Medical Folk-Lore Connected with Them', *The Caledonian Medical Journal*, vol. 15, **1932–36**, pp. 190–200

Dinneen, Rev. Patrick S., *Foclóir Gaedhilge agus Béarla: An Irish-English Dictionary*, new edn, Irish Texts Society, Dublin, **1927**

Dixon, John H., *Gairloch*, Edinburgh, **1886** [repr. Gairloch 1974]

D. M., 'Air an Àirigh I', *The Celtic Review*, vol. 5, **1908–09**, pp. 235–37

D. M., Stafainn (D. A. Maclean, Staffin), 'Gealach nan Sealgairean', *An Gaidheal*, vol. 59, **1964**, pp. 124–25

D. M. R., 'The Kennedys of Lianachan', *The Oban Times*, 1 February **1913**

Dòmhnallach, an t-Urr. Tormod, *MacAidh Thiridhe*, 2nd edn, Carinish [**1970**, 1st edn Carinish 1964]

——, see also **MacDonald**, Rev. Norman

Domhnullach, Iain Tormad, 'Sgeulachdan mu Ghilleasbuig Aotrom', in Macleod **1911**, pp. 10–11

Donaldson, M. E. M., *Wanderings in the Western Highlands and Islands*, 2nd edn, Paisley, **1923** [1st edn 1920]

Dorson, Richard M., *The British Folklorists: A History*, London, **1968**

DOST *A Dictionary of the Older Scottish Tongue*, Chicago, Aberdeen, Oxford, 1937–2002

D[ouglas], W., 'The Brocken Spectre', *The Scottish Mountaineering Club Journal*, vol. 1, **1891**, p. 326

[Drummond, John, of Balhaldy], *Memoirs of Sir Ewen Cameron of Locheill, Chief of the Clan Cameron*, Abbotsford Club, Edinburgh, **1842**

Drummond-Norie, William, *Loyal Lochaber*, Glasgow, **1898**

Duckworth, Christian L. D., **and Langmuir**, Graham E., *Clyde and Other Coastal Steamers*, 2nd edn, Prescot, **1977** [1st edn Glasgow 1939]

Dughallach, Ailein, *Orain Ghaidhealacha*, Edinburgh, **1798** [2nd edn Inverness 1829]

Duncan, David Ewing, *The Calendar*, London, **1998**

Dundes, Alan, ed., *The Evil Eye: A Casebook*, Madison (Wisconsin), **1992**

[Dwelly, Edward], *Am Feillire agus Leabhar-Poca Gàidhlig, 1907*, Herne Bay

[——], *Am Feillire agus Leabhar-Poca Gàidhlig 1908*, Herne Bay

Dwelly, Edward, *The Illustrated Gaelic-English Dictionary*, 9th edn, Glasgow, **1977** [1st edn Herne Bay 1902–11]

——, *Appendix to Dwelly's Gaelic-English Dictionary*, ed. by Douglas Clyne and Derick Thomson, Glasgow, **1991**

Eberly, Susan Schoon, 'Fairies and the Folklore of Disability', in Narváez **1997**, pp. 227–50

Ellice, Edward C., *Place-Names of Glengarry and Glenquoich and Their Associations*, 2nd edn, London, **1931**, repr. Invergarry, 1999 [1st edn London 1898]

Elton, Charles, *Origins of English History*, London, **1882**

Ewing, Rev. William, *Annals of the Free Church of Scotland 1843–1900*, 2 vols, Edinburgh, **1914**

Eyre-Todd, George, *History of Glasgow*, vol. 3, Glasgow, **1934**

Fagg, M. C., *Rock Music* (Pitt Rivers Museum, University of Oxford, Occasional Paper on Technology No. 14), Oxford, **1997**

Farmer, D. H., ed., *Bede: Ecclesiastical History of the English People*, new edn, London, **1990**

Fear Bha Ann, 'A Highland Wedding in Bygone Days', *Celtic Magazine*, vol. 13, **1887–88**, pp. 509–11

Fear nan Sgeul, 'Saobh-Chràbhadh na Gaidhealtachd', *Highland News*, 14 March **1896**, partially repr. as 'Na Sithichean', *Mac-Talla*, 4 April 1896

Fenton, Alexander, *Scottish Country Life*, Edinburgh, **1976**

Ferguson, Malcolm, Callander, 'The Spanish Princess', *The Celtic Monthly*, vol. 3, **1894–95**, pp. 91–93

Ferguson, Mary, **and Matheson**, Ann, *Scottish Gaelic Union Catalogue*, Edinburgh, **1984**

Fergusson, Charles, 'The Gaelic Names of Trees, Shrubs, and Plants', *TGSI*, vol. 7, **1877–78**, pp. 127–56

——, 'The Early History, Legends, and Traditions of Strathardle', *TGSI*, vol. 21, **1896–97**, pp. 326–68

Fine, Gary Alan, 'Joseph Jacobs: A Sociological Folklorist', *Folklore*, vol. 98, **1987**, pp. 183–93

Fionn (Henry Whyte), 'The Mams of Mull', *The Oban Times*, 23 February **1889a**

——, 'Macintosh's Lament. Cumha Mhic-an-Toisich', *The Oban Times*, 14 September **1889b**

——, 'Bealach a' Mhorbheinn', *The Celtic Monthly*, vol. 4, **1895–96**, pp. 68–69

——, 'A Lochaber Hag. The Glaistig of Lianachan', *The Celtic Monthly*, vol. 9, **1900–01a**, pp. 188–89

——, 'The Kennedys of Lochaber', *The Celtic Monthly*, vol. 9, **1900–01b**, pp. 203–05

——, *Naigheachdan Firinneach II*, Glasgow, **1907**

——, 'Guth na Bliadhna (The Voice of the Year) Being Notes on the Gaelic Calendar', *Guth na Bliadhna*, vol. 5, **1908**, pp. 187–96, 285–97

——, 'Ronald Mac Donell of Morar. A Famous Piper', *The Celtic Monthly*, vol. 19, **1911**, pp. 167–69

——, 'Notes on the Celtic Year', *The Celtic Monthly*, vol. 20, **1912a**, pp. 34–36, 52–54, 68–69, 96–97, 118–19, 134–35, 160, 177–78, 188–89, 216, 236

——, 'The Kennedys of Lianachan and the Lochaber Hag', *The Oban Times*, 21 December **1912b**

——, 'Kennedys of Lianachan and the Lochaber Hag', *The Oban Times*, 11 January **1913**

Fleming, Maurice, 'Tales of the Shiels', *The Scots Magazine*, July **1997**, pp. 65–70

——, *Not of this World*, Edinburgh, **2002**

Fodor, Eugene, ed., *Germany*, n.p., **1964** edn

Fojut, Noel, 'Wallace and the Pass of Awe', *West Highland Notes & Queries*, series 3, no. 6, November **2003**, pp. 25–26

Forbes, Alexander Robert, *Gaelic Names of Beasts (Mammalia), Birds, Fishes, Insects, Reptiles, etc.*, Edinburgh, **1905**

——, *Place-Names of Skye and Adjacent Islands*, Paisley, **1923**

Forbes, Rev. Robert, *The Lyon in Mourning*, ed. by Henry Paton, 3 vols, Scottish History Society, Edinburgh, **1895–96** [repr. Edinburgh 1975]

Forsyth, Rev. William, *In the Shadow of Cairngorm*, 2nd edn, Aviemore, **1999** [1st edn Inverness 1900]

Fraser, Rev. James, *Chronicles of the Frasers: The Wardlaw Manuscript*, ed. by William Mackay, Scottish History Society, Edinburgh, **1905**

Fraser-Mackintosh, Charles, 'Minor Highland Septs, No. 2. The Macdonalds of Morar, Styled "Mac Dhughail"', *TGSI*, vol. 15, **1888–89**, pp. 63–75

——, *Antiquarian Notes, Historical, Genealogical, and Social, Second Series*, Inverness, **1897**

Frazer, Sir James, *The Golden Bough, 3rd Edition, Part II: Taboo and the Perils of the Soul*, London, **1911a**

——, *The Golden Bough, 3rd Edition, Part III: The Dying God*, London, **1911b**

——, *The Golden Bough, 3rd Edition, Part V: Spirits of the Corn and of the Wild*, 2 vols, London, **1912**

——, *The Golden Bough, 3rd Edition, Part VI: The Scapegoat*, London, **1913**

Freer, Ada Goodrich, 'The Powers of Evil in the Outer Hebrides', *Folk-Lore*, vol. 10, **1899**, pp. 259–82

——, 'More Folklore from the Hebrides', *Folk-Lore*, vol. 13, **1902**, pp. 29–62

——, *Outer Isles*, Westminster, **1903**

Gaffney, Victor, 'Shielings of the Drumochter', *Scottish Studies*, vol. 11, **1967**, pp. 91–99

Gaskell, Philip, *Morvern Transformed*, Cambridge, **1968** [repr. Colonsay 1996]

Geddie, John, *Thomas the Rymour and his Rhymes*, The Rymour Club, Edinburgh, **1920**

Gibson, Rosemary M., *The Appin Murder: In Their Own Words*, Edinburgh, **2003**

Gillies, Dr H. Cameron, *The Place-Names of Argyll*, London, **1906**

Gillies, John, ed., *A Collection of Ancient and Modern Gaelic Poems and Songs*, Perth, **1786**

Gillies, William, 'Alexander Carmichael and Clann Mhuirich', *SGS*, vol. 20, **2000**, pp. 1–66

Gillies, Rev. William A., *Kenmore, In Famed Breadalbane*, Perth, **1938**

Glenmore (Donald Shaw, Inchrory, Glen Avon), *Highland Legends and Fugitive Pieces of Original Poetry*, Edinburgh, **1859**

Godden, Gertrude M., 'The Sanctuary of Mourie', *Folk-Lore*, vol. 4, **1893**, pp. 498–508

Goodare, Julian, 'The Statutes of Iona in Context', *Scottish Historical Review*, vol. 77, **1998**, pp. 31–57

——, ed., *The Scottish Witch-Hunt in Context*, Manchester, **2002**

Gordon, Cosmo A., ed., 'Professor James Garden's Letters to John Aubrey 1692–1695', in *The Miscellany of the Third Spalding Club*, vol. 3, Aberdeen, **1960**, pp. 1–56

Gordon, Sir Robert, *A Genealogical History of the Earldom of Sutherland*, Edinburgh, **1813**

Gordon, Seton, *Highways and Byways in the West Highlands*, London, **1935**

——, *Highways and Byways in the Central Highlands*, London, **1949**

[**Gordon**, William,] *Tables of Pedigree of the Family of Gordon in Scotland*, n.p., **1784**

Gowans, Linda, *Am Bròn Binn: An Arthurian Ballad in Scottish Gaelic*, Eastbourne, **1992**

——, 'Sir Uallabh O Còrn: A Hebridean Tale of Sir Gawain', *SGS*, vol. 18, **1998**, pp. 23–55

Graham, Henry Grey, *The Social Life of Scotland in the Eighteenth Century*, London, **1906** [1st edn London 1899]

Graham, Rev. Dr Patrick, *Sketches Descriptive of the Picturesque Scenery of Perthshire*, Edinburgh, **1810** [1st edn 1806]

Grant, Mrs Anne, *Essays on the Superstitions of the Highlanders of Scotland*, 2 vols, London, **1811**

Grant, Francis J., ed., *The Register of Apprentices of the City of Edinburgh, 1583–1666*, Scottish Record Society, Edinburgh, **1906**

Grant, Isabel F., *The MacLeods*, London, **1959** [repr. Edinburgh 1981]

——, *Highland Folk Ways*, London, **1961** [repr. London 1975]

Grant, Rev. John, 'Parish of Kirkmichael', **1791**, in *The Statistical Account of Scotland*, ed. by Sir John Sinclair, vol. 12, Edinburgh, 1794, pp. 425–74 = new edn, vol. 16, Wakefield, 1982, pp. 264–313

Grant, Mrs Katherine Whyte, 'The Influence of Scenery and Climate on the Music and Poetry of the Highlands', *The Caledonian Medical Journal*, vol. 5, **1902–04a**, pp. 105–41

——, 'Old Highland Therapy', *The Caledonian Medical Journal*, vol. 5, **1902–04b**, pp. 356–78

——, *Myth, Tradition and Story from Western Argyll*, Oban, **1925**

Grant, Rev. Ludovick, 'United Parishes of Ardchattan and Muckairn', **1792**, in *The Statistical Account of Scotland*, ed. by Sir John Sinclair, vol. 6, Edinburgh, 1793, pp. 174–82 = new edn, vol. 8, Wakefield, 1983, pp. 1–9

Gray, Affleck, *Legends of the Cairngorms*, Edinburgh, **1987**

Green, Miranda J., *The Gods of the Celts*, Stroud, **1986** [repr. Stroud 1993]

——, *Dictionary of Celtic Myth and Legend*, London, **1992**

Greene, David, 'Miscellanea', *Celtica*, vol. 2, **1954**, pp. 146–49

Gregor, Rev. Walter, 'Stories of Fairies from Scotland', *The Folk-Lore Journal*, vol. 1, **1883a**, pp. 25–27, 55–58

——, 'Kelpie Stories from the North of Scotland', *The Folk-Lore Journal*, vol. 1, **1883b**, pp. 292–94

Gregory, Lady Augusta, *The Kiltartan Wonder Book*, Dublin, [**1911**]

——, *Visions and Beliefs in the West of Ireland*, 2nd edn, Gerrards Cross, **1970** [1st edn New York 1920; repr. 1992]

Gregory, Donald, *History of the Western Highlands and Isles of Scotland*, Edinburgh, **1836** [2nd edn London 1881, repr. Edinburgh 1975]

Grimble, Ian, *The World of Rob Donn*, Edinburgh, **1979**

Grimm, Jacob, *Deutsche Mythologie*, 4th edn, vol. 1, Berlin, **1875** [repr. Darmstadt 1965]

——, *Teutonic Mythology*, trl. by James Steven Stallybrass, 4 vols, London, **1880–88**

—— and Wilhelm, *Deutsche Sagen*, part 1, Berlin, **1816**

Grosjean, Paul, S.J., 'The Life of St. Columba from the Edinburgh MS.', *SGS*, vol. 2, **1927**, pp. 111–71

Guraig, 'The Airds and Mams of Mull', *The Oban Times*, 9 February **1889**

Guthrie, E. J., *Old Scottish Customs, Local and General*, London, **1885** [repr. Felinfach 1994]

Gwyndaf, Robin, 'Fairylore: Memorates and Legends from Welsh Oral Tradition', in Narváez **1997**, pp. 155–95

Gwynn, E. J., **and Purton**, W. J., 'The Monastery of Tallaght', *Proceedings of the Royal Irish Academy*, vol. 29, **1911–12**, Section C, pp. 115–79

Haldane, A. R. B., *New Ways through the Glens*, Newton Abbot, **1962**

Halliday, W. R., review of N. Penzer, ed., *The Ocean of Story*, in *Folk-Lore*, vol. 37, **1926**, pp. 105–08

Halliwell, James Orchard, ed., *Illustrations of the Fairy Mythology of A Midsummer Night's Dream*, The Shakespeare Society, London, **1845**

Hamilton, David, *The Healers: A History of Medicine in Scotland*, Edinburgh, **1981**

Hamp, Eric P., 'Varia', *SGS*, vol. 15, **1988**, pp. 150–52

Hanham, Alison, 'The Scottish Hecate', *Scottish Studies*, vol. 13, **1969**, pp. 59–65

Hanks, Patrick, **and Hodges**, Flavia, *A Dictionary of Surnames*, Oxford, **1988**

Hardy, James, 'Wart and Wen Cures', *Folk-Lore Record*, vol. 1, **1878**, pp. 216–28

Harman, Mary, *An Isle Called Hirte*, Lusta (Skye), **1997**

Harrison, Alan, *The Irish Trickster*, The Folklore Society, Sheffield, **1989**

Hartland, Edwin Sidney, *The Science of Fairy Tales: An Inquiry into Fairy Mythology*, London, **1891**

Hemming, Jessica, 'Bos primigenius in Britain', *Folklore*, vol. 113, **2002**, pp. 71–82

Henderson, Rev. Dr George, ed., *Fled Bricrend*, Irish Texts Society, vol. 2, London, **1899**

——, *The Highlanders' Friend: Second Series*, Edinburgh, **1901**

——, 'Sgeulachd Cois' O' Cein', *TGSI*, vol. 25, **1901–03**, pp. 179–265

——, 'Lamh-Sgriobhainnean Mhic-Neacail', *TGSI*, vol. 27, **1908–11**, pp. 340–409

——, *The Norse Influence on Celtic Scotland*, Glasgow, **1910**

——, *Survivals in Belief among the Celts*, Glasgow, **1911**

Henderson, Hamish, 'The Women of the Glen', in *The Celtic Consciousness*, ed. by Robert O'Driscoll, Edinburgh, **1982**, pp. 255–64

Henderson, Lizanne, **and Cowan**, Edward J., *Scottish Fairy Belief*, East Linton, **2001**

——, see also **Cowan and Henderson**

Henderson, T. F., ed., *Sir Walter Scott's Minstrelsy of the Scottish Border*, vol. 4, Edinburgh, **1902**

Herbert, Máire, *Iona, Kells, and Derry*, Oxford, **1988**

Heron, Rev. James, *The Church of the Sub-Apostolic Age*, London, **1888**

Higgitt, John, *The Murthly Hours*, London, **2000**

Hogan, Edmund, S.J., *Onomasticon Goedelicum*, Dublin, **1910** [repr. Dublin 1993]

Hogg, James ('The Ettrick Shepherd'), *Winter Evening Tales*, 2nd edn, 2 vols, Edinburgh, **1821** [1st edn Edinburgh 1820]

——, *A Tour in the Highlands in 1803*, Paisley, **1888** [repr. Edinburgh 1986]

——, *The Spy: A Periodical Paper of Literary Amusement and Instruction, Published Weekly in 1810 and 1811*, ed. by Gillian Hughes, Edinburgh, **2000**

Holbourn, Ian B. Stoughton, *The Isle of Foula*, 2nd edn, Edinburgh, **2001** [1st edn Lerwick 1938]

HSD: *A Dictionary of the Gaelic Language, compiled and published under the direction of the Highland Society of Scotland*, 2 vols, Edinburgh, **1828**

Hull, Eleanor, 'In Memoriam: Alfred Nutt (1856–1910)', *The Celtic Review*, vol. 7, **1911–12**, pp. 143–46

Hunter, Michael, *The Occult Laboratory*, Woodbridge (Suffolk), **2001**

Hutchings, John, 'Folklore and Symbolism of Green', *Folklore*, vol. 108, **1997**, pp. 55–63

Hutchinson, Roger, *Camanachd!* Edinburgh, **1989**

Hutton, Ronald, *The Rise and Fall of Merry England: The Ritual Year 1400–1700*, Oxford, **1994**

——, *The Stations of the Sun: A History of the Ritual Year in Britain*, Oxford, **1996**

——, 'The Global Context of the Scottish Witch-Hunt', in Goodare **2002**, pp. 16–32

Innes, Cosmo, ed., *The Black Book of Taymouth*, Edinburgh, **1855**

Jackson, Kenneth, 'Four Local Anecdotes from Harris', *Scottish Studies*, vol. 3, **1959**, pp. 72–87

——, 'Cailleach a[n] Struth Ruaidh ('The Hag of the Red Stream)', *Scottish Studies*, vol. 6, **1962**, pp. 184–93

Jacobs, Joseph, ed., *Celtic Fairy Tales*, London, **1892** [repr. Bath 2003]

——, *More Celtic Fairy Tales*, London, **1894** [repr. under same cover as *Celtic Fairy Tales*, Bath 2003]

Jamieson, John, *An Etymological Dictionary of the Scottish Language*, new edn, vol. 1, Paisley, **1879**

Jamieson, Robert, *Popular Ballads and Songs*, 2 vols, Edinburgh, **1806**

J. M., 'Aig an Teine I', *The Celtic Review*, vol. 5, **1908–09**, pp. 250–52

J. McG., 'The Kennedys of Lianachan', *The Oban Times*, 18 January **1913**

Johnson, Samuel, *A Journey to the Western Islands of Scotland*, 1st edn, London, **1775**

——, see also **Chapman**, R. W., and **Levi**, Peter

Jones, W. H. S., ed., *Pliny: Natural History*, vol. 8 (books 28–32), London, **1963**

Keightley, Thomas, *The Fairy Mythology*, London, **1850** [1st edn London 1828]

Kemble, John Mitchell, *The Saxons in England*, new edn, 2 vols, London, **1876**

Kennedy, Rev. John, Caticol, 'Arran Gaelic Dialect', *TGSI*, vol. 20, **1894–96**, pp. 126–41

——, 'Unpublished Gaelic Ballads from the Mac-Lagan MSS.', *TGSI*, vol. 24, **1899–1901**, pp. 156–84

Kennedy-Fraser, Marjory, *Songs of the Hebrides*, vol. 1, London, **1909**

Kermack, W. R., 'Emblems of the Gael', *Scottish Gaelic Studies*, vol. 7, **1953**, pp. 184–92

Kerr, Cathel, 'Fishermen and Superstition', *The Celtic Magazine*, vol. 13, **1887–88**, pp. 101–11

Kidd, Sheila M., 'Social Control and Social Criticism', *Scottish Gaelic Studies*, vol. 20, **2000**, pp. 67–87

Kilgour, William T., *Lochaber in War and Peace*, Paisley, **1908**

Kirk, Rev. Robert, Aberfoyle, *The Secret Common-Wealth*, ed. by Stewart Sanderson, The Folklore Society, Cambridge, **1976**

Knockfin, 'New Year in the Old Style in the Highlands', *The Celtic Magazine*, vol. 1, **1876**, pp. 106–11

Lamont, Rev. Donald, Strath, *Strath: In Isle of Skye*, Glasgow, **1913** [repr. Strath 1983]

Lang, Andrew, *Angling Sketches*, London, **1891**

Larner, Christina, *Enemies of God: The Witch-Hunt in Scotland*, Oxford, **1983** [repr. Edinburgh 2000]

Larner, Christina, **Lee**, Christopher Hyde, **and McLachlan**, Hugh V., *A Source-Book of Scottish Witchcraft*, Glasgow, **1977**

Lauder, Sir Thomas Dick, *Highland Rambles*, vol. 2, Edinburgh, **1837**

[**Lawson**, Bill, ed.], *Chi Mi 'n Tir*, Northton, **1996**

Lawson, Bill, *The Isle of Taransay*, Northton, **1997**

——, *Harris in History and Legend*, Edinburgh, **2002**

Lee, Maurice, *Government by Pen: Scotland under James VI and I*, Urbana, **1980**

Leitch, Roger, 'Hogg, Scott, and the Gaick Catastrophe', in *Studies in Hogg and his World*, ed. by Gillian H. Hughes, no. 1, **1990**, pp. 126–28

Levi, Peter, ed., *A Journey to the Western Islands of Scotland and the Journal of a Tour to the Hebrides* by Samuel Johnson and James Boswell, **1984** edn, London

Leyden, Dr John, *The Poetical Works of Dr John Leyden*, ed. by Thomas Brown, London, **1875**

——, *Journal of a Tour in the Highlands and Western Islands of Scotland in 1800*, ed. by James Sinton, Edinburgh, **1903**

Lhuyd, Edward, *Archæologia Britannica*, vol. 1, Oxford, **1707** [repr. Shannon 1971]

——, 'Observations in Natural History and Antiquities', *Philosophical Transactions*, vol. 28, **1713**, pp. 93–101

Liddell, Henry, **and Scott**, Robert, *A Greek–English Lexicon*, **1996** edn, Oxford [1st edn Oxford 1843]

Lindsay, Keith, 'The Rhymer was Real', *The Scots Magazine*, February **1995**, pp. 193–97

Lindsay, William Alexander, **Dowden**, John, **and Thomson**, John Maitland, eds, *Charters and Other Documents Relating to the Abbey of Inchaffray*, Scottish History Society, Edinburgh, **1908**

Livingston, William (Uilleam Mac Dhunléibhe), *Duain agus Òrain*, Glasgow, **1882**

Livingstone, Colin, Fort William, 'Lochaber Place Names', *TGSI*, vol. 13, **1886–87**, pp. 257–69

Lobban, Maighread Dhòmhnallach, ed., *Lachann Dubh a' Chrògain*, Iona, **2004**

——, see also **MacDonald**, Margaret

Lockhart, J. G., ed., *The Poetical Works of Sir Walter Scott*, Edinburgh, **1869** [1st edn Edinburgh 1841]

Lockwood, W. B., 'Noa Terms of the Gaelic Fishermen', *SGS*, vol. 11, **1966–68**, pp. 85–99

Logan, James, *The Scottish Gaël*, 2 vols, Edinburgh, **1976** [1st edn London 1831]

——, *McIan's Highlanders at Home*, 2nd edn, Glasgow, **1900** [1st edn London 1848, see **McIan**]

Lorne, the Marquis of, K.T. (J. D. S. Campbell), *Adventures in Legend*, Westminster, **1898**

Loudon, Joseph Buist, ed., *The Mull Diaries: The Diary of James Robertson*, Dunoon, **2001**

Love, John A., 'Shielings of the Isle of Rum', *Scottish Studies*, vol. 25, **1981**, pp. 39–63

Lyle, Emily B., 'The Dark Days and the Light Month', *Folklore*, vol. 95, **1984**, pp. 221–23

Lysaght, Patricia, 'The Banshee's Comb (MLSIT 4026)', *Béaloideas*, vol. 59, **1991**, pp. 67–82

——, *The Banshee: The Irish Supernatural Death-Messenger*, 2nd edn, Dublin, **1996** [1st edn Dún Laoghaire 1986]

——, 'Fairylore from the Midlands of Ireland', in Narváez **1997**, pp. 22–46

MacAlpine, Neil, *A Pronouncing Gaelic Dictionary*, new edn, Glasgow, **1929** [1st edn Edinburgh 1832]

MacAmhlaigh, Domhnall, *Seobhrach as a' Chlaich*, Glasgow, **1967**

Mac an Toisich, Fearchar, 'Laithean Sona agus Laithean Dona', *TGSI*, vol. 42, **1953–59**, pp. 214–39

Mac-an-Tuairneir, Paruig, *Comhchruinneacha do dh' Orain Taghta, Ghaidhealach*, Edinburgh, **1813**

[**Mac Aonghais**, Fionnladh] (Rev. Dr Norman MacLeod), 'Litir o Fhionnladh Piobaire', *An Teachdaire Gaelach*, no. 9, Jan. **1830**, pp. 190–93

MacAonghais, Prainnseas, 'Cigein agus Cuaigein', *An Gaidheal Og*, pp. 9–10, in *An Gaidheal*, vol. 50, **1955**

MacAonghuis, Iain, 'Samhla na Craoibhe', in *Sar Ghaidheal: Essays in Memory of Rory Mackay*, Inverness, **n.d.**, pp. 64–69

——, see also **MacInnes**, Dr John

Mac a' pharsuinn, Seumas, 'Bardachd a Baideanach', *Gairm* 99, An Samhradh **1977**, pp. 207–19

Mac a Phì, Eoghan, ed., *Am Measg nam Bodach*, Glasgow, **1938**

——, 'Sgeul o Ghleann Baile Chaoil', *TGSI*, vol. 49, **1974–76**, pp. 277–308

MacArthur, E. Mairi, 'A' Bhliadhna a dh'Fhalbh am Buntata', *TGSI*, vol. 57, **1990–92**, pp. 135–51

——, *Columba's Island*, Edinburgh, **1995**

——, *Iona*, 2nd edn, Edinburgh, **2002** [1st edn Edinburgh 1990]

Macaulay, A., 'The Battle of Cremona', *The Piping Times*, vol. 21, no. 2, November **1968**, pp. 14–17

Macaulay, Thomas Babington, *The History of England*, ed. by Charles Firth, vol. 4, London, **1914**

Macbain, Alexander, 'Highland Superstition', *TGSI*, vol. 14, **1887–88**, pp. 232–72

——, 'Badenoch: its History, Clans, and Place Names', *TGSI*, vol. 16, **1889–90**, pp. 148–97

——, 'Gaelic Incantations', *TGSI*, vol. 17, **1890–91**, pp. 221–66

——, 'Incantations and Magic Rhymes' (pp. 117–25) and 'Gaelic Incantations' (other pages), *The Highland Monthly*, vol. 3, **1891–92**, pp. 117–25, 174–81, 222–31, 290–97, 341–48

——, *An Etymological Dictionary of the Gaelic Language*, Inverness, **1896**

——, 'Further Gaelic Words and Etymologies', *TGSI*, vol. 21, **1896–97**, pp. 306–26

——, 'Early Highland Personal Names', *TGSI*, vol. 22, **1897–98**, pp. 152–68

Macbean, Lachlan, *The Songs and Hymns of the Scottish Highlands*, Edinburgh, **1888**

MacCallum, Donull, Arisaig, *Sop as Gach Seid*, a Cheud Bhoitean: Bardachd, Edinburgh, **1883**

——, *Sop as Gach Seid*, an Dara Boitean: Bardachd, Edinburgh, **1884**

[**MacCallum**, Duncan, ed.,] *Co-Chruinneacha Dhàn, Òrain, &c.*, Inverness, **1821**

Mac Calum, Domhnull, 'Sruth nam Fear Gorm', in Macleod **1913**, p. 12

——, 'Gruagach Airidh-na-h-Aon-Oidhch'', in Macleod **1913**, p. 26

Mac Cárthaigh, Críostóir, 'The Ship-Sinking Witch', *Béaloideas*, vol. 60–61, **1992–93**, pp. 267–86

McCaughey, T. P., 'Cumha le Iain Dhùn Ollaidh?' *Scottish Gaelic Studies*, vol. 17, **1996**, pp. 213–20

Mac-Choinnich, Iain, *Eachdraidh a' Phrionnsa, no Bliadhna Thearlaich*, Edinburgh, **1844**

——, see also **Mackenzie**, John

McColl, Rev. Archibald, 'Parish of Tiry', **1792**, in *The Statistical Account of Scotland*, ed. by Sir John Sinclair, vol. 10, Edinburgh, 1794, pp. 393–418 = new edn, vol. 20, Wakefield, 1983, pp. 255–80

Mac Cormaic, Iain, 'An Rìghinn Spainnteach', in Macleod **1913**, pp. 10–12

MacCulloch, Donald B., *Romantic Lochaber*, Spean Bridge, **1996** [1st edn Edinburgh 1939]

MacCurdy, Edward, 'Norman Macleod', *TGSI*, vol. 39/40, **1942–50**, pp. 229–42

MacDhòmhnaill, Dòmhnall Iain, *Uibhist a Deas*, Stornoway, **1981**

——, 'A' Srùdhan', *Gairm* 128, Am Foghar **1984**, pp. 301–04

MacDhomhnaill, Iain, 'Imrich Luain', *An Gaidheal Og*, p. 22, in *An Gaidheal*, vol. 54, **1959**

Mac-Dhonuill, Alastair, *Ais-Eiridh na Sean Chánoin Albannaich*, Edinburgh, **1751**

Mac Dhughaill, Eachann, 'Tigh Lianachain, Loch-Abar', in Macleod **1911**, p. 33

——, 'Buidseach Lagain', in Macleod **1913**, pp. 31–32

MacDhùghaill, Eachann M., 'Beachdachadh mu Ainmhidhean na Gàidhealtachd. Earann II', *TGSI*, vol. 35, **1929–30**, pp. 98–144

Mac Dhun-Leibhe, Uilleam, *Duain Ghaelic*, Edinburgh, **1858**

MacDiarmid, James, 'Fragments of Breadalbane Folk-Lore', *TGSI*, vol. 25, **1901–03**, pp. 126–48

——, 'More Fragments of Breadalbane Folklore', *TGSI*, vol. 26, **1904–07**, pp. 31–59

McDiarmid, Matthew P., ed., *Hary's Wallace*, 2 vols, Scottish Text Society, Edinburgh, **1968–69**

MacDonald, Revs A. and A., eds, *The MacDonald Collection of Gaelic Poetry*, Inverness, **1911**

MacDonald, Aidan, ' "Annat" in Scotland', *Scottish Studies*, vol. 17, **1973**, pp. 135–46

Macdonald, Alexander, 'Presidential Address', *The Caledonian Medical Journal*, vol. 3, **1897–99**, pp. 331–47

Macdonald, Alexander, 'Some Legends of the Macneils of Barra', *The Celtic Review*, vol. 1, **1904–05**, pp. 264–67

Macdonald, Alexander, 'Fragments of Gaelic Song and Lilt', *TGSI*, vol. 29, **1914–19**, pp. 95–119

——, 'Shinty', *TGSI*, vol. 30, **1919–22**, pp. 27–56

——, *Story and Song from Loch Ness-Side*, 2nd edn, Inverness, **1982** [1st edn Inverness 1914]

McDonald, Fr Allan, Eriskay, 'Piobairean Smearcleit', *The Celtic Review*, **1908–09**, pp. 345–47

——, 'Cluich na Cloinne – Children's Games', *The Celtic Review*, vol. 7, **1911–12**, pp. 371–76

——, 'Children's Rimes from the MSS. of the Rev. Father Allan Macdonald', *The Celtic Review*, vol. 8, **1912–13**, pp. 166–68

——, *Gaelic Words and Expressions from South Uist and Eriskay*, ed. by J. L. Campbell, Dublin, **1958**

MacDonald, Rev. Archibald, 'Some Hebridean Singers and their Songs', *TGSI*, vol. 15, **1888–89**, pp. 255–79, and vol. 16, **1889–90**, pp. 253–66

——, 'Notes on the Religion and Mythology of the Celts', *TGSI*, vol. 19, **1893–94**, pp. 37–49

——, *The Uist Collection*, Glasgow, **1894**

——, 'Stories Told when on Ceilidh, being Gleanings from the MSS. of the Late Miss Frances Tolmie', *TGSI*, vol. 37, **1934–36a**, pp. 184–207

Macdonald, Rev. D. J., Killean, 'Jottings, Legendary, Antiquarian, and Topographical, from West Kintyre', *TGSI*, vol. 20, **1894–96**, pp. 53–66

MacDonald, Donald, *Lewis*, Edinburgh, **1978**

——, 'Lewis Shielings', *Review of Scottish Culture*, no. 1, **1984**, pp. 29–33

Macdonald, Dr Donald, Gisla, *Tales and Traditions of the Lews*, Edinburgh, [**2000**]

MacDonald, Donald (Dòmhnall Aonghais Bhàin), *Smuaintean fo Éiseabhal: Thoughts under Easaval*, ed. by Ronald Black, Edinburgh, **2000**

MacDonald, Donald Archie, 'A Uist Legend', *Scottish Studies*, vol. 7, **1963**, pp. 209–15

——, 'Righ Eilifacs', *Scottish Studies*, vol. 16, **1972**, pp. 1–22

——, 'Migratory Legends of the Supernatural in Scotland', *Béaloideas*, vol. 62–63, **1994–95**, pp. 29–67

MacDonald, Duncan, Sandwickhill, 'Some Rare Gaelic Words and Phrases', *TGSI*, vol. 37, **1934–36b**, pp. 1–54

MacDonald, Duncan, Peninerine, S. Uist, *Fear na h-Eabaid*, Stornoway, **1953**

Macdonald, James, *Character Sketches of Old Callander*, new edn, Callander, **1938**

Macdonald, Rev. James, Reay, 'Stray Customs and Legends', *TGSI*, vol. 19, **1893–94**, pp. 272–86

Macdonald, John, 'An Elegy for Ruaidhrí Mór', *SGS*, vol. 8, part 1, **1955**, pp. 27–52

MacDonald, Dr Keith Norman, *MacDonald Bards from Mediæval Times*, Edinburgh, **1900**

——, *Puirt-a-Beul – Mouth-Tunes*, Glasgow, **1901**

Macdonald, Kenneth, *Peat Fire Memories*, East Linton, **2003**

MacDonald, Margaret, 'Growing up on Lismore', *The Scots Magazine*, January **1995**, pp. 59–68

——, see also **Lobban**, Maighread Dhòmhnallach

Macdonald, Martin, *Skye Camanachd*, Portree, **1992**

MacDonald, Rev. Norman, 'Gaelic Folklore: Natural Objects with Supernatural Powers', *Scottish Studies*, vol. 2, **1958a**, pp. 140–48

——, 'Notes on Gaelic Folklore', *Arv: Tidskrift för Nordisk Folkminnesforskning*, vol. 14, **1958b**, pp. 118–62, and vol. 17, **1961**, pp. 180–97

——, *Occult Elements Common to Celtic and Oriental Folklore*, Inverness, **n.d.** [*c.* 1963]

——, see also **Dòmhnallach**, an t-Urr. Tormod

Macdonald, Sheila, 'Old-World Survivals in Ross-shire', *Folk-Lore*, vol. 14, **1903**, pp. 368–84

M[acDonald], T[homas] D[onald], *Puirt mo Sheanamhar*, Stirling, **1907**

MacDonald, Thomas Donald, *Gaelic Proverbs and Proverbial Sayings*, Stirling, **1926**

MacDonogh, Steve, *Green and Gold: The Wrenboys of Dingle*, Dingle, **1983**

MacDougall, Betty, *Folklore from Coll*, n.p., **1978a**

MacDougall, Hector, **and Cameron**, Rev. Hector, *Handbook to the Islands of Coll and Tiree*, Glasgow, **n.d.**

MacDougall, Rev. James, Duror, ed., *Folk and Hero Tales* (Waifs and Strays of Celtic Tradition, Argyllshire Series, No. III), London, **1891**

——, 'Ùruisg Choire-nan-Nuallan', *Zeitschrift für Celtische Philologie*, vol. 1, **1897**, pp. 328–41

——, *Highland Fairy Legends*, ed. by Rev. George Calder and Alan Bruford, Ipswich, **1978b** [new edn of MacDougall and Calder 1910]

——, **and Calder**, Rev. George, *Folk Tales and Fairy Lore*, Edinburgh, **1910**

MacEchern, Rev. Dugald, 'Place-Names of Coll', *TGSI*, vol. 29, **1914–19**, pp. 314–35

MacFadyen, John, 'The Ards and Mams of Mull', *The Oban Times*, 2 March **1889**

——, *Sgeulaiche nan Caol*, Glasgow, **1902**

MacFarlane, Rev. Angus M., 'Gaelic Names of Plants', *TGSI*, vol. 32, **1924–25**, pp. 1–48

——, 'Myths Associated with Mountains, Springs, and Lochs', *TGSI*, vol. 34, **1927–28**, pp. 135–52

Macfarlane, Walter, *Geographical Collections Relating to Scotland*, ed. by Sir Arthur Mitchell, 3 vols, Scottish History Society, Edinburgh, **1906–08**

Mac Ghill Eathain, Somhairle, *Dàin do Eimhir agus Dàin Eile*, Glasgow, **1943**

Mac Gill-Eain, Somhairle, *Ris a' Bhruthaich:*

Criticism and Prose Writings, ed. by William Gillies, Stornoway, **1985**
Mac Gilleathain, Calum Iain, 'Sgéalta as Albain', *Béaloideas*, vol. 15, **1945**, pp. 237–46
——, 'Cas Shiubhail An T-Sleibhe', *Gairm* 25, Am Foghar **1958**, pp. 67–70
Mac Gille Sheathanaich, Niall, 'Na Sithichean', *Gairm* 27, An t-Earrach **1959**, pp. 216–25
McGinty, Stephen, 'Present and Incorrect', *The Scotsman*, 9 January **2004**
Macgregor, Alastair, 'Second Sight', *The Caledonian Medical Journal*, vol. 3, **1897–99**, pp. 42–56, 141–56, and vol. 4, **1899–1901**, pp. 258–71, 297–308
MacGregor, Rev. Alexander, *Highland Superstitions*, Stirling, **1901**
MacGregor, Amelia Georgiana Murray, *History of the Clan Gregor*, 2 vols, Edinburgh, **1898–1901**
MacGregor, George, *The History of Glasgow*, Glasgow, **1881**
McGregor, Rev. Gregor, 'United Parish of Lismore and Appin', **1841**, in *The New Statistical Account of Scotland*, vol. 7, part 2, Edinburgh, 1845, pp. 223–56
McGregor, Richard E., *Gregor Willox the Warlock*, Aberdeen & N.E. Scotland Family History Society, Aberdeen, **1994**
McHardy, Stuart, *The Quest for the Nine Maidens*, Edinburgh, **2003**
MacIain, 'A Long Island Witch', *The Celtic Magazine*, vol. 10, **1884–85**, pp. 433–34
McIan, R. R., **and Logan**, James, *The Clans of the Scottish Highlands*, vol. 2, London, **1847**
——, *Gaélic Gatherings; or, The Highlanders at Home*, London, **1848** [2nd edn Glasgow 1900, see **Logan**]
Mac'illeathain, Iain C., 'Sgeulachdan nan Uamh', *TGSI*, vol. 39/40, **1942–50**, pp. 36–62
MacilleDhuibh, Raghnall, *West Highland Free Press*
——, 'Naming the Winds of Spring', 13.3.87
——, 'The Storm of the Borrowing Days', 22.4.88
——, 'Ploughing a Lonely Furrow', 7.4.89
——, 'The Gaick Disaster – Part 2', 12.1.90
——, 'The Isle of the Nine Virgins', 27.7.90
——, 'When was the Shieling Season?' 10.8.90
——, 'Reading the Bone', 14.12.90, 28.12.90
——, 'The Moon and the Tides', 20.9.91
——, 'The Moon, the Weather – and MacNeil', 4.10.91
——, 'The Sighs and the Laughter of Spring', 21.2.92
——, 'The Trouble with *Carmina*', 29.5.92
——, 'In Search of May-Day Wells', 30.4.93
——, 'At the End of a Month of Autumn', 20.8.93
——, 'The Night when Water Turns to Wine', 4.3.94
——, 'The *Carmina* and the Stars', 24.6.94
——, 'Warband on Point, Dollars Down . . . ', 31.3.95
——, 'So the Gaelic for Chess is . . . ', 14.4.95
——, 'A Book about Brigid and Bears', 2.2.96
——, 'Down to the Year of the Black Spring', 28.3.97
——, 'Your brains the next time!' 1.8.97
——, 'A Century of Coded Messages', 13.2.98
——, 'The Biggest Animal in the World?' 12.3.99
——, 'The Big Beast of Loch Awe', 7.5.99
——, 'Kelpie the Lowland Water-Horse', 21.5.99
——, 'Willox the Wizard', 10.9.99
——, 'Whose Calendar but the Cursed Campbells'!' 25.2.00
——, 'The Lady of Lawers', 19.5.00, 2.6.00, 16.6.00
——, 'The Silent Goddess Tà', 12.1.01
——, 'When Each Waterfall is Pregnant', 9.3.01
——, 'The Trees of Easter Week', 6.4.01
——, 'The Flowers of Death', 20.4.01
——, 'Keep the Cat Turning!' 29.6.01
——, 'The Summons by Water', 13.7.01
——, 'The Wrapping in the Hide', 27.7.01
——, 'The Bin Laden of the Gael?' 16.11.01
——, 'What does the Devil Look Like?' 8.3.02
——, 'The Two Easter Beetles', 22.3.02
——, 'The Eagle of Loch Tréig', 3.5.02
——, 'The Women behind King Lear', 26.7.02
——, 'The Woman who Ran with the Deer', 20.9.02
——, 'How the Fairies Got into the Bible', 18.10.02
——, 'Kidnapping Women', 15.11.02, 29.11.02
——, 'From Rory Mor's Cup to the Fairy Flag', 13.12.02
——, 'Sniffing the Sacred Dewlap', 10.1.03
——, 'Bramble Berries in the Wolftime', 24.1.03
——, 'A Smell of Honied Apples', 7.2.03
——, 'The Ghost of Coilig Ravine', 21.2.03
——, 'The Underbelly of History', 7.3.03
——, 'Now You See Him, Now You Don't', 21.3.03
——, 'Robert Mac Iain Ghiorr from Mull', 4.4.03
——, 'The Pursuit through the Kyles', 18.4.03
——, 'The Hairs of your Head are Numbered', 30.5.03
——, 'The Knotted Black Silk Handkerchief', 13.6.03
——, see also **Black**, Ronald
Macinnes, Allan I., *Clanship, Commerce and the House of Stuart, 1603–1788*, East Linton, **1996**
MacInnes, Rev. Duncan, Oban, *Folk and Hero Tales* (Waifs and Strays of Celtic Tradition, Argyllshire Series, No. II), London, **1890**
——, 'Notes on Gaelic Technical Terms', *TGSI*, vol. 19, **1893–94**, pp. 212–16
MacInnes, Dr John, 'Sgeulachd Mhicheil Scot', *Scottish Studies*, vol. 7, **1963**, pp. 106–14
——, 'MacMhuirich and the Old Woman from Harris', *Scottish Studies*, vol. 10, **1966**, pp. 104–08
——, 'Twentieth-Century Recordings of Scottish Gaelic Heroic Ballads', in *The Heroic Process*, ed. by Bo Almqvist, Séamas Ó Catháin and Pádraig Ó Héalaí, Dún Laoghaire, **1987**, pp. 101–30
——, 'Gleanings from Raasay Tradition', *TGSI*, vol. 56, **1988–90**, pp. 1–20
——, 'The Seer in Gaelic Tradition', in *The Seer*, ed. by Hilda Ellis Davidson, Edinburgh, **1989**, pp. 10–24
——, 'Clan Sagas and Historical Legends', *TGSI*, vol. 57, **1990–92**, pp. 377–94
——, 'Preface', in Carmichael **1994**, pp. 7–18
——, 'Looking at Legends of the Supernatural', *TGSI*, vol. 59, **1994–96**, pp. 1–20
——, review of Donald Meek, *Tuath is Tighearna*, in *Béaloideas*, vol. 64–65, **1996–97**, pp. 413–17
——, see also **MacAonghuis**, Iain
MacInnes, Rev. Dr John, *The Evangelical Movement in the Highlands of Scotland*, Aberdeen, **1951**
Mac Intoisich, Donncha, *Co-Chruinneach dh' Orain Thaghte Ghaeleach*, Edinburgh, **1831**

Macintosh, Rev. Donald, *A Collection of Gaelic Proverbs, and Familiar Phrases*, Edinburgh, **1785**
——, *Mackintosh's Collection of Gaelic Proverbs, and Familiar Phrases; Englished A-New*, ed. by Alexander Campbell, Edinburgh, **1819**

Macintyre, Rev. Joseph, 'United Parishes of Glenorchay and Inishail', **1792–93**, in *The Statistical Account of Scotland*, ed. by Sir John Sinclair, vol. 8, Edinburgh, 1793, pp. 335–61, 651–52 = new edn, vol. 8, Wakefield, 1983, pp. 109–36

Mac Iomhair, Domhnull, Garrabost, 'Cuid de na h-Atharraichean a Thainig air Leodhas', *TGSI*, vol. 34, **1927–28**, pp. 337–51

MacIver, Donald, *Place-Names of Lewis and Harris*, Stornoway, **1934**

Maciver, Iain F., ed., *Lamplighter and Story-Teller: John Francis Campbell of Islay*, Edinburgh, **1985**
——, 'A 17th Century Prose Map', in *Togail Tìr*, ed. by Finlay MacLeod, Stornoway, **1989**, pp. 23–31

Mack, Douglas S., ed., *James Hogg: Selected Poems*, Oxford, **1970**

Mackay, Alexander, 'The Fairies and Domhnull Duaghal', *Celtic Magazine*, vol. 1, **1876**, pp. 339–42
——, 'Fairies in Sutherland', *The Celtic Magazine*, vol. 9, **1883–84**, pp. 207–09

Mackay, John, 'Oidhche Shamhna', *TGSI*, vol. 9, **1879–80**, pp. 136–41
——, 'Sutherland Place Names', *TGSI*, vol. 16, **1889–90**, pp. 39–59

[——], 'Aimsirean na Bliadhna', *Guth na Bliadhna*, vol. 5, **1908**, pp. 340–41, and vol. 6, **1909**, pp. 76–104

Mackay, J. G., 'Social Life in Skye from Legend and Story', *TGSI*, vol. 29, **1914–19**, pp. 260–90, 335–50, and vol. 30, **1919–22**, pp. 1–26, 128–74
——, trl., 'Tòmas Reumair: Thomas the Rhymer', *The Celtic Monthly*, vol. 24, **1916**, pp. 76–80, 91–94
——, 'Gruagach an Eilein Uaine: The Gruagach of the Green Isle', *SGS*, vol. 1, **1926**, pp. 156–87
——, *The Tale of the Cauldron*, Dundee, **1927a**
——, 'Féileagan Ruadh nan Spòg', *Scottish Gaelic Studies*, vol. 2, **1927b**, pp. 34–68
——, 'An Tuairisgeal', *TGSI*, vol. 34, **1927–28**, pp. 1–112
——, 'Comh-Abartachd eadar Cas-Shiubhal-an-t-Sléibhe agus a' Chailleach Bheurr', *Scottish Gaelic Studies*, vol. 3, **1929–31**, pp. 10–51

[**MacKay**, Mackintosh], *Reminiscences*, n.p., **n.d.**

Mackay, Margaret A., 'Here I am in Another World', *Scottish Studies*, vol. 32, **1998**, pp. 119–24

Mackay, William, ed., *Records of the Presbyteries of Inverness and Dingwall 1643-1688*, Scottish History Society, Edinburgh, **1896**
——, *Urquhart and Glenmoriston*, 2nd edn, Inverness, **1914** [1st edn Inverness 1893]

Mackay, William, *Gaelic Place Names of Upper Strathglass*, Inverness, **1968**

McKean, Thomas A., *Hebridean Song-Maker: Iain MacNeacail of the Isle of Skye*, Edinburgh, [**1997**]

Mackechnie, Rev. John, ed., *The Dewar Manuscripts*, Glasgow, **1964**
——, *Catalogue of Gaelic Manuscripts*, vol. 1, Boston (Mass.), **1973**

Mackellar, Mrs Mary, 'The Waulking Day', *TGSI*, vol. 13, **1886–87**, pp. 201–17
——, 'The Sheiling: Its Traditions and Songs', *TGSI*, vol. 14, **1887–88**, pp. 135–53, and vol. 15, **1888–89**, pp. 151–71
——, 'Traditions of Lochaber', *TGSI*, vol. 16, **1889–90**, pp. 266–76

Mackenzie, Alexander, *The Prophecies of the Brahan Seer*, Inverness, **1877**; 2nd edn, Inverness, **1878**; 3rd edn, Inverness, **1882**; 4th edn, Stirling, **1899**; 5th edn, Stirling, **1945**; 6th edn, ed. by Elizabeth Sutherland, London, **1977**
——, *History of the Chisholms*, Inverness, **1891**
——, 'Mairi Nighean Alastair, Rory Mor's Cup and Horn, and Unpublished Macleod Traditions', *TGSI*, vol. 22, **1897–98**, pp. 43–67

Mackenzie, A. Donald, 'Some Notes', *Appin Historical Society Newsletter*, no. 17, **2003**, pp. 18–30

MacKenzie, Ann, *Island Voices, Air Bilibh an t-Sluaigh: Traditions of North Mull*, Edinburgh, **2002**

MacKenzie, Annie M., ed., *Òrain Iain Luim*, Scottish Gaelic Texts Society, Edinburgh, **1964**

Mackenzie, Dan, 'Euthanasia in the Folk-Medicine of Britain', *The Caledonian Medical Journal*, vol. 15, **1932–36**, pp. 304–10

MacKenzie, Donald A., 'The Glaistig and the Black Lad', *The Celtic Review*, vol. 5, **1908–09**, pp. 253–58
——, 'The Fians in their Cave', in Macleod **1911**, p. 41
——, *Tales from the Moors and the Mountains*, London, **1931**
——, *Scottish Folk-Lore and Folk Life*, London, **1935**

MacKenzie, Donald W., *As It Was, Sin Mar a Bha: An Ulva Boyhood*, Edinburgh, **2000**

Mackenzie, John, *Eachdraidh Mhic-Cruislig, Sgialachd Ghàëlach*, Glasgow, **1836**
——, *Sar-Obair nam Bard Gaelach: or, The Beauties of Gaelic Poetry*, 1st edn, Glasgow, **1841**
——, *A' Bheithir-Bheuma*, January **1845**
——, *An English–Gaelic Dictionary*, Glasgow, **1930** [1st edn Edinburgh 1847]
——, see also **Mac-Choinnich**, Iain

Mackenzie, Rev. Neil, 'Bardachd Irteach', *The Celtic Review*, vol. 2, **1905–06**, pp. 327–42

Mackenzie, Osgood, *A Hundred Years in the Highlands*, new edn, Edinburgh, **1980** [1st edn 1921]

M[a]ck[enzie], W[illiam], 'Cumha', *The Celtic Magazine*, vol. 2, **1876–77**, p. 235

Mackenzie, William, 'Leaves from my Celtic Portfolio', *TGSI*, vol. 7, **1877–78**, pp. 52–76, 100–26; vol. 8, **1878–79**, pp. 18–32, 100–28; vol. 9, **1879–80**, pp. 19–74, 95–113
——, 'Gaelic Incantations, Charms, and Blessings of the Hebrides', *TGSI*, vol. 18, **1891–92**, pp. 97–182
——, 'The Seal in Hebridean and Northern Lore', *The Highland Monthly*, vol. 4, **1892–93**, pp. 467–74
[——], 'Fourteenth Annual Dinner', *TGSI*, vol. 12, **1885–86**, pp. 98–117

MacKenzie, William, *Skye: Iochdar-Trotternish and District*, Glasgow, **1930**
——, *Old Skye Tales: Traditions, Reflections and Memories, with a Selection from Skye: Iochdar-*

Trotternish and District, ed. by Alasdair Maclean, Aird Bhearnasdail, **1995** [1st edns 1934 and 1930]

Mackenzie, W. C., 'Pigmies in the Hebrides: A Curious Legend', *The Scottish Geographical Magazine*, vol. 21, **1905**, pp. 264–68

Mackenzie, W. M., *The Book of Arran*, vol. 2, Glasgow, **1914** [repr. Brodick 1982]

McKerracher, Archie, *Perthshire in History and Legend*, Edinburgh, **1988**

——, 'The Great Gormshuil', *The Scots Magazine*, April **1994**, pp. 374–81

MacKillop, Donald, 'The Place Names of Berneray', *TGSI*, vol. 53, **1982–84**, pp. 115–64

Mackinlay, James M., *Folklore of Scottish Lochs and Springs*, Glasgow, **1893** [repr. Felinfach 1993]

——, 'Traces of River-Worship in Scottish Folk-Lore', *PSAS*, vol. 30, **1895–96**, pp. 69–76

——, 'Traces of the Cultus of the Nine Maidens in Scotland', *PSAS*, vol. 40, **1905–06**, pp. 255–65

Mackinnon, Donald, 'Hector Maclean, M.A.I.', *The Celtic Monthly*, vol. 1, **1892–93**, pp. 105–07

——, *A Descriptive Catalogue of Gaelic Manuscripts*, Edinburgh, **1912**

MacKinnon, Fiona E., *Tiree Tales*, Kirkapol, **1992**

MacKinnon, Lachlan, *Place Names of Lochaber*, Fort William, **1973**

MacKintosh, Angus, 'Ewen MacPhee, the Outlaw', *The Celtic Monthly*, vol. 11, **1902–03**, pp. 162–63

Maclagan, Dr Robert Craig, 'Notes on Folklore Objects Collected in Argyleshire', *Folk-Lore*, vol. 6, **1895**, pp. 144–61, 302–03

——, 'Corn-Maiden in Argyleshire', *Folk-Lore*, vol. 7, **1895–96**, pp. 78–79

——, *The Games & Diversions of Argyleshire*, The Folk-Lore Society, London, **1901**

——, *Evil Eye in the Western Highlands*, London, **1902**

——, 'Charms, etc., Figured on Plate IX', *Folk-Lore*, vol. 14, **1903**, pp. 298–300

——, 'Latha na Caillich', *The Caledonian Medical Journal*, vol. 7, **1907–09**, pp. 233–41

——, 'Calluinn – Hogmanay', *The Caledonian Medical Journal*, vol. 9, **1912–14**, pp. 3–42

McLaren, Moray, *Lord Lovat of the '45*, London, **1957**

MacLauchlan, Rev. Dr Thomas, 'Gaelic Literature, Language, and Music', in *A History of the Scottish Highlands*, ed. by John S. Keltie, vol. 2, Edinburgh, **1882**, pp. 66–115

Maclean, Alasdair, *Night Falls on Ardnamurchan*, London, **1984** [repr. Edinburgh 2001]

McLean, Angus, *The Place Names of Cowal: Their Meaning and History*, Dunoon, **n.d.** [*c.* 1980]

Maclean, Calum I., 'Death Divination in Scottish Folk Tradition', *TGSI*, vol. 42, **1953–59**, pp. 56–67

——, 'Am Ministear agus an Claban', *Scottish Studies*, vol. 1, **1957**, pp. 65–69

——, 'Traditional Beliefs in Scotland', *Scottish Studies*, vol. 3, **1959**, pp. 189–200

——, 'The Last Sheaf', *Scottish Studies*, vol. 8, **1964**, pp. 193–207

——, *The Highlands*, Inverness, **1975** [1st edn London 1959]

Maclean, Charles, *The Isle of Mull: Placenames, Meanings and Stories*, Dumfries, **1997**

MacLean, Rev. Donald, Duirinish, *Typographia Scoto-Gadelica*, Edinburgh, **1915**

Maclean, Rev. Donald, Edinburgh, 'The Literature of the Scottish Gael', *The Celtic Review*, vol. 7, **1911–12**, pp. 345–60, and vol. 8, **1912–13**, pp. 51–74

——, 'The Effect of the 1745 Rising on the Social and Economic Condition of the Highlands', *The Celtic Review*, vol. 10, **1914–15**, pp. 1–23

—— 'The Life and Literary Labours of the Rev. Robert Kirk, of Aberfoyle', *TGSI*, vol. 31, **1922–24**, pp. 328–66

Maclean, Rev. Duncan, 'Parish of Glenurchy & Inishail', 1843, in *The New Statistical Account of Scotland*, vol. 7, Edinburgh, **1845**, part 2, pp. 82–103

MacLean, J. P., *A History of the Clan MacLean*, Cincinnati, **1889** [repr. Bruceton Mills, WV, 1986]

——, *History of the Island of Mull*, 2 vols, Greenville (Ohio) and San Mateo (California), **1923–25**

Maclean, [John], *Reminiscences of a Clachnacuddin Nonagenarian*, **1886** edn, Inverness [1st edn Inverness 1842]

Maclean, John, 'Am Pìobaire Dall', *TGSI*, vol. 41, **1951–52**, pp. 283–306

MacLean, Lachlan, *The History of the Celtic Language*, London, **1840**

MacLean, Rev. Malcolm, 'Extracts from a Lewis MS.', *TGSI*, vol. 39/40, **1942–50**, pp. 141–66

Maclean, Rev. Neil, 'Parish of Tiree and Coll', **1843**, in *The New Statistical Account of Scotland*, vol. 7, Edinburgh, 1845, part 2, pp. 195–222

MacLean, Rev. Norman, *Set Free*, London, **1949**

MacLean, Sorley, 'Some Raasay Traditions', *TGSI*, vol. 49, **1974–76**, pp. 377–97

Maclean-Bristol, Nicholas, *Warriors and Priests: The History of the Clan Maclean, 1300–1570*, East Linton, **1995**

——, ed., *Inhabitants of the Inner Isles Morvern and Arnamurchan 1716*, Scottish Record Society, Edinburgh, **1998**

——, *Murder under Trust: The Crimes and Death of Sir Lachlan Mor Maclean of Duart*, East Linton, **1999**

——, 'MacFadyen's Cave', *West Highland Notes & Queries*, series 3, no. 5, November **2002a**, p. 22

——, 'The Seed of the Goldsmith', *West Highland Notes & Queries*, series 3, no. 5, November **2002b**, p. 23

McLeay, Alison, *The Tobermory Treasure: The True Story of a Fabulous Armada Galleon*, London, **1986**

MacLellan, Angus, *Stories from South Uist*, ed. by J. L. Campbell, London, **1961** [repr. Edinburgh 1997]

MacLennan, Hugh Dan, 'Shinty: Some Fact and Fiction', *TGSI*, vol. 59, **1994–96**, pp. 148–274

——, *Not an Orchid . . .*, North Kessock, **1995**

MacLennan, Lt. John, 'Notices of Pipers', *The Piping Times*, vol. 23, no. 10, **July 1971**, pp. 22–28

——, 'Notices of Pipers', *The Piping Times*, vol. 24, no. 2, **Nov. 1971**, pp. 25–30

MacLeod, Angus, *Sàr Òrain*, Glasgow, **1933a**

——, ed., *The Songs of Duncan Ban Macintyre*, Scottish Gaelic Texts Society, Edinburgh, **1952**

Macleod, Donald John, 'Gaelic Prose', *TGSI*, vol. 49, **1974–76**, pp. 198–230

——, *Twentieth Century Publications in Scottish Gaelic*, Edinburgh, **1980**

MacLeod, Finlay, *The Healing Wells of the Western Isles*, Stornoway, **2000**

——, see also **MacLeòid**, Fionnlagh

MacLeod, Fred T., 'Observations on the Gaelic Translation of the Pentateuch', *TGSI*, vol. 36, **1931–33**, pp. 346–407

——, *The MacCrimmons of Skye*, Edinburgh, **1933b**

Macleod, J. F. M., 'A Boyhood in An Gearasdan', *TGSI*, vol. 57, **1990–92**, pp. 224–72

McLeod, Rev. Dr John, 'Parish of Morvern', **1843**, in *The New Statistical Account of Scotland*, vol. 7, Edinburgh, 1845, part 2, pp. 163–95

Macleod, Rev. Kenneth, 'Am Bannach Bearnach', *The Celtic Magazine*, vol. 13, **1887–88**, pp. 368–70

——, 'Gaisgeach na Sgeithe Deirge', *The Celtic Review*, vol. 3, **1906–07**, pp. 257–66, 346–60

——, 'Nighean Righ Eireann', *The Celtic Review*, vol. 4, **1907–08**, pp. 313–16

——, 'An Ossianic Fragment', *The Scottish Historical Review*, vol. 5, **1908**, pp. 253–54

Macleod, Malcolm C., ed., *The Celtic Annual 1912*, Dundee, **1911**

——, ed., *The Celtic Annual 1913*, Dundee, **1913**

——, ed., *The Celtic Annual*, Dundee, **1915**

Macleod, M. D., 'Amadain agus Oinsichean', *The Caledonian Medical Journal*, vol. 4, **1899–1901**, pp. 308–14

McLeod, Rev. Norman, 'Parish of Morven', **1793**, in *The Statistical Account of Scotland*, ed. by Sir John Sinclair, vol. 10, Edinburgh, 1794, pp. 262–76 = new edn, vol. 8, Wakefield, 1983, pp. 361–75

MacLeod, Rev. Dr Norman, Barony, *Reminiscences of a Highland Parish*, 5th edn, London, **1882** [1st edn London 1867; new edn, ed. by Iain Thornber, Edinburgh, **2002**]

MacLeod, Rev. Dr Norman, Campsie, **and Dewar**, Rev. Dr Daniel, Glasgow, *A Dictionary of the Gaelic Language*, Glasgow, **1831** [repr. Edinburgh 1901]

[MacLeod, Rev. Dr Norman, Campsie], 'Sgeul' mu Mhàiri Nighean Eoghainn Bhàin', *An Teachdaire Gaelach*, vol. 1, **1829–30**, pp. 97–102

——, 'Clann-'ic-Chruimein', *Cuairtear nan Gleann*, vol. 1, **1840–41**, pp. 134–37

——, 'Lachunn Mór Dhubhairt', *Cuairtear nan Gleann*, vol. 2, **1841–42a**, pp. 191–96, 219–23, 243–46

——, 'Saobh-Chràbhadh nan Gàidheal', *Cuairtear nan Gleann*, vol. 2, **1841–42b**, pp. 309–12

MacLeod, Rev. Dr Roderick, 'Ministearan an Arain? A Profile of Nineteenth Century Hebridean Moderates', *TGSI*, vol. 52, **1980–82**, pp. 243–69

MacLeòid, Fionnlagh, *Tobraichean Slàinte anns na h-Eileanan an Iar*, Stornoway, **2000**

——, see also **MacLeod**, Finlay

MacLeòid, Niall, *Clàrsach an Doire*, 6th edn, Glasgow, **1975** [1st edn Edinburgh 1883]

MacMillan, Hugh, *The Highland Tay*, London, **1901**

MacMillan, Somerled, *The MacMillans and Their Septs*, Glasgow, **1952**

——, ed., *Sporan Dhòmhnaill*, Scottish Gaelic Texts Society, Edinburgh, **1968**

——, *Bygone Lochaber*, Paisley, **1971**

Mac-na-Ceàrdadh, Gilleasbuig, ed., *An t-Òranaiche*, Glasgow, **1879**

McNaughton, William, *The Scottish Congregational Ministry 1794–1993*, Glasgow, **1993**

——, *Early Congregational Independency in the Highlands and Islands and the North-East of Scotland*, Ruaig, Tiree, **2003**

MacNeacail, Calum, *Bardachd Chaluim Ruaidh*, Glasgow, **1975**

MacNeil, Joe Neil, *Sgeul gu Latha, Tales until Dawn*, ed. by John Shaw, Edinburgh, **1987**

Macneil, Robert Lister, of Barra, *The Clan Macneil*, New York, **1923**

——, *Castle in the Sea*, 2nd edn, New York, **1975** [1st edn London 1964]

MacNeill, Eoin, ed., *Duanaire Finn*, part 1 (Irish Texts Society, vol. 7), London, **1908**

McNeill, F. Marian, *The Silver Bough*, 4 vols, Glasgow, **1957–68**

——, *Hallowe'en*, Edinburgh, **1970**

MacNeill, Máire, *The Festival of Lughnasa*, Oxford, **1962**

McNicol, Rev. Donald, *Remarks on Dr. Samuel Johnson's Journey to the Hebrides*, London, **1779**

——, 'United Parishes of Lismore and Appin', **1790**, in *The Statistical Account of Scotland*, ed. by Sir John Sinclair, vol. 1, Edinburgh, 1791, pp. 482–502 = new edn, vol. 20, Wakefield, 1983, pp. 345–65

McOwan, Rennie, 'Murder Mystery Tour', *The Scots Magazine*, March **2004**, pp. 280–84

MacPhail, Iain M. M., 'Gunboats to the Hebrides', *TGSI*, vol. 53, **1982–84**, pp. 531–67

——, *The Crofters' War*, Stornoway, **1989**

MacPhail, Rev. Malcolm, Kilmartin, 'Traditions, Customs, and Superstitions of the Lewis', *Folk-Lore*, vol. 6, **1895**, pp. 162–70, 303–04

——, 'Folklore from the Hebrides', *Folk-Lore*, vol. 7, **1896**, pp. 400–04; vol. 8, **1897**, pp. 380–86; vol. 9, **1898**, pp. 84–93; vol. 11, **1900**, pp. 439–50

Macpherson, Alan Gibson, *A Day's March to Ruin*, Newtonmore, **1996a**

Macpherson, Alexander, 'Sketches of the Old Ministers of Badenoch', *TGSI*, vol. 14, **1887–88**, pp. 193–216, and vol. 15, **1888–89**, pp. 216–38

——, 'Selections from the MSS. of the Late Captain Macpherson, Biallid', *TGSI*, vol. 16, **1889–90**, pp. 207–28

——, *Glimpses of Church and Social Life in the Highlands in Olden Times*, Edinburgh, **1893**

——, *Captain John Macpherson of Ballachroan and the Gaick Catastrophe of the Christmas of 1799 (O.S.): A Counter-Blast* (Clan Chattan Papers, no. 4), Kingussie, **1900**

MacPherson, Donald C., *An Duanaire*, Edinburgh, **1868**

——, see also **Abrach** and **Diarmad**

Macpherson, James, *The Poems of Ossian*, ed. by Howard Gaskill, Edinburgh, **1996b**

Macpherson, Rev. Dr John, Sleat, *Critical Dissertations*, London, **1768**

Macpherson, John, *A History of the Church in Scotland*, Paisley, **1901**

MacPherson, John, Northbay, *Tales of Barra Told by the Coddy*, ed. by J. L. Campbell, Edinburgh, **1960**

McPherson, J. M., *Primitive Beliefs in the North-East of Scotland*, London, **1929**

Macpherson, Malcolm, et al., *Legends of Badenoch*, 3rd edn, Kingussie, **1925** [5th edn Kingussie 1965]

Mac Philib, Séamas, 'The Changeling (ML 5058)', *Béaloideas*, vol. 59, **1991**, pp. 121–31

MacQuarrie, Duncan M., *The Placenames of Mull*, Tobermory, **1983**

MacRae, Norman, *Highland Second-Sight*, Dingwall, **1908**

MacRitchie, David, *The Testimony of Tradition*, London, **1890**

——, 'Stories of the Mound-Dwellers', *The Celtic Review*, vol. 4, **1907–08**, pp. 316–31

——, 'A New Solution of the Fairy Problem', *The Celtic Review*, vol. 6, **1909–10a**, pp. 160–76

——, 'Druids and Mound-Dwellers', *The Celtic Review*, vol. 6, **1909–10b**, pp. 257–72

——, 'The House of the Dwarfs', *The Celtic Review*, vol. 8, **1912–13**, pp. 289–95

MacRury, Rev. John, Snizort, 'Old Gaelic Songs', *TGSI*, vol. 16, **1889–90**, pp. 97–110

——, 'Màirnealachd agus Rud no Dhà Eile', *TGSI*, vol. 17, **1890–91**, pp. 17–31

——, 'Taillear Ghearraidh-bo-Stig', *TGSI*, vol. 19, **1893–94a**, pp. 25–37

——, 'An Teine Mòr – (Will o' the Wisp)', *TGSI*, vol. 19, **1893–94b**, pp. 158–71

——, 'Briathran nan Daoine 'dh' Fhalbh', *TGSI*, vol. 20, **1894–96**, pp. 141–51

——, 'Seana Bheachdan agus Seana Chleachdaidhean. No. I', *TGSI*, vol. 21, **1896–97**, pp. 368–79

——, 'Turus Ruairidh do 'n Exhibition', *TGSI*, vol. 25, **1901–03**, pp. 35–54

MacSween, Malcolm, **and Gailey**, Alan, 'Some Shielings in North Skye', *Scottish Studies*, vol. 5, **1961**, pp. 77–84

MacThòmais, Ruaraidh, *Smeur an Dòchais: Bramble of Hope*, Edinburgh, **1991**

Mac Thomais, Seumas, 'Uirsgeulan Leodhais', *TGSI*, vol. 38, **1937–41**, pp. 177–93

McWhannell, Dr Donald C., 'Mac Gille Chonaills and the Elusive Conall', *The Scottish Genealogist*, vol. 44, **1997**, pp. 25–30

——, 'Who Was the Eponym of the Clann Mhic Gille Chonaill?' *West Highland Notes & Queries*, series 2, no. 19, March **1999**, pp. 21–23

MacWhite, Eóin, 'Early Irish Board Games', *Éigse*, vol. 5, 1945–47 [**1948**], pp. 25–35

Maddrell, Breesha, 'Speaking from the Shadows', *Folklore*, vol. 113, **2002**, pp. 215–36

Maier, Bernhard, '*Sugere mammellas*: A Pagan Irish Custom and its Affinities', in *Celtic Connections*,

ed. by R. Black, W. Gillies and R. Ó Maolalaigh, East Linton, **1999**, pp. 152–61

Mair, Craig, *Mercat Cross and Tolbooth*, Edinburgh, **1988**

Malcomson, Robert, 'Notice of a Book Entitled "Beware the Cat"', *The Journal of the Historical and Archaeological Association of Ireland*, Third Series, vol. 1, no. 4, October **1868**, pp. 187–92

Maloney, Clarence, ed., *The Evil Eye*, New York, **1976**

Martin, Martin, *A Description of the Western Islands of Scotland*, 2nd edn, London, **1716** [repr. Edinburgh 1981]

——, *A Description of the Western Islands of Scotland ca 1695 and A Late Voyage to St Kilda*, **1999** edn, Edinburgh

——, see also **Robson**, Michael

Marwick, Sir James David, *List of Markets and Fairs Now and Formerly Held in Scotland*, London, **1890** (offprint paginated 1–116 = UK Parliamentary Papers 1890–91, vol. 37, pt 7, pp. 559–674, see Black 2000, pp. 4–5)

Masson, Rev. Donald, **and Aitken**, Dr [Thomas], 'Popular Domestic Medicine in the Highlands Fifty Years Ago', *TGSI*, vol. 14, **1887–88**, pp. 297–313

Matheson, Angus, 'A Traditional Account of the Appin Murder', *TGSI*, vol. 35, **1929–30**, pp. 343–404

——, 'Gleanings from the Dornie Manuscripts', *TGSI*, vol. 41, **1951–52a**, pp. 310–81

——, 'Some Words from Gaelic Folktales', *Éigse*, vol. 8, **1956–57**, pp. 247–58

——, 'Traditions of Alasdair Mac Colla', *Transactions of the Gaelic Society of Glasgow*, vol. 5, **1958**, pp. 9–93

Matheson, Norman, 'The Ghosts and Apparitions of the Isle of Skye', *TGSI*, vol. 18, **1891–92**, pp. 8–16

Matheson, Rev. William, ed., *The Songs of John MacCodrum*, Scottish Gaelic Texts Society, Edinburgh, **1938**

——, 'Notes on Mary MacLeod', *TGSI*, vol. 41, **1951–52b**, pp. 11–25

——, 'The Historical Coinneach Odhar', *TGSI*, vol. 46, **1969–70**, pp. 66–88

——, ed., *The Blind Harper*, Scottish Gaelic Texts Society, Edinburgh, **1970**

——, 'The MacLeods of Lewis', *TGSI*, vol. 51, **1978–80**, pp. 320–37

——, 'Notes on North Uist Families', *TGSI*, vol. 52, **1980–82**, pp. 318–72

——, review of Ó Baoill 1979, in *Scottish Gaelic Studies*, vol. 14, part 1, **1983**, pp. 129–36

Mattingly, H., **and Handford**, S. A., eds, *Tacitus: The Agricola and the Germania*, Harmondsworth, **1970** [1st edn 1948]

Meek, Domhnall, 'Aimhreit an Fhearainn an Tiriodh, 1886', in *Oighreachd agus Gabhaltas*, ed. by D. MacAmhlaigh, Aberdeen, **1980**, pp. 23–31

Meek, Donald E., 'Gaelic Poets of the Land Agitation', *TGSI*, vol. 49, **1974–76**, pp. 309–76

——, 'The Prophet of Waternish', *West Highland Free Press*, 8 July **1977**

——, ed., *The Campbell Collection of Gaelic Proverbs and Proverbial Sayings*, Inverness, **1978**

——, ed., *Tuath is Tighearna: Tenants and Landlords*, Scottish Gaelic Texts Society, Edinburgh, **1995a**

——, 'Farquharson, Archibald', in *The Blackwell Dictionary of Evangelical Biography 1730–1860*, vol. 1, ed. by D. M. Lewis, Oxford, **1995b**, pp. 379–80

——, ed., *Caran an t-Saoghail: Anthology of 19th Century Scottish Gaelic Verse*, Edinburgh, **2003**

Mercer, John, *Hebridean Islands: Colonsay, Gigha, Jura*, Glasgow, **1974**

Meyer, Kuno, ed., *The Cath Finntrága or Battle of Ventry*, Oxford, **1885**

——, 'The Edinburgh Gaelic Manuscript XL', *The Celtic Magazine*, vol. 12, **1886–87**, pp. 208–18

——, 'Neue Mitteilungen aus Irischen Handschriften', in *Archiv für Celtische Lexikographie*, ed. by W. Stokes and K. Meyer, vol. 3, Halle, **1907**, pp. 215–46

——, *Fianaigecht* (Royal Irish Academy, Todd Lecture Series, vol. 16), Dublin, **1910**

Mhàrtainn, Cairistìona, ed., *Òrain an Eilein*, Breacais Àrd, **2001**

Milford, H. S., ed., *The Poetical Works of Leigh Hunt*, Oxford, **1923**

Miller, Hugh, *Scenes and Legends of the North of Scotland*, Edinburgh, **1994** [1st edn 1835]

Miller, Ronald, 'Land Use by Summer Shielings', *Scottish Studies*, vol. 11, **1967**, pp. 193–221

Mitchell, Arthur, 'On Various Superstitions in the North-West Highlands and Islands of Scotland, Especially in Relation to Lunacy', *PSAS*, vol. 4, **1860–62**, pp. 251–88

Mitchell, Ian R., 'Ewan MacPhee of Loch Quoich', *West Highland Free Press*, 12 May **1995**

——, *Mountain Outlaw*, Edinburgh, **2003**

——, 'The Curse of Gaick', *The Scots Magazine*, February **2004**, pp. 136–39

Mitchell, Joseph, *Reminiscences of my Life in the Highlands*, 2 vols, Chilworth, **1883–84**

Mitchison, Rosalind, **and Leneman**, Leah, *Girls in Trouble: Sexuality and Social Control in Rural Scotland 1660–1780*, Oxford, **1989**; 2nd edn, Edinburgh, **1998**

Moir, James, ed., *The Actis and Deidis of . . . Schir William Wallace Knicht of Ellerslie by Henry the Minstrel*, Scottish Text Society, Edinburgh, **1889**

Moncreiffe, Sir Iain of that Ilk, *The Highland Clans*, London, **1967**

Moodie, Mrs R., 'Highland Therapy', *The Caledonian Medical Journal*, vol. 5, **1902–04**, pp. 320–41

Morgan, Prys, 'A Welsh Snakestone, its Tradition and Folklore', *Folklore*, vol. 94, **1983**, pp. 184–91

Morris, Ruth and Frank, *Scottish Healing Wells*, Sandy, **1982**

Morrison, Alexander, 'Uist Games', *The Celtic Review*, vol. 4, **1907–08**, pp. 361–71

Morrison, Alick, *Orain Chaluim, Being the Poems of Malcolm MacAskill, Bard of Berneray, Harris*, Glasgow, n.d. [*c.* **1965**]

——, *The Chiefs of Clan MacLeod*, n.p., **1986**

Morrison, Hew, ed., *Songs and Poems in the Gaelic Language by Rob Donn*, Edinburgh, **1899**

Morrison, John, ' "Drumming Tunes": A Study of Gaelic Rat Satires', *TGSI*, vol. 57, **1990–92**, pp. 273–364

[**Muir**, Thomas Smyth], *Characteristics of Old Church Architecture*, Edinburgh, **1861**

Muller, Sylvie, 'The Irish Wren Tales and Ritual', *Béaloideas*, vol. 64/65, **1996–97**, pp. 131–69

Munro, Joyce Underwood, 'The Invisible Made Visible', in Narváez **1997**, pp. 251–83

Munro, Neil, *The Lost Pibroch and Other Sheiling Stories / Jaunty Jock and Other Stories / Ayrshire Idylls*, Inveraray Edition, Edinburgh, **1935**

Munro, R. W., *Monro's Western Isles of Scotland and Genealogies of the Clans, 1549*, Edinburgh, **1961**

Murchison, Rev. Dr Thomas Moffatt, 'The Macleods of Morvern', *An Gaidheal*, vol. 52, **1957**, pp. 55, 66–68, 74–75

——, ed., *Prose Writings of Donald Lamont 1874–1958*, Scottish Gaelic Texts Society, Edinburgh, **1960**

——, 'The Presbytery of Gairloch (or Lochcarron) 1751–1827', *TGSI*, vol. 47, **1971–72**, pp. 1–66

——, ed., *Sgrìobhaidhean Choinnich MhicLeoid*, Scottish Gaelic Texts Society, Edinburgh, **1988**

Murphy, Gerard, ed., *Duanaire Finn*, part 2 (Irish Texts Society, vol. 28), London, **1933**

——, ed., *Duanaire Finn*, part 3 (Irish Texts Society, vol. 43), Dublin, **1953**

——, ed., *Early Irish Lyrics*, Oxford, **1956**

Murray, Iain, ed., *The Happy Man: The Abiding Witness of Lachlan Mackenzie*, Edinburgh, **1979**

Murray, James A. H., ed., *The Romance and Prophecies of Thomas of Erceldoune*, Early English Text Society, London, **1875** [repr. Felinfach 1991]

Nagy, Joseph Falaky, *The Wisdom of the Outlaw*, Berkeley, **1985**

[**Napier**, Lord], *Evidence taken by Her Majesty's Commissioners of Inquiry into the Condition of the Crofters and Cottars in the Highlands and Islands of Scotland*, 4 vols, Edinburgh, **1884**

Narváez, Peter, ed., *The Good People: New Fairylore Essays*, 2nd edn, Lexington (Kentucky), **1997** [1st edn New York 1991]

Nether-Lochaber (Rev. Alexander Stewart, Onich), 'Murder of Colin Campbell of Glenure', *The Celtic Magazine*, vol. 9, **1883–84**, pp. 352–54

Newall, Venetia, *An Egg at Easter*, London, **1971**

Newton, Michael, 'The MSS of Donald MacGregor', *TGSI*, vol. 61, **1998–2000**, pp. 280–305

——, 'Coille Mhòr Chailleann ann am Beul-Aithris nan Gàidheal', in *Cruth na Tìre*, ed. by W. McLeod and M. Ní Annracháin, Dublin, **2003**, pp. 180–94

——, 'Dancing with the Dead', conference paper (unpublished), 'Rannsachadh na Gàidhlig 3', University of Edinburgh, 22 July **2004**

Newton, Norman, *The Shell Guide to the Islands of Britain*, Newton Abbot, **1992**

Ní Anluain, Éilís, 'The Cardplayers and the Devil (ML 3015)', *Béaloideas*, vol. 59, **1991**, pp. 45–54

Nicolson, Alexander, *Gaelic Proverbs*, 2nd edn, Edinburgh, **1882**; 3rd edn, Glasgow, **1951**

Nicolson, Alexander, *Gaelic Riddles and Enigmas*, Glasgow, **1938**

——, 'Shinty (Iomain)', *An Gaidheal*, vol. 58, **1963**, pp. 45–47

——, *History of Skye*, 2nd edn, ed. by Dr Alasdair Maclean, Bernisdale, **1994** [1st edn Glasgow 1930]

Nicolson, C., 'Roots and Branches: The Name Game', *The Scots Magazine*, March **2004**, pp. 306–07

N[icolson], J[ohn], 'John Sands', *The Shetland Times*, 3 July **1937**

Ní Dhonnchadha, Máirín, '*Caillech* and Other Terms for Veiled Women in Medieval Irish Texts', *Éigse*, vol. 28, **1994–95**, pp. 71–96

Ní Dhuibhne, Eilís, 'The Old Woman as Hare', *Folklore*, vol. 104, **1993**, pp. 77–85

Nixon, Ingeborg, ed., *Thomas of Erceldoune*, 2 vols, Copenhagen, **1980–83**

N. M., 'Oidhche na Calainn', *The Celtic Review*, vol. 5, **1908–09**, pp. 243–44

Nutt, Alfred, 'Notes on the Tuairisgeul Mòr', *The Scottish Celtic Review*, November **1881**, pp. 137–41

——, 'The Campbell of Islay MSS. at the Advocates' Library', *Folk-Lore*, vol. 1, **1890**, pp. 369–83

——, review of SHIS, in *Folk-Lore*, vol. 11, **1900**, pp. 422–23

Oates, Caroline, 'Cheese Gives you Nightmares', *Folklore*, vol. 114, **2003**, pp. 205–25

Ó Baoill, Colm, ed., *Bàrdachd Shìlis na Ceapaich*, Scottish Gaelic Texts Society, Edinburgh, **1972**

——, 'Some Notes on "*An Aigeannach*"', *Scottish Gaelic Studies*, vol. 13, part 1, **1978**, pp. 103–11

——, ed., *Eachann Bacach and Other Maclean Poets*, Scottish Gaelic Texts Society, Edinburgh, **1979**

——, 'Norman MacLeod, *Cara na nGael*', *Scottish Gaelic Studies*, vol. 13, part 2, **1981**, pp. 159–68

——, 'Caismeachd Ailean nan Sop: The *Literatim* Text', *SGS*, vol. 17, **1996**, pp. 295–97

——, *Duanaire Colach 1537–1757*, Aberdeen, **1997**

——, '*Caismeachd Ailean nan Sop*: Towards a Definitive Text', *SGS*, vol. 18, **1998**, pp. 89–110

——, and McGuire, Nancy R., eds, *Rannsachadh na Gàidhlig 2000*, Aberdeen, **2002**

O'Brien, Michael A., 'Miscellanea Hibernica', *Études Celtiques*, vol. 3, **1938**, pp. 362–73

——, *Corpus Genealogiarum Hibelniae*, vol. 1, Dublin, **1962** [repr. Dublin 1976]

Ó Buachalla, Breandán, 'Aodh Eanghach and the Irish King-Hero', in *Sages, Saints and Storytellers*, ed. by Donnchadh Ó Corráin, Liam Breatnach and Kim McCone, Maynooth, **1989**, pp. 200–32

Ó Catháin, Séamas, 'Tricking the Fairy Suitor (ML 6000)', *Béaloideas*, vol. 59, **1991**, pp. 145–59

——, *The Festival of Brigit*, Dublin, **1995**

——, and Watson, Seosamh, 'An Easter Ross Mermaid', *Béaloideas*, vol. 64–65, **1996–97**, pp. 339–41

Ó Cathasaigh, Tomás, *The Heroic Biography of Cormac Mac Airt*, Dublin, **1977**

——, 'The Semantics of "Síd"', *Éigse*, vol. 17, **1977–79**, pp. 137–55

O'Connor, Anne, *Child Murderess and Dead Child Traditions: A Comparative Study*, FF Communications No. 249, Helsinki, **1991**

Ó Corráin, Donnchadh, and Maguire, Fidelma, *Irish Names*, 2nd edn, Dublin, **1990** [1st edn Dublin 1981]

Ó Crualaoich, Gearóid, *The Book of the Cailleach: Stories of the Wise-Woman Healer*, Cork, **2003**

Ó Cuív, Brian, 'Modern Irish *Slinnéanacht*', *Celtica*, vol. 2, **1954**, p. 277

Ó Duilearga, Séamus, ed., *Seán Ó Conaill's Book*, translated by Máire MacNeill, Dublin, **1981**

——, see also Delargy, J. H.

OED: *Oxford English Dictionary*

O'Grady, Standish Hayes, ed., *Silva Gadelica*, 2 vols, London, **1892**

Ó hÓgáin, Dáithí, 'An É an t-Am Fós É?' *Béaloideas*, vol. 42–44, **1977**, pp. 213–308

——, *Fionn Mac Cumhaill*, Dublin, **1988**

—— 'Has the Time Come?' *Béaloideas*, vol. 59, **1991**, pp. 197–207

O'Keefe, J. G., ed., 'Cáin Domnaig: The Epistle Concerning Sunday', *Ériu*, vol. 2, **1905**, pp. 189–214

Ó Lúing, Seán, *Kuno Meyer 1858–1919*, Dublin, **1991**

Ó Madagáin, Breandán, 'Gaelic Lullaby', *Scottish Studies*, vol. 29, **1989**, pp. 29–38

Omond, R. T., 'Notes on Brocken Spectre', *The Scottish Mountaineering Club Journal*, vol. 3, **1895**, pp. 92–94

Ó Murchú, Máirtín, *East Perthshire Gaelic*, Dublin, **1989**

O'Neill, Áine, '"The Fairy Hill is on Fire!" (MLSIT 6071)', *Béaloideas*, vol. 59, **1991**, pp. 189–96

Ó Néill, Eoghan Rua, 'The King of the Cats (ML 6070B)', *Béaloideas*, vol. 59, **1991**, pp. 167–88

Opie, Iona, and Tatem, Moira, eds, *A Dictionary of Superstitions*, **1992** edn, Oxford

O'Rahilly, T. F., 'Etymological Notes. II', *Scottish Gaelic Studies*, vol. 2, **1927**, pp. 13–29

O'Reilly, Barry, 'Now You See It, Now You Don't', *Béaloideas*, vol. 62–63, **1994–95**, pp. 199–209

Ó Súilleabháin, Seán, *Irish Wake Amusements*, Cork, **1967** [repr. Cork 1997]

Parman, Susan, 'Curing Beliefs and Practices in the Outer Hebrides', *Folklore*, vol. 88, **1977**, pp. 107–09

Paton, Henry, ed., *Kingarth Parish Records: The Session Book of Kingarth 1641–1703*, n.p., **1932**

Paton, Sir Noel, 'Notes on Clach-na-Bratach', *PSAS*, vol. 21, **1886–87**, pp. 226–36

Peacock, Edward, 'Stone Celts', *The Folk-Lore Journal*, vol. 1, **1883**, p. 191

Peacock, William F., *Everybody's New Guide, Companion, & Associate (for both Summer and Winter) to the Isle of Man*, Manchester, [**1863**]

Pennant, Thomas, *British Zoology*, vol. 2, London, **1768**

——, *A Tour in Scotland; MDCCLXIX*, 3rd edn, Warrington, **1774** [repr. Perth 1979]

——, *British Zoology*, 2nd edn, 4 vols, London, **1812**

——, *A Tour in Scotland and Voyage to the Hebrides 1772*, new edn by Andrew Simmons, Edinburgh, **1998** [1st edn Chester 1774–76]

Pinkerton, John, ed., *A General Collection of the Best and Most Interesting Voyages and Travels in All Parts of the World*, vol. 3, London, **1809**

Pitcairn, Robert, *Criminal Trials in Scotland*, 3 vols, The Bannatyne Club, Edinburgh, **1833**

Plummer, Charles, ed., *Miscellanea Hagiographica Hibernica*, Brussels, **1925**

Polson, Alexander, *Our Highland Folklore Heritage*, Dingwall, **1926**

——, *Scottish Witchcraft Lore*, Inverness, **1932**

Puhvel, Martin, 'The Legend of the Devil-Haunted Card Players in Northern Europe', *Folklore*, vol. 76, **1965**, pp. 33–38

Purser, John, *Scotland's Music*, Edinburgh, **1992**

Ramsay, D[onald], 'Stratherrick', *TGSI*, vol. 10, **1881–83**, pp. 197–202

Ramsay, John, of Ochtertyre, *Scotland and Scotsmen in the Eighteenth Century*, ed. by Alexander Allardyce, 2 vols, Edinburgh, **1888**

Rankin, Effie, ed., *As a' Bhràighe: The Gaelic Songs of Allan the Ridge MacDonald*, Sydney (N.S.), **2004**

Rankin, Robert A., 'Place-Names in the *Comhachag*', *Scottish Gaelic Studies*, vol. 18, **1998**, pp. 111–30

——, 'Addendum to Place-Names in the *Comhachag*', *Scottish Gaelic Studies*, vol. 19, **1999**, p. 257

RCAHMS (Royal Commission on the Ancient and Historical Monuments of Scotland), *Argyll, An Inventory of the Monuments, Vol. 3: Mull, Tiree and Northern Argyll*, Edinburgh, **1980**

——, *Argyll, An Inventory of the Monuments, Vol. 4: Iona*, Edinburgh, **1982**

Rea, F. G., *A School in South Uist*, ed. by J. L. Campbell, 2nd edn, Edinburgh, **1997** [1st edn London 1964]

Reeves, William, 'The Island of Tiree', *The Ulster Journal of Archæology*, vol. 2, **1854**, pp. 233–44

——, 'Saint Maelrubha: His History and Churches', *PSAS*, vol. 3, **1857–60**, pp. 258–96

Renton, Ronnie, **and Beaton**, James, eds, 'A Stone on the Cairn of Neil Munro', *ParaGraphs, The Neil Munro Society Journal*, no. 8, winter **2000**, pp. 6–8

Rhŷs, John, *Celtic Folklore: Welsh and Manx*, vol. 1, Oxford, **1901** [repr. London 1980]

Riddell, John F., *Clyde Navigation*, Edinburgh, **1979**

Rieti, Barbara, ' "The Blast" in Newfoundland Fairy Tradition', in Narváez **1997**, pp. 284–97

Robertson, Boyd, **and MacDonald**, Ian, *Teach Yourself Gaelic Dictionary*, London, **2004**

Robertson, Rev. Charles M., 'Perthshire Gaelic', *TGSI*, vol. 21, **1897–98a**, pp. 4–42

——, 'Topography and Traditions of Eigg', *TGSI*, vol. 22, **1897–98b**, pp. 192–210

——, 'Skye Gaelic', *TGSI*, vol. 23, **1898–99**, pp. 54–89

——, 'The Gaelic of the West of Ross-Shire', *TGSI*, vol. 24, **1899–1901**, pp. 321–69

——, 'Folk-Lore from the West of Ross-Shire', *TGSI*, vol. 26, **1904–07**, pp. 262–99

——, 'Scottish Gaelic Dialects', *The Celtic Review*, vol. 3, **1906–07**, pp. 97–113, 223–39, 319–32; vol. 4, **1907–08**, pp. 69–80, 167–83, 273–80, 335–48; vol. 5, **1908–09**, pp. 79–90

Robertson, Hamish, 'Studies in Carmichael's Carmina Gadelica', *SGS*, vol. 12, part 2, **1976**, pp. 220–65

Robertson, James, 'Memories of Rannoch', *TGSI*, vol. 51, **1978–80**, pp. 199–319

Robertson, Rev. James, 'Parish of Callander', **1791**, in Sir John Sinclair, ed., *The Statistical Account of Scotland*, vol. 11, Edinburgh, 1794, pp. 574–627 = new edn, vol. 12, Wakefield, 1977, pp. 137–90

Robertson, J. Logie, ed., *Scott: Poetical Works*, London, **1904** [repr. 1971]

Robertson, R. Macdonald, *Selected Highland Folktales*, Colonsay, **1995** [1st edn Edinburgh 1961]

Robertson, Sylvia, **and Young**, Patricia, *Daughter of Atholl: Lady Evelyn Stewart Murray 1868–1940*, The Abertay Historical Society, Dundee, **1997**

Robinson, Mairi, ed., *The Concise Scots Dictionary*, new edn, Aberdeen, **1987**

Robson, Michael, ed., *Curiosities of Art and Nature*, Port of Ness, **2003**

Rogers, Rev. Charles, *Social Life in Scotland from Early to Recent Times*, vol. 3, Edinburgh, **1886**

[**Rorie**, David], 'An Obstetric Girdle', *The Caledonian Medical Journal*, vol. 9, **1912–14**, p. 46

Rose, John, ed., *Metrical Reliques of "The Men" in the Highlands*, Inverness, **1851**

Ross, Alexander, 'Notes on Superstitions as to Burying Suicides in the Highlands', *The Celtic Magazine*, vol. 12, **1886–87a**, pp. 349–54

Ross, Alexander, 'Notes on the Formation of the Caledonian Canal', *TGSI*, vol. 13, **1886–87b**, pp. 313–35

Ross, Anne, 'Cutting the "Maiden" on Loch Tayside', *Scottish Studies*, vol. 8, **1964**, pp. 229–30

——, 'Hallowe'en at Fortingall, Perthshire', *Scottish Studies*, vol. 9, **1965**, pp. 204–06

——, *The Folklore of the Scottish Highlands*, London, **1976**

Ross, James, 'A Classification of Gaelic Folk-Song', *Scottish Studies*, vol. 1, **1957**, pp. 95–151

Ross, Rev. Dr Neil, *Heroic Poetry from the Book of the Dean of Lismore*, Scottish Gaelic Texts Society, Edinburgh, **1939**

Rust, Rev. James, Slains, *Druidism Exhumed*, Edinburgh, **1871**

Sage, Rev. Donald, Resolis, *Memorabilia Domestica*, 2nd edn, Wick, **1899** [1st edn Wick 1889; repr. Edinburgh 1975]

Sands, John, 'Notes on the Antiquities of the Island of St Kilda', *PSAS*, vol. 12, **1876–78**, pp. 186–92

——, 'Life in St Kilda', *Chambers's Journal*, **1877**, pp. 284–87, 312–16, 331–34

——, *Out of the World; or, Life in St Kilda*, 2nd edn, Edinburgh, **1878** [1st edn Edinburgh 1876]

——, *Sketches of Tranent*, Edinburgh, **1881a**

——, *Frank Powderhorn*, London, **1881b**

——, 'Notes on the Antiquities of the Island of Tiree', *PSAS*, vol. 16, **1881–82**, pp. 459–63

——, *King James' Wedding and Other Rhymes*, Arbroath, **1888**

Sands, John Sim, *Report of the Speech of Horatio Ross, Esq. M. P.*, Arbroath, **1832**

——, *Poems on Various Subjects*, Arbroath, **1833**

Santino, Jack, ed., *Halloween and Other Festivals of Death and Life*, Knoxville (Ten.), **1994**

Schofield, William Henry, *Mythical Bards and the Life of William Wallace*, Harvard Studies in Comparative Literature, vol. 5, Cambridge (Mass.), **1920**

Scott, Archibald B., 'Saint Maolrubha', *The Scottish Historical Review*, vol. 6, **1908–09**, pp. 260–80

Scott, Hugh, *Fasti Ecclesiæ Scoticanæ*, new edn, 8 vols, Edinburgh, **1915–50**

Scott, James E., 'The MacIntyre Pipers of Rannoch', *The Piping Times*, vol. 20, no. 9, June **1968**, pp. 14–15

Scott, Sir Walter, *Minstrelsy of the Scottish Border*, 2nd edn, 3 vols, vol. 1, Edinburgh, **1803**

——, *Ballads and Lyrical Pieces*, Edinburgh, **1806**

——, *The Lady of the Lake*, 1st edn, Edinburgh, **1810**

——, *The Lay of the Last Minstrel*, 13th edn, London, **1812**

——, 'On the Supernatural in Fictitious Composition', *The Foreign Quarterly Review*, vol. 1, **1827**, pp. 60–98

——, *Rob Roy*, Parker's Edition, Waverley Novels, 2 vols, Boston, **1830**

——, *Letters of Sir Walter Scott; addressed to the Rev. R. Polwhele; D. Gilbert, Esq.; Francis Douce, Esq. &c. &c.*, London, **1832**

——, *The Prose Works of Sir Walter Scott, Bart.*, vol. 18, Edinburgh, **1835**

——, *The Complete Poetical and Dramatic Works*, London, **1883**

——, *Waverley*, Border Edn, 2 vols, London, **1892**

——, *The Monastery*, Border Edn, 2 vols, London, **1893a**

——, *Rob Roy*, Border Edn, 2 vols, London, **1893b**

——, *Manners, Customs, and History of the Highlanders of Scotland*, New York, **1993**

——, *Letters on Demonology and Witchcraft*, The Folklore Society, London, **2001** [1st edn 1830]

Scrope, William, *Days of Deer-Stalking in the Scottish Highlands*, Glasgow, **1894**

Sellar, W. D. H., **and Maclean**, Alasdair, *The Highland Clan MacNeacail (MacNicol)*, Lochbay, **1999**

Shackleton, G[illian], 'The Appin Banner', *Appin Historical Society Newsletter*, no. 4, **1997**, pp. 3–5

Sharpe, Henry, 'Brocken Spectres, Bows, and Glories', *Scottish Mountaineering Club Journal*, vol. 3, **1895**, pp. 85–91

Shaw, Donald, see **Glenmore**

Shaw, John, 'Sgeulachd a' Chait Bhig 's a' Chait Mhóir', *Scottish Studies*, vol. 30, **1991**, pp. 93–106

——, ed., *Brìgh an Òrain, A Story in Every Song*, Montreal, **2000**

——, 'What Alexander Carmichael did not Print', *Béaloideas*, vol. 70, **2002**, pp. 99–126

Shaw, Rev. Lachlan, *The History of the Province of Moray*, Edinburgh, **1775**; new edn, Elgin, **1827**

Shaw, Margaret Fay, *Folksongs and Folklore of South Uist*, 2nd edn, Oxford, **1977** [1st edn London 1955]

Sibbald, Robert, *Scotia Illustrata*, Edinburgh, **1684**

S[im], R[obert], *Legends of Strathisla . . . and Strathbogie*, 2nd edn, Elgin, **1862** [1st edn Keith 1849]

Simmons, Andrew, ed., *Burt's Letters from the North of Scotland*, 3rd edn, Edinburgh, **1998** [1st edn London 1754]

Simpson, Eric, 'Auld Handsel Monday', *The Scots Magazine*, January **1979**, pp. 376–79

Simpson, J. Y., 'Notes on some Scottish Magical Charm-Stones', *PSAS*, vol. 4, **1860–62**, pp. 211–24

Sinclair, Rev. Alexander Maclean, 'An Co-Chruinneachadh Muileach', *An Gaidheal*, vol. 6, **1877**, pp. 50–52

——, *Clarsach na Coille*, Glasgow, **1881**

——, *The Gaelic Bards from 1411 to 1715*, Charlottetown, **1890**

——, 'The Macintyres of Glennoe', *TGSI*, vol. 18, **1891–92**, pp. 289–95

——, *Na Bàird Leathanach: The Maclean Bards*, 2 vols, Charlottetown, **1898–1900**

——, *The Clan Gillean*, Charlottetown, **1899**

——, 'The MacNeils of Barra', *The Celtic Review*, vol. 3, **1906–07**, pp. 216–23

——, 'The Clan Fingon', *The Celtic Review*, vol. 4, **1907–08**, pp. 31–41

——, 'The Macneills of Argyllshire', *The Celtic Review*, vol. 6, **1909–10**, pp. 55–64

Sinclair, Colin, *The Thatched Houses of the Old Highlands*, Edinburgh, **1953**

Sinton, Rev. Thomas, 'Gaelic Poetry from the Cluny Charter Chest', *TGSI*, vol. 23, **1898–99**, pp. 247–81

——, *The Poetry of Badenoch*, Inverness, **1906**

Sithiche, 'A' Bhean-Nighe', *Guth na Bliadhna*, vol. 9, **1912**, pp. 195–221, 333–66

Skjelbred, Ann Helene Bolstad, 'Rites of Passage as Meeting Place: Christianity and Fairylore in Connection with the Unclean Woman and the Unchristened Child', in Narváez **1997**, pp. 215–23

Slade, Harry Gordon, 'Three Early Croft Houses in Gairloch, Wester Ross', in *Vernacular Building 18: Scottish Vernacular Buildings Working Group 1994*, **1995**, pp. 34–47

Smith, Rev. Colin, Inveraray, 'Parish of Glassary', *The New Statistical Account of Scotland*, vol. 7, part 2, Edinburgh, **1845**, pp. 675–700

Smith, Rev. Dr John, *Sean Dana*, Edinburgh, **1787**

Smith, John A., *et al.*, eds, *Aithris is Oideas*, Scottish Council for Research in Education, London, **1964**

Speke, John Hanning, *Journal of the Discovery of the Source of the Nile*, Edinburgh, **1863**

Spence, Lewis, *The Fairy Tradition in Britain*, London, **1948**

Staniforth, M., **and Louth**, A., eds, *Early Christian Writings: The Apostolic Fathers*, London, **1987**

Stark, Suzanne J., *Female Tars: Women Aboard Ship in the Days of Sail*, London, **1996**

Stevenson, David, *The Hunt for Rob Roy: The Man and the Myths*, Edinburgh, **2004**

Stewart, A. and D., eds, *Cochruinneacha Taoghta de Shaothair nam Bard Gaëleach*, Edinburgh, **1804**

Stewart, Rev. Alexander, 'Parish of Killin', in *The New Statistical Account of Scotland*, vol. 10, **1845**, pp. 1076–94

Stewart, Rev. Alexander, Onich, *'Twixt Ben Nevis and Glencoe*, Edinburgh, **1885**

Stewart, Alexander, *A Highland Parish or The History of Fortingall*, Glasgow, **1928**

Stewart, Rev. Charles, 'United Parishes of Strachur and Stralachlan', **1791**, in Sir John Sinclair, ed., *The Statistical Account of Scotland*, vol. 4, Edinburgh,

1792, pp. 555–78 = new edn, vol. 8, Wakefield, 1983, pp. 397–420

Stewart, Charles, *The Killin Collection of Gaelic Songs*, Edinburgh, **1884**

Stewart, James, *Settlements of Western Perthshire*, Edinburgh, **1990a**

Stewart, John H. J., **and Stewart**, Lt-Col. Duncan, *The Stewarts of Appin*, Edinburgh, **1880**

Stewart, John, of Ardvorlich, *The Camerons*, 2nd edn, n.p., **1981** [1st edn 1974]

Stewart, R. J., *Robert Kirk: Walker between Worlds, A New Edition of The Secret Commonwealth of Elves, Fauns and Fairies*, Longmead, Shaftesbury, **1990b**

Stewart, William Grant, Congash, *The Popular Superstitions and Festive Amusements of the Highlanders of Scotland*, Edinburgh, **1823**; London, **1851**

——, *Lectures on the Mountains*, 2 vols, London, **1860**

Stokes, Whitley, ed., 'Find and the Phantoms', *Revue Celtique*, vol. 7, **1886**, pp. 289–307

——, ed., 'The Prose Tales in the Rennes Dindshenchas', *Revue Celtique*, vol. 15, **1894**, pp. 272–336, 418–84

——, 'Irish Etymologies', *Revue Celtique*, vol. 27, **1906**, pp. 85–92

——, **and Strachan**, John, eds, *Thesaurus Palaeohibernicus*, 2 vols, Cambridge, **1901–03**

Story, Elma, ed., *Am Bolg Solair*, Glasgow, **1907**

Stott, Rebecca, *Darwin and the Barnacle*, London, **2003**

Strachan, P. D., 'Life in a Hebridean Island Half a Century Ago', *The Caledonian Medical Journal*, vol. 15, **1932–36**, pp. 523–32, 579–87

Sutherland, Elizabeth, *Ravens and Black Rain*, Ealing, **1987** [1st edn 1985]

Sutherland, Rev. George, *Folk-Lore Gleanings and Character Sketches, from the Far North*, Wick, **1937**

Sutherland, Ian, 'Willox the Warlock', *The Scots Magazine*, July **1997**, pp. 63–64

Taylor, William, *The Military Roads in Scotland*, 2nd edn, Colonsay, **1996** [1st edn Newton Abbot 1976]

Temperley, Alan, *Tales of the North Coast*, London, **1977**

Tennyson, Hallam, Lord, ed., *The Works of Tennyson*, London, **1913**

Thiele, Just Matthias, *Danske Folkesagn*, 4 vols, Copenhagen, **1818–22**

Thomas, Capt. F. W. L., 'Traditions of the Macaulays of Lewis', *PSAS*, vol. 14, **1879–80**, pp. 363–431

——, 'On Islay Place-Names', *PSAS*, vol. 16, **1881–82**, pp. 241–76

Thomas, N. W., 'The Scape-Goat in European Folklore', *Folk-Lore*, vol. 17, **1906**, pp. 258–87

Thompson, Francis G., 'John Francis Campbell', *TGSI*, vol. 54, **1984–86**, pp. 1–57

——, *The Supernatural Highlands*, 2nd edn, Edinburgh, **1997** [1st edn London 1976]

Thompson, Stith, ed., *Motif-Index of Folk-Literature*, 6 vols, Copenhagen, **1955–58**

Thoms, William J., 'Divination by the Blade-Bone', *Folk-Lore Record*, vol. 1, **1878**, pp. 176–79

Thomson, Derick S., *The Gaelic Sources of Macpherson's 'Ossian'*, Edinburgh, **1951**

——, 'The MacMhuirich Bardic Family', *TGSI*, vol. 43, **1960–63**, pp. 276–304

——, *New English–Gaelic Dictionary*, Glasgow, **1981**

——, 'The McLagan MSS in Glasgow University Library', *TGSI*, vol. 58, **1992–94**, pp. 406–24

——, ed., *The Companion to Gaelic Scotland*, 2nd edn, Glasgow, **1994** [1st edn Oxford 1983]

——, ed., *Alasdair Mac Mhaighstir Alasdair: Selected Poems*, Scottish Gaelic Texts Society, Edinburgh, **1996**

Thomson, Duncan, *The Life and Art of George Jamesone*, Oxford, **1974**

Thomson, James, *The Works of James Thomson*, 3 vols, London, **1788**

Thomson, J. Maitland, ed., *Inventory of Documents relating to the Scrymgeour Family Estates, 1611*, Scottish Record Society, Edinburgh, **1912**

Thomson, R. L., ed., *Foirm na n-Urrnuidheadh*, Scottish Gaelic Texts Society, Edinburgh, **1970**

Thomson, Rev. Thomas, ed., *The Works of the Ettrick Shepherd: Poems and Life*, London, **1874**

Thornber, Iain, 'Rats', *TGSI*, vol. 55, **1986–88**, pp. 128–47

——, 'The Saving of the Banner', *The Scots Magazine*, July **1991**, pp. 404–08

——, *Dail na Cille, the Field of the Church: Kingairloch Graveyard, Ardgour and its Inscribed Stones*, n.p., **2000**

Thorndike, Lynn, *Michael Scot*, London, **1965**

Thorpe, Lewis, ed., *Geoffrey of Monmouth: The History of the Kings of Britain*, **1966** edn, London

T. M., 'Air an Àirigh II', *The Celtic Review*, vol. 5, **1908–09**, pp. 237–39

Todd, James H., ed., *Cogadh Gaedhel re Gallaibh: The War of the Gaedhil with the Gaill*, London, **1867**

Tolmie, Frances, *One Hundred and Five Songs of Occupation from the Western Isles of Scotland*, Llanerch, 1997, repr. from *Journal of the Folk-Song Society*, vol. 4, part 3, **1911**, pp. iv–xiv, 143–276

Tolmie, P. G., 'Remains of Ancient Religion in the North', *TGSI*, vol. 6, **1876–77**, pp. 88–102

T[ormod] O[g] (Rev. Dr Norman MacLeod, Campsie), 'Eoghann a Chinn Bhig', *An Teachdaire Gaelach*, vol. 2, **1830–31a**, pp. 92–94

T[ormod] O[g] (Rev. Dr Norman MacLeod, Campsie), 'M'an *Florida*, an Long Mhòr Spainndeach', *An Teachdaire Gaelach*, vol. 2, **1830–31b**, pp. 135–36

Train, Joseph, *An Historical and Statistical Account of the Isle of Man*, 2 vols, Douglas, **1845**

Trevarthen, Geo Athena, 'Brightness of Brightness: Seeing Celtic Shamanism', unpublished PhD thesis, Edinburgh, **2003**

Vallancey, Gen. Charles, ed., *Collectanea de Rebus Hibernicis*, 4 vols, Dublin, **1786**

Vendryes, Joseph, *et al.*, eds, *Lexique Étymologique de l'Irlandais Ancien*, Paris, **1959–96**

Waldron, George, *A Description of the Isle of Man*, The Manx Society, Douglas, **1865**

Wallace, Mrs Jessie, 'Am Fomhair agus an Gille Ruadh: The Giant and the Fair Man-Servant', *The Celtic Magazine*, vol. 13, **1887–88a**, pp. 20–28

——, 'An Iobhal Gheal 's an Iobhal Fhionn 's an Iobhal Dhonn 's an Iobhal Charrach bu Mhathair Dhoibh: The Snow-White Maiden, and the Fair Maid, and the Swarthy Maid, and Frizzle, or Bald Pate their Mother', *The Celtic Magazine*, vol. 13, **1887–88b**, pp. 454–65, 493–95

——, 'The Highland Chieftain, and How he Won his Wife', *The Highland Monthly*, vol. 1, **1889–90**, pp. 622–33

Walters, Michael, 'Curing of Warts', *Folklore*, vol. 103, **1992**, p. 114

Watson, E. C., 'Highland Mythology', *The Celtic Review*, vol. 5, **1908–09**, pp. 48–70

——, see also **Carmichael**, E. C.

Watson, James Carmichael, ed., *Gaelic Songs of Mary MacLeod*, Scottish Gaelic Texts Society, Edinburgh, **1965** [1st edn London 1934]

Watson, Lyall, *Heaven's Breath: A Natural History of the Wind*, Sevenoaks, **1985** [1st edn 1984]

Watson, Seosamh, 'Deascán Ábhair Thraidisiúnta ó Oirthear Rois', *Béaloideas*, vol. 69, **2001**, pp. 145–57

Watson, William J., *Place-Names of Ross and Cromarty*, Inverness, **1904**

——, 'Topographical Varia – V', *The Celtic Review*, vol. 7, **1911–12**, pp. 361–71

——, 'Topographical Varia – VI', *The Celtic Review*, vol. 8, **1912–13**, pp. 235–45

——, 'The Celtic Church in its Relations with Paganism', *The Celtic Review*, vol. 10, **1914–16**, pp. 263–79

——, 'Marbhnadh Dhonnchaidh Duibh', *An Deò-Gréine*, vol. 12, **1916–17**, pp. 132–34, 149–51

——, *The History of the Celtic Place-Names of Scotland*, Edinburgh, **1926a**

——, 'Varia', *SGS*, vol. 1, **1926b**, pp. 78–82, 210–14

——, ed., *Scottish Verse from the Book of the Dean of Lismore*, Scottish Gaelic Texts Society, Edinburgh, **1937**

——, ed., *Bàrdachd Ghàidhlig*, 3rd edn, Inverness, **1959** [1st edn Inverness 1918]

——, *Scottish Place-Name Papers*, London, **2002**

Watt, Eilidh, *Gun Fhois*, Edinburgh, **1987**

——, 'Some Personal Experiences of the Second Sight', in *The Seer in Celtic and Other Traditions*, ed. by Hilda Ellis Davidson, Edinburgh, **1989**, pp. 25–36

Welch, Robert, ed., *W. B. Yeats: Writings on Irish Folklore, Legend and Myth*, London, **1993**

Wentz, W. Y. Evans, *The Fairy-Faith in Celtic Countries*, Oxford, **1911** [repr. Gerrards Cross 1977]

Wheater, Hilary, *A Guide in Hand to Kenmore and Loch Tay*, n.p., **1980**

Whitaker, Ian, 'Some Traditional Techniques in Modern Scottish Farming', *Scottish Studies*, vol. 3, **1959**, pp. 163–88

White, Gilbert, *The Natural History of Selborne*, ed. by Thomas Brown, 4th edn, Edinburgh, **1835** [1st edn London 1789]

Williams, Noel, 'The Semantics of the Word *Fairy*: Making Meaning out of Thin Air', in Narváez **1997**, pp. 457–78

Willis, Douglas P., 'That Special Island', *The Scots Magazine*, November **1989**, pp. 145–50

——, 'The Cult of the Clootie Well', *The Scots Magazine*, May **1995**, pp. 527–30

Wilson, Daniel, *Prehistoric Annals of Scotland*, 2nd edn, 2 vols, London, **1863** [1st edn 1851]

Wilson, John, *CB: A Life of Sir Henry Campbell-Bannerman*, London, **1973**

Winberry, John J., 'The Elusive Elf: Some Thoughts on the Nature and Origin of the Irish Leprechaun', *Folklore*, vol. 87, **1976**, pp. 63–75

Winchester, Rev. Hugh, *Traditions of Arrochar and Tarbet and the MacFarlanes*, n.p., *c.* **1916**

Windisch, Ernst, ed., *Irische Texte mit Wörterbuch*, Leipzig, **1880**

Yarwood, R. E., 'Hogmanay 1443 in West Yorkshire', *Folklore*, vol. 95, **1984**, pp. 252–53

Youngson, Rev. Peter, *Ancient Hebridean Tales of Jura Collected from 1908 to 1914 by Rev. Charles Robertson*, Kirriemuir, **n.d.**

——, *Jura: Island of Deer*, Edinburgh, **2001**

OTHER ABBREVIATIONS

AC	Alexander Carmichael
Adv.	Advocates'
beg.	beginning
CW	Carmichael–Watson
EUL	Edinburgh University Library
f.	folio *or* feminine
ff.	folios
fl.	floruit
GROS	General Register Office for Scotland
gs.	genitive singular
GUL	Glasgow University Library
JFC	John Francis Campbell
JGC	John Gregorson Campbell
m.	masculine
NAS	National Archives of Scotland
n.d.	no date given
n.p.	no place given
NS	New Style [Gregorian]

OPR	Old Parish Register
OS	Old Style [Julian]
PSAS	*Proceedings of the Society of Antiquaries of Scotland*
r	recto (right-hand page)
SA	Sound Archive
SGS	*Scottish Gaelic Studies*
SHIS	*Superstitions of the Highlands & Islands of Scotland*
SoSS	School of Scottish Studies
s.v.	sub verbum ('under the word')
SWHIHR	Society of West Highland and Island Historical Research
TGSI	*Transactions of the Gaelic Society of Inverness*
v	verso (left-hand page)
WSS	*Witchcraft & Second Sight in the Highlands and Islands*

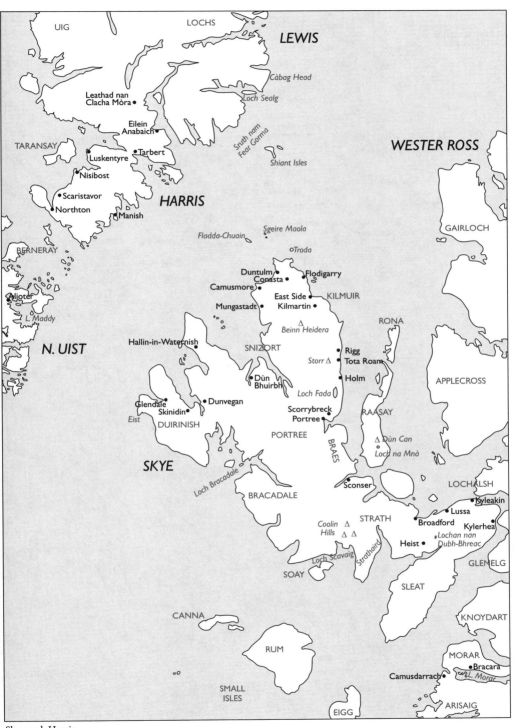

Skye and Harris

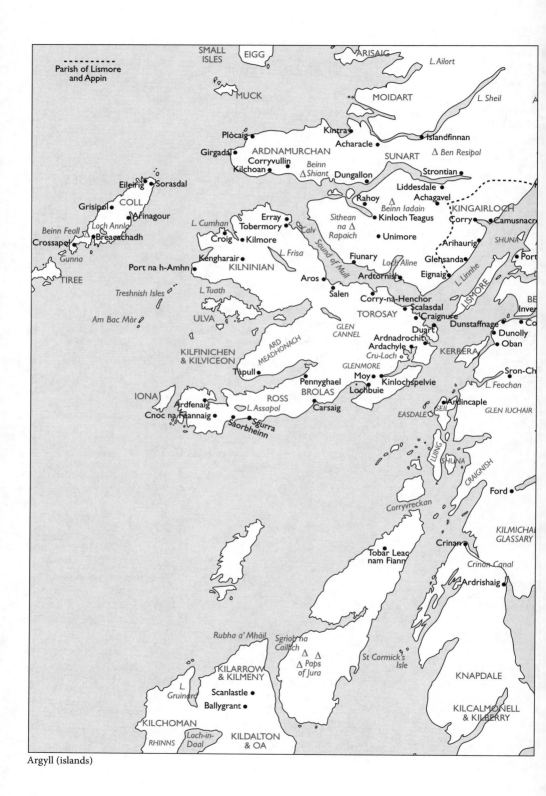

Argyll (islands)

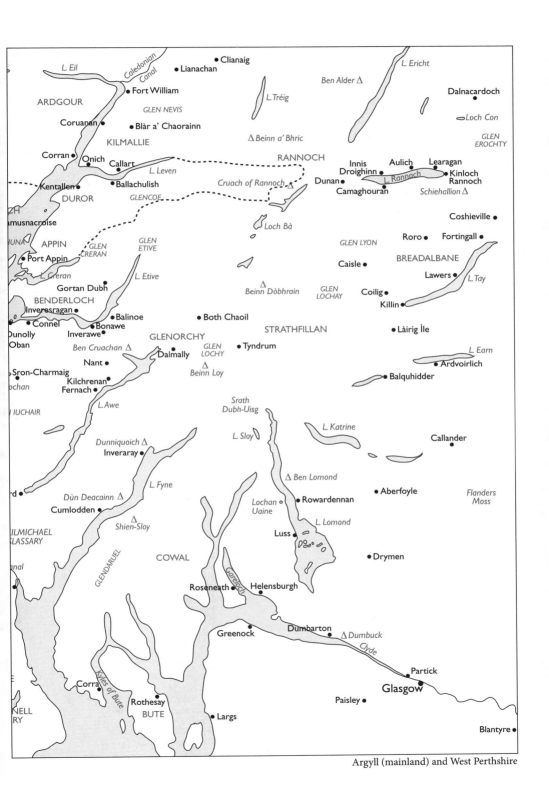

Argyll (mainland) and West Perthshire

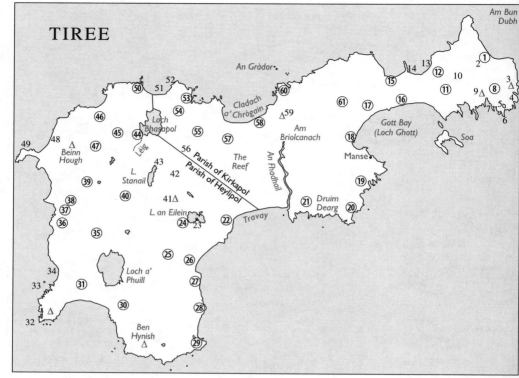

TIREE

Am Bun Dubh

An Gràdor

Cladach a' Chrògain

Loch Bhasapol

Am Briolcanach

Gott Bay (Loch Ghott)

Soa

Lèig

Parish of Kirkapol
Parish of Heylipol

The Reef

An Fhadhail

Beinn Hough

Manse

L. Stanail

Druim Dearg

L. an Eilein

Travay

Loch a' Phuill

Ben Hynish

INDEX TO TALES

This is a digest of the principal tale-types found above, with the pages on which they occur. The motif numbers on the left relate to the following sources:

AT   Thompson 1955–58; Antti Aarne and Stith Thompson, *The Types of the Folktale* (FF Communications 184), Helsinki, 1961

F   Fairy legends as listed in MacDonald 1994–95, pp. 43–59, 68–78

ML   Reidar Th. Christiansen, *The Migratory Legends* (FF Communications 175), Helsinki, 1958

MLSIT   Migratory legend, suggested Irish type (cited in MacDonald 1994–95)

Other   Unnumbered items in MacDonald 1994–95, pp. 65–66

W   Witch stories as listed in Bruford 1967, pp. 15–36, and MacDonald 1994–95, pp. 35–42

Also worth consulting are *CG*6, pp. 166–78 (indexed list of motifs in *CG* arranged by AT classification, corresponding closely to the range of motifs which appear in the present work); Henderson and Cowan, pp. 218–23 (list of Fairy motifs extracted from ML, AT and Bruford 1997); Seán Ó Súilleabháin and R. Th. Christiansen, *The Types of the Irish Folktale* (FF Communications 188), Helsinki, 1963.

AT 726 The oldest on the farm. Wayfarer asks for night's lodging; meets a very old man outside, but is shown to his father who has to decide, and so on up to the seventh generation (AT F571.2): pp. 34–35.

AT A151.1.1 Home of gods inside hill: see MLSIT 8009 below.

AT A2231.1.2 Discourteous answer (flounder's crooked mouth): pp. 120–21.

AT A2231.7.1.1 Beetle cursed for betraying Holy Family: pp. 123–24.

AT B81 Mermaid: p. 108.

AT D1960.2 King asleep in mountain will awake one day to succour his people: see MLSIT 8009 below.

AT E502 The sleeping army: see MLSIT 8009 below.

F1B Fall with Lucifer: angels become Fairies or seals: pp. xxv, xxx–xxxi, 107, 156.

F9 Language of Fairies: pp. 34, 48.

F11B Request by Fairy woman that household should stop throwing out dirty water / potato water at door, as it is a nuisance / damaging furniture / endangering children: pp. 7, 51.

F11C Person tethering horse or cow is asked to do so elsewhere as the hole made by the tether-pin is letting water in / has almost injured one of the Fairy household: pp. 7, 33, 51.

F12 Music heard from hill: p. 73.

F15 Musician enters cave, is heard playing and never returns: cf. p. 74.

F22 Man goes into Fairy dwelling, spends year or more there dancing with cask/basket on his back: p. 33.

F27A Midwife, taken into Fairy dwelling to deliver child, gets ointment/water in one of her eyes, and can afterwards see Fairies with that eye. She meets and recognises a Fairy. On revealing which eye she can see Fairy with he/she blinds that eye: p. 77.

F29 Man sticks knife, or limpet pick, in seal, which escapes. Later old man in Norway gives him back the weapon. The old man is the seal: p. 157.

F32A Fairy host seen travelling: horseback procession: p. 77.

F32B Fairy host seen travelling as eddy of wind: pp. 13, 46.

F34 Man taken by *sluagh* and made to wound someone (woman, animal) with Elf-shot: pp. 37, 47.

F37 Other tales of person shifted by Fairy host: pp. 37–39.

F51B Abduction of woman: she appears to husband and tells him she is really with Fairies, who have buried a dead leaf, log, etc.: tells him how to save her but he does not dare: p. 78.

F54 Woman abducted into Fairy hill and set to work baking: p. 36.

F57 Woman meets water-horse in human form and goes with him. He carries her off into loch. Heart and lungs on loch: p. 109.

F58A Woman meets water-horse in human form and goes with him, but finds grains of sand in his hair when combing it and realises what he is. Runs away: pp. 113–14.

F61A / AT F321.1.1.1 'The brewery of eggshells.' Changeling discovered by his astonishment at mother 'brewing' with eggshells: p. 21.

F61B Changeling discovered by other remark betraying his old age: pp. lvi–lvii, 20.

F62 Changeling sits up in cradle and plays pipes or tongs to travelling tailor at work in kitchen: p. lxvi.

F64 Changeling: *Muc Dhearg* (its cry) taken to magician (MacMhuirich) who drives away the false child with a sword: pp. 48–49.

F65 Changeling: other stories of how driven away (fire, water, other threats): pp. lii, lviii–lix, 20, 48–49.

F68 Children carried off into loch when they ride on water-horse. Numbers of children destroyed by riding on 'extensible' water-horse, to which they stick fast. One may escape by cutting off finger: p. 112.

F75 Man captures Fairy woman by hiding her seal's etc. skin. After many years she finds skin (usually through one of children) and goes: pp. 156–57.

F88 Loan of sieve (etc.) asked for in curious language: p. 48.

F91 Fairy (or sea) cattle caught (with churchyard mould or iron between them and water, or other trick, or just appear) and breed: p. 72.

F94E Water-horse caught and harnessed. Carries off master when he omits some precaution: pp. 110–11.

F96 / ML 6045 Luran steals gold cup from Fairy dwelling. Pursued by Fairies but escapes. Hears verse saying that if Luran ate porridge he would be even faster. Follows advice and becomes heavy and slow (see also F128): pp. 28–30.

F98 Kettle borrowed by Fairies: wife away, husband omits to ask for it back; wife goes to Fairy dwelling and carries it off. Various tricks to throw off pursuing dogs, and verses: p. 31.

F101A Young piper enters Fairy hill and is taught to play by Fairies: p. 74.

F101C Young piper is taught to play by Fairies through gift of Fairy chanter: p. 74.

F103A Fairy song overheard and learned: p. 73.

F103B Fairy tune overheard and learned: p. 74.

F106A Fairies give good fortune (general): p. 81.

F106B Fairies give good fortune (Fairy flag of Dunvegan): p. 3.

F111 One of two companions wishes for drink (food) after hearing sounds of churning from Fairy hill. Woman appears, offers buttermilk/milk (food). The one who made the wish refuses. The other accepts, enjoys long and prosperous life. The other is cursed and dies, or is otherwise unfortunate: pp. 72–73.

F112 Wish for female company; MacPhee's black dog: pp. 58–64.

F115B Fairies help with harvest. Farmer allows them as much as can be got into one bundle. They bind the whole harvest in one rope. It breaks when farmer names God or days when ploughing/sowing were done: pp. 51–52, 317.

F115C Fairies help with harvest. Helpers finish work, demand more; sent to make ropes of sand: p. 51.

F118 Fairies help with cloth-working: pp. 39–40.

F120 Fairies help about house (brownies): pp. 83–85, 100–01, 102–03.

F120A / ML 7015 Brownie disappears when given clothes (pay): pp. 101–02, 360.

F124 Young ('whelp', 'chick') of the Muilidheartach (or other name) captured. Parent comes demanding its release and is made to perform tasks as a condition: p. 95.

F128 Luran chases Fairy who is pestering his wife, stealing his cows, etc.: told (in rhyme) that if he ate porridge he would be even faster (cf. F96 above). This advice is designed to make him slower: p. 30.

F130A Fairy as omen (*bean nighe*): pp. 22–23, 237.

F130B Fairy as omen (family banshi): pp. 23, 82–86.

F132 Stories of Fairies killing or crippling: p. 45.

F133 Man captures supernatural which promises to leave area if released; sometimes it performs tasks. It asks to shake hands; man holds out red-hot implement and it disappears with a shriek. Sometimes curses man and descendants: pp. 88–92.

F134 Wrestling match with supernatural/ghost: pp. xlviii–li, 273–76, 281–89.

F142A 'The Fairy Hill on Fire!' Supernaturals (unwelcome cloth-workers) got rid of by this cry: pp. 39–40.

F150 Dogs drive away supernatural, return hairless or not at all: pp. 63–64, 76–77, 515.

ML 3015 The card-players and the devil: pp. 160–61.

ML 3025 Carried to Rome by the devil or by evil spirits: pp. 162–63, 546.

ML 3030 / AT 673 The white serpent's flesh: pp. 121–22, cf. p. 504.

ML 6070B The king of the cats: pp. 190–91.

MLSIT 8009 'Has the time come?' (Barbarossa): pp. 148–49, 329–30, 402.

Other The princess of Lochlann appears to graveyard watchers: pp. 133, 185.

Other The tailor in the haunted church(yard): pp. 278–79.

Other The cannibal corpse: pp. 197–98.

Other *Colann gun cheann* (headless body): pp. 276–77.

W1 The witch hare: p. 188, cf. p. 175.

W3 The swelling hag, the hair and the hunter's dogs: pp. 65–66, cf. pp. 77, 337.

W5 Man drowns witches who are sailing in sieves: p. 180.

W7A The witch's daughter and her father: pp. 182–83.

W8 Witch delays birth of child: pp. 194–95.

W9 Attack by slighted lover: p. 193.

W10 Dubh a' Ghiuthais / An Dubh Ghiuthsach burns the forests: p. 653.

W20 Man tries to fly by imitating witches but comes to grief: pp. 179–80.

W21 'Off to London': p. 189.

W31 The three knots: pp. 180–81 and cf. pp. 181–82.

W40A The ship-sinking witch: pp. 184–86.

W41 The witch in the eggshell: cf. p. 180.

GLOSSARIAL INDEX

GENERAL INDEX

abbeys 399; Dull 508; Inchaffray 351; Iona 519; Lismore 508; Melrose 418

Aberdeen 279, 428, 542, 679; Aberdeenshire xliii, lviii, lxviii, 391, 399, 406, 415, 494, 615

Aberfoyle (Perthshire) xxii–xxiv, 296, 345, 729

Aberlour, presbytery of 414

Abernethy, presbytery of 414

Abhainn Cam Linne (Lorn) 417

Abhainn Chonnain, River Conon (Skye) 416

Abhainn Dalach (Lorn) 346

Abhainn Muileann Iain Duibh (Benbecula) 413

Abhainn na Fadhlach (Tiree) 647

Abhainn na Feàrna (Kingairloch) 616

Achabeg (Morvern) 38, 320

Achagavel (Morvern) 222, 486, 613, 728

Acharacle (Ardnamurchan) 267, 625, 674, 690, 697

Acharn (Appin) 520

Achdaliew, *Achadh da-Liubha* (Lochaber) 461

Achindarroch, *Acha nan Darach* (Appin) 85

Achintore (Lochaber) 337

Achluachrach (Brae Lochaber) 352, 353

Achnacarry (Lochaber) xciv, 653

Achnahannait, *Achadh na h-Annaid* (Skye) 15, 308

Achnarrow (Glenlivet) 415

Ailein mac Eachainn 167–68, 425, 426

Ailein Mòr Cheannacoille 218–19, 482–83

Ailein nan Creach, see Cameron, Allan

Ailein nan Sop or *Ailean nan Sop* 194, 356, 444

Ailsa Craig (Firth of Clyde) xciv, 177, 432

Àird an Runnair (N. Uist) 411

Aird Nisabost (Harris) 407

Airds (Appin) 345–46

Airigh Bhoidheach (Coll) 412

Airigh Mhaoraich (Coll) 412

Àirigh mhic Mharoich (Coll) xiv, 187, 438

Àirigh na h-Aon Oidhche 115, 370, 371–72, 730

Àirigh nan Cioch (Glen Lochy) 363

Àirigh O Dhùin (Islay) 436

Alastair na Béiste 'Alexander of the Monster' 112

Aldcheardie (Rannoch) 500

Aline, River (Morvern) 324

Alioter, *Àth Leòdair* (N. Uist) 291, 493, 525, 727

Alison, Rev. John (Newington) 620, 623

Allt a' Chaiginn (Kingairloch) 613

Allt an Lòin (Lochaber) 351

Allt an t-Snaige (Glen Nevis) 338

Alltaogain, *Allt Aogainn* (Lismore) 94, 355

Allt Chaisle (Glen Lyon) 525

Allt Choire an Eòin (Lochaber) 351

Allt Dhùn Croisg (Glen Lochay) 523

Allt Dòmhna(i)ch (Atholl) 564

Allt Féith Chiarain (Lochaber) 338

Allt nam Bruach (Lochaber) 353

Alves, parish of (Moray) 388–89

Amie, Lady, wife of John, Lord of the Isles 393

amulets 116, 119, 150, 199, 200, 219–24, 227, 294, 305, 483, 486

Anderson, Margaret (Alves) 388

angels xxv–xxvi, xxx–xxxi, lxxviii, 107, 156, 204, 210, 301, 445, 471, 477, 480, 554, 576, 680, 691, 731

Angus, county of xciv, 494, 696

Angus, Andrew (Alves) 388

annaid, annat 308; Annat (Lochaber) 400

Aodann Mòr 'Big Face' (Liddesdale, Morvern) 52

Appin, *Apainn nan Stiùbhartach* (Argyll) lxvii, xciv, 80, 85, 92, 161, 162, 178, 250, 256, 291, 322, 327, 345–46, 356, 408, 417, 430, 431, 478, 492, 508, 520–21, 522, **609–11**, 612, 614, 615, 616, 637, 729; Braes of 346; Strath of 346, 609, 611; Appin House 417; Appin Murder 281, 520, 613

Appin of Menzies, *Apainn nam Mèinnearach* (Perthshire) xiii, 256, 285, 508, 522, 567

Applecross (Ross-shire) xxiv, 121, 133, 727

Arbroath (Angus) 696; Declaration of (1320) 399

Ardachyle (Mull) 70, 111, 728

Ardchattan (Lorn) 446

Ardeas (Caolas, Tiree) 692

Ardersier (Inverness-shire) xciv

Ardfenaig (Mull) 636, 640, 728

Ardgour (Argyll) 729

Ardincaple (Seil) 728

Ardiura (Mull) 368

Ardlamont (Cowal) 623

Ardlàraich, Ardlarich (Rannoch) 38, 320, 520, 521

Ardmeanach, *Ard Mheadhonach* (Mull) 55, 322, 728

Ardmore (Islay) 636, 640, 663, 690, 696

Ardnacallich (Ulva) 96, 355

Ardnacross (Mull) 367

Ardnadrochit (Mull) 94, 103, 355, 728

Ardnamurchan (Argyll) lxiii, lxxxii, 28, 29, 97, 98, 122, 193, 195, 197, 200, 228, 247, 337, 346, 347, 356, 381, 451, 504, 609, 641, 670, 690, 691, 697

Ardrishaig (Argyll) 450, 621, 630, 682, 728

Ardsheal (Appin) lxvi, 281, 431, 520

Ardtornish (Morvern) 501, 613, 728

Ardtun (Mull) 322

Ardvo(i)rlich (Perthshire) 224, 487, 729

Ardvourlie Bay (Harris) 319

Argyll xlii, lxv, xciv, 20, 33, 44, 67, 99, 100, 107, 118, 120, 122, 147, 149, 155, 189, 199, 274, 292, 305, 318, 329, 346, 354, 359, 363, 372, 373, 390, 406, 408, 409, 426, 430, 438, 492, 494, 507, 508, 510, 518, 522, 567, 609, 613, 616, 621, 623, 626, 684, 685, 691, 693, 699; earls *or* dukes of 292, 510; 2nd earl of 373; 7th earl of 354, 438; 9th earl of 356; 5th duke of 349; 7th duke of 627; 8th duke of 620, 621, 622, 626, 627, 633–34, 635, 636, 640, 641, 647–48, 650, 661, 663, 674, 679, 691, 693; 9th duke of, formerly marquis

735

eyebrows 480, 481, 499; eyes 293, 301, 310, 312, 313, 334, 345, 377, 394, 398, 403, 425, 426–27, 428, 450, 453–54, 466, 481, 485, 488, 494, 498, 515, 516, 731; face 310, 489; feet 293, 472, 506, 511, 514; fingers, fingertips 397, 453, 504, 732; fists 483; flanks 511; flesh 278–79, 474, 526; genitals 449, 497; gullet 519; hands 394, 395, 506; head 489, 506, 515, 517, 518; heart 378, 450, 458, 474, 479, 731; hips 410; jaw 404, 515; knees 385, 410, 460–61, 463, 466, 473, 484, 489, 511; legs 385, 446, 455, 512, 513; lips 394; livers 369, 378; loins 456; lungs 731; marrow 44, 155, 205, 206, 283, 451; menstrual fluid 392; mouth 489, 493; neck 466, 474, 489, 499, 514; nose 394, 485, 515; nostrils 301, 334; palate 485; palms 394, 502, 511; ribs 496; shoulders 453, 466, 482, 502, 506; sinews 426; skull lxxviii–lxxix, 6, 127, 149, 151, 267, 280, 404, 442–43, 510, 686; snout 423, 488, 491; soles 466, 472, 477, 502; spine 506; spleen 473, 474; stomach 468, 492; tail 364, 412, 513, 515; teeth 20, 102, 144, 163, 194, 221, 274–75, 404, 411, 459, 485, 486, 493, 515, 526; testicles, *magairlean* 398, 669; throat 466, 519; thumbs 310, 397, 398, 404, 460–61; toes 397; tongue 313, 428, 481, 482; veins 451, 458; weasand 519; webbed feet 514, 515; windpipe 519; womb 392; wrists 453; *see also* blood, hair, nails, saliva, urine

Bogha Eilean t-Somhairle (Tiree) 319, 730

bogs, *féithean*, swamps 438–39, 486, 647; bog-oak 352; *Féith Chiarain* (Lochaber) 66, 338; 'Feith Mhoire' 445

Bohuntin (Lochaber) 423

Bonar Bridge (Ross-shire) 513

Bonawe (Lorn) lxxii–lxxiii, 250, 729

Bonskeid (Atholl) 289, 524

books 151, 161, 178, 281, 310, 314, 417, 418, 434, 520, 610, 635, 637, 638, 643–44, 675, 683; chapbooks 313; diaries 506; dictionaries 613, 621; red books 400, 417; Black Book of Taymouth 408; Book of Invasions, *Lebor Gabála* 485; Book of Leinster 347; Little Book of Clanranald 339; Red Book of Appin 161, 178, 417, 418; Red Book of Balloch 151; book-keeping 610; booksellers 396, 418; devil's *or* Satan's books 417; libraries 638; 'Matthew and Plilon' 610

borrowing, lending 386; 'The Borrowed Peats' 385

Borve, *Borgh* (Barra) 558, 598; Upper Borve 305

Boswell, James 368, 505

Bourtie (Aberdeenshire) 628

Bousd (Coll) 38, 320

Bowie, Master James (Taymouth) 408

Bowmore (Islay) 515

Bowriefauld (Angus) 696

Boyd, Rev. A. K. H. (St Andrews) 619

Boyd, Margaret, *see* Wallace, Mrs Margaret

Boyds 310

Boyle, Robert 504

Bracadale (Skye) 342, 727

Bracara (Morar) 276, 727

Brackletter (Lochaber) 30, 316

Brae-Glen, *Bràighleann* (Lorn) 264, 510

Brae Lochaber 350, 352, 353

Braes of Portree (Skye) 15, 53, 73, 182, 258, 263, 291, 308, 342, 358, 444, 620, 727

Bragar (Lewis) 388

Brahan (Ross-shire) 157; *see also* Coinneach Odhar

Breacachadh xii, 87, 187, 292, 349, 490, 510, 525, 728

bread, cakes 10, 11, 18, 19, 25, 28–30, 36, 39, 127, 128, 137, 139, 257, 299, 309, 314, 316, 320, 334, 342, 384–85, 404, 411, 433, 489, 498–99, 530, 532, 546, 553, 576, 609; breads 302; bread-sticks 301; leg cakes, *bonnaich lurgainn* 128; loaves 332

Breadalbane (Perthshire) 71, 105, 151, 223, 229, 234, 363, 451, 493–94, 576, 729; 1st earl of 408; 'Curse of the Breadalbanes' 410

brewing 731; brewery of eggshells 311, 731

Brian Boru, *Brian Brugh* 59, 62, 67–69, 335, 339, 349, 466, 483, 497

Bridge of Allan (Stirlingshire) 683

Bridge of Awe (Lorn) lxxiii–lxxiv, 47

Bridge of Lochay (Perthshire) 524

bridges 324, 444, 445, 446, 452; drawbridges 348

Briolcanach, Am (Tiree) 646, 647, 730

Broadford (Skye) 284, 369, 405, 698, 727

Brodick (Arran) 654

Brolas (Mull) 64, 501, 728

Brown, Christina (Tiree) 681

Brown, D. (Tiree) 622

Brown, John (Glen Lochay) 524

Brown, John (Kilmoluag) 513, 664–65

Brown, Mary (Balevullin) 632

Brown, May 699

Brown, Murdoch (Mannal) 682, 699

Brown, Murdoch, RN 699

Brown, Neil (Tiree) 632

Brown, Peter, *Par Lonach* (Glen Lochay) 287–88, 524

brownies liii–lv, lxxxix, 83, 100–03, 105, 106, 347, 348, 359, 364, 413–15, 732

Browns 622, 640, 664; *Macilduinn* 190

Bruce, —— (East Side, Skye) 277, 516

Bruce, Marion 620

a' Bhuaile Bheag (Coll) 412

Buail Uachdrach (S. Uist) 482

Buchanan, Alexander (Baugh, Tiree) 649, 654, 661, 673, 681, 683, **694**

Buchanan, Michael (Barra) 305

Buchanans 427

Buies 398

bulls 24, 136, 162, 176, 177, 178, 211, 227, 332, 341, 373, 571, 597; bullocks 328; bull's head 500; bulls' hooves 179, 230; *Tarbh Boibhre* 373; *see also* dàir

Bunacaimb (Arisaig) 440

Bun Dubh, am, Gunna Sound 260, 730

Bunessan (Mull) 355, 370, 418

Bunroy (Brae Lochaber) 351, 353

Burg (Mull) 322

burial 409, 424; burial-grounds, burying-grounds 267, 329, 367, 405, 486, 494, 508, 511

Burnet, John, advocate (Edinburgh) 625, 627

Burt, Capt. Edmund 189, 400, 440

Bute, isle of 427, 455, 729; marquess of 698

butter 17, 18, 42, 122, 127, 128, 134, 139, 173, 175, 178, 210, 237–38, 280, 322, 324, 342, 410, 411, 426, 430, 433, 439, 463, 520, 549, 553, 557, 578, 580, 593, 618; butterfat 449; buttermilk 72, 439, 732

Cabag, Càbag Head (Lewis) 182, 436, 727